This isn't
the only place
ICI appears
on the
golf course...

—Peter Jacobsen

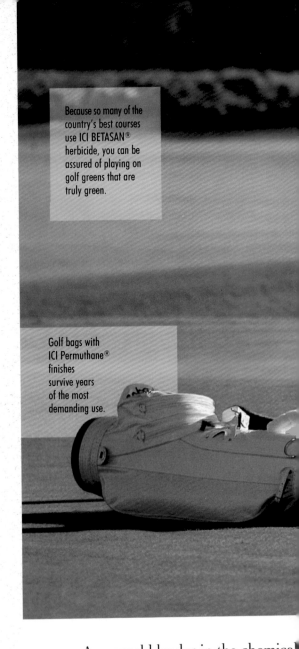

...We're with you from tee to green.

Because so many of the country's best courses use ICI BETASAN® herbicide, you can be assured of playing on golf greens that are truly green.

Golf bags with ICI Permuthane® finishes survive years of the most demanding use.

As a world leader in the chemical industry, ICI provides materials to serve you from tee to green. Whether it's a protective coating, graphite epoxy tape, herbicide, or synthetic fiber, each ICI product helps you play longer, better, and

Durable, easy-care Tactel® textile fiber helps your golf shirts stay dry and comfortable.

ICI Fiberite® graphite epoxy tape strengthens club shafts without adding weight.

ICI Resins special-purpose polymer strengthens the protective coating on your golf balls to keep moisture out and give them a longer life.

—Billy Andrade

A Permuthane® coating on your shoes keeps their good looks in and water out.

more comfortably.

Yet golf is only one area that benefits from ICI's expanding technology. The broad range of ICI products is constantly improving our lives, whether we're in the office, at home, or playing a lei-surely round of golf.

You might not see us the next time you tee off, but we're there to help you win.

ICI is proud to be a corporate sponsor of Peter Jacobsen and Billy Andrade on the 1990 PGA Tour.

Discover who we are...

Presents

Mark H. McCormack's World of Professional Golf 1990

Photographs by Lawrence Levy

1990

First published in 1990
by Sackville Books Ltd.
Stradbroke, Suffolk, England

© International Merchandising Corp. 1990

Designed and produced by Davis Design

British Library Cataloguing in Publication Data

McCormack, Mark H.   (Mark Hume)
    Mark McCormack's World of Professional Golf - 1990 -
    1. Golf
    796.352

    ISBN 0-948615-38-9

Printed and bound in the United States of America.

Contents

1. The Sony Ranking

The Sony Ranking achieved universal acceptance in 1989, the final major hurdle being the approval of the PGA Tour in the United States, which came at year's end, along with some relatively minor modifications in the method for determining the ranking. Starting in 1990, the Sony Ranking will be distributed along with the PGA Tour money list and other official statistics.

While the PGA Tour's approval was important, there were no better endorsements of the Sony Ranking in 1989 than the performances of the leading golfers in the four major championships. All four championships were won by players who were among the top eight in the Sony Ranking.

There were 19 players who completed 72 holes in all four championships, and 12 of those were in the top 20 of the Sony Ranking. (Of the remaining eight in the top 20 of the Sony Ranking, three were not entered in all the majors, and five missed the cut in only one major.) Of the 19 players who completed every round of all the majors, all were among the Sony Ranking's top 50 with the exceptions of Hall of Famers Raymond Floyd (presently 74th on the Sony Ranking) and Jack Nicklaus (presently 124th).

Following is a chart of those 19 major championship leaders, with their scores listed in the order of the championship; Masters, U.S. Open, British Open and PGA Championship:

Name	Sony Ranking	Tournament Scores				Total Score
Greg Norman	1	284	289	275	282	1130
Nick Faldo	2	283	285	281	281	1130
Payne Stewart	5	292	284	280	276	1132
Curtis Strange	4	291	278	292	277	1138
Ian Woosnam	9	290	279	290	279	1138
Chip Beck	11	288	279	285	286	1138
Tom Watson	20	290	291	277	281	1139
Tom Kite	6	291	283	283	286	1143
Don Pooley	39	290	287	283	286	1146
Larry Mize	19	293	289	283	283	1148
Peter Jacobsen	46	296	282	286	285	1149
Jack Nicklaus	124	291	290	286	285	1152
Jodie Mudd	49	287	292	278	296	1153
Scott Simpson	36	298	281	285	290	1154
Steve Pate	41	293	292	282	287	1154
Seve Ballesteros	3	285	290	299	282	1156
Raymond Floyd	74	298	287	288	288	1161
Mark McCumber	18	300	279	289	294	1162
Bernhard Langer	16	293	294	309	292	1188

In the spring of 1986, the Sony Corporation announced the launch of this world ranking system for professional golf. The Sony Ranking is sanctioned by the Championship Committee of the Royal and Ancient Golf Club of St. Andrews, and is a specially developed computerized system which provides an authoritative reference source to the relative performances of the world's leading players. Some of the most respected people in golf worldwide bring their opinions to bear on the workings of the system. The Sony Ranking Advisory Committee meets at St. Andrews each October, and its recommendations are passed on to the R&A for approval. In addition to myself, the Sony Ranking Advisory Committee consists of:

Brenda Blumberg, advisor to the South African PGA
Peter Dobereiner, golf correspondent for *The Observer* (London)
Taizo Kawata, member of the International Committee of the Japan Golf Association
Graham Marsh, executive of the Australian PGA
Colin Phillips, secretary of the Australian Golf Union
Richard Rahusen, chairman of the European Golf Association Technical Committee
Pat Rielly, president of the PGA of America
Ken Schofield, executive director of the PGA European Tour
Frank Tatum, past president of the United States Golf Association
Peter Townsend, former British Walker and Ryder Cup player and a member of the PGA European Tour Tournament Policy Board

All tournaments from the world's golf tours are taken into account and points are awarded according to the quality of the players participating in each event. The number of points distributed to each player is dependent upon his finishing position. The four major championships and The Players Championship are weighted separately to reflect the greater prestige of the events and the strong fields participating.

The Sony Ranking is based on a three-year "rolling" period, weighted in favor of more recent results, and a divisor is used to take into account the number of tournaments played by each ranked golfer. Points accumulated over the current 52-week period are multiplied by four, points earned over the previous 52-week period are doubled, and points from the first 52-week period are simply added to the total. Each golfer is then ranked according to his point average, which is determined by dividing his total number of points by the number of starts he has made over the three-year period. A golfer must, however, play in at least 60 tournaments over the three-year period. Should he play in fewer tournaments, his divisor is still 60.

Fifty points are awarded to the winner of a major championship, then 30 points for second place, 20 for third, 15 for fourth, 12 for fifth and down to at least one point for every golfer completing the final round. The winner of The Players Championship is awarded 40 points, then down to one point for 50th place. All other events have a points system based upon the number and rank of top-100 ranked players participating in that event.

For this purpose, each top-100 ranked player is assigned ratings points, ranging from 65 for the No. 1 player to one for the No. 100 player, and the total of the points is then used to adjust the Sony Ranking points to reflect the quality of the field. The points vary from a maximum of 40 for the winner down to one point for 50th place in a high-quality championship, to two points for the winner and one point to the player finishing fourth in a minor tournament.

Minimum points safeguards for winners of official tour events have been set at four points for events in Asia and Africa, six points for Australia, New Zealand and Japan, and eight points for Europe and the United States. In addition, the Volvo PGA Championship in Europe has a minimum points level of 32 for the winner.

The Sony Ranking is compiled and released to the news media and to the governing bodies of professional golf each Monday from London.

The final Sony Ranking of 1989 is listed at the end of this chapter, along with a table of the system for determining the Sony Ranking points to be distributed in each event. A more detailed listing of the Sony Ranking may be found in the Appendixes.

As can be noted in the final 1989 calculations, Greg Norman regained the No. 1 position which he had held almost continuously from mid-September, 1986, until the end of October, 1988, when the loss of points effected by being sidelined for almost two months after a wrist injury in the 1988 U.S. Open deprived him of the No. 1 spot. His playoff loss at the British Open boosted Norman from third to second place, then he took over first place by winning The International and solidified his position in the two following weeks by placing fourth in the NEC World Series of Golf and winning the Greater Milwaukee Open. For the year, Norman had five victories, two in the United States, two in Australia and one in Japan.

The previous No. 1 player, Seve Ballesteros, dropped to third place despite three victories in Europe, while Nick Faldo advanced from fourth to second place with his Masters Tournament victory and four titles in Europe, including the Volvo PGA Championship and Suntory World Match Play Championship. Curtis Strange successfully defended his U.S. Open Championship and climbed one position to fourth place, and Payne Stewart jumped from 19th to fifth place after winning the PGA Championship and MCI Heritage Classic. The Player of the Year in the United States, Tom Kite, who won three tournaments including The Players Championship, rose to No. 6 from 13th place, then came young European star Jose-Maria Olazabal at No. 7, an improvement from 15th place, and British Open champion Mark Calcavecchia at No. 8. Ian Woosnam (No. 9) and Paul Azinger completed the top 10.

Overall in the Sony Ranking for 1989, Stewart made the greatest gain, and Sandy Lyle, who got off to a reasonable start in the year then completely lost his game, had the largest loss of points. Calcavecchia, who also won two early-season tournaments in America (plus one unofficial event), had the second-largest gain of points, while Ballesteros' relatively poor performances in the major championships resulted in the second-greatest loss of points. The Sony Ranking also underlines the dramatic improvement of Blaine McCallister, Tim Simpson and Steve Jones in the United States, and of Ronan Rafferty and Craig Parry in Europe, as well as the disappointing showings of some others, especially of David Ishii, Tsuneyuki Nakajima and Masahiro Kuramoto in Japan. Consider the tables noting major movements which follow the final 1989 ranking.

Detailed Structure For Allocation of Sony Ranking Points

Pos.	MAJOR CHAMPIONSHIPS	Players Championship	776-825	726-775	676-725	626-675	576-625	526-575	501-525	476-500	451-475 Europe PGA Champ. Minimum	426-450	401-425	376-400	351-375	326-350	301-325	276-300	251-275	226-250	201-225	176-200	151-175	141-150	131-140	121-130	111-120	101-110	91-100	81-90	71-80	61-70	51-60	41-50	31-40 Europe & USA Minimum	26-30	21-25 Aust/NZ & Japan Minimum	16-20	11-15 Asa, SAf & Safari Minimum	6-10	0-5 SAm, Can & Regional Minimum
1st	50	40	40	39	38	37	36	35	34	33	32	31	30	29	28	27	26	25	24	23	22	21	20	19	18	17	16	15	14	13	12	11	10	9	8	7	6	5	4	3	2
2nd	40	24	24	23	23	22	22	21	20	20	19	19	18	17	17	16	16	15	14	14	13	13	12	11	11	10	10	9	8	8	7	7	6	5	5	4	4	3	2	2	1
3rd	30	16	16	16	15	15	14	14	14	13	13	12	12	12	11	11	10	10	10	9	9	8	8	8	7	7	6	6	6	5	5	4	4	4	3	3	2	2	2	1	1
4th	20	12	12	12	11	11	11	11	10	10	10	9	9	9	8	8	8	8	7	7	7	6	6	6	5	5	5	5	4	4	4	3	3	3	2	2	2	2	1	1	1
5th	15	9	9	9	9	8	8	8	7	7	7	6	6	6	5	5	5	5	4	4	4	4	4	4	3	3	3	3	3	3	2	2	2	2	2	2	2	1	1	1	1
6th	12	8	8	8	7	7	7	6	6	6	6	6	6	5	5	5	5	4	4	4	4	3	3	3	3	3	3	3	2	2	2	2	2	2	2	2	2	1	1	1	1
7th	9	7	8	7	7	7	6	6	6	5	6	6	6	5	5	5	4	4	4	4	4	3	3	3	3	3	3	3	2	2	2	2	2	2	2	2	1	1	1	1	
8th	8	7	8	7	7	6	6	6	5	5	5	5	5	5	4	4	4	4	4	4	3	3	3	3	3	3	2	2	2	2	2	2	2	2	1	1	1	1	1		
9th	8	6	7	7	6	6	6	6	5	5	5	5	5	4	4	4	4	4	3	3	3	3	3	3	2	2	2	2	2	2	2	2	2	1	1	1	1	1			
10th	7	6	7	7	6	6	5	5	5	5	5	5	4	4	4	4	4	3	3	3	3	3	3	3	2	2	2	2	2	2	2	2	1	1	1	1	1				
11th	6	6	6	6	6	5	5	5	5	5	4	4	4	4	3	3	3	3	3	3	3	3	2	2	2	2	2	2	2	2	2	1	1	1	1	1					
12th	6	6	6	6	5	5	5	5	4	4	4	4	3	3	3	3	3	3	3	3	2	2	2	2	2	2	2	2	2	1	1	1	1	1	1						
13th	5	5	5	5	5	5	4	4	4	4	3	3	3	3	3	3	3	3	2	2	2	2	2	2	2	2	2	2	1	1	1	1	1								
14th	5	5	5	5	5	4	4	4	4	3	3	3	3	3	3	3	3	2	2	2	2	2	2	2	2	2	2	1	1	1	1	1									
15th	5	5	5	4	4	4	4	4	3	3	3	3	3	3	3	2	2	2	2	2	2	2	2	2	2	1	1	1	1	1	1										
16th	5	4	4	4	4	4	3	3	3	3	3	3	3	3	2	2	2	2	2	2	2	2	2	1	1	1	1	1	1												
17th	4	4	4	3	3	3	3	3	3	3	3	2	2	2	2	2	2	2	2	2	2	2	1	1	1	1	1	1													
18th	4	4	3	3	3	3	3	3	3	2	2	2	2	2	2	2	2	2	2	2	2	1	1	1	1	1	1														
19th	4	3	3	3	3	3	3	3	3	2	2	2	2	2	2	2	2	2	2	2	2	1	1	1	1	1	1														

TOTAL RATING POINTS

RATING POINTS

Current Rank of Players	Rating Points
1st	65
2nd	60
3rd	55
4th	50
5th	45
6th	40
7th	35
8th	30
9th	25
10th	20
11th to 15th	5 x 15
16th to 25th	10 x 10
26th to 50th	25 x 6
51st to 75th	25 x 2
76th to 100th	25 x 1

51st plus all making 36-hole cut in major championships

20th
21st
22nd
23rd
24th
25th
26th
27th
28th
29th
30th
31st
32nd
33rd
34th
35th
36th
37th
38th
39th
40th
41st
42nd
43rd
44th
45th
46th
47th
48th
49th
50th

The Sony Ranking
(as of December 31, 1989)

POS.	PLAYER, TOUR	POINTS	POS.	PLAYER, TOUR	POINTS
1	Greg Norman, ANZ 1	17.76	47	Fuzzy Zoeller, USA 29	4.22
2	Nick Faldo, Eur 1	16.25	48	Naomichi Ozaki, Jpn 3	4.20
3	Seve Ballesteros, Eur 2	15.03	49	Jodie Mudd, USA 30	4.17
4	Curtis Strange, USA 1	13.79	50	Bill Glasson, USA 31	4.15
5	Payne Stewart, USA 2	12.82	51	Joey Sindelar, USA 32	4.07
6	Tom Kite, USA 3	12.41	52	Gordon Brand, Jr., Eur 9	4.07
7	Jose-Maria Olazabal, Eur 3	12.00	53	Eduardo Romero, SAm 1	3.96
8	Mark Calcavecchia, USA 4	11.81	54	Peter Fowler, ANZ 6	3.94
9	Ian Woosnam, Eur 4	11.56	55	Jeff Sluman, USA 33	3.93
10	Paul Azinger, USA 5	10.95	56	Graham Marsh, ANZ 7	3.92
11	Chip Beck, USA 6	10.49	57	Howard Clark, Eur 10	3.83
12	Masashi Ozaki, Jpn 1	10.00	58	Hal Sutton, USA 34	3.79
13	David Frost, Afr 1	9.39	59	Ian Baker-Finch, ANZ 8	3.76
14	Sandy Lyle, Eur 5	9.37	60	Sam Torrance, Eur 11	3.74
15	Fred Couples, USA 7	8.85	61	Gil Morgan, USA 35	3.71
16	Bernhard Langer, Eur 6	8.47	62	Jose-Maria Canizares, Eur 12	3.58
17	Ben Crenshaw, USA 8	8.31	63	Jay Haas, USA 36	3.55
18	Mark McCumber, USA 9	8.04	64	Donnie Hammond, USA 37	3.53
19	Larry Mize, USA 10	7.08	65	Davis Love, USA 38	3.50
20	Tom Watson, USA 11	6.81	66	Tsuneyuki Nakajima, Jpn 4	3.48
21	Ronan Rafferty, Eur 7	6.73	67	Wayne Levi, USA 39	3.41
22	Mike Reid, USA 12	6.57	68	Mike Harwood, ANZ 9	3.39
23	Larry Nelson, USA 13	6.46	69	Brian Jones, ANZ 10	3.27
24	Scott Hoch, USA 14	6.42	70	Jose Rivero, Eur 13	3.27
25	Lanny Wadkins, USA 15	6.35	71	Christy O'Connor, Jr., Eur 14	3.27
26	Peter Senior, ANZ 2	6.35	72	Brett Ogle, ANZ 11	3.26
27	Mark O'Meara, USA 16	6.20	73	Dave Rummells, USA 40	3.21
28	Steve Jones, USA 17	6.09	74	Ray Floyd, USA 41	3.19
29	Craig Parry, ANZ 3	6.03	75	David Ishii, USA 42	3.13
30	Craig Stadler, USA 18	5.90	76	Andy Bean, USA 43	3.13
31	Mark McNulty, Afr 2	5.82	77	Des Smyth, Eur 15	3.09
32	Bruce Lietzke, USA 19	5.68	78	Mark Wiebe, USA 44	3.07
33	Ken Green, USA 20	5.47	79	David Feherty, Eur 16	3.03
34	Isao Aoki, Jpn 2	5.45	80	Gene Sauers, USA 45	3.01
35	Tim Simpson, USA 21	5.44	81	Roger Mackay, ANZ 12	2.96
36	Scott Simpson, USA 22	5.33	82	Michael Allen, USA 46	2.95
37	Mark James, Eur 8	5.27	83	John Mahaffey, USA 47	2.88
38	Nick Price, Afr 3	4.87	84	Tateo Ozaki, Jpn 5	2.80
39	Don Pooley, USA 23	4.75	85	Corey Pavin, USA 48	2.78
40	Bob Tway, USA 24	4.69	86	David Edwards, USA 49	2.76
41	Steve Pate, USA 25	4.67	87	Vijay Singh, Asa 1	2.62
42	Wayne Grady, ANZ 4	4.62	88	Dave Barr, Can 1	2.57
43	Rodger Davis, ANZ 5	4.42	89	Fulton Allem, Afr 4	2.57
44	Dan Pohl, USA 26	4.36	90	Mike Hulbert, USA 50	2.54
45	Blaine McCallister, USA 27	4.30	91	Tze Chung Chen, Asa 2	2.46
46	Peter Jacobsen, USA 28	4.28	92	D.A. Weibring, USA 51	2.45

POS.	PLAYER, TOUR	POINTS
93	Mike Sullivan, USA 52	2.35
94	Mats Lanner, Eur 17	2.35
95	Derrick Cooper, Eur 18	2.34
96	Clarence Rose, USA 53	2.33
97	Roger Chapman, Eur 19	2.31
98	Hale Irwin, USA 54	2.31
99	Barry Lane, Eur 20	2.31
100	Jim Carter, USA 55	2.30
101	Andrew Murray, Eur 21	2.30
102	Tom Purtzer, USA 56	2.29
103	Gary Koch, USA 57	2.29
104	Ted Schulz, USA 58	2.26
105	Loren Roberts, USA 59	2.25
106	Brad Faxon, USA 60	2.25
107	Philip Walton, Eur 22	2.25
108	Tom Byrum, USA 61	2.20
109	Masahiro Kuramoto, Jpn 6	2.12
110	Frank Nobilo, ANZ 13	2.11
111	Doug Tewell, USA 62	2.10
112	Robert Wrenn, USA 63	2.10
113	John Bland, Afr 5	2.09
114	Gordon J. Brand, Eur 23	2.04
115	Jeff Hawkes, Afr 6	2.04
116T	Ove Sellberg, Eur 24T	2.00
116T	Eamonn Darcy, Eur 24T	2.00
118	Bob Gilder, USA 64	1.95
119	Kenny Perry, USA 65	1.91
120	Tony Johnstone, Afr 7	1.88
121	Nobuo Serizawa, Jpn 7	1.87
122	Denis Durnian, Eur 26	1.87
123	Mike Donald, USA 66	1.86
124	Jack Nicklaus, USA 67	1.85
125	Jim Benepe, USA 68	1.81
126	Ronnie Black, USA 69	1.81
127	Bobby Wadkins, USA 70	1.80
128	John Huston, USA 71	1.78
129	Ed Fiori, USA 72	1.76
130	David Ogrin, USA 73	1.73
131	Koichi Suzuki, Jpn 8	1.73
132	Hubert Green, USA 74	1.72
133	Mark Mouland, Eur 27	1.71
134	Bob Lohr, USA 75	1.69
135	Yoshiyuki Yokoshima, Jpn 9	1.68
136	Kenny Knox, USA 76	1.68
137	Peter O'Malley, ANZ 14	1.67
138	Mark Lye, USA 77	1.65
139	Akihito Yokoyama, Jpn 10	1.64
140	Hajime Meshiai, Jpn 11	1.64
141	Curt Byrum, USA 78	1.63
142	Steve Elkington, ANZ 15	1.62
143	Hugh Baiocchi, Afr 8	1.62
144	Morris Hatalsky, USA 79	1.59
145	Saburo Fujiki, Jpn 12	1.59
146	Roger Maltbie, USA 80	1.59

POS.	PLAYER, TOUR	POINTS
147T	Lee Trevino, USA 81	1.58
147T	Bob Shearer, ANZ 16	1.58
149	Jay Don Blake, USA 82	1.56
150	Yoshimi Niizeki, Jpn 13	1.56
151	J.C. Snead, USA 83	1.55
152	David Graham, ANZ 17	1.55
153	Toru Nakamura, Jpn 14	1.53
154	Mac O'Grady, USA 84	1.51
155	Katsunari Takahashi, Jpn 15	1.51
156	Dan Forsman, USA 85	1.51
157	Mark Roe, Eur 28	1.51
158	Jim Gallagher, USA 86	1.48
159	John Cook, USA 87	1.48
160	Scott Verplank, USA 88	1.45
161	Chris Perry, USA 89	1.44
162	Colin Montgomerie, Eur 29	1.42
163	Brian Claar, USA 90	1.41
164	Ken Brown, Eur 30	1.41
165	Tommy Armour, USA 91	1.40
166	Andrew Magee, USA 92	1.40
167	Terry Gale, ANZ 18	1.38
168	Greg Twiggs, USA 93	1.35
169	Johnny Miller, USA 94	1.32
170	Tadami Ueno, Jpn 16	1.31
171	Yoshitaka Yamamoto, Jpn 17	1.29
172	Mark Brooks, USA 95	1.28
173	Akiyoshi Ohmachi, Jpn 18	1.28
174	Anders Forsbrand, Eur 31	1.25
175	Jim Hallet, USA 96	1.24
176	Magnus Persson, Eur 32	1.23
177	Larry Rinker, USA 97	1.22
178	Miguel Martin, Eur 33	1.19
179	Seiichi Kanai, Jpn 19	1.18
180	Carl Mason, Eur 34	1.17
181	Ossie Moore, ANZ 19	1.14
182	Brian Tennyson, USA 98	1.14
183	Russell Claydon, Eur 35	1.13
184	Buddy Gardner, USA 99	1.13
185	Billy Andrade, USA 100	1.13
186	Katsuyoshi Tomori, Jpn 20	1.11
187	Mike Clayton, ANZ 20	1.10
188	Tom Sieckmann, USA 101	1.10
189	Tsukasa Watanabe, Jpn 21	1.09
190	Hiroshi Makino, Jpn 22	1.09
191T	Hideki Kase, Jpn 23	1.08
191T	Jeff Woodland, ANZ 21	1.08
193	Richard Boxall, Eur 36	1.08
194	Phil Blackmar, USA 102	1.08
195	Leonard Thompson, USA 103	1.08
196	Peter Baker, Eur 37	1.08
197	Lance Ten Broeck, USA 104	1.06
198	Tze Ming Chen, Asa 3	1.05
199T	Mike Colandro, USA 105	1.05
199T	Manuel Pinero, Eur 38	1.05

1989 Sony Ranking Review

Major Movements Within Top 50

	Upward				Downward		
Name	Net Points Gained	Position 1988	Position 1989	Name	Net Points Lost	Position 1988	Position 1989
Payne Stewart	403	19	5	Sandy Lyle	435	3	14
Mark Calcavecchia	312	9	8	Seve Ballesteros	368	1	3
Nick Faldo	248	4	2	Lanny Wadkins	261	10	25
Jose-Maria Olazabal	228	15	7	Ben Crenshaw	204	7	17
Tom Kite	219	13	6	Mark McNulty	196	22	32

Major Movements Into Top 50 — Major Movements Out of Top 50

Name	Net Points Gained	Position 1988	Position 1989	Name	Net Points Lost	Position 1988	Position 1989
Blaine McCallister	314	161	45	David Ishii	267	26	75
Tim Simpson	304	113	35	Joey Sindelar	257	27	51
Steve Jones	287	76	28	Tsuneyuki Nakajima	172	36	66
Ronan Rafferty	276	57	21	Corey Pavin	151	49	85
Craig Parry	275	65	29	Jeff Sluman	148	40	55

Other Major Movements

	Upward				Downward		
Name	Net Points Gained	Position 1988	Position 1989	Name	Net Points Lost	Position 1988	Position 1989
Eduardo Romero	230	281	53	Masahiro Kuramoto	170	60	109
Peter Fowler	221	123	54	Anders Forsbrand	143	79	174
Mike Harwood	197	153	68	D.A. Weibring	140	58	92
Michael Allen	189	319	82	Mac O'Grady	138	71	154
Ted Schulz	186	603	104	Bobby Wadkins	138	73	127

2. The Year In Retrospect

You would have a hard time convincing anyone that 1989 was Greg Norman's year in professional golf. Even Norman might not believe that. He did nearly everything except what matters most and what he wants most, to win major championships. Yet in comparing the records, especially the major championships and the Sony Ranking, no one achieved more than Norman on a worldwide basis.

Norman came within a whisker of winning both the Masters and the British Open, and tied Nick Faldo for the lowest cumulative score in the major championships. He won five tournaments (again tied with Faldo, and second only to Masashi (Jumbo) Ozaki's seven wins in Japan): Australian Masters, Australian TPC, Chunichi Crowns in Japan, and The International and Greater Milwaukee Open in the United States, and won the Vardon Trophy for low scoring average.

He won $1,351,761 worldwide, his best-ever earnings year and the third best in the world for 1989. According to the Sony Ranking, there was no contest, anyway you figured it. Norman was the best in the three-year period on which the system is based, and the best for this past year alone.

Here's what others did that Norman might wish he had:

—Faldo completed one of the greatest comebacks in Masters Tournament history after starting the last round in ninth place. He shot 65 with nine birdies, and won on the second playoff hole with a 25-foot birdie putt, after Scott Hoch missed a two-foot downhill putt to win on the first extra hole.

—Curtis Strange became the first golfer since Ben Hogan in 1950-51 to win back-to-back U.S. Opens, shooting 64 in the second round to put himself in position, then enduring a stretch of 35 holes without a birdie—including 15 straight pars on the final day while others were making mistakes—and nailing an 18-foot birdie putt on No. 16 to secure his gutsy triumph.

—Mark Calcavecchia, who on the 12th hole hit a chip shot too thin, but the ball hit midway up the flagstick and fell into the hole for a birdie, scored another two astonishing birdies on the 18th hole to win the British Open. The first was in regulation with an eight-iron shot to three feet, and the second in a four-hole playoff after he drove into the rough then hit the best shot of his life, and of the year in professional golf, a five iron to within six feet of the hole.

—Payne Stewart birdied four of the last five holes—including putts of 18 feet at No. 16 and 12 feet at No. 18—for 67, then was in position to benefit from Mike Reid's mistakes and win the PGA Championship. Reid bogeyed No. 16, double-bogeyed No. 17 and missed a seven-foot birdie try on the final hole.

—Tom Kite hit a four iron into the water on No. 18 at Bay Hill, but survived that double bogey because his closest challenger, Davis Love III, also double-bogeyed there, and Kite won The Nestle Invitational. The next week, Kite won The Players Championship then overcame the greatest disappointment of his career—78 in the final round when he was leading the U.S. Open—to win the Nabisco Championship, set a PGA Tour money record and become U.S. Player of the Year.

But Norman was simply the best golfer in the world while, as Jaime Diaz wrote in *Golf Digest*, the golf cognoscenti took "to bashing Norman nearly as hard as the Queenslander can crack a 350-yard drive." It's been said that Norman is over-rated, too aggressive, doesn't have the short game, cannot think on the course, puts too much pressure on himself, and has done less with more talent than anyone in his era. Earlier, that same magazine (different writer) included this line about the man who has won 59 tournaments worldwide in his career: "Greg Norman doesn't know how to play golf."

That obviously was a ridiculous statement. What Norman has not done is live up to other people's, and probably his own, expectations. Every time Norman gets into position to win a major championship, and then does not, the criticism becomes harsher, and even from some other players.

He was one stroke out of the Masters playoff between Faldo and Hoch, after a bogey on the final hole. He came from nowhere in the last round of the British Open, shot 64 to earn a playoff berth along with Calcavecchia and Wayne Grady, then birdied the first two holes in the four-hole playoff— that's 10 under par for 20 holes—and again did not finish the job. He chipped 12 feet past the hole for a bogey on the next hole, hit an extraordinarily long drive into a bunker at No. 18, then lost to Calcavecchia's epic five-iron shot for birdie.

Of course, it was not the first time Norman had been the victim of someone else's incredible play. Bob Tway holed a bunker shot in the 1986 PGA Championship, and Larry Mize holed a 140-foot chip in the 1987 Masters. Greg could use a bit of luck. He has been second in majors five times, three times in playoffs and once in regulation by a single stroke. Tom Watson, who has experience of such things, says "I think Greg is just snakebit. There is nothing wrong with his game. It's just that you can't win without luck. I know Tom Watson has had more than his share of luck in his career. Greg hasn't. And there is no rule that says it will even out in the end."

Norman has held up remarkably well to the bad luck, disappointment and criticism. "I would miss that stuff if I didn't hear it," he says. "It's a credit to my ability that there is so much focus on what I do." But Greg turned 35 years of age in February, 1990, and had only the 1986 British Open on his major championship record. While it's true Ben Hogan did not win his first major until age 34, Jack Nicklaus had 14 by then. Arnold Palmer won his last at 34, and Watson, his last at 33. Norman, however, did not begin playing golf until late, age 17, and considers his "golf age" more like 28. He is looking to the next decade for his greatest success. "I look at the 1980s as a complete learning experience, and the learning curve was very high," he says. "I feel like I've just turned the front nine and shot about 33. I'm looking to shoot 31 or 30 on the back nine. All I see for the 1990s is my best golf."

A development in 1989 that will impact the game in 1990 and beyond were the lawsuits brought by Karsten Manufacturing Co. against the United States Golf Association, Royal and Ancient Golf Club of St. Andrews, and the U.S. PGA Tour. The USGA and R&A had banned Karsten's U-grooved Ping Eye-2 irons effective January 1, 1990, for its competitions and effective January 1, 1996, for the general public. Karsten sued for $100 million. The PGA Tour banned not only the Ping Eye-2, but all U-grooved irons—actually the rule required the use of traditional V-grooved irons—and again Karsten sued, joined this time by nine golfers, but significantly not either Calcavecchia or Tim Simpson, a two-event winner in 1989, who also endorse the irons. As of this writing, Karsten had obtained a temporary injunction to prevent the ban from taking effect.

These lawsuits place the game at great risk. Can the USGA and the R&A continue to write and interpret the Rules of Golf? If not, then will any organization ever again have that right? Can the PGA Tour establish the rules for that circuit? "The PGA Tour, as a rule-making sanctioning body, must be able to set standards," said commissioner Deane Beman. "Should a manufacturer be able to make those decisions? I don't see how that can work."

Without going into technical detail, the U-grooved irons provide more backspin and control over shots, especially when used by skilled professionals and particularly shots out of high grass. "I tested the clubs for the USGA in 1986," Norman said. "I hit 300 balls and didn't hit one flier. No one will ever convince me they don't make a big difference." Many others including Calcavecchia, who endorses the Ping Eye-2 irons, say the same thing. "My wedge is my savior," Calcavecchia said. "I probably use it 90 percent of the time when I miss a green."

Beman says, "This is just the beginning. We have to protect the integrity of golf. There are, no doubt, many devices and innovations that can affect the basic skills of the game. When you change that, we think that's wrong. We believe a player should have to develop a skill to play a shot, not pull it off because of something he bought in a pro shop."

The Karsten lawsuits were not unexpected, nor was another challenge presented to the PGA Tour for the 1990s, with the announcement in early January that RJR Nabisco was severing most of its ties with the circuit after 1990. It involved a commitment of $6 million annually—the $2.5 million Nabisco Championship, $1 million individual bonus program, $2 million team charity program and sponsorship of the statistical program. There was a large settlement because a long-term deal, reportedly for 10 years, had been signed in the autumn of 1985. There apparently was a change of corporate philosophy after RJR Nabisco was taken over by Kohlberg Kravis Roberts and Co. in 1988.

"This is a business and marketing decision," said T. Wayne Robertson, senior vice president for sports marketing for RJR Nabisco. "We concluded that although our golf sponsorship was good for our companies, the programs had grown so rapidly in the last couple of years they received a disproportionate share of Nabisco's marketing dollars. Therefore, it was necessary to shift some of those funds to other areas."

RJR Nabisco's sponsorship of electronic scoreboards on the PGA Tour was to be continued beyond 1990, as would the corporation's entire involvement with the Senior PGA Tour, which included the $1.5 million Vantage Championship, $750,000 individual bonus program, $750,000 team charity program, $1 million Vantage Classic program for players over age 60, and presenting sponsorship of tournaments in Lexington, Kentucky, and San Antonio, Texas.

In his report to PGA Tour members and sponsors, Beman said that RJR Nabisco's decision was expected "to have very little impact on the continuation" of the programs. "With the substantial income derived from the contract settlement, the Tour will have sufficient revenues to continue most of the programs on its own for several years, with or without an alternate corporate partner to replace Nabisco. Substitute commercial sponsorship is an option that we will review over the next couple of years, but the Tour will definitely continue some or all of these programs in some form.

"While the final determination of exact makeup of the programs will ultimately be subject to Tournament Policy Board approval, we would certainly anticipate a continuation of such components as the team charity competition, the official statistics program, and the season-ending championship (currently the Nabisco Championship). In summary, we view this new arrangement in a very positive light, and we are committed to continuing on a long-term basis the components of the Nabisco relationship which have become so popular over the past several years."

Meanwhile, the PGA Tour was expanding in 1990, with the introduction of the Ben Hogan Tour, a $3 million circuit consisting of 30 events to serve as a minor league to give young players an opportunity to develop their games, sponsored by the Ben Hogan equipment company.

1989 World Money List

David Frost led the 1989 World Money List with $1,650,230, including the $1,000,000 first prize from the Million Dollar Challenge in Sun City, Bophuthatswana. The record is $1,793,268 won in 1987 by Ian Woosnam, who was also a winner of the Million Dollar Challenge that year. A total of seven players won more than $1,000,000 in 1989, not including the Nabisco, Volvo and other such bonus, appearance and endorsement awards. This brought to 16 the number of golfers to have won $1,000,000 or more in prize money in one year, Greg Norman having been the first in 1986. Norman and Curtis Strange are the only golfers to have done it twice. The complete World Money List appears in the Appendixes of this annual.

The leading money winners of 1989 were:

Pos.	Name	Money	Pos.	Name	Money
1.	David Frost	$1,650,230	11.	Nick Faldo	945,679
2.	Tom Kite	1,491,164	12.	Masashi Ozaki	867,649
3.	Greg Norman	1,351,761	13.	Jose-Maria Olazabal	865,236
4.	Payne Stewart	1,283,515	14.	Fred Couples	793,983
5.	Mark Calcavecchia	1,258,946	15.	Wayne Grady	777,548
6.	Curtis Strange	1,176,443	16.	Bob Charles	767,253
7.	Paul Azinger	1,046,915	17.	Steve Jones	766,534
8.	Scott Hoch	990,548	18.	Mark O'Meara	744,654
9.	Chip Beck	984,417	19.	Orville Moody	718,235
10.	Tim Simpson	975,597	20.	Ronan Rafferty	713,730

The Ryder Cup was hailed as the golf event of the year, or even of the decade, with an astonishing 12 matches concluding the event, between heroes and tragedians with all the tension of a major championship. No tournament in the year was more eagerly anticipated, and this one delivered all anyone could have expected. It was tremendous theater, and so typical of professional golf in the 1980s. The notion was reasserted that too many Americans don't know how to win anymore, as Stewart, Calcavecchia, Fred Couples and Ken Green lost after all had been even on the 18th tee of the final-day singles. The American winners that day were Paul Azinger, Chip Beck and then a parade of old soldiers: Kite, Watson, Mark McCumber, Lanny Wadkins and finally Strange, birdieing the last four holes to prevent the loss and secure the tie, 14 to 14, even though Europe, as the Ryder Cup holder, retained the cup.

The Europeans were not without their regrets. Two of their major champions, Seve Ballesteros and Faldo, also slashed shots into the water on the 18th. Saving the Ryder Cup for Europe were such unlikely heroes as Jose-Maria Canizares, who had the clinching victory over Green, and perhaps most of all, Christy O'Connor, Jr., who delivered one of the biggest strokes of the last day, a two iron that covered 229 yards and settled gently scant feet from the cup at No. 18. Captain Tony Jacklin had told O'Connor, "Get to the green in two, and something will happen." It did—Couples shanked a nine iron, missing the green, and his chip was six feet short. He missed the putt, and O'Connor raised his hands to the sky, overwhelmed. He was swarmed by his teammates and buried his tearful face in Jacklin's shoulder. "This has got to be the greatest and most emotional moment of my whole life," O'Connor said.

It marked the voluntary end of Jacklin's tenure as European captain after four Ryder Cup encounters, an era of unprecedented success in which Europe won in 1985 at The Belfry and again in 1987 in the United States, the first-ever American loss on home soil. The European leaders were the Spaniards, young Jose-Maria Olazabal with a 4-0-1 record and Ballesteros (3-1-1), the inspirational leader, as well. For captain Raymond Floyd's American team, Beck (3-0-1) and Azinger (3-1-0) supplied the most points, including Azinger's 1-up defeat of Ballesteros on the final day, which was the first of those 12 spell-binding duels.

The real winner was golf. You heard that over and over, at the presentation ceremony, in press interviews and in conversations among the spectators at The Belfry in Sutton Coldfield, near Birmingham, England. And in a literal sense it was true: The Ryder Cup has become an occasion of major significance, and golf is the better for it, but how important can it be when so few in America care about it, outside of the players, officials and some press people?

Perhaps the Ryder Cup will become a more popular event, as it deserves to be, but I doubt that it will before the next playing in 1991 at Kiawah Island, South Carolina, on a course that is only now under construction. It will again be held in the autumn, and even if American enthusiasm were to multiply, that would not be apparent because of the overriding interest in football at that time of year.

The Ryder Cup in America can hardly fare better than it did in 1987 at Muirfield Village Golf Club in Columbus, Ohio, home of the enormously successful Memorial Tournament and a city hungry for sports attractions, having only that golf tournament and Ohio State University games. Around 20,000 tickets and 15 hospitality tents were sold, but the television ratings were 1.5 on Saturday and 2.1 on Sunday, versus 14 ratings for football on those days.

The noted American columnist Dan Jenkins says the 1989 Ryder Cup was not shown on network television—it was on the minor USA cable system instead—because American television executives are lazy and stupid. I would not disagree entirely with that assessment but remember, Dan, it would not have been on network television in 1987 had Muirfield Village not sold the advertisement time. In light of the previous ratings, who would have taken that risk in England?

Financially, it's a different matter on the other side of the Atlantic. At The Belfry, there were 27,000 tickets and over 200 hospitality marquees sold, and estimates of the gross revenues were $5 million or more. Even there, because of the money, the Ryder Cup is in danger of being ripped apart in a dispute between the British PGA and the PGA European Tour over sharing the income. John Lindsey, executive director of the British PGA, says "This decade has seen a transformation in the situation. We are now very, very successful, but it was a different animal 10 years ago. Our success has brought about our problems."

Ballesteros offers this opinion: "The profit from the Ryder Cup should not go just to the British PGA. It should be used to help golf in Spain, France and even Switzerland. Lots of things need to be changed about the Ryder Cup, and where the money goes is one of them." Besides that, Ballesteros does not want the Ryder Cup to be held in Britain every fourth year, as it always has been. He wants Spanish courses added to the rota, and suggests that if not, he might not play. Lindsey contends that if the Ryder Cup left Britain, Ireland would have a better claim, and if it were then held in Spain, it would not return to Britain until 2001. "I'm not at all sure that would be acceptable," Lindsey said.

Some have suggested that the Ryder Cup be held every year. "I think that would be regarded as overkill," Lindsey said. "I didn't notice anyone asking for an annual Ryder Cup when we were losing for 28 years in succession."

There are nine non-Americans in the following Sony Ranking list, and only two, Norman and Frost, will be members of the 1990 U.S. PGA Tour. (Another prominent non-American, former Masters and British Open champion Sandy Lyle, who is No. 14 on the overall Sony Ranking, will also be on the American circuit.) But Faldo and Langer have decided to join Ballesteros, the fourth of Europe's major championship winners, in declining membership. This means that they may play only eight events in America: five PGA Tour events with sponsor exemptions and the Masters, U.S. Open and PGA Championship, which are independent of the tour. One can assume that Olazabal, Woosnam, Ozaki and Rafferty, just four among many capable players, are discouraged from even trying the U.S. tour for the same reasons that the others found it unacceptable.

In order to be a member, a golfer must play 15 tournaments in America each year, and some overseas players, especially those with young and growing families, such as Faldo and Langer, found that commitment was too

1989 Sony Ranking Points

The Sony Ranking, the universally accepted ranking system for professional golf, is based upon a three-year "rolling" average. While the results of one year alone are not considered sufficient data for the Sony Ranking, a review of the points earned and averages for any single year is useful in determining the relative performances of various golfers.

The leaders in Sony Ranking points earned in 1989 were:

Pos.	Name	Total Points	Average Points	Pos.	Name	Total Points	Average Points
1.	Greg Norman	844	33.76	11.	Seve Ballesteros	452	18.08
2.	Payne Stewart	816	30.22	12.	Masashi Ozaki	504	18.00
3.	Nick Faldo	832	28.69	13.	Mark McCumber	356	16.95
4.	Tom Kite	656	27.33	14.	Fred Couples	488	16.27
5.	Curtis Strange	656	26.24	15.	Bernhard Langer	440	15.71
6.	Mark Calcavecchia	744	24.80	16.	Ronan Rafferty	492	15.38
7.	Jose-Maria Olazabal	592	23.68	17.	David Frost	436	14.53
8.	Ian Woosnam	548	21.08	18.	Steve Jones	404	13.93
9.	Paul Azinger	496	19.08	19.	Tim Simpson	428	13.81
9.	Chip Beck	496	19.08	20.	Larry Mize	356	12.71

much. They asked that the minimum be reduced to 12 tournaments. In a series of meetings over the year, one suggestion which the PGA Tour put forth was that nine of the tournaments be of the player's choice and the other three assigned, to bolster weaker tournaments. This was declined, because those other three tournaments would surely have been in the autumn, the time of many significant international events.

"The U.S. tour is a tough tour that advances your game, but you can't do both (U.S. and European) tours," Faldo said. "I tried to play both tours since 1981, and it can't be done. The time has come to concentrate and build a schedule around the majors. But we (Europeans) won't be able to have the build-up to the majors like a Curtis Strange, so it's got to hurt us."

It must be noted that the opposition to a more reasonable change for the non-American players came not from the top level but from the rank-and-file of the PGA Tour. "The top-level players on the U.S. tour were for us," Faldo said, "but the middle and lower levels are much more numerous and that is where the opposition comes from." It's unfortunate that, in an instance such as this, the majority rules to the detriment of golf, for they are jeopardizing the appeal and the stature of the PGA Tour. Once a player wins a major championship, he should be entitled to special privileges, and the more majors won, the more privileges, but the majority will never see it that way. "There's a simple solution," Norman says. "Increase their sponsor exemptions to 10."

Beman says the absence of these stars is "no big deal," but it's doubtful that tournament sponsors or television audiences would see it that way. The irony of the situation is that because the world's best golfers will now have fewer opportunities to all compete in the same tournaments, those in which they do compete—the four major championships, which the PGA Tour does not control—will be even more important.

Jose-Maria Olazabal said of Seve Ballesteros during the Ryder Cup, "When Seve gets his Porsche going, not even San Pedro in heaven could stop him."

Unfortunately for Ballesteros, he stalled in the Masters and never really got going again. Even though he won three times on the PGA European Tour—Cespa Madrid Open, Epson Match Play Championship and Ebel European Masters-Swiss Open—Ballesteros was not a threat again in the majors except briefly in the PGA Championship, and was 11th in Sony Ranking points earned for the year, falling from first to third place. He won $541,300 and was 38th on the World Money List and, despite the off-year, took over No. 1 on the Career World Money List with $6,573,553.

On Saturday at the Masters, Ballesteros was paired with then-leader Ben Crenshaw, his game was falling apart as darkness fell after a rainstorm, before play was suspended for the day. He snap-hooked a drive into the trees on No. 13 and made bogey-six. "The hot blood went through, you know?" Ballesteros said later of that hole. By Sunday morning, the Augusta National course was left defenseless, because there was no wind and the lightning-fast greens had been slowed by the heavy rains.

Ballesteros made the first move of the day. He birdied three of the last five holes in the delayed third round to get back into the tournament, and was tied for fourth place, three strokes behind Crenshaw. He bolted into the lead in the fourth round that afternoon, birdieing four of the first five holes en route to a first-nine 31. Alas, Seve bogeyed No. 10, did not birdie either of the par-five holes, Nos. 13 or 15, and lost hope of his third Masters title when he double-bogeyed No. 16 after his six-iron shot missed the green and rolled into the water. He placed fifth with 69, two strokes out of the playoff.

That was by far Ballesteros' best showing in the major championships. He tied for 43rd in the U.S. Open, tied for 77th in the British Open and tied for 12th in the PGA Championship. Could it be that Ballesteros loses interest, that he quits when winning is out of his grasp, at times when other players such as Strange and Norman would be clawing for birdies? Take the British Open, where Ballesteros was the defending champion. His scores were 72-73-76-78, and he shared 77th place with an amateur from Sweden. Langer, another of the world's best, was playing so badly that he finished 83-82 and was dead-last, but it seems to happen too often to Seve.

Only Lyle lost more Sony Ranking points than Ballesteros, falling from third to 14th, while Faldo succeeded Lyle as Masters champion, with one Brit passing the green jacket to another, and climbed from fourth to second. It's hard to write about Faldo or Lyle without mentioning the other. Sarah Ballard wrote for *Sports Illustrated* the best golf article of the year, and these were her closing paragraphs:

"So it went, measuring one another and being measured, always against each other. Faldo was first to win in the U.S., but Lyle was first to win the British Open. Then Faldo won the British, but Lyle won the Masters. Then Faldo won the Masters . . .

"As inseparable in their time as Hogan and Snead or Nicklaus and Palmer were in theirs, Faldo and Lyle are like a pair of old vaudevillians. They feed each other lines and then, with a deft bit of business, like a seven-iron shot from a fairway bunker or a 25-foot putt in approaching darkness, one steals the spotlight from the other, but the show goes on. Even in this new golden age of golf, when all the world's a stage and other stars shine equally bright, theirs will be an act to remember."

In that same article, Lyle said, "One year I'm up and the next year Nick is." While Faldo wasn't exactly down in 1988 (He lost a playoff in the U.S. Open, one of eight runner-up finishes, had the lowest total score in the major championships for the first of two successive years, and won two tournaments), Sandy was most definitely off-stride in 1989. He started the year well enough, with three top-three finishes in his first five tournaments, but lost his game while the tour was in Florida. From Bay Hill through the U.S. Open, a span of 11 tournaments, he made the 36-hole cut only twice. He later decided to forego a place on the Ryder Cup team, rather than risk hurting Europe's chances to win, but played much more respectably in his last several tournaments. His 1989 worldwide earnings were $514,346 for 41st place. No one was particularly concerned about Lyle, however. When he's playing at his worst, he's most dangerous, on the verge of more impressive victories.

Faldo won five times in 1989 as he rose to No. 2 in the world behind Norman. Never did it seem less likely that Faldo would do so than on Sunday morning at the Masters, when he completed the third round, losing two strokes to par. "I was really despondent about my putting. As soon as I finished I went to the locker room and got a new putter," Faldo said. "But then I thought, 'You're only five shots back. This is the hardest tournament in the world to win if you lead after three rounds.'"

Right off, Faldo knocked in a 50-foot birdie putt on the first hole, went out in 32, then bogeyed No. 11 but followed with more birdies on Nos. 13, 14, 16 and 17, the last two from 18 and 35 feet for his 65. He also holed that 25-footer in the playoff, and on Friday he had holed a 100-footer at No. 2. That was the longest putt in Masters history, according to historian Herbert Warren Wind, exceeding the 65-footer that Cary Middlecoff, the 1955 Masters winner, rolled in on the 13th green that year, also in the second round.

(Hoch's missed two-foot putt on the first playoff hole, which gave Faldo another chance, was possibly the shortest putt ever missed with a chance to win a major. Sam Snead missed from 30 inches to give the 1947 U.S. Open to Lew Worsham, and Doug Sanders missed from three and one-half feet to send the 1970 British Open into a playoff, which Jack Nicklaus won. Sure, Faldo was lucky, but if he had made any putts, he might have won the 1988 U.S. Open.)

After the Masters, Nick played four more events without contending then, with his American schedule complete except for the majors, he returned to Europe. His first event there was the Volvo PGA Championship at Wentworth, his home course. He led by one stroke while playing No. 17, and nearly threw the victory away, trying to fade a four-iron shot to the green. The ball crossed the out-of-bounds stakes, hit a tree and rebounded onto the course. He escaped with a two-stroke win over Woosnam and his record fourth PGA title. Faldo then won the Dunhill British Masters (succeeding Lyle again) and, after two weeks away for the U.S. and Canadian Opens, made it three straight in Europe by winning the Peugeot French Open.

Including his victory in the Volvo Masters at the end of 1988, Faldo had won four in succession there, but the string ended with his tie for 20th in the Bell's Scottish Open.

His fifth victory of the year, resulting in worldwide earnings of $945,679 for 12th place, was second in importance only to the Masters for Faldo. It was the Suntory World Match Play Championship, back at Wentworth, and he again beat Woosnam. The only time Faldo led in the 36-hole match was at the 36th hole, when he scored an eagle-three from 20 feet after Woosnam had already been given his birdie-four. His leap in delight and the crowd's mighty roar when the putt fell in was reminiscent of the Masters. To top it off, Faldo announced at the presentation that he was donating his £100,000 check—Europe's first six-figure first prize—to benefit sick children.

For the third time this year, Faldo had succeeded Lyle in winning a tournament. This one had special meaning. Several times before, they had gone head-to-head in the World Match Play, with Lyle inflicting some of Faldo's most painful defeats. There was Lyle's 2-and-1 win in the 1988 final, and their epic duel in a first-round match in 1982. Then, Faldo was six holes up after the first 18, but Lyle came back to win 2 and 1. Later Faldo said, "There are some defeats that take a long time to get over. That was one of them, because you begin to question your ability."

What a performance Faldo gave this time: He was 38 under par for 105 holes in his three matches, six better than Woosnam's 32 under par record in 1987, which was achieved in 141 holes and four matches. His 65.2 average per round was 1.5 strokes below the previous record. His 64 was two strokes better than any previous score in a final.

"It's been a long wait. I have been here 10 times but this has a place of its own," Faldo said. "It's match play and it has fantastic tradition. It's been won by all the greatest players, and joining them means everything. Cups, trophies, championships, they are what matter."

It would be easy to say that Curtis Strange did not have as good a year as he did in 1988, when he won the U.S. Open and four other tournaments. This year, Curtis won twice—the Open again and the Palm Meadows Cup in Australia—plus the unofficial RMCC Invitational with Mark O'Meara, which was part of his impressive autumn performance in team events. He won $1,176,443 for sixth place, $8,332 less than he won in 1988, when his total included a victory in the rich Nabisco Championship.

Arguably, Strange had as good or better a showing this year than last. In 1988, Curtis had six really good chances to win, and did so all but once. This year, he was a top-10 finisher 10 times and was third or better six times, including a tie for second in the PGA Championship. He advanced one place in the Sony Ranking to fourth, whereas he remained fifth despite those five victories in 1988. Not included in the Sony Ranking were his 1989 team events. After the Ryder Cup, in which he won his last-day singles match, Strange won the Dunhill Cup for the United States (with Kite and Calcavecchia), the Four Tours Championship (six-man American team) and the RMCC Invitational.

As Strange knows, however, his place in the game's history will be determined not by the number of titles won so much as the major titles. "It's not so much that I've done what Ben Hogan did, but it's what so many others haven't done. It feels fantastic," Strange said after securing those back-to-back U.S. Open titles at Oak Hill Country Club in Rochester, New York.

Strange tied Hogan's record from 1942 at Oak Hill with 64 in the second round, but played badly on Saturday and his three-over-par 73 left him in third place, three strokes behind Kite and two behind Scott Simpson, a former champion. Kite played the first four holes of the last round in one under par, then drove into a creek and made a triple-bogey seven. Two bogeys and two double bogeys followed, and Kite limped in with 78.

"When I saw the scoreboard I knew they were playing into my hands," Strange said. He continued to make pars, and finally got the birdie putt he needed on No. 16. Simpson and another challenger, Jumbo Ozaki, fell back and the eventual runners-up were Woosnam, Beck and Mark McCumber, as Strange could afford a bogey on the final hole for an even-par 70. "It was emotional last year," Curtis said, thinking back to dedicating that victory to his deceased father. "This year it's more a feeling of satisfaction, I guess, a feeling of accomplishment . . . I've put myself in position to do something in this game."

Before 1989, Mark Calcavecchia had won three tournaments in seven years on the PGA Tour and perhaps was best known as a proponent of the Ping Eye-2 irons, or as the fellow who placed second in the 1988 Masters after Lyle scored a birdie on the final hole from a fairway bunker. Calcavecchia gained a great deal more respect, and much less was heard about his U-grooved clubs, when he won the British Open and two other tournaments this year, totaling $1,258,946 in worldwide earnings for fifth place. He also was instrumental in the United States victory in the Dunhill Cup at St. Andrews, where he will try in 1990 to defend his British Open title.

Calcavecchia got the year off to a smashing start after fading while in contention at the Bob Hope Chrysler Classic. He came back with a seven-stroke victory the next week in the Phoenix Open and two weeks later he won the Nissan Los Angeles Open, which was especially pleasing because he had to beat Lyle there. He had four more top-10 finishes through June, but almost did not enter the British Open. His wife, Sheryl, was expecting their first child, but she insisted that he go to Troon, Scotland. "I have some good vibrations about you there," she said.

While Calcavecchia called her three times a day—and false contractions Friday and Saturday had him reaching for his plane tickets—he played rounds of 71, 68 and 68 to be in contention on the final day, starting in a tie for fourth place, three strokes behind Wayne Grady, with Watson and Stewart in between. One stroke behind, Watson was probably the sentimental favorite to win his sixth British Open and first since 1983, but Tom finished two strokes out after shooting 72, and Stewart finished with 74. Meanwhile, Norman blistered the course for 64, leaving Calcavecchia and Grady to try to keep the pace.

Grady needed four pars over the last four holes to win. He got only three, bogeying the 17th for his 71. Calcavecchia knocked the ball in from 50 feet on No. 11 to save par, then chipped-in on the fly at No. 12. "I've always said, 'When it's your time to win, you're going to win. You're picked,'" Mark said. When Calcavecchia was on the 18th tee, Norman was in his hotel room next to the 18th fairway, and said to his caddy, Bruce Edwards, "Here's the one. We've got a bullet to dodge." Calcavecchia needed a birdie, and got it with an eight-iron shot to three feet.

What followed was the first scheduled four-hole playoff in major championship history. Norman birdied the first hole, and Calcavecchia rolled in a 25-footer for birdie at No. 2. Norman matched that with a 20-foot birdie. Calcavecchia said that he thought to himself, "If he doesn't deserve to win, then who does?" But Norman chipped too strongly on the par-three 17th and bogeyed, while Calcavecchia got his par. They were tied and Grady, incidentally, was by then two strokes behind and out of it.

On the 18th, Calcavecchia hit an awful drive into the crowd on the right. Then Norman hit his drive into a seemingly-unreachable bunker, 325 yards from the tee. Calcavecchia followed with that perfect five-iron shot to six feet. "I just stood there watching it," Mark recalled. "And I said, 'I don't care where it ends up, because that's the best shot I've ever hit.'" Norman went from bunker to bunker to out of bounds, and Calcavecchia had three putts from six feet to win the British Open. He only needed one putt, a birdie. "I'm getting home as quick as I can," he said. The baby, a girl they named Britney Jo, arrived a few weeks later.

Like Calcavecchia, Payne Stewart earned more respect in 1989, and not just because he won the PGA Championship over a faltering Mike Reid. Stewart, who like Calcavecchia had previously won three times in seven years on the PGA Tour, had an excellent year and made the biggest gain of anyone in the Sony Ranking, from 19th to fifth place. He won twice—his other win was a wire-to-wire, 16-under-par triumph in the MCI Heritage Classic—was second three times, third twice and had a total of 11 finishes in the top 10. He was third behind Norman and Faldo in major championship scoring, and was a contender in the British Open until that final-round 74 dropped him to a tie for eighth place. He was fourth on the World Money List with $1,283,515.

During the year, Stewart undertook a conditioning and weight-loss program after experiencing back pains, which began when the tour was in Los Angeles. Age 32, Payne reduced his weight from 190 to 175 pounds, among other ways by cutting his beer consumption. "I realized if I wanted to continue my career, enjoy the success I was having, I would have to start exercising, watching my weight and taking better care of myself," Stewart said. "Now I have an exercise program that's part of my everyday life. I'm making the effort and seeing the results."

Stewart won the PGA Championship at Kemper Lakes, near Chicago, despite starting with 74. He had subsequent rounds of 66 and 69, then played the first nine on Sunday in 36.

He was playing three groups ahead of Reid and trailed the leader by five strokes. ABC commentator Jerry Pate was following Stewart's threesome, and Stewart told Pate if he could shoot a five-under 31 on the back nine, he might still win.

That's exactly what Payne did. He parred No. 10, sank a 12-foot birdie putt on No. 11, and saved par on Nos. 12 and 13 after missing the greens. Then Stewart caught fire, birdieing four of the last five holes. Dressed in the orange and dark blue of the Chicago Bears—under an endorsement deal with the National Football League, he wears the colors of NFL teams—Stewart chipped in from just off the green on No. 14, hit a nine iron to within two feet of the flagstick on No. 15, sank an 18-footer on No. 16, the most difficult hole on the course, and capped his magnificent rally by holing a 12-footer on No. 18.

In the process, Stewart passed eight players, but he didn't catch the leader. When Stewart completed play, Reid was two strokes ahead with three holes to play. "The last nine holes of a major, some really strange things happen," Stewart said later. "I just stood in that tent and said a little prayer."

Reid met misfortune for the second time in the majors this year. He led the Masters with six holes remaining, but wound up in sixth place. In the PGA Championship, his opening-round 66 shared the lead with Leonard Thompson, then he held the lead outright after the second and third days with scores of 67 and 70, heading into the final day's play with a margin of three strokes over second-place Dave Rummells and six strokes over Stewart, who was in 10th place.

About the same time that Stewart was finishing with a birdie, Reid found a water hazard for the first time all week. The 35-year-old Reid, nicknamed "Radar" because of his accuracy, drove into the water off the 16th tee, but sank a 10-foot putt for a bogey, and needed two pars for only the third victory of his career. He fluffed a chip shot on the 17th, however, then three-putted for the first time in the tournament. After that double bogey, Reid needed to birdie the 18th to tie Stewart, but he pushed a seven-foot putt left of the cup and finished second with 74. "Where can you go around here to have a good cry?" Reid asked when he began his press-room interview. Moments later, he found the place.

The PGA Championship will also be remembered for Arnold Palmer's charge, a month before his 60th birthday. In the opening round, Palmer reeled off five straight birdies and was tied for the lead at six under par after 16 holes. He bogeyed the last two holes for 68, but even that was the lowest score he had shot in the PGA—the only major championship he never won— since 1968. Palmer finished at five over par, tied for 63rd place, but he infused the tournament with more excitement than anyone else.

In his 17-year career, Tom Kite had probably experienced no greater highs or lows than he did this past year. He had won 10 tournaments, but only once had he won two in the same year. He had won tournaments every year for seven years until being shut out in 1988. Kite won successive titles early in 1989, The Nestle Invitational and The Players Championship, only to endure a gut-wrenching 78, his worst round in longer than he could remember, to lose the U.S. Open.

Then, in a playoff against Stewart with all the year-end honors at stake, Kite won the Nabisco Championship for his third title of the year. He got a first-prize check of $450,000 plus a Nabisco bonus of $175,000 (not included in the World Money List in this annual) for being the leading money-winner for a total of $1,395,278, a record for the American tour. His World Money List total was $1,491,164 for second place behind David Frost. He also went to top of the U.S. career money list ahead of Nicklaus and Watson with $5,600,691. "It's a distorted statistic," Kite acknowledged. "I would be foolish to say this makes me a better player than Jack or Tom."

Along with those spoils also went Player of the Year recognition, honors which Stewart could also have gained with a victory. He started the final round as if he would, over the same Harbour Town course at Hilton Head Island, South Carolina, where he earlier won the Heritage. Payne birdied the first five holes to overtake previous leader Wayne Levi and was out in 29 strokes for a three-shot margin over Kite, Levi and Donnie Hammond. Stewart's three-putt bogey on No. 18 reduced his lead to one stroke and opened the door for Kite, who was then playing the 17th. In a fierce wind, Kite struck a perfect seven-iron shot three feet past the hole for a birdie to tie Stewart. Pars from there on were all Kite needed, as Stewart bogeyed the second extra hole.

"Does this make up for my fiasco at Oak Hill?" Kite asked afterward. "No, nothing will ever change the fact I had such a poor round at the U.S. Open. But I'm sure a lot of people thought that would end my victories on the PGA Tour, and that I wouldn't be able to come back and play well. I knew better. And now everybody knows."

Sheepishly, Stewart added, "Ain't life a bitch? I'm complaining and I just made two hundred and something thousand dollars."

Others who won more than once on the American tour were Steve Jones, with three victories, and Blaine McCallister and Tim Simpson, with two each. All three were among the major gainers in the Sony Ranking. Jones advanced from 76th to 28th place, Simpson from 113th to 35th place, and McCallister from 161st to 45th place.

Although Jones first qualified for the tour in 1982, he had only one previous victory, at Pebble Beach in 1988. He suffered a thumb injury during his first year, and didn't requalify until 1985. He was eighth on the official money list with $745,578, nearly three times his previous best. "I guess I'm the type who has to have things sink in gradually," said Jones, who at 6-foot-4 was an all-state basketball player in high school, but focused on golf once he entered the University of Colorado. "I wasn't a good junior player right away, I wasn't a good college player right away, and it's taken me a while on the tour."

It didn't take Jones long in 1989. He won the first two tournaments of the year, the MONY Tournament of Champions and Bob Hope Chrysler Classic, and later won the Canadian Open. Simpson was just ahead of Jones on the money list with $761,597 with his victories in the USF&G Classic and Walt Disney World/Oldsmobile Classic, along with two seconds and a third-place finish. McCallister won the Honda Classic and Bank of Boston Classic, but also missed the 36-hole cut 11 times while earning $523,891.

Other winners of special note included Paul Azinger, who was third on the money list behind Kite and Stewart with $951,649 and won the Canon-Greater Hartford Open, placed second twice and third four times; Scott Hoch, who came back from his Masters disappointment to win the Las Vegas Invitational (donating $100,000 from that purse to the Arnold Palmer Children's Hospital), and also performed well in both the U.S. Open and PGA Championship; Mark O'Meara, who won the AT&T Pebble Beach Pro-Am for the second time in his career, and Mark McCumber, winner of the Beatrice Western Open just two weeks after he made such a fine effort and came away one stroke short in the U.S. Open.

The year's results confirmed the axiom that professional golfers "drive for show and putt for dough." The leader of the putting statistics was Jones, while the leader in driving distance, Ed Humenik, finished 168th on the money list and lost his playing card. The top five in driving distance won a total of $517,623, which was less than Kite received in the Nabisco

Championship. "Guys come out here and think they have to bust it 300 yards to win," Azinger said. "All you have to do is look at players like Strange and Kite. Accuracy is the name of the game, not distance."

The Byrum brothers (Curt and Tom) became the first brothers to win events in the same year on the U.S. tour since the Hills (Dave and Mike) each claimed victories in the 1972 season. Donnie Hammond's 258 total in the Texas Open was one stroke off the all-time record of 257 by Mike Souchak in the 1955 Texas Open. It was a good year for the Australians as Norman, Grady and Ian Baker-Finch all claimed victories, as did South Africa's David Frost. Gene Sauers, age 26, was the youngest winner of the year and Leonard Thompson, age 42, was the oldest. Thompson went 12 years between victories, a record.

Wrapping up the American circuit, two non-winners who should not be overlooked are Andy Bean, a joint runner-up in the PGA Championship, and Chip Beck, a joint runner-up in the U.S. Open for the second time, as well as second in the Phoenix Open and The Players Championship. After the Masters got away from Ben Crenshaw, he didn't win either, nor did such notables as Hal Sutton, Craig Stadler, Bruce Lietzke, Larry Mize, Tom Watson, Lanny Wadkins, Fuzzy Zoeller and Larry Nelson. Mize and Nelson did win in Japan, and Peter Jacobsen narrowly dodged that list by winning the late-season unofficial Kapalua International.

There were a couple of new stars, Ronan Rafferty and Craig Parry, emerging on the PGA European Tour while Jose-Maria Olazabal continued to develop his game at age 23, advancing from 15th to seventh in the Sony Ranking. Rafferty climbed from 57th to 21st, and Parry, from 65th to 29th.

In addition to being unbeaten in the Ryder Cup, Olazabal had three victories in the Tenerife Open, KLM Open and in Japan's Visa Taiheiyo Club Masters, and was second four times. He has seven career victories in seven countries since turning professional for the 1986 season. He was No. 2 (behind Rafferty) on the European money list with £336,239 and 13th on the World Money List with $865,236. There is little doubt Olazabal has the potential to be a world-class star, and the Spaniard fared well in his first American ventures, having an eighth-place finish in the Masters and a tie for ninth in the U.S. Open. In other majors, Jose-Maria was tied for 23rd in the British Open and missed the cut in the PGA Championship.

While leading the European money list with £400,311, and placing 20th worldwide with $713,730, Rafferty won three times in the Lancia Italian Open, Scandinavian Enterprise Open and the season-ending Volvo Masters. Those were Rafferty's first European victories, although he had won four times previously, twice in Australia, once in New Zealand and once in Venezuela. It was in the Volvo Masters that Rafferty took the money title from Olazabal, winning by one stroke over Faldo with Olazabal in third place, five strokes behind. "There was so much at stake for me besides the money," said Rafferty, a 25-year-old Northern Irishman who has been on the European circuit since 1982. "There were invitations to the Masters, the U.S. Open and the PGA Championship. So far, I've played in only the British Open. And it means everything to a golfer to play in the majors."

Parry, at age 23, joined the ranks of Australia's successful international golfers with his victories in the Wang Four Stars National Pro-Celebrity and German Open, plus the Bridgestone Aso in Japan. He was third in Europe with £277,321 and 30th worldwide with $604,006. A native of Kardinya, Western Australia, Parry is a protege of Graham Marsh. After two Australian triumphs in 1987, he came to the European circuit and had five top-10 finishes his first year, including a runner-up place to Norman in the 1988 Italian Open. Like the other two young stars of the 1989 European season, Parry is anxious for his chance to play the majors. He played in none this past year.

Like them, Ian Woosnam wanted to prove himself in America in 1988, after he had won eight tournaments and led the World Money List the previous year. But Woosnam had a disappointing and somewhat embarrassing performance then, arriving with a lot of publicity and leaving with a string of missed cuts. He left no doubt of his ability this past year, coming within one stroke of the U.S. Open title, and placing sixth in the PGA Championship and 14th in the Masters. He tied Strange for the fourth best record overall in the majors.

Woosnam, who was sixth in Europe with £210,100 and 22nd worldwide with $679,489, held to a top-10 place in the Sony Ranking although dropping from sixth to ninth. He played his best golf in May and June, securing his only victory in the Carrolls Irish Open, in playoff over Irishman Philip Walton, just after he had lost a playoff to Parry in the Wang Four Stars. He also was second in the Volvo PGA Championship and tied for second in the Bell's Scottish Open.

Aside from the play of Ballesteros, Faldo and Lyle, previously mentioned, other notable results of the 1989 European season included two victories each by Mark James and Bernhard Langer. James won the Karl Litten Desert Classic, a new event which stretched the European circuit to Dubai, and the NM English Open, placing fifth on the money list with £245,916 (and $461,737 worldwide). He advanced from 48th to 37th on the Sony Ranking. Langer maintained his No. 16 ranking with victories in the Peugeot Spanish Open and German Masters, winning £205,194 for eighth place in Europe and $623,284 for 29th place worldwide. He had three top-10 finishes in America.

Finally, the European season was memorable for 10 first-time winners, including Rafferty and Parry, as well as Eduardo Romero of Argentina, who won the Lancome Trophy and followed countrymen Roberto De Vicenzo and Vicente Fernandez in excelling at this level of play, and Vijay Singh, the winner of the Volvo Open and the first Fiji Islander ever to win on the European circuit. Both made huge advances in the Sony Ranking, Romero rising from 281st to 53rd place, and Singh, from 271st to 87th. Romero earned $278,193 worldwide and Singh, $239,452. Both also won on other tours, Romero taking the Argentina Open, and Singh, three events in Africa. Singh, who scored his first-ever victory in the 1988 Nigerian Open, won that title again, along with the Zimbabwe Open and Ivory Coast Open.

Singh was, of course, the Safari Tour money leader. The two other events were won by newcomers, David Jones of Northern Ireland in the Kenya Open and Craig Maltman of Scotland in the Zambia Open. The Sunshine Tour in South Africa provided a mix bag, the old and the new, with victories by several young golfers as well as by familiar players such as Jeff Hawkes, who won twice; John Bland, Tony Johnstone, Fulton Allem and Hugh Biaocchi, who ended the decade with a victory, as he had started the 1980s.

As noted earlier, David Frost came home to win the Million Dollar Challenge by three strokes over Scott Hoch for his second triumph of the season and the World Money List title.

The early-year portion of the Australasian Tour was highlighted by the victories of two of the world's best players, Strange in the Daikyo Palm Meadows Cup followed by Norman in the Australian Masters and Tournament Players Championship. By year's end, however, there was another and unlikely hero, Peter Senior. The 30-year-old Senior, who had six Australian victories and eight overall in his career, romped to three wins in five weeks. He rose from 47th to 26th on the Sony Ranking for the year, and had earnings of $670,656 for 26th place on the World Money List.

The first win for Senior was the Australian PGA, where he avoided a playoff when Jim Benepe three-putted the 18th hole. Then, two weeks later, Senior cruised to a seven-stroke victory in the Australian Open and followed that with a five-stroke triumph in the Johnnie Walker Classic. Senior uses one of those extra-long putters popularized by U.S. Senior PGA Tour players, and that got much attention, but he has long been known as one of Australia's best iron players, and his driving was exceptionally straight during his streak. "I know how to win now and I want to win more consistently," said Senior, who was on the U.S. circuit in 1986, but lost his player's card. "This sequence of golf has given me confidence to play the quality of golf necessary to win major tournaments."

Other Australasian winners included overseas players Isao Aoki and Nick Price, and promising young Australians Brett Ogle and Brad King. The two New Zealand events were won by Don Bies, on leave from the U.S. Senior PGA Tour, and another young golfer, Greg Turner.

On the Asia/Japan Tour, the Ozaki brothers again dominated, remarkably holding the same final positions that they held in 1988. Masashi (Jumbo) Ozaki was No. 1 on the money list, Naomichi (Joe) Ozaki was No. 2 and Tateo (Jet) Ozaki was No. 7. Jumbo, the oldest of the brothers at 41, won seven tournaments, one more than he had last year, including the Japan Open, Japan PGA and Japan Match Play. Joe won once, but had six runner-up finishes, and Jet won twice. Their worldwide earnings were $867,649 for Jumbo, $665,057 for Joe and $395,795 for Jet.

Together, they have won 22 tournaments and $4,220,747 worldwide in the past two years. They were the first brother trio in the British Open since the Whitcombes in the 1930s, and Jumbo was a final-round contender in the U.S. Open before placing sixth, three strokes behind. Jumbo retained his No. 12 spot on the Sony Ranking, while Joe rose from 64th to 48th place, and Jet slipped from 68th to 84th.

Aoki, at age 47, returned to form with two victories to go along with his triumph in Australia, and won $571,623 worldwide, advancing three places to 34th on the Sony Ranking. Japan's only other golfer in the top 100, Tsuneyuki (Tommy) Nakajima, went from 36th to 66th place as he was winless for the year. He didn't fare well overseas, and missed several good opportunities for victories in Japan. He blew a four-stroke lead in the final round of the Japan Series, and earlier finished second three times in a month. His worldwide winnings were $375,562.

Elsewhere on the Asia/Japan circuit, three players—Akiyoshi (Aki) Omachi, Koichi Suzuki and Yoshikazu Yokoshima—had two victories each.

Six different Australians also had victories: Norman, Parry, Marsh, Terry Gale, Roger Mackay and Brian Jones. On the early-year Asia circuit, Brian Claar, who would later regain his player's card for the U.S. tour, won two events, and Americans Emlyn Aubrey and Jeff Maggert each won once. Lu Chien Soon won twice.

On the U.S. Senior PGA Tour, Bob Charles duplicated his great success of 1988. He won seven tournaments for the second straight year—five on that circuit plus the Volvo Seniors British Open and the Fuji Electric Grand Slam in Japan. His worldwide earnings were $767,253, bringing his two-year total to $1,545,382, not including seasonal bonus awards. Charles' primary rival was Orville Moody, whose two victories were the U.S. Senior Open and the Mazda Senior Tournament Players Championship. Moody was just behind Charles in worldwide earnings with $718,235.

Seven more seniors won two tournaments each and six more exceeded $500,000 in worldwide earnings. One of those, Don Bies, also had two other wins, one in South Africa and, as just noted, another in a regular tour event in New Zealand. The other two-time winners were Miller Barber, Gary Player, Jim Dent, Larry Mowry, Dave Hill and Bruce Crampton. Player, a six-time winner in 1988, earned his largest check ever, $202,500 from the RJR Championship, and Mowry won the PGA Senior Championship.

George Archer joined the circuit in October and won in his first start, he and Dent being among seven first-time winners. Lee Trevino reached age 50 in time for one 1989 tournament, but the great anticipation was for 1990 when Trevino and Jack Nicklaus, who would turn 50 in January, would both be on the $14 million tour.

Betsy King was the dominant player on the American LPGA circuit. She won six tournaments, including three of the most important—U.S. Women's Open, Nestle World Championship and McDonald's Championship—and had official earnings of $654,132, an LPGA record. This was by far the best year ever for the 34-year-old King, who was the LPGA's Player of the Year once before, in 1984. She had entered the season with 14 career victories and won nearly half as many again, and exceeded her best previous earnings year by nearly $200,000.

Her closest rival was another product of Furman University, Beth Daniel, who was a star from the outset of her career in 1979, but who had not added to her 14 career victories since 1985. Daniel was far behind on the money list, placing second with $504,851, but won four tournaments and matched King statistically with 20 finishes in the top 10 in 25 starts.

Besides King and Daniel, only Nancy Lopez and Juli Inkster won more than one tournament. Lopez won three times, including the Mazda LPGA Championship, and was third on the money list with $487,153. Inkster's two wins included the Nabisco Dinah Shore, and Tammie Green also had a major victory in the du Maurier Classic.

Worldwide, King was the money leader with $675,964, while Taiwan's Tu Ai Yu was second with $643,397. Marie-Laure de Lorenzi won three times on the European circuit and earned $124,166, which put her in 55th place. The major European event, the Weetabix Women's British Open, was won by an LPGA player, Jane Geddes. England's Laura Davies had one victory each on the LPGA and European tours.

This was Bill Blue's first year as commissioner, and the LPGA moved its headquarters from Houston, Texas, to Daytona Beach, Florida.

Before turning to the 1989 season in detail, we recall the passing of . . . Glenna Collett Vare, 85, six-time winner of the U.S. Women's Amateur, and runner-up to Joyce Wethered in the 1929 British Women's Amateur, one of the greatest golf tournaments ever . . . Claude Harmon, 73, winner of the 1948 Masters and longtime professional at Winged Foot Golf Club and Seminole Golf Club . . . William (Wild Bill) Melhorn, 90, a pioneer of the U.S. PGA Tour and winner of 47 tournaments . . . Tony Manero, 84, winner of the 1936 U.S. Open and seven other tournaments . . . Dick Mayer, 65, winner of the 1957 U.S. Open . . . Aubrey Bloomer, 91, the last survivor of the first British Ryder Cup team in 1927 . . . Jess Sweetser, former U.S. Amateur and British Amateur champion, and a member of the first U.S. Walker Cup team in 1922 . . . Jack Grout, 79, former professional at Scioto Country Club, where he taught the game to Jack Nicklaus . . . Herb Graffis, 95, a prominent writer, editor and publisher, and founder of the National Golf Foundation.

3. The Masters Tournament

Professional golfers begin thinking about the Masters Tournament in January at the Tournament of Champions, and as each week passes and Masters week looms, it becomes more and more a part of their thoughts and conversations.

They wouldn't miss being there for anything. Great theater must have its stars and its proper stage. What would Carnegie Hall be without a Leonard Bernstein or the Met without an Opera? Yankee Stadium is more than just a baseball park when New York is playing a World Series.

Augusta National Golf Club is that way, also. For 51 weeks each year, its hallowed grounds are closed off to all but club members. But come the first full week in April, its splendor bursts forth in azaleas and dogwood. And people. Only then does it come alive.

At the Masters.

Someone once said, "There are no bad Masters. Some are just better than others." Certainly the 1989 one was a classic. Yes, equal to Larry Mize's chip shot that beat Greg Norman on the second hole of sudden death in 1987; and yes, better than the one in 1988, where Sandy Lyle hit a wonderful seven-iron shot from the bunker at No. 18 on Sunday, then sank the birdie putt to break the heart of Mark Calcavecchia, who stood waiting for an expected playoff.

1989 had it all—Lee Trevino leading for two days, storms that delayed play in round three, Ben Crenshaw looking like a winner on Saturday and wearing the look of a loser late Sunday afternoon.

In the end, it had Nick Faldo as its champion, marking the first time in Masters history that foreigners had won back-to-back. It was no easy run. He had to fight back from being five down when the final round began and he had the agony of watching Scott Hoch line up a two-foot par putt on the first hole of the playoff, then the ecstasy as he missed.

Finally, in the gloaming, Faldo sank a 25-foot putt on No. 11, down in Amen Corner where so many previous championships have been decided. It could not have gone another hole. It was that dark.

When golf's best came to Augusta on Monday, it was with memories of 1988's hard and fast greens still very much in place. It was after the third round on Saturday a year earlier, after he had shot 66, that Fuzzy Zoeller leveled the most severe criticism of Augusta National's greens, calling them, among other things, "tricked up."

It took only one practice round this year, however, for players to see that it might be a different story. Yes, the greens were still fast, but not as firm. Shots were holding. Four-foot putts, while still dangerous and nerve-wracking, did not have to be lagged. Pitch-and-run shots did not run and run. The course wasn't losing the respect it had held. The fear, however, was gone.

"It's a different golf course this year," said Tom Kite, who for the umpteenth time came in as one of the favorites. "It shouldn't be a pansy and it isn't, but it's set up properly now. The greens are still fast and firm, but not hard. It's the kind of situation now where comes Saturday and Sunday, you'll have the opportunity to see some guy shoot a score and make a charge.

"The last couple of years here it was a battle not to lose it. In 1986, we had the most exciting Masters ever. The greens weren't hard then. The past two years have not been exciting."

What Kite foresaw was one of those old-fashioned Masters, complete with the crowd roars late in the tournament, the ones that start down in Amen Corner and roll up to the clubhouse as a fast finisher reels in the leaders.

"The course is perfect right now," said Hubert Green after Monday's practice round. "If they leave it like it is, it could be exciting. But I've been coming here too long and know better than that. The greens may be mowed to the same height they'll be all week. But tell me if you see them putting any water on them."

Kite came to the Masters in a no-nonsense mood and free of the pressure of having been so close in Masters past. He had won the Players Championship two weeks earlier and the Nestle Invitational the week before that. He felt he could win.

"Good players should play well anywhere, no matter the course," he said. "And I like to think I'm a good player. I've never been intimidated by this course. I just haven't won. I'm anticipating a good week. I feel good mentally and physically, and I've never come here playing as well as I am now. Whether that translates into winning, I can't say."

Pressure, however, was riding the backs of defending champion Lyle and Norman, who had finished second in two of the last three years. Lyle had missed the cut in three straight tournaments coming in and Norman's patience was beginning to wear thin with those in the media who were beginning to question if he was overrated.

Making the Masters even more stressful for Norman was the memory of 1987 when Mize stole the championship in a playoff. Earlier in the year, Norman admitted that Mize's chip at No. 11 ruined him for most of the next two years.

"I didn't realize how much that, added to the one at the PGA Championship the preceding year, depressed me until I bottomed out at the Nabisco last November," Norman said, referring to his last-place finish. "I had been in a two-year trough because of that."

On Monday, the media hoards descended on Norman as he spoke to British television. "It's Monday, guys. Don't start over-loading me on Monday. There's still two days of hype left."

On Tuesday, when asked by Australian television if the U.S. media was suffocating him, he said, "No matter how good you tell them you're playing, they say you're playing bad. The media does that here. They emphasize the bad instead of the good. Media always wants to put pressure on you that way."

On Wednesday, in front of mostly U.S. media, Norman said there were more expectations in Australia, where he is expected to win every week.

The rest of the field went about its merry way of preparing. There was no clear-cut favorite, not like in the late 1970s when Jack Nicklaus or Tom Watson or Gary Player held that place, or the early 1980s when Severiano Ballesteros became The Man. A pre-tournament poll of sportswriters showed 13 different players as the most likely to succeed.

One of Britain's leading bookmaking services had Ballesteros and Norman at 8-1, which came as no surprise, and Curtis Strange at 12-1. Lyle was no better than 14-1.

One prediction came from Tim Simpson, who admitted he had rather win one Masters than ten U.S. Opens. But he didn't like his chances.

"There aren't many guys here who have a chance because they (Masters officials) want certain people to win," Simpson said. "They make the greens firm and fast for the start of the tournament every year. They get the field where they want it and then they slow down the greens for Saturday and Sunday. Certain players putt fast greens very well. Jack (Nicklaus) grew up in Ohio on fast greens and he's a master at it. I know when Bobby Jones set up this golf course, he didn't design it to embarrass the greatest players in the world."

Masters chairman Hord Hardin had other concerns than those of Simpson. Escalating purses on the PGA Tour cast a gloom over his stewardship of the Masters. And he said so.

"We fear someone may look at our million dollar purse, or whatever it will become later, and come up with a two-million dollar event opposite us. Do you think the players would come here? We don't want to 'turn pro,' to go commercial. We don't want to get monies out of putting TV rights up for bidding or take on a corporate sponsor because we don't want to be dictated to."

Strange had heard it before and enough was enough. "I can't believe Mr. Hardin is really serious about this. He knows what he's got here, one of the best, and some say the best, tournaments in the world. No matter what could happen in the future, we'd all be pointing towards the Masters. When I practice in the early season, the Masters is on my mind. I'll be making a couple of shots and think, 'That will work at the 16th on Sunday,' and I've got to tell you, you never think that way about any other tournament. Because we come back to the same place, we can prepare in such a fashion. And we all look forward to coming back or coming for the first time. You hear guys say all the time after they win a tournament, 'That's great. It gets me in the Masters.' For some players, the season doesn't really start until Augusta."

The last order of business before Thursday's liftoff was the annual Par-Three contest. And in keeping with the 28-year tradition of this event—no player has ever won the Par-Three and gone on to win the Masters the same year—Bob Gilder won the little one and finished 37th in the big one.

First rounds at major championships hardly ever cause much excitement. This Masters was an exception. Only two men could have caused such a stir. Jack Nicklaus didn't. Trevino did.

Given the time, the place and the event, Trevino was one of the last players in the field expected to be the first on the leaderboard after the field of 85 had made one lap around Augusta National. Forget that at age 49 with his 67, he became the oldest player ever to lead the Masters. He's never been overly fond of the course, the tournament, or those who run it.

It was Trevino's best-ever round at the Masters and good enough for a one-stroke lead over Faldo's 68 and two over Hoch, who birdied the final hole for 69. At 70 were Andy Bean and Don Pooley. Only 10 players broke par and in with 71s were Crenshaw, Ballesteros, T.C. Chen, Jumbo Ozaki and Tom Purtzer.

For 20 years, Trevino and the Masters had been carrying on like feuding spouses. It was a marriage that had no chance, but somehow the two kept kissing and making up. Four times he refused to play. Two times he stated that his attitude toward the Masters had been the greatest mistake of his golf career. And in 1988, he missed the cut and said, "I hope to God they don't invite me back."

Trevino came back, playing on the final year of a five-year exemption earned from his 1984 PGA Championship, and he wasn't expected to make a ripple, at least not during the tournament.

But this was a more serious Trevino than the one who had trashed this course and tournament in both words and performance. Off the course, he changes his shoes in the parking lot, a sign of his personal boycott of the clubhouse. On the course, he has been known to go through the motions and had not broken 80 in three of his last four rounds.

"Well, I guess I'm the last guy you expected here today," Trevino said to a standing-room only crowd of media in the interview room. "But I'm here. That's the important thing."

For the first time in his Masters career, Trevino took a more scientific approach to the course. He didn't try to overpower it, one of his failings in the past. "I tried to place the ball in spots, which I've never done before," he said. "I've really never been here mentally, which is my fault. But that's what carried me today, not my swing."

That and some of the best shotmaking and putting seen around Augusta National in years. He made no bogeys, but escaped quite a few, making birdie from the lip of the bunker at No. 4, and pars on the two closing holes after bouncing his approach shots over the greens. He needed only 12 putts on the front side and 27 overall.

Trevino's deft putting touch was rediscovered after he looked at a picture of himself taken in the 1968 Masters. It showed his right elbow tucked in on his stomach. Until seeing that, his posture had been extending his arms, making for a much wider take-away.

"On fast greens like this, you have to decelerate your putts," the Merry Mex said. "I was taking the putter back too far away from the ball before. But I never hit a putt on this course this year until Thursday.

"I'm getting ready for the Senior Tour, and this round means a tremendous amount to me. Man, I was making putts from everywhere. If I hit it like I did today and putt like that, yes, I can win it. On the other hand, I may come back with three 88s, but it won't bother me. It lets me know that there still is a spark in the fireplace."

Several of Trevino's competitors weren't surprised at his performance. Tom Watson was one of them. "I think his attitude here has hurt him in the past. I'm not surprised by his score. He can play well anywhere."

While Trevino was having the time of his life and showing it, Faldo was his usual conservative self. He did get off one good line, saying, "Lee talks a lot on the golf course and he played well. I talked a lot and I played well;" this from the man who might say 10 words in 18 holes and whose idea of golf course chatter is, "I think you're away."

A change in putters keyed Faldo's good round. After finished 42nd the week before in Houston, he took a half dozen with him to the practice putting green and replaced the Ping he had been using for five years with a

Bullseye, one he hadn't used since his amateur days.

"I think I found something I can use," Faldo said after his one eagle, three birdies and one bogey round. "I've been practicing two months for this tournament and to say the least, this is my most satisfying round of the year. I changed putters and made a little adjustment in my stroke and the results were gratifying."

Before the week was over, Faldo was back on the practice green with another handful of putters, but more on that later.

Hoch came on late to challenge for the first-round lead. He was even par through No. 14, then rolled in a 60-foot eagle putt at No. 15 and made a 12-footer for birdie at No. 18.

Pooley had six birdies, but four bogeys; Bean ran into a four-putt on No. 6, the last one of those coming from inside a foot; Ballesteros birdied the first two holes, but bogeyed Nos. 6 and 13 before getting it back under par with a birdie at No. 17. Larry Nelson played the first 10 holes in one-under 35 and the next four in seven-over 23 on the way to a devastating 77.

Then there was four-time champion Nicklaus. He popped up his drive on the first hole, barely making it to the cross walk, leaving him 200 yards from the green. A one iron and two putts later, he had his par on the way to a safe 73.

First round scores were hardly on the low side. The wind blew just hard enough to make club selection guesswork; the greens were decidedly quicker than during the practice rounds, and only 11 players broke par of 72. And several of the game's leading lights didn't come close.

Lyle shot five-over 77, becoming the fourth consecutive defending champion to not break par in the first round. Lyle had seven bogeys and only two birdies.

The round for Lyle could be compressed to No. 13, which for him should be no more than a driver and four iron. Lyle hit a good drive, but then hit the four iron into the water guarding the front of the green.

"Just stupid," Lyle said. "I was thinking birdie or eagle and suddenly I had a six on the hole. That's how screwy my game is right now. I can't put two good shots together. I was feeling a bit anxious about getting started today. I had easy birdie putts—if there's any such thing as an easy birdie putt around here—and missed them. My short game is just terrible. It wasn't a good day; I made a few silly shots. But if I had putted or chipped half-decently, I could have scored a 71 or 72."

Strange was on the leaderboard at two under after 11 holes, then took triple-bogey six at No. 12 and finished with a 74; Norman bogeyed Nos. 16 and 18 for 74, and Arnold Palmer finished at 81 with bogeys on four of the last five holes.

The first-round par-breakers:

Lee Trevino	67	Tom Purtzer	71
Nick Faldo	68	Ben Crenshaw	71
Scott Hoch	69	T.C. Chen	71
Don Pooley	70	Seve Ballesteros	71
Andy Bean	70	Jumbo Ozaki	71

Augusta's weather turned ugly on Friday. The temperature was 51 degrees and it was pouring rain when the first groups went off, and 19-mile-per-hour winds, with gusts to 25, made it seem like 35 degrees. The rain stopped before noon, but the wind blew harder. No lead was safe, no putt a sure thing as those conditions turned Augusta National into a game of dungeons and dragons.

When the final shot was fired, only five players had broken par and Trevino with a 74 and Faldo with a 73 staggered in tied for the lead at three-under 141. They led by two over five others—Hoch (74), Ken Green (69), Mike Reid (71), Crenshaw (72) and Ballesteros (72). There was horror story after horror story, as the players straggled in, wearing dazed, worn-out looks.

"I've been coming here for 25 years and these were the toughest conditions I've seen," said Raymond Floyd after shooting 75 and barely making the cut at 151. "If I had played like I did Thursday, I'd have shot 95."

The general consensus was that par was 76 and some pin placements were used for the first time, especially in these kinds of conditions. The players could see them, they just couldn't get to them, Nos. 7 and 8 in particular. "Those are holes where you don't want to hit downwind and we were hitting downwind," said Fuzzy Zoeller. "And they set the pins up like it was a perfectly calm day."

There was this assessment from Nick Price, who just a few years ago toured Augusta National in a record 63 strokes, yet took 82 this time, which with his opening 76 sent him packing.

"We play in wind and rain all the time in Europe; it's no big deal," Price said. "But we don't have greens like this in Europe and you usually know where the wind is coming from—behind you going out, into you coming in, or vice versa. Today, it was behind you, then in your face. All the while you're standing over a shot. It's tough as hell. I lost all my confidence out there."

The second round could have been scarier, most everyone agreed, if not for rain late Thursday night and Friday morning. Rain softens greens. Soft greens hold shots.

"If not for that rain Thursday night and this morning, I hate to think what it could have been," said Tom Kite. "Last year, if we had this wind with the greens as hard as they were, we would still be playing the 1988 tournament right now."

Shots in the air and on the ground were affected by the strong wind. Some putts were blown off line by as much as six inches. Three-putting was common and four putts not rare.

Ballesteros was one of them. He had climbed to within a stroke of Faldo with a birdie at No. 13 and appeared ready to mount a charge. But two holes later, the two-time Masters champion was floundering.

From 25 feet below the hole at No. 15, he four-putted for double-bogey seven and three of those putts came from just outside three feet. And at No. 17, he three-putted from 25 feet.

"I played as good as I can play today and ended up even par," Ballesteros said. "The wind was close to being the toughest I've ever played in. Concentration was very, very difficult. There were no easy putts today; no tap-ins. Only seven players are now under par for the championship. That shows you how tough it was."

While 10 players broke par on Thursday, only five bettered it Friday, and

11 of them couldn't break 80, including Arnold Palmer for the second straight day. The cut came at seven-over 151 and among the notables who missed it were defending champion Sandy Lyle, 1982 champion Craig Stadler, Hal Sutton, Bob Tway, Larry Nelson and all the amateurs.

"I'm no good at defending titles," said Lyle, who shot rounds of 77-76. "I missed the cut here, at the Players Championship and nearly missed at last year's British Open. I just played rubbish golf. The only good job I've done this week is make a perfect fool of myself."

Somehow Trevino and Faldo managed to escape Lyle's disease. Trevino started the round a shot in front of Faldo but surrendered it on the fourth hole. The 1987 British Open champion extended the margin to three at the turn, but gave a share of it back to the Merry Mex. His slide began with a bogey at No. 11 where he came off a four-iron approach and left it in the swale. And he finished rather weakly, bogeying No. 16, with a poor chip after missing the green short, and No. 17, where his tee shot caught Ike's tree and left him 200 yards from the green.

"Despite the conditions, the round went well until I messed up at the end," said Faldo, managing a slight smile. "It's not a precise game. I hit 90 percent of the shots where I was aiming and that's all you can ask. I'm pleased to be right there now, and that's the object, isn't it?"

He wouldn't have been right there had not Trevino given him a boost. After making about every putt he looked at in the first round, he didn't make anything in the second until a 20-footer from above the hole found the cup at No. 12. He had only 27 putts on Thursday, but 35 Friday, and if he had made only half of the difference, he would have been singing in the rain.

"I knew it was going to be a tough day so I just hung in there," Trevino said. "Par was about 75 and I thought if I shot 75 or 76, I would be okay. In these kinds of conditions, nobody's going to do a whole lot, not in this wind and on these greens. I didn't think anyone was going to run away and hide. I can play this course under these conditions. If it keeps raining, I'll have a shot at it."

While nobody at the top broke away, some others picked up ground on the leaders. Kite shot 72 and gained two strokes; Strange had 71 and picked up three, as did Mark O'Meara.

But it was Ken Green, who made the biggest charge and along the way was one of the few players in Masters history to be booed. That came at the second hole where, after mis-hitting a sand wedge shot, he hurled the offending club against his golf bag.

He wasn't all that excited, either about being booed or his round. His best previous finish before the Masters was 17th and he wasn't sure whether the 69 meant he was playing well again, or just a momentary thing. "The way I'm swinging at it, it could go away at any particular moment. The thing I did today was make a bunch of five or six-foot putts for pars and you don't do that every day around this place."

More quietly than Trevino or Faldo, and certainly less than Green, Hoch continued to be a factor. On Thursday, he completed his round of 69 at 7 p.m., after most of the columnists were long gone.

Friday, though, he was even for the day until he made a double bogey at No. 16. And there were other places where he might have nose-dived, which everyone thought he might do. On Nos. 11 and 12, he needed seven-foot putts just to save par. By the 14th hole, he was so weak, he needed another lunch.

And at No. 16, his nerves were so taut that when a television technician, who was kneeling just inside the ropes, lost his balance just as Hoch started his downswing, he chunked the shot into the water, then gave the man a long, hard look, but held his temper in check.

"I didn't do what I normally do," Hoch said. "I usually don't hold things back too much and normally he would have gotten a piece of my mind. But I figured the cameras were still rolling and my father was watching at home, so I figured I had better not say anything. But I wanted to."

The leaders after two rounds were:

Lee Trevino	67-74—141	Mark O'Meara	74-71—145
Nick Faldo	69-73—141	Curtis Strange	74-71—145
Seve Ballesteros	71-72—143	Tom Watson	72-73—145
Ben Crenshaw	71-72—143	Mark Calcavecchia	74-72—146
Ken Green	74-69—143	T.C. Chen	71-75—146
Scott Hoch	69-74—143	Jumbo Ozaki	71-75—146
Mike Reid	72-71—143	Dan Pohl	72-74—146
Tom Kite	72-72—144	Jeff Sluman	74-72—146

As bad as Friday's second round was, Saturday's third round was worse. At least the players finished play on Friday.

The weather was "iffy" from the start and became just plain miserable shortly after noon as heavy rain hit the course. Play was suspended at 3:30 p.m. due to lightening and wasn't resumed until 5:10 before it was finally called due to darkness at 6:45.

By then, the wind had shifted, the greens became softer and everyone in the field was chasing a new leader, Crenshaw.

Crenshaw got in 13 holes before play was suspended for the day and he played them in three under par to take a four-stroke lead over Faldo, Hoch and Reid. Norman, who finished his round with a four-under 68, and Jumbo Ozaki were five back.

Crenshaw didn't need reminding that in 1984 he was on the 14th hole when the third round was suspended. Nor did he need reminding that the next day he won his first major championship.

"I feel comfortable and confident here," Crenshaw said. "I tried to slow everything down today and remain patient. Now, I want to come back out Sunday and try to build on my lead. You never have enough on this course."

The one difference between this year and 1984 was that five years ago Crenshaw trailed Kite by three strokes. This time, he was the only player under par.

Ballesteros lost five shots in nine holes, including consecutive bogeys at Nos. 11, 12 and 13, and trailed Crenshaw by seven. Faldo lost three in eight holes and his playing partner and first-round leader Trevino was five over after eight. Strange crept to within a shot of the lead, then bogeyed four holes in a row.

Only Crenshaw seemed unaffected by the elements. He had 10 pars and three birdies, at Nos. 2, 4 and 7 and missed three more that would have gone, he said, if he had hit them a bean harder.

"It was pretty bad out there, but I can't say they should have stopped it earlier than they did," Crenshaw said. "There wasn't any casual water until the last. It was just getting very dark. It was pitiful that you had all that rain coming down and it wasn't gathering itself in places where they could call the round because of casual water."

Faldo and Ballesteros felt Masters officials crossed the line between good and bad judgement.

"I asked an official for relief on the green at No. 11 because there was water between my ball and the hole. He turned me down," said Faldo, who three-putted from 50 feet. "I think they went too far in allowing play to continue. It was very difficult out there. The wind blew, it rained hard, it got dark. There was no way to get any rhythm. At one point, it took us one hour to play three holes. We see weather like this all the time in Europe, but we don't play golf courses like this over there. This course is designed for good conditions."

One man not caught up in all the controversy was Norman. He was too busy catching up. He had started the third round eight strokes behind Crenshaw on rounds of 74-75, then did his usual weekend number, a sparkling 68 that could have been better except for a botched birdie opportunity at No. 13 and an even worse bogey at No. 14.

"Now, we'll just have to wait and see how it all ends today, if they are able to finish, which I doubt," Norman said. "I don't know why I wait so long here. I've tried to analyze that and work that out right when I get here. When the time comes for the final two days, I would rather play good on the weekend than play good on Thursday. I just hope I haven't dug myself too deep a hole before now.

"Every shot around here on the weekend is important, putting for eagle or putting for bogey. I don't think people realize the importance of every shot on this golf course. I mean, there's not an easy shot out here."

One man who no longer figured he was a contender was Trevino. When he laced up his spikes in his van earlier that morning, he was tied for the lead at three under par. When he placed his soggy socks on the driver's seat more than five hours later, he was four over. One minute he was thinking about winning, the next he was talking about finishing in the top 24.

"It was my putting today," Trevino said. "I putted awful. Just a bad day on the greens. I had 20 of them on the front side, shot 41 and it didn't get any better. Only the weather was worse. Man, it was miserable out there. I'll bet even the ducks stayed under cover today. Looks like it didn't bother Ben any. He must have really golfed his ball to get three under."

And one man who had high hopes early then saw them dashed almost as quickly was Strange. After finally moving under par with back-to-back birdies at Nos. 2 and 3 to move to within a stroke of Crenshaw, he went bogey, bogey, bogey, bogey.

"I don't know what happened," Strange said. "Those bogeys came as easy as the birdies. I'm not in good shape certainly, but I'm not out of it, either. But obviously, I have to really play some good golf. Ben was able to do it today. Most of us didn't. He's got a big edge, especially if this stuff (weather) stays like it is."

Before leaving the course for dry clothes and a warm bed, Crenshaw noted of his position: "There's a great opportunity here for me now," he said. "I want to come back out Sunday and add to my lead because you never have enough. You can drop strokes so quickly on this course."

Crenshaw didn't lose his lead when the third round resumed Sunday, but didn't add to it either. He finished with a 70 but was now one ahead of Hoch and Reid, who had 71s. Ballesteros made the biggest move, scoring birdies on three of his final five holes for a 73 and closed to within three strokes.

Faldo went the other way, finishing his five holes in two over and fell five behind Crenshaw.

"It was perfectly calm when we came back Sunday morning to finish the third round," Crenshaw said. "Conditions were right to make a couple of birdies and I didn't. I played the holes one over, made a bogey on No. 18. I hope that's not a bad omen. But I still have the lead. They've still got to take it away from me."

Faldo was in no mood to talk of his finish. He went straight from the 18th green to his locker, pulled out three putters and spent 45 minutes on the practice green before returning to his room.

So as the final round began, the top 10 looked like this:

Ben Crenshaw	71-72-70—213
Scott Hoch	69-74-71—214
Mike Reid	71-71-71—214
Seve Ballesteros	71-72-73—216
Ken Green	74-69-73—216
Tom Kite	72-72-72—216
Greg Norman	74-75-68—217
Mark O'Meara	74-71-72—217
Larry Mize	72-77-69—218
Paul Azinger	75-75-69—219
Jumbo Ozaki	71-75-73—219
Tom Watson	72-73-74—219

There have been too many dramatic final rounds in too many Masters to say that one stands out over another. There was Gary Player's 64 in 1978 that beat Hubert Green. And undoubtedly Nicklaus's back nine 30 that produced a 65 and his record sixth championship in 1986 is one few will ever forget because of the man himself and the magnitude of his accomplishment.

And for pure drama, the one played out on soggy Augusta National on April 9, 1989, was theater at its best. Known for its improbable finishes, the 53rd Masters added another one where so many of them have ended before, down in Amen Corner.

This time it was Faldo sinking a 25-foot birdie putt on No. 11, the second hole of a playoff, to break the heart of Hoch. With that one stroke, Faldo succeeded his countryman Lyle and marked the first time in Masters history that foreigners had won back-to-back.

With a marvelous round of seven-under-par 65, the 31-year-old Englishman came from five shots behind to add this major title to his 1987 British Open and took the $223,739 winner's share of the $1.1 million purse.

Hoch shot a 69 and could have won it himself on the first extra hole, but he missed a par putt of two feet. Third-round leader Crenshaw bogeyed the final hole for 71 and tied for third with Norman, who played 17 great holes in a round of 67, but bogeyed the one he needed to par, No. 18, to make the playoff.

But back to Amen Corner. The Masters only went to sudden death to decide a winner in 1979 and there now have been four of them. It was on No. 11 in sudden death that Fuzzy Zoeller won over Ed Sneed and Tom Watson in 1979, and two years ago, Mize sank his chip shot there to stun Norman. Craig Stadler won his Masters on No. 10, defeating Dan Pohl.

"I've seen other guys do this, like Nicklaus, and to do it yourself is a tough feeling to handle," Faldo said. "You dream it's going to happen to you. It means the world to me. It makes up for the U.S. Open last year."

In that one, Faldo happened to get in the way of Strange's destiny and lost 75-71 in an 18-hole playoff at The Country Club in Brookline, Massachusetts.

Hoch was all but fitted for the Green Jacket on the first hole of the playoff. Faldo hit his approach shot into the bunker that guards the right front of the green, while Hoch's approach was on the green, 30 feet away. Faldo's bunker shot was a testy one. Too much and the ball could roll over the green; too little and it could stop short. It did the latter, trickling about six feet out of the bunker and stopping eight feet short.

Here was where Hoch made the first of two critical mistakes. He hit a marvelous putt, which stopped barely two feet from the hole. Strategy dictated that he knock it in, making Faldo's putt for par much more difficult. But Hoch marked it. Faldo missed and taped in for bogey-five.

Now Hoch's second mistake. Normally a fast player, Hoch did everything but pull out a slide rule as he studied that two-footer. It was the length that most weekend golfers would have walked up to, given it a quick glance and tapped it in.

Hoch had gotten this far because he had played the tournament of his life on Sunday under the kind of pressure that finally had reduced Norman, Ballesteros and Crenshaw to spectators in front of television sets in the Augusta National clubhouse. Finally, Hoch was ready.

He stepped up to the putt, then took one more look at it. And missed. The ball rolled a good four feet past the hole, and this one he hit quickly, dead center for a halving bogey.

"I stood over that first putt and said, 'This is for all the marbles. Hit it firm,'" Hoch said. "I couldn't believe it didn't go in. I looked at it longer than normal and there was a split second of indecision on my part before I putted it. I saw it one way, then putted it another way.

"The message between my brain and my hands got crisscrossed. It was a poor effort on my part. I hadn't three-putted all week until then."

It was only the second bogey of the day for Hoch. The first came on the 17th and was just as deadly. He hit his approach over the green, then almost holed the chip coming back, leaving himself a five-footer for par. He played it to break, it didn't. Bogey.

After Hoch missed his par putt at No. 10, you could feel the advantage shifting to Faldo as they moved to the 11th tee. Given a reprieve, Faldo split the fairway with his drive, then hit the three iron of his life into the green. Shaken, Hoch missed the green to the right, leaving him with a long pitch shot.

"I had visions of Larry Mize and his winning chip," Hoch said. "I hit it right on line, but the green was slower than we usually play it."

It was all academic a second later. Faldo stroked his 25-footer and as if riding a rail, the ball rolled dead center into the cup. Faldo looked disbelieving at first, then raised both arms into the misty, darkening sky.

Faldo figured to be only a bit player as the final round began after his poor finish earlier that day of the third round which left him five behind Crenshaw. His putting was as ordinary as a weekend hacker.

"I was in a poor mood after my finish this morning," he said. "I was looking to play those last five holes two-under and I played them two-over. I played so well and putted so poorly. But I went back to my room, got myself together and came out determined to make a better showing."

As it was, he was only a member of the supporting cast for much of the final 18. The limelight was first on Ballesteros, who birdied four of the first five. Then the steady Reid with birdies on Nos. 8 and 9 moved into a tie before taking it alone with another one on 12.

"There was so much going on out there, it was tough to know what was happening, who was where," Faldo said. "I just kept trying to make birdies. It's so difficult to win from the lead here because this golf course asks for perfection and perfection is difficult under all this pressure."

Crenshaw had lost the lead early to Ballesteros's charge, and Ballesteros handed it to Reid and Hoch in the middle of the round. Reid looked like a possible winner when he left the 13th hole with a one-stroke lead, but two holes later he was gone, done in by a three-putt bogey at No. 14 and a double bogey at No. 15.

"It seemed like things happened so quickly, no faster than the blink of an eye," Reid said. "Just like that—bogey, double bogey. But that's baseball. I'll be back here next year. Life goes on."

Ballesteros, who has won two Masters and lost a third in a playoff, showed his majestical powers over Augusta National's front side with birdies at Nos. 1, 2, 4, 5 and 8 to turn in 31. But the Masters is won over Augusta's back nine, which he played in 38. He bogeyed No. 10, didn't birdie the par-five 13th or 15th and a closing birdie at No. 18 was too late. He had taken care of that with a double bogey at No. 16.

"I told my caddy if I played one under on the back nine I would have a very good chance to win the tournament," Ballesteros said. "Unfortunately, I played it two over. The shot at No. 16 did that. I had 175 yards to the pin and when I saw the ball fly off the tee it looked like a great shot, fantastic. I couldn't believe it went in the water. It was only a matter of a couple of yards. After that, though, the tournament was over for me."

Faldo, Norman and Crenshaw were there to pick up the pieces. Faldo had come quietly through the pack. He was three behind after 14 holes, but birdied Nos. 15, 16 and 17. Norman made a similar charge with birdies at Nos. 13, 15, 16 and 17, as did Crenshaw with birdies at Nos. 16 and 17.

For a while, it appeared a foursome would go into the playoff—Faldo, Hoch, Norman and Crenshaw. The 18th eliminated all but the two who did.

First Norman. With 180 yards to the green and tied for the lead, Norman hit a five iron that fell well short onto the fringe and spun back. He then flubbed the chip shot and missed a 12-footer for par.

Norman defended the selection to the press. "You guys are making it sound like I hit a crappy five iron," he said. "I hit it perfect. It was the perfect club. It just didn't fly; it hung up in the breeze. I actually thought about hitting the four iron, but the way I was feeling, it was a five.

"Maybe it was the right club, maybe it wasn't. At this point, sitting here now, it doesn't make too much difference. The truth is I put myself in a comeback position the first two days, especially on the front nine each day. If I can figure out a way to play the first two rounds better, I might be able to win this S.O.B. one of these days."

Now Crenshaw. He had 172 yards to the hole, five iron all the way. As he struck the ball, the grip moved on his glove hand and you could see the sick look on his face as the ball found the bunker guarding the front left of the green. From there, he blasted out 12 feet past the hole and his tying putt never came close.

"I was very happy to have a chance to win, very proud of the two birdies there on Nos. 16 and 17," he said. "But I ran out of equipment. I ran out of towels and it cost me. My left hand slipped as I hit the shot. It hurts to be this close. I'm laughing right now, but when you think of the tournament in retrospect, when it boils down to one shot, it's painful. Believe me."

Hoch's pain was double that of Crenshaw. The tournament was his to win at No. 17. "I hit the chip of my life, then thought I'd made the putt. I just misread it. It usually breaks more, but I guess the green was wet. I can't second-guess myself on that one.

"I felt good about myself all day. I figured that this must be my time. I wasn't nervous, not even that putt at No. 10. I didn't look at the scoreboard until I birdied No. 15 and saw I had a one-shot lead. Then I felt it was mine."

It was Faldo's. His tournament, Faldo confessed, hadn't been a model of consistency. The first 27 holes were eight under par, the next 27 eight over. But the final 18 were all that counted and he played those in 65 strokes on a day where the pressure was as heavy as the air.

The putt that got him in the playoff was in some ways bigger than the putt that won it. It came at No. 16, a 15-foot downhiller on the slickest green on the course.

"It was about exactly the same spot that Sandy (Lyle) made his birdie from in last year's final round. It was a joke, really. There was a piece of mud on my ball that I couldn't wipe off because I was just off the green. I couldn't believe how I could hole that one. It was 15 feet, but it must have been six to eight feet of break on it. I just touched it like I would a two-foot putt. I just started it rolling. After I made that, I thought I could win."

Although Faldo couldn't believe his eyes when Hoch's putt didn't fall at No. 10, he wasn't shocked. "I never thought I was out of it, even when Scott had that two-footer," he said. "I know what was going through his mind. He's got to make that to win the Masters. That doesn't make it easy. This one was a battle of emotions. I think I won that, too. This is a day I'll never forget."

Masters officials will forever be grateful for Faldo ending it when he did. They had pushed Sunday's starting times back to the limit to accommodate television. The game could not have gone on another hole. And it didn't stop raining in Augusta until Wednesday.

4. The U.S. Open

Years ago, as the Twentieth Century approached maturity, Walter Hagen laid down his doctrine. It states, roughly, "Anybody can win the Open once, but only a great player can win it twice."

With the obvious exception of Andy North, who indeed won the U.S. Open twice, but absolutely nothing else, the Hagen Doctrine has held up remarkably well; the others who won two Opens rank at the top of American golf. Eighty-nine Opens had been played through 1989, but only 16 remarkable men had won the championship more than once. Indeed, they make up an all-star cast. Look at who they are:

Willie Anderson	Cary Middlecoff
Alex Smith	Julius Boros
John McDermott	Billy Casper
Walter Hagen	Jack Nicklaus
Gene Sarazen	Lee Trevino
Bob Jones	Hale Irwin
Ralph Guldahl	Andy North
Ben Hogan	Curtis Strange

Even more surprising, until Curtis Strange shot 278 at the Oak Hill Country Club, in Rochester, New York, in June, only five men had won the Open in successive years—Anderson, who won three in succession, in 1903, 1904, and 1905, Johnny McDermott (1911-12), Bob Jones (1929-30), Ralph Guldahl (1937-38) and Ben Hogan (1950-51). A case could be made for Hogan's actually having won three in succession, since he won in 1948, didn't play in 1949 because he had nearly been killed in an automobile accident early in the year, then won the 1950 and 1951 championships.

Sitting before an audience of reporters shortly after he had checked and signed his scorecard, Strange put what he had just accomplished into a different perspective, "It's not so much that I've done what Ben Hogan did, but it's what so many others haven't done. It feels fantastic."

Looking at it from that standpoint, what Curtis had done grows in stature. Sarazen couldn't do it, or Hagen, or Trevino, and not even Nicklaus. Only those few of the game's leading figures, and in most of those incidents, the circumstances had to be right. Anderson, a Scot who came to the United States as a teenager, was simply the best golfer in American during his time, but he won the 1903 Open because David Brown, the 1886 British Open champion and a former chimney sweep from Musselburgh, close by Anderson's native North Berwick, played worse than Willie in a playoff, shooting 84 against Anderson's 82. Anderson won the next year with ease, then made it three successive championships by nipping Alex Smith the following year. If he hadn't, Smith might have won successive championships himself, because he won in 1906, beating his brother Willie. It works both ways.

Like Anderson before him, Johnny McDermott won the 1911 championship because both Mike Brady and George Simpson played worse than he in a playoff. Scores in the 80s were fairly common in those early years, but both Brady and Simpson had played four rounds in the 70s, yet slipped to 82 and 85 in the playoff, while McDermott shot 80. McDermott won the following year by shooting 294 and beating Brady by two strokes.

The wonder of it all is that Jones didn't win two in succession more than once. Over a period of nine years, for 1922 through 1930, he won four Opens and placed second in four others, losing twice in playoffs, once to Willie Macfarlane, in 1925, then winning the following year. Earlier, he had missed tying Sarazen for the 1922 championship by one stroke, then won his first Open in 1923.

A slow-moving, deliberate man, Guldahl won his first Open in 1937, playing the last 11 holes in 41 strokes and beating Sam Snead, the dashing newcomer, by two strokes. Sam was playing in his first Open, and he thought he had won when he shot 283, since his score missed the 72-hole record by one stroke. With a lightning backswing and a powerful thrust through the ball, delivered with the force of a sledgehammer, Guldahl was the most dangerous big-time player of his time. He won with ease the following year, shooting 284 at Cherry Hills, in Denver, beating Dick Metz by six strokes.

Thirteen years passed before Hogan won his two successive Opens, years that spanned the Second World War, when the championship was suspended for four years. Ben won his first Open in 1948, shooting 276 at Riviera, in Los Angeles, lowering the record by five strokes, but he couldn't defend his championship the following year, because he hadn't recovered from his automobile accident. He came back in 1950, at Merion, near Philadelphia, played the last 18 holes in pain, once nearly falling to the ground as he lashed into his drive on the 12th hole, dropped three strokes over the last six holes, staggered home in 74, tied Lloyd Mangrum and George Fazio, then beat them the next day in a playoff.

The following year Hogan played perhaps the best single round of his career, shooting 67 at Oakland Hills, near Detroit, a course he called a monster, shooting 35 on the first nine, then ripping Oakland Hills apart with 32 coming back.

Since then no one had been able to win two in succession, although several could have. Nicklaus had his best chance in 1971 and 1972. He lost a playoff to Trevino at Merion in 1971, then won at Pebble Beach the next year. Strangely, this was Trevino's best chance as well. Lee had had an attack of bronchial pneumonia and had been released from an El Paso, Texas, hospital on Thursday, flown to Pebble Beach on Wednesday, and begun play on Thursday. Playing through high winds, Nicklaus shot 74, but Trevino was worn out and couldn't keep up, closing with 78 and dropping to fourth place.

Only Tom Watson had threatened since then, winning at Pebble Beach in 1982 by holing his spectacular pitch on the 17th hole and nipping Nicklaus, then bogeying the 17th at Oakmont in 1983 and losing by a stroke to Larry Nelson, who was breaking a 51-year-old record by playing the last 36 holes in 65-67—132.

In a way Strange's achievement mirrors Hogan's, since they both won over difficult courses, and in Strange's case, under trying circumstances.

Merion, where Hogan won in 1950, is one of the country's classic courses, and Oakland Hills of 1951 was perhaps the most difficult the Open had ever seen, with high rough, narrow fairways pinched in by bunkers in the drive zone, and lightning fast greens. Conditions have eased somewhat since then. While it is still a significant factor in an Open, the rough is cut shorter; with the added distance built into the ball since Hogan's day, the courses play shorter; and although the greens putt as fast as ever, with advances in agronomy, the ball rolls truer.

Nevertheless, The Country Club, where Francis Ouimet had defeated Harry Vardon and Ted Ray in a playoff for the 1913 Open, and where Julius Boros had beaten Arnold Palmer and Jacky Cupit 50 years later, had turned out to be a superb test of the game in 1988. It was there that Strange won his first Open, beating Nick Faldo in another playoff.

The United States Golf Association took the 1989 Open to the Oak Hill Country Club, a heavily wooded course on the outskirts of Rochester, New York, 10 or 15 miles south of Lake Ontario. Twenty-one years had passed since Trevino had won the last previous Open there, and the club had been looking forward to it for some time, but neither the club nor the USGA was quite prepared for what happened—a week of rain that flooded parts of the course, causing administrative nightmares along with the valiant, backbreaking labor by the grounds crew in turning what at times looked like a rice paddy into a playable golf course; four holes-in-one in a period of less than two hours at the same hole, which defies any kind of odds; a champion who played the last 37 holes with only one birdie; and the destruction of Tom Kite's hopes when he played his worst round of the year at the worst possible time. It was indeed an eventful week.

The 1989 renewal was the third Open played at Oak Hill. The championship went there first in 1956, when Hogan was still chasing his fifth Open, and when the field included Sam Snead, Tommy Bolt, Julius Boros, Jack Burke, the Englishman Henry Cotton, Jimmy Demaret, Ted Kroll, and lean and tall Cary Middlecoff, who shot his 281 early, then waited two agonizing hours while others took their shots at beating him. They all failed. With chances to win, Hogan fell a stroke behind by bogeying the 17th, Boros' putt for birdie on the 18th caught the lip of the cup but spun out, and Kroll hit his ball under a low-growing spruce tree on the 16th and made seven.

When the Open returned for another unforgettable week, in 1968, we had our first glimpse of Trevino's wonderful promise. Locked in a battle with Bert Yancey, whose elegant swing made Trevino's look primitive, Lee played the more elegant golf, shot four rounds in the 60s, and won by four strokes over Nicklaus, after Yancey had fallen apart in the last round and sank to third place with a closing 76. Trevino matched the Open's 72-hole record by shooting 69-68-69-69—275 a year after Nicklaus had set it at Baltusrol. Trevino turned out to be one of the great players of the age, but Yancey dropped from sight and didn't figure in another significant event.

Oak Hill, however, did. The course had been laid out in the middle 1920s by Donald Ross, the most famous of our early designers of golf courses. He was given about 350 acres and told to give the club two golf courses. On barren, treeless ground he created two gems, the East Course and the West Course.

Looking over the land, Ross found it hard to believe the fields had once been heavily wooded. Like much of western New York, the ground had been stripped of its oak forests during colonial times, the trees cut down to build ships, or burned to ashes to produce the caustic potash used to make soap in England.

Conversely, surveying Oak Hill's tree-lined fairways, and its ivy-covered Tudor-style clubhouse rising among tall, aging oaks, it is difficult to believe this ground ever lay bare. How the forest was restored is the story of Dr. John Williams, an Oak Hill member of years past.

A well-known Rochester physician, Dr. Williams dabbled in botany and horticulture. Obsessed with restoring those old oak forests, he threw himself into the job, studied not only the scientific, but the historical issues, learned all he could about oaks, collected acorns and planted them in his own small garden. The acorns came from all over—black oaks from Mount Vernon, planted by George Washington himself; from Kew Gardens, in London; from West Point; from the Shakespeare Oak, in Stratford-on-Avon, in England; from wherever he could find them. As they sprouted and matured, Williams transplanted them to Oak Hill.

His was not a one-man job, though. Others joined in the reforestation program and planted thousands of trees. Some are clustered around high ground rising from behind the 13th green of the East Course. The knoll is named the Hill of Fame; many of those oaks have been dedicated to those who have made outstanding contributions to the game. One of those trees is dedicated to Dr. Williams, others to such truly outstanding people in golf as Richard S. Tufts, a former USGA president, the man who created the manual for setting up Open courses; to President Eisenhower, to Bob Hope, Ben Hogan, Bobby Jones, Francis Ouimet, Cary Middlecoff, Babe Zaharias, Walter Hagen, Gene Sarazen, Chick Evans, and Joseph C. Dey, for many years the Executive Director of the USGA, and the first Commissioner of the PGA Tour. Just before the 1989 Open began, another tree was dedicated to Robert Trent Jones, who brought new fame to golf course design.

Becoming enshrined, so to speak, at Oak Hill is particularly fitting for Jones, because it was there that he was smitten with the idea of becoming a golf course architect. He was 18 years old in 1924, had grown up in Rochester, and had won the city's golf championship a year earlier, shooting 69 in the last round during a time when scores in the 60s were rare indeed. He was another Bobby Jones, becoming a very good player at a time when the game was dominated by the other Bobby Jones. He dreamed his dreams, but as he thought of greater achievements ahead, his doctor told him he had developed an ulcer and had to give up competitive golf.

As he relived that day years later, Trent recalled, "That was a terrible blow to someone who lived and breathed golf as I did."

Jones had heard of the two courses under construction at Oak Hill, and unable to play, he ran out one day to see what was going on. With a lifelong inclination to head for the man in charge, Jones approached Ross. After a few minutes of conversation had convinced him that Jones was seriously interested in the subject and not simply an inquisitive pest, Ross took the time to explain the reasons behind the earth moving and dirt piling.

Jones recalls that Ross let him walk the site with him.

"I remember he told me the green was the most important feature of every hole, and that every effort should be made to place it in the most natural location possible. 'Always remember, Laddie,' he told me, 'the green is the heart of the hole.'"

In his meetings with Ross, Jones was given an insight into golf course architecture, decided to make it his life's work, and entered Cornell University, designing his own curriculum in three of the university's colleges.

"I'll always be indebted to Donald Ross," Jones said, "because he planted the germ in me to become a golf course architect."

Jones, of course, developed into our most widely known designer, laying out courses throughout the world. He returned to Rochester in the early 1950s, after he had won wide recognition for turning Oakland Hills, near Detroit, into such a severe test for the 1951 Open that only Ben Hogan and Clayton Heafner broke 70.

The stronger of the two, Oak Hill East became the club's tournament course; it had indeed been the site of the old Rochester Open, a tour tournament that had been played in the early 1940s but had died a casualty of the Second World War. The demands of the Open go beyond those for weekly tour events, though. When the USGA awarded the 1956 Open to Oak Hill, the club realized it must strengthen the East Course and called on Jones for revisions. He brought about extensive changes, affecting every hole but the 14th, a short par four of 342 yards played across a valley to a green set atop a rise. He extended its length several hundred yards, stretching it out to 6,902 yards, built new tees, re-routed Allen's Creek, a stream that powered a mill in colonial times, and planted even more trees.

With all his changes, Jones didn't touch the greens; they belonged to Donald Ross.

Other alterations followed periodically with each succeeding championship. Two par threes, for example, haven't been the same in any of Oak Hill's three Opens, and what was the sixth in 1989 not only hasn't been in the same place twice, it hasn't even been the sixth hole in each Open. On the other hand, the 15th has remained the 15th, but it has been moved around in the same general area, changing from a little par three of 133 yards in 1956 to a stronger 163-yard hole in 1968.

By 1975, after discouraging responses to Oak Hill's tentative approaches to the USGA asking for another Open, the club brought in George and Tom Fazio for further alterations. They concentrated mainly on that troublesome par three that had gone from the sixth to the fifth, and on the par four that had switched back and forth with the par three. In some minds, the Fazios' solution turned out to be worse than the problem. The par four had been a wonderful hole, a slight dogleg right of 440 yards with the creek running along the right, then swinging across the fairway and bordering the left side of the green. The revised layout cut its yardage back to 406 yards by setting the shallow green directly behind the creek, where it swings across the fairway, broadening the creek somewhat, and raising the green above fairway level.

The creek continues past the fifth green, then swirls to its right, forming a hazard for the par three, which became the sixth once again, its green nestled behind and to the right of the stream. The hole measures 167 yards from the championship tees, but with the tee set well above the level of the green, it plays much shorter; it was only a seven iron for the Open field.

It played considerably easier as well.

In addition to the work they did on those two holes, and the revision to the 15th, the Fazios brought the 18th green forward to the edge of a deep gully that had never been in play under the old design; it had been a walking hazard, coming so late in the round, rather than a playing hazard, since the second shot, if it wasn't topped, simply soared overhead on its way to the target. Now, though, the under-clubbed shot or one snuffed out by the deep and tangled rough, could tumble to the bottom of the hill, leaving a pitch back to the green. The change also reclaimed enough ground for a grandstand between the back of the green and the clubhouse.

The 18th is the anchor of a swing of three particularly strong finishing holes, whose strength may have been forgotten over the years. The 16th, which plays straightaway, measures 439 yards, the 17th, a slight dogleg to the right, measures 458 yards, and the redone 18th plays to 440 yards. They had been even longer in the previous two Oak Hill Opens, measuring 441, 463, and 449 yards in both 1956 and 1968. They had nearly ruined Middlecoff. He had played them in eight strokes over par over the four rounds, and he had made seven on the 17th in the second round. Hogan had played them in four over, but Boros had played them in just one over. The 16th destroyed Kroll when he made his seven.

They were no more forgiving in 1989. Of those who were in position to win the championship, only Scott Simpson played them under par. Strange, Ian Woosnam, Mark McCumber, Chip Beck, Jumbo Ozaki, and Kite were all two over.

Through all the changes, the course itself retained its character. When the PGA Championship came to Oak Hill, in 1980, it was won by Jack Nicklaus, who had won his fourth Open only a month earlier, equaling the record held by Willie Anderson, Bobby Jones, and Ben Hogan. (His PGA Championship, by the way, was his fifth, matching the record held by Walter Hagen; Nicklaus is alone, however, with six Masters Tournaments.)

If the quality of the men who had won there indicated the quality of the golf course, then Oak Hill stood at the top. The last five times Oak Hill had been host to the game's greatest players, the tournaments had been won by the best of them. Sam Snead won the 1940 Rochester Open, and Ben Hogan the 1942 renewal; then Cary Middlecoff won the 1956 Open, followed by Lee Trevino in 1968; and Nicklaus won the 1980 PGA. You can't do better than that. Those who knew this record could assume, then, that the 1989 Open would be won by a player of the stature of Strange, Faldo, Ballesteros, or by someone about to climb to that level.

Early in the week the old course looked lovely in the warm, springtime sun. The trees had grown more mature than I remembered, closing in and narrowing the fairways, but at the same time framing them and laying out precise lines of play, and the *poa annua* and bentgrass fairways lay green and lush from the heavy rainfall that had soaked upper New York State through the previous two months. At times the rain overshadowed the golf, and it certainly affected how the Open was played.

Five-and-a-half inches of rain had fallen on Rochester in May, and another 2.3 inches through the first week and a half of June. With the crowds flocking through the gates early in Open week hoping to catch a glimpse of the practice rounds, another inch and a half fell on the course Monday and Tuesday, and at noon Wednesday, with the course crowded with spectators, rain began falling heavily once again. The storm lasted for quite some time; the course was being turned into a bog; and, with more rain forecast for Thursday, those who run the championship wondered if the first round might have to be postponed.

Thursday, however, turned out better than the forecast. Although clouds hung low and threatening throughout the day, and a good part of the round was played through a drizzle, the full-scale rainstorm that had been promised didn't develop, and the round was completed. The players began the day wearing sweaters, but shed them as the temperature rose.

We've seldom seen a day like this in the Open. The galleries had churned the ground beyond the restraining ropes into slippery, slimy mud through the early days. Spectators slipped and slid as they followed the players, occasionally losing their balance and falling to the ground, embarrassing them and ruining their clothes. Attempting to help the galleries get around and to help preserve the course, the grounds crew spread 500 cubic yards of tanbark in the worst areas, and where the muck lay deepest, oozing over shoetops, they laid four-by-eight sheets of plywood, which would cause trouble later.

The crewmen worked into exhaustion, arriving at four o'clock in the morning and remaining until 10 at night. Without this kind of effort, though, this Open couldn't have been played.

With the ground so soft, routine shots embedded, and with pools of water lying about, balls seemed to be in the players' hands as often as they lay on the ground. They were continually lifted and cleaned as the players took relief, walking them away from casual water, and incidentally moving them clear of the rough and other trouble, or dropping from plugged lies. Constantly on the move, rules officials sped from one trouble spot to another, offering relief to one player, denying it to another.

Seve Ballesteros had pulled his drive into the trees on the seventh hole, a 431-yard straightaway par four. The ground was sodden where his ball lay, and he felt he was entitled to drop from casual water. Mac England, a USGA official who ranked among the game's leading authorities on the rules, rushed to the spot, spoke briefly with Seve, and told him he could have relief. Ballesteros dropped the ball, and then England said, in his West Virginia twang, "Drop it again."

"Why's that?" Ballesteros asked.

A tall, lean, fun-loving man who enjoyed people and delighted at working any level of a golf tournament, England grinned and said, as if he were explaining the rules to a new golfer, "Because it rolled closer to the hole."

Seve lifted his ball and dropped it once again, looked at England, England nodded his head, and then, grinning his mischievous, disarming grin, Seve said, "Tough official." The gallery laughed.

This may have been the last time Mac was in action on a golf course. He died in October, at 73, while he was playing in Pensacola, Florida.

Ballesteros has always been an enigma in the U.S. Open. One of the most versatile and best all-around players in the game since the middle 1980s, he had never performed at his best in the U.S. Open. He often appears angry at appearing at all, and plays with none of the assurance and confidence he shows at the Masters or the British Open. He is, of course, more at home in Europe, but a golfer of his ability should play well everywhere. He seems to become disgusted when his ball finds the deep, severe U.S. Open rough, and gives the impression he loses interest.

He certainly has the strength to play from Open rough as well as anybody. For example, playing his approach to the second hole, a strong par four of 401 yards, Seve took a vicious swipe at the ball, ripped it from the rough, and carried it over the bunkers that pinch the opening down to a narrow neck, and onto the green. He made his par, but Ballesteros was not on his game this day. After birdieing the third hole, a solid par three of 211 yards, he shanked his approach to the fifth, the ball shot off to the right, hit the high branches of one tree, and dropped among a copse of others on the far side of the creek. He made six there, made up one of those strokes with a birdie-two on the sixth, bogeyed the seventh after his ruling from England, then made his four at the eighth. He stood one stroke over par on the ninth tee, another par four that starts out on low ground, begins a gradual rise to the green in the drive zone, and turns gently right, swinging around a grove of trees on the right, standing atop a steep but not very high hill.

The hole measures only 419 yards, hardly more than a drive and a pitch for Open-caliber players; the object here is to place the drive in a position that offers a clear line to the green. For reasons beyond comprehension, Ballesteros lashed into the shot as if he were trying to drive the green, hair flying, teeth gritting as if life itself hung in the balance. Predictably, the ball slipped off to the right toward a grove of trees, and rolled to the base of the abrupt rise. He had no shot. He couldn't advance his ball toward the green, and was left only with a pitch back to the fairway. Even then he took the riskier line, aiming toward the lower branches of the tree closest to the fairway and punching his shot through the leaves. He was lucky to have made it, but it saved him nothing. He bogeyed, made the turn in 37, came back in 38, and didn't have a part in the outcome, shooting 70, 76, and 69 in the subsequent rounds, 290 for the 72 holes, 12 strokes behind Strange.

While Ballesteros might have had his problems, a great many others didn't. Within hours after the start, it began to look as if the 72-hole record of 272, which Nicklaus had set at Baltusrol in 1980, might fall. With the ground so soft, both drives and approaches could be controlled more easily than under normal Open conditions, the players throwing their shots as the flagsticks. Emlyn Aubrey, a 25-year-old ex-college golfer from Louisiana State who had played the Asian tour the previous two years, teed off at 7:27 in the fourth group to start. He moved through the first nine in 36, attracting no attention at all, but suddenly the putts began to fall. A birdie on the 10th, another on the 11th, then two more on the 13th and 16th, and he dropped to three under par before most of the gallery had arrived.

A double-bogey-six on the devilishly difficult 17th brought him back to earth, but he still finished with 69, the clear leader before lunchtime. Still, he didn't stay atop the leaderboard for long. Bernhard Langer came in about an hour and a half later with 66, a stroke better than Scott Simpson, who was grouped with him, then in quick order came Nicklaus with 67, Kite with 67, Payne Stewart with 68, and then tall, lean Jay Don Blake with another 66. By day's end 21 men had broken Oak Hill's par of 70, and three men shared the lead at 66, one stroke ahead of four others at 67.

The Open had never seen scoring like that. Nine years earlier 19 men had broken par in the first round at Baltusrol, setting a record, but we had gone beyond that on this day. Talk sped through the gallery that for the first time the 72-hole score might fall below 270.

Langer's round was particularly impressive, built around superb iron play that left him constantly within birdie range, and sensational putting. He had 11 one-putt greens, even though he uses an odd grip (standing up to the ball in the right-handed position, he holds the putter grip with his left hand low down the shaft while he clamps the upper part of the grip against his left forearm with his right hand). He had his ball inside 20 feet on nine greens, birdied five of those, holed another putt from 25 feet, and still another from 60 feet. Out in 31, he played the second nine in even par 35 with four birdies, four bogeys, and one lone par.

Grouped with him, Scott Simpson, the 1987 Open champion, said, "This was one of the best putting rounds I've ever seen."

Finding Langer among the leaders, especially with such a good round, was surprising, for this was his best round of an unsatisfactory year. With a bad back that caused him constant pain, he had had only three reasonably good finishes on the American tour all year, placing eighth in the Hope in January, 12th at Pebble Beach two weeks later, and then third in the Heritage Classic a week after the Masters.

He had his first indication that this would not be his year late in February, when he missed the cut at Doral. That was only the beginning, though. March was terrible; in a three-week period he placed 70th, 67th, and 66th, climbed to 25th at Houston, then 26th at the Masters.

He had played slightly better in Europe, winning the Spanish Open, just after the Masters, but then placing 21st in Belgium, and 20th in the Volvo PGA, in England. He had, therefore, given no indication he could become a threat to win the Open. He wasn't; his 66 turned out to be a mirage.

Like Langer, Payne Stewart has a back problem as well. It hurt him so badly he withdrew from the Westchester Classic the week before the Open, and played at Rochester wearing an inflatable brace.

Playing more consistent golf than Blake, he too went out in 33 with two birdies and no bogeys, dipped to four under par after the 14th hole, the drive and pitch par four, but he lost strokes on both the 15th and 16th, falling two strokes behind Langer, playing an hour ahead. With those three punishing finishing holes ahead of him, Stewart's chance of catching up didn't look good, but he rifled five irons to six feet on the 17th, and 20 feet on the 18th and holed both putts, picking up the birdies he needed, and catching Langer.

How Blake turned up among the leaders defied logic. Once a promising young golfer, winner of the NCAA Championship, he failed to qualify for the tour in his first attempt, and almost gave up the game, taking a job in a hardware store and then in a golf shop, trying to support a wife and two children, and pay off a mortgage. He qualified for the tour in 1986, but his life away from the golf course had turned bitter. His father died in December of 1987, and he and his wife were divorced a month later.

"It was pretty hectic," Blake explained following his round. "It's been a struggle, but these things happen."

Great rounds happen as well, and this was among them. Blake birdied seven holes, four of them on the first nine, where he placed a three iron within six feet on the third, a six iron within eight feet on the sixth, both par threes, and nearly holed a five iron on the eighth, stopping it within three feet of the cup just after chipping in from 30 feet on the seventh. He ruined what could have been a sensational nine holes by double-bogeying the fifth. Out in 33, he came back in 33 as well, with three more birdies and one bogey. Except for the shot he chipped in, he made no unreasonable birdies; a 15-footer on the 13th and a 16-footer on the 18th the longest.

A one-stroke lead at this stage is meaningless, of course, particularly with three players who are shaky at best. Neither Langer nor Blake belonged on top—and indeed they would disappear soon enough—and Stewart had never shown he could play at his best level when it mattered most. Furthermore, Simpson, Nicklaus, and Kite stood just behind them.

Even though Nicklaus was 49 at the time, he couldn't be dismissed. No one had played golf at the highest level longer than Jack, and only Harry Varden matched him. Jack won his first Open in 1962 and his last Masters in 1986, and Vardon won his first British Open in 1896 and finished one stroke behind Ted Ray, another Englishman, in the 1920 U.S. Open. Both covered 24 years.

Those ahead of Nicklaus might have felt even more unsettled had they known he had opened with a better round than 67 only once in his Open career; he had shot 63 in the first round at Baltusrol nine years earlier, and had won with the record score of 272. To go even further, he had bettered 67 at all only then and 13 years earlier, when he had closed with 65 over the same course, setting the record 275 that he broke in 1980. Like Langer, though, Nicklaus's threat turned out to be less than it looked.

Nevertheless, strong players were grouped within reach of the leaders. Nick Faldo, who had lost to Strange in the playoff a year earlier, stood at 68, and Scott Hoch, whom Faldo had beaten in the Masters playoff earlier in the year, lurked another two strokes behind, at 70, along with Ian Woosnam, the chunky little Welshman, and Mark McCumber.

Others, however, weren't doing nearly as well, particularly Sandy Lyle, who had done nothing right all year. In perhaps the most dismal season of his career, Sandy shot 78, followed with 74, and missed the cut.

The leaders:

Bernhard Langer	66	Tom Pernice	67
Payne Stewart	66	Larry Nelson	68
Jay Don Blake	66	Nick Faldo	68
Scott Simpson	67	Raymond Floyd	68
Jack Nicklaus	67	Dillard Pruitt	68
Tom Kite	67	Kurt Beck	68
Joey Sindelar	67		

The second round began with one of those strange incidents that cannot be explained, and perhaps had never happened before in the history of tournament golf—at least no one can remember its having been done before. No one had made a hole-in-one in an Open since Ben Crenshaw on the ninth hole at Oakland Hills in 1985, but within about an hour and a half on Friday morning, four men holed their tee shots on the sixth.

The hole that morning was set in a hollow toward the front of the two-level fan-shaped green, in a position where shots that fell within relatively close range would funnel toward the cup. Doug Weaver, playing in the first group off the tee that day, at seven o'clock, had opened with 72, and had come to the sixth tee that second morning three over par for the day after a double-bogey-five on the third, and a bogey-six on the fourth.

He had made his par-four on the fifth, though, and in the company he was keeping, that was good enough to take the honor on the sixth. He was, then, the first man on the sixth tee that day. Drawing his seven iron, Weaver hit a high, lazy shot that carried past the flagstick, hit against the gentle slope that rises toward the upper level, took the backspin, then drew back down the hill and into the cup for an ace. It wasn't quite nine o'clock then, but a good-sized gallery had gathered in the grandstand to the right of the green, and they jumped and cheered as the ball dropped into the hole. It was quite a treat for those who had arrived early enough. When word spread, others wandered over, hoping they might see another. They didn't know what they were in for; a little more than an hour later there were three holes-in-one in less than 20 minutes.

Six other groups played through after Weaver's, and then Mark Wiebe arrived. He had started an hour and 10 minutes after Weaver, at 8:10. He played a seven iron as well, and hit a shot that drifted a little left of the flagstick, spun right when it hit the green, and dropped into the cup. Another roar, this time with the sense the gallery really didn't believe what it had seen.

Another group passed, then Jerry Pate climbed onto the tee. Pate carried his seven iron six or eight feet past the hole, and once again the ball hit into the slope and rolled back down and into the cup. The field had backed up by then, and another group, which included Nick Price, stood on the tee as Pate played his shot. After Pate, David Graham, and Hale Irwin, who were grouped together, had left the green (Irwin and Graham each made threes), Price chose a seven iron as well, played his ball about 10 feet to the right of the flagstick, and watched it jump forward, then curl back and into the cup, the fourth ace, three of them within four groups.

The gallery had grown with each succeeding ace, until spectators crowded eight deep behind the green, and three deep along the ropes leading from the tee. It was also becoming jaded. When Pate's shot dropped into the cup, someone cried out, "So what!," one assumed in jest. When Ken Green followed with a birdie-two, he was given light applause.

Called to account for why we had been blessed with this phenomenon, P.J. Boatwright, who set up the course, explained that each day he and the championship committee try to balance the relative difficulty of the hole locations throughout the course, placing some of them in easy positions, some in difficult spots, and assigning numbers ranging from one for the easier through four for the most testing.

Someone asked him what degree of difficulty he had assigned to the cup on the sixth. Boatwright smiled in a sheepish sort of way and said, "Obviously, very easy."

The hole-in-one kept Weaver in the Open; he shot 145, the highest score to qualify for the final 36 holes. Wiebe shot 71 and remained among the leaders, at 140, but neither Pate nor Price made the cut.

While the sixth hole was playing rather easily, the rest of Oak Hill wasn't. Where 21 men had broken par in the first round, only 15 shot sub-par rounds in the second, and when the day ended, only six men remained under par for the first 36 holes. Ian Woosnam was the first of these to finish, rushing to the turn in 33, then struggling home in 35, with three birdies, three holes to play, but then three-putted the 16th from 25 feet and had a six-footer slip past the cup on the 17th after his approach had missed the green. His 68 gave him 138 for the first 36 holes, and a clear lead that would last into late afternoon, for the first-round leaders all went out after lunch. When they did, only Blake played reasonably well, shooting 71 and hanging within reach of the lead.

Langer didn't; he had nothing left, bogeyed three holes on the first nine, double-bogeyed another, shot 40, then came back in 38. His 78 dropped him to 144, and he kept sinking from sight through the last two rounds. Ironically, he double-bogeyed the sixth, where four others had scored holes-in-one, by dropping his tee shot into the creek.

Stewart played only marginally better, holding at one over par through 14 holes, but then losing strokes on three of the last four, shooting 75, and falling to 141, but Simpson had held fast, played a not-too-steady four-birdie, four-bogey 70, and with 137, passed Woosnam.

Simpson had left the first tee at 1:22; within an hour after he finished, the lead was out of his reach, for Curtis Strange had rushed to the front.

Strange had opened with a dull 71, ruined by double-bogey-six on the 17th, but he is capable of wild bursts of scoring, and he played the second round as if he not only might break both the 18- and 72-hole scoring record, but run away with the championship as well.

One of the last starters, beginning a little after two o'clock, Curtis opened by reeling off four straight threes, dropping a five iron on the first and an eight iron on the second within ten feet, and holing both putts for birdies. A par on the third, and then he came to the fourth, at 570 yards the first of the two par-five holes. A 260-yard drive, then a safe four iron left him within 115 yards of the green. A pitching wedge flew straight at the cup, hit short of the pin, checked, then tumbled into the cup for an eagle-three.

Four under for the round then, Strange knew he was closing in on the lead.

"Don't back off now," he told himself. "This is the Open. Let's keep it going."

He didn't, following with five routine pars, missing one putt from six feet and another from 15 that might have been birdies. A 20-footer fell on the 10th and a 15-footer on the 14th. Six under now. A missed green at the 15th, but a chip to one foot to save par, and then an eight iron to four feet on the 16th, and another putt fell. Clearly leading the Open now, he stood seven under; par in and he would match the Open's scoring record of 63, set by Johnny Miller at Oakmont back in 1973, and matched by Nicklaus and Tom Weiskopf at Baltusrol in 1980.

Oak Hill's 17th was playing harder in relation to par than any other hole; the field averaged half a stroke over par that day, and it cost Strange a shot at the record. Still, he brought his problems on himself, missing the first fairway he had failed to hit all day, and finding his ball in a bad lie. A four-iron second caught the right greenside bunker, and he missed a saving putt from five feet. Back to six under. Another four iron to the 18th set him up with a chance to win that stroke back, but his putt from 15 feet barely slipped past the cup. A 64.

Not only did Strange's 18-hole score miss the Open record by one stroke, but so also did his 36-hole score of 135. Both Nicklaus, in 1980, and T.C. Chen, in 1985, shot 134s. Mike Souchak had shot 135 in 1960, the year Arnold Palmer came from seven strokes behind and won at Cherry Hills; Bert Yancey had matched it in 1968, the last previous Open at Oak Hill; and then Tom Watson had equaled it in 1975, George Burns in 1981, and Scott Simpson at The Country Club in 1988. Strangely enough, only Nicklaus had won the Open in those years.

While Strange was ripping the course apart, he barely kept ahead of Kite, plodding along two groups behind him. Caught in one of those days that separate the good players from the not-so-good, Kite wasn't playing particularly well; even though he seldom placed his approaches within birdie range, he made his figures, and indeed scored reasonably well. He had a bad break on the sixth; he hit a stunning shot that covered the flagstick all the way, but where what seemed like half the field holed in one, Kite's ball rolled within three inches of the cup, then stopped. A two, which by then must have seemed like a bogey.

He gave that stroke back by mis-hitting his drive on the ninth so badly he could only pitch back to the fairway from among the trees and take his bogey. Even par now, he held his position through the 13th, then played a nice soft pitch to the 14th, holing a 15-footer for his second birdie of the day, and followed up with an even better seven iron to six feet on the 15th, and holing that for a birdie-two.

Two under now, but he still had those three hard holes to play. They nearly ruined him. He lost a stroke at the 16th, where his punch shot from the right rough overran the green, and he struggled with the last two holes, pulling his approach into the 17th left greenside bunker and holing from six feet for his par, then driving into the rough again at the 18th, leaving his approach short, and chipping within a foot. With 69 and 136, he had climbed into second place.

Kite's putting had been impeccable. He hadn't three-putted a green during the first two rounds, even though he had begun putting cross-handed only a week earlier, at Westchester.

"I've practiced putting cross-handed for years," he explained, "just trying to get the left arm going. It's not that big a deal." Perhaps.

The leaders after 36 holes:

Curtis Strange	71-64—135	
Tom Kite	67-69—136	
Scott Simpson	67-70—137	
Jay Don Blake	66-71—137	
Ian Woosnam	70-68—138	
Mark McCumber	70-68—138	

While the rain had held off through most of the day, it had pounded down so heavily just before five o'clock that the USGA had suspended play for about 15 minutes. At its worst, the delay was inconvenient; everyone finished, which, as it turned out, was about the best break the USGA had all week. No one could guess what would have happened if some players would have had to return the following morning, because they simply could not have played. Worse lay ahead.

Heavy, drenching rains dumped another two inches on Oak Hill overnight. Already swollen, the creek over-flowed and swept away some of those four-by-eight plywood sheets laid down to help spectator traffic, floating them toward three huge culverts that cross under the club's driveway and drain the water off the property. Caught broadside in the current, the plywood couldn't fit through, became flattened against two culverts, and acted like corks in a bottle. The water backed up, and before long the fifth, sixth, and eighth fairways lay under water, at some points a foot deep.

Arriving at the club at perhaps 4:30, Rusty Madden, the assistant superintendent, looked about and decided his best move might be to go to breakfast, because nobody could possibly play golf that day.

Two and a half hours later, P.J. Boatwright drove through the gates.

"I was half-asleep when I got here," he said later, "but that Mississippi River coming down No. 8 woke me up."

Play was to have begun at 8:45, but Boatwright alerted the USGA's championship committee to make other plans; that wouldn't be possible.

The back wall of a bunker behind the 13th green had collapsed from water cascading down the slope rising behind it, and a rivulet ran across the green from back to front, runoff from the clubhouse area. Where the water lay ankle deep in the landing zone of the fifth, a family of ducks—a mother and five or six chicks—swam about. Deep pools lay on the landing zone of the seventh, which runs parallel to the fifth and eighth, and a great pond collected near the big culvert that carries the flow of the creek off the Oak Hill property by the eighth hole. A beaver was seen swimming through the flow near the sixth hole.

Walking about without boots was impossible. Where a week earlier it had been possible to walk across some parts of the creek without getting your feet wet, several small footbridges spanning the creek lay under water, and the tanbark floated about the fairways and the rough.

The grounds crew swollen to about 50 men for the week of the Open, had been struggling since about five o'clock. The rain had stopped by then, but the conditions were growing no better. Oak Hill is located in the village of Pittsford. Asked to give whatever help it could, the fire department sent a pumper. It sat along the driveway and sucked out 1,000 gallons a minute from the lake in front of the blocked culverts and spewed it across the road, and into the creek on the other side.

It made a spectacular show, but the conditions didn't begin to ease until Tim Moraghan, the USGA's agronomist on the scene, wrestled the plywood sheets free of the culverts. Once the culverts stood free, the water rushed through the huge tubes, and the water level fell. The grounds crew manned their squeegees, pushing standing water into the creek, where it was carried away, some of the footbridges rose above the tide, and within a short time were clear, but still every footstep raised water.

Surveying the course as best he could in the conditions, Boatwright said, "I've never seen a course so badly damaged by the weather as this one. I mean the places where there has been spectator and vehicular damage. I sympathize with the Oak Hill members."

While the grounds crew struggled to make the course playable, the USGA struggled to solve what had become a major problem. How should the Open proceed? Play could be cancelled for the day, and the championship could wind up with a double round of 36 holes on Sunday, or it could finish on Monday. Of course, it might be possible to work in the round on Saturday.

Considering the alternatives, Boatwright said, "Our philosophy is to play when you can." They would try to play Saturday afternoon.

Pairings were rearranged, splitting the 71-man field into two groups, the higher scorers beginning from the 10th tee, the lower scorers from the first. Instead of grouping them in pairs, the customary procedure, they would be grouped in threes, and play would begin at 12:51, if it would indeed be possible.

No one could be sure at this point, and the USGA set two deadlines. First, at 11 o'clock it would say whether play would begin at 12:51 or whether the start would be delayed another hour. Second, at noon it would decide if the round would be played at all or be put off until Sunday.

As each hour passed, and the rain held off, the course became more and more playable, principally through the mammoth effort of the grounds crew, which labored without let-up. Players had begun arriving in mid-morning, the deadlines passed, and the field was able to begin on time.

The course was a bog. Some low-lying areas, for instance the valley separating the 14th tee from the green, wouldn't drain, and in some areas, like the 11th, a par three, the ground seemed to give way and sink under your feet.

With the courses so soft, and with balls occasionally picking up mud, speculation arose that the USGA might permit the players to lift, clean, and place the ball in the fairway, a local rule often put into effect when the tour runs into this kind of weather. The speculation was wrong: the USGA had never bent before difficult conditions in the past, and it wouldn't now. The Open would be played according to the rules.

Strange was in the last group to start, at 2:30, along with Kite and Simpson, and just behind McCumber, Woosnam, and Blake. Play was painfully slow, partly because the field had been grouped in threes, but principally because the ball became embedded so often, allowing the players to lift, clean, and drop a plugged ball, and also because so much casual water lay about, which gave them the same option. The Strange-Kite-Simpson group played the first nine in a little more than two hours and 45 minutes. Had they continued at that rate the round would have taken five and a half hours, but the pace picked up somewhat coming in, and the round was completed in about five hours and 25 minutes.

Furthermore, a slight wind had come up, which, combined with the sodden ground, turned Oak Hill into a more difficult challenge. Under the circumstances, some scores ran lower than we might have expected. Fred Couples shot 67, the best round of the day, and Brian Claar and Tom Pernice 68. They had begun the day too far behind for their hot rounds to affect the standing, but Larry Nelson and Jumbo Ozaki shot 68 as well, thrusting them into contention, at 209.

Whether it was the conditions, or the pace of play, Strange wasn't the golfer this day he had been on Friday. The shots didn't ring from his clubs with the old authority, he couldn't establish his rhythm, missing fairways and greens, along with a number of shots that could have saved him. For example, where he had hit 13 of the 14 fairways on driving holes in the second round, he hit only eight in the third, and where he had needed only 25 putts in the second round, he used 33 in the third.

Out in 37, he continued to struggle coming back, seldom in position to birdie, and missing those few where he had remote chances. He looked as if he might live through the home nine in par, but the 17th cost him another stroke. Once again he drove badly, and missed from 15 feet. In three rounds, he had dropped four strokes there. With a par four at the 18th, Curtis had come home in 36, and shot 73 for the round. Where he had birdied five holes on Friday, he had birdied none on Saturday, and he fell from the lead.

Meantime, others were having troubles as well. Blake played reasonably well through the 14th hole, standing one under par, but suddenly he lost strokes on three consecutive holes, one on the 15th, the par three, where he overshot the green, chipped all the way off the green, then had to chip once more—a two-chip green. Blake shot 72, and finished with 209, one stroke behind Strange, with 208.

While both Strange and Blake were laboring, so were Woosnam and McCumber. Woosnam shot 73 and fell to 211 for 54 holes, and McCumber shot 72, moving a stroke ahead of Woosnam, at 210. Simpson, though, kept up his steady, first-class golf, shaving one stroke from par with 69, and 206 for the 54 holes.

Tom Kite shot 69 as well, which thrust him into the lead, at 205. With earlier rounds of 67 and 69, he was running a stroke ahead of the pace Lee Trevino had set at Oak Hill 21 years earlier, and he had played so steadily it seemed possible that like Lee he might play all four rounds in the 60s.

Kite's 69 wasn't easily won though; it reflected his determination. Off to a shaky start, he bogeyed the fourth, the par five, by overshooting the green with a sand wedge, then missing an 18-inch putt after chipping close, then bogeyed the fifth, a hole that would cause him even more problems later, three-putting from 60 feet.

He was playing loose, uninspiring golf until he came to the ninth, where he curled in a 35-footer for a birdie. He seemed to perk up after that, and his shots took on some of their usual authority. A six iron to 18 feet on the 10th and another birdie, an eight iron to 10 feet on the 12th, and a nine iron to five feet on the 14th. The putts dropped, and Kite had slipped two strokes under par with four holes to play. A stroke lost at the 15th, where he three-putted once again, missing from four feet, but then he saved his four at the difficult 17th, and closed out his round with a routine par on the 18th. Back in 33 after an indifferent 36 going out, he had moved ahead of the field.

Kite was having a good year. He had already won at Bay Hill and the Players Championship a week later, placed second at Pebble Beach, and fifth at Westchester the week before the Open. Always a steady player, his record in the Open didn't reflect how well he had played through most of his career. Kite had placed among the top 10 scorers in only one of the 17 he had played, and that had been 15 years earlier, when he had finished in eighth place at Winged Foot, in 1974. He had missed the cut in six Opens, once as an amateur, but again as late as 1984, when the Open had returned to Winged Foot, and in the last three years had placed 35th at Shinnecock Hills, 46th at Olympic, and 36th at The Country Club. He had never been in better position than now, though. He stood one stroke ahead of Simpson, and three ahead of Strange.

The third-round leaders:

Tom Kite	67-69-69—205
Scott Simpson	67-70-69—206
Curtis Strange	71-64-73—208
Larry Nelson	68-73-68—209
Jumbo Ozaki	70-71-68—209
Jay Don Blake	66-71-72—209
Tom Pernice	67-75-68—210
Mark McCumber	70-68-72—210
Ian Woosnam	70-68-73—211
Chip Beck	71-69-71—211
Brian Claar	71-72-68—211
Jose-Maria Olazabal	69-72-70—211

Oak Hill had dried somewhat by Sunday morning, although the ground was still mushy in spots. Pools of water still collected in some low areas, and the grounds crew was still pumping bunkers dry as the crowd began filing through the gates in early morning. A cool breeze swept over the course, and the dull grey overcast began breaking up. Soon the sun shone through, and it was a warm, pleasant Sunday afternoon, filled with growing drama and broken dreams.

As the leader, Kite was paired with Simpson, the last two men off the tee, just behind Strange and Nelson. Blake and Ozaki played together in the third-from-last pairing, and McCumber and Pernice ahead of them. Of those who would matter in the final round, Woosnam and Beck played first, at 1:25, ahead of Olazabal and Claar.

Off to a fast start with good birdies on the first two holes, Woosnam was making a run at the lead, but he stumbled on the ninth, overshooting the green, then taking three putts. His double-bogey-six left him too much ground to make up, but he hung on until the very end, birdieing three holes on the second nine, including the 18th, a 440-yard hole he played with a drive and nine iron (his drive *carried* 290 yards). He shot 68 for the day, and 279 for the 72 holes, exceptionally good for a man playing in his first Open.

McCumber and Beck found themselves in about the same positions, playing good rounds of 69 and 68, but needing something better than that. They tied Woosnam at 279.

The drama of the day would be played out among the last two groups, and through the first four holes at least, it looked as if Kite would walk away with the championship. Although he began with a shaky first hole, driving into the left rough, then holing a 15-foot putt to save his par, Kite played the first few holes with confidence he's seldom shown in one of the four major competitions.

After a routine par-four on the second, he rifled a two iron perhaps 20 feet right of the hole on the third, then rolled in the putt for a birdie-two. Simpson, meanwhile, had missed the green badly, pulled his iron well left of the green and down a hill. When he bogeyed, Kite had suddenly dropped to six under par for 57 holes, and had shot into a three-stroke lead, which at the time looked safe, for Kite had seldom played with the assurance he was showing here.

A routine par-five at the fourth, and then Kite stepped onto the fifth tee, the 406-yard par four where the creek borders the fairway before swinging across in front of the green. Here Kite threw away the Open.

What happened with his drive is difficult to say. He seemed to have thrust his hips into the shot too quickly, causing him to block it out. Whatever the cause, his ball shot off to the right in a high, arching parabola, and came down into the center of the creek, never touching land. Kite seemed stunned. He stood on the tee, his feet not moving, still clutching his driver, and stared after the ball, as if he couldn't believe what he had done. Barring a miracle shot, he's lose at least one stroke here, maybe more, for when he dropped clear of the water, his ball lay in the rough, blocked from a direct line to the green by a billowy tree. Although he had dropped his ball into a decent lie, and might conceivably have sliced a ball around the tee and onto the green, the wind was blowing from right to left, which would work against the shot; should he miss the green, there was no limit to the strokes he might take.

Kite chose the safer approach, feeling that with his wedge game, he could save a bogey. He played onto the fairway short of the creek, then lofted a lovely pitch that hit the green, then drew back about level with the flagstick, perhaps 12 feet to the right. Seeing how well he had played that shot, and remembering he had holed almost every putt he had had to over the first three days, I felt sure Tom would make his five, leave the green five under par for the distance, and still hold a two-stroke lead over Simpson, three strokes over Strange.

Standing up to the ball with his cross-handed grip, Kite stroked the ball nicely; it ran toward the hole at just the right pace, but it slipped past the low side of the cup and rolled not much more than two feet past. A six, we thought. That would hurt, but he'd hang onto the lead. Now Kite stunned us all; his second putt grazed the edge of the cup but somehow stayed out. Now instead of a six, he'd made seven, and fallen into a tie with Simpson.

As Tom's second putt eased past the cup, the gallery groaned, and spectators turned away, embarrassed for him. Although he had to be shocked, Tom showed hardly any emotion. His face turned blank, and his lips pressed together in a grim, straight line. He handed his putter to his caddy, who had been holding the flagstick, said something quietly, then walked toward the sixth tee.

We didn't know it then, but that was the end of Kite. Not only had he fallen into a tie for first place, he had given new hope to those behind him, particularly to Curtis Strange, who by then had played through the seventh and stood two under par, just one stroke back now, along with Ozaki.

Strange had realized that so long as Kite had played as he had through the first three rounds, he would have to make birdies to catch him, and the birdies simply would not come. Now, though, when Kite made his seven, Strange said to himself, "Now I have a chance, a real, real chance. Now I can play my game and still win the Open."

He had indeed been playing his game, hitting fairways and greens, parring hole after hole. When he made his four at the ninth, he had parred 17 of the last 18 holes he had played; only the bogey on the 17th hole of the third round had interrupted his string of regulation golf.

At about the time Strange had passed the ninth, Kite had bogeyed the eighth, and now Strange was tied for first place. When Kite bogeyed the 10th he fell out of a tie and began a slide that would drop him into a tie for eighth place. He had gone out in 38, followed his bogey at the 10th with double bogeys at the 13th and 15th, came back in 40, and finished with 78, which he said was "by far the worst round I've had for five or six years. You don't build a reputation for consistency like I have by having rounds like this." He had, however, shot 77 in the first round of the Memorial, in May, and had shot 75s in the last rounds at Doral and in the Masters, and indeed had not shot a final round in the 60s since the Los Angeles Open, in January.

Kite has a history of somewhat weak finishes in the Open. He had closed with 75 in 1988, and 76 in 1987. He had had a worse finish early in his career, shooting 77 at Cherry Hills in 1978, a year after finishing with 76 at Southern Hills.

Furthermore, this had been the third major tournament he might have won with a strong closing round. He had come to the 18th hole of the 1986 Masters needing a birdie-three to tie Jack Nicklaus, but his putt from perhaps 12 feet slipped past the cup.

While it was disappointing, we can't call that a collapse, but his seven at the fifth at Oak Hill brought to mind his six at the 10th at Royal St. George's in the 1985 British Open. Tom had shot 67 in the third round, then 32 on the first nine of the fourth round, and had come to the 10th hole in command of the championship, leading by two strokes. There he pulled a nine-iron approach far left of the green, stubbed his pitch and dropped his ball into a bunker, bladed his bunker shot across the green, pitched back on close enough to hole out for a double bogey. He shot 40 on the home nine, 285 for the championship, and Sandy Lyle won with 282.

It is a shame that this has happened to Kite, a genuinely likeable man. By the end of 1989, he had won more money on the PGA Tour than anyone— more than $5 million, passing both Jack Nicklaus and Tom Watson—but never a tournament of lasting significance. It is a pity, because winning an Open, a British Open, or a Masters would mean so much to him, and at 40, he hasn't much time left.

When Kite bogeyed the eighth, Simpson made six, then bogeyed the ninth, but where Kite continued his fall, Simpson righted himself. He stood at even par for the distance with nine holes to play, just two strokes behind Strange and Ozaki, who had birdied the 10th to climb into the tie, at two under par. The Open wasn't over just yet, and Simpson would hang on a bit longer. He played a nice pitch to the 12th to pull back to one under par, but he could go no further. Bogeys on the 14th and 15th ruined whatever chance he might have had, and he finished with 75 for the round, 281 for the 72 holes.

Strange, meantime, had hit eight of his first nine greens and made one par after another. His face bearing an expression of grim determination, he played one superb stroke after another—drives into fairways, irons onto greens; no one could have asked for better tee-to-green golf. But the putts wouldn't fall. A three wood and an eight iron to 12 feet on the 12th, his best chance yet, and the putt slipped past. Three good shots onto the long 13th, and still another par, and then a two iron and wedge to the 14th, but another missed putt from 15 feet.

Still two under, but by now the field had bunched up. It was 5:10 in the afternoon, and six men stood within one stroke of one another. After bogeying the 13th McCumber had birdied the 16th to dip one under par; Ozaki had bogeyed the 14th and fallen a stroke behind; Woosnam was finishing up with birdies on both the 15th and 18th, again falling to one under for 72 holes; Beck had birdied the eighth, 11th, and 12th, but then could make nothing but pars; and with his birdie on the 12th, Simpson had moved back to one under. It was still a tight, tense battle; one mistake could cost anyone the championship, and a few birdies could win it.

Strange seemed to have made an error on the 15th, the 177-yard par three. Playing away from a pond crowding against the right of the green, Strange pulled his four iron onto the left fringe, and his chip curled slightly right and rolled perhaps six feet past the cup. Now he might lose a stroke and fall back into a tie, leaving those last three tough holes to play. Curtis studied his putt, and rolled it into the hole. A par three; still one stroke ahead with those demanding finishing holes lying ahead.

For a time Strange's drive to the 16th looked as if it might bound into the rough. He pulled it slightly, and when it came to earth it continued moving left, stopping just on the edge of the fairway. From there Strange played a six iron that seemed to fly directly at the flagstick. It came down on the green, and pulled up 16 to 18 feet short of the hole, leaving him a straight, uphill putt.

Strange had birdied the 16th on Friday, on his way to shooting his 64. He hadn't had a birdie since, and had played 35 holes in three over par. Now, with the Open still to be won, he stroked the ball right into the hole. A birdie at last. He stood three strokes under par, and had opened his lead to two strokes, leaving some breathing room for those last two trying holes.

Now for the 17th, the hole that had given him so much trouble through the first three rounds. He hadn't made a four yet, and stood four over par on this one hole alone. Now he threaded a drive into the fairway, then ripped into a three iron, carrying the bunker boring in from the left, and onto the green. Two putts, and he had his par.

One hole to play now, holding a two-stroke cushion. Another drive into the fairway, then a six iron left and above the hole. Strange strode toward the green to the rising cheers of the gallery, bunched deep around the green. It had been 38 years since a man had won two consecutive Opens, and the crowd wanted to share the moment. Climbing the grade leading to the green, Strange waved to the spectators, then made a fist and thrust it high above his head, smiling and reacting to the acclaim. Only some unthinkable error could cost him the Open. He would take no chances here.

Strange's ball had settled 25 feet or so left and beyond the hole, which was cut into the lower right corner. Since the ball would run downhill on a slick green, he couldn't afford to leave the ball short and risk a second downhill putt. He didn't; a firm stroke rolled the ball six or eight feet past the hole, but now he could come at it uphill. His second putt rolled true to the cup, but stopped short, and then he tapped it in. A bogey-five, but a round of 70, and a 72-hole score of 278, enough to win.

Later in the day, with the trophy in hand once again, Strange climbed onto the platform in the press center and sat before the reporters as he had done a year earlier. There was a difference, though. He had dedicated the

1988 championship to his late father, Tom Strange, who had died when Curtis and his twin brother, Allan, were 14.

"It was emotional last year," he said, thinking back to his comments at The Country Club. "This year it's more a feeling of satisfaction, I guess; a feeling of accomplishment, because to win the Open two years in a row is really something. It's hard to describe the feeling."

Speaking of his last round, Curtis said, "I played very well today." Then, shaking his head, he continued, "To go so long as I did without making a birdie . . . It's tough to play an Open course."

Thinking of his two Opens, and reflecting that so many exceptional players had failed to win in consecutive years, Strange said, "I've put myself in position to do something in this game."

He has indeed, but considering how the game has evolved, he must win something other than the Open. In Hogan's time and, to a lesser extent, in Palmer's and Nicklaus's time, the U.S. Open might have been enough, but the world has moved on. The British Open has made remarkable progress since the time Palmer gave life to what had become a moribund championship, and the Masters has become the goal of every player of quality; just to play in it signifies a golfer has arrived. The game has become more balanced; Strange must win at least one of those others as well.

For the moment, however, two consecutive U.S. Opens was quite enough, but he felt it needed a dedication. Winding up his talk, Curtis said, "This one's for me and Sarah and Thomas and David," his wife and two sons. "You sacrifice a lot to play this game; I sacrifice and they sacrifice. It's a team effort."

5. The British Open

Arnold Palmer, whose magnetism and bold game changed golf forever, is credited with reviving the British Open simply by playing in it. Palmer's first visit was in 1960, and though he was only the runner-up, the American conquest had begun. In the 24 years from 1960 through 1983, Americans won 16 times. The end of American domination began with the emergence of a flamboyant Spaniard, Severiano Ballesteros, who won the Open in 1979. Europeans discovered they could play this game, and some of them became as good as any Americans who stepped out on the tee. The American grip was broken. Beginning with 1984, the Open was won by Ballesteros (twice), Britons Sandy Lyle and Nick Faldo, and Australian Greg Norman. The Americans used to cover the leaderboard, but even that had pretty much ended.

The reversal came in the person of another small-town American. Mark Calcavecchia, 29, a strapping guy with auburn hair and freckles; born in the flat, windswept expanses of Laurel, Nebraska; at age 13, moved with his family to West Palm Beach, Florida, which he learned to love when he found he could play golf even on Christmas Day. As a pro, he struggled for five years, even caddied a few times for his friend, Ken Green, then broke through with a victory in 1986. He won once each in each of the next two years, then exploded in 1989, winning both the Phoenix Open and the Los Angeles Open. He is one of that growing group of Americans who feel they must play overseas, and especially in the Open, to stamp themselves as world golfers. This 118th Open was his third. He tied for 11th in 1987, and he missed the cut in 1988.

With the victory at Royal Troon, Calcavecchia won his first major championship in nine years on the PGA Tour. He scored the first victory by an American in six year. And one other thing—he beat the stork. He played the entire Open with one ear listening for the squall of a new arrival back across the Atlantic. His wife, Sheryl, was at home near Phoenix, Arizona, awaiting the birth of their first child. (It was a girl, and she arrived about three weeks later.)

And he helped make Open history. He was not even a factor in this Open until he birdied the 72nd hole after a monumental eight iron. That tied him with two Australians—Norman, the 1986 Open champion, who returned a course-record 64, and Wayne Grady, who led for about two and a half rounds, and who would finish second for the 27th time in his career. They became the first three-way playoff in Open history, and also the first under the four-hole aggregate adopted by the Royal and Ancient Golf Club in 1985. Then Calcavecchia won on another incredible shot to the 18th after Norman bunkered his tee shot on the final playoff hole. So this Open became notable for another reason. It completed Norman's Grand Slam of Disappointments. Fuzzy Zoeller beat him in an 18-hole playoff in the 1984 U.S. Open; Bob Tway beat him by holing out a bunker shot on the last hole of the 1986 PGA Championship; Larry Mize beat him again in the 1987 Masters, holing out a 120-yard pitch on the second playoff hole. And now Calcavecchia at the British Open.

Tom Watson, seeking a record-tying sixth Open, was more like his old self than at any time since losing to Ballesteros at St. Andrews in 1984. But the rest of the usual all-star cast were not their usual selves. Ballesteros, the defending champion, finished third from last, Bernhard Langer did finish last, and Nick Faldo, Sandy Lyle, and Ian Woosnam couldn't get off dead center. Low-European honors went to an opera-loving Irishman named David Feherty. And Royal Troon, holding its sixth Open, also wasn't its old self. Gripped by warm, dry, windless weather, the old links took an awful beating, most of all from Calcavecchia, who speaks the way he plays, flat-out and forthright: "I played great golf, but I got awful lucky, too."

If you wanted to find the soon-to-be Open champion after the first round, you would have had to rummage around in the pack. There were seven men tied for second, jammed two strokes off the lead. He wasn't one of them. There were eight others three strokes back, and he wasn't there, either. And another seven four strokes back, and still no Calcavecchia. Finally—there he was, five behind, in that crowd at 71. No one was paying attention to him. A 71 didn't mean much. It was four strokes back and a tie for 24th. The mild weather had turned Royal Troon into a cakewalk. A total of 41 players—more than one-fourth of the field—broke par and another 19 matched it. Calcavecchia's 71 was hardly an indifferent one. After a birdie at No. 2, he started to stumble. He bogeyed three of the next four holes and seemed ready to crash. He righted himself with a birdie at No. 8 and made the turn in one-over-par 37. After a bogey at No. 10, he brought his game under control and made three birdies the rest of the way. He was done for the day and forgotten long before the day's key figure teed off.

Every Open seems to have a mystery man. He didn't take long to emerge in this one. He did it by smashing his way giddily into the first-round lead on a six-under-par 66 in his first Open. How big was his gallery? "Well, at first," he said, "there was my father . . ." This was Wayne Stephens, or as some wag in the press center put it, "Wayne Stephens, MC." The "MC" didn't stand for Military Cross. It stood for "Missed Cut." Stephens was a long-suffering golfer. His career was a collection of disasters. Condensed, it read this way: Age 28; seven times through the PGA European Tour qualifying school, starting in 1978; won his playing card (for the third time) in 1988; missed the 36-hole cut in 16 of his 17 starts in 1988; in 1989, up to the British Open, made it in eight of 15 starts, his finishes ranging from 22nd to 66th.

"It's a marvelous feeling I have at the moment," Stephens said, meeting the press for the first time in his 11 years as a pro. "I don't think it's sunk in yet." Stephens not only returned a 66, he did it without a bogey, a remarkable accomplishment on Royal Troon for anyone, much less a golfer of his modest credentials. Nick Faldo, the 1987 Open champion and reigning Masters champion, was the only other man in a field of 156 to come through the first round without a bogey—17 pars and a birdie for a 71.

This is the secret to Troon: Make hay going out, then hold on coming in. Stephens, a late starter, went it one better. Taking advantage of the benign conditions, he made four birdies going out, from two, five, eight, and 30 feet. He added two more coming in, from 12 feet at No. 15 and 18 feet at the intimidating 223-yard 17th. But coming down the stretch, the screws started to tighten, he said. The legs were going. He was working on his 15th cigarette, more than double his daily ration. Try as he might, he couldn't blank things from his mind. He knew he was leading. Just one hole to go. And he hit his drive into the rough. But he pulled himself together, chopped out with a sand wedge, then dropped an 85-yard pitch to within four feet of the hole, and saved his par for the bogey-free 66. "I think I'll be able to sleep quite well tonight," Stephens insisted. Not that anyone really expected him to hold up the next day. But if he did, could he still hold off the pack at his heels? Which, by the way, may have been the oddest mix in recent Open history.

Lumped at four-under-par 68 were two-time Open champion Lee Trevino, big-hitting Fred Couples, 1987 runner-up Paul Azinger, and the always-threatening Jose-Maria Olazabal, along with Eduardo Romero, the Argentinian who seems to play his best in the Open; Wayne Grady, an Australian on the American tour, and Miguel Martin, a little-known Spaniard.

Trevino was 49 now, still his bubbly self, and the crowd favorite, as usual. His 68 was good for a share of the lead until Stephens came in late in the day, so this Open was the 1989 Masters revisited. Just some three months earlier, he led the Masters for a while in the first round. Overall, it was one of his best showings at Augusta National. He finished 18th on a course he doesn't like, in a tournament he doesn't like. The British Open is a different matter. Trevino, who won in 1971 and 1982, found flat Royal Troon much to his liking. The dry, hard fairways were "running"—giving plenty of roll. And the rough was thin and patchy, a blessing to his low-flying, left-to-right shots. "The rough was my problem in the past," he said. "I hit a low 'cut,' and the ball would run right off the fairway and I couldn't get to the green."

How many fairways did you hit today? someone asked. "Just about all of them," Trevino said, grinning. "Just didn't stay on 'em. But with this rough, you could get to the green with an iron or a wood, even." He was dazzling on the greens. "Really had the flat stick working," is the way he puts it. He needed just 27 putts—nine one-putt greens, six of them for his six birdies, and coming in he one-putted the last five holes for three birdies and two pars. "The putting is good because I'm playing more," he said. He had played in only 10 tournaments in all of 1988, concentrating instead on his job as a commentator on golf telecasts. But he had already played in 10 so far in 1989, including the Hartford Open two weeks earlier, where he tied for fourth. The week before that, he was a joint fifth in the Western Open, on the long and grueling Butler National. All of this was done, he said, in the name of the wildly popular Senior PGA Tour, which he planned to join when he turned 50 in December. "I'd join right now if they'd let me," he said. Would you join the seniors if you won this British Open? came the question. Trevino cackled. "I was born at night, but not *last* night," he said. "Why should I play with the flat-bellies when I can play with the round-bellies?"

Two of the American flat-bellies were among those tied with him at 68—Couples and Azinger. Couples was more impressed with his playing partner, Nick Faldo, than with his own score. "I enjoyed playing with Nick—just the way he plays," Couples said. "He didn't make a bogey." Couples made only one himself, when he three-putted the par-three eighth from 15 feet, missing a four-footer for his par. That was an astonishing miss, considering he had holed from 20, 45, and eight feet for three consecutive birdies, starting at No. 4. As for Azinger, after his opening tee shot, he did well just to get his mind back on his game. Planning to fall short of the fairway bunkers at No. 1, he hit a three iron off the tee, and found a bunker. That cost him a bogey right off the bat. He made one other, at No. 13. He far offset those with six birdies, and came within a whisker of taking sole possession of second place. His five-iron approach at the 18th was rolling right for the hole, about to become an eagle-two for a 67. But it lipped out and came to rest about an inch from the cup. He shrugged it off and looked ahead to the final round. "I just hope that by Sunday, I have a number [three-round total] that will allow me to shoot an achievable number to win the tournament," he said.

The parade of the unknown golfers started early. It was almost two hours before Stephens even teed off that Gene Sauers, 29, an American tour pro with two victories in his six years, lit up the scoreboard with a six-under-par 30 going out. But he came back in 40, though with nothing worse than a bogey. Argentina's Eduardo Romero, also at 68, was not unknown to Open-watchers. He was 13th in 1988. He put his 300-yard drives to good use and mauled Troon's four par-fives—an eagle and three birdies. He led off with the eagle at the 557-yard No. 4, on a drive, a three iron, and a nine-foot putt. For the birdies, he holed from two feet after chipping at No. 6, two-putted from 12 feet at No. 11, and dropped a 16-footer after a wedge at No. 16. Also at 68, and the biggest surprise after Stephens himself, was Miguel Martin, the unknown and diminutive (5-foot, 1-inch) Spaniard who was lucky just to be in the Open. He had missed by a stroke in the qualifier, and was an alternate, a determined one. "I was prepared to stand around the first tee all day, just in case somebody didn't show up," Martin said. Sure enough, someone didn't. On Tuesday, Jay Haas withdrew, and Martin was summoned. He didn't get much practice. "But I have been playing good for a month," said Martin, who had yet to win in his eight years on the European Tour. His outward 33 included a bogey at No. 5, a birdie at No. 8, and a birdie at No. 9 from 45 feet.

Jose-Maria Olazabal, crediting a change in his putting stance—"I put the ball closer to my feet, so that my eyes were over it"—barged into the group at 68. A bunkered tee shot at No. 6 and a bunkered approach at No. 10 cost him his only bogeys. But a pair of superb four-iron shots took some of the sting out of them. He put one to 24 feet at the 13th, the other to 12 feet at the 15th, and holed both for birdies. That's the stuff of championships. "I'm getting closer," the 23-year-old said.

Another Wayne popped up—there were four in the field—this one Grady, an Australian in his fifth year on the American tour. He was best known as "Mr. No. 2" for his many second-place finishes, but he finally broke through early in June. "My victory in the Westchester Classic helped me to be the best I've ever been coming into the Open," Grady said. "It made me feel a lot better." Grady was out in 32 in a bogey-free front nine. He made his big move with three consecutive birdies from No. 6, on putts of 10, 12, and 20 feet. His lone bogey was at No. 17, where he missed the green with his tee shot.

The obscure and the underdogs made for toothsome talk at the champagne tent, but the real attention was reserved for the Best-In-The-World Derby. And here's how that went:

Greg Norman (69) was concerned about the baked fairways. "I had two extremely good drives—at No. 4 and No. 6—350, 360 yards," he said. The problem, he said, is keeping those shots on the fairway. (Three days later, and there would be a fatal echo to that comment.)

U.S. Open champion Curtis Strange (70) spent the day gnashing his teeth. "I was 30, 40 feet away all day," Strange said. But it cost him only one bogey, when he missed the green at the par-three 14th. "But I was pleased with my start," he said. "It was a hell of a lot better than that 79 last year."

Nick Faldo (71) ground out 17 pars and one birdie—two putts from 40 feet at the 11th. It recalled his final round in the 1987 Open, when he won the cup by rolling over the faltering Paul Azinger with 18 consecutive pars. "I was frustrated with the putter," Faldo said. He was also frustrated at the par-five holes. "They were reachable," he said. "It's just that I hit lousy drives."

Seve Ballesteros (72), the defending champion, logged two birdies, three lip-outs, two bogeys, and a vintage Ballesteros save. At the par-three 17th, his tee shot ended up in the TV cables next to a spectator fence. He got a free drop, for all the good it did him. He had to drop in chewed-up sand. He had an awful lie. Master of the short game, the best he could do was chip to 35 feet. Then he holed it. "Nice putt," he muttered, walking off the green.

Disasters snuffed out two other promising rounds. Sandy Lyle, in the slump of his life, and Tom Kite, still aching from losing the U.S. Open, both made triple-bogey sevens. Kite's was particularly galling. He was five under par and in the lead coming to No. 15, a fairly straightforward par four of 457 yards. Like a sea captain avoiding reefs, Kite tried to steer his drive away from a fairway bunker on the left. "And my right foot slipped just as I hit the ball," he said. The ball went shooting off to the right, out of bounds. At the other end of this wreck, he two-putted from three feet. The seven not only knocked him out of the lead, it opened a fresh wound—the triple-bogey at the fifth hole in the final round that cost him the U.S. Open a month earlier. Lyle, on the other hand, was not leading, but he was playing some of his best golf in a long time. He was two under par coming to the 18th. A good drive put him right in the fairway, 181 yards from the flag. Then he took his seven iron, the club that set up his 1988 Masters victory from the fairway bunker at Augusta's 18th. The ball ended up on a gravel path just behind the green and only a few yards from the clubhouse. Lyle started up the fairway. Then he stopped. Someone was telling him something strange: The ball had gone out of bounds. His face fell. He turned and walked wearily back to his starting point. He dropped and hit his fourth, and it landed in a television cart to the left of the green. He got a free drop, chipped to 10 feet, and two-putted. "I played well," Lyle said. "But I just feel sick."

When it came to disasters, British Amateur champion Stephen Dodd found one in a hurry. Perhaps playing with Arnold Palmer—who would struggle to a day's worst 82—unnerved him as much as playing in the Open. Dodd hit his opening drive onto Troon beach, fluffed his second into the rough, and shanked his third into the whin bushes. Somehow, he held the damage to a double-bogey six. But his troubles were just starting. At the short eighth, he left his first try in the bunker, and bladed the second across the green into another. He finally got on the green, then two-putted for his six. He was out in 43, but settled down and came home in nine consecutive pars for a 79. Another amateur had a far better time of it. This was Russell Claydon, 23, runner-up in the Australian Masters and 11th in the English Open. Claydon shook off a three-putt bogey at No. 2, made four birdies in seven holes starting at No. 6, and posted a 70. The last came at No. 12, on a 25-foot putt, and as he left the green, he got his biggest thrill. "Seeing my name on the leaderboard in the Open," he said.

The thrill for Ireland's Philip Walton, in the crowd at 69, seemed to come from something approaching divine intervention. Walton, playoff runner-up to Ian Woosnam in the Irish Open a month earlier, missed the green at No. 8. But he escaped with a breathtaking up-and-down for par. As he was leaving the green, he spotted a priest in the gallery. "Keep praying, father," Walton said. Then at the par-five 11th, not once but twice voices came just in time to bail him out. He probably would never have found his tee shot if it hadn't been for a friend who happened to be perfectly positioned downrange. The friend showed him where his ball had ended up in the bottom of a bush. It was unplayable. He was about to take a penalty drop, until a voice from the gallery reminded him he was entitled to line-of-sight relief from a television tower some 50 yards ahead. He got a free drop, and he turned a sure bogey into a birdie with a 12-foot putt. He didn't get off free, though. The fates took one back at No. 18, where he needed three putts from 70 feet for a bogey. At that, it was only a 29-putt day for Walton.

For all of the heroics, disasters, and struggles, the 13-hour day ended up belonging to Wayne Stephens, a late starter who was finishing shortly before twilight fell. He would have a night to think about where he was—leading the British Open. "I've failed dismally one year after another," Stephens said, looking back over his disappointing experiences. "In 1984 I really thought I should give it up. The trouble is that I've repeatedly lost my swing under duress. But tomorrow? Well, I'm going out there to enjoy myself. I'll keep to my game plan, which is to play my normal game. I'll sleep well tonight."

The first-round leaderboard:

Wayne Stephens	66	Philip Walton	69
Lee Trevino	68	Brian Marchbank	69
Fred Couples	68	Derrick Cooper	69
Eduardo Romero	68	Greg Norman	69
Paul Azinger	68	Steve Pate	69
Miguel Martin	68	Mark James	69
Wayne Grady	68	Tom Watson	69
Jose-Maria Olazabal	68	Gavin Levenson	69

In the 1982 Open at Royal Troon, waiting played a dramatic role. There was Tom Watson, standing beside No. 18 green, waiting to see what Nick Price would do over the last few holes. When Price stumbled and fell, Watson was the champion. Now, in the second round of the 1989 Open, waiting again was the stuff of drama, only this was a six-hour wait, and for a much different reason: Would the slumping Sandy Lyle make the 36-hole cut? No matter what else was happening on the course, it was the Lyle question that knitted the entire day together. Sympathy favored the personable Scot. But there is never any sympathy in those cold, impersonal numbers. He had missed nine cuts in his past 13 outings. Would he make it 10-for-14?

Lyle teed off at 9:25 a.m. and finished about 2 p.m. with a 73—146, two over par. Ordinarily, 146 ought to make the cut comfortably. But there was nothing ordinary about the way Troon was playing. The weather continued warm, and there was just a smidgen of rain at midday, enough to make the course even more agreeable. So Lyle would have to wait until all the returns were in to see whether his 146 was any good. Finally, it was—but with no room to spare. It was the first cut he would make in the 1989 majors. Eighty players at 146 and under made it. Among those who did: Two of the 10 amateurs, Russell Claydon (74—144) and Sweden's Robert Karlsson (70—145), and all three of the Japanese Ozaki brothers—Naomichi (71—142), Masashi (73—144), and Tateo (71—146), better known as Joe, Jumbo, and Jet, respectively. They were the first trio of brothers to make the cut since Reg, Ernest, and Charles Whitcombe did it in 1938. Reg, incidentally, won the championship.

Among those who didn't: 1988 runner-up Nick Price (73—147), 1987 co-runner-up Rodger Davis (79—157), and 1986 runner-up Gordon J. Brand (73—151). Three former champions also were swept away—Tom Weiskopf, 1973 (73—147); Gary Player, who won in three decades, 1959, 1968, and 1974 (73—152); and Arnold Palmer, 1961-62 (last at 82—164).

Another subject occupied much of the day—would Wayne Stephens, the unknown who had the audacity to take the first-round lead, fall to pieces the way unknowns are supposed to? You could make book on it. The local betting shops did, offering odds of 10-1 that he couldn't even make par or better in the second round. And they took a pasting. Stephens couldn't match his opening 66, but he did make that par 72 for a 138 and a tie for fourth at the end of the day. He started out with a big gallery this time, but they melted away when he went bogey, double bogey at the 13th and 14th. He rewarded his faithful immediately, with a pair of birdies. He still thought he could win, but even if he didn't he felt he had already been rewarded beyond his dreams. "You know what's best?" he said. "The respect from my fellow professionals. When they congratulate me, it's as if they're saying, 'Hey, you can actually play the game.'"

But Stephens had to stand aside for some interesting developments. To sum them up: Another Wayne—this one Grady, of Australia—posted a 67 and took a two-stroke lead at 135. Just behind him were Payne Stewart (65), the man in the plus-two trousers, sharing second place with none other than the long-dormant Tom Watson (68), who won the Open at Troon in 1982. Then there was Mark McCumber (68—139), who charged into the picture with about as wild a show as an Open will ever see. It was hard to believe. He went out in 34, and had parred only one hole.

Grady would turn 32 shortly after the Open. He took up golf at age 15, turned professional in 1978 and won the West Lakes Classic that year in Australia. Before he won again, six year later in the 1984 German Open, he had 17 second-place finishes. He had 26 overall, until he finally broke through on the U.S. tour and won the 1989 Westchester Classic. He had played the Asian circuit for five years and the European tour for five, but, he said, "I always wanted to play in the States and enjoy the lifestyle there." Grady's 67 was comparatively trouble-free. Hot putting has a way of calming trouble. He had six birdies—one from three feet, the others from 15, 25, 30, 25, and 40 (two putts). In all, he needed just 27 putts, and then explained, "I drove the ball well." He missed just two greens. At No. 9, it cost him his only bogey, a weak chip and two putts from 15 feet. At the par-three 17th, he escaped a possible disaster. His tee shot plugged in a bunker. "I could see myself hitting the lip and coming back in," he said. "It would have been a shame to let it get away on the last two holes." The determination got him through. He blasted the ball out to 20 feet, then logged the sixth of his seven one-putts. He had discovered the joys of full concentration. "Lately, I have had a lot of good rounds, but tend to get a little bit ahead of myself on the last few holes and thinking about finishing rather than concentrating on the shot at hand," he said. "I'm sure I'll be jittery when I tee off tomorrow, but I hope it will make me concentrate harder."

It seems it would. Just two strokes behind him were two men who could give any golfer nightmares—Tom Watson and Payne Stewart. Watson, 39, had been snoozing for years. His 68 was no work of art. It was a scrambling, battling mix of power and finesse. "I had a mixed grill," was the way Watson put it, with that famous gap-toothed smile. "Some luck, some magic, some bad shots, some good shots—a typical Tom Watson round." For magic, there was the birdie at No. 11. He pulled his drive into the whins, somehow got a six iron out of there, then pitched to four feet, and holed the putt. As for luck, he bunkered his second at the par-five 16th, then holed out a 60-foot blast for an eagle-three. Watson, whose best finish so far in 1989 was a tie for third at Westchester, seemed to be snapping out of his slump. He had consulted a number of gurus, and his game had improved, but he wasn't sure why. He was equally at a loss to explain his slump. "The reason I haven't played well is that I haven't played well," he said.

Stewart had finished just minutes ahead of Grady and about an hour before Watson and had put up the score for everyone to shoot at, a 65 that was announced as the record for the revised course. Since the revision consisted of lengthening No. 1 by 30 yards, to 452, most observers discounted talk of a record, and Stewart himself was hardly impressed. "Course records don't mean much," he said, "unless you win the tournament." There was no disputing that 65, though—an eagle, six birdies, and a bogey. Compared to Watson's hole-out from the bunker, Stewart's eagle was routine—a 60 foot putt from 10 yards off the green for a three at the 577-yard sixth. Stewart needed just 28 putts overall, and three of his birdies came in the last five holes. So did his lone bogey, after an out-of-bounds approach shot at No. 15 and two putts from 20 feet, his only two-putt in the last five holes. "Once I got on the greens, I felt I could make it from anywhere," Stewart said. "And that little bit of rain meant you could be aggressive with your putts."

It was a remade David Feherty who came charging into a share of fourth on 67—138. "I have changed my attitude," said Feherty, 30, a two-time winner in his 11 years on the European Tour. He had had enough of putting yips. "You get very fed up with it," he said. "I've had them on and off for most of my career. It all comes from the fear of missing." Feherty fought back by seeing a sports psychologist, and he also switched his stance from open to closed. For relaxation off the course during a tournament, Feherty, a former opera student, listens to grand opera—Puccini's "Turandot," mostly. He's possibly the only real opera-lover on the tour. There was certainly nothing yippy about his 67. He went out in a 31, a five-birdie, no-bogey performance on putts ranging from six to 25 feet. Just when he was in sight of home, his swing got away from him. At the 16th, he drove into the rough, pitched into a bunker, and missed a four-foot par putt. At the 18th, he drove into the rough again, and two-putted from 12 feet. Except for those errors, he would have been breathing down Grady's neck, just a stroke behind. Feherty started early, and was already finished when the day's wildest round was just getting started near 2 p.m.

As a simple figure, Mark McCumber's 68 looked like nothing more than a solid four-under-par performance. Look closer. He went out in two-under-par 34, but he parred just *one* hole. And that was the first. The next eight were a real adventure. He went birdie-bogey-birdie-bogey-birdie-bogey-birdie-birdie. "Then I went and messed things up," McCumber said, grinning. "I parred No. 10." The question was, how long would he last with that sore back? He was all right for now, at least. "I didn't have to wear my corset or take 12 painkillers a day," McCumber said. "Two lagers at night and I'm OK."

Two quiet men moved into contention, both in the pileup at 139. One was Scott Simpson, the 1987 U.S. Open champion. There was nothing quiet about his nine-birdie 66. He stumbled through the turn with three bogeys, then played the last eight holes in five birdies and three pars. The other was Mark James, a three-time winner on the European Tour so far this year. James is famous for the sharp brevity of his wit and interviews, and he didn't hurt that reputation after his 70 on Friday:

It seems you do well in Opens. Why?

"Don't know."

How did you play?

"Average."

What's been the big factor this week?

"Everything is all right."

How far did you top your drive at No. 18?

"I was looking for it, not pacing it."

The outburst of the day belonged to Howard Clark (68—140), who exploded for five consecutive birdies, starting from No. 11. The shot of the day belonged to Derrick Cooper (70—139). Thanks to a sweaty glove and wet hands, he shanked his one-iron second at No. 11. The ball rocketed to the right, bounced off the railway line and back into the fairway. Reprieved, Cooper made his par and slipped away. And the crash of the day belonged to Sam Torrance. He four-putted No. 9 for a double-bogey six, then bogeyed five of the last six holes, the last four in succession. A 77 knocked him out by a stroke.

Seve Ballesteros all but conceded he could not repeat as champion. His 73—145 put him 10 strokes off the lead. "If I had made that birdie at No. 16, who knows?" he said. But the five-footer got away. He shook his head. Was he too far behind now? "I think so," he said. "I play early tomorrow.

I would need 66 or 67, and bad weather in the afternoon . . ." He recalled that his final-round 64 in 1986 at Turnberry vaulted a huge part of the field, but he still fell eight strokes short of Greg Norman, who was busy winning that Open. Lee Trevino figured he was out of it, too, after a five-bogey 73 carried him to 141, six strokes astern. "Bad ball-striking," Trevino explained. "I'd have to make a good score tomorrow and hope for bad weather. When you're that far behind against these guys, you need some weather." Hopes were about to dim for some other prominent names. Tom Kite returned 74 for 144, and tied a slipping Curtis Strange (74—144), who bogeyed two of the first four holes, and limped in with a double-bogey five at No. 17, where he missed the green, then hit a bunker. "I played badly and I putted badly," Strange said. "I want to go practice." Ireland's Philip Walton got no divine help this time and took 74—143, tying with Gene Sauers (73), who went out in 38 this time, not 30. Paul Azinger had a nondescript 73 for 141, as did Miguel Martin.

Despite that spot of rain about midday, or perhaps because of it, Royal Troon was again a wonderfully hospitable place. The cut, at a low two-over-par 146, left 80 players in the field. And of those, 43 were under the par of 144, and through the two days there were 31 rounds in the 60s.

Into this quickening mix stepped, for the first time, Mark Calcavecchia. A 68 lifted him out of the pack and into contention, four strokes off the halfway lead at 139, after which he made an odd observation. "I missed three greens," he said, "but I think I did better missing them than hitting them." Oh? But the facts bear him out. At No. 1, his wedge approach rolled off the back of the green, 35 feet from the flag. He holed it out with his putter. At No. 3, he did hit the green, but it did him no good. He three-putted from 30 feet for a bogey. So it was back to missing them, the two consecutive birdies. At the par-five fifth, he was short in two, chipped to 10 feet, and made the birdie putt. At the par-three fifth, his tee shot missed to the left. No matter—he chipped in for the birdie. He added a birdie at No. 7 to get to three under, then got to five under with consecutive birdies coming down the stretch. At the 15th, he put an eight iron to five feet, and at the 16th, he recovered from the rough, chipped to three feet. He gave a stroke back at the par-three 17th. A gust of wind carried his tee shot left of the green, and a heavy-handed chip cost him two putts. "Overall, I feel pretty good," Calcavecchia said. "I should have made birdies on six, eight, and 11, but I guess the other holes evened it out." Someone noted that Ballesteros, Trevino, and even Greg Norman, were hoping for some nasty weather to separate the contenders from the pretenders. "Whatever it does," Calcavecchia said, "it's fine by me." He's an agreeable sort. Here was a man about to become a father for the first time. There was some turmoil down there, but he never showed it and never mentioned it.

Calcavecchia and everyone else went comparatively unnoticed. The fans were tuned in on Watson. Had his game really returned? If nothing else, he was good business. The local betting shop had him at 66-1, an attractive proposition. "I tried to get some of that," Watson said. "But the bookie found out who it was, and he'd give me only 40-1." Watson accepted. He also took the precaution of betting "each way," a bet that covers the first four places. He got his money down just in time. His second-round 68 dropped him to 6-1. The time was right for him. Four of his five Opens had come in Scotland, so he not only had his game back, he had the inspiration. He needed just one more thing. "I'd like to see the wind blowing," he said. "The field is bunched up because of the benign conditions. That will change Sunday, because of the choke factor. Add wind to the choke factor, and you've got to have 'bottle.'" Watson had been at it so long, he was speaking the native tongue. In America, the word is "guts."

The leaderboard after 36 holes:

Wayne Grady	68-67—135	Greg Norman	69-70—139
Payne Stewart	72-65—137	Steve Pate	69-70—139
Tom Watson	69-68—137	Mark James	69-70—139
Eduardo Romero	68-70—138	Scott Simpson	73-66—139
David Feherty	71-67—138	Mark McCumber	71-68—139
Wayne Stephens	66-72—138	Mark Calcavecchia	71-68—139
Derrick Cooper	69-70—139	Fred Couples	68-71—139

Larry Mize was wearing a silly smile when he met the press after the third round Saturday. He took one look at the scores and said. "Is this the Bob Hope Classic or something?" Everyone had a good chuckle. "Well, it's hard to think of 11 under par winning the British Open," Mize added, meaning that Royal Troon was being taken apart. Mize had just joined the sub-par stampede with 66, which was a precipitous drop after his 71-74 start. He came in at 211, five under par, and was among the leaders at that point. He was contemplating what another 66 tomorrow, in the final round, might do for him. Well, it would put him at 11 under par and—he figured—that might be enough to win the Open. Ordinarily, that would be a very good supposition. But this wasn't an ordinary British Open.

Mize didn't know the half of it. He had started early, and finished about 1:30 p.m. Most of the names on the leaderboard hadn't even gone out yet. By the time they had finished early in the evening, 11 under par wasn't even good enough for the first round lead, much less the championship. Tom Watson, who won at four under par in 1982, was now 11 under par with 68—205, and that was only second behind Wayne Grady, whose 69 gave him a 12-under total of 204. Mize, at five under, was buried in the pack. "We're seeing a tame, benign Troon," said Watson, remembering that it was neither in 1982. "The course is giving away a lot this week." A year ago, at Lytham, play was washed out in the third round, and fire trucks had to be called out to pump water off the course. Troon, on the other hand, with no rain and hardly any wind, was still defenseless, as the 54-hole breakdown showed: Of the 80 players, 46 were under par, another eight matched it (216), and only 26 were over. This wasn't the Bob Hope Desert Classic, but it sure didn't seem like a British Open.

Wayne Grady wasn't interested in comparisons at the moment. He returned a brow-mopping 69 for a 12-under-par 204 and held on to the lead by a stroke over Watson, two over Payne Stewart. He stood them off in the second round, and now he had done it again while he could not only feel, but see them breathing down his neck. Stewart was his playing partner in the final twosome of the day, and Watson was with Eduardo Romero just ahead. Grady definitely was not playing in a vacuum.

"I got out of the round very well," he said. "I hit my irons poorly, and had to scramble to keep the lead."

What it came down to was Grady's chipping. It was sensational. It was his salvation. It got him a bogey-free round, one of seven in the third round. He went out in nine pars. Two of them he saved with chips—to 18 inches at No. 5 and six inches at No. 6. He added a 15-foot putt for another save at No. 9. Inward-bound, he chipped in from 20 feet for a birdie at No. 10, and chipped to three feet and holed for a birdie at No. 11. At the 14th, he ran in a 40-foot putt to save par, and at the 16th he pitched to three inches and set up a birdie. He had one last chip in him before he would call it a day. At the par-three 17th, he missed the green by 30 feet. So he chipped to four inches and saved the par. As Lee Trevino once noted, when you're chipping and putting to save pars, you're like a dog chasing cars—not much of a future. But Grady was content to count his blessings and hope for better times. One more good day, and he might be the British Open champion.

Of course, it was looking more and more as though it was the old Tom Watson he would have to beat. "My game got a little bit sloppy," Watson said. Even so, he managed to get around without a bogey, and even gain a stroke on Grady with a 68, which was a stroke lower than his best round in 1982. "My short game rescued me at 15, 16, and 18," Watson said. Those were three pars—a pitch to four inches at the 15th, a 15-foot putt after a poor bunker shot at the 16th, and a chip and a three-foot putt at the 18th. They saved a four-birdie effort. His putter had been working—a pair of 15-footers going out, two putts from 20 feet at the par-five 11th, and an eight-footer at No. 13.

Payne Stewart had no reservations about his 69. "I played very well," he said. "And if I had been a little stronger with a few putts, I would have been 10 under. Anyway, this is the best position I've ever been in in a major." Stewart missed only one green, the 14th, and it cost him his only bogey, two putts from 15 feet after his only poor chip shot of the day. He chipped to three feet at No. 4, and to six inches at the 11th, and birdied both, and got two more coming in. He holed an 18-foot putt at No. 9, and took his caddie's advice at No. 17. "I've holed 30-footers every day at 17," Stewart said. "I was 30 feet again, and my caddy said, 'You know how to putt this green, knock it in,' and I did."

David Feherty still showed no sign of the shakes or the yips. His 69, for a share of fourth at 207, looked more like a man who was finding himself. Even his lone bogey at the 13th showed good putting. He three-putted from 90 feet, and the last one, for the bogey, was from 12. Two of his four birdies came on 15-footers, and the one at No. 12 was a breathtaker—a 50-footer. "I have very little experience being so close in a major," Feherty said. "I want to go out tomorrow with a chance of winning. I'm not saying I am going to win, but I want to know what it's like to be in that position."

Fred Couples (68, also at 207) did know, and like Larry Mize, he was puzzled. "On other courses, if you were even par after six or seven holes, you were doing great," he said. "Here, you're in trouble. In other U.S. and British Opens, it seems the guys hitting the fairways are the leaders. Here, it's the guys making the putts." His three birdies going out were from three, 15 and 10 feet, and coming in, a two-putt at the 11th and an 18-footer at the 16th. That put him at 10 under par. Just one final par and he would be tied for third with Payne Stewart, who was playing an hour behind him. The

18th had other ideas. Couples drove into a pot bunker, and had to two-putt from 40 feet to scratch out a bogey-five, his second there in succession. "I've got to go out and hit the ball hard," Couples said, "and more or less straight."

Mark Calcavecchia, who played with Couples and matched him with 68—207, was facing an entirely different problem: Which club to leave out of the bag for the final round. Like Couples, Calcavecchia had birdied No. 16 and was also 10 under par coming to the 223-yard 17th, and he also bogeyed it. "I needed a three iron off the tee and I didn't have it in the bag," Calcavecchia said. "I just never figured I'd need it at that hole. I figured a one iron was too much and a three iron wasn't enough, so I took the two iron again." Wrong again. He bogeyed No. 17 in the second round, and now again in the third. "I hit it left—which is death," he said. He chipped on and two-putted for his third and final bogey of a day that didn't start out with much promise.

After two routine pars to start, Calcavecchia had a 30-inch putt for a birdie at No. 3. He missed it. He tapped in for a par that felt like a bogey, but at No. 4 he got a real bogey—a 10-foot par putt that lipped out. He shrugged and marched on, and birdied three of the next four holes—a three-foot putt at No. 5, two putts from 50 feet at No. 6, and a 10-footer at No. 8. Coming in was a different story. It wasn't a wild ride, like Mark McCumber's front nine in the second round, but it would do. Calcavecchia two-putted from 50 feet for a birdie at the 11th, gave the stroke back at the 12th with a two-putt bogey from 30 feet. He birdied three of the next four holes, a 15-footer at No. 13, a three-footer at No. 14, and tap-in at the par-five 16th. That put him at 10 under. Then came the club problem at the 17th, and the bogey. The obvious question from the press corps: Which club will you carry in the final round, the two iron or the three iron? Calcavecchia laughed. "Good question," he said. "I hadn't thought about it. I'm not sure. I may decide to take both of them and leave my one iron out." Then his face brightened. "In fact," he said, "I just did."

At the end of the day, there was still that peculiar feeling about this Open, a sense of disquiet. It was as though you were at a party and couldn't find someone who ought to be there. Then you finally put your finger on it: The top Europeans, and especially the British, hadn't shown up. In a golf sense, that is. Three days now and the leaderboard showed no Ballesteros, no Faldo, no Woosnam, no Lyle, no Langer.

Ballesteros shot 76 on Saturday. He had glum written all over his expressive face. "One day you go to bed feeling you are the best in the world," he said, "and the next day you look as though you have never played that game before. That's what happened to me."

Faldo, the 1987 champion and the reigning Masters champion, also was gloomy, despite having his best round yet, a 70. The trouble was, he was out in 32. A hot round had slipped through his fingers. "I am very depressed," Faldo said. "I'm fed up. It was a waste. I got myself going, then went backwards." He two-putted from eight feet at No. 10, and from six feet at No. 12, and bogeyed both. "I lost my confidence in my putting with those," he said. "And when I hooked at No. 15, I lost confidence in my swing as well, and that was it."

Lyle also had his best round yet, a 71, but the signs of trouble were still there. He made three bogeys, plus a double bogey-six at the 15th, where his tee shot was so wild, he said, "that it was out of bounds before it had gone a hundred yards."

Woosnam was also in a pathetic struggle, despite an innocent-looking 73. "It's strange," he said. "You feel it going and you put too much pressure on yourself to get it back. You start to get the bad breaks and your confidence goes as well. You find you can't stop yourself. You start thrashing at the ball. You start guessing at the line of your putts. You feel like you are being left out of the things that matter. Something has gone," he added, "and I don't know when I'll get it back."

As for Langer, a 71-73 start raised hopes that his agonizing slump was easing. Then came an 83.

Another big name missing: Curtis Strange, U.S. Open champion. A second consecutive 74 put him at 218, out of the picture. So the field was pretty sharply defined for the final battle. They left the third round with these thoughts:

Wayne Grady, on leading a major into the final round for the first time: "I'll be nervous, for sure. But I'd rather be where I am than four behind."

Tom Watson, on reaching for his sixth British Open championship where he won his fourth: "When you win on a course, it's easier to win the second time. I've never forgotten the feeling I had in 1982."

Payne Stewart, on predicting the winner: "I'd probably have to pick Tom— if I wasn't picking myself."

Fred Couples, on what he has to do: "If I have to hit driver on some holes where I haven't, just to make something happen, then I will."

David Feherty, on contemplating his finest position ever in a major: "What will I be thinking of tomorrow? Puccini."

Mark Calcavecchia, on the last piece that has to fall into place: "I'm pretty happy with the way I'm playing. If I get my putter straightened out, I'll be all right."

The third-round leaderboard:

Wayne Grady	68-67-69—204
Tom Watson	69-68-68—205
Payne Stewart	72-65-69—206
Fred Couples	68-71-68—207
Mark Calcavecchia	71-68-68—207
David Feherty	71-67-69—207
Paul Azinger	68-73-67—208
Jodie Mudd	73-67-68—208
Jose-Maria Olazabal	68-72-69—209
Mark McCumber	71-68-70—209
Steve Pate	69-70-70—209
Mark James	69-70-71—210

Contenders are generally in a high state before the last round of a major. They toss and turn the night before, find little room for breakfast in the morning, and go off and sit by themselves in the locker room. Not Mark Calcavecchia. This may be the British Open, but as far as his exercise regimen was concerned, it was just another day. Calcavecchia was converted to exercise when he married Sheryl, an aerobics exercise instructor. And so on the morning of what was to become the biggest day of his golfing life to date, Calcavecchia went out and ran three and a half miles. "I didn't even realize I ran it," he said. "I was just wondering how it would feel to win." Just a few hours later, he did know.

For most of the day, however, Wayne Grady seemed like the only man who would know that feeling. He started out 12 under par, one stroke ahead of Tom Watson, two ahead of Payne Stewart. Calcavecchia was three behind and gave no hint he would be a factor. Nor did Greg Norman. At seven strokes off the pace, he was out of it. He didn't know it, though.

The British Open is an unlikely place to discuss what dreams mean. Norman made this one an exception. "In my dream last night, I saw three 3s in my mind," Norman said. "I interpreted this to mean that I would start out with three straight birdies." He tuned out on the dream too soon. Actually, he birdied the first *six* holes, and posted a number for the rest to shoot at—64, and a 13-under-par total of 275. Norman changed the picture completely. But it took agonizingly long for this dream to weave itself. Norman had teed off at 1:05 p.m., and there were still 20 players out on the course who could beat him. "I don't wish any ill on anybody," Norman said, with a little grin, "but I hope they fall over out there."

Norman's opening birdie rampage read 3-3-3-4-2-4, and included two putts from 35 feet at the par-five fourth, a brilliant 45-footer at No. 5, and a four-footer at the par-five sixth. The Postage Stamp, the little 126-yard No. 8, cooled him down. He bunkered his nine-iron tee shot, blasted out, and two-putted for his only bogey of the day. As things turned out, one of the tiniest holes in golf kept him from one of the biggest championships. Norman came home in 33 for the 64, and stepped aside. Like Tom Watson in 1982, all he could do now was wait. "I've had a few majors taken from me," Norman said. "Maybe it's my turn to have one handed to me." Someone wondered about the ones that got away: Does fate owe you one? Norman grinned, "It owes me *four*."

Norman hadn't cornered the disappointment market. There was the woebegotten Bernhard Langer. "I'm hitting the ball sideways," he said. "You can't use these two days to count as the average for my year." He meant the awesome 83-82 crash (after the 71-73 start) that left him 80th and last at 21-over-par 309. Seve Ballesteros, it seems, just lost interest. He started 72-73, finished 76-78 for 11-over-par 299, third from the last, tied for 77th, his worst Open performance ever. "I just didn't feel comfortable at all over the ball," he said, "and when I feel that way, the confidence is not there and it is very difficult for me to trust my swing." Britain's Big Three were a quick study in contrasts. Nick Faldo finished 69—281, tied for 11th, and was glad it was finally over. "That's it," he said. "Get my flight. I'm going fishing." Sandy Lyle played his best golf in months, finishing 72—289 and a tie for 46th. "I'm not playing badly," he said, "but a few holes in every round have killed me." This time, it was four consecutive bogeys coming in. Ian Woosnam had his best day of the Open, a 71 for a tie for 49th at 290. He shook his head.

The top European was David Feherty, tied for sixth at 72—279, nine under. He never made a move on the lead, but he shook off a rocky stretch of three bogeys over four holes coming in and birdied the 16th. "At least

I proved to myself that I can hold up under pressure," he said. "Now I know I can compete with the best in the world. It's been a tournament I'll remember for the rest of my life."

The vast crowd of some 34,000 didn't lack for diversion. Brian March-bank, a native Scot, went out in 30, tying the record set by American Gene Sauers in the first round. Unfortunately, he also matched Sauers' perform-ance coming in, stumbling to a 40. The 70 gave him 286 and a share of 30th place. Mark McNulty burst from the pack with birdies on the last four holes for 66—next best of the day after Norman's 64—to tie for 11th at 281. Mark McCumber's delicate back kicked up, and he dropped like a stone, from a tie for ninth after the third round to a tie for 46th finish, at 80—289. Fred Couples fell off the leaderboard with an outward 40, then closed with four consecutive birdies for a 72—279 and a share of sixth. Payne Stewart, playing with him in the next-to-last group, suffered a fatal slide into the turn—a bogey at No. 8, a double bogey at No. 9, and he was out of it. He finished with 74—280, a tie for eighth.

Others left different kinds of marks. Lanny Wadkins played some of the best golf in the Open, but got the least out of it. His only blots were one double bogey and six single bogeys. He even went 31 consecutive holes without a bogey. All he got out of it was a three-under-par 285 and a joint 26th. Vijay Singh, the first Fijian to play in the Open, was impressive for any kind of first-timer. His highest round was 73, and he finished at four-under 284, a tie for 23rd. American Jodie Mudd, also a first-timer, came within a whisker of making the playoff, but bogeys at the 14th and 17th stalled him. He finished at 70—278, tied for fifth. Ken Green (292) proved the Royal Troon Theorem again. He was eight under par on the outward nine for the week, and 12 over on the inward.

When it came to frustration, Tom Watson was no worse than second to Greg Norman. Watson started the round at 11 under par, a stroke behind Grady. He birdied the first and the sixth, and still lost ground to Grady's three birdies. Then Watson's dream of Open title No. 6 died when he bogeyed three out of four holes through the turn. He three-putted No. 7 from 25 feet, hit a poor approach at No. 9, and drove into the rough at No. 10. A birdie at the 11th helped him to a 72—277, and fourth place. "The key shot was a bad eight iron at No. 9," Watson said. "I felt it was slipping away right there. I was on the upslope and tried to get it going left, and blocked it. I was thinking of a birdie and made bogey instead. Well, my score is disap-pointing, but I played well for four rounds, and I got a little money off the bookies." The fourth place was his best since his runner-up finish in 1984. From 1985 to now he was tied for 47th, 35th, solo seventh, and tied for 28th.

They say golf tournaments are won over the last nine holes, which means one of three things happens: The leader holds up under the pressure and wins; or he folds; or someone gets hot and catches him from behind. Wayne Grady's case was a mix. He didn't fold completely—a one-under-par 71 isn't folding—but he did drop a couple of crucial shots down the stretch. And because of this, he did get caught. It was almost an echo of Nick Price in 1982, including the wait.

Norman put up that 64—275, then waited to see whether they would all fall over out there. A bunch did. Mark Calcavecchia did not. But you couldn't be sure at times. His birdie at No. 2, from two feet, merely balanced Grady's birdie at No. 1. He was still three strokes down. The same at No. 4. Calcavecchia chipped to five feet and birdied, going to 11 under, but Grady followed with one of his own there. Then things started looking really grim. Grady birdied No. 5, going three ahead of Watson and four up on Calcavecchia. And then Calcavecchia fell five behind with a bogey at No. 7. He drove into the left rough, but put a sand wedge to 18 feet. "Then brain-lock set in," he said. "I missed the hole by one inch and went five feet past, then missed coming back."

Grady bogeyed No. 9, his first bogey in 35 holes, but got the stroke back on a birdie at No. 12, staying four ahead of Calcavecchia. He would have been six ahead, but for what Calcavecchia conceded were "miracles from God."

At the par-five 11th, everyone's birdie hole, Calcavecchia was about to self-destruct. "I hit a duck slice into the right gunch," Calcavecchia said. "Then I got greedy and made a mistake. I tried to hit a three iron, but I couldn't get it up. The ball bounced off the hump in front of me and into a thorn tree. It hurt in there, but I slashed an eight-iron out, got it to 40 feet." And then he holed the putt for his par. Miracle No. 1.

Miracle No. 2 came moments later, at the par-four 12th. First, another bad drive, this one into the right rough. "I was hanging back, not shifting my weight," Calcavecchia was to say, and he would correct the error later, but first he had to get out of this mess. His five-iron second ended up on a hill above the green. Now he was looking at no better than par, and probably bogey. He was 60 feet from the hole. He needed a good chip shot, but he never dreamed of what he got. "The ball hit about two feet in front of the hole," he said, "and bounced up and hit the stick—and dropped right in. I was embarrassed more than anything else. My God, how lucky can you get?" The birdie put him 11 under par and still four behind after Grady also birdied the 12th a short while later. Then Grady began to slip. At the 14th, he missed a four-footer and bogeyed, and Calcavecchia made it a two-stroke swing with a bold birdie at the 16th. He hit a one iron off the tee to get a good grassy lie, then with 275 yards left to the hole, he hit his driver off the fairway. "All I had, one of the all-time great drivers." He ended up 30 feet past the hole. Two putts got him the birdie and dropped him to 12 under. Moments later, there was another two-stroke swing. Grady bunkered his tee shot to the par-three 17th and lipped out a four-foot par putt. Meanwhile, up ahead, Calcavecchia was hitting another miracle shot.

Calcavecchia had come to No. 18, his last chance. "I told myself, I've got to make birdie or it's history," he said. But he drove into the right rough, 161 yards from the green. But from there—and this was the shot—he smacked an eight iron to four feet. "Never a doubt that putt was going in," he said. And Calcavecchia was in the lead, or at least sharing it, for the first time. That's when Norman first noticed him. "Until then," Norman said, "I never even thought of Mark. That's when I told my caddy, 'Here's where we've got to dodge a bullet.'"

Calcavecchia's 68 tied Norman at 275, 13 under par. Moments later, Grady, who led from about lunchtime in the second round until now, parred the 18th for a 71 and joined them for the Open's first three-way playoff, first four-hole aggregate playoff.

Norman, who had to wait almost an hour and a half, was awesome at the start. At No. 1, he hit a 45-yard pitch-and-run to six feet and holed for a birdie. At No. 2, Calcavecchia drained a 35-footer for a birdie, but Norman matched him with a 10-footer. So he led by one over Calcavecchia (par-birdie) and by two over Grady (par-par). Then he stumbled at the third playoff hole, the 223-yard, par-three 17th. His three-iron tee shot was too strong. In Calcavecchia's language, "He over-pured it, he over-smoked it, I'd say." The ball stopped in the back fringe, about 45 feet from the hole. From there, he chipped about 10 feet past, and he two-putted for a bogey-four. (He had played it in two pars and two birdies in regulation.) Calcavecchia parred and tied him, and Grady bogeyed and fell two strokes behind. Then came the decisive moment.

They went to No. 18, 452 yards, par four, the fourth playoff hole. Calcavecchia drove first and put his ball into patchy rough at the right. Norman hit second, a tremendous shot that bounced and rolled down the right side of the hard, dry fairway, some 325 yards into a fairway bunker. The ball was almost up against the front lip. "I hit driver there every day," Norman said. "I didn't think I could reach it." A simple shot wouldn't do now. He was forced to try for the green, after what Calcavecchia did.

Just an hour earlier, Calcavecchia had hit that magnificent eight iron to four feet to set up the birdie that got him into the playoff. Now he had a less agreeable lie, 201 yards from the hole, and under the severest pressure. "Ordinarily, it was a four iron," Calcavecchia said. "But it looked like a five might go." He hit a majestic five iron that arched so beautifully against the early evening sky that even he was captivated by it. "It's a shot I'll never forget," he said. "I watched it, and I said I don't care where it ends up, because that's the best shot I've ever hit." It ended up seven feet below the hole.

Seeing this, Norman had to go for the green from the bad lie in the bunker. But he merely made it into another bunker, downrange. He tried to get his next close to set up a par and hope Calcavecchia would two-putt. But his shot went over the green and onto the gravel path in front of the clubhouse, the one Sandy Lyle had hit back in the first round. Norman began marching toward the green. An official came up and said something. Norman's face fell. The ball was out of bounds. He could never catch Calcavecchia now. He gave up and walked in.

Calcavecchia finished like a champion. He didn't need a birdie now, but he ran that seven-footer in—only the sixth at No. 18 all day, including his own in regulation. In the playoff, it was Calcavecchia 13 (two under par), Grady 16 (one over), and Norman, no score.

Grady had just finished second for the 27th time in his career, but he enjoyed his best finish in a major. "Well, I'm very happy with myself," he said. "It was the first time I'd found myself in such a position, and I hung in there. I all but did it."

He also managed to retain some sense of humor, though it had a jagged edge to it.

"Are you disappointed?" one writer asked him.

"No, I'm over the moon, mate," Grady said.

"Do you throw clubs?" another asked.

"Do you break pencils?" he replied.

Norman had reason to be bitter. Disappointment showed, but bitterness didn't. "Destiny has a funny way of saying, 'Hey, this is the way it's got to be,'" he said. "But we all accept fate. It's what keeps us coming back, hoping. You've got to think positively. I have to believe my time will come soon."

Mark Calcavecchia, the man whose time had come, arrived before the press corps with a small confession.

"I had no idea what kind of playoff it was," he said. "I asked my caddy, and he said it was sudden-death. Then we found out it was a four-hole aggregate, and I thought, great. It's much more relaxing to play four holes.

"Happy as I was for myself," he added, "I felt very bad for Greg, for the things that happen to him in the major championships. On the other hand, Greg has to know he's lucky. If Wayne doesn't shoot that 71, he's not in a playoff."

A tough question came from an American writer, asking him to review what he had said earlier in the year.

"Sure," Calcavecchia said, grinning. "I said I'd rather win the Ryder Cup than a major. That's because back then, I didn't think I had a chance to win a major, and I did think we have a hell of a chance to win the Ryder Cup."

He also thanked his family for their sacrifices, especially his dad, who died in 1985. "He gave me money when we didn't have money," Calcavecchia said, "and he sent me places to play golf when we couldn't afford it."

And finally he revealed that he had played with at least half his mind in Phoenix, Arizona, where his wife, Sheryl, was awaiting the arrival of their first child. Imminent babies have no concept of time, so there had been a good chance all week that Calcavecchia would not be around to win the Open. So he no sooner dropped the winning putt than he called home. "She was crying all over the place," Calcavecchia said. "She'd been watching on television. And just as I was about to ask, she said, 'No! I haven't had the baby yet!'"

He had been calling all week, three times on Saturday. "I asked God, please, help Sheryl hang on just a little longer," Calcavecchia said. "Because if I had got a phone call Saturday night, that she had gone into labor, I'd have been on a plane out of here. There are things more important than a golf tournament."

And so there are. Britney Jo Calcavecchia arrived a few weeks later, and Mark Calcavecchia passed up the PGA Championship to be at home to greet her.

6. The PGA Championship

As one of the four majors, the PGA Championship normally can stand on its own without added hype. The PGA hangs like a yoke around the necks of Arnold Palmer and Tom Watson because it is the one major title they have not won, despite their many golfing accomplishments. So it is important, both for personal and financial considerations.

In 1989, however, the pot of gold at the end of this rainbow contained more than prestige and the $1.2 million purse, of which $200,000 went to the winner. The champion also had a spot reserved for him on the U.S. Ryder Cup team, unless he was a foreigner or had already qualified. And since the Europeans had beaten the Americans in both 1985 and 1987, and seemed to delight in bringing it up at every opportune moment, making the Ryder Cup ranked right up there with Remembering the Alamo.

Larry Nelson put the PGA Championship in this prospective. "For most of us here, it's a 72-hole qualifier for one spot on the Ryder Cup team. I can't imagine an American in this field who hasn't already qualified not having that on his mind when we tee off Thursday," said Nelson, a three-time Ryder Cupper but far down on the 1989 qualifying list.

It hardly mattered that the championship was being played on a public course, Kemper Lakes, named for a corporation whose headquarters were less than a par-five hole away, or that it was stuck so far outside Chicago that access was by a single two-lane road. These guys would have teed it up on Rush Street and played around the Loop for a chance to make the U.S. Ryder Cup team and compete against the Europeans.

"It's payback time," said U.S. Ryder Cup captain Raymond Floyd. "They beat us over there in 1985, over here in 1987 for the first time ever. They've dominated some of our majors and their own Open. The PGA Championship is the vehicle for a lot of guys to right the ship."

Outwardly, Floyd pulled against no one. Inwardly, however, he was in the corner of any of the eight already assured of spots on the team since that would give him two wild-card choices rather than one.

Thus on Sunday afternoon when Mike Reid went to the 16th hole with a seemingly safe, three-stroke lead, Floyd's options seemed halved. But golf tournaments are 72 holes as Reid discovered, and one of Floyd's own, Payne Stewart, strode in the back door to win the title.

The only other topics of note leading up to the championship were how Kemper Lakes would play and how in the name of Bobby Jones had Greg Norman let another major championship—the British Open three weeks earlier—slip away.

First, the course. Only those who had participated in exhibition matches called the Grand Slam of Golf had played the course previously. And practice rounds told them little, especially about greens as large as those at Augusta National and almost as intimidating with their slopes. The rough was high, but uniform; only one par five could be reached in two and, depending on the wind, No. 16 could be played with a driver and seven iron, or a driver and three wood, and it wasn't any fun no matter what the conditions.

"The 16th and 17th holes are very difficult and I think they will say a lot about this tournament," said Seve Ballesteros prophetically. "No. 17 is especially tough when the pin is back left. It will be very difficult to make par three unless you play aggressively and make a great shot."

Curtis Strange picked the 16th as the pivotal hole. "That's a hell of a hole," he said. "It's so long and narrow. You've got to drive in beside the water, then go in over the water. I don't think you'll see a fluke winner here. You won't see anybody back in, especially Sunday on Nos. 16 and 17. This is a lot of golf course."

Because of his length, Norman figured to be among the favorites. But some questioned his state of mind so soon after the British Open. Since a majority of the U.S. media wasn't there, it was second-guessing time when Norman arrived at Kemper Lakes. And he was testy.

"It's easy to sit back and be an armchair critic," he said, not smiling. "I don't care what anybody says, I have to hit the shot I think I need to hit at the time. What's been lost in the way it turned out is what I did to get there. I lost because I gave myself the opportunity to win by shooting 64 Sunday to get back into the tournament. I've played with a lot of guys who give up when they get three, four shots behind. I'm proud of my ability to be able to not do that. I made 11 birdies in 22 holes, but nobody wants to talk about that."

It was difficult to come up with a leading contender because nobody really knew how the course would play under tournament conditions. Most were saying it would take a couple of tournament rounds before the cream would rise.

"It's gonna take a good ball-striker, that's a definite," Floyd said. "A lot of guys here are going to be hitting one irons and three woods into some of these par fours. For the average hitter to do well, he's going to have to hit the ball awfully sound."

One thing was certain. Mark Calcavecchia wasn't going to add the PGA to his British Open victory. He became the father of a baby girl on Tuesday morning and withdrew from the championship to be with his wife Sheryl. "At this time, being with Sheryl is more important than any golf tournament, even a major," Calcavecchia said.

Ryder Cup talk, Calcavecchia's absence and Norman bashing was second-page stuff compared to the news generated in the tournament's first round.

Golf fans yearning for the good old days skipped easily past the names of Mike Reid and Leonard Thompson, who led the first round, and settled on those of Arnold Palmer, Tom Watson and Jack Nicklaus. Reid and Thompson shot six-under-par 66s, but Watson was only one stroke back with Tom Kite and Chris Perry. The next two on the leaderboard sent a charge of excitement through the large gallery—Palmer and Nicklaus with 68s, tied with five others.

They all broke the course record of 69 established by Larry Nelson the year before in the Grand Slam of Golf. In all, 49 players, almost a third of the field, broke par and another seven players matched it.

"I'm flabbergasted the scores are so low," Nicklaus said. "I thought earlier this was the longest, toughest PGA course we've played. I thought, 'You've got to be kidding,' when I heard so many players broke the course record."

With Watson, Palmer and Nicklaus among the leaders, it sent golf historians searching for the last time these three greats, with 34 major championships among them, enjoyed such status. They're still searching.

"Ten years ago I would have wanted them to shoot 76s," Nicklaus said of his old rivals. "But as you get older, you're happy to see them shoot the scores they did today. But we're not leading the golf tournament. Mike Reid and Leonard Thompson are, and they have to be given their due."

Reid figured to be the least likely to lead any round at Kemper Lakes, which measures 7,197 yards. But he played near flawless golf with six birdies, no bogeys and only one save on his card.

"It was like Jack and the Beanstalk and I'm Jack," Reid said of the tough Kemper Lakes course. "But I was able to tackle the monster today. I never thought I'd be in this position, but I missed only one fairway and one green. Perfect golf is perfect distance and direction and I had both today."

Thompson, who won his first tournament in 12 years two weeks before the PGA, played his round in six birdies, an eagle and two bogeys. "I'm lucky to be in a major, never mind leading one. But I'll enjoy it while I can," he said.

That must have been the attitude of the large galleries following Palmer, Nicklaus and Watson.

Watson, who has won the other three Grand Slam events but not the PGA, drove poorly, but as in his glory days saved par from the most unlikely places and capped his round by chipping in for birdie on No. 18.

"I got jumpy the last couple of holes," Watson said of challenging for the lead. "But this is where I want to be. My game is getting there and that excites me. I feel close to a second coming."

It was more than that for Palmer. One month shy of his 60th birthday, Palmer turned the calendar back 35 years to when he was 24, young, strong and almost unbeatable. It had been that long since he had shot 68 in the opening round of the PGA Championship and he couldn't remember the last time he made five consecutive birdies. He did both in one round this day and it brought goose bumps to those leathery, still powerful arms.

Palmer didn't win that PGA, or any other year, but his round rekindled the spark that, except on rare occasions, has made him golf's eternal optimist and the winner of seven major championships and 61 overall before he joined the Senior PGA Tour.

Two of those rare occasions came this year. After shooting 81-80 in the Masters, he talked about not coming back because he no longer could compete. He had the same feeling when he shot 82-82 in the British Open three weeks ago.

"When you play in two major championships and can't break 80, you have those thoughts," Palmer said. "But they are passing things. The great thing about golf is you get another chance. I always think I'm going to play well."

Palmer said that feeling of optimism began during the practice rounds and his performance left him confident for the rest of the week. "I feel if I can play and feel like I did today for the four days, yes, I can win," he said.

Palmer parred the first three holes. Then the magic began. And by the time he had made his third straight birdie on No. 6, the crowd, his faithful

Arnie's Army, was really into it. And so was Palmer. He made it five straight on the next two and as his numbers went up on the leaderboard, his gallery grew.

"I asked myself the question before I played today, 'What's so much different now than when you were 30? You feel good, your health is good. So why can't you still do it? Just go out and play a good round of golf.' That got me started on a positive note and it carried through most of the day," Palmer said.

Even his playing partners, two-time PGA champion Nelson and defending champion Jeff Sluman, got excited.

"I feel like a gallery person," Nelson said at one point during the round. And later, "It was fun, exciting for me watching him make all those birdies. It was hard not to get caught up in what he was doing."

As the birdies kept falling, it motivated the crowd and the crowd motivated Palmer, who said, "I had some emotion about keeping it going and leading the PGA. I won't say it didn't enter my mind. The fans let me know how I stood and after I birdied No. 14, it caused me to look up and see the leaderboard and see that I was tied. I said, 'This is great. Don't screw up now.'"

He did stagger coming in, however. He missed an uphill 12-foot birdie putt at No. 16 and finished bogey-bogey.

"The last two holes were disappointing," he said, "but after playing so poorly for so long, I can't be too disappointed. As I walked up the 18th fairway, I looked at the big leaderboard and saw Tom Watson's name up there, Jack's up there and mine up there. Golf and history have a way of repeating themselves. We're three decades apart and we used to go head-to-head some years ago. And I thought, 'Wouldn't it be something if we stayed up there until the end on Sunday?'"

It was almost an hour later when Nicklaus finished, and when he rolled in a 15-foot birdie putt on No. 18 to tie Palmer, he smiled. For much of the day he'd been too busy with his own game to notice what others were doing, but now he could enjoy it.

"It's special to see the guys who were champions play well," Nicklaus said. "Even me. I hit some of the worst-looking shots you've ever seen today, but somehow I escaped. I hit my first putt of the day six feet past the hole and made it coming back for par. That set the tone for the day, and the tone was that I made everything I looked at. I hit only seven fairways and 10 greens, but made only one bogey. That hasn't happened in a while."

It didn't seem to bother Reid that the leader of the golf tournament was getting less attention than the followers. "Shoot, what those guys did today excites me, too," he said. "It's good for golf. I'm happy with what I did today, too."

Several other players made a run at the lead. Mike Hulbert was five under at the turn, then self-destructed with a double bogey on No. 10 and bogeys at Nos. 12 and 13 to finish with 71. Blaine McCallister had it four under after nine but double-bogeyed the 11th and also shot 71; club pro Lindy Miller was four under after five and shot 73.

Norman put himself in position to require another comeback. After shooting two-under 34 on the front side, he needed 40 strokes on the back and shot 74. But that was nothing compared to the trials and tribulations of David

Ogrin. He was two under after No. 10 then took a quadruple-bogey nine on No. 11 and bogeyed Nos. 12, 15 and 16 to finish the backside in 43.

Then there was Seve Ballesteros. He birdied Nos. 1 and 3, eagled No. 4 to get to four under, then bogeyed eight and nine. "My putting was terrible," he said. "I missed four putts from less than seven feet on the back side. My confidence is no good today."

The first-round leaderboard:

Mike Reid	66	Arnold Palmer	68
Leonard Thompson	66	Jack Nicklaus	68
Tom Watson	67	Ian Woosnam	68
Tom Kite	67	Dave Rummells	68
Chris Perry	67	Mark O'Meara	68
Ben Crenshaw	68	Phil Blackmar	68

The nostalgia of the first round gave way to reality as the PGA Championship hit the 36-hole mark. Where Reid suffered in silence on Thursday while overshadowed by the Palmer-inspired wave of days gone by, there was no denying him the headline Friday.

The man the players call "Radar" for his pinpoint accuracy from tee to green tacked on a 67 to his opening 66 and moved to 11-under-par 133. That was good for a two-stroke lead over his first-round co-leader Thompson, who came back with a 69, and the Walrus, Craig Stadler, who carved out a course-record 64.

At eight-under 136 was Watson, who had 69, while Rummells (69), Perry (70), Ed Fiori (67) and Andy Bean (67) were at 137. U.S. Open champion Strange shot 68 and was tied at 138 with Scott Hoch (69) and Wales' Ian Woosnam (70).

A thunderstorm caused a two-hour delay and darkness left 24 players to complete the second round on Saturday, but none of them were a threat to Reid's lead.

Almost no one noticed Reid's 66 on Thursday. They were too caught up in the play of 59-year-old Palmer and 49-year-old Nicklaus. So was Reid, who joked, "There won't be anybody at the Cubs game Friday. They'll all be out here watching Arnold and Jack. It doesn't bother me. Heck, if I wasn't playing, I'd probably be out there watching them, too."

There was none of that to get in his way Friday, however. Both Palmer and Nicklaus had completed their rounds of 74 and 72, respectively, when Reid teed off. Thompson and Stadler had posted their 135s and Reid was three behind before he started.

Reid quickly closed in with birdies at Nos. 2 and 4, caught them with another birdie at No. 10 and moved into the lead for good at the 15th. As twilight closed in on Kemper Lakes, he knocked in a 14-foot birdie putt at No. 18, then asked one of the marshals if a pizza could be delivered to the club.

"I'm a little bit tired and a whole lot hungry," Reid said. "It's been a long day with the rain delay and all. Today's round wasn't as pretty as yesterday's, but I hung in there and made the most of it."

This was Reid's second run at a major championship in 1989. He led the Masters after 13 holes on Sunday, but bogeyed the 14th and double-bogeyed the 15th to eventually finish sixth. "Call it a learning experience, a stepping stone rather than a tombstone," he said of the Masters. "I learned to handle pressure and apply it to other situations. I didn't view it as a defeat or letdown. As Fuzzy Zoeller says, 'I was happy to be in the position to choke.'"

While Reid's game is so routine it often borders on boredom, Thompson's is anything but. He was all over the place—a birdie on No. 1, a bogey on No. 3, an eagle on No. 4, a bogey on No. 6. "If I hadn't putted well early, you wouldn't find my name on the leaderboard," he said. "But winning two weeks ago (Buick Open) has given me a lot of confidence. I needed it today."

Stadler, who was a regular winner on the PGA Tour until 1984, was close to being perfect as he moved up. He turned in 33 then blitzed the back side with birdies at Nos. 11, 14, 15, 16 and 18. And when he missed a green, he chipped inside five feet and saved par.

"I'm beginning to get fired up again," said Stadler, who won eight times between 1980 and 1984, including the 1982 Masters. "My career has seen it all, the good, the bad and the ugly. I've had a lot of chances to win the last couple of years and when I didn't a lot of people wrote me off, but I didn't."

Stadler's victory drought started after the Byron Nelson Classic in 1984. He won a couple of times overseas, but in the States kept coming only close. "I think I finished second probably eight or 10 times since then, but if you don't win those are remembered about as much as missing the cut," he said.

Speaking of the cut, it came at 145, one over par, and among those "down the road" were three U.S. Ryder Cuppers—Paul Azinger, Fred Couples and Mark O'Meara. Also getting the weekend off were former PGA champions Lee Trevino, Lanny Wadkins, Bob Tway, Hal Sutton and John Mahaffey.

Palmer safely made it, but he was grim and emotionally spent. Gone was the bounce in his step and the smile on his face from a day earlier when he was the darling of the tournament. He shot 74 and looked like he hadn't broken 80. A 74 isn't bad for a man almost 60, but Palmer never has hidden behind his age, and he wasn't doing so now.

"Age has nothing to do with it," he said. "I didn't feel any differently physically today than I did yesterday. I kept up with my playing partners walking down the fairways, hit my drives out there with them, didn't need to rest. As I said yesterday, I don't see any reason why I can't play as well as I once did."

The difference was on the greens. In the first round, he hit eight greens on the front side and made five birdies. Friday, he hit eight greens and made one birdie. The round got away from him on the 11th hole, where he three-putted from 24 feet. He followed that by missing a five-foot birdie putt at No. 12 and made double bogey on No. 13.

"The three-putt at No. 11 threw me off track," Palmer said. "I felt I needed another birdie there to keep me going, and to walk away with a bogey, well . . . ."

Thursday's other legend, Nicklaus, wasn't happy, either. Many years ago, the immortal Bobby Jones said of Nicklaus, "He plays a game with which I am not familiar." Nicklaus hasn't recognized it all week, but for the wrong reasons.

"I've been all over this place for two days and hit some of the worst shots of my life. If not for my putting, I would have vaulted right over 80, never touched it," Nicklaus said of his scramble-filled rounds of 68 and 72. "I couldn't hit this place (Kemper Lakes) if I aimed for it."

Thompson felt the same way after the middle six holes of his 69. He saved par on the seventh with a 30-foot putt and did it again on the eighth after driving into the water. "I didn't play nearly as well as I did yesterday, but I settled down in the middle of the round and was pretty solid the last eight or nine holes," he said. "My putter saved me. Am I going to sleep with it? No, but I'm not going to get far from it."

Still very much in contention were Watson and Strange. "I'm in a better position right now than I thought I would be in two months ago," Watson said. "If you had asked me then if I could win the PGA I would have said no. Now it's just a matter of holding my concentration for two more rounds."

Strange, who began the day two under, made the turn at five under and got it to seven under through No. 11, but missed a 10-foot birdie on No. 12 and bogeyed No. 13.

"I hit the ball pretty well the first 12 or 13 holes but not so well at the end," Strange said. "But I'm not too far back. I have to shoot a good round Saturday. When I came here after taking two weeks off, I expected to hit some bad shots. Now that the weekend is here and I'm in contention, I will be expecting more of myself."

He was also expecting more from PGA officials. He wasn't happy that it took them so long to halt play because of the thunderstorm. "We should not have teed off on the seventh hole at all," said Strange, who was on the seventh green when play was suspended. "We could have quit at any time. We tried to finish the hole. Howard (Twitty) and I both had five-footers. A bolt hit right then, and we just took off running. It seemed like a bolt of lightning went between everybody's legs and they still hadn't called it."

As they left the course late Friday afternoon, none of the contenders were down-playing Reid's position at the top, Strange among them. "He's playing awfully well, which doesn't surprise those who know him. He's won only two tournaments, but he's a much better player than two wins would show."

From Watson: "A lot of people might be surprised to see Mike Reid up there. Not me. Radar can play."

Reid hardly figured to be there, however. In his last three tournaments, prior to the PGA, he missed the cut in the U.S. Open, tied for 72nd in the Western Open and was 70th in the British Open.

"That's the great thing about sports, isn't it?" Reid asked. "The Cubs shouldn't be in first place in August, either."

The leaderboard at the halfway point:

Mike Reid	66-67—133		Ian Woosnam	68-70—138
Craig Stadler	71-64—135		Scott Hoch	69-69—138
Leonard Thompson	66-69—135		Tommy Armour	70-69—139
Tom Watson	67-69—136		Tim Simpson	69-70—139
Dave Rummells	68-69—137		Payne Stewart	74-66—140
Chris Perry	67-70—137		Ben Crenshaw	68-72—140
Ed Fiori	70-67—137		Dan Pohl	71-69—140
Andy Bean	70-67—137		Jack Nicklaus	68-72—140
Curtis Strange	70-68—138		Loren Roberts	71-69—140

There was a lot of confusion and thunder, lightning and rain but not much golf played at Kemper Lakes on Saturday. Play was halted at 4:25 p.m. and finally suspended at 7:20 p.m., with only 31 of the 70 players having completed play. The leaders were not among them.

When the lightning bolts got really nasty, second-round leader Reid had just putted out on the ninth hole, and Strange was on the 10th tee, telling PGA of America President Pat Rielly that he wasn't going to continue play. Rielly, trying to make the best of a bad situation, made it worse by using an old joke to get Strange moving. "Why don't you go ahead and hit a one iron? Even God can't hit a one iron."

Strange was not amused. "There's lightning all over the place, and he's standing there making jokes like that? I didn't appreciate it," Curtis said later.

This little scene began unfolding almost 10 minutes before play was called. Strange looked back toward downtown Chicago at the thickening and rolling darkness and suggested to Rielly that the PGA go ahead and suspend play before the storm got on top of them.

It seemed to Strange that it wasn't a matter of if the storm would hit, but when. "Why don't you call it now?" Strange asked.

"There's no lightning in the area," Rielly replied.

"What's that?" Strange asked, pointing to a flash on the horizon.

In a matter of minutes, the storm hit with such fury that some players still had not reached the safety of the clubhouse. Asked why the PGA did not see the danger as soon as Strange did, rules committee chairman Larry Startzel said, "I assume personalities. I don't know. We got them (players) off at the right time."

If Strange hated to see the bad stuff coming, think how Reid looked at it. He was playing his usual flawless golf—drive in the fairway, hit the green in regulation—until the ninth. He birdied the first, fifth and seventh to pull four ahead of Stadler and Thompson. Then on the ninth he drove into a rough, hit his second shot into a bunker and needed a blast and two putts for only his second bogey in the 45 holes he had completed.

Stadler picked up a shot with a par, but Thompson lost one, making double bogey, which would signal the beginning of his end. Still, Reid was not out of danger, especially with a night to think about it and 27 holes to play on Sunday.

"It's happened so much, I'm sort of numb to it," Reid said. "Of course, I'd rather have finished today, but it was obvious we couldn't. This thing came in fast. On the eighth tee, everything looked fine, but by the time we got in the middle of the ninth fairway it was all over us.

"Lightning is pretty frightening, especially in view of recent events with all these golfers being hit on courses around here. People should be careful. When He wants to play through, you let Him."

Watson, who started the round just three behind Reid, birdied the third hole, then likely played himself out of contention with bogeys on three of the next four. He welcomed the suspension. It was time to regroup. "I played very poorly," Watson said. "I missed five short putts and they cost me three pars and two birdies. I didn't have any feel with my putter today. Obviously, I need to come out Sunday and make something happen quickly."

Reid began his round with a spurt, making a two-footer for birdie on No. 1, a 15-footer at No. 5 and a 12-footer on the seventh. The bogey at No. 9 was only his second of the tournament.

"I was happy with the way I started, but I can't relax," he said. "There are a lot of good players just a few strokes behind. No, I don't look at the bogey on nine as a bad omen. It wasn't a bad bogey. That hole is 448 yards long and playing into the wind. The bogey seemed like a par to me anyway."

Before the storms came, Isao Aoki shot the tournament's best round, 65, to move into contention at eight-under 208. And Norman, with an inspirational lift from his pal, Jamie Hutton, shot a too-late 67. A total of 37 players did not complete their rounds. Included in that group was Palmer, who through 14 holes was now 18 shots behind Reid, and Ballesteros, who was five under on his round and seven under for the tournament with two holes remaining.

Although now in contention, Aoki saw little hope in winning the championship. "He is going to win," Aoki said of Reid. "He hits the ball always straight, straight, straight. Maybe someone can catch him, but I am too far back."

For Norman, it again appeared he waited too long to make his move. He barely made the cut of 145 and was so sure he didn't that he cleaned out his locker. But he was a new man Saturday. After hitting his practice balls, he spotted Hutton, the 18-year-old leukemia victim who was Norman's inspiration in his 1988 MCI Heritage Classic victory.

"I wanted to get back into contention and Jamie showing up today gave me a little more motivation to do so," Norman said. "I didn't know he was coming, but was awfully glad to see him."

Norman then played like the best player in the world. He birdied four of the first five holes on the backside before a double-bogey six on the 16th ended his surge. He drove into the bunker, hit his second over some trees, was long on his third, chipped strong and two-putted for six.

"I looks like I've done it again, waited too long to give myself a chance to win," Norman said. "I really don't know why. I get off to a slow start. Maybe I like the challenge more, but I don't like the idea. I'd rather shoot 67, 68 the first couple of days and be there on Saturday and Sunday and be in the last few groups."

Before he left the course, Reid was asked about having to play 27 holes on Sunday. "I like to think I won't get fatigued," he said. "There will be plenty of time, three or four hours, between rounds, and that's enough to rest."

Reid finished his third round Sunday morning with nine pars and still had a three-stroke lead over Rummells. Hoch and Stadler were next, four behind, while Woosnam and Strange lurked five behind. The man on the move, however, was Stewart. For 47 holes he had been just another guy in the field, with rounds of 74-66, and was one over par on his third round through 11 holes. He came back Sunday morning, however, and played his remaining seven holes four under, but at seven under and six back, seemed the longest shot of the top 10.

"I didn't play too well when I came back out this morning, but I don't think I hurt myself much," Reid said of 70.

The top 10 after 54 holes:

Mike Reid	66-67-70—203
Dave Rummells	68-69-69—206
Scott Hoch	69-69-69—207
Craig Stadler	71-64-72—207
Chris Perry	67-70-70—207
Ian Woosnam	68-70-70—208
Curtis Strange	70-68-70—208
Seve Ballesteros	72-70-66—208
Isao Aoki	72-71-65—208
Payne Stewart	74-66-69—209

"I just want to say that I've never felt so bad for anyone in my life. You played too well not to win."

Those words were spoken by one of the greatest to ever play the game to one of the least known deep in the bowels of the Kemper Lakes clubhouse late Sunday afternoon. Jack Nicklaus, the man who had won 20 major championships, said them to Mike Reid, a man who was two holes away from winning his first and didn't.

For 69 holes, Reid had his game on cruise control and his destination in sight. Then he had wrecked, and Stewart slipped past him to win the PGA Championship.

Reid's three-stroke lead after 69 holes was erased quicker than the week's thunderstorms struck. He bogeyed the 16th and double-bogeyed the 17th, giving the title to Stewart, who was pacing around the scorer's tent after shooting a final-round 67, including 31 over the final nine holes.

Stewart finished at 12-under-par 276 to win his first major title, while Reid was 277 and tied for second with Strange, who had 69, and Andy Bean with a late-charging 66.

It was Stewart's fifth career victory and the $200,000 winner's share of the purse raised his season earnings to $747,087, far and away his career best. It also gave Ryder Cup captain Floyd two wild-card choices rather than the one he expected, as Reid wore the look of a champion before disaster struck.

Though Reid lost it more than Stewart won it, the victor wasn't in an apologizing mood.

"This is a dream I've been working on for a long time," Stewart said. "I'm a patient man, but I've wondered when it was going to happen. I've been so close before, and I can't describe the feeling I have. It's a big deal for me, and I'll cherish it a long time. I know exactly how Mike Reid feels. I've messed up a couple of golf tournaments in my time. I feel for him, leading as long as he did. But, on the other hand, I'm happy I won."

Prior to the PGA, Stewart's closest brush with major fame came in the 1986 U.S. Open at Shinnecock Hills. He led by two shots after 12 holes in the final round, but three-putted the 13th for bogey and eventually tied for sixth.

"I've been living with that a long time," he said. "But today more than makes up for it. I played my heart out and was rewarded."

For Reid, it was another major disappointment. He led the Masters after

13 holes on Sunday, but three-putted the 14th for bogey and double-bogeyed the 15th and finished sixth.

"I made it through 14 holes with the lead at the Masters and I got through 16 here. One of these days I'll get it right," said Reid, fighting back tears. "This hurts."

Stewart was given hardly a nod through the first 54 holes, but final rounds of major championships have a way of heating up. This one did that midway Sunday. Reid struggled early, made only his third bogey of the tournament on No. 5 to fall to 12 under par. Suddenly five players were within two strokes of the lead.

Strange, Ballesteros, Woosnam, Rummells and Hoch were at 10 under, while Stewart was still a distant four strokes behind, playing three groups ahead.

"I wasn't playing particularly well, but I felt in control of my game," Reid said. "When I needed a gut check, I got it, except for the bogey on No. 5. I thought if I ever got my rhythm, watch out."

When the field turned for home, Reid was still two shots up on Hoch and Strange, while Rummells, Ballesteros and Woosnam had dropped another stroke back. And when Strange pulled within one with a birdie on No. 10— his final birdie as it turned out—the game was on.

Then just as suddenly, it appeared to be off again, when Reid birdied Nos. 10 and 11 to regain his three-stroke lead. Ballesteros disappeared with bogeys at Nos. 11, 13 and 16, while Strange, Woosnam, Hoch and Rummells flattened out with a string of pars.

"I couldn't hit my iron shots close enough to have any makeable putts," Strange said. "For five minutes I was within a stroke of the lead, then Mike went birdie-birdie and I couldn't do anything about it."

Stewart could. Earlier on the 10th tee, he made a casual remark to ABC roving reporter Jerry Pate: "I can shoot 31 on the back nine and still win."

Although he had birdied No. 11, Stewart's surge began oddly enough with a scrambling par from 15 feet on the No. 13. He then ran off three straight birdies of 20 feet, two feet and 18 feet. Now 11 under par, he was within three, and when he walked off the 18th green after his fifth birdie on the back, he had pulled to within two. It became only one a minute later, after Reid bogeyed No. 16.

"I was trying to cut my drive into the middle of the fairway and the Russians must have been transmitting. My radar got zapped," Reid said. "But when I made that putt for bogey (a curling, knee-knocking five-footer), I thought I was okay."

There was indication of the doom to come when his four-iron shot to the par-three 17th green rolled just off the collar, 25 feet above the hole. What happened next didn't seem possible.

Rather than chipping and running the ball to the hole, Reid attempted a lob shot, which came up 15 feet short. His first putt grazed the cup and stopped two feet away. His second putt hit the right side of the hole and spun out. He made a five, a double bogey, and his lead was gone.

"I couldn't putt the ball from the fringe because sometimes it will pop right up, so I tried to play it like a bunker shot, but I didn't follow through with it," said Reid. "I thought I hit a good first putt, but it was too hard. The second one, I hit too hard and right through the break."

Up ahead, in the scorer's tent, Stewart was pacing nervously, stopping occasionally to watch a television monitor. When Reid made his mess of the 17th, Stewart wore the look of a winner. "After he missed his first putt at No. 17, I assumed he would make the second," he said. "When he didn't, my heart definitely started beating faster."

That look of victory turned to one of concern when Reid drove into the middle of the 18th fairway then hit his approach just seven feet from the hole.

"There was a big crowd around the 18th tee and they cheered for me," Reid said. "They wanted me to do it, to birdie the hole and tie the guy in the Bears outfit (Stewart). I had never heard that before. I remember being paired with Tom Watson once and me leading and it being so quiet. Then he overtook me and everybody roared and my stomach about dropped out. I've always been so anonymous out here for 13 years. But today . . . all four days, really . . . these people were great to me. I can't really figure out why."

But Reid couldn't tie the guy in the Bears outfit. He played the putt for the left-center of the cup and pulled it.

"I thought he was going to make the putt and we would go into sudden death," Stewart said. "Yeah, I was worried. Anybody who knows my playoff record (0-4) knows it's not worth a damn."

When Reid missed, Stewart dashed out of the scorer's tent, high-fiving everyone in sight, including one he got from Reid on his way into the tent.

An hour later, Reid visited the press tent and his reputation of being unflappable caved in. He wore a glazed look and the first words out of his mouth were, "Oh, boy. Where can you go around here to have a good cry."

And then he did. Right there, with television cameras rolling and hardened writers suddenly softened by his genuine emotion. He had lost the PGA Championship and he knew it. And it hurt. He wept shamelessly.

Finally, Reid broke the silence. "It's okay," he said. "I cry at supermarket openings." It was a tension breaker and got a laugh. Then he choked up again.

"I'm happy for Payne, but sad for me. It's only a game, right? Everybody can identify with failure out here. You can't play textbook golf. Sports is like life with the volume turned up. The friendships are tighter, the laughter is louder and some nights seem a little longer, like tonight's going to be when I'm trying to figure out what happened. I'll go back to the hotel and cry, yeah, I'll cry big time."

There were no tears in the eyes of either Stewart or Floyd. While they felt for the kind, 35-year-old Reid, there were other considerations.

For Stewart, it was retribution. He probably leads the PGA Tour in tournaments blown, finishing second so many times (11), that the caddys call him "Avis." Two weeks before the PGA, he bogeyed the final hole to lose the Buick Open. At the time, he said, "You keep giving me the chance and I'll beat your butt. I guarantee it."

What he did Sunday was charge, post a number, then let others shoot at it. It's easier to win coming from behind than to hold a lead—ask Reid— but it says something that he came from six behind and passed nine other players in the process. Still, it wasn't until his two-foot birdie at No. 15 that he seriously considered himself a contender.

"At that point, I thought if I could make two more birdies, I had a chance," he said. "Realistically, it wasn't a good chance, but I've seen a lot of weird things happen in this game, some of them to me. So what you do is you shoot the very lowest number you can, put it up there and say, 'If you can beat this, good for you.'"

Knowing what he had to do, he did it.

"Nothing against Mike, but my only real worry was Curtis," he said. "I figured if I could beat him, I could win. Then I saw that Curtis wasn't making any birdies and that gave me hope. Then when Mike made such a poor shot from just off the green at No. 17, I started to get excited."

When Reid did not birdie the 18th and force a playoff, Stewart said his first reaction was one of disbelief. He had finally won a major championship.

"Hey, I know," he said of his near-misses. "My patience was running thin, too. I'm 32. I hadn't won a major, and everybody all over the world is always asking me why. They did the same thing to Curtis and look what happened. He won back-to-back U.S. Opens. Now maybe I'll repeat next year at Shoal Creek."

Then there was Floyd. All day long, as Reid continued his steady play, he began to consider the names for the one wild-card choice he would have for his Ryder Cup team. When suddenly it was two, Floyd's first reaction was a feeling of sadness for Reid, then one of "what-do-I-do-now?"

"My condolences to Mike Reid," Floyd said immediately after it was over. "He looked in control of the tournament and it was so unlike him to finish the way he did. He's normally so steady. That's why we call him 'Radar.' I would have been happy to have him on the team, and I really mean that. His loss, however, will make my day more difficult with two choices rather than one."

There was another loser Sunday, and although it wasn't of the magnitude of Reid's, it was still a hurting thing. Hoch needed to finish fifth or better to make the top 10 and oust Mark McCumber from the Ryder Cup team. He started the day in third place and appeared to have fifth place sewn up until he finished bogey-bogey and tied for seventh.

"I knew what I had to do and I didn't do it," Hoch said. "I've had rotator cuff problems the last couple of months, and when it went out on me on the fourth hole, it was just a matter of trying to hold on. I came close, but close doesn't count. I'm very disappointed."

Oh, one more thing. A championship that began with nostalgia—Palmer and Nicklaus in contention—ended with a nice touch for those two greats.

Some players who were still on the course in mid-afternoon thought they heard thunder coming from the direction of the 18th green. They did as in thunderous applause for Palmer and Nicklaus, in that order.

The first came as Palmer walked up to the green, his ball 25 feet from the pin. "The ovation coming up was probably as great as I've ever had," he said. "It got me thinking about making that last putt. I wondered what would happen if I got that one in the hole."

He quickly found out as the ball rolled dead center, prompting an even greater ovation for his final-round 70.

That putt and ovation inspired Nicklaus—Palmer always inspires Nicklaus—who followed Palmer to the 18th a few minutes later. Not to be outdone, Nicklaus made a 40-footer of his own.

7. The Ryder Cup

The Americans came into the 1989 Ryder Cup Match with their hackles up. For two solid years, ever since their loss in 1987 at Muirfield Village—their second in succession—critics were saying they were no longer the best, and in fact could hardly win outside their own tour. Only Mark Calcavecchia, a new American force, showed the old Yankee muscle. Americans had won the British Open almost routinely since Arnold Palmer took his first in 1961, but they had been shut out for five years, until Calcavecchia broke through in July at Royal Troon. Even so, the critics ground on, right up to the Ryder Cup. Said Raymond Floyd, the American non-playing captain, "I'm not tired of hearing about it—I'm *sick* of it."

So on their way to The Belfry, at Sutton Coldfield, England—the site of the European victory in 1985—the Americans decided they would show the world and go win the Ryder Cup. They even sounded a little like the late American movie hero, John Wayne. "Let's go kick some butt," Tom Watson said. "And take names," said Lanny Wadkins. In current American vernacular, this was super-confidence with a dash of swagger.

"I don't think I've ever seen determination and dedication like this team has," said Floyd, who played in six Ryder Cups, including the only other tie, in 1969, when Jack Nicklaus conceded a short putt to Tony Jacklin for a tie on the final hole.

So the Ryder Cup, still a matter of high indifference to the American public, had become really important to the American golfers. Early in the year, Calcavecchia, a veteran of the losing 1987 team, said he would rather bring back the Ryder Cup than win a major. And after he won the British Open, his first major, just two months earlier, an American writer asked whether that was still the case. He laughed. "That was when I thought I didn't stand a chance to win a major," he said. But he still wanted that cup.

Said Jacklin: "We have a side that is as strong, if not stronger, than in 1987. We've won twice, and we're playing at home. The cup isn't going anywhere." Still, the Americans were favored.

But the cup did stay in Europe, thanks to one of the most stunning collapses in Ryder Cup history. The Americans had put on a furious charge in singles the last day, and had the cup wrapped up and ready for shipping home. If they had so much as halved one of the four matches that got away, they would have won it. But Jack Nicklaus' words came echoing back from 1987—Americans don't know how to win anymore. "The Europeans are tougher," he said. In a carbon copy of 1987, the Americans folded at the 18th hole. Down went Calcavecchia, PGA champion Payne Stewart, Fred Couples and Ken Green. It took a four-birdie finish by U.S. Open champion Curtis Strange to beat Ian Woosnam in the final singles match and salvage the tie. And under the rules, in case of a tie, the cup remains with the previous winners.

The big shock coming into this Ryder Cup was Sandy Lyle, a member of the last five European teams, scratching himself from this one. Lyle had been playing badly since early in the season, and couldn't qualify off points, but it was a given that he would be one of Jacklin's three wild-card selections. But he was still off form late in August, and so he telephoned Jacklin from the World Series of Golf, at Firestone Country Club in Akron, Ohio. His message was simple: Scratch me.

"It was my decision," Lyle said. "The mental scars of missing cuts over the year have been too much. It's not fun when you're not playing well, especially when you're trying to support a team."

"I take my hat off to him," Jacklin said. "He said the team must come before any individual."

Abruptly, the picture cleared. Jacklin announced his three wild-card selections: Bernhard Langer, Howard Clark, and Christy O'Connor, Jr. The first two met with no disagreement in the press, even though Langer, 32, a member for the fifth time, was battling a severe recurrence of the yips, and Clark, 35, was also slumping. But Jacklin caught a lot of flak for picking O'Connor, whose record was less than shimmering. O'Connor, 41, broke a 14-year drought when he won the Jersey Open in April, the second European Tour victory in his 20-year career. He had played on just one Ryder Cup team, 1975, and was 0-2 in his two matches.

At the German Open, both the No. 8 man, Seve Ballesteros, and No. 9, Philip Walton, could still be knocked off the points list. Now, it was a given that Ballesteros would be on the team, even if he had to be a wild-card pick. But otherwise, the situation was so fluid that someone as far down the list as 21st, Mats Lanner, could take a spot if Walton were to miss the cut. Walton did miss it, but Jose-Maria Canizares, No. 10 coming into the German Open, made sure no one else got that spot. Canizares tied the course record with a 62 in the final round for a tie for fifth. That kind of grit would serve Europe well. And critics would find that O'Connor had his supply of grit, too.

Jacklin's team contained only one newcomer, Ronan Rafferty, winner of the Italian and Scandinavian Opens. The rest of the European team: Seve Ballesteros, Gordon Brand, Jr., Nick Faldo, Mark James, Jose-Maria Olazabal, Sam Torrance, and Ian Woosnam.

A change in the American selection process, brought on by the European victory in 1987, gave Floyd as many as two wild-card picks. Payne Stewart was already qualified for the American side, so when he won the PGA Championship, the automatic berth that went with that title became Floyd's second wild-card choice. He surprised no one, choosing Tom Watson, a three-time Ryder Cup veteran who had been slumping, and Lanny Wadkins, who had a sparkling record of 13-7-1 in his five appearances.

If Ryder Cup experience is crucial, then the Americans were at a great disadvantage. Europe had one rookie, Rafferty, but the Americans had five—Paul Azinger, Ken Green, Chip Beck, Mark McCumber, and Fred Couples. The rest of Floyd's team: Calcavecchia, Tom Kite, Mark O'Meara, Stewart, and Strange.

The Americans held a top-heavy 21-5-1 record in the matches, but Floyd reminded his men that they had lost the last two.

"The first time, here at The Belfry four years ago," Floyd said, "everybody said it was inevitable, it had to happen some time. The Europeans had a lot of luck. All the things that losers say. Then two years ago, we went to Muirfield Village. It was what's called an American course. There was no way the Europeans could win. But they beat us handily. All the excuses were thrown aside. Now it's a matter of pride and respect."

On that point, Floyd drew some flak at the Wednesday night banquet when he borrowed from Ben Hogan's proclamation in the 1967 Ryder Cup and announced his team as "the 12 best golfers in the world." To which Jacklin later replied, "I suppose that makes Seve Ballesteros No. 13?"

Floyd said he was just trying to get his boys excited. As for strategy, Floyd again said all 12 of his men would play in the team matches on Friday and Saturday (everybody would play in the singles finale on Sunday). Jacklin saw it another way. "In an ideal world, it would be nice if everyone could play every day," he said. "But this is about winning the Ryder Cup."

Next question, the pairings.

"Tony would be foolish to change," Floyd said. "They worked for him the last time, and I would do the same thing. So I think Tony will play the Spanish pair, Ballesteros and Olazabal, and Woosnam and Faldo." Jacklin would not disappoint him.

And long before the opening gun, it was conceded by all concerned—including the crowds swarming to their vantage points—that this Ryder Cup would turn on the 10th and 18th holes. The 10th is a 275-yard par-four, with a narrow green protected by water in the front and to the left, and with trees and bunkers behind and to the right. Ballesteros drove the 10th back when it was something over 300 yards, but that definitely was not the recommended way for everybody. Now, in its shortened form, it was not a mere temptation but practically a must gamble. It could be reached with a three wood, but an excellent one. Who didn't take a crack at it was just about giving away the hole. The 18th was a different matter. It's a par-four of 474 yards, dogleg left, with a lake cutting across the fairway up ahead, then curling back and in front of the green. Thus the golfer had to carry water twice. But if the drive was off a tad, or if a good breeze was coming in, the second shot almost had to be a lay-up. Of course, if the golfer were desperate, or recklessly bold, he might try to cross anyway. Some great Ryder Cup drama would be played out on these two holes.

The ingenuity award for the opening day crowd of some 25,000 on the relatively flat course went to the five people who got the most out of a stepladder. One sat on top of it, two others stood on either side, and the remaining two stood on their shooting sticks and held on to the ladder. That's a hard way to spend a day on the golf course, but this one was off and running from the opening gun. It sure wasn't boring.

Jacklin led off the Friday morning foursomes with two of his big guns, Faldo and Woosnam. Floyd countered with Strange and Kite, who were 2-down before they had really warmed up. But then the Britons had an awful time going through the turn. The Americans won four consecutive holes. Actually, they won just one, No. 7, where Strange cut the deficit to one hole with a 22-foot birdie putt. Then Woosnam and Faldo lost the next three. They bogeyed the eighth and ninth, two-putting both from short range, then crashed at the tempting 10th, both of them chipping into the water and finally conceding a winning birdie to the Americans. Woosnam got one hole back with a seven-foot birdie putt at the par-three 14th, and then he dropped a nine iron to within a foot at No. 15 for a conceded birdie that squared the match. It ended that way, a half-point for each side, but not without regrets. "We would have won if I had played a decent shot at No. 17," Strange said. He had put his five-iron approach into a bunker. "I should have hit my irons better." Said Kite, "Yeah, but then I drove into a couple of bunkers." Things were really tight at the 18th. Kite, putting first, coolly ran in an eight-footer for par. Woosnam faced a six-footer for a half. "I was really nervous," he said. "I thought I wasn't going to get that putt." But he did, and the match was halved.

Lanny Wadkins got the U.S. a point with a sensational eagle at No. 17. He and Stewart couldn't shake Clark and James in the second match. The lead changed hands four times, on birdies, and the match was square coming to the 575-yard 17th, where things didn't look good for the Americans. The Europeans were lying two on the green, 70 feet from the hole, and Stewart just missed the green with his three-iron approach. Wadkins, who had caught the Europeans with an 18-foot birdie putt at the 14th, now sank them when he chipped in from 25 yards for an eagle-three at the 17th. "All four of us played really great, and there's nothing better than when all four play well," Wadkins said. At stroke play, it would have been the Americans, 68-71. Wadkins reserved his highest compliment for Stewart. "He's a beautiful shotmaker," he said. The 1-up victory gave the Americans a 1-1/2—1/2 lead.

Next came Jacklin's other two men-of-war, Ballesteros and Olazabal. After their 3-1 performance together in 1987, with Olazabal then a Ryder Cup rookie, fans all but conceded every outing to them. But Tom Watson and his rookie partner, Chip Beck, decided otherwise, even though they were in deep trouble for a while. At the inviting 10th, Olazabal drove the green and was about eight feet from the hole. The Americans, meanwhile, were going from trees to bunker to water. Ballesteros drilled home the putt for an eagle-two and a 3-up European lead. But Ballesteros was not happy with what happened at the next three holes. "The Americans were very lucky," he said. At No. 11, Watson cut the European lead to two holes with a birdie from 12 feet. The 12th was halved in bogeys, and the Europeans conceded the 13th after making a bogey. Then Watson squared the match at the 14th with a 27-foot birdie. The Americans had wiped out a three-hole deficit in four holes. But it wasn't over yet. Both sides stumbled in, the Americans with a bogey at the 15th, the Europeans with one at the 16th, their third three-putt of the day. And finally both sides bogeyed the 18th to halve the match. The Americans led, 2-1.

In playing his big guns first and third, Jacklin clearly was looking for at least a 2-1 lead coming to the final foursomes match, where he was gambling with a risky mix—the yip-plagued but seasoned Langer to offset Rafferty, young and talented, but a rookie. They were up against Mark Calcavecchia, who had played only in 1987 (1-0 in singles, 0-1 in fourball), and his old pal, the outspoken Ken Green, a raw rookie. Jacklin's worst fears materialized. Langer and Rafferty were rocky from the start. They missed the first five fairways, double-bogeyed the fifth, and didn't make a birdie going out. They were five over par at the turn. The Americans failed to take full advantage of their wobbly opponents, going out in three birdies and three bogeys, but they were 3-up at the turn en route to a 2-and-1 win. The opening foursomes were over. The 1989 Ryder Cup had begun the way the 1985 match did at the Belfry, with the Americans leading, 3-1.

"It's been a marvelous morning," said Floyd.

Said Jacklin: "After this morning, we were subdued but not down. Three matches going down to the last hole. It could just as easily go the other way this afternoon."

He never dreamed how easily. Now came a duplicate of the 1987 victory, a European sweep of the afternoon fourball matches, but with a historic wrinkle. Fourballs is supposed to be an American strong suit, but they never led in any of the four matches, and statistics buffs said that was a first. Of more interest to the Europeans—they had vaulted from a 3-1 deficit to a 5-3 lead.

"I'm so proud of them all," Jacklin said. "It was marvelous to see them in full flow."

Observers were about evenly divided on whether Floyd's play-them-all approach had opened the door to the Europeans. True to his word, he played all 12 of his men on Friday. Perhaps more to the point, he changed each of his pairings, sitting out four of the morning men and sending in the four who didn't play in the morning. Golf writers pressed the point—why had he broken up winning combinations? "There's more to the Ryder Cup than winning or losing," Floyd said. "There's the spirit of play. If I have 12 men on the team, then 12 should play. I feel strongly about that."

Even Jacklin was asked. "What Raymond does is of no concern to me," he said. "I've got to worry about what I come up with." For the afternoon fourballs, Jacklin stuck with his strong suits, making only one switch. Sam Torrance and Gordon Brand, Jr., replaced Langer and Rafferty.

The afternoon sweep ended with Spanish fireworks, another one of those breathtaking Ballesteros rampages. Starting from No. 10, Ballesteros ripped through an eagle-birdie-birdie-birdie streak that snuffed out Tom Watson and Mark O'Meara, 6 and 5, tying the record for a European fourball win. "When Seve gets his Porsche going," said Olazabal, his astounded partner, in unabashed hyperbole, "not even San Pedro in heaven could stop him."

Watson and O'Meara never had a chance. Olazabal birdied the first two holes, Ballesteros the fourth, and Watson bogeyed the fifth. The Americans were 5-down after five holes. It looked like a shutout in the making. But O'Meara ended that possibility with his winning birdie at No. 6. Nor were the Spaniards supermen. They made a bogey, at No. 8, but even that was for a half. Watson's birdie at No. 9 left the Spaniards 3-up at the turn. Then came the explosion. Both Ballesteros and Olazabal drove the green at No. 10. Olazabal was only six feet from the hole. But he never got the chance to putt. Ballesteros was putting first, and he dropped his 20-footer for an eagle-two. Next, he birdied No. 11 from six feet, No. 12 from two, and then for a stupendous coup de grace, he drove the 395-yard 13th and two-putted from 40 feet for a birdie.

After a performance like that, what's left to say? Ballesteros just shrugged. "The way we played today, there was no way anyone could beat us," he said.

Ballesteros and Olazabal started last but finished first. Finally, there was just one match still on the course, and the day hung on it. "When we saw that on the scoreboards," Woosnam said—he and Faldo were struggling against Calcavecchia and Mark McCumber—"I knew we dare not lose our match."

The day also started with fireworks, but of a different kind. Floyd benched Tom Kite and sent rookie Paul Azinger out with Curtis Strange to meet Torrance and Brand. In stroke play, the Americans shot 67, the Europeans 66, and there was only one bogey between the two teams. It was Azinger's, on the very last hole, and it decided the match, but only because of Brand's heroics out of a bunker. It was a dramatic moment. Strange had just squared the match with an eagle at the 17th (drive, five iron, 25-foot putt). And so the 18th would be the decisive hole. It was especially nasty at the moment. Having to cross water with both the tee shot and the approach is tough enough, but doing it against a dangerous wind might be above and beyond the call. Azinger and Strange both laid up short of the water in front of the green, but Brand and Torrance went for it. Torrance hit a stunning two iron to the back of the green, and Brand hit a three wood—"I was trying to hit a snaker, and it got away from me"—into the right bunker. He seemed to be out of it when Azinger hit a sharp four iron to 14 feet, in good shape for his par. But Brand followed with a spectacular 50-yard sand shot to 10 feet. Azinger missed, but Brand didn't. The roar from the crowd was deafening.

Actually, Brand had a great day at the beach. "The real key were shots out of the traps—three great shots," he said. He opened with two birdies, the second set up by a 92-yard bunker shot to five feet. At the 13th, a 110-yard shot to about 30 feet, from where he saved par. And then the 18th. "The single most difficult shot in golf," Jacklin marveled. "A soft lie, and 50 yards to the pin." The masterful shot cut Europe's deficit to one point, 3-2.

James and Clark evened the match at 3-3 with bogey-free golf in beating Wadkins and Fred Couples, 3 and 2. "As the Americans would say, we 'ham-'n-egged-it,'" said Clark. "We fitted together very well." James chipped in from 45 feet for a birdie at No. 2. Wadkins squared the match with a two-foot birdie putt at No. 3. At the fifth, Clark chipped in from 40 feet for a birdie and the Europeans were in the lead for good. Couples' watery bogey at No. 8 put the Americans 2-down, and at the 12th, Europe went 3-up when James saved par with two putts from 70 feet. A string of four halves in pars ended the match at the 16th. "We played well in the morning, but we didn't get the breaks," James said. "But we got them this afternoon."

The third match of the afternoon, Faldo and Woosnam against Calcavecchia and McCumber, was a dogfight. The Europeans took the lead on Faldo's birdie from six feet at No. 7, then fell back to even on his two-putt bogey at No. 8. It stayed that way until the 13th, where Woosnam holed a 40-foot bunker shot for a birdie. The decisive edge came when McCumber ran into trees and water and bogeyed the 15th. By now, this was the last match on the course, and the entire day hung in the balance. Would the Europeans boost their lead or fall back into a tie?

It wasn't coming easily. Calcavecchia dropped a 15-foot birdie putt at the 16th. That kept the Americans alive. They were still alive after the 17th, on a half in two-putt birdies. Now the Americans had to win the last hole or it was all over. Calcavecchia gave it a big try. But a stiff gust of wind brought his three-wood second down short, into the mud and water on the bank in front of the green. He took a sand wedge, and it was all he could do to get the ball out of the goop. A wedge shot to five feet set up his bogey-five, an excellent save. But Woosnam wiped it out. He had cleared the water with his three wood, put an eight iron to three feet and made the par for a two-hole victory and the afternoon sweep. Faldo and Woosnam, who first teamed up in 1987, were still unbeaten, and Europe led the first day of the Ryder Cup, 5-3.

"But we still have a lot of hard work to do," Woosnam cautioned. Said an unbelieving Jacklin, "No wise man counts his chickens before they hatch." And said Floyd, puzzled by the American weakness in fourballs: "I'm stunned. It doesn't make sense to me or to anybody on the team. They've won hundreds of tournaments and millions of dollars. Possibly they're helping each other out too much. They got where they are on their own."

Whatever it was, if Floyd could straighten it out, he had one night to do it. There would be more of the same on Saturday, and time was running out.

But on Saturday, time stood still.

The first Ryder Cup was played in 1927, and counting time off for World War II, there had been 27 of them. In this, the 28th, the second round would take its place in history. For the sheer, raw struggle all day long, for the paralyzing intensity, it was the equal of anything that had gone on before, and maybe even better. For one thing, there was simply no stopping the Spanish Armada.

"Nobody can beat us—we can beat anyone!" said Seve Ballesteros, in a high state after a good day's work. And who's to argue? Ballesteros and Jose-Maria Olazabal beat two of America's best in the morning foursomes, Tom Kite and Curtis Strange. And in the afternoon fourballs they drew as flinty a pair as there is, Ken Green and Mark Calcavecchia. No matter. Nothing the Americans did could work. On the other hand, Paul Azinger and Chip Beck, two of the five American rookies, collided with the mighty Faldo-Woosnam pairing and put on a show in the fourballs that some said was the greatest match ever played. They got no argument. Faldo and Woosnam fell for the first time, but it was hard to believe. They were nine under par through 17 holes—nine birdies and not one bogey—and they lost. Beck and Azinger were 11 under—11 birdies, and also no bogeys. In fact, there were no bogeys at all, on either side, all afternoon. Sixteen players, 68 holes of golf, and not one bogey. That's how it was on Saturday.

Jacklin, savoring a 5-3 lead, again played a strong suit first, looking to pad that lead immediately. He led off with Faldo and Woosnam. Floyd, anticipating the move, responded with that wily gunfighter, Lanny Wadkins, and Payne Stewart. The Americans made two early errors and never saw the lead. A chance to win No. 1 died when Wadkins missed a birdie from six feet, and a chance to halve No. 4 died when Stewart missed a three-foot par putt. Still, the match was square through the turn, and then came the decisive 10th. Stewart's drive found water. The Europeans seized the opportunity. Faldo, rather than make a needless try for the green, laid up off the tee, and Woosnam wedged on to about 11 feet. The Americans eventually bogeyed, and Faldo and Woosnam had the lead for good. They made four more threes in succession, two of them birdies on longish putts that gave them a 3-up lead that ended the match at the 16th. The victory made Faldo the biggest European winner ever, with 16 Ryder Cup wins. (The American leaders were Arnold Palmer, 22; Billy Casper, 18; and Jack Nicklaus and Lee Trevino, 17 each.) Faldo shrugged. "I just had to get Ian into the right place," he said, "and he did the rest."

In the second Saturday morning match came a pairing everyone wanted to see—the rookie team of Paul Azinger and Chip Beck. They had debuted separately the day before, Beck getting a half-point with Tom Watson against the Spanish Armada in foursomes, and Azinger and Curtis Strange falling to Sam Torrance and Gordon Brand, Jr., in fourballs. Now Azinger and Beck were a team for the first time, and they surprised everybody but themselves and Floyd with a six-birdie, 4-and-3 romp over Brand and Torrance. "They played that way in practice," Floyd said. "I just wanted them to get over the first-day jitters."

They didn't start convincingly, though. Azinger put his opening drive into the hospitality tents, and Beck had to play a blind recovery shot to the edge of the green, setting up a saving par. The Scots led just once, on a birdie at No. 2, the first of only three the entire round. The Americans then went 1-up with three consecutive birdies from No. 3 on some sensational iron play and putting, getting winners from eight feet and two feet, then a half at No. 5 from eight feet. The Scots couldn't get going, and the Americans wouldn't stop. They birdied the 11th from 14 feet, the 12th from three, and closed out the match with a birdie from seven feet at the 15th.

"It's obvious," Floyd was to say, "that Beck and Azinger are going out again." Their victory brought the Americans to within two points at 6-4. Things were looking up for the Americans, for in the next match, Calcavecchia and Green got them within one on a 3-and-2 victory over the Irish twosome of Ronan Rafferty and Christy O'Connor, Jr., who was seeing his first action.

"Ken and I played well," Calcavecchia said. "We made a couple of mistakes, but we were 5-up by then, and if you're going to make mistakes, that's a good time to make them." He also spoke of the "good chemistry" Floyd said there was between them. "We get out of each other's way and give the other guy some room," Calcavecchia said.

Rafferty and O'Connor led once, after the Americans took a three-putt bogey from 10 feet on the second, then went to 3-up through No. 9 on one birdie of their own and two bogeys by the Irish. The demoralizing blow came at the inviting 10th. Green's drive just missed the green and was 35 feet from the flag. Calcavecchia holed it for an eagle and a 4-up lead. They went 5-up with a par at the 12th, then delayed the end with two bunkered shots and a bogey at No. 13, and a bunkered approach and a losing par at the 15th. Two putts from 45 feet got them a par, the win at the 16th, and a big boost to American hopes.

"Our goal is to go into the singles even," Calcavecchia said. "Although 1- or 2-down wouldn't be a big problem." Such talk, by the way, is why some British writers called him "arrogant." Calcavecchia delivered those words as a statement of belief in the Americans' strength in head-to-head play, and he delivered them in the same near-monotone that he used in the emotionally charged moments back at the British Open when he spoke of his late father and of the impending arrival of his first child. He simply comes right to the point, like many Americans—Azinger, Strange and Kite among others.

Just when a tie was within the Americans' reach, the Spanish Armada snatched it away again. Seve Ballesteros and Jose-Maria Olazabal met their third set of opponents in three outings, Curtis Strange and Tom Kite this time. The Spaniards frittered away a three-hole lead down the stretch, but ducked out with a one-hole victory. They got to 3-up at the 11th, where Ballesteros hit a thunderous drive, Olazabal hit a seven iron to nine feet, and Ballesteros dropped the birdie putt. Then came two crucial errors that threatened to swing the match around. At the par-three 12th, Olazabal bunkered his two-iron tee shot, triggering a two-putt bogey from eight feet, and at the 13th, the Spaniards hit two bunkers from the fairway, and bogeyed again, dropping two holes to the American pars. Their lead was down to one hole. They nursed it home through four halves, and it all came down to the 18th. Both sides bunkered their approach shots. Olazabal blasted out to seven feet, but the gritty Kite topped him, coming out to four feet. Now it was up to Ballesteros, who had already saved them with a clutch five-footer at the 17th. He stalked this seven-footer from all sides, then drilled it in, saving a half. "I just had to sink that last putt," he said. "I just had to."

And so after all the fireworks and gut-wringing tension, nothing had changed, except for one thing. The morning round was over, and the Europeans, though still leading by two points, 7-5, were a half-day closer to success. As for the Americans—as they say in the United States, the meter was running.

The Saturday afternoon fourballs opened on an alarming note for the Europeans. Their unbeaten twosome, Faldo and Woosnam, with a record of 5-1/2—1/2 dating back to their first pairing in the 1987 matches, were finally beaten. They ran into that new American buzz saw, Azinger and Beck, a most un-rookie-like set of rookies. This was the match of the ages. On a statistician's chart, it would look like this: Across 17 holes, there were 20 birdies total, no bogeys; five holes were halved in birdies, and three in pars, which is to say that only three holes escaped being birdied by one side or the other. The Americans were 11 under par (Azinger making six of the 11 birdies), and the Europeans nine under (Woosnam making five of the nine).

It was a 2-and-1 victory, but only some miracle shots kept it that close. Woosnam chipped in from 60 feet at No. 1, rescuing a half with a birdie. Faldo holed a 40-foot bunker shot from a nasty lie for a winning birdie at No. 7. And at the 10th, Woosnam saved a half with a birdie the hard way. He hit a tree with his drive, wedged out of trouble, then holed a 15-foot chip shot. "From 50 yards in, we started believing we had to hole every shot," Faldo said. "Sometimes for a half," he added. Said Jacklin: "They ran into some unbelievable golf. When that happens, all you can do is put your hand out and say, 'Right, man.'" At any rate, the European lead was cut to a point, 7-6. And then that, too, was gone in the next match.

Tom Kite and Mark McCumber squared everything at 7-7, beating Bernhard Langer and Jose-Maria Canizares 2-and-1 in a classic example of fourballs play—one player taking the gamble as soon as his partner is safe. "I know it looks as if I'm doing it all," McCumber said, after making five birdies and a conceded eagle (a brilliant three-wood tee shot to seven feet at No. 10), "but with Tom hitting the fairway and the greens every time, I can go for it. I feel so comfortable. I'm loving it."

Kite made just one birdie, a 30-foot putt at the par-three 12th. McCumber's birdies came from six, 30, 10, 18, and 12 feet. "Mark was hot," Kite said.

"I'll take him as a partner any day."

So the Americans were stirring. The Europeans had just lost the first two afternoon matches. They needed something to stem that fast-turning tide. And they got it in the most unlikely way—from silent Mark James, who was having a good year, and the slumping Howard Clark. In a five-hour, 20-minute dogfight that will take its place alongside any in Ryder Cup history, they beat Curtis Strange and Payne Stewart by one hole. But it took a European surge and two stunning American errors to do it. First, Clark dropped a 10-foot birdie putt at the 16th to square a bitter, seesaw battle. Then at the vulnerable 575-yard 17th, a birdie chance for everyone, a weird thing happened: Stewart and Strange both hit their second shots into the trees to the right.

"Pressure will affect the greatest player in the world at times," Floyd said later. "Sometimes it has a good effect, sometimes a bad one. They were very poor shots. What more can you say?"

At any rate, James hit a wedge to five feet, holed the birdie putt for a 1-up lead, and set the stage for a heart-stopping finish at the 18th. Clark hit a huge and nearly fatal tee shot. It was too far left, and heading for a watery grave. But somehow it carried the trees. "And it must have cleared the water by only inches, and it left me with 154 yards to the flag," he said. He had only an eight iron left. But the silent James saved him the trouble. James' tee shot ended up on the flat lip of a bunker, part on grass, part on sand. It would take an absolutely precise shot to get it safely across the water. And that's what he hit—one of the finest shots of this Ryder Cup. He picked it off with a magnificent three iron, 205 yards, to within 14 feet of the flag. He two-putted for a half in pars and a European win. Said James, "I never want to be that nervous again."

Now Europe led, 8-7, and it came down to the Spaniards again. And Ballesteros, for one, never ceases to amaze Jacklin. "Seve has never had a rest in my time as captain," Jacklin said. "He hinted last week he wouldn't mind a rest this time. But he said, well, maybe Jose-Maria is a bit better player now, and now he can carry me." But Ballesteros didn't need any carrying. This time the Spaniards faced a new pairing, Mark Calcavecchia and Ken Green. The outcome was the same. Or, as Ballesteros put it, "Nobody can beat us—we can beat anyone!" Even the Calcavecchia-Green chemistry didn't work. Olazabal birdied the first from 15 feet, Ballesteros birdied the third from 14 and the fourth on a tap-in after nearly holing out a wedge approach, and they were on their way—3-up at the turn, 4-up at the 10th (Ballesteros on a tap-in again after nearly holing a wedge). It was a 4-and-2 runaway. "We missed a few putts," Olazabal said, "otherwise we would have won by a larger margin." It was Ballesteros at his best again. He made five of their seven birdies in the 16 holes. After a few shaky moments, the Europeans had put down the American uprising.

"This afternoon was more than I could have expected," Jacklin said. "To come back like that shows what human beings can do when they dig deep. As a captain, I couldn't have expected more." Jacklin could sleep more peacefully that night. His lads had given him a 9-7 cushion to put his head on.

They had come to the singles, and the fans had come to a simple conclusion. If the Ryder Cup were played in the logic classroom, the Americans could have stayed home and had the cup mailed to them. On paper, the Europeans just couldn't match up. Jacklin had no depth to work with, which is why he played his big guns—Faldo, Woosnam, Ballesteros, and Olazabal—every day. Beyond them, he had the two oldest men in the field, Christy O'Connor, Jr., 41, and Jose-Maria Canizares, 42, neither of whom had a great record on the European Tour to begin with. Jacklin also had three men who were slumping badly—Clark, Langer, and Torrance. And they were up against the cream of the American tour. So in the paper match-ups, it was no contest. But golf isn't played on paper.

Jacklin parceled out his strength carefully. He sent Seve Ballesteros out first, going for that instant, demoralizing point at the top of the lineup. Ballesteros would meet Paul Azinger. Jacklin then had Jose-Marie Olazabal third (against Payne Stewart), and threw his other two hammers last, Nick Faldo No. 11 (against Lanny Wadkins), and Ian Woosnam No. 12 (against Curtis Strange). Oddly enough, the players helped to shape the lineup. "At the meeting last night, Jacklin asked Ian to play in the first match," Ballesteros said. "But Ian said he'd rather not because he did it the last time and it didn't work. So I said I would play in the first match."

This was the situation, then, that final day. The Europeans went out into the sunny, still, warm weather with a 9-7 lead. They needed five points to tie and keep the cup (14 points, total). A half-point more would give them their third consecutive victory. But it would be an awesome job. Aside from an apparent imbalance in the match-ups, singles figured to be the Americans' strong suit. Each man on his own, just like back home in a $1 million tournament. "We're going for a clean sweep," Paul Azinger said. And that's what it looked like from the start. This was the way the day unfolded, in chronological order:

• Tom Kite, who Floyd said would be at a disadvantage because of his lack of distance, spotted Howard Clark about 30 yards a shot and wiped him out with one of the worst beatings in Ryder Cup history, 8 and 7. Kite had seven birdies (only one conceded) in the 12 holes they played, and never lost a hole. What made the outlook grim for Europe was that they were the fifth match off, but the first finished, in just two hours and 11 minutes, and Kite's work was so sudden and decisive that it might set a tone for the other Americans. Kite was this hot: Clark made three bogeys, but only one of them cost him a hole. This was a blitz, pure and simple. Europe's lead was down to one, 9-8.

• Chip Beck again played like a crusty veteran, not a rookie. He turned in a museum piece in his 3-and-1 victory over Bernhard Langer. Aside from his one bogey, he was brilliant. He made seven birdies, the longest from nine feet and the shortest from three. (He ended up the top American point-winner, with 3-1/2, and fellow rookie Paul Azinger was next, with a 3-1-0 record.) The Americans had drawn even, at 9-9, for the first time since Friday afternoon.

• Next came Paul Azinger, the other half of the American one-two rookie punch. This was the lead-off match, and a dazzling one at that. It even had a flash of Spanish temper. At the second hole, Azinger refused to allow Ballesteros to change his ball to putt. Ballesteros glared. "It's your nerves against his nerves," Azinger said. "You can't let anything he does get to you. There's a ton of pressure. It's unbelievable. There was a bit of gamesmanship there. Seve was trying to get into my head, and until I pulled myself out of it after the third hole, he succeeded."

It was a seesaw battle. Ballesteros lost an early 2-up lead, fell two behind at the turn, then twice battled back to be all-square coming in. Azinger took what proved to be the decisive lead at the 15th, where he holed a 12-footer from off the green for a birdie. They halved the 17th in birdies, and then came one of the stranger episodes in Ryder Cup history. Azinger pulled his tee shot into the water well to the left. He took his penalty drop amid trees and high grass, then hit a brilliant Ballesteros-special recovery across the water and into a greenside bunker. He seemed done for anyway, until an incredible thing happened: Ballesteros, who was high and dry with his tee shot, proceeded to hit his three-iron second into the water in front of the green. He hit his next to 20 feet, holed the putt, and Azinger, who had blasted out to five feet, holed his for a half in bogeys and a one-hole victory. The Americans led, 10-9, and were ahead for the first time since Friday morning.

"I can't believe it," the lanky, boyish Azinger said. "Seve is the best player in the world. I am just thrilled."

It was, by the way, Ballesteros' first loss in singles since his rookie defeat by Larry Nelson in 1979. He shrugged it off.

"He gave me a gift with his tee shot," Ballesteros said, "and I gave it back to him with my second shot."

• The American lead didn't last long. In the sixth match, the fourth to finish, Mark James whipped Mark O'Meara, 3 and 2, to tie the match at 10 points each. O'Meara played well—three birdies and only one bogey. But James was hot. He birdied four out of five holes, going from 1-down at No. 2 to 2-up by the turn. "I'm disappointed," O'Meara said. "It's been very tough because I only played the first day, and we were beaten by Seve and Olazabal." James gave one of his longest statements. "I feel very, very pleased," he said. "I played well, I putted well, I did everything well."

Now the American collapse began ...

• Olazabal leaped ahead on birdies at the first two holes and Payne Stewart squared it with birdies of his own at the fourth and fifth. They seesawed down the stretch. Stewart was 1-up with three to play. Olazabal squared the match with a two-putt birdie from nearly 40 feet at the 17th, and then came Stewart's fatal mistake. At No. 18, he drove into the water, and he put on his rain suit and tried to hit the ball out. He took swipe after swipe. "How many's that?" he asked, exasperated. The answer was three. Olazabal had a one-hole victory, and Europe an 11-10 lead.

• Mark Calcavecchia and Ronan Rafferty also hooked up in a tug-of-war. The match could have gone either way, but the surprise was that it went this way: They were all-square coming to the 18th. Then with Rafferty safe in the fairway, Calcavecchia caught water not only off the tee but with his second shot as well. "He had just hit his first bad shot of the day," Rafferty said. "He said, 'Thanks for the last couple of days. Enjoy your moment.' This," Rafferty added, "is great." Europe led, 12-10.

(But with six matches still out on the course, Europe was leading in one, the U.S. in one, and two others were all-square. It was anybody's cup.)

• Christy O'Connor's time had come. At 41, O'Connor, the unwanted, was the second-oldest man on the course, and his opponent, Fred Couples, was just about a week from his 30th birthday. It looked like a mismatch. But Couples couldn't shake the gritty Irishman. O'Connor led once, on a seven-foot birdie putt at No. 2. He trailed twice, squared it twice, the last at the 16th, where he put a wedge to four feet and holed the birdie putt. Couples had a chance to take the lead at the 17th, but missed a five-foot birdie putt. And so it came to the last hole. At the 18th, Couples, nicknamed "Boom-Boom" for his immense power, hit a tremendous drive. There was no way O'Connor could stay with him. The role of the captain came into play here. Whatever it was—instruction, inspiration, cheering—it worked. Jacklin had been walking with O'Connor for a few holes, a kind of mother hen. "Tony said on the 18th tee that if I put the pressure on, he wouldn't be able to take it," O'Connor said.

O'Connor found a way to put the pressure on. The shot is now part of golf lore. With everything riding on his "unworthy" shoulders, he whistled a two-iron second 229 yards to about three feet from the flag. Couples had only a nine iron left, but he missed the green. He pitched on, six feet short, and two-putted for his bogey. He knew O'Connor wasn't going to three-putt from three feet. He conceded the birdie and the match, and there were two men crying. As Couples walked away, tears streaming, O'Connor—who was four under par with five birdies and one bogey—looked heavenward, a hallelujah on his face, and then he, too, began to cry. His wife raced up and hugged him, leading his teammates in tribute while the crowd thundered. Europe led, 13-10.

"This has got to be the greatest and most emotional moment in my whole life," said O'Connor. Not surprising. The man had proved himself. "I felt terrible at breakfast this morning, because of an article in one of the Sunday newspapers," he said. "The pressure it put on me was too much, unfair on one man." He didn't realize it at the time, but obviously there wasn't too much pressure for him.

• Next came the oldest man on the course, 42-year-old Jose-Maria Canizares against Ken Green, 31. Their match was so dead even that both would return four-under-par 68s on six birdies and two bogeys. Green went 1-up at the 13th on a four-foot birdie, and Canizares squared it with a birdie at the 15th, tapping in after his wedge approach. They halved the 17th in birdies, Green two-putting from 75 feet, Canizares from 50. It foreshadowed what was to come next.

At the 18th, Canizares put his approach shot 70 feet past the hole. His first putt stopped three feet short. Green, lying 40 feet away, rammed his first putt six feet past. It was still his turn. And he missed the par. Canizares sized his up carefully, stood over it rock-still, then stroked gently. The ball rolled to the hole, and dropped. And when it did, Canizares charged across the green, fist pumping into the air, into the arms of his teammates. He had clinched a tie for Europe. The cup would stay. "That point not only meant a lot to me, it meant a lot to the whole team," Canizares said. "I am very proud that I got it."

The European counterattack had been electrifying. Trailing by 10-9, Europe had won five consecutive matches, and the last four at the 18th hole. Now Europe led, 14-10, and the Americans were against the wall. They had to win the last four matches. The slightest slip, so much as a half, even, meant the third consecutive defeat.

• Tom Watson was not the man to let that happen. He raced past Sam Torrance, 3 and 1. Europe now led, 14-11.

• Mark McCumber and Gordon Brand, Jr., were locked in a quiet, heated struggle. McCumber led three times, never by more than one hole, and Brand squared the match three times. Three holes were halved in birdies, and each man made only one bogey. McCumber's came early, a three-putt from 65 feet at the 12th, and squared the match. Brand's came at the last instant, and decided it. At the 18th, he bunkered his approach, blasted out to 15 feet, and two-putted for his bogey five. McCumber two-putted from 60 feet for a par and a one-hole victory. Europe's lead was down to two, 14-12.

• The water at the 18th claimed yet another victim, but it was a European this time—Nick Faldo. Lanny Wadkins spotted Faldo the first hole on a bogey, then won four of the next nine holes on birdies—one-putts of six, seven and 10 feet, and a two-putt from eight feet at the 10th. Faldo could get nothing stirring. He won two holes back on Wadkins' bogeys, and squared the match on his lone birdie of the day, a 16-foot putt at No. 17. Then he watered his drive at the 18th, gamely finished the hole for a six, but Wadkins two-putted from 60 feet for his par and a one-hole victory. Faldo surveyed a card that showed one bogey, one double bogey, and one birdie, and said, "My game was no good." The European lead was down to one, 14-13.

• Curtis Strange and Ian Woosnam met in the closing match, and for a final act, the drama was equal to any. Strange took a 2-up lead on Woosnam's bogey at No. 5 from a bunker and his own birdie at No. 6, on a 16-foot putt. They got back to all-square when Woosnam won No. 7 on a four-foot birdie putt and No. 8 on Strange's watery bogey. Woosnam then won his third consecutive hole and went one ahead with a three-foot birdie at the ninth. And he held that lead, and the fate of the Ryder Cup, for the next six holes. It was then that Strange, battling desperately with one eye on the scoreboard, started a four-birdie streak born of a magical short game.

First was a 12-footer at No. 15 for a half. Then Strange squared the match at the 16th on a four-foot putt. He plunked a sand wedge to a foot at the 17th and went 1-up. At the 18th, Strange fired a two-iron approach that almost rolled over the hole. The ball stopped six feet away. Woosnam missed the green and chipped on. He realized he couldn't make birdie, so in an act reminiscent of the Nicklaus-Jacklin scene in the 1969 tie, he picked up Strange's ball and handed it to him, conceding the hole and the match. Strange had a two-hole victory, and the 1989 Ryder Cup had ended in a 14-14 tie.

But there were differing views of that tie. To many American observers, it was a loss, principally because a team conceded to be the stronger collapsed in the middle matches. And, of course, the cup was staying in Europe. For the underdog Europeans, who had been teetering on the brink earlier in the day, it was a victory.

What was the difference? Nicklaus' words from 1987 continue to hang in the air. Maybe he's right. Maybe the Americans simply aren't tough enough any more. On the other hand, there's no question the Europeans have improved immensely. Now maybe they simply refuse to be beaten. It's an argument that should last until 1991, when the Ryder Cup is due for Kiawah Island, South Carolina, on a course that as of autumn, 1989, was not yet built.

And what of the American collapse?

"It's the pressure," Raymond Floyd said. "You have a lot of world-class players who will fold under pressure. But all these players will be better players because of what happened here this week."

Said Jacklin: "They crack like we all crack. They're only human."

As if he had proof in hand, it was noted that three of his four big guns—Ballesteros, Faldo, and Woosnam—all lost. And all three went 18 holes. In fact, eight of the 12 singles went to the 18th hole, and in half of them, someone hit into the water.

"We're not really happy with a tie," Floyd said. "But early on, I'd have felt like a tie was a defeat. Later on, I thought we had no chance at all. To come back after that—I'm tickled to death. I'd like to have won, but I'd hate to go home a loser. But we're going home with fond memories of a great match. All along, I said golf would be the winner. So I'm not going back a loser. The match was a credit to both sides."

The match closed on a somber note. "You've got to know when to say goodbye," said Jacklin, affirming that this, his fourth captaincy, was his last. Obviously, his was the most successful European (or British) tenure ever. He opened with a one-point loss in 1983, he won in 1985 and 1987, and now had a tie.

"It's been a wonderful feast of golf," Jacklin said. He was speaking of what had just happened at The Belfry. But the words would stand for his four turns at the helm.

8. The Dunhill Cup

The Ryder Cup was over. The cup would stay in European hands, thanks to a tie at The Belfry. The cheers had died away, and nothing was left but the rosy glow of the European side, having come back from the brink of defeat, and the disappointment of the Americans, stumbling on the verge of success. The combatants packed up their gear and left Sutton Coldfield, England, and went their separate ways. Twelve of them headed to St. Andrews, Scotland, for the fifth playing of the Dunhill Cup. Three Americans remained teammates: Curtis Strange, Tom Kite, and Mark Calcavecchia. Nine Europeans had to shift gears, forget their allegiance of the previous week, and join with countrymen in a new common purpose: Howard Clark and Mark James for England; Ronan Rafferty and Christy O'Connor, Jr., for Ireland; Gordon Brand, Jr., and Sam Torrance for Scotland; Jose-Maria Olazabal and Jose-Maria Canizares for Spain, and Ian Woosnam for Wales.

This Dunhill Cup was without two of its usual headliners, both Ryder Cup stars—Seve Ballesteros and Nick Faldo. Ballesteros had said earlier that he would not play, but Faldo withdrew shortly after the Ryder Cup, saying he was "emotionally drained." He was replaced by Clark.

The press immediately flocked to Calcavecchia, for two reasons. First, he's a forthright and willing talker, and second, he was probably the most noticeable of all the Americans who slipped in the Ryder Cup. The Americans were charging through the singles that last day when four of them faltered coming in, allowing Europe to tie, 14-14, and keep the cup. At the final hole, Calcavecchia hit his tee shot into the water, then hit his approach in, and finally conceded the hole and the match to Rafferty.

"I'm tired," Calcavecchia said at St. Andrews. "Really tired, and really sore. My legs hurt. And I'm not very happy, either. We didn't win. We didn't lose, either, but we wanted to win. I hit that bad drive at No. 18—popped it up. It only happens to me twice a year, and it happened there. I feel it cost us the Ryder Cup. That was a great downer. I had been pointing at that one for two years."

There was one other reason the press flocked to him. He would be defending his British Open championship at the Old Course in 1990. This was his first visit to it. What did he think of it?

"I don't like it yet," Calcavecchia said, echoing the first impression of so many golfers. "But I don't dislike it. And I thought I'd like it less than I do. Anyway, I'm excited about playing here this week. And a win here definitely would take a lot of the sting out of last week."

Not that the Americans were dwelling on the disappointment. "The Ryder Cup is gone, it's past," Strange said. "No, there's no revenge motive here this week. We just want to go out and play golf."

And so they did, marching past Korea, Argentina, Ireland, and Japan to their first Dunhill Cup championship and finally justifying their No. 1 seeding. Greg Norman and the Australians were seeded No. 2, Scotland with the rejuvenated Sandy Lyle No. 3, Spain No. 4, defending champion Ireland No. 5, England No. 6, Japan No. 7, and Wales No. 8. The unseeded teams were

Argentina, Sweden, New Zealand, France, Canada, Taiwan, and the two that won berths in the preliminary round, South Korea and Italy. Korea, led by Park Nam Shin's 67, beat Colombia, 3-0; and Italy, led by Alberto Binaghi's 67, defeated Zimbabwe, 3-0.

This Dunhill Cup barely got started before the spectators knew it was going to be one for the books. In the first round, three seeded teams got knocked out and two others escaped by the skin of their teeth. Part of the reason, of course, was what possibly is the meanest hole in golf—No. 17, the Road Hole.

Spectators again pretty well filled the stands at the green of that old dragon to witness some of the keenest anguish in golf. Through the first four Dunhill Cups, the course as a whole played to a total of 65 under par, but No. 17 was at 269 *over* par. Nothing happened to damage its reputation in the 1989 Dunhill Cup, despite the warm and almost totally calm days. In 102 rounds, No. 17 played to a total of 70 over par. It took no blockbuster scores, nothing over a triple-bogey seven, but it also yielded only three birdies. No. 17 was in good working order from the start. In the very first match, all three Welshmen and one Argentinian bogeyed it.

The first round was a time of pithy quotes or cries from the wilderness, depending on the author. Ireland's O'Connor, for example: "All this excitement is making me very old." And Wales' Woosnam: "I am still tired." Said France's Gery Watine, "I think it's a big thing." And most telling of all, Australia's Norman: "I'll see you guys next year. I'm going fishing early."

That's a good cross-section from the most startling first round in the five years of the Dunhill Cup. Never before had the world powers been treated with such impunity. Three seeded teams were knocked out by unseeded teams—No. 2 Australia, by the French; No. 4 Spain, by Sweden, and No. 8 Wales, by Argentina. Two others had to escape by playoffs—No. 8 Ireland, the defending champion, and No. 6 England. This one-day outburst didn't prove anything, of course. But it was another indication that as the 1980s were drawing to a close, golf was on the rise throughout the world, and more and more quality players were emerging.

The best example in the first round was the young Frenchman, Marc Pendaries, 23, who came to the Dunhill No. 137 on the European order of merit and who was struggling to keep his playing card for 1990. No one would rank him with Greg Norman. Yet he beat Norman, 71-73. Maybe the story was not so much that Pendaries won, but that he could even function under the circumstances. France, 0-9 in three previous appearances, had taken a surprising 1-0 lead in the first game on Emmanuel Dussart's 72-73 victory over Ian Baker-Finch. Now Pendaries could give France its first-ever match in the Dunhill Cup. All he had to do, this little-known and inexperienced Frenchmen, was beat one of the very best players in the world. By all accounts, he should have buckled. Not only was he playing Norman head-to-head, but he had fallen four strokes behind through No. 7, thanks to his two bogeys and two Norman birdies. It helped only slightly that he had gained a stroke at the turn, after Norman bogeyed No. 8. "It looked as though I was cruising right along," Norman said. "But strange things happen in this game."

The first was Pendaries' eagle-two at No. 10, a wedge shot from 98 yards out. That pulled him to within one stroke. Then came Norman's crash at the par-five 14th. "I was trying to fade my tee shot down the middle," Norman said, "but I got ahead of it and blocked it out." The ball rocketed out of bounds to the right, costing him a double-bogey seven and dropping him a stroke behind the cool Frenchman. Pendaries added to his margin at No. 15, with a birdie from 25 feet, and Norman's three-putt bogey at No. 17 merely underlined his frustration. He saluted Pendaries. "He played good, solid golf, very intelligently," Norman said. He left with a 14-3 record in Dunhill play. Pendaries had joined some distinguished company. Only Strange and Woosnam had beaten Norman before. Pendaries restrained his emotions. "It was a great day to beat Norman, but it was only one day in my life," he said simply. Pendaries, another in the long line of Europeans who seek to hone their games in American collegiate golf, was a scholarship player at the University of Houston, a perennial powerhouse.

Wayne Grady, co-runner-up in the British Open just a few months earlier, salvaged a little something for the Aussies with a 67-70 win over Gery Watine in the final match. It was the Aussies' worst showing ever in the Dunhill Cup. They won in 1985 and 1986, finished fourth in 1987, and were runner-up to Ireland in 1988.

"Golf is growing in France, and we need something like this to make it grow more," Watine said. "This will be a big thing in France." Indeed—one of the biggest days for French golf fans since Arnaud Massy won the British Open in 1907.

The French win, coming in the seventh of the eight matches, was merely the biggest surprise of the day. For shock value, though, unseeded Sweden's 2-1 ouster of No. 4-seeded Spain wasn't far behind. Granted, the absence of Ballesteros made a difference. But this was not a weak, inexperienced Spanish team. In 1987, this identical team reached the second round without Ballesteros. With him, Spain reached the second round in 1985, lost in the first round in 1986, and finished third in 1988. Sweden, on the other hand, never got beyond the first round.

They did this time when Magnus Persson held on to beat Jose Rivero, 71-72, in the final game. But a Swedish upset had to be the furthest thing from one's mind, especially after Olazabal's 67-70 run over Mats Lanner in the first game. Olazabal, who had been averaging 29 putts a round on the European tour up to the Ryder Cup just the week before, stayed hot on the greens at the Old Course. Thanks, in part, to a superb short game. He birdied No. 1 from six feet, then ran off three in a row from No. 4, from one, three, and six feet, for a four-stroke lead at the turn, and he was on his way.

Spain's lead disappeared in the next game when Ove Sellberg birdied No. 18 for a 71-72 victory over Ryder Cup hero Canizares. But it was No. 17 that set it up. "I didn't hole any putts until I got to No. 17," Sellberg said. "I holed my second from 13 feet." That was a par, and when Canizares bogeyed, they were tied. At the last hole, Canizares missed his birdie try from eight feet, and Sellberg holed from five, and that was it. In the final game, Persson was out in a three-birdie, one-bogey 34 for a two-stroke lead. Rivero birdied the 18th to cut Persson's victory margin to one, 71-72. So Sweden, for the first time in five Dunhill Cups, was through the first round.

Argentina's pre-1989 record wasn't much better—one victory in two appearances. But it improved in a hurry on the strength of the first upset on Thursday.

The engaging, boyish-looking Philip Parkin, the first Welsh victim, was troubled by his game from the outset. It couldn't have come at a worse time. He was matched against Eduardo Romero, the veteran campaigner who plays so well in the British Open and who just a few weeks earlier scored his first European tour victory in the Lancome Trophy. "I hit horrendous shots from start to finish," Parkin said. "After duffing my opening drive, I was just short of the burn in two at the first hole. At the second, I hooked it into the rough." So he opened with two bogeys. Romero, on the other hand, was inspired by uncomfortable memories. "In 1988, I lost to Zimbabwe (Morgan Shumba), 73-75, in the preliminary round," Romero said. "I was determined not to make the same mistake this time." And he didn't. Romero raced out in 32 on four birdies ranging in length from three to eight feet, and led by 32-38 at the turn. Poor Parkin. If nothing else, he found a new way to double-bogey the par-three 11th. "How often," Parkin pleaded with a sheepish grin, "are you on a green with your tee shot, and plugged in a bunker with your second?" Once is enough. Parkin was about 50 yards from the flag, and he decided to chip with a sand wedge. But he pulled the shot into the bunker. Romero won, 68-75, and Argentina led, 1-0.

Wales stayed alive in the second game, but only just, when Mark Mouland birdied No. 18 to tie Vicente Fernandez, 70-70. It had looked like a Welsh victory at the turn, with Mouland up by three strokes. But Fernandez rattled off three birdies through the first six incoming holes, and parred No. 17 for good measure for an inward 33. Now it was up to the Welsh captain, Woosnam, in the last game. But Woosnam wasn't up to it.

Woosnam and Miguel Fernandez were bogey-free going out, Woosnam leading, 32-34. He was still one stroke ahead through No. 13, then fell utterly to pieces. He bogeyed the 14th, double-bogeyed the 15th, and bogeyed the 17th, and was beaten 69-72. It was his third defeat against nine victories in Dunhill Cup play, and it was the second-worst Welsh showing since they were ousted in the qualifier in 1987. "I think the result is a reflection of last week (Ryder Cup)," Woosnam said. "I am still tired. I lacked concentration, and I am tired." He said that at No. 15, he hit a shot 100 yards off line, slicing into the bushes. He had to take a drop, then was short of the green, chipped up, and two-putted from 35 feet for his double-bogey six. And Argentina advanced, 2-1/2—1/2.

There was some question whether fifth-seeded Ireland had enough muscle to repeat as champions. Rafferty was the only returnee from the 1988 championship team, Walton was largely untested in such events, and O'Connor was 41 years old. But there was no doubt they'd get through the first round handily. They were playing Taiwan. And Walton's breezy 69-76 win over Lu Chien-Soon proved this outing was a mere formality. Someone forgot to tell the other Taiwanese.

Yu Chin-Han was steady in beating Rafferty, the Ryder Cup star, 71-73, to even the match at 1-1. Yu was out in pars for a one-stroke edge against Rafferty's two-bogey, one-birdie 37. Then Rafferty made the expected comeback. Birdies at No. 11 and No. 12 wiped out Yu's two-stroke lead, and the spectators awaited the predictable result. Except that Rafferty got torpedoed by No. 13. His tee shot buried in a bunker, leaving him only a sideways escape. But he left his first try in the bunker. It cost him a double-bogey six. Rafferty caught Yu at No. 14, birdie to bogey. Now he would come sailing home. Not so. He bunkered his tee shot at No. 16 and two-putted from four feet for a bogey to fall one behind. Yu locked up the win with a birdie at No. 18. "You have to play well to win," Rafferty said. "And I didn't play well." (His 73, by the way, was the first time in five Dunhill Cup matches that the Irish were over par. Rafferty, Des Smyth, and Eamonn Darcy were under par in all four matches in winning the 1988 champion-ship.) With Rafferty's fall, the Irish hopes rested on O'Connor, playing Hsieh Chin-Sheng, and things didn't look good.

O'Connor lost his one stroke lead when he double-bogeyed No. 11 after his tee shot plugged in a bunker. "I was just 20 feet from the pin, and I had to play out backwards," he said. "It was so unjust, and that was what drove me. I said, 'You're not going to lose after that hole.'" Well, he didn't, but he came close. He trailed by two strokes with two holes to play when Hsieh birdied No. 16. But Hsieh gave a stroke back with a bogey at the Road Hole, where O'Connor saved his par with a nine-foot putt. And then at No. 18, O'Connor birdied from six feet to square the game at 73 and the match at 1-1/2 each. It was sudden death. They battled for four holes—Nos. 1, 2, 17, and then 18, where O'Connor repeated his earlier birdie, this time from 20 feet. Hsieh missed from six. O'Connor had come through again. The Irish, 2-1 winners, mopped their brows.

Next on the tightrope: No. 6-seeded England against Canada in the eighth and final match of the day. The suspense came early. England's Denis Durnian squandered a two-stroke lead with a double-bogey seven at No. 14—the hole that destroyed Norman just a few minutes earlier—and was tied by Richard Zokol, 72-72. They stood by to watch the finish, not realizing that they would be it, the second playoff of the day.

James, another of the Ryder Cup heroes, started shakily and finished worse, and was bounced by Dave Barr, 71-73. It wasn't really that close. Barr was three under par and three ahead until he double-bogeyed No. 17. James was now within one, but he bogeyed No. 18, and Canada led, 1-1/2—1/2. England had been knocked out in the first round only once before, in 1986 (by Argentina). Would it happen again?

Clark did his bit to prevent it. He settled a gritty battle against Dan Halldorson with birdies at the 15th and 16th for a 71-72 victory that squared the match. It was playoff time. Nothing new to Zokol. He went five extra holes before losing to Greg Norman in 1987. This one was much quicker. At No. 2, Zokol bunkered his tee shot and Durnian hit a four iron to 10 feet and got down in two putts for the winning par. But he didn't see how. He had begun using the elongated putter about a month earlier, and he was disturbed at how he could hear his heart thumping as he held the handle to his chest. "It was the worst pressure I've ever known in my life," he said.

The other three matches went according to form, though not without some difficulty.

The second match of the day pitted unseeded South Korea against top-seeded United States. And in the first game, a battle of newcomers to St. Andrews, South Korea's Park Nam Shin scored a 70-71 victory over Cal-cavecchia. Was yet another top-seeded American team going down?

"This will make me a national hero," said Park, 33, a former caddy. Park jumped in front immediately with birdies at the first and third, but bogeys at the fourth and fifth left him at level par through the turn. Calcavecchia bogeyed the second and fourth, but could offset only one of them, with the birdie at No. 3. Angry with himself, he marched right off to the practice tee after his loss. But the Americans were in no trouble. In the second game, despite five three-putt greens, Kite rolled up a 72-75 victory over Choi Yoon Soo. "I missed only one green in regulation," the surprised Kite said. "I'm sure glad we're seeded, because although we're not coasting, this match helps get our feet back on the ground. The Ryder Cup took a lot out of everybody." Strange wrapped it up for the United States in the final game, a 67-69 win over Choi Sang Ho. "I made a few putts on the back nine, but no real mistakes," Strange said. Five of his six birdies came on par-four holes, the longest putt from 15 feet, the shortest four. As the day wore on, he had to work to keep his mind on the match. "Once Tom and I were pretty well ahead, I concentrated on getting ready for tomorrow," he said. "But you can't take anyone lightly." If he needed to remind himself, he had only to go back a year, to when the lightly regarded Irish knocked off the Americans and everybody else, and took the cup.

In Match 5, third-seeded Scotland against New Zealand, yet another upset was brewing. "It was ridiculous," said Scotland's Torrance. "Midway through the first nine we were down in all three matches." Things improved just slightly by the turn. Brand, the lead-off Scot, was one down to Simon Owen, Torrance had tied Grant Waite at 34, and in a barn-burner, Lyle led Frank Nobilo, 31-32.

New Zealand took a 1-0 lead when Brand broke down coming in, bogeying the last three holes and four of the last seven to fall to Owen, 72-76. Torrance shook free for an incoming 33 to beat Waite, 67-70, and tie the match. Just behind them, the deciding match was a real battle. The old Sandy Lyle showed up in the nick of time.

He came exploding out of his long slump with an outward, five-birdie 31, and led Nobilo by only one. Nobilo caught him with a birdie at No. 12. Both were five under. The tension broke two holes later. At No. 14, Nobilo was too strong with a chip and bogeyed. Lyle two-putted from 90 feet for a birdie, and just that fast, he was leading by two. Lyle bogeyed No. 17 but still gained a stroke, thanks to Nobilo's mortifying error. Nobilo ran his birdie putt five feet past the hole, then left his par putt two inches from the hole. And then incredibly, ". . . he hit at it one-handed," Lyle said, "and hit the ground first and missed. As he came off he said, 'That's six,' and I said 'Are you sure?' I didn't even see him do it." Lyle birdied No. 18 for a 66, the best of the day, a four-stroke win, and a 2-1 Scottish victory.

A footnote to this first round underlined how competition is increasing worldwide. Seventh-seeded Japan beat Italy as expected, but the score was 2-1. Thus for the first time in the Dunhill Cup's five years, there were no shutouts in the first round. And insignificant as it may seem, that one little victory was Italy's first in three visits to the tournament proper. It came from Alberto Binaghi, 25, a professional since 1987 and a rookie in the Dunhill Cup. He's known for both power and touch, with drives in the 290-yard range, and an average of 28.5 putts per round this season coming into the Dunhill Cup. Binaghi met Hajime Meshiai in the last game, and came back from an early deficit to win, 72-73, with a birdie on the final hole. Kouichi Suzuki led off with a 74-76 win over Massimo Mannelli, and Naomichi "Joe" Ozaki won the match with his 68-73 victory over Costantino Rocca.

Now the fun would begin. Five seeds came through the first round, and two of them had to escape via playoffs. Three ambitious underdogs had tasted victory, and suddenly, there was a new undercurrent in international golf.

On Friday, conditions were ideal for more of the same. The day blossomed into another autumn jewel. The weather would not be a factor in the second round, so all eyes were on the inexperienced French. Any unseeded team that could send Norman and the Aussies packing was bound to be the center of attention. They were playing the seventh-seeded Japanese, and doubtless the Japanese remembered Gery Watine's words from the day before. "Maybe the Australians thought we would be too easy," Watine had said. The Japanese were not about to make the same mistake.

Their strategy wasn't to counter strength with strength, but to get points as quickly as possible. So Ozaki, the Japanese captain, sent himself out first, against Dussart rather than Pendaries, the man who slew the Norman giant in the first round. The strategy paid off immediately. Ozaki won easily, 71-73. He could even afford the luxury of a triple bogey at No. 17—a seven that included an out-of-bounds drive, a nine iron off the road, and two putts from eight feet. "It could have changed at No. 17," Ozaki said. But Dussart couldn't cash in the opportunity. In fact, he picked up only one stroke because he stumbled there himself. After a risky wedge shot from the edge of the Road Bunker, he needed three putts to get down from 70 feet. That was for six.

In the second game, Suzuki opened with a bogey and still had a one-stroke lead. Pendaries put his wedge second shot into Swilcan Burn and took seven. And there weren't any eagles in his clubs this time. He made just two birdies, one at No. 2, the other at No. 18. Suzuki double-bogeyed No. 16 and bogeyed No. 17 and still won by two, 73-75. Japan was the winner, 2-0. In the last game, Meshiai came from under a two-stroke deficit at the turn and made it a 3-0 sweep with a 72-74 victory over Watine. But this Dunhill Cup already was something of a moral victory for the French. "We expected to be going home after the first day," Pendaries said, "so we have done a good job in getting this far."

Strange also decided to go for the quick points. Since Calcavecchia was still unsure of the Old Course, Strange decided to send out the seasoned Kite against Argentina's Vicente Fernandez. Strange's strategy also paid off immediately. Kite was out in a three-birdie 33, and Fernandez double-bogeyed the sixth after a bunkered drive and trailed by three at the turn. Kite's bogey at No. 17—three putts from 60 feet—left him with a 70-72 victory and the Americans with a 1-0 lead.

Calcavecchia wrapped up the American victory, beating Miguel Fernandez, 72-77. Calcavecchia had an especially tough time early on the inward half, making bogeys at Nos. 10, 11 and 13. But it was his swing, not the Old Course, that was troubling him. The turning point came at No. 13. "I hit what I thought was a pretty solid drive," said the big-hitter, "and it went straight into the wind. It didn't go 240 yards. I thought about what was causing it, and then it dawned on me—I was hanging back." That meant keeping his weight back on his right foot, instead of powering through the ball, he explained. He corrected the error on the spot, birdied the 14th and 16th, and walked off a relieved man.

Strange gave America a 3-0 sweep, but his 68-70 victory over Romero was a lot closer than it looked. Strange missed just one real birdie opportunity, a two-putt from seven feet at No. 17. Romero missed a bunch—from five feet at No. 3, from seven at No. 5, and from three at No. 18. Said Strange: "I was just trying to get through and survive to the next day. I'm just happy not to make more mistakes than the other guy."

Ireland also advanced without incident. It was a gift as much as anything. The Swedes were having their problems. Not one of them got near par, and they averaged a whopping 76 for the day. Lanner, in the first game, was typical. He bogeyed the second, third, and fourth holes, and was quickly on his way to a 72-74 loss to Walton. Sellberg broke down on the back nine for a 42 and Rafferty won in a walk, 68-78. And O'Connor bogeyed five of seven holes on the inward nine for a 39, and still beat Persson easily, 73-76.

The day had gone too smoothly. Leave it to the Scots and English.

They had met twice before in the Dunhill Cup, and England took both—2-1 for the championship in 1987, 2-1 in the second round in 1988. It was 2-1 again this time, to the surprise of the victorious English. "We're overjoyed that we've come through today, especially after seeing the scoreboard, seeing one in front and the other two well behind . . . ," said leadoff man Clark, who had about written his side off. "I was walking up the 18th just to say to Sam, 'Good luck tomorrow,' and Sam said, 'Look at the scoreboard.'"

Before that, it looked grim for the English. Clark was in control all the way against Torrance for a 67-69 victory set up by a burst of four consecutive birdies from No. 9. But Durnian crashed to a 41 coming in, and Scotland's Brand squared the match, 71-78. It looked like a lock for Scotland now, with the revived Lyle rolling beautifully against a flu-stricken James, who was dosing himself with "antibiotics, nose sprays, pain-killers, whatever."

With superb iron play and deadly putting, Lyle had posted five birdies and was leading James by four strokes with four holes to play. James, hardly a stranger to pressure, stood his ground. Back at the 342-yard 10th, for example, he refused to shake when the powerful Lyle drove the green. He calmly pitched on and holed his seven-footer, matching Lyle's two-putt birdie from 60 feet. "But standing on No. 15 tee," said James, "I would have wanted at least 25-to-1 if I were betting on me." Actually, 250-to-1 might be more realistic. But now something broke down for Lyle. At No. 15, he left an eight iron 70 feet from the flag, and three-putted. First bogey. At No. 16, his seven-iron approach finished 48 feet away, and he three-putted again. Second bogey. And at No. 17, he was short of the green with a six iron, pitched to 12 feet, and two-putted. Third bogey. There went three strokes of his lead. James made up the rest of it with a birdie-bogey-birdie finish—the last a clutch eight-footer at No. 18—to tie the game at 70 and force a playoff, England's second of the tournament. It was brief. At No. 1, Lyle missed his birdie and James dropped a 15-footer for his. It was England, 2-1.

And it was Clark's insight that did it. He had detected a new flaw in Lyle's game. "Last year and the year before and every year before, if you thought of someone to hang on under pressure, it was Sandy," Clark said. "But now we felt he was not so well equipped as he has been in the past.

That's the reason Mark played last. We felt Sandy might crack if Mark could get him under pressure."

"It was just like my match against Nick Faldo last year," Lyle said. "I made the mistakes. That's it."

So the lineup was set for the semifinals on Saturday. England would meet Japan for the first time ever in the Dunhill Cup. But for the United States and Ireland, it would be a rematch. In their only previous meeting, in 1988, the Irish breezed, 2-1/2—1/2, on their way to the title. The top-seeded Americans had been knocked out again. And here they were, top-seeded again.

"It will be lovely to take on the Americans tomorrow," O'Connor said. "We have a lot of confidence. They'll be optimistic, but it won't be a walkover for anybody."

If he thought the Americans were overconfident, he was misreading them. "You don't take anyone lightly," Strange said again, and that was evident in the study he was giving his lineup for the next day. He simply wasn't sending his men out and saying, "Play." "I'll have to talk with Tom and Mark before deciding the lineup," Strange said. "But I guarantee you I will go last. If it comes down to two or three holes, I'd as soon be out there as anyone."

The next day, it wasn't Strange and it didn't come down to the last few holes. It came down to a playoff, the fourth of the tournament, and the second for Ireland and for O'Connor, who also came through in the clutch at the Ryder Cup a week earlier. Maybe this was one time too many in the pressure cooker.

"As much as you want to win, and anyway you can get it," Kite was saying, "you hate to see the match end on that type of catastrophe." The catastrophe was a simple approach shot that went fatally bad in a playoff. It made the United States the winner, and Ireland the loser. But to set the stage . . .

Calcavecchia went out first, against Walton, and after an early exchange of birdies, jumped in front to stay at the 564-yard fifth. A driver and a three wood got him home, and two putts from 30 feet got him a birdie four. Walton bunkered his approach and settled for a par. He would get no closer than one stroke. But a big chance got away. "At No. 13, Mark had no shot," Walton said. "He was standing with his feet on the edge of a bunker to play his second, and topped it 20 yards. I hit a seven iron and got a desperate kick off a mound and was left with a putt of 62 yards." So a golden opportunity had turned into a three-putt bogey. Calcavecchia also bogeyed, and they matched bogeys again at No. 17. Calcavecchia's 25-foot birdie at No. 18 gave him the final margin, 69-71.

In the second game, Kite and O'Connor battled to a draw that didn't come to full drama until they had to go back out in the playoff. But it looked like anything but a draw for a while. O'Connor went two up with an outward no-bogey 33. The jewel of his three birdies was a nine iron to two feet at No. 7. Kite matched two of his birdies, but then gave him another stroke with a bogey at No. 9, after a bunkered tee shot. The pivotal exchange took place early coming in. Kite birdied No. 10 from 15 feet, and O'Connor bogeyed No. 11 with three putts from 60, and they were all square. The gods twitted both of them at the Road Hole. Kite drove into the rough, missed the green with his second, and his pitch still left him 20 feet from the flag. O'Connor's second finished just left of the green, only 30 yards from the cup, but with the Road Bunker lurking just to the right. To get anywhere near the flag, he would have to putt up over the big shoulder of the bunker. His intended line was just a hair to the left, so that the ball could fall off onto the green when it lost speed. But he missed that line by a fraction. His putt was just a hair to the right. The ball climbed the shoulder, teased him for a moment, then peeled off to the right and plunged into the bunker. Kite's hopes brightened. But then O'Connor made a great bunker shot to four feet. Kite two-putted and bogeyed, and O'Connor holed his four-footer to match him. They parred No. 18, tied at 71-71, and stepped aside and waited. They didn't wait long.

Strange and Rafferty, in the final game, had an odd finish. Rafferty caught Strange at No. 12, a six-foot birdie putt leaving them tied at three under par. Then Strange missed a four-foot par putt at No. 13 while Rafferty was three-putting from 20 feet. It was Rafferty's turn at the 16th. Against Strange's three-putt bogey, all he needed was two putts from 30 feet for a par. But he missed. It was worse at No. 17. Strange three-putted from 20 feet, and Rafferty now needed just a three-footer for a par to go one ahead. He missed again. And so at the last hole, what he couldn't do at short range he now did from long range. He dropped a 25-foot birdie putt for a 71-72 decision, handing Strange only his second loss after seven Dunhill Cup victories. Now the match was all square, Kite and O'Connor had to go back out.

At No. 1, the first playoff hole, O'Connor had 91 yards left to the green. But his sand wedge second traveled only about 81 yards. The ball fell short, bounced, and plunged into meandering Swilcan burn, that menacing little stream, the only water hazard on the Old Course. O'Connor slumped. He knew about great shots. He made one just a week ago, a 229-yard two iron on the last hole of the Ryder Cup. But that was then. This was now. Kite was on in two, about 15 feet from the flag. O'Connor decided that he couldn't afford a penalty drop. His ball was in the middle of the burn, in very shallow water, and he elected to hit it out. Nervously, he took practice swing after swing. Then he finally hit. And the ball hit the wall and bounced back in. He splashed it out this time, some 25 feet beyond the flag. Kite two-putted for his par, and it was over, a 2-1 victory that put the United States into the final for the second time in five Dunhill Cups.

O'Connor was distressed. "I had the same yardage as this morning, 91 yards, downwind, and hit it 26 feet past the flag," O'Connor said. "I hit a sand wedge again. I couldn't believe it went into the burn. And someone said why didn't I go for the safe shot to the back of the green. But I haven't done that all week. It's not my style. Besides, I was trying to make three, because I know how deadly Tom can be."

"What was that you did with the ball at the end?," someone asked. "I threw it back in," O'Connor said. "I said, 'Here, you can have it now. It's over.'"

His teammates had no regrets. "Without Christy," Rafferty said, "we would have been watching it on TV today."

Kite offered his sympathies, and added, "I'll take a win any way I can, but I'll tell you this: Winning ugly beats the heck out of losing pretty."

Even as Kite was speaking, the question of an opponent for the title had been settled—abruptly. It would be Japan, 2-1 winner over England in the other semifinal. Japan locked up the berth in the shortest possible time, taking the first two games for a 2-1 victory. Japan also was in the final for the second time in the five Dunhill Cups.

Ozaki, facing Durnian in the first game, rode a hot putter for a 32 and a four-stroke lead at the turn, the birdies coming from 10, 20, 12, and four feet. Durnian was out in 36, after two three-putt bogeys canceled out his two birdies. Ozaki had some trouble coming home, taking two bogeys and getting no birdies. But Durnian gained no ground. His long putter failed him. He missed two five-foot birdie putts. Ozaki's 70-72 win gave Japan a 1-0 lead.

Suzuki wrapped it up with a 66-70 romp over Clark, and figured a little gamesmanship did the trick. "I watched Clark playing on television and saw that he is a very deliberate player," Suzuki said. "I am a quick player, and I realized that if I played my natural game, I might have an unsettling effect on him." Clark wouldn't know about this until much later, but perhaps that's what undid him. Not that he played badly—he made only one bogey—but maybe his game lacked a crisp edge. "I really did not float today," he said. Suzuki left out one point: He played superb golf. Not a bogey, and seven one-putt greens, six of them for birdies.

In the final game, James saved England from a sweep, beating Meshiai, 71-73. All that was left was the postmortem. "We knew we had to play well, because they're good," Clark said. "We were just scraping matches anyway, not firing on all cylinders. We probably made the wrong decisions, or played the wrong players, I don't know. I played the best I could, and that was about it."

So it was on to the final, and if anybody had conceded the championship to the powerful American team, it certainly wasn't the Americans. "We're going to have to play really well against them," Kite said. "They've played better than anyone in the tournament. They've shot lower scores." (This was a slight overstatement. The Japanese were an aggregate eight under par to this point. The Americans were 16 under.) "They have a never-say-die attitude," Calcavecchia said. "They know how to play." He would be the first to find out.

"They are tough, don't let anybody kid you," Strange said. "Tom and I have played against all three, and Mark has played against Meshiai. Anyway, Mark is going off first tomorrow. He wants it that way. He likes to play first and that's OK with me."

Once Calcavecchia got his swing straightened out, it didn't take him long to develop a fondness for the Old Course. The more he played it, the better he liked it. Come Sunday and the Dunhill Cup's first-ever 36-hole finale, the Old Course had him wrapped around its little finger—and vice versa. "I'm getting to like it, I really am," Calcavecchia was saying Sunday afternoon, just after he had demolished Japan's Meshiai for the second time that day and locked up America's first Dunhill Cup. Strange had decided Calcavecchia would go out first in both rounds that day because he was the least experienced at the Old Course. Thus, if he were to fall victim to the ancient dangers, then his seasoned teammates could steer the ship home. Strange wasn't alone in his thinking. "Mark wants to go first, too," Strange had said.

Calcavecchia seemed quite at home Sunday morning. Leading off, he got the Americans their first point with a 67-68 victory over Meshiai. It wasn't easy. Meshiai took the lead with three consecutive birdies from the start, on putts of one, one, and 10 feet. Calcavecchia offset only one of them, at No. 1, from 10 feet, and he trailed by two strokes until the seventh, where Meshiai needed two pitches to get on and two putts to get down from six feet. Calcavecchia then caught him with a birdie at No. 9 and didn't waste the reprieve. He took the lead for good with a birdie at No. 10, matched Meshiai's at No. 12, then delivered an awesome knockout punch—an eagle-three at the 567-yard 14th. Kite had said that Calcavecchia was the only one of them who could stay with the long-hitting Japanese, but even knowing that, it's doubtful Meshiai was ready for this. Calcavecchia hit a drive of over 280 yards, and even though he still had about 280 to go, he found his position too tempting. "I took the driver out again," he said, "and I smoked it." He had reached the old brute with two mighty thunderclaps. He was 25 feet from the cup. The stunned Meshiai needed two putts from 40 feet for his par. Calcavecchia ran in his eagle and walked off with a three-stroke lead. The three-putt bogey at No. 15 didn't shake him, nor did Meshiai's impressive birdie at No. 17, a six-iron to five feet. It was Meshiai's first birdie there, and the 1989 Dunhill Cup's third and final birdie in 102 cracks. The Americans led, 1-0.

"I don't think the Old Course is too hard to understand in weather like this," Calcavecchia said, after a morning round in benign conditions. "The course is based on wind, and now, without wind, it isn't too hard to figure out." Would he find weather like this in the 1990 British Open? "I sure hope so," Calcavecchia said, grinning. Of course, he knows better.

It was No. 18 that made the difference in the second match. Kite ended a desperate rally with a birdie there to catch Ozaki for a 68-68 tie, winning the half point that was to make his life so much easier in the afternoon. Ozaki had got on a roll for an outward 32 that threatened to crush Kite by the turn. As golfers like to say, he was making everything he looked at. He led by three through the turn, and still by three at No. 10, where both birdied. It was in the middle of the inward half that Kite finally began to pick up some ground. At No. 13, an eight iron put him 33 feet from the cup, and at No. 16, a wedge settled him just four feet away. He birdied both and was within a stroke. They halved the 17th—in bogeys, of course, both two-putting from long range. So Kite came to No. 18 trailing by a stroke. He badly needed some dash. He got it with his approach shot, a pitch to within four feet of the hole. Ozaki lobbed his pitch to six feet. But where he two-putted for the par, Kite took cool aim, stroked, and willed the ball in—a birdie. They tied at 68, leaving the morning decision to Strange and Suzuki.

That one would end on a curious note. Suzuki parred No. 18 on a driver, eight iron, and two putts from 30 feet. But he signed for a five and a five it stayed. Not that it made any difference. It gave him a 75 instead of a 74 against Strange's 72. Both men were rocky coming home in the face of rising breezes. They had tied at one-under-par 35 through the turn, then—with treacherous going up ahead—Strange got his winning margin early. A six-foot putt gave him a birdie and a one-putt edge at No. 10. Then Suzuki contributed a stroke to Strange's lead when he ran afoul of the nasty par-three 11th. His five-iron tee shot left him 45 feet from the hole, and he three-putted. Strange led by two.

They both literally staggered home, but Strange staggered less. Starting at No. 14, he went bogey-birdie-bogey-bogey (6-3-5-5). A three-hole crash did Suzuki in. From No. 16, he went bogey-double bogey-bogey (5-6-5). The double bogey at No. 17 was especially galling. Suzuki's four-iron approach ended up in the Road Bunker. He got the ball out on the first try, but was 28 feet from home. And he three-putted. He was two behind with No. 18 to play. Strange was not about to let him off the hook. The Americans took a 2-1/2—1/2 lead into the afternoon finale. Now—just one more win in the afternoon. That's all they needed.

And that's what they got from their rookie. In fact, Calcavecchia was awesome. He was against Meshiai again, and the poor guy never had a chance. Meshiai was three strokes down almost before he got started. Calcavecchia birdied No. 1 from nine feet, and Meshiai double-bogeyed No. 2 after hitting into the bushes. The thing was, Meshiai didn't play badly at all. He shook off that double bogey and played the next seven holes in three under par for an outward 35 that included a 28-foot birdie at No. 4 and a 34-footer at No. 8. But Calcavecchia was simply too much. He walked off with a seven-stroke win, 66-73, and America had its first Dunhill Cup victory.

"I'm a great putter," Calcavecchia said, "and sometimes I'm an incredible putter." Discounting the three-putt bogey from 60 feet at No. 4 and the two-putter from 16 at No. 12, this was one of those times. He dropped the six outward birdies from nine, three, 39 (two putts), six, 10, and 12 feet. He cooled off a little coming in, and though he was in no danger from the laboring Meshiai, he didn't let up. He finished in style, a birdie at No. 15 from 18 feet, and at No. 18, another from 18 before a roaring crowd in the stands.

Calcavecchia's victory had a backlash effect on Kite and Strange, still out on the course. It was as though someone had opened a valve and let the pressure blow off. Both lost their meaningless matches, Kite to Suzuki, 71-74, and Strange to Ozaki, 69-71. The final score: U.S. 3-1/2, Japan 2-1/2.

Calcavecchia, on the failed American hopes in the Ryder Cup, took some consolation with this victory. "I came here with the thought of winning, and not settling for anything less," he said. And he could almost have predicted his performance. "It seems every time, after a big disappointment, losing a tournament, I've come back and won," he said.

Calcavecchia's scores had dropped steadily: 71-72-69-67-66, a total of 15 under par. Through all five rounds, he made nothing worse than a single bogey, and only 12 of those. He was phenomenal in the two-round finale— 12 birdies, one eagle, three bogeys, a total of 11 under par. His favorite hole was No. 1. He brutalized it all week—four birdies and a par. Six holes refused to yield to him. No birdies at Nos. 2, 4, 7, 11, 13, and, of course, 17. But he played No. 17 better than anyone who went the distance—four pars and one bogey.

So this was Calcavecchia in October, 1989, a good 10 months before his date with history: "I'm really getting excited about the Open next year," he said. "I know I've played the course in perfect conditions for six days. And I know if it gets windy and rainy, it will be a completely different course. But I'm from Florida, and we play in wind and rain, and I have confidence I can play this course. Anyway, I'm getting really excited about the Open and about coming back here next year."

9. The World Match Play Championship

Somehow the World Match Play Championship, now sponsored by Suntory, always has something up its sleeve. Not a year has gone past since it began at the Wentworth Club near London in 1964 has there failed to be some epic match, drama, collapse or recovery, and this year was no exception, the best in many respects being left until last.

It was won by Nick Faldo, who thereby completed what must go down as his greatest year. In April he had followed Sandy Lyle as the winner of the Masters and now in October he followed him again with his first victory in the World Match Play. Nor were these the only occasions on which Faldo had followed Lyle's footsteps. He also succeeded him as the Dunhill Masters champion.

This was Faldo's fifth victory of the year, the Volvo PGA Championship and the French Open titles being the others. Just as Lyle had been the outstanding British golfer of 1988, so Faldo stood supreme in 1989.

It took 24 years before the first British golfer, Ian Woosnam in 1987, won the World Match Play, and now in quick succession he has been followed by Lyle and Faldo, a Welshman, a Scotsman and an Englishman in turn, fending off the challenge of many of the best golfers in the world. Gone are the days when the overseas players used to take this title almost as if by right, indeed it now being 10 years since an American, Bill Rogers, made off with the trophy.

What made Faldo's victory so special, however, was that no one has ever played the sort of golf he played, either in the final, when he beat Woosnam on the last green, or throughout the championship. Scores in match play golf must be approximate, because not every putt is holed, some being given that might not have been holed after the opponent has conceded. Even so, Faldo's rough 38 under par for his 105 holes—better than a birdie every three holes—eclipsed Woosnam's 32 under for 141 holes in 1987. In three games Faldo was 12 under par, 13 under and 13 under again thanks in total to five eagles, 31 birdies and only three bogeys. In the final he had eagles at all four of the par fives and that had never been done either.

Yet only once in those three games did Faldo have everything his own way, when he beat Severiano Ballesteros by 6 and 5 in the semi-finals. In the quarter-finals he was 3-down with 11 to play against David Frost of South Africa, before winning at the second extra hole, and in the final against Woosnam he was 3-down with only seven to play.

An accusing finger can almost invariably be pointed at anyone who loses after being 3-up and seven to play. Not Woosnam. Already 3-up, he played those last seven holes in one under par and still lost. What he had to take was some golf by Faldo that came almost from another world. Those same seven holes Faldo completed in seven under par, two eagles, three birdies and two pars. He was home in 30 and no one had ever done that before over the Burma Road.

The only time Faldo led was when he won, and when he did win it was with an eagle-three at the last hole, a putt of 20 feet or so finding its mark after Woosnam had already been given his birdie-four. There just cannot be better finishes than that, and the leap of delight Faldo made as his ball disappeared from sight to a mighty roar from the crowd almost exceeded the jump he had made when he won the Masters, then holing a birdie putt at Augusta's 11th, the second extra hole, in a playoff against Scott Hoch.

If this took the breath away, so again it was also squeezed from the lungs when immediately afterwards on being presented with the trophy, Faldo announced, in a voice filled with emotion, that he was going to donate the whole of his £100,000—the first six-figure check ever to have been on offer in Europe—to sick children.

"It is just something I want to do," Faldo said later. In a quiet way he had been involved with them for some time and appreciated not only how they suffered but also how their parents suffered. As a parent himself, he knew what it must be like and he had made up his mind the night before when he discussed the matter with his wife, Gill. No matter that Faldo's earnings for the year were close on £500,000. By donating a fifth of it to those in need, he won himself a legion of admirers, made front-page headlines, and was the subject within the next 24 hours of countless features. He was revealed to be a man who cared.

Even as he came to those last nine holes at Wentworth, Faldo still believed he could win, even though Woosnam was both playing and putting well. "Ian really had the grips on me," said Faldo later. "But all the time I kept sticking in and I tried an old trick of thinking only of the flags and aiming at them all the time. Everything else was blotted out.

"It's been a long wait. I have been here 10 times, but this has a place all its own. It's match play and it has a fantastic tradition. It's been won by all the greatest players and joining them means everything. Cups, trophies, championships, they are what matter."

Such was the high quality of the final that it must be discussed first. Apart from one brief spell of rain on Thursday morning, this record-breaking summer of little rain held its course, and most of the early indications were that Woosnam would repeat his triumph of two years earlier. He drew first blood with a birdie-two at the second, holing from 14 feet and though a bunkered drive at the next swiftly allowed Faldo to catch him again, Woosnam went 2-up by taking the fifth and seventh, both in birdies.

A four iron to five feet did the trick for Woosnam at the short fifth hole, after Faldo had missed from not much further away, and on the two-tiered seventh green Woosnam holed from 12 feet. He was out in 32 to Faldo's 34 and pressed home his advantage with an eagle-three at the 12th, holing from 40 feet as Faldo, who had hit an unplayable shot off the tee, was heading for a five anyway.

All was going according to plan so far as Woosnam was concerned, and it came very much as a surprise when he lost three holes in a row to go back to all-square. At the 15th it was of his own doing. This is a much better hole as a par-four than it used to be as a par-five, and though playing very short this year, there was still trouble to be found. Faldo, in fact, cut his drive and had to bend his second shot sharply left to right, which he managed successfully to do.

Woosnam, on the other hand, had gone left, and though it seemed he could get a swing at the ball right-handed, he chose to give it a full belt left-handed, and succeeded only in knocking his ball into an adjacent bush, at which point he conceded. It was just the break Faldo needed. At the 16th he got inside Woosnam with a sand-wedge second shot and safely sank the putt for a birdie-three. Then at the 17th he cracked a magnificent one-iron second to 25 feet and holed that for an eagle-three. The match was alive again.

Woosnam played the 18th better, two wood shots lacing their way to the green for a birdie-four that Faldo could not match. Faldo partially blocked himself out close to the trees on the right from the tee, overdid a heavily cut second shot, and was scrambling around even to make five. Even so, Faldo shot 67 and, at 1-down, was very much back in the hunt.

For six holes in the afternoon, the situation did not dramatically change. Woosnam, though again driving into the fairway bunker at the third, still got his four with the aid of a longish putt and that put him 2-up again. Faldo came back with an eagle-three at the fourth, a four-iron second shot and 30-foot putt doing the trick, as Woosnam missed from a little closer. And so the exchange went on.

Woosnam won back the short fifth with a two, after both had peppered the flagstick with their tee shots, only to lose the next hole. Close to the trees on the right with his drive, Woosnam could not attack the flag with his second shot. With Faldo likely to get a birdie, the little Welshman charged his first putt and then missed the one back. Woosnam put the lapse behind him, and at the seventh he hit both the better drive and approach shot, his seven iron coming to rest some 12 feet from the flag, and his putter did the rest.

Two down once again, Faldo must have lost a good deal of heart on the next two holes. He had had a good chance of getting back to only 1-down, and instead faced the last nine holes 3-down. At the eighth, he played much the superior second shot, a seven iron to six feet, but failed to take advantage of it, missing the putt. Then at the ninth, Faldo erred with his second shot. Nine times out of 10, Faldo would have got up and down for his four, but this time he chipped too strongly and his ball skidding forward off a bare patch on the green.

Faldo hung back before walking to the 10th tee, trying the putt again and recomposing himself. It could have been 4-down on the 10th, because Woosnam was putting for a birdie-two while Faldo was having to putt from off the green to save his par. However, the 10th hole was halved and so was the 11th. Time, it seemed, was running out. At the 12th, with both almost equidistant from the flag, Faldo sank the marginally longer putt, from nearly 40 feet, for his eagle-three, and a hope was there to be clutched.

As at the sixth hole, Woosnam lost the 13th by three-putting, but again the pressure was on him because Faldo was very close in two after a nine-iron second. He was credited with a birdie he did have to make. He also had the better of the 14th without making it count, but saved himself the 15th, where his approach putt, swinging right to left downhill, ran dangerously far past the hole. He was still 1-down, with three holes to play.

Faldo drew level at the 16th, hitting a perfectly judged sand wedge from the fairway beyond the flag and drawing it back to three feet for his birdie. Here then was the perfect climax. They were all square after 34 holes and two par-fives to play.

The drive at the 17th, swinging right to left against the slope of the fairway, favored Woosnam's natural draw and he hit much the longer drive, though dangerously close to the bushes flanking the fairway. Faldo, further back, needed a one iron against his opponent's three iron and it tumbled down the big slope to the right of the green, leaving him a difficult pitch if he was to get his birdie.

Faldo's shot was made even more difficult because Woosnam hit a glorious three iron which, to a growing roar from the crowd massed around the green, ran 12 feet beyond the flag for a certain birdie and a possible eagle. Faldo's thoughts were that he had to get his pitch close enough to make Woosnam at least putt first, to keep the pressure on. He judged it well, got his ball to six feet and, after Woosnam had missed for his eagle, holed out for the half.

Here was a crucial moment. At the 18th, Faldo's more natural fade of the ball left him with the shorter second shot, admittedly made more difficult, when Woosnam rifled a three wood to the edge of the green pin high. All week Faldo's one iron had stood him in good stead and it was for this club that he reached, so much depending on it.

Just as Faldo's five iron to Muirfield's 18th green in 1987 had won the British Open for him, and a three iron to Augusta's 11th had won the 1989 Masters, now Faldo found another perfect stroke as his ball covered the flag all the way and finished some 20 feet beyond the flag. Woosnam, from twice that distance, was just short for his eagle; and so here was Faldo with his one chance. He read the putt perfectly and the title was his. It was the only time in 36 holes that he had led and he had completed those last 18 holes in an approximate 64.

Four days earlier there had been speculation that this could be the most open World Match Play in years. Faldo's form had lost some of its early-season gloss, Woosnam's was patchy, Severiano Ballesteros was claiming never to having felt so tired in his life, and Sandy Lyle, the defending champion, was still in the midst of a slump.

Such a scenario indicated that this was a fine opportunity for the un-seeded, all of whom had to play an extra round before joining the big guns. The general feeling was that Ronan Rafferty, the leader at the time of the European Tour's Order of Merit; Jose-Maria Olazabal, who had taken five and a half points out of six in the Ryder Cup; Chip Beck, the star of the American side; and David Frost, of South Africa, were the greatest threats. So it was proven, as each won their preliminary games.

The unusual aspect of this championship was that seven of the 12 players were receiving their first invitations to the World Match Play. Olazabal had played once before, in 1986, but Rafferty, Beck and Frost were all newcomers, as too were Mike Reid and Scott Hoch, both of the United States, Aki Ohmachi from Japan, and Ian Baker-Finch of Australia. Each were on preliminary-round duty and there was a good deal of interest in all of them.

Hoch was familiar to the British only via their television screens, since he was the man Faldo beat in the playoff for the Masters, the putt he had missed at the second extra hole being probably the shortest on which a major championship had hung, even shorter than the one Doug Sanders let slip away for the 1970 British Open. Reid was also remembered for the "wrong" reasons in that he had thrown away a three-stroke lead with three holes to play in the 1989 PGA Championship at Kemper Lakes, being beaten by Payne Stewart.

Baker-Finch was the best-known of the overseas players. He had spent a number of seasons in Europe and in 1984 had led the field going into the final round of the British Open at St. Andrews. His one victory was in the Scandinavian Enterprises Open in 1986, but he had been much more successful in his home country, and when he took the plunge in America, he was quickly rewarded when he won the 1989 Colonial at Fort Worth.

Ohmachi was the unknown quantity, but he too had earned his American tour card in 1986 and held it for two years with three top-10 finishes in 1987. When he returned to Japan in 1989 he immediately won the Mizuno Open. As it happened, Ohmachi's appearance in the World Match Play was very brief. He was knocked out by Chip Beck by the almost indecently wide margin of 8 and 6, Beck confirming the high regard in which he was held after his performance in the Ryder Cup.

So wide a margin was not at once apparent. Ohmachi had led twice in the morning, after the fourth and 13th holes, even though Beck had gone out in 32. It was over the last five holes that the American began to impose himself, drawing level at the 14th, where his opponent took three putts, and taking the lead at the next where the Japanese went out of bounds. This set the pattern. Beck was 2-up at lunch with a birdie at the 18th and in the afternoon he drew further and further away as Ohmachi could do no right. "He can play much better than that," said Beck afterwards as he looked eagerly forward to meeting Ballesteros.

There was no doubt as to the match of this first day and that was the one in which Rafferty defeated Reid by 3 and 2. It was sparkling stuff with hardly an eyebrow between them as they swapped birdies and eagles in profusion, Rafferty being 12 under par for the 34 holes and Reid nine under. The American was justified if he felt unfortunate. Against anyone else, he would have won. But this is match play.

Both were out in 33 in the morning, Rafferty winning three of the first four holes and Reid getting them all back in quick succession from the sixth. A par at the 10th from off the green was sufficient to restore the Irishman's lead, he went 2-up again at the 13th with a birdie but then lost both the 14th and 16th. However, Rafferty still led at lunch, getting down in two for his birdie at the 18th.

Briefly the lead changed hands early in the afternoon, Reid drawing level at the second, where Rafferty was bunkered, and then taking the third with another par. An important blow was the eagle putt Rafferty holed on the fourth green to restore his lead, both being home with four-iron second shots and the Irishman sinking substantially the longer putt.

The balance began to shift around the turn as Rafferty made birdies at the eighth and ninth. He was out in 32, 2-up again and in control. Reid won back the 10th with a birdie, chipping into the hole, but lost the next to a three and Rafferty remained rock solid over the remaining holes, closing his man out with a fine birdie-three at the 15th where he holed from 25 feet. It was a telling moment, for the chances had been that it was the American who would make the birdie since he had hit a six-iron second to three feet. So shaken was he by Rafferty's "bolt from the blue" that he then missed for the half.

Well though he had played, Rafferty tended to dismiss it. He was full of praise for Reid who, he felt, had not hit a loose shot all day. Nor was the American, not the longest of hitters, under any disadvantage on fairways still bearing the scars of the long hot summer. His low-ball flight gave him a lot of run on the ball and there was not the disparity of clubbing for the second shots there otherwise might have been.

Olazabal, who beat Hoch by 4 and 2, did so despite a raging headache and what he suspected was a fever. No doubt it was because of this that he played rather poorly in the morning, no better than 72 but still 2-up, which hardly reflected well on the golf of the American. Hoch was struggling from first to last and at no stage did he lead.

Hoch did not give up either. Though 2-down after six holes, he made the most of errors by Olazabal at the seventh and ninth to turn all square. Then, after the Spaniard had taken the 10th with a two, Hoch got his first birdie at the 11th to square again. The 12th and 13th were also exchanged and it was not until the 17th and 18th that a firm pattern began to emerge.

Three putts by the American started his ultimate slide, and he compounded it by bunkering his second to the 18th. Within four holes in the afternoon, Olazabal was 4-up and coasting. Unexpectedly, however, it all changed as Hoch, with two birdies and a par, took the next three holes to stand only 1-down again. Briefly it was a match once more.

It might indeed have been a different story had Olazabal not sunk a putt of 35 feet for a birdie at the eighth, for Hoch was already very close in two for an almost guaranteed three as well. The Spaniard made good his escape when the ninth was handed to him on a plate. Both were out in 34, which was much better, and Olazabal at last found a higher gear as he completed the remaining seven holes in three under par, his two at the 14th and three at the 16th being something to which Hoch had no answer.

Frost's defeat of Baker-Finch by 4 and 3 was predictable right away for he took three of the first four holes and only once was he subsequently as little as only 1-up. The tall Australian was not at his best, perhaps the more nervous of the two. Frost was round in 71 in the morning and still 3-up and he must have been caught by surprise by Baker-Finch's revival in the afternoon as the Australian went to the turn in 31. Yet it only gained him one hole, the fourth, fifth, sixth and ninth all being halved in birdies. The only hole Baker-Finch won back was the third, with a par.

The match was not without minor incident, though it could have had some bearing on the result. At the 13th Frost, after missing for his birdie, quickly tapped the ball into the hole. In fact the putt had not been given and Baker-Finch was not sure of the ruling. All he could have asked was for the ball to be replaced and putted again. Nevertheless it may have had some effect on Baker-Finch, for he had putted two feet beyond the hole and then missed the one back to go 2-down again. What is more, he took three putts at the 14th as well and his time was soon up.

So the quarter-final line-up was very much as expected with Rafferty now facing Lyle, the defending champion; Olazabal playing Woosnam, the champion of 1987; Beck meeting Ballesteros, who was going for a record-equalling fifth title; and Frost opposing Faldo, who obviously had ambitions of repeating Lyle's feat of winning the Masters and the World Match Play in the same year. There was a wide suspicion that the four seeds would not have things all their own way and, with the exception of Ballesteros, they did not. The Spaniard swamped Beck by 9 and 8, which made a mockery of his claim a couple of days earlier that he had never felt so tired in his life.

Nevertheless, only Lyle was beaten as he went down by one hole to Rafferty. Faldo came back after being 3-down with 11 to play against Frost before winning in extra holes, and Woosnam from 1-down at lunch to defeat Olazabal.

Even though Rafferty was then the leader of the European Tour, a title he was to clinch a week or two later, and Lyle was still wracked by poor form, it was the Northern Irishman's performance that took most attention, particularly since it was not until the 32nd hole of the day that he got in front.

The early indications were that the "old Lyle" was back. He was out in 32, round in 66 and 2-up at lunch, as he had been after the first four holes when he had two birdies. Rafferty won back the eighth with a birdie and the 13th with another, after Lyle had scrambled a four with a single putt after driving into the trees. The Irishman was four under par at that point, but he had to concede the 16th following an errant drive, and lost the 17th, where Lyle revealed his enormous strength, reaching the green with no more than a three wood from the tee and then a four iron to the green.

Rafferty's response was to take the 18th, where he was home in two with a four wood whereas Lyle was short, but within four holes in the afternoon the defending champion had apparently taken charge. A four at the third was sufficient to restore his two-hole lead and Rafferty was twice in ditches at the long fourth, at which point he conceded. He won back the seventh with a birdie-three and then chipped in for a two at the 10th to get back to 1-down.

At once Lyle showed his fallibility, pitching very weakly into a bunker at the 11th. Rafferty sensed his chance and, with a two at the 14th, he led for the first time. Two holes later he was 2-up as Lyle made a mess of his drive. Although the champion retrieved the 17th and was home in two at the last, Rafferty got down in two from off the green to preserve his one-hole lead and secure his victory.

Faldo had a terrific tussle with Frost in a match between two pupils of David Leadbetter. Not only was he 3-down with 11 to play, but it was not until the 17th hole in the afternoon that he led. The South African had birdies at both the first and second holes in the morning. It was not until the ninth that Faldo won a hole with a birdie-three, though he soon drew level, his opponent being bunkered by the green at the 11th and losing it to a four.

The next four holes were halved, but Frost's birdie at the 16th restored his lead and he was round in 66 to remain 1-up at the break. Though the match was quickly level again in the afternoon, Faldo drawing level with a two at the second, Frost suddenly won three holes out of the next four, first with an eagle at the fourth and then with birdies at the sixth and seventh.

At the eighth Faldo was given a glimmer of daylight, profiting as the South African took three putts. Still 2-up at the turn, Frost was caught within the next two holes as Faldo went 2, 3 with putts of 30 and 15 feet.

The deadlock remained until the 17th, where Faldo was home in two to lead for the first time. With victory there for the taking, Faldo was timid with his approach putt at the 18th, mis-read his next and was into extra holes.

Faldo had gone round in 66 to Frost's 67 and though he had in the end wasted a golden opportunity, he got away with it. At the second in the playoff, Faldo played an almost identical tee shot to the one he had hit earlier, though this time even closer to the hole, and the putt was a formality.

Woosnam was given a hard time by Olazabal, even though he had made the better start, winning two of the first three holes and then exchanging the next two. Out in 32, Woosnam had his lead cut to one at the 10th, where he missed the green from the tee, and when some rather miserable rain set in down the closing stretch, he got in trouble off the tee at the 15th, and also lost the 18th where he was bunkered beside the green.

Woosnam was unhappy with his putting and he forfeited his lunch for a long session on the practice green. He admitted to letting too many thoughts enter his head. It was Olazabal who began to miss the putts in the afternoon, particularly on the first two greens, and by the fourth Woosnam was level, home there with a drive and five iron.

At once the tide began to turn Woosnam's way. Birdies at the sixth and ninth put him out in 33 and he was 2-up. Then he followed with a two at the 10th, hitting a six iron very close. It began a very impressive spell. He was four under par for the next eight holes, losing only one of them, the 15th, where Olazabal had one of three birdies over the same stretch. Woosnam was seven under par for his 17 holes in the afternoon and there was no Spanish answer to that.

Ballesteros's annihilation, if not his defeat, of Beck was totally unpredictable. He was simply at his very best while the bemused American, who could hardly hit a shot all day, reflected colorfully that he had been "tested in the crucible of humiliation." The Spaniard had holed some good putts in the morning, when he was round in 66. Four birdies in five holes, beginning at the fourth, put him in control. Out in 32 and 4-up, he had increased it to five by the 16th and then won the first three holes in the afternoon to stand 8-up.

By the seventh it was 10-up and the record books began to come out for the record margin, 11 and 9 by Tom Watson against Dale Hayes in 1978. It seemed assured when across the pond at the eighth, Ballesteros holed from 20 feet for a three. Beck had a putt of only marginally less than that to save himself from being beaten 11 and 10. But he got it in and even won the ninth with another birdie. His cause was hopeless, however, and on the 10th green they shook hands.

In 28 holes Ballesteros had had only one bogey, a five at the 13th in the morning. He had also taken five, a par at the 18th, but otherwise he was all fours and threes and nine under par altogether. He was able to enjoy much of the afternoon off, resting for the confrontation that lay ahead with Faldo, who was having to go into overtime.

There is something of Walter Hagen about Ballesteros. He seldom does anything by halves. Having walked all over Beck in the quarter-finals, he was in turn beaten out of sight by Faldo in the semi-finals, losing 6 and 5. At the same stage 12 months earlier, Ballesteros had also lost to Sandy Lyle by the even wider margin of 7 and 6. An omen, since Lyle had gone on to take the title? Indeed it was. Meanwhile the other semi-final was more evenly contested, Woosnam overcoming some marginal early difficulties to defeat Rafferty by 2 and 1 to reach his second final in three years.

Having had his escape against David Frost, Faldo was back on a high again, playing his best golf since the spring and early summer. It had taken more out of him than many people realized. "I really was exhausted," he admitted, "at around the time of the Open" and it was reflected in his ability to find the spark that had briefly given him some claim to being the best golfer in the world.

However, the World Match Play had always been dear to Faldo's heart and he wasted no time in getting the upper-hand over Ballesteros. Two woods through the slightly chilly early morning air safely reached the first green and he was 1-up, Ballesteros hitting the longer drive but failing to get home in two. The next two holes were exchanged, Ballesteros making a two at the second with a seven iron to six feet, but losing the next where he took three putts.

The Spaniard looked like he was going 2-down at the fourth, where his drive left him having to play left-handed from close to the trees, but Faldo rather let him off the hook by taking five as well. Ballesteros had a good chance to square the match at the fifth but missed from eight feet, and another lapse followed at the sixth where, after Faldo had holed from 10 feet for a three, Ballesteros missed from inside three feet.

This was very unlike Ballesteros, who was still 2-down at the turn, Faldo being out in 33. Ballesteros again failed to sink another very short putt for a two at the 10th after a lovely six-iron tee shot, Faldo rubbing it in by getting down in two from off the green for his par. At the 11th it happened again, Ballesteros again missing from three feet for his birdie, and it was an enormous relief to him when at last he did get one in, from some 25 feet for an eagle-three at the 12th.

It was a brief reprieve, because Faldo played much the better tee shot up the hill to the 14th and holed from 10 feet for his two. Another birdie followed at the 15th—now a six iron to 12 feet—for him to stand 3-up and at the 17th it became four as Ballesteros, tight to some bushes on the right of the fairway, pulled a three-iron second out of bounds. Certainly the Spaniard had the better of the 18th, but Faldo got up and down in two for a matching birdie and at 4-up at lunch, he was well in command, round in 65.

Almost like two prize fighters, both came out of their corners for the second round with a flurry of punches. Faldo caught his man squarely on the chin at the first with a one iron to 18 feet and holing the putt for a three. Then he sank another for a two at the second for 15 feet, only for Ballesteros to follow him in from much closer. At the third Ballesteros, home with a huge drive and then a five iron, sank a putt of 40 feet for a three, but Faldo made a birdie at the fourth. Between them they were five under par for those first four holes and Faldo was 5-up.

It was hard to see Ballesteros getting back from there, and his goose was cooked at the eighth and ninth, Faldo making further birdies with long putts of 20 feet or more. He was out in 30 and 7-up and though Ballesteros, whose 33 to the turn was decidedly not to be sneezed at, had two more birdies still up his sleeve (a two at the 10th and then a four at the 12th), Faldo matched the second of them and did not have to go beyond the 13th.

Ballesteros blamed his putting, and justly so. "You cannot do that against a great champion like Nick," he said. For his part, Faldo said that he had "just kept motoring on. The long putts I holed at the eighth and ninth were the killers. I've always had trouble hitting through the ball at a good speed, and I concentrated on a tip from David Leadbetter, hitting the ball 'on the up,' almost topping it. It clicked."

So Faldo reached the final for the third time. He had lost to Greg Norman in 1983 and to Lyle in 1988. Now he was to meet his Ryder Cup foursomes partner, Woosnam, who had less difficulty in disposing of Rafferty than had appeared likely. The Irishman had quickly gone ahead in the morning with a par at the first. He was caught straightaway by Woosnam's comfortable two at the second, but moved ahead again with an eagle at the fourth, a four iron to four feet.

Both holed big putts for birdies at the seventh, Rafferty from off the green, but Woosnam was beside the flag in two at the eighth to square the match, and they were square at the turn, both out in 33. Both made birdies from close range at the 10th and it took an eagle from Woosnam at the 12th to get his nose in front after a glorious two iron to within three feet of the flag. When Rafferty found the trees with his drive at the 13th, he became 2-down and, though he got back the 17th with a chip-and-putt birdie, he three-putted the 18th and was 2-down again. Woosnam was round in 66, Rafferty in 68.

There was no change for five holes in the afternoon, but at the drive-and-pitch sixth, Rafferty stuck a wedge to a foot and was back to 1-down again. If a flame flickered, it quickly seemed to die. He was in trouble off the tee at the seventh and lost it to a four and at the eighth went 3-down, when Woosnam holed the longer of two substantial putts.

Even so, Rafferty was far from finished. Though having to take a wood for his second shot at the ninth, he hit it to 10 feet for a birdie and followed that with a two at the 10th with a putt of around the same length. Once again they were at one another's throats, and the 12th was critical. Though Rafferty was never going to make better than five, Woosnam had a badly plugged ball in a bunker and it took all his strength to extricate it. Nor could he even get his ball on the green, having next to chip and then hole from eight feet for the half.

It was Rafferty's turn to get away with the 13th, where he had to chip out of the trees. But he still got down in two after a nine-iron third shot and Woosnam must have begun to wonder when he would ever shake this man off. It was his five iron to 10 feet for a two at the 14th that was the telling blow for it put him 2-up again, a bridgehead that was not further threatened as the remaining holes were halved with fours at the 15th, 16th and 17th.

So the stage was set for a Faldo-Woosnam final and it is difficult to imagine there being a better. Mind you, we have thought that before.

10. The U.S. Tour

Tom Kite ended the 1988 PGA Tour in the United States as a sympathetic figure. His streak of consecutive years with a victory ended at seven as he finished second three times, twice in playoffs. If 1988 was a bummer for Kite, 1989 was . . . well, what's the opposite of bummer—hummer?

At 39 and in his 17th year on the tour, Kite reached the apex of his career. He won three tournaments and set a money-winning record of $1,395,278 (including Nabisco performance bonuses), topping the mark of $1,147,644 set a year earlier by Curtis Strange. Under the PGA of America's system, Kite was crowned player of the year although some might dispute that recognition. Kite has yet to win a major. Indeed, with the U.S. Open within his grasp, Kite crumbled and Strange won for the second year in a row.

Much of Kite's winnings came in the year-end Nabisco Championship, when he defeated Payne Stewart in a playoff, but let's not nit-pick. It was another year of spiraling paychecks, and if a man played well enough, it was difficult to avoid winning half a million dollars or so. Fifteen players won that much and another came within $708. Stewart also broke Strange's one-year record with $1,201,301, picking up a big chunk of his earnings in the Nabisco tournament. It was a breakthrough year for Stewart. He won his first major title in the PGA Championship at Kemper Lakes, near Chicago, when Mike Reid stumbled on the closing holes.

A case for Player of the Year could be made for Strange or Mark Calcavecchia. In addition to his victory in the U.S. Open, Strange tied for second in the PGA Championship with Reid and Andy Bean, and his sensational four-birdie finish in the Ryder Cup Matches helped gain the United States a tie with the Europeans. Calcavecchia won twice on the American tour, at Phoenix and Los Angeles, and scored a dramatic triumph in the British Open with a sensational shot out of the rough at the final hole of the four-hole playoff after Greg Norman, who was leading, got into inextricable trouble by hitting his tee shot into a fairway bunker. Calcavecchia's British Open winnings were not included in his official U.S. tour earnings, but he still finished fifth with $807,741. Norman later won twice in America, at The International and Milwaukee Open, and placed fourth among the money winners with $835,096.

For consistency, no one could match Paul Azinger, who won at Hartford and tied for second in the Bob Hope Desert Classic and Texas Open. Azinger led the tour in top-10 finishes with 14 in 25 starts and ended the season as the No. 3 money winner with $951,649. He set a record with his 64-62 start in the Texas Open.

Other record-setters: Kenny Knox's 93 putts for 72 holes in the MCI Heritage Classic broke George Archer's record by one, and Knox tied the record for fewest putts in a round (18) and fewest in nine holes (eight); Tom Watson tied Jack Nicklaus' record for consecutive $100,000 seasons with his 16th, but his 12-year streak for $200,000 seasons came to an end, and Strange took over as the leader with 10 in a row; Mike Sullivan set a record for sand saves with a percentage of .660 (the old mark was .654 by Bob

Eastwood in 1980); Leonard Thompson set a record for the most years between victories, his tearful triumph in the Buick Open ending a 12-year drought; Donnie Hammond's 258 in the Texas Open was just one stroke off the record set by Mike Souchak in the 1955 Texas Open.

There were nine first-time winners: Greg Twiggs (Shearson Lehman Hutton), Tom Byrum (Kemper), Ian Baker-Finch (Southwestern Bell Colonial), Curt Byrum (Hardee's Classic), Wayne Grady (Westchester), Mike Donald (Anheuser-Busch), Stan Utley (Chattanooga), Ted Schulz (Southern) and Bill Britton (Cental). The victories for the Byrums marked the first time brothers have won on the U.S. tour in the same year since the Hill brothers, Dave and Mike, did it in 1972.

Steve Jones, who scored his first victory in 1988, came out blazing in 1989, winning the MONY Tournament of Champions and the Bob Hope Desert Classic the next week. He later added the Canadian Open, tying with Kite for the most tournaments won in 1989. (Kite won The Nestle Invitational and The Players Championship in addition to the Nabisco.) The only other multiple winners were Calcavecchia, Stewart, Norman, Blaine McCallister and Tim Simpson who each won twice.

Perhaps the most bizarre day of the year came in the second round of the U.S. Open at Oak Hill in Rochester, New York. Doug Weaver, Mark Wiebe, Jerry Pate and Nick Price all made holes-in-one at the No. 6 hole in the morning, all with seven irons. Tom Watson, Gil Morgan and Billy Mayfair all made aces in the same round of the AT&T Pebble Beach Invitational, but they weren't at the same hole or on the same course—Watson and Morgan made theirs at Spyglass Hill, and Mayfair, at Pebble Beach.

The U.S. tour saw little of Seve Ballesteros in 1989 and probably will see him, and some other foreign stars, no more often in the future. The long-simmering debate of requiring players to compete in at least 15 tournaments came to a head when the Tour Policy Board rejected a proposal to reduce the minimum to 12 tournaments for foreign players. A compromise had been offered in which foreign players could play in 12 tournaments, but three had to be designated events that suffer for the lack of big-name players. Ballesteros rejected the plan, as did Masters champions Nick Faldo and Bernhard Langer.

MONY Tournament of Champions—$750,000
Winner: Steve Jones

When Steve Jones won the MONY Tournament of Champions at LaCosta Country Club, he became the third consecutive first-year man to win the meeting of the previous year's tournament winners.

One theory of why this has transpired is that in the first week in January the veterans are not ready to compete as they might later on. Jones, who won at Pebble Beach for his first victory in 1988, figured the veterans might not be ready, and his own preparations paid off as he won by three strokes over David Frost and Jay Haas with a nine-under-par 279 total.

LaCosta is in the desert country of Southern California, and even in early January the sun usually shines and the weather is warm. Not so in 1988, and not so in 1989. The first round finished in rain, the second round was played in a cold wind, the start of the third round was delayed by frost on the greens, and the fourth round also had a touch of frost. The conditions didn't seem to bother Jones, who shot 69 in every round except the third, in which he took 72.

With Larry Nelson missing because of an ankle injury and Seve Ballesteros absent because of his recent wedding, the field consisted of 32 players. Among them was Andrew Magee, the Pensacola Open winner who was awed by his company. Determined not to make his debut an embarrassment, Magee, the last man off in the first round, opened with 68 to overtake Jones and Chip Beck, who had 69s. A second 69 gave Jones a one-stroke lead over Beck after 36 holes, and he held his lead after 54 holes, although he had to come from behind to reclaim it. When Jones' driving got him in trouble, Beck moved ahead, but Beck bogeyed the final three holes and Jones' newest threats were Lanny Wadkins and Ben Crenshaw, only two strokes behind. Crenshaw had birdies at seven par-three holes in the first three rounds, but too often his ball came up with a glob of mud on it after hitting a fairway, and that prevented him from mounting a serious challenge.

Jones got his driving back on line again in the final round and never gave his pursuers an opening as he shot a 69. Wadkins (73) and Crenshaw (75) faded. Frost and Haas slipped into second place with 68s and Greg Norman matched their score to take fourth place at 283.

Bob Hope Chrysler Classic—$1,000,000
Winner: Steve Jones

Steve Jones could be classified as a slow starter. His debut on the PGA Tour in 1982 was interrupted by thumb surgery and he didn't regain his player's card until 1985. He was just another visored face in the crowd until he won the Pensacola Open late in 1988. His adult life also got off to a sputtering start. A basketball player in college, he said, "I was a boozer and hard to get along with." Then he got religion.

It took him awhile to win but once he did, it seemed to open the floodgates. Jones, 30, began the 1989 season with a victory in the MONY Tournament of Champions. The following week he won again, scoring an impressive triumph in the million-dollar Bob Hope Chrysler Classic.

Jones made three double bogeys and shot a 76 in the first round of the five-round tournament and "I never expected to make the cut." His getaway plans were put on hold by a 68 in the second round and he went from there to a $180,000 payday with a playoff victory over Sandy Lyle and Paul Azinger. "I never thought in my wildest dreams I would win this tournament," he said after he holed the four-foot birdie putt at the 14th green of Bermuda Dunes Country Club that finished his comeback. He was the first to win the first two official tournaments of the year since Gil Morgan in 1983.

The Hope Classic is played over four desert courses and in the first round Bermuda Dunes and Indian Wells produced the lowest scores. Fred Couples opened with a 65 at Indian Wells, putting Jones 11 strokes behind. But Jones played the last four rounds in 21 under par, finishing with a 17-under 343 total.

His 68 in the second round narrowed his deficit to seven strokes and a 67 in the third round left him eight behind, as Scott Verplank took the lead. In the pivotal fourth round, Jones shot a tournament-record 63 at Eldorado and vaulted into a tie for second place at 274 with Lyle, Azinger and Tom Kite. Mark Calcavecchia's third straight 67 put him two strokes ahead.

Calcavecchia maintained the lead until he tried to hit a driver from the fairway at the par-five No. 13 at Bermuda Dunes and hit it out of bounds. Azinger took over and went from one to two ahead with a birdie at the 15th hole. Jones was still in the hunt and Calcavecchia refused to be counted out. Both chipped in for birdies at the par-three No. 17, Jones from 17 feet, Calcavecchia from 20 yards. Jones was within a stroke of Azinger and Calcavecchia was another stroke behind. Nobody seemed to be aware that Lyle had to be reckoned with. "I didn't know Sandy was involved in the playoff until we got to the tee," Jones said.

There would have been no playoff had Azinger not fouled up the 18th hole. He muffed his third shot at the par-five hole, then pitched to within four feet of the hole. He was four feet from a par and victory, but his putt broke off at the hole. The playoff was quick and sweet for Jones. Lyle pushed his second shot about 30 feet to the right of the hole. Azinger hit his to within 15 feet. Jones' seven iron checked up seven feet from the hole. After Azinger and Lyle missed, Jones holed his winning putt.

Phoenix Open—$700,000
Winner: Mark Calcavecchia

The picture of Mark Calcavecchia is of a sturdy man digging up a considerable amount of turf with a mighty swing while getting his ball out of the rough and onto the green. He puts his all into the effort to win. Sometimes it doesn't work, as when he blew a two-stroke lead in the final round of the Bob Hope Classic. Sometimes it does work, as a week later when Calcavecchia won the Phoenix Open by seven strokes with a combination of powerful drives, awesome iron shots and scintillating putting.

Calcavecchia has been accused of getting the most mileage out of the controversial U-shaped grooved clubs, but nobody could point to his clubs as the reason for his fourth victory since he joined the PGA Tour in 1981. He shots rounds of 66-68-65-64—263, a 21-under-par score that broke by five strokes the course record for the three-year-old Scottsdale, Arizona, Tournament Players Course. Chip Beck got to within four strokes of Calcavecchia on the final nine and placed second, but really it was a one-man show.

Ken Green took the first-round lead with 63, but Calcavecchia gave a hint of what was to come when he birdied the 14th, 15th and 16th holes on putts of 30, 40 and 30 feet. Mark McCumber and Bill Glasson led after 36 holes with 133, but Calcavecchia was only a stroke behind.

Late in the third round, Calcavecchia exploded. It began with a fizzle. At the 195-yard 12th hole, Calcavecchia hit his tee shot into the lake, but recovered for a bogey. "I hit one bad shot and I was even par. After I made that bogey I just wanted to shoot 68 or 69."

The bogey must have had a calming effect. He reached the green at the

576-yard No. 13 with a four iron and two-putted for birdie. He sank a 20-footer for birdie at No. 14. At the 501-yard No. 15, he hit a six iron to within six feet of the hole and sank the eagle putt. He birdied Nos. 16 and 17. In six holes he had gone from three strokes behind to three ahead. McCumber and Gary Hallberg were the closest to him.

Some began looking for a blowup by Calcavecchia when he began the final round by topping his tee shot at the first hole and having his lead reduced to two strokes. The drive was embarrassing, but it was humorous, too. And once again Calcavecchia relaxed. He birdied Nos. 2, 4 and 5 and unleashed some prodigious drives as he birdied four of the five holes beginning at No. 12, leaving his pursuers behind. Calcavecchia was three under par for the front nine during the tournament and 18 under on the back nine.

AT&T Pebble Beach National Pro-Am—$1,000,000
Winner: Mark O'Meara

Mark O'Meara hadn't won a PGA Tour Event since the Hawaiian Open in 1985. But to say the three years between that victory and the 1989 AT&T Pebble Beach Pro-Am were a bust would be incorrect. In that time, O'Meara had earned about a million dollars in prize money. But victories are what count, and O'Meara ended his drought on one of his favorite areas, the Monterey Peninsula.

The tournament was played on three courses: Pebble Beach, Spyglass Hill and Cypress Point. All are difficult courses, usually made more so by capricious weather. This time the weather was marvelous for every round except the third and the scoring reflected that. O'Meara was over par on only one round, the third, as he won by one stroke over Tom Kite with 66-68-73-70—277.

The third round ruined 49-year-old Jack Nicklaus, who took an 80 that blemished an otherwise immaculate 289 that included rounds of 69, 69 and 71. Dave Stockton, 47, shot a 78 the third day, yet tied for 10th at 282. "I can still play," said Stockton, the 1970 and 1976 PGA champion who spends most of his time playing corporate outings.

O'Meara, 32, also can still play, especially at Pebble Beach. He won the California Amateur there in 1979 and took the Pebble Beach Pro-Am in 1985. It is Kite's favorite course, as well. Two months earlier, Kite lost to Curtis Strange in a playoff for the Nabisco championship. His placing behind O'Meara marked the fourth time since 1987 he had come in second. "I gave the tournament away by three-putting the seventh and eighth holes," Kite lamented.

O'Meara's opening round included a bit of luck. At the 12th hole, O'Meara's ball flew the green, hit a spectator and fell into light rough. O'Meara parred, a big save in his 66, which left him a stroke behind Stockton, and a 73 the third day left him tied for the lead at 207 with Nick Price, who moved up with 67.

Sandy Lyle and Jim Carter advanced with 68 and 69, respectively, in the final round, and Price faded away with 73. Greg Rita, who had caddied for Strange in his Nabisco triumph two months earlier, helped steer O'Meara around Pebble Beach, and when O'Meara reached the green at No. 18 he was tied for the lead with Kite, who took 69 for 278. The victory came with a slightly downhill putt from 10 feet. O'Meara hit the putt perfectly for a birdie and 70, worth $180,000.

Nissan Los Angeles Open—$1,000,000
Winner: Mark Calcavecchia

Hale Irwin almost got knocked out in the preliminaries and Mark Calcavecchia won by a knockout over a man who has become his No. 1 rival in the Los Angeles Open at Riviera Country Club in Pacific Palisades, California. It was the second victory of the year for Calcavecchia; he won the Phoenix Open two weeks earlier.

At Phoenix, Calcavecchia won by seven strokes. His triumph in Los Angeles was much slimmer—by one stroke—but it might have been a little more satisfying because of the man he beat. Calcavecchia came from two strokes behind Sandy Lyle with 68 for a 272 total. The $180,000 paycheck pushed his earnings for the year to almost $359,000.

During the pro-am, Rich Saul, a former pro football player, hit a wild three wood and yelled "fore!" as the ball headed toward the adjacent fairway. Irwin heard the cry and covered his face with his hands. The ball hit him between the hands, almost squarely between the eyes. He never lost consciousness, but it required 16 stitches to close the wound. It could have been worse. Irwin normally wears glasses, but on this day he was wearing contact lenses. The accident had no effect on Irwin's game; he stayed in contention, placing third, two strokes behind Calcavecchia.

Calcavecchia had had his bid for a Masters victory in 1988 taken from him by Lyle's marvelous bunker shot at the final green. It was not that shot so much as the Americans' loss to the British-European team in the Ryder Cup Match in 1987 that ate at Calcavecchia. He couldn't wait for the renewal in England in September. Until then, he would take the decision against Lyle.

Perhaps astrologers could explain why Calcavecchia and Lyle play so well at the same time. Their charts for the Los Angeles Open would be interesting. They both opened with 68s that left them one stroke behind. Both came back with 66s that left them tied for the lead. They were fortunate that they played early in the day. A steady rain made conditions miserable and caught 71 players on the course when play was halted. They finished Saturday before the field was cut and the third round began.

It was Lyle's first appearance at Riviera and he quickly fell in love with the course. A 68 in the third round put him two strokes in front of Calcavecchia and four ahead of Irwin. Suddenly Lyle's putter went sour and Calcavecchia, booming his drives and chipping and putting magnificently, slowly eased past. Irwin led briefly, but couldn't hold on, a bogey at the final hole dropping him into third place. Calcavecchia chipped in from the fringe at No. 12 to tie Lyle and Lyle fell behind to stay when he three-putted No. 14 for a bogey. Sandy added a little suspense at the final green when he chipped out of the rough to within inches of the hole to save par. But Calcavecchia easily two-putted from 15 feet.

Hawaiian Open—$750,000
Winner: Gene Sauers

Gene Sauers, whose only triumph in five years came in 1986, got an emotional boost from the birth of his first child three weeks earlier and rode it to a one-stroke victory over David Ogrin in the Hawaiian Open.

The tournament was reduced to 54 holes because of rain, and Sauers won with 65-67-65—197. "I just shot 18 under at Waialae Country Club and I didn't win," Ogrin lamented. Dave Rummells closed with a 64 for third place at 199.

Rummells' opening 70 put him seven strokes behind Brad Fabel, whose nine-under-par 63 gave him a one-stroke lead on Jim Carter and two over Sauers, Ogrin and Dick McClean, a club professional. The rainy weather moved in Friday, bringing with it doubt that everybody would finish the round that day. Carter was one of those who finished, completing his 66 moments after the horn sounded to suspend play. A total of 66 players failed to complete their rounds. Saturday was not much better, as those who were caught on the course Friday attempted to finish their rounds.

Sauers was among those who finished on Friday, his 67 leaving him two strokes behind Carter, who led with 66—130. Ogrin played one hole on Saturday and birdied it for 67 that tied him with Sauers. Carter had a full day off and the rest seemed detrimental. He got off to a slow start in the third and final round Sunday. Sauers and Rummells both played the front nine in 31 and Rummells' 64 for 199 gave the later starters a score to shoot for. Sauers' concern was not Rummells' score, but Ogrin, and with four holes to go Sauers seemed to have that situation well in hand. But Sauers bogeyed No. 15 and Ogrin birdied No. 16, and suddenly they were tied for the lead.

Sauers birdied the par-three No. 17 to take a one-stroke lead to the 552-yard No. 18. Ogrin's third shot stopped 10 feet below the hole. Sauers' approach went over the green, but he got a break. Instead of running down the side of the hill, it hit a photographer and stopped in the short rough just off the green. A one-stroke swing for a tie or a two-stroke swing for a loss still seemed possible. Because he had a poor lie to putt the ball, Sauers chipped from 20 feet, and the ball went into the hole.

Shearson Lehman Hutton Open—$700,000
Winner: Greg Twiggs

When he was a youngster, Greg Twiggs lined up to play the Torrey Pines course near San Diego, often dreaming what it would be like to play in a tournament there. When he attended San Diego State College, Torrey Pines was his home course. Before the 1989 Shearson Lehman Hutton Open, he had played the North and South courses more than 200 times.

Even with the friendly surroundings, Twiggs was a long shot to win the Shearson Lehman Hutton Open. The South course was not as Twiggs remembered it; an extensive remodeling job had given the public course a facelift. But Twiggs used his 64 in the third round to vault to a 17-under-par 271 total and a two-stroke victory. Mark Wiebe, Mark O'Meara, Steve

Elkington and Brad Faxon tied for second, O'Meara leaping into the dead-lock with 66.

David Peoples, Mark Lye and Frank Connor opened with 65s, then re-treated. As they did, Elkington took over, moving up from five strokes be-hind with 63 and 67 in the middle rounds. Elkington's approach at the 499-yard 18th hole nearly rolled back into the lake. He chipped up and holed a 15-foot putt for birdie and a 54-hole total of 200. Twiggs' 64 brought him to second place, two strokes behind, and Wiebe pulled into third, three back, with a 70.

Twiggs' caddy had pulled out before the tournament began, so at the last moment Twiggs conscripted his nephew, Bret Finley, not to caddy but just to carry his bag. "He doesn't know a par-four from a par-five," Twiggs said. Finley handed Twiggs the clubs he asked for and Twiggs used them to build a lead in the final round as Elkington slipped back to a 73. He had a little help. At No. 15, Twiggs missed a 15-foot putt for birdie. Wiebe, facing a birdie putt from 18 inches at the same hole, failed to gain ground as he missed it. That left Twiggs three ahead with three to go and he parred in as Wiebe futilely tried to overtake him.

Doral-Ryder Open—$1,300,000
Winner: Bill Glasson

When he was a boy growing up in Fresno, California, Bill Glasson's day-care center was a golf course. His mother, working two jobs to keep the family intact, deposited him at 7 a.m. and picked him up at 5 p.m. He played 54 holes a day. That polished Glasson's game, and it also gave him a target. "I wanted to make one million by the time I was 30."

Glasson reached that goal a year early when he won the Doral Ryder Open against the strongest field so far in 1989 at Doral Country Club's Blue Monster course. Glasson's 13-under-par 71-65-67-72—275 beat Fred Couples by one stroke and made him the PGA Tour's 100th millionaire. The victory was his third in nine starts—he won the B.C. Open and Centel Classic late in 1988—but Glasson was not overjoyed with it. He had a good chance for the tournament record of 18 under par with 10 holes to play.

Winter came to Miami, for the first two rounds, with night-time tempera-tures dropping into the 30s and a wind making the chill factor during play feel like 20 degrees below the actual mid-50s. Under the circumstances, the 65s by Mark Calcavecchia in the first round and by Glasson in the second round were viewed at outstanding. Glasson opened with 71 and when Cal-cavecchia came back with 73 he slipped two strokes behind Glasson and a stroke behind Wayne Levi, who got off to a 68-69 start.

Glasson was to lead the rest of the way, but he gave his pursuers a chance on the final nine. A 67 in the third round put him at 203 and gave him a one-stroke lead on Calcavecchia, who bounced back with 66. Couples, with 69-69-70, trailed by five strokes and seemingly was out of the picture.

The final round was primarily a battle between Glasson and Calcavec-chia, who were paired. Calcavecchia caught Glasson a few times, but never could overtake him. Glasson played the first eight holes in three under par and with nine holes to play they were in a deadlock for the lead. They both began to fade. Glasson made four bogeys and a birdie over the last 10 holes, only a birdie at the 16th hole provided his margin of victory.

When they stepped to the tee at the 18th hole, one of the toughest finishing holes on the tour, Calcavecchia trailed by one stroke. Glasson hit his second shot over the green, avoiding the water on the left. "I knew he would probably make par, so I was thinking birdie all the way," said Calcavecchia, who went for the pin with a six iron from 171 yards. The ball fell into the lake. He made a double bogey. Meanwhile, Couples, who had finished with 68 for 276, was looking on and kicking himself for the double bogey he had taken after hitting his ball into the water at the fourth hole. Couples needed a bogey from Glasson to force a playoff. "I played very poorly over the last 10 holes. I'm very dissatisfied," Glasson said afterward. He wasn't about to make it a total embarrassment, getting a par at No. 18 for 72 and a $234,000 payday.

Honda Classic—$800,000
Winner: Blaine McCallister

In his first victory, the 1988 Hardees Classic, Blaine McCallister proved he was able to shoot low numbers as he matched the PGA Tour's 36-hole record with 62-63—125 in the middle rounds. He demonstrated that again in his second triumph as he finished with 65-64 on the way to a four-stroke decision in the Honda Classic at the Tournament Players Club at Eagle Trace in Coral Springs, Florida.

Mid-week rain and virtually no wind made an easy mark of Eagle Trace. McCallister and Dan Pohl led a record-breaking onslaught. The 36-hole cut came at 140, four under par. McCallister's 70-67-65-64—266 total, 22 under par, broke by three strokes the tournament record when it was played at nearby Inverrary and was nine better than the course record set by Curtis Strange in 1985. And McCallister had to come from nine strokes behind after 36 holes.

For the first two rounds it was difficult to figure out who was the tournament leader. Tom Byrum opened with 65 that was low round on Thursday, but about half the field was still on the course when play was halted. Morning fog, then lightning in the afternoon delayed play for nearly three hours. Buddy Gardner and Rex Caldwell tied Byrum after completing their opening rounds Friday morning, but that was quickly forgotten as Pohl strung together an impressive array of birdies. Pohl birdied four of the 10 holes he played Friday morning to complete a 66. It was just a warm-up. Starting his second round on the back nine shortly afterward, Pohl opened with an eagle at the 10th hole and played that nine in 29 on the way to a 62—128 total and a three-stroke lead over Gardner and Ted Schulz.

Pohl set tournament records for nine holes, 18 holes and 36 holes, but that was a pace he couldn't maintain. A 75 in the third round proved disastrous, as Pohl placed fifth, six strokes behind McCallister.

When the rain stopped the winds came and the scores went up. As Pohl faded, the tournament became wide-open. Steve Pate shot 64 in the third round and took a one-stroke lead to the final round. Payne Stewart, two strokes behind, birdied Nos. 2, 3, 4 and 5 to take over the lead, but McCallister tied him with an eagle at the fifth. Then McCallister moved in front by himself with birdies at Nos. 9 and 10. Stewart made three birdies on the back nine, but he also had two bogeys, and when McCallister birdied Nos. 13 and 14 he had a four-stroke lead. He still had that margin as he teed off at the 18th and he never lost it. Stewart's 67 gave him second place for the third year in a row.

The Nestle Invitational—$800,000
Winner: Tom Kite

With three second-place finishes in 1988, Tom Kite had acquired a growing reputation as a runner-up. An unwarranted label, to be sure, since Kite had 10 victories on his career resume. But even Kite was thinking second place again after he hit his second shot at the 72nd hole of The Nestle Invitational at Bay Hill. Kite's four iron from 190 yards came up short, into the lake in front of the green. Tied for the lead with Davis Love, Kite placed an arm across the end of his club and buried his head in it, figuring he had thrown away his chance for victory.

But this was to be one of the most bizarre endings of the season, Kite took a double bogey, but so did Love, and moments later Kite ended his 18-month drought with a par on the second extra hole. "So often I've played well in the last round of a tournament and I would come up short. Today I played poorly on the back nine and won. It's very strange," said Kite after his 68-72-67-71—278 total.

Kite's opening 68 left him two strokes behind Loren Roberts, whose six-under-par 66 in the cold and windy Orlando, Florida, weather was called "awesome" by host Arnold Palmer. Roberts came back with 73 that tied him for the 36-hole lead with Mark Calcavecchia and Love, who had 69 and 67, respectively. Kite trailed by one stroke. Love's 66 in the third round gave him the lead by two strokes over Kite, while Roberts and Larry Rinker were another stroke back.

Love and Kite reversed their positions on the front nine of the last round, Kite shooting a 32 to take a two-stroke lead. Love caught him with a five-foot birdie putt at No. 16, setting up the 18-hole follies. Kite, not regarded as a long hitter, was hitting his drives with growing authority and he hit a good one at the difficult 18th. Love, a recognized long hitter, drove it well past him, about 30 yards. Kite had a four iron shot; Love was an eight iron away. After Kite hit his ball into the lake, many assumed Love would do no worse than hit the green and three-putt for a bogey. That probably would be enough.

Roberts was an example of what could happen at the hole. He needed a par to finish at 278, but took four to get down from off the green and the double bogey dropped him to a tie for sixth place with Payne Stewart and Don Pooley, one stroke behind Curtis Strange.

So Love hit his approach over the green into the short rough. After taking a drop, Kite hit his fourth shot 12 feet from the hole, setting up a possible bogey. "I figured Davis would make five and I had a reasonable chance to make five," Kite said. Love chipped weakly, leaving his ball short of the green. His next chip stopped four feet above the hole. Not a tap-in, but a great opportunity for victory after Kite missed his putt. But Love pulled the putt, and as the ball slipped past the hole Kite and the crowd began a walk to the 15th hole, the start of the playoff. Both parred the 15th, then at the 446-yard 16th Love hit his approach 45 feet from the hole and left his first putt eight feet short. Kite putted close and made par, then Love missed.

The Players Championship—$1,350,000
Winner: Tom Kite

Tom Kite's victory in The Players Championship in Ponte Vedra, Florida, gave an indication of how fickle golf can be. For seven years, Kite won at least one tournament each year. In 1988, he came away empty. Then Kite was virtually handed the winner's trophy by Davis Love in The Nestle Invitational at Bay Hill, and followed that with a triumph in the TPC—only the second time in his 17-year career that he won two tournaments in one year.

Kite's victory in the TPC bore little resemblance to that in Orlando. It put to rest his reputation as a conservative player. Well, one hole did, as Kite beat Chip Beck by one stroke with a nine-under-par 279 total that was worth $243,000.

Since opening in 1982, the TPC at Sawgrass had received a torrent of criticism for its greens. They were too severe for the shots demanded and the penalty for missing the greens was too high, the pros said. The greens had undergone several changes through the years, and after the 1988 tournament they received another facelift. The top 18 inches were removed and replaced with a new drainage foundation. While retaining the original contours, the bent grass was replaced with a Bermuda variety, and the high grass around the greens was drastically reduced. "We felt we were losing chipping and putting, those fine skills that were so important and very much a part of traditional golf," said PGA Tour commissioner Deane Beman.

So the greens were more playable, and when the wind didn't blow, the course was not villainous either. When the wind began to blow, the greens got harder and the scores went up. The wind was calm in the first round, as was reflected in the scoring: Keith Clearwater 65, Steve Pate 66, David Frost 66, Bruce Leitzke 66, Ben Crenshaw 67. Kite was one of several at 69. Clearwater could have broken the course record of 64 set by Fred Couples in 1984. Playing the back nine first, he went out in 31 and with two holes to play he was nine under par. He bogeyed the 215-yard No. 8 and the 582-yard No. 9. Crenshaw also had end-of-the-round troubles, losing two strokes on his last three holes.

A slow-play warning seemed to throw Clearwater off his game in the second round and he limped out of contention with 76. Clearwater and companions Phil Blackmar and Mark Wiebe were informed at the 12th tee that they had fallen a hole behind, and Clearwater went bogey, double-bogey, bogey on the next three holes. Lietzke stepped into the lead and the 16th hole came into prominence. The 16th is a par-five dogleg hole with water to the right and back of the green. Trying to reach it in two shots was a gamble, but a ball going over the green did not carry a severe penalty. A player could drop a ball on the fringe where it went over and still chip and putt for par. Lietzke went for the green in two and lost a ball. His 69—135 total gave him a two-stroke lead over Frost, and Kite was at 139, after a 70.

Lietzke appeared on his way to a rout in the third round, but, of course, a rout seldom takes place in the third round of a tournament. Lietzke was 12 under par as he made the turn and had a five-stroke lead. He began the back nine with a bogey and double bogey. He also bogeyed the 14th and 18th. When the round ended, he trailed Beck by two shots and Kite by one. Lietzke had 74, Beck 68 and Kite 69. Crenshaw was another shot behind Kite after a 70.

With the greens hardening, the course became its old self, a great condition for a steady player such as Kite in the final round. Kite kept playing par and let the others self-destruct. Crenshaw followed an eagle at the ninth hole with a triple bogey at the 10th. Beck went out in 41. Kite birdied the second, sixth and 10th and bogeyed the fifth and 14th. At the 426-yard 15th he chopped his way out of a grass bunker and sank a six-foot putt for par and said, "That was the one that kept me going."

Then came the 16th. A week earlier, Kite hit his approach into a lake fronting the 18th green at Bay Hill and thought he had thrown away his chances to win. Faced with a shot of 227 yards, he never hesitated. He went for the green with a four wood, and the ball rolled across the green to the collar behind it, stopping about 18 inches from the edge. He hit a poor chip and two-putted for par, but with two holes to go and a two-stroke lead, Kite had the victory in hand. Beck reduced the lead to one stroke at the final hole, sinking a 25-foot birdie putt that completed a 32 on the back nine, but Kite had hit his first putt to within two feet of the hole and he had no trouble sinking the winning shot.

USF&G Classic—$750,000
Winner: Tim Simpson

With four holes left in the USF&G Classic, Greg Norman trailed Tim Simpson by one stroke. The 15th hole, a 542-yard par-five with an island green, was going to be the turning point. Norman would reach the green in two strokes, make an eagle or a birdie while Simpson parred or bogeyed, and Norman would go on to a victory. Indeed, No. 15 was the pivotal hole, but it didn't turn out the way Norman or his followers expected.

As expected, Norman reached the green with a 228-yard one-iron shot and Simpson played short, more than 100 yards from the green. Simpson hit a wedge to within 12 feet, while Greg was 40 feet from an eagle or an almost-certain birdie. Norman's eagle putt barely missed, stopping four feet past the hole. Simpson sank his birdie putt. Norman missed his comeback putt, three-putting for a par. Simpson had a two-stroke lead and won by two strokes with a 68-67-70-69—274 total.

Simpson made the necessary putts; Norman and Hal Sutton didn't. "I feel like I would have been about 10 shots in front had I putted well," Norman said. He took 35 putts in his final-round 72 and Sutton, constantly missing birdie opportunities, putted 34 times for a 70 that tied him for second place.

It was odd that Norman and Sutton, not Simpson, sang songs of putting blues, for it was Simpson who wrestled with that problem between the third and fourth rounds. Trailing Norman by one stroke after 54 holes, Simpson called Dr. Bob Rotella, the sports psychologist from the University of Virginia, then practiced with a teach aid.

The USF&G Classic was making its initial appearance at the Jack Nicklaus-designed English Turn course, carved out of swampland near New Orleans, and the course received high approval from the players.

Simpson stayed close to the lead for the first three rounds. His opening 68 left him two strokes behind Dan Forsman, as only eight players broke 70. Scoring was much lower in the second round. Simpson's 67 put him in a tie for the lead with Forsman at 135. Norman shot his third consecutive 68 in the third round to pull a stroke ahead. But Simpson, whose only previous victory came in the Southern Open in 1985, refused to back off.

The last round was mostly a two-man affair—Simpson and Norman. Sutton began sinking some putts only when it became obvious his chances were about over. After Simpson doubled his lead at the 15th hole, Norman had one more chance, and he fumbled it. Norman sank a 12-footer to save par at the 16th hole and it looked as if momentum had swung his way when Simpson missed the green at the 200-yard No. 17. But Norman hit his tee shot over the green and both were unable to sink par putts, Simpson from 15 feet, Norman from 12. Simpson clinched his victory with a four iron out of the rough to the green at the 471-yard No. 18.

Independent Insurance Agent Open—$800,000
Winner: Mike Sullivan

After the 36-hole cut in the Independent Insurance Agent Open, Mike Sullivan was one of the longest of long shots. His 147 total was the cutoff figure. In what used to be called the Houston Open, the winner had never opened with a score higher than par-72. Yet Sullivan won after starting with 76. He won even though after 54 holes he still trailed the leaders by seven strokes.

Sullivan knew he could play The Woodlands. Three years earlier, he set the course record with a nine-under 63. From his position after 54 holes, even a 63 might not be enough for a victory. Then those in front began to retreat, and Sullivan won by one stroke over Craig Stadler with a final-round 65—including a bogey at No. 18—that gave him eight-under 280 total.

For two rounds, it seemed that Mike Donald was headed for his first victory. He took the first-round lead with 67 and padded his margin to four strokes with another 67. Shadowing Donald were such figures as defending champion Curtis Strange, Seve Ballesteros and Hal Sutton, in addition to Stadler.

The Woodlands is the type of course where one can gain ground with a modest 68 or two. Sullivan shot 68 in the third round and picked up six strokes on Donald, who remained in the lead despite his 74. "I was a long way back. I was thinking about going fishing," Sullivan said.

His thinking didn't change until late in the final round. He began the day birdie-birdie and ended the front nine the same way and grieved over short birdie putts he missed at the fifth and sixth holes. But he birdied Nos. 11, 12 and 13 and when he birdied No. 13, an island green, thoughts of winning surfaced. The shot that ultimately won for him was a four iron to the par-three No. 16 that set up a 12-foot birdie putt. He plugged his approach in a bunker at the 445-yard No. 18, bogeyed and "I thought that might cost me."

Those with a shot of overtaking Sullivan aimed and missed. Ballesteros got to eight-under with an eagle at No. 13 and a birdie at No. 14, but he hit a second-shot three wood out of bounds at No. 15. Strange and Sutton couldn't get anything started, and Stadler failed to convert birdie opportunities as he shot 70 and finished a stroke behind at 281. It was the second tour victory in 13 years for Sullivan. His other win came in the 1980 Southern Open.

Deposit Guaranty Classic—$200,000
Winner: Jim Booros

The weather at the Deposit Guaranty Classic in Hattiesburg, Mississippi, was worse than that at the Masters, which was played at the same time in Augusta, Georgia. Like the Masters, it ended in a playoff, with Jim Booros playing the part of Nick Faldo, and Mike Donald, the role of Scott Hoch. Unlike the Masters, the Deposit Guaranty Classic was trimmed from four rounds to three because of the weather.

The first three rounds were played in mostly pleasant weather. Booros took the first-round lead with a six-under-par 64. A 69 in the second round tied him at 133 with Donald, who had 68-65. They both shot 66s in the third round and stayed tied at 199.

When the bad weather moved in, it was as bad as it had ever been in the 22-year history of the tournament. Lightning forced the first suspension of play, after 14 players had completed their rounds. When it was determined that not everyone would finish the round, the PGA Tour decided that Booros and Donald would have a playoff for the title over the 10th and 18th holes.

Donald had his chances. At the first playoff hole, he missed a 15-foot birdie putt. At the next, he failed on an eight-foot birdie putt. At the third, Donald sank a 20-footer for birdie, but Booros matched him with another 20-footer. Back to No. 18. Donald's tee shot landed in a divot, about 175 yards from the green. His five-iron approach nearly went into a lake, stopping 50 yards from the green. Booros reached the green in two shots, 18 feet from the hole. Donald's chip stopped eight feet from the hole, and when he missed that putt, Booros won by sinking a two-footer.

MCI Heritage Classic—$800,000
Winner: Payne Stewart

Payne Stewart is one of the best players on the PGA Tour, but it's hard to convince him. His victory in the MCI Heritage Classic at the Harbour Town Links on Hilton Head Island, South Carolina, should have helped. On a course that was in poor condition because of cold weather, and with an ailing back, Stewart won by five strokes with a 65-67-67-69—268 total.

The only time Stewart seemed to be in trouble was the last day. Rain had stopped play with 18 players still on the course in the third round. One was Stewart, who still had seven holes to play. He was forced to complete those seven and the final 18 on Sunday. "I've got an 18-hole back. I'm not sure about handling seven more in one day," said Stewart, who has degenerative disks. Handle it he did, so well that Kenny Perry, who placed second admitted early in the round that he was aiming to be runner-up.

Stewart and Perry got out to identical 65-67 starts. Some of the attention in the first round was diverted to Kenny Knox, who shot 69. Knox chipped in three times and needed only 18 putts as he opened an assault on the record for putts in a tournament. He finished the 72 holes with 93, one fewer than the record held by George Archer, and tied for fifth place.

The rains came on Saturday, delaying the start for the leaders until 5 p.m. and assuring they wouldn't finish before darkness set in. When play was called off, Stewart had a two-stroke lead. Stewart finished his third round with 67, giving him a three-stroke lead over Perry and five over Mark McCumber. The skies had cleared, the weather was brilliant and so was Stewart. That became obvious to Perry, who played conservatively, shooting for the middle part of greens in an effort to maintain his second-place position.

Stewart, holing almost every putt, built a good-sized lead before his back started to bother him with two holes to play. He had a par-three and a par-four hole left and his caddy said, "You've got only three full shots left. You can handle it." He could and did, finishing with 69, and Perry took second place with 71.

K-Mart Greater Greensboro Open—$1,000,000
Winner: Ken Green

After a player misses victory by a bad break, a poor putt, or a shot that somehow comes up short, the lament often is "the course owes me." When Ken Green three-putted the 72nd green, then lost to Sandy Lyle in a playoff in the 1988 Greater Greensboro Open, he changed that to a vow: "I owe the course." In 1989, Green paid it back.

Green and Lyle tied with 17-under-par 271 at River Oaks Country Club in Greensboro, North Carolina, in 1988. Green had a chance to duplicate that fine score in 1989, but he didn't have to, winning by two strokes over John Huston with 277. It was his fifth victory in eight years on the PGA Tour.

With two victories, two playoff losses and a near-playoff (he three-putted the final green and missed tying for first place in the Pensacola Open) in 1988, Green placed fourth in money winnings and only a couple shots away from being named Player of the Year.

The fans at Greensboro are often rowdy, greeting players at the 17th hole with shouts and the noise of pop-top cans. They are the kind of fans the brash and uninhibited Green enjoys. Formerly a pre-Masters fixture, the tournament was moved to two weeks after the Masters to avoid the foul weather that often accompanied it. As a result, the weather was good and the course well groomed. The scores reflected the conditions. Tom Sieck-mann, Jim Booros, David Ogrin, Don Shirey and Bill Glasson led the first round with 69s.

Green shot 66 in the second round that tied him for the lead at 139 with Booros (70), Duffy Waldorf (68) and Dave Eichelberger (67). Green hit only seven fairways—two more than he found in the second round—en route to another 66 in the third round and led Huston, who had 67, by two strokes. Green made up for his misdirection off the tee by using only 55 putts in his middle two rounds. Huston birdied the second hole and Green bogeyed the third in the final round, putting them in a tie. But Huston bogeyed No. 4 and Green birdied No. 5, and for all intents and purposes the race was over. Green birdied Nos. 9, 13, 14 and 15 to get to 14 under par and five strokes ahead, then relaxed for 72 and his two-stroke victory margin over Huston, who also shot 72 that held off charging Ed Fiori (67) for second place.

Las Vegas Invitational—$1,250,000
Winner: Scott Hoch

With each two- or three-foot putt he faced, the memory sat there on his shoulder like a malevolent devil, grinning foolishly, waiting for him to miss. Earlier in the month he had missed a two-foot par at the first hole of a playoff that would have won the Masters. "It's something my wife and my friends and I have had to live with," said Scott Hoch.

Hoch had many chances to duplicate that tragedy in the 90-hole Las Vegas Invitational. The memory was just there; it didn't guide his arms or his hands. He showed the mistake at Augusta might have been due to major championship nervousness or Augusta National's difficult greens instead of intestinal fortitude as he defeated Robert Wrenn for the Las Vegas title with an eight-foot birdie putt on the fifth playoff hole. Hoch and Wrenn survived a tense duel with Craig Stadler, Dan Pohl and Gil Morgan to tie with a 336 total, 24 under par.

Hoch shot 69-64-68-65 over the Las Vegas, Desert Inn and Spanish Trail courses to take a one-stroke lead into the final round. Wrenn, with 69-66-66-69, trailed by one stroke along with Pohl. Stadler and Morgan were right behind them. Hoch opened the final round with birdies on three of the first four holes, but was unable to gain any ground. At one point on the back nine, Hoch, Wrenn, Stadler, Morgan and Brad Bryant, who closed with 64 and tied for fifth place, were tied for the lead at 23 under par.

After Wrenn finished with 66 for 336, the target score was up. Pohl virtually erased his chances by three-putting the 17th green. Morgan and Stadler needed birdies at the 524-yard finishing hole, but Morgan took three from a back bunker and Stadler missed a 15-foot birdie putt. That left only Hoch, who in nine years on the PGA Tour had won only three times, twice in the Quad Cities Open. His most recent victory was in that tournament in 1984. Hoch went for the green with his second shot and made it, but his putt for an eagle just missed. His birdie gave him a 70 and put him in his second playoff in the month of April.

Both parred the first playoff hole, No. 15, then both got a break at the next hole. Wrenn's drive was headed out of bounds to the right when it hit a spectator on the arm, ricocheted off a tree and landed in the fairway. Hoch's approach to the green was long, but an unwitting spectator reached out and stopped it. Both parred, Hoch after a magnificent chip shot after taking a free drop. At the par-three 17th, Hoch's tee shot went into a bunker and he played "one of the best shots of my life," saving par with a blast three feet from the hole. As he had on the previous hole, Wrenn missed a birdie putt. Wrenn outdrove Hoch at the long No. 18, but as he had done in regulation, Hoch went for the green from about 225 yards and made it. Both two-putted for birdie. The fifth playoff hole was No. 12 and Wrenn put his ball on the fringe to the left of the hole. Hoch's sand-wedge second shot stopped eight feet from the hole. Wrenn's birdie putt barely missed. Hoch sent his birdie putt into the center of the cup, and the devil on his shoulder hopped away.

Hoch's victory was worth $225,000, but he took only $125,000. The other $100,000 he donated to the Orlando (Florida) Regional Medical Center. "It's something I've wanted to do for a long time, but I kept putting it off. I had the idea I would do it when I won," he said. Two and a half years earlier, Hoch's son, Cameron, was treated at the hospital for what was first believed to be bone cancer in a leg. Doctors diagnosed it as an inflammation of the bone marrow and treated it successfully.

GTE Byron Nelson Classic—$1,000,000
Winner: Jodie Mudd

As the Byron Nelson Classic went into its final nine holes, many observers remarked what a coincidence it was that the winner might have the same last name as the Hall of Famer for whom the tournament was named. Larry Nelson had played the front nine in 31, a birdie at the ninth hole putting him 16 under par for the tournament. And Nelson was not known as a man to let opportunity slip from his grasp.

But while many noted the Nelson connection, they also seemed to over-look the correlation between Jodie Mudd and the conditions at the TPC course at the Las Colinas Sports Club in Dallas, Texas. The tournament began in weather that threatened to blow the area off the map and ended with a man named Mudd shaking off the mud to claim his second victory— the first came nine months earlier—in eight years on the PGA Tour. Mudd, three strokes behind with nine holes to play, made two outstanding pars on the final nine, as he tied Nelson at 15-under-par 265 with a final-round 65 to Nelson's 67, then beat him with a birdie on the first playoff hole.

That the tournament would be played at all loomed as unlikely after the Wednesday pro-am was washed out. Winds measured as high as 110 miles an hour scoured the course and the storm, which knocked out electrical power in the Dallas-Fort Worth area, dropped about five inches of rain on the course. Another storm Thursday morning delayed the start of the first round until 11:30 a.m. As a result, 56 players were still on the course when play was stopped because of darkness and were forced to complete their rounds Friday morning.

From the weather problems emerged some of the best scoring of the year, since the course was tailored to allow for the wet conditions. Nelson opened with 63, but Wayne Levi sank a 13-foot putt in fading light for an 8-under-par 62 that tied the course record. Nine others began with 64s. A total of 67 broke par, setting up a 36-hole cut the next day at 137, three under par. Levi added 67 to take a one-stroke lead after 36 holes. Nelson, with 68, trailed by two and Mudd, with a 68-66 start, was five behind.

Levi remained in the lead after 54 holes by shooting 68 for a 197 total, but now he had to share his position with Larry Mize, who had 63. Nelson, with 67, was one back and Mudd, with a second straight 66, was three in arrears. Levi, bothered by the unexpected early tee times for a leader in the final two rounds because of television commitments, stayed in the chase until the final nine holes, then faded with 38. When Nelson birdied the ninth hole to go 16 under, he seemingly had the victory in his pocket. But he bogeyed the 13th hole and could only par the other holes.

Mudd, meanwhile, began the back nine by three-putting the 10th green, but three birdies brought him back. Two great pars helped give him a 265 total, a target score for Nelson. At the 390-yard No. 14, Mudd's approach came up short and stuck in the embankment, only inches above the water. He blasted 20 feet past the hole, then, without cleaning the mud off his ball, sank the putt for par. At the 18th hole, Mudd's approach came to rest on a peninsula of grass between a bunker and the green and after "one of the best chips of my life," he sank a five-footer for par. Nelson, too, made some great saves coming in, the last from almost the same spot as Mudd at No. 18.

The playoff began at the par-five 16th, an advantage for the longer-hitting Mudd. Nelson outdrove him, but his ball rolled into the rough. Mudd's three-wood second shot left him only 15 yards away from the green. Nelson had to lay up and was left with a 140-yard approach. Nelson's third shot left him 45 feet from the hole. Mudd played a pitch-and-run to within 10 feet. After Nelson's birdie attempt went eight feet past, Mudd said he told himself "I can make this thing and get out of here." And he did.

Memorial Tournament—$930,250
Winner: Bob Tway

Who will ever forget Bob Tway's elation after he blasted his bunker shot into the hole at the 72nd green and beat a startled Greg Norman in the 1986 PGA Championship? Until the 1989 Memorial Tournament, Tway had only the memory to look back on. For two and a half years, he had gone winless on the PGA Tour.

Tway underwent some changes in his game, primarily going to a more upright swing, and in 1988 he lost twice in playoffs. The breakthrough finally came in the Memorial, when he birdied four of the last six holes and beat front-running Fuzzy Zoeller by two strokes.

Jack Nicklaus moved up his tournament two weeks to the second weekend in May in order to avoid television conflicts with the National Basketball Association playoffs. All it got Nicklaus was cold and wet weather, complaints about the condition of the course, and the tournament still was bumped off television on Saturday, this time by an auto race. But the Memorial turned out to be a good one, spiced by Zoeller's remarks about slow play, principally aimed at Curtis Strange, who was warned four times during the third round. It had rained heavily Friday night, and the players were permitted to lift and clean their balls in the final two rounds, accounting for the slow play and the low scores.

Zoeller was the only player to break 70 on the cold and windy first round, taking a one-stroke lead over Payne Stewart and Fred Couples with a three-under-par 69. Using a home-made putter a fan had sent him, Zoeller had 15 birdies in the first two rounds. In the second round he had nine in a 66 that gave him a five-stroke lead. But it wasn't the putter that paid off so much as his driver and his irons—"I'm hitting so far I can get that baby in close."

After the Friday night rain, the birdies began to fade for Zoeller and the field bunched up behind him. Tway, who had a 68 after 71-69, might have caught or passed him except for Zoeller's alert caddy. Zoeller was short of the 18th green on his approach, facing a chip from a poor lie below the green. He faced a likely bogey until his caddie noticed he was permitted to lift and place the ball. Zoeller did, then chipped in for a 72 that kept him one stroke ahead of Tway.

Stewart, who finished with 65, Bruce Lietzke and Mark Calcavecchia threatened in the final round, but Zoeller's biggest problem was Tway. Bob bogeyed the second and third holes and Zoeller birdied the fourth, putting four strokes between them, but Zoeller bogeyed the seventh and eighth holes and his grip was broken. Tway caught him with a birdie at No. 13 and, with four holes remaining, it looked like a four-man battle. Stewart, playing ahead of Tway and Zoeller, missed a four-footer at No. 17 and settled for 65 and 281. Then Tway got hot. He hit an iron almost into the hole at No. 15 and took the lead. Zoeller caught him with a birdie at No. 16.

At the 17th, Tway duplicated his iron shot of two holes earlier and took the lead again. He looked as if he might lose the lead again after his drive at No. 18 barely bounced onto the edge of the fairway and Zoeller hit a long tee shot to the center. Tway's approach left him with a 25-foot downhill putt. Zoeller's approach was long and left him little chance for a birdie. It didn't matter anyway, as Tway rolled in his birdie putt for a 69—277 and a two-stroke victory.

Southwestern Bell Colonial National Invitation—$1,000,000
Winner: Ian Baker-Finch

Ian Baker-Finch was not well known to Americans before the Southwestern Bell Colonial National Invitation tournament in Forth Worth, Texas. Some remembered him for leading the 1984 British Open after the second and third rounds. Some might have recalled he played in some PGA Tour events. Others might have placed him as the Australian who placed third in the 1988 World Series of Golf. But Baker-Finch was better known in other parts of the world, a 28-year-old who competed in 1988 on four major tours—United States, Europe, Japan and Australia.

His World Series showing prompted Baker-Finch to give the U.S. tour his full attention in 1989. "You're never going to know in your heart that you are one of the best players unless you do it here," he said. Baker-Finch proved he's one of the best by winning the Colonial by four strokes, leading from start to finish, the first such triumph since Curtis Strange won the Nabisco Championship six months earlier.

Once again, weather played an important role. More than four inches of rain fell on Colonial Country Club on Tuesday and Wednesday and in its wake came winds that reached 25 miles an hour. The only hole that showed the aftereffects of the rain was the 18th, where a lift-and-clean rule was put into effect, but the course played longer than its nearly 7,100 yards. Baker-Finch's opening 65 gave him a one-stroke advantage on Isao Aoki and Fulton Allem. He threatened to turn the tournament into a one-man show in the middle of the second round before he stumbled at the end for 70 that left him at 135, one stroke in front of Nick Price and David Frost, each of whom had 66.

The tournament became a two-man affair in the third round—Baker-Finch vs. Price. Ian's lead dwindled to one stroke when he bogeyed the 14th hole, but he birdied No. 15 from 25 feet, birdied No. 17 from 10 feet and Price bogeyed 17. Baker-Finch finished with another 65 that put him four strokes ahead at 10-under-par 200.

Baker-Finch admitted he didn't know how he would handle being in the lead going into the final round. "I believed I could win; I just didn't know how to go about doing it," he said. All he had to do, as it developed, was handle adversity and capitalize on others' mistakes. He failed to birdie the par-five opening hole and three-putted the second hole, and when Price went birdie-par, Baker-Finch's lead was cut in half. But Price retreated on the next three holes and the only threat Baker-Finch got after that was from Tim Simpson. Simpson birdied four of the first six holes, and when he birdied No. 13 he trailed Baker-Finch by only two strokes. Simpson double-bogeyed the 14th hole, three-putting from six feet, and afterward could only say, "Well, I put a little fear in him." Baker-Finch shot 70 for 270, and even though Simpson offered him final challenge, second place went to David Edwards, who shot an unobtrusive 65.

Bellsouth Atlanta Classic—$900,000
Winner: Scott Simpson

Before Scott Simpson won the U.S. Open in 1987, he was regarded as a solid, if unspectacular, player. When he won at The Olympic Club in San Francisco, it moved him up a notch. But Simpson had to wait almost two years for his next victory, and when it came in the Bellsouth Atlanta Classic, it was almost as if Simpson were one of the boys in what had been for the most part a no-name tournament.

For three rounds the contenders had names such as Jay Don Blake, Duffy Waldorf, Wayne Grady, Kent Kluba and Ray Stewart. Not easily recognizable. Bob Tway, winless for two and a half years from the 1986 PGA Championship until the 1989 Memorial, and Simpson brought order to the final round. Both finished with 67—278 totals, and Simpson won the playoff on the first hole with a par.

"It's been a long, long time. I would have been happy to finish second. But winning means a lot," Simpson said.

Until the dramatics of Simpson and Tway, the tournament was one for the usual supporting cast. Blake, a former NCAA champion from Utah State, led the first round with a six-under-par 66. Grady's 66 in the second round gave him the lead at 136, one stroke ahead of five, including Blake, who shot a 70 in the third round and regained the lead at 207, one stroke ahead of Waldorf.

Meanwhile, Simpson and Tway lurked in the second echelon. Simpson had 72-68-71 and Tway kept in step with him with 70-70-71. After 54 holes, they were in a group that trailed by four strokes.

Blake held tough for seven holes in the final round. Then the first cracks appeared: bogeys at the next three holes. He birdied Nos. 11 and 13 before he finally retreated with a bogey at No. 15 and a double bogey at No. 16 and a birdie at No. 17 left him needing an eagle at the final hole to tie. His 72 left him in a deadlock with Davis Love (70) for third place at 279.

Simpson and Tway shot matching 67s to tie at 278, but Simpson had to birdie the final hole to do it. The playoff began at the 206-yard No. 16 and Tway put himself in trouble by hitting his tee shot over the green. Simpson hit a three iron three feet from the hole. Simpson missed his birdie putt, but the miss came after Tway failed on a par putt.

Kemper Open—$900,000
Winner: Tom Byrum

Tom Byrum is an example that experience really is the best teacher. In his fourth year on the PGA Tour, he was winless when the Kemper Open began at the TPC at Avenel in Potomac, Maryland, but there had been two close brushes with victory: the 1986 Western Open, when he blew a lead with five holes to play, and the 1988 Pensacola Open, when he frittered away a four-stroke lead.

It was the memory of the Western Open, Byrum said, that led to his five-stroke victory in the Kemper Open, the first on the tour for the brothers from Oneida, South Dakota. (Older brother Curt had yet to win.) "It was a good way to lose and make myself stronger," Tom said after his steady 66-65-69-68—268, a 16-under-par score that broke the Avenel course record. Byrum began the final round with a two-stroke lead, expanded it to five strokes with birdies at the fourth, fifth and sixth holes, and nobody got closer than three strokes after that.

His record score was not unexpected. Avenel was in top condition, the greens were soft and the weather was hot, humid and calm. So it was no surprise when D.A. Weibring, fresh off a $120,000 victory in a two-day tournament in Pittsburgh, came out of the chute with a course-record 64. Fred Funk, golf coach at the University of Maryland, was right behind him at 65. Jay Don Blake and Don Pooley matched Weibring's record in the second round, Blake taking the lead at 132 and Pooley slipping a stroke behind him.

The leaders of the first two rounds stepped aside as the contenders over-took them in the last two rounds. Tommy Armour III turned in the fourth 64 of the week on Saturday and Byrum shot his 65. Now Byrum led at 200 and Armour, who three-putted twice, was two strokes back. Byrum capped his round with a 30-foot birdie putt at the final hole, a stroke that seemed to be a tip-off of what was to come the next day. After Byrum built his lead to five strokes in the final round, it was clear sailing until he hit a ripple at the 15th hole. Jim Thorpe birdied the hole and moments later Byrum bogeyed it, reducing Byrum's lead to three strokes. But Byrum, following teacher David Leadbetter's instructions to relax, hit an approach to within 15 inches for a cinch birdie at the 16th hole and all doubt disappeared.

Manufacturers Hanover Westchester Classic—$1,000,000
Winner: Wayne Grady

After four years on the PGA Tour, Wayne Grady was becoming discouraged that he had not won. He gave some thought to returning to his native Australia and playing there. Then came the Manufacturers Hanover Westchester Classic and after he won, Grady told the other players, "You're stuck with me now."

Grady's first U.S. triumph was as much a survival as it was a victory. With one round to play, 19 players were within four strokes of the lead; nine others were another stroke behind. And Westchester is a course that customarily yields low scores. But the Rye, New York, course was not its old self. The rough was thick and was made more difficult by rain Friday, and the wind that followed that rain put even more muscle into the tree-lined course.

All but Grady and Ronnie Black went by the wayside during the final round. Black birdied the 18th hole for 68 and 277, then damned himself for the bogey he made at No. 17 while waiting for the others to finish. Only Grady caught him, birdieing the 18th for 72. Their 277s matched the tournament high set by Jack Renner in 1979.

The playoff was over quickly. It began at the 314-yard No. 10, a hole with trouble mainly around the green. Black eschewed a driver and played his tee shot about 65 yards short of the green. Grady went with his driver and left himself a pitch of about 25 yards. Blake's approach was about 25 feet from the hole and he two-putted. Grady hit a wedge to five feet and birdied.

It looked like it would be another low-scoring tournament when Tom Sieckmann opened with 64 and Rocco Mediate, 65, but they moved out of the picture as the weather took a turn for the worse. Grady added 65 to his opening 69 to tie Sieckmann and Dick Mast for the lead after 36 holes. Curtis Strange, who was preparing to defend his U.S. Open title the following week, was among those that rain forced to finish their second rounds on Saturday, and he pulled to within three strokes of the lead with 65. A 74 that afternoon dropped him out of contention.

Grady, finishing just before nightfall, shot 71 and tied for the lead with J.C. Snead, who had 70, and Mast, who had 71. The race was tight, then people began to self-destruct. Snead triple-bogeyed the par-three No. 14. Mast started the day triple bogey, bogey. When Grady three-putted the 11th hole, Mark Lye was tied for the lead. But at No. 17 he hit his tee shot into the trees and triple bogeyed. Tom Watson double bogeyed the first hole, and he failed to birdie the par-five 18th after birdieing Nos. 16 and 17 and finished a stroke out of the playoff in a tie with Clarence Rose, who also failed to birdie the 18th.

Now it was Grady's tournament to win or lose. It looked as if it would be a win until he bogeyed the 16th hole, dropping him into a tie with Blake, who had finished. Grady's eight-iron approach went over the green at No. 17, putting him a stroke behind. But at No. 18 his three-wood second shot went to the back fringe of the green, and he nearly ended matters with a chip shot. However, he had to sink an eight-foot putt to force the playoff. "I was thinking, you've been leading this tournament since Friday afternoon. You can't blow it now."

Canadian Open—$900,000
Winner: Steve Jones

Steve Jones, who won the first two tournaments of the year, claimed the Canadian Open title at Glen Abbey in Oakville, Ontario, by virtually demolishing the last three holes on the course the last three days. Jones' scores were 67-64-70-70—271. That's 17 under par. Of the 83 players who made the 36-hole cut (two under par), all finished under par for 72 holes.

Glen Abbey is not usually so kind, but there were extenuating circumstances. Thunder clouds rolled in Thursday morning and broke loose before play began. As a result, the first players teed off at 12:45 p.m., and when darkness fell the last groups had just passed the ninth hole. Jim Gallagher, Jr., led those who finished with an eight-under-par 64, a score that was posted every day.

The finish of the first round Friday was delayed for 90 minutes by fog. When the last shot was fired, it was dark and the 64 shooter of the day was Jones, whose 36-hole 131 total gave him a one-stroke lead over Gallagher. With a prediction of more rain Saturday, players started on both nines, a prudent decision. The rain broke again just as the last players finished and this day the 64 was posted by Clark Burroughs, giving him a two-stroke lead over Jones.

The weather and the resultant easier pin positions made Glen Abbey an easy track, and the tournament was still wide open with 18 holes to play. The daily 64 on Sunday was shot by Mike Hulbert, but the showdown was between the players who started one-two at the outset of the round. Hulbert's 64 gave him a 273 and a tie for second place, but he was hopeless as Jones and Burroughs came down the stretch.

Burroughs, a second-year player without a victory, made a double bogey at the seventh hole after hitting his ball into the water and Jones took the lead. Burroughs got the stroke back with a birdie at the next hole. When they teed off at the 16th, Jones trailed Burroughs by a stroke, but up ahead were the three holes he played the best. He had birdied Nos. 16, 17 and 18 the previous two days. At the 516-yard 16th, Jones hit a sand wedge to within eight feet of the hole and the birdie putt tied him for the lead. At No. 17, Jones hit a 182-yard eight iron out of the rough to within nine feet and birdied, as Burroughs bunkered and bogeyed. Jones played the par-five No. 18 conservatively after Burroughs hit his second shot over the green, but nearly rued his decision when Burroughs almost birdied. Burroughs' 74 tied him for second place.

Beatrice Western Open—$1,000,000
Winner: Mark McCumber

The Beatrice Western Open at Butler National Golf Club was again a scene of disappointment for Peter Jacobsen. Needing a par at the last hole to win in 1988, Jacobsen hit his approach into the water and his double bogey gave the victory to Jim Benepe. This time, Jacobsen carried his misery into an extra day, three-putting the first playoff hole on Monday, missing the second putt from four feet, after he had tied Mark McCumber at 275 for 72 holes.

McCumber had won the Western Open in 1984, sinking an 18-foot birdie putt at the final hole. This time, he faded a five iron over the trees and water at No. 18 and into a greenside bunker. He needed a par to tie Jacobsen and got it with a six-foot putt after blasting out of the sand. That finished off a 69—Jacobsen had shot a 68—and normally they would have headed for the No. 10 tee for a playoff. But the final round had been delayed for more than three hours and both players agreed they would have been able to play only one more hole, so why not delay the playoff to the next morning? It was a short morning as McCumber picked up his seventh career victory.

Earlier in the day, it looked as if McCumber might be the most likely not to make a playoff from among the multitude that began the round in contention. McCumber had back spasms at the 12th hole of the first round. A rain storm hit as McCumber strode to the tee at the par-three eighth hole. "The delay scared me. That's the last thing I needed, to sit down for three hours," McCumber said. When play resumed, McCumber hit his tee shot into the trees, but saved par by chipping in. The spasms began again at the ninth hole, but he dropped a par putt from 10 feet there, a big putt. His caddy sprayed his back with a freezing agent at the 10th tee and he had no more trouble with his back the rest of the way.

The trouble, instead, came from Jacobsen and Paul Azinger. A bogey at the ninth hole had dropped Azinger three strokes back. He birdied Nos. 10 and 11 to close in. Then Jacobsen began a charge, birdieing Nos. 12 and 14 to take a two-stroke lead. McCumber birdied No. 13. Jacobsen bogeyed No. 15. At No. 17, Jacobsen came out of a bunker to sink an 18-footer for par, then parred the troublesome 18th for 68. McCumber was faced with a six-foot par putt at the 18th hole to send the tournament into overtime and he made it for 69. Azinger nearly made a three-man playoff, missing a birdie putt at No. 18 and settling for third place with 69—276.

McCumber and Jacobsen bettered the Butler National record of 276 set by Tom Weiskopf in 1982. In the first round, Chip Beck played his first six holes in six under par, including putts of 60 feet (for eagle) and 32, 30 and 30 feet for birdies, as he grabbed the lead with an eight-under 64. Azinger (67-68) and McCumber (68-67) took the 36-hole lead as Beck slipped to 71. Larry Mize shot 67 in the third round and tied for the lead with McCumber, who had 69. Mize stayed in contention in the final round until the 13th hole, where he hit his tee shot into the water and took double bogey. Then it became a showdown among McCumber, Jacobsen and Azinger.

Canon Greater Hartford Open—$1,000,000
Winner: Paul Azinger

Although Mark McCumber won the Western Open, Paul Azinger felt just as happy placing one stroke behind. "I played awesome today. I thought I was going to win," Azinger said. The feeling persisted through the Canon Greater Hartford Open, which Azinger did win with a startling shot. Facing a possible playoff with Wayne Levi after blowing a comfortable lead, Azinger chipped in from 45 feet at the final hole to win his first tournament in more than a year.

Azinger's victory on rounds of 65-70-67-65—267 was worth $180,000, but of even greater benefit in his estimation was it clinched a place for him on the U.S. Ryder Cup team.

Kenny Knox, Wayne Grady and Levi led the field into the final round, but 20 players were within four shots of the lead. Azinger was one stroke behind. He hit a pitching wedge to five feet at the first hole for a birdie and was off on a run. He birdied Nos. 2, 4, 5, 7 and 9, playing the front nine in 30, and suddenly was three strokes in front.

The touch left Azinger as quickly as it came, especially his touch with the wedge. He missed a five-foot birdie putt at the 10th hole and sank a six-footer to save par at the 11th and began to question himself. "It was a real Jekyll and Hyde round," he said. "After the 10th hole I became unsure about myself. My frame of mind changed."

As Azinger struggled to make pars, Levi began making birdies—at Nos. 8, 9, 10 and 12—and when Grady looked at another birdie putt at No. 13 for a share of the lead, Azinger and his caddy talked about how "Levi was a gambler and wouldn't back up." So Azinger immediately bogeyed No. 16. But Levi bogeyed it, too, and when Azinger teed off at No. 18 he and Levi, playing a group behind him, were tied for the lead.

Azinger drove into the right rough, leaving himself with a poor lie from 187 yards. Azinger's six iron went to the right, but the ball hit the hillside and bounced down into the short grass behind the green. Azinger had cut his ball with the shot and after playing companion Bill Britton agreed, he placed a new ball, then chipped it into the hole.

Levi, lining up a 15-foot birdie putt at the 17th green, heard the roar and said to himself, "I'd better make this." His putt brushed the edge of the cup. Levi drove into the fairway at No. 18, but he pushed his approach and, like Azinger's ball, it hopped and skipped down the hillside, only into a better position, 15 feet above the hole. But he missed the putt.

Azinger's opening 65 had tied Knox and Bob Gilder for the lead. He dropped back with 70 on the second day, a round that belonged to 49-year-old Lee Trevino, whose 64 put him in a tie for second place at 134, two strokes behind Knox. Trevino ultimately finished in a tie for fourth place at 271.

Anheuser-Busch Classic—$850,000
Winner: Mike Donald

Before the Anheuser-Busch Classic in Williamsburg, Virginia, Mike Donald hadn't won in nine years on the PGA Tour. He finally won, but had to survive a lengthy playoff.

Rain sent the playoff into a second day. It also may have prevented the playoff from involving four men instead of three. Mike Hulbert took the lead in the final round with an eagle at the par-five 15th hole, but dropped back into a tie with Donald, Hal Sutton and Tim Simpson with three putts at the next hole. The rain came down as Sutton and Hulbert reached the 18th tee and Simpson was on the green. Simpson putted out for a par, but Sutton and Hulbert had to wait on the tee for about 15 minutes to let the rain subside. Then they both hit poor tee shots. Both recovered nicely, Sutton saving par with an eight-foot putt, but Hulbert failed on a five-footer and had to settle for fourth place, a stroke behind Donald, Sutton and Simpson, who finished at 16-under-par 268. Donald had 65, Sutton 68, Simpson 67 and Hulbert 70.

Donald, Sutton and Simpson began the playoff with pars at the 16th hole and had just hit their tee shots at the par-three 17th when the skies let loose again. After waiting nearly an hour, all got pars. Sutton dropped out of the playoff at the third hole, No. 18, which had troubled him all week, with a bogey after a poor tee shot. By now it was too dark to continue, so Donald and Simpson put their clubs aside until the next morning. They didn't have them out very long Monday morning as Donald ended it at the fourth (16th) hole by sinking a 10-foot birdie putt.

Perhaps the strength of the field also had something to do with Donald's first triumph. Many of the top players were in Scotland preparing for the British Open, leaving only four of the top 25 money winners to play at Williamsburg. Among them was U.S. Open champion Curtis Strange, the Kingsmill touring pro. The course played longer than its 6,776 yards because of heavy rains, but it also played easier. The players took advantage of it from the start. Simpson and Sutton each reeled off five birdies and an eagle in the first round for 64s, one better than Hulbert and Chris Perry. Donald had 67. Wind toughened the course for the second round, but some were able to cope with it, most notably Hulbert, whose 66—131 total gave him a one-stroke edge on Tim Norris, Don Shirey and Roger Maltbie, who escaped missing the cut with a record-tying 63.

Hulbert held onto his lead in the third round with 68 for a 199 total, but the field bunched up behind him. Simpson was at 201, Maltbie and Norris at 202 and Donald, with 70, was at 203. Hulbert took his one-stroke lead into the final nine holes. Then the race really became tight, with Donald, Sutton, Simpson and Blaine McCallister battling for the lead. McCallister eventually backed up, leaving the chase to Donald, Simpson, Sutton and Hulbert.

Hardee's Classic—$700,000
Winner: Curt Byrum

When his brother, Tom, won the Kemper Open in June, the monkey jumped on Curt Byrum's back. Curt, two years older than Tom, was always the "one that was one-up." Now here was Tom winning a PGA Tour event before his older brother. Unthinkable. So driven by a desire not to let his brother show him up, Curt Byrum turned what had been a trying year into a good one by winning the Hardee's Classic by one stroke over Bill Britton and Brian Tennyson.

The Hardee's Classic, formerly the Quad Cities Open, is played at the same time as the British Open. Thus it often produces a winner of no great reputation, possibly a star of the future, if you will. Curt Byrum had been on tour for seven years and, after placing second in the Hardee's Classic in 1986 and the Memorial in 1987, he was regarded as a man with a bright future. Still, Tom had won first.

"I said, 'Let's see if we can go out and win this thing.' I had my mind set on the trophy all the way," Byrum said after shooting 66-67-69-66—268 at unusually tough Oakwood Country Club in Coal Valley, Illinois.

Wind inflated the scores on Thursday, although Blaine McCallister managed a five-under-par 65 that gave him a one-stroke lead over Byrum and two newcomers, Cary Hungate and David Toms. Byrum leaped ahead of McCallister and into the lead with his 67 in the second round, even though McCallister shot 69. McCallister, the defending champion, regained the lead with 67 in the third round, but Byrum was among three players just a stroke back.

Byrum had taken a two-stroke lead into the final round in 1986 and finished second. "I was a lot more nervous then," he said. The final round looked as if it would be bad for anybody with shaky nerves. Barry Jaeckel, seven strokes out of the lead after 54 holes, shot 63 and finished with 271. And Jim Gallagher, Jr., Tom Sieckmann and Andrew Magee were making overtures. Amid all the jockeying for the lead, Byrum scored five birdies in six holes and suddenly had a four-stroke lead. When he got to the 18th tee, only Britton and Tennyson had realistic chances of catching him. All he needed at the final hole was a bogey to win. He played the tight, 378-yard 18th conservatively, using an iron off the tee. His approach left him 40 feet from the hole, and he safely three-putted for victory.

The victories by Curt and Tom marked the first time brothers had won on the PGA Tour in the same year since Dave and Mike Hill did it in 1972.

Buick Open—$1,000,000
Winner: Leonard Thompson

As the eight-foot par putt dropped at the 18th hole at Warwick Hills Golf Club in Grand Blanc, Michigan, Leonard Thompson raised his head and smiled through teary eyes, lifting an arm into the air to indicate he could make a pressure putt of that length. Most everyone understood the gesture, because Thompson had a feeling he might have blown the victory when he missed a putt of shorter length while three-putting the 17th green.

Payne Stewart and Hal Sutton were on the course behind Thompson. "I thought if I birdied 18, then they'd have to come after me," he said. "I never thought they would bogey the last hole, not both of them."

Sutton and Stewart were tied for the lead with Thompson as they stepped to the tee at the 17th hole, a par-three. Sutton had even more trouble on the green than Thompson, four-putting and burying his chances. Stewart parred and now he needed a par to force a playoff, a birdie to win. His approach at No. 18 found a bunker and he came out long, his ball stopping at about the spot from where Thompson had made his saving putt. Stewart's putt failed to drop.

Leonard could hardly believe it. The last time he had won a tournament was in 1977—the 12-year gap between victories is a PGA record— and the $180,000 he won represented not only his biggest paycheck but more than he had won the two previous years combined. At 42, Thompson's career had seemed to be fading although in his two tournaments before the Buick Open he had played well.

Nevertheless, when he opened with 65, he caused Bernie Smilovitz, a Detroit television sportscaster, to comment "the Tigers lost again and Leonard Thompson is leading the Buick Open and I can't explain either one." Thompson saw the telecast and, a self-described redneck, he took the heat. Still, there was nothing in Thompson's resume that justified his protest. He had struggled just to stay on tour for five years, losing his exempt status for a 147th place finish in 1987, and was 154th on the money list going into the Buick Open.

Thompson followed his opening 65 with 71 that dropped him a stroke off the pace, as Sutton and Doug Tewell took over. Stewart carved out 64 in the third round and Thompson, with 69, trailed by three strokes. It looked as if all he had to play for was a good payday. But Thompson birdied the first two holes in the last round, saved par on a couple other holes and when he birdied Nos. 13 and 15—a 457-yarder rated as the toughest hole on the course—he began thinking of victory. "I knew I was close," he said, although he kept his eyes off the leaderboard.

So Thompson gambled. At the 580-yard No. 16, he was about 280 yards from the green after a good drive. "If it hadn't been the last round, I would have laid up, but it's been 12 years since I was in this position and who knows if I'll be there again?" Thompson said. He went for the green with a driver from the fairway. It didn't quite make the green but it left him with an easy chip to about a foot, and the birdie putt gave him the lead. Then he looked at the leaderboard, saw his position and promptly three-putted, missing a two-footer for par. Then he sweated out the threats by Sutton and Stewart, thankful neither tied him. He said, "I couldn't have beaten either one of them in a playoff."

Federal Express St. Jude Classic—$1,000,000
Winner: John Mahaffey

John Mahaffey admitted that winning the Tournament Players Championship in 1986 had an effect on his career. "I became complacent for a year or so and when I decided I really wanted to play golf, I couldn't play as well as I wanted," he said. "I almost wrote off this year." So Mahaffey became just a face in the crowd, a 41-year-old veteran apparently destined to just make a living before beginning a second career as a senior.

When Leonard Thompson won the Buick Open at 42, the competitive juices started flowing. The result was a victory in the Federal Express St. Jude Classic at the new TPC course at Southwind near Memphis, Tennessee, his first since his Tournament Players Championship.

For three rounds, he was just a veteran player, apparently just trying to make a paycheck.

It was a week for veterans. Doug Tewell, approaching 40, started with a nine-under-par 63. Ed Fiori, 36, took the lead after 36 holes with 65-67—132. And Hubert Green, one of the consultants on the design of the course, finished with 63 that jumped him into a tie for second place, three stokes behind Mahaffey's 16-under-par 272.

Fiori, the leader by two strokes after 36 holes, got to 11 under par in the third round then crashed, the final blow coming when he hit his ball out of bounds at the 13th hole and double-bogeyed. As Fiori stepped aside, Bernhard Langer, Bob Gilder, Mike Donald, Bob Tway and Billy Ray Brown battled for the lead, and Gilder and Langer emerged on top by a stroke with birdies at the 16th hole. Mahaffey shot a 66 and was virtually unnoticed, three strokes behind the leaders.

On the first hole of the final round, Mahaffey hit an eight iron to within 15 feet of the hole. "I thought, 'Let's be aggressive,'" he said. The ensuing birdie touched off three more birdies on the front nine and put him in pursuit of Langer, who had the lead at the time. Mahaffey bogeyed No. 11 but birdied Nos. 12 and 13. Langer, playing behind him, double bogeyed the 13th after hitting his tee shot into the water, and suddenly Mahaffey was in front. His lead lasted only one hole as he found the water at No. 14 and had to sink a good putt just to save bogey. Donald, parred with him, hit the green at the par-three hole and could have tied with par, but he three-putted. "That was the turning point for me," Donald said.

Unperturbed by the bogey, Mahaffey sank a 20-foot putt for birdie at No. 15 that erased everybody but Gilder. Mahaffey took care of him by sinking an 18-foot birdie putt at No. 17 that doubled his lead to two strokes. Gilder birdied No. 16, but he three-putted No. 17 and Mahaffey's 65 gave him a comfortable three-stroke victory. Green tried to make it uncomfortable. He went out in 30 and was 11 under par for the round with two holes to go. He began the day nine strokes behind and now here he was in contention and threatening to tie the PGA 18-hole record of 59 set by Al Geiberger in this same tournament at Colonial Country Club in 1977. But Green bogeyed the final holes for 63 that tied him with Tway, Langer and Gilder for second place. Mahaffey was aware of what Green was doing and afterward he said jokingly, "Even if he shoots 59, he loses by a stroke."

The International—$1,100,000
Winner: Greg Norman

Greg Norman's showing in the PGA Championship after opening with a 74 was typical of his recent play. Open with a poor round, then get better every day, ending with "I'm not so far back a 60 wouldn't help." Then he goes out in the last round and tries to shoot 60 . . . and sometimes comes pretty close.

It's the type of approach that can pay off with an avalanche of birdies. Which made Norman a prime candidate to win The International at Castle Pines Golf Club in Castle Rock, Colorado. The International uses a revised Stableford scoring system that awards points for eagles and birdies and subtracts points for bogeys and double bogeys. Pars mean nothing.

So it was that two weeks after the PGA Championship, Norman put his game in gear and won the tournament that seemed to be made for him. His nine points for the first two rounds and his 11 points in the third round merely put him in position to make one of his runs in the final round. Given that opportunity, Norman fought off challenges from Clarence Rose, Chip Beck and Billy Andrade to win on the final day with 13 points.

Under the tournament's Stableford system, eight points are awarded for a double eagle, five for an eagle, two for a birdie, none for a par, minus one for bogey and minus three for double bogey or worse. Under the tournament's original format, there were cuts every day, but that was changed to allow everyone to play at least 36 holes, with the points for the first two days being added together. In the third and fourth rounds, only the points made those days count. The change was applauded by the players. What wasn't applauded was a pairing system that gave starting times in the next round based on the previous day's scores, a format which proved to be detrimental to, among others, Nick Price, the leader after the first two rounds.

Price gathered 12 points in the first round and eight in the second for a total of 20 points for a one-point edge on Steve Elkington and Doug Tewell. Norman made the cut with nine. Defending champion Joey Sindelar, who with Bruce Lietzke were the only players to make the finals in all three previous tournaments, failed to make the cut. Price was in the final pairing the next day and that proved to be a disadvantage. The early players had relatively calm conditions; Price and other later players were faced with intermittent rain and wind. Price got only two points and missed the cut.

"I just think it (the pairing system) stinks," Price said. "I've never been in a tournament where I've been penalized for playing well, but I feel like I was penalized today."

Meanwhile, Rose was just hanging on. He tied with six others and went into a playoff for the last six spots after the first two rounds. A double bogey at the first hole left Rose and Dave Eichelberger as the sole contenders for one spot and they went four more holes before Rose won with a birdie. After Saturday's third round, Rose was again in a playoff and he, Steve Pate, Ian Baker-Finch and Chris Perry advanced as Trevor Dodds was eliminated. Norman qualified comfortably with 11 points, three behind leader Ted Schulz.

All of the previous scoring didn't count, of course, when the final round began with a field of 24 players. Norman came out storming, birdieing the first two holes for four points. Halfway through the round he had 10 points and it looked as if he could walk in. Rose, Beck and Andrade made runs at him to make it interesting. But Norman was not to be denied. He made only one bogey, sinking a four-footer at the 15th hole for what he called "probably the shot that won the tournament," and finished with 13 points, two ahead of Rose.

Fred Meyer Challenge—$700,000
Winners: Joey Sindelar and Craig Stadler

Joey Sindelar and Craig Stadler won the Fred Meyer Challenge, a better-ball event hosted by Peter Jacobsen that has grown into one of the most outstanding unofficial tournaments. But Arnold Palmer and Bob Gilder provided the crowd with the biggest thrills on the final day of the 36-hole event in Portland, Oregon.

Palmer brought the house down by sinking a 25-foot birdie putt at the final hole that gave him and teammate third place with 65-62—127. The putt provided a bonus for Palmer and Jacobsen. They had a side bet of $100 each with Curtis Strange and Greg Norman, and Palmer's putt beat them, 62 to 63. "Can you imagine Peter and I beating the two greatest golfers in the world?" said Palmer with a laugh.

Sindelar and Stadler had a two-stroke lead and both had 12-foot birdie putts at the final green. It looked as if both could two-putt and win. Then Gilder almost spoiled their celebration when he hit a 50-yard wedge shot that missed falling for an eagle by scant inches. Sindelar and Stadler both parred to finish off a 62-63—125 total, but had Gilder's pitch fallen into the hole, they would have needed a birdie at the 558-yard finishing hole to avoid a playoff with Gilder and Mark Calcavecchia, who placed second at 62-64—126. The 19-under-par score of Sindelar and Stadler tied the tournament record set by Paul Azinger and Bob Tway a year earlier and earned them $50,000 each.

NEC World Series of Golf—$1,000,000
Winner: David Frost

The first time David Frost came from South Africa to play in the United States was in the 1983 World Series of Golf at the Firestone Country Club in Akron, Ohio. He went home impressed with both the tournament and the course. So it was that when he won the World Series in 1989, beating Ben Crenshaw in a playoff, he said, "It's very thrilling. The most thrilling feeling is to beat Ben Crenshaw, Payne Stewart and Greg Norman."

Firestone South always plays like a championship course, no matter the weather. For this tournament the weather was perfect. Yet Frost, with 70, 68, 69, 69, was the only player to shoot par or better every round, finishing with a four-under-par 276 total. Crenshaw, who opened with a six-under 64, hit the ball all over the course in the next three rounds. Only his putter—he used only 99 putts—kept him in contention, pulling him through for a 68 in the final round.

Crenshaw's erratic play got him into the trouble on the second playoff hole, and this time he had no time to recover. Frost, on the other hand, showed he can scramble, too. At the first playoff hole Frost drove into a fairway bunker, yet got a par after hitting a six iron to the green. Crenshaw drove into the rough, but a fine chip to three feet led to a par. At the 18th, Crenshaw drove into a difficult lie in the rough and failed to reach the green in two. Frost's approach stopped in the fringe to the right of the green. It wasn't a difficult shot and Frost managed it magnificently, chipping to two feet. Crenshaw hit a good chip to within nine feet, but after he failed to sink his par putt, Frost had little trouble sinking his putt for the victory.

It was the seventh defeat in seven playoffs for Crenshaw. "I'm beginning to have a real aversion to them," he said.

The World Series brings together most of the best players in the world—Seve Ballesteros was a notable exception—and included 20 of the top 25 money winners on the PGA Tour. U.S. Open champion Curtis Strange played 27 holes, then withdrew because of a neck ailment. His withdrawal cost him a chance to win the Vardon Trophy, given for low scoring average, and Player of the Year honors.

Three-time winner Steve Jones turned in a great 63 in the second round, but he had opened with 76 and Crenshaw maintained his lead with a scrambling 72. Another 72 in the third round dropped Crenshaw back behind Frost, who had a 69; Stewart, who had 68, and Paul Azinger, who had 67. That set up a tense final round in which Frost's steadiness off the tee and Crenshaw's ability to escape from trouble and putt left them the survivors.

Three bogeys and a double bogey on the first five holes removed Azinger from contention. Crenshaw hit a wild hook at the fourth hole and the resultant double bogey seemed to eliminate him, too, but he wasn't done. Crenshaw birdied the long 16th, giving him a one-stroke lead, but Frost birdied No. 17 from 18 feet and Stewart birdied the 16th, making it a three-way tie for the lead. Stewart's bid ended when he bogeyed the 17th after driving into the rough. Norman, meanwhile, was closing in until the 16th hole, where he dropped two back when Crenshaw birdied, and a drive into the rough at No. 17 negated a necessary birdie.

That left Crenshaw and Frost, and Crenshaw hung on doggedly. At No. 17, Crenshaw drove into the rough, failed to reach the green in two, yet made par with a chip shot to three feet. At No. 18, his approach went into a bunker, but he saved par with an explosion to three feet. Frost needed a birdie to win, a par to tie when he got to No. 18, which gave up only seven birdies all week. His approach went over the green into deep grass, but he hit a perfect shot out and got his par. After that, the playoff became almost academic.

Chattanooga Classic—$500,000
Winner: Stan Utley

Stan Utley, a former All-America at the University of Missouri, became one of the few players without a PGA Tour card to win a sponsored tournament when he won the Chattanooga Classic with a 17-under-par 263 at the short Valleybrook Country Club course in Chattanooga, Tennessee. Utley, who received a sponsor's exemption, had played in only seven previous tour-related events, twice in the U.S. Open.

He won with outstanding play on the final two rounds (64, 64) and with a nerveless birdie putt on the final green. Ray Stewart had finished the long final day with 63 for 264 and was anticipating a playoff when Utley came to the 18th green. But Utley, who had two-putted for birdie at the par-five 17th hole to tie Stewart for the lead, hit a five iron to within 12 feet of the hole at No. 18 and avoided a playoff by sinking the birdie putt.

The Chattanooga Classic, sponsored by Hamilton County, was a low-scoring, tightly contested tournament featuring a number of little-known players while most of the big names competed in the World Series of Golf. Mark Hayes opened with 62, then gave way to Ted Schulz, who shot 66, 63. Utley, with 69, 66, trailed by six strokes. Then the tournament became an endurance contest as rain halted play with a number of players still on the course in the third round. Utley had played only three holes and was forced to return the next morning to complete the round before starting the final round. John Daly had to do the same and, after taking the lead with 63 in the third round, the long day caught up with him.

Utley completed his third round with 64, then got involved in a battle for the lead. He took the lead for the first time with a birdie at the 10th hole, lost it, regained it with a birdie at No. 15, then had to birdie the last two holes to overtake Stewart, who eagled the 17th hole.

Greater Milwaukee Open—$800,000
Winner: Greg Norman

Milwaukee's golf fans were excited. Greg Norman had entered the Greater Milwaukee Open for the first time and they turned out in droves at Tuckaway Country Club to see him win. They weren't disappointed. Neither was Jamie Hutton, the leukemia victim whom Norman befriended at The Heritage Classic a year earlier. Norman won The Heritage and he won at Milwaukee, too, a classic case of a golfer coming through in style.

Norman unloaded with his driver on a 7,030-yard course that was tailored for unloading and that ability paid off handsomely. Norman was 11 under par on the par-five holes, as he won by three strokes over Andy Bean with 64, 69, 66, 70 for a 269 total. It was his second victory in three weeks, coming on the heels of The International, and his fifth of the year worldwide.

Norman's opening 64 gave him a one-stroke lead and he dropped into a tie for the lead with Wayne Grady and Mark Lye at 133 with his 69 in the second round. His position excited the crowd even more, and Norman responded with 66 in the third round that opened up a four-stroke lead. "I don't know if we can beat him," said Wayne Levi, who gave it a try in the final round. Levi played the front nine in 32 on Sunday and tied with Norman, who missed a putt of less than three feet at the sixth hole on the way to a 36. It was beginning to look as if, instead of having someone hole a miraculous shot to beat him, Norman might beat himself. He missed a 12-foot putt for par at the 11th hole, but instead of deflating him, that mistake fired him up. "It got my juices flowing," he said.

He birdied the par-five 12th hole and, as Levi slipped to 71, the only man to overcome was Bean, who finished with 66 for 272. Norman took care of him by sinking a 25-foot birdie putt at the 13th hole and birdieing the par-five 16th.

B.C. Open—$500,000
Winner: Mike Hulbert

As children, Mike Hulbert and Joey Sindelar were friends in Horseheads, New York, which is about a 45-minute drive from Endicott, site of the B.C. Open. Sindelar was always the better golfer. Two weeks older than Hulbert, Sindelar had won five tournaments before the start of the 1989 season, including the B.C. Open twice; Hulbert had won only once.

The circumstances—the proximity to his home, his pal's victories—made Hulbert's triumph in the B.C. Open that much sweeter. "I never dreamed I would shoot 16 under here," he said after he beat Bob Estes on the first hole of a playoff after they had tied with 268 totals. Sindelar was two strokes behind Hulbert after 36 holes, but 74 in the third round relegated him to being a cheerleader.

Hulbert had spent time with teacher David Leadbetter two weeks before the tournament, working on his short game, and the schooling paid off. "I chipped and putted incredibly this week," Hulbert said. The last chip and putt came at the playoff hole, where he chipped to within 10 inches of the hole for an easy birdie that was the winner after Estes hit his ball over the green into a poor lie from which he hit his ball 18 feet past the hole.

Keith Clearwater led the first two rounds with rounds of 65 and 68, then marked time until he double-bogeyed the first hole in the final round. Estes, who had opened 66-68, came back with another 66 in the third round and took a one-stroke lead. Hulbert trailed by three strokes. Hulbert began the final round with a bogey that dropped him five behind, but he birdied the next four holes to move to within a stroke of Estes and Dave Eichelberger. Birdies at the eighth and 10th holes got him in a tie for the lead with Estes, Eichelberger and Steve Elkington. Estes birdied No. 11, then could do nothing but par the rest of the way. Elkington came in with a sensational 62, but that left him a stroke shy of Estes' 268 total. Eichelberger bogeyed No. 14, then hit into the water and double-bogeyed No. 15 and he was gone. Hulbert caught Estes with a 25-foot birdie putt at No. 16 and saved par at the final two holes, hitting a bunker shot to within 18 inches of the hole at No. 17 and making a good chip at No. 18.

The playoff ended quickly when Estes hit his shot over the green at the first hole. "I knew not to go over that green, but with a sand wedge I wasn't even sure I could carry the green," he said. "It's a dream come true, to win here, so close to home," Hulbert said.

Bank of Boston Classic—$700,000
Winner: Blaine McCallister

In the 1986 Bank of Boston Classic, Gene Sauers birdied the third hole of a playoff to beat old buddy Blaine McCallister, but the defeat was not a total disaster for McCallister. "That tournament proved to me that I could play on the PGA Tour, and that's what I wanted to do," McCallister said. After several starts and stops, McCallister found himself, finally winning the 1988 Hardee's Classic. So when McCallister came back to Sutton, Massachusetts, for the Bank of Boston this year, he said he was on a mission to win.

And win he did, surviving a virtual gang charge in the final round to win by one stroke over Brad Faxon with 67-67-71-66—271. It was his second victory of the year; his first came in the Honda Classic in March and, like his earlier career, his last two rounds were a struggle.

Don Pooley started 66-65, a record for Pleasant Valley Country Club, but McCallister was only three strokes behind and he had plenty of company. Pooley slipped to 72 in the third round, dropping into a tie for the lead with Faxon, one ahead of Mark Calcavecchia, tuning up for the Ryder Cup matches, and Peter Jacobsen.

Calcavecchia, the defending champion, opened the final round with birdies at the first two holes and threatened to make it a runaway, but the runaway never developed. Nick Price, too far behind to make a charge for the victory, blasted out 62 in the final round, but in the final stages it looked as if the winner would come from the group of McCallister, Faxon, Calcavecchia, Fuzzy Zoeller, Pooley and Chris Perry, who at one time shared the lead.

Calcavecchia bogeyed Nos. 13 and 16 and retreated, Perry's 66 wasn't enough and finally it was just McCallister and Faxon. With help from the crowd—"the putt is straight in"—McCallister sank a 25-foot birdie at the 17th hole to go 12 under par and he finished 13 under with a three-foot birdie putt at No. 18 after nearly reaching the green with two drivers at the 583-yard par-five. Faxon was facing a 10-foot birdie putt at No. 16 when McCallister's putt dropped at No. 18 and knew he had to birdie two of the last three holes to force a playoff. He got the birdie at No. 16, but didn't get the necessary second one, finishing with 69 for 272.

Southern Open—$400,000
Winner: Ted Schulz

Ted Schulz had won more than $230,000 for the year prior to the Southern Open, but he had to be one of the least-known $200,000 winners on the tour. He had played the tour with little success in 1986, lost his card, spent 1988 on the Asian Tour and regained his card at the end of the year. He finally got his first victory in the Southern Open in Columbus, Georgia, the 11th first-time winner in 20 years of the tournament.

Schulz had led at Pebble Beach earlier in the year, which probably prepared him for the pressure he would receive in the Southern Open. He shot 66, 66, 68 in the first three rounds, yet trailed David Canipe by one stroke. Canipe and Jay Haas, who was tied with Schulz after 54 holes, both shot 64s in the third round. Canipe collapsed in the final round with a 76. Haas, on the other hand, wouldn't go away, briefly holding the lead in the final round. Haas and Tim Simpson stayed on Schulz' heels after Schulz took the lead with two birdies on the first three holes, although Simpson didn't do it until later in the round. Simpson, who began the round six strokes out of the lead, shot a seven-under-par 63, his 10-foot putt at the final hole putting him in a tie for the lead with Schulz, who was still on the course. Haas managed 68 that tied him with Simpson at 267.

Schulz birdied No. 11 to get to 13 under par, Simpson's finishing score. He made a nice save of par at No. 16, then sank the decisive birdie putt at No. 17, a 15-footer following a neat seven iron.

Centel Classic—$750,000
Winner: Bill Britton

Bill Britton picked a good place to take a special niche in PGA Tour history by winning the Centel Classic in Tallahassee, Florida. His first victory in nine years on the tour made him the last winner of the Centel Classic and he achieved it while sitting in his hotel room. Britton took a four-stroke lead over Ronnie Black when he shot a 63 in the third round and never had to hit another shot as rain washed out the fourth round.

Britton was just a face in the crowd in the first two rounds amid a controversy over Tom Pernice. Tournament director Mike Shea had prevailed upon teaching pro Peter Kostis to give up his sponsor's exemption to allow Pernice a shot at gaining an exemption for the 1990 tour. Some players thought Shea was out of line and might have set a precedent, but Pernice made him look good by starting out 68-65 to take a one-stroke lead over Black (67-67) and Jim Carter (73-61).

Britton, with 71-66, trailed by four strokes but quickly reversed that margin with 63 Saturday as Black slipped to 70 and Carter crumbled to 74. Britton hadn't left for the course when he learned he had won the next day. Pernice tied for fourth, six strokes behind Britton, and the $31,000 he won was a big boost toward his exemption hopes.

Centel dropped the Tallahassee venue to become sponsor of the Western Open in 1990, but it also signed an agreement to sponsor an LPGA tournament in Tallahassee.

Texas Open Presented By Nabisco—$600,000
Winner: Donnie Hammond

If this is Texas, it must be time for some records to be broken and the players didn't disappoint in the Texas Open at Oak Hills Country Club in San Antonio.

Donnie Hammond won by seven strokes with 65-64-65-64—258, just one stroke off the tour record for 72 holes of 257 set by Mike Souchak in the 1955 Texas Open at Brackenridge Park. The portent of things to come was given in the first round when Lanny Wadkins, Tom Sieckmann and Mark Wiebe all matched the course record with eight-under-par 62s. In the second round, Paul Azinger shot 62 that gave him a total of 126, equaling Tommy Bolt's record for 36 holes set in the 1954 Virginia Beach Open.

Azinger hadn't planned on competing in the Texas Open. The fish weren't biting back home in Florida, so he put his fishing gear aside. Azinger followed his 62 with 70, which is like six over par instead of even-par in the Texas Open, and slipped to two strokes behind Hammond, along with Bob Lohr and Duffy Waldorf. Azinger birdied the first hole on Sunday to cut the margin to one stroke, but three straight bogeys defused his charge. Hammond's only birdie on the front side came at the par-five No. 5, where he two-putted.

Hammond marched in place as the others retreated, and as he turned for home his lead was up to four strokes. Hammond sank a 30-foot putt for eagle at No. 10 and he widened his lead to six strokes with a 12-foot birdie putt at No. 12. Now the only questions were how much would he win by and would he break the tour record. A four iron to three feet at No. 15 got him to 21 under par and a 20-foot birdie putt at No. 17 put him 22 under, one stroke away from Souchak's record. He drove into the rough at No. 18 and had to sink an eight-foot par-saving putt just to finish one stroke shy of the record for his second tour victory.

Walt Disney World/Oldsmobile Classic—$800,000
Winner: Tim Simpson

In the past, golf was No. 1 with Tim Simpson. He was engrossed in it. Everything else was a distant second. But in recent years his perspective and his priorities were changed by several incidents. There was his daughter Katie, who lingered near death after her birth three years ago; there was the daughter of his tailor, who was paralyzed from the chest down in an auto accident. Katie lived, and the tailor's daughter graduated from high school and entered college, and Simpson learned that golf should be enjoyed, that it's not a life-and-death matter.

So it was when Paul Azinger began reeling off birdies in the final round of the Walt Disney World/Oldsmobile Classic in Orlando, Florida, Simpson was able to concentrate on his own game. When it came down to Simpson and Donnie Hammond, Tim was able to sink a crucial putt at the 17th hole for his second victory of the year and his third since joining the tour in 1977.

Simpson's week started with another tragedy. During the Shootout that preceded the tournament, a spectator died in Simpson's gallery. "I got chills up my back and tears in my eyes," he said. "It's a lot easier to win when you think life is so fragile."

Simpson was undeterred when he opened the tournament with 65 and found himself four strokes behind Bob Tway, who made almost every putt he faced. Tway had one of those lucky days, and did not break 70 again. Simpson took the lead with 67 for a 132 total, and Hammond shot 65 that put him five strokes behind. The weather for the third round, played on Friday, turned windy and cold and the scores reflected the conditions. Only 11 players broke 70. Hammond's second successive 65 was a marvel and moved him into a tie for the lead with Simpson, who had 70.

Azinger went on a tear early in the final round. He birdied seven of the first nine holes, and nine of the first 12, and moved in front. He didn't move out of reach, his putter costing strokes at the sixth, 10th and 13th holes. When he hit his drive under a tree and bogeyed No. 14, then hit his ball into the lake at No. 16 for another bogey, he faded to 68 and tied for third. Curtis Strange also made a charge, birdieing seven of the first 12 holes to move from eight back to one back, but a bogey at No. 15 stopped him. He settled for 66 and a tie for eighth place. Kenny Knox also threatened but was unable to birdie any of the last five holes and tied Azinger and Fred Couples at 274.

So it came down to Simpson and Hammond, who were two strokes ahead of the field with two holes to play. At No. 17, Simpson had a 60-foot putt for birdie and hit it 12 feet past the hole. Hammond made an easy par. With the pressure on, Simpson made his putt for par to remain in a tie. At No. 18, Hammond hit his drive into the rough and his shot to the green was blocked by a small tree. Simpson reached the green in two, 10 feet from the hole. Hammond hit his approach into a bunker next to the green and blasted to 20 feet. Hammond failed to sink his putt, and Simpson won with 70—272 by two-putting. "I didn't expect Tim to make that putt," said Hammond of Simpson's 12-footer at No. 17. "It surprised me." But Hammond's $86,400 check for second place earned him some consolation, a place in the rich Nabisco Championship.

Nabisco Championship—$2,500,000
Winner: Tom Kite

Tom Kite won $450,000 in prize plus a $175,000 bonus for being the No. 1 money winner of the year in the Nabisco Championship. That moved him to first place on the all-time earnings list with $5,600,691, ahead of Tom Watson. It was Kite's third victory of the year—he also won The Nestle Invitational and The Players Championship—and was his 13th triumph in 17 years on the tour.

The field consisted of the top 30 money winners and determined both the year's leading money winner and the PGA Player of the Year. Kite won the money title with $1,395,278, nearly $195,000 more than Payne Stewart, who could have traded places with Kite with some better putting on the closing holes. Kite also was named Player of the Year under the PGA point system.

Stewart won the MCI Heritage Classic in the spring on this same Harbour Town Links on Hilton Head, South Carolina. When he played the front nine of the final round in 29 strokes it looked as if no one would catch him. Even with a marvelous 66, Stewart left the door open and Kite walked in, while Wayne Levi stumbled on the doorstep.

Greg Norman, who won the 1988 Heritage, got off to a fast start, his 67 leaving him tied with Mark O'Meara, two strokes behind Donnie Hammond. Norman failed to cope with the winds that swirled over the course Friday and Sunday and finished eight strokes back at 284.

Kite, who cut his golfing teeth on the winds of Texas, found the conditions very much to his liking in the second round. He shot 65 that gave him a 36-hole 134 total. Hammond slipped to second place, four strokes behind, by bogeying the last three holes, and O'Meara joined him with a double bogey at the 18th hole after hitting into the marsh. "I hope the wind blows the next two days," Kite said. It didn't blow on Saturday, and Kite shot 74 that dropped him to one behind Hammond, who had 69, and two behind Levi, who shot a course record-tying 63.

Meanwhile, Stewart had shot 69, 70, 71 and was lingering four shots off the lead. The wind kicked up again on Sunday, but for nine holes it didn't seem to bother Stewart. He birdied the first five holes, including an 18-foot putt at No. 3 and a 20-footer at No. 4, and sank a pitching wedge from 121 yards for an eagle-two at the ninth hole. He went out in 29 and had gone from four behind to three ahead. The back nine had given Stewart trouble all week. He lost a stroke from his lead with a bogey at No. 11 and parred until he reached the pivotal 18th.

O'Meara, Fred Couples, Norman, Hammond and Curtis Strange had made tentative stabs at the lead, but when Stewart reached No. 18 the only ones who concerned him were Kite and Levi. Stewart hit the green, about 25 feet from the hole. Two putts would almost certainly clinch the victory. He left his first putt more than three feet short and pulled the next one. That cut his lead to one stroke, and Kite wiped it out when he rode the wind with a 189-yard seven iron to within three feet of the hole at the par-three No. 17, and sank the birdie putt. Kite missed the green at No. 18, but chipped to within three feet and was perfect on the tying par putt. He tied Stewart at eight-under 276 with 68 to Stewart's 66. Levi, who needed a birdie at the final hole to tie them, hit his approach shot over the green and his bogey gave him a tie for third place at 278 with Paul Azinger.

The playoff began at the par-four 16th, and they tied with pars, Stewart after hitting the green from a fairway bunker and Kite by chipping to within three feet of the cup. Stewart failed to reach the green at the par-three No. 17, and Kite knocked his tee shot into the middle of the green, about 25 feet from the hole. Stewart was strong with his putt from the fringe, his ball going nearly five feet past the hole. Kite chipped close and tapped in. Stewart's attempt went past the cup on the right.

"This doesn't make up for the fiasco at Oak Hill (U.S. Open)," Kite said. "But a lot of people probably thought the Open was the end of my career, or the end of my winning on tour. I knew I would win in my heart and now everyone knows."

Isuzu Kapalua International—$650,000
Winner: Peter Jacobsen

Peter Jacobsen had a lot of fun on the Hawaiian island of Maui during the Isuzu Kapalua International. During the day he put together the shots that led to the tournament victory, and at night he teamed with Mark Lye and Payne Stewart to form Jake Trout and the Flounders, a musical threesome. But the tournament triumph was more enjoyable for a man who has seldom tasted victory—official or unofficial—since his last victory in 1984.

It took extra holes to do it. Jacobsen and Steve Pate tied at 270, Jacobsen with 66 and Pate, 67, the final day. The playoff began at the 16th hole, and Pate almost ended it there. His birdie putt lipped out. At No. 17, Jacobsen sank a 12-foot par putt for a half. Both players left their approaches about 30 yards short of the green at the par-five No. 18. The next shot decided matters. Jacobsen chipped to within a foot of the hole; Pate left his ball about 25 feet short and failed to hole his putt.

Jacobsen shot 69s in the first two rounds, trailing Donnie Hammond by five strokes after 18 holes and by seven after 36 holes. Robert Wrenn, who shot 64 in the second round, came back with 67 the next day to take the lead, one stroke ahead of Pate and two ahead of Jacobsen. Jacobsen's 66 got a boost with a hole-in-one at the 12th.

RMCC Invitational Hosted By Greg Norman—$1,000,000
Winners: Curtis Strange and Mark O'Meara

With Mark O'Meara as his partner this time, Curtis Strange continued adding to his bankroll in autumn team events by winning the inaugural $1 million Ronald McDonald Children's Charities Invitational Hosted By Greg Norman.

The team of Strange and O'Meara led every round of the 54-hole tournament, which was played under different formats each day—alternate shot, best-ball and finally scramble. They had rounds of 66, 62, 62 for a 190 total and a six-stroke victory at 26 under par on the new Sherwood Country Club course in Thousand Oaks, California. Since the Ryder Cup—in which Strange birdied the last four holes to win his singles match—the two-time defending U.S. Open champion had won the Dunhill Cup ($100,000), Four Tours Championship ($65,000) and now the RMCC Invitational, which paid $125,000 each to Strange and O'Meara.

The runners-up were the teams of Tom Weiskopf and Lanny Wadkins, and Bernhard Langer and John Mahaffey (196), then tied for fourth were Raymond Floyd and Chip Beck along with the host, Norman, and Jack Nicklaus (197), who designed the course. Norman and Nicklaus, who finished poorly in the first round for a 74, shot a remarkable 58 in the scramble format on the last day. They shot 10-under 26 on the last nine, with two eagles and six birdies, including Norman's chip-in from the fringe at the finish, after which he bowed to the delighted crowd.

If anyone in such circumstances ever deserved a bow, it was Norman, who was ever the gracious host, down to slicing the pork at the Saturday night Aussie Barbecue. The RMCC Invitational was Norman's idea, inspired by his victory three years ago in the Bay Hill Member-Guest, with photographer/friend Lawrence Levy, under similar formats. He took the concept to the McDonald's Corporation, one of his sponsors, and six other sponsors were eventually enlisted (Dole, Lexus, American Airlines, Penske, Reebok and Spalding), along with television coverage by ESPN and ABC. The tournament, a PGA Tour-sanctioned event, raised $1 million for the various children's charities funded by RMCC.

J.C. Penney Classic—$1,000,000
Winners: Bill Glasson and Pat Bradley

Bill Glasson and Pat Bradley were a team that had overcome adversity. Glasson had undergone four operations on his sinuses since winning the Doral Open in March, and Bradley had made a marvelous recovery from hyperthyroidism. When Bradley faced a 12-foot putt on the third hole of their playoff with Duffy Waldorf and Patty Sheehan in the J.C. Penney Classic, it was just another obstacle to overcome. Bradley sank the putt, then sank a 10-foot eagle putt after Glasson's great three-iron shot to win the tournament at the next hole.

The J.C. Penney event is an alternate-shot event in which PGA Tour players are paired with LPGA members. Each hits a drive at every hole, then each hits his or her partner's ball on the second shot, then they alternate shots with a chosen ball. It's a break from the usual stroke play, and much of the success of a team depends on the ability of the woman with her tee shot.

Glasson said he wasn't going to play until he learned he could be paired with Bradley. Sheehan also wasn't going to play, but her house had been destroyed in the California earthquake, and she thought it might be good therapy to compete. Glasson and Bradley shot 68-68-65-66—267 at the Bardmoor Country Club in Largo, Florida, but they never led until the final round. Jay Don Blake and Tracy Kerdyk opened with 63, then fell a stroke behind four teams with 72 in the second round. Blake and Kerdyk bounced back with 64 in the third round, giving them a share of the lead with Gene Sauers and Beth Daniel, who had 63. Waldorf and Sheehan, with 64, were only a stroke behind, and Glasson and Bradley trailed by two strokes.

Sauers and Daniel bogeyed the first two holes of the final round and never recovered. Blake and Kerdyk couldn't make birdies and finished in a tie for third place with Sherri Turner and Ken Perry. Waldorf and Sheehan could only watch as their playing partners, Glasson and Bradley, birdied five of the first seven holes and pulled away to a four-stroke lead. "It looked like they were going to run away with it, but I had a feeling they would cool off," said Sheehan. They did, and when Waldorf sank a 20-foot putt at the 16th hole they were tied. Glasson sank a 10-foot birdie putt at No. 17 to give his team the lead again, but Sheehan sent the tournament into extra holes with a magnificent sand shot at No. 18 that allowed Waldorf a two-foot tap-in for birdie. Both teams were birdie-par on the first two extra holes before Bradley sank the clutch 12-footer at the third hole. When Waldorf failed to reach the green at the par-five No. 16 and Glasson put his shot 10 feet from the hole, the outcome was virtually settled. Sheehan missed a birdie putt from 30 feet, but it didn't matter as Bradley sank the 10-foot eagle putt.

Chrysler Team Championship—$600,000
Winners: David Ogrin and Ted Schulz

After David Ogrin and Ted Schulz had won the Chrysler Team Championship, David Ogrin professed to being one of the most surprised people on the course. "I thought we would need at least 62. I figured Mike and Bob could shoot 65 falling out of bed." But Mike Hulbert and Bob Tway, who had finished second-first-second in the previous three years, fell apart in the final round. Ogrin sank a 35-foot birdie putt at the final green to clinch their two-stroke victory over Blaine McCallister and Charlie Epps.

The Chrysler event is a better-ball tournament played on three Florida courses. The teams of Clark Burroughs and Lance Ten Broeck and Jim Rutledge and Mike Smith tied for the first-round lead with 60s. Epps, a 45-year-old who is golf director of a Texas company that operates five public courses and is on the teaching staff of *Golf Digest* magazine, and McCallister tacked 60 onto their opening 63 to take the 36-hole lead. The weather turned windy, wet and cold in the third round, and the team that handled the conditions best was Hulbert and Tway. They shot a 64 following rounds of 62 and 62 and moved into the lead, apparently ready to stay there.

Meanwhile, Ogrin and Schulz just stayed in position for three rounds, trailing by four strokes with 63-64-65. Schulz made four of their six birdies on the first 12 holes of the final round and suddenly they were tied for the lead. Then Hulbert and Tway bogeyed the 13th and 14th holes—one bogey can be a disaster in better-ball play—and Ogrin's 35-footer at the final hole wrapped it up. McCallister and Epps slipped past Hulbert and Tway with a 65 to claim second place with 259.

Spalding Invitational Pro-Am—$250,000
Winners: Bob Gilder and Mark Calcavecchia

The Spalding Invitational Pro-Am was held twice in 1989, on its traditional January dates and a second time over the last four days of the year to avoid a conflict with the early start of the 1990 PGA Tour schedule.

The venues were different but the winners' scores were the same—276 totals produced two-stroke victories for Bob Gilder in January over three Monterey Peninsula, California, courses, and for Mark Calcavecchia in December over the Desert Highlands layout in Scottsdale, Arizona.

What the two champions had most in common was their attitude. Glider, unable to obtain good results when he pressed, decided to accept whatever happened, which has been Calcavecchia's philosophy all along.

Gilder's triumph took place at the Golf Club of Quail Ridge, Carmel Valley Ranch and Poppy Hills. In rainy and cold conditions, Gilder shared the first-round lead with 66, fell one stroke behind with 72 in the second round, then went three strokes ahead after 54 holes with 68. Gilder finished with 70 and club professional Rob Boldt, who made a 123-yard wedge shot for eagle-two at the 15th hole, took second place.

Calcavecchia started with 69 at Desert Highlands and trailed LPGA pro Colleen Walker, who shot one of four 65s that were posted during the week. Calcavecchia didn't come close to that number but followed with rounds of 69 again and 67 to lead after 54 holes. While Calcavecchia finished with 71, Dave Barr shot a closing 66 to tie Bill Glasson for second place.

11. The U.S. Senior Tour

Not since the first years of the Senior PGA Tour has a player put together two such outstanding years in a row as Bob Charles did in 1988 and 1989 when he had seven victories in each year and led both season's money-winners with record amounts. In 1989, the New Zealander didn't nose in front of Orville Moody, his only real rival for the money title, until the final weeks of the season on the U.S. Tour. However, he had seven titles—five on the circuit plus victories in the Seniors British Open and the Fuji Electric Grand Slam in Japan—compared to Moody's prestigious wins in the U.S. Senior Open and the Mazda Tournament Players Championship. Only Don Bies, with four, scored more than a pair of victories during the 1989 season, in which there were a record 22 different winners for the year.

Charles was a remarkably consistent and busy senior during 1989, when his senior competitive earnings from all sources were $653,387, not to mention his $112,500 bonus as Senior Tour leading money-winner. He finished in the top 10 in all except four of his 30 starts and was fifth or better in 21 tournaments.

Bies, who like Moody employs the long putter and pendulum stroke on the greens, scored back-to-back victories in the Murata Reunion in Dallas and the new Tradition tournament at Desert Mountain in Arizona and repeated as winner in the rain-shortened GTE Kaanapali in December, the week after he won a "regular tour" event, the Air New Zealand/Shell Open.

In addition to Moody, six men were double winners. Gary Player, a six-time victor in 1988, won twice late in the season, but one was the RJR Championship that gave the Hall of Famer $202,500, his biggest check ever. Miller Barber, senior golf's biggest winner, ran his total of individual senior titles to 29 with early-season victories in the Tournament of Champions and Vintage Invitational in California. Jim Dent joined the circuit in May and won the Newport Cup and Syracuse Classic en route a near $400,000 half-year. Larry Mowry, Dave Hill and Bruce Crampton also added pairs of titles to their records, Mowry capturing the PGA Seniors Championship in February.

George Archer impacted the Senior Tour immediately upon arrival, winning the Gatlin Brothers Southwest Classic in his first outing, he and Dent being among seven first-time winners. Tom Shaw, Rives McBee and the surprising John Paul Cain also were rookie winners, while Homero Blancas and Charles Coody got their initial senior victories a little farther along.

The United States team regained the Chrysler Cup at Prestancia in Sarasota, the Americans' third victory in the four-year-old international competition patterned generally after the Ryder Cup. Perhaps, though, the biggest single subject of conversation during the season was about 1990, when the battle for shares of the $14 million in prize money was to be joined by Jack Nicklaus and, after his end-of-year debut, Lee Trevino.

MONY Senior Tournament of Champions—$250,000
Winner: Miller Barber

Miller Barber took care of one of his most impressive records early in 1989. When Barber won the MONY Senior Tournament of Champions for the second time the first week of January in California, he extended his unmatched accomplishment of having won at least one title in every one of his nine seasons on the Senior PGA Tour.

Barber's 25th individual Senior Tour victory in the 1989 opener at the plush LaCosta Country Club near San Diego, where the regular and senior champions of the year play separate events at the same time, came with shocking suddenness when he holed a long chip shot for a par 72 and an eight-under-par 280. The birdie gave Miller a one-stroke victory over a disappointed Dale Douglass, who appeared to have at least a playoff shot at the title, despite a closing bogey when Barber put his approach at the final hole just off the green, 40 feet from the cup. With seven birdies over an 11-hole stretch, Douglass had closed the six-shot gap he faced at the start of the round. Dale posted 67—281, then watched as Barber's transcontinental chip rolled into the cup. Miller had never won a tournament with a final-hole chip-in before. Nobody else was even close, with Bruce Crampton taking third place with 287 after a closing 76.

Those three players had things pretty much to themselves among the 14 seniors in the field. (Sixteen had qualified with 1988 wins, but Gary Player and Bob Charles declined invitations, Charles because of a recent hernia operation.) Douglass shot his first of two 67s Thursday and jumped off to a three-stroke lead over Crampton and Walt Zembriski and retained first place Friday with 72—139, leading Barber (73-67) and Crampton (70-70) by a shot. The second-day's play was punctuated by two-stroke penalties against Arnold Palmer and Harold Henning that stirred up a continuing argument of Palmer and others that the seniors should play from the same tees as the regular tour players in the Tournament of Champions. Tour officials shorten LaCosta's 7,012 yards more than 200 yards for the seniors and, on one of the affected holes, Palmer and Henning inadvertently teed off from the wrong area and incurred the penalties.

Barber added a 68 Saturday and took a three-shot advantage over Crampton with his 208, which, incidentally, was three strokes better than Steve Jones' leading 210 in the concurrent battle. Douglass struggled to 75 and bogeyed the first hole Sunday before mounting his near-miss charge.

General Foods PGA Senior Championship—$400,000
Winner: Larry Mowry

In 1987 and 1988, Larry Mowry established himself among the upper crust of the Senior PGA Tour with three victories in regular 54-hole circuit events, making a successful return from domination of the Florida mini-tours to competition against his old peers of the regular PGA Tour, circa 1960s. Mowry reached the top plateau in early February when he hung on for a one-stroke victory in the General Foods PGA Senior Championship, a circuit major that had had a distinguished list of victors in the 1980s.

The 53-year-old Mowry seized a three-stroke lead on the Champions course at the PGA National Golf Club with a third-round 65, the best score of the week at Palm Beach Gardens, and nosed out Miller Barber and Al Geiberger by a stroke with his final-round 73 for 281 and the $72,000 first prize. Actually, Larry lost and regained the lead from Barber twice during the final round before holing a winning six-foot putt at the 72nd hole.

Mike Hill, the youngest senior in the field just 13 days beyond his 50th birthday, shot a 67 in his first serious competition in eight years and seized a two-stroke lead over Geiberger Thursday. (Hill, a three-tournament winner during his PGA Tour career and Dave's brother, operated a golf course in Michigan through most of the 1980s.) He followed Friday with 71 and retained the lead, then by one over Geiberger and three over Barber, Mowry moved up with 69 after an opening 74. Hill's nerves lacked tournament toughness, and his putting tailed off the last two days, but he still managed a fourth-place-tie finish, six behind Mowry.

Larry's 65 on Saturday—seven birdies, no bogeys—was the only sub-70 round of the day as he raced from five behind to three in front of Geiberger and Barber, with Al taking a double-bogey at the last hole. The final round came down to three putts on the last green, Geiberger and Barber missing birdie efforts and Mowry canning the six-foot par putt. Larry had lost most of his lead when he bogeyed two of the first four holes, then went back in front to stay when he birdied the 10th and 11th. That two-shot margin enabled him to absorb one more bogey coming in to victory in a tournament that he had watched as a spectator in 1987 after failing to qualify for a spot in the field.

GTE Suncoast Classic—$300,000
Winner: Bob Charles

Stretches of brilliant shotmaking and putting combined with a shocking catastrophe to produce one of the most exciting finishes in the history of the Senior PGA Tour or, for that matter, of tournament golf, period, when the GTE Suncoast Classic came to its conclusion in Tampa, Florida, in mid-February.

The late Sunday theatrics obscured all that had gone before in the 54-hole tournament at Tampa Palms Golf and Country Club, but, for the record, Don Massengale led by two after 18 holes with 66, and Dave Hill took over after two rounds with 68-69—137, a stroke better than Bob Charles, the eventual winner; Doug Sanders and Chi Chi Rodriguez.

As the tournament neared its end Sunday, the fireworks began. Jim Ferree birdied eight times, including the 15th, 16th and 17th holes, to post an early 65 and 207. After a double bogey at the 13th hole, Harold Henning seemed out of it despite five earlier birdies, but he birdied the last four holes, the 18th from 30 feet for 67 to tie Ferree. Next, Charles. Seemingly en route to a bogey or worse at the 16th, he pitched in from 20 yards off the green, then birdied Nos. 17 and 18 for 69 and yet another 207.

Until moments before, these all appeared to be good for a three-way tie for second. Hill was confidently playing the 17th hole with a four-shot lead in hand at the time. Suddenly, his irons deserted him. He put two straight shots to the green in the water on the par-five hole and made a tough putt for a triple-bogey eight. The once-volatile Hill maintained his composure and sank a 15-foot birdie putt at the 18th for 70—207 and a spot in the playoff.

However, Dave and Ferree went out with pars at the first playoff hole as Henning made his fifth straight birdie and Charles his third. Both birdied the 18th again, Bob with a match of Harold's earlier monster there, and Charles, who has always been a great putter, holed from 15 feet for the victory when they returned to the 17th. It was his 10th official individual win on the Senior Tour since he arrived in 1986 and paid him $45,000.

Aetna Challenge—$300,000
Winner: Gene Littler

With his swing, rustiness is hard to spot in Gene Littler's game, but he contended that he was mentally rested but not mechanically solid when he made his first start of 1989 in the Aetna Challenge at Naples, Florida. Regardless, Littler scored one for the older players on the Senior PGA Tour at the Club at Pelican Bay, getting an assist from playing partner Harold Henning, his only serious rival in the stretch.

Littler shot 70-70-69—209, seven under par, in scoring his 14th individual victory in senior golf, eight of them considered official wins on the circuit. He did not win in 1988, the first season since he helped start the senior tour in 1980 that he failed to post a victory.

Littler and Henning locked up in the head-to-head battle after sharing the second-round lead with 70-70 starts for 140 and a two-stroke advantage over Bruce Crampton. Unseasonably cold and windy weather invaded Naples that late February weekend and the scores reflected it. The best score Friday was 70, the number posted by Miller Barber and Chick Evans along with Littler, Henning and Crampton.

The weather improved Sunday, but nobody took a run at the top three players in the standings. Crampton mounted a threat when he eagled the eighth hole, but he came back with a double bogey at the next hole and fell out of contention. Meanwhile, Henning had built a three-stroke lead over Littler on the front nine with 34 to Gene's 37. Harold still led by two after Littler had birdied the 11th and 12th and he birdied the 13th, but the South African came a cropper at the par-three 16th. He trapped his tee shot, took two blows to escape the sand, and double-bogeyed. Gene made it a three-stroke swing and took the lead when he holed an eight-foot birdie putt there. Another birdie from 10 feet on the final green established his two-stroke victory margin over Henning and brought him the $45,000 winner's check.

Vintage Chrysler Invitational—$370,000
Winner: Miller Barber

When Miller Barber began to pick off victories almost as soon as he joined the Senior PGA Tour in 1981, he said he felt like Jesse James. In the same frame of reference in 1989, Barber must feel like Jesse's father, especially after he heisted his second title of the young season with his one-stroke victory in the Vintage Chrysler Invitational at Indian Wells, California, in early March.

With the $55,500 first prize, Miller had stashed away more than $2 million in loot in those eight seasons, the first senior to pass that mark. The victory tied him with Don January, both with 26 individual titles to their credit. How much longer will he continue the "holdups?" Responds the 58-year-old Barber: "I'll just play as long as I feel competitive."

Miller was two strokes off the pace after the opening round over the Vintage Club's 6,819-yard Mountain Course as Bob Charles, another early-season winner despite off-season hernia surgery, shot 68 on the windy Thursday in the Southern California desert resort area. J.C. Goosie, the maestro of the mini-tours, moved into a tie with the southpaw Friday at 139, as Barber shot his second straight 70 for 140 and tour newcomer Tom Shaw and January posted 141s. Things tightened up at the top Saturday with three of golf's most successful players—Charles, Barber and two-time Vintage winner Gene Littler—holding the lead at 212 and Don Bies, Larry Mowry and Goosie sitting just a shot off the lead.

Charles, Mowry, Littler and Bies jockeyed with the lead on the front nine Sunday, Barber biding his time as he ran off eight pars. A five-iron approach to two feet brought Miller his first birdie at the ninth and it tied him with Mowry and Bies for the lead. Barber birdied the 11th and Mowry the 12th to move seven under and Miller birdied again at the 15th from four feet to go in front to stay. However, after his closing 69, his margin was just one stroke and he watched Mowry, needing an eagle from 18 feet, and Charles and Bies, needing birdies from 20 feet, all miss those chances on the last green.

MONY Arizona Classic—$300,000
Winner: Bruce Crampton

Bruce Crampton had won victories in just about every way imaginable among his 15 on the PGA Tour, 15 others on the Senior PGA Tour and a few assorted others, but he had never done it quite like he did in capturing the MONY Arizona Classic at The Pointe Golf Club in Phoenix. A phlegmatic player by nature, the transplanted Australian shook off apparent disaster late in the final round and bounced back to take the Arizona Classic title by a stroke with a 16-under-par 200.

Crampton emerged from a back-nine dogfight Sunday to take the lead with a birdie at the 12th hole. However, he gave it back when he bogeyed the 14th, 15th and 16th holes, falling a stroke behind Bobby Nichols, who had led for two days. Bruce then birdied the 17th from 10 feet and reached the green at the par-five finishing hole in two while Nichols was forced to play short of the green because of the poor position of his tee shot. After Bobby pitched 18 feet short of the cup, Crampton rolled his 65-foot putt to virtual tap-in range and knocked in the winning birdie after Nichols missed the 18-footer.

Low scores were fairly commonplace in the early going. Nichols led the way on Friday with a tournament-record 62 that gave him a three-stroke lead over Al Geiberger and five over Crampton. Nichols shot 67 Saturday for 129 and a two-stroke lead over Crampton (67-64), with Gene Littler (67-65) and Bob Boldt (70-62) another shot back. Boldt, a 52-year-old Californian who never won a penny on the regular tour, followed with another 70 and tied for third, his best showing yet on the Senior PGA Tour. Nichols shot 72 Sunday for his runner-up finish. Geiberger (69) and Littler (70) matched Boldt's 202.

Fuji Electric Grand Slam—$370,000
Winner: Bob Charles

Double winners are becoming rather commonplace in the Fuji Electric Grand Slam, the international senior tournament that draws heavily from the PGA Senior Tour for its stand at Oak Hills Country Club at Katori, Japan. When Bob Charles scored his second straight victory in the Japanese-based event, he joined Gene Littler and Lee Elder as two-time winners of the Grand Slam.

Late arrivals from South Africa, Charles and Orville Moody shared the first-round lead in the late March tournament with 67s, as Arnold Palmer shot 68 and Larry Mowry and Gene Littler posted 69s. Charles moved ahead to stay Saturday when he added 71 for 138 and a three-stroke lead over Mowry (72—141) as Moody soared to 76 and Palmer fell out of contention with 75. The New Zealand left-hander breezed to victory Sunday, his closing 69 giving him a four-stroke triumph over Mowry, Charles Coody and Don January, who had 211s. Mowry had 70, January 69 and Coody 68 Sunday. Coody had joined the ranks of the long-putter players after taking 38 putts with his regulation-sized putter the first day.

Attendance for the week topped 29,000, significant of the growing interest in senior golf in Japan. The crowds were the largest in the seven-year history of the tournament, which changed sponsorships to Fuji Electric from Coca Cola in 1988.

Murata Seniors Reunion—$300,000
Winner: Don Bies

Don Bies erased any doubts about the validity of his fast 1988 start on the Senior PGA Tour when the 1989 circuit reached Dallas (prematurely, tournament officials complained) for the Murata Seniors Reunion at Stonebriar Country Club. Switching to an Orville Moody-style tall putter, Bies made a runaway of the competition, the only player in the field seemingly able to cope with the winds of early spring and inferior course conditions caused by the event's late March dates. Even with a closing 73, the Seattle pro breezed to a six-stroke victory with his eight-under-par 208. Said Harold Henning, the runner-up: "I didn't even think about catching the guy. Catching him was like trying to fly a kite to the moon."

Don, who joined the senior circuit with little fanfare at the start of the 1988 season and rolled to two victories and 11th position on the final money list, never trailed at Stonebriar, where Don January, the long-time star of both tours is golf director. Bies shot 68 on a quite-chilly Friday and was the only man to break 70 in the PGA Senior Tour's counterpart of the "Crosby" format in which each pro has an amateur partner. Bruce Crampton and Gary Player were next with 71s.

Wielding the oversized putter as though he had been using it for years, Bies broke things wide open Saturday. With wind gusts recorded up to 50 miles per hour, 50 of the 70 pros in the field shot 78 or worse, but Bies calmly racked up five birdies and 13 pars for 67 that gave him an eight-stroke lead, by three the Senior Tour record for 36 holes. Despite two early bogeys, Bies was never in serious trouble Sunday as Saturday runner-up Crampton, his playing partner, headed toward a final 78 and sixth place. Don made no other bogeys, birdied the 12th with a 25-footer and coasted to the 73 and $45,000. Henning, who had started the day nine back, shot 70 to finish second for the third time in 1989. His 214 was the only other sub-par total as January placed third at 217 and Mike Hill and Al tied for fourth at 220, 12 strokes behind the winner, who had just one three-putt green for the distance.

The Tradition At Desert Mountain—$600,000
Winner: Don Bies

With the guidance and clout of two former presidents of the PGA of America and the wide-open checkbook of developer Lyle Anderson, the Tradition at Desert Mountain debuted on the Senior PGA Tour in mid-April in the high desert outside of Scottsdale, Arizona, a cut above the normal circuit tournament. Hopeful that they can turn the event with the optimistic title into a Senior Tour major counterpart to the Masters, the tournament directors established a four-round format with no pro-amateur and the season's third largest individual purse of $600,000.

Whatever the Tradition turns out to be, Don Bies got it started this year with a hard-won victory in a stretch battle with Gary Player, becoming the season's first back-to-back winner in the process. The second-year senior from Washington came from a shot off the lead in Sunday's fourth round at the Jack Nicklaus-designed Desert Mountain Course, shooting a closing 66 for 275 and a one-shot triumph over Player, the third-round leader. Bies had 13 birdies in his last 36 holes as he posted his fourth Senior Tour victory in 10 months and made it $135,000 in winnings in 14 days. His overall winnings in just 16 months on the circuit were fast approaching his $538,209 career total on the PGA Tour.

Bies may have gotten his victory impetus at the end of the opening round. He eagled the par-five finishing hole to salvage a one-under-par 71 and stay in the ballpark with the Thursday leaders—Gene Littler at 66, Player at 67 and Walter Zembriski at 68. Don's 70 on Friday left him five behind Player (69) and Littler (70) at 136. His move came Saturday as he posted a solid 68 that included seven birdies, all from within 15 feet, and the 209 put him just a shot behind when Player inexplicably bogeyed the last two of the course's three back-nine par-fives for 72 and 208.

With four birdies on the first 11 holes Sunday, Bies forged a two-shot margin over Player, only to have Gary come back with an eagle three at the

12th to overtake him. Don went back in front when he birdied the par-five 15th off a huge drive and hung on with one-putt pars at the next two holes and nailed the rich victory with a par five as Player missed a tying birdie putt from 11 feet. The consistently high-finishing Harold Henning took third place with 280.

Chrysler Cup—$600,000
Winner: United States

American pros have been giving way to International stars of late in most of the important competitions, but in the Senior realm the United States continues to hold sway in the team events; specifically, the Chrysler Cup competition with its Ryder Cup-like format. In fact, the American seniors scored their third victory in the four-year history of the event, played for the third time this year at the TPC at Prestancia in Sarasota, Florida, by the most decisive score yet.

The U.S. victory margin of 71-29 prompted some expressions of concern for the competitive future of the event, considering that Jack Nicklaus and Lee Trevino will be eligible for the 1990 matches and the International team has no newcomers of consequence on the horizon.

Depth was certainly a factor this year at Prestancia. All eight U.S. players brought strong credentials to Prestancia, but the Internationals, unable to attract several able seniors from abroad who don't play on the Senior PGA Tour, had to go as eighth man with Doug Dalziel, a native Scot who has been a club pro throughout his career, mostly in this country, and a non-winner in tour competition. To boot, the Internationals' hottest players coming in—Bob Charles, Harold Henning, Bruce Crampton and Captain Gary Player—had mediocre weeks at best, participating in only three wins and three ties among them.

In four-ball competition the first day, the U.S. took a 10-6 lead after four close matches, the most decisive the 3-and-1 victory of Gene Littler and Al Geiberger over Henning and Bruce Devlin during which Geiberger made a double-eagle at the par-five 15th hole. In Friday's singles matches, the Americans won five and tied another to open a 21-11 lead, capturing three of the matches with two birdies and a par on the 18th green.

The U.S. picked up 17-1/2 of the available 28 points in the four-ball stroke play competition Saturday and carried a 38-1/2—21-1/2 margin into Sunday's stroke-play singles. The decision came early as Chi Chi Rodriguez, then Geiberger and, for the clincher, Walt Zembriski won the first three matches to put the U.S. over the needed 50-point total. Captain Arnold Palmer, Miller Barber and Dave Hill also won and Orville Moody tied with Roberto De Vicenzo in later-finishing matches, Peter Thomson getting the only International victory Sunday.

Liberty Mutual Legends of Golf—$650,000
Winners: Al Geiberger and Harold Henning

Al Geiberger and Harold Henning tried to give away the 12th Liberty Mutual Legends of Golf but found no takers. So, they went ahead and won it anyway, the first victory of the season for either player and $60,000 apiece for their bank accounts. Their winning total—29-under-par 251 on the par-70 Onion Creek Country Club course in Austin, Texas—equalled the tournament record.

The American/South African tandem and the Down Under pairing of New Zealander Bob Charles and Australian Bruce Devlin had things pretty much to themselves the first three days. Those two teams jumped in front Thursday with 61s, then Geiberger and Henning took things into their own hands, firing another 61 to move three strokes in front of Charles and Devlin. The latter duo chipped one stroke off the margin with a 61 Saturday to the 62 posted by Al and Harold for 184. Nobody else was within six shots of the lead.

"We opened the door and four or five teams slipped in," said Henning of the team's poor performance Sunday. Geiberger/Henning didn't make a birdie until the ninth and that just got them back to even after a bogey at the fourth. Fortunately for them, Charles and Devlin weren't playing much better, though they did nose in front on the first nine before almost running out of birdies. Dale Douglass and Charles Coody shot the week's best score—60—and wound up third, just two shots behind the winners. Bruce Crampton and Orville Moody, who had won the Legends the previous two years, also made a late charge before settling for 64 and 254, a stroke behind Douglass/Coody and tied with Dave Hill and Gardner Dickinson.

Henning and Geiberger pulled themselves together at the 16th, changing their batting order (Henning hitting first) for the first time all week. Henning promptly birdied from four feet and they tied for the lead at the par-three 17th, where Geiberger put his nine-iron shot eight feet from the hole and dropped the putt. Al was the hero at the 18th as well: Driver and four wood onto the green and two careful putts for birdie at the par-five with his partner's ball in the pocket. That left it in the hands of Charles, but the deadly putter missed from 14 feet after reaching the green in three and it was over.

RJR At The Dominion—$250,000
Winner: Larry Mowry

Things have rarely "come easy" for Larry Mowry in his golfing career and the pattern continued this year for him on the Senior PGA Tour. He had to hole a six-foot putt on the final green to win the PGA Senior Championship in February. Three months later, he scored his second one-stroke victory of the season, nipping Gay Brewer with a birdie on the last hole in the RJR at the Dominion in San Antonio, Texas. His winning 15-under-par 201 was a record score in the five-year old event.

The outcome was a particular disappointment for Brewer. The 57-year-old pro had not posted an individual victory since scoring his lone triumph on the Senior PGA Tour at Lexington, Kentucky, in 1984. He appeared to be on his way Friday when he opened with 65, a shot off the Dominion course record, and took a one-stroke lead over Mowry, Miller Barber, Don Massengale and Lou Graham. He had a run of six threes late in the round. Mowry eased in front Saturday, working a 67 from his second straight bogey-less round and 133 as Brewer shot 69 for 134, Harold Henning 65 and Barber 70 for 136. Larry posted four of his birdies on the back nine after nearly holing a wedge approach at No. 6 and took the lead when Gay three-putted at the 17th.

Mowry's putting was a bit shaky Sunday as the finish settled into a three-way fight with Brewer and Barber. After 12 holes, Larry had a two-stroke advantage on Brewer, but Barber birdied the 13th to catch Mowry at 15 under. Three holes later, all three were tied after Brewer birdied and the other two bogeyed the 16th hole. However, Barber, playing ahead of the final twosome, plugged his seven-iron tee shot in a bunker at the par-three 17th and took himself out of it with a double-bogey. Mowry had the best drive at the 18th and was able to rifle a two-iron shot just short of the green on the par-five hole. Brewer was 50 yards short with his second shot and failed to get close with his pitch. Larry then chipped to tap-in range and had the victory when Gay's 30-footer for a tie was off-line. All three contenders had 68s Sunday, Mowry's giving him the $37,500 first prize and his fifth Senior Tour title.

Bell Atlantic St. Christopher's Classic—$400,000
Winner: Dave Hill

Dave Hill evened his 1989 playoff record and snared his sixth Senior PGA Tour title when the circuit jumped east for its fifth appearance at Chester Valley Country Club near Philadelphia. Among the three losers in the GTE Suncoast Classic playoff in February after blowing a big lead, Hill came out the winner over Chi Chi Rodriguez after three holes of overtime in the Bell Atlantic St. Christopher's Classic.

Although the long putters were the talk of the week at Chester Valley and Rodriguez toyed with one the first day, he and Hill were using conventional putters as they battled for the title Sunday. Chi Chi carried two putters Friday, using his normal one just five times as he took the first-round lead with a three-under-par 67, a stroke better than Mike Hill, Orville Moody, Deray Simon and Tommy Aaron. Dave Hill, who had opened with a two-over 72, and big Jim Dent, making his first Senior Tour start, seized the second-round lead, Hill with 66 and Dent with a pair of 69s. With 72, Rodriguez was just a shot off the lead along with six other players.

Hill needed help from his putter on the back nine Sunday and got it. His tee shots with his three-wood strayed but he came up with clutch par putts four times in the closing stretch. One was from 35 feet at the 11th, but the key roller was on the 18th green, where he forged the tie with Rodriguez at 206 with a 10-foot par putt after Chi Chi had bogeyed the hole for 67 to Dave's 68. Harold Henning birdied the 17th but missed the playoff by a stroke when he parred the 18th for 68—207.

Rodriguez, the 1987 winner in Philadelphia and in serious contention for the first time this season, matched pars with Hill on the first extra hole and birdies on the second before an errant tee shot did him in. Chi Chi missed the green from the left rough and bogeyed the hole while Hill was registering a routine, two-putt par for the victory and $60,000 in prize money.

NYNEX/Golf Digest Commemorative—$300,000
Winner: Bob Charles

The week and the NYNEX/Golf Digest Commemorative tournament belonged to Bob Charles, who accomplished a feat that may be unprecedented in tour golf of any sort. Charles shot an opening round of 63 at Sleepy Hollow Country Club for the second year in a row and, just as he did in 1988, rolled to a wire-to-wire victory. Memory fails to produce a match for that. This time, his remarkable final score of 193 set not only a tournament record but also was the lowest 54-hole total in the history of the Senior PGA Tour, bettering by a stroke Don January's winning score in the 1984 du Maurier Champions event in Canada. Charles set the Commemorative record of 196 last year.

The five-stroke runaway of Charles went like this:

First Round—His opening, seven-under-par 63 gave him a two-shot edge over Don Bies, Frank Beard and Billy Casper, the tournament honoree this year. Bob birdied five in a row from the 11th through the 15th holes.

Second Round—Bob shot 65 for 128, tying the tour record for 36-hole starts. Even Bruce Crampton's blazing 64—five birdies on the first eight holes—failed to untrack the brilliant New Zealander. It merely moved him into a tie with Bies four strokes off the torrid pace of Charles. Dave Hill was another stroke back at 133.

Final Round—Charles didn't really have things to himself early Sunday, his deft putter keeping him well ahead even though Crampton and Bies each birdied three of their first six holes. When Bruce and Don birdied the seventh and Bob bogeyed the eighth, the margin was down to two. But, with Bies ready for a tap-in birdie at the ninth, Charles holed from 45 feet to maintain the margin and was never seriously threatened after that, before and after a 45-minute delay for a thunderstorm to come and go. He birdied the 13th after the rain and finished with 65 for the 193. Bies and Crampton shot 66s for 198s and joint possession of second place. The $45,000 triumph was the third of the season for the 1988 leading money-winner, following the GTE Suncoast Classic on the circuit and the Fuji Electric Grand Slam in Japan. He then had 11 official victories on the Senior Tour and several other non-circuit senior titles.

Southwestern Bell Classic—$300,000
Winner: Bobby Nichols

Even though he had not remained tour-active in the years immediately preceding his 50th birthday, most observers expected Bobby Nichols to become one of the more successful players on the Senior PGA Tour after he arrived in the spring of 1986. A former PGA champion and winner of

12 PGA Tour titles through 1974, Nichols had not played particularly well since he and two other pros suffered effects from a nearby lightning strike at the 1975 Western Open.

His early appearances and first-year victory in the then-team Showdown Classic with partner Curt Byrum indicated his game was reasonably sharp again. Yet he had to settle for five runner-up finishes and several other runs at victory over two years before finally nailing the elusive first individual win in the Southwestern Bell Classic at Oklahoma City's Quail Creek Golf and Country Club in late May. "I feel like I've played my best golf since joining the seniors, but I couldn't beat anybody," Nichols observed after the victory on the course where he and George Archer won the old National Team Championship in 1968. "I had a lot of opportunities and then something would happen."

Bobby had little reason to expect victory to happen at Quail Creek, since he had not made a single birdie in his last previous start at Philadelphia two weeks earlier. However, he made a few during the first two rounds in windy weather to keep himself in position behind leader Al Geiberger, who opened with 66-71 despite a heavy cold and was a shot ahead of Nichols and his pair of 69s. Orville Moody, Jim Dent and Paul Moran were at 139. Bobby moved in front early Sunday with birdies on the first two holes and, despite a bogey at the fifth, never trailed with his following 13 consecutive pars in winds that reached 35 mph. However, Moody rolled in a seven-foot birdie putt on the 18th green to force the tournament's second straight playoff . . . Player over Henning in 1988.

Nichols just missed a birdie putt on the first extra hole, Moody kept himself alive with a 15-foot par putt at the next hole after two errant shots, and Nichols ended it with a 12-foot birdie putt at the par-five 18th after a spectacular recovery shot over trees. Moody had also reached the green circuitously in three, but was 55 feet from the pin and missed that remote birdie chance.

Doug Sanders Kingwood Celebrity Classic—$300,000
Winner: Homero Blancas

The victory had to be doubly sweet for Homero Blancas. The second-year player on the Senior PGA Tour, competing in the city where he grew up, learned the game and starred in collegiate golf, held off the late threats of Bob Charles and Walter Zembriski and captured the Doug Sanders Kingwood Celebrity Classic at the Deerwood Club. It was the first Senior Tour victory for Blancas, who had left the PGA Tour early in the decade for a club job in Tucson, Arizona, and had not competed seriously in national tournaments for years until just before he turned 50 in March of 1988. He had last won in tour golf in the 1973 Monsanto Open at Pensacola, Florida.

Blancas got away weakly in Friday's opening round of the hybrid event that keeps amateurs in action that day and celebrities in the competition through Saturday. Homero shot 73, six strokes off the opening-day of leader Gary Player, but jumped into the fray Saturday with the round's best score of 65, his 138 leaving him just a stroke behind Player (67-70) and Al Geiberger (68-69). Blancas made his move on the strength of eight birdies as Player struggled with a balky putter.

An early three-putt bogey did not unsettle Homero, but, when he offset two quick birdies with two more bogeys, he was out in 37. Both Player and Geiberger were faltering toward closing 74 and 75, respectively, but Bob Charles had entered the picture. Gunning for his fourth 1989 victory, Charles had birdied four of his first six holes and moved momentarily into the lead from a five-stroke deficit. Bob bogeyed the seventh, though, and Blancas grabbed the lead when he wedged to 18 inches at the 11th and sank a 20-footer at the 12th for birdies. He made the last birdie of his closing 70 with a 40-footer from the fringe at the 15th and took a two-stroke lead to the 18th tee. He drove into the trees there and had to pitch out, but pumped a seven-iron 180 yards to eight feet and dropped the par putt for 70—208, the victory and its $45,000 paycheck, the second straight week that the Senior Tour saw one of its former PGA Tour winners take his first title on the over-50 circuit. Charles shot 68, and Zembriski shot 69 to tie for second at 210.

Mazda Senior TPC—$700,000
Winner: Orville Moody

Orville Moody had a peculiar record on the PGA Tour, his only official victory in his many seasons of campaigning being the very major U.S. Open Championship in 1969. On the other hand, Moody turned into a frequent winner of regular-stop events when he joined the Senior PGA Tour in 1984 and didn't put a "major" on that record until he made this year's Mazda Senior TPC his eighth individual victory. Two weeks after losing a playoff to Bobby Nichols at Oklahoma City, Orville rolled to a relatively easy win in the Senior TPC's final stand in Jacksonville, Florida. In 1990, the championship moves to Detroit.

The final edition on the Valley course at the TPC at Sawgrass brought the stars to the top, although on Sunday it was Charles Coody, rather than Gary Player and Arnold Palmer from among the contenders, who threw the only serious challenge at Moody, who had put together rounds of 67-69-64 and staked himself to a six-shot lead going into the final day. He eventually beat Coody by two with his 17-under-par 271.

Moody had shared the first-round lead at 67 with Palmer, Butch Baird, Lou Graham, Tom Shaw and Dick Howell, then yielded after two thunderstorm delays to Player, who shot 68-66—134 and led Baird by one, Moody, Palmer and Miller Barber by two. Orville went on a tear during the third round, which was once again rain-interrupted. After five holes, he was tied with Palmer, Player and Baird at nine under. Two birdies on the next four holes put him in front by a stroke, then he birdied five of the next six holes to go eight strokes on top of Player and Coody before parring in for the 64, a course and tournament record. Palmer had a 9-7-5-4-6 finish while Player and Coody picked up two strokes on the leader on the last two holes and trailed Moody by six after 54 holes.

Nobody ran at Moody on the front nine Sunday and he turned in 34, his six-shot lead intact. Coody began his belated charge at the 12th with a three-foot birdie putt, parred Nos. 13 and 14, birdied again at No. 15 and eagled the par-five 17th when he fired a five-iron shot 197 yards to gimme range.

Meanwhile, Moody had bogeyed the 16th from off the back edge. However, he responded to Coody's eagle with a birdie of his own at the 17th and parred the home hole to secure the two-stroke triumph with a 71. Moody, interestingly, acknowledged that it was nice to win a "major" on the Senior Tour but was more impressed with the $105,000 first-place check, his biggest ever. Player, with 68—274, finished third, while Palmer had a closing 67 for 278 and finished in a five-way tie for fourth, his best showing of the year.

Northville Long Island Classic—$350,000
Winner: Butch Baird

You've surely heard that old comment golfers make when expressing their surprise about a particularly low score: "He must have skipped a couple of holes." Well, make it "they" and you have it right about this year's Northville Long Island Classic. Butch Baird won the Northville tournament with an astonishing 183 (and a playoff) that really wasn't that astonishing because he and the rest of the field played only 48 holes to get into the overtime battle.

What happened that will probably put some asterisks into the Senior PGA Tour record book was that, with two greens unplayable and not repairable at the rain-soaked Meadow Brook Country Club, Senior Tour officials decided to declare the ninth and 14th out of play and go with a 16-hole, par-64 course. So, Baird was just nine under par in posting his second Senior Tour victory, the other coming in his rookie 1986 season in the now-defunct Cuyahoga International at Hilton Head, S.C.

Baird "broke" Al Geiberger's long-standing 18-hole record of 59 in the opening round at Meadow Brook after the continuing early-week downpours had washed out the Thursday pro-amateur. Butch shot *58 for a one-stroke lead over Paul Moran, George Lanning, Frank Beard, Orville Moody and Don Bies, then yielded first place to the ever-present Bob Charles Saturday. With 60-59—119, nine under, Charles moved into a one-shot advantage over Baird (62) and fellow lefty George Lanning (59-61).

Early problems, including a double-bogey at the sixth hole, took Charles out of contention, but few of the others. Defending champion Bies had a one-stroke lead until he drove under a tree at the 16th and bogeyed. Moody and Baird birdied there and Beard's par created a four-way tie at the top, which remained that way through the last two holes, Beard catching the corner of the cup with a seven-foot putt for the win on the last green. The playoff went only one hole, as Baird and Beard put their approaches so close together—3-1/2 feet from the cup—on the 10th green that a coin flip was necessary to determine who would putt first after Moody missed his birdie putt from 22 feet and Bies from 15. Beard missed, Baird made and collected the $52,500 first-place check.

MONY Syracuse Classic—$300,000
Winner: Jim Dent

Jim Dent became the newest member of the "Better With Age Club" on the Senior PGA Tour shortly after he qualified by passing his 50th birthday. In nearly 20 years on the regular PGA Tour, Dent frequently attracted attention with his prodigious length off the tee, but never converted that asset into a victory on the circuit. The only win he managed during that period was in a "minor league" event in Chattanooga in 1983. Yet, it took him little more than a month after joining the Senior Tour to put an official victory in his column, outracing Al Geiberger to the title in the MONY Syracuse Classic in late June.

Dent didn't seem to be a factor during the first two rounds as Dick Hendrickson, a 6'-7" former club professional from the Philadelphia area, dominated the tournament. Outplaying a somewhat talent-shy field for two days, the towering Hendrickson produced a pair of 66s to take a four-stroke lead over Harold Henning, as the No. 5 money winner the top player in the field, and Phil Rodgers, a prominent PGA Tour player of the 1960s who devoted the more recent years to teaching the game and a second-year man on the Senior Tour. Rodgers achieved his second-round 66 despite starting the day with a triple-bogey. Dent, a one-time caddy in his native Augusta, Georgia, was then five back after rounds of 69-68 and Geiberger seemed out of range entirely at 73-66—139.

But Lafayette Country Club, playing at 6,540 yards with five par-five holes, is always ripe for hot rounds, particularly from big hitters, and Jim made the most of it Sunday. He was four under on the par-fives and took the lead for keeps when a drive and a six iron to three feet set up an eagle at the 17th hole. His par at the 18th for 64 and 201 gave him a one-stroke advantage over Geiberger, who had dropped a 10-footer on the 18th green for his 10th birdie of the day, a 63 and 202. Hendrickson, who played a fairly good round for a man not accustomed to national tournament golf, still had a chance to tie at the final hole, but bogeyed and dropped to 203 with his 71, getting third place. Dent's final-round rally for the $45,000 first prize was the biggest final-round comeback of the season.

USGA Senior Open—$450,000
Winner: Orville Moody

Orville Moody joined an exclusive group at Laurel Valley, the distinguished golf club in Western Pennsylvania, when he captured the 10th U.S. Senior Open Championship on the second of July. Before him, only Arnold Palmer, Gary Player and Billy Casper had won both the U.S. Open and the U.S. Senior Open. Moody, the 1969 U.S. Open champion, who had taken another major—the Senior TPC—the month before, took charge of the final round with a sixth-hole eagle and went on to a two-under-par 70 and a 279, finishing two strokes in front of playing partner Frank Beard.

The tournament at Laurel Valley, which, along with more-famous Oakmont, brings national/international tournament golf periodically to Western Pennsylvania, was a rousing success. It was more or less dedicated to its one and

The Masters

Scott Hoch tosses his putter in despair after missing a two-foot putt for the Masters title.

Given a reprieve, Nick Faldo won with a 25-foot putt in the gloaming at No. 11, the second playoff hole.

The men to watch were first Seve Ballesteros (left), then Mike Reid (right) in the final round.

The agony of Greg Norman at Augusta is a now-familiar scene.

To everyone's surprise, especially his own, Lee Trevino was an early leader.

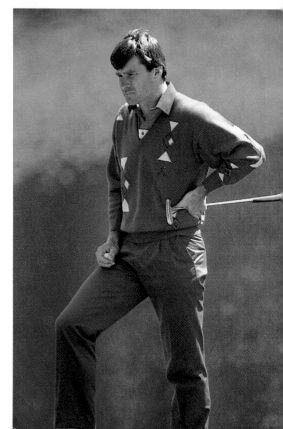

For Nick Faldo, a victory in the Masters did not come easily.

U.S. Open

Third-round leader Tom Kite struggled to a closing 78.

Holes-in-one were scored at No. 6 in the second round by Doug Weaver, Jerry Pate, Nick Price and Mark Wiebe, who were then called The Four Aces.

Although his first victory was more emotional, Curtis Strange obviously
relished his second U.S. Open title.

Runners-up in the U.S. Open
were (clockwise, from left)
Chip Beck, Ian Woosnam
and Mark McCumber.

British Open

Mark Calcavecchia's great play at No. 18—at the end of regulation and in the playoff—earned him the British Open trophy.

Greg Norman stormed
to a final-round 64,
birdied the first two
playoff holes, then lost
to Calcavecchia.

Tom Watson was one
shot off the pace enter-
ing the last round and
placed fourth.

The 36- and 54-hole leader, Wayne Grady was a British Open playoff victim.

A strong contender until his closing 74, Payne Stewart tied for eighth place.

PGA Championship

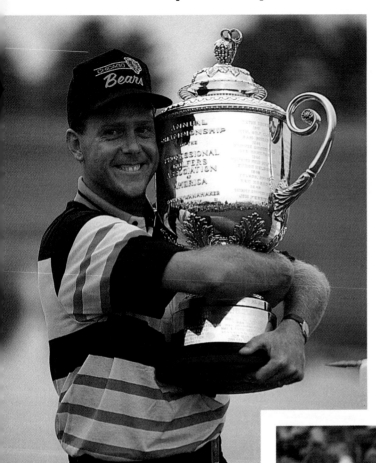

Payne Stewart became PGA champion—and a popular one in the colors of the home-town Chicago Bears.

The final blow for Mike Reid was this missed putt at No. 18.

Arnold Palmer excited the
crowds in the early rounds.

Andy Bean finished with 66 for a
second-place tie.

Tied for second, Curtis Strange could not get the break he needed.

Ryder Cup

The Ryder Cup ended in a tie, but the Europeans retained the cup.

Wives of the American players were in star-spangled apparel.

Photo: Danielle Fluer

Christy O'Connor, Jr., was overwhelmed by his success in the singles.

The American stalwarts included veteran Tom Watson (left) and Chip Beck, who won the most points.

There were some tense moments for European captain Tony Jacklin (with radio), alongside his stars, Seve Ballesteros and Jose-Maria Olazabal.

Dunhill Cup

Americans Curtis Strange, Mark Calcavecchia and Tom
Kite pose with the Dunhill Cup on the Swilken Bridge.

Greg Norman and the Australians were beaten
by France in the first round.

Christy O'Connor could not escape the Swilken
Burn in losing to Tom Kite in extra holes.

After a poor start, Mark Calcavecchia led the Americans to their Dunhill Cup triumph, scoring the final point against Japan.

World Match Play

After many disappointments, Nick Faldo finally took the Suntory World Match Play Championship.

Seve Ballesteros ranks behind only Gary Player in the World Match Play annals.

Ian Woosnam got to the final in pursuit of a second title.

only tournament professional, Arnold Palmer, a life-long resident of nearby Latrobe, who had deftly remodeled the course for the championship and was to celebrate his 60th birthday two months later. In fact, Palmer's poor play in front of the home folks—312 and a tie for 53rd place—was the only negative in a week that saw heavy June rains quit just in time for excellent course conditions.

Moody didn't really become a contender until the third round. Al Geiberger opened with 68 for a one-stroke lead over Harold Henning and unknown amateur Frank Boydston, a restaurant owner from Arizona. Beard jumped into the lead Friday with his 70-69, heading Bobby Nichols (70-70), Don Bies (74-66) and Geiberger (68-72) by a shot. At that point, Moody was six back after ho-hum rounds of 72-73, but the Sarge got it going Saturday. He fashioned a Senior-Open-record 64 which he called "one of the best rounds I've ever played . . . under these conditions (on) a championship golf course" and climbed into a first-place tie with Beard at 209, seven under par, leaving the rest of the field at least four strokes back. Orville had six birdies and an eagle in the 64, finishing with three birdies and an eagle on the last five holes, considered one of the tougher finishing stretches in golf.

The final round was head to head, Moody versus Beard, and it turned on the sixth hole, where Sarge rolled in a 30-foot eagle with his elongated putter to go a stroke in front. He stretched the lead to its final two strokes with a 12-foot birdie putt at No. 11. Beard's last chance at the spectacular and reachable par-five 18th—a gallery delight—ended when a poor drive prevented him from going for the green in two and a possible eagle.

Digital Classic—$300,000
Winner: Bob Charles

No surprise that Bob Charles was the first man of the Senior PGA Tour to score three 1989 victories. The most consistent player on the circuit the last two years, Charles annexed his third official title of the year and fourth overall (Fuji Electric Grand Slam in Japan) when he broke the stranglehold of Chi Chi Rodriguez on the Digital Classic at Concord, Massachusetts. These four victories during the first six-and-a-half months of 1989 followed seven 1988 triumphs, including five on the Senior Tour, as Charles' overall U.S. earnings topped $2 million for his career.

Though he opened reasonably with 69, it was apparent that a hurting Rodriguez was not about to become the first man in U.S. tournament golf to win the same event four years in a row since Walter Hagen's 1924-1927 run of PGA Championships. Clearly, a pinched-nerve problem contributed to a mediocre showing 13 strokes behind winner Charles. The great lefthander put a pair of 65s around a 70 for 200 and a three-shot victory over Mike Hill, another Senior Tour newcomer having a fine season.

With the opening 65, Charles trailed only Dale Douglass, who fired an eight-under 64 over the flat and wide-open Nashawtuc Country Club course on which 43 of the starters shot par or better. Bob lost his swing Saturday, shot 70 and wound up two strokes off the leading pace of Bruce Crampton (66-67—133) and Douglass (64-69—133). A long evening session on the practice tee apparently remedied Charles' troubles. All he had to do Sunday, it turned out, was wait for his putter to ignite as he hit every green and the 18th in two. Bob birdied the first hole, then not again until the ninth as Crampton, Douglass and Hill jockeyed for the lead. The putts began to drop for Charles at the 11th and he made four more on the way in for the closing 65. Hill shot 69 for 203 to edge into second place, a stroke in front of Crampton and Douglass, who both shot 71s Sunday.

Greater Grand Rapids Open—$300,000
Winner: John Paul Cain

On Monday, July 10th, John Paul Cain was just one of a group of over-50 golfers trying to win a spot in the field of the Greater Grand Rapids Open on the Senior PGA Tour. On Sunday, July 16th, he was the winner of the tournament in perhaps the most unlikely development in the 10-year history of the tour. It wasn't that he was the first man to come out of a Monday qualifier to win on the circuit. Larry Mowry did that at Richmond in 1987. But, Mowry had a solid professional background even though a non-winner on the PGA Tour. The 53-year-old Cain not only never played on the PGA Tour, but he was an amateur until 1988, talked into turning pro by Texas friend Bruce Crampton and John Brodie at the 1988 U.S. Senior Open.

Cain had fine amateur credentials, including victory in the Texas State Amateur and enshrinement in the Texas Golf Hall of Fame, but the Houston securities broker finished 15th in the national qualifier for the 1989 tour, so had no easy entrances to the Senior Tour tournaments. In the seven events into which he gained spots, he won less than $25,000 and placed no better than 10th before teeing off at the Elks Country Club in Grand Rapids.

John Paul attracted no attention Friday despite a 69 as Orville Moody fired in front with 64 and eight others were better than his two-under-par group.

Moody, the defending champion, settled for 70 Saturday and was tied for the lead with Walter Zembriski (68-66). Cain was then three back after a second-round 68. As it turned out, he got a great break in the pairings when he wound up grouped with Crampton and another friend from his amateur days in Texas, Bruce Devlin, who also were at 137 and obviously were the most likely to make moves Sunday. Instead, the 53-year-old Texan birdied the first two holes, five of the first nine and had the lead at the turn. After falling back with three-putt bogeys at the 10th and 11th, Cain came back with birdies at the 14th and 15th, parred Nos. 16, 17 and, with a clutch four-footer, No. 18 for 66 and 10-under 203. Charley Sifford, now 67, was already in with 204 after an astonishing 65, and Cain had the title and all of its spoils for a non-exempt player when Dave Hill, who had birdied the 14th, 15th and 16th holes, missed his birdie bid for a tie from 12 feet on the 18th green. Who knows how stockbroker Cain invested his $45,000 winner's check?

Ameritech Open—$500,000

Winner: Bruce Crampton

Bruce Crampton knew he could play Canterbury Golf Club when he arrived in Cleveland for the inaugural Ameritech Open, and he proved it by week's end. Crampton had finished second to Jack Nicklaus when Canterbury hosted the 1973 PGA Championship and to Chi Chi Rodriguez when the Senior TPC was last played there in 1986. Victory came in mid-July when Bruce fought off the bids of leading money-winner Orville Moody and Jim Ferree, who roared home with an eight-under-par 64 and fell one stroke short. Crampton shot 68 for 205 and his second 1989 victory on the Senior PGA Tour. It was his 17th Senior Tour title in less than four years on the circuit.

Two unlikely leaders—Chick Evans and Dick Rhyan—opened with 66s Friday on a rain-softened Canterbury that played "the easiest it's ever played," a Ferree opinion shared by most of the other veterans of previous visits to the Cleveland club. Evans and Rhyan were supplanted Saturday by Harold Henning, who was trying to shed a runner-up syndrome (three seconds, two thirds) and put an individual title beside his victory with Al Geiberger in the Legends of Golf. Henning had a 67-68—135 start, leading Jimmy Powell (68-68) by one and Crampton by two going into the final round.

The plateau-green 15th hole proved the decisive one Sunday. Crampton holed a 15-foot birdie putt there to move a stroke in front of Ferree after an in-and-out performance earlier in the round that included an eagle at the par-five sixth, two birdies and two bogeys. His finish was a struggle as he one-putted the long 16th and the par-three 17th, the latter after a bunkered three-wood tee shot and a 50-foot sand blast to six feet. At the 18th, he got a seven-iron onto the green from the right rough and two-putted for the win, knowing he needed the par because Ferree and Moody, who birdied the 18th for 67 and his 206, had already finished.

The rich tournament, which paid the winner $75,000, his biggest check ever, was operated by the Chicago-based Western Golf Association for Ameritech, a Windy City company. Next year's site was not immediately announced, but the tournament takes up permanent residence in Chicago in 1991 after the city has hosted this year's PGA Championship and 1990's U.S. Open at Medinah.

Newport Cup—$275,000

Winner: Jim Dent

Multiple winners abounded on the Senior PGA Tour during the first seven months of 1989. When Jim Dent repeated his come-from-behind pattern that had brought him his first circuit victory in June in Syracuse and won the Newport Cup in Rhode Island in late July, he became the seventh man with at least two victories this year. At that point, the Senior Tour had more multiple winners than it had single victors—six.

Dent's unexpected triumph—"I was just trying to finish in the top 10"— came at the expense of a frustrated Harold Henning, who once again was unable to muster a finishing kick in a final round and had to settle for his fourth runner-up closing of the season. The South African had a two-stroke lead when he started Sunday and led by three after 11 holes. "But I blew another one," he remarked disgustedly. Unaware of Dent's charge, Harold faltered. He barely parred the 12th from a trap, bogeyed the 13th and 15th, managed a tough par at the 16th and another at the 17th, where he first learned that Dent was in with 66 and 206 and that he needed a birdie to tie. When his approach at the 18th fell short of the green in heavy grass, Henning was fortunate to get down in two for another par to salvage second place by a shot over Tom Shaw, another first-year senior.

The winner had an up-and-down tournament, actually. He opened with 67 and tied journeyman Gordon Jones for the lead. Both fell away Saturday, Dent to 73—140 and Jones to 77—144, as Henning took charge. Harold shot 65 for 135 and a two-shot lead over Dick Hendrickson, three over Shaw and Chick Evans. Shaw birdied the first three holes Sunday to pull within a stroke of Henning, but never got closer, missing self-described makeable putts on the last two holes. Meanwhile, the long-hitting Dent was on the move. He reached the par-five second and seventh holes in two and two-putted for birdies and scored another from just short of the green at the par-five 12th with a fine chip. He had holed a 20-footer at the ninth and was four under when he reached the 17th, where he wedged to 12 feet, made it, and sank another 12-footer for the winning birdie on the final green. The win paid $41,500.

Volvo Seniors British Open—£150,000
Winner: Bob Charles

Bob Charles showed admiring Scottish galleries why he has been the most successful senior golfer in the world the last two years when he put the Volvo Seniors British Open championship onto a 1989 record that already sported three victories on the Senior PGA Tour in America and the Fuji Electric Grand Slam in Japan on the heels of a 1988 season during which he won seven times and was the U.S. tour's leading money winner.

The weapon for which the New Zealand lefthander has long been famous—the putter—led Charles to victory at Turnberry over its reputed Ailsa course. Bob needed just 29 putts Sunday as he crushed the field with his closing 66 for 269 and a massive, seven-stroke victory over Billy Casper, who ran out of gas Sunday after leading the way for three days in his best showing of the year. The Charles triumph in the Seniors British Open came 26 years after he won the British Open. Gary Player had been the only other to hold both of those titles.

Casper shot 67 the first day, jumping off to a three-stroke lead over Charles, Neil Coles and Agim Bardha, the pleasant native of Albania (and perhaps its only golfer) who has been a pro only since turning 50 two years ago and battling his way into quite a few events on the U.S. circuit. Casper, another putter of long-time repute who found his stroke with a new implement at Turnberry, remained in front on Friday with 69—136, but Charles shaved the margin to two shots with 68. Casper added 65 Saturday with six birdies and bogey, while Charles matched the score to keep pace and Babe Hiskey, a first-year senior from the U.S., took third place with yet another 65. Despite his position and fine play for three rounds, Casper seemed doubtful about it all, commenting: "How can a guy of 58 be shooting these scores?"

He didn't Sunday, although his near-collapse was a bit surprising. It all turned around at two holes on the front nine. At the fifth hole, Casper found an unplayable lie and took six to Bob's birdie three; then Billy dropped two more strokes when he bunkered and three-putted at the par-three sixth. Still, Casper only trailed by two strokes until he bogeyed the 15th hole from a trap and Charles holed a 35-foot birdie putt. It was all over when Casper's approach at the 16th drew back off the front edge of the green into water. Double bogey again. He finished with 75 and 276, still three shots better than Hiskey, the third-place finisher.

Showdown Classic—$350,000
Winner: Tom Shaw

Tom Shaw had little doubt that he could win on the Senior PGA Tour, but first he had to convince the powers-that-be that he belonged on that circuit. Less than a year after producing the documents that proved he had harmlessly falsified his age early in his pro career, Tom did just that, capturing the Showdown Classic at Jeremy Ranch outside of Salt Lake City in early August.

In his first years as a tournament player, the youthful-faced pro had so much trouble convincing the media and others of his real age that he quietly cranked it back four years and few were the wiser. However, with a 1942 birth date in official recordbooks, Tom's application for playing privileges on the Senior Tour was put on hold until he submitted his birth certificate verifying his December 13, 1938 birthday to Tour officials.

Surely the youngest-looking man out there, Shaw played respectably through the early months of 1989 before breaking through with his one-stroke victory at Jeremy Ranch, his first professional win since he captured his fourth and last victory on the PGA Tour, the 1971 Bing Crosby back to back with a triumph in the Hawaiian Open during his finest season. A half-dozen players were in the stretch-run Showdown, Tom finally edging Larry Mowry with a closing 70 for a nine-under-par 207 as Homero Blancas (69) and Lou Graham (70) fell back on the final holes.

Gene Littler was the first-round leader at 67, but Shaw moved into the top spot with Mowry Saturday when he put a 68 with his opening 69 to match Larry's 73-66. By the 70th hole Sunday, the two were still dead-locked, and both birdied there to go nine under, two ahead of Blancas. Both were long at the par-three 17th and Shaw left his first putt eight feet from the cup, but Mowry three-putted and Tom dropped his par-saver. Larry made Shaw work on the last hole, saving par from a greenside trap, but Tom wrung in a four-footer for the win, becoming the season's fourth first-time victor on the Senior Tour.

Rancho Murieta Gold Rush—$350,000
Winner: Dave Hill

Dave Hill added another chevron to his sometimes-underrated reputation when he put the 1989 Rancho Murieta Gold Rush title into his personal collection. In little more than two years on the Senior PGA Tour, Hill amassed seven victories. Throw in the 12 victories he posted during his career on the regular PGA Tour and you have a record that stacks up extremely well against those of all but the game's superstars and a handful of others. Yet, if you want to believe this amusingly-opinionated Michigan native, he has accomplished all this without any real devotion to the game but rather as strictly a way to make a living.

Hill, who had won in May in Philadelphia at the Bell Atlantic St. Christopher's Classic, became the season's eighth double winner in the Sacramento tournament, edging Orville Moody by a stroke as both closed with 68s. In fact, it would be fair to say that Dave won by a foot—the distance of a par putt that Moody missed at the 16th hole in the final round. Hill finished at 207, nine under par, at Rancho Murieta Country Club, the 68 following a 69-70 start. With a closing 65, Don Bies fell two shots shy of the top.

John Paul Cain, the surprise winner of the Greater Grand Rapids Open in July, occupied center stage the first two days at Rancho Murieta. Cain, the Houston stockbroker who just became a pro in 1988, opened with 67, a stroke better than Ken Still and two in front of Hill and three others. After 12 holes Saturday, Cain had expanded his lead to four, but two incoming bogeys forced him to settle for 72—139 and a share of the lead with Still, Hill and Quinton Gray. Moody was a shot back after his 72-68 start. Hill moved in front by himself with virtual tap-in birdies on the first two holes Sunday. Phil Rodgers ran off a five-birdie string to seize the lead at the 11th hole, then yielded it to Moody, who had won and placed third in the two previous tournaments at Sacramento. Hill regained a share of the lead with Moody with an eagle at the 11th and a birdie at the 12th and accepted sole possession when Orville's one-footer at the 16th slipped off line over a faultily-repaired ballmark. Both parred in, Dave canning a four-footer for the win on the last green.

GTE Northwest Classic—$350,000
Winner: Al Geiberger

Al Geiberger came out winging when he joined the Senior PGA Tour in late 1987 and won four times in the first six months. Eighteen months later, Geiberger's victory total was unchanged, although he didn't exactly disappear from sight as a money-winner and did pick up a team victory with partner Harold Henning in the 1989 Legends of Golf. Unquestionably, the tragic accidental death of his two-year-old son in the summer of 1988 had a lot to do with the slippage.

The affable Californian, claiming he had been goaded into adopting a killer instinct that week, ended the victory drought in Seattle with his three-stroke triumph in the GTE Northwest Classic. With his 21-year-old son

John, a two-handicapper serving as his caddy and observer of his game, Al strung three 68s together for a 12-under-par 204 that took him to the barn an easy victor over runner-up Frank Beard, who had rounds of 69-70-68 for his 207. Orville Moody, then the tour's leading money-winner and the previous week's runner-up, finished third at 208.

Miller Barber had the quickest start at Inglewood Country Club in the Seattle suburb of Kenmore in the first round Friday. Barber birdied six of the first seven holes, turned in 31 and seized a three-stroke lead with his 65. Dave Hill and Don Massengale matched Geiberger's first 68. An early double-bogey headed Miller toward a 74 Saturday, and Geiberger jumped into a two-shot lead over Dave (70) and Mike (66) Hill. Remaining aggressive Sunday, Geiberger eagled the par-five first hole and was seriously threatened thereafter only by Beard, who birdied five of the first seven holes to pull within a stroke. However, Frank three-putted the 11th green and fell three shots back when he bogeyed the 15th. He birdied the 18th for a 68 match to Geiberger's final-round score and edged Moody by a stroke.

Sunwest Bank/Charley Pride Classic—$300,000
Winner: Bob Charles

Since he hails from New Zealand, Bob Charles probably had a little spelling problem when the city of Albuquerque, New Mexico, took a place on the Senior PGA Tour in 1986. You can safely bet that he handles it now with no trouble at all and considers Albuquerque one of his favorite towns in all the world. Consider his accomplishments there at Four Hills Country Club in his four appearances in the Sunwest Bank/Charley Pride Classic:

—Victories there the last three years, something he had never done before in his 30-year pro career.

—Twelve consecutive sub-par rounds in the tournament. (Bob finished third in the 1986 event before starting the winning streak.)

—Second player in Senior Tour history to win the same tournament three years in a row. Chi Chi Rodriguez won the 1986-87-88 Digital events, Charles breaking that streak earlier in the 1989 season.

The game's greatest left-hander outfought Charles Coody in a head-to-head confrontation in Sunday's final round to score his fourth Senior PGA Tour victory and sixth triumph of the year at Four Hills in late August. Charles entered the final round with a 66-69—135 total and a one-stroke lead over Coody and Jim Dent, slipped as much as three shots behind Coody, winless as a senior, but persevered and won by a stroke. Both he and Coody finished with 68s for totals of 203 and 204. Mike Hill (206) and Gene Littler (207) were next after shooting 65s.

Coody, who had shared the first-round lead at 66 with Charles, got the upper hand in the middle of the final round. He roared three strokes in front with birdies at the seventh, eighth and 10th holes and a 20-foot eagle putt at the 11th. His 40-foot birdie putt at the 15th gave him a two-shot advantage with three to play. But the famous Charles putting stroke and his own failures on the greens did Coody in in the stretch. Bob holed an eight-foot birdie putt at the 16th, got back to even when Coody three-putted the 17th and won the match when he dropped an eight-foot par putt before Coody missed his from five feet.

RJR Bank One Classic—$300,000
Winner: Rives McBee

Rives McBee did it the hard way, just as Larry Mowry and John Paul Cain did before him on the Senior PGA Tour. When the week of the RJR Bank One Classic began in Lexington, Kentucky, the little-known McBee was not even in the field, just one of 116 men shooting for one of the eight spots available in the Monday qualifier. Never successful enough on the regular PGA Tour back in the 1960s to merit a direct spot on the Senior Tour, he had the Monday qualifiers as his only entranceways.

That late August Monday at Griffin Gate Golf Club, McBee shot his first sub-par round of the week—67—to land a place in the tournament, then followed at the end of the week with three more rounds in the 60s to win the title with an eight-under-par 202. The 50-year-old Texan, who at one time shared one of the more important U.S. Open scoring records when he shot 64 at Olympic Club in 1966, became the fifth player to score a first Senior Tour victory in 1989, following Homero Blancas, Tom Shaw, Jim Dent and Cain. With the victory, his first since winning the PGA Club Pro Championship in 1973, he had exemptions for the next 12 months on the Senior Tour.

Rives (pronounced Reeves) moved in front Saturday when he tacked a five-under 65 to his opening 68 for 133 and a one-shot lead on Harold Henning after Walter Zembriski and Jim O'Hern, long a leading club pro player in Kentucky, opened with 66s. McBee never trailed Sunday, jumping his lead over Henning to three when he birdied and Harold bogeyed the par-five third hole. He maintained that margin with birdies at the 11th and 12th but then over Orville Moody. However, Moody faltered with bogeys at the 14th and 15th, eventually finishing fourth at 206. McBee played the last six holes in one-over with a bogey at the 17th for 69 and a two-shot victory over Henning, who shot 70. Larry Ziegler, another first-year senior pro, closed with 67 to register his best finish in third place at 205.

GTE North Classic—$350,000
Winner: Gary Player

Gary Player was not exactly bubbling with optimism when he arrived in Indianapolis in early September to defend his championship in the GTE North Classic. He had not won since that victory in 1988, had been off the PGA Senior Tour and in Great Britain and back in his native South Africa for two months and had "warmed up" for his return to action in Sarasota working on the site of a golf course he had designed in Florida. His appraisal of his chances: "It would take a mini-miracle."

Maybe his subsequent victory at Broadmoor Country Club was something of a miracle, but the fact that even 36 holes were played that weekend amid repeated rainstorms was much more remarkable. Thunderstorms harassed first-round play, wiped out the Saturday round and threatened the final day's action but passed by.

The first bad weather caused a one-hour delay in the first round Friday and may have contributed to the mass bunching of leaders at day's end. Player, who began to contradict himself with a 64 in the Thursday pro-amateur, shot a five under-par 67 and found himself in a seven-way tie for the lead with Dale Douglass, Jim Dent, Billy Casper, Gene Littler, Walter Zembriski and Mike Hill. Six others—Al Geiberger, Joe Jimenez, Larry Mowry, Dave Hill, Bob Charles and Tommy Aaron —were just a shot behind. Thirty-three pros in all were under par after 18 holes.

Officials delayed Saturday's start for two hours and put the players off both the first and 10th tees. All for naught. A violent thunderstorm flooded the course and blew down concession and media tents, forcing the year's first cancellation of a round and shortening the event to 36 holes. (Monday carry-overs and 36-hole days are barred on the Senior Tour.)

Although Jimenez, Geiberger and Casper finished in a second-place tie at 136, Douglass and Dent were Player's strongest challengers Sunday on the 6,670-yard course which drained well overnight. Gary made three birdies and a bogey on the front nine, trailing Douglass and Dent by a stroke at that point. Dent had the lead when Douglass bogeyed the 14th, but turned it over to Player when he double-bogeyed the par-three 15th. Ahead of the other two, Gary birdied from six feet at No. 15 and almost holed his nine-iron approach at No. 16 to get to nine under. He parred in, making a shaky par from short of the green at the last hole. Dent and Douglass finished at 137 with Mike Hill, two behind the winner of his 13th Senior Tour title.

Crestar Classic—$350,000
Winner: Chi Chi Rodriguez

The Crestar Classic put a sort of ditto on the Senior PGA Tour record. For the second week in a row, one of the circuit's star players ended a lengthy winless stretch. It was Gary Player at Indianapolis preceding the first victory of Chi Chi Rodriguez in nearly 14 months (1988 Digital Classic) with his one-stroke triumph at the Hermitage Country Club at Richmond, Virginia in mid-September.

Rodriguez, a 12-tournament winner on the Senior Tour in his first three seasons and the leading money-winner in 1987, attributed his long dry spell to a pinched nerve in his neck that had forced him to play hurt for some nine months. Finally pain-free at the Hermitage, Chi Chi surged from two strokes off the pace in the final round, posting a four-under-par 68 for 203 to edge Dick Rhyan and Jim Dent by a stroke and capture his second Crestar Classic title. The first was in 1986.

"Maybe I'm on my way back," Rodriguez observed when he opened with 66 and followed with a second bogey-less round Saturday, a 69 for 135. The 66 put him a shot off Jim Dent's pace-setting 65, and the 135 sent him into the final round two behind Jim Ferree, who had started 67-66—133. Chi Chi's early moves Sunday included a chip-in birdie at the sixth hole, which he considered a victory omen—"I always used to win when I chipped one in"—were obscured by the 32 front-nine charge of Arnold Palmer, the defending champion, who had not won since the 1988 victory and was to come back in 37 for 69 and place eighth at 206.

Three other birdies with the chip-in put Chi Chi out in 32, too, and he was two shots in front until he bogeyed the 14th and dropped into a three-way tie with Rhyan and Dent, who birdied the hole right behind him. However, Chi Chi regained the lead with an eight-foot birdie putt at the par-five 16th and parred in. Both Rhyan, from long range, and Dent had birdie putts for ties on the last green but missed, Rhyan finishing with 70—204 and Dent with 69—204.

PaineWebber Invitational—$325,000
Winner: Hurricane Hugo

For the first time in 40 years of professional golf in the United States, weather wiped a tournament out completely when Hurricane Hugo devastated Quail Hollow Country Club and the city of Charlotte in the early morning before the first round of the PaineWebber Invitational.

Though Charlotte is almost 200 miles from Charleston, South Carolina, where the powerful hurricane came ashore, the storm retained most of its punch as it crossed South Carolina and struck North Carolina's biggest city almost dead center. Besides the heavy damage to trees, a portion of club-house roof, trailers, tents and television equipment at Quail Hollow, Hugo left Charlotte virtually without power, partially flooded and badly damaged by fallen trees. Tournament officials had no choice except to cancel the tournament, concluding that it would not be possible to reschedule it during the remainder of the Senior PGA Tour season.

It was to have been the final PaineWebber at Quail Hollow, since the 1990 tournament had already been announced for the new TPC at Piper Glen course in Charlotte. Piper Glen, an Arnold Palmer/Ed Seay-designed course, also sustained heavy hurricane damage, worse than absorbed by Quail Hollow.

The only other tournament ever completely cancelled was the 1949 Colonial National Invitation, which was called off well before the scheduled week after the flooding Trinity River destroyed a major section of the Fort Worth, Texas, course. The 1966 Houston Champions International was called off after four days of futile efforts to play, but was rescheduled and played later in the year.

Fairfield Barnett Space Coast Classic—$300,000
Winner: Bob Charles

It was about time for another victory for Bob Charles. The consistent southpaw had spaced his first six wins of 1989 rather evenly through the year, from Tampa in February to Albuquerque in August. So, when the Fairfield Barnett Space Coast Classic came up on the schedule at the end of September, it seemed almost likely that Charles would put No. 7 onto his brilliant 1989 record. And he did.

Charles' victory at Suntree Country Club in Melbourne, Florida, was one of his most decisive. Keeping the ball out of Suntree's clutching rough, Bob led from wire to wire (for the second time in 1989) and, with rounds of 66-70-67 for 203, 13 under par, he won by six strokes. The victory was his fifth on the Senior PGA Tour. He also won the Seniors British Open and the Fuji Electric Grand Slam in Japan. The title was his 14th in four seasons of senior golf on the U.S. circuit.

Charles stepped off in front Friday, hitting 16 greens en route to a six-under-par 66 and a one-stroke lead over Butch Baird, two over Larry Mowry, Dale Douglass, Jim Dent and Bruce Devlin. Saturday came up tough, and only Al Geiberger with 67 broke 70, the score Charles shot to maintain his one-stroke lead over Baird with Dent just another stroke back.

Bob gave nobody an opening Sunday. He opened the round with birdies on the first two holes and, when he turned with 31, he had a four-stroke margin in hand. Another birdie at the 11th widened the gap to five and even led the conservative man to conclude, "That's when I thought I had it won." The battle then turned to second place and Baird, the wire-to-wire runner-up, secured it when he sank a 15-foot birdie putt on the 18th green to finish at 209, a shot ahead of Mowry and Harold Henning. Dent faded to 76.

RJR Championship—$1,350,000
Winner: Gary Player

Put him into a tournament that has a little something extra going for it like prestige or big money and you can count on Gary Player to elevate his game and his intensity to its peak. Major titles and national championships dot his brilliant record of 138 victories as testimony to that. So, it was no surprise when, entering a tournament with the biggest first-place prize he had had a shot at in senior golf, Player emerged as the victor in the RJR Championship in Winston-Salem, North Carolina.

With his one-stroke victory over Rives McBee, Gary collected the $202,500 first-place check, which actually was the biggest of his fabled career. One perspective—he never won that much in any of his many fine seasons on the regular PGA Tour. Player opened with 65 and added a pair of 71s for his three-under-par 207. McBee, who led Gary by a stroke after two rounds with his 68-67—135, finished with 73 and 208, the only other man to break par on a Tanglewood Park course with rebuilt, immature greens that plagued the field on a soggy course that had experienced the fringe rains of Hurricane Hugo and torrential downpours the weekend before the tournament. The win was Player's 14th in four years on the Senior PGA Tour, not counting the 1988 Seniors British Open.

The first nine holes set the tone for the talented South African. He shot 29, then 36 coming in for the 65 as an afternoon player on badly-spiked-up greens. It gave him a two-stroke lead over non-winners Quinton Gray and Paul Moran, three over McBee and Ben Smith. After two rounds, only one other player besides McBee and Player was under par—Doug Dalziel, three behind Player at 139. Sunday's finale was virtually a two-man battle between the Hall of Famer and the man who had just escaped Monday qualifiers a month earlier. Gary quickly got the upper hand and a four-stroke lead with birdies at the third and fourth holes as Rives was going bogey, double-bogey. However, he made three bogeys and lost all except one shot of his lead through the 10th hole. McBee caught up with a five-foot birdie putt at the 15th, then muffed an 18-inch par putt at the 16th that proved the deciding stroke. Rives couldn't muster a birdie against Gary's two solid pars on the last two holes, but was still delighted with the $145,000 second-place check, a sum greater than the sum total of all of his previous winnings on the PGA and Senior PGA Tours.

Gatlin Brothers Southwest Classic—$300,000
Winner: George Archer

The cognoscenti of tournament golf insisted on a qualifier to constant remarks during the year about the impact Jack Nicklaus and Lee Trevino would be making on the Senior PGA Tour in 1990. "Don't forget," they cautioned, "George Archer will be out there, too." Archer proved them to be sages even before the arrival of Trevino and Nicklaus, winning his first start as a senior in the Gatlin Brothers Southwest Classic two weeks after turning 50. Only Arnold Palmer and Gary Player before him had won the first time out as a senior, Arnie in the 1980 PGA Seniors and Gary in the 1985 Quadel Classic.

Not that it was a breeze for the 6'-5" Californian, who played on the regular tour with adequate performances almost up to his 50th birthday. After two rounds at Fairway Oaks Golf and Racquet Club in Abilene, Texas, Archer was five shots off the pace of Mike Hill, who posted rounds of 69-67—136 to take over the lead from Gary Player and Butch Baird, who opened with 68s. Five under par for the day through 17 holes, Archer had the lead Sunday, but bogeyed the par-five 18th for 68 and 209, seven under par. That dropped him into a tie with Jimmy Powell, who had made an even greater rally with a closing 66 but missed a four-foot birdie putt on the last green. Orville Moody joined them when he birdied the 18th for 69 and his 209.

The three men—former Masters champion Archer, former U.S. Open champion Moody and non-winner Powell—parred the first extra hole, the 15th, in the Senior Tour's first playoff since mid-June. At the par-three 16th, a 150-yard water hole where Bruce Crampton had blown the lead not long before, Archer had the honors and put his seven-iron tee shot 16 feet behind the hole. Moments later, he routinely two-putted for the victory when, first, Powell, then Moody put their tee shots in the drink. So, Archer, a 13-tournament winner over the years on the PGA Tour, had a $45,000 start in senior golf.

Five players—John Paul Cain, Jim Dent, Player, Crampton and Hill—missed the playoff by a stroke, and Charles Coody, the Abilene resident who was director of golf at Fairway Oaks for a decade before joining the senior circuit, made a strong run at the title before the treacherous little 16th slapped him with a double-bogey.

Transamerica Championship—$400,000
Winner: Billy Casper

Natural disasters seemed to be on the trail of the Senior PGA Tour in the late season. Hurricane Hugo wiped out the PaineWebber Invitational in September, and a month later the circuit had a close brush with the devastating San Francisco earthquake that struck without warning as the players gathered for the first Transamerica Championship just north of the heavy tremors in the Napa Valley of California.

Then, too, it was not earthshaking when Billy Casper emerged as the winner that Sunday, considering his fine record of 61 victories on the regular and Senior PGA Tours, even though the last victory had occurred 16 months earlier. Casper was a realist after scoring his three-stroke victory at Silverado Country Club, where he had won the 1971 Kaiser International during the PGA Tour's 13-year series at Silverado through 1980. "Any time you win now, you know there aren't going to be too many more wins in your life," the 58-year-old pro observed.

The Transamerica title was up for grabs after two rounds. Charles Coody and 6'-7" Dick Hendrickson, a former club pro, fought biting winds to post 67s for the first-round lead with Casper, Dave Hill and Bruce Devlin at 69. A logjam developed at the top Saturday. Both Casper and Hill eagled the 18th hole for 70s that put them into a first-place tie with Coody (72) and Al Geiberger (70-69) at 139, a shot ahead of Bob Charles and Jim Ferree. Hill's wild round included the eagle, five birdies, three bogeys and a double-bogey. Geiberger got away fast Sunday with birdies on the first two holes, but Casper caught him with two brilliant iron shots that set up easy birdies at the third and sixth holes. Geiberger three-putted the seventh, and Billy was in front to stay, his putter handling matters well as in his days of yore.

Casper finished with 68 for his nine-under-par 207 and the $60,000 first-prize check. Geiberger shot 71 for 210, nosing out Coody (72) and Larry Ziegler (70) for second by a stroke.

General Tire Classic—$300,000
Winner: Charles Coody

A long, long victory vigil ended when Charles Coody became the seventh and last first-time winner of 1989 on the Senior PGA Tour with a playoff triumph in the General Tire Classic at the Desert Inn Country Club in Las Vegas. It wasn't just that Coody was nearing the end of his third season on the Senior Tour without a victory on the record. He hadn't won anywhere since 1973 in Europe or since 1971 in the United States when he captured the coveted Masters championship.

With his pro son Kyle as caddy and wife Lynette in the gallery, Coody moved himself into position for the win over the first two rounds, just as he had in the two previous circuit events at Abilene and Napa. This time, he had the lead going into the final day after rounds of 67-69, sitting a shot in front of Tom Shaw and Al Geiberger. However, Bob Charles and Chi Chi Rodriguez mustered the challenges to Coody Sunday. Charles birdied four of the first five holes on the back nine to go 11 under par and overtake the

52-year-old Texan. Playing partner Rodriguez then birdied the 15th hole for an 11-under position, but Charles bogeyed the hole. Bob re-forged the three-way tie with a 10-foot birdie putt at the 17th, and he and Chi Chi watched as Coody made a hard par at the final hole, leaving a 110-yard pitching wedge shot short of the green and dropping a six-foot par putt to make the playoff, his first ever, a three-way affair.

After pars at the starting 16th hole, Charles and Coody put their approaches on the 17th green but Rodriguez missed it. His bullseye chip hit the flagstick but stayed out, Charles missed his birdie putt from 12 feet and Coody canned his from eight feet for the long-awaited victory. Coody collected $45,000 and Charles' share of second/third money—$24,625—cushioned his No. 1 position on the Senior PGA Tour money list.

Du Pont Cup—$450,000
Winner: United States

A select group of U.S. senior pros traveled to Japan in mid-November to inaugurate a new event on the Senior PGA Tour schedule and made the most of the trip, scoring a resounding victory in the Du Pont Cup competition at Batoh on a Japanese version of a Tournament Players Club.

In a peculiar format, the 10 pros on each team played pairs matches but the win or loss was meaningless. Instead, each team used its seven best scores in each of the three rounds, the cumulative totals being all that counted. The Americans wound up with 1,493 strokes at the end of the three-day event, the Japanese 34 strokes higher at 1,527. With the victory, each U.S. team member won $27,000, while the Japanese players each received $13,000.

Two first-time senior winners—Charles Coody (just the week before in Las Vegas) and Rives McBee—and first-year senior Frank Beard paced the U.S. team as the only men whose scores counted all three days. However, Don Bies shared medalist honors at 210 with Coody and Teruo Sugihara, the long-time Japanese star who was clearly his country's leading player. Sugihara shot 70 each day and only Kesahiko Uchida bettered that score for Japan all week with his Saturday 69.

The U.S. led from start to finish. With four players under Batoh's 72 par—Coody and Bies at 69, Beard and McBee at 71—and Sugihara the only member of his team under par, the Americans began with a 503-to-513 advantage. The margin rose to 22 Saturday (483 to 495) as Orville Moody, Tom Shaw and McBee led the way with 68s. Gusty winds blew up the scores Sunday, but the U.S. pros still got the better of things, compiling the final total by adding 12 strokes to the margin. Bies and Sugihara were the only par-breakers Sunday.

GTE West Classic—$300,000
Winner: Walter Zembriski

At 6,190 yards, the resort course at Ojai Inn and Country Club in the foothills northwest of Los Angeles was rather easy pickings for the pros on the Senior PGA Tour at the end of November in its solo appearance as site of the GTE West Classic. Among those who rubbed his hands in joy at first sight of the track was Walter Zembriski, whose 1989 season had been a bit of a comedown from the big year he had enjoyed in 1988. A two-time winner and Chrysler Cup qualifier that season, Zembriski was still looking for No. 3 when he arrived at Ojai. He had it in hand when he left.

Zembriski, the 54-year-old hero of the "common man," who found his first real success in senior golf, fired a 13-under-par 197 in the GTE West Classic to become the circuit's 22nd different winner of 1989. He finished two shots in front of George Archer and Jim Dent as 26 players broke Ojai's par of 70.

Butch Baird shot a closing 63 and four players had 64s in the assault on the Ojai course. Zembriski and Homero Blancas had two of the 64s Thursday to lead after the first 18 holes. Bob Charles, Frank Beard and Dent had 66s. Zembriski got away fast Friday in the second round with an eagle and three birdies in the first seven holes and surged to a five-shot lead over Blancas and Archer. However, his putting went sour for the rest of the round, and he wound up with a 68 and a one-stroke lead over Archer, who shot 64, and Al Kelley, a Monday qualifier shooting for a exempt spot in 1990.

Walter repeated his fast start in Saturday's final round. With birdies at the first, sixth, seventh and eighth holes and a bogey at the ninth, he was out in 32. He added birdies at the 11th and 15th holes, took his first look at the on-course scoreboards and realized he had a three-stroke lead. He parred in and won easily, since both Archer, who shot 64, and Dent, who had a 66, had to birdie the 18th to get that close. Charles, in fourth place, was five behind Zembriski.

GTE Kaanapali Classic—$300,000
Winner: Don Bies

The focus of television, media and gallery attention at the GTE Kaanapali Classic, the final official event on the Senior PGA Tour schedule, was on the debut of Lee Trevino six days after his 50th birthday. Virtually ignored in all of this was the defending champion, Don Bies, even though the quiet man from Washington was having another fine year and had just beaten the regulars in the Air New Zealand/Shell Open before coming to Hawaii.

Although Trevino performed creditably in the rain-shortened tournament at Royal Kaanapali Golf Club on Maui, Bies grabbed the final headlines by capturing the title while sitting in the clubhouse as torrential rains beat down on the course, forcing cancellation of the scheduled final round that December Saturday. He thus became the fourth successful title defender of the season (Bob Charles did it twice—Fuji Electric Grand Slam and Charley Pride Sunwest—and Gary Player won again in the GTE North Classic) and, with his third 1989 win, Don matched Player and trailed only Charles in the victory-total department for the year.

While Trevino was starting his senior career with two bogeys, then bouncing back with enough birdies for a three-under 69, Joe Jimenez was putting together a 64 that was just a shot over his age. Jimenez, the king of the over-60 set with nine victories in that auxiliary "Super Senior" competition during the year, took a two-stroke lead over Dale Douglass, four over Bies, Homero Blancas and Bob Boldt. The 63-year-old Missourian, who would have been the oldest Senior Tour winner ever by some six months, kept that possibility alive for six holes in Friday's second round, getting to 11 under with birdies at the fourth, fifth and sixth. But his putting stroke deserted him with four three-putts that brought about a 73, dropping him into a tie for fifth at day's end. Meanwhile, Bies was ripping out a 64 of his own, making five of his eight birdies in a six-hole stretch on the back nine. He posted his 132, a shot better than Douglass, who had no bogeys while shooting 66-67. Trevino had another 69 for 138, and he wound up in a three-way tie for seventh and collected $9,258.33 when the downpour ended the tournament Saturday before the leaders even reached the first tee.

Mauna Lani Challenge—$300,000
Winner: Dale Douglass

Dale Douglass was frustrated. He had played well enough but gone without a victory during the 1989 Senior PGA Tour season, capping his exasperation when he played bogey-less golf, shot 133 and still didn't win in the GTE Kaanapali Classic, finishing second to Don Bies in the final official circuit event. He changed islands in Hawaii and gained some solace six days later when he won the unofficial, limited-field Mauna Lani Challenge at the Mauna Lani Golf Club on the Kohala Coast of the island of Hawaii.

It took a playoff to settle things as Douglass and Jim Ferree finished with 209s. Dale won the title and the $45,000 first prize on the first extra hole. Thirty pros cut up the $300,000 purse.

Mazda Champions—$900,000
Winners: Mike Hill and Patti Rizzo

In better-ball competition, a double-bogey is usually as sure death as was the hemlock cocktail quaffed by Socrates those many centuries ago. You just can't give away two strokes to the field in such events as the Mazda Champions and still finish first, the rule of thumb tells us. Mike Hill and Patti Rizzo proved that it isn't always so, overcoming a freak-penalty double-bogey in the first round of the season-ending special event in mid-December at the Hyatt Dorado Beach course in Puerto Rico to win the huge first-place purse in the Mazda's final event of the five-year-old series. With rounds of 65-60-66—191, they edged the teams of Don Bies/Tammie Green and Charles Coody/Sherri Turner by a stroke and picked up their individual checks of $250,000.

Hill, whose older brother Dave had won the 1988 event with his LPGA partner Colleen Walker, and Rizzo were lightly regarded in pre-tournament speculation. Both were playing in the Seniors/LPGA team event for the first time, the 50-year-old Hill had not won during his first season on that circuit and Patti Rizzo had scored her only 1989 victory back in April. Then came that apparent killer at the 17th hole in the first round. Hill's approach struck the ball of Harold Henning, already on the green, but, before Mike arrived,

Henning replaced the wrong ball—Hill's—and marked it. Mike marked the remaining ball—Henning's—without noticing it. The mistake hurt only Hill because Henning's partner, Patty Sheehan, already had par. Rizzo, however, was already "in the pocket" when Hill discovered after his first putt that he was playing the wrong ball. He made six with the penalty and two putts, dropping the team from eight to six under. They birdied the 18th for 65, but trailed leaders Bies and Green by four shots.

With hardened resolve, Hill and Rizzo shot a 12-under-par 60 Saturday and inched into a one-stroke lead at 135 over Bies/Green, Gene Littler/Jane Geddes and Orville Moody/Beth Daniel. They stayed in front through Sunday's final round, their 66 just enough to nip Bies/Green (66) and Coody/Turner (65).

Mazda announced the termination of its sponsorship of the event and its place on the Senior PGA Tour schedule will be taken by a regular Senior Tour tournament. The LPGA had no replacement for 1990.

12. The European Tour

The year 1989 was a fitting finish to the greatest decade in the history of European golf. Like the entire decade, 1989 was big and booming—a year of growth and thrills, and also of puzzles and pain. Nick Faldo won the Masters, his second major championship, then exploded in Europe. Sandy Lyle fell from grace like a stone. Bernhard Langer was afflicted by the putting yips and a bad back, but suddenly saw light at the end of the season. Seve Ballesteros was his volatile self, a man of dazzling highs and deep lows. The young players were on the march, led by Ronan Rafferty, who rocketed from his first win to the top of the Order of Merit. And perhaps the most significant event didn't happen in Europe at all, but in America. To the delight of spectators and tournament sponsors, it meant the stars would be staying home more.

It started in June, when Faldo, Ballesteros, Langer, Lyle and Japan's Isao Aoki met with PGA Tour Commissioner Deane Beman at the U.S. Open at Oak Hill Country Club in Rochester, New York. They wanted a reduction in the American tour's requirement that foreign members play at least 15 events. Faldo, Lyle, Langer, and Aoki were members of the U.S. tour. Ballesteros used to be, until he balked some years earlier and was suspended. They argued that 15 events was too much time to spend away from their home tour.

"I've tried to play both since 1981, and it can't be done," Faldo said. Jack Nicklaus, Tom Watson, Ben Crenshaw, and other American golfers long had advocated an open-door policy for foreign players, but their view was not shared by the Tournament Policy Board, which ultimately kept the requirement at 15. Faldo and Langer quit the American tour, and Ballesteros and Woosnam would not join. Sandy Lyle was the only prominent European left on the American tour. The door wasn't completely closed, however. Foreign golfers could still play in up to nine American events—the U.S. Open, the Masters, and the PGA Championship (by either qualifying or by special invitation); the World Series of Golf (by qualifying); and five regular events through sponsors' exemptions.

By an interesting coincidence, this issue dovetailed beautifully with the European tour's own efforts to keep Europeans at home. Said Executive Director Ken Schofield, "My first consideration must be to the European tour in the nineties, otherwise we will just stagnate." To this end, the tour added the £400,000 American Express Mediterranean Open early in March, 1990, at Las Brisas, Spain.

Whatever the 1990s held, they would be hard-pressed to match the 1980s. Take growth alone: In 1979, the tour's total prize fund was about £1.5 million. In 1989, with a schedule now stretching from February to November, the total was some £12 million. And when it came to players, the tour was priceless in 1989.

First, there were the old faithfuls. Faldo played the American tour in the first half of the season, and won only once—the Masters. He returned to Europe and went on a rampage, winning his first three starts—the Volvo

PGA Championship, the Dunhill British Masters, and the Peugeot French Open. Ballesteros made big news by missing two cuts. But he also won three times (Cepsa Madrid Open, Epson Grand Prix, Ebel European Masters - Swiss Open). Ian Woosnam, after a tentative start, won the Carrolls Irish Open and had three seconds. Langer won his first start, the Peugeot Spanish Open, then sank with the yips. He tried a new grip that looked weird but seemed to work. He would hold the putter with his left hand far down, then with the top of the grip braced well up his left forearm, wrap his right hand around both the grip and his arm. He hit rock bottom in the British Open in July, when he started 71-73 then finished dead last on 83-82—309. He wound up the season with some high finishes capped by a victory in the German Masters.

Sandy Lyle was another matter altogether. This truly was the year of his discontent. He had a promising start on the U.S. tour, scoring two seconds early in the year. Then came the slide. In The Nestle Invitational in March, he walked off the course in disgust. Then, beginning with The Players Championship the following week, he missed the 36-hole cut in seven of his next eight starts. These included the Masters, where he was defending champion, and the U.S. Open. Things weren't much better back in Europe. In 11 starts, he missed the cut twice, and the rest were distant finishes except for a tie for eighth in the European Open and a solo fourth in the Volvo Masters, the last event on the schedule. Things got so bad that he scratched himself from Ryder Cup consideration, not wanting to hurt the team. Through it all he sought the help of various gurus. Nothing helped. And he got tons of unsolicited help, including a call from a Scottish psychiatrist. "I didn't even speak to the man," Lyle said. "My dad answered the phone, and told him he was speaking a lot of hooey."

These weren't the only names to draw attention. There were the 10 first-time winners, led by Ronan Rafferty, only 25 and already in his ninth year on the tour. He was stamped as a comer when he first stepped out, and he lived up to that billing with a vengeance. He won the Italian Open in May, his first tour victory, then added the Scandinavian Enterprise Open in August and the Volvo Masters in October, and vaulted over Jose-Maria Olazabal to the top of the Order of Merit with £400,311. Rafferty only led the march: Craig Parry won the Wang Four Stars and the German Open; Paul Broadhurst, Cannes Open; Colin Montgomerie, Portuguese Open; Mark Roe, Catalan Open; and Vijay Singh, not only a first-time winner (Volvo Open) but the first Fiji Islander ever to win in Europe. Other first-timers: Michael Allen, an American, in the Scottish Open; the veteran Gordon J. Brand, the Belgian Open; Argentina's Eduardo Romero, the Lancome Trophy; and the veteran Andrew Murray (European Open), whose career is threatened by a crippling form of arthritis.

There were two postscripts on the state of European golf in 1989. The first was in the tour's Satellite Tour, a circuit for hopefuls. The nationality breakdown showed (in round numbers) Britain with some 115 golfers; Sweden 75; France 50; Italy 30; West Germany 20; and a handful from Switzerland, Spain, Denmark, Holland, Austria, and Finland.

The second postscript occurred in amateur golf. It was part of the phenomenal geopolitical developments in Eastern Europe, with the spread of the first economic and political freedom since World War II. It wasn't much, but it was remarkable that it happened at all: In the summer of 1989, a group of some 10 Soviet youngsters, who had learned their golf swings on the first driving range in Russia, went to Sweden and played their first round of real golf.

Tenerife Open—£200,000
Winner: Jose-Maria Olazabal

The PGA European Tour kicked off the 1989 season with the Tenerife Open, and nothing could have been newer—a brand-new tournament on a brand-new golf course, the Golf del Sur on the island of Tenerife. The first to catch the golfers' attention was the course, because it had only just opened. It measured 6,384 yards, par 72, with fairways making their way through fields of black volcanic ash. It also offered such oddities as the 203-yard second, a par-three calling for a blind shot to a 50-yard long green surrounded by lava.

It took the golfers no time at all to catch on to it, however. Ian Woosnam posted a seven-under-par 65 in the first round. That stood as the course record for all of five hours. Along came Jim Rutledge, 29, from British Columbia, Canada, with a 64. Rutledge erupted for eight birdies in nine holes, starting at No. 8, including six of the first seven inward holes. "I just went out and let it fly when I saw the winds had dropped," Rutledge explained. That was his career-best round, and only a closing 74 kept him from a career-best finish. Rutledge, whose best was fifth in the 1988 Cannes Open, was tied for 12th this time. This week belonged to another man.

If it seems strange to continue to call Jose-Maria Olazabal "young," it's only because we're accustomed to him. But he is young. He only turned 23 on February 5 of the new season. But he was entering his fourth year of a PGA European Tour career that already was outstanding. He won twice in his debut season, 1986, and was named Rookie of the Year at age 20. The following year, 1987, went by with good money but no victories, and he made up for that with two victories in 1988. He made sure he wouldn't come up empty in 1989, a Ryder Cup year.

Olazabal returned a 69 in the first round and was five strokes astern of Rutledge's record 64. He also had some pretty strong sharpshooters between him and the lead—Woosnam at 65, Des Smyth and Peter Teravainen at 66, and Mark Roe and Denis Durnian at 68. Woosnam, who had labored for most of 1988, seemed troubled again. A 73 in the second round and then a 77 in the third took him out of the running. He would finish tied for 33rd. Rutledge held firm in the second round, a 72 leaving him tied for the lead with Jose-Maria Canizares (66) at eight-under-par 136. Olazabal began his move with a 68 and rose to tie for third behind the leaders. Another 68 put him into a one-stroke lead through the third round, at 11-under-par 205. He slipped slightly in the fourth round, but it didn't dent him. His challengers slipped even more.

While Canizares was working on a 72 in the last round, and Mark Roe a 75, Olazabal came out firing. He exploded for birdies on the first three holes, and no one was going to catch him. He was on his way to a 13-under-par 275 total and a comfortable three-stroke victory. The only thing approximating a challenge came from a man who was too far back to begin with. This was David Gilford, former English amateur champion and Walker Cupper. Gilford carded an eagle and three birdies for a final-round 67 and a share of second with Canizares at 278.

Karl Litten Desert Classic—£250,000
Winner: Mark James

A new week, another new tournament, and as if to prove that golf is played by almost everyone, everywhere, this one was in a desert in the Middle East. So doesn't it make sense that a Dane should step forward, topping a scrambled leaderboard?

The inaugural Desert Classic was staged at the Emirates Golf Club in Dubai, a southern Persian Gulf state, and up popped Steen Tinning, 26, of Copenhagen, in his third year on the PGA European Tour and looking for his first victory. He breezed across the 7,100-yard, par-72 layout for a course-record 66, and discovered it was just barely enough. Right on his heels were a Swede, Magnus Persson (67), and behind him, all jammed at 68, were two Britons Malcolm Mackenzie and David Williams; an Italian, Alberto Binaghi; and an American, Peter Teravainen.

Tinning's record 66 wouldn't be touched for, oh, one day. Newcomer Paul Broadhurst, 23, the promising English rookie, matched it in the second round. And Robin Mann, also from England, did it in the fourth. It was too little for Tinning, who immediately jumped into the mid-70s and tied for 19th. It was much too late for Mann. The 66 was his best score by seven strokes, and he was tied for 24th. Broadhurst, a graduate of the 1988 tour qualifying school, made some hay out of his 66, adding a 70 and two 72s for an eight-under-par 280 and a solo third-place finish, the best of his young career.

It wasn't the outburst that paid off in the desert, however. It was quality over the long haul, and that came from the English veteran, Mark James, 35, and the Australian newcomer, Peter O'Malley, 23. James returned 69-68-72-68, and O'Malley 71-68-68-70, tying at 11-under-par 277. So the first Desert Classic came down to a playoff. It went to the vastly more experienced James, on a birdie-three on the first extra hole.

James had been one perplexed golfer. His swing was hardly a classic one, and observers said it wouldn't hold up. Their prophecies seemed to come true in 1987, when he missed 13 halfway cuts. So off he went to his original teacher, Gavin Christie, to have it rebuilt. The hard work paid off in 1988 in Peugeot Spanish Open and South African TPC victories. James opened the 1989 season rock-steady, a tie for 12th at Tenerife with 71-71-70-70—282. In the Desert Classic, James was three strokes back after the first round, then rose to the top on 68—137 through 36 holes. But the kids were hard on his heels. Broadhurst birdied the last four holes for 66—138, and O'Malley was at 68—139. In fact, it seemed a rookie shootout was in the offing after O'Malley took the third-round lead on 68—207, with Broadhurst (70) just a stroke behind. James was two strokes off the pace at 209 after his only round above the 60s, a par 72.

It was time for experience to pay off. O'Malley's toughest assignment to date was the American tour qualifying school, which he failed to crack. James was older, and nine European victories in seven seasons had prepared him for tough times. This was one. At the first extra hole, he dropped a wedge shot to within six feet of the flagstick and sank the birdie putt for the win. For him, a spot on the Ryder Cup team didn't seem so distant at the moment. Said European captain Tony Jacklin, "He's playing well and is the kind of man who would be a terrific asset to the side." For O'Malley, a spot on the European tour suddenly didn't seem so far away.

Renault Open de Baleares—£225,000
Winner: Ove Sellberg

European Ryder Cup captain Tony Jacklin keeps saying that a Swede is going to crack his team one of these years. By mid-March in the new Ryder Cup year, Ove Sellberg was the one saying, "I'm your man." Sellberg, 29, in his seventh year on the European tour, put in a bid to make this the year when he came from behind after 36 holes and turned away a strong field to take the Renault Open de Baleares, at Majorca. That made him the first Swede to win twice on the European tour. He became the first Swede to win when he took the 1986 Epson Grand Prix Match Play.

He stood up to some intense pressure to pluck this one. Look who finished second: Jose-Maria Olazabal, winner of the season-starting Tenerife Open just three weeks earlier; Mark McNulty, the win-everywhere Zimbabwean, and Philip Parkin, the lean and hungry Welshman looking for his first victory. They were all at 281, no closer than two strokes. And look who was behind them: Ronan Rafferty at 282, Eamonn Darcy at 289, Ian Woosnam at 290, and Seve Ballesteros at 295. Sellberg toured the 7,152-yard, par-72 Santa Ponsa course in 68-71-69-71—279, nine under par. It was the end of an odd week.

First, there was the out-of-sorts Ballesteros, who was both competitor and promoter in this event. He was still suffering from a virus infection that forced him to return early from a foray into the American tour. He was getting a lot of attention that he didn't want. "Don't ask me any more questions," he said, finally. His 295 was seven over par, 16 strokes behind Sellberg, and tied for 54th. The stage was set early for the hopefuls. The first-round lead was shared at 67 by a Swede—this one Anders Forsbrand—and Tony Charnley, a lanky Englishman whose caddy is his Dutch wife. Charnley was alone in the lead after 36 holes, at eight-under 136 and three strokes up on Sellberg, McNulty, and Bill Malley. He had real hope. "People like me put the stars on pedestals," Charnley said. "But last year, a lot of first-time winners came through, and that gives us all hope. If I play well, I'm as good as anybody." Then things went sour (74-75), and Charnley's first victory would have to wait for another time. He tied for 13th.

Missing the cut, by the way, was auto racing star Nigel Mansell, who was last with 87-82—169, 25 over par.

Sellberg took the 54-hole lead at 69—208, a stroke ahead of Malley. He held on, despite some real heat. Olazabal, runner-up in this event in 1988, birdied three homeward holes for a closing 67, matching the low round of the tournament. Sellberg was relentlessly steady. He made 17 pars, and one birdie, which he made at the 341-yard fifth, where he put a sand wedge to eight feet. His closing 71 was his fourth consecutive sub-par round. You could almost read his mind: Were you watching, Mr. Jacklin?

Massimo Dutti Catalan Open—£200,000
Winner: Mark Roe

Golf can be fun, Mark Roe will tell you. And to prove it, he and fellow fun-lover Robert Lee once entertained British Open fans by pulling paper bags over their heads and hitting exploding golf balls. The Royal and Ancient Golf Club of St. Andrews was not amused. The twosome also entered a charity mixed foursomes at the 1988 English Open—Roe wearing a skirt and makeup. For real fun, though, Roe, 26, discovered that nothing beats winning. And this he did for the first time in his six years on the PGA European Tour at the Massimo Dutti Catalan Open at the par-73 Pals Golf Club at Gerona, some 50 miles north of Barcelona. He was the first new winner on the 1989 circuit. All he had to do was outgun local favorite Jose-Maria Olazabal with a 32 on the final nine. Roe returned 69-70-69-71—279, 13 under par, to beat Olazabal, Colin Montgomerie, and Gordon Brand Jr. by a stroke.

"Jose taught me a lot about coping with pressure in Tenerife," Roe said. "And it's a great honor to beat such a great player down the finishing stretch for my first win." Olazabal was turning into something of a man-who-came-to-dinner in these early weeks of the 1989 season. You couldn't get rid of him. He played three of the four events so far, and had a victory and two seconds. At the Tenerife Open, he led going into the final round, and Roe was a stroke behind. Olazabal shot 70 and won. Roe stumbled to a 75 and tied for eighth.

Pals Golf Club, a 6,800-yarder tightly lined with Mediterranean pines, was seeing its first tournament action since the 1972 Spanish Open, won by Antonio Garrido (he tied for 57th on this visit). The first round belonged to an unlikely pair at five-under-par 68. Manual Calero, 36, non-winning European tour veteran who made his debut in the 1972 Spanish Open and who was preparing to start a club job in Barcelona, birdied four of his first six holes. Australian David Ecob, who did not have a European tour card, was playing under a sponsor's exemption as a former European Amateur champion. He was also playing without a caddy. Unable to understand Spanish, he dismissed the caddy and handled his own clubs on a pull cart. They didn't stay on top, but it was a good outing for both men. Calero finished ninth, his best in years, and Ecob tied for 10th.

Roe, a stroke back after the first round, got his teeth into the tournament with a second-round 70 that tied him with Grant Turner (66) for a one-stroke lead on 139 after 36 holes. A third-round 69 gave him a 208 total and a one-stroke lead over Olazabal (68) and Turner (70). Then came the strange finale.

As one might logically expect, the pressure was too much for Roe. He started to stumble. Olazabal jumped to the opportunity, eagled No. 8, and held a three-stroke lead with nine holes to play. Then as one might not logically expect, Roe suddenly came back from the dead. He birdied the

10th and 12th, and 15th, and holed a 30-foot bunker shot for an eagle-three at No. 16, and he was back in the lead. He didn't let go this time. Whatever it was he learned about pressure from Olazabal, he learned it well.

AGF Open—£137,457
Winner: Mark James

If ever a man was destined to win, it was Ronald Stelten, 32-year-old American out of La Quinta, California. He was in his fifth year on the European circuit, and he had never finished higher than 10th. In 1988 he won only $12,600, 144th on the Order of Merit. Now, in the AGF Open at La Grande Motte, at Montpelier, France, his time had come. His suffering was about to end. After that first round, what else could you think?

"In three holes, I hadn't hit a green and I'd gone four under," the astonished Stelten said. "It was an incredible streak!" He turned that streak into a seven-under-par 65 for a three-stroke lead. But, unfortunately, the gods were just taunting him. Stelten was unaccustomed to the rarefied air at the top, but he managed to hang on gamely until the final round. Then a 77 caved him in, and a veteran, Mark James, stepped out. James, who won the Desert Classic in Dubai just three weeks earlier and nursing a sore left wrist, returned 69-67-69-72—277, 11 under par. He won by three over Mark Mouland, who charged to a 65 finish and a 280 total.

Stelten had to settle for a tie for fourth, but first he gave everyone a thrill—especially himself. Look at that opening 65—five birdies and an eagle. Only once was he threatened with a bogey, and he turned that into a birdie. First came the eagle. Stelten, playing the inward nine first, got it at the 12th, holing a 100-yard nine-iron shot. At No. 13, he faced the very probable bogey. His ball was lying badly in a bunker. But he went after it confidently, flicked the shot delicately, and the ball dropped into the cup for a birdie-two. Back-to-back successes, and he didn't even have to use his putter. He didn't need it at the 14th, either. He chipped in from five yards for another birdie. In a span of three consecutive holes, he missed all three greens, and he went four under par. Under that head of steam, the 65 was almost a formality. It put him three strokes up on Sam Torrance and Mark Davis, both at 68.

Stelten held the lead through 36 holes on 68—133, 11 under par—two ahead of Sam Torrance (67—135), and three up on James (69—136). You could almost predict Stelten's coming doom from the steady rise in his scores. He reached par 72 in the third round, and James caught him with a 69. The two of them were tied for the lead on 11-under-par 205. With Torrance three behind on 73—208, it looked like a James-Stelten shootout in the final round. It didn't work out that way.

Stelten opened the final round with a birdie, but it did nothing for his nerves. He missed a three-foot putt at No. 2, then double-bogeyed the fourth, suffering a six after he drove into the water. He was on his way to a 77—282 and a share of fourth. "It's my best finish and biggest money, but it's a tough way to get it," Stelten said. "I guess I just lost control out there."

James jumped to the front at the fourth with a decisive three-stroke swing, posting a birdie against Stelten's double bogey. He escaped disaster at the

558-yard, par-five seventh. He pulled his second shot close to the trees, then ignored safe play and hit a big, sweeping eight-iron hook over water to the green. "It was just a question of grinding out par," said James, who had done just that, a 72. "I really wasn't in control today, but two titles in five tournaments is great."

Volvo Open—£200,000
Winner: Vijay Singh

Gary Player long has insisted that a golfer has to play around the world to be recognized. For a golfer from Fiji, that's more than a working definition. It's a necessity. There's not much for a tournament golfer to do in that Pacific island nation. At all events, Vijay Singh, the 26-year-old Fijian who won his European tour card in the December, 1988, qualifying school, has a leg up on Player's dictum. When the slender six-footer took the Volvo Open in Sardinia—the first time for the event there—that gave him victories in Malaysia, Africa, and now on the European tour. What's next? Well, his goals for 1989 were to qualify for the British Open and to finish in the top 10 of the Order of Merit.

Those goals seem modest, even anticlimactic, after the way he took the Volvo Open. Singh, who finished second in the qualifying school, has a high-powered, attacking game, remindful of Seve Ballesteros. After an unimpressive start, Singh rolled to the championship on 72-68-68-68—276, a 12-under-par total on the 7,080-yard, par-72 Is Molas course. He led by one going into the final round, and came out winning by three over Australian Peter Fowler. His bold approach to the game was the other part of the story. Singh carded 23 birdies over the 72 holes, an average of 5.75 per round. Put those 23 birdies against his 12-under-par finish, and simple arithmetic tells you that his flamboyant play also cost him.

"When I see the chance, I go for it," Singh said. "I can't play any other way." Just the week before, en route to a tie for fourth in the AGF Open, he scored 19 birdies and a hole-in-one. Before the AGF, he was having a lackluster time of it. In the first four events of the season, he finished 41st, 87th, 89th, and 46th. Then his game clicked in the AGF and exploded in the Volvo Open. Some may argue that his victory was diluted, having come when the big European guns were in the United States getting ready for the Masters the following week. But there are two things no one can argue with: Singh's name is on the trophy, and it's on the check. His portfolio now showed the Volvo Open, the 1984 Malaysian PGA, the 1988 Nigerian Open, the 1988 Swedish PGA, and the 1989 Zimbabwe Open.

With his opening par 72, Singh was four strokes off the pace set by Carl Mason and American Charlie Bolling, co-leaders at 68. Andrew Chandler moved to the top in the second round, his 69—138 giving him a one-stroke lead. Singh was two behind on 68—140. He finally broke through to the top in the third round with 68—208, and was leading Mason by one.

Then came the clincher. Mason stumbled early, and if that eased the pressure, Singh didn't seem to notice. He was playing his game. After two pars, he opened up at No. 3, holing a curling 40-foot putt for a birdie, the first of six in that final round. He turned in 32 and stumbled immediately, three-putting No. 10. He got revenge with a birdie at No. 11, then got his 23rd of the week at No. 16. If there had been any doubts, that one erased them.

Jersey European Airways Open—£147,000
Winner: Christy O'Connor Jr.

Of all the people telling Christy O'Connor Jr. "I told you so," Ann O'Connor was doing it best. As a wife, she turned out to be quite a prognosticator, to say nothing of a comfort.

"It's been a long time," O'Connor was saying, with great relief after winning the Jersey European Airways Open, "but my wife has never stopped telling me for the last two years that I can win again."

Actually, it was some 14 years, if you go back to his last individual title, the 1975 Irish Open (he also had a tie for the Martini International that year). His last victory of any sort was the two-man Sumrie-Bournemouth Better-Ball he and Eamonn Darcy won in 1978, and 1976 before that. He joined the pro tour in 1970, and his first victory was the 1974 Zambian Open. So the Jersey Open was a big step for the personable Irishman. At least as big to him as winning the Masters was to Nick Faldo that week.

Ann O'Connor didn't realize how close she was cutting it with her prediction. O'Connor left this one up in the air until the last moment. He lost a one-stroke lead at the final hole, got caught by Denis Durnian, and had to go to a playoff to win. O'Connor did it with a par on the first extra hole. O'Connor had returned 73-70-66-72, a seven-under-par 281 at the 6,797-yard, par-72 La Moye course. Durnian had 70-71-67-73.

Neither man looked like much of a winner when the tournament got under way. The first-round lead was split five ways at 69—Peter Mitchell, David Feherty, Rick Hartmann, David A. Russell, and Colin Montgomerie. Durnian, with his 70, seemed lost in the crowd. O'Connor had saddled himself with a 73. Around came the second round, and still neither man appeared on the leaderboard. David Llewellyn (69) and Russell (70) shared the 36-hole lead at 139, just ahead of a small pack at 140. Durnian hung tight with 71—141, but O'Connor still seemed no threat at 70—143. If he was to figure in this tournament, he would have to make a move soon. And he did.

It came in the form of the best round of the week, a six-under-par 66 that put him a stroke behind Durnian, who took the lead going into the final round with 67—208. Now it was time for the fates to taunt Durnian, 38, who gave up his club pro job in 1987 in the belief that "I can compete with the Ballesteroses and the Langers." Durnian began entering tour events in 1971, and was still looking for his first victory. Jersey almost was it.

O'Connor had taken the lead from Durnian and was ahead by a stroke coming to the finish, when the nerves hit. "I was nervous on the last hole for the first time today," he said. "My drive was fine, but I didn't want to go over the green or leave myself a 35-foot putt." Instead, he found a bunker. He blasted out to six feet, then two-putted for a bogey and a par 72. Durnian tied him with a 73. They went to a playoff in a harsh rain. This time, it was Durnian who made the error. His approach went off the back of the green, and O'Connor got his par and his victory. Next question: In this Ryder Cup year, did Ann O'Connor have any more predictions?

Credit Lyonnais Cannes Open—£209,110
Winner: Paul Broadhurst

Paul Broadhurst, only 23 and a raw rookie on the European tour, had to figure that this was his week when he birdied off a tree in the first round and got washed out in the last. The birdie helped him into a lead he never gave up, and when heavy rains wiped out the final round, he was declared the winner. He was the first rookie winner on the European tour since Jose-Maria Olazabal, who won twice in 1986. Broadhurst also staked a claim to Ryder Cup consideration. In the first eight weeks of the tour, he owned a victory and two thirds. This was the same Paul Broadhurst who was the only amateur to survive the cut in the 1988 British Open. The six-foot, three-inch redhaired Englishman left his part-time job as a glass fiber technician and, with $210 in his bank account, turned pro. He entered the tour qualifying school in December and won his card with room to spare, 18th out of 50.

His victory, despite coming in three rounds, was hardly chintzy. First, the field had muscle—among others, Ian Woosnam, American veteran Bill Glasson, and two new champions, the Renault Open's Ove Sellberg, and the Volvo Open's Vijay Singh (who missed the cut here).

Second, there was Broadhurst's own performance. He led all the way on the 6,786-yard, par-72 Cannes Mougins course, on 65-70-72—207, nine under par. He won by a stroke over Jimmy Heggarty, Brett Ogle, and Peter Senior.

Broadhurst was saved at any number of places. For one, at No. 15 in the first round, when his wild tee shot bounced off a tree and back onto the green, some 20 feet from the cup, Broadhurst didn't look at that gift horse very long. He holed the putt for his birdie. He had just birdied No. 11 from 15 feet, and No. 12 from 12. Before that, he holed a 30-foot bunker shot at No. 9 to go four under through the turn. The 65 left him shaking his head.

"When I hit the greens, I made the putt, and when I missed the greens, I got up and down in two," he said. "It was ridiculous. In fact, what's happened to me so far on the pro tour has been silly. I feel as though any minute I'm going to wake up, and find that all this hasn't happened."

Broadhurst was pretty much the entire Cannes story. There were a few sidelights. Howard Clark, back in action after getting his swing rebuilt for a month, was disgusted with his opening 79 and got himself disqualified by not signing his scorecard. Then there was Derrick Cooper, tying the course record in the second round with a 64, just the inspiration for defending his Madrid Open title the next week.

In the third round, Broadhurst came up with another semi-miracle. At the par-five 16th, he hit his first ball out of bounds, then pulled himself together and made a four on his second, escaping with a six. When Senior followed with a six at No. 17, and Ogle with a six at No. 18, Broadhurst found himself the leader. And when rain washed out the final round, he found himself the champion. He was prepared for the critics.

"People may say I didn't really win," Broadhurst said. "But that won't worry me. It was out of my hands. And all I care about is that it's in the record books."

Cepsa Madrid Open—£225,000
Winner: Seve Ballesteros

When last heard from, Howard Clark was stalking out of the Cannes Open, fuming over his first-round 79 and refusing to sign his card. Now it was the Cepsa Madrid Open, and Clark was miffed again. Not at the score this time, but at Seve Ballesteros.

Ballesteros and Clark have a long-running battle in the Madrid Open. Twice before, Ballesteros needed an eagle at the final hole to tie, but couldn't do it, and Clark won both times, in 1984 and 1986. It was Clark who needed the eagle this time. He did birdie, but that merely cut his final deficit to one stroke. Ballesteros scored his first victory on the season and his third Madrid title with 67-67-69-69, a 16-under-par total of 272 at the 6,941-yard, par-72 Puerta de Hierro course. Clark returned 65-68-70-70—273. Then the fireworks started.

"He tried to intimidate me," Clark said. "He continually walked around while I was putting, but it seemed every time he did that, I sank it. At the end, he was generous. He said, 'Well done.' Maybe he doesn't like me. He's not very gracious. He doesn't say 'Good shot' very often. Maybe he thought he was going to lose."

That was an echo of Bernhard Langer's comments at the Suntory World Match Play a few years earlier. And Ballesteros, as he was back then, was surprised by the sharp criticism. "It is incredible he said that," Ballesteros said, after having praised Clark as a tremendous player. "I can't believe it. I've never had anything against him. I always say nice things about him. Maybe he has the wrong impression of me. When he was walking around on the greens, I was reading my putts. As soon as he was ready to putt, I stopped. The best way to concentrate is not to watch the other player."

So much for the fireworks off the golf course. The fireworks on the course went this way:

The first round belonged to two Swedes, Jesper Parnevik and Magnus Persson, on eight-under-par 64s. Clark was at 65, Ballesteros at 67. The rematch began in the second round. Clark took the lead on 68—133, and Ballesteros (67) was tied for second with 134 with Persson (70). Things heated up in the third round. Clark went to two under for the round and 13 under for the tournament with a 25-foot birdie putt at No. 7. But he bogeyed the 10th and 11th, and Ballesteros went ahead with birdies at No. 13 and No. 15. Meanwhile, defending champion Derrick Cooper was having a wild time. He birdied three of the first four holes and three of the last six in a 67 that left him three strokes off the lead. He was tied at 206 with Mark James, who shook off a bogey, triple-bogey start for a 68 that included four birdies and an eagle.

A three-way fight was developing in the last round with Ireland's Philip Walton, who made the turn in 33 and then tied for the lead at 13 under par with a birdie at No. 10. But he fell out with bogeys at No. 11 and No. 14. A couple of late birdies got him third place on 68—275. The way was clear for the two main characters.

Ballesteros and Clark were tied through the turn, going out in par 36s. Then Ballesteros went ahead for good. Clark bogeyed the 12th, and Ballesteros birdied the par-four 13th after hitting a sand wedge to three feet. Ballesteros locked up the title with a downhill, 20-foot birdie putt at the par-three 17th. Clark needed that eagle at No. 18 to tie. He didn't get it, but he did drop a 15-foot putt for the next best thing. Then he got a load off his chest.

Peugeot Spanish Open—£250,000
Winner: Bernhard Langer

Bernhard Langer, a walking clinic on the dreaded yips, found peace and happiness at possibly the toughest inland course in Europe, El Saler, at Valencia. "It certainly seems like my problems are behind me," said Langer. "I'm putting consistently and holing my share of the big ones." For the soft-spoken West German, that represented an absolute outburst. What inspired it was the five-under-par 67 he fired in the third round. That put him into what had become strange country for him—the head of the pack. It gave him a two-stroke lead going into the final round of the Peugeot Spanish Open. Then an extraordinary thing happened: He went on to win it. It was his first victory in a year, but more important—to his state of mind—it meant relief from the yips. Perhaps only temporary, given the strange nature of the yips, but relief nonetheless.

Early on, Langer showed no sign that he might win. On the other hand, he gave no sign that he wouldn't. There is a huge difference between the two. Langer erased that difference with 70-72-67-72—281, seven under par. It gave him a three-stroke win over Jose-Maria Canizares and Paul Carrigill.

Carrigill, who won back his European tour card in December, broke into the 36-hole lead with 69—139. For a while, that was encouraging news back home in Leeds. He said the landlady of a public house there bets £1 on him each week at 100-to-1 odds with his father, who is a bookmaker. "The only time she collected," Carrigill said, "was when I won the Zambian Open in 1987." It took Derrick Cooper's crash to get Carrigill up there. Cooper, playing the course for the very first time—even without practice—returned an eight-birdie 66 in the first round, and led by three strokes over Mark Davis and Mariano Aparicio. A second-round 75 shoved Cooper aside. Some big names also didn't find El Saler quite so amenable. Seve Ballesteros returned a 75, and Ian Woosnam a 78, and neither was a factor.

Langer, meanwhile, was unnoticed with his 70-72—142 start. It left him just three strokes off the 36-hole lead. The marvel was that he made the cut at all. He was suffering his third bout of the yips. His earlier solution was to putt cross-handed from about 20 feet on in. That worked for a few years. But the yips returned with a vengeance. Who can forget that pathetic five-putt in the final round of the 1988 British Open? Now his solution was a split grip that maybe no one had ever seen before. He moves his left hand far down the shaft, then clutches the upper part of the grip against the underside of his left forearm. It worked especially well in the third round. He needed just 27 putts, including a pair of birdies from 16 and 25 feet at the first two holes. He did that much of the day. He tripped only once, a three-putt at No. 4, and finished the day with a 50-foot chip-in for a birdie at No. 18. In the fourth round, things went sour early. He birdied No. 4, but followed that with a six at No. 5, where he needed a penalty drop after hitting his second into trees, then made a three-putt bogey at No. 6. Eventually, he fell into a tie with Canizares and Carrigill. He broke free with a 50-foot birdie putt at No. 16, and followed that at No. 17 with a tap-in birdie after missing a hole-in-one. He was a winner for the 18th time in his 14 years on the European tour. It was a fitting end to a strange week.

It began with Langer coming to the defense of Ballesteros, whom Howard Clark had sharply criticized a week earlier at the Madrid Open. Langer had said pretty much the same things at the 1985 Suntory World Match Play. "I know him better now, and he's a very nice guy," Langer said. "It might come over as if he doesn't like you, but it's just that he's so competitive, so intense. He wants to win so badly." Then there was the hearsay report that Ryder Cup captain Tony Jacklin was supposed to have said that Langer ought to give up the game. "I know Tony too well," Langer said. "It had to be a translation mix-up. I admit to having slight doubts late last year that I might never win again. A lot of guys have failed to come back from problems like mine. But I always knew I was better than most, even playing badly, and too good to retire. I never lost faith in myself . . . "

Perhaps, figuratively speaking, a little home cooking is what he needed. He had spent the early part of the season on the American tour. This was his first European tournament of the year. In 1988, his first European outing was the Epson Grand Prix, and he won that. "Maybe," he cracked, "I'll stay in the States until British Open time next year."

Epson Grand Prix of Europe Match Play—£300,000
Winner: Seve Ballesteros

"It's wide open now," Des Smyth was saying, with a hint of satisfaction. He had been somewhat inspired by the third-round massacre, which wiped the remaining big guns out of the Epson Grand Prix of Europe. Then a dark thought struck him. "Except," he said, "for Ballesteros."

Good thinking. With Seve Ballesteros on the prowl, no event is entirely wide open. This one was no exception. Ballesteros lost his very first hole back on Friday, shook off one tough match on Saturday, and came barrelling home in the final one for a 4-and-3 decision over Denis Durnian and the Grand Prix victory. It was his second victory of the European season. If there was any doubt who was in command, Ballesteros erased it on the first hole, hitting his three-wood approach shot 275 yards, to within inches of the hole.

"That was awesome," Durnian said.

"I was lucky," Ballesteros protested.

The match play tournament opened with its most decisive victory ever, Mats Lanner's 8-and-6 win over Manual Pinero. "I didn't play badly," Pinero said. "Mats was fantastic." The eight top seeds—including top-seeded Ballesteros, defending champion Bernhard Langer, No. 2, and Ian Woosnam, No. 4—drew byes on Thursday. Things went pretty much according to form in their first outings, on Friday. Ballesteros lost his first hole, then played the next 14 in six under par to sink Australian Mike Clayton, 4 and 3. Langer bumped Christy O'Connor Jr., 2 and 1. Woosnam needed some heroics, and he couldn't have chosen a better place than his homeland. He was the local favorite at St. Pierre Golf and Country Club at Chepstow, Wales, and he gave his boosters a thrill. He was all but dead, trailing Richard Boxall by two with three holes to play. He birdied No. 16, halved the 17th, then squared the match by holing a long birdie putt on the final hole of regulation. He wrapped up the win on the first extra hole with yet another birdie, his third in four holes. "I really didn't think I was going to win," he said.

Woosnam's luck ran out the next day. Australian Mike Harwood ousted him on the final hole. Des Smyth lost the first two holes, then one-putted the last five to beat Jose-Maria Olazabal. Ken Brown tripped Langer, then himself was spilled by Durnian, who also beat Mark James. It was at this point that Smyth decided the tournament was wide open. Durnian closed it for him in the morning semifinal, 4 and 3. Ballesteros took the other final berth, walloping Harwood, 6 and 5.

The final was decided almost before it started.

Ballesteros fired that three-wood approach to inches at No. 1. That stunned Durnian. He was lying three and still short of the green. He conceded the hole. Ballesteros won the next three as well. Durnian, former English club pro champion, was giving a creditable account of himself, but Ballesteros was on one of his rampages. Durnian won just two holes. Ballesteros made the turn in five-under-par 30 and kept his four-hole lead. He wrapped up the victory with a signature shot—a 145-yard nine-iron to within a foot at No. 15. It was nearly a carbon copy of his great approach to No. 16 that helped wrap up the 1988 British Open. All told, Ballesteros was 29 under par for the 73 holes he played, and in that span made just two bogeys and 27 under-par scores.

"Seve is the greatest player in the world, without question," Durnian said. "When he is on that kind of form, there is no one who would beat him."

Volvo Belgian Open—£200,000
Winner: Gordon J. Brand

Gordon J. Brand—the Brand from England, not from Scotland—has been described over the years as pleasant, reserved, frustrated, and patient. You may now add "rewarded."

Brand, 33, had known the taste of victory in his 13 years, but only in Africa, never in Europe. So the Volvo Belgian Open at Royal Waterloo, near Brussels, goes down as landmark achievement for him. Brand wasted little time getting a leg up on this one. He birdied three of the last six holes in the first round to tie Australia's Peter McWhinney at five-under-par 67 for a one-stroke lead on a traffic jam at 68. Brand added rounds of 69-68-69 for a 273 total, 15 under par and a four-stroke victory over English club pro Kevin Dickens.

"I've won six times on the Safari Tour in Africa and had five seconds in Europe," Brand said. His seconds included the 1986 British Open, to Greg Norman at Turnberry. "Finishing runner-up to Greg convinced me I was good enough," Brand said. "And with greatest respect to the lads who have won, I know I'm as good or better than they are."

Playing in Africa is not the same as playing in the British Open, Brand conceded. "Winning isn't just a matter of how well you swing the club," he said. "When I had my chance at Turnberry, I wilted under the pressure. But this time I was always in control."

That he was. He did not trail in the tournament. He was tied twice, with McWhinney in the first round and with Dickens in the third. He led by a stroke in the second, and he ran off and hid in the fourth. There was no room for doubt.

Brand's first-round 67 included six birdies, two of them for deuces from 10 and 20 feet on the outward nine. He started his powerhouse finish at No. 13, where he cut his drive around the corner of the dogleg and holed a 10-footer for a birdie-three. He birdied the 17th and 18th after chip-and-runs to within four feet. His second-round 69 included a stunning three-birdie outburst—from 20 feet at No. 16, three feet at No. 17, and 15 at No. 18. He clinched it in the final round with his own 69, especially with his outward 33 against the 37 by the collapsing Dickens. Nor did Brand sneak home. After a bogey-six at No. 17, he boldly hit two woods to reach the green at No. 18, setting up a birdie-four finish.

If Brand's victory wasn't enough of a thrill for the fans, then Peter Baker's astounding 65 ought to have been. He was robbed. He came within an eyelash of three holes-in-one—six inches at No. 7, eight inches at No. 15, and at No. 12, he hit the hole with his tee shot. There went the new Volvo offered as a prize. He also just missed the Perrier prize for the first sub-64 round—25,000 new European Economic Community monetary units, said to be worth US$25,000. But he bogeyed No. 13 after hitting his drive into the trees, and he missed a five-foot birdie attempt at No. 18. No whimpering from Baker, though. In his past nine outings, he missed four 36-hole cuts, and finished 66th, 70th, and 72nd in three other events. His 283 was good for a tie for 16th here.

Brand and Baker finished 10 strokes apart, but had one thing in common—the Ryder Cup dream. "I don't expect to be picked unless I win again," said Brand. "So I must concentrate on making the top nine in the points table, to get one of the automatic spots."

Lancia Italian Open—£255,450
Winner: Ronan Rafferty

You knew this Lancia Italian Open was going to be a mass tightrope walk when 46 of the 142 starters broke the par of 72, and 17 of those shot in the 60s. No one could afford the slightest misstep. The 6,960-yard Monticello course, near Como, had become a shooting gallery. Another 15 broke 70 in the second round, and the 36-hole cut was made at a tight one-over-par 145. They were firing full-bore, so it would take an error to decide this one. Sam Torrance, trying to win his second Italian Open, was the one who made it. And Ronan Rafferty, trying to win his first big event of any kind, was there to pick up the spoils. He had already done his part—a closing 65. He had waited eight years-plus for this moment, since joining the European tour in

1981. Then he had to wait a century—actually, 20 minutes—for it to come true.

Rafferty had already finished. He had put up 71-69-68-65—273, 15 under par. Then his fate rested in Torrance's hands, out there on the course some 20 minutes behind him. Torrance started the day with a two-stroke lead, and now he came to the final hole needing a five-foot putt for his par four and a tie. But he missed. Finally, Rafferty was a winner.

"You thoroughly deserved to win," Torrance told him.

"Winning my first 72-hole open in Europe has proved a big barrier to break through," Rafferty said. "Everyone has expected me to win since I turned pro. I've been in position several times without being able to take my chances, but after a nervous start to the last round, I finally made it."

Torrance, 35, fighting the yips, had taken up the elongated putter so popular on the American Senior PGA Tour. The golfer holds the top near his chest and sweeps, broom-like, with the other hand halfway down. His last victory, ironically, was the 1987 Italian Open on the very same course—with the regular putter—when he beat Jose Rivero in a six-hole playoff. Torrance used the long one to deadly effect in the third round. He dropped an 18-footer and a 25-footer to make the turn in 33, then birdied four of the last five holes for a 65. The surge lifted him into the 54-hole lead by two strokes over David Feherty (the first-round leader with 65) and unknown Briton Paul Carman, former assistant pro to Denis Durnian. Rafferty was warming up. He birdied No. 12 on a spectacular eight-iron recovery shot from a bunker and a 25-foot putt, and he saved par with a 20-footer at No. 18.

The final day, Torrance led by two with nine holes to play, then his rollercoaster ride began. He birdied the 10th and 11th, bogeyed the next two, then birdied No. 14 and No. 15. He saved par from a bunker at No. 17, then stumbled to that bogey at No. 18 for a 70, hardly a bad score. But Rafferty had just torn through the course for a 65.

Rafferty got rolling fast, dropping a 15-footer for a birdie at No. 1. He picked up three more and made the turn in 32, holing putts of 25 feet at No. 6 and 20 feet at No. 7. He also chalked up a beauty at the par-five 14th, where he blasted from a bunker and sank an 18-footer. He was having the kind of putting day Torrance was dreaming of—all told, only 29 putts, and holing five times from between 15 and 25 feet.

Rafferty, who helped the Irish team win the 1988 Dunhill Cup, had finally cracked the tournament he had flirted with. He lost the 1986 Italian Open to David Feherty in a playoff, and was third to Greg Norman in 1988. But he was not the only happy man at Monticello. There was Carman. Unable to afford a caddy, he used a pull cart until the third round, when officials informed him he would have to hire a caddy because he had been paired with Seve Ballesteros, the British Open champion. "I haven't earned much so far," Carman said. "I'm not thinking of a victory here. I hope to finish among the top five." And with 70-69-67-72—278, and £9,885, that's precisely what he did.

Volvo PGA Championship—£350,000
Winner: Nick Faldo

The signal came late in the final round, but as signals go, they don't come any stronger. This one said the Volvo PGA Championship belonged to Nick Faldo.

Faldo had his record fourth PGA title in hand—or so it seemed. All he needed, there at Wentworth, was an untroubled finish. But the gods of golf were welcoming him back to European action for the first time since his Volvo Masters victory in October, also welcoming him back from winning the U.S. Masters just seven weeks earlier, and they had one more little thrill left for him. They gave it to him at No. 17, a par-five.

Faldo drove to the right, near the trees. Faced with an uphill-and-downhill flight path, and trying to protect his lead, he decided to fade a four iron to the green. It was good, bold thinking, but the shot misfired. Faldo held his breath as he watched the ball rocket over the out-of-bounds stakes, headed for a garden next to the course. Then the ball hit a tree and bounced back in. Faldo took a deep breath and said thanks. Then he chipped to 45 feet, got down in two putts for his par, and one hole later he added the PGA title to his resume. He returned 67-69-69-67 for a 16-under-par 272 and a two-stroke victory over Ian Woosnam, the 1988 champion. Faldo is a member at Wentworth, and lives near the club. He had finally beaten his own course.

"It's taken long enough," he said. "I must have had 30 attempts to win in PGA Championships and World Match Plays, but it has always eluded me. So this one is gratifying."

Faldo led all the way, but never alone until the end. Someone dogged him all the way. Woosnam matched his 67 in the first round. Faldo called it "my best putting round since Augusta." After fives at No. 1 and No. 3, he ran off four consecutive birdies from the fifth, three of them on good-sized putts. Woosnam missed a number of makeable putts. And as if to signal a return of Britain's Big Three to full health, slumping Sandy Lyle posted a two-under-par 70, his best score in weeks. But things got worse for him in a hurry. He just made the cut at 75—147, then finished dead last with 78-77 for a 300 total.

In the second round, it was Craig Parry who stayed with Faldo, his 68 knotting them at eight-under-par 136. Faldo bogeyed the second and third, but rebounded for birdies at the fourth, fifth, and eighth and a 69. He was nine under par and the lone leader by No. 13, but Parry kept the pressure on with an outward 31. Woosnam (72) was in a group at 139. Seve Ballesteros, unable to get things moving, returned a 74 and just made the halfway cut at 147. He would make a fierce finish, though—65-66—131—zooming to a share of fourth place.

Parry dogged Faldo in the third round, too, both getting 69—205, 11 under par, and not without drama. At the par-three 10th, Parry's tee shot missed the green to the right and bounced down the bank and into thick grass near a ditch. He was 20 yards from the hole and nose-to-nose with a sure bogey. But somehow he popped the ball up the hill, under some branches, and it hit the green and rolled into the hole. Said Faldo, "Some shot from there." Then he holed a 12-footer for a birdie of his own. Parry was threatening to run away, getting to three ahead with six holes to play on the hot, dry day. But he bogeyed No. 13 and No. 17. "It was probably the most frustrating round I've ever played in my life." Parry said. "I made so many birdies and bogeys." Actually, the 23-year-old Aussie had seven birdies, four bogeys. He finished third on 71—276.

It was all Faldo in the final round. Remember the gift miracle at No. 17? Well, he created one of his own at No. 15. His tee shot ended up in an awkward lie. But he had plenty of breathing room—three ahead of Woosnam, four ahead of Parry. He could afford to waste a play-safe shot and settle for a five. Instead, he bent a beautiful three-iron shot around the trees to within five feet of the hole. He dropped that one for a fourth consecutive birdie, and eased on home, pausing only for that little bank shot off the tree at No. 17.

Dunhill British Masters—£300,000
Winner: Nick Faldo

At least things started differently this time. Ian Young, never higher than fifth in his seven years on the European tour, ignored the cold and rain to shoot seven-under-par 65 in the first round. He was leading the Dunhill British Masters by one. "I've decided it's about time I got going," he said. (The fates decided otherwise. A closing 81 left him tied for 63rd.)

The second round belonged to the Irish. Ronan Rafferty, who had scored his first tour victory in the Italian Open two weeks earlier, matched the 65. Christy O'Connor Jr., the Jersey Open winner in April, posted a 66. So they shared the 36-hole lead on 135. The supporting cast having had their say, the rest of the tournament belonged to Nick Faldo despite the fearful drubbing the field put on Woburn—1,006 birdies and 44 eagles by the other 68 players who played all four rounds.

And so came the question again: Who's the best in the world? Faldo says there are actually five or six "best" players, depending on who's hot. "We keep handing it back and forth," he said. Well, nobody handed anything to Faldo this time. He simply went out and took it. After a 71 in the first round, he shot 65 in the second round, took the lead in the third with another 65, and closed with a 66 for a 21-under-par 267 and a runaway, four-stroke victory over Rafferty. Counting the Volvo Masters in 1988, this was his third consecutive European win. And don't forget the U.S. Masters victory in April.

This time, the putter did it, Faldo said, crediting a stroke change. "I found it almost by accident during the first round at No. 15," Faldo said. "I decided to widen my stance, and all of a sudden the penny dropped. From then on, I just swung the putter at the hole and I missed nothing important."

It was a week of extremes. For defending champion Sandy Lyle, it was a short visit—76-70 and his seventh missed cut in nine events. For Faldo, it was an affair of state, with a dinner at No. 10 Downing Street with Prime Minister Margaret Thatcher and President George Bush. Golf had come a long way since the day pros were barred from the clubhouse.

Faldo wasted no time making his move. In the second round, he birdied three of the first four holes, setting up his 65. But it was a par that highlighted his card. At No. 14, he had to chop his way back to the fairway, and then a 90-yard wedge shot to seven feet and a cool putt saved his par. In the third round, Faldo staked an early claim to his second 65, dropping long birdie putts at the first and second.

Faldo was on automatic pilot for his closing 66. The key shot came at the 502-yard No. 11, a seven-iron second to within two feet of the hole for an easy eagle-three. Rafferty's chances died when he bunkered shots at No. 15 and No. 16. Faldo wrapped it up, and the bookkeepers figured out the damages: He had played eight sub-par rounds in a row; he was 37 under par for 144 holes, of which he birdied 48 and eagled one; he won £108,330 in prize money, an average of £200.98 per stroke.

Rafferty deserved better with his 17-under-par performance, but he didn't seem to notice. "I loved today," he said. "It was not only an honor, but a pleasure to play with Nick. He is to my mind the best in the world."

Wang Four Stars National Pro-Celebrity—£200,000
Winner: Craig Parry

It seems more and more Australians are making England their home, the better to play the European tour. It also seems they're staking out the Wang Four Stars National Pro-Celebrity as their own event. It was Rodger Davis in 1988, making the Wang his first victory in 18 months (a pinched neck nerve forced him out of this one). This time it was Craig Parry, a second-year man, making the Wang his first European tour victory and also giving the European tour its sixth first-time winner of the year. And also leaving Ian Woosnam to shake his head, wondering "What do you have to do to win?"

A reasonable question. Woosnam closed with a six-under-par 66 at the par-72 Moor Park course in Rickmansworth, Hertfordshire. That ought to have been enough. But Parry, 23—who almost hauled in the Great White Shark, countryman Greg Norman, in the 1988 Italian Open—is a never-say-die type. He needed birdies on the last two holes to stay alive. He got them. Then he got a third in the sudden-death playoff, and Woosnam was runner-up for the second time in three weeks and still looking for his first victory of the year. Both came out of the pack. Parry (67-71-66-69—273, 15 under par), first led in the third round. Woosnam (67-72-68-66) trailed by one in the first, and by three in the second and third before that 66 finish. Between them, they made 41 birdies and four eagles.

The Australian parade began immediately when Mike Harwood, the newcomer in a group of countrymen (including Parry) living at Bagshot near London, powered his way into the first-round lead on 66. Harwood, 1988 Portuguese Open champion, set it up with the tournament's first eagle-three on a four-iron to 10 feet at No. 3. Woosnam, starting at No. 10, was out in 32, with three birdies, including a two-putt at No. 17. Parry, also starting from No. 10, had a birdie-bogey finish. The drama didn't really take shape until the third round.

Woosnam notched a pair of eagles to take the early 54-hole lead, on 68-207, nine under par. He got overrun quickly. Bob Shearer, another Aussie, topped him with 65—206, and himself was topped by Harwood (67) and England's David Gilford (65), both at 205. Then along came Parry with a

66—204, and a one-stroke lead. In the final round, Woosnam tore through in 66 despite a sore leg that required pain killers. Parry found himself trailing by two with two holes to play. Then he birdied the par-five 17th. He trailed by one with one to play. But he bunkered his tee shot at No. 18. No matter. He hit a five iron to 15 feet, and made that one, too. He had caught Woosnam, who had no trouble finding the seeds of his self-destruction—the quest for instant riches.

A prize of £1 million—half to the golfer, half to charity—was being offered for a hole-in-one at the 184-yard 14th. "I went all out for it," Woosnam said. "But I caught my tee shot a bit fat, found a terrible lie in the bunker, and took four. That cost me the title." That and Parry's determination. In the playoff, Woosnam was short of the green and ended up needing a birdie from 20 feet to stay alive. He didn't get it, nor another chance. Parry hit a two iron to the back of the green and got down in two for his third consecutive birdie; and to his wins in Australia, Canada, and Japan, he added his first European victory.

NM English Open—£250,000
Winner: Mark James

When time and circumstance came together at the NM English Open, the result was predicable: The Ryder Cup started to boil. The European tour's 1989 season had reached about the halfway point. While its big guns were in the U.S. Open, the English Open was being played, this third week of June, on the Brabazon Course of The Belfry, where the Ryder Cup Match would be played September 22-24.

Add another reason: European captain Tony Jacklin was in the field. Nobody expected much from his game (he would miss the cut by a mile, 77-79), but everyone was watching him. "The team is shaping up as I thought it would," Jacklin said. "The cream is surfacing. But there are still a couple of players I would like to see among the leaders on the list." Jacklin would have three free choices to add to the nine automatic qualifiers. He mentioned Gordon Brand Jr. and Jose Rivero as two he was watching. He didn't have to mention Mark James. Mark James tapped him on the shoulder anyway, to remind him he had a certified Ryder Cupper right under his nose.

This James did by scoring his third victory of the season, coming from behind to take the English Open by a stroke from two 1987 Ryder Cuppers, Eamonn Darcy and Sam Torrance, as well as Craig Parry, winner of the Wang Four Stars the week before. James, by adding the English Open to the Desert Classic and the AGF Open, not only assured himself of his best season in 14 years on the tour, but also put himself right at the top of Jacklin's automatic Ryder Cup list.

"I'll be looking forward to coming back here for the matches," James said. "I've had a long wait." James, 35, was last in the Ryder Cup in 1981, another in a long string of American victories, and before that, in the 1979 matches, he was fined £1,500 for various offenses, including refusing to wear the official uniform at the flag raising ceremony. James (72-70-69-68—279, nine under par) never so much as smelled victory in the English Open until the final round. He trailed by six strokes after the first round, then four, then three. And the final round didn't exactly start with promise. He bogeyed No. 2 after his wedge shot missed the green. But he shook it off and cruised home without another error. He also put on the kind of chipping clinic that warmed Jacklin's heart. Three times he chipped to within inches of the hole.

That put a strain on the men he just passed. Darcy birdied the last three holes for a 72, and Torrance, using his 48-1/2-inch anti-yip pendulum putter, dropped a 35-footer on the last hole for a 71. Both fell short, as did Parry, but not for lack of trying. Starting the day five strokes off the lead, he birdied three of the last four holes for a 67 and a share of second. Meanwhile, the two men under Jacklin's Ryder Cup microscope lurched badly. Rivero missed the cut wildly (78-75—153) by seven strokes. Brand missed by three (77-72—149), but also spectacularly. In that first round 77 was a crushing 11 at No. 17. It took him seven whacks to get out of knee-deep rough.

Carrolls Irish Open—£262,697
Winner: Ian Woosnam

Ian Woosnam couldn't bear the thought. But what if just a couple putts had dropped in the Volvo PGA? What if he had holed that birdie in the Wang Four Stars playoff? How about a little break, here or there, in the U.S. Open? If those "what-ifs" had come true, Woosnam would have been the king of the hill by late June, when in a five-week span he capped a string of three near-misses with a victory in the Carrolls Irish Open.

In the Volvo PGA, foiled by his putter, he was second to Nick Faldo by two strokes. Two weeks later, in the Wang Four Stars, he caught Craig Parry with a final-round 66, only to lose in the playoff. Then he was tied for second to Curtis Strange by a mere stroke in the U.S. Open. Then the next week, he won his second consecutive Irish Open title at Portmarnock. But it didn't look like his week at first.

In fact, it started out as Sandy Lyle's week. The suffering Scot was fresh from missing the 36-hole cut at the U.S. Open. That was nine misses in his last 11 outings. But he arrived at Portmarnock saying he was feeling "lean and mean." It seemed so. At his first hole, the 341-yard 10th, his tee shot stopped just 20 yards short of the flag. It was an easy birdie, triggering a course-record, eight-under-par 64 and a one-stroke lead. Woosnam was six behind.

They reversed roles quickly. Lyle slipped away (64-73-74-76) to a tie for 15th at 287. Woosnam was headed in the other direction—70-67-71-70—278, tying Ireland's Philip Walton (68-69-69-72) then beating him on the first hole of a playoff with a birdie from 10 feet at No. 18, where moments earlier he missed a winning seven-footer in regulation.

"I was shaking all over as I tackled both of those putts," Woosnam said. "But at least I knew the line the second time around." Woosnam had his first victory of the season. Walton, 27, former Walker Cup player, had the best finish of his seven years on the tour.

An Irishman win the Irish Open? It would be the headiest moment on the Emerald Isle since the Irish team of Eamonn Darcy, Des Smyth, and Ronan

Rafferty won the Dunhill Cup back in October. This would be a great setting for Walton's first victory. He used to sneak onto Portmarnock as a 10-year-old and get in a few shots before someone could run him off. In the second round, he joined Woosnam and Lyle at the lead on 69—137, but wasn't entirely happy. "Had I putted at all well, it would have been a 66," Walton said. What hurt the most was that missed four-footer at No. 11. The next day, he did birdie No. 11, and that spurred him to another 69 for 206 and a two-stroke lead over Woosnam. But it disappeared immediately the next day.

"I was a bundle of nerves, knowing that my own people were desperate for me to win," Walton said. And so he bogeyed the first two holes in the fourth round. He got the strokes back with birdies at the next two, and from there on, it was a match-play battle. Woosnam broke out of the deadlock at No. 16 with what he called his best shot of the week. He came out of light round 265 yards to within 15 feet of the flag. "That impressed me, that one did," he said. But he squandered his one-stroke lead at No. 18, where he needed three to get down from just short of the green.

Woosnam's opponent in the playoff was not only Walton, but the some 30,000 partisan spectators. "They were very excitable," Woosnam said. "But I knew that if Philip hadn't been there, they would have been rooting for me as the defending champion." Moments later, they were.

Peugeot French Open—£313,405
Winner: Nick Faldo

Nick Faldo made his year by winning the Masters in April. Then he returned to Europe and won his first two outings, the Volvo PGA and the Dunhill British Masters, back-to-back. He put his feet up for three weeks, then made it three-for-three with the French Open. He got a lot of help, though. Ronan Rafferty suffered an awful crash in the last round. Faldo returned 70-70-64-69—273, seven under par, for a one-stroke victory over Mark Roe, Hugh Baiocchi, and Bernhard Langer, whose pains with the putter seemed to be easing. He had nine one-putts in a closing 66.

Faldo looked like an also-ran early in the tournament. "I played great and putted lousy," he said, after a par 70. Jose-Maria Olazabal took the lead with 66, and despite two birdies from about 30 feet, also complained about his putting, but not his putter. "It's not the arrow," said Olazabal. "It's the Indian who's to blame." A stroke behind him was Ian Woosnam (67), fighting a cold and the pressure of a superhuman pace. With his victory in the Irish Open the week before, he had a win and three seconds in five weeks.

The best that could be said for Faldo's second 70 was that it cost him only one stroke against the lead through 36 holes. At 140, he was five behind Seve Ballesteros (64—135), who had his eye three weeks down the road—on the British Open. "I'm very pleased with how I'm striking the ball," the normally grudging Ballesteros said. "I wish the Open were next week." He was striking it especially well with his new putter. He ran off five birdies in six holes, starting with a tap-in at No. 8, then putts of 10, 30, 15, and 12 feet over the next five holes. He led by one over a crowd of eight, including the doomed Rafferty (67), little-known American Mike

Allen (69), and less-known Frenchman Jean-Ignace Mouhica (64).

Rafferty, who scored his first victory in the Italian Open just six weeks earlier, got a leg up on a second with a third-round 66 for 202 and a two-stroke lead on a group that included Faldo, who made his move with a 64. Rafferty set the tone with an inspired recovery at No. 2, where he threaded a shot through the trees after getting line-of-sight relief from a scoreboard, then holed an 18-foot birdie putt. Faldo got off to a running start at No. 1, smacking an eight iron 154 yards downwind to within a foot of the hole for an easy birdie-three. He got another from 20 feet at No. 5, a two-putt birdie at No. 8, but bogeyed No. 9 when he blew a four-foot par putt after a bunkered approach. No. 10 was almost a carbon copy of No. 1—a nine-iron approach to a foot. He came home in 31, adding birdies from 10, 12, and six feet.

In the final round, Faldo (69) made a last-gasp birdie, but the real drama came from Rafferty. His drives got away from him at No. 10 and No. 11, and cost him double-bogey sixes. Faldo, always dangerous, leaped through the crack. He got up and down from under the lip of a bunker and birdied the par-five eighteenth, edging into the lead that would win for him. Rafferty (74—277) dropped to a tie for 11th.

Torras Monte Carlo Open—£289,715
Winner: Mark McNulty

"The secret here is patience," Mark McNulty was saying. If it isn't gusting winds or crazy bounces on Mont Agel, then it's fog—actually, low-lying clouds—delaying play. All told, it's one grand conspiracy by nature to keep anyone from winning the Monte Carlo Open. But McNulty did keep his wits about him and picked up his eighth European tour victory. There was also a little zip in his game. Or as he put it, "I really hit some crackers."

McNulty was talking about the third round, but he might as well have meant all four. Twice a Monte Carlo runner-up, McNulty ran off with this one, a six-stroke victory over Jose-Maria Canizares and Jeff Hawkes. McNulty shot 68-64-64-65—261, 15 under par on the 6,198-yard, par-69 course.

That opening 68 left him five strokes off the lead. Little-known British professionals Robin Mann and Grant Turner shared it with 63s, leading the way as the course took a pounding: 31 of the 145 starters broke par. Actually, Mann was happy just to be playing. The operator of a golf school in England, he failed to regain his European tour card in December. The day he learned he was in the Monte Carlo field, his passport was stolen. He had to scramble for a temporary one, then was in an auto accident on the way to Heathrow Airport, near London. Playing golf was anticlimactic. Mann went on to tie for 39th, Turner tied for 20th.

Seve Ballesteros was another vexed soul. First, he was coughing and sniffling from a bad cold. Then he lost his opening tee shot in the trees. That triggered a 75, and there were only 12 rounds higher. "I never recovered from that lost ball," Ballesteros said. "I felt bad mentally and physically, and I played and putted badly." A second-round 67 was not enough to save him. At 142, he missed the 36-hole cut for the first time since April, 1988.

McNulty (64) and Peter Senior (66) took over at the halfway point, and at 132 shared a one-stroke lead on a small crowd that included Denis Durnian, who was one off the course record with 62. McNulty put on the kind of show that was so common in his near-monopoly on the Sunshine Tour in South Africa. He was on course for a 27 over his last nine holes after four successive birdies from No. 13. But he "settled" for a 30 after missing the last two greens.

The issue was settled rather early in the fourth round—at the par-three 12th. McNulty and his closest challenger, Canizares, both missed the green. But where Canizares chipped up and missed his par from three feet, McNulty holed out a 60-foot chip from the trees for a birdie. "I felt that chip was the make-or-break shot, and I willed it into the hole," McNulty said. "Sometimes you feel you can do that. It really put the pressure on Jose-Maria." McNulty birdied the next two hole to go four strokes clear. The rest was mere formality.

Bell's Scottish Open—£300,000
Winner: Michael Allen

Nick Faldo was going after his fifth consecutive European victory. Ian Woosnam was looking strong. Sandy Lyle seemed to be shaking his deep slump. Except for Seve Ballesteros, anyone who was anyone was at the Bell's Scottish Open at Gleneagles' Kings Course, chasing a national title and warming up for the British Open the next week.

Enter someone named Michael Allen, unknown American. In the very last round, mind you.

Allen, 30, from San Francisco, studied finance at the University of Nevada, in the state that is home to the glitzy gaming halls of Las Vegas. What were the odds against his winning the Scottish Open? After all, he had failed "three or four times" trying to get on the American tour. It took him two cracks to get on the European tour. And in six years as a professional, he hadn't made an impression, much less won.

And what are the odds against a finish like this: Allen started the final round five strokes out of the lead, Gordon Brand, Jr., Jose-Maria Olazabal, and Ian Woosnam between him and the top. He lost even more ground in the first five holes, then ran off seven birdies and an eagle over the last 13 holes, zipping home in 30 for an eight-under-par, career-best 63. He used only 22 putts all day. That's a deceptive figure. Because coming down the stretch, he putted only once in a three-hole span.

"It was a magical day," Allen said. "I was spinning from the whole experience." He had just made up 15 strokes on Brand, the third-round leader, who blew to 78, and he beat Woosnam and Olazabal by two. With 73-66-70-63—272, 12 under par, Allen was the season's newest winner.

The tournament certainly didn't start with any surprises. Woosnam, at 65, held the first-round lead by two over Olazabal and Des Smyth. American Mike Smith notched two eagles for 68, tying with Joe Ozaki, who led a six-man Japanese contingent. Lyle and Faldo were at 70.

In the second round, the suffering Lyle was the big news. A 66 carried him to within a stroke of the 36-hole lead, shared by Woosnam (70—135) and Ozaki (67). "I was just going through a stale period," Lyle said. "I've got my teeth back in the game now." (Lyle would tie for 10th, his best in a long time. Faldo's bid for a fifth straight win never materialized. He tied for 20th.)

Next up in a week that wouldn't hold still was Gordon Brand, Jr., who birdied four of his last five holes for 67—204 and a one-stroke lead over Olazabal (68) and Peter Senior (68) through three rounds. Meanwhile, Allen, whom the fates would soon summon to center stage, returned 70 that left him five strokes behind, at 209. He didn't stay there long.

After that stumbling start in the fourth round, came that breathtaking rush, especially that one-putt stretch. At the 164-yard 14th, he drove the green with a two iron and holed a 22-foot putt for an eagle-two. At No. 15, he sank a 30-foot bunker shot for a birdie. And if he didn't already understand that it was his time, he had to know it at the par-three 16th. His tee shot, headed for trouble, hit a woman spectator and bounced into the fringe of the green. He chipped in for his birdie.

He showed nerve, too. At No. 18, he missed the green and was facing a 25-foot putt for his birdie when the leaderboard suddenly told him that Woosnam was just a stroke behind with four holes to play. Allen badly needed to put Woosie two strokes behind. And he did, calmly rolling in that 25-footer. Now both Woosnam and Olazabal had to eagle the last hole to tie him. They didn't, and he was the winner.

"Incredible," Allen said. And it was.

KLM Dutch Open—£275,000
Winner: Jose-Maria Olazabal

Gordon Brand, Jr., was hoping history would repeat itself in the KLM Dutch Open at the Kennemer Golf and Country Club. Not recent history, of course. He was fresh from missing the 36-hole cut at the British Open, and the week before that he was all set to win the Scottish Open until he exploded to a final-round 78. No, what he had in mind was 1987-style history, when he won the Dutch Open, then the Scandinavian Enterprise Open, and a spot on the Ryder Cup team. He seemed headed that way again in this Dutch Open, solo leader in the first round (65), joint leader through the second (68—133). But a third-round 74 ended his hopes. Anyway, the gods had other fish to fry.

Jose-Maria Olazabal and Ronan Rafferty ended up in the longest playoff in European tour history, a nine-hole struggle through a driving rain and howling wind. Play was almost impossible. Then came a finish as raw as the weather. On the ninth extra hole, Olazabal needed an 18-inch putt for a bogey. Incredibly, he missed it and took a double bogey-six. Rafferty moved in for the kill. The victory was just four feet away. Two putts would do it. But Rafferty three-putted.

"I was just luckier than Ronan," said Olazabal, bagging his second win of the season. "When I missed that 18-inch putt, I sat on my bag and held my head in my hands. But Ronan's putt was downhill and downwind, and he hit it a little to hard, then missed the one coming back."

Olazabal could have won it outright in regulation play. Despite an eight back at No. 2, he needed only a par at No. 18 to take it all. But he three-putted the hard way, knocking his first putt seven feet to the left of the hole. It was his fourth three-putt of the round, and it was on to the playoff. Actually, it was a three-way playoff. Olazabal (76), Rafferty (73), and Roger Chapman (69) tied at three-under-par 277. Chapman bowed out on the first extra hole, No. 16, when his approach bounced over the green.

Olazabal and Rafferty kept plowing around the 16-17-18 loop, through the wind and rain. It ended about 8:30 p.m., and Olazabal's playoff score told you everything you needed to know about the weather. Against a par of 33 for those nine extra holes, he shot a 40. "I have never played before in conditions as bad as that," he said. "I hope I never have to go through anything like that again."

The Dutch Open was not without other forms of misery. Consider Swedish rookie Jesper Parnevik, who led the 1988 tour qualifying school. He was three under par for his first three holes, but bogeyed the last three. He missed the playoff by a stroke and finished fourth at 70—278. Another victim was 1988 Benson & Hedges winner Peter Baker. He was four under par (one better than the leaders' final score) playing No. 10 in the last round. His approach bounced over the green and into the dense growth. The ball was found just before the five-minute search period expired, but he had to take a drop to get a club on it. Then he needed five chops to reach playable ground. Next, he two-putted for a 10, for 83—288 and a tie for 36th. But he forgot to sign his card. He was disqualified.

Scandinavian Enterprise Open—£335,000
Winner: Ronan Rafferty

If Ronan Rafferty suffered any lasting wounds from that nine-hole playoff loss in the Dutch Open the week before, they didn't show in the Scandinavian Enterprise Open at Drottningholm Golf Club, near Stockholm. Rafferty put on a hot finish, shrugged off Michael Allen's threat, and breezed to the championship, thus raising a big question: Was another superstar emerging on the European tour?

It was far too early for an emphatic yes, but certain signs were there. The career that was tagged as "promising" when it began in 1981 enjoyed four top-five finishes in 1988, and was starting to bear real fruit in 1989. Rafferty finally scored his first victory in the Italian Open in May, and when he took the Scandinavian title, he had posted his 13th top-10 finish of the season. And two of them were seconds. It should be noted, by the way, that Rafferty is only 25 years old.

The Scandinavian title was hardly a walk in the park. In the first two rounds, despite good-looking scores of 70-69, Rafferty was laboring back in the pack. Then he caught fire, shooting 64-65 in the last two rounds for a 268 total, a whopping 20 under par, for a two-stroke victory over the ambitious Allen, the surprise Scottish Open winner three weeks earlier.

Rafferty had his work cut out for him from the start. His opening two-under-par 70 paled against the course record-tying 64s returned by Peter Senior and Philip Harrison. Senior, who uses the awkward pendulum-style putter so popular on the U.S. Senior PGA Tour, had nine birdies and one bogey, and Harrison had six birdies and an eagle-three at the 566-yard No.

18 for his career-low. In the rain-plagued second round, Harrison bogeyed his first four holes and slipped to a 71 that dropped him to second place. Senior, who started on the inward nine, bogeyed his 12th and 13th holes but shook them off and scored three birdies in his last four holes for 70—134, 10 under par. Rafferty was five strokes back at 69—139.

Rafferty broke out with a vengeance in the third round, suffering only one bogey in a season-low 64. It was a real rampage, a nine-birdie assault that included six birdies in the span of eight holes in an outward 30. Gordon Brand, Jr., in front of him, also made six birdies and a 30 going out, and tied for the lead with another birdie at No. 12. Then he three-putted No. 14 for a bogey, and missed eight-foot birdie putts at No. 16 and No. 18. A 66 left him at 206, one behind Allen, and three behind Rafferty.

Allen, who came from nowhere in the final round to win the Scottish Open, made another charge—five birdies in the last six holes for a 65—270. But he had to settle for second place because Rafferty had already put on a charge of his own, getting three birdies in the first four holes on putts of 15, five, and eight feet. He also birdied five of the first eight holes, going out in 31. He was five strokes clear at that point, the kind of edge that had been a problem for him.

"Too often in the past, when I've threatened to win, I've backed off and played safe," Rafferty said. "But this time I played positive golf."

Benson & Hedges International Open—£300,000
Winner: Gordon Brand, Jr.

For Gordon Brand, Jr., the dream was delayed but every bit as sweet, maybe more so. Two weeks earlier, he was hoping that history would repeat itself, to wit: That he would win the Dutch Open again, and be on his way to the Ryder Cup matches. That's the way it happened in 1987. But in the 1989 Dutch Open, victory slipped away on a third-round 76. He also missed in the Scottish Open, with a closing 78. The clock was running. But Brand stopped it cold at the Benson & Hedges International Open at Fulford. Derrick Cooper had the title all but wrapped up, a three-stroke lead going into the final round. But Brand came rocketing from seven strokes behind and grabbed that dream—the victory and the Ryder Cup berth. Happy birthday, Gordon. He was just days from his 31st birthday.

Cooper didn't fold. That was a solid 72 he posted in the final round. But Brand went roaring by with a 64, for a matched set of scores—64-72-72-64, for a 272 that edged Cooper by a stroke and won him that coveted Ryder Cup spot.

"It would have been a nothing year if I hadn't made it," Brand said. "I got such a buzz out of my debut in American two years ago, and I hope to be a much more valuable asset this time." For another European star, however, the Ryder Cup situation was gloomy. Sandy Lyle, everybody's favorite, had received a vote of confidence from captain Tony Jacklin just before the tournament. But Lyle gave no sign that his slump was ending. In the first round, he had four bogeys, one triple bogey, and 77. He would miss the 36-hole cut—again.

Ironically, while the famed Lyle was struggling, an unknown Australian newcomer, Bradley Hughes, took center stage in the first round, tying the course record 62. Hughes, 22, a former Melbourne dock clerk, had switched to a crosshanded putting grip only four days earlier, and his 10 birdies included putts of 15 feet (twice), 25, and 30. Hughes turned professional in September, 1988. Newcomers often blow up, but Hughes didn't. His worst was a final-round 74, leaving him tied for ninth at 278.

Hughes had to share the second-round lead with Cooper, who fought off a battering wind for seven birdies for a 66—133 and a one-stroke lead on Malcolm Mackenzie (68). Mackenzie would have had company at 134 except for one of golf's ironies. Mark Mouland signed for a four instead of a birdie-three at No. 17, leaving himself one stroke poorer at 68—135.

Cooper, the 1988 Madrid Open winner, took the third-round lead with the only bogey-free round among the challengers, a 68 for 201, three ahead of the determined Hughes (71). Brand seemed mired in mediocrity at this point. His 72 leaving him seven strokes astern at 208. Then he regrouped.

The final round was buffeted by stiff winds and heavy rain, but Brand did not drop so much as one stroke. He logged four birdies from between five and 15 feet, and added an eagle-three from 40 feet at No. 9, and another from 18 feet at No. 18. Cooper had dropped four strokes in the first six holes, but fired back with five birdies. He needed an eagle at the last to tie. But his 25-foot putt just missed. Brand was in the winner's circle, and in the Ryder Cup.

Denmark's Steen Tinning provided a curious footnote. At the 438-yard No. 2, he hit four consecutive fairway irons out of bounds and took 13. Later, at the 161-yard No. 14, he holed an eight iron and won a £13,000 Volvo.

PLM Open—£300,000
Winner: Mike Harwood

Peter Senior had to be wondering what it takes to win. Fellow Australian Mike Harwood didn't lead the PLM Open at any time—until the very last shot. Which, of course, was quite enough. Harwood eagled the final hole from a bunker, leaped from one stroke behind to one ahead, and scored the second victory of his four years on the European tour. He broke through in the 1988 Portuguese Open, and had been threatening earlier this year. He was fifth in the French Open, fourth in the Epson Grand Prix, and third in both the Dunhill British Masters and Wang Four Stars.

Harwood, 30, toured Bokskogen, at Malmo, Sweden, in 66-70-67-68, for a 17-under-par 271. Senior, the 1986 PLM winner, returned 68-67-65-72—272. And perhaps of more interest to European fans, Sam Torrance, who had gone to the long, pendulum putter in his battle against the yips, was a solid third at 273 to lock up a Ryder Cup berth. "I'm disappointed not to have won," Torrance said, "but my main target all summer has been to retain my Ryder Cup place." Five others who already had won their Ryder Cup berths finished behind Torrance—Ronan Rafferty, joint sixth on 276; Jose-Maria Olazabal, 279; Ian Woosnam, 282; Mark James, 282; and Gordon Brand, Jr., 284.

Barry Lane, the 1988 Scottish Open champion, made a move on a Ryder

Cup berth with a course record-tying 64, eight under par, for a two-stroke lead in the first round. That was despite a bogey at No. 1 after a watered one-iron tee shot. He regrouped and ran off nine birdies the rest of the way on a series of eight-to-10 foot putts with his new crosshanded putting. But a second-round 74 put an end to the dreaming. And at that moment, Bernhard Langer, another man looking to keep his Ryder Cup place, took a one-stroke lead on 66—134 through 36 holes. Langer, well-known yip victim, seemed to be pulling out of his prolonged slump. He had finished second in the St. Jude Classic on the American tour two weeks earlier.

In the third round, Langer's sin was nothing worse than a 69, but it was enough to drop him to a tie for second with Torrance and Harwood behind the charging Senior, who took the lead with 65—200. Senior is another of the converts to the pendulum putters so popular on the American senior tour. "I've been fighting the yips for 10 years," Senior said. "They destroyed me. This new putter has restored my confidence." The more so here. He one-putted the first five holes for birdies.

It wasn't putter trouble that hurt him in the final round. It was Harwood's sand wedge. Senior led by three strokes going into the last round. Harwood cut that lead to one with birdies at the 14th and 15th, and he still trailed by one coming to the 540-yard, par-five No. 18. There, Senior's troubles began with a drive into the rough. Then he found himself in a bunker next to the green. Harwood was also bunkered. But where Senior had to make do with a par, Harwood holed a 40-foot sand shot for an eagle-three and the win.

And so it was on to the German Open at Frankfurt, the climax of the Ryder Cup year—last chance to lock up one of the nine automatic berths on the 1989 Ryder Cup team.

German Open—£325,470
Winner: Craig Parry

Two men were in the frying pan at the 1989 German Open. One was Philip Walton, the seven-year European tour veteran from Ireland. This tournament, at the Frankfurt Club, Frankfurt, in the final week of August, was the last of the the points events for the European Ryder Cup team. The ninth and final automatic berth on the team was at stake, and Walton stood ninth on the points list. He could fall either way here. The other man was Russell Claydon. Just a few weeks earlier he helped Great Britain-Ireland beat the United States in the Walker Cup match. Now he had ended a bright amateur career and was making his professional debut on a sponsor's exemption. With only some two months left to the season, Claydon would have to win about £15,000 to get his player's card without having to go to the qualifying school. It would be a sour week for both men. They missed the 36-hole cut.

That ninth and final automatic Ryder Cup berth was taken by Jose-Maria Canizares, who had staked his claim with a dynamite third-round 62, tying the course record. He tied for fifth at 269. (A sign of the future?—German amateur Sven Struever also shot a 62. He tied for ninth at 270.)

And while many were focused on ninth place, the people watching first place were having a dandy time. Craig Parry, 23, came charging from six strokes back to catch Mark James, then beat him in a playoff. Some sort of justice was served. In the English Open back in June, Parry birdied three of the last four holes for what would have been a tie for the lead until James birdied two of the last four to win. So Parry balanced the scale here. He returned 66-70-66-64 against James' 65-66-65-70 to tie at 18-under-par 266. They halved the first extra hole, No. 17, in birdie-fours. Then James' putter broke down on the second, No. 18. His first putt was five feet past the hole, he missed coming back, and took a bogey-five.

Parry, in only his second year on the tour, thus picked off his second European victory—both this year and both by playoffs, after coming from behind. In the Wang Four Stars early in June, Parry birdied the last two holes to tie Ian Woosnam, then birdied the first extra to win.

James was having his best year ever. He had already won three times— the Desert Classic, the AGF Open, and the English Open. Win No. 4 was all but in the bag. He went into the final round leading by two strokes over Mike Allen, the obscure American who made his name in a hurry when he won the Scottish Open, and Mike Harwood, who won the PLM Open just a week earlier. It was six strokes and eight more players back to Parry. So no one even saw him coming.

James had left himself something of a sitting duck when he took a double bogey-six at No. 2, then a bogey-five at No. 3. Parry wasn't yet a force to be noticed. James got the strokes back, but then bogeyed the par-three 16th. He couldn't afford it. Now the charging Parry was right on him.

By now, the only suspense left was the Ryder Cup team—that is, Jacklin's three wild card picks. The point positions were taken, in order, by: Ronan Rafferty, James, Jose-Maria Olazabal, Nick Faldo, Woosnam, Gordon Brand, Jr., Seve Ballesteros, Sam Torrance, and Canizares. Now Jacklin had to pick the final three.

First came a blockbuster announcement from America. Sandy Lyle, playing there this week in the World Series of Golf, ruled himself out of consideration because he'd been playing so badly all year. Jacklin, reluctantly accepting Lyle's decision, then made his three selections—Bernhard Langer, Howard Clark, and Christy O'Connor, Jr. The campaign had ended. There was a lot of golf left on the European tour, but the feverish Ryder Cup chase was no longer part of it.

Ebel European Masters-Swiss Open—£414,315
Winner: Seve Ballesteros

Seve Ballesteros, that master of escapes, thrills, and mind-boggling scoring bursts, outdid even himself in winning the Ebel European Masters-Swiss Open for the third time. It came down to a blazing finish at Crans-sur-Sierre, Switzerland. Two birdies and a brilliant save over the final three holes capped a performance that amazed even veteran Ballesteros-watchers—a total of 22 birdies and two eagles on a card of 65-68-66-67—266, 22 under par for a two-stroke victory over Australian Craig Parry. And all because Ballesteros took his own advice.

He had been frustrated since winning the Epson Match Play and the Madrid Open back in the spring. He finally visited Bob Torrance, the noted teacher and father of Sam, and discovered he had been shutting the clubface on the backswing. "I tried hard to stop it, but I couldn't," Ballesteros said. "Then in Switzerland, I was reading one of my own instruction books and realized why. I was too open at address. Once I closed up my stance a little bit, I was able to do what Bob wanted me to do naturally. How easy it is to forget the fundamentals of this game."

Ballesteros led only at the beginning and at the end. A seven-under-par 65 put him in a five-way tie for the first-round lead. The group included the troubled Bernhard Langer, but this ray of sunshine for him was extinguished the next day by a 75. Ballesteros had 68 that included three birdies, an eagle, and a complaint. "I didn't play very well," he insisted. And he was aching. He had to take aspirin for a sore back before he could play. He lost ground on that 68, slipping to fourth place, three strokes behind, thanks to Jose Rivero's outburst. Rivero shook off a heavy rain, birdied the last five holes, and posted 64—130. Stephen Bennett rang up seven birdies for 67 for a share of second with Barry Lane (65) at 132. Emmanuel Dussart, one of the few French on the tour, played himself into excellent position with a 67 to tie with Ballesteros at 133 (a 76-76 close would drop him all the way to a tie for 56th).

Rivero, whose last victory was in the 1988 Monte Carlo Open, stuck to his guns and led through 54 holes, with 67—197, a healthy 19 under par. But his lead shrank. Bennett (66) closed to within one, on 198, and Ballesteros (66) and Lane (67) shared third at 199. Parry, in only his second European season, who won the German Open the week before and the Wang Four Stars in June, was an unknown factor to this point. A 66 in the third round left him on the fringe, at 201, four strokes back. Then the right combination hit. Rivero folded with an eight at No. 9, and Parry, out in 31, and Ballesteros (33) made it a two-man chase.

Parry took the lead with a birdie at the 14th, then made a fatal error at the 15th: He ran his first putt 25 feet past the hole, and ended up with a four-putt six. Ballesteros charged through the opening. He birdied the 16th from 15 feet, the 17th from 10, and then saved par at the 18th with one of his miracle shots—a big curve to get his ball out from behind the wall where he put his tee shot.

Panasonic European Open—£350,000
Winner: Andrew Murray

No one noticed when Andrew Murray took the first-round lead in the Panasonic European Open. For one thing, he didn't figure to last. The slender 33-year-old Englishman with the big smile hadn't won in his 11 years on the European tour, and he hadn't finished higher than 18th this year. Moreover, the big news at Walton Heath Golf Club was the slumping Sandy Lyle. Just two weeks removed from a poor showing in the World Series of Golf— that's when he withdrew himself from Ryder Cup consideration—Lyle played his best golf since June, returning 69, tied for fourth, three strokes behind Murray. Before long, though, everyone was watching Murray as a combination fairy tale and Hollywood story unfolded.

Murray joined the tour in 1979, the year Seve Ballesteros won his first

British Open. His best finish ever was a tie for seventh in the 1987 Jersey Open, and his most profitable year was 1988, with £44,301. It was only his second year in five-figure winnings. If his golf weren't sluggish enough, there was his health to consider. Murray is a victim of spondylitis, a crippling form of arthritis, in his left hip. In July, shortly after he missed qualifying for the British Open, doctors told him his career probably had only one or two more years to go.

"I've been looking around, thinking what I might do for a second career," he said. "I'd like it to be in golf, maybe teaching or administration." Whatever it is, he'll come equipped with a great tale to tell, of the time when, against a field that included Sandy Lyle, Sam Torrance, Ian Woosnam, and Nick Faldo, he took the lead and held it, and won the European Open. Murray returned 66-68-71-72—277, 11 under par, for a one-stroke victory over Frank Nobilo. Torrance was third, three behind; Woosnam tied for fourth (281); Lyle tied for eighth (284), and Faldo tied for 20th (288). Murray led by one in the first round, four in the second, and three in the third.

"I've been a bag of nerves all week," Murray said, after his victory. "But making three birdies in seven holes settled me down. The one at the 12th, where Frank had knocked in a big putt, kept me one in front and probably was the key to victory." First, however, he had to rescue himself at the 11th, where he pushed his one-iron second shot into the trees. Nobilo cut his deficit to one stroke with a birdie. They halved their way home, starting at the 12th, where Nobilo dropped a 15-footer for a birdie-three and Murray matched him from five feet.

At the 18th, a par four of 432 yards, Murray hit a perfect drive, then fired a six iron to 10 feet, made his par, and claimed the victory of his life. It won him £53,330, more than he ever won in a year, and it got him a place in the Lancome Trophy. And most important, he said: "To win in such a style earns me the respect of my fellow professionals, and that means more than money."

Lancome Trophy—£410,000
Winner: Eduardo Romero

Can a man who jumps out of airplanes for fun keep his nerve in a game played on the ground? Argentinian Eduardo Romero's answer at St. Nom la Breteche was a resounding "yes" in the Lancome Trophy. There, he capped a long, painful climb with an eagle at the 16th hole and held on to score his first-ever victory in three years on the European tour, and his first outside South America. Back home, he had won 25 times, including two Argentine PGAs. Now a European title. He couldn't stop the tears.

"I can't speak about this," Romero said. "I am too moved. This is my most important win, by a long way. There were so many big players here." Indeed, there was nothing cheap about this victory. Romero, 35, who lists parachuting and hunting as his favorite hobbies, entered the final round two strokes off the lead of Peter Fowler. After making only two birdies in the first 15 holes, he chipped in from 50 yards for an eagle-three at the par-five 16th to take the lead for the first time. Danger threatened at the next, the

386-yard 17th. He was bunkered close to the green, but he blasted out delicately—"That was where I won it," he said—saved his par, and beat Bernhard Langer and Jose-Maria Olazabal by a stroke. He was the 10th first-time winner on the tour this year. He shot 69-65-66-66—266, 14 under par on the 6,780-yard par-70 composite of the Red and Blue courses. Langer and Olazabal both closed with 65s for 267.

But for 69 holes, it was anyone's tournament. Andrew Murray's, for example. Murray, 33, who won the European Open just a week earlier, took a two-stroke lead in the first round on 64 that included a little magic. He holed out from a badly plugged lie in a bunker for a birdie at the par-three seventh. At the par-four ninth, he more than made up for a so-so drive by holing a 100-yard wedge shot for an eagle-two. The next day, reality hit in the form of a 78. Fowler solved the winds and the rain-soaked course for a 64—130 and a four-stroke lead over Romero. Fowler was the magician this time, with two eagle-threes—a one iron to three feet at No. 8, and a three iron to 20 feet at No. 16. Romero made hay with his eight iron, setting up four of his birdies with it.

Fowler kept the lead through the third round, once he shook off that ugly start. He lost three strokes of his four-stroke lead in the first four holes, but he pulled himself together for a 68—198 and a two-stroke lead over Romero. Other remarkable accomplishments in the third round: Mats Lanner returned a 62 (for 208, 10 strokes off), and Grant Turner (76) and U.S. Open champion Curtis Strange (72) both took eight at the par-three 18th.

In the fourth round, as Fowler faded, Langer turned up the heat with a birdie-eagle-birdie run from the seventh. Olazabal almost matched him with an eagle-par-birdie finish. But both fell just short. Indeed, Romero had beaten so many big players. Not only Strange and Greg Norman, who finished tied for 16th at 277, but 11 of the 12 men (Ian Woosnam was playing in Japan) who would make up the European Ryder Cup team at The Belfry later that week.

German Masters—£331,950
Winner: Bernhard Langer

Bernhard Langer was not exactly the perfect host at this third edition of the German Masters. He was the winner, too. If there was an element of poetic justice in that outcome, there also was plenty of fireworks for the spectators who turned out at the Stuttgarter Golf Club at Monsheim, West Germany. There was also a sense of redemption for the personable West German, who had to fight an ailing game and a bad back most of the season. This one came down to the final shots on the final green.

Payne Stewart, the U.S. PGA champion, was leading by two strokes over Langer and defending champion Jose-Maria Olazabal coming into the final round. Then the fun began. Langer went out in 33 and took the lead. The faltering Stewart, wearing mittens between shots on the cold and rainy day, fired back with two 25-foot birdie putts coming in, but he bogeyed the par-three 15th, where both Langer and Olazabal birdied. Langer came to the 552-yard, par-five 18th a stroke ahead but also in big trouble. He could hardly have found more. He missed the fairway with his drive, had to lay up with his approach, then put his third into a greenside bunker. But he came out beautifully to three feet and got his par, then had to watch as both Stewart and Olazabal took aim at birdies that would tie him. But Stewart (71) missed his 12-footer by a hair, Olazabal (69) just missed a 10-footer, and Langer won by a stroke at 67-71-70-68—276, 12 under par.

What a relief. Between a chronic bad back and a recurrent case of the putting yips, it had not been a banner year for him. He had won his first European outing of the season in April, the Spanish Open, then tailed off into troubled times. He was especially desperate in the British Open in July, finishing 83-82 for a 309 total, 21 over par and in last place. It seems that his back had acted up. He was already battling the yips with an odd grip: He'd hold the putter low with his left hand, and with his right clench the top of the shaft against his left forearm.

Langer led the first round on 67, then slipped into the background. In the second, Nick Faldo notched four birdies and an eagle for 66 and took the 36-hole lead on 135, which helped knock two prominent names out of the tournament. Both Seve Ballesteros (75-75) and Mark Calcavecchia (72-78) missed the halfway cut. Olazabal, who seemed destined for the same fate after an opening 73, birdied the 15th and 16th, then eagled the 18th with a bunker shot for a 66—139. Langer birdied two of the last four holes for 71—138. The stage for the roaring finish was set in the third round when Stewart took the lead on 70—206, to lead by two over Langer (70—208) and Olazabal (69).

"I played really well all week," Langer said. "My putting troubles seem to be over, 12 months after I changed to my present grip. And it was a great thrill for me to win in Germany, especially for the first time in my own tournament."

BMW International Open—£275,000
Winner: David Feherty

When last seen, David Feherty was listening to grand opera at the British Open in July, trying to turn the inspirational art of Puccini into success on the links of Royal Troon. He did a pretty good job of it, too. He was the low European, tied for sixth. Next we find him in the inaugural BMW International Open at Munich in mid-October, in a different situation—golf's equivalent of the loneliness of the long distance runner. It was a new tournament on a new course, the four-month-old Golfplatz Munchen Nor-Eichenreid, and Feherty was so far ahead he was all but playing by himself.

Feherty burned up the 6,910-yard course with a 10-under-par 62 for a three-stroke lead in the first round, then added 66-68-73, and successively led by six, then eight, and finally took a five-stroke victory over Fred Couples at 19-under-par 269. Not that he lacked for pressure. Some big guns didn't even make the 36-hole cut of one-under-par 143: Bernhard Langer (70-74—144), who won the German Masters the week before; British Open champion Mark Calcavecchia (74-71—145), and Sam Torrance (71-76—147).

Feherty made 11 birdies in that 62, the last of them in deep gloom. Darkness was falling about 5 p.m. at this time of the year. A 30-foot putt at No. 5 was merely the longest of his early birdies, and a 15-footer at No.

8 and an eight-footer at No. 9 wrapped up an outward 30. He escaped trouble at the par-three 12th, where his tee shot ended up in shallow water. He splashed it out to 12 feet and saved his par. Big-hitting Davis Love III had five birdies and an eagle for a 65 and second place.

Peter Mitchell, an Englishman and a 10-year veteran seeking his first victory, took over second place in the second round with 67—134. That became the question: Who would finish second? Feherty boosted his lead to six strokes with 66—128, 16 under par, despite a late tee time that gave him the worst of the young greens. "It seemed the worse they got, the better I putted," Feherty marveled. He started on No. 10 and ran in a 65-footer for a birdie. Was another 62 in the offing? Not quite. He missed short putts on the uneven greens at the 12th and 13th. "You just have to accept that," he said. "The ball will jump and bobble on these new surfaces."

Another thought struck him during the second round—the lonely feeling that goes with being so far ahead. It got lonelier in the third round when he went to 18 under and nine ahead at No. 9, chipping stiff for a birdie, then 19 under with a birdie at the 12th. Eventually, he slipped into a frame of mind that displeased him. "I was trying not to lose," he said.

This was the fifth victory of Feherty's career. He had won twice before in 11 years on the European tour, the Italian Open and Scottish Open, both in 1986. He also had won two Sunshine Tour events in South Africa, the 1984 ICL International and 1988 Lexington PGA. But this was by far his most decisive. By the second round, this one was reminding him of an 18-stroke win he had once in a small tournament back in Ulster. "The difference here," he noted, "is that there is a host of players entirely capable of catching me." Which is what made this one all the sweeter.

Portuguese Open TPC Championship—£275,000
Winner: Colin Montgomerie

For Colin Montgomerie, failing to qualify for the British Open in July—at Royal Troon, no less, where his father is secretary—was the last straw. He had also missed 10 halfway cuts, five of them in succession. Off he went to his boyhood coach, Bill Ferguson, to get help for his erratic game. The problem was simple: he had the ball too far forward in his stance. So when he arrived at the Portuguese Open, he was armed with a stronger game. And also with the painful memory of how he had let the Catalan Open get away from him in March. Not this one. Even though he was leading by four strokes going into the final round, he wasn't about to coast home. A 63 isn't coasting.

Montgomerie, 26, former Walker Cupper and the European tour's rookie of the year in 1988, thus became the 11th first-time winner of 1989. And he did it in spectacular fashion. He shot 67-65-69-63—264, and in those figures were these facts: The 63 was the record for the 7,095-yard, par-72 Quinta do Lago course, knocking a stroke off the one that had stood for five years. The 264 total, 24 under par, was the tournament record, six strokes lower than the previous one. And his 11-stroke margin over Manuel Moreno, Rodger Davis and Mike Smith (all at 275) was the biggest in five years.

The tournament got off to an odd start—the Case of the Shrunken Hole.

In the first round, Mark McNulty stopped playing at the 16th and called for an official to complain that the hole had become smaller than the regulation 4-1/2 inch diameter. Apparently the cup had been sunk too low, and the turf had bent over the rim. Play was delayed for nearly a half-hour while the situation was repaired. McNulty then missed his 12-foot birdie try and settled for a 68, two strokes behind Davis's 66 lead. Montgomerie, Luis Carbonetti, and Mark Mouland shared second on 67. It was the only time Montgomerie didn't lead, and when he did step forward, it was with a vengeance. In the second round, he posted a 65 for 132 and a four-stroke lead over Carbonetti, Mouland and Juan Quiros. Nothing would budge him. His challengers got the idea in a hurry. He held firm in the third round, and in that final-round 63, he started with four birdies in the first five holes.

This might have been Mongomerie's second victory, at the least, if he hadn't frittered away the Catalan Open in mid-March. Back then, he was leading by two coming to the last hole, but his chip was 40 foot short, and then he three-putted for a bogey-six, allowing Mark Roe to take the win. (That made Roe, incidentally, the first of the 11 first-time winners.) Montgomerie had been miffed at himself ever since. "I hope I've learned from the experience," he said. It would seem he had.

Volvo Masters—£400,000
Winner: Ronan Rafferty

Ronan Rafferty, age 25, started 1989, his ninth year on the European tour, still looking for his first victory. He not only got it, he got two others as well, played on his first Ryder Cup team, and ended up atop the Order of Merit. He did it with his third and final win in the tour's final event, the Volvo Masters at Valderrama, Spain. Rafferty shot 72-69-70-71—282, six under par, for a one-stroke victory over 1988 champion Nick Faldo. Jose-Maria Olazabal, the Order of Merit leader coming into the tournament, finished third, five strokes behind.

"There was so much at stake for me besides the money," Rafferty said. "There were invitations to the Masters, the U.S. Open, and the PGA Championship. So far, I've played in only British Opens. And it means everything to a golfer to play in the majors."

Rafferty left no doubt in racking up this one. First off, he beat a fine course. Many consider Valderrama the toughest course on the tour. That reputation wasn't hurt when only three men could break par 72 in the first round. Olazabal, making two of his five birdies on long putts he was trying to lag on the swift greens, took the lead on 69. Sandy Lyle had 70, and Ian Woosnam, 71. Faldo ran afoul of the greens and posted a 74. Rafferty (72) offset a shaky start with an inward 34, thanks to a pair of birdies, one of them a holed bunker shot at No. 14.

The Order of Merit duel came to a boil in the second round. Rafferty came to within a stroke, and Olazabal responded with a superb birdie at the 18th—a seven iron to one foot and a tap-in birdie for 70—139. He led by one over Ian Woosnam (69) and two over Rafferty (69) and Parry (68). "It was a very trying day," said Rafferty. It had started at No. 2, where he went out of bounds but made a "birdie" on his second ball and lost only one stroke. He ran off three birdies, starting at No. 6, and he got three more in the space of four holes from the 10th. Then came two bogeys, a three-putt at the 14th and a missed green at the 15th. Faldo (68—142) was out in 32, then coming in, canceled out three birdies with three bogeys. "I wasn't swinging very well," he said.

Rafferty forged into the lead in the third round on a one-bogey 70 for 211 and a two-stroke edge on Olazabal (74—213). Faldo moved into third on 72—214, and Woosnam slipped to 75—215, tying with Lyle (69), all of which set up a wild and wooly finish.

Rafferty, the overnight leader, went out in a rocky 39, including a double-bogey six at No. 8, where he drove into the trees. Faldo, then, seemed headed for a repeat championship when he birdied the 10th and 11th and took a two-stroke lead. Rafferty fired back with a birdie at the 10th, holing a 15-footer.

Olazabal faded away on bogeys at the 13th and 15th. Rafferty carded birdie-twos at the 12th, from 20 feet, and the 15th from 30. He finally caught Faldo with a birdie-four at the 17th. Up ahead at the 18th, Faldo's recovery from behind some trees caught a greenside bunker. The lost shot would prove fatal.

Rafferty closed like a champion. At the 18th, he boldly cut over the trees at the dogleg. He put his approach on the left edge of the green, ran the first putt five feet past, then cooly dropped the return for the one-stroke victory. "I turned professional to win tournaments, and that's the first priority," Rafferty said. "I couldn't have asked for a better year—with three victories, the Ryder Cup, and the Order of Merit bonus."

World Cup—$910,000
Winner: Australia

The storms that hit the Costa del Sol in mid-November weren't exactly what the composers had in mind when they wrote "The Rain in Spain." There were some serious doubts that the World Cup at Las Brisas, Marbella, could even be played. Not only was the course waterlogged, but roads were washed out and airports closed. The marvel was that all 32 two-man teams made it there, some just barely. Ironically, it was the eventual winners who had the worst of it. It took Australians Peter Fowler and Wayne Grady 70 hours to make the trip, part of it on foot. They had to walk in front of their rented car with a flashlight Tuesday night, to make sure they wouldn't hit a mud-slide. "We had plenty to think about, and we concentrated on the course," Grady said. The first time either had played it was in Thursday's first round. It seemed made for them.

Fowler shot 66, one stroke shy of the course record, for the individual first place, and Grady was second with 68. Fowler made six birdies, Grady five, and both of them eagled the 495-yard, par-five 12th. Grady did it with a 15-foot putt, and Fowler followed him in from four feet. Their aggregate 134 gave them a whopping seven-stroke lead over Spaniards Jose-Maria Olazabal (70) and Jose-Maria Canizares (71). The threat from the defending champion Americans—Paul Azinger and Mark McCumber this time—never materialized. Azinger (70) and McCumber (73) were fourth behind the

Swedes, Mats Lanner (69, individual third place) and Ove Sellberg (73). Fifth place, on 145, was shared by England's Denis Durnian (74) and Mark Roe (71) and Ireland's Des Smyth (72) and Christy O'Connor, Jr. (73).

The torrential rains returned and washed out Friday's second round, reducing the tournament to 54 holes. This news was sunshine to Fowler and Grady. Their comfortable seven-stroke lead was even cozier now that they were one round farther out of reach.

The second round was played on Saturday, and the Aussies finally slipped. Both bogeyed the par-three 11th and were 11 under par. The Spaniards both birdied the hole and dropped to seven under. The Aussie lead was down to four. It was the only battle on the course. At day's end, Fowler had 66-71—137 and Grady 68-73—141. Canizares was 71-67—138 and Olazabal 70-73—143, and that's where it ended. The rains hit again on Sunday, and play was abandoned. Australia, with a 278 total, was declared the winner. Spain was second at 281, Sweden and the United States were tied for third at 287, Wales fifth at 288, and Argentina and New Zealand shared sixth at 290.

Fowler was the individual champion, and Denmark's Anders Sorensen (70-68—138) shared second with Canizares. Argentina's Miguel Fernandez was fourth at 71-69—140, and Azinger (70-71) and Roe (71-70) shared fifth at 141.

13. The African Tours

When last heard from, Vijay Singh, the personable, ubiquitous, and unlikely Fiji Islander, was busy doing his bit for history. That was in 1988, when Singh, functionally a nobody in world golf, became a somebody by becoming the first Fijian to win an important tournament outside of Fiji. That was the Nigerian Open. Come the Safari Tour of 1989, and Singh was like the man who came to dinner. He liked things so much he decided to stick around.

If anybody thought Singh was a club pro with a lucky hand in 1988, he soon enough straightened out the picture. He led off the 1989 Safari Tour late in January by winning the Zimbabwe Open, a two-stroke victory over Mark Mouland. (A month later, Singh celebrated his 26th birthday.) The five-event tour was on a split schedule this time, and when it resumed for the final two tournaments in November, Singh won them both—the Nigerian Open (a repeat) and the Ivory Coast Open. That made him the king of African golf. He sat comfortably atop the Safari throne with £39,344, more than doubling the winnings of No. 2, Jeffrey Pinsent.

(Critics could argue that it's one thing to win on the Safari circuit, quite another to win in faster company. OK, said Singh. Is Europe fast enough? He was a rookie on the PGA European Tour in 1989, No. 2 in the qualifying school. He ran off with the Volvo Open by three strokes, thus becoming—of course—the first Fijian ever to win in Europe.)

The other two Safari events went to first-timers. David Jones, of Northern Ireland, won the Kenya Open by three over Mark Mouland. And Craig Maltman, a Scot, won the Zambia Open, an event that made a bit of history of its own. Rain knocked out not only a round, but also a hole. The final day was reduced to 17 holes, and so Maltman's victory was over the unusual and probably unprecedented length of 53 holes.

On the Sunshine Tour in South Africa, it was a mixed bag of the old, the new, and the invader. Veterans John Bland and Tony Johnstone exerted their authority early, Bland winning the year-opening Dewar's White Label Trophy in January and Johnstone the Lexington PGA two weeks later. Then the Americans took over. Stuart Smith won the Palabora Classic, beating Ian Palmer in a playoff, and the following week, Fred Wadsworth took the Protea Assurance Open by a stroke over another American, Tom Lehman. South Africa's Jeff Hawkes, who scored his first victory in 1988, seemed bent on running away with the rest of 1989. He won the AECI Charity Classic and Swazi Sun Classic back-to-back, and was heading for a third in succession until American Jay Townsend surfaced to take the Trust Bank Tournament of Champions, the final event of the Sunshine's early segment.

When the tour resumed in November, newcomer Desmond Terblanche won the Bloemfontein Classic, and then it was business as usual for the South African veterans. Fulton Allem won the Minolta Match Play, American-based David Frost the embattled Million Dollar Challenge, and Hugh Baiocchi the Twee Jongegezellen Masters, his first Sunshine victory since 1980.

The year also marked the debut of a South African newcomer who will bear watching. He should at least be the hero of headline writers all over the world. His name: Ernie Els. Els, 20, former South African amateur champion, first drew attention when he led the qualifier in the Minolta Match Play. Then he came within a stroke of tying Baiocchi in the Twee Jongegezellen Masters. Els finished as co-runner-up, and in the process graphically re-exposed a problem hurting golf.

Els said that he intends to play elsewhere, but probably not the European tour, since it is all but closed to South Africans. As a method of bringing pressure on the South African government to change the national policy of apartheid, several European countries, home of tournament sites, have banned South African golfers from playing. Spain is the most crucial of these. Since it's the site of the tour's qualifying school, South Africans are effectively banned from that route to the tour. And so, Els said, he may try the American tour. (The fight against apartheid has been going on for years in business and politics, and also in all sports. The sanctions in other sports are more severe than in golf, falling not only on South Africans outside their country, but on foreign athletes who compete in South Africa.)

In golf, the anti-apartheid campaign is being felt most severely in the Million Dollar Challenge in Sun City, Bophuthatswana. Sandy Lyle, shaking off the pressure, was the lone European to accept an invitation to the 1989 edition. The American tour has no anti-apartheid prohibitions, but some American stars stayed away. Consequently, the 1989 Million Dollar Challenge, except for Lyle, was devoid of the world's brightest marquee names. Americans who did accept, such as Scott Simpson, argued that boycotting sports is not the way to encourage change.

Whatever the answer, it seems the problem is destined to haunt and shape the game for years to come.

Dewar's White Label Trophy—R250,000
Winner: John Bland

The Sunshine Circuit opened 1989 looking more like a branch of the U.S. circuit. Some 42 Americans turned up at Durban Country Club for the Dewar's White Label Trophy the first week of January, all of them looking to ring in the New Year with a victory. And for a while, it seemed one of them would do just that. Americans dominated the leaderboard in the first three rounds. "I knew when I went out today I'd need at least a 67 to win, and that was my goal," said South African John Bland, 42, a Sunshine veteran, who had two victories and two seconds in 1988. His guess was a stroke too high, but his score wasn't. He solved the windy, storm-battered course in the final round for a 66 and a one-stroke victory—it came on the final hole—over his old rival, Tony Johnstone. Bland returned 70-66-71-66—273, 13 under par, to Johnstone's 67-70-69-68—274.

The American parade started in the first round, with Rick Morton and John Daly returning 65s to share a one-stroke lead. Then the tournament turned into a steeplechase. Alan Pate, 35, a former American tour player, shrugged off the wind for a 67—135 and a one-stroke lead on two rookie pros, South African Ben Fouchee (70) and American Tom Tolles (69), along with Phil Simmons (69), and Bland (66). "So many players panic in the wind," said Pate, who made six birdies. "But I try to use it to my advantage by inventing shots—for instance, soft, low shots downwind as well as into the wind." Fouchee recovered from a two-bogey start, and Tolles, just two months a pro, carded five birdies. Bland had to shake off a pair of early three-putts before he got rolling.

Only Johnstone interrupted an all-American outing in the third round. A 69 put him at 206, a joint third with Tolles (70), and another American, Carl Cooper (68). They were one off the 205 lead shared by Pate (70) and American Stuart Smith (68), a Californian making his fourth Sunshine visit. Johnstone, who had three wins and two seconds in 1988, had four birdies and one bogey, then headed for the practice tee. "I have to sort out a kink in my swing," he said. "Then I should be OK out there tomorrow." It would seem so. Bland was still more or less quiet, a 71 leaving him two strokes off the lead on 207.

The weather stole the show in the final round. Heavy overnight rains flooded parts of the course, forcing the PGA to cut the field to 50 players, and to rearrange the golf course into two nine-hole loops. The golfers played holes one through seven twice, and the 17th and 18th, a patchwork course with a par of 70.

Bland wasn't worth a bet when the final round started. "I three-putted the first hole for a bogey, which was a big disappointment early on," he said. "But it woke me up. I didn't do much wrong after that, except for driving into the trees at the 16th, where I also dropped a shot." He fought his way through the foul weather, and Johnstone kept pace as the pretenders fell away. It came down to the last hole. Johnstone put his approach at about 15 feet from the flag, and Bland put his at about half that distance. Johnstone missed the birdie try, Bland didn't.

ICL International—R250,000
Winner: Chris Williams

You didn't need a handicapper's crystal ball to figure the favorites as the Sunshine Tour entered its second week of 1989 with the ICL International at Zwartkops Golf Club, Pretoria. There was John Bland, of course, the winner the week before. And Tony Johnstone, the previous week's runner-up, 1987 and 1988 ICL winner, and the tour's dominant character. There were the Americans, among them Alan Pate, Stuart Smith, and Tom Tolles, who made such a run the week before. And the British were restless after their disappointment. If nobody noticed Chris Williams, it shouldn't be surprising.

Williams, Liverpool-born and a resident of South Africa since 1963, had done little for four years. In the most recent ICLs he had just modest success—tied for 18th in 1987, tied for ninth in 1988. He was last really heard from in the 1985 Lexington PGA, when he did it all: four strokes off the lead in the first round, 10 behind after the second, and then that stunning 63 in the third, which set him up to win. And win he did, with a 30-foot putt on the final hole to edge Denis Watson, Jay Townsend, and Mark McNulty by a stroke. He didn't sneak up on anybody this time.

Williams broke on top with an eight-under-par 64 for a one-stroke lead on Bland. American J.C. Anderson, the only one who would keep the pressure on Williams, held third at 66. Johnstone returned a 68, but never got up to speed.

In the second round, Williams held firm with a 68—132, but the field behind him reshaped in a hurry. Bland's try for a second successive title evaporated, in with nothing worse than a par-72, and he was on his way to a tie-10th finish. Hugh Baiocchi, who had opened on 68, came charging up with a 66 to take second on 134, two strokes behind Williams. Anderson continued to cling to third place on 70—136.

It is reasonable to conclude that a man who hadn't won since 1985 and who hadn't done much since, would not stand up much longer under the pressure of holding the lead. People who reasoned that way would have to wait at least one more day. Williams returned a 69 in the third round and actually padded his lead. At 201, he was now three ahead of Baiocchi (70) and American John Chaffee (67), both at 204. And Williams would disappoint the watchers for yet another day, the final one. In the last round, he left the 60s for the first time, but his 71 was good enough for a one-stroke victory over the persistent Anderson (68), 272-273. For others, it was too little, too late.

American Timothy Robinson (66) vaulted to 274 and share of third with David Feherty (67), who was left to look ahead to the next outing. "I'm playing well," Feherty said, "and I'm looking forward to defending my title in the PGA." Jeff Hawkes, after middle rounds of 71-72, surged with a 65 to tie for sixth at 275, and Mark James was finally heard from, a resounding 64 that lifted him to eighth on 276.

Lexington PGA Championship—R250,000
Winner: Tony Johnstone

In a week of intense heat, low scores, and high frustration, Tony Johnstone was one of few challengers in the Lexington PGA Championship not to post a round under 65. He enjoyed another distinction that nobody else had—he won, picking up in 1989 where he left off in a three-victory 1988. It took a playoff to do it, though. Johnstone got a birdie-two at the first extra hole to beat Chris Williams, winner of the ICL International a week earlier, after they tied at 11-under-par 269 at the par-70 Wanderers, in Johannesburg.

Johnstone was one of the pre-tournament favorites—until it started. A 71 in the first round left him eight strokes off the lead. The parade of low-60s had begun. At the end, there were three 63s, and six 64s. What saved Johnstone and Williams was that nobody got more than one of either. Johnstone returned 71-65-66-67, and Williams 67-68-67-67.

First came an unknown American, Dan Walsworth, who surfaced with a 63, for a one-stroke lead in the first round. It was practically an all-British show behind him. Britons held six of the first 11 spots on the leaderboard, and three of them were right on Walsworth's heels, all at 64—Phil Harrison, Ian Mosey, and Stuart Little, along with South African Phil Jonas. Harrison, erratic tee-to-green, was saved by his putter. "I made everything I looked at," he said. Mosey experimented with his set-up and made a discovery.

"I've just found," he said, "that I can hit the ball better and farther by moving forward in my stance."

(A quick look forward: Mosey's new-found confidence didn't last. His 73-77 in the middle rounds doomed him to a tie for 45th with Harrison, who finished 75-72. Walsworth and Jonas slipped to 74s in the second round and tied for 13th. A closing 74 helped drop Little to a tie for 41st.)

Next up for a 63 was Mark Wiltshire, 26, the former South African Amateur champion who lost his right eye in a childhood accident. He got his in the second round for a 132 total and a two-stroke lead on American Bruce Vaughan (69) and J.C. Anderson (64). European Masters champion Chris Moody made a run at it, with two bursts of three birdies in four holes for a 66—136. Defending champion David Feherty's hopes of repeating died on his seventh hole (No. 16), when he drove into the trees and took a triple-bogey seven. A 71 put him nine strokes behind, at 141. Johnstone stirred, but still wasn't scaring anybody. A 65, his best round of the tournament, put him at 136 and four off the pace after 36 holes.

Wiltshire kept the lead through 54 holes with a 67—199, and Johnstone (66) and Williams (67) closed in and shared second place with Anderson (68), three strokes back at 202.

At last Feherty was heard from, but too late. He closed with a 63, and shared seventh on 274. Wiltshire shook, but barely, closing with his worst round, a 71 for 270, missing the playoff by one stroke. One extra hole later, Johnstone had his first win of 1989, his third in three months, and his fourth in 13 months.

Palabora Classic—R250,000
Winner: Stuart Smith

The 1989 Palabora Classic started out more like a nature walk than a golf tournament. First, there was a lion, spotted not far from Hans Merensky Country Club just a week before the tournament. Then there was a problem at the 11th hole. This was not your average hazard. It seems that anybody hitting over the green had to contend with a cantankerous bull buffalo. Game rangers had to come in and cart him away. In addition, there was the usual compliment of wildlife—herds of buck roaming the course, and a few hippo families and a number of crocodiles inhabiting the pools at No. 17. Add to this a prolonged lack of rain that left the rough thin, which in turn allowed balls to run off into the bush, and also add heat in the 100-degree range, then powerful winds, and this tournament would not be a walk in the park.

Phil Harrison put things into perspective after posting a one-under-par 71 in the first round. "I'm as pleased with that," he said, "as with my 64 in the PGA at the Wanderers last week. That's the comparison." With the heat and the wind beating away, only 25 players out of 161 in the field were below par for the first round. These included a local player, Len O'Kennedy, and an American, Scott Dunlap, who returned 67s to share a one-stroke lead. David Feherty was three strokes off the pace and still was a happy man. "A 70 is a very good round under these conditions," he said.

The nationalities remained the same, but the names changed in the second round. This time, Stuart Smith, 27, an unknown American from Sacramento, California, returned a dazzling seven-under-par 65, and South African Ian Palmer a 67 to share the 36-hole lead at 135. These were remarkable scores, coming under the relentless pressure of 100-degree heat. Their performances also did fatal damage to some hopefuls, bringing in the 36-hole cut at two-over-par 146 and sweeping out, among others, Ian Mosey, Ian Young, and Brian Evans, all at 147, and Denis Durnian at 148.

Palmer, whose only win came in the 1985 Wild Coast Classic, surged into the solo lead with a 68 for a 203 total after three rounds. This put him three strokes clear of Smith, who returned a 71, and Feherty, who finally found the touch he was looking for, with a 67. The fates of golf robbed Feherty of a better showing. "I hit my best shot of the day at the 17th," he said. "It was a five iron, right at the flag. But it rolled over the green and into a bunker." That ultimately cost him a bogey-four. Mark Davis, former English Amateur international, ran off six birdies but made two bogeys and turned in a 68 for 208, five strokes off the lead. So the Palabora seemed headed for a routine wrap-up. Well, for those who like their finishes neat, this one was anything but.

Feherty's bid in the final round was cooled quickly by a bogey at the second hole. He settled for a 71 and a share of fourth place on 276. Trevor Dodds, who had a 65 in the second round, came out of nowhere with a closing 66 to claim third place at 275. First and second place were a matter of unexpected dispute. Palmer acquitted himself well with a closing 71, but his three-stroke advantage disappeared under Smith's 68. They tied at 14-under-par 274. Then Smith beat Palmer with a birdie on the first hole of their playoff. Thus Smith not only had his first victory of his four-year career, he became the first overseas player to break the South African monopoly on the current Sunshine Tour.

Zimbabwe Open—£49,550
Winner: Vijay Singh

Vijay Singh's days of "sneaking up on people" are long over. Singh, the slender Fijian, surprised everybody in 1988 when he scored his first victory in the Nigerian Open. That started the season. If he seemed a fluke, he dispelled the notion with a couple of other high finishes, the No. 1 position on the Safari money list, and the No. 2 spot in the PGA European Tour Qualifying School at La Manga, in Spain. So he was no surprise when he kicked off the 1989 Safari season the way he had a year earlier—with a victory. This time it was the Zimbabwe Open at the par-72 Royal Harare course, and he did it authoritatively. He trailed by five strokes in the first round, took the lead in the second, and stayed there. He returned 72-67-71-72—282, six under par, for a two-stroke victory over Mark Mouland. There was a little sense of revenge, too. Singh was edged out of the 1988 Zimbabwe Open when Roger Chapman birdied the final hole to win by a stroke. He wasn't about to let this one get away.

"It was easier than I expected," said Singh. He wasn't being brash. "I was confident of success," he explained, "after finishing second in the European Tour qualifying event in December." That little exercise in masochism had taken place barely seven weeks earlier.

People who chart golf events as snippets of history might wonder whether another career was budding in Zimbabwe, much as Singh's had a year earlier. This golfer was Welshman David Wood, 25, the 1982 Welsh Amateur champion, who turned professional after failing to make the 1987 Walker Cup team. He also missed, by a stroke, in winning his tour card in the 1988 qualifying tournament. But he looked like a seasoned veteran in the Zimbabwe Open, when he took the first-round lead with a five-under-par 67. Wood works part-time in insurance, ". . . in case golf doesn't work out," he said. Insurance seemed a good idea after he returned a pair of 75s in the middle rounds. Then he closed strong with a 68 and finished third with three-under-par 285, a stroke out of second place.

Singh took a grip on this one in the second round, when he logged six birdies in his first 14 holes. Of course, there is always weather to contend with. At No. 18, Singh had no sooner hit the green than the heavy rains came. He three-putted through water for a bogey-five and a 67 for a 139 total and a two-stroke lead over Wayne Stephens. Gordon J. Brand, the pre-tournament favorite, was four under par with two holes to play but ran into trouble under darkening skies. He three-putted the 17th for one bogey-five and drove into the trees at the last hole for another, and settled for a 69—142, three off the lead. Brand finished a joint fourth on 287.

Singh's biggest worry in the final round had to be Mouland, who started the day only a stroke behind. But with Mouland unable to mount a real challenge—he closed with 73—284—Singh got safely home with a steady par 72. Fiji's star golfer had just won the Safari Tour's opener for the second consecutive year. New year, same story. But it would never get old for him.

Protea Assurance South African Open—R300,000
Winner: Fred Wadsworth

They had the word of no less an authority than Tony Johnstone: The Glendower course at Johannesburg, venue for the Protea Assurance Open, is the toughest course in South Africa. David Feherty pretty much seconded the motion on the par-72 course. "If you miss the fairway," Feherty said, "you're dead." The reasons for these warnings: if Glendower's thick rough doesn't get you, there's water waiting on 14 holes. Johnstone, the dominant force of the Sunshine Tour, delivered his message after the second round, when a 67—136 left him a solid second, a stroke off the lead. Feherty managed just two birdies for a 71 that left him at 140, five strokes off the lead. Before long, Andre Cruse would add his endorsement in the form of disappointment.

Cruse, a 23-year-old South African, had good reason to think of winning. He broke the course record with a bogey-free 65 in the second round, taking a one-stroke lead at 135 over Johnstone. But his dreams sagged with a 76 in the third round, then died with another in the fourth. He finished tied for 11th.

The Protea turned into an American scramble over the last two rounds, and a battle over the last two holes between two former American tour pros. At the end, it was Fred Wadsworth fighting past a faltering Tom Lehman to grab the title. Lehman, 29, out of Los Angeles, a three-year veteran of the American tour, made his big move in the second round with a 66, one stroke off the new course record, to move within three of the lead. Wind and rain battered the field in the third round, but Lehman ignored them. After a bogey at No. 3, he eagled the fourth and added three birdies for a 68—206 that gave him a four-stroke lead over Johnstone (74), and two Americans who had been all but silent, Charles Bolling (70) and Wadsworth (70).

In the final round, Wadsworth kept the pressure on and finally caught the slipping Lehman on the 17th. And when Lehman three-putted No. 18, Wadsworth had the victory by a stroke. Wadsworth returned 72-68-70-68—278, 10 under par. Lehman's card was 72-66-68-73—279. Jack Ferenz, yet another American, took third with a strong finish, 67—281. The American monopoly was interrupted by Ernie Els, a South African amateur, who took fourth on 69—282. Johnstone's hopes for yet another Sunshine victory sank in the final two rounds. After a solid 69-67 start, he faded to 74-73 and finished fifth on 283.

Wadsworth, 26, a rangy blond out of Columbus, Georgia, won his U.S. tour card in Hollywood style. He had missed by a stroke in the qualifying school in the fall of 1985. In the autumn of 1986, he had made it through the first stage of the qualifying school, the sectional qualifier. The next step was the regional qualifier some weeks later. He would just have time to play in the Southern Open, in his home town, if he could get one of the Monday spots available through the Monday qualifier. He got in with a 68, and then to everyone's surprise, he won the tournament. The victory also conferred a tour card on him. Unfortunately, the magic didn't last. "I had a miserable 1988," he said. It cost him that precious card.

Zambian Open—£75,000
Winner: Craig Maltman

What do you do with a 53-hole tournament? Statisticians will just have to shrug and stick an asterisk on the rain-battered 1989 Zambian Open. It won't matter to Craig Maltman, though. Whatever they do, it will still bear his name—the first big victory ever for the 35-year-old Scot. Maltman, who led all the way, shook off a poor second round and pulled himself together just in time in the third and final round for a two-stroke victory over Mark Roe, even par 215 for the 53 holes to Roe's 217.

The big problem was rain, sheets of it. The week opened with a torrential downpour. Some five inches fell in 72 hours before the tournament even began, denying the field the chance to practice on the par-73 Lusaka course, a long brute at 7,217 yards, but longer still because of the wet conditions. Maltman was the only one who didn't seem to notice. He solved the soggy stretches in the first round for a six-under-par 67 while the best anyone else could manage was the 72 by Jeff Pinsent. Gordon J. Brand and Vijay Singh, the pre-tournament favorites, were barely within shouting distance at 76 and 75, respectively. Maltman, it developed, really needed that five-stroke cushion. Without it, his second-round 76 might have destroyed him.

And in the third and final round—actually, the final 17 holes, with the submerged 18th having been declared unplayable—he was showing signs of strain. That three-stroke lead looked healthy until his driver balked. Errant tee shots cost him strokes at the third, fifth, eighth, and ninth. He got only one birdie in that stretch, at No. 2. But he was safe. Nobody else could get up any steam, so that shaky front nine cost him only one stroke. He led Roe by two through the turn.

A cooly scrambled par at No. 12 settled Maltman down. He had got off yet another unruly drive, this one far to the right, then dropped a seven iron short of the green. Another bogey was at hand. But he chipped to 10 feet and holed his par, and he was on his way. He saved a little drama for the home stretch. He birdied the par-five 14th, three-putted for a bogey at the short 16th, and then missed the green at No. 17, the final hole, but saved his par with a chip and putt for 72.

His 67 in the first round was a jewel, especially given the setting of a mushy course and a struggling field. While everyone else was baffled by the sodden greens, Maltman dropped a half-dozen putts of between five and 20 feet. Pinsent, on his way to the second-place 72, conquered four of the five par-fives for birdies from 10 feet and less, but the 17th set him back with a double bogey-six after he drove into the trees. Overnight storms didn't help matters for the next day. Maltman, who made seven birdies in the first round, got just one in the second, and staggered home in 76—143. But 74 was the best Pinsent could muster, and that kept him second at 146. He closed on 75 and slid back to fifth, while Roe, crippled by an opening 76, took second with a closing 70. Brand was third on 218, Singh fourth at 220.

AECI Charity Classic—R250,000
Winner: Jeff Hawkes

The AECI Charity Classic was as much an exercise in crowd control as a golf tournament. A field of 257—the Sunshine Tour's biggest yet—turned out and forced the event to be spread over two courses for the first two rounds. Basic arithmetic says that meant nearly two full regular fields descended on Randpark and adjoining Windsor Park near Johannesburg. Things got no simpler at the end. A severe storm washed out the final round Sunday, leaving Jeff Hawkes the winner of a 54-hole tournament on 67-64-70—201, 15 under par and two strokes better than runner-up Tony Johnstone. It was the second victory in his 14-year career.

Hawkes secured his position in the Saturday round, carding four birdies in seven holes to go to 17 under par and four ahead of Johnstone. Others were giving him a lot of breathing room. Andrew Chandler, for one, began the day in a bright mood after two successive 69s, then dropped six strokes on the 10 holes he played. This included a triple bogey-seven at No. 9, where it took him three tries to escape a bunker. Play had to be suspended when several Randpark greens were water.

Hawkes was three strokes astern of the lead in the first round, his 67 barely noticeable alongside the 64s returned by South Africans Paul Simmons and Kevin Stone at Winter Park. A second-round 64 carried him right to the top at 131, a stroke ahead of American Stuart Smith, the Palabora winner two weeks earlier, who tied the course record with a 63.

British golfers were trying to make a move. Brian Evans did it the hard way, returning a 66 with a brand-new set of clubs. "I haven't played so well the past few weeks," Evans said. "But I took the new clubs out of the box for the pro-am on Tuesday, and they are really helping my game." In turn, Evans helped someone else. "I've been having trouble with my swing," said Chandler, after his second 69, "and Brian sorted it out in five minutes for me last night." But it was all futile. This one had Jeff Hawkes' name on it.

It became a more familiar name in 1988. Hawkes, a sailboat maker when he's not on tour, broke through for his first career victory in the Bloemfontein Classic on the Sunshine circuit. He was already known as something of a giant-killer. In the 1987 Epson Grand Prix match play tournament, he swept through David Feherty, Howard Clark, Tommy Armour, and Sam Torrance, and then whipped Seve Ballesteros in the semifinals, 4 and 3. Mats Lanner finally cooled him off, beating him for the championship.

Kenya Open—£69,230
Winner: David Jones

First, you had Vijay Singh, winning the Zimbabwe Open to start the season. It's not every day that a Fijian wins a tournament. So the year was off to a great start. Next, you had a first-time winner. That was Craig Maltman, a 35-year-old Scot, who made the Zambian Open his first big pro victory. So why wouldn't there be room for a 41-year-old Irishman to finally make his mark?

The man was David Jones, from Ulster, and the event was the Kenya Open, at Muthaiga. And Jones left no doubt about it. He posted a course-record-tying 13-under-par 271 (69-69-65-58) for a comfy three-stroke victory over Mark Mouland, who was second to Singh in the Zimbabwe Open just two weeks earlier.

It was the first victory in Jones' 20 years as a professional, and it pretty much clinched his decision, of about a year ago, not to retire. Jones was coaching the Irish national squad, a position that gives a man responsibility, prestige, and little time to practice. "My own game suffered through neglect," Jones said. "And it was very frustrating because every suggestion I made was turned down. I finally resigned the job." Jones was on the verge of retiring, but friends talked him out of it. "I decided to go back to the PGA school in December," he said. He won his credentials with ease, finishing eighth in the school.

It fitted Jones' non-existent existence that he did not figure prominently early in the tournament. Maltman looked as though the spirits were with him in the first round, when he took a one-stroke lead with 67 with a big boost from a peculiar eagle he himself wanted to disown. Maltman, who doubles as a grocery store operator in Eyemouth, Berwickshire, pushed his drive into the rough at the par-five second. He hit a six iron out of the tall grass that seemed on its way over a wall. But it hit fluffy grass in front of the green, a 190-yard shot that lost its steam and rolled obediently across the green, some 25 yards, and dropped into the hole. "It was a complete fluke, and I was embarrassed," Maltman insisted. "I've rarely played worse and rarely scored better."

The furies got even with him the next day. Maltman returned a most respectable 70—even with two three-putt greens—and it dropped him into third place behind Mouland and little-known Clive Tucker. Mouland birdied only one of the four par-five holes and missed three putts inside two feet, and still managed a 69 that gave him a share of the lead at 136 with Clive Tucker, who gave lessons for three years at a City of London golf club. Tucker returned a 66, playing the back nine in 32. He made two twos, one from a few feet and the other from 25. Maltman was a stroke back, at 137. Jones was steady, but hardly a looming threat when he put together a 69 that left him a joint third at 138.

A third-round 65 boosted him to a three-stroke lead through 54 holes, and he had to be more than steady for the final round. Now the big guns were lobbing their final shots at him. But there was new trouble for Mouland. He birdied all of the par-five holes this time, but on the other hand, missed a number of putts inside 15 feet. He had to close with two consecutive birdies for the 67 that would give him second place at 274. But the destiny-bound Jones had the luxury of a three-stroke lead going into the final round. What he needed down the stretch was the experience of all those days plus the memories of all those barren years. Jones kept his composure, his swing, and his three-stroke lead. The final-round 68 gave him a 271 total and the victory by three strokes.

Hosken Hollard Swazi Sun Classic—R250,000
Winner: Jeff Hawkes

For Ian Mosey in the Hosken Hollard Swazi Sun Classic, if it wasn't one thing, it was another. The PGA European Tour would start its 1989 season in a week—the last week of February—and all other British card-holders had flown home. Mosey decided to remain in South Africa. He felt a certain affinity for the Swazi tournament. The shortish Royal Swazi course at Mbabane, Swaziland, seemed to lend itself to his game. A year earlier, a six-foot putt on the final green would have put him into the playoff for the championship. But the putt didn't drop, and he missed out by a stroke. Don Levin went on to beat Alan Pate for the crown. Mosey settled for third place. He had only one round out of the 60s, and that was a 70, which means that once he got over the disappointment, he saw a lot of promise in a performance like that. And so he stayed for the 1989 edition. And a rainy one it was.

The rain was so severe on opening day that not only was the first round washed out, the tournament immediately was cut to 54 holes. In the second round, Mosey was one under par with two holes to play when rain stopped play. John Daly, 22-year-old American, a pro of only 18 months, held the lead at the end of the day with 67-67—134. It didn't last long.

The next day, Sunday, Jeff Hawkes, who won the AECI Charity Classic the week before, came out at 6 a.m. to complete his second round. And he did it with a flourish, wrapping up a 66 for a 133 total and a one-stroke lead through 36 holes. Hawkes then took his second title in two weeks with a final-round 69 for a 202 total. Daly (67) and Swaziland's Joe Dlamini (67) shared second a stroke back. Poor Ian Mosey. Impressive as rounds of 70-72-71 may look, they left him 11 strokes off the lead.

Trust Bank Tournament of Champions—R250,000
Winner: Jay Townsend

Jay Townsend, 26-year-old Floridian who had been unable to win his playing card on the American PGA Tour, enjoyed something of a consolation when he fought off rainy weather, uncut fairways, and a host of fellow Americans to take the Trust Bank Tournament of Champions. Townsend romped over the Kensington course in Johannesburg in 13-under-par 275, on a card of 67-70-67-71, and won by two from another American, Bruce Vaughan.

The Trust Bank event, falling in the last week of February, was the finale of the early segment of the 1989 Sunshine Tour, and Townsend's success gave Americans victories in three of the eight events—in fact, three of the last five. Stuart Smith won the Palabora Classic in the last week of January, and Fred Wadsworth the Protea Assurance Open in the first week of February.

Not that Townsend had a cakewalk to the Trust Bank winner's circle. He was challenged to the end by some of the Sunshine circuit's finest. Tied for third at 279 were Dewar's White Label Trophy champion John Bland; double-winner Jeff Hawkes (AECI, Swazi Sun), going for his third consecutive win; Ian Palmer, runner-up to Smith in the Palabora playoff, and the veteran Gavin Levenson. Palmer closed with 65, Bland 67, Levenson 68, and Hawkes 70.

Are Americans better rain players? The question was at least raised in the Trust Bank. The tournament opened in a steady drizzle, and the course was already soaked by weeks of rain. Some fairways, too soft to support the mowers, had to go uncut, and some tees had to be moved to give golfers more playable areas to hit into. For all of this, the Trust Bank looked like an all-American affair from the start. Jon Chaffee, a Texan who spent four years on the U.S. tour, grabbed the first-round lead on 66. Townsend was right behind, tied for second with Swaziland's Joe Dlamini at 67. Two more Americans were tied for fourth at 68, and seven others were at 70, in a logjam that included Bland.

Townsend moved into the lead in the second round on 70—137, a one-stroke edge on a cluster that included Hawkes and Americans Chaffee and J.C. Anderson. Townsend all but wrapped it up in the third round with a 67 that powered him to a four-stroke lead at 204. Hugh Royer, another American, led the pursuit with a blistering 63, but after a 71-74 start, it could get him only a tie for second after 54 holes. Then it was just a matter of holding on, and this Townsend did very well with his closing one-under-par 71. Vaughan and Palmer made the big moves with their 65s, but it was too little and too late.

Railfreight Bloemfontein Classic—R250,000
Winner: Desmond Terblanche

Back in 1983, Desmond Terblanche, then just 18, was stamping himself as a young man to watch. He capped this early promise by winning the World Junior championship. Six years later, at age 24, he was stamping himself again, this time with his first Sunshine Tour victory. It came in the Bloemfontein Classic in mid-November at Bloemfontein's Schoeman Park, when he climbed painfully from deep in the pack on 74-67-67-70—278, for a two-stroke victory over Wayne Westner and John Bland.

But Terblanche's prospects looked bleak to start with. His 74 in the first round was anemic compared to a land-rush start that left six men tied for the lead on 69. These were Bland, who led off the year by winning the Dewar's White Label Trophy early in January: Tony Johnstone, Lexington PGA champion; Fred Wadsworth, who won the Protea Assurance Open early in February; Jeff Hawkes, winner of the AECI Charity Classic and the Swazi Sun Classic, back-to-back, in February, and Bobby Lincoln and Mark McCann. Terblanche's position was more tenuous than it looked. Consider these raw facts: His 74 wasn't as strong as it seemed. He was one of nine at that figure, and only 17 others were worse, from 75 through 77. And although he was only five strokes off the lead, there were 38 players crammed ahead of him between 70 and 73. At that, it was a small wonder that the first round was played. A cloudburst and hailstorm halted play, leaving about half the field to complete the round the next day.

The field shook itself out in the second round. Bland had another 69 for 138 and a one-stroke lead over Wadsworth (70), Westner (69), and Nico Van Rensburgh (68). Terblanche started his rise, coming to within three strokes at 141, returning a tournament-low 67. He matched it the next day, the second of only six 67s in the tournament, and sat one behind Wadsworth, who took the third-round lead on 68—207. Westner and Bland killed their chances in the third round, Westner with a 74, Bland a 73. Then Wadsworth followed them in the final round, blowing to a 77. That set the stage for Terblanche. A solid 70 in the final round—only nine scores were better—carried him to his first victory.

First Bank Nigerian Open—£63,211
Winner: Vijay Singh

Vijay Singh, a rookie on the PGA European Tour, was already renowned as the first Fiji Islander to win on that tour. If there was still any doubt that he could perform under pressure, he cleared it up with authority in the First Bank Nigerian Open when the Safari Tour resumed late in November. He had come to the Ikoyi Club at Lagos, Nigeria, as defending champion, but his chances of repeating didn't look promising when he got to the final round trailing co-leaders Jeff Pinsent and Chris Platts by two strokes. And if that deficit weren't enough, he had the additional obstacle of a pressure-tested veteran immediately in front of him, in the person of Gordon J. Brand, who was one stroke off the lead.

But the slender 26-year-old Fijian proceeded to brush aside the odds and race home with a three-under-par 68 for the victory. On a card of 71-68-72-68—279, five under par, he took a one-stroke victory over Brand (70), Pinsent (71), and England's Ian Spencer, who closed with a 67. The low honors for the day went to Stephen Richardson, English Amateur champion, who was sharpening his game for the PGA European Tour Qualifying School. Richardson closed with a five-under-par 66 for a one-over-par total of 285 and a tie for eighth.

But Singh was the man of the hour. Not only did he repeat as the Nigerian Open champion, he also posted his third victory of the year, adding it to the Zimbabwe Open at the start of the Safari season in January and the Volvo Open championship on the PGA European Tour in April. The young man from the far Pacific—who is of Indian background and who learned his golf from his father—had come a very long way, literally and figuratively.

Ivory Coast Open—£82,859
Winner: Vijay Singh

If Vijay Singh surprised the odds-makers by making the Nigerian Open his third victory of 1989, then he must have stunned them completely by taking the Ivory Coast Open the very next week. He double-stamped himself with that one: Not only was he now known as the first Fijian ever to win on the European tour, but he also had crowned himself king of the Safari Tour.

Indeed, on the Safari, they heard of little else. The five-tournament Safari circuit was played in two segments—the first three early in the year, the other two late. Singh, 26, won three of the five, and with a dramatic sense of timing. He won the first one, the Zimbabwe Open, late in January, then the last, the Ivory Coast Open, late in November (the week after he won the Nigerian Open). In between, Singh made himself one of the 10 first-time winners on the European tour with his victory in the Volvo Open in April.

The Ivory Coast victory was a little scarier. In the Nigerian Open, he had to come from two strokes behind in the final round. In this one, he led by four strokes going into the final round, and almost let it get away. He was saved by a set of powerful middle rounds. Singh shot 70-65-65-74—274, 14 under par, for a one-stroke victory over Jeff Pinsent, co-runner-up to him the week before in the Nigerian Open.

It was almost a year earlier, in the first week of December, 1988, that Singh was going through the perils of the European tour qualifying school at La Manga, in Spain. He ground away for six rounds—71-68-72-69-69-71—420, finishing tied for second, four strokes behind Jesper Parnevik. Only once, with the par 72 in the third round, did he fail to break par. There's a lot of promise in a performance like that. It would seem Singh more than fulfilled it. In Europe alone, he had one victory and four other top-10 finishes. Almost lost in that impressive rookie performance was his "iron man" display. Singh played in 32 of the 34 tournaments, more than anybody else on the European tour. And where most golfers say they need a break from the strain every four or five weeks, Singh played in the last 23 events in succession, and enjoyed two of his four top-10 finishes in that span. Maybe the victories weren't the measure of Singh's year. Maybe survival was.

Minolta Match Play Championship
Winner: Fulton Allem

The scene and the format shifted, but the faces were familiar in the Minolta Match Play Championship at Gary Player Country Club. Of most recent fame, there was Desmond Terblanche, who scored his first Sunshine Tour victory the week before in the Bloemfontein Classic. His dreams of winning two in succession ended abruptly in the second round, thanks to Dale Hayes. Then there were the old standbys—David Frost, John Bland, Fulton Allem, and defending champion Tony Johnstone.

The week began with Ernie Els leading the qualifier on 68, only to be bounced out in the second round by Trevor Dodds, who in turn was knocked out by Frost, the pre-tournament favorite. The bracket also included the rest of the Bloemfontein supporting cast—co-runners-up Wayne Westner and John Bland. Frost defeated Westner for one semifinal berth, but not without a tense moment. Frost was on the verge of a comfortable win, but suffered a double-bogey six at the 18th, fell into a tie with Westner on 72, and had to birdie the second playoff hole to take one of the semifinal berths. Bland took the other with a 69-70 win over Allan Henning. Bland then spilled Frost to gain the final.

In the other bracket, Johnstone got no further than the third round. That bracket also contained the burly and congenial Allem, fresh from his third season on the American tour. Allem cruised through the field, rolling over Hendrik Buhrman, Dale Hayes, Hugh Baiocchi (a four-stroke decision on a course record-tying 65), and a five-stroke romp over George Reid, 73-78. The final had the touch of a scriptwriter. Allem and Bland tied at three-under-par 69 in regulation. Allem ended the shootout with a par on the first playoff hole.

Million Dollar Challenge—$2,360,000
Winner: David Frost

This was a tale of a man trying to play golf with his mind in two countries. David Frost had come home to his native southern Africa for the Million Dollar Challenge, but part of him was still back in Dallas, Texas, where his wife, Linda, was in a hospital with pre-natal complications. Their second child was due in two months. Maybe the combination of playing in front of the home folks plus worrying about Linda was inspiration as much as pressure. Whatever the reason, Frost never left the lead in the 10-man field, touring the Sun City course in Bophuthatswana in 67-66-75-68—276, 12 under par, for a three-stroke victory and a $1 million first prize. "I can't tell you what a thrill it is to win in front of your own people," he told the press, but only after he had telephoned Linda in the hospital back in Dallas.

Frost became the third South African in four years to win the event. Fulton Allem, the 1988 champion, was well down the list in this one. The final scoreboard: Frost, 276; Scott Hoch, 279; Tim Simpson, 280; Don Pooley, 291; Chip Beck, 294; Andy Bean, 295; Sandy Lyle, 298; Fulton Allem, 299; Ken Green, 301, and Scott Simpson, 301.

The tournament opened with fireworks. Hoch and Tim Simpson went out in 32s, including eagles on the par-five ninth, and posted 67s. Frost birdied five of the last nine holes to catch them and share the first-round lead. They were the only players to break par in the first round, a fact that gave rise to conflicting observations. "The greens are super and fast, and I'm full of confidence," said Frost. Countered Scott Simpson (72): "There is a point where the greens can be just too severe to be fair, and it's close to that now." Lyle shot 75 that included a spectacular crash, a triple-bogey eight at No. 9, where he had to lay up after driving into the rough, then pitched short of the island green, into the rocks. Allem had 76, and a woeful Bean was last with an 81. "I can't see me playing any better," Bean said.

Frost zoomed three strokes ahead in the rain-interrupted second round with a 66—133, two of his birdies coming on bold putts of 15 and 25 feet at the last two holes. He was three ahead of Tim Simpson (69), six ahead of Hoch (72). Now a villain emerged: the par-five ninth hole, with its island green, where Lyle became victim No. 1 with that eight in the first round. It cost Frost the solo lead in the third round. He hit his second shot into the water behind the green and took seven, en route to a 75. Other victims: Beck (76) took nine, and Don Pooley (76) took eight. Tim Simpson, with 72, was co-leader with Frost at 208.

The tie was short-lived. Frost opened the final round with birdies on the first two holes, and he was on his way to a 68—276 and a three-stroke victory over Hoch (69—279). It might have been a tie for second for Tim Simpson (72—280) except for a belated reversal on a ruling. Hoch's final round score was reduced from 70 to 69 when officials decided that his penalty drop at No. 9 actually should have been a free drop for line-of-sight relief from a television tower. Had Hoch and Tim Simpson tied, each would have won $275,000. But when the tie was broken, Hoch received second-place money of $300,000, and Simpson was dropped to third place and $250,000.

Twee Jongegezellen Masters
Winner: Hugh Baiocchi

For Hugh Baiocchi, it was—as they say of the camel—a long time between drinks. Baiocchi, 43-year-old South African, came from behind in the final round to win the Twee Jongegezellen Masters, and when his final putt dropped, he was one happy man. It had been nine years since he last won on the Sunshine Tour—the 1980 South African PGA and the Val Reefs Open, along with the Zimbabwe Open—and six since his last victory of any kind, the 1983 State Express Classic on the PGA European Tour. Little wonder that when he closed out 1989, his 19th year as a professional, he gave a sigh of relief. Baiocchi won by a stroke on 69-68-74-70—281, seven under par.

This was the final Sunshine Tour event of 1989, and one of the tougher Masters fields had assembled at Stellenbosch Golf Club, near Cape Town, in mid-December. European tour regulars Denis Durnian and David Feherty stopped by, joining such Sunshine veterans as Tony Johnstone and John Bland. As things turned out, neither European developed into much of a threat. Feherty, jet-lagged after a long trip from Australia, returned 75 in the first round. Durnian, well-rested but perhaps rusty after several weeks off, had a 74. After that, neither man was a factor. Despite high winds that buffeted the course and lifted scores, Baiocchi, Bland, and Johnstone all returned three-under-par 69s and shared a one-stroke lead in the first round.

Baiocchi was alone at the 36-hole point. He shot a second-round 68 for a 137 total and a two-stroke lead over Bland (70) and Tommy Tolles (67), a young American. Johnstone slid back on 71—140. In the third round, a young newcomer stole the show. This was Ernie Els, 20, former South African Amateur champion, who logged an eagle and six birdies in a 65 that carried him into a share of the third-round lead with Johnstone (69) at 209. Tolles was a solo third on 71—210, and Baiocchi slid to fourth on 74—211. It seemed an old story—nice try, no cigar.

But not this time. In the last round, Els and Johnstone faltered, and no one else got anything going. No one but Baiocchi. He had a wild two-under-par 70, with seven birdies and five bogeys, for a 281 total and a one-stroke victory over Els (73), Tertius Claassens (70) and American Rick Hartman (67). Baiocchi had rung out the old year, and the old decade, in fine fashion.

14. The Australasian Tour

A new and highly unlikely hero emerged in the second half of the Australian circuit when Peter Senior produced some marvelous shots to enthuse the galleries and win three events in five weeks, including the Australian Open. Greg Norman couldn't match him, nor could anyone else from either Australia or overseas, and the man whose career has twice suffered setbacks because of serious putting problems, not only won the tournaments but, as well, swept to the top of the Order of Merit.

Quietly spoken, courteous and possessed of bulldog courage and determination, Senior is a wonderful example to young Australian golfers. He goes about his golf in exemplary fashion and was not in the slightest overawed by the massive amount of attention he received following his success. He was particularly pleased to have edged out Norman, for whom he has always had the highest regard. "Greg has done an enormous amount for Australian golf and is a wonderful player. I have always enjoyed playing against him and it's a real thrill to have jumped to the top of the Order of Merit," Senior said.

Norman played well at times, but Senior was too good for everyone, wielding his extra long putter with comfortable skill, instead of using the orthodox type with shaky and twitching fingers. His success came after several years of very solid golf where he more than once gently complained, with some justification, that the media were inclined to concentrate more on 70 from a young star than 68 from him. Although many instantly equated Senior's success with the putter, first brought to notice by Orville Moody and others, it was his play from tee to green which brought the victories. He has long been regarded as one of Australia's finest iron players, and his consistent iron shots, along with straight driving, was certainly the main reason for his wonderful run.

There were other stars in the group of promising players. Lucien Tinkler, recently the recipient of the PGA Encouragement Award, climbed more than 20 places in the Order of Merit and again underlined his potential. Mike Harwood had a splendid finish in Europe and then jumped to seventh in the Australian Order of Merit, while Peter Fowler showed the benefit of playing the European Tour by gaining 11 places to finish in the top three in Australia. The effervescent Brett Ogle lifted himself to fifth with his win in the Queensland Open, the last event on the 1989 circuit. New Zealander Frank Nobilo, along with Peter O'Malley and Craig Parry, all played well during the year.

Parry played mostly overseas, and he rose from 65th to 26th in the Sony Ranking, confirming predictions in Australia that he could be the next outstanding Australian player on the world circuits.

Of the more experienced players, Bob Shearer had a great season. Rodger Davis had a horrible year, not because of his golf, but because of the lack of it after a serious shoulder injury sidelined him. A good finish towards the end of the circuit in the Australian PGA, followed by a win in the Johnnie Walker Classic, showed he is on the way back. Don Bies, a U.S. senior, beat the juniors at their own game in the Air New Zealand-Shell Open, and Greg Turner had a splendid win in the AMP New Zealand Open, a proper reward for a fine player who had been going through a rough time.

David Graham, one of Australia's greatest-ever players, announced his retirement to concentrate on golf course designing, and the question of appearance money flared again towards the end of the season, with Greg Norman and five-time British Open champion Peter Thomson exchanging words through the media on the question of whether appearance money should be paid for the Australian Open. The issue was unresolved, but there is no doubt it will again be very prominent in 1990.

Daikyo Palm Meadows Cup—A$600,000
Winner: Curtis Strange

U.S. Ryder Cup captain Raymond Floyd had a close look at the skills of one of his potential star players over the concluding stages of the Daikyo Palm Meadows Cup, when Curtis Strange defeated him by two strokes with an eight-under-par 280 total. A crucial six-foot putt for par on the 10th hole on the last afternoon allowed Strange to hold off Floyd, but neither was able to tame the course, each shooting final-round 73s. Nor, for that matter, was any other player in the field able to make a charge, 70s by Ossie Moore and Mike Ferguson being the best rounds of the last day.

The suspense of the final afternoon revolved around whether Floyd could catch Strange and whether Terry Price, a young red-haired Queenslander, could hold his short game together after the brilliant golf he had played for rounds of 65 and 70 on the second and third days. Price fell away with 74 and, like most of the other players, was unable to handle the enormous overnight change in the quality of the greens.

Strange said, "It was a real puzzle out there. When we played the third round it was like throwing darts into the greens, but today they were crusty and hard. It was one of the most odd turnabouts I have seen." In fact, the grounds staff, disturbed that the game might be appearing too easy for the professionals, overnight had cut all the greens several times and it certainly made life more difficult. The day before the tournament, Greg Norman had described the greens as, "the slowest I have putted on anywhere in the world in a professional tournament."

None of that deterred Strange, though, as he shot 66 for a one-stroke lead in the opening round against Norman's 75, a score which included several three putts, possibly a legacy from the Australian's pre-tournament worries about the greens. There was no shortage of incident around the clubhouse on the opening day with Australian PGA Executive Director, Don Johnson, making a dramatic exodus from the job claiming, "I can't be a puppet any longer!" On the course harsh words were exchanged between Mike Colandro and Brett Ogle, his marker. Colandro hit his tee shot into the water hazard at the 18th and argued that he should have a drop a considerable distance down the fairway.

Strange had a 70 and led by two shots on the second day over U.S. player Jeff Maggert, then still by two after a 71 on the third day, over Floyd and Price but, after a splendid second-day 68, Norman again slipped in the third round with 73, which began with him hitting his tee shot into a bamboo thicket for double bogey and then three-putting the second hole. With only four players breaking par on the final day, Strange's task was merely to repel the challengers, which he achieved in his usual solid fashion.

Coca-Cola Golf Classic—A$600,000
Winner: Isao Aoki

Isao Aoki may not have played the 18th hole at Royal Melbourne as Dr. Alister Mackenzie designed it, but his brilliant victory showed fierce determination and great skill derived from his many years at the top level of golf. This wonderful composite course has seen many brilliant finishes over the years, but few better than when Aoki, while the play was beamed to millions of television watchers in Japan, stood on the last tee, needing a par-four to win.

His tee shot did nothing to ease the minds of his fans, as it flew away to the right and bounced off a car in the parking area behind the hospitality tents. He was given a free drop away from the cars and from the television cherry-picker. He was then faced with one of the hardest shots in golf to make par, from the right-hand side of the 18th, over a giant bunker with grass at its center, and onto a green with a pin placement close to the bunker.

Aoki struck the ball perfectly, but could do nothing to stop it going to the back of the green, leaving him far enough from the hole that the four other players waiting to see if it would be a five-way playoff began their stretching and swinging exercises. Aoki has not become known as one of the best putters in the world for nothing. He coaxed the ball down and across the treacherous slope to dash the hopes of those already in the clubhouse with scores of 280.

When asked about it at the prize-giving, Aoki laughed and said, "I was confident about winning here and even had my speech made out on Saturday night. And I couldn't afford to three putt, otherwise I would have missed my flight to Hawaii." One of those potentially in the playoff, Rodger Davis, said later, "He is the most marvelous putter, just wait until he gets onto the American Senior Tour!"

Although Aoki shot 69 in the opening round, such was the quality of the play in benign conditions that he was five shots behind the leader, Peter O'Malley. Worse was to come in the second round because O'Malley, with 70, remained four shots ahead of the field and Aoki, with 73, was now eight shots behind.

The turnaround came in the third round, with O'Malley shooting 77 and Aoki hitting the front with a blistering 66, with players like Davis, Peter Fowler and Grant Waite also making their charges. Once Aoki started the back nine holes in the lead, he was going to be difficult to catch, even though Fowler continued his good play on the final day with 68 and O'Malley fought back from his disappointing third round with 69. Aoki, though, stole the show with his intense determination and last-hole triumph, once again claiming victory outside his own country.

Asthma Foundation Victorian PGA—A$100,000

Winner: David Ecob

There was nothing mundane about the Victorian PGA. It gave David Ecob his first victory since turning professional, after Peter Senior missed a three-foot playoff putt on the 18th to allow Ecob to pick up the $18,000 check.

Drama abounded in the event, with four players being penalized. First Phillip Glass, on his way to an opening-round 68 and a share of the lead, was disqualified when he holed a chip shot but the ball stuck between the flagstick and the edge of the hole. Glass allowed his caddy to go forward and grab the ball, rather than remove the stick and allow the ball to fall into the hole.

Glass, who was responsible for the infringement by not knowing the rules, then was handed an invitation to the following week's Victorian Open and was flooded with offers of financial assistance while Tod Power, the man who correctly protected the field by calling the penalty, was made to look like the bad guy.

Then Canadian Kelly Murray signed an incorrect card and was disqualified, but his troubles didn't stop there. The incorrect signing came about because he took an unauthorized drop from thick black scrub without bothering to refer the matter to his marker, Jack Larkin, and he then didn't include the penalty on his card. Murray's explanation was that he was in a hurry. Other players on an adjoining fairway questioned the score when they saw he had listed par for the hole. Murray's invitation to play the Australian circuit was withdrawn.

Wayne Case was disqualified on the opening day when he forgot to sign his card, and Peter Krauss went the same way after signing incorrectly for an 84 in the second round.

Through all this Ecob played very steady golf, never quite able to force his way onto the leaderboard on the first three days with rounds of 72, 69, 71, but then in the last round he blasted the field with a brilliant 67 for a 279 total and a one-stroke margin over Senior. He relished the hot conditions in gusting winds and he and Craig Parry, also with 67, were the only players in the field to break 70. The win provided Ecob with the incentive to try again for his European players' card.

Victorian Open—A$100,000

Winner: Mike Clayton

A golfer holing in one but missing the $50,000 prize because he was an amateur, a green resembling a patch of sand dune, and a professional who had not picked up a winner's check for five years all provided an unusual week in the Victorian Open at the famous Kingston Heath Golf Club.

Back in 1984, Mike Clayton won the Tasmanian Open, Korean Open, and then the Timex Open in France, but since then has only seen the winner's platform from a distance. In the normal course of events, last rounds of 75, 74 would be unlikely to help him improve that record, but conditions were so difficult on the last two days that his challengers found even more trouble than Clayton.

Lucien Tinkler, having led into the fourth day, crashed with 81, David Merriman had 82 and John Clifford 83, and the strong winds accounted for almost all the rest of the field, other than Ossie Moore, whose last-round 69 put some pressure on Clayton over the final nine holes. But Clayton's 285 total, including his 69-67 start, provided a two-stroke margin over Moore.

"When you haven't won for five years, some very strange things start going through your head when suddenly you get in contention," Clayton said later. "I decided the best thing to do was just keep the ball on the fairway. It may not have looked all that pretty, but it worked. Being raised in Melbourne, I'm used to these conditions, but it certainly is much more pleasant playing on a nice day than what we had to go through today."

Kingston Heath is one of Australia's greatest courses and was in near immaculate condition, but course superintendent Graeme Grant had some problems after trying to rid the third green of poa grass four weeks before the event. The treatment didn't quite work and the putting surface, after being top-dressed, was almost all sand with only a sparse grass covering.

Victorian amateur Stephen McCraw, on the way to a splendid opening-round 71, aced the par-three 15th on the first day, something of a waste from the financial point of view, as a prize of $50,000 was on offer, but was of course restricted to professionals. He then shot 69 and followed this with creditable rounds of 78, 75 to finish as the leading amateur, eight strokes behind.

Australian Match Play Championship—A$150,000
Winner: Ossie Moore

Ossie Moore took quick revenge for being runner-up to Mike Clayton in the Victorian Open by winning the Australian Match Play Championship at Kingston Heath a week later. On the way to collecting his $32,000 check he defeated Clayton 3 and 2 in the quarter-final, beat John Clifford by the same margin in the semi-final and played some brilliant golf to defeat former champion Peter Fowler 1-up in the final.

Moore, with magnificent approach shots and deadly putting, posted 66 for the first 18 holes of the 36-hole last day and, despite having played some great golf in shooting 69, Fowler went to lunch three down. He came out firing after the break with four birdies and a three-under-par 33 to be even after nine holes, and the match then fluctuated until Fowler bogeyed the 35th to allow Moore to go 1-up.

After both parred the last hole to give Moore his victory, Fowler had the added disappointment of being fined $750 by the PGA because his caddy did not wear the regulation uniform. His troubles didn't end there. The PGA also considered suspending him, a penalty which would have removed him from the field for the Australian Masters the following week; fortunately for Fowler, only the fine was imposed.

During the same week as the Match Play, a Skins Game was staged at Port Douglas in the north of Queensland with the participants Greg Norman, Jack Nicklaus, Curtis Strange and Isao Aoki. Sponsored and televised by Christopher Skase's Channel 7 Network and Mirage Resorts, it provided some excellent and exciting golf, with Nicklaus winning almost US$300,000.

Australian Masters—A$450,000
Winner: Greg Norman

Greg Norman staged a magnificent comeback to win the Australian Masters for the fifth time and, in so doing, destroyed the fairy-tale hopes of the English amateur Russell Claydon. Claydon finished second, a marvelous performance from someone who had never before played golf in front of galleries the size seen at Huntingdale over the four days.

The long 14th hole started the Norman victory at a time when many players were locked on the leaderboard, seemingly at the mercy of the cold southerly wind which had battered them throughout the day. The 14th is over 600 yards long, and Norman hit the most fantastic one-iron shot as his approach. The ball finished just 35 feet short of the pin. He two-putted for birdie and then, on the 15th, a tough par-three, he hit his tee shot into an awkward lie in the right-hand bunker. Admonishing himself to be positive, he stepped up to the ball and blasted it into the hole.

There were 42,000 spectators present on the last day and the roars resounded around the course, as the leaderboards flashed the news that Norman had now jumped out of the pack. He then birdied the next two holes, parred the last and finished the back nine in 31 strokes to the clear disbelief of the other competitors, who struggled to stay within range.

Claydon, who plays his golf at Gog Magog near Cambridge in England, bogeyed two holes at the same time. The burly Englishman had previously confessed to the fairy-tale dream of being the amateur to beat Norman and the rest of the field. Instead, Claydon's 285 total left him five strokes behind Norman, whose 280 included rounds of 69, 69, 74 and a closing 68.

As Claydon could not accept prize money, which would have been $48,000, his caddy received only $100, but had one of the most exciting four days of his life, toting a bag for a player who not only distinguished himself by his play, but also his demeanor.

Hard luck stories abounded. Bob Shearer looked to be a winner until the 14th, and then his touch disappeared and he dropped three shots in the last four holes. The previous evening he had the chance to take a three-stroke lead through to the final round, but drove into the trees on the last hole and had to be content with a one-stroke lead over Japan's Tsuyoshi Yoneyama.

The latter disappeared with a last-round 78 after fighting on the third day through the hot northerly winds for 70. He wasn't the only casualty. Peter Fowler, who led on the first and second days with 67, 68, had 80 on the third day, then finished with 73 for sixth place.

Claydon, with opening rounds of 66, 69, captivated the galleries and led the field by a shot on a golf course that rarely does the players any favors. The greens are large, but perfectly prepared, and the fairways are lined with tall gum trees hundreds of years old. Many players hardly look at their driver during the week, let alone use it, but the length of the course, almost 7,000 yards, requires distance from many of the tees, as well as pinpoint accuracy into the greens.

Norman said after his win, "It is a course which encourages the creative player and it can be rewarding. Every time you step onto the tee at Huntingdale you know you have to work the ball either to the left or right and, if you don't keep it in play, you simply don't get it on the greens."

For Norman, it was a welcome return to good form. He had listened before the tournament to Jack Nicklaus and to his own coach, Charlie Earp, and they seemed to have ironed out the abbreviated swing which had crept into his game since his wrist injury the previous June in America.

Tournament Players Championship—A$500,000
Winner: Greg Norman

Greg Norman's astonishing 275-yard one-iron shot at Huntingdale on the last day spread-eagled his opposition and here, at Riverside Oaks in the Tournament Players Championship, he did it again, this time with driver. At Huntingdale, he two-putted for birdie; here, at the par-four 12th hole, 310 yards, he hit the ball a yard from the hole and tapped in for an eagle, and that was the finish of the challengers. His closing 67 and 276 total produced a two-stroke victory over Roger Mackay.

Norman was in no doubt about the quality of the shot, nor were those at the hole or watching on television. First of all, he had to negotiate a carry of 267 yards to clear the water and then the pin was another 43 yards. "As soon as I hit it, I bent down to pick up the tee; it was like hitting a good putt where you know from the moment it leaves the club it is in the hole unless bad luck intervenes. It was my best tee shot for a couple of years. It might even be the straightest tee shot I have ever hit in my life; it never wavered and went straight for the pin."

Up to that moment not everything had been going well for the Shark. Several times he had let frustration show through, notably where a spike mark had not been repaired on the eighth hole, leaving a quarter-inch hump just in front of his ball as he stepped up to the putt. Then the layout of the 17th once again angered him. He has been vocal about the fact that although it is a par-five, it is impossible to see where to hit the ball and, although changes are to be made, Norman contends they may make the hole even more frustrating.

It wasn't until the back nine that Norman began to place his stamp on the tournament. Opening rounds of 70, 70, left him fuming that he had not been able to convert chances with his putter and even a third-round 69 pushed him only into third place behind Jeff Woodland and David De Long and left him equally annoyed. "I should have shot 63 or 64 out there today," he said. "The pin positions were easy, the fairways are good and the conditions just about perfect, but it was difficult to lift oneself with such small crowds in contrast to the wonderful audiences we had last week in Melbourne."

Norman's problems, though, were minor compared with those encountered by 20-year-old Victorian rookie Robert Edmond, who, after starting on the 10th tee on the second day turned in a dashing par 36, which included three birdies. He then took 19 strokes on the next hole, normally the first on the course. He managed that by hooking his drive into the water, took a penalty drop and then produced a saga of mis-hits into the water and incurred more penalties which, while totally bemused, included two for marking his ball when it wasn't on the green. Finally, he three-putted, which was just about the best thing to happen to him on the hole.

Monro Interiors Nedlands Masters—A$100,000
Winner: Louis Brown

A 25-year-old American golfer, Louis Brown of Newnan, Georgia, played four rounds of controlled golf to take the Nedlands Masters by one stroke over Ken Trimble, Wayne Smith and Garry Merrick.

Scores were low in the perfect conditions over the four days, and Brown's winning total was 274, 14 under par, with scores of 70, 68, 68, 68.

Brown's first professional victory was set up with a 14-foot putt on the 18th hole. "I had to putt up over a tier and I just tried to get it somewhere close to the hole for par," he said. "Instead it went in for birdie which was a massive bonus and I was able to sit in the clubhouse and watch the others try to catch me."

When Brown sank that putt, Garry Merrick was on the 16th hole, also 14 under par, and he maintained the score until reaching the 18th tee. Then he hooked his drive into the trees, hit more trees in attempting too ambitious a recovery and his third shot finished off the green, leaving him needing a chip-in for a tie with Brown.

This was a fine performance by Brown, who was in Australia for experience and along the way collected an $18,000 check. There were some very good players in the field, notably Terry Gale, seeking his ninth Masters' title, Craig Parry and Roger Mackay.

Town & Country Joondalup PGA Classic—A$100,000
Winner: Brad King

One of Australia's most promising young golfers is Brad King, a 23-year-old from Perth, and he absolutely blitzed this field at the picturesque Joondalup Country Club. King is a former Australian Amateur champion, a splendid shotmaker and skillful short-game player who has been frustrated by his inability to break through in the professional ranks, even though he has been playing only a short time.

On the way to his victory, King broke the course record by shooting 65 and then broke his own record by one stroke the following day in the third round. After his second-round 65 he said, "I went home and thought that I had never hit the ball better, but I did strike it even better in the third round. I had nine birdies and one bogey, and although in the past few weeks I haven't been getting the putts in the hole, today my stroke felt good and they just kept dropping."

When King came to the final day he confessed to being very nervous at the start of the round, but spectators would never have guessed as he reeled off seven pars, then a string of four birdies from the eighth hole onwards. He then parred every hole on the way home and gave no one else a chance, finishing with a rock-solid 68 for his 271 total and a nine-stroke win.

Joondalup is a very difficult golf course and the 280 totals of the second-place finishers, Ken Trimble and Peter Senior, would normally be regarded as excellent scores. Seventeen under par was enough to have locals marvelling at King's consistency on a layout that penalizes to the ultimate the wayward stroke.

Tattersall Tasmanian Open—A$100,000
Winner: Ian Stanley

Stories abound of players having their swing or putting stroke improved by fellow competitors on the practice tee, and this type of benevolence almost cost Ian Stanley the first Tasmanian Open title. Stanley had been runner-up in four previous tournaments in Tasmania, and the recipient of his excellent putting advice here was Peter O'Malley, a rising young star whom he finally defeated at the first hole of a playoff.

Both finished with 279s after sub-par last rounds, O'Malley challenging all the way and firing a 67 in perfect conditions to leave Stanley with a two-foot putt for a 69 to force the playoff. They were paired on the final day, with Stanley two strokes behind the leader, Stephen Taylor of Queensland, and one shot behind American Roy Hunter, who was combining the golf tour with his honeymoon. O'Malley surged past Taylor and Hunter, and held a two-stroke lead over Stanley when they reached the 17th hole. O'Malley pulled his drive into the trees and could only play a little punch shot back on to the fairway. He hit the green with his third, but two-putted for a bogey and had to watch as Stanley played a nine iron to six feet and sank the putt for a two-stroke swing.

There was more trouble in the trees for O'Malley on the 18th, where Stanley forced the playoff, and then O'Malley was faced with playing the 17th again as the first extra hole. Stanley birdied, O'Malley bogeyed and had to be content with second place, having jumped ahead of 10 players in the final round. The putting lesson Stanley gave him might have been worthwhile because, after rounds of 72 and 73, where he couldn't make a putt of any consequence, he played the last two days in 67 and 67.

Zoran Zorkic and Jeff Woodland shared third place, with Jeff Wagner another shot behind in fifth place. Zorkic, a Queenslander, is an interesting rookie, 23 years old, a graduate of the University of Houston and rated highly by those who have watched him. The week prior to the Tasmanian Open he won the Queensland PGA Championship which, although not on the Order of Merit list because of low prize money, boasted a strong field.

Air New Zealand-Shell Open—NZ$200,000
Winner: Don Bies

Don Bies struck a wonderful blow for the seniors when he raced away from a strong field in the Air New Zealand-Shell Open, winning by four strokes and, at the same time, boosting the confidence of those who have troubles on the putting green. The pendulum putter may not be the prettiest sight, even in the hands of expert users, but there is no doubt it has rejuvenated the careers of those who have come under the influence of the dreaded yips; two notable beneficiaries are Sam Torrance in Europe and Peter Senior in Australia.

Bies has won twice using it on the U.S. Senior PGA Tour, and the club was deadly on the final day at Titirangi, where he shot a five-under-par 65 and blew away the chances of the youngsters. His wedge shot on the 16th did him no harm either. He hit a good drive into perfect position down the left-hand side of the fairway and his 110-yard pitch with the wedge bounced past the cup and then spun back into the hole. This came at a time when he was fighting for the lead with Stewart Ginn, but Ginn bogeyed the hole and suddenly there was a three-shot swing. It was all Bies needed, and he played error-free golf on Nos. 17 and 18 for a five-under-par 65 and 275 total and a four-shot triumph over Brad Andrews and Glenn Joyner. Ginn, Kevin Burton and Tony Maloney tied for fourth place at 280.

Not least of the congratulations for Bies came from fellow senior Bob Charles, who had persuaded Bies and the tournament organizers that it would be a good idea for him to play, along with other veterans Miller Barber, Billy Casper and Peter Thomson. There were some early mutterings from the younger golfers about the seniors taking places in "their" tournament, but none of this was heard afterwards.

The Alister Mackenzie-designed Titirangi course is only a par-70 layout but, like all of Dr. Mackenzie's great creations, puts a premium on positioning of the ball off the tee and accuracy of the short game. As the pressure mounts, there is also a real test of temperament. Bies showed no sign of nerves, nor did Andrews, the young Sydney professional who shot 64 to jump past 31 players on the final day and into a tie for second place. With him was another young player, Joyner, whose last-round 68 gave him the biggest check of his short career.

There were two hard luck stories, the first from Ginn, who held the lead from the sixth to the 14th holes and then suffered that three-stroke swing on No. 16, and the second to do with John Clifford. Clifford, at the par-three 14th hole, with a Toyota car on offer for a hole-in-one, saw his tee shot spin back down the hill towards the hole. It rolled slowly to the edge of the cup when the very stiff breeze suddenly bent the flagstick and knocked it out.

AMP New Zealand Open—NZ$150,000
Winner: Greg Turner

Greg Turner could be excused for breathing not one, but many sighs of relief when victory came in the AMP New Zealand Open at Paraparaumu. Before the celebrations began, Turner said, "I've been right to the bottom of the ladder in recent times and I just hope this will be the start of the way back." Things had been so bad that when Turner was asked how long it was since he had been within two shots of the lead before the last round of a tournament, he replied, "You know, I honestly cannot answer that. It's been so long since I was in any kind of contention I simply can't recall the last day I was able to challenge in this manner."

Turner teed off in the next-to-last group, having spent the early hours of the morning watching the direct telecast of the New Zealand-Wales Rugby International at Cardiff Arms Park. Rugby Union is the national game of New Zealand and Turner after his victory confessed to being thoroughly inspired by the All Blacks' performance.

That may have been the inspiration, but Turner also was quick to pay tribute to his coach, Dennis Pugh, who is a partner of David Leadbetter, the coach who has been working with Nick Faldo and others in recent years. "I went to him in desperation after the British Masters and asked him to throw the book at me. I've had two hard and miserable years and I hope now this win is a portent of things to come."

With Frank Nobilo two shots ahead of Turner at the start of the day, there was no real hint of what was to come when both players made pars at the opening two holes. Then Turner birdied the third and fourth while Nobilo triple-bogeyed the fifth, and the galleries thronging the course carried Turner through on a wave of emotion. More birdies came at the seventh, ninth and 12th, then Nos. 14 and 18 fell to him as well. He shot five-under-par 66 for a 277 total. It was a superb exhibition of golf, marked by spectacular putting and magnificent approach work to the greens. Nobilo's 78 saw him slump from the lead to a tie for 13th. Only 10 players broke par on the final day despite the good conditions. Richard Gilkey finished in second place, six shots behind Turner, and Graeme Trew and Jim Benepe tied for third, a further stroke away.

Australian PGA Championship—A$500,000
Winner: Peter Senior

There was a comedy of errors in the Australian PGA, where Peter Senior won his first significant Australian title. There was no playoff because Jim Benepe three-putted the last green, but either of them could have won the event outright with ease. Bogeys and birdies dominated their scorecards and, although Senior shot one-under-par 71 and Benepe 72, the spectators, the millions of television viewers and the players themselves were bemused by the errors under pressure.

Senior is a wonderful competitor, one of the most under-rated golfers in Australia, and it was a good, tight tussle up to the time he walked on to the 12th tee, but then his drive slid off the fairway and into a small ornamental garden covered with bark, from which there was no relief. To hit the ball he had to stand on a rock which wobbled alarmingly when he perched himself on it.

With Benepe on the green after a great second shot, Senior decided against taking a penalty drop, but managed only to splash the ball into the water 30 feet short of the green. Benepe sank his putt for birdie, Senior double-bogeyed, and the three-stroke swing took the American to a two-shot lead in the tournament and what seemed to be a winning margin.

Then on the next hole, the 13th, Benepe took the wrong club and over-shot the green by a long way for bogey, a mistake that seemed to matter little because at the same time Senior, having found one fairway bunker, hit into another with a very ordinary stroke. He too bogeyed. Then Senior brought cheers from the galleries with birdies on the 14th and 16th holes to draw even with Benepe and saved par on the 17th after hitting his approach to the fringe of the green. When Senior parred the last hole, Benepe was left with two putts to force the playoff, but couldn't manage it, and the Australian was moved to say, "I felt for Jim. It's no way to win a golf tournament, but that's the way the game goes sometimes."

The Riverside Oaks course is the home of the Australian PGA. It has new owners these days, the Japanese company GGS, who not only have taken over the magnificent complex but also the sponsorship of this event. It was an excellent tournament, although the PGA came under criticism on the opening day for the placement of the pins. Rodger Davis asked for a meeting after his opening 69 and explained with annoyance that the placing of the pins in many cases bore no relation to their positioning on the chart the players had been given. He described that as "an absolute disgrace."

Davis, recovering from a shoulder injury, took a share of fourth place with Peter Fowler at 10 under par. Another young Australian, Mike Harwood, finished third at 11 under.

Ford New South Wales Open—A$300,000
Winner: Rodger Davis

After finishing fourth in the Australian PGA, Rodger Davis said that not only did he feel he had recovered from his shoulder injury, but that he was also ready to win. Then, in difficult conditions, he raced away from the strong field in the Ford New South Wales Open, shooting 15-under-par 277 and winning by nine shots and confirming his place in Australian golf as one of the most outstanding players in windy weather. While others were unable to handle the Lakes course and the strong southerlies, Davis relished the problems they created.

Even on the last day, when Davis was in no danger and could have been forgiven for relaxing, his three-under-par 70 was a magnificent performance and, of the 65 players, only Peter McWhinney, with 69, was able to shoot better. An indication that Davis was back on track was that his 277 total equalled Ian Baker-Finch's course record, and he was the only player in the field not to have a bogey on the final day. The stiff 30 mile-per-hour wind, which because of the layout was mostly a crosswind, blew everyone else off course. Davis was of the opinion after the round that, in such conditions, he had never played better, nor hit the ball more solidly.

The irony of the opening day was that Davis couldn't even make it on to the leaderboard although he fired 71. Americans Jeff Maggert and David De Long, and Killara professional Greg Hohnen shared the lead with 67s. Maggert had entered the tournament by claiming the last spot in a seven-hole shootout at the neighboring Eastlakes course in the pre-qualifying. He was realistic enough to know that 67 posted in the benign conditions, prior to the storms and heavy rain, could change instantly if the wind blew. "It's a pretty tough course, and if the wind gets up it will sort everyone out," he said.

In fact, Maggert played brilliantly on the second day, this time in rain, for his 69, but ominously was joined in the lead by Davis who shot 65 in a bogey-free round. In the final two rounds Davis showed his mastery of the strong winds, with the other competitors unable to cope with the conditions which had balls moving on the greens and putts affected after the ball was struck. None of this worried Davis, who steadily drew away from the field.

West End South Australian Open—A$150,000
Winner: Nick Price

Four years is a long time between tournament victories for a top-class golfer like Nick Price, but he broke the drought in the West End South Australian Open with a 15-under-par score of 277. Price won the Lancome Trophy in France in 1985 and earlier, in 1983, had been successful in the World Series of Golf, but there had been some agonizing near-misses in between. He was runner-up to Seve Ballesteros in the 1988 British Open.

On the Alister Mackenzie-designed Royal Adelaide course, Price added 71 to his first-round 70, then blitzed the field with six-under-par 67 to take a two-stroke lead over Paul Foley and four over one of Australia's most promising young players, Lucien Tinkler. Tinkler and Foley held their places on the last day with 70 and 72 respectively, and Price's 69 allowed him to ease further and further ahead. He had two lapses in concentration with a double-bogey on the 10th, which he put down to "sheer stupidity," and a bogey on the 12th, but on the way home he settled in to play some delightful golf.

Price provided a high-class finish to the round with birdies on the last two holes, the long par-five 17th and the difficult 18th where he sank a 60-foot putt. It was the 18th where, on the second day of the tournament, Brad Hughes was faced with a 20-foot putt, also for birdie, which would have taken him to the outright lead, and he five-putted.

Price is another of the ever-increasing number of golfers who have put their golf swings in the hands of Florida-based coach David Leadbetter. Nick Faldo is perhaps the best known, but Price said in Adelaide, "This win has told me that all the work I have put in with David on my swing has been worthwhile. It has given my confidence a tremendous boost, and I have now won on four continents, Australia, Africa, America and Europe."

The most surprised golfer of the week was Burma's Kyi Hla Han, who took out a three wood on the tee of the 227-yard 12th and, after playing the shot towards the green, bent down, picked up his tee and turned away. He didn't see the ball bounce into the hole and earn him a $20,000 car.

Australian Open Championship—A$500,000
Winner: Peter Senior

Australians filled the three top places in the Australian Open at Kingston Heath, providing the greatest golfing day in many years for home-grown players. Against one of the strongest fields ever assembled for the event, Peter Senior won by an astonishing seven shots over Peter Fowler, who won the tournament on the same course in 1983; Brett Ogle, with a final-round 69, was in third place. British Open champion Mark Calcavecchia was fourth, and Nick Faldo, the 1989 Masters champion, sixth, but on that last day neither managed to pose the slightest problem for Senior.

Senior became only the sixth man to win both the Australian Open and PGA in the same year, following Dan Soutar, Ossie Pickworth, Norman von Nida, Kel Nagle and Greg Norman. Having the 18 leading players finish under par for the Open was a record, and Senior's 271, 17 under par, was also a course record for Kingston Heath. It put the finishing touch to a remarkable comeback. Already it has been chronicled how his putting was so poor at one stage of his career that he thought of giving up the game. Then came the elongated putter and Senior was a born-again golfer.

There was no doubt Senior putted well in this event, but putting alone could not finish the job. He hit the ball from tee to green, and time after time he selected the right club on holes where the wind played a significant role. This was a crucial factor at Kingston Heath, where the eucalyptus and ti-trees will provide some form of wind buffer, then suddenly a gap in the trees in front of a green will form a tunnel where the ball will drop very quickly.

Fowler also showed excellent judgement and worked his way through the field on the final day to the point where he was the main challenger. "I managed to get myself into the position where if Peter made a mistake I was in with a chance, but he simply didn't make an error," Fowler said.

After the first hole on the last day, it was doubtful anyone would catch Senior, unless he managed to find some way to pose problems for himself. On the opening par-four hole, Calcavecchia double-bogeyed and Senior slotted an eight-foot putt for birdie and a three-stroke swing which suddenly lifted his lead from four shots to seven.

By modern-day standards, Kingston Heath, at 6,814 yards, might appear on the short side, but positioning the ball is all-important, particularly when allied to some of the pin placements. Greg Norman hasn't often played well on the course and finished two over par for the event, including a last-round 77. He shot 72 on the opening day when others like Curtis Strange, 65, and Peter Senior, 66, were already setting up their places.

Strange began the second day with four successive bogeys, then fought back with four consecutive birdies, had two more bogeys and then three birdies. He said later, "I simply don't know how to describe the round. I need to go away and dissect it and think about what happened. It's the first time I've ever had a round like that, and I never felt comfortable at any time. But I kept fighting and that's the important thing."

By that time Senior had added a second 66 and was in a wonderfully buoyant mood. "I don't want to sound over-confident, but I've just played 36 holes on a difficult course and haven't had a bogey. The secret of the two rounds was that I drove well and then hit most of my approach shots close to the flagstick and, in the circumstances, these have been the best two rounds of my life. The ultimate goal is to play 72 holes without a bogey, and you never know."

Nick Faldo seemed to be a real threat at that stage, just three strokes behind Senior but not completely happy with his swing. He said at the end of his second-round 67 that he was still experimenting and trying to get lateral rotation. None of that seemed to happen in his third-round 74, and Senior really spaced out the field with 69 in difficult conditions. He had his first bogey of the event on the 16th hole on the third day, but finished with a four-stroke lead over Calcavecchia.

Johnnie Walker Classic—A$1,000,000
Winner: Peter Senior

Peter Senior, on his way to three victories in five tournaments at the end of the Australian circuit, turned in another magnificent performance in winning the Johnnie Walker Classic by five shots over Greg Norman and giving no one more than a whisper of hope on the final day. Norman, as so often happens, shot the best round of the last day, but his 67 was never going to be good enough, providing Senior kept his head. Senior did that, the only real problem coming on the 11th hole where, in a moment of caution, he took an iron off the tee and pulled the ball into a fairway bunker. In the end he had to settle for bogey but, such was his play from then on, that on the 18th green he could afford the luxury of three putts and still win by five strokes. Once more Senior putted well with the implement which, by now, was being called anything from a broomstick to a shortened fishing rod, but it was his superb iron play which set him up for par saves as well as birdies.

The astonishing thing about this victory for Senior was that once again he led all the way. His opening round was played against a backdrop of mutterings from the professionals that the pin placements were too difficult. Senior subscribed to that theory and stuck to it even when his answer to the question, "What did you shoot?" was, "Oh, I had a seven-under-par 65. I started today where I left off at Kingston Heath last week, holing a couple of quite decent putts, but generally hitting the ball straight off the tee and my iron play set up some good chances. Believe me, though, the pin positions today were the most difficult I have ever encountered in any tournament at Royal Melbourne."

The field was without Mark Calcavecchia, who flew back to America because of an illness in his family, and only seven players in the field broke 70 on the opening day. It was significant that most of them remained on the leaderboard at the tournament's conclusion, but Senior's fast start kept his opponents fully stretched throughout the four days. His double bogey at the fifth hole on the second day was his first in four weeks.

Senior was three strokes ahead on the first day but only one on the second, with Mike Clayton having carded two 69s. Chris Moody of Britain and New Zealander Frank Nobilo were another stroke behind at 139, but it was Senior who grabbed the headlines again because he had only 72.

He increased his lead to three shots with his third-round 70, but Rodger Davis suddenly appeared as his main threat with a solid 68. Greg Norman continued to be at odds with his putter on the lightning fast Royal Melbourne greens, so much so that his coach, Charlie Earp, watching on television in Brisbane, called him in the evening to point out how he was crowding the ball in addressing his putts. Norman added 70 to his earlier rounds of 73, 71, but still didn't have the putter working with the magic touch needed to pose problems for Senior. Norman at that stage was seven shots behind Senior and needed one of his famous last-round rushes if he were to have any chance at all. Even then, Norman needed 65, providing Senior restricted himself again to 72, and that would have meant a playoff, rather than an outright victory.

In the end, 67 against 69 was not good enough to produce the upset, and Senior's only problem was in trying to ensure he didn't three-putt the last green, as he said, "So I wouldn't feel like a dill in front of all these people. In fact, I missed it and did indeed feel like a dill!"

The win capped a marvelous return to Australia for Senior, who had done well in Europe but not won. Norman commented that he had never seen Senior play better golf, and Norman had no doubt Senior was now ready to try the U.S. tour as well as the European, Australian and Japanese circuits. Senior was more circumspect. "I know how to win now and I want to win more consistently. The sequence of victories has given me confidence to play the quality of golf necessary to win major tournaments."

Mirage Queensland Open—A$300,000
Winner: Brett Ogle

Brett Ogle, one of Australia's finest young golfers, led from start to finish in the Queensland Open played at Royal Queensland, one of the most difficult courses in the country. Ogle's 14-under-par 278 was a stunning performance which lifted him to fifth place in the Australian Order of Merit and denied Peter Senior his fourth major victory in six weeks.

It was the old story of "beware the injured golfer," for Ogle was lucky even to make it to the first tee on opening day, because of a back injury he sustained in the pro-am before the tournament. He advised officials that he might have to pull out, but his hotel's resident masseuse performed magic on his back that night, to the extent that he decided an all-out attack was the way to conquer the course. The main problems were in the positioning of the bunkers, between 260 and 280 yards from the tee, and the fact that the fairways had been narrowed to such an extent the players complained they had to walk in single file.

Ogle's plan worked perfectly the first two days, when he ripped his drives past every bunker on the par fours and fives, leaving only wedges or sand wedges to the greens, while his opponents sometimes used seven or eight irons. John Clifford stayed with him in those opening rounds, shooting 68 and 69, against Ogle's 66 and 68, but some notable players missed the cut.

The third round was an entirely different matter with Ogle nervously, and occasionally irritably, losing the lead to Clifford and then grabbing it back, finishing with a 71 against Clifford's 70 to retain a two-stroke advantage, while Senior, with 69, had a chance despite being seven shots off the pace. Senior started the round with birdie-eagle, but bogeys at the seventh and ninth holes set him back.

Nerves were always likely to be the main problem for Ogle on the final day, but he was lucky he was paired with Senior, who is a calm and happy character. Ogle's game was solid enough, although lacking the brilliance which brought him 16 birdies on the two opening days. He settled down to a steady even-par round, and over the last 36 holes he carded only four birdies and an eagle. The vital swing came at the 152-yard 14th, where Ogle hit an eight iron to six feet and holed the putt, while Clifford bogeyed.

The two-stroke swing put him three shots in front of Clifford, and he held that lead to the end. This was only Ogle's second tournament victory but, at 25 and already with good performances in Europe to his credit, he seems to have a splendid future.

15. The Asia/Japan Tour

If one didn't know better, he would have thought he was looking at instant replay on a golf telecast when he was sizing up the 1989 Japan Tour at season's end. Here were the Brothers Ozaki again in the top strata of the money standings in exactly the same positions in which they had finished the 1988 season and, in Japanese currency, with just about the same huge amounts of money. Masashi (Jumbo) Ozaki, 43, again the runaway No. 1 man on the circuit money list . . . Naomichi (Joe) Ozaki, 33, again the No. 2 player in Japanese winnings . . . Tteo (Jet) Ozaki, 35, who repeated in the No. 7 spot even though bothered for a time with a leg injury.

In terms of victories, Jumbo improved on his 1988 performance by one with seven wins, including a rare sweep of the Japan Open, the Japan PGA Championship and the Japan Match Play Championship, and moved well in front as the all-time tournament titleholder with the 64 he has accumulated since turning from baseball to golf in 1971. Jet picked up a pair of wins, including a playoff victory over brother Joe in the Jun Classic, one of six tournaments in which Ozaki the Youngest had runner-up finishes to go with his lone early-season victory in the Setonaikai Open. (He also won two pre-season unofficial events.) That mass of high finishes, including back-to-back second places in the plush Pacific Masters and Dunlop Phoenix, brought Naomichi his repeat second-place spot on the money list. The comparison of earnings in U.S. terms between the two seasons must be weighed against the dollar/yen evaluations, since we used 140 yen to the dollar as the average for 1989 but just 125 yen to the dollar in 1988. While his official total atop the Japan Tour money list was ¥108,715,733 compared to ¥125,162,500 in 1988, the U.S. equivalent was $776,541 compared to $1,001,300 in 1988. Joe's official winnings in 1989 were $569,220, while Jet banked $357,467 . . . in summary, over $4 million in two years for the three men.

The resemblance to 1988 pretty much ended with the Ozakis, though. Masahiro Kuramoto, a 25-tournament winner who had added five of them in 1988, went without a victory and dropped to 27th on the money list. On the other hand, the veteran superstar Isao Aoki returned to form, though playing only half the year in Japan. Shut out in 1988, Aoki came back with victories in the Tokai Classic and Casio World Open, the first win by a Japanese pro in the nine-year history of the latter tournament. That gave him 55 titles in Japan to go with his international wins in the United States, Britain and Australia. At age 47, he will have a tough time, though, over-taking Ozaki in the total-wins department. Tsuneyuki (Tommy) Nakajima continued to be frustrated at home and abroad. He didn't fare well overseas in the early months, then frittered away chances to win several times later in the year in Japan, most notably in the Japan Series, in which he blew a four-shot lead in the final round. Back in June, he finished second three times in four weeks.

Only three other players—the promising Akiyoshi (Aki) Omachi, Koichi Suzuki and Yoshikazu Yokoshima—were multiple winners, each with two. Omachi, who obviously profited from two seasons on the U.S. PGA Tour, was the most impressive with his come-from-behind victories in the Mizuno

Open and Japan Series, which is considered the fourth "major" on the circuit. Six different Australians scored victories in Japan, headed by Greg Norman's in the rich, early-season Chunichi Crowns, one of his five 1989 triumphs. Terry Gale won the Dunlop International, Craig Parry the Bridgestone Aso, Graham Marsh the Sapporo Tokyu (his 24th in Japan), Roger Mackay the Bridgestone and Brian Jones the big-money Lark Cup in the late fall. Larry Mize was the most successful American, winning the big Dunlop Phoenix and finishing second in the Casio World the following week when Hubert Green came apart in the final round. Larry Nelson earlier took the Suntory Open and Jose-Maria Olazabal, the new Spanish star, scored his first Japanese victory in the Taiheiyo Club Masters. The six-man United States team won the five-year-old international event now called the Asahi Glass Four Tours Championship in a tough final match against Europe via a total-strokes tie-breaker.

U.S. pros won four of the tournaments on the early-year Asia Circuit, which expanded for the first time in 15 years with the addition of the Pakistan Open as its 11th event. Brian Claar, who was later to regain playing privileges on the U.S. Tour, led the American contingent and the circuit's overall standings, winning the Hong Kong and Thailand Opens back to back in February. His wins followed the season-opening victory of Emlyn Aubrey, another subsequent PGA Tour qualifier, in the Philippines Open. Jeff Maggert picked up the other U.S. victory in the Malaysian Open. Two of Taiwan's top players scored victories, Lu Chien Soon bagging his sixth and seventh career Asia Circuit wins in Singapore and Taipei and Lu Hsi Chuen his 11th in Korea. Remi Bouchard, a Canadian, won in India and Frankie Minosa in the new Pakistan Open, along with Gale's victory in the joint Dunlop event in Japan, but the surprise of the year in Asia was the triumph in the Indonesia Open by a home-grown player with the single name of Kasiyadi.

San Miguel/Coca Cola Philippines Open—US$140,000
Winner: Emlyn Aubrey

Emlyn Aubrey took advantage of the final-round collapse of Sweden's Mats Lanner to score his first Asia Circuit victory in the San Miguel/Coca Cola Philippines Open at the Puerto Azul Beach and Country Club in early February. The 27-year-old Aubrey, a Pennsylvanian who turned pro in 1986 and was starting his second swing on the Asia Circuit, closed with a four-under-par 67. His 276 total gave him a two-stroke victory over home-favorite Mario Siodina, who finished fast, too, with 65, a course-record-tying effort. Lanner, a European Tour regular, who had set the record with his 65 Saturday for 203 and a five-stroke lead, stumbled to 77 Sunday, winding up in a third-place tie with Craig McClellan.

Aubrey remained close in the early rounds of Asia's oldest tournament. At 69 Thursday, he trailed the leader, defending champion Hsieh Chin Sheng by two shots. His par round Friday for 140 left him three strokes off the pace of fellow Americans Brian Mogg and Mark Aebli, a three-time winner in Asia, with Lanner, Edward Kirby and Frankie Minosa, a top Philippines pro, at 138. He fell six back Saturday with his 69 as Lanner's 65—203 put him five in front of Aebli and Minosa.

Johnny Walker Hong Kong Open—US$175,000
Winner: Brian Claar

A long quest for victory on one of the regular golf tours ended for 29-year-old Brian Claar when he captured the Johnny Walker Hong Kong Open. Claar, a pro since 1981 who had campaigned without winning on the U.S. PGA Tour and the Asia Circuit in past seasons, came from four shots off the lead in the final round. He emerged with a six-under-par 274 to win by a stroke in an exciting finish with four other players all having a shot at at least a tie on the final holes of the composite course created for the tournament at Royal Hong Kong Golf Club.

The American from Tampa, who was the PGA Tour's Rookie of the Year in 1986 but lost his playing privileges two years later, birdied the 17th hole and sank a seven-foot par putt at No. 18 for 67 and the victory when British Ryder Cupper Howard Clark, the third-round leader (203), and Hsieh Yu Shu, the 36-hole co-leader (136) with American Todd Hamilton, both took bogeys on the final hole. Hamilton, who was in front after 18 holes with 67, put a ball in the water at the last hole for 69 and fell back into a tie at 276 with Clark, Hsieh and Jean-Louis Lamarre. Gary Rusnak of the U.S. and Mats Lanner of Sweden finished second at 275. Lanner, who had blown a five-stroke lead the previous week in the Philippines, birdied the last two holes for 66 and Rusnak finished with 67. The veteran Clark, unsettled by the big Sunday crowds on the unroped course, blew his chances with a closing 73.

Thai International Thailand Open—US$150,000
Winner: Brian Claar

The taste of victory in Hong Kong carried over for Brian Claar when the Asia Circuit moved on to the Pinehurst Golf and Country Club course for the Thai International Thailand Open. Once Japan's Hiroshi Ueda came back to the field after his record 63 in the opening round, Claar was pretty much in command. With Tracy, his bride of four months, looking on, Claar took the second-round lead with 66-67—133 and went on to a three-stroke victory with following rounds of 68-71. His 16-under-par 272 was just two strokes off Ben Arda's tournament record at Navatanee Golf Club in 1976.

In running America's fast start on the 1989 Asia Circuit to three straight, Claar moved a stroke in front of Ueda (63-71) and Mike Hammond (67-67) at the halfway mark, then took the lead for keeps Saturday with the 68, going three ahead of Ueda. His closing 71 maintained that margin and other U.S. players finished in three of the next four spots in the standings. E.J. Pfister, the 1988 NCAA Champion from Oklahoma State, shot 68 to take second and Gary Webb of Dallas had 72 for 277 and third place. Emlyn Aubrey, the Philippines Open winner, added 68 to three 70s and tied for fourth with Esteban Toledo at 278.

Pakistan Open—US$120,000
Winner: Frankie Minosa

The Asia Circuit added a new tournament for the first time since the Indonesian Open came into being in 1974, inserting the new Pakistan Open into the lineup as the fourth event in early March. Frankie Minosa of the Philippines was the major beneficiary, scoring his third career victory on the circuit. He was merely two-under-par at 286 and overcame a 74-77 start as the Lahore Gymkhana Golf Club proved a stern test for the circuit travelers.

Minosa trailed by five strokes after the first day as only Tray Tyner and Remi Bouchard broke 70 with their 69s and, when he followed with the 77 for 151, he was 10 strokes behind the American, Tyner, the 1988 Malaysian Open champion. Then, the Filipino went to work. He shot 65 Saturday, the best score (by four) shot all week, and chopped seven strokes off Tyner's margin, as Tray shot 72. A two-under-par 70 against Tyner's 74 finally produced the one-stroke victory in the two-man battle Sunday. Eddie Kirby finished third, three shots behind Tyner.

Wills Indian Open—US$120,000
Winner: Remi Bouchard

Remi Bouchard became the second Canadian to win on the Asia Circuit when he scored a one-stroke victory in the Wills Indian Open at New Delhi, and the pattern was remarkably similar to his predecessor countryman, Tony Grimes, who also recorded his victory in India. Like Grimes, Bouchard was making his first golfing trip abroad and, at 25, was just a year older. Finally, his nine-under-par 279 matched the 72-hole total Grimes had posted four years earlier at Delhi Golf Club.

The key to Bouchard's victory was his course-record 64 in the second round, when he stormed into the lead after opening with 73 and trailing Carlos Espinosa by eight strokes. Remi had nine birdies in the record round as he took a one-shot lead over U.S. pros Greg Bruckner, the 1988 Singapore Open winner, and Gary Rusnak. Espinosa, the 1988 China Open victor, slipped to 75 and 140. Little change occurred Saturday as Bouchard matched par and retained a one-stroke margin on Bruckner, two on Espinosa. It came down to an exciting finish with Espinosa posting a birdie for 69 at the last hole, finishing a group ahead of Bouchard, who nearly holed his tee shot at the par-three 17th and rolled a 40-foot putt within inches of the cup at the 18th for a tap-in victory.

Singapore Open—US$220,000
Winner: Lu Chien Soon

Lu Chien Soon completed a sort of "daily double" when he prevailed in the Singapore Open at Tanah Merah Country Club in mid-March. Two weeks earlier, the 1988 Asia Circuit champion, having passed up the trip to Pakistan and India, won the Rolex Masters, a non-tour event on the Bukit course of

Singapore Island Country Club. The Open victory was Lu's second in that event and his sixth since 1983 on the Asia Circuit, more than any other player during that period.

The 30-year-old Taiwanese star, who won at Singapore in 1983, his rookie season as a pro, slipped into the lead at Tanah Merah with a 67 in Saturday's third round and hung on for a one-stroke victory over Carlos Espinosa, when the Mexican, runner-up for the second week in a row, three-putted the final green. Both had 72s, Lu for 11-under-par 277, Carlos for 278. Four strokes farther back was American E.J. Pfister, who had opened the tournament with a course-record 65 and remained in front the second day with 71—136. He finished with 75 for 282 as Lu rallied from an outgoing 38 Sunday to nail the title.

Shizuoka Open—¥40,000,000
Winner: Koichi Suzuki

Koichi Suzuki liked the idea of starting the Japanese Tour season in his home area so much that he went out and won the tournament. The 33-year-old Shizuoka native led, lost and regained the lead en route to his second circuit victory, closing with a one-under-par 71 in the final round to take the Shizuoka Open by one stroke with his 285. Suzuki's only other victory in his 13-year pro career came in the 1986 Yomiuri Open.

Koichi jumped in front Thursday, shooting 67 on the Hamaoka course of Shizuoka Country Club to lead by a stroke over Isao Isozaki. However, on a Friday when nobody shot better than 71, he took 78 and dropped three strokes off the pace of Toru Nakamura, Yoshikazu Yokoshima and Isozaki. Back Suzuki came Saturday with a 69 that pushed him into a two-stroke lead at 214 over Nobumitsu Yuhara and Eduardo Herrera, and he clung to first place Sunday, his 71 giving him a final one-stroke margin over Yuhara and Naomichi Ozaki.

Indonesia Open—US$120,000
Winner: Kasiyadi

The surprise of the Asia Circuit season sprang up in the Indonesian Open when Kasiyadi (his full name), a 26-year-old former caddy with no international credentials at all, came from four strokes off the pace to claim the title, shooting a 66 in the final round for an 11-under-par 269 on the Rawamangun course of Jakarta Golf Club. It was the first victory ever for an Indonesian pro on the Asia Circuit.

The major victim of Kasiyadi's late charge was Jeff Maggert, the U.S. winner of the 1988 Malaysian Open. With rounds of 65-64-70, Maggert had carried a two-stroke lead into the final round, but stumbled to 74 and dropped into a tie for fifth. While he was fading, Kasiyadi was surging, eventually finishing with nine birdies, three bogeys and a double-bogey. Coming up two strokes short at 271 was Kirk Triplett of the U.S. and Frankie Minosa of the Philippines, who had won the Pakistan Open three weeks earlier.

Setonaikai Open—¥40,000,000
Winner: Naomichi Ozaki

Naomichi Ozaki was in top form at the start of the Japan PGA Tour and quickly put his name on the victory list with a two-stroke victory in the Setonaikai Open at Shido Country Club. The win, his 11th circuit victory, followed his runner-up finish in the previous week's Shizuoka Open and earlier triumphs in two small non-tour events. Ozaki broke from a first-place tie going into the final round, posting 71 for 282 and a two-shot victory over Kinpachi Yoshimura.

The youngest of the remarkable Ozaki brothers opened with 68 for a one-shot lead over three other men, then yielded first place to Nobumitsu Yuhara, another hot player at the time. Yuhara, with 70-69—139, led by one over Pete Izumikawa and Ozaki was three back after shooting 74. Naomichi's 69 and Yuhara's 72 forged a first-place tie at 211 after 54 holes, setting up the tight finish. Yuhara fell away to 75, tying for fifth at 286.

Benson & Hedges Malaysian Open—US$175,000
Winner: Jeff Maggert

Jeff Maggert shook off the disappointment of a blown tournament the previous Sunday in Indonesia and rolled to an impressive victory in the Benson & Hedges Malaysian Open. Maggert closed with a 68 for a five-under-par 283 and a five-stroke triumph over fellow Americans Greg Bruckner, Bob Lendzion, Craig McClellan and Hawaiian Casey Nakama. The victory gave the U.S. forces four of the first eight titles as the Asia Circuit entered the month of April.

Ayer Koroh Country Club, a new site for the long-standing Malaysian Open in Malacca, yielded few rounds in the 60s all week. Bruckner was the only player to break 70 twice. His middle rounds of 69-67, coupled with his opening 75, put him a shot ahead of McClellan and four in front of Maggert and Liao Kuo Chie of Taiwan.

But the two leaders went in the wrong direction Sunday, opening the door for an easy victory to Maggert, a third-year pro from Texas. Bruckner took a 77 and McClelland shot 76, Lendzion and Nakama joining them in second place with 71s for their par 288 totals.

Republic of China Open—US$200,000
Winner: Lu Chien Soon

The gallery of champions of the Republic of China Open is studded with virtually all of the prominent Taiwanese players of the last quarter century and another of the country's top stars—Lu Chien Soon—joined the ranks in early April. Lu may have gotten some help from the weather in scoring his second Asia Circuit victory of the season and seventh of his career, as heavy fog blanketed Linkou International Golf and Country Club Sunday morning, forcing a cancellation of the final round at 1 o'clock when it failed to lift. With that, Lu, the third-round leader with rounds of 70-69-68, nine under par at 207, was declared the winner.

For two days, the lead was in the hands of Australia's George Serhan. The Australian shattered by three strokes the Linkou 18-hole record with his opening 64 over the 7,008-yard course. He led Kuo Chi Hsiung, a three-time China Open winner, and three Americans—Casey Nakama, Kyle Coody and Steve Veriato—by four strokes and maintained that margin with his second-round 70 for 134. Kuo remained in second place, then with Chen Liang Hsi and Andrew Debusk. Lu Chien Soon was at 139, then moved in front with the 68 as Serhan plunged with 76 for 210, tied for fourth with four others, including defending champion Carlos Espinosa. Chen Liang Hsi shot 70 to hold the runner-up spot and Lio Kuo Chie took third place with 70—209.

Pocari Sweat Open—¥50,000,000
Winner: Yoshikazu Yokoshima

Naomichi Ozaki and Nobumitsu Yuhara were in the midst of things again in the season's third official event in early April, but were the losers in a three-way fight for the Pocari Sweat Open title at Hakuryuko Country Club to Yoshikazu Yokoshima, a veteran pro with three previous victories to his credit. Yokoshima shot a one-under-par 70 for 274 to defeat Ozaki by one stroke and Yuhara and Noboru Sugai by two.

Kinpachi Yoshimura started the tournament in strange but exciting and effective fashion. He double-bogeyed the first hole, but came back with 10 birdies over the remaining 17 holes for an eight-under-par 63 and a two-shot lead. Even though he broke par by a shot the second day, Yoshimura, the 1987 Pocari Sweat champion, yielded first place to Ozaki, who started 66-65 for 131. Naomichi seemed headed for a solo run Sunday. He had built a two-shot margin through 17 holes Saturday, but double-bogeyed the 18th to drop into a three-way tie with Yokoshima and Yuhara.

Maekyung Korean Open—US$150,000
Winner: Lu Hsi Chuen

Lu Hsi Chuen took over second place on the all-time victory list on the Asia Circuit with his one-stroke win in the Maekyung Korean Open. Never out of the lead at Nam Seoul Country Club in Seoul, Lu nosed out countryman Chen Liang Hsi, the 1987 Korean Open winner, to post his 11th victory in 11 seasons on the Asia Circuit, his first in three years. Hsieh Yung Yo, now a senior, has 13 tour titles on his record.

Twice Lu shared the lead at Nam Seoul. His opening 67 was equalled by American Steve Bowman and Aaron Meeks, then he moved in front by two with 69—136. Brian Claar, the season's other two-time winner at Hong Kong and Thailand, was solo second with 70-68—138. Chen came up with 66 in the third round to overtake Lu (70) at 206, 10 under par, with Korea's Bong Tae Ha a stroke back. Lu's closing 71 for 277 produced the one-shot win over Chen, who posted a par 72 round. Rick Gibson jumped into third place at 280 with a 69-69 finish.

Bridgestone Open—¥40,000,000
Winner: Craig Parry

Another country was heard from in the Bridgestone. After Japanese pros had won the first three official events on the circuit, Craig Parry won one for Australia, rolling to a six-stroke victory at Aso Golf Club with rounds of 67-69-70-66 for 272, 16 under par. As champion, he succeeded countryman Ian Baker-Finch and was the third Australian winner of the event in the last four seasons, Brian Jones having triumphed in 1986.

The 23-year-old Parry ran within a stroke of a wire-to-wire victory, which was his first in Japan. His opening 67 locked him with Toru Nakamura and Hisao Inoue atop the heap and he had the lead to himself when he birdied the last two holes for 69 in the second round. At that point he had a stroke on Yoshiyuki Isomura and two on Fujio Kobayashi. Isomura, 33, a one-time winner on the circuit, shot a solid 68 Saturday and jumped ahead of Parry and Kobayashi, but was no match for the young Aussie Sunday. Parry quickly seized the lead and salted it away with four birdies on the last five holes for the 66. Despite shooting 73, Isomura placed second at 278. Kobayashi and Nakamura were tied for third at 280.

Dunlop Open—¥60,000,000
Winner: Terry Gale

Two men who had followed the entire Asia Circuit to its concluding Dunlop Open in Japan stole the early headlines, but in the end the title went as usual to a pro affiliated with the Japan Tour, for which the tournament near Tokyo serves as the start of its swing of important spring/summer events. That winning pro was Terry Gale, the veteran Australian who has played in the past on the Asia Circuit but in 1989 was making his first start outside his native country. Gale, who started the tournament at Ibaraki Golf Club with 73, five shots behind co-leaders Greg Bruckner and Steve Bowman, and was tied for 48th place after 36 holes when he followed with 74, came back with rounds of 68-69 for 284 and a one-stroke victory over fellow Aussie Peter Senior and Chen Tze Ming.

In between, Masashi (Jumbo) Ozaki, coming off his brilliant 1988 season, held sway through the middle rounds. He shot 67 Friday and, at 137, had a one-stroke lead over Hsieh Chin Sheng and two over Bruckner (71—139). Ozaki moved closer to a successful title defense in the Dunlop on a blustery Saturday, overcoming a double-bogey, double-bogey start to shoot 72 and open a three-shot lead over Senior. The 42-year-old Gale was six back starting out on the rainy Sunday, but his 69 was good enough for his second victory in Japan and sixth in Asia Circuit events when Ozaki struggled to a 77 and tied for fourth two shots behind Gale.

Brian Claar shot an even-par 288, tied for eighth and captured the overall championship of the 1989 Asia Circuit. It was the third time in six years that the tour title went to an American.

Chunichi Crowns—¥100,000,000
Winner: Greg Norman

Several international players showed up in Nagoya for the big-money event of the early Japanese season—the ¥100,000,000 Chunichi Crowns—and the biggest name among the arrivals—Greg Norman—joined the distinguished list of winners of the 30-year-old tournament that launched the growth of the Japan Tour from its domestic-events nucleus. Norman trailed only once through the four rounds at Nagoya Golf Club in late April and wound up with an eight-under-par 70 and a three-stroke victory, his third of the season following two February wins in Australia.

Norman shared the first-round lead (65) with Tadao Nakamura and the 36-hole lead (133) with Koichi Suzuki, the Shizuoka Open victor. Then, the flamboyant Aussie gave up first place Saturday when Blaine McCallister, the American winner of the Honda Open in Florida in early March, fired a 65 and took a two-stroke edge on Norman and Suzuki, who both shot 71s. Greg birdied the first two holes Sunday and rolled to a 68 and his three-shot win, his first official title in Japan. He had won the 36-hole Kuzuha back in 1977. McCallister also started well Sunday with an eagle at the second hole, but a string of four bogeys starting at the fourth hole killed his chances. He shot 73 and tied for second with Suzuki, who added another 71 for his 275.

Fuji Sankei Classic—¥60,000,000
Winner: Masashi Ozaki

Masashi Ozaki put himself on track for another big season in Japan with a two-shot victory in the Fuji Sankei Classic, one of his favorite tournaments. Jumbo, a six-tournament winner in 1988, picked up his first 1989 title on the Fuji course at the Kawana Hotel at Ito, where he had scored previous victories in 1980, 1986 and 1987.

Starting the tournament two strokes off the lead, Ozaki moved into a first-place tie with defending champion Ikuo Shirahama with his second 68 while Shirahama posted 69-67, then took over the lead Saturday with 70—206 and a three-shot margin over Shirahama (73). Two weeks earlier, a high finishing round dropped Jumbo down the standings in the Dunlop Open. Another poor-scoring fourth round hit him Sunday at Kawana, but his 76 came in rugged, windy weather and didn't cost him. His two-under-par 282 placed him two strokes ahead of runner-up Katsunari Takahashi in the final standings. Two more strokes back were Masanobu Kimura, Eduardo Herrara of Colombia and Jeff Sluman, the 1988 U.S. PGA champion.

Japan Match Play Championship—¥50,000,000
Winner: Masashi Ozaki

The Japan Match Play Championship of 1989 was a dual milestone for Masashi Ozaki. With his 3-and-2 final victory over Hiroshi Makino at Green Academy Country Club, Ozaki reached the 60-win mark in his outstanding career. It also gave him a career sweep of Japan's four recognized majors (the Open, PGA, Series and Match Play). Isao Aoki, Tsuneyuki Nakajima and Takashi Murakami are the only others to have accomplished that feat before him.

Ozaki and Makino reached the final through quite-different degrees of difficulty. Jumbo was never really pressed in his first four matches, taking Haruo Yasuda, 5 and 4; Tomohiro Maruyama and Noboru Sugai, 4 and 3, and Nobumitsu Yuhara, 5 and 4. On the other hand, Makino, with only the 1983 Pocari Sweat title on his record, had only one easy match in reaching the final. He nipped Ikuo Shirahama, 1-up, then Katsunari Takahashi, 2 and 1, before handling Yoshitaka Yamamoto, 5 and 3. Saburo Fujiki carried the 33-year-old Makino to the last hole before bowing, 2-up, in the semi-finals. Makino was never really close in the 36-hole final after Ozaki took the second, third and fourth holes in the morning. Jumbo was 6-up when they finished the first 18. Hiroshi rallied with birdies at the 20th, 23rd and 24th, but never got closer than that before the match ended on the 34th green.

Pepsi Ube Kosan—¥50,000,000
Winner: Akihito Yokoyama

The season's first playoff gave Akihito Yokoyama his first national exposure as a tournament winner. Yokoyama, whose only previous victory was in the 1988 Kanto Open when that event was one of six played that weekend, prevailed over Yoshimi Niizeki on Ube Country Club's Mannenike East course at Ajisucho when his bogey on the second extra hole was the winning score against Niizeki's double-bogey.

The two men had been close to the top through the three rounds that were played, the Friday activity having been washed out by heavy rains. Niizeki opened with 66, Yokoyama with 67 Thursday as Australia's Wayne Smith tied the course record with 64 and led by two. Both playoff participants had 69s when play resumed after the rainout Saturday and ranked two-three behind Tadami Ueno's 132 as Smith took 75 and fell from contention. Yokoyama made up his one-stroke deficit against Niizeki Sunday with consecutive birdies at the 14th, 15th and 16th holes, finishing with 67 to Yoshimi's 68 to forge the tie at 203 and force the playoff. Ueno had a 72, tying for third at 204 with Nobuo Serizawa.

Mitsubishi Galant—¥70,000,000
Winner: Tateo Ozaki

Tateo (Jet) Ozaki joined his brothers in the 1989 winners' circle in late May when he captured the Mitsubishi Galant tournament at the Kumamoto Airport Country Club in Kikuyomachi. Ozaki, who won two of his nine previous titles during the brothers' remarkable season in 1988, seized the lead in the second round of the Mitsubishi Galant and never trailed thereafter, finishing with a four-under-par 284 and a two-stroke win over Masanobu Kimura.

Toyotaka Nakao had his day in the sun Thursday. He holed a 218-yard three-wood shot for a double-eagle two at the par-five finishing hole for 68 and the first-round lead. As he faded over the weekend to a tie-for-32nd finish, Ozaki took over. He added 67 to his opening 72 for 139 and a one-stroke lead over three other players, including eventual runner-up Masanobu Kimura. Scores were high Saturday and Ozaki's 74 still left him two strokes in front of Kimura and Haruo Yasuda. Four birdies and three bogeys produced a closing 71 for Jet Ozaki that gave him his 10th career win. Kimura also shot 71 for 286, one stroke in front of Yoshimi Niizeki, Masahiro Kuramoto and Ikuo Shirahama.

Sendai Hoso Classic—¥45,000,000
Winner: Masashi Ozaki

One of the tournaments in which Masashi (Jumbo) Ozaki enjoyed particular success early in his career was the Tohoku, which he won three years in a row in 1973-4-5. The name and the course have changed since then, but Ozaki hasn't lost the winning touch in the event. Jumbo won what is now called the Sendai Hoso Classic the first week of June at Omote Zeo Golf Club at Shibatamachi, blazing home in the final round with a five-under-par 66 for 272 and a three-stroke victory.

Low scores were common all week. Australia's Roger Mackay and Taijiro Tanaka shot 65s in the opening round to lead after 18 holes, a shot in front of Hajime Meshiai. Ozaki matched that score in the second round and, coupled with his opening 70, he moved into a tie for first place with Tanaka at 135. Norio Mikami, 42, an 18-year circuit veteran, jumped into first place by a stroke Saturday when he shot 67 for 205. Ozaki took 71 for 206, joined at that score by Meshiai (70). Ozaki birdied four of the first seven holes Sunday and was never in serious trouble after that. Another 66, by Katsunari Takahashi, and a 65 by Tsuneyuki Nakajima merely advanced them into a second-place tie at 275. Jumbo's third win of the season fattened his victory record in Japan to 61.

Sapporo Tokyu Open—¥50,000,000
Winner: Graham Marsh

Graham Marsh brought back memories of his early international career when he scored his first Asia Circuit victory in almost two years in the Sapporo Toyku Open at the Sapporo International Golf Club. The most successful non-Asian pro ever on the Japan Tour, Marsh counts the Sapporo Tokyu among his early victories, having won that tournament in 1975. This year's win was his 24th in Japan, far more than any other player from outside the country.

Marsh, now 45, played like he did in his younger days in Japan, too. After trailing Katsuyoshi Tomori by a stroke with his opening 71, Graham roared into a six-stroke lead in the Friday round with a seven-under-par 65 for 136, Yasuo Sone his closest pursuer after pairing 71s over the 36 holes. Nobody broke 70 Saturday, so Marsh's 76—two birdies, six bogeys—merely reduced his margin to four strokes over Yoshitaka Yamamoto, Katsuji

Hasegawa and Yurio Akitomi. His total was 212. The final margin was three as Marsh closed with 70 for 282. Tsuneyuki Nakajima, winless in Japan in 1989, made a late run at the title for the second week in a row, again tying for second place. At Sapporo, he fired a final-round 67 to tie Hasegawa for the runner-up spot at 285.

Yomiuri Sapporo Beer Open—¥70,000,000
Winner: Hajime Meshiai

Hajime Meshiai established his strength early in the Yomiuri Sapporo Beer Open and proceeded to a two-stroke victory in the rain-shortened tournament in mid-June at Osaka's Yomiuri Country Club. Meshiai jumped off to a two-shot lead in Thursday's first round with an eight-under-par 64 and outfought Naomichi Ozaki in leading the rest of the way. His winning 54-hole score was 11-under-par 205, and it brought him his first 1989 victory and fifth of his career on the Japan Tour.

Meshiai, 35, made two eagles in his course-record-tying 64, which put him two ahead of Ozaki. After four hours of play in the rain Friday, low portions of the Yomiuri course flooded and the round was cancelled. In the restart Saturday, Meshiai widened his margin to three with a 71 for Naomichi's 72. Chen Tze Chung, a recent U.S. tour regular, matched Ozaki's 138 with 67 and Yoshitaka Yamamoto and Yoshinori Kaneko joined them at that score. Hajime's 70 on Sunday—three birdies and a bogey—carried him to a two-stroke victory as Ozaki shot 69 to finish second, a stroke ahead of Chen and Brian Jones.

Mizuno Open—¥65,000,000
Winner: Akiyoshi Omachi

It appeared that a long-expected victory by Tsuneyuki Nakajima, the outstanding Japanese player who was winless since 1987, was at hand when he surged into the lead in the Mizuno Open on the front nine of Tokinodai Country Club's Mijodai course in Sunday's final round. But it was not to be. Nakajima gave three strokes back coming in and Akiyoshi (Aki) Omachi surged past him with a closing 69 for 283 and a two-stroke victory over Nakajima and three other players.

Omachi, 30, who gained valuable experience in the crucible of the U.S. PGA Tour in 1987 and 1988, entered the final round two shots off the pace of Chen Tze Ming, whose third-round 69 for 212 had given him a single-stroke lead over Nakajima, Yoshikazu Yokoshima, Eiichi Itai and defending champion Yoshimi Niizeki. Omachi birdied the first two holes Sunday to establish his bid, but Australian transplant Brian Jones had the lead after Nakajima's slip until Aki made his third and last birdie at the 16th and parred in for the 69. Nakajima finished with 72 for his 285 and was tied there with Jones, Fujio Kobayashi and Masahiro Kuramoto, all 71 shooters Sunday.

Kanto PGA Championship—¥40,000,000
Winner: Saburo Fujiki

The Japan Tour split into two sections the last week of June for the staging of the regional PGA Championships in the eastern and western sectors of the country. Akiyoshi Omachi, riding the momentum of his Mizuno Open victory, came within a stroke of a chance for two in a row in the Kanto (Eastern Japan) PGA, missing a playoff opportunity when Saburo Fujiki birdied the 72nd hole for 70, 277 and a one-shot win at Prestige Country Club at Tochigi, north of Tokyo.

Tsuneyuki (Tommy) Nakajima made another futile bid to end his long victory slump in Japan dating back to the fall of 1987 with a strong start in the Kanto PGA. He shot 67 and shared the first-round lead with three others, then followed with 71, settling in a stroke behind new leaders Fujiki (69-68) and Yutaka Hagawa (68-69). However, the 39-tournament winner disappeared from view after that, and Omachi strengthen his run at the title Saturday with a 67 that jumped him a stroke in front of the field at 11-under-par 205. Fujiki shot 70 to drop two strokes off the pace with Noboru Sugai in between. Omachi could manage just a 73 Sunday, opening the door for Fujiki's winning birdie. It was Saburo's ninth tour victory and first since he won the season-finale Daikyo Open in 1988.

Kansai PGA Championship—¥30,000,000
Winner: Hajime Matsui

Hajime Matsui, who had scored his first tour victory in the 1988 Hiroshima Open, surged to a final-round 68 and captured the Kansai (Western Japan) PGA Championship by three strokes with his 12-under-par 276 at Yamaguchi Golf and Country Club in Toyota. Matsui's final rush contrasted with the Sunday collapse of veteran Toru Nakamura, a 24-tournament career winner with only a 63-hole victory in the rain-shortened 1988 Jun Classic in the last three seasons.

After unknown Isamu Sugita opened with 65, then began fading to a 35th-place finish, Nakamura took charge. With 68-69—137, he moved into the second-round lead, a stroke in front of Matsui, Masanubo Kimura and the two other tour-playing Nakamuras, Tadao and Teruo. Toru widened his lead to three strokes Saturday with a seven birdie-two bogey 67, his 204 giving him the three-shot edge over Tadao Nakamura (69) and four over Matsui (70) and Nobuhiro Yoshino (69). However, Toru put the title up for grabs when he crumbled to 79, and Matsui seized the lead quickly with three front-nine birdies. Yoshino shot 71 for 279, three better than Toru and Tadao Nakamura and Hisashi Kaji.

Yonex Hiroshima Open—¥50,000,000
Winner: Masashi Ozaki

After just a one-month gap, during which he made a strong showing in the U.S. Open, Masashi (Jumbo) Ozaki resumed his title collection on the Japan

Tour with a resounding victory in the Yonex Hiroshima Open on the Happonmatsu course of Hiroshima Country Club. It was familiar ground for Ozaki, who won there in his rookie season in 1971 and subsequently in 1976, 1978 and 1984. None were as decisive as his six-stroke victory for the fifth one and his 62nd title overall.

Nobuo Serizawa stirred things up in Thursday's first round with a course-record-tying 63, a flawless nine-birdie round. At that point, Ozaki was six strokes behind with Teruo Sugihara and Pete Izumikawa in the runner-up slot at 66. Serizawa came back to the field with a par round Friday for 135, his lead reduced to a single shot over Ozaki (67) and Hiroshi Ueda (67-69). Jumbo jumped into a two-stroke lead Saturday, birdieing the first two holes and scoring 32 on the front nine. He shot 68 for 204. Serizawa carded 71 and shared second place at 206 with Satoshi Higashi. Ozaki made short work of any opposition Sunday with birdies on the first two holes and five on the front nine en route to 66 and his 18-under-par 270. With 70, Serizawa tied for second with veterans Seiichi Kanai and Seiji Ebihara.

NST Niigata Open—¥50,000,000
Winner: Katsuyoshi Tomori

Katsuyoshi Tomori was the beneficiary of a rare occurrence in modern-day tournament golf. Par won . . . and Tomori had that 288 score after four rounds on the Sanjo course of Dainiigata Country Club in the NST Niigata Open in late July. The victory was Katsuyoshi's fourth in his six-year career, the most recent previous win having come in the 1988 Kyushu Open.

On the other side of the coin was Toru Nakayama, frustrated again in his quest for victory over the last 13 seasons. Nakayama, 43, eagled the par-five 18th hole Friday to swoop into a tie at 141 with Tomori, who had led the first round with 71 and followed with 70 to Toru's 68. Saturday's best score was 71, which enabled Nakayama to open a two-stroke lead despite shooting 74. Tomori shot 76 and shared the runner-up position with Shigeru Kawamata, then won the tournament with a one-under 71 Sunday as Nakayama's game came apart. He was fortunate to salvage 76 and a tie-for-sixth finish as he had a quadruple-bogey and a double-bogey during the round. Tomohiro Maruyama finished second at 289, and three veterans took third-place-tie money with 290s—Seiichi Kanai, Teruo Sugihara and Kikuo Arai, who had a double-eagle on the par-five ninth hole.

Japan PGA Championship—¥70,000,000
Winner: Masashi Ozaki

Eighteen years after highlighting his first season on the Japan Tour with victory in the prestigious Japan PGA Championship, Masashi (Jumbo) Ozaki won it for a third time in early August at Karasuyamajo Country Club, scoring the fifth victory of his sensational season and 63rd of his brilliant career. This major win came by a single stroke with a six-under-par 278, as he just survived a 66 finish by little-known Hideki Kase amid stormy weekend conditions spawned by the fringes of a typhoon.

Ozaki, who likened conditions the last day to those usually faced at British Opens, grabbed the lead on Friday and never trailed after that. He had opened with 68, three behind leader Nozomu Kamatsu, and moved in front with another 68, the score greatly aided by his hole-in-one at the second. Toru Nakamura was then second at 137. Ozaki shot an in-and-out 71 with five birdies in the high winds Saturday, widening his lead over Nakamura (72) to two strokes. However, as had happened three weeks earlier when he led the Kansai PGA after 54 holes, Nakamura fell apart Sunday, tumbling down the standings with an 80. Instead, Kase mustered the challenge to Jumbo. Winner of just two non-tour events in his seven years on the circuit, Kase came from four strokes back to catch Ozaki at the eighth hole Sunday when Jumbo double-bogeyed after registering just one par before then. However, Jumbo rebounded from the double-bogey and established the slim final margin with three birdies and a bogey over the last 10 holes. The tournament marked the return to action in Japan of Isao Aoki, who had campaigned in America during the first six months. He tied for 11th at 287, nine strokes behind Ozaki. Jumbo Ozaki succeeded younger brother Tateo (Jet) as the PGA champion. Jet had been forced out of the tournament in the second round with a hamstring pull in his left leg.

Nikkei Cup—¥60,000,000
Winner: Yoshimi Niizeki

Yoshimi Niizeki has a thing going with playoffs. The 34-year-old Niizeki scored his first and at the time only Japan Tour victory when he rolled in a 40-foot birdie putt on the second extra hole of the 1988 Mizuno Open. Eleven months later, in his best bid for a 1989 victory, Niizeki tied Akihito Yokoyama in the Pepsi Ube tournament, but lost in the playoff when he double-bogeyed the second extra hole. So, how does he land his second tour title? In a playoff, of course. This time, in the Nikkei Cup, his par on the first overtime hole—the par-five 18th—brought the win over Saburo Fujiki.

Australian Roger Mackay, who was to be a challenger until a final-round 80, opened the Nikkei Cup with a six-under-par 64, but led three players, including Fujiki, by just a single shot. Yutaka Hagawa (65), Norikazu Kawakami (68) and Yoshiyuki Isomura (69) forged a three-way tie for the lead at 134 at the halfway mark, Isomura frittering away a four-stroke lead on the back nine. Hagawa and Kawakami shot 67s Saturday to remain on top at 201 with Niizeki and Fujiki two back after posting 68s. They shot 68s again Sunday to set up the playoff as Hagawa triple-bogeyed the 15th hole and dropped three shots off the pace into third place with 73 and Kawakami had 74 for 275 to tie for fourth with Isomura.

Maruman Open—¥80,000,000
Winner: Koichi Suzuki

With Jumbo Ozaki in a class by himself, the titles on the Japan Tour had been evenly distributed among 15 other pros during the first six months of the season. Finally, in the Maruman Open at Higashi Matsuyama Country

Club in mid-August, Koichi Suzuki became the year's second multiple winner, eking out a one-stroke victory to go with his season-opening triumph in the Shizuoka Open. Interestingly, Ozaki had won two of the three immediately previous Maruman Opens.

Suzuki stormed into the lead with a course-record 63 in the second round, coming from four shots off Tsukasa Watanabe's opening pace of 66. Koichi had nine birdies in the record round, four in a row from the 13th to 16th, to jump four strokes in front of Watanabe. He remained four ahead with a 71 Saturday, but the runner-up was then Taijiro Tanaka, who shot 68 for 207. Watanabe was at 208 after a 72, then made a strong bid for victory Sunday against an erratic Suzuki. After a double-bogey at the 10th, a birdie at the 12th and bogeys at the 14th and 16th, Koichi had dropped into a deadlock with the Tsukasa Watanabe from Eastern Japan at nine under par. But, Suzuki birdied the par-five 18th to nail the victory by a shot over Watanabe and Satoshi Higashi, two over Ozaki, who closed with a 66. Tanaka fell to a tie for sixth with a 77.

Daiwa KBC Augusta—¥100,000,000
Winner: Teruo Sugihara

Teruo Sugihara, Japan's answer to Sam Snead, just keeps rolling along.

In 1965, the remarkable Snead won the Greater Greensboro Open on the U.S. PGA Tour at the age of 52. Twenty-four years later, the diminutive Sugihara, at the same age, won the Daiwa KBC Augusta tournament on the Japan Tour. In both cases, they are the oldest-ever winners on the respective circuits. Sugihara, who played extensively on both the regular and senior tours in Japan in 1989, beat the best in the KBC Augusta at Kyushu Shima Country Club, finishing two strokes in front of Graham Marsh and Tsuneyuki Nakajima and three ahead of Jumbo Ozaki. He didn't shoot his age, but he has won his age with 52 titles in his 33-year career.

Most of the fireworks occurred in the final round as the early leaders and strongest contenders faded and the stars came to the fore. Hiroshi Ueda had the lead after the first and third rounds with his 67-72-70 start; Kiyoshi Murota was on top the second day (69-68—137) and Harumitsu Hamano shared the 54-hole lead with Ueda. All fell quickly out of the picture, as Sugihara, starting the day four shots off the pace, recovered from a front-nine 36 with five birdies coming home, the last one at the 18th for 68 and seven-under-par 281. Marsh also shot 68 to tie Nakajima (70) for second at 283. Ozaki finished another stroke back with 68 after virtually ending his chances with a third-round 78.

Kanto Open—¥30,000,000
Winner: Yoshinori Mizumaki

Kansai Open—¥20,000,000
Winner: Yoshitaka Yamamoto

Chu-Shikoku Open—¥20,000,000
Winner: Tadami Ueno

Hokkaido Open—¥10,000,000
Winner: Mamoru Takahashi

Chubu Open—¥15,000,000
Winner: Tadao Nakamura

Kyushu Open—¥20,000,000
Winner: Shinji Kuraoka

Yoshitaka Yamamoto and five lesser lights on the Japan Tour picked up victories during the circuit's usual six-tournament weekend of small-purse events at the end of August.

Yamamoto scored his 16th career victory in the Kansai Open, one of two long-standing tournaments on the busy schedule that week. Ahead of three others by a single stroke after 54 holes, Yamamoto gained the title for the second time when heavy Sunday rains washed out the final round. His score was 67-74-70—211, with Toru Nakamura, Kazuo Kanayama and Toshiaki Nakagawa at 212. Yamamoto had won his earlier Kansai Open in 1977.

Yoshinori Mizumaki outlasted four-time Kanto Open winner Isao Aoki for the first tour victory in his five-year career. He shot a final-round 70 for 281, seven under par at Hidaka Country Club to edge Aoki by a stroke after both started the final round three strokes behind defending champion Akihito Yokoyama. Yokoyama skied to 81 in high winds Sunday, and Aoki opened the gates for Mizumaki by absorbing four bogeys on the back nine after making four early birdies and taking the lead.

Playoffs decided the victories of Mamoru Takahashi (over Katsunari Takahashi) in the Hokkaido Open and Shinji Kuraoka (over Katsuyoshi Tomori) in the Kyushu Open. Tadami Ueno edged Norio Mikami and Yoshikazu Sakamoto, 283 to 284, in the Chu-Shikoku Open, and Tadao Nakamura beat Masahiro Shioda by a stroke, 210 to 211, in the Chubu Open, which was shortened to 54 holes because of bad weather.

Suntory Open—¥80,000,000
Winner: Larry Nelson

The Japan Tour swung into its rich fall segment with the Suntory Open, a stretch that always attracts leading players from the United States and Europe. Larry Nelson, a frequent visitor and two-time winner, came to Narashino Country Club for the Suntory and left with the title after a playoff. Nelson, who had lost a Suntory playoff to Tateo Ozaki in 1985, bumped off Saburo Fujiki this time around when he sank a 20-foot birdie putt on the first playoff hole—No. 18. It was Fujiki's second playoff loss of the season, the Nikkei Cup defeat the other.

Nelson and Fujiki rode the top rung throughout the Suntory. Fujiki's opening 68 gave him a one-stroke lead over Nelson, Chen Tze Chung (T.C.

Chen in the U.S.) and three other Japanese pros, who fell from contention during the middle rounds. Chen and Nelson shot 67s Friday and Fujiki a 68, forming a three-way first-place tie at 136. It was still that way 24 hours later as the three leaders all mustered 70s. Nelson and Fujiki repeated the 70s Sunday, setting up the playoff, as Chen struggled to 77 and dropped into a three-way tie for fifth at 283.

All Nippon Airways Open—¥70,000,000
Winner: Masashi Ozaki

Once again, Masashi Ozaki reprised early success on the Japan Tour when he recorded his sixth victory of the season in the All Nippon Airways Open at Sapporo Golf Club. Jumbo won that Sapporo tournament two years in a row in the early 1970s, neither victory in 1972 and 1973 as convincing as his six-stroke triumph in 1989, the 63rd of his career.

Ian Woosnam, the brilliant Welsh shotmaker who led the World Money List in 1987, provided Ozaki's only serious challenge in the final going. He and Ozaki stood together a stroke off the lead of Tsukasa Watanabe after 36 holes. The Eastern Japan pro had 72-68—140 while Ozaki was shooting 71-70 and Woosnam 74-67 during the first two rounds. Norikazu Kawakami was the first-round leader with 70 but took himself out with a third-round 80. Ozaki went in front to stay with a four-under-par 68, carrying a four-stroke lead over Woosnam into the final round. The Welshman pulled within two strokes of Jumbo early Sunday, but ran into a series of bogeys and finished with 73 to Jumbo's 71, edging Watanabe and Brian Jones for second place by a shot.

Jun Classic—¥70,000,000
Winner: Tateo Ozaki

A rarity in tournament golf came as the 1989 winner of the Jun Classic was decided in late September at Jun Classic Country Club—brother against brother in a playoff for the title. Who else but the Ozakis. Middle brother Tateo (Jet) came from three strokes off the pace in the final round to catch younger brother Naomichi (Joe) and then defeated him in the subsequent playoff.

Joe Ozaki had taken the third-round lead with a 69 for 210, six under par, after Yoshikazu Yokoshima held first place the first day with 67 and Norio Mikami and Koichi Suzuki the second day with 140s, Joe Ozaki one stroke back. The third Ozaki—the mighty Jumbo—joined Jet at 213 going into the final round, but, while Jet was firing a final-round 66 to create the deadlock, his older brother, who had won the Jun Classic three times in the previous five years, could manage only a par round and finished in a three-way tie for sixth. Yokoshima and Seiji Ebihara tied for third at 281 after closing 68s, and Toru Nakamura placed fifth at 282.

Tokai Classic—¥60,000,000
Winner: Isao Aoki

Perhaps Isao Aoki was getting tired of Jumbo Ozaki widening the career victory gap between the two of them on the Japan Tour. The No. 1 man just two years ago, Aoki went winless in 1988 and through the first nine months of 1989, his total remaining at 53 while Ozaki had run his to 64. Regardless of the motivation, Aoki put on one of his typical performances of old in swallowing the field in the Tokai Classic, rolling to a five-stroke victory with his 13-under-par 275 on Miyoshi Country Club's West course. Actually, it was Aoki's second 1989 victory, since he won his third overseas title in January in Australia.

Isao broke up a tight duel with Pete Izumikawa with a closing 68 as Pete slipped to 74, barely holding onto second place, a stroke ahead of Tsuneyuki Nakajima and Akiyoshi Omachi at 281. Aoki led through the first two rounds with his 67-69 start, sharing first with Izumikawa when he fired 64 in the second round for his 136. Pete followed with 70 Saturday and took a one-stroke lead at 206 when Aoki bogeyed the final hole for 71—207. Izumikawa birdied four of the last eight holes to overcome a shaky start. On Sunday, Isao began his winning charge with birdies on the first three holes, although Pete kept pace with two of his own on the front nine. Aoki then broke his back with another three-birdie spurt in the middle of the back nine while he was stumbling with four bogeys.

Japan Open Championship—¥60,000,000
Winner: Masashi Ozaki

Masashi (Jumbo) Ozaki staged a successful defense of one of his proudest titles—the Japan Open Championship—as he scored his seventh victory of the 1989 season and, with his third Open crown, became the first player in 31 years to have such a triple on his record. Torakichi (Pete) Nakamura, the first post-war star of Japanese golf, won his third Open championship in 1958.

The 1989 win did not come easily to Ozaki. Aussie Brian Jones battled him to the final hole at the Wago course of Nagoya Golf Club, annual site of the early-season Chunichi Crowns tournament, and was in hot pursuit from the start, even though Kiyoshi Okura, a 28-year-old amateur from Fukuoka, shot 65 for the first-round lead, the first amateur leader at the Open in 11 years. Jumbo began shakily with a double-bogey but bounced back with six birdies for 66 on the 6,473-yard, par-70 course. Jones and Akihito Yokoyama, the Pepsi Ube champion, had 67s. Okura skied to 78 Friday as Ozaki moved in front with 68—134. Jones matched Jumbo's Friday score and trailed by a stroke. Ozaki's solid 67 on a drizzly Saturday widened his lead over Jones to three shots with Yokoyama and Noboru Sugai two strokes farther back.

Ozaki gave Jones his shot at the championship Sunday when he triple-bogeyed the par-four ninth hole. The two traded birdies at the 10th and 14th holes, then Jumbo fell a stroke behind with a bogey at the 15th. However, he regained the deadlock when he holed a 66-foot bunker shot at the 17th and retained the winning margin despite a bogey at the last hole when Jones knocked his second shot out of bounds and took a double-bogey for 71 and 275. Ozaki's finish was 73—274.

Polaroid Cup Golf Digest—¥60,000,000
Winner: Yoshikazu Yokoshima

Yoshikazu Yokoshima broke a logjam from the early rounds with a six-under-par 65 the third day and breezed to a six-stroke victory in the Polaroid Cup Golf Digest tournament at Susono's Tomei Country Club. In a solid, 16-under-par performance, Yokoshima posted rounds of 67-67-65-69 for 268 as he scored his second 1989 victory and fifth of his career. He was the Pocari Sweat winner in April.

Things were crowded the first two days. Five players—Masaji Kusakabe, Takeshi Kubota, Graham Marsh, Norikazu Kawakami and Chen Tze Ming—opened the tournament with 66s and six others, including Yokoshima, were at 67. It barely thinned out Friday. Yokoshima shared the 36-hole lead with Chen, Kawakami and Akihito Yokoyama at 134, then seized the lead for good Saturday. Ultimately, three players deadlocked for second place—Kiyoshi Muroda, Kusakabe and Bill Glasson, in Japan from the U.S. tour for two weeks. Glasson shot four rounds in the 60s, but the 274 was no threat to Yokoshima.

Bridgestone—¥80,000,000
Winner: Roger Mackay

Two Australians wrestled through four rounds for the title in the Bridgestone tournament, but at the end a veteran Japanese pro nearly snuck in and stole it away from both of them. Roger Mackay prevailed by a stroke, however, winning his first tournament in Japan.

Brian Jones, the Australian who has played regularly in Japan for many years and has eight Japan Tour titles on his record, started the tournament at Sodegaura Country Club at Chiba with an eight-under-par 64 and a two-shot lead over Mackay. Roger crept a stroke closer Friday with a 70 to Brian's 71—135 and was joined at 136 by Tadao Nakamura. Mackay birdied the final hole Saturday for 68 and moved into a first-place tie with Jones, who shot a bogey-free 69 for his 204. The two Aussies held a three-stroke lead over American Bill Glasson and Kinpachi Yoshimura, who had 68s. Yoshitaka Yamamoto, who earlier in the year had won his 16th title in the Kansai Open, entered the final round four shots off the pace and made a strong run with two birdies and no bogeys, his 70 leaving him a shot behind Mackay, who finished with 73 for 277. Jones stumbled to a 75 and dropped into a four-way tie for third at 279 with Glasson, Nakamura and Katsuji Hasegawa.

Lark Cup—¥160,000,000
Winner: Brian Jones

Brian Jones couldn't have picked a better time for a rebound. On October 22, Jones started the day tied for the lead and shot a final-round 75 in the Bridgestone tournament. One week later, he had shrugged off that bad experience so well that he expanded on a third-round lead and laid claim to ¥28,800,000/US$205,000, one of the two largest first-place checks of the 1989 season, as winner of the second Lark Cup.

Three Americans crossed the Pacific for the rich tournament, and one of them—Doug Tewell—was a strong contender from the start until unravelling in the final round. Tewell, a four-tournament winner on the U.S. PGA Tour, opened with 67 and shared the first-round lead with veteran Taiwanese star Hsieh Min Nan. Doug followed with 71 and retained a piece of the lead, then with another Taiwanese pro, Chen Tze Ming (69-69). Jones advanced into a four-way tie for third at 139 with 70-69, joining Hsieh (72), Satoshi Higashi (71-68) and Yasuhiro Funatogawa (69-70). Another 69 on the ABC Golf Club course at Tojocho elevated Jones two strokes ahead of the field Saturday with a 208 total. Tewell posted a par round for 210 and was joined there by virtual unknown Toshiaki Sudo and Hiroshi Makino, who eagled the 18th hole. Both shot 66s. A steady par round Sunday gave Jones a 280 total and four-stroke victory, his ninth in Japan. Even though shooting 74, Sudo finished second and won more by far in one tournament than he had in his entire career—¥16,000,000 or US$114,285. Tewell collapsed with a 79 and plunged to 13th place.

Asahi Glass Four Tours Championship—US$1,020,000
Winner: United States

The name changed and the tournament returned to Japan, but the United States scored its fourth victory in the five-year history of the round-robin, stroke match play team event that is now called the Asahi Glass Four Tours World Championship. The Sunday championship match between the six-man teams of the U.S. and Europe was reminiscent of the September Ryder Cup Matches in that they wound up in a 6-6 points deadlock. In the Four Tours, though, the Americans won the total-strokes tie-breaker, 404 to 416.

The first three rounds determined finalists as each team from the "Four Tours"—U.S., Europe, Australia/New Zealand and Japan—played each other and totaled their points. The U.S. and Europe also tied, 6-6, in the first round as Ken Green, Mark Calcavecchia and Curtis Strange won for America, Bernhard Langer, Gordon Brand Jr. and Ronan Rafferty for Europe. Wayne Grady, Ian Baker-Finch, Greg Norman and Brian Jones won in Australia/New Zealand's 8-4 victory over Japan, which got triumphs from Masashi and Naomichi Ozaki.

Both the U.S. and Europe scored big victories Friday, halves by Peter Senior and Grady saving their team from a shutout. Jumbo Ozaki's win over Ian Woosnam and Koichi Suzuki's halve with Mark James were Japan's only point-makers in a 9-3 loss. The Americans (Chip Beck, Payne Stewart and Tom Kite were the other team members) routed Japan, 10-2, and Europe edged Australia/New Zealand, 7-5, to qualify for the title match. With the Sunday matches going three/three for another 6-6 tie, the 62 of Beck in his rout of Langer and Kite's 65 in his triumph over Woosnam played big parts in the total-score tie-breaking that gave the six Americans $65,000 checks. The Europeans each received $40,000, while the Japanese (Tateo Ozaki, Toru Nakamura and Katsunari Takahashi were the other team members) defeated Australia/New Zealand in the third/fourth-place consolation for $35,000 apiece. The losers each got $30,000.

Visa Taiheiyo Club Masters—¥100,000,000
Winner: Jose-Maria Olazabal

Severiano Ballesteros had an uncharacteristically bad tournament when he came to Japan to defend his Visa Taiheiyo Club (Pacific) Masters title, so his younger Spanish compatriot, Jose-Maria Olazabal, picked up for him, retaining the strong play that saw him win three of four matches the previous weekend in the Asahi Glass Four Tours elsewhere in Japan.

When play began at the Taiheiyo Club's Gotemba course Friday after the scheduled first round was rained out, Olazabal fashioned a solid eagle-four birdie 66 to take a one-stroke lead over England's Barry Lane, who also had an eagle, and Yoshiyuki Isomura. Congestion at the top developed Saturday as Olazabal (70) was joined at 136 by Naomichi Ozaki (70-66), Nobuo Serizawa (69-67), Ryoken Kawagishi (69-67) and Ken Green, the U.S. Ryder Cupper who tied the course record of 65 set by Lon Hinkle in 1981.

Olazabal broke from the five-way tie Sunday with 67 for a 13-under-par 203 and a three-stroke victory, his first in Japan. It wasn't as easy as the margin indicates. Isao Aoki got into the act by matching the course record as Green had done the day before and missed three short birdie putts in a row starting the back nine. In that same stretch, Olazabal built his winning margin with birdies at the 10th, 11th and 13th holes. However, Joe Ozaki kept his hopes alive to the par-five 18th where, bidding for a tying eagle, he bunkered his second shot and wound up three-putting for a bogey that dropped him into a second-place tie with Aoki. Green wound up in a three-way tie for fourth with Lane and Serizawa.

Dunlop Phoenix—¥160,000,000
Winner: Larry Mize

Nothing is likely to ever top his sensational victory in the 1987 Masters, but his mid-November triumph in one of Japan's two richest tournaments fits easily into the next notch of the ladder of success for Larry Mize, a four-stroke victor in the Dunlop Phoenix tournament. In fact, Mize has countered a victory drought in America since that memorable Masters with two wins in Japan—the Dunlop Phoenix and the 1988 Casio World Open.

Mize made his move at Phoenix Country Club in the second round, jumping two strokes into the lead with an eight-under-par 64 for 133 and held onto first place the rest of the way. Naomichi Ozaki, challenging for a title the second week in a row, climbed within a stroke of Mize Saturday. Ozaki, who scored his only 1989 victory in the Setonaikai Open back in March, had been the first-round leader by a stroke over Tom Watson with 66 and came back with 69 Saturday after a Friday 70 for his 205, and Mize shot 71 for 204. Larry shot a flawless 68 Sunday in wrapping up the victory, the fourth straight by an American in the Dunlop Phoenix, in which foreign players have won every year since the tournament's infancy except for Tsuneyuki Nakajima's triumph in 1985. Mize was 16 under par at 272.

Ozaki finished with 71 for 276, as Americans occupied three of the next four places in the final standings. Blaine McCallister was alone at 278, Tateo (Jet) Ozaki at 279 and Mike Reid and Jeff Sluman paired at 280. Larry Nelson, the Suntory winner in September, tied for seventh with Yoshikazu Yokoshima, the 54-hole runner-up who closed with 75.

Casio World Open—¥100,000,000
Winner: Isao Aoki

Considering the high calibre of the leading tournament players of Japan, one of the most incongruous of circumstances on the Japan Tour was the total monopoly of the Casio World Open by foreign players through its first eight years. Appropriately, Isao Aoki, one of the country's all-time greats, ended that negative string in the 1989 tournament. He did it in record fashion, though winning by a single stroke over defending champion Larry Mize, the previous week's victor in the Dunlop Phoenix.

For a while, it appeared one of the former Casio winners—43-year-old Hubert Green—might keep the tournament's all-foreigners string alive and score his first victory since that Casio triumph in 1985. Green slid one stroke in front in Friday's second round with 68-67—135 after Naomichi Ozaki, again a contender, opened in front with 66. Hubert held his lead with a 69 Saturday, then at 204 just a stroke in front of Mize (67-71-67) and Aoki (70-70-65) with a handful of other strong players close behind them.

Green couldn't maintain his pace Sunday and managed just a 75. That left the race for the title in the season's last big-money tournament to Aoki and Mize, who were tied through most of the round and never were more than a stroke behind at any time. Isao made the final birdie with a 15-foot putt at the 16th hole and hung on for the victory as Mize barely missed eight-footers there and at the 17th and three-putted for par after reaching the green in two on the par-five finishing hole. He missed a four-foot second putt that would have forced a playoff. Instead, Aoki rang up his 55th victory on the Japan Tour and second of the season, besting Lee Trevino's record 275 in the inaugural Casio.

Japan Series Hitachi Cup—¥60,000,000
Winner: Akiyoshi Omachi

Elation for Akiyoshi Omachi . . . frustration again for Tsuneyuki Nakajima . . . three out of four "ain't bad" for Masashi (Jumbo) Ozaki. That was the story line of the Japan Series Hitachi Cup, the season-climaxing, split-course tournament bringing together the winners and top 20 money-winners of the year on the Japan Tour.

Omachi's joy was in the victory as he came from seven strokes off the pace in the final round at Tokyo's Yomiuri Country Club with a six-under-par 66 to capture his third and most important title. The 31-year-old Omachi, who qualified for the tournament with his victory in the Mizuno Open, finished with a 278, rounds of 70-73-69 preceding the blazing final rush.

Nakajima's frustration deepened as he blew a four-stroke lead after leading from the start, once again failing in his quest for his first tour victory since the 1987 Tokai Classic, a puzzling drought for a player of Nakajima's ability. Ironically, his best earlier chance in 1989 came in the Mizuno, in which Omachi also passed him and won in the final round. In the Series, Nakajima posted rounds of 69-68 at Osaka's Yomiuri Country Club for a three-stroke lead over Aussies Graham Marsh and Brian Jones, then widened the gap to four with another 68 for 205 when the tournament resumed after the travel day at the Tokyo Yomiuri. His closest pursuers then were Katsuyoshi Tomori at 209 and Larry Nelson at 210. Omachi was virtually unnoticed at 212 before his Sunday charge and Nakajima's retreat.

Jumbo Ozaki had eyes on a Grand Slam sweep of Japan's four major prestige titles with the Match Play, PGA and Open already in the bag, but an opening 74 blunted his chances, and he eventually tied for seventh at 284.

Daikyo Open—¥80,000,000
Winner: Nobuo Serizawa

Nobuo Serizawa put some fancy finishing touches on Japan's 1989 season in the Daikyo Open at Daikyo Country Club on Okinawa, overpowering the field almost from start to finish in registering a four-stroke victory with a 17-under-par 271, one of the lowest winning scores of the year. The win was his second on the circuit, complementing his victory in the 1987 Nikkei Cup.

With his first of three consecutive 67s, Serizawa shared the first-round lead with Toshimitsu Kai, Brian Jones, Noriichi Kawakami and Motomasa Aoki, then opened a monstrous six-stroke lead with the 134, with Jones, Hiroshi Makino and Yoshimi Niizeki at a distant 140. The margin went to seven Saturday with the third 67 for 201, David Ishii shooting 66 for 208 and Masahiro Kuramoto 64 for 210. They finished in that order as Nobuo closed with 70. Ishii made up three strokes with his 67 for 275, and Kuramoto finished seven behind at 278 after a 68. Ishii and Kuramoto, two frequent winners on the circuit, thus came close but missed in final bids for a 1989 victory.

16. The Women's Tours

When future historians of women's professional golf look back on the 1989 season, surely they will be amazed at what they find. The name of Betsy King will keep showing up on every page they turn.

The 34-year-old product of Furman University won six times on the U.S. LPGA Tour on the way to a record $654,132 in earnings and Player-of-the-Year honors. All this without a visit to victory circle in any of the season's final eight tournaments or even participating in the finale, the Mazda Japan Classic where in most years season honors are determined.

Her earnings eclipsed by over $150,000 the previous record set by Pat Bradley in 1986, and her six victories were the most since Nancy Lopez won eight times in 1979. King won the first event of the year, the Jamaica Classic, and along the way added such important tournaments as the U.S. Women's Open and Nestle World Championship.

Sharing the spotlight with King in 1989 was fellow Furman graduate Beth Daniel. She had gone almost four years without a victory before winning four of the season's final 10 events, and she did not play in three of the other six. Daniel also finished second four times and won the Vardon Trophy with a stroke average of 70.38.

So dominating were King and Daniel that only two other players won more than once: Nancy Lopez with three, including the LPGA Championship, and Juli Inkster with two, the Nabisco Dinah Shore being one of them. The other major title, the du Maurier Classic, was won by Tammie Green.

In the only other significant news of 1989, the LPGA pulled up stakes in Houston, Texas, and moved its corporate headquarters to Daytona Beach, Florida.

On the European Tour, Marie-Laure De Lorenzi took top honors with three consecutive victories early in the year, and finished with £77,534. Alison Nicholas also had three wins and was second with £56,528. Others on the 20-event circuit with more than one triumph were Kitrina Douglas (who was third for the year with £48,534) and Dennise Hutton.

Among the 10 one-time winners were superstar Laura Davies and American Jane Geddes, who claimed the biggest prize, the Weetabix Ladies British Open.

Jamaica Classic—$500,000
Winner: Betsy King

The Ladies Professional Golf Association gathered for the inaugural Jamaica Classic in early January and found that the island was still intact from the past September's onslaught of Hurricane Gilbert. Also very much intact after a short off-season was the game of Betsy King.

Just as Gilbert made a shambles of the island for a few days, so did King of the field for three days over the Tryall Resort, a course that played 6,200 yards and to a par of 71. King literally had one of those weeks, 17 birdies, six bogeys, and led wire-to-wire with rounds of 64-68-70—202 to win by six strokes over Nancy Lopez.

The course and conditions did as much as King to keep the elite field of last year's top 72 money winners on the verge of nervous breakdowns. The greens were fast, very fast, the winds blew a gale and rainstorms raged in the morning. Never have so few hit so many balls out of bounds, and four-putts were as common as rum and Coca-Cola at the island's favorite watering hole.

"No doubt my 64 in the first round set up the whole week," said King, who on the first hole sank a putt so long that if she had measured it would have brought a warning for delay of play. "It was one of the best starts I've had anywhere."

She played catch-me-if-you-can and nobody came close. When she followed that 64 with a 68 and led Lopez seven, you could hear the fat lady singing from one end of the island to the other. The party was over.

King won an easy $75,000, Lopez $46,250. The LPGA was a bigger winner when new commissioner William Blue announced the Jamaica Tourist Board was picking up the $500,000 season-long bonus points pool abandoned by Mazda.

Oldsmobile Classic—$300,000
Winner: Dottie Mochrie

Those who took in the new Oldsmobile Classic at Stonebridge Country Club didn't know whether to be happy for Dottie Mochrie or feel sorry for Beth Daniel.

On the one hand, Mochrie, in her second year, won for the first time. On the other, the veteran Daniel lost for the second time in less than a year in a playoff, ran her streak of runner-up finishes to five in just over two years and extended her non-winning streak to three years and one month.

Both players had to sleep on this one an extra night. They were tied at 9-under 279 after 72 holes and were still tied four playoff holes later.

Mochrie had anything but a restful night. She had bogeyed the 18th hole to let Daniel into the playoff and that's the hole where play was to be resumed. But it was Daniel who bogeyed it in the early morning dew and victory went to the 23-year-old New Yorker who, like Daniel, is a graduate of Furman University.

"I always thought I could win out here," Mochrie said. "This takes the pressure off for the rest of the year. Who knows, maybe I'll win two or three times."

Her victory was impressive. She not only had to beat a veteran in the playoff, but had to chase down Hall-of-Famer Nancy Lopez in the final round. Lopez finished third and Sandra Palmer a distant fourth.

ORIX Hawaiian Open—$300,000
Winner: Sherri Turner

After all the wondrous things she accomplished in 1988, Sherri Turner sort of wondered what she could expect in 1989. She didn't have to wait long; only three weeks, in fact, before winning again.

No. 1 came in the $300,000 ORIX Hawaiian Open at the Turtle Bay Resort. And it was a blowout, four strokes over Sara Ann McGetrick and five over Deb Richard and Colleen Walker.

"It's difficult for me after last season. I'm trying to pretend it's still 1988," Turner said at the 36-hole mark, one shot out of the lead. "I haven't set any goals this year, because, what kind of goals do you set after a year like last year?"

In 1988, Turner won twice, had a couple of seconds and thirds and was the leading money winner with $350,821. In some circles, she was named LPGA Player of the Year.

Turner started the final round one shot off the lead of Alice Ritzman and McGetrick. After nine holes, she was three up and cruising.

"Sometimes it's tough to be out front early in the round and still win," she said. "But I'd done so once last year and that really helped me today. I had a very positive attitude."

Some of that rubbed off on McGetrick, who said she learned a lot by watching Turner during the final round. "That's going to help me somewhere. I just know it is," McGetrick said.

It was also a pretty good week for Sue Ertle and Sherri Steinhauer, despite finishing well back in the pack and making only $468 and $322, respectively. Sponsor ORIX (Orient Leasing Group of Japan) gave each of them $10,000 for scoring holes-in-one on the 153-yard par-three 17th.

Women's Kemper Open—$400,000
Winner: Betsy King

If ever there was a week to try the patience of these LPGA nomads, this was it. Rather than fun in the sun at the Mirage-Princeville Resort, it was pain in the rain.

The Helen Curtis Pro-Am was forced indoors and played on carpet, not grass, the tournament itself reduced to 52 holes and in the first round nearly everyone shot 60-something because they played only 16 holes.

None of this seemed to bother Betsy King, however. She won the title for the second straight year and became a two-time winner after only four events. She shot 63-72-67—202 and beat Jane Geddes by two strokes.

"I've been lucky so far. I've been in position (to win) and taken advantage of it," King said. "I'm sure things will even out before the season is over. I just hope I'm not going to flatten out."

King shared the first-round lead at 63 with Jody Rosenthal. That was only two under par of 65 for the 16-hole layout. She gave way to Nancy Brown after 36, then took control of the tournament midway during Sunday's final 18. She couldn't relax, however, until both Geddes and Nancy Lopez failed to reach the 18th green in two shots to set up possible tying eagle attempts.

Lopez hit her second shot fat and into the lake that fronts the green, and Geddes came up just short of the putting surface.

"Having to make eagle just to tie shows you how good Betsy was playing," Geddes said. "She has fond memories of this place and played very, very well considering the conditions."

King won the season's first event in Jamaica, starting a string of four straight victories by graduates of Furman University.

Circle K Tucson Open—$300,000
Winner: Lori Garbacz

It took Lori Garbacz more years than she likes to remember, but she finally scaled the peak of her personal mountain in the Circle K Tucson Open. Not only did she win her first career LPGA event, but outlasted her nemesis, Nancy Lopez, in doing it.

Garbacz had gone 10 years and 245 tournaments without winning, then took this one in a walkaway. With rounds of 69-68-67-70—274, she won by four over Lopez, who hadn't been a factor all week before shooting a final round 67.

"We've been friends and rivals since junior golf days," Garbacz said of Lopez, "but before today I was always the one doing the congratulating. Every time we went head-to-head, she won."

Martha Nause carried the banner the first 64 holes, holding onto a one-shot lead with eight to play. But she bogeyed Nos. 12, 14, 15 and 16 and slipped into a tie for third.

"After No. 15, I knew it was my tournament to win or lose," Garbacz said. "Then I looked at the leaderboard and there was Nancy. This time, though, it had a different ending."

Lopez was only four back after 36, but a Saturday 72 left her trailing by seven. At one point, she strung together 23 straight pars before making a birdie.

"Par used to be pretty good out here, but not anymore," Lopez said. "I'm excited for Lori. I've known her for a long, long time, and it was neat the way it happened because I finished second to her."

It was quite an emotional moment for the 30-year-old Indiana native. She had struggled with her game since the death of her teacher, Davis Love, Jr., in November. "I was devastated and it's taken me a long time to get over it." Then she brushed back the tears that had formed in her eyes and said, "This one is for you, Davis."

Standard Register Turquoise Classic—$400,000
Winner: Allison Finney

There's something about the Standard Register Turquoise Classic that seems to bring out the best in players seeking their first LPGA victory. The latest of those was Allison Finney, who ended a six-year drought and became the sixth woman to make this tournament her first victory.

Fact is, Finney had never won more than $66,972 in a season, but the

$60,000 winner's share of the $400,000 purse took care of that, also. With rounds of 66-69-74-73—282, she beat Beth Daniel by a stroke at Moon Valley Country Club in Phoenix.

Finney was never far out of the lead. She led after the first round, second round, trailed Daniel only a stroke to start the fourth round, but moved ahead on the second hole with a par to Daniel's double bogey. Along the way in that final round, she had to withstand a slight rally by Penny Hammel who drew to within one before playing the back nine in 45.

As had been the case all week, the tournament eventually came down to Finney and Daniel. On the final hole, leading by one, Finney's approach stopped 25 feet from the hole; Daniel got within birdie range with a nice approach to nine feet. Finney lagged to within two feet, then watched Daniel miss her birdie attempt.

"When Beth was putting, my only thoughts were I wish I had a tap-in situation," Finney said. "It was only two feet, but it looked like 20 to me."

Of her missed tying putt, Daniel said, "I thought it was going to break right, but it was a straight putt. I misread it, but I hit it where I wanted."

Nabisco Dinah Shore—$500,000
Winner: Juli Inkster

When Juli Inkster is bad, not even she knows where the next shot is going. But when she's good, well, you get almost perfection. And she was good, very, very good in the Nabisco Dinah Shore, the LPGA's first major championship of the year.

With rounds of 66-69-73-71—279, Inkster led wire-to-wire and cruised in with a five-stroke victory over JoAnne Carner and Tammie Green for her second Dinah Shore triumph. She won her first in 1984.

There was little to indicate that this would be Inkster's week. During the first six weeks of the LPGA Tour, Inkster had won only $11,313 in the four tournaments she played, just 49th on the money list. At Mission Hills, she won $80,000.

The 28-year-old former three-time U.S. Amateur champion from Northern California led by two after the first round, by four at the halfway point and by five beginning the final round. Only three times over the final 36 holes was she seriously challenged, once by Daniel and twice by Carner.

Daniel eliminated herself by making double bogey on the third hole on Saturday and by playing the final five in four over. On Sunday, Big Mamma Carner kept nipping at Inkster's heels. On the sixth hole, Inkster drove directly behind a large palm, but lifted a nine-iron shot over it to 12 feet and made par. On the 12th, leading by three, Inkster needed three shots to reach the front of the green, then sank a 20-footer for par.

That was the tournament. She birdied Nos. 16 and 18 to come home like a champion.

"I was getting a little wobbly halfway through the final round," Inkster said. "The putt at No. 12 was big. No lead is too big in this tournament. If I miss that point, my lead is two and there's Big Mamma nipping at my heels."

Carner, just two weeks shy of her 50th birthday, played like the Carner of old. She hit 33 of the last 36 greens after hitting only five in the second round.

"I'm happy with the way I played," Carner said. "Juli was just too good this week. I had two chances to pick up ground, two places where she looked to be in serious trouble. But she survived them both and certainly deserved to win."

Green, a third-year pro from Ohio, would have been a bigger factor except for a third-round 75. Still, it was her best finish on the tour.

"It was a great week for me," Inkster said. "I never was real nervous, on edge, even before the last round. I hit my irons great all week and I putted well. To win a major, you have to putt well."

With her victory, Inkster became the first player to qualify for the Nestle World Championship later in the year at Stouffer PineIsle Resort outside Atlanta.

"I'm looking forward to that," she said. "For some reason, I've not done well there and I'm determined to make a better showing there this year."

Red Robin Kyocera Inamori Classic—$300,000
Winner: Patti Rizzo

When Patti Rizzo hit the LPGA Tour in 1982, she had superstar written all over her game: her swing, her touch around the greens, and her course management.

That hasn't happened. Every once in a while, she'll give you a glimpse of it, though. One such glimpse came in the hills just outside San Diego, in the Red Robin Kyocera Inamori Classic, where with a final-round 67, she won for the fourth time in seven years.

Oddly, Rizzo is more comfortable playing in Japan than in the United States. She has won six times in Japan, where she's instantly recognized wherever she goes. In America, she considers herself just one of those in "the pack of ants" who make up the LPGA Tour.

"I've always tended to concentrate better in Japan and get better energy from the people," she said. "In Japan, it's fun because I'm the intimidator, not the intimidated."

The most intimidating thing about this stop on the LPGA Tour was the heat. It was in triple figures for the first three rounds and it seemed hotter considering the hilly terrain of Stone Ridge Country Club. As a result, there was a short field of only 138, rather than the normal 144.

Rizzo opened with an ordinary 73, five strokes behind the pace-setters Cindy Rarick, Deedee Lasker and Dale Eggeling. She shot 67 on Friday, but still trailed Nancy Brown and defending champion Laura Davies by four strokes. Rizzo moved into second place after a third round 68 left her only two behind Brown. Martha Nause was third, another shot back.

It was all Rizzo and Nause on Sunday, however. Brown disappeared with a bogey-riddled 78. And Rizzo nailed down the title midway of the back nine with a couple of birdies for a two-stroke victory.

An interesting sidelight to the tournament was the play of 14-year-old Emilee Klein, the reigning California Women's Amateur champion. She opened with an 82, but came back with a respectable 74 on Friday.

Al Star/Centinela Hospital Classic—$450,000
Winner: Pat Bradley

It was like old times at 43-year-old Rancho Park, a municipal course outside Los Angeles. The names on the leaderboard after 54 holes in the Centinela Hospital Classic had a familiarity to them—Pat Bradley, Hollis Stacy and Nancy Lopez.

And none was happier, or more worthy than Bradley when her name topped the list after 54 holes. Forget the $67,500 first-place check, even if it was her largest since 1986.

For at last, Bradley had made it all the way back from over a year-long bout with hyperthyroidism. Only a year ago, at this same tournament, Bradley shot 82-87 and left dispirited and very sick. A couple of weeks later, her disease was diagnosed and she began to treat it.

"I'm a very lucky person," said a tearful Bradley, who shot rounds of 72-67-69—208 to win by a single stroke over Stacy and Lopez. "Until my disease was diagnosed, I thought I was having a nervous breakdown and they were coming to take me away."

It was the old Bradley who took control of this tournament on the 12th hole of the final round. At one point Sunday, eight players were tied for the lead, but at the 12th, Bradley made birdie, Lopez made bogey and there was no catching her.

Bradley became ill late in the 1987 season. At first, she dismissed it as just fatigue, but as the weeks and months rolled along, it only got worse. She considered giving up the game and going back to Massachusetts to work in the family ski and tennis shop.

"The harder I worked at my golf, the worse I got," she said. "I was ashamed of the way I was playing. Now, I'll never take my career and the game for granted again. I've been granted a second chance at my profession."

USX Classic—$250,000
Winner: Betsy King

When Betsy King arrived at the USX Golf Classic in Gulfport, Florida, she wasn't particularly dazzled by the Pasadena Yacht and Country Club course. It was too easy.

Four days later, she counted her blessings that it was. King came from four strokes behind—tied for third—caught Lynn Adams with a final round 66, then won on the first hole of a playoff.

The first-place check wasn't much, only $37,500, but it was enough to push King into a rather select group of career $2-million money winners that included Pat Bradley, Nancy Lopez, Amy Alcott and JoAnne Carner. It also was her third victory of the year.

"You have to shoot low scores here," King said upon arriving at the Florida resort, "and I don't know if I like that. You feel you have to make every one. You're going to see a lot of low numbers."

It didn't hurt King's chances that she was the big fish in this little pond. Only eight of the top 20 money winners were entered in the $250,000 tournament. The field consisted of two amateurs, three club pros and 60 other players from outside the top 100 money winners.

The USX was hurt by two things. One, the LPGA had just completed a seven-tournament West Coast swing, and two, it fell between the $450,000 Al Star/Centinela and the $425,000 Sara Lee Classic. Plus, it was a 72-hole event.

It didn't lack for dramatics, however. Adams hadn't won since the 1983 Orlando Classic and had made a remarkable recovery from disc and nerve damage in her back that same year. She opened with three solid rounds of 69-68-68 and led Lori Garbacz by three with one to play, with King tied for fourth.

Here's where the ease of Pasadena came to King's rescue. On any other course she might have been too far behind, but this was birdie paradise.

Sara Lee Classic—$450,000
Winner: Kathy Postlewait

As household names go on the LPGA Tour, Kathy Postlewait's would draw puzzled looks when mentioned in the same context as those of Nancy Lopez, Patty Sheehan, Betsy King and Colleen Walker.

But when the final putt had fallen in the Sara Lee Classic, this nice 39-year-old veteran reduced the "names" to also-rans and slipped away with the $63,750 first-place check. Entering the final round, 14 players, including those big names, were within five shots or less.

Postlewait never gave them a chance, however. She birdied three of the first five and said adios to those who would deny her fourth career victory and third in three years. She shot a final round 69 and beat Val Skinner by one, Sheehan and Lopez by three and King by seven.

King, who has won three times this year, started one stroke back and shot 75; first-round leader Colleen Walker was only two behind, but shot 73; Lopez began three behind and shot 70 to tie for third with Sheehan, who made up ground with a 67.

"I played solid all week," said Postlewait, whose biggest victory was the 1987 Mazda LPGA Championship. "I hadn't played very well lately, but everything came into place here."

She had played so badly—three missed cuts and a withdrawal in eight events—that she consulted a sports psychologist prior to coming to Hermitage Golf Club in Nashville and his prescription was to relax, have fun and be patient. It worked like a charm.

"Golf was getting to be frustrating," she said. "It wasn't fun. I was treating it like a job. Seeing the psychologist has helped me appreciate the game more. Now I don't let things bother me the way they did. Golf is just a game. That's the attitude I have to keep."

Postlewait moved into the lead with a second round 66 and never lost it.

"It has taken me a long time to learn how to play this game," she said. "Golf is a difficult game by itself, but when you put pressure on yourself, it becomes almost impossible. It takes some people longer to reach the level you need to be at to win."

Crestar Classic—$300,000
Winner: Juli Inkster

There's something about being a defending champion that brings out the best in Juli Inkster. Take the Crestar Classic in Chesapeake, Virginia, for example. Or the Nabisco Dinah Shore, Safeco Classic or Atlantic City. She won them one year, then did it again the next.

The latest of these was the Crestar Classic. In 1988, she eagled the first hole of a playoff to beat Nancy Lopez, Rosie Jones and Betsy King at Sleepy Hole in Suffolk, Virginia.

This time, though, there were no such dramatics as Inkster breezed home with a five-stroke victory over Beth Daniel at Greenbrier Country Club. She did it on rounds of 69-72-69—210, then gave herself a much deserved pat on the back.

"I've been out here six years and have won 13 tournaments, including three majors," said the 28-year-old Californian. "I think I'm doing pretty well. I don't think anyone out here in her 20s has won as many as I have. In fact, I know nobody has."

She was right. Closest to Inkster was Jane Geddes, who was a year older and six victories short of that mark.

There was more for Inkster to deal with than being the defending champion in the Crestar. There was cold and rain and wind Friday and Saturday and having to play 28 holes on Sunday before her week's work was done.

When the final round began, she was tied for third with Daniel and Liselotte Neumann, a stroke behind Jody Rosenthal and Cindy Figg-Currier.

Before high winds, lightening and rain forced her to complete Saturday's second round on Sunday morning, Rosenthal had two five-year-old LPGA records in sight. She had strung together six straight birdies, two short of Mary Beth Zimmerman's record of eight, and had eight birdies overall, three shy of the 11 Vicki Fergon made in 1984.

The moment was lost with the delay, however. She parred her first hole when play resumed Sunday, made only one more birdie and ended the round bogey, bogey to fall back into a tie with Figg-Currier, who resumed play by going birdie, eagle, birdie.

All except Inkster, however, gave in to the elements during the final round, leaving her to coast home. Daniel and Neumann shot 74s, Rosenthal 77 and Figg-Currier 76.

Daniel was second for the third time in the young season and it was her eighth runner-up finish since her last victory, in 1985.

"I feel for Beth," Inkster said. "At one point two years ago, I went 16 months without winning and started asking myself, 'When am I going to win again?' When Beth does win, I think they will come in bunches."

Chrysler Plymouth Classic—$275,000
Winner: Cindy Rarick

Cindy Rarick hadn't experienced much success in 1989 until she came to the Chrysler-Plymouth Classic. She had won only $41,000 and change. Then in the space of three days, the blonde Arizonian won everything in sight.

Rarick started her week's Triple Crown on Wednesday, winning the pre-tournament shootout and $3,000. Then she led wire-to-wire with rounds of 70-72-72—214, 5-under on the par-73 Bamm Hollow Country Club course in Lincroft, New Jersey, for her first victory of the year. And on top of the $41,250 winner's share of the purse, came a $2,700 solid gold pin bordered by diamonds, given in memory of Peter Busatti, founder of the tournament.

"A great, great week," said Rarick afterwards. "Leading all the way was special because I didn't give in to the pressure of all the great players who were chasing me."

Rarick was the only player to tour the 6,410-yard course in sub-par numbers each day, and over the final 18 holes was unflappable in the presence of playing partner Laura Davies, who eventually finished second. Defending champion Nancy Lopez and Alice Ritzman tied for third.

Rarick shared the first-round lead with Davies and Marci Bozarth and went into round three tied with Davies and Sherri Steinhauer. Bozarth couldn't maintain her first-round pace and shot 77-75 to finish 15th, while Steinhauer faded to 76 on Sunday with a bogey, bogey, bogey finish and wound up fifth.

Rarick got herself clear of the co-leaders on the first hole of Sunday's final round and though tied twice by Davies never was out of the lead. She took it for good with a par on No. 11 and sealed the victory with a par on No. 16, making a miracle four-iron recovery shot that had to get around a small tree, over a bigger one and carry a creek. It did all those things and came to rest 22 feet from the hole.

"When you play a hole like that, it makes you tingle all over," Rarick said.

Mazda LPGA Championship—$500,000
Winner: Nancy Lopez

If, as reports indicate, the LPGA is moving its championship out of Kings Island, Ohio, and leaving Jack Nicklaus's Grizzly Course to the PGA Senior Tour, it did so with a bang in 1989.

Few will likely forget this Mazda LPGA Championship won by Nancy Lopez with a dash of magic over the final eight holes that finally wore down Japan's Ayako Okamoto.

Lopez didn't lead after any of the first three rounds, shooting 71-69-68, but nobody did it better on Sunday as she finished with a 66 for a 14-under total of 274 and won by two over Okamoto to capture her 40th career LPGA victory.

"I was not aware at all what I had scored," Lopez said. "I was taking it one shot at a time. It was a shock when I got into the scoring tent and added it up to 66. Then, I got excited."

The first round belonged to a couple of other veterans, Pat Bradley and Sandra Haynie, both with 67s. On Friday, it was a different pair as Betsy King added a 67 to her opening 69 for 136 and a one-stroke lead over Okamoto's 137 on rounds of 69-68. Lopez was hanging around, tied for fourth, four strokes back.

Moving day is always Saturday and it produced a leaderboard you could take to the Hall of Fame. Okamoto led the parade with Patty Sheehan, who had 66, just one back, followed by Lopez two back and King, Bradley and Allison Finney only four in arrears.

By the time the field turned for home on Sunday, however, it was a two-player tournament—Lopez and Okamoto. Sheehan disappeared with a 78, as did King. Bradley couldn't make a birdie and shot 73 along with Finney. Susan Sanders came out of the pack to shoot a closing 68, the best in her 27 years and would eventually finish third.

But the leaders hardly noticed. They were too involved in winning the tournament, which tilted Lopez's way as the result of a three-putt bogey on No. 10 that dropped her out of the lead, one stroke behind Okamoto.

"I got mad after three-putting for bogey on No. 10," Lopez said. "That got my attention. I needed to turn my game up a notch, concentrate more, and I guess I did that."

Obviously. She chipped in for birdie on No. 11, made a 12-footer for another birdie at 12, nearly holed out from the fairway at 14 and finished birdie, birdie at 17 and 18.

"I figured I needed at least to par in from 16 and make Ayako make birdies," Lopez said. "Seventeen and 18 aren't really birdie holes. What a feeling it was after making a birdie at 17. I had to contain myself. And what a feeling it was when I came up 18 and knew I had it won, all those wonderful people cheering and calling my name. Then I birdied and the hugging began."

Okamoto simply became swamped in the Lopez wave. At the 15th, needing a birdie to remain within a stroke, Okamoto missed from five feet.

"Nancy is No. 1, the best," a gracious Okamoto said after the round. "When she is playing like that, not many people can beat her. I take my hat off to her."

With her victory, not only did Lopez win the $75,000 winner's share of the purse, she received another Mazda, her 10th.

Corning Classic—$325,000
Winner: Ayako Okamoto

Only a week after she came up three shots shy of Nancy Lopez in the Mazda LPGA Championship, Japan's Ayako Okamoto had 'em waving the white flag of surrender in the Corning Classic.

Okamoto shot rounds of 69-66-67-70—272 over the Corning (New York) Country Club course and won by a whopping six strokes over Beth Daniel, who finished second for the fourth time in 1989.

The victory put to rest the whatever-happened-to-Okamoto questions. She had played poorly early in the year due to recurring tendonitis in her left elbow, then taken almost a month off to let it heal before returning to the tour for the LPGA Championship.

Oddly, Okamoto had not planned to play in the Corning Classic, but buoyed by her play in the LPGA decided at the last moment to do so, which cost her $100, the amount of the fine for a late entry. That became mere peanuts when she picked up the $48,750 winner's share of the purse.

This was vintage Okamoto, especially in the final two rounds. She needed only 26 putts in Saturday's third round of 67, enabling her to take a five-shot lead over Daniel. And Sunday's 27 putts kept anyone from making a charge.

"When she's playing the way she's playing now, I think she's unbeatable," said Daniel before the final round. "She's a better chipper and putter than I am anyway, but if she keeps putting like that, there's no way I'll catch her."

Okamoto's biggest challenge came from within. There was the memory of blowing a six-shot lead in the final round of the 1987 du Maurier Classic and losing to Jody Rosenthal. It seemed to be working against her when Daniel cut her lead to two with a birdie to Okamoto's bogey at No. 10.

"When that happened, I thought I had no chance to win this week," Okamoto said. "I remembered what happened in the du Maurier and thought it was happening again. Lucky for me, it didn't."

Daniel had a hand in that. She bogeyed No. 11, Okamoto birdied it and then played the next seven holes three under par.

"I showed up, but my golf game didn't," Daniel said. "It was a struggle."

Rochester International—$300,000
Winner: Patty Sheehan

Patty Sheehan described it as 72 holes of "blood, guts and dirt," after putting the Rochester International into her ledger book at Locust Hill Country Club. What she was saying was that while it wasn't pretty, she wasn't going to apologize.

It was the first victory of the year for Sheehan and the 20th of her career. More importantly, though, it was sweet revenge for the sudden-death loss she suffered here a year earlier after carrying a one-shot lead to the final hole.

Even more enjoyable was the fact the victory came in a playoff, just as did the defeat in 1989. Her victim was Ayako Okamoto, on the first hole. Sheehan had rounds of 68-73-66-71—278 and won $45,000.

"I can't believe I won this tournament the way I played," Sheehan said. "For three days, I was playing catch-up golf and only on one day was I rock solid. But I didn't steal it. I deserved it."

To put it in proper perspective, Sheehan played 70 holes and one playoff hole in five under par. She matched that on one hole, the 459-yard, par-five 17th. On Saturday, she made a rare double-eagle two there and on Sunday, when she needed it most, she eagled it and tied Okamoto for the lead.

At No. 18, Sheehan missed the green long and it looked bad for her when Okamoto's shot stopped five feet from the hole. Making things worse was the previous year she also missed the green long while holding a stroke lead, and when she failed to get up and down, it dropped her into a three-way tie with Nancy Lopez and Mei-Chi Cheng, which Cheng eventually won.

"I wasn't even thinking about that because this shot was a different kind of shot," Sheehan said. "The one last year was more difficult."

The result was different this time because Sheehan did get up and down and Okamoto missed her five-foot putt for a winning birdie. And on the first playoff hole, No. 18, again, it was Okamoto who failed to get up and down for par and Sheehan two-putted for hers.

Sheehan's double eagle was the first of the year on the LPGA Tour and the first since Chris Johnson recorded one in the 1987 Circle-K Tucson Open.

"To make a double eagle anytime is really something, but what made this one so special was that it came at a time when I needed to make something happen," Sheehan said. "It was the greatest shot of my life."

Planters Pat Bradley International—$400,000
Winner: Robin Hood

In 1988, it was Martha Nause who came to the Pat Bradley International without a career victory and left with her first. And in 1989, 24-year-old Robin Hood followed Nause to the winner's circle after having won the grand total of just over $34,000 in the two years since leaving Oklahoma State.

And like Nause the year before, Hood survived a first-hole playoff in the third round just to make the final shootout, under the Stableford scoring system. She went out early Sunday, made three birdies early and three late to post a score of 16 points and let the field shoot at it. Nobody came close. Finishing second with 11 were Patti Rizzo and Kathy Postlewait.

In the beginning, this wasn't a field guaranteed to excite fans of women's golf. It lost Nancy Lopez because of her father's illness and never had Betsy King, Beth Daniel, Patty Sheehan, Juli Inkster or Sherri Turner. As Lopez said, "I know a couple of players who didn't come here this year because of the Stableford. I'm here because I enjoy the people and I like the golf course. I'll probably always come back, but I like the format better the old way."

The Stableford works this way. An eagle is worth five points, birdie three, bogey minus one and anything worse minus two. Shoot 18 straight pars and you're out because par is worth nothing. One day Dawn Coe shot even-par 72, but did it with five birdies and five bogeys, plus 15 for the birdies, minus 10 for the bogeys for a net five and survival. Kris Monaghen also shot even par, one birdie, one bogey, and was eliminated.

The first-round leader was Myra Blackwelder with 21 points and Patti Rizzo led after two with 28, good for $4,000. Debbie Massey compiled 13 points on Saturday, the same day that Hood got only three. Still they all started even on Sunday, including the host, Pat Bradley, who just made it with birdies on two of the final three holes. For the round, Bradley was four over par and a lot of non-survivors had done better in regards to par. But old man par doesn't mean anything in this format.

"That's what this format is all about," Bradley said. "That's the way it's supposed to be."

Lady Keystone Open—$300,000
Winner: Laura Davies

Put the longest hitter on the LPGA Tour together with one of the most savvy and give them the opportunity to go head-to-head for a championship and you have golf at its finest.

And that's what it came down to in the closing holes of the Lady Keystone Open in Hershey, Pennsylvania—big Laura Davies and wily Pat Bradley. This time, strength won out over experience as Davies birdied the last hole for a one-stroke victory.

Davies, who made the U.S. Women's Open her first LPGA victory two years ago, and Bradley were just two of five golfers who held a share of the lead heading down the final nine holes. Betsy King was there with Liselotte Neumann and Ok-Hee Ku.

But King and Neumann couldn't make anything but pars the rest of the way and finished tied for third, and Ku ran into a couple of bogeys and fell to seventh. That left it to Davies and Bradley to fight it out for the $45,000 first-place check. They went to the 18th tied at eight under par.

And in the end, it came down to Davies' touch, not power, as she sank a 35-foot putt for the victory.

"To be honest, I didn't think she would make that putt," said Bradley, who had scrambled from the trees to get in position for what she thought would be a par and sudden death. "I thought all I had to do was make my par and we'd play some more."

Davies wasn't the most confident person when she struck the putt. She was hoping to get it close and turned away after striking the ball.

"I looked at my caddy and he was jumping up and down, and that's when I knew it had gone in," Davies said.

Davies' caddy also was her cousin, who had taken Davies' putter after one of her victories in Great Britain. "I felt more confident with it and he's not getting it again," said Davies, who shot rounds of 67-73-67—207.

Although disappointed by the sudden turn of events, Bradley walked across the green and gave Davies a high-five. "I didn't win, but my performance sends a message—'Pat is back,'" Bradley said.

McDonald's Championship—$500,000
Winner: Betsy King

If the LPGA should come up with a fifth major to go with the Women's Open, Nabisco Dinah Shore, du Maurier Classic and its own LPGA Championship, McDonald's Championship would be it.

It has the purse of a major: $500,000, is run like a major, has the field of a major, and more times than not the winner has won a major championship.

And so it was in 1989, also. Betsy King—her again—came from four shots behind after three rounds to shoot 67 on Sunday and win by two, breaking the heart of Shirley Furlong, who for three days threatened to run away with the first prize.

It was King's fourth victory of the year, pushed her earnings to $365,000 and made her the odds-on-favorite to win Player of the Year honors.

But this wasn't the Betsy King story until the final round. The first and third round leads belonged to Furlong after a pair of robust 66s and in the middle of that Pat Bradley showed up with a 66 of her own to once again prove her illness is ancient history. Also taking a share of the spotlight was 31-year-old Deborah McHaffie, a six-foot blonde, dressed to kill, who's been playing golf only seven years.

As they headed into Sunday's finale, it was Furlong up by four over King and five in front of Bradley and McHaffie.

"It might be my turn to come from behind," said King, who in the last month had opportunities to win the LPGA, Rochester and Lady Keystone only to falter in the final round. "I'm due."

Furlong birdied the first two holes on Sunday, however, and went six ahead. It proved to be something she could not overcome. Never having been there, she didn't know how to act.

"All week I thought about one shot at a time and that kept me going," Furlong said. "But after those two birdies, all I could think about was my lead."

As they turned for home, Furlong's lead had dwindled to one over Bradley and King. Bradley got no closer with nine straight pars coming in, but King grabbed the lead on a two-shot swing at No. 11, then turned it on with birdies at Nos. 13, 14 and 17.

"I won this time with patience," King said. "I didn't have any choice because Shirley went up by six early. All I could do then was play like there was nobody else out there but me. Golf's a crazy game sometimes."

Furlong shot a final-round 73 and had to share second with Bradley, who had 68. McHaffie was alone in fourth and won $28,750, only $10,000 less than she'd made in three seasons.

du Maurier Classic—$600,000
Winner: Tammie Green

Sometimes it's the little things that turn also-rans into champions. For Tammie Green it was a pledge to "play this tournament totally relaxed and without fear," and then the act of writing it down and signing it at the insistence of her caddy, Jimmy Gilmour.

From that simple act, Green went on to victory in the du Maurier Classic, which not only was her first major championship but her first championship, period.

It wasn't easy, however. She had to be totally relaxed and without fear to come through with veterans like Betsy King, Nancy Lopez, Pat Bradley, Patty Sheehan and Amy Alcott, who were never more than a shot or two away.

"When I first came out here, these women were my idols," Green said. "I was afraid."

But she was not intimidated this time. King shot 67 to lead the first round, Green shot 68. King shot 69 on Friday, and Green did, too. She'd stared down the tour's leading money winner for 36 holes and it was King who finally blinked with a Saturday 74 to Green's 70. The three-shot cushion was just enough.

"I'm going to make birdies tomorrow," Green said after Saturday's third round. "I've never been in this position before, leading the final round, and the more birdies I make the more fun I'm going to have. I feel great."

She defended her statements with pride. When Bradley eagled No. 6 to pull within a shot, Green also eagled it a few minutes later and added a birdie on No. 7. When Lopez birdied No. 12 to move to within one, Green responded with one of her own.

And when it was over, Green, with her final round 72, had won by one over King and Bradley and two over Sheehan and Alcott.

"The only time I looked at the leaderboard was at nine and 18. I had nerves all day," said Green, who went to qualifying school four times before getting her card.

Jamie Farr Toledo Classic—$275,000
Winner: Penny Hammel

They say a lesson learned is one never forgotten, and to that Penny Hammel will say "Amen."

After taking the second-round lead in the Jamie Farr Toledo Classic with a six-under-par 66, she went home and remembered what happened at Phoenix earlier this year. Tied for the lead with nine to play, Hammel shot an embarrassing 45.

"I thought of that and told myself, 'You can win. You can win. Don't choke. Don't go out and shoot 80.'"

The next day, Hammel put herself in that zone where nothing can penetrate and shot even-par 71 to win for the first time since 1985, ironically the Jamie Farr Classic. The $41,250 first-place check was her largest.

Hammel needed tunnel vision in that final round. Breathing down her neck were Betsy King, Nancy Lopez, Liselotte Neumann and Hollis Stacy. "I just played the golf course; I wasn't thinking about who was behind me. This is a big stepping stone for me."

When Hammel won here in 1985, it took a final-round 65 to overtake Lopez, who was there again this year. She finished second, her fourth in four appearances in this tournament. Her final-round 68, as well as that of Stacy, brought them from five back but one short.

Lopez got to within one stroke after No. 15, but bogeyed the 16th after missing her four-foot par putt. Stacy hit 17 greens, but made only four birdies.

The tournament also produced one course record and an oh-so-close run at the LPGA all-time scoring record of 62, set by Mickey Wright in 1964. Chris Johnson shot the course record, a 64, which vaulted her past 34 players and into a tie for fifth. Laura Davies flirted with the second when she went out in 29, but a double bogey, par, bogey finish ended it.

U.S. Women's Open Championship—$450,000
Winner: Betsy King

Just when it appeared the Women's U.S. Open was becoming a haven for foreign players new to the LPGA Tour, up stepped Betsy King to restore order, and on a course that looked more Scottish than American.

And King did it in the familiar style that had brought her four other LPGA victories this year. She opened with a 67, closed with a 68 and in between shot 71-72 for 278 and once again Nancy Lopez was denied the one major championship she hasn't won. Lopez finished second, four strokes behind.

It had been two years since an American had won the Women's Open. Laura Davies of England took it in 1986 and Liselotte Neumann won it in 1988. But this was King's show all the way; a masterpiece of shot-making and putting.

When it was over, nobody asked if she felt she was the best woman golfer in the world. Nobody needed to. It was her fifth victory of the year and she had finished in the top five in her last eight tournaments. The $80,000 winner's share of the $450,000 purse pushed her season earnings to an LPGA single-season high of $503,794, easily eclipsing Pat Bradley's 1986 total of $492,021.

"This is my 15th Open and you feel like you should win at some point," King said. "It's something you dream about as a kid and work for. For me, there's more history in this event than in any other."

As dominating as it was, it could have been more so. She led de Taya by one stroke after the first round, increased it to three strokes in the second round, and was four strokes ahead with four holes to play on Saturday. But she finished bogey, bogey, bogey, bogey and fell into a tie with Patty Sheehan. That lapse in concentration also gave Lopez new life. She was eight back after finishing her round, but only four behind when King finished hers.

"I can't wait for tomorrow night," said King after stumbling in with a 72. "I'm tired. I've had a chance to win every tournament the last nine holes the last five weeks. It wears you out. I'll be happy Sunday night, no matter what happens."

What happened was that King went out Sunday morning and birdied four of the first seven holes and put her game on cruise control on No. 8 after Sheehan, who had hung tight, made a triple-bogey seven. There were no more serious challenges. France's Marie-Laure de Lorenzo de Taya made an early charge with two quick birdies, but faded with a triple bogey on No. 9. Bradley moved up with a 68, but King was long gone.

Normally unemotional on the course, King almost lost it as she walked up the 18th fairway, her first Open firmly in hand. "The thing I get choked up about is when I'm at a concert or something and somebody gets a standing ovation. I always start crying then. It's funny when you get one yourself. I almost did cry at 18," King said.

Boston Five Classic—$350,000
Winner: Amy Alcott

Those who had whispered that maybe 33-year-old Amy Alcott was over the hill were nowhere to be found after the LPGA Tour and the Alcott Express rolled out of Danvers, Massachusetts, site of the Boston Five Classic.

With four rounds of 68, Alcott won for the first time in 1988, put an end to the slowest start of her career, proved the shoulder she hurt early in the year in Hawaii was healed, and moved to within two victories of entrance into the LPGA Hall of Fame.

This was vintage Alcott. She trailed Kathy Postlewait and Penny Hammel by one after the first round before joining a four-way jam at the top on Friday with Hammel, Cathy Marino and Shirley Furlong. On Saturday she birdied three of the first seven to break away from the pack by two.

There was no catching Alcott on Sunday. She birdied the second and fourth to stretch her lead to four and no one got within three after that. The players expected to wilt first—Marino and Marta Figueras-Dotti—handled the pressure well and shot 68 each to finish second and third. The players expected to challenge—Patty Sheehan and Jody Rosenthal—stumbled early. And the players who staged the best rallies—Beth Daniel and Ayako Okamoto—started too far back to cause Alcott much concern.

With her fourth straight 68 and 16-under 272, Alcott broke by two the tournament record set a year earlier by Colleen Walker. She called the victory almost inevitable.

"It was destiny," she said. "You can't play as well as I have the past couple of weeks and not win. When you're hurt and you start slow, you wonder whether you can get it going again. People have been saying all year they didn't think I could win again, but I didn't care what other people thought. I knew what I thought."

Atlantic City Classic—$225,000
Winner: Nancy Lopez

Odds are long that a string of six straight pars in the final round is good enough to win when you have four players tied for the lead. But considering this was Atlantic City, New Jersey, where odds are what it's all about, and the players in question were Hall-of-Famer Nancy Lopez, Chris Johnson, Vicki Fergon and Jennifer Wyatt, anything is possible.

Guess who won?

Lopez.

Wyatt and Johnson were the first to make it easier for Lopez. They both bogeyed the 15th hole. The 16th took care of Fergon. It wasn't even close. She pulled her tee shot into deep rough, left her second in the rough, No. 3 sailed wide of the green onto a sandy lie, No. 4 was chunked, No. 5 was 30 feet from the pin. Two putts later, she had made double bogey.

Lopez cruised in.

It was only Lopez's second victory of the season and plodding as it was, she wasn't complaining. She had been playing well since winning the LPGA Championship, but coming up short.

"I was beginning to wonder if I was snake-bit," Lopez said. "I had been playing so well, but finishing second and third so often. I certainly didn't think I could win with only pars, but everyone else faltered enough to let me."

Lopez opened with a 67 to lead by one over Betsy King, Johnson and Elaine Crosby. Round two went to Fergon, who had 66, and Johnson, by a stroke over Lopez and by two over King and Amy Alcott.

But on Sunday, it was Lopez, Johnson and Wyatt all the way.

It was the 41st victory of Lopez's career and her fifth in the state of New Jersey.

Greater Washington Open—$300,000
Winner: Beth Daniel

As victory droughts go, Beth Daniel's was a dandy. From her Rookie-of-the-Year beginning in 1979 to the Inamori Classic in 1985, the tall, slender South Carolinian won 14 times. Greatness was predicted. Maybe even the Hall of Fame.

No one would have predicted at the time that Daniel would not win again for four years. Certainly not Daniel.

But she didn't.

Those four years, three months and 23 days of frustration ended in the Greater Washington Open, where Daniel blitzed the field with opening rounds of 66-68, then cruised home with 18 pars on Sunday for an easy four-stroke victory over Sherri Turner.

"It was getting old. All those questions of 'Why aren't you winning?'" Daniel said. "I always knew I would win again, but as each year goes by you wonder more and more when it might happen."

Coming to Bethesda, Maryland, Daniel had been second four times and 10 times had finished in the top five. One of them was a five-hole playoff loss to Dottie Mochrie in the Oldsmobile Classic way back in January.

The winner's check of $52,500 sent Daniel past the $345,000 mark for the year and pushed her to within less than $125,000 of becoming the LPGA's seventh player to earn $2 million.

After building a four-shot lead through 36 holes, Daniel's final round strategy was fairways and greens. It became sound strategy when Penny Hammel, her closest competitor at that point, double-bogeyed the first hole.

"Making 18 pars is not my idea of the way to win a tournament," Daniel said. "But when Penny doubled the first hole, I knew as long as I didn't make any stupid mistakes, everybody else was pretty much out of it. Before we started, though, even leading by four I felt some pressure. I didn't want to read those 'Daniel Chokes' headlines."

Turner did her best to put pressure on Daniel. But she started too far back after opening 73-71, 10 shots behind Daniel's 134 total. Still, her closing 65 was only one off the course record.

"Halfway to the Hall of Fame," Daniel joked afterwards regarding the 30 victories it takes for entry. "At the rate I'm going, four years between victories, it will take me until I'm 90."

Nestle World Championship—$265,000
Winner: Betsy King

The Betsy King show came to the shores of Lake Lanier, Georgia, for what would be the final Nestle World Championship at Stouffer PineIsle Resort and left with little doubt about who should be the LPGA Player of the Year.

For three rounds King insisted she was hanging on by her fingernails, but in the end she had a firm grasp on her sixth victory of the year and the $83,500 winner's share of the $265,000 purse.

King opened with a six-under-par 66 to share the lead with defending champion Rosie Jones, came back with a shaky 71 on Friday to fall one behind Patty Sheehan, claimed the top spot again on Saturday with a 70 and eventually won by three over Sheehan and Pat Bradley with a closing 68.

The show began with a question. Would King continue her domination or would Nancy Lopez make this event her springboard to Player-of-the-Year honors? These two were 1-2 or 2-1 in just about every category the LPGA keeps. In the end, it was no contest. Lopez broke par in only one of the four rounds and finished a disappointing 15th in the elite field of 16. But before King could add this one to her already bulging portfolio, she had to survive several anxious moments during the middle of the final round.

Starting with a one-stroke lead over Sheehan and Bradley, King burst from the gate with birdies at Nos. 3 and 4, eagled the fifth and birdied the seventh to move to 14 under and four ahead of the field.

"Right about then, I started rehearsing my acceptance speech and my game went from pure to putrid," King said. "It looked like it was going to be easy and then it became very difficult."

Starting at No. 9, King popped up her tee shot and made bogey; escaped with a shaky par at No. 10, then pulled sand wedge shots at Nos. 11 and 12, again making bogeys. The lead was all but gone as Laura Davies had put on her own power display to pull to within one and Sheehan and Bradley were only two behind.

But at the level King plays, she can make on-course repairs and she did.

"As much as I practice, I know what's happening and I'm not afraid to make adjustments to get back on track," King said.

King birdied Nos. 13, 15 and 16 to regain control, and with it her pursuers began to falter. Davies could only par the 405-yard, par-five No. 16, and her party was over when she double-bogeyed the par-three 17th. Bradley bogeyed the 16th and Sheehan didn't make a birdie after No. 14.

When it was over, it was runner-up Bradley (with Sheehan) who first gave a hole-by-hole of the champion's round. "It didn't matter whether I put shots inside hers, five feet or 20 feet, you just knew she was going to make them," Bradley said. "And when she got into a little trouble in the middle of the round, she corrected the problem and does what she's done all year, finish strong."

A few weeks after the tournament, Nestle announced it was dropping its sponsorship after five years.

"It's a nice setting for a tournament, the people are great, but really I think this tournament should be played on a more difficult course," King said after her victory. "It's beautiful to walk around here, but not much fun to play. I think for a tournament of this calibre we need a bigger challenge."

Mitsubishi Motors Ocean State Open—$150,000
Winner: Tina Barrett

While the best in women's golf were competing for big bucks in the Nestle World Championship, the rest of women's golf were up in Cranston, Rhode Island, for the Mitsubishi Motors Ocean State Open, a testing ground for rookies and faltering veterans.

And this is where Pam Barrett made a career decision. The world would have to survive without another stockbroker and with another professional golfer.

The 23-year-old rookie from Longwood College in Farmville, Virginia, led almost from start to finish on the way to a six-under-par 210 and a two-stroke victory over Nancy Brown. Her previous best finish was a tie for 18th in the Planters Pat Bradley, and her winnings of $22,500 were easily the highest of her brief career.

Barrett's expectations were hardly optimistic. After shooting a first-round leading 67, she said, "No matter what happens from here, I can say I once led a tournament."

When she still had a share of the lead with Dottie Mochrie after Saturday's second round, she explained, "I've got nothing to lose. Look at the other people who are up there and a lot of them have been there before. I'll be nervous, but I'll give it my best."

Her best was a final-round 70 in which she hit 16 greens, made 16 pars and two birdies. She shook Mochrie at No. 4 with a par while the co-leader self-destructed with a double-bogey seven.

Maggie Will, another rookie, made a courageous run at Barrett with six birdies in a seven-hole stretch, from No. 8 to No. 14, but she ran out of momentum with a three-putt bogey at No. 15 and eventually finished tied for third.

"I'm shocked," Barrett said after her victory. "I expected to come out my first year and learn what it's all about, maybe contend my second and win the third year. This is great."

Rail Charity Classic—$250,000
Winner: Beth Daniel

The way Beth Daniel sees it, there's magic in the numbers game. Like the No. 32.

She won the Rail Charity Classic 32 years after being born in Charleston, South Carolina, 32 days after her back-from-obscurity return to the winner's circle in the Greater Washington Open and with a pair of 32s in the final round. And if you want more, her locker number was 32 in each of the two years she won the U.S. Amateur title.

For two rounds, however, Daniel was but a bit player as first Cathy Gerring, then Alice Ritzman grabbed hold of the lead. And when the final day did roll around, she went out six shots behind as Gerring, Ritzman and Betsy King were the players to watch, a rematch of sorts of the 1986 four-hole playoff from which King walked away the winner.

Aside from the weather, which was awful, the early story of the week was

King, who sliced open her left index finger instead of the breakfast bagel she was holding. She almost withdrew, but got around in 71 and when she added 66 to it, the injury was all but forgotten.

So was Daniel until she started the final round with birdies at Nos. 2 and 3 and ended the front side in 32 with another pair at Nos. 8 and 9. And by the time she ended her surge with a two-putt birdie at No. 13, she had moved past the fading Ritzman and King. But enough is never enough with King in pursuit, so Daniel put an exclamation point on her round with another birdie at No. 16 and finished with 64.

She still wasn't sure it was enough until King bogeyed the 16th. "You can't be comfortable with any kind of lead if Betsy's behind you and has a chance," Daniel said.

The victory was Daniel's second of the year, both coming within a month, to go with a remarkable 17 top 10s, including four seconds, in 22 tournaments.

"Everybody kept asking me early when I thought I would win again and I didn't have an answer for them then," Daniel said. "I knew it was going to happen. It's been a good month."

Cellular One-Ping Championship—$300,000
Winner: Muffin Spencer-Devlin

Even before the final round of the Cellular One-Ping Championship began, Muffin Spencer-Devlin pretty much had it handicapped. She stood four shots behind Dawn Coe and summed it up this way: "No one runs away with a tournament on this golf course."

She was right. Coe, who had romped to that big lead with scores of 68 and 71, shot a final-round 76, while Spencer-Devlin prevailed with a closing one-under-par 71 and a one-stroke victory over Nancy Lopez, Tammie Green and Susan Sanders.

It was Spencer-Devlin's third career victory, but her first since 1986, and the $45,000 check that went with it was her largest payday.

"I feel so incredibly good," said Spencer-Devlin, who missed three months of the 1988 season with back problems and earlier this year had missed six cuts. "I was more survivor than winner today. That's why it's so sweet."

It all came down to the final hole, where she nursed in a three-foot downhill putt that if she had missed would have thrown the tournament into a five-way playoff. Seven players led or shared the lead in the scramble to the finish line, and collapses came in droves.

Coe three-putted twice for double bogeys to land with a thud. Patty Sheehan led going to No. 9, but staggered back with 76. Sanders seemed to have it in her grasp, leading by two after No. 11. But she bogeyed No. 14, missed a tap-in birdie at No. 15, three-putted No. 16 and hit a six-iron approach into the lake at No. 17.

"It was my tournament to lose and I lost it," Sanders said.

Spencer-Devlin might have been in the group, too, except for a lucky break on No. 16, where her tee shot appeared headed into the lake before it hit a spectator's foot and stayed in the light rough.

"I kind of thought then it was my day to win," she said.

Safeco Classic—$300,000
Winner: Beth Daniel

Beth Daniel kind of figured it was going to be her day in the final round of the Safeco Classic, when she hooked three of her first four tee shots into the woods and walked away from that experience with three pars and a birdie.

She was right. Starting with a four-shot lead, Daniel won by six with a 15-under-par 273 for her second consecutive victory, her third in her last four tournaments and 17th in an 11-year LPGA career. Her closing 70 was her 18th sub-par round in a row, worth $45,000 and left her less than $32,000 short of the $2 million mark in career LPGA Tour earnings.

Cindy Rarick broke out of a pack of five with a closing 69 to take second and Pat Bradley finished third.

"After the first four holes, I easily could have been three over," Daniel said. "It was scary, especially when you're hooking the ball. But one of the best things about it was that I was able to scramble. I had a tough day and I scored. I went out there today with the attitude that I couldn't try to protect a lead on this kind of course."

Daniel was never far from the lead. She trailed Shirley Furlong and Chris Johnson by three strokes after the first day, moved to only one back at the halfway point behind Rarick and Bradley. A third-round seven-under 65, which included only 24 putts, moved her to the top by four shots over Bradley and five over Danielle Ammaccapane.

During the final round, Rarick kept Daniel dimly within sight, going out in 32, but she had too far to go and not enough holes to get there.

"At No. 10, I thought anything was possible, but Beth was playing so well you don't think it's really going to happen," Rarick said. "She was just too good for us this week."

Nippon Travel - MBS Classic—$300,000
Winner: Nancy Lopez

The more things change, the more they stay the same. While the LPGA has bounced around the Los Angeles area like a homeless child, it hasn't seemed to bother Nancy Lopez.

Take the MBS Classic in Buena Vista, for instance. She made it her third victory of the year, 42nd of her career and seventh as a professional in Southern California. It also made up for the second-place finish she had last year in what was the Al Star Classic.

Lopez shot rounds of 73-69-65-70—277 to win by two strokes over Alice Ritzman and relative unknown Pam Wright and collected $45,000. The victory kept her in sight, though barely, of the absent Betsy King in the Player-of-the-Year sweepstakes.

This wasn't one of those Lopez wire-to-wire things. Fact is, she was a distant six strokes behind Lisa Walters and Sherri Turner, who took the first-round lead with 67s, and trailed second-round leaders Cindy Rarick, Amy Alcott and Pat Bradley by four. But a seven-under-par 65 got her to within one of rookie Wright after the third round.

Lopez didn't remember Wright's first name, and apologized for that before the two teed off on Sunday. "I told her with two children, it's easy to lose your mind," Lopez said.

That out of the way, Lopez then lost those who would deny her victory. Ritzman came closest, moving into a tie early over the final nine holes, but couldn't sustain her charge.

"It's still exciting to win," Lopez said. "I didn't feel good when I got here this week, as my scores indicate, so this was especially nice."

Konica San Jose Classic—$325,000
Winner: Beth Daniel

Earlier this year, Beth Daniel was the object of sympathy from many of her fellow LPGA Tour members as her winless streak stretched on and on. But as the season hit its domestic end in California, a Break-Up-Daniel mood had set in.

Daniel put another "W" in her column in the Konica San Jose Classic, the fourth victory in her last six events after having gone almost four years since the last one. She shot rounds of 65-67-73—205 and won by one stroke over Pat Bradley.

Her victory was achieved with one eye on the task at hand and the other on her home in Charleston, South Carolina, where Hurricane Hugo landed.

"It was tough concentrating," Daniel said. "I went 36 hours without being able to contact my family. It was very stressful. I was pretty much a zombie all week."

Daniel didn't play like one, however. An opening round seven-under-par 65 was one better than Bradley. She moved three ahead of Bradley with a 67 in the second round. As it turned out, she needed every stroke of that cushion.

On Sunday, Bradley caught Daniel at the 12th hole and the two were tied going to No. 17. A playoff loomed until Daniel saved par after almost driving out of bounds and Bradley bogeyed, three-putting from 50 feet.

"I don't think I've ever been so tired in my life," Daniel said. "I didn't have anything left on Sunday. I was lucky to win. My drive on No. 17 couldn't have been more than 15 feet from going out of bounds."

Mazda Japan Classic—$500,000
Winner: Elaine Crosby

Anti-climactic is the best way to describe the LPGA's season-ending event. But anyone would have trouble convincing Elaine Crosby of that fact. To Crosby, it was climactic.

First the anti-climactic part. Two weeks before the Mazda, it appeared this would be for all the honors—money title, Player of the Year, Vardon Trophy. A likely showdown involving Betsy King and Beth Daniel, clearly the two best players of 1989.

It was nothing of the sort. Daniel, pleading fatigue, withdrew from the tournament a week earlier, leaving King with both Player-of-the-Year and money titles, and when King injured her wrist and also withdrew, Daniel won the Vardon trophy.

Even without its billboard players, the Mazda did not lack for excitement and surprises. The biggest surprise was Crosby, who had never won anything in five years on the LPGA Tour. She shot rounds of 71-64-70—205 and won by two strokes over Dawn Coe.

The 31-year-old Floridian had an entire country pulling against her on Sunday, as local hero Ayako Okamoto began the final round only two behind Crosby. But the best Okamoto, playing with a painful right elbow, could do was 73 in the finale, while Crosby played her first 10 holes in two under par, and parred in.

"I knew it was going to be a tough day with all the people following Ayako, but I ignored the noise and commotion, concentrated on my game and played good, steady golf," Crosby said.

The $75,000 winner's share of the purse lifted Crosby's season earnings to $126,899, almost $500,000 less than King. But Crosby could have cared less. "This is the perfect way to end the season," she said. "It's a great, great Christmas present."

The Women's European Tour

Rome Ladies Classic—£65,000
Winner: Sofia Gronberg

Sweden's Sofia Gronberg notched her first win as a professional when she came from behind to take the opening event of the European season, the Rome Ladies Classic at Ogliata. England's Debbie Dowling opened with 70 to share the lead with Gronberg and South Africa's Alison Sheard, despite having to contend with rain, wind and even hail.

If the weather was bad on the first day, it was impossible on the second day, when tournament director David Hughes was forced to cancel the round and reduce the tournament to 54 holes. The third day dawned sunny and dry, and Dowling shot 69 to retain a one-stroke lead over Scotland's Gillian Stewart and two over Gronberg.

The final round brought out the crowds who were treated to spectacular golf. Dowling slipped out of contention, dropping nine shots in the first nine holes, and finished in eighth place. The door was left open for Gronberg, who took advantage, going ahead of Stewart and holding off a challenge from Marie-Laure De Lorenzi. Stewart arrived at the final green needing a birdie to force a playoff, but she just missed, and Gronberg's 69 for a three-under-par total of 210, was enough to give her the title by one shot over De Lorenzi, who had a last-round 68, and by two over Stewart.

Ford Ladies Classic—£50,000
Winner: Marie-Laure De Lorenzi

Marie-Laure De Lorenzi quickly showed the talent which had won her eight titles in 1988 when she began a marvelous run by winning the Ford Ladies Classic at Woburn. She opened with 67 to take a four-shot lead over England's Beverley New. A second-round 74 might have seen her lead disappear, if not for horrendous conditions, and she found herself six shots ahead of Janet Soulsby and Gillian Stewart.

De Lorenzi continued with a third-round 73 for an eight-shot lead over Soulsby. The final round was a formality, with De Lorenzi producing a 72 for a total of 286 and an eight-shot victory over Stewart, who had 71 to finish runner-up. Although a convincing victory, it was not a record, but the French professional did win with the lowest score in the eight-year history of the event.

Hennessy Ladies Cup—£80,000
Winner: Marie-Laure De Lorenzi

Continuing a superb run, Marie-Laure De Lorenzi defended her Hennessy Ladies Cup title at St. Germain, Paris. Australia's Corinne Dibnah opened with 67. De Lorenzi was at her shoulder with 68, while former winner Kitrina Douglas was a further shot back at 69, tied with Britain's Laura Davies.

De Lorenzi made her move in the second round when she matched her own course-record 66 to take the lead at 134. She was three strokes ahead of Davies, who had 68, and four ahead of Dibnah. It was beginning to look like a one-women show, but Davies, playing with De Lorenzi in the third round, staged a comeback to make a contest of it. While De Lorenzi struggled to 72, Davies had 70 to cut the deficit to just one shot going into the last round.

The crowds turned out for the final round, excited by the prospect of a duel between Europe's top two players. They were not disappointed, as De Lorenzi dropped a shot at the first hole to be tied with Davies. The tables soon turned and De Lorenzi found herself three shots in front. She went four ahead with a birdie at the 13th, but then dropped shots at the next three holes to be only one ahead of Davies, Dibnah and American Jody Rosenthal.

De Lorenzi then holed a 30-foot birdie at the 17th to go two in front with one hole to play. A safe par at the last meant the title was hers. Dibnah and Rosenthal tied for second place, and Davies, who had a last-round 75, was a further shot back. De Lorenzi now had an enormous lead at the top of the Woolmark money list with £26,100, nearly double the earnings of second-place Sofia Gronberg.

BMW Ladies Classic—£70,000
Winner: Marie-Laure De Lorenzi

Marie-Laure De Lorenzi won her third event in a row, the BMW Ladies Classic at Hubbelrath. She had now won more than £36,000—an average of £2,440 for each round she had played.

Belgium's Florence Descampe set the target on the opening day with 68, a nice celebration for her 20th birthday. It was brief, however, as France's Corinne Soules and American Susan Moon came in with rounds of 67 to share the lead. Australian Dennise Hutton came in the second day with 69 for a 138 total and it was not until the end of the day that Soules overtook her with 69 to add to her earlier 67 for 136.

Another Australian, Corinne Dibnah, has a reputation for coming out of the pack just when you least expect her. This was one such event, when a third-round 68 put her at 208 while Soules slipped to 74 and dropped back. Dibnah was caught by Hutton when she birdied the last holes and the two were two shots ahead of Soules, Moon, Descampe and, of course, De Lorenzi.

Hutton began the final round with five birdies in the first six holes, then began to falter. De Lorenzi later said, "I knew I had to be patient and wait for the more difficult last nine holes and it paid off." It certainly did. She came home in 34 against Hutton's 39 for 67 to finish one stroke ahead of the Australian. She played the last 36 holes without exceeding par.

Ladies French Open—£60,000
Winner: Suzanne Strudwick

England's Suzanne Strudwick ended Marie-Laure De Lorenzi's streak of victories by notching her first win as a professional in the Ladies French Open at Fourqueux. Strudwick started with 70 and was one stroke behind Laurette Maritz, while De Lorenzi had a horrendous 78 and for once looked well out of things.

Strudwick, the Staffordshire professional, took the halfway lead with 69, and was four strokes ahead of her nearest rivals. De Lorenzi shot 73 and had to wait to see if she had made the cut, finally doing so by one stroke. A course-record 64 in the third round suddenly put De Lorenzi back in the picture. Strudwick slipped to 74, and found herself playing with Marie-Laure on the last day with a two-stroke lead.

The crowds turned out to cheer their French heroine in a tense and thrilling final round. Strudwick was three shots ahead with six holes to play, but dropped one at the 13th and the French professional drew level with birdies at the next two holes. Strudwick nosed one shot ahead as they went to the par-three 18th, but made bogey there while De Lorenzi collected her par to force a playoff.

It was the first playoff of Strudwick's career, but she displayed no nerves as she hit a fine drive at the first hole, then a marvelous approach shot to six feet. The birdie putt looked almost a formality as she rolled it into the hole for the £9,000 first prize.

St. Moritz Ladies Classic—£70,000
Winner: Kitrina Douglas

A set of clubs purchased just days before the St. Moritz Ladies Classic in Switzerland helped England's Kitrina Douglas win her first event of the season. Douglas, who had traveled to Switzerland in style on the Orient Express, having missed the cut at the French Open the previous week, took a gamble using the clubs, but it certainly paid off.

The Bristol professional finished tied with Suzanne Strudwick, who had won in France, with a two-under-par total of 286. Douglas won on the first playoff hole with a par-three for her first victory since 1987.

Sweden's Marie Wennersten-From led on the opening day with 70, while New Zealander Joanne Green was celebrating for a different reason, having aced the 17th hole to win an £18,000 car. The young Belgian, Florence Descampe, played her way into contention the second day with 69 for a 141 total, one shot ahead of Strudwick, who had 68, with Douglas three shots further back.

Douglas made her move in the third round with 71 to be two strokes off the lead held by Descampe and France's Elizabeth Quelhas at 214, while Strudwick stumbled to 75. But Strudwick set the target on the final day with 69, and Douglas had to finish with three birdies in the last five holes for 70 to force a playoff. Douglas found the green with her tee shot to the par-three first playoff hole and, although Strudwick played a fine shot to four feet from a greenside bunker, she failed to make the putt, and a par was enough to give Douglas the title and take her earnings to more than £14,000.

TEC Players Championship—£75,000
Winner: Anna Oxenstierna

A new star was born when Anna Oxenstierna of Sweden won the prestigious TEC Players Championship at the Tytherington Club, Cheshire, the headquarters of the Women's European Tour. Not bad for someone who had originally entered a pro-am at Tytherington by mistake, and had to pay double the entry fee for the Players Championship as a late entrant.

She opened with 75 and then added 74, but another Swede, Helen Alfredsson, led at 141, one stroke ahead of South African Laurette Maritz. From then on, Maritz and Oxenstierna captured all the attention.

The young Swede came through with a course-record 66 in the third round, including six birdies. This superb score put her level with Maritz going into the final round, and the stage was set for an exciting finale to this prestigious event, regarded as one of the "majors" on the European Tour.

Oxenstierna, a former Swedish Amateur champion, who had only turned professional two years earlier, remained remarkably cool to win her first event. She began with three birdies in four holes, and by the turn was four strokes ahead of Maritz. From that point it was a matter of who would finish second, as Oxenstierna romped to a two-shot victory over Maritz with 71 for a 286 total to win £11,250.

Bloor Homes Eastleigh Classic—£60,000
Winner: Debbie Dowling

Beginning five strokes off the lead, England's Debbie Dowling had a last-round 62 and a birdie at the third extra hole to win the Bloor Homes Eastleigh Classic, near Southampton. Dowling survived the playoff against America's Melissa McNamara and Britain's Rae Hast and Cathy Panton. All had finished at two-under-par 261, but Dowling settled the issue when she pitched to 10 feet for a birdie to pick up a check for £9,000.

American Susan Moon set the pace on the first day with a four-under-par 62, with McNamara two shots further back. Scotland's Panton shot 65 for a 131 halfway total, one stroke behind McNamara, while Hast and Dowling were four shots off the lead at 134. A third-round 63 from Panton enabled the Scottish Open champion to take the lead, this time reversing the tables on McNamara who was one shot behind, with Hast and Dowling four and five shots off the pace respectively.

While Panton slipped to a final-round 67, McNamara managed 66 to leave the two tied, while Dowling had come out of the pack with a 62 and Hast a 63 to force the playoff.

Lufthansa German Open—£80,000
Winner: Alison Nicholas

Alison Nicholas produced a fantastic seven-under-par 65 to win her first title of the season in the Lufthansa German Open and collect the £12,000 first prize, taking her earnings to more than £18,000. The British professional got the better of the Worthsee course, near Munich, breaking 70 in all four rounds for a 19-under-par total of 269, one shot off the record shared by Nancy Lopez, Laura Davies and Dale Reid.

Nicholas started with 67 to share the lead with two Americans on a two-week stint on the European Tour, Jane Geddes and Patti Rizzo. Three birdies on the closing holes and her second-round 69 put Nicholas one stroke behind Rizzo, who took the lead with a total of 135. A new name came on the leaderboard in the third round, when Colombia's Patricia Gonzalez had 66 for a 205 total. But Nicholas remained undaunted and a hard-earned 68, including four birdies and an eagle, gave her the lead at 204, with Rizzo two shots back after a disappointing 71.

Playing with Gonzalez in the final round, Nicholas went on the attack but, despite three birdies for an outward 33, was only two strokes ahead of the Colombian. An eagle-three at the 12th gave her the edge she needed, and Gonzalez began to go backwards with bogeys at the 15th and 17th. Nicholas finished with a five-shot victory over Gonzalez, with England's Suzanne Strudwick and Rizzo way back in third spot at 279.

Weetabix Ladies British Open—£120,000
Winner: Jane Geddes

Jane Geddes more than made up for the fine she faced for taking leave from the LPGA Tour to play in Europe for two weeks when she won the Weetabix Ladies British Open at Ferndown, Dorset. The 29-year-old professional, who made no secret of her desire to win the event, collected a check for £18,000. She joined Laura Davies as the only players to have won both the British and U.S. Open titles and became the first American to win the British Open since Betsy King in 1985.

After her victory she spoke of her high regard for the title. "It will mean a lot to me taking this trophy back to America. I will be back to defend the title next year, fine or no fine," Geddes said. "The Americans here think this is now a major championship, and should be recognized by our own tour."

Geddes finished two strokes ahead of Florence Descampe, the 20-year-old from Belgium, having led from the first day. She opened with 67 to share the lead with two others, and another 67 on the second day left her at 10-under-par 134, three strokes ahead of her nearest rival, American Peggy Conley. Descampe made her challenge in the third round with eight birdies in a round of 66, which left her sharing third place. Geddes faltered with 72, and Europe's No. 1, Marie-Laure De Lorenzi, made her move with 67 to share the lead at 206.

The battle was on, and the pressure was clearly telling, as both players dropped shots in the opening holes of the final round. But Geddes made eagle at the long sixth, and two more birdies put her 12 under par and three strokes ahead of the field at the turn. Descampe then made a dramatic move, with fourth birdies and an eagle from the ninth to move just one stroke behind Geddes. The American refused to give, and two more birdies left her with the two-shot cushion she needed to secure the title.

Ladies Danish Open—£65,000
Winner: Tania Abitbol

The fourth first-time winner of the season emerged at the Ladies Danish Open in Rungsted, when Spain's Tania Abitbol led from start to finish to pick up her first professional title. She had to beat the formidable Marie-Laure De Lorenzi in a playoff to do it, and won the admiration of the crowds of spectators for her plucky determination. Abitbol, who turned professional just a year earlier, had been rated as a potential winner, and her performance in Denmark confirmed those thoughts.

Abitbol looked determined from the start, opening with 69 and then following with another 69 to share the 36-hole lead with Peggy Conley. A third-round 73 gave her the outright lead, while De Lorenzi had made her move with 68 to be just two shots behind.

The young Spaniard, whose previous-best finish had been sixth in the Rome Classic, looked like a winner as she began the final round, and went on to play the last nine holes in strict par figures despite the pressure. She needed a four at the par-five 18th to win, but her second shot found a bunker. She made a good recovery, but her birdie putt just lipped out, leaving her tied with De Lorenzi at 285.

In the playoff, pars at the first hole saw the hole halved, as did birdies at the second. De Lorenzi missed the green at the third, but Abitbol was able to get up and down in two for a winning birdie.

Gislaved Open—£65,000
Winner: Alison Nicholas

Britain's Alison Nicholas claimed her second victory of the season, and the seventh of her career, when she won the Gislaved Ladies Open in Sweden. However, it was not all plain sailing for the Yorkshire professional, who had to fight off a last-minute challenge from former U.S. Open champion Liselotte Neumann, making a rare appearance in front of her home fans. Nicholas was clearly delighted with her win. She received a check for £9,750 to take her into second place on the money list with £34,240.

Strong winds made play difficult on the opening day, and eventually the top of the leaderboard looked like a bus stop, with eight players, including Nicholas, sharing the lead at one-over-par 73. Neumann was well down the field at 77, but a flawless 68 in the second round enabled her to move into a share of the lead with Nicholas, who shot 72, and Scotland's Jane Connachan, all at 145.

Nicholas grabbed the edge on the third day with 69, while Neumann slipped to 74, to take a three-shot lead over her nearest rivals going into the last round. She began five strokes ahead of Neumann, but the Swede closed the gap to just one stroke after a birdie at the fifth, while Nicholas dropped shots at two of the opening four holes. She recovered with birdies at the ninth and 14th on her way to a final-round 74 for a level-par total of 288, and two-stroke victory.

Variety Club Celebrity Classic—£50,000
Winner: Corinne Dibnah

After 12 months on the European Tour without a victory, Australia's Corinne Dibnah won the Variety Club Celebrity Classic at Calcot Park. Dibnah had not won since her British Open victory the previous year and admitted it had been a great relief to end the drought. The event was unusual in that each round was played in a pro-am format with some of Britain's top television and show business stars competing to raise money for charity.

American Peggy Conley set the target on the first day with 68, but Dibnah later matched it with five birdies and an eagle. Fellow Australian Dennise Hutton shot a course-record 66 to finish at 138 alongside Dibnah, but ten minutes later England's Rae Hast added another 66 to her first-round 70 for a two-stroke lead. Dibnah could clearly smell victory and a third-round 70 gave her back the lead, two ahead of Hast, with Conley one stroke further back.

The familiar attacking style of the Australian was in evidence early in the final round, where she moved into a four-stroke lead after just seven holes. A marvelous run by Conley soon cut that to one, but Dibnah weathered the onslaught with three more birdies for a closing 71 for a 13-under-par total of 279, two shots ahead of Conley, with England's Sally Prosser third thanks to a closing 65, a course record.

Godiva European Masters—£110,000
Winner: Kitrina Douglas

England's Kitrina Douglas proved that she is one of the best players on the European Tour when she won the Godiva European Masters in Belgium against one of the best fields ever assembled at a European women's golf event. All the top players were there, lured by the title and £16,500 first prize—second only to the winner's prize in the Ladies British Open.

If there was anything to mar the event it was the demise of Marie-Laure De Lorenzi in a playoff, the fourth she had lost so far that season. Both players were tied at one-under-par 287 and facing a weary walk—at least for Lorenzi—to another playoff hole. Douglas must have been feeling more confident, having already won one title in a playoff that season, the St. Moritz Classic in Switzerland.

They halved the first extra hole, but a par at the next was enough for victory, after De Lorenzi had again blown her chances by missing the green and failing to get up and down in two. Douglas' victory was crucial in the battle for the top three places in the money list. De Lorenzi was now in an almost unassailable position at the top of the Woolmark Order of Merit, with Douglas in second place, just £1,000 ahead of Alison Nicholas.

Douglas and De Lorenzi had been neck and neck from the start in Belgium, sharing the first-round lead at 69. Douglas wavered slightly in the second round, when she dropped shots at four of the closing holes for 75, while De Lorenzi's 72 left her three strokes ahead. A third-round 73 compared with De Lorenzi's 76 left the two tied going into the final round, and they matched each other virtually shot-for-shot for closing rounds of 70.

Expedier European Open—£70,000
Winner: Jane Connachan

One of the most popular wins of the season took place when Jane Connachan romped to victory in the Expedier European Open at Kingswood, Surrey. It was impressive to say the least, as the 25-year-old Scot opened with a course-record-equalling 65 and never looked like being caught. It was one of the best rounds of her career and marked a comeback for Connachan, who had nearly quit at the start of the season because she was so fed up with her play.

Connachan, who had not won since 1987, led by four strokes and even 73 in the second round saw her retain a three-shot lead as everyone else seemed to go backwards. A third-round 70 firmly set her up for victory, as she found herself six shots ahead of her nearest rivals. With six holes in the final round remaining, she led by seven shots and it seemed a matter of not if she would win, but by how many. Only a last-minute challenge by Gillian Stewart prevented a run-away victory. With a haul of four birdies and an eagle for 67, Stewart moved to within three strokes. Connachan continued to battle on, and her 71 for a nine-under-par 279 total was enough to give her the title and the £10,500 first prize.

Italian Open—£80,000
Winner: Xonia Wunsch

Spain proved to be a force on the Women's European Tour when the Spaniards produced yet another winner in the shape of Xonia Wunsch. She joined compatriot Tania Abitbol as the season's fifth first-time winner with her victory in the Italian Open at Carimate. She displayed a cool nerve to win the £12,000 first prize, and those watching predicted Wunsch would be a name often seen on the leaderboard in the future.

She started the final round one shot behind leaders Jane Connachan, fresh from victory in the European Open, and Trish Johnson, following a long spell on the LPGA circuit. Johnson dropped strokes at the first two holes to leave Wunsch and Connachan tied. They continued to match each other until the 13th, where the Spaniard holed a 90-foot putt for a birdie to take the lead. Wunsch never once exceeded par and made another birdie at the 18th for 68 and a six-under-par total of 278, for a two-shot victory. She had coped with the pressure admirably and was more than delighted.

It was a good tournament for Johnson, who had suffered two lean years on the LPGA circuit and who regained much of her confidence in Italy where she was always in contention. Marie-Laure De Lorenzi was briefly up with the leaders and, although she finished in 12th place, she now had a £30,000 lead at the top of the Woolmark money list, having earned £75,000, and looked certain to be Europe's No. 1 for a second successive year.

Laing Ladies Classic—£60,000
Winner: Laura Davies

Laura Davies at last broke her 1989 winless streak on the European Tour when she won the Laing Ladies Classic at Stoke Poges. The Surrey professional had been desperate to keep up her record of at least one win every year since she turned professional in 1985, and to add to her Lady Keystone Open victory on the LPGA Tour earlier in the season.

It was a convincing win by any standards, and the crowd was delighted to see her launching her drives with the carefree abandon which has endeared her to spectators all over the world. She admitted the course had a lot to do with it. "I just love being able to stand and look down a wide-open fairway and have a go at it," she said.

An American and a Swede shared the honors on the opening day, with Susan Moon and Sofia Gronberg both scoring 67s to take a one-shot lead, while Davies had to settle for 72. The former British and U.S. Open champion hit her best form in the second round, when a new putter was used only 28 times on her way to a course-record-equalling 64. It gave her a total of 136 and a one-shot lead over Moon. There was not much change at the top of the leaderboard after the third round, when Davies shot 72 for a 208 total, while Moon failed to make her move, also shooting 72 to remain a stroke behind.

At the start of the final round, Davies immediately threw down the gauntlet at the opening hole, where she rolled in a 35-foot putt for an eagle-three. Another birdie followed at the fifth and at the 407-yard ninth, where she only needed a wedge for her second shot. She was now three strokes clear of Moon, Jane Connachan and Federica Dassu from Italy, who had gone out in 31. Davies eventually finished with 68 for a 16-under-par total of 276 and three-shot victory over Connachan, Moon, Corinne Dibnah and Dale Reid.

Woolmark Ladies Match Play Championship—£70,000
Winner: Dennise Hutton

A bunch of bananas and advice from her husband, John, saw Australia's Dennise Hutton defeat Ireland's Maureen Garner in the final of the Wool-mark Match Play Championship at Vallromanas, Spain, and become the European Tour's sixth first-time winner of the season. Hutton relied on bananas to keep herself going through the fiercely contested final, having already had to survive a tense semi-final earlier in the day.

Both Hutton and Garner had yet to win on the tour and both clearly felt they had a lot to prove as they halved the first 11 holes. Hutton then went 1-up with a birdie at the 12th and another at the 16th put her two ahead. Garner pulled her drive into trouble at the 18th and, when Hutton hit her second shot to just five feet from the pin, it was all over.

The winner's check for £12,000 took her earnings to more than £32,000, and Hutton was clearly delighted, considering it was a last-minute decision to stay on the tour for the match play event. "We usually go back home before this event, but I felt I was really starting to play well enough to win and so decided to stay on for a while," she said. "I'm glad I did."

Hutton had beaten the Swedish rookie Helen Alfredsson in her semi-final, which did not finish until the 20th hole, while Garner had a much easier time against Australian Anne Jones, winning by 7 and 6. Alfredsson had knocked out favorite Marie-Laure De Lorenzi in the fourth round, and Garner had dispatched the second seed, Alison Nicholas, in the third round. Laura Davies, who hates match play, lost to Colombia's Patricia Gonzalez in the second round.

AGF Biarritz Open—£60,000
Winner: Dennise Hutton

Dennise Hutton made it two in a row when she won the AGF Biarritz Open. Having taken two seasons to secure her first victory on the European Tour, Hutton now seemed unstoppable as she banked the £9,000 first prize taking her fortnight's earnings to £21,000.

It was another frustrating event for veteran American Peggy Conley, who was still looking for her first win of the season, and matters were made even worse by the fact she had found herself four shots ahead with only five holes left to play. Not only did she let that lead slip away to finish tied with

Hutton at two-under-par 274, but also Conley at the first hole of the playoff could only manage a par-five while Hutton rolled in a five-foot putt for birdie.

Swedish rookie Helen Alfredsson stole the limelight on the first day when she shot a course-record, five-under-par 64. Conley made her challenge in the second round when she equalled that record to take the lead. The big disappointment was the withdrawal of local girl Marie-Laure De Lorenzi, due to the tendonitis in her wrist, which meant she did not play again for the remainder of the season.

Conley added a third-round 70 to go into the last round with a three-stroke lead over Hutton, and many felt the 42-year-old American's moment had arrived at last, with her first victory of the season just around the corner. But Conley never looked comfortable and, as Hutton plugged away, her lead rapidly dwindled until Conley needed two putts on the last hole to win by a shot. She took three putts, and went on to lose in the playoff for her second runner-up spot of the season.

Qualitair Ladies Classic—£50,000
Winner: Alison Nicholas

Britain's Alison Nicholas celebrated her third victory of the year and in doing so confirmed her position as No. 2 in the Woolmark Order of Merit, when she won the Qualitair Ladies Classic at La Manga, Spain. Marie-Laure De Lorenzi, having already assured the No. 1 spot for a second successive year, took a week's break, leaving the rest of the field to fight it out in the last event of the season.

Only a few thousand pounds separated Nicholas from another Brit, Kitrina Douglas, in third place, and both were looking to win to grab the all-important No. 2 ranking, which entitles them to automatic entry to events such as the U.S. Women's Open.

Nicholas took the title with a six-under-par total of 213 in the 54-hole event, while Douglas could do no better than 12th place to remain third in the rankings. Britain's Suzanne Strudwick made a last-minute return to form to lead after the first round with 68, with Peggy Conley and Nicholas tied in second place at 69.

The Union Jacks were flying high at the end of the second round, when three British players led the way at 143: Strudwick, Nicholas and Scot Gillian Stewart. Nicholas set out in determined fashion at the start of the final round, and three birdies in the first four holes put her well on the way to victory.

Conley briefly challenged when she tied with Nicholas at six under par after 15 holes. It was another case of "what might have been" for the American, who bogeyed the 16th to tie with Sofia Gronberg, while Nicholas also cruised to 70 and the £7,500 winner's check. It took her earnings to £56,528, with De Lorenzi comfortably at the top with £77,534, and Douglas in third with £48,534.

APPENDIXES

World Money List

This listing of the 200 leading money winners in the world of professional golf in 1989 was compiled from the results of all tournaments carried in the Appendixes of this edition, along with other non-tour and international events for which accurate figures could be obtained and in which the players competed for prize money provided by someone other than the players themselves. Skins games, shootouts and seasonal bonus money are not included. Leading money-winner David Frost's total includes $1,000,000 from the Million Dollar Challenge.

In the 24 years during which World Money Lists have been compiled, the earnings of the player in the 200th position have risen from a total of $3,326 in 1966 to $162,158 in 1989. The top 200 players in 1966 earned a total of $4,680,287. In 1989, the comparable total was $77,951,401.

Because of the fluctuating values of money throughout the world, it was necessary to determine an average value of non-American currency to U.S. money to prepare this listing. The conversion rates used for 1989 were: British pound = US$1.60; 140 Japanese yen = US$1; South African rand = US40¢; US$1 = Australia/New Zealand 80¢.

POS.	PLAYER, COUNTRY	TOTAL MONEY
1	David Frost, South Africa	$1,650,230
2	Tom Kite, U.S.	1,491,164
3	Greg Norman, Australia	1,351,761
4	Payne Stewart, U.S.	1,283,515
5	Mark Calcavecchia, U.S.	1,258,946
6	Curtis Strange, U.S.	1,176,443
7	Paul Azinger, U.S.	1,046,915
8	Scott Hoch, U.S.	990,548
9	Chip Beck, U.S.	984,417
10	Tim Simpson, U.S.	975,597
11	Nick Faldo, England	945,679
12	Masashi Ozaki, Japan	867,649
13	Jose-Maria Olazabal, Spain	865,236
14	Fred Couples, U.S.	793,983
15	Wayne Grady, Australia	777,548
16	Bob Charles, New Zealand	767,253
17	Steve Jones, U.S.	766,534
18	Mark O'Meara, U.S.	744,654
19	Orville Moody, U.S.	718,235
20	Ronan Rafferty, Northern Ireland	713,730
21	Blaine McCallister, U.S.	696,787
22	Ian Woosnam, Wales	679,489
23	Peter Senior, Australia	670,656
24	Naomichi Ozaki, Japan	665,057
25	Bill Glasson, U.S.	660,512
26	Peter Fowler, Australia	660,054
27	Mike Hill, U.S.	647,104
28	Mark McCumber, U.S.	630,017
29	Bernhard Langer, West Germany	623,284

POS.	PLAYER, COUNTRY	TOTAL MONEY
30	Craig Parry, Australia	604,006
31	Al Geiberger, U.S.	595,693
32	Harold Henning, South Africa	588,163
33	Isao Aoki, Japan	571,623
34	Larry Mize, U.S.	569,251
35	Dave Hill, U.S.	568,791
36	Mike Hulbert, U.S.	553,471
37	Gary Player, South Africa	544,916
38	Severiano Ballesteros, Spain	541,300
39	Brian Jones, Australia	539,194
40	Bob Tway, U.S.	532,086
41	Sandy Lyle, Scotland	514,346
42	Peter Jacobsen, U.S.	506,529
43	Donnie Hammond, U.S.	501,885
44	Don Bies, U.S.	500,451
45	Mike Reid, U.S.	494,842
46	Wayne Levi, U.S.	493,492
47	Ken Green, U.S.	485,948
48	Charles Coody, U.S.	484,780
49	Craig Stadler, U.S.	482,701
50	Steve Pate, U.S.	470,154
51	Scott Simpson, U.S.	468,490
52	Ben Crenshaw, U.S.	468,455
53	Hal Sutton, U.S.	466,353
54	John Mahaffey, U.S.	462,342
55	Mark James, England	461,737
56	Bruce Crampton, Australia	460,148
57	Ted Schulz, U.S.	455,305
58	Don Pooley, U.S.	439,874
59	Jodie Mudd, U.S.	436,860
60	Dave Rummells, U.S.	432,904
61	Mike Donald, U.S.	428,396
62	Miller Barber, U.S.	427,292
63	Andy Bean, U.S.	422,847
64	Ian Baker-Finch, Australia	421,733
65	Koichi Suzuki, Japan	398,747
66	Dale Douglass, U.S.	397,979
67	Tateo Ozaki, Japan	395,795
68	Nick Price, Zimbabwe	392,510
69	Graham Marsh, Australia	387,237
70	Tsuneyuki Nakajima, Japan	375,562
71	Nobuo Serizawa, Japan	362,125
72	Jim Carter, U.S.	359,422
73	Gordon Brand, Jr., Scotland	352,865
74	Larry Nelson, U.S.	352,369
75	Mike Harwood, Australia	352,033
76	Chi Chi Rodriguez, U.S.	351,914
77	Tom Byrum, U.S.	347,096
78	Akiyoshi Omachi, Japan	347,094
79	Jose-Maria Canizares, Spain	346,667
80	Gene Sauers, U.S.	341,479
81	Yoshikazu Yokoshima, Japan	341,396
82	Larry Mowry, U.S.	340,788
83	Bruce Lietzke, U.S.	339,987
84	Walter Zembriski, U.S.	328,861
85	Howard Clark, England	328,432
86	Davis Love III, U.S.	328,108

POS.	PLAYER, COUNTRY	TOTAL MONEY
87	Jim Dent, U.S.	325,191
88	Bill Britton, U.S.	321,578
89	Saburo Fujiki, Japan	317,875
90	Gene Littler, U.S.	314,516
91	Bob Gilder, U.S.	314,427
92	Jay Haas, U.S.	312,381
93	Roger Mackay, Australia	304,532
94	Sam Torrance, Scotland	303,589
95	Yoshimi Niizeki, Japan	303,481
96	Loren Roberts, U.S.	302,598
97	Robert Wrenn, U.S.	302,058
98	Mark Wiebe, U.S.	301,929
99	Lanny Wadkins, U.S.	301,643
100	Gil Morgan, U.S.	300,395
101	David Ogrin, U.S.	296,946
102	Teruo Sugihara, Japan	296,513
103	David Feherty, Northern Ireland	296,373
104	Billy Casper, U.S.	281,229
105	Mark McNulty, Zimbabwe	280,533
106	Mike Sullivan, U.S.	279,887
107	Eduardo Romero, Argentina	278,193
108	Leonard Thompson, U.S.	277,422
109	Rives McBee, U.S.	273,987
110	Tom Shaw, U.S.	273,823
111	Brett Ogle, Australia	273,769
112	Jim Gallagher, Jr., U.S.	273,222
113	Yoshitaka Yamamoto, Japan	271,586
114	Mats Lanner, Sweden	269,873
115	Clarence Rose, U.S.	269,766
116	Ronnie Black, U.S.	269,138
117	Toru Nakamura, Japan	266,597
118	Hajime Meshiai, Japan	264,044
119	David Ishii, U.S.	263,842
120	Jeff Sluman, U.S.	261,932
121	Ove Sellberg, Sweden	260,849
122	Tom Watson, U.S.	258,769
123	Rodger Davis, Australia	254,483
124	David Edwards, U.S.	253,551
125	Steve Elkington, Australia	253,178
126	Kenny Knox, U.S.	251,175
127	Arnold Palmer, U.S.	249,973
128	Mark Lye, U.S.	249,529
129	Dave Barr, Canada	247,780
130	Michael Allen, U.S.	247,231
131	Kenny Perry, U.S.	247,224
132	Christy O'Connor, Jr., Ireland	246,086
133	Lee Trevino, U.S.	244,846
134	Fulton Allem, South Africa	244,056
135	Lou Graham, U.S.	243,777
136	Philip Walton, Ireland	242,979
137	Fuzzy Zoeller, U.S.	241,992
138	Chris Perry, U.S.	240,490
139	Denis Durnian, England	239,940
140	Brad Faxon, U.S.	239,931
141	Vijay Singh, Fiji	239,452
142	Jay Don Blake, U.S.	235,499
143	Bobby Nichols, U.S.	233,147

POS.	PLAYER, COUNTRY	TOTAL MONEY
144	Hiroshi Makino, Japan	232,861
145	Butch Baird, U.S.	232,513
146	Katsuyoshi Tomori, Japan	230,700
147	Hale Irwin, U.S.	230,341
148	Billy Andrade, U.S.	229,112
149	Curt Byrum, U.S.	228,702
150	Akihito Yokoyama, Japan	226,117
151	Terry Gale, Australia	219,003
152	D.A. Weibring, U.S.	218,686
153	Joey Sindelar, U.S.	216,842
154	Frank Nobilo, New Zealand	214,262
155	Duffy Waldorf, U.S.	214,045
156	Jim Ferree, U.S.	212,242
157	John Huston, U.S.	211,232
158	Mark Roe, England	211,181
159	Ed Fiori, U.S.	211,062
160	Ray Floyd, U.S.	210,464
161	Frank Beard, U.S.	208,655
162	Brian Tennyson, U.S.	206,720
163	Tommy Armour, U.S.	203,795
164	Mark Mouland, Wales	202,731
165	George Archer, U.S.	202,446
166	Katsunari Takahashi, Japan	202,290
167	Derrick Cooper, England	201,259
168	Gordon J. Brand, England	196,417
169	Dan Pohl, U.S.	196,332
170	Doug Tewell, U.S.	195,449
171	Chen Tze Chung, Taiwan	193,072
172	Bruce Devlin, Australia	191,585
173	Hubert Green, U.S.	191,419
174	Masahiro Kuramoto, Japan	191,143
175	Joe Jimenez, U.S.	189,473
176	Katsuji Hasegawa, Japan	188,986
177	Tadao Nakamura, Japan	187,885
178	Nobumitsu Yuhara, Japan	187,204
179	Tom Purtzer, U.S.	187,177
180	Corey Pavin, U.S.	182,684
181	Brad Bryant, U.S.	181,393
182	Toshiaki Sudo, Japan	181,154
183	Brian Claar, U.S.	180,139
184	Colin Montgomerie, Scotland	178,951
185	Homero Blancas, U.S.	175,032
186	Seiichi Kanai, Japan	172,339
187	Tsukasa Watanabe, Japan	172,096
188	Gary Hallberg, U.S.	172,003
189	Jimmy Powell, U.S.	171,498
190	Billy Ray Brown, U.S.	170,464
191	Masanobu Kimura, Japan	170,446
192	Chen Tze Ming, Taiwan	168,707
193	Bobby Wadkins, U.S.	167,461
194	Tadami Ueno, Japan	166,874
195	Barry Lane, England	166,864
196	Rocco Mediate, U.S.	166,751
197	Andrew Murray, England	166,537
198	Kiyoshi Muroda, Japan	163,658
199	Lon Hinkle, U.S.	162,163
200	James Hallet, U.S.	162,158

The Sony Ranking
(as of December 31, 1989)

Pos.	Player	Tour	Points Average	Total Points	No. of Events	86/88 Total	86/88 Minus	1989 Plus
1 (2)	Greg Norman	ANZ 1	17.76	1385	78	1366	-825	844
2 (4)	Nick Faldo	Eur 1	16.25	1365	84	1117	-584	832
3 (1)	Seve Ballesteros	Eur 2	15.03	1097	73	1465	-820	452
4 (5)	Curtis Strange	USA 1	13.79	1172	85	1102	-586	656
5 (19)	Payne Stewart	USA 2	12.82	1115	87	712	-413	816
6 (13)	Tom Kite	USA 3	12.41	993	80	774	-437	656
7 (15)	Jose-Maria Olazabal	Eur 3	12.00	864	72	636	-364	592
8 (9)	Mark Calcavecchia	USA 4	11.81	1146	97	834	-432	744
9 (6)	Ian Woosnam	Eur 4	11.56	948	82	877	-477	548
10 (8)	Paul Azinger	USA 5	10.95	898	82	863	-461	496
11 (14)	Chip Beck	USA 6	10.49	860	82	788	-424	496
12 (12)	Masashi Ozaki	Jpn 1	10.00	850	85	795	-449	504
13 (11)	David Frost	Afr 1	9.39	836	89	868	-468	436
14 (3)	Sandy Lyle	Eur 5	9.37	862	92	1297	-687	252
15 (20)	Fred Couples	USA 7	8.85	814	92	677	-351	488
16 (16)	Bernhard Langer	Eur 6	8.47	720	85	725	-445	440
17 (7)	Ben Crenshaw	USA 8	8.31	673	81	877	-476	272
18 (23)	Mark McCumber	USA 9	8.04	619	77	548	-285	356
19 (24)	Larry Mize	USA 10	7.08	595	84	538	-299	356
20 (17)	Tom Watson	USA 11	6.81	429	63	519	-294	204
21 (57)	Ronan Rafferty	Eur 7	6.73	666	99	390	-216	492
22 (30)	Mike Reid	USA 12	6.57	565	86	508	-267	324
23 (18)	Larry Nelson	USA 13	6.46	465	72	596	-315	184
24 (41)	Scott Hoch	USA 14	6.42	610	95	467	-261	404
25 (10)	Lanny Wadkins	USA 15	6.35	489	77	750	-413	152
26 (47)	Peter Senior	ANZ 2	6.35	641	101	433	-232	440
27 (29)	Mark O'Meara	USA 16	6.20	564	91	547	-311	328
28 (76)	Steve Jones	USA 17	6.09	518	85	231	-117	404
29 (65)	Craig Parry	ANZ 3	6.03	531	88	256	-129	404
30 (32)	Craig Stadler	USA 18	5.90	460	78	486	-270	244
31 (22)	Mark McNulty	Afr 2	5.82	483	83	679	-396	200
32 (35)	Bruce Lietzke	USA 19	5.68	386	68	403	-221	204
33 (21)	Ken Green	USA 20	5.47	509	93	692	-375	192
34 (37)	Isao Aoki	Jpn 2	5.45	518	95	527	-321	312
35 (113)	Tim Simpson	USA 21	5.44	506	93	202	-124	428
36 (25)	Scott Simpson	USA 22	5.33	474	89	532	-282	224
37 (48)	Mark James	Eur 8	5.27	437	83	345	-188	280
38 (33)	Nick Price	Afr 3	4.87	404	83	461	-253	196
39 (34)	Don Pooley	USA 23	4.75	380	80	467	-263	176
40 (43)	Bob Tway	USA 24	4.69	441	94	495	-330	276
41 (38)	Steve Pate	USA 25	4.67	467	100	543	-284	208
42 (85)	Wayne Grady	ANZ 4	4.62	434	94	255	-133	312
43 (31)	Rodger Davis	ANZ 5	4.42	402	91	582	-344	164
44 (28)	Dan Pohl	USA 26	4.36	327	75	502	-295	120

( ) : Figures in brackets indicate 1986/88 positions.

Pos.	Player	Tour	Points Average	Total Points	No. of Events	86/88 Total	86/88 Minus	1989 Plus
45 (161)	Blaine McCallister	USA 27	4.30	456	106	142	-78	392
46 (62)	Peter Jacobsen	USA 28	4.28	338	79	302	-164	200
47 (39)	Fuzzy Zoeller	USA 29	4.22	274	65	337	-215	152
48 (64)	Naomichi Ozaki	Jpn 3	4.20	395	94	341	-198	252
49 (53)	Jodie Mudd	USA 30	4.17	375	90	347	-196	224
50 (94)	Bill Glasson	USA 31	4.15	349	84	214	-117	252
51 (27)	Joey Sindelar	USA 32	4.07	391	96	648	-357	100
52 (51)	Gordon Brand, Jr.	Eur 9	4.07	395	97	401	-222	216
53 (281T)	Eduardo Romero	SAm 1	3.96	265	67	35	-18	248
54 (123)	Peter Fowler	ANZ 6	3.94	418	106	197	-111	332
55 (40)	Jeff Sluman	USA 33	3.93	381	97	529	-276	128
56 (54)	Graham Marsh	ANZ 7	3.92	298	76	327	-193	164
57 (56)	Howard Clark	Eur 10	3.83	318	83	317	-195	196
58 (52)	Hal Sutton	USA 34	3.79	322	85	344	-226	204
59 (46)	Ian Baker-Finch	ANZ 8	3.76	399	106	484	-281	196
60 (82)	Sam Torrance	Eur 11	3.74	303	81	208	-121	216
61 (59)	Gil Morgan	USA 35	3.71	252	68	254	-134	132
62 (88)	Jose-Maria Canizares	Eur 12	3.58	222	62	153	-91	160
63 (45)	Jay Haas	USA 36	3.55	327	92	431	-236	132
64 (74)	Donnie Hammond	USA 37	3.53	307	87	257	-158	208
65 (91)	Davis Love	USA 38	3.50	301	86	230	-129	200
66 (36)	Tsuneyuki Nakajima	Jpn 4	3.48	320	92	492	-308	136
67 (97)	Wayne Levi	USA 39	3.41	266	78	193	-111	184
68 (153)	Mike Harwood	ANZ 9	3.39	325	96	128	-71	268
69 (69)	Brian Jones	ANZ 10	3.27	327	100	322	-175	180
70 (44)	Jose Rivero	Eur 13	3.27	219	67	307	-168	80
71 (84)	Christy O'Connor, Jr.	Eur 14	3.27	232	71	184	-104	152
72 (131)	Brett Ogle	ANZ 11	3.26	264	81	115	-63	212
73 (106)	Dave Rummells	USA 40	3.21	308	96	219	-115	204
74 (42)	Ray Floyd	USA 41	3.19	204	64	335	-223	92
75 (26)	David Ishii	USA 42	3.13	288	92	555	-311	44
76 (66)	Andy Bean	USA 43	3.13	219	70	252	-193	160
77 (50)	Des Smyth	Eur 15	3.09	238	77	325	-179	92
78 (70)	Mark Wiebe	USA 44	3.07	301	98	326	-185	160
79 (127)	David Feherty	Eur 16	3.03	297	98	168	-99	228
80 (78)	Gene Sauers	USA 45	3.01	265	88	278	-157	144
81 (89)	Roger Mackay	ANZ 12	2.96	210	71	163	-85	132
82 (319)	Michael Allen	USA 46	2.95	215	73	26	-15	204
83 (61)	John Mahaffey	USA 47	2.88	271	94	358	-219	132
84 (68)	Tateo Ozaki	Jpn 5	2.80	263	94	299	-176	140
85 (49)	Corey Pavin	USA 48	2.78	242	87	393	-231	80
86 (107)	David Edwards	USA 49	2.76	199	72	156	-89	132
87 (271T)	Vijay Singh	Asa 1	2.62	204	78	32	-16	188
88 (67)	Dave Barr	Can 1	2.57	216	84	297	-161	80
89 (55)	Fulton Allem	Afr 4	2.57	203	79	286	-159	76
90 (140)	Mike Hulbert	USA 50	2.54	272	107	178	-118	212
91 (75)	Tze Chung Chen	Asa 2	2.46	204	83	268	-152	88
92 (58)	D.A. Weibring	USA 51	2.45	189	77	329	-188	48
93 (190)	Mike Sullivan	USA 52	2.35	193	82	87	-58	164
94 (133)	Mats Lanner	Eur 17	2.35	169	72	115	-62	116
95 (202T)	Derrick Cooper	Eur 18	2.34	187	80	75	-40	152
96 (108)	Clarence Rose	USA 53	2.33	235	101	236	-137	136
97 (110)	Roger Chapman	Eur 19	2.31	206	89	191	-101	116

( ) : Figures in brackets indicate 1986/88 positions.

Pos.	Player	Tour	Points Average	Total Points	No. of Events	86/88 Total	86/88 Minus	1989 Plus
98 (83)	Hale Irwin	USA 54	2.31	162	70	205	-107	64
99 (103)	Barry Lane	Eur 20	2.31	199	86	184	-93	108
100 (139)	Jim Carter	USA 55	2.30	228	99	138	-70	160
101 (264)	Andrew Murray	Eur 21	2.30	175	76	42	-23	156
102 (81)	Tom Purtzer	USA 56	2.29	181	79	233	-140	88
103 (63)	Gary Koch	USA 57	2.29	176	77	297	-173	52
104 (603T)	Ted Schulz	USA 58	2.26	190	84	4	-2	188
105 (205)	Loren Roberts	USA 59	2.25	205	91	92	-47	160
106 (132)	Brad Faxon	USA 60	2.25	200	89	159	-83	124
107 (138)	Philip Walton	Eur 22	2.25	182	81	124	-66	124
108 (175)	Tom Byrum	USA 61	2.20	220	100	125	-69	164
109 (60)	Masahiro Kuramoto	Jpn 6	2.12	189	89	359	-210	40
110 (194)	Frank Nobilo	ANZ 13	2.11	203	96	90	-47	160
111 (72)	Doug Tewell	USA 62	2.10	172	82	289	-185	68
112 (128)	Robert Wrenn	USA 63	2.10	176	84	160	-80	96
113 (93)	John Bland	Afr 5	2.09	180	86	230	-134	84
114 (101)	Gordon J. Brand	Eur 23	2.04	184	90	199	-135	120
115 (126)	Jeff Hawkes	Afr 6	2.04	163	80	132	-69	100
116T (144)	Ove Sellberg	Eur 24T	2.00	152	76	116	-72	108
116T (87)	Eamonn Darcy	Eur 24T	2.00	164	82	196	-104	72
118 (115)	Bob Gilder	USA 64	1.95	179	92	196	-105	88
119 (201)	Kenny Perry	USA 65	1.91	164	86	80	-40	124
120 (99)	Tony Johnstone	Afr 7	1.88	175	93	239	-132	68
121 (122)	Nobuo Serizawa	Jpn 7	1.87	174	93	151	-77	100
122 (136)	Denis Durnian	Eur 26	1.87	198	106	156	-78	120
123 (195)	Mike Donald	USA 66	1.86	203	109	110	-63	156
124 (105)	Jack Nicklaus	USA 67	1.85	111	60	141	-110	80
125 (90)	Jim Benepe	USA 68	1.81	141	78	162	-81	60
126 (167)	Ronnie Black	USA 69	1.81	150	83	112	-70	108
127 (73)	Bobby Wadkins	USA 70	1.80	178	99	316	-194	56
128 (174)	John Huston	USA 71	1.78	144	81	88	-44	100
129 (143)	Ed Fiori	USA 72	1.76	153	87	142	-77	88
130 (219)	David Ogrin	USA 73	1.73	154	89	80	-46	120
131 (151)	Koichi Suzuki	Jpn 8	1.73	145	84	129	-76	92
132 (197T)	Hubert Green	USA 74	1.72	127	74	82	-55	100
133 (116)	Mark Mouland	Eur 27	1.71	161	94	179	-98	80
134 (109)	Bob Lohr	USA 75	1.69	166	98	231	-121	56
135 (168)	Yoshiyuki Yokoshima	Jpn 9	1.68	155	92	113	-58	100
136 (125)	Kenny Knox	USA 76	1.68	181	108	198	-125	108
137 (252T)	Peter O'Malley	ANZ 14	1.67	100	60	40	-20	80
138 (238)	Mark Lye	USA 77	1.65	157	95	73	-44	128
139 (314T)	Akihito Yokoyama	Jpn 10	1.64	120	73	24	-12	108
140 (96)	Hajime Meshiai	Jpn 11	1.64	162	99	223	-117	56
141 (95)	Curt Byrum	USA 78	1.63	163	100	216	-117	64
142 (163T)	Steve Elkington	ANZ 15	1.62	159	98	114	-63	108
143 (120)	Hugh Baiocchi	Afr 8	1.62	131	81	176	-109	64
144 (102)	Morris Hatalsky	USA 79	1.59	116	73	187	-99	28
145 (166)	Saburo Fujiki	Jpn 12	1.59	146	92	115	-69	100
146 (114)	Roger Maltbie	USA 80	1.59	119	75	168	-105	56
147T (157)	Lee Trevino	USA 81	1.58	95	60	84	-61	72
147T (124)	Bob Shearer	ANZ 16	1.58	114	72	116	-74	72
149 (185)	Jay Don Blake	USA 82	1.56	142	91	92	-46	96
150 (119)	Yoshimi Niizeki	Jpn 13	1.56	145	93	169	-92	68

( ) : Figures in brackets indicate 1986/88 positions.

Pos.	Player	Tour	Points Average	Total Points	No. of Events	86/88 Total	86/88 Minus	1989 Plus
151 (118)	J.C. Snead	USA 83	1.55	127	82	171	-96	52
152 (77)	David Graham	ANZ 17	1.55	119	77	241	-146	24
153 (104)	Toru Nakamura	Jpn 14	1.53	144	94	211	-119	52
154 (71)	Mac O'Grady	USA 84	1.51	118	78	256	-150	12
155 (121)	Katsunari Takahashi	Jpn 15	1.51	142	94	185	-103	60
156 (112)	Dan Forsman	USA 85	1.51	148	98	206	-122	64
157 (223)	Mark Roe	Eur 28	1.51	134	89	72	-42	104
158 (305)	Jim Gallagher	USA 86	1.48	135	91	39	-24	120
159 (92)	John Cook	USA 87	1.48	127	86	244	-145	28
160 (86)	Scott Verplank	USA 88	1.45	135	93	217	-118	36
161 (220)	Chris Perry	USA 89	1.44	140	97	85	-45	100
162 (308)	Colin Montgomerie	Eur 29	1.42	114	80	28	-14	100
163 (387)	Brian Claar	USA 90	1.41	116	82	22	-18	112
164 (98)	Ken Brown	Eur 30	1.41	114	81	204	-114	24
165 (159)	Tommy Armour	USA 91	1.40	139	99	118	-63	84
166 (111)	Andrew Magee	USA 92	1.40	137	98	212	-111	36
167 (148)	Terry Gale	ANZ 18	1.38	116	84	126	-82	72
168 (410)	Greg Twiggs	USA 93	1.35	89	66	13	-8	84
169 (135)	Johnny Miller	USA 94	1.32	79	60	102	-59	36
170 (180)	Tadami Ueno	Jpn 16	1.31	97	74	78	-41	60
171 (158)	Yoshitaka Yamamoto	Jpn 17	1.29	121	94	123	-66	64
172 (130)	Mark Brooks	USA 95	1.28	122	95	168	-86	40
173 (321)	Akiyoshi Ohmachi	Jpn 18	1.28	124	97	35	-23	112
174 (79)	Anders Forsbrand	Eur 31	1.25	111	89	254	-147	4
175 (134)	Jim Hallet	USA 96	1.24	113	91	130	-65	48
176 (183)	Magnus Persson	Eur 32	1.23	81	66	72	-43	52
177 (218)	Larry Rinker	USA 97	1.22	107	88	82	-47	72
178 (149)	Miguel Martin	Eur 33	1.19	89	75	103	-54	40
179 (129)	Seiichi Kanai	Jpn 19	1.18	111	94	164	-93	40
180 (147)	Carl Mason	Eur 34	1.17	96	82	123	-63	36
181 (210)	Ossie Moore	ANZ 19	1.14	111	97	95	-60	76
182 (186)	Brian Tennyson	USA 98	1.14	96	84	80	-40	56
183 (688T)	Russell Claydon	Eur 35	1.13	68	60	0	0	68
184 (162)	Buddy Gardner	USA 99	1.13	112	99	141	-77	48
185 (323)	Billy Andrade	USA 100	1.13	98	87	29	-15	84
186 (226)	Katsuyoshi Tomori	Jpn 20	1.11	98	88	63	-33	68
187 (179)	Mike Clayton	ANZ 20	1.10	111	101	110	-63	64
188 (146)	Tom Sieckmann	USA 101	1.10	102	93	153	-83	32
189 (155)	Tsukasa Watanabe	Jpn 21	1.09	98	90	120	-66	44
190 (154)	Hiroshi Makino	Jpn 22	1.09	101	93	134	-73	40
191T (412T)	Hideki Kase	Jpn 23	1.08	65	60	12	-7	60
191T (260)	Jeff Woodland	ANZ 21	1.08	65	60	37	-20	48
193 (197T)	Richard Boxall	Eur 36	1.08	92	85	82	-42	52
194 (206)	Phil Blackmar	USA 102	1.08	95	88	88	-61	68
195 (332)	Leonard Thompson	USA 103	1.08	111	103	36	-25	100
196 (100)	Peter Baker	Eur 37	1.08	85	79	172	-87	0
197 (288)	Lance Ten Broeck	USA 104	1.06	82	77	32	-18	68
198 (145)	Tze Ming Chen	Asa 3	1.05	97	92	134	-73	36
199T (172)	Mike Colandro	USA 105	1.05	63	60	75	-40	28
199T (117)	Manuel Pinero	Eur 38	1.05	63	60	123	-72	12

( ) : Figures in brackets indicate 1986/88 positions.

World's Winners of 1989

Spalding Invitational Pro-Am	Bob Gilder
MONY Tournament of Champions	Steve Jones
Bob Hope Chrysler Classic	Steve Jones (2)
Phoenix Open	Mark Calcavecchia
AT&T Pebble Beach National Pro-Am	Mark O'Meara
Nissan Los Angeles Open	Mark Calcavecchia (2)
Hawaiian Open	Greg Sauers
Shearson Lehman Hutton Open	Greg Twiggs
Doral-Ryder Open	Bill Glasson
Honda Classic	Blaine McCallister
The Nestle Invitational	Tom Kite
The Players Championship	Tom Kite (2)
USF&G Classic	Tim Simpson
Independent Insurance Agent Open	Mike Sullivan
Masters Tournament	Nick Faldo
Deposit Guaranty Classic	Jim Booros
MCI Heritage Classic	Payne Stewart
K-Mart Greater Greensboro Open	Ken Green
Las Vegas Invitational	Scott Hoch
GTE Byron Nelson Classic	Jodie Mudd
Memorial Tournament	Bob Tway
Southwestern Bell Colonial National Invitation	Ian Baker-Finch
Bellsouth Atlanta Classic	Scott Simpson
Kemper Open	Tom Byrum
Manufacturers Hanover Westchester Classic	Wayne Grady
U.S. Open Championship	Curtis Strange (2)
Canadian Open	Steve Jones (3)
Beatrice Western Open	Mark McCumber
Canon Greater Hartford Open	Paul Azinger
Anheuser-Busch Classic	Mike Donald
Hardee's Classic	Curt Byrum
Buick Open	Leonard Thompson
Federal Express St. Jude Classic	John Mahaffey
PGA Championship	Payne Stewart (2)
The International	Greg Norman (4)
Canadian PGA	Jean-Louis Lamarre
Fred Meyer Challenge	Craig Stadler/Joey Sindelar
NEC World Series of Golf	David Frost
Chattanooga Classic	Stan Utley
Greater Milwaukee Open	Greg Norman (5)
B.C. Open	Mike Hulbert
Bank of Boston Classic	Blaine McCallister (2)
Southern Open	Ted Schulz
Centel Classic	Bill Britton
Texas Open Presented By Nabisco	Donnie Hammond
Walt Disney World/Oldsmobile Classic	Tim Simpson (2)
Nabisco Championship	Tom Kite (3)
Isuzu Kapalua International	Peter Jacobsen
RMCC Invitational Hosted By Greg Norman	Curtis Strange (3)/Mark O'Meara (2)
J.C. Penney Classic	Bill Glasson (2)/Pat Bradley (2)
Chrysler Team Championship	David Ogrin/Ted Schulz (2)
Spalding Invitational Pro-Am	Mark Calcavecchia (4)

U.S. SENIOR TOUR

MONY Senior Tournament of Champions	Miller Barber
First National Bank Classic (S. Africa)	Harold Henning
General Foods PGA Senior Championship	Larry Mowry
GTE Suncoast Classic	Bob Charles
Aetna Challenge	Gene Littler
Vintage Chrysler Invitational	Miller Barber (2)
MONY Arizona Classic	Bruce Crampton
Fuji Electric Grand Slam (Japan)	Bob Charles (2)
Murata Seniors Reunion	Don Bies
The Tradition At Desert Mountain	Don Bies (2)
Chrysler Cup	United States
Liberty Mutual Legends of Golf	Al Geiberger/Harold Henning (2)
RJR At The Dominion	Larry Mowry (2)
Bell Atlantic St. Christopher's Classic	Dave Hill
NYNEX/Golf Digest Commemorative	Bob Charles (3)
Southwestern Bell Classic	Bobby Nichols
Doug Sanders Kingwood Celebrity Classic	Homero Blancas
Mazda Senior Tournament Players Championship	Orville Moody
Northville Long Island Classic	Butch Baird
MONY Syracuse Classic	Jim Dent
USGA Senior Open	Orville Moody (2)
Digital Classic	Bob Charles (4)
Greater Grand Rapids Open	John Paul Cain
Ameritech Open	Bruce Crampton (2)
Newport Cup	Bob Charles (5)
Volvo Seniors British Open	Jim Dent (2)
Showdown Classic	Tom Shaw
Rancho Murieta Gold Rush	Dave Hill (2)
GTE Northwest Classic	Al Geiberger (2)
Sunwest Bank/Charley Pride Classic	Bob Charles (6)
RJR Bank One Classic	Rives McBee
GTE North Classic	Gary Player
Crestar Classic	Chi Chi Rodriguez
Fairfield Barnett Space Coast Classic	Bob Charles (7)
RJR Championship	Gary Player (2)
Gatlin Brothers Southwest Classic	George Archer
Transamerica Championship	Billy Casper
General Tire Classic	Charles Coody
Du Pont Cup	United States
GTE West Classic	Walter Zembriski
GTE Kaanapali Classic	Don Bies (4)
Mauna Lani Challenge	Dale Douglass
Mazda Champions	Mike Hill/Patti Rizzo (2)

EUROPEAN TOUR

Tenerife Open	Jose-Maria Olazabal
Karl Litten Desert Classic	Mark James
Renault Open de Baleares	Ove Sellberg
Massimo Dutti Calalan Open	Mark Roe
AGF Open	Ronald Stelten
Volvo Open	Vijay Singh (2)
Jersey European Airways Open	Christy O'Connor, Jr.
Credit Lyonnais Cannes Open	Paul Broadhurst
Cepsa Madrid Open	Seve Ballesteros
Peugeot Spanish Open	Bernhard Langer
Epson Grand Prix of Europe Match Play	Seve Ballesteros (2)
Volvo Belgian Open	Gordon J. Brand
Lancia Italian Open	Ronan Rafferty

Volvo PGA Championship	Nick Faldo (2)
Dunhill British Masters	Nick Faldo (3)
Wang Four Stars National Pro-Celebrity	Craig Parry (2)
NM English Open	Mark James (2)
Carrolls Irish Open	Ian Woosnam
Peugeot French Open	Nick Faldo (4)
Torras Monte Carlo Open	Mark McNulty
Bell's Scottish Open	Michael Allen
British Open Championship	Mark Calcavecchia (3)
KLM Open	Jose-Maria Olazabal (2)
Scandinavian Enterprise Open	Ronan Rafferty (2)
Benson & Hedges International Open	Gordon Brand, Jr.
PLM Open	Mike Harwood
German Open	Craig Parry (3)
Ebel European Masters - Swiss Open	Seve Ballesteros (3)
Panasonic European Open	Andrew Murray
Lancome Trophy	Eduardo Romero
Ryder Cup	Europe/United States Tied
Dunhill Cup	United States
Motorola Classic	David Llewellyn
German Masters	Bernahrd Langer (2)
Suntory World Match Play	Nick Faldo (5)
BMW International Open	David Feherty
Portuguese Open - TPC Championship	Colin Montgomerie
Volvo Masters	Ronan Rafferty (3)
Benson & Hedges Trophy	Miguel Angel Jimenez/Xonia Wunsch-Ruiz (2)
World Cup	Australia

AFRICAN TOURS

Dewars White Label Trophy	John Bland
ICL International	Chris Williams
Lexington PGA Championship	Tony Johnstone
Palaboro Classic	Stuart Smith
Zimbabwe Open	Vijay Singh
Protea Assurance South African Open	Fred Wadsworth
Zambian Open	Craig Maltman
AECI Charity Classic	Jeff Hawkes
Kenya Open	David Jones
Hosken Hollard Swazi Sun Classic	Jeff Hawkes (2)
Trust Bank Tournament of Champions	Jay Townsend
Railfreight Bloemfontein Classic	Des Terblanche
First Bank Nigerian Open	Vijay Singh (3)
Ivory Coast Open	Vijay Singh (4)
Minolta Match Play Championship	Fulton Allem
Million Dollar Challenge	David Frost (2)
Twee Jongegezellen Masters	Hugh Baiocchi

AUSTRALASIAN TOUR

Daikyo Palm Meadows Cup	Curtis Strange
Coca-Cola Golf Classic	Isao Aoki
Asthma Foundation Victorian PGA	David Ecob
Victorian Open	Mike Clayton
Australian Match Play Championship	Ossie Moore
Australian Masters	Greg Norman
Tournament Players Championship	Greg Norman (2)
Monro Interiors Nedlands Masters	Louis Brown
Town & Country Joondalup PGA Classic	Brad King
Tattersall Tasmanian Open	Ian Stanley
Air New Zealand-Shell Open	Don Bies (3)

AMP New Zealand Open	Greg Turner
Australian PGA Championship	Peter Senior
Ford New South Wales Open	Rodger Davis
West End South Australian Open	Nick Price
Australian Open Championship	Peter Senior (2)
Johnnie Walker Classic	Peter Senior (3)
Mirage Queensland Open	Brett Ogle

ASIA/JAPAN TOUR

San Miguel/Coca Cola Philippines Open	Emlyn Aubrey
Johnnie Walker Hong Kong Open	Brian Claar
Thai International Thailand Open	Brian Claar (2)
Pakistan Open	Frankie Minosa
Wills Indian Open	Remi Bouchard
Singapore Open	Lu Chien Soon
Shizuoka Open	Koichi Suzuki
Indonesia Open	Kasiyadi
Setonaikai Open	Naomichi Ozaki
Benson & Hedges Malaysian Open	Jeff Maggert
Republic of China Open	Lu Chien Soon (2)
Pocari Sweat Open	Yoshikazu Yokoshima
Maekyung Korean Open	Lu Hsi Chuen
Bridgestone Open	Craig Parry
Dunlop Open	Terry Gale
Chunichi Crowns	Greg Norman (3)
Fuji Sankei Classic	Misashi Ozaki
Japan Match Play Championship	Misashi Ozaki (2)
Pepsi Ube Kosan	Akihito Yokoyama
Mitsubishi Galant	Tateo Ozaki
Sendai Hoso Classic	Misashi Ozaki (3)
Sapporo Tokyu Open	Graham Marsh
Yomiuri Sapporo Beer Open	Hajime Meshiai
Mizuno Open	Akiyoshi Omachi
Kanto PGA Championship	Saburo Fujiki
Kansai PGA Championship	Hajime Matsui
Yonex Hiroshima Open	Misashi Ozaki (4)
NST Niigata Open	Katsuyoshi Tomori
Japan PGA Championship	Misashi Ozaki (5)
Nikkei Cup	Yoshimi Niizeki
Maruman Open	Koichi Suzuki (2)
Daiwa KBC Augusta	Teruo Sugihara
Kanto Open	Yoshinori Mizumaki
Kansai Open	Yoshitaka Yamamoto
Chu-Shikoku Open	Tadami Ueno
Hokkaido Open	Mamoru Takahashi
Chuba Open	Tadao Nakamura
Kyushu Open	Shinji Kuraoka
Suntory Open	Larry Nelson
All Nippon Airways Open	Misashi Ozaki (6)
Jun Classic	Tateo Ozaki (2)
Tokai Classic	Isao Aoki (2)
Japan Open	Misashi Ozaki (7)
Polaroid Cup Golf Digest	Yoshikazu Yokoshima (2)
Bridgestone	Roger Mackay
Lark Cup	Brian Jones
Asahi Glass Four Tours Championship	United States
Visa Taiheiyo Club Masters	Jose-Maria Olazabal (3)
Dunlop Phoenix	Larry Mize
Casio World Open	Isao Aoki (3)
Japan Series Hitachi Cup	Akiyoshi Omachi (2)
Daikyo Open	Nobuo Serizawa

SOUTH AMERICAN TOUR

Sao Paulo Open	Mike Cunning
Argentina Open	Eduardo Romero (2)
Los Leonas Open	Mark Aebli

THE LPGA TOUR

Jamaica Classic	Betsy King
Oldsmobile Classic	Dottie Mochrie
Orix Hawaiian Open	Sherri Turner
Women's Kemper Open	Betsy King (2)
Circle K Tucson Open	Lori Garbacz
Standard Register Turquoise Classic	Allison Finney
Nabisco Dinah Shore	Juli Inkster
Red Robin Kyocera Inamori Classic	Patti Rizzo
Al Star/Centinela Hospital Classic	Pat Bradley
USX Classic	Betsy King (3)
Sara Lee Classic	Kathy Postlewait
Crestar Classic	Juli Inkster (2)
Chrysler Plymouth Classic	Cindy Rarick
Mazda LPGA Championship	Nancy Lopez
Corning Classic	Ayako Okamoto
Rochester International	Patty Sheehan
Planters Pat Bradley International	Robin Hood
Lady Keystone Open	Laura Davies
McDonald's Championship	Betsy King (4)
du Maurier Classic	Tammie Green
Jamie Farr Toledo Classic	Penny Hammel
U.S. Women's Open Championship	Betsy King (5)
Boston Five Classic	Amy Alcott
Atlantic City Classic	Nancy Lopez (2)
Greater Washington Open	Beth Daniel
Nestle World Championship	Betsy King (6)
Mitsubishi Motors Ocean State Open	Tina Barrett
Rail Charity Classic	Beth Daniel (2)
Cellular One-Ping Championship	Muffin Spencer-Devlin
Safeco Classic	Beth Daniel (3)
Nippon Travel - MBS Classic	Nancy Lopez (3)
Konica San Jose Classic	Beth Daniel (4)
Nichirei Cup	Colleen Walker
Mazda Japan Classic	Elaine Crosby

THE WOMEN'S EUROPEAN TOUR

Rome Ladies Classic	Sofia Gronberg
Ford Ladies Classic	Marie-Laure de Lorenzi
Hennessy Ladies Cup	Marie-Laure de Lorenzi (2)
BMW Ladies Classic	Marie-Laure de Lorenzi (3)
Ladies French Open	Suzanne Strudwick
St. Moritz Ladies Classic	Kitrina Douglas
TEC Players Championship	Anna Oxenstierna-Rhodin
Bloor Homes Eastleigh Classic	Debbie Dowling
Lufthansa German Open	Alison Nicholas
Weetabix Ladies British Open	Jane Geddes
Ladies Danish Open	Tania Abitbol
Gislaved Open	Alison Nicholas (2)
Variety Club Celebrity Classic	Corinne Dibnah
Godiva European Masters	Kitrina Douglas (2)
Expedier European Open	Jane Connachan
Italian Open	Xonia Wunsch-Ruiz

Laing Ladies Classic	Laura Davies (2)
Woolmark Ladies Match Play Championship	Dennise Hutton
AGF Biarritz Open	Dennise Hutton (2)
Qualitair Ladies Classic	Alison Nicholas (3)

Multiple Winners of 1989

PLAYER	WINS	PLAYER	WINS
Bob Charles	7	Kitrina Douglas	2
Misashi Ozaki	7	David Frost	2
Betsy King	6	Al Geiberger	2
Nick Faldo	5	Bill Glasson	2
Greg Norman	5	Jeff Hawkes	2
Don Bies	4	Harold Henning	2
Mark Calcavecchia	4	Dave Hill	2
Beth Daniel	4	Dennise Hutton	2
Vijay Singh	4	Juli Inkster	2
Isao Aoki	3	Mark James	2
Seve Ballesteros	3	Bernhard Langer	2
Steve Jones	3	Lu Chien Soon	2
Tom Kite	3	Blaine McCallister	2
Nancy Lopez	3	Orville Moody	2
Marie-Laure de Lorenzi	3	Larry Mowry	2
Alison Nicholas	3	Akiyoshi Omachi	2
Jose-Maria Olazabal	3	Mark O'Meara	2
Craig Parry	3	Tateo Ozaki	2
Ronan Rafferty	3	Gary Player	2
Peter Senior	3	Patti Rizzo	2
Curtis Strange	3	Eduardo Romero	2
Miller Barber	2	Ted Schulz	2
Pat Bradley	2	Tim Simpson	2
Brian Claar	2	Payne Stewart	2
Bruce Crampton	2	Koichi Suzuki	2
Laura Davies	2	Xonia Wunsch-Ruiz	2
Jim Dent	2	Yoshikazu Yokoshima	2

Career World Money List

The following is a listing of the 50 leading money-winners for their careers through the 1989 season. It includes active and inactive players. The World Money List from this and the 23 previous editions of this annual and a table prepared for a companion book, THE WONDERFUL WORLD OF PROFESSIONAL GOLF (Atheneum, 1973), form the basis for this compilation. Additional figures were taken from official records of major golf associations, although the shortcomings in records-keeping in professional golf outside the United States in the 1950s and 1960s and exclusions from U.S.

records in a few cases during those years prevent these figures from being completely accurate. Conversions of foreign currency figures to U.S. dollars are based on average values during the particular years involved.

POS.	PLAYER, COUNTRY	TOTAL MONEY
1	Severiano Ballesteros, Spain	$6,573,553
2	Greg Norman, Australia	6,375,988
3	Tom Kite, U.S.	6,287,853
4	Jack Nicklaus, U.S.	6,232,285
5	Tom Watson, U.S.	6,158,145
6	Curtis Strange, U.S.	6,110,108
7	Isao Aoki, Japan	5,374,652
8	Lanny Wadkins, U.S.	5,202,375
9	Gary Player, South Africa	5,118,997
10	Ben Crenshaw, U.S.	5,075,719
11	Miller Barber, U.S.	5,023,756
12	Lee Trevino, U.S.	4,995,754
13	Raymond Floyd, U.S.	4,923,625
14	Masashi Ozaki, Japan	4,739,210
15	Bernhard Langer, West Germany	4,373,636
16	Sandy Lyle, Scotland	4,361,744
17	Nick Faldo, England	4,253,264
18	Gene Littler, U.S.	4,224,790
19	Billy Casper, U.S.	4,242,039
20	Payne Stewart, U.S.	4,161,523
21	Craig Stadler, U.S.	4,072,813
22	Arnold Palmer, U.S.	4,056,608
23	Bob Charles, New Zealand	4,045,813
24	Hale Irwin, U.S.	4,039,900
25	Ian Woosnam, Wales	4,008,022
26	Tsuneyuki Nakajima, Japan	3,960,180
27	Andy Bean, U.S.	3,921,462
28	Graham Marsh, Australia	3,878,618
29	Johnny Miller, U.S.	3,777,730
30	Don January, U.S.	3,698,521
31	Bruce Crampton, Australia	3,610,235
32	John Mahaffey, U.S.	3,553,839
33	David Frost, South Africa	3,537,606
34	David Graham, Australia	3,522,035
35	Mark O'Meara, U.S.	3,509,406
36	Scott Hoch, U.S.	3,454,173
37	Fred Couples, U.S.	3,441,116
38	Larry Nelson, U.S.	3,420,180
39	Chip Beck, U.S.	3,346,214
40	Bruce Lietzke, U.S.	3,307,935
41	Chi Chi Rodriguez, U.S.	3,091,076
42	Scott Simpson, U.S.	3,077,945
43	Fuzzy Zoeller, U.S.	3,075,461
44	Hubert Green, U.S.	3,053,423
45	Paul Azinger, U.S.	3,004,446
46	Hal Sutton, U.S.	2,976,264
47	Mark Calcavecchia, U.S.	2,930,832
48	Orville Moody, U.S.	2,924,006
49	Al Geiberger, U.S.	2,866,580
50	Gil Morgan, U.S.	2,812,503

These 50 players have won $207,803,958 in their lifetimes playing professional tournament golf.

Women's World Money List

This list includes winnings of the three tours—U.S., Europe and Japan—along with J.C. Penney, Nikkei Cup, Mazda Champions, Spalding and several other unofficial events. Of note, Marie-Laure de Lorenzi, the leader on the European LPGA money list, ranks 55th on this World Money list.

POS.	PLAYER	TOTAL MONEY
1	Betsy King	$675,964
2	Tu Ai Yu	643,397
3	Patti Rizzo	582,489
4	Hiromi Kobayashi	561,845
5	Beth Daniel	554,551
6	Pat Bradley	541,214
7	Nancy Lopez	495,153
8	Ayako Okamoto	418,789
9	Fukumi Tani	409,623
10	Patty Sheehan	320,605
11	Aiko Takasu	320,044
12	Sherri Turner	314,903
13	Colleen Walker	305,166
14	Yuko Moriguchi	297,881
15	Mayumi Hirase	275,145
16	Tammie Green	250,973
17	Jane Geddes	250,950
18	Laura Davies	237,475
19	Cindy Rarick	221,736
20	Erika Nakajima	220,677
21	Atsuko Hikage	212,580
22	Huang Yueh Chyn	204,855
23	Kathy Postlewait	196,647
24	Michiko Okada	194,551
25	Junko Yasui	194,527
26	Penny Hammel	194,336
27	Holly Hartley	191,316
28	Miki Oda	191,006
29	Alice Ritzman	190,632
30	Fusako Nagata	185,677
31	Huang Bie Shyun	185,411
32	Nayoko Yoshikawa	183,293
33	Juli Inkster	180,848
34	Amy Alcott	175,089
35	Wu Ming-Yeh	171,743
36	Allison Finney	171,377
37	Chikayo Yamazaki	170,457
38	Jody Rosenthal	160,583
39	Mitsuko Hamada	160,231
40	Amy Benz	159,736
41	Ritsu Imabori	159,548
42	Lori Garbacz	154,726
43	Martha Nause	151,405
44	Dawn Coe	150,423
45	Liselotte Neumann	148,000
46	Danielle Ammaccapane	141,524
47	Hiromi Takamura	139,455

POS.	PLAYER	TOTAL MONEY
48	Dottie Mochrie	137,820
49	Hollis Stacy	137,610
50	Shirley Furlong	135,774
51	Ikuyo Shiotani	134,973
52	Nancy Brown	133,337
53	Tomiko Ikefuchi	131,478
54	Elaine Crosby	126,899
55	Marie-Laure de Lorenzi	124,166
56	Hiroko Inoue	121,458
57	Reiko Kashiwado	118,852
58	Val Skinner	117,839
59	Susan Sanders	116,276
60	Vicki Fergon	113,534

The U.S. Tour

Spalding Invitational Pro-Amateur

Golf Club at Quail Lodge
Par 71; 6,515 yards

January 5-8
purse, $250,000

Carmel Valley Ranch
Par 70; 6,175 yards

Poppy Hills
Par 72; 6,850 yards

Pebble Beach, California

	SCORES				TOTAL	MONEY
Bob Gilder	66	72	68	70	276	$50,000
Rob Boldt	68	69	74	67	278	30,000
Mark Hayes	69	72	70	69	280	14,250
Sam Randolph	72	69	69	70	280	14,250
J.C. Snead	72	73	66	69	280	14,250
Lennie Clements	72	67	70	71	280	14,250
Dave Barr	68	75	70	68	281	6,250
Jeff Wilson	75	68	68	70	281	6,250
Donnie Hammond	71	69	73	69	282	4,000
Loren Roberts	69	68	76	70	283	3,233
Keith Fergus	71	72	70	70	283	3,233
Dave Stockton	73	68	71	71	283	3,233
George Archer	69	69	74	72	284	2,800
Ted Goin	68	73	77	67	285	2,500
Danny Edwards	74	69	66	76	285	2,500
Roger Maltbie	68	78	72	68	286	1,975
Johnny Miller	69	76	70	71	286	1,975
Bruce Summerhays	72	70	71	73	286	1,975
Bob Ford	73	67	72	74	286	1,975

	SCORES				TOTAL	MONEY
Sonny Skinner	70	75	75	67	287	1,500
Alan Tapie	66	72	77	72	287	1,500
David Ogrin	70	71	75	71	287	1,500
George Burns	70	71	73	73	287	1,500
Keith Clearwater	69	70	75	73	287	1,500
Duffy Waldorf	72	73	72	71	288	1,200
Adam Armagost	71	73	73	71	288	1,200
Craig Stadler	68	75	70	75	288	1,200
Rod Curl	71	74	71	73	289	1,025
Jay Delsing	70	76	68	75	289	1,025
Ron Stelten	74	76	72	68	290	920
Mark Lye	73	69	75	73	290	920
Russ Cochran	74	69	73	74	290	920
Barry Jaeckel	71	74	70	75	290	920
Bob Lunn	74	73	72	72	291	900
Robert Huxtable	68	70	79	74	291	900
Kenny Perry	72	73	72	74	291	900
Shawn McEntee	73	72	77	70	292	840
Charlie Gibson	69	74	77	72	292	840
Mark Pfeil	77	72	70	73	292	840
George Daves	70	79	72	72	293	793
John Elliott Jr.	75	72	74	72	293	793
Greg Powers	66	71	78	78	293	793
David Edwards	70	69	75	79	293	793
Howie Johnson	77	73	71	73	294	777
Roy Vucinich	74	72	74	74	294	777
Chuck Milne	74	79	69	73	295	770
Dave Eichelberger	71	75	79	71	296	760
Warren Chancellor	69	76	76	75	296	760
Robert Meyer	71	75	75	75	296	760
Peter Oosterhuis	77	77	68	75	297	743
Glen Stubblefield	72	77	71	77	297	743
Andrew Blossom Jr.	75	72	71	79	297	743
Gary McCord	70	78	70	79	297	743

MONY Tournament of Champions

LaCosta Country Club, Carlsbad, California
Par 36-36—72; 7,002 yards

January 5-8
purse, $750,000

	SCORES				TOTAL	MONEY
Steve Jones	69	69	72	69	279	$135,000
David Frost	72	70	72	68	282	67,000
Jay Haas	75	67	72	68	282	67,000
Greg Norman	71	72	72	68	283	37,000
Chip Beck	69	70	74	71	284	31,000
Morris Hatalsky	74	74	70	67	285	26,500
Lanny Wadkins	71	70	71	73	285	26,500
Jeff Sluman	70	71	73	71	285	26,500
Bill Glasson	75	73	67	71	286	23,000
Ben Crenshaw	70	72	70	75	287	20,000
Bob Lohr	70	74	70	73	287	20,000
Sandy Lyle	71	71	71	74	287	20,000
Curtis Strange	77	70	69	71	287	20,000
Phil Blackmar	73	74	71	70	288	17,000
Mike Reid	74	73	71	70	288	17,000
Steve Pate	73	75	71	70	289	14,500

	SCORES				TOTAL	MONEY
Tom Sieckmann	71	74	71	73	289	14,500
Joey Sindelar	71	75	74	69	289	14,500
Bruce Lietzke	77	73	72	69	291	12,750
Corey Pavin	74	74	72	71	291	12,750
Blaine McCallister	74	72	74	72	292	11,750
Tom Purtzer	74	71	77	70	292	11,750
Jim Benepe	75	74	74	71	294	11,200
Mark Calcavecchia	72	69	75	78	294	11,200
Gary Koch	77	72	73	73	295	10,600
Andrew Magee	68	75	79	73	295	10,600
Mark McCumber	75	73	73	74	295	10,600
Scott Verplank	74	75	72	74	295	10,600
Paul Azinger	75	79	73	69	296	10,000
Ken Green	77	72	73	74	296	10,000
Mark Brooks	71	79	77	75	302	9,700
Jodie Mudd	77	76	79	72	304	9,500

Bob Hope Chrysler Classic

Bermuda Dunes Country Club
Par 36-36—72; 6,927 yards

Eldorado Country Club
Par 36-36—72; 6,708 yards

Indian Wells Country Club
Par 36-36—72; 6,478 yards

PGA West, Palmer Course
Par 36-36—72; 6,924 yards

January 11-15
purse, $1,000,000

	SCORES					TOTAL	MONEY
Steve Jones	76	68	67	63	69	343	$180,000
Sandy Lyle	70	68	68	68	69	343	88,000
Paul Azinger	69	68	70	67	69	343	88,000
(Jones defeated Lyle and Azinger on first extra hole.)							
Lanny Wadkins	68	70	68	70	68	344	39,375
Kenny Knox	68	71	69	67	69	344	39,375
Mark Calcavecchia	71	67	67	67	72	344	39,375
Fred Couples	65	71	71	68	69	344	39,375
Hubert Green	73	70	65	68	69	345	29,000
Tom Kite	68	69	68	69	71	345	29,000
Bernhard Langer	70	68	68	69	70	345	29,000
Dave Rummells	75	68	67	67	69	346	23,000
Tim Simpson	68	71	71	67	69	346	23,000
Donnie Hammond	73	68	67	67	71	346	23,000
Howard Twitty	72	71	70	67	67	347	17,500
Ted Schulz	70	68	68	69	72	347	17,500
Bruce Lietzke	73	71	65	69	69	347	17,500
Brad Bryant	67	68	73	67	72	347	17,500
Jodie Mudd	72	66	68	70	72	348	12,171.43
Corey Pavin	70	69	71	68	70	348	12,171.43
J.C. Snead	71	67	70	69	71	348	12,171.43
Peter Jacobsen	67	70	69	71	71	348	12,171.43
Davis Love III	73	71	67	68	69	348	12,171.43
Chip Beck	71	71	69	66	71	348	12,171.43
Scott Verplank	70	68	65	72	73	348	12,171.42
Brian Tennyson	72	73	69	67	68	349	7,800

	SCORES					TOTAL	MONEY
Larry Mize	70	74	68	67	70	349	7,800
James Hallet	74	68	69	66	72	349	7,800
Bill Glasson	73	67	70	69	70	349	7,800
Mike Donald	71	73	68	66	71	349	7,800
Payne Stewart	70	72	68	72	68	350	6,650
Bobby Wadkins	71	68	70	70	71	350	6,650
Steve Pate	81	71	62	69	68	351	5,300
Hal Sutton	69	71	68	72	71	351	5,300
Ken Green	72	72	72	68	67	351	5,300
John Mahaffey	70	69	71	70	71	351	5,300
Rocco Mediate	70	70	73	69	69	351	5,300
John Cook	74	70	70	68	69	351	5,300
Tommy Armour	68	75	68	70	70	351	5,300
Jay Don Blake	68	70	69	73	71	351	5,300
Don Reese	68	71	72	70	71	352	3,504.45
David Ogrin	68	72	71	69	72	352	3,504.45
Tim Norris	74	70	69	68	71	352	3,504.45
Billy Ray Brown	70	73	69	69	71	352	3,504.45
Jeff Sluman	69	68	74	72	69	352	3,504.44
Jack Kay Jr.	76	71	70	65	70	352	3,504.44
Johnny Miller	74	69	70	68	71	352	3,504.44
Gil Morgan	75	70	70	67	70	352	3,504.44
Jim Benepe	68	68	76	69	71	352	3,504.44
Bob Tway	73	69	69	68	74	353	2,443.34
Buddy Gardner	71	69	71	71	71	353	2,443.34
Mike Sullivan	74	71	72	68	68	353	2,443.33
Lon Hinkle	74	74	68	69	68	353	2,443.33
Gary Koch	68	70	74	71	70	353	2,443.33
David Canipe	74	71	69	69	70	353	2,443.33

Phoenix Open

TPC of Scottsdale, Scottsdale, Arizona
Par 35-36—71; 6,992 yards

January 19-22
purse, $700,000

	SCORES				TOTAL	MONEY
Mark Calcavecchia	66	68	65	64	263	$126,000
Chip Beck	67	70	66	67	270	75,600
Scott Hoch	64	70	69	68	271	36,400
Bill Glasson	65	68	73	65	271	36,400
Paul Azinger	68	68	68	67	271	36,400
Mark McCumber	64	69	69	70	272	25,200
Steve Elkington	66	73	64	70	273	21,087.50
Jim Carter	68	68	70	67	273	21,087.50
Ted Schulz	64	70	61	68	273	21,087.50
Larry Mize	70	69	67	67	273	21,087.50
Gary Hallberg	68	68	66	72	274	14,840
Ben Crenshaw	66	69	70	69	274	14,840
Tim Simpson	66	72	70	66	274	14,840
Kenny Perry	69	72	67	66	274	14,840
Davis Love III	69	72	68	65	274	14,840
Fred Couples	68	74	67	66	275	10,500
Tommy Armour	67	70	70	68	275	10,500
Fuzzy Zoeller	70	72	70	63	275	10,500
Joey Sindelar	67	73	67	68	275	10,500
Mike Swartz	66	71	73	65	275	10,500

	SCORES				TOTAL	MONEY
Jim Gallagher, Jr.	65	71	68	72	276	7,560
Fulton Allem	70	68	69	69	276	7,560
Nick Price	68	71	67	70	276	7,560
Mark Lye	65	76	68	67	276	7,560
Billy Ray Brown	72	69	68	68	277	5,460
Curtis Strange	66	70	72	69	277	5,460
Clarence Rose	68	71	72	66	277	5,460
Hal Sutton	72	70	69	66	277	5,460
Bruce Lietzke	69	71	68	69	277	5,460
Ken Green	63	73	72	70	278	4,347.20
Corey Pavin	65	71	72	70	278	4,347.20
Larry Rinker	72	67	69	70	278	4,347.20
Gil Morgan	72	69	70	67	278	4,347.20
Kenny Knox	69	72	65	72	278	4,347.20
Nick Faldo	71	72	65	71	279	3,450.80
Bob Gilder	70	72	71	66	279	3,450.80
Jim Thorpe	70	71	72	66	279	3,450.80
Jeff Sluman	71	72	66	70	279	3,450.80
Rocco Mediate	72	69	67	71	279	3,450.80
Jack Kay Jr.	69	73	68	70	280	2,660
David Edwards	73	70	70	67	280	2,600
Curt Byrum	69	72	69	70	280	2,660
Robert Wrenn	68	70	72	70	280	2,660
Mike Sullivan	71	72	69	68	280	2,660
Blaine McCallister	66	75	69	70	280	2,660
Ed Fiori	67	73	71	70	281	1,844.50
Peter Jacobsen	66	74	70	71	281	1,844.50
Brian Tennyson	68	73	68	72	281	1,844.50
Dan Pohl	71	72	68	70	281	1,844.50
Richard Zokol	70	73	70	68	281	1,844.50
David Ogrin	69	70	72	70	281	1,844.50
Andrew Magee	71	71	71	68	281	1,844.50
Sandy Lyle	68	68	76	69	281	1,844.50

AT&T Pebble Beach National Pro-Am

Pebble Beach Golf Links
Par 36-36—72; 6,799 yards

Cypress Point Golf Club
Par 36-36—72; 6,506 yards

Spyglass Hill Golf Club
Par 36-36—72; 6,810 yards

Pebble Beach, California

January 26-29
purse, $1,000,000

	SCORES				TOTAL	MONEY
Mark O'Meara	66	68	73	70	277	$180,000
Tom Kite	67	70	72	69	278	108,000
Sandy Lyle	68	72	72	68	280	52,000
Jim Carter	70	72	69	69	280	52,000
Nick Price	66	74	67	73	280	52,000
Steve Jones	71	69	71	70	281	32,375
Lanny Wadkins	73	69	72	67	281	32,375
Steve Pate	72	72	66	71	281	32,375
Hal Sutton	70	73	70	68	281	32,375

	SCORES				TOTAL	MONEY
Dave Stockton	65	70	78	69	282	26,000
Loren Roberts	67	72	76	67	282	26,000
Bernhard Langer	70	68	71	74	283	21,000
Mark Brooks	73	66	71	73	283	21,000
David Ogrin	68	70	72	73	283	21,000
Mike McCullough	69	71	71	73	284	17,500
Scott Simpson	70	72	73	69	284	17,500
Gary Hallberg	73	72	72	68	285	14,500
Ken Green	68	71	71	75	285	14,500
Dennis Trixler	69	72	75	69	285	14,500
Gil Morgan	70	69	73	73	285	14,500
Bob Eastwood	75	66	72	73	286	10,000
George Archer	69	72	75	70	286	10,000
John Cook	67	76	70	73	286	10,000
Howard Clark	71	70	73	72	286	10,000
Bobby Clampett	69	74	70	73	286	10,000
Fuzzy Zoeller	71	71	73	71	286	10,000
John Mahaffey	69	77	69	72	287	6,516.67
Rocco Mediate	71	69	78	69	287	6,516.67
Johnny Miller	70	72	73	72	287	6,516.67
Chris Perry	69	72	73	73	287	6,516.67
Tim Simpson	68	76	73	70	287	6,516.67
Ted Schulz	68	70	74	75	287	6,516.67
Brad Fabel	70	71	73	73	287	6,516.66
Mike Hulbert	76	69	72	70	287	6,516.66
Billy Andrade	71	71	69	76	287	6,516.66
Roger Maltbie	69	74	74	71	288	4,305.56
John Inman	70	70	73	75	288	4,305.56
Brad Faxon	74	75	68	71	288	4,305.56
John Adams	71	72	72	73	288	4,305.56
Andy Bean	74	72	71	71	288	4,305.56
Andrew Magee	74	75	67	72	288	4,305.55
Davis Love III	70	72	73	73	288	4,305.55
Hubert Green	74	73	71	70	288	4,305.55
Keith Clearwater	72	69	73	74	288	4,305.55
Jack Nicklaus	69	69	80	71	289	2,928
Brad Bryant	72	72	72	73	289	2,928
Craig Stadler	70	73	72	74	289	2,928
Bob Tway	70	73	71	75	289	2,928
Brian Tennyson	74	69	74	72	289	2,928
Mark Lye	74	71	72	73	290	2,377.15
Kenny Perry	73	72	73	72	290	2,377.15
Greg Ladehoff	69	70	75	76	290	2,377.14
Mark Calcavecchia	71	72	75	72	290	2,377.14
Chen Tze Chung	73	75	70	72	290	2,377.14
D.A. Weibring	73	70	74	73	290	2,377.14
Mike Reid	73	74	69	74	290	2,377.14

Nissan Los Angeles Open

Riviera Country Club, Pacific Palisades, California
Par 35-36—71; 6,946 yards

February 2-5
purse, $1,000,000

	SCORES				TOTAL	MONEY
Mark Calcavecchia	68	66	70	68	272	$180,000
Sandy Lyle	68	66	68	71	273	108,000
Hale Irwin	70	67	69	68	274	68,000

	SCORES				TOTAL	MONEY
Gene Sauers	67	70	72	67	276	41,333.34
Steve Pate	67	71	68	70	276	41,333.33
Phil Blackmar	68	72	67	69	276	41,333.33
Fred Couples	69	68	69	71	277	33,500
Tom Kite	73	70	66	69	278	31,000
Mike Reid	68	69	73	70	280	25,000
Tom Purtzer	71	66	73	70	280	25,000
Johnny Miller	71	70	70	69	280	25,000
Donnie Hammond	68	73	68	71	280	25,000
Ben Crenshaw	70	71	70	69	280	25,000
D.A. Weibring	70	72	71	68	281	18,500
Peter Jacobsen	70	69	72	70	281	18,500
Bobby Wadkins	71	68	73	70	282	14,500
Mark O'Meara	75	68	70	69	282	14,500
James Hallet	72	70	70	70	282	14,500
Mark Brooks	67	71	73	71	282	14,500
Jay Don Blake	71	71	70	70	282	14,500
Fulton Allem	70	71	71	70	282	14,500
Howard Twitty	68	71	73	71	283	10,400
Rocco Mediate	70	71	70	72	283	10,400
Nick Faldo	72	68	68	75	283	10,400
Tim Simpson	70	75	68	71	284	7,471.43
Craig Stadler	71	67	73	73	284	7,471.43
Nick Price	73	67	73	71	284	7,471.43
John Huston	70	70	75	69	284	7,471.43
Andrew Magee	71	71	71	71	284	7,471.43
Gary Hallberg	71	69	71	73	284	7,471.43
Don Reese	72	68	70	74	284	7,471.42
Hal Sutton	70	73	71	71	285	5,414.29
Bernhard Langer	70	71	72	72	285	5,414.29
Ray Floyd	69	75	71	70	285	5,414.29
John Inman	69	76	70	70	285	5,414.29
Loren Roberts	69	70	72	74	285	5,414.28
Chris Perry	71	69	72	73	285	5,414.28
Mark Lye	72	72	74	67	285	5,414.28
Dan Pohl	72	73	74	67	286	3,900
Corey Pavin	72	71	73	70	286	3,900
Clarence Rose	71	73	71	71	286	3,900
Scott Simpson	73	70	71	72	286	3,900
Bill Sander	72	71	73	70	286	3,900
Steve Elkington	74	71	75	66	286	3,900
Tommy Armour	71	71	71	73	286	3,900
Willie Wood	71	71	74	71	287	2,835
Brian Tennyson	76	69	68	74	287	2,835
Curtis Strange	73	71	68	75	287	2,835
David Frost	73	69	72	73	287	2,835
J.C. Snead	72	70	73	73	288	2,377.15
Bruce Lietzke	69	70	75	74	288	2,377.15
Fuzzy Zoeller	72	69	74	73	288	2,377.14
Lanny Wadkins	72	73	72	71	288	2,377.14
Webb Heintzelman	69	74	74	71	288	2,377.14
Lon Hinkle	70	75	74	69	288	2,377.14
Andy Bean	69	75	72	72	288	2,377.14

Hawaiian Open

Waialae Country Club, Honolulu, Hawaii
Par 36-36—72; 6,975 yards

February 9-12
purse, $750,000

(Shortened to 54 holes because of rain delays.)

	SCORES			TOTAL	MONEY
Gene Sauers	65	67	65	197	$135,000
David Ogrin	65	67	66	198	81,000
Dave Rummells	70	65	64	199	51,000
Jim Carter	64	66	70	200	36,000
Chip Beck	69	64	69	202	28,500
Don Reese	69	69	64	202	28,500
Rex Caldwell	69	67	67	203	25,125
Paul Azinger	68	70	66	204	21,000
Kazunari Takahashi	70	67	67	204	21,000
Lon Hinkle	66	70	68	204	21,000
Bill Glasson	67	67	70	204	21,000
Bobby Wadkins	66	68	71	205	13,821.43
Billy Pierot	68	69	68	205	13,821.43
Craig Stadler	67	71	67	205	13,821.43
Brian Tennyson	74	65	66	205	13,821.43
Scott Simpson	67	69	69	205	13,821.43
Buddy Gardner	68	69	68	205	13,821.43
Ben Crenshaw	69	66	70	205	13,821.42
Ed Fiori	70	69	67	206	7,067.31
Danny Edwards	71	67	68	206	7,067.31
Mike Donald	67	69	70	206	7,067.31
Joel Edwards	69	69	68	206	7,067.31
Steve Elkington	66	70	70	206	7,067.31
Rick Pearson	71	66	69	206	7,067.31
Corey Pavin	70	68	68	206	7,067.31
James Hallet	68	71	67	206	7,067.31
Mark Hayes	71	68	67	206	7,067.31
Larry Nelson	71	66	69	206	7,067.31
George Archer	68	66	72	206	7,067.30
Fulton Allem	66	68	72	206	7,067.30
Tim Simpson	66	67	73	206	7,067.30
Jim Gallagher, Jr.	68	68	71	207	3,891.67
David Canipe	70	66	71	207	3,891.67
Miguel Martin	70	67	70	207	3,891.67
Scott Hoch	68	68	71	207	3,891.67
Ed Humenik	69	71	67	207	3,891.67
Billy Mayfair	69	68	70	207	3,891.67
Mark Brooks	68	65	74	207	3,891.66
Bill Buttner	70	71	66	207	3,891.66
Lance Ten Broeck	70	70	67	207	3,891.66
David Frost	72	68	68	208	2,486.67
Lennie Clements	66	71	71	208	2,486.67
Brad Bryant	74	64	70	208	2,486.67
Bob Wolcott	70	70	68	208	2,486.67
Don Shirey, Jr.	70	69	69	208	2,486.67
Masanobu Kumura	70	69	69	208	2,486.67
Jay Don Blake	71	70	67	208	2,486.66
John Adams	66	74	68	208	2,486.66
Loren Roberts	72	69	67	208	2,486.66
Curt Byrum	72	69	68	209	1,752
Bill Britton	67	73	69	209	1,752
Ronnie Black	68	73	68	209	1,752

	SCORES			TOTAL	MONEY
Dan Forsman	71	67	71	209	1,752
Jay Delsing	70	70	69	209	1,752
Tony Sills	72	67	70	209	1,752
Duffy Waldorf	67	72	70	209	1,752
J.C. Snead	69	72	68	209	1,752
John Inman	68	69	72	209	1,752
Kenny Knox	70	70	69	209	1,752

Shearson Lehman Hutton Open

Torry Pines Golf Club, La Jolla, California
South Course
Par 36-36—72; 7,021 yards
North Course
Par 36-36—72; 6,659 yards

February 16-19
purse, $700,000

	SCORES				TOTAL	MONEY
Greg Twiggs	68	70	64	69	271	$126,000
Mark Wiebe	68	65	70	70	273	46,200
Mark O'Meara	68	67	72	66	273	46,200
Steve Elkington	70	63	67	73	273	46,200
Brad Faxon	67	69	69	68	273	46,200
Sam Randolph	71	69	66	68	274	23,450
John McComish	68	69	67	70	274	23,450
Dan Forsman	73	64	70	67	274	23,450
Duffy Waldorf	68	69	69	69	275	18,900
John Cook	70	68	69	68	275	18,900
Phil Blackmar	69	68	70	68	275	18,900
Dave Rummells	68	66	73	69	276	14,175
Johnny Miller	69	69	66	72	276	14,175
John Adams	71	68	68	69	276	14,175
Fred Couples	68	69	68	71	276	14,175
Robert Wrenn	70	70	71	66	277	11,200
Mike Hulbert	68	70	69	70	277	11,200
Keith Clearwater	71	68	70	68	277	11,200
Bob Tway	66	73	71	68	278	7,147
Dennis Trixler	66	74	67	71	278	7,147
Ray Stewart	70	68	71	69	278	7,147
Lance Ten Broeck	69	68	70	71	278	7,147
Craig Stadler	68	72	69	69	278	7,147
Pat McGowan	68	72	68	70	278	7,147
Steve Pate	70	71	67	70	278	7,147
David Peoples	65	72	71	70	278	7,147
Billy Ray Brown	69	68	70	71	278	7,147
Dave Barr	66	68	71	73	278	7,147
Scott Simpson	70	68	69	72	279	4,081
Bill Sander	70	65	70	74	279	4,081
Tony Grimes	70	68	71	70	279	4,081
Wayne Grady	72	66	73	68	279	4,081
Ray Barr, Jr.	68	70	70	71	279	4,081
Dave Eichelberger	70	68	70	71	279	4,081
Tommy Armour	68	68	72	71	279	4,081
George Archer	69	69	71	70	279	4,081
Jim Booros	68	72	68	71	279	4,081
Bill Buttner	70	68	68	73	279	4,081
Dave Stockton	72	66	70	73	281	3,010
John Mahaffey	69	71	72	69	281	3,010
Fred Funk	70	69	70	72	281	3,010

	SCORES			TOTAL	MONEY
Clarence Rose	71	70	68	73	282	2,252.25
Brian Tennyson	69	68	75	70	282	2,252.25
Jodie Mudd	68	69	71	74	282	2,252.25
Mark Lye	65	70	74	73	282	2,252.25
Gary McCord	71	69	70	72	282	2,252.25
Curt Byrum	68	70	71	73	282	2,252.25
Jay Don Blake	72	66	70	74	282	2,252.25
Rick Fehr	67	73	70	72	282	2,252.25
Tony Sills	68	70	74	71	283	1,722
Billy Mayfair	68	73	71	71	283	1,722
Ed Fiori	69	72	70	72	283	1,722

Doral-Ryder Open

Doral Hotel and Country Club, Blue Course, Miami, Florida

Par 36-36—72; 6,939 yards

February 23-26

purse, $1,300,000

	SCORES			TOTAL	MONEY
Bill Glasson	71	65	67	72	275	$234,000
Fred Couples	69	69	70	68	276	140,400
Mark Calcavecchia	65	73	66	74	278	67,600
Curtis Strange	73	67	69	69	278	67,600
Bruce Lietzke	68	71	68	71	278	67,600
John Huston	69	69	70	71	279	43,550
Wayne Levi	68	69	73	69	279	43,550
Dan Pohl	69	71	73	66	279	43,550
Buddy Gardner	70	68	69	74	281	35,100
Paul Azinger	73	71	66	71	281	35,100
Ben Crenshaw	67	72	72	70	281	35,100
Jim Carter	71	73	69	69	282	23,957.15
Billy Mayfair	75	72	69	66	282	23,957.15
Steve Elkington	69	72	68	73	282	23,957.14
Dave Barr	71	73	67	71	282	23,957.14
Bob Tway	69	72	71	70	282	23,957.14
Gil Morgan	74	68	70	70	282	23,957.14
David Ogrin	71	71	69	71	282	23,957.14
Jay Haas	72	73	72	66	283	15,756
Chen Tze Chung	72	72	69	70	283	15,756
Seve Ballesteros	73	69	71	70	283	15,756
Gene Sauers	73	74	67	69	283	15,756
Mark Lye	75	72	66	70	283	15,756
Steve Jones	70	74	71	69	284	10,790
Dan Halldorson	70	69	74	71	284	10,790
Keith Clearwater	72	71	68	73	284	10,790
Bobby Wadkins	69	74	72	69	284	10,790
Nick Price	72	73	73	66	284	10,790
David Frost	71	76	70	68	285	8,645
John Inman	74	71	72	68	285	8,645
Mike Hulbert	71	75	72	67	285	8,645
Mark O'Meara	70	77	68	70	285	8,645
Ed Fiori	69	73	74	70	286	6,722.86
Kenny Knox	75	70	71	70	286	6,722.86
David Edwards	73	74	69	70	286	6,722.86
Robert Wrenn	71	73	73	69	286	6,722.86
Dave Rummells	71	74	71	70	286	6,722.86
Tom Kite	69	73	69	75	286	6,722.85
Bobby Clampett	70	73	71	72	286	6,722.85
Lon Hinkle	69	74	74	70	287	5,330

	SCORES				TOTAL	MONEY
Brad Bryant	72	69	72	74	287	5,330
Hal Sutton	71	71	77	68	287	5,330
Sandy Lyle	74	71	71	72	288	3,958.50
Mike Donald	72	74	71	71	288	3,958.50
Curt Byrum	72	74	73	69	288	3,958.50
Billy Ray Brown	74	71	73	70	288	3,958.50
Lennie Clements	69	75	74	70	288	3,958.50
Isao Aoki	71	75	72	70	288	3,958.50
Ray Floyd	74	71	72	71	288	3,958.50
Denis Watson	72	71	73	72	288	3,958.50

Honda Classic

TPC at Eagle Trace, Coral Springs, Florida
Par 36-36—72; 7,037 yards

March 2-5
purse, $800,000

	SCORES				TOTAL	MONEY
Blaine McCallister	70	67	65	64	266	$144,000
Payne Stewart	68	65	70	67	270	86,400
Curtis Strange	68	71	67	65	271	46,400
Steve Pate	70	67	64	70	271	46,400
Dan Pohl	66	62	75	69	272	32,000
Paul Azinger	67	66	72	68	273	27,800
Tom Byrum	65	69	70	69	273	27,800
Fuzzy Zoeller	70	66	70	68	274	24,800
Nick Price	69	66	69	71	275	20,800
Gary Koch	69	68	68	70	275	20,800
Mike Hulbert	71	67	67	70	275	20,800
Davis Love III	70	67	68	70	275	20,800
J.C. Snead	68	69	71	68	276	14,133.34
Mark McCumber	68	67	72	69	276	14,133.34
Gene Sauers	68	72	66	70	276	14,133.33
Larry Rinker	67	68	67	74	276	14,133.33
John Huston	68	66	73	69	276	14,133.33
Bruce Lietzke	68	69	69	70	276	14,133.33
Ted Schulz	66	65	71	75	277	10,800
Fulton Allem	66	68	72	71	277	10,800
Joey Sindelar	68	64	73	73	278	8,000
Roger Maltbie	69	68	68	73	278	8,000
Jim Carter	67	67	69	75	278	8,000
Ed Fiori	67	68	72	71	278	8,000
Ken Green	70	68	70	70	278	8,000
Buddy Gardner	65	66	73	74	278	8,000
Mark Wiebe	67	68	71	73	279	5,440
Steve Jones	69	70	71	69	279	5,440
Sandy Lyle	67	73	67	72	279	5,440
Rick Pearson	72	68	72	67	279	5,440
Andy North	70	66	71	72	279	5,440
Nick Faldo	67	72	69	71	279	5,440
Fred Couples	66	73	70	70	279	5,440
Jim Thorpe	69	71	69	71	280	4,220
Tim Simpson	70	69	70	71	280	4,220
Andrew Magee	70	70	68	72	280	4,220
John Inman	68	69	71	72	280	4,220
Bob Gilder	66	68	73	74	281	3,760
Kenny Perry	69	69	71	73	282	3,200
Ed Humenik	73	67	68	74	282	3,200

	SCORES			TOTAL	MONEY
Rocco Mediate	69	66	73	74	282	3,200
Brad Fabel	67	71	71	73	282	3,200
Brad Bryant	70	70	69	73	282	3,200
Bill Britton	69	68	72	73	282	3,200
Scott Hoch	71	67	70	75	283	2,560
Greg Ladehoff	69	71	73	70	283	2,560
Scott Simpson	70	69	71	74	284	2,152
Larry Nelson	71	69	72	72	284	2,152
Jim Booros	67	73	70	74	284	2,152
Rex Caldwell	65	70	75	74	284	2,152

The Nestle Invitational

Bay Hill Club and Lodge, Orlando, Florida
Par 36-35—71; 7,103 yards

March 9-12
purse, $800,000

	SCORES			TOTAL	MONEY
Tom Kite	68	72	67	71	278	$144,000
Davis Love III	72	67	66	73	278	86,400
(Kite defeated Love on second extra hole.)						
Curtis Strange	73	72	69	65	279	54,400
Don Pooley	69	73	68	70	280	33,066.67
Payne Stewart	76	69	65	70	280	33,066.67
Loren Roberts	66	73	69	72	280	33,066.66
Dan Pohl	70	70	71	70	281	26,800
Larry Rinker	72	68	68	74	282	24,000
Nick Price	67	77	71	67	282	24,000
Tommy Armour	75	69	69	70	283	20,000
Blaine McCallister	71	73	74	65	283	20,000
Larry Mize	70	71	69	73	283	20,000
Brad Faxon	74	68	74	68	284	14,133.34
Greg Norman	71	73	73	67	284	14,133.34
Fred Couples	72	69	73	70	284	14,133.33
Brad Bryant	75	72	68	69	284	14,133.33
Ted Schulz	68	74	70	72	284	14,133.33
Steve Jones	73	72	67	72	284	14,133.33
Hal Sutton	74	71	67	73	285	11,200
Tom Sieckmann	75	70	68	73	286	9,320
Tom Purtzer	68	75	73	70	286	9,320
Corey Pavin	74	71	72	69	286	9,320
David Ogrin	77	71	71	67	286	9,320
Jim Carter	71	78	68	70	287	5,920
James Hallet	73	74	69	71	287	5,920
Fulton Allem	71	73	72	71	287	5,920
Ray Floyd	71	74	71	71	287	5,920
Ian Baker-Finch	72	70	73	72	287	5,920
Mike Hulbert	74	73	72	68	287	5,920
Rocco Mediate	78	70	71	68	287	5,920
Steve Pate	69	74	75	69	287	5,920
John Mahaffey	74	73	71	69	287	5,920
Billy Mayfair	74	73	71	69	287	5,920
Dave Barr	77	71	68	72	288	4,128
Paul Azinger	73	75	70	70	288	4,128
Bobby Wadkins	75	69	69	75	288	4,128
Leonard Thompson	75	74	66	73	288	4,128
Mark O'Meara	75	73	73	67	288	4,128
Donnie Hammond	72	74	69	74	289	3,280

	SCORES				TOTAL	MONEY
Scott Hoch	76	69	71	73	289	3,280
David Frost	74	75	72	68	289	3,280
Tom Watson	76	69	73	71	289	3,280
Howard Twitty	76	73	70	70	289	3,280
Kenny Knox	74	75	68	73	290	2,560
Mark Calcavecchia	70	69	75	76	290	2,560
D.A. Weibring	74	74	71	71	290	2,560
Dave Rummells	74	71	70	75	290	2,560
Phil Blackmar	76	73	73	69	291	1,988.58
Keith Clearwater	73	74	71	73	291	1,988.57
Gary Koch	72	77	71	71	291	1,988.57
Greg Twiggs	70	74	74	73	291	1,988.57
Mark Lye	76	73	71	71	291	1,988.57
Chris Perry	70	74	76	71	291	1,988.57
Roger Maltbie	77	71	68	75	291	1,988.57

The Players Championship

TPC at Sawgrass, Ponte Vedra, Florida
Par 36-36—72; 6,881 yards

March 16-19
purse, $1,350,000

	SCORES				TOTAL	MONEY
Tom Kite	69	70	69	71	279	$243,000
Chip Beck	71	68	68	73	280	145,800
Bruce Lietzke	66	69	74	72	281	91,800
Greg Norman	74	67	69	72	282	59,400
Fred Couples	68	70	71	73	282	59,400
Mark McCumber	69	70	70	74	283	46,912.50
Gil Morgan	71	69	70	73	283	46,912.50
Gary Koch	70	69	70	75	284	39,150
David Frost	66	71	75	72	284	39,150
Andy Bean	68	76	69	71	284	39,150
Rocco Mediate	73	71	69	72	285	31,050
Ben Crenshaw	67	72	70	76	285	31,050
Tom Watson	71	73	71	70	285	31,050
Paul Azinger	68	71	74	73	286	24,300
Fulton Allem	70	69	75	72	286	24,300
Loren Roberts	72	73	69	72	286	24,300
Brad Faxon	72	71	69	75	287	19,575
Mike Sullivan	72	71	70	74	287	19,575
Mark Wiebe	74	71	71	71	287	19,575
Tim Simpson	70	71	71	75	287	19,575
Chris Perry	70	75	70	73	288	12,673.13
Kenny Perry	68	77	72	71	288	12,673.13
D.A. Weibring	70	74	72	72	288	12,673.13
Larry Rinker	71	72	72	73	288	12,673.13
David Edwards	71	73	69	75	288	12,673.12
Ken Green	70	71	73	74	288	12,673.12
Mike Donald	68	72	73	75	288	12,673.12
Craig Stadler	70	72	69	77	288	12,673.12
Jack Nicklaus	71	72	68	78	289	8,775
Mike Reid	73	71	71	74	289	8,775
Hal Sutton	71	71	78	69	289	8,775
Bob Tway	69	73	72	75	289	8,775
Ted Schulz	73	72	73	71	289	8,775
Corey Pavin	70	70	77	73	290	6,672.86
Jim Gallagher, Jr.	70	72	74	74	290	6,672.86

	SCORES				TOTAL	MONEY
Bob Gilder	73	71	73	73	290	6,672.86
Doug Tewell	70	75	72	73	290	6,672.86
Curtis Strange	68	76	72	74	290	6,672.86
Steve Pate	66	78	71	75	290	6,672.85
Joey Sindelar	72	73	68	77	290	6,672.85
Roger Maltbie	75	71	71	74	291	5,130
Steve Jones	68	75	73	75	291	5,130
Keith Clearwater	65	76	74	76	291	5,130
Lanny Wadkins	73	73	71	74	291	5,130
John Mahaffey	73	73	73	73	292	3,952.80
David Ogrin	72	74	74	72	292	3,952.80
Masashi Ozaki	75	68	70	79	292	3,952.80
Jim Carter	74	70	73	75	292	3,952.80
Fuzzy Zoeller	74	72	71	75	292	3,952.80
Wayne Levi	75	71	68	79	293	3,256.20
Clarence Rose	72	71	75	75	293	3,256.20
Dan Pohl	69	70	75	79	293	3,256.20
Gary Hallberg	74	72	71	76	293	3,256.20
Richard Zokol	71	74	72	76	293	3,256.20

USF&G Classic

English Turn Golf and Country Club, New Orleans, Louisiana   March 23-26
Par 36-36—72; 7,106 yards   purse, $750,000

	SCORES				TOTAL	MONEY
Tim Simpson	68	67	70	69	274	$135,000
Hal Sutton	71	68	67	70	276	66,000
Greg Norman	68	68	68	72	276	66,000
Mark Hayes	72	71	67	68	278	36,000
Mark O'Meara	72	67	72	68	279	26,343.75
Payne Stewart	70	69	69	71	279	26,343.75
Bill Sander	68	71	70	70	279	26,343.75
P.H. Horgan III	70	70	67	72	279	26,343.75
Lanny Wadkins	72	70	67	71	280	18,750
Pat McGowan	68	70	71	71	280	18,750
Dan Forsman	66	69	71	74	280	18,750
David Edwards	72	68	72	68	280	18,750
Chip Beck	74	67	68	71	280	18,750
Ted Schulz	71	69	69	72	281	12,750
Wayne Levi	74	67	72	68	281	12,750
Jim Gallagher, Jr.	72	70	70	69	281	12,750
Tony Grimes	73	65	72	71	281	12,750
Curt Byrum	73	69	72	67	281	12,750
Robert Wrenn	70	71	71	70	282	9,750
Rick Dalpos	72	73	68	69	282	9,750
David Graham	72	71	71	68	282	9,750
Tom Watson	71	69	69	74	283	7,800
Rick Pearson	72	72	68	71	283	7,800
Brian Tennyson	72	65	75	71	283	7,800
Larry Rinker	74	68	73	69	284	5,850
Jack Nicklaus	73	69	70	72	284	5,850
Don Pooley	72	69	72	71	284	5,850
Nolan Henke	75	70	69	70	284	5,850
Ed Humenik	71	71	71	71	284	5,850
Dave Rummells	73	71	70	71	285	4,556.50
Peter Jacobsen	75	69	68	73	285	4,556.50

	SCORES				TOTAL	MONEY
John Mahaffey	71	70	71	73	285	4,556.50
Seve Ballesteros	72	72	70	71	285	4,556.50
Phil Blackmar	72	71	71	71	285	4,556.50
Tom Byrum	68	70	72	75	285	4,556.50
Chris Perry	75	70	69	72	286	3,456
Jeff Sluman	75	70	73	68	286	3,456
Tom Kite	70	69	74	73	286	3,456
George Archer	72	73	71	70	286	3,456
Lee Chill	68	73	75	70	286	3,456
Mark Brooks	71	75	70	70	286	3,456
Scott Verplank	76	66	77	68	287	2,413.13
Bill Britton	74	72	72	69	287	2,413.13
Billy Andrade	74	70	72	71	287	2,413.13
Tommy Armour	73	70	75	69	287	2,413.13
James Hallet	69	75	71	72	287	2,413.12
Steve Hart	72	71	71	73	287	2,413.12
Kenny Knox	73	70	72	72	287	2,413.12
Jim Booros	71	71	73	72	287	2,413.12
Ed Fiori	76	67	70	75	288	1,795
Karl Kimball	72	72	70	74	288	1,795
Mike Hulbert	70	75	73	70	288	1,795
Ray Barr, Jr.	75	68	74	71	288	1,795
Billy Ray Brown	74	71	71	72	288	1,795
David Canipe	75	68	74	71	288	1,795

Independent Insurance Agent Open

TPC at The Woodlands, The Woodlands, Texas
Par 36-36—72; 7,042 yards

March 30-April 2
purse, $800,000

	SCORES				TOTAL	MONEY
Mike Sullivan	76	71	68	65	280	$144,000
Craig Stadler	72	71	68	70	281	86,400
Mike Reid	72	69	71	70	282	41,600
Mike Donald	67	67	74	74	282	41,600
Seve Ballesteros	69	69	72	72	282	41,600
Hal Sutton	74	69	68	72	283	26,800
Curtis Strange	69	70	72	72	283	26,800
David Frost	70	74	70	69	283	26,800
Gil Morgan	70	77	69	68	284	21,600
Bob Gilder	70	71	71	72	284	21,600
Mike Hulbert	68	76	71	69	284	21,600
D.A. Weibring	71	74	69	71	285	16,200
Bruce Lietzke	70	72	70	73	285	16,200
Billy Ray Brown	71	70	72	72	285	16,200
Brad Bryant	69	72	72	72	285	16,200
Ian Woosnam	73	71	71	71	286	11,600
Calvin Peete	71	72	73	70	286	11,600
Ron Streck	73	70	70	73	286	11,600
John Inman	69	75	66	76	286	11,600
Roger Maltbie	69	73	73	71	286	11,600
Fred Couples	75	70	69	72	286	11,600
Steve Hart	70	72	70	75	287	8,320
Wayne Grady	70	70	75	72	287	8,320
Ben Crenshaw	73	70	69	75	287	8,320
Brad Fabel	73	72	72	71	288	5,977.15
Bernhard Langer	74	71	72	71	288	5,977.15

	SCORES				TOTAL	MONEY
Lance Ten Broeck	70	72	68	78	288	5,977.14
Loren Roberts	73	71	70	74	288	5,977.14
Fred Funk	71	73	74	70	288	5,977.14
Jack Kay, Jr.	71	76	71	70	288	5,977.14
Ed Fiori	71	73	72	72	288	5,977.14
Don Shirey, Jr.	69	72	76	72	289	4,840
Lennie Clements	71	73	76	69	289	4,840
Gary Koch	73	71	74	72	290	3,870
Steve Jones	75	72	68	75	290	3,870
Rocco Mediate	73	69	75	73	290	3,870
Lon Hinkle	72	74	69	75	290	3,870
Jose-Maria Olazabal	72	73	68	77	290	3,870
Jim Gallagher, Jr.	70	70	75	75	290	3,870
Phil Blackmar	73	72	73	72	290	3,870
Russ Cochran	71	76	72	71	290	3,870
J.C. Snead	71	72	74	74	291	2,800
John Mahaffey	77	68	73	73	291	2,800
Roy Biancalana	70	72	76	73	291	2,800
Joel Edwards	74	69	73	75	291	2,800
Nick Faldo	73	70	72	76	291	2,800
Tony Sills	71	70	75	76	292	2,054.86
David Ogrin	72	74	72	74	292	2,054.86
John Adams	71	76	72	73	292	2,054.86
Bill Buttner	73	72	73	74	292	2,054.86
Keith Clearwater	74	69	73	76	292	2,054.86
Chris Perry	70	76	74	72	292	2,054.85
Tony Grimes	73	72	75	72	292	2,054.85

Masters Tournament

Augusta National Golf Club, Augusta, Georgia
Par 36-36—72; 6,905 yards

April 6-9
purse, $1,067,600

	SCORES				TOTAL	MONEY
Nick Faldo	68	73	77	65	283	$200,000
Scott Hoch	69	74	71	69	283	120,000
(Faldo defeated Hoch on second extra hole.)						
Greg Norman	74	75	68	67	284	64,450
Ben Crenshaw	71	72	70	71	284	64,450
Seve Ballesteros	71	72	73	69	285	44,400
Mike Reid	72	71	71	72	286	40,000
Jodie Mudd	73	76	72	66	287	37,200
Jeff Sluman	74	72	74	68	288	32,200
Jose-Maria Olazabal	77	73	70	68	288	32,200
Chip Beck	74	76	70	68	288	32,200
Mark O'Meara	74	71	72	72	289	25,567
Fred Couples	72	76	74	67	289	25,567
Ken Green	74	69	73	73	289	25,567
Tom Watson	72	73	74	71	290	19,450
Don Pooley	70	77	76	67	290	19,450
Ian Woosnam	74	76	71	69	290	19,450
Paul Azinger	75	75	69	71	290	19,450
Jack Nicklaus	73	74	73	71	291	14,000
Curtis Strange	74	71	74	72	291	14,000
Masashi Ozaki	71	75	73	72	291	14,000
Lee Trevino	67	74	81	69	291	14,000
David Frost	76	72	73	70	291	14,000

	SCORES				TOTAL	MONEY
Tom Kite	72	72	72	75	291	14,000
Payne Stewart	73	75	74	70	292	10,250
Tom Purtzer	71	76	73	72	292	10,250
Steve Pate	76	75	74	68	293	8,240
Fuzzy Zoeller	76	74	69	74	293	8,240
Lanny Wadkins	76	71	73	73	293	8,240
Larry Mize	72	77	69	75	293	8,240
Bernhard Langer	74	75	71	73	293	8,240
Dave Rummells	74	74	75	71	294	6,900
Mark Calcavecchia	74	72	74	74	294	6,900
Steve Jones	74	73	80	67	294	6,900
Bruce Lietzke	74	75	79	68	296	6,000
Hubert Green	74	75	76	71	296	6,000
Peter Jacobsen	74	73	78	71	296	6,000
Bob Gilder	75	74	77	71	297	5,400
Scott Simpson	72	77	72	77	298	4,900
Tommy Aaron	76	74	72	76	298	4,900
Charles Coody	76	74	76	72	298	4,900
Ray Floyd	76	75	73	74	298	4,900
Dan Pohl	72	74	78	75	299	4,300
Greg Twiggs	75	76	79	70	300	3,900
George Archer	75	75	75	75	300	3,900
Mark McCumber	72	75	81	72	300	3,900
D.A. Weibring	72	79	74	76	301	3,125
Mike Sullivan	76	74	73	78	301	3,125
Jay Haas	73	77	79	72	301	3,125
Bob Lohr	75	76	77	73	301	3,125
Corey Pavin	74	74	78	76	302	2,800
Andy Bean	70	80	77	77	304	2,700
Chen Tze Chung	71	75	76	84	306	2,600

Out of Final 36 Holes

	SCORES		TOTAL
Tim Simpson	75	77	152
Mark Wiebe	77	75	152
Andy North	77	75	152
Gary Player	76	77	153
Andrew Magee	73	80	153
Blaine McCallister	76	77	153
Billy Casper	75	78	153
Joey Sindelar	75	78	153
Sandy Lyle	77	76	153
Craig Stadler	74	79	153
Gene Sauers	74	79	153
Larry Nelson	77	76	153
Bob Tway	77	77	154
Tom Sieckmann	79	75	154
Hal Sutton	72	82	154
Bill Glasson	77	77	154
Mark Brooks	77	78	155
Mark McNulty	80	75	155
Ralph Howe III	77	79	156
Gary Koch	76	80	156
Jim Benepe	82	75	157
Tsuneyuki Nakajima	76	81	157
P. Daniel Yates III	81	77	158
Doug Tewell	77	81	158

	SCORES			TOTAL
Nick Price	76	82		158
Scott Verplank	79	79		158
Morris Hatalsky	78	81		159
Arnold Palmer	81	80		161
Eric Meeks	83	79		162
David Eger	84	78		162
Doug Ford	81	82		163
Christian Hardin	85	85		170
Gay Brewer	83	WD		

(Professionals who did not complete 72 holes received $1,500 each.)

Deposit Guaranty Classic

Hattiesburg Country Club, Hattiesburg, Mississippi
Par 35-35—70; 6,594 yards

April 6-9
purse, $200,000

	SCORES			TOTAL	MONEY
Jim Booros	64	69	66	199	$36,000
Mike Donald	68	65	66	199	21,600
(Booros defeated Donald on fourth extra hole.)					
Robert Thompson	65	71	65	201	9,600
Lance Ten Broeck	69	65	67	201	9,600
Fred Funk	71	65	65	201	9,600
David Peoples	68	68	65	201	9,600
P.H. Horgan III	69	69	64	202	6,233.34
Bob Wolcott	70	66	66	202	6,233.33
Steve Lowery	68	69	65	202	6,233.33
Perry Arthur	69	68	67	204	5,400
Barry Jaeckel	67	73	65	205	4,240
Rocco Mediate	65	72	68	205	4,240
Ray Barr, Jr.	69	69	67	205	4,240
Clark Burroughs	68	68	69	205	4,240
Rex Caldwell	69	70	66	205	4,240
Larry Ziegler	70	66	70	206	3,000
Steve Hart	68	70	68	206	3,000
Barry Cheesman	65	72	69	206	3,000
Jim Dent	72	68	66	206	3,000
Terrance Dill	69	71	66	206	3,000
Ron Streck	71	71	65	207	2,080
Chris Kite	71	70	66	207	2,080
Ed Humenik	67	71	69	207	2,080
Larry Silveira	70	68	69	207	2,080
Rick Fehr	70	65	72	207	2,080
Billy Tuten	71	70	67	208	1,390
Harry Taylor	70	71	67	208	1,390
David Jackson	68	70	70	208	1,390
Dewey Arnette	69	69	70	208	1,390
Bill Buttner	69	68	71	208	1,390
Gregory Chapman	71	67	70	208	1,390
Rick Dalpos	70	69	69	208	1,390
Joel Edwards	72	68	68	208	1,390
David Ogrin	67	73	69	209	1,055
J.L. Lewis	67	71	71	209	1,055
Billy Andrade	73	68	68	209	1,055
Antonio Cerda	70	70	69	209	1,055
Doug Weaver	67	71	72	210	900

	SCORES			TOTAL	MONEY
Nolan Henke	72	73	65	210	900
Trevor Dodds	71	69	70	210	900
Dennis Trixler	72	69	70	211	720
Jim Thorpe	70	70	71	211	720
John Inman	70	72	69	211	720
Mike Bender	72	67	72	211	720
Frank Conner	73	71	67	211	720
Bob Estes	70	72	69	211	720
Jack Kay, Jr.	74	71	67	212	502.23
Forrest Fezler	76	69	67	212	502.23
Fred Wadsworth	70	69	73	212	502.22
Clarence Rose	69	72	71	212	502.22
Karl Kimball	76	69	67	212	502.22
Steve Thomas	70	73	69	212	502.22
Roy Biancalana	72	72	68	212	502.22
Tom Garner	74	67	71	212	502.22
Kelly Gibson	75	69	68	212	502.22

MCI Heritage Classic

Harbour Town Golf Links, Hilton Head Island, South Carolina
Par 36-35—71; 6,657 yards

April 13-16
purse, $800,000

	SCORES				TOTAL	MONEY
Payne Stewart	65	67	67	69	268	$144,000
Kenny Perry	65	67	70	71	273	86,400
Bernhard Langer	69	70	67	71	277	46,400
Fred Couples	71	72	69	65	277	46,400
Lanny Wadkins	72	69	70	67	278	29,200
Craig Stadler	70	70	70	68	278	29,200
Kenny Knox	69	70	67	72	278	29,200
Tim Simpson	75	68	68	68	279	23,200
Mark McCumber	71	64	69	75	279	23,200
Tom Kite	72	67	70	70	279	23,200
Mike Reid	69	70	70	71	280	17,600
David Ogrin	70	72	68	70	280	17,600
David Edwards	73	68	70	69	280	17,600
Nick Faldo	68	77	67	68	280	17,600
Corey Pavin	73	71	67	70	281	13,200
Jodie Mudd	73	71	67	70	281	13,200
Billy Mayfair	70	70	69	72	281	13,200
Jay Don Blake	69	71	71	70	281	13,200
Rocco Mediate	67	68	75	72	282	10,040
Larry Nelson	72	71	72	67	282	10,040
Tom Byrum	72	69	68	73	282	10,040
David Canipe	72	72	69	69	282	10,040
Tom Watson	76	66	70	71	283	6,920
Peter Jacobsen	71	68	70	74	283	6,920
George Archer	73	71	71	68	283	6,920
Dave Barr	74	69	69	71	283	6,920
Chip Beck	71	71	68	73	283	6,920
Mike Donald	71	68	76	68	283	6,920
Johnny Miller	71	69	75	69	284	5,560
Donnie Hammond	75	65	70	74	284	5,560
Gene Sauers	73	72	70	70	285	4,537.15
Mark Wiebe	76	69	70	70	285	4,537.15

	SCORES				TOTAL	MONEY
Bob Tway	73	71	71	70	285	4,537.14
Loren Roberts	69	69	70	77	285	4,537.14
Larry Rinker	72	70	74	69	285	4,537.14
Jim Carter	72	73	71	69	285	4,537.14
Bob Eastwood	67	75	71	72	285	4,537.14
Doug Tewell	71	72	71	72	286	3,680
Blaine McCallister	77	68	70	71	286	3,680
Lee Trevino	72	73	70	72	287	2,960
Mike Sullivan	71	73	70	73	287	2,960
Larry Mize	73	72	70	72	287	2,960
John Mahaffey	73	69	75	70	287	2,960
Gil Morgan	73	70	72	72	287	2,960
Ted Schulz	74	71	70	72	287	2,960
Bill Britton	70	75	69	73	287	2,960
Buddy Gardner	69	74	70	75	288	2,152
Wayne Grady	72	73	68	75	288	2,152
Billy Ray Brown	69	73	74	72	288	2,152
Jim Gallagher, Jr.	73	72	67	76	288	2,152

K-Mart Greater Greensboro Open

Forest Oaks Country Club, Greensboro, North Carolina
Par 36-36—72; 6,984 yards

April 20-23
purse, $1,000,000

	SCORES				TOTAL	MONEY
Ken Green	73	66	66	72	277	$180,000
John Huston	71	69	67	72	279	108,000
Ed Fiori	70	71	73	67	281	68,000
Dave Eichelberger	72	67	72	71	282	48,000
Mike Sullivan	70	74	70	69	283	36,500
Greg Norman	73	72	70	68	283	36,500
Jim Booros	69	70	72	72	283	36,500
Mark Wiebe	72	69	71	72	284	30,000
Kenny Perry	70	70	72	72	284	30,000
Dave Barr	71	69	73	73	286	27,000
Don Pooley	71	74	75	67	287	22,000
Payne Stewart	71	69	76	71	287	22,000
Bob Gilder	74	73	72	68	287	22,000
Donnie Hammond	75	70	72	70	287	22,000
Tom Sieckmann	69	76	71	72	288	14,066.67
Mark McCumber	73	73	71	71	288	14,066.67
Tom Purtzer	72	73	72	71	288	14,066.67
Curtis Strange	75	73	70	70	288	14,066.67
David Edwards	70	71	75	72	288	14,066.67
John Adams	70	75	72	71	288	14,066.67
Robert Thompson	73	73	69	73	288	14,066.66
Chip Beck	74	70	70	74	288	14,066.66
Fred Couples	75	71	68	74	288	14,066.66
David Ogrin	69	76	69	75	289	8,525
Gene Sauers	75	70	69	75	289	8,525
Larry Silveira	70	75	68	76	289	8,525
Davis Love III	73	69	75	72	289	8,525
Nick Price	72	75	72	71	290	6,368.75
Bill Sander	77	71	72	70	290	6,368.75
Scott Verplank	71	71	76	72	290	6,368.75
J.C. Snead	71	69	75	75	290	6,368.75

	SCORES				TOTAL	MONEY
Ray Stewart	70	75	68	77	290	6,368.75
Dan Pohl	72	74	71	73	290	6,368.75
Dave Rummells	76	72	73	69	290	6,368.75
Bobby Clampett	71	74	73	72	290	6,368.75
Larry Mize	72	72	74	73	291	4,608.34
Jim Gallagher, Jr.	75	72	72	72	291	4,608.34
Tony Sills	75	70	74	72	291	4,608.33
Lance Ten Broeck	72	72	75	72	291	4,608.33
Don Shirey, Jr.	69	74	77	71	291	4,608.33
Scott Hoch	73	73	75	70	291	4,608.33
Doug Tewell	71	73	71	77	292	3,217.50
Lon Hinkle	75	70	74	73	292	3,217.50
Blaine McCallister	76	72	72	72	292	3,217.50
Bob Eastwood	71	75	75	71	292	3,217.50
George Archer	72	76	73	71	292	3,217.50
Mike Donald	74	71	70	77	292	3,217.50
Billy Ray Brown	72	73	76	71	292	3,217.50
Russ Cochran	76	71	72	73	292	3,217.50
Loren Roberts	73	71	76	73	293	2,348.89
Billy Pierot	76	70	76	71	293	2,348.89
Tony Grimes	75	73	73	72	293	2,348.89
John Inman	72	73	74	74	293	2,348.89
Mark Lye	71	76	72	74	293	2,348.89
Rocco Mediate	74	74	73	72	293	2,348.89
Ronnie Black	70	73	73	77	293	2,348.89
Bill Buttner	74	70	72	77	293	2,348.89
Larry Rinker	77	71	75	70	293	2,348.88

Las Vegas Invitational

Las Vegas Country Club
Par 36-36—72; 7,162 yards

Desert Inn Country Club
Par 36-36—72; 7,111 yards

Spanish Trail Country Club
Par 36-36—72; 7,088 yards

April 26-30
purse, $1,250,000

	SCORES					TOTAL	MONEY
Scott Hoch	69	64	68	65	70	336	$225,000
Robert Wrenn	69	66	66	69	66	336	135,000
(Hoch defeated Wrenn on fifth extra hole.)							
Craig Stadler	69	67	65	69	67	337	72,500
Gil Morgan	70	63	73	64	67	337	72,500
Mark Wiebe	71	67	66	68	66	338	43,906.25
Dan Pohl	69	66	64	68	71	338	43,906.25
Brad Bryant	67	68	69	70	64	338	43,906.25
Russ Cochran	70	70	66	64	68	338	43,906.25
Tony Sills	67	69	69	68	67	340	33,750
Gene Sauers	65	69	72	66	68	340	33,750
Jim Carter	70	67	65	67	71	340	33,750
Nick Price	74	65	66	68	68	341	28,750
Steve Pate	66	69	67	70	70	342	25,000
John Mahaffey	67	73	66	65	71	342	25,000
Joey Sindelar	71	69	66	70	67	343	17,583.34

		SCORES				TOTAL	MONEY
Webb Heintzelman	73	70	66	68	66	343	17,583.34
Steve Elkington	73	67	67	72	64	343	17,583.34
Dave Rummells	67	73	67	69	67	343	17,583.33
Tom Purtzer	66	66	75	67	69	343	17,583.33
John Inman	70	69	66	68	70	343	17,583.33
Bob Estes	69	71	67	66	70	343	17,583.33
David Edwards	69	69	69	69	67	343	17,583.33
Donnie Hammond	70	66	67	72	68	343	17,583.33
Steve Jones	73	68	69	69	65	344	10,656.25
Bill Glasson	65	67	70	74	68	344	10,656.25
Trevor Dodds	70	70	71	68	65	344	10,656.25
Lennie Clements	69	67	69	72	67	344	10,656.25
Don Shirey, Jr.	74	70	67	67	67	345	7,961.25
Hal Sutton	72	72	67	66	68	345	7,961.25
David Love III	72	68	69	69	67	345	7,961.25
Bob Gilder	69	69	69	68	70	345	7,961.25
Hubert Green	70	68	68	69	70	345	7,961.25
Bill Britton	71	68	67	72	67	345	7,961.25
Curt Byrum	68	70	70	73	64	345	7,961.25
Mark Calcavecchia	69	71	66	72	67	345	7,961.25
Rick Pearson	67	69	71	70	69	346	5,381.67
Kenny Knox	73	68	70	69	66	346	5,381.67
Jodie Mudd	74	67	69	71	65	346	5,381.67
Rick Fehr	70	70	69	71	66	346	5,381.67
Jim Gallagher, Jr.	70	71	69	67	69	346	5,381.67
Ken Green	71	71	67	69	68	346	5,381.67
Ted Schulz	70	70	66	68	72	346	5,381.66
Larry Silveira	67	69	72	68	70	346	5,381.66
Mark O'Meara	66	70	73	68	69	346	5,381.66
Bob Tway	67	73	70	70	67	347	3,875
Wayne Levi	72	68	66	70	71	347	3,875
Rocco Mediate	66	72	68	71	70	347	3,875
Leonard Thompson	69	69	70	70	70	348	3,107.15
Mac O'Grady	68	73	69	70	68	348	3,107.15
Roger Maltbie	72	68	69	68	71	348	3,107.14
Chris Perry	66	69	73	69	71	348	3,107.14
Peter Jacobsen	69	73	65	67	74	348	3,107.14
John McComish	71	71	67	68	71	348	3,107.14
Ed Fiori	68	68	70	71	71	348	3,107.14

GTE Byron Nelson Classic

TPC at Las Colinas, Irving, Texas
Par 35-35—70; 6,767 yards

May 4-7
purse, $1,000,000

		SCORES			TOTAL	MONEY
Jodie Mudd	68	66	66	65	265	$180,000
Larry Nelson	63	68	67	67	265	108,000
(Mudd defeated Nelson on first extra hole.)						
Mark O'Meara	67	68	65	66	266	68,000
Loren Roberts	65	68	66	68	267	48,000
Wayne Levi	62	67	68	71	268	36,500
Chris Perry	65	65	70	68	268	36,500
Larry Mize	67	67	63	71	268	36,500
Dave Rummells	64	68	67	70	269	29,000
Payne Stewart	64	70	68	67	269	29,000

	SCORES	TOTAL	MONEY
Ted Schulz	69 66 66 68	269	29,000
Craig Stadler	65 66 72 67	270	24,000
Blaine McCallister	67 67 68 68	270	24,000
Mark Wiebe	70 67 67 67	271	18,200
Howard Twitty	66 71 66 68	271	18,200
Steve Jones	68 69 66 68	271	18,200
Mark Calcavecchia	70 67 66 68	271	18,200
Russ Cochran	67 67 71 66	271	18,200
Mark McCumber	66 71 69 66	272	12,600
Doug Tewell	66 69 71 66	272	12,600
Duffy Waldorf	64 68 71 69	272	12,600
Kenny Knox	64 72 67 69	272	12,600
Wayne Grady	67 70 68 67	272	12,600
Brad Bryant	66 71 68 67	272	12,600
Tim Simpson	65 70 68 70	273	7,914.29
Steve Hart	66 68 69 70	273	7,914.29
Robin Freeman	66 71 67 69	273	7,914.29
Isao Aoki	68 69 67 69	273	7,914.29
Dan Halldorson	65 65 70 73	273	7,914.28
Nick Faldo	67 66 69 71	273	7,914.28
Jim Carter	67 67 68 71	273	7,914.28
Tony Sills	66 69 71 68	274	5,433.34
Mark Lye	67 67 72 68	274	5,433.34
Billy Andrade	65 69 73 67	274	5,433.34
Clarence Rose	68 68 67 71	274	5,433.33
Greg Ladehoff	66 66 71 71	274	5,433.33
Steve Elkington	66 69 69 70	274	5,433.33
Dick Mast	66 70 67 71	274	5,433.33
Tommy Armour	68 69 68 69	274	5,433.33
Bobby Clampett	68 67 68 71	274	5,433.33
Sam Randolph	64 73 70 68	275	3,504.45
Mike Sullivan	64 73 70 68	275	3,504.45
Buddy Gardner	69 68 68 70	275	3,504.45
Ian Baker-Finch	65 71 69 70	275	3,504.45
Corey Pavin	69 68 67 71	275	3,504.44
Bob Tway	69 68 66 72	275	3,504.44
Tom Kite	70 63 71 71	275	3,504.44
John Mahaffey	65 68 69 73	275	3,504.44
Jay Don Blake	67 70 67 71	275	3,504.44
Billy Pierot	64 73 69 70	276	2,468
Mike Reid	71 65 73 67	276	2,468
Ken Green	69 66 70 71	276	2,468
Ray Floyd	67 66 69 74	276	2,468
David Edwards	66 71 70 69	276	2,468

Memorial Tournament

Muirfield Village Golf Club, Dublin, Ohio
Par 36-36—72; 7,104 yards

May 11-14
purse, $930,250

	SCORES	TOTAL	MONEY
Bob Tway	71 69 68 69	277	$160,000
Fuzzy Zoeller	69 66 72 72	279	96,000
Payne Stewart	70 73 73 65	281	60,440
Bruce Lietzke	73 70 69 71	283	40,835
Mark Calcavecchia	72 68 73 70	283	40,835

	SCORES				TOTAL	MONEY
Scott Verplank	72	73	69	70	284	32,610
Mark O'Meara	75	68	72	69	284	32,610
Larry Nelson	72	72	72	69	285	26,610
Scott Hoch	72	76	69	68	285	26,610
Ray Floyd	73	67	73	72	285	26,610
David Frost	75	71	72	67	285	26,610
Dave Rummells	72	72	72	71	287	19,722.50
Donnie Hammond	72	70	75	70	287	19,722.50
Greg Norman	75	68	73	71	287	19,722.50
Tom Byrum	76	71	72	68	287	19,722.50
Corey Pavin	71	74	73	70	288	15,056
Larry Mize	72	74	73	69	288	15,056
John Mahaffey	74	75	67	72	288	15,056
Dave Barr	74	72	72	70	288	15,056
Fred Couples	70	72	70	76	288	15,056
Mark Wiebe	71	75	75	68	289	11,680
Curtis Strange	78	69	69	73	289	11,680
David Edwards	71	73	73	72	289	11,680
Tim Simpson	73	74	71	72	290	8,921.67
Lanny Wadkins	77	73	69	71	290	8,921.67
Craig Stadler	77	71	69	73	290	8,921.67
Kenny Knox	71	76	72	71	290	8,921.67
Clarence Rose	75	74	67	74	290	8,921.66
Keith Clearwater	71	74	70	75	290	8,921.66
Johnny Miller	73	72	77	69	291	7,367.50
David Ogrin	73	76	72	70	291	7,367.50
Ed Fiori	73	73	74	71	291	7,367.50
Wayne Grady	73	73	70	75	291	7,367.50
Peter Jacobsen	75	73	74	70	292	6,115.72
Jim Carter	71	79	72	70	292	6,115.72
Brad Faxon	77	73	75	67	292	6,115.72
Billy Mayfair	72	74	73	73	292	6,115.71
Hale Irwin	76	70	74	72	292	6,115.71
Mike Reid	72	75	71	74	292	6,115.71
Paul Azinger	73	73	73	73	292	6,115.71
Mike Sullivan	72	74	74	73	293	5,100
Sandy Lyle	76	73	73	71	293	5,100
Davis Love III	75	75	70	73	293	5,100
Ben Crenshaw	73	76	72	72	293	5,100
Andrew Magee	76	72	69	77	294	4,265
Larry Rinker	74	70	74	76	294	4,265
John Huston	72	77	72	73	294	4,265
Ian Baker-Finch	74	74	74	72	294	4,265
Brad Bryant	71	78	72	73	294	4,265
James Hallet	81	69	73	71	294	4,265

Southwestern Bell Colonial National Invitation

Colonial Country Club, Fort Worth, Texas
Par 35-35—70; 7,096 yards

May 18-21
purse, $750,000

	SCORES				TOTAL	MONEY
Ian Baker-Finch	65	70	65	70	270	$180,000
David Edwards	72	69	68	65	274	108,000
Tim Simpson	71	71	66	68	276	58,000
David Frost	70	66	71	69	276	58,000

	SCORES				TOTAL	MONEY
Curtis Strange	74	71	66	66	277	36,500
Nick Price	70	66	68	73	277	36,500
Lon Hinkle	74	69	66	68	277	36,500
Payne Stewart	70	70	70	68	278	28,000
Scott Simpson	71	67	70	70	278	28,000
Isao Aoki	66	74	66	72	278	28,000
Paul Azinger	70	74	69	65	278	28,000
Doug Tewell	71	71	68	69	279	19,600
David Ogrin	72	69	68	70	279	19,600
Fulton Allem	66	73	69	71	279	19,600
Chip Beck	74	72	66	67	279	19,600
Mike Donald	70	74	69	66	279	19,600
Mike Sullivan	67	70	74	69	280	13,533.34
Davis Love III	73	72	66	69	280	13,533.34
Joey Sindelar	72	68	71	69	280	13,533.33
Mike Hulbert	70	69	71	70	280	13,533.33
Clarence Rose	67	71	69	73	280	13,533.33
Mark Calcavecchia	68	72	71	69	280	13,533.33
Steve Pate	71	70	72	68	281	9,600
Billy Mayfair	71	73	67	70	281	9,600
Nick Faldo	72	72	68	69	281	9,600
Chris Perry	71	74	70	67	282	7,400
Tom Purtzer	76	70	66	70	282	7,400
Gil Morgan	70	68	74	70	282	7,400
Steve Elkington	70	70	73	69	282	7,400
Brad Faxon	72	68	70	72	282	7,400
Robert Wrenn	73	71	68	71	283	5,800
Andy North	70	75	71	67	283	5,800
Mark O'Meara	73	68	70	72	283	5,800
Dave Barr	74	69	66	74	283	5,800
Morris Hatalsky	69	74	68	72	283	5,800
Keith Clearwater	68	72	70	73	283	5,800
Loren Roberts	71	72	71	70	284	4,800
Tom Byrum	73	69	70	72	284	4,800
Corey Pavin	70	73	68	74	285	4,100
Bruce Lietzke	75	69	70	71	285	4,100
D.A. Weibring	69	77	70	69	285	4,100
Mark Wiebe	70	71	75	69	285	4,100
Jim Carter	75	69	69	72	285	4,100
Mark Brooks	72	70	75	69	286	3,023.34
Donnie Hammond	71	70	73	72	286	3,023.34
Mike Reid	72	71	69	74	286	3,023.33
Andy Bean	69	72	71	74	286	3,023.33
Ben Crenshaw	71	73	69	73	286	3,023.33
Buddy Gardner	71	73	69	73	286	3,023.33
Peter Jacobsen	71	73	73	70	287	2,490
Tom Kite	72	69	73	73	287	2,490

Bellsouth Atlanta Classic

Atlanta Country Club, Marietta, Georgia
Par 36-36—72; 7,007 yards

May 25-28
purse, $900,000

	SCORES				TOTAL	MONEY
Scott Simpson	72	68	71	67	278	$162,000
Bob Tway	70	70	71	67	278	97,200
(Simpson defeated Tway in playoff on first extra hole.)						
Davis Love III	71	69	69	70	279	52,200
Jay Don Blake	66	71	70	72	279	52,200
David Peoples	70	71	70	69	280	34,200
David Canipe	71	70	70	69	280	34,200
Ray Stewart	69	68	75	69	281	28,050
Wayne Levi	72	70	72	67	281	28,050
Wayne Grady	70	66	75	70	281	28,050
Don Pooley	68	72	74	68	282	19,950
Gene Sauers	72	70	71	69	282	19,950
Tim Simpson	75	68	71	68	282	19,950
Mike Miles	71	73	66	72	282	19,950
Larry Mize	71	69	69	73	282	19,950
Ronnie Black	71	68	72	71	282	19,950
Duffy Waldorf	70	67	71	75	283	14,400
Dave Rummells	68	71	75	69	283	14,400
Bill Britton	70	70	73	70	283	14,400
Payne Stewart	69	73	71	71	284	10,157.15
Hubert Green	69	70	74	71	284	10,157.15
Lance Ten Broeck	71	73	68	72	284	10,157.14
Ronnie McCann	71	73	74	66	284	10,157.14
Kenny Perry	72	71	76	65	284	10,157.14
Calvin Peete	69	72	70	73	284	10,157.14
Tommy Armour	72	71	68	73	284	10,157.14
Jim Thorpe	74	69	69	73	285	6,390
Larry Silveira	71	66	76	72	285	6,390
Brad Faxon	71	68	76	70	285	6,390
Dick Mast	73	71	72	69	285	6,390
Kenny Knox	69	71	71	74	285	6,390
Kent Kluba	70	70	69	76	285	6,390
Paul Azinger	74	69	69	73	285	6,390
Steve Pate	71	70	73	72	286	4,972.50
Nolan Henke	76	69	69	72	286	4,972.50
Gary Hallberg	70	73	74	69	286	4,972.50
Dewey Arnette	70	69	74	73	286	4,972.50
Don Shirey, Jr.	72	72	73	70	287	3,690
Doug Tewell	72	70	73	72	287	3,690
Rick Pearson	73	70	72	72	287	3,690
John Inman	74	71	68	74	287	3,690
Buddy Gardner	73	72	70	72	287	3,690
Robin Freeman	71	69	72	75	287	3,690
Steve Lowery	74	71	76	66	287	3,690
John McComish	75	69	70	73	287	3,690
Dave Barr	72	67	75	73	287	3,690
Bobby Wadkins	75	69	68	76	288	2,551.50
Larry Nelson	70	73	68	77	288	2,551.50
Tim Norris	75	70	72	71	288	2,551.50
Jodie Mudd	71	73	71	73	288	2,551.50
Billy Andrade	72	73	71	73	289	2,191.50
Rex Caldwell	72	71	70	76	289	2,191.50
Bob Eastwood	68	75	75	71	289	2,191.50
Lennie Clements	72	72	73	72	289	2,191.50

Kemper Open

TPC at Avenel, Potomac, Maryland
Par 36-35—71; 6,867 yards

June 1-4
purse, $900,000

	SCORES				TOTAL	MONEY
Tom Byrum	66	69	65	68	268	$162,000
Jim Thorpe	70	69	67	67	273	67,200
Tommy Armour	68	70	64	71	273	67,200
Billy Ray Brown	69	67	70	67	273	67,200
Gil Morgan	70	71	68	66	275	36,000
Mark McCumber	69	69	66	72	276	31,275
Andrew Magee	73	69	65	69	276	31,275
Lon Hinkle	68	70	68	71	277	26,100
Mike Hulbert	68	72	67	70	277	26,100
Jay Don Blake	68	64	75	70	277	26,100
Robert Wrenn	70	67	71	70	278	18,450
Howard Twitty	69	67	71	71	278	18,450
Gary McCord	70	67	73	68	278	18,450
Don Pooley	69	64	71	74	278	18,450
Jeff Hart	71	68	65	74	278	18,450
Brian Claar	70	68	70	70	278	18,450
Morris Hatalsky	70	71	69	69	279	14,400
Duffy Waldorf	72	69	67	72	280	10,200
Clarence Rose	69	69	70	72	280	10,200
Tony Sills	70	69	72	69	280	10,200
Wayne Grady	69	70	68	73	280	10,200
Brad Faxon	68	72	68	72	280	10,200
Hale Irwin	69	70	70	71	280	10,200
Billy Mayfair	73	70	67	70	280	10,200
Dave Barr	67	70	73	70	280	10,200
Ronnie Black	70	69	69	72	280	10,200
Roger Maltbie	72	65	73	71	281	5,990.63
Fred Funk	65	72	74	70	281	5,990.63
Tom Kite	68	75	68	70	281	5,990.63
Steve Jones	76	65	70	70	281	5,990.63
D.A. Weibring	64	72	70	75	281	5,990.62
P.H. Horgan III	70	68	69	74	281	5,990.62
Phil Blackmar	74	69	68	70	281	5,990.62
Bill Buttner	66	72	68	75	281	5,990.62
Leonard Thompson	70	67	74	71	282	4,635
Scott Hoch	71	69	68	74	282	4,635
Bill Britton	68	72	70	72	282	4,635
Craig Stadler	73	68	71	71	283	3,690
Tom Pernice, Jr.	70	71	73	69	283	3,690
Mike Sullivan	70	68	69	76	283	3,690
Larry Silveira	70	73	70	70	283	3,690
Donnie Hammond	66	73	70	74	283	3,690
Mike Miles	69	72	72	70	283	3,690
Mike Donald	71	72	67	73	283	3,690
Corey Pavin	68	75	69	72	284	2,635.20
Don Shirey, Jr.	77	66	72	69	284	2,635.20
Billy Tuten	71	71	71	71	284	2,635.20
Bob Lohr	70	71	74	69	284	2,635.20
Fred Couples	71	69	69	75	284	2,635.20
Richard Zokol	70	70	73	72	285	2,114
Scott Simpson	70	72	71	72	285	2,114
Mark Hayes	68	70	71	76	285	2,114
Pat McGowan	71	72	70	72	285	2,114
Tim Norris	69	71	72	73	285	2,114

U.S. Tour

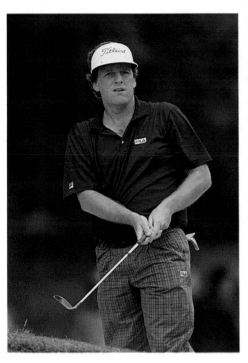

After starting cold here at Bay Hill, Greg Norman warmed to two U.S. victories, and five overall.

Mark Calcavecchia won twice in the first five PGA Tour events.

Shown here after winning The Players Championship, Tom Kite also won The Nestle Invitational and Nabisco Championship, and was the No. 1 money-winner and Player of the Year.

Steve Jones won the first two
1989 events.

Mark O'Meara was the winner at Pebble
Beach.

The Colonial was the venue for
Ian Baker-Finch's first U.S.
triumph.

A win at Hartford highlighted Paul
Azinger's year.

Chip Beck (left) and Mark McCumber both provided excitement during the year.

Despite some obstacles, Payne Stewart won twice and nearly overtook Tom Kite in the Nabisco Championship.

His loss in the Masters was a huge disappointment, but Scott Hoch came back
quickly to win in Las Vegas.

David Frost (left) and Fred
Couples (above) both had
steady performances.

Tim Simpson won two events.

His U.S. Open victory was the crowning moment, but Curtis Strange had many highlights in 1989.

Peter Jacobsen bowed out a winner at the Kapalua International.

European Tour

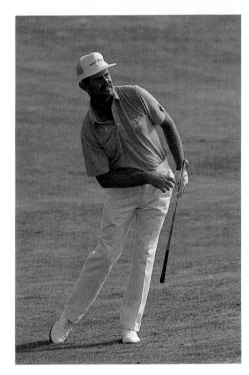

Mark James had two European victories.

Despite three wins in Europe, Seve Ballesteros had a below-standard year.

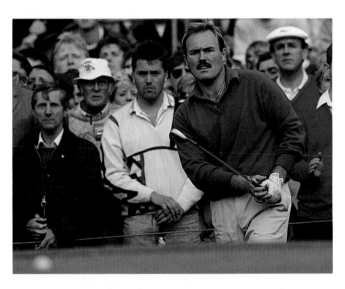

Three victories—including the season-ending Volvo Masters—took Ronan Rafferty to No. 1 on the European Order of Merit.

The No. 2-ranking Spaniard, Jose-Maria Olazabal proved to be among the world's best.

Australian Craig Parry emerged with two wins in Europe and one in Japan.

In short order, Nick Faldo returned from Augusta to win the Volvo PGA, Dunhill British Masters and French Open titles.

Australia's Mike Harwood won in Sweden at the PLM Open.

Ian Woosnam's big victory was in the Carrolls Irish Open.

Photo: Danielle Fluer

Monte Carlo was the scene of Mark McNulty's sole European win.

Sam Torrance was effective with a long putter under his chin.

Peter Senior's putter provided four wins – one in Europe and three in Australia.

Gordon Brand, Jr., won the Benson & Hedges International, despite this awkward shot.

Argentina's Eduardo Romero took the Lancome Trophy.

It was a discouraging year for Sandy Lyle, after his great 1988 campaign.

Photo: Danielle Fluer

Vijay Singh became the first golfer from Fiji to win in Europe, and had three African victories.

Despite his putting problems, Bernhard Langer won the Spanish Open and German Masters.

Senior Tour

Harold Henning's wave has become his trademark.

The rich RJR Championship capped Gary Player's year.

Bob Charles had a seven-victory year, including wins in Japan and Britain.

The PGA Senior Championship was one of Larry Mowry's two victories.

Orville Moody added the U.S. Senior Open to his U.S. Open title.

Bruce Crampton continued his Senior Tour success with two triumphs.

Al Geiberger had two victories.

Billy Casper won the Transamerica Seniors.

Back-to-back victories early in the year sparked
Don Bies to an outstanding season.

LPGA Tour

Betsy King won the U.S. Women's Open and five other titles.

Nancy Lopez won three times and entered the World Golf Hall of Fame.

In a comeback year, Beth Daniel had four victories.

Taking leave from the LPGA Tour,
Jane Geddes claimed the Weetabix
Ladies British Open title.

Juli Inkster won the Nabisco
Dinah Shore.

Marie-Laure De Lorenzi won
three in a row on the European
circuit.

Asia/Japan Tour

With seven victories, Jumbo (right) led the Ozaki clan. Golf's most formidable brother trio also includes Jet (below left) and Joe.

	SCORES				TOTAL	MONEY
Rick Dalpos	69	72	73	71	285	2,114
Ian Baker-Finch	74	67	76	68	285	2,114
Jim Benepe	70	69	72	74	285	2,114
Jim Carter	70	70	73	72	285	2,114

Manufacturers Hanover Westchester Classic

Westchester Country Club, Rye, New York
Par 36-35—71; 6,769 yards

June 8-11
purse, $1,000,000

	SCORES				TOTAL	MONEY
Wayne Grady	69	65	71	72	277	$180,000
Ronnie Black	69	71	69	68	277	108,000
(Grady defeated Black on first extra hole.)						
Tom Watson	71	69	70	68	278	58,000
Clarence Rose	72	69	67	70	278	58,000
J.C. Snead	67	68	70	74	279	35,125
Tom Kite	70	67	72	70	279	35,125
Billy Andrade	69	69	70	71	279	35,125
Fred Couples	66	72	70	71	279	35,125
Nick Price	74	67	69	70	280	27,000
Mike Reid	69	72	68	71	280	27,000
Mark Lye	66	70	71	73	280	27,000
Don Pooley	72	71	69	69	281	21,000
Paul Azinger	71	67	70	73	281	21,000
Chip Beck	70	70	72	69	281	21,000
Curtis Strange	72	65	74	71	282	17,000
Gary Hallberg	72	71	67	72	282	17,000
Scott Hoch	68	72	67	75	282	17,000
Larry Mize	68	71	69	75	283	13,040
Craig Stadler	66	74	68	75	283	13,040
Joey Sindelar	70	70	73	70	283	13,040
Mark O'Meara	69	72	72	70	283	13,040
Tom Byrum	68	72	69	74	283	13,040
Bob Tway	69	71	70	74	284	8,428.58
Doug Tewell	69	72	69	74	284	8,428.57
Greg Norman	69	71	69	75	284	8,428.57
Scott Simpson	71	68	71	74	284	8,428.57
Ted Schulz	70	69	70	75	284	8,428.57
Kenny Perry	69	68	72	75	284	8,428.57
Bill Buttner	70	70	70	74	284	8,428.57
Hal Sutton	70	73	71	71	285	6,650
Donnie Hammond	71	69	72	73	285	6,650
Jeff Sluman	72	69	70	75	286	5,787.50
Larry Nelson	69	69	73	75	286	5,787.50
Steve Pate	72	70	75	69	286	5,787.50
Dick Mast	66	68	71	81	286	5,787.50
Dan Pohl	67	71	75	74	287	4,710
Brad Faxon	71	72	72	72	287	4,710
David Frost	70	67	75	75	287	4,710
Kenny Knox	66	70	74	77	287	4,710
Fulton Allem	73	68	71	75	287	4,710
Loren Roberts	73	70	72	73	288	3,600
James Hallet	71	70	69	78	288	3,600
John Adams	71	68	75	74	288	3,600
Seve Ballesteros	71	70	72	75	288	3,600
Bob Estes	72	68	68	80	288	3,600

	SCORES				TOTAL	MONEY
Ben Crenshaw	67	76	71	74	288	3,600
Bill Britton	73	67	73	76	289	2,568.58
Scott Verplank	73	69	73	74	289	2,568.57
Jay Haas	70	72	75	72	289	2,568.57
Dan Halldorson	71	72	74	72	289	2,568.57
Rocco Mediate	65	74	75	75	289	2,568.57
Mark Brooks	69	72	74	74	289	2,568.57
Curt Byrum	69	74	73	73	289	2,568.57

U.S. Open Championship

Oak Hill Country Club, Rochester, New York   June 15-18
Par 35-35—70; 6,902 yards   purse, $1,049,089

	SCORES				TOTAL	MONEY
Curtis Strange	71	65	73	70	278	$200,000
Ian Woosnam	70	68	73	68	279	67,823
Mark McCumber	70	68	72	69	279	67,823
Chip Beck	71	69	71	68	279	67,823
Brian Claar	71	72	68	69	280	34,345
Scott Simpson	67	70	69	75	281	28,220.50
Masashi Ozaki	70	71	68	72	281	28,220.50
Peter Jacobsen	71	70	71	70	282	24,307
Jose-Maria Olazabal	69	72	70	72	283	19,968.50
Tom Kite	67	69	69	78	283	19,968.50
Hubert Green	69	72	74	68	283	19,968.50
Paul Azinger	71	72	70	70	283	19,968.50
Larry Nelson	68	73	68	75	284	15,634.20
Payne Stewart	66	75	72	71	284	15,634.20
Tom Pernice, Jr.	67	75	68	74	284	15,634.20
Scott Hoch	70	72	70	72	284	15,634.20
Mark Lye	71	69	72	72	284	15,634.20
David Frost	73	72	70	70	285	18,013
Nick Faldo	68	72	73	72	285	13,013
Jay Don Blake	66	71	72	76	285	13,013
D.A. Weibring	70	74	73	69	286	11,306
Nolan Henke	75	69	72	70	286	11,306
Bill Glasson	73	70	70	73	286	11,306
Fred Couples	74	71	67	74	286	11,306
Steve Elkington	70	70	78	68	286	11,306
Don Pooley	74	69	71	73	287	9,983.67
Ray Floyd	68	74	74	71	287	9,983.67
Robert Wrenn	74	71	73	69	287	9,983.66
Dan Pohl	7]	71	73	73	288	9,006.50
Hal Sutton	69	75	72	72	288	9,006.50
Scott Taylor	69	71	76	72	288	9,006.50
Emlyn Aubrey	69	73	73	73	288	9,006.50
Mark Wiebe	69	71	72	77	289	7,576.60
Joey Sindelar	67	77	74	71	289	7,576.60
Edward Kirby	70	70	73	76	289	7,576.60
Billy Mayfair	72	69	76	72	289	7,576.60
Larry Mize	72	72	71	74	289	7,576.60
Davis Love III	71	74	73	71	289	7,576.60
Greg Norman	72	68	73	76	289	7,576.60
Isao Aoki	70	70	75	74	289	7,576.60
Brad Faxon	73	70	75	71	289	7,576.60
Dan Forsman	70	70	76	73	289	7,576.60

	SCORES				TOTAL	MONEY
Jack Nicklaus	67	74	74	75	290	6,281
Seve Ballesteros	75	70	76	69	290	6,281
Clark Dennis	72	72	72	74	290	6,281
Richard Zokol	71	69	76	75	291	5,485.80
Tom Watson	76	69	73	73	291	5,485.80
Steve Jones	69	75	77	70	291	5,485.80
John Mahaffey	77	68	74	72	291	5,485.80
Ken Green	73	72	71	75	291	5,485.80
Steve Pate	74	69	73	76	292	4,690
Tom Sieckmann	73	71	74	74	292	4,690
Jodie Mudd	73	71	74	74	292	4,690
Chris Perry	76	67	72	78	293	4,299.80
Hale Irwin	74	70	79	70	293	4,299.80
David Ogrin	73	72	73	75	293	4,299.80
Webb Heintzelman	72	70	75	76	293	4,299.80
Ronnie Black	71	74	76	72	293	4,299.80
Clarence Rose	70	75	73	76	294	4,120
Bernhard Langer	66	78	77	73	294	4,120
David Graham	73	72	77	73	295	4,099
Mark Calcavecchia	74	70	74	77	295	4,099
Tony Sills	72	72	71	81	296	4,099
Dan Halldorson	72	70	76	78	296	4,099
*Gregory Lesher	70	72	76	78	296	
Bobby Wadkins	73	72	75	77	297	4,099
Dillard Pruitt	68	74	81	75	298	4,099
Ed Humenik	73	72	76	77	298	4,099
Doug Weaver	72	73	80	75	300	4,099
John Daly	74	67	80	79	300	4,099
Kurt Beck	68	73	83	77	301	4,099

Out of Final 36 Holes

	SCORES		TOTAL
Leonard Thompson	75	71	146
Dennis Trixler	73	73	146
Jeff Sluman	75	71	146
Lanny Wadkins	73	73	146
James Hallet	73	73	146
Bob Mann	72	74	146
Nick Price	74	72	146
Bob Proben	73	73	146
Mac O'Grady	73	73	146
John Adams	71	75	146
Bill Buttner	71	75	146
Bob Gilder	71	75	146
Ben Crenshaw	73	73	146
Dave Eichelberger	73	73	146
Mark McNulty	73	74	147
John Huston	73	74	147
Mike Reid	72	75	147
Loren Roberts	72	75	147
Gary Player	78	69	147
Andy North	72	75	147
Bill Sander	72	75	147
Fred Funk	72	75	147
Jay Haas	69	78	147
Steve Bowman	76	71	147
Jim Carter	73	74	147
David Edwards	74	73	147
Roger Gunn	71	76	147

	SCORES		TOTAL
Bob Tway	74	74	148
Stan Utley	74	74	148
Tim Simpson	74	74	148
Ken Schall	72	76	148
Jerry Pate	74	74	148
Jack Ferenz	70	78	148
Gordon J. Brand	76	72	148
Steve Lamontagne	78	71	149
Wayne Grady	75	74	149
Bill Britton	71	78	149
Jim Gallagher, Jr.	74	75	149
*Eric Meeks	75	75	150
Ed Fiori	73	77	150
Denny Hepler	77	73	150
Keith Clearwater	74	76	150
Brian Tennyson	75	76	151
Duffy Waldorf	78	73	151
Fuzzy Zoeller	78	73	151
Mark O'Meara	78	73	151
John Mazza	80	71	151
Dan Oschmann	77	74	151
Tommy Armour	74	77	151
Jim Booros	75	76	151
Sandy Lyle	78	74	152
Jim McGovern	79	73	152
Danny Mijovic	76	76	152
*Greg Reid	76	76	152
Jimmy Roy	77	75	152
Brian Fogt	77	75	152
Michael Brisky	76	76	152
John Burckle	80	72	152
Michael Burke Jr.	77	75	152
P.H. Horgan III	77	75	152
Lee Trevino	74	79	153
Mike Walton	79	74	153
*Jay Sigel	77	76	153
Andy Bean	70	83	153
*Eric Hogg	74	79	153
Mike Donald	80	73	153
Martin Schiene	77	77	154
Steve Schroeder	79	75	154
Buddy Gardner	76	78	154
Ken Krieger	76	78	154
Steve Hart	74	80	154
Gary Koch	74	81	155
Scott Williams	81	75	156
David Glenz	79	77	156
Paul Oglesby	77	79	156
Don Reese	76	80	156
Jeff Fairfield	78	79	157
John Fleischer	76	82	158
Kevin Healy	76	82	158
Rick Flesher	76	83	159
Jon Fiedler	77	84	161
Jeffrey Bloom	81	80	161
Gregory Chapman	78	84	162
*Jonathon Yarian	90	88	178
Gil Morgan	71	WD	

(All professionals who did not complete 72 holes received $1,000 each.)

Canadian Open

Glen Abbey Golf Club, Oakville, Ontario, Canada
Par 35-37—72; 7,102 yards

June 22-25
purse, $900,000

	SCORES				TOTAL	MONEY
Steve Jones	67	64	70	70	271	$162,000
Mike Hulbert	71	66	72	64	273	67,200
Clark Burroughs	69	66	64	74	273	67,200
Mark Calcavecchia	67	69	68	69	273	67,200
Joey Sindelar	69	72	65	68	274	32,850
Mark McCumber	69	69	69	67	274	32,850
Mark Brooks	67	73	68	66	274	32,850
Jim Gallagher, Jr.	64	68	71	72	275	27,000
Dave Barr	69	69	69	68	275	27,000
Corey Pavin	70	70	69	67	276	18,675
David Ogrin	68	69	68	71	276	18,675
Jack Nicklaus	68	69	69	70	276	18,675
Bill Sander	67	69	70	70	276	18,675
Lon Hinkle	69	68	66	73	276	18,675
Dan Halldorson	68	70	67	71	276	18,675
John Adams	70	70	69	67	276	18,675
Fred Couples	73	67	69	67	276	18,675
Larry Silveira	69	67	69	72	277	10,575
Loren Roberts	72	70	69	66	277	10,575
Don Shirey, Jr.	70	70	68	69	277	10,575
Lee Trevino	68	68	70	71	277	10,575
Ken Green	70	69	67	71	277	10,575
Nick Faldo	68	70	69	70	277	10,575
David Edwards	71	66	69	71	277	10,575
Jim Carter	69	68	72	68	277	10,575
Jodie Mudd	67	71	71	69	278	6,390
Tom Purtzer	70	72	67	69	278	6,390
Rocco Mediate	66	69	71	72	278	6,390
Jeff Sluman	72	70	66	70	278	6,390
Greg Norman	70	70	68	70	278	6,390
Bruce Lietzke	69	69	67	73	278	6,390
Tom Byrum	71	67	70	70	278	6,390
Curtis Strange	68	66	72	73	279	4,972.50
Bill Glasson	69	68	71	71	279	4,972.50
Jeff Hart	73	67	71	68	279	4,972.50
Gary Hallberg	68	71	69	71	279	4,972.50
Mark Wiebe	68	69	74	69	280	4,050
Craig Stadler	68	69	72	71	280	4,050
Johnny Miller	71	67	69	73	280	4,050
Nick Price	68	67	72	73	280	4,050
Blaine McCallister	69	72	69	70	280	4,050
Richard Zokol	69	70	71	71	281	2,895.75
Larry Rinker	69	72	71	69	281	2,895.75
Gene Sauers	70	71	66	74	281	2,895.75
Scott Verplank	72	69	69	71	281	2,895.75
Bob Lohr	70	68	73	70	281	2,895.75
Rick Gibson	70	68	69	74	281	2,895.75
Isao Aoki	71	69	71	70	281	2,895.75
Billy Rae Brown	69	71	70	71	281	2,895.75
Brian Tennyson	70	69	74	69	282	2,214
Rick Fehr	71	70	72	69	282	2,214
Morris Hatalsky	67	72	67	76	282	2,214

Beatrice Western Open

Butler National Golf Club, Oak Brook, Illinois
Par 36-36—72; 7,097 yards

June 29-July 2
purse, $1,000,000

	SCORES				TOTAL	MONEY
Mark McCumber	68	67	71	69	275	$180,000
Peter Jacobsen	69	69	69	68	275	108,000
(McCumber defeated Jacobsen in playoff on first extra hole.)						
Paul Azinger	67	68	72	69	276	68,000
Jim Gallagher, Jr.	71	72	70	66	279	48,000
Lance Ten Broeck	68	71	72	69	280	38,000
Lee Trevino	73	71	67	69	280	38,000
Jodie Mudd	69	73	72	67	281	30,125
Joey Sindelar	71	71	70	69	281	30,125
Larry Mize	69	70	67	75	281	30,125
Chip Beck	65	71	75	70	281	30,125
Tim Simpson	74	71	67	70	282	18,666.67
Jeff Sluman	70	71	70	71	282	18,666.67
Wayne Levi	71	72	71	68	282	18,666.67
Isao Aoki	73	72	69	68	282	18,666.67
Bill Buttner	72	68	71	71	282	18,666.67
Bobby Clampett	68	75	69	70	282	18,666.67
Tom Kite	71	71	69	71	282	18,666.66
Mike Hulbert	71	72	67	72	282	18,666.66
Curt Byrum	71	72	67	72	282	18,666.66
Lanny Wadkins	73	69	73	68	283	10,428.58
Mark Wiebe	69	70	69	75	283	10,428.57
Greg Norman	68	70	73	72	283	10,428.57
J.C. Snead	71	72	69	71	283	10,428.57
Roger Maltbie	68	73	71	71	283	10,428.57
Tommy Armour	68	73	68	74	283	10,428.57
Russ Cochran	71	67	75	70	283	10,428.57
Payne Stewart	66	74	73	71	284	6,380
Leonard Thompson	68	69	74	73	284	6,380
Doug Tewell	70	70	74	70	284	6,380
Chris Perry	71	72	71	70	284	6,380
Loren Roberts	73	66	74	71	284	6,380
John Mahaffey	73	69	70	72	284	6,380
Blaine McCallister	66	73	72	73	284	6,380
Ian Baker-Finch	70	75	71	68	284	6,380
Brad Bryant	72	72	73	67	284	6,380
Clark Burroughs	72	72	71	69	284	6,380
Don Shirey, Jr.	69	74	68	74	285	4,400
Dan Halldorson	71	73	73	68	285	4,400
Nolan Henke	73	71	71	70	285	4,400
Mark Lye	74	68	71	72	285	4,400
Jim Carter	73	68	72	72	285	4,400
Mike Donald	68	75	68	74	285	4,400
Gene Sauers	75	68	70	73	286	3,045
Tom Sieckmann	72	73	68	73	286	3,045
Howard Twitty	73	70	74	69	286	3,045
Nick Price	70	71	71	74	286	3,045
Bobby Wadkins	71	71	74	70	286	3,045
Tim Norris	72	72	71	71	286	3,045
Bill Glasson	71	72	74	69	286	3,045
Steve Jones	72	71	71	72	286	3,045
*Chris Dimarco	72	73	70	71	286	

Canon Greater Hartford Open

TPC of Connecticut, Cromwell, Connecticut
Par 36-35—71; 6,786 yards

July 6-9
purse, $1,000,000

	SCORES				TOTAL	MONEY
Paul Azinger	65	70	67	65	267	$180,000
Wayne Levi	69	68	64	67	268	108,000
Dave Rummells	70	67	67	66	270	68,000
Jim Carter	66	68	71	66	271	41,333.34
Lee Trevino	70	64	70	67	271	41,333.33
Mark Calcavecchia	67	68	67	69	271	41,333.33
Hal Sutton	67	71	68	66	272	29,100
Roger Maltbie	66	69	69	68	272	29,100
Blaine McCallister	69	69	67	67	272	29,100
Don Shirey, Jr.	70	67	68	67	272	29,100
Clark Burroughs	66	67	70	69	272	29,100
Wayne Grady	69	67	65	72	273	22,000
Rick Fehr	71	67	65	70	273	22,000
Brian Tennyson	66	71	66	71	274	18,000
Clarence Rose	68	72	66	68	274	18,000
Jay Haas	70	68	67	69	274	18,000
Mark Lye	70	70	68	67	275	12,222.23
Pat McGowan	71	68	69	67	275	12,222.23
John Mahaffey	67	68	70	70	275	12,222.22
Doug Tewell	69	66	68	72	275	12,222.22
Loren Roberts	67	69	71	68	275	12,222.22
Tim Simpson	73	66	68	68	275	12,222.22
Scott Hoch	70	69	66	70	275	12,222.22
David Frost	69	65	70	71	275	12,222.22
Ronnie Black	66	70	71	68	275	12,222.22
Robert Wrenn	68	66	73	69	276	6,950
Bobby Wadkins	71	67	69	69	276	6,950
Ted Schulz	67	70	67	72	276	6,950
Russ Cochran	69	70	65	72	276	6,950
Dave Barr	72	67	67	70	276	6,950
Bill Britton	67	67	68	74	276	6,950
Mark Brooks	70	66	70	70	276	6,950
Ben Crenshaw	70	66	71	69	276	6,950
Mac O'Grady	69	71	68	69	277	4,942.86
Gary McCord	68	69	70	70	277	4,942.86
John McComish	68	69	71	69	277	4,942.86
Howard Twitty	67	68	75	67	277	4,942.86
Ed Humenik	68	69	71	69	277	4,942.86
Kenny Knox	65	67	69	76	277	4,942.85
Mike Hulbert	68	70	69	70	277	4,942.85
Steve Pate	69	68	69	72	278	3,600
Tom Pernice, Jr.	69	68	72	69	278	3,600
Bob Gilder	65	74	69	70	278	3,600
Jim Gallagher, Jr.	70	68	68	72	278	3,600
P.H. Horgan III	70	67	71	70	278	3,600
Curt Byrum	69	69	72	68	278	3,600
Brett Upper	70	70	73	66	279	2,568.58
Leonard Thompson	68	70	69	72	279	2,568.57
Tim Petrovic	67	72	70	70	279	2,568.57
Ed Fiori	67	69	74	69	279	2,568.57
Tony Grimes	69	70	65	75	279	2,568.57
Ken Green	71	67	68	73	279	2,568.57
Billy Ray Brown	71	67	68	73	279	2,568.57

Anheuser-Busch Classic

Kingsmill Golf Club, Williamsburg, Virginia
Par 36-35—71; 6,776 yards

July 13-16
purse, $850,000

	SCORES				TOTAL	MONEY
Mike Donald	67	66	70	65	268	$153,000
Hal Sutton	64	71	65	68	268	74,800
Tim Simpson	64	70	67	67	268	74,800
(Donald defeated Sutton on third extra hole, Simpson on fourth.)						
Mike Hulbert	65	66	68	70	269	40,800
Tom Byrum	70	70	64	66	270	34,000
Roger Maltbie	72	63	67	69	271	28,475
Blaine McCallister	67	70	66	68	271	28,475
Brian Tennyson	67	71	67	66	271	28,475
Chris Perry	65	73	65	69	272	22,950
Ron Streck	68	67	69	68	272	22,950
John Mahaffey	69	67	69	67	272	22,950
Curtis Strange	68	71	66	68	273	18,700
Jim Gallagher, Jr.	68	72	67	66	273	18,700
Bobby Wadkins	71	68	69	66	274	14,450
Peter Jacobsen	67	68	69	70	274	14,450
Scott Hoch	69	65	70	70	274	14,450
Ed Humenik	67	69	68	70	274	14,450
Curt Byrum	71	68	70	65	274	14,450
Fuzzy Zoeller	66	70	71	68	275	8,943.89
John McComish	69	66	70	70	275	8,943.89
Leonard Thompson	68	71	68	68	275	8,943.89
Jeff Hart	71	66	71	67	275	8,943.89
Steve Hart	69	70	68	68	275	8,943.89
John Adams	68	68	71	68	275	8,943.89
Ian Baker-Finch	66	72	71	66	275	8,943.89
Brad Bryant	67	70	72	66	275	8,943.89
Webb Heintzelman	69	69	65	72	275	8,943.88
Calvin Peete	70	68	67	71	276	5,413.63
Mark Brooks	70	71	66	69	276	5,413.63
Steve Elkington	69	69	72	66	276	5,413.63
Keith Clearwater	71	69	68	68	276	5,413.63
Corey Pavin	70	69	65	72	276	5,413.62
J.C. Snead	67	70	67	72	276	5,413.62
Don Shirey, Jr.	66	66	72	72	276	5,413.62
Tim Norris	65	67	70	74	276	5,413.62
Buddy Gardner	69	68	68	72	277	4,270.50
Ronnie Black	69	71	68	69	277	4,270.50
Kenny Perry	68	68	70	72	278	3,400
Dennis Trixler	70	66	71	71	278	3,400
Steve Pate	67	70	69	72	278	3,400
Jay Haas	69	72	69	68	278	3,400
Kenny Knox	67	70	72	69	278	3,400
Rick Fehr	71	64	70	73	278	3,400
Billy Ray Brown	72	69	71	66	278	3,400
Lennie Clements	69	69	69	71	278	3,400
Tom Sieckmann	70	70	71	68	279	2,312
Ted Schulz	70	68	71	70	279	2,312
Dick Mast	70	69	68	72	279	2,312
Hubert Green	72	69	70	68	279	2,312
Dan Forsman	70	70	72	67	279	2,312
Fred Funk	70	71	70	68	279	2,312

Hardee's Classic

Oakwood Country Club, Coal Valley, Illinois
Par 35-35—70; 6,606 yards

July 20-23
purse, $700,000

	SCORES				TOTAL	MONEY
Curt Byrum	66	67	69	66	268	$126,000
Brian Tennyson	69	69	67	64	269	61,600
Bill Britton	70	65	69	65	269	61,600
Jim Gallagher, Jr.	69	68	69	65	271	30,800
Barry Jaeckel	70	71	67	63	271	30,800
Dan Forsman	74	65	68	65	272	24,325
John Adams	67	68	67	70	272	24,325
Andrew Magee	71	69	67	66	273	19,600
Tom Sieckmann	69	68	69	67	273	19,600
Jay Haas	72	68	67	66	273	19,600
Greg Ladehoff	69	65	69	70	273	19,600
Blaine McCallister	65	69	67	73	274	12,512.50
John McComish	73	65	67	69	274	12,512.50
Buddy Gardner	71	69	66	68	274	12,512.50
John Huston	69	71	66	68	274	12,512.50
Bill Glasson	71	70	66	67	274	12,512.50
James Hallet	72	66	69	67	274	12,512.50
Dave Barr	73	65	65	71	274	12,512.50
Lennie Clements	69	66	67	72	274	12,512.50
Gil Morgan	70	67	67	71	275	8,155
Dan Halldorson	67	71	67	70	275	8,155
Brad Bryant	71	69	65	70	275	8,155
Barry Cheesman	72	67	67	69	275	8,155
David Peoples	71	69	66	70	276	5,068.73
Leonard Thompson	70	70	69	67	276	5,068.73
Jim Thorpe	70	68	68	70	276	5,068.73
Ron Streck	70	67	68	71	276	5,068.73
Ernie Gonzalez	73	64	70	69	276	5,068.73
David Jackson	71	66	70	69	276	5,068.73
Lon Hinkle	68	73	67	68	276	5,068.73
Mike Donald	72	65	69	70	276	5,068.73
Tom Pernice, Jr.	68	70	68	70	276	5,068.72
Bob Lohr	70	69	66	71	276	5,068.72
Keith Clearwater	69	68	72	67	276	5,068.72
Calvin Peete	69	67	71	70	277	3,304.86
Dick Mast	72	66	71	68	277	3,304.86
Bob Eastwood	68	68	70	71	277	3,304.86
Russ Cochran	70	69	69	69	277	3,304.86
Andrew Debusk	71	66	70	70	277	3,304.86
Tim Norris	73	66	66	72	277	3,304.85
Bob Estes	74	67	68	68	277	3,304.85
Roger Maltbie	70	69	71	68	278	2,450
Pat McGowan	71	67	67	73	278	2,450
Webb Heintzelman	71	68	69	70	278	2,450
Steve Elkington	72	69	67	70	278	2,450
Mark Brooks	70	71	69	68	278	2,450
Harry Taylor	70	70	70	69	279	1,776.25
Bob Proben	69	69	69	72	279	1,776.25
Steve Hart	68	72	69	70	279	1,776.25
Billy Mayfair	71	66	68	74	279	1,776.25
Mike McCullough	70	70	73	66	279	1,776.25
Phil Blackmar	68	69	71	71	279	1,776.25
Brian Fogt	72	67	70	70	279	1,776.25
Brian Claar	73	67	69	70	279	1,776.25

Buick Open

Warwick Hills Country Club, Grand Blanc, Michigan
Par 36-36—72; 7,014 yards

July 27-30
purse, $700,000

	SCORES				TOTAL	MONEY
Leonard Thompson	65	71	69	68	273	$180,000
Doug Tewell	69	66	70	69	274	74,666.67
Bill Andrade	67	71	69	67	274	74,666.67
Payne Stewart	71	67	64	72	274	74,666.66
Hal Sutton	67	68	68	72	275	36,500
Mark O'Meara	66	70	71	68	275	36,500
Bob Eastwood	73	66	66	70	275	36,500
Tom Kite	69	70	71	66	276	29,000
Gil Morgan	71	70	67	68	276	29,000
Wayne Grady	67	69	72	68	276	29,000
James Hallet	71	70	68	68	277	23,000
Steve Elkington	70	71	65	71	277	23,000
Dave Barr	70	71	67	69	277	23,000
Robert Wrenn	70	69	72	67	278	16,500
Lanny Wadkins	70	70	70	68	278	16,500
Pat McGowan	68	69	69	72	278	16,500
Joel Edwards	67	69	72	70	278	16,500
Dan Forsman	70	67	70	71	278	16,500
George Archer	69	71	67	71	278	16,500
Brian Watts	67	72	70	70	279	9,272.73
Brian Tennyson	70	70	69	70	279	9,272.73
Duffy Waldorf	68	72	69	70	279	9,272.73
Tom Sieckmann	72	67	71	69	279	9,272.73
Don Shirey, Jr.	66	73	70	70	279	9,272.73
Bill Sander	70	69	70	70	279	9,272.73
Lon Hinkle	67	73	70	69	279	9,272.73
Greg Ladehoff	70	71	69	69	279	9,272.73
Davis Love III	72	70	67	70	279	9,272.72
Brad Fabel	66	71	71	71	279	9,272.72
Fulton Allem	68	71	69	71	279	9,272.72
Howard Twitty	69	71	71	69	280	5,100
Ron Streck	68	73	71	68	280	5,100
Richard Zokol	66	74	70	70	280	5,100
J.C. Snead	71	70	71	68	280	5,100
Hale Irwin	71	69	71	69	280	5,100
Lee Janzen	67	72	69	72	280	5,100
Billy Mayfair	68	72	72	68	280	5,100
Rick Fehr	68	70	73	69	280	5,100
Ed Fiori	69	70	69	72	280	5,100
Bill Glasson	69	71	70	70	280	5,100
Mark Hayes	71	68	71	70	280	5,100
Jay Delsing	73	68	73	66	280	5,100
Lee Trevino	72	66	72	71	281	3,300
Barry Jaeckel	70	67	71	73	281	3,300
Robin Freeman	69	72	74	66	281	3,300
Jim Booros	70	71	69	71	281	3,300
Fred Couples	70	67	74	70	281	3,300
Jim Thorpe	73	68	72	69	282	2,580
Bob Wolcott	71	70	69	72	282	2,580
Ray Stewart	70	72	69	71	282	2,580
Tim Norris	71	67	70	74	282	2,580

Federal Express St. Jude Classic

TPC at Southwind, Germantown, Tennessee
Par 35-36—71; 7,006 yards

August 3-6
purse, $1,000,000

	SCORES				TOTAL	MONEY
John Mahaffey	70	71	66	65	272	$180,000
Bob Tway	66	72	68	69	275	66,000
Bernhard Langer	67	69	68	71	275	66,000
Hubert Green	70	69	73	63	275	66,000
Bob Gilder	68	66	70	71	275	66,000
Jay Haas	70	70	68	69	277	32,375
Rick Fehr	71	71	69	66	277	32,375
James Hallet	70	70	71	66	277	32,375
Mike Donald	70	67	69	71	277	32,375
Bob Lohr	69	73	72	64	278	27,000
Jim Gallagher, Jr.	64	70	75	70	279	23,000
Jay Don Blake	69	71	68	71	279	23,000
Billy Ray Brown	68	66	71	74	279	23,000
Tim Simpson	73	67	70	70	280	18,000
Mark Wiebe	72	70	69	69	280	18,000
David Canipe	69	72	72	67	280	18,000
Lance Ten Broeck	73	66	73	69	281	14,000
Brian Watts	65	70	73	73	281	14,000
David Peoples	72	70	72	67	281	14,000
Ed Fiori	65	67	76	73	281	14,000
Dan Halldorson	70	73	70	68	281	14,000
Jodie Mudd	70	71	71	70	282	9,014.29
Gary Hallberg	73	70	70	69	282	9,014.29
Billy Andrade	68	74	71	69	282	9,014.29
Rex Caldwell	74	70	68	70	282	9,014.29
Corey Pavin	72	71	67	72	282	9,014.28
Fulton Allem	67	70	72	73	282	9,014.28
Phil Blackmar	73	67	70	72	282	9,014.28
Bobby Wadkins	70	69	75	69	283	6,500
Doug Tewell	63	75	72	73	283	6,500
Andrew Magee	69	68	71	75	283	6,500
Webb Heintzelman	70	71	72	70	283	6,500
Trevor Dodds	69	75	69	70	283	6,500
Tony Sills	71	70	71	72	284	4,942.86
Jeff Sluman	74	66	71	73	284	4,942.86
Kenny Perry	71	71	73	69	284	4,942.86
Bob Estes	72	70	72	70	284	4,942.86
Buddy Gardner	72	71	74	67	284	4,942.86
Mark Lye	66	74	67	77	284	4,942.85
Rick Dalpos	70	72	69	73	284	4,942.85
Hal Sutton	70	68	72	75	285	3,500
Howard Twitty	70	69	73	73	285	3,500
Pat McGowan	69	74	71	71	285	3,500
Ted Schulz	73	71	69	72	285	3,500
Barry Jaeckel	72	69	76	68	285	3,500
Mike Hulbert	73	70	69	73	285	3,500
George Cadle	72	72	73	68	285	3,500
Ray Stewart	72	71	69	74	286	2,544
Dick Mast	68	72	72	74	286	2,544
Donnie Hammond	71	68	71	76	286	2,544
Steve Hart	71	71	71	73	286	2,544
Brian Claar	70	72	74	70	286	2,544

PGA Championship

Kemper Lakes Golf Club, Hawthorn Woods, Illinois   August 10-13
Par 36-36—72; 7,197 yards   purse, $1,200,000

	SCORES				TOTAL	MONEY
Payne Stewart	74	66	69	67	276	$200,000
Andy Bean	70	67	74	66	277	83,333.34
Mike Reid	66	67	70	74	277	83,333.33
Curtis Strange	70	68	70	69	277	83,333.33
Dave Rummells	68	69	69	72	278	45,000
Ian Woosnam	68	70	70	71	279	40,000
Craig Stadler	71	64	72	73	280	36,250
Scott Hoch	69	69	69	73	280	36,250
Tom Watson	67	69	74	71	281	30,000
Ed Fiori	70	67	75	69	281	30,000
Nick Faldo	70	73	69	69	281	30,000
Mark Wiebe	71	70	69	72	282	21,900
Mike Sullivan	76	66	67	73	282	21,900
Greg Norman	74	71	67	70	282	21,900
Jim Gallagher, Jr.	73	69	68	72	282	21,900
Seve Ballesteros	72	70	66	74	282	21,900
Chris Perry	67	70	70	76	283	15,000
Larry Mize	73	71	68	71	283	15,000
Blaine McCallister	71	72	70	70	283	15,000
Davis Love III	73	69	72	69	283	15,000
Buddy Gardner	72	71	70	70	283	15,000
Isao Aoki	72	71	65	75	283	15,000
Ben Crenshaw	68	72	72	71	283	15,000
Dan Pohl	71	69	74	70	284	10,000
Jeff Sluman	75	70	69	70	284	10,000
Tommy Armour	70	69	73	72	284	10,000
Howard Twitty	72	71	68	74	285	7,535.72
Jack Nicklaus	68	72	73	72	285	7,535.72
Mike Hulbert	70	71	72	72	285	7,535.72
Tim Simpson	69	70	73	73	285	7,535.71
Brian Tennyson	71	69	72	73	285	7,535.71
David Frost	70	74	69	72	285	7,535.71
Peter Jacobsen	70	70	73	72	285	7,535.71
Leonard Thompson	66	69	73	78	286	5,750
Loren Roberts	69	71	72	74	286	5,750
Don Pooley	70	71	72	73	286	5,750
Bob Gilder	72	72	74	68	286	5,750
Tom Kite	67	73	72	74	286	5,750
Ian Baker-Finch	74	68	70	74	286	5,750
Chip Beck	73	71	69	73	286	5,750
Steve Pate	70	72	74	71	287	4,260
Bob Lohr	75	69	69	74	287	4,260
Bill Britton	75	67	71	74	287	4,260
David Edwards	69	72	72	74	287	4,260
Steve Elkington	69	75	71	72	287	4,260
Nick Price	70	72	72	74	288	3,220
Larry Nelson	71	74	68	75	288	3,220
Wayne Grady	70	75	72	71	288	3,220
Bruce Lietzke	70	72	73	73	288	3,220
Ray Floyd	73	71	70	74	288	3,220
Kenny Perry	71	74	70	74	289	2,750
Steve Jones	71	74	71	73	289	2,750
Scott Simpson	70	74	75	71	290	2,490
Doug Tewell	73	69	72	76	290	2,490

	SCORES				TOTAL	MONEY
Tom Purtzer	69	73	74	74	290	2,490
Clarence Rose	74	71	72	73	290	2,490
Phil Blackmar	68	75	75	72	290	2,490
Gene Sauers	76	68	75	72	291	2,380
Andy North	69	75	77	70	291	2,380
Brad Bryant	70	70	72	79	291	2,380
Bernhard Langer	74	71	75	72	292	2,330
Gary Koch	71	72	77	72	292	2,330
Arnold Palmer	68	74	81	70	293	2,290
Greg Twiggs	71	73	74	75	293	2,290
Mark McCumber	70	73	74	77	294	2,260
Hubert Green	69	73	76	77	295	2,240
Jodie Mudd	71	70	80	75	296	2,220
Dave Stockton	76	69	75	77	297	2,200
Ronnie Black	73	70	74	82	299	2,180
Curt Byrum	73	71	76	87	307	2,170

Out of Final 36 Holes

	SCORES		TOTAL
Hal Sutton	76	70	146
Scott Verplank	73	73	146
Ted Schulz	72	74	146
Stu Ingraham	70	76	146
James Hallet	72	74	146
Gil Morgan	73	73	146
Billy Andrade	73	73	146
Dave Barr	76	70	146
Fred Couples	73	73	146
Robert Wrenn	73	74	147
Fuzzy Zoeller	75	72	147
John Huston	74	73	147
Mark O'Meara	68	79	147
Chris Mitchell	74	73	147
Jose-Maria Olazabal	73	74	147
Andrew Magee	74	73	147
Ken Allard	76	71	147
Lanny Wadkins	74	74	148
Steve Spray	74	74	148
Joey Sindelar	71	77	148
Roger Maltbie	74	74	148
Kenny Knox	79	69	148
Gregg Jones	77	71	148
Naomichi Ozaki	75	73	148
Bob Betley	73	75	148
Jay Don Blake	74	74	148
Mike Donald	76	72	148
Bob Tway	78	71	149
Lee Trevino	74	75	149
Corey Pavin	75	74	149
Jack Lewis	73	76	149
Rick Morton	74	75	149
Bob Boyd	77	72	149
Bobby Heins	75	74	149
Billy Ray Brown	74	75	149
John Mahaffey	73	77	150
Shawn McEntee	74	76	150
Lindy Miller	73	77	150
Sammy Rachels	76	74	150

	SCORES		TOTAL
Dan Forsman	75	75	150
Jay Haas	80	70	150
Tom Byrum	73	77	150
Russ Cochran	77	73	150
Scott Davis	76	74	150
Donnie Hammond	75	75	150
Ron Vlosich	77	74	151
Bobby Wadkins	75	76	151
Gary Robtson	80	71	151
Ray Freeman	74	77	151
Jim Carter	80	71	151
John Jackson	75	76	151
Bob Ford	79	72	151
Bob Mann	77	75	152
Brad Faxon	75	77	152
Jeff Jackson	73	79	152
Fulton Allem	79	74	153
David Graham	79	74	153
Paul Azinger	74	79	153
Jim Cichra	75	78	153
Jerry Tucker	77	78	155
Robert Gibbons	77	78	155
Mark Brooks	75	80	155
Ed Terasa	77	79	156
Ed Whitman	79	77	156
Bruce Lehnhard	82	74	156
David Ogrin	77	80	157
Don Brigham	77	80	157
Bill King	83	74	157
Gene Fieger	76	81	157
Bob Groff	78	80	158
Wally Kuchar	81	77	158
Lonnie Nielson	80	80	160
Bob Klein	78	82	160
Ralph Landrum	79	82	161
Mark Gardner	80	81	161
Rick Meskell	81	82	163
Greg Frederick	82	83	165
John Traub	92	79	171
Emil Esposito	87	87	174
Ken Green	75	WD	

(All players who did not complete 72 holes received $1,200 each.)

The International

Castle Pines Golf Club, Castle Rock, Colorado
Par 36-36—72; 7,503 yards

August 17-20
purse, $1,000,000

FINAL ROUND

13	Greg Norman, $180,000.
11	Clarence Rose, $108,000.
9	Chip Beck, $68,000.
8	Mark Lye, Billy Andrade, $44,000 each.
7	David Frost, $36,000.
6	Jim Carter, Dan Forsman, $32,250 each.
5	Jack Nicklaus, $29,000.

4   Mac O'Grady, Ray Stewart, $26,000 each.
3   Tom Kite, Mike Hulbert, $22,000 each.
1   Brad Fabel, $19,000.
E   Chris Perry, $18,000.
-1 Ian Baker-Finch, Tom Watson, $16,500 each.
-3 Lance Ten Broeck, $15,000.
-4 Steve Pate, John Inman, Ted Schulz, Ben Crenshaw, $12,550 each.
-6 Bob Lohr, $10,400.
-7 Hale Irwin, $9,600.

NON-QUALIFIERS - FINAL ROUND

6   Trevor Dodds, $8,800.
    (lost playoff for final round 24th spot)
5   Ronnie Black, Rick Pearson, Jay Haas, Ken Green, Bob Gilder, Gary Hallberg, $7,250 each.
4   Greg Ladehoff, Robert Wrenn, Richard Zokol, Bob Estes, Doug Tewell, $5,660 each.
3   Nolan Henke, Jim Hallet, Larry Silveira, Lee Trevino, Steve Jones, $4,500 each.
2   Brad Bryant, Billy Ray Brown, Duffy Waldorf, John Mahaffey, Bill Britton, Nick Price, Steve Elkington, $3,305.72 each.
1   D.A. Weibring, Clark Burroughs, Mark Brooks, Wayne Grady, Gil Morgan, Bill Glasson, $2,443.34 each.

Fred Meyer Challenge

Portland Golf Club, Portland, Oregon   August 21-22
Par 36-36—72; 6,612 yards   purse, $700,000

	SCORES		TOTAL	MONEY (Each)
Craig Stadler/Joey Sindelar	62	63	125	$50,000
Bob Gilder/Mark Calcavecchia	62	64	126	40,000
Arnold Palmer/Peter Jacobsen	65	62	127	35,000
Andy Bean/Raymond Floyd	65	63	128	30,000
Greg Norman/Curtis Strange	66	63	129	27,500
Ben Crenshaw/Payne Stewart	68	62	130	25,000
Fred Couples/Lee Trevino	67	63	130	25,000
Chip Beck/Tom Kite	63	67	130	25,000
Jay Haas/Jeff Sluman	67	65	132	23,500
David Ishii/Scott Simpson	65	67	132	23,500
Paul Azinger/Bob Tway	66	67	133	23,000
Fuzzy Zoeller/Chi Chi Rodriguez	70	67	137	22,500

NEC World Series of Golf

Firestone Country Club, Akron, Ohio   August 24-27
Par 35-35—70; 7,136 yards   purse, $1,000,000

	SCORES				TOTAL	MONEY
David Frost	70	68	69	69	276	$180,000
Ben Crenshaw	64	72	72	68	276	108,000
(Frost defeated Crenshaw on second extra hole.)						
Payne Stewart	72	67	68	71	278	68,000
Greg Norman	73	65	70	71	279	48,000
Larry Mize	73	66	70	71	280	38,000
Mike Reid	68	71	70	71	280	38,000

	SCORES			TOTAL	MONEY
Paul Azinger	72	68 67	74	281	33,500
Mark Calcavecchia	71	67 74	70	282	29,166.67
Bill Glasson	69	74 73	66	282	29,166.67
Steve Jones	76	63 69	74	282	29,166.66
Corey Pavin	71	70 68	75	284	25,000
Brian Claar	70	69 72	74	285	22,000
Scott Hoch	74	69 70	72	285	22,000
John Mahaffey	69	72 71	74	286	19,000
Phil Blackmar	75	73 73	67	288	16,000
Scott Simpson	75	73 68	72	288	16,000
Tom Kite	76	70 73	69	288	16,000
Blaine McCallister	70	70 77	71	288	16,000
Mark O'Meara	72	70 75	71	288	16,000
Leonard Thompson	72	72 72	73	289	11,800
Nick Faldo	72	68 73	76	289	11,800
Bob Lohr	73	70 71	75	289	11,800
Tim Simpson	76	70 69	74	289	11,800
Bob Tway	71	74 74	72	291	9,766.67
Mark McCumber	77	67 72	75	291	9,766.67
Ronan Rafferty	74	70 72	75	291	9,766.66
Ian Baker-Finch	73	72 72	75	292	9,100
Gene Sauers	73	73 74	72	292	9,100
Ken Green	69	75 75	73	292	9,100
Curt Byrum	70	75 73	75	293	8,650
Fred Wadsworth	70	72 73	78	293	8,650
Wayne Grady	74	71 70	79	294	8,450
Greg Twiggs	73	71 73	77	294	8,450
Tony Johnstone	72	75 73	75	295	8,250
Tom Purtzer	74	75 70	76	295	8,250
Bob Boyd	77	69 79	71	296	8,100
Sandy Lyle	74	74 77	72	297	7,950
Chris Moody	75	72 73	77	297	7,950
Andrew Magee	76	75 76	71	298	7,800
Mike Sullivan	74	75 73	78	300	7,700
Jodie Mudd	67	74 82	81	304	7,600
Ian Woosnam	73	77 77	79	306	7,450
Mike Donald	75	76 74	81	306	7,450
Tom Byrum	78	77 77	75	307	7,300
Curtis Strange	76	80WD			

Chattanooga Classic

Valleybrook Golf and Country Club, Chattanooga, Tennessee
Par 35-35—70; 6,641 yards

August 24-27
purse, $500,000

	SCORES			TOTAL	MONEY
Stan Utley	69	66 64	64	263	$90,000
Ray Stewart	71	63 67	63	264	54,000
Bobby Wadkins	67	67 65	66	265	29,000
Don Shirey, Jr.	65	65 68	67	265	29,000
Richard Zokol	68	67 65	66	266	17,562.50
John Inman	66	68 67	65	266	17,562.50
Bob Estes	69	65 66	66	266	17,562.50
Russ Cochran	66	67 67	66	266	17,562.50
Ted Schulz	66	63 70	68	267	12,500
Steve Lowery	66	69 67	65	267	12,500
Kenny Perry	70	67 66	64	267	12,500

	SCORES				TOTAL	MONEY
Fred Funk	68	64	67	68	267	12,500
Lennie Clements	70	65	67	65	267	12,500
Don Reese	66	68	66	68	268	8,500
Joel Edwards	66	69	68	65	268	8,500
Brad Fabel	64	72	66	66	268	8,500
Jay Delsing	69	64	66	69	268	8,500
John Daly	65	66	63	74	268	8,500
Duffy Waldorf	68	66	68	67	269	5,850
Dave Rummells	67	68	66	68	269	5,850
Rick Pearson	67	69	68	65	269	5,850
Pat McGowan	65	67	68	69	269	5,850
Jim Gallagher, Jr.	64	71	68	66	269	5,850
Bill Buttner	68	67	67	67	269	5,850
Andy Bean	68	67	69	66	270	4,083.34
Morris Hatalsky	65	66	69	70	270	4,083.33
Jim Booros	67	69	66	68	270	4,083.33
Lance Ten Broeck	66	70	67	68	271	3,253.58
Brian Tennyson	68	69	66	68	271	3,253.57
Bill Sander	68	67	67	69	271	3,253.57
Dan Halldorson	73	65	63	70	271	3,253.57
Mark Hayes	62	71	71	67	271	3,253.57
Charles Bowles	73	66	64	68	271	3,253.57
David Canipe	70	69	64	68	271	3,253.57
Ronnie McCann	68	65	68	71	272	2,518.75
Jim Thorpe	70	68	65	69	272	2,518.75
Tommy Armour	67	70	65	70	272	2,518.75
Brad Faxon	63	73	65	71	272	2,518.75
J.C. Snead	69	65	69	70	273	2,150
James Hallet	68	69	66	70	273	2,150
Keith Clearwater	67	70	68	68	273	2,150
Brian Mogg	68	69	63	74	274	1,800
Robert Thompson	70	67	65	72	274	1,800
Harry Taylor	67	66	69	72	274	1,800
Jim Carter	69	70	66	69	274	1,800
Dick Mast	65	71	69	70	275	1,317.50
Mike McCullough	68	71	67	69	275	1,317.50
David Peoples	65	73	69	68	275	1,317.50
Dillard Pruitt	67	69	71	68	275	1,317.50
Clark Burroughs	67	68	69	71	275	1,317.50
Jeff Coston	69	68	67	71	275	1,317.50
Gibby Gilbert	68	71	70	66	275	1,317.50
Rick Dalpos	69	66	70	70	275	1,317.50

Greater Milwaukee Open

Tuckaway Country Club, Franklin, Wisconsin
Par 36-36—72; 7,030 yards

August 31-September 3
purse, $800,000

	SCORES				TOTAL	MONEY
Greg Norman	64	69	66	70	269	$144,000
Andy Bean	70	69	67	66	272	86,400.00
Ted Schulz	68	69	68	68	273	46,400.00
Mark Lye	67	66	72	68	273	46,400.00
Tom Purtzer	72	67	66	69	274	30,400.00
Wayne Levi	69	66	68	71	274	30,400.00
Steve Pate	65	71	70	69	275	21,657.15
Jeff Sluman	70	71	66	68	275	21,657.15

	SCORES				TOTAL	MONEY
Duffy Waldorf	68	67	69	71	275	21,657.14
Joey Sindelar	70	69	67	69	275	21,657.14
Loren Roberts	69	67	68	71	275	21,657.14
Larry Mize	68	67	70	70	275	21,657.14
David Frost	67	67	70	71	275	21,657.14
Bill Sander	71	68	66	71	276	12,800.00
Clarence Rose	69	69	67	71	276	12,800.00
P.H. Horgan III	68	67	68	73	276	12,800.00
Phil Blackmar	65	69	74	68	276	12,800.00
Jay Don Blake	72	66	69	69	276	12,800.00
Curt Byrum	65	70	72	69	276	12,800.00
Keith Clearwater	70	70	68	68	276	12,800.00
J.C. Snead	68	71	67	71	277	6,780.00
Larry Rinker	71	67	66	73	277	6,780.00
Mark Hayes	71	68	70	68	277	6,780.00
Wayne Grady	65	68	72	72	277	6,780.00
Webb Heintzelman	70	67	68	72	277	6,780.00
Bob Lohr	69	68	66	74	277	6,780.00
Hale Irwin	67	69	68	73	277	6,780.00
Fulton Allem	70	70	69	68	277	6,780.00
Ian Baker-Finch	70	66	74	67	277	6,780.00
Dave Eichelberger	72	69	69	67	277	6,780.00
Jim Carter	71	67	71	68	277	6,780.00
Russ Cochran	68	71	71	67	277	6,780.00
Richard Zokol	70	70	70	68	278	3,796.37
Larry Silveira	70	70	70	68	278	3,796.37
Tom Pernice, Jr.	70	71	71	66	278	3,796.37
Corey Pavin	69	70	71	68	278	3,796.37
Stan Utley	71	66	72	69	278	3,796.36
Blaine McCallister	69	69	70	70	278	3,796.36
Nick Price	67	68	69	74	278	3,796.36
Buddy Gardner	69	69	70	70	278	3,796.36
Andrew Magee	67	72	68	71	278	3,796.36
Joel Edwards	72	67	67	72	278	3,796.36
Brad Fabel	68	71	70	69	278	3,796.36
Pat McGowan	68	73	67	71	279	2,640.00
Mike Hulbert	73	68	68	70	279	2,640.00
Rick Fehr	70	66	70	73	279	2,640.00
Gil Morgan	71	68	72	69	280	2,082.67
Steve Jones	73	67	69	71	280	2,082.67
Steve Lowery	66	70	73	71	280	2,082.67
David Jackson	70	67	72	71	280	2,082.67
Wayne Westner	70	71	68	71	280	2,082.66
Tommy Armour	68	70	70	72	280	2,082.66

B.C. Open

En-Joie Golf Club, Endicott, New York
Par 37-34—71; 6,966 yards

September 7-10
purse, $500,000

	SCORES				TOTAL	MONEY
Mike Hulbert	69	66	68	65	268	$90,000
Bob Estes	66	68	66	68	268	54,000
(Hulbert defeated Estes on first extra hole.)						
Steve Elkington	68	72	67	62	269	34,000
Fuzzy Zoeller	69	67	66	69	271	22,000
Dave Eichelberger	67	67	67	70	271	22,000

	SCORES			TOTAL	MONEY
Wayne Levi	69	73	64	66	272	18,000
Gil Morgan	67	67	71	68	273	16,750
Nolan Henke	69	67	73	65	274	15,500
Tom Pernice, Jr.	71	68	67	69	275	11,571.43
Jeff Sluman	69	68	69	69	275	11,571.43
Barry Jaeckel	70	67	68	70	275	11,571.43
Mark Lye	69	69	72	65	275	11,571.43
Steve Lowery	69	69	70	67	275	11,571.43
Mark Hayes	71	68	68	68	275	11,571.43
Jim Booros	70	65	68	72	275	11,571.42
Steve Pate	70	70	69	67	276	8,000
Nick Price	68	70	70	68	276	8,000
Jay Haas	69	69	70	68	276	8,000
Rocco Mediate	68	72	69	68	277	5,642.86
Lanny Wadkins	71	67	71	68	277	5,642.86
Webb Heintzelman	70	71	71	65	277	5,642.86
Jim Gallagher, Jr.	69	65	74	69	277	5,642.86
Mike Donald	70	69	71	67	277	5,642.86
Jim Thorpe	69	71	65	72	277	5,642.85
Bobby Clampett	70	69	69	69	277	5,642.85
Doug Tewell	74	65	68	71	278	3,475
Doug Weaver	69	67	74	68	278	3,475
Joey Sindelar	69	68	74	67	278	3,475
Bobby Wadkins	68	72	68	70	278	3,475
Buddy Gardner	73	69	67	69	278	3,475
Bill Glasson	71	71	67	69	278	3,475
Bill Britton	72	70	71	65	278	3,475
Keith Clearwater	65	68	70	75	278	3,475
Blaine McCallister	70	72	69	68	279	2,700
John Inman	69	71	68	71	279	2,700
Tommy Armour	70	67	72	70	279	2,700
Mike Miles	69	72	70	69	280	2,300
Sam Randolph	73	69	72	66	280	2,300
Bill Sander	71	69	70	70	280	2,300
Billy Tuten	72	70	69	69	280	2,300
Tom Sieckmann	68	72	70	71	281	1,800
Ronnie McCann	69	69	73	70	281	1,800
Greg Ladehoff	71	71	68	71	281	1,800
P.H. Horgan III	73	68	73	67	281	1,800
Fulton Allem	67	75	72	67	281	1,800
Ed Dougherty	69	67	73	72	281	1,800
Loren Roberts	70	72	70	70	282	1,233.64
Wayne Westner	68	71	72	71	282	1,233.64
Greg Powers	69	73	72	68	282	1,233.64
Doug Martin	69	73	72	68	282	1,233.64
Dick Mast	69	72	71	70	282	1,233.64
Fred Funk	74	66	71	71	282	1,233.64
Bill Buttner	71	70	70	71	282	1,233.64
Robert Thompson	70	71	68	73	282	1,233.63
Larry Rinker	69	68	71	74	282	1,233.63
Duffy Waldorf	72	69	69	72	282	1,233.63
Brad Bryant	71	69	70	72	282	1,233.63

Bank of Boston Classic

Pleasant Valley Country Club, Sutton, Massachusetts
Par 36-35—71; 7,110 yards

September 14-17
purse, $700,000

	SCORES				TOTAL	MONEY
Blaine McCallister	67	67	71	66	271	$126,000
Brad Faxon	66	67	70	69	272	75,600
Don Pooley	66	65	72	70	273	36,400
Chris Perry	68	69	70	66	273	36,400
Mark Calcavecchia	67	68	69	69	273	36,400
Nick Price	70	68	74	62	274	22,662.50
Fuzzy Zoeller	68	67	70	69	274	22,662.50
Mark Lye	68	71	66	69	274	22,662.50
Steve Jones	68	70	71	65	274	22,662.50
Wayne Grady	69	70	71	65	275	18,200
Webb Heintzelman	68	69	69	69	275	18,200
J.C. Snead	65	69	73	69	276	12,900
Loren Roberts	67	72	73	64	276	12,900
Duffy Waldorf	70	69	71	66	276	12,900
Pat McGowan	69	69	68	70	276	12,900
Peter Jacobsen	68	68	68	72	276	12,900
Jim Gallagher, Jr.	69	67	73	67	276	12,900
Bill Britton	68	71	72	65	276	12,900
Steve Pate	65	70	72	70	277	8,785
Wayne Levi	68	66	72	71	277	8,785
Chip Beck	73	67	69	68	277	8,785
Trevor Dodds	67	71	71	68	277	8,785
D.A. Weibring	71	71	69	67	278	7,000
Rocco Mediate	69	72	70	67	278	7,000
Larry Silveira	72	66	71	70	279	5,230
Mark Wiebe	71	71	73	64	279	5,230
Jim Thorpe	65	74	73	67	279	5,230
Tom Pernice, Jr.	71	66	73	69	279	5,230
Mark O'Meara	70	71	71	67	279	5,230
John Mahaffey	65	71	73	70	279	5,230
Rex Caldwell	67	72	71	69	279	5,230
Howard Twitty	70	72	72	66	280	3,790
Joey Sindelar	71	70	72	67	280	3,790
John McComish	69	70	73	68	280	3,790
Lon Hinkle	67	70	72	71	280	3,790
Donnie Hammond	74	67	71	68	280	3,790
Bill Kratzert	67	71	69	73	280	3,790
Billy Ray Brown	68	71	72	69	280	3,790
Doug Weaver	72	68	70	71	281	2,590
Bob Wolcott	73	68	74	66	281	2,590
David Peoples	70	71	72	68	281	2,590
Dan Forsman	70	70	75	66	281	2,590
Fred Funk	71	68	74	68	281	2,590
Nolan Henke	67	74	72	68	281	2,590
Bob Lohr	67	72	69	73	281	2,590
Roger Maltbie	69	71	74	67	281	2,590
George Burns	69	69	71	72	281	2,590
Larry Mize	71	68	75	68	282	1,709.56
Joel Edwards	70	70	73	69	282	1,709.56
Brian Claar	69	70	75	68	282	1,709.56
Lennie Clements	70	72	73	67	282	1,709.56
Rick Fehr	69	73	72	68	282	1,709.56
Leonard Thompson	68	74	69	71	282	1,709.55
Dan Halldorson	71	71	71	69	282	1,709.55

	SCORES				TOTAL	MONEY
Fulton Allem	71	70	70	71	282	1,709.55
Ed Fiori	73	69	71	69	282	1,709.55

Southern Open

Green Island Country Club, Columbus, Georgia
Par 35-35—70; 6,791 yards

September 21-24
purse, $400,000

	SCORES				TOTAL	MONEY
Ted Schulz	66	66	68	66	266	$72,000
Tim Simpson	66	73	65	63	267	35,200
Jay Haas	68	67	64	68	267	35,200
Bob Tway	69	69	65	67	270	16,533.34
Lance Ten Broeck	70	66	65	69	270	16,533.33
Larry Rinker	70	68	64	68	270	16,533.33
Steve Pate	64	68	70	69	271	12,466.67
Andrew Magee	66	70	66	69	271	12,466.67
Kenny Knox	65	68	67	71	271	12,466.66
Dave Rummells	68	64	67	73	272	10,400
Mike Donald	68	70	66	68	272	10,400
Billy Tuten	66	69	69	69	273	8,800
Jim Benepe	69	67	66	71	273	8,800
Corey Pavin	66	69	69	70	274	6,600
Hal Sutton	67	68	67	72	274	6,600
Webb Heintzelman	67	69	67	71	274	6,600
Jim Gallagher, Jr.	67	69	71	67	274	6,600
Scott Hoch	68	70	67	69	274	6,600
David Canipe	69	65	64	76	274	6,600
Rick Fehr	64	68	72	71	275	4,826.67
Robert Gamez	68	68	69	70	275	4,826.67
Ronnie Black	69	68	67	71	275	4,826.66
Rocco Mediate	68	69	68	71	276	3,560
Billy Andrade	64	72	70	70	276	3,560
Jim Booros	69	70	69	68	276	3,560
Bill Britton	66	71	67	72	276	3,560
Brian Claar	68	71	67	70	276	3,560
Robert Wrenn	67	70	68	72	277	2,660
Bill Sander	68	66	68	75	277	2,660
Bob Lohr	68	71	68	70	277	2,660
Dan Halldorson	68	70	68	71	277	2,660
John Inman	68	67	67	75	277	2,660
Bobby Clampett	67	64	72	74	277	2,660
Hugh Royer	66	70	71	71	278	1,893.34
Buddy Gardner	69	70	69	70	278	1,893.34
Jay Delsing	70	70	72	66	278	1,893.34
Kenny Perry	72	68	67	71	278	1,893.33
Chris Perry	68	67	71	72	278	1,893.33
Ronnie McCann	71	65	68	74	278	1,893.33
Bill Kratzert	66	71	69	72	278	1,893.33
David Edwards	70	66	69	73	278	1,893.33
Russ Cochran	70	70	66	72	278	1,893.33
Larry Silveira	69	70	69	71	279	1,320
Gene Sauers	67	73	70	69	279	1,320
Larry Mize	71	67	70	71	279	1,320
Mark Hayes	67	68	73	71	279	1,320
Rex Caldwell	69	71	69	70	279	1,320
Scott Verplank	69	71	69	71	280	994.29

	SCORES				TOTAL	MONEY
Tom Pernice, Jr.	68	70	71	71	280	994.29
J.C. Snead	69	70	70	71	280	994.29
Mike Hulbert	71	67	72	70	280	994.29
Larry Nelson	71	68	65	76	280	994.28
Steve Lowery	67	70	70	73	280	994.28
Richard Crawford	70	70	67	73	280	994.28

Centel Classic

Killearn Golf and Country Club, Tallahassee, Florida
Par 36-36—72; 7,098 yards
(Final round cancelled - rain.)

September 28-October 1
purse, $750,000

	SCORES			TOTAL	MONEY
Bill Britton	71	66	63	200	$135,000
Ronnie Black	67	67	70	204	81,000
Gary Hallberg	68	71	66	205	51,000
Mike Reid	69	68	69	206	31,000
Tom Pernice, Jr.	68	65	73	206	31,000
Bill Buttner	69	66	71	206	31,000
Leonard Thompson	72	70	65	207	20,303.58
Tim Simpson	68	69	70	207	20,303.57
Tim Norris	70	68	69	207	20,303.57
Kenny Knox	69	69	69	207	20,303.57
Hale Irwin	67	73	67	207	20,303.57
Peter Jacobsen	69	69	69	207	20,303.57
Tom Byrum	68	69	70	207	20,303.57
Bobby Wadkins	69	70	69	208	10,920
Stan Utley	71	65	72	208	10,920
Dave Rummells	73	67	68	208	10,920
Mark Lye	72	67	69	208	10,920
Billy Mayfair	72	68	68	208	10,920
Ed Fiori	70	67	71	208	10,920
Tommy Armour	66	71	71	208	10,920
Brad Bryant	69	66	73	208	10,920
Jim Carter	73	61	74	208	10,920
Mike Donald	70	71	67	208	10,920
Hal Sutton	71	67	71	209	5,430.82
Brian Tennyson	69	71	69	209	5,430.82
Rick Pearson	71	67	71	209	5,430.82
Jeff Hart	71	68	70	209	5,430.82
John Adams	69	69	71	209	5,430.82
Dave Eichelberger	68	69	72	209	5,430.82
Jim Benepe	71	67	71	209	5,430.82
Jay Don Blake	71	69	69	209	5,430.82
Russ Cochran	71	68	70	209	5,430.82
John McComish	69	68	72	209	5,430.81
Greg Ladehoff	66	70	73	209	5,430.81
Brian Watts	74	67	69	210	3,540.86
Kenny Perry	68	72	70	210	3,540.86
Ronnie McCann	68	73	69	210	3,540.86
Chris Perry	70	72	68	210	3,540.86
Billy Ray Brown	72	69	69	210	3,540.86
Andrew Magee	67	70	73	210	3,540.85
Roy Biancalana	72	67	71	210	3,540.85
Don Reese	70	69	72	211	2,355
Loren Roberts	71	70	70	211	2,355
Mike Hulbert	70	72	69	211	2,355

	SCORES			TOTAL	MONEY
Mark Hayes	70	67	74	211	2,355
Barry Jaeckel	72	68	71	211	2,355
Davis Love III	72	68	71	211	2,355
Clark Burroughs	70	70	71	211	2,355
Bob Estes	73	69	69	211	2,355
Lennie Clements	68	72	71	211	2,355

Texas Open Presented By Nabisco

Oak Hills Country Club, San Antonio, Texas
Par 35-35—70; 6,576 yards

October 5-8
purse, $600,000

	SCORES				TOTAL	MONEY
Donnie Hammond	65	64	65	64	258	$108,000
Paul Azinger	64	62	70	69	265	64,800
Bob Lohr	66	64	66	71	267	31,200
Duffy Waldorf	67	63	66	71	267	31,200
Mark Wiebe	62	68	70	67	267	31,200
Jay Don Blake	67	65	68	68	268	20,100
Bill Britton	67	65	67	69	268	20,100
Lanny Wadkins	62	68	68	70	268	20,100
Bob Eastwood	66	68	65	70	269	15,000
Davis Love III	67	68	65	69	269	15,000
Don Pooley	64	66	67	72	269	15,000
Loren Roberts	66	64	72	67	269	15,000
Hal Sutton	66	66	69	68	269	15,000
Webb Heintzelman	71	66	68	65	270	10,200
Hale Irwin	65	66	69	70	270	10,200
Kenny Knox	67	67	69	67	270	10,200
Wayne Levi	67	66	69	68	270	10,200
Steve Pate	64	66	72	68	270	10,200
Jim Gallagher, Jr.	66	69	69	67	271	8,100
Jodie Mudd	72	65	64	70	271	8,100
Billy Andrade	70	65	68	69	272	5,802.86
Dave Barr	67	67	67	71	272	5,802.86
Steve Elkington	68	68	66	70	272	5,802.86
Bob Estes	68	69	68	67	272	5,802.86
Tim Norris	71	65	67	69	272	5,802.86
Clark Burroughs	67	68	65	72	272	5,802.85
Tom Sieckmann	62	69	67	74	272	5,802.85
Russ Cochran	70	67	71	65	273	3,904.29
Mike Donald	69	64	71	69	273	3,904.29
Ray Floyd	67	69	69	68	273	3,904.29
Tom Kite	66	68	73	66	273	3,904.29
Tommy Armour	66	69	68	70	273	3,904.28
Jim Booros	65	68	69	71	273	3,904.28
J.L. Lewis	68	66	70	69	273	3,904.28
Jay Delsing	68	69	67	70	274	3,022.50
Brad Faxon	69	64	68	73	274	3,022.50
Rick Fehr	70	65	70	69	274	3,022.50
Scott Hoch	65	68	71	70	274	3,022.50
John Adams	69	68	68	70	275	2,400
David Canipe	68	68	70	69	275	2,400
Brad Fabel	70	67	70	68	275	2,400
Billy Mayfair	66	71	68	70	275	2,400
Mike Sullivan	68	69	68	70	275	2,400
Bobby Wadkins	68	67	68	72	275	2,400

	SCORES				TOTAL	MONEY
Hubert Green	69	67	67	73	276	1,920
David Ogrin	67	67	72	70	276	1,920
Billy Ray Brown	68	66	75	68	277	1,614
Morris Hatalsky	67	68	72	70	277	1,614
Corey Pavin	68	66	72	71	277	1,614
Robert Wrenn	69	67	66	75	277	1,614

Walt Disney World/Oldsmobile Classic

Walt Disney World, Lake Buena Vista, Florida   October 18-21
Magnolia Course, Par 36-36—72; 7,190 yards   purse, $800,000
Palm Course, Par 36-36—72; 6,967 yards
Lake Buena Vista Course, Par 36-36—72; 6,706 yards

	SCORES				TOTAL	MONEY
Tim Simpson	65	67	70	70	272	$144,000
Donnie Hammond	72	65	65	71	273	86,400
Paul Azinger	65	70	71	68	274	41,600
Fred Couples	70	65	69	70	274	41,600
Kenny Knox	70	65	71	68	274	41,600
Jay Haas	71	66	70	68	275	27,800
Ted Schulz	65	69	72	69	275	27,800
Bob Gilder	70	65	69	72	276	24,000
Curtis Strange	72	66	72	66	276	24,000
James Hallet	72	69	69	67	277	19,200
Mike Hulbert	68	69	69	71	277	19,200
Roger Maltbie	71	63	74	69	277	19,200
Nick Price	72	69	67	69	277	19,200
Bob Estes	67	71	71	69	278	14,400
Dave Rummells	66	68	76	68	278	14,400
Lance Ten Broeck	67	71	72	68	278	14,400
Loren Roberts	68	68	71	72	279	12,800
Peter Jacobsen	69	66	77	68	280	9,066.67
Mark O'Meara	75	68	71	66	280	9,066.67
Chris Perry	70	69	72	69	280	9,066.67
Craig Stadler	68	69	74	69	280	9,066.67
Bobby Wadkins	68	72	73	67	280	9,066.67
Mark Wiebe	69	74	67	70	280	9,066.67
Lennie Clements	67	69	73	71	280	9,066.66
Bruce Lietzke	69	68	73	70	280	9,066.66
Tom Sieckmann	71	69	70	70	280	9,066.66
John Mahaffey	69	69	74	69	281	4,996.37
Rocco Mediate	66	72	74	69	281	4,996.37
Kenny Perry	73	66	73	69	281	4,996.37
Don Shirey, Jr.	67	71	73	70	281	4,996.37
Chip Beck	70	67	73	71	281	4,996.36
David Edwards	67	70	73	71	281	4,996.36
Buddy Gardner	68	71	70	72	281	4,996.36
Larry Mize	69	67	74	71	281	4,996.36
Corey Pavin	67	70	71	73	281	4,996.36
Tom Purtzer	68	73	69	71	281	4,996.36
Lanny Wadkins	73	67	68	73	281	4,996.36
Bobby Clampett	69	72	72	69	282	3,520
Lon Hinkle	73	67	70	72	282	3,520
Wayne Levi	69	68	74	71	282	3,520
Gil Morgan	69	71	73	69	282	3,520
Jim Benepe	69	70	72	72	283	2,800

	SCORES				TOTAL	MONEY
Bill Britton	67	68	74	74	283	2,800
Billy Ray Brown	69	68	74	72	283	2,800
Bob Tway	61	77	71	74	283	2,800
Fuzzy Zoeller	72	69	69	73	283	2,800
Andy Bean	73	67	74	70	284	2,008.89
Jay Don Blake	71	71	73	69	284	2,008.89
Tom Byrum	69	71	75	69	284	2,008.89
Dan Forsman	72	69	69	74	284	2,008.89
Morris Hatalsky	73	66	71	74	284	2,008.89
Davis Love III	69	70	73	72	284	2,008.89
Steve Pate	69	71	72	72	284	2,008.89
Payne Stewart	67	70	76	71	284	2,008.89
Larry Silveira	66	69	75	74	284	2,008.88

Nabisco Championship

Harbour Town Golf Links, Hilton Head Island, South Carolina   October 26-29
Par 36-35—71; 6,657 yards   purse, $2,500,000

	SCORES				TOTAL	MONEY
Tom Kite	69	65	74	68	276	$450,000
Payne Stewart	69	70	71	66	276	270,000
(Kite defeated Stewart on second extra hole.)						
Paul Azinger	71	73	67	67	278	146,250
Wayne Levi	71	72	63	72	278	146,250
Donnie Hammond	65	73	69	72	279	100,000
Mark O'Meara	67	71	71	71	280	90,000
Fred Couples	68	74	67	72	281	82,500
Scott Hoch	71	71	68	71	281	82,500
Chip Beck	71	68	73	71	283	73,000
Mark Calcavecchia	70	75	68	70	283	73,000
David Frost	70	76	67	71	284	64,166.67
Curtis Strange	68	75	68	73	284	64,166.67
Greg Norman	67	74	68	75	284	64,166.66
Ben Crenshaw	73	72	71	69	285	53,400
Mike Hulbert	73	75	70	67	285	53,400
Steve Jones	72	69	71	73	285	53,400
Jodie Mudd	72	72	70	71	285	53,400
Craig Stadler	71	75	72	67	285	53,400
Mark McCumber	74	70	68	74	286	48,000
Dave Rummells	72	70	69	75	286	48,000
Ted Schulz	73	69	69	75	286	48,000
Wayne Grady	75	67	71	74	287	44,000
Blaine McCallister	70	75	74	68	287	44,000
Tim Simpson	75	75	67	70	287	44,000
Hal Sutton	70	73	73	71	287	44,000
Bob Tway	72	70	73	72	287	44,000
John Mahaffey	80	68	68	72	288	41,500
Mike Donald	70	74	72	73	289	41,000
Bill Glasson	74	71	74	71	290	40,500
Mike Reid	73	75	71	72	291	40,000

Isuzu-Kapalua International

Kapalua Resort, Bay Course, Maui, Hawaii
Par 36-36—72; 6,671 yards

November 8-11
purse, $650,000

	SCORES				TOTAL	MONEY
Peter Jacobsen	69	69	66	66	270	$150,000
Steve Pate	67	68	68	67	270	84,000
(Jacobsen defeated Pate on third extra hole.)						
Nick Price	68	70	69	65	272	53,000
Donnie Hammond	64	67	73	70	274	34,400
Robert Wrenn	71	64	67	72	274	34,400
Ted Schulz	70	69	68	68	275	19,333.34
Loren Roberts	70	68	67	70	275	19,333.33
Chris Perry	70	68	67	70	275	19,333.33
Davis Love III	73	67	71	65	276	11,875
Ed Fiori	69	68	71	68	276	11,875
Leonard Thompson	74	66	68	68	276	11,875
John Mahaffey	72	69	66	69	276	11,875
Blaine McCallister	70	72	70	65	277	8,825
Dave Rummells	69	71	71	66	277	8,825
Lennie Clements	74	67	69	67	277	8,825
Brad Faxon	71	69	67	70	277	8,825
Mike Hulbert	71	69	70	68	278	7,600
Billy Andrade	71	71	68	68	278	7,600
Bob Gilder	73	65	69	71	278	7,600
Jim Carter	70	68	71	70	279	6,700
David Ogrin	71	67	71	70	279	6,700
Wayne Levi	70	72	67	70	279	6,700
Corey Pavin	71	71	69	69	280	5,600
Tom Byrum	73	70	68	69	280	5,600
John Cook	69	69	71	71	280	5,600
David Edwards	71	68	70	71	280	5,600
Tom Purtzer	69	71	68	72	280	5,600
Bob Estes	72	68	66	74	280	5,600
Mac O'Grady	70	69	72	70	281	4,975
Kenny Perry	71	68	68	74	281	4,975
Mark Wiebe	72	72	69	69	282	4,600
Gary McCord	68	72	72	70	282	4,600
Lon Hinkle	70	70	71	71	282	4,600
Steve Elkington	73	70	72	69	284	4,225
Craig Stadler	70	64	73	77	284	4,225
John Huston	73	76	69	67	285	3,900
Billy Mayfair	71	72	69	73	285	3,900
Ben Crenshaw	69	69	72	75	285	3,900
Brian Tennyson	76	70	70	71	287	3,650
Hale Irwin	70	72	70	75	287	3,650
Dick McClean	73	73	74	70	290	3,500
Mats Lanner	76	74	69	72	291	3,262.50
Jim Gallagher	71	73	76	71	291	3,262.50
Mark Seki	71	74	71	75	291	3,262.50
Kenny Knox	73	71	71	76	291	3,262.50
Mark Lye	74	77	72	74	297	3,075
Mike Sullivan	77	71	76	73	297	3,075
Mark Rolfing	77	77	74	78	306	3,000

RMCC Invitational Hosted By Greg Norman

Sherwood Country Club, Thousand Oaks, California
Par 36-36—72; 7,025 yards

November 17-19
purse, $1,000,000

	SCORES			TOTAL	MONEY (Each)
Curtis Strange/Mark O'Meara	66	62	62	190	$125,000
Tom Weiskopf/Lanny Wadkins	71	65	60	196	59,000
Bernhard Langer/John Mahaffey	70	67	59	196	59,000
Raymond Floyd/Chip Beck	72	63	62	197	42,750
Greg Norman/Jack Nicklaus	74	65	58	197	42,750
Hale Irwin/Steve Jones	71	66	62	199	39,000
Tom Kite/Hal Sutton	71	68	63	202	36,500
Mark Calcavecchia/Bruce Lietzke	72	69	62	203	34,000
Arnold Palmer/Peter Jacobsen	75	68	61	204	31,000
Lee Trevino/Andy Bean	74	64	66	204	31,000

(Note: First round - foursomes; second round - fourball; third round - scramble.)

J.C. Penney Classic

Bardmoor Country Club, Largo, Florida
Par 36-36—72; 6,892 yards - men, 6,434 yards - women

November 30-December 3
purse, $1,000,000

	SCORES				TOTAL	MONEY (Each)
Bill Glasson/Pat Bradley	68	68	65	66	267	$100,000
Duffy Waldorf/Patty Sheehan	69	67	64	67	267	60,000
(Glasson/Bradley defeated Waldorf/Sheehan on fourth extra hole.)						
Jay Don Blake/Tracy Kerdyk	63	72	64	72	271	35,000
Kenny Perry/Sherri Turner	70	64	69	68	271	35,000
Gene Sauers/Beth Daniel	70	66	63	73	272	24,700
Gary Hallburg/Liselotte Neumann	72	66	68	69	275	15,750
Mark McCumber/Debbie Massey	71	67	68	69	275	15,750
Rocco Mediate/Missie Berteotti	71	69	65	70	275	15,750
Mike Hulbert/Val Skinner	67	67	70	71	275	15,750
Wayne Levi/Dale Eggeling	69	69	68	70	276	9,500
Kenny Knox/Nancy Brown	69	67	68	72	276	9,500
Billy Andrade/Penney Hammel	72	67	69	69	277	7,000
Dave Barr/Dawn Coe	67	72	69	69	277	7,000
Brad Bryant/Chris Johnson	72	67	68	70	277	7,000
Hale Irwin/Amy Alcott	72	70	67	68	277	7,000
Robert Wrenn/Vicki Fergon	67	72	67	71	277	7,000
Tommy Armour/Lori Garbacz	65	70	68	74	277	7,000
Ted Schulz/Allison Finney	68	67	68	74	277	7,000
Steve Jones/Jane Crafter	70	71	64	73	278	4,950
Andy Bean/Laura Davies	68	66	70	74	278	4,950
Steve Pate/Sandra Palmer	72	66	69	72	279	4,550
Roger Maltbie/JoAnne Carner	70	68	69	72	279	4,550
Bill Britton/Donna White	68	66	72	73	279	4,550
Stan Utley/Myra Blackwelder	73	67	70	69	279	4,550
Joey Sindelar/Lauri Merten	73	68	70	68	279	4,550
David Ogrin/Robin Walton	67	71	65	76	279	4,550
Leonard Thompson/Cathy Gerring	73	70	64	73	280	4,150
Jim Gallagher/Cindy Figg-Currier	70	69	69	72	280	4,150
Gary Koch/Deb Richard	71	69	67	74	281	3,750
Brad Faxon/Jody Anschutz	72	71	66	72	281	3,750

	SCORES				TOTAL	MONEY
John Huston/Amy Benz	71	73	65	72	281	3,750
Curt Byrum/Colleen Walker	68	68	70	75	281	3,750
Jim Hallet/Sally Quinlan	72	72	66	71	281	3,750
Tom Byrum/Susan Sanders	70	75	65	71	281	3,750
Lon Hinkle/Martha Nause	71	71	67	73	282	3,350
Dan Forsman/Dottie Mochrie	73	69	68	72	282	3,350
Donnie Hammond/Tammie Green	71	69	71	72	283	3,150
Jay Haas/Hollis Stacy	70	72	69	72	283	3,150
Brian Tennyson/Marci Bozarth	73	67	69	75	284	2,975
Bob Gilder/Cindy Rarick	71	70	68	75	284	2,975
Doug Tewell/Betsy King	74	69	70	71	284	2,975
Chris Perry/Caroline Keggi	73	70	70	71	284	2,975
Mike Sullivan/Sally Little	70	73	71	72	286	2,850
Andy North/Sherri Steinhauer	72	68	72	75	287	2,775
Jim Carter/Danielle Ammaccapane	72	71	70	74	287	2,775
Mike Donald/Judy Dickinson	73	70	69	76	288	2,700
Clarence Rose/Shirley Furlong	70	72	72	75	289	2,625
Jeff Sluman/Jane Geddes	74	68	72	75	289	2,625
Larry Rinker/Laura Rinker	71	73	70	79	293	2,550
Greg Twiggs/Jan Stephenson	60	72	66	DQ		2,500

Chrysler Team Championship

Palm Beach Polo and Country Club
Cypress Course: Par 36-36—72; 7,085 yards
Dunes Course: Par 36-36—72; 7,050 yards
Wellington Club: Par 36-36—72; 6,850 yards
West Palm Beach, Florida

December 7-10
purse, $600,000

	SCORES				TOTAL	MONEY (Each)
David Ogrin/Ted Schulz	63	64	65	65	257	$50,000
Charlie Epps/Blaine McCallister	63	60	71	65	259	28,500
Mike Hulbert/Bob Tway	62	62	64	72	260	17,500
Mark Brooks/Scott Verplank	65	66	66	64	261	12,400
Jim Booros/Bill Britton	64	65	70	63	262	9,050
Steve Elkington/Dick Harmon	66	65	66	65	262	9,050
Rick Fehr/Kent Kluba	63	61	66	72	262	9,050
Clark Burroughs/Lance Ten Broeck	60	69	67	66	262	9,050
Jim Rutledge/Mike Smith	60	68	70	65	263	7,250
Steve Hart/Ed Humenik	65	65	66	67	263	7,250
Peter Jacobsen/Johnny Miller	60	64	66	65	264	5,750
Nolan Henke/Joel Edwards	67	64	69	64	264	5,750
Stan Utley/Bob Wolcott	64	66	68	66	264	5,750
Bob Lohr/Chris Perry	67	63	66	68	264	5,750
Jim Carter/Rocco Mediate	70	64	66	65	265	4,250
Mike McCullough/Kenny Perry	63	67	69	66	265	4,250
Billy Pierot/Don Reese	65	66	68	66	265	4,250
Fred Funk/Mike Miles	65	64	68	68	265	4,250
Kenny Knox/Keith Kulzer	64	65	69	67	265	4,250
Curt Byrum/Tom Byrum	64	67	70	65	266	3,250
Fred Couples/Mike Donald	67	64	70	65	266	3,250
Dave Barr/Ronan Rafferty	66	63	68	69	266	3,250
Jim Hallet/P.H. Horgan	66	66	68	67	267	2,750
Bob Ford/Larry Rinker	68	67	65	68	268	2,375
Tommy Armour/Dave Eichelberger	63	66	71	68	268	2,375
Jay Haas/Jerry Haas	61	67	72	69	269	1,900
Greg Ladehoff/Dave Rummells	64	70	67	68	269	1,900

	SCORES				TOTAL	MONEY (Each)
Pat McGowan/Jim Nelford	66	67	67	70	270	1,600
David Canipe/Greg Twiggs	64	70	67	70	271	1,450
Dick Mast/David Peoples	64	68	69	70	271	1,450
Joey Sindelar/Jim Thorpe	65	66	69	72	272	1,300

Spalding Invitational Pro-Amateur

Desert Highlands Country Club, Scottsdale, Arizona
Par 72

December 28-31
purse, $250,000

	SCORES				TOTAL	MONEY
Mark Calcavecchia	69	69	67	71	276	$60,000
Dave Barr	71	73	68	66	278	26,300
Bill Glasson	69	72	67	70	278	26,300
David Edwards	68	72	70	69	279	8,250
Steve Pate	73	65	71	71	280	8,250
Bob Ford	72	65	73	70	280	8,250
Bill Malley	71	73	70	68	282	6,500
Brian Mogg	70	73	68	72	283	5,750
Colleen Walker	65	73	73	72	283	5,750
John Adams	72	74	70	68	284	4,150
Ronnie Black	70	71	74	69	284	4,150
Kenny Knox	68	72	72	72	284	4,150
Gary McCord	70	69	73	72	284	4,150
Loren Roberts	76	67	68	73	284	4,150
Tim Norris	73	73	69	70	285	3,300
Bob Gilder	74	68	72	71	285	3,300
Jeff Thomsen	72	70	71	72	285	3,300
Cindy Rarick	71	74	70	72	287	3,100
Andrew Magee	74	73	71	70	288	2,900
George Burns	73	75	65	75	288	2,900
Duffy Waldorf	70	72	69	77	288	2,900
Gene Sauers	67	74	69	79	289	2,650
Mark Lye	72	73	69	75	289	2,650
David Glenz	72	77	71	70	290	2,450
Jim Nelford	71	72	74	73	290	2,450
Mike Reid	74	72	73	72	291	2,200
Roger Maltbie	69	72	76	74	291	2,200
Jay Overton	73	74	71	73	291	2,200
Barry Jaeckel	77	73	72	70	292	1,660
J.C. Snead	70	75	73	74	292	1,660
Al Geiberger	67	74	76	75	292	1,660
Lon Hinkle	70	74	72	76	292	1,660
Don Levin	70	76	75	71	292	1,660
Danny Briggs	73	73	74	73	293	1,625
Jeff Brehaut	73	73	76	72	294	1,550
Charlie Gibson	75	72	73	74	294	1,550
Howie Johnson	75	71	73	75	294	1,550
Rob Boldt	70	77	77	71	295	1,450
Bob Pancratz	75	74	72	75	296	1,390
Howard Twitty	68	73	77	78	296	1,390
Danny Edwards	71	75	75	76	297	1,350
Billy Casper	73	72	72	80	297	1,350

The U.S. Senior Tour

MONY Senior Tournament of Champions

LaCosta Country Club, Carlsbad, California
Par 36-36—72; 6,815 yards

January 5-8
purse, $250,000

	SCORES				TOTAL	MONEY
Miller Barber	73	67	68	72	280	$50,000
Dale Douglass	67	72	75	67	281	30,000
Bruce Crampton	70	70	71	76	287	25,000
Orville Moody	72	75	72	70	289	20,000
Billy Casper	72	79	71	68	290	17,000
Al Geiberger	71	77	72	71	291	16,000
Dave Hill	73	73	75	71	292	15,000
Chi Chi Rodriguez	73	76	71	75	295	13,500
Walter Zembriski	70	77	72	76	295	13,500
Larry Mowry	75	77	72	72	296	12,000
Don Bies	73	75	77	75	300	10,500
Arnold Palmer	75	74	74	77	300	10,500
Lee Elder	76	77	74	79	306	9,000
Harold Henning	75	78	81	73	307	8,000

General Foods PGA Senior Championship

PGA National Golf Club, Champion Course,
Palm Beach Gardens, Florida
Par 36-36—72; 6,530 yards

February 9-12
purse, $400,000

	SCORES				TOTAL	MONEY
Larry Mowry	74	69	65	73	281	$72,000
Miller Barber	72	69	70	71	282	35,200
Al Geiberger	69	70	72	71	282	35,200
Mike Hill	67	71	74	75	287	16,533.34
Joe Jimenez	72	70	72	73	287	16,533.33
Dave Hill	73	72	70	72	287	16,533.33
Harold Henning	72	73	70	73	288	13,400
Gary Player	70	76	72	71	289	11,600
Ben Smith	72	73	71	73	289	11,600
Bruce Crampton	72	73	71	73	289	11,600
Arnold Palmer	71	74	74	71	290	8,800
Walter Zembriski	76	72	73	69	290	8,800
Bob Brue	75	70	73	72	290	8,800
Doug Dalziel	73	72	72	73	290	8,800
Stan Thirsk	73	76	72	70	291	7,000
Gay Brewer	79	70	70	72	291	7,000
Orville Moody	70	75	72	75	292	6,200
Jim Ferree	79	72	70	71	292	6,200
Chi Chi Rodriguez	75	75	75	68	293	4,848
Billy Maxwell	73	71	74	75	293	4,848
Don Massengale	78	74	70	71	293	4,848
Lee Elder	74	76	72	71	293	4,848
Bobby Nichols	78	71	73	71	293	4,848
Jimmy Powell	78	69	74	73	294	3,520

	SCORES				TOTAL	MONEY
Tom Shaw	74	76	70	74	294	3,520
Bob Charles	71	80	71	72	294	3,520
Tommy Aaron	80	72	70	73	295	2,900
Jim O'Hern	75	73	78	69	295	2,900
Don Bies	72	74	74	75	295	2,900
Dick Hendrickson	74	75	76	70	295	2,900
Paul Moran	71	73	76	76	296	2,480
Gardner Dickinson	74	72	74	76	296	2,480
Dale Douglass	74	77	74	71	296	2,480
George Lanning	76	76	73	72	297	2,160
John Brodie	73	73	77	74	297	2,160
Bruce Devlin	78	75	73	71	297	2,160
Rives McBee	76	74	73	75	298	1,880
Butch Baird	78	75	75	70	298	1,880
Joe Carr	74	75	73	76	298	1,880

GTE Suncoast Classic

Tampa Palms Golf and Country Club, Tampa, Florida   February 17-19
Par 36-36—72; 6,631 yards   purse, $300,000

	SCORES			TOTAL	MONEY
Bob Charles	68	70	69	207	$45,000
Jim Ferree	72	70	65	207	21,833.34
Dave Hill	68	69	70	207	21,833.33
Harold Henning	73	67	67	207	21,833.33
(Charles defeated Hill and Ferree on first extra hole, Henning on third.)					
Doug Sanders	68	70	70	208	14,500
Chi Chi Rodriguez	68	70	72	210	11,100
Arnold Palmer	70	71	70	211	10,000
Miller Barber	71	69	73	213	7,855
Bruce Crampton	70	71	72	213	7,855
Dale Douglass	74	69	70	213	7,855
Ray Beallo	71	73	69	213	7,855
Gene Littler	73	69	71	213	7,855
Joe Jimenez	73	70	71	214	5,675
Lee Elder	75	68	71	214	5,675
Don Massengale	66	74	74	214	5,675
Gary Player	75	71	68	214	5,675
Al Kelley	72	74	69	215	4,450
Orville Moody	73	72	70	215	4,450
Doug Dalziel	79	68	68	215	4,450
Larry Mowry	73	71	71	215	4,450
Mike Hill	71	73	72	216	3,725
Bruce Devlin	71	74	71	216	3,725
Jim O'Hern	71	70	76	217	3,425
Tom Shaw	73	72	72	217	3,425
Phil Rodgers	73	73	72	218	3,125
Paul Moran	73	73	72	218	3,125
Al Geiberger	70	75	74	219	2,681.25
Lou Graham	76	72	71	219	2,681.25
Bob Erickson	78	70	71	219	2,681.25
Paul Harney	75	73	71	219	2,681.25
George Lanning	70	80	70	220	2,083.34
Richard Rhyan	76	75	69	220	2,083.34
J.C. Goosie	75	72	73	220	2,083.33
Billy Casper	73	76	71	220	2,083.33

	SCORES			TOTAL	MONEY
Butch Baird	71	75	74	220	2,083.33
Charles Owens	72	74	74	220	2,083.33
Charles Coody	77	70	74	221	1,700
Gay Brewer	72	75	74	221	1,700
Dick Hendrickson	73	76	72	221	1,700
Tommy Aaron	74	76	72	222	1,475
Don Bies	73	72	77	222	1,475
Walter Zembriski	76	74	72	222	1,475

Aetna Challenge

The Club at Pelican Bay, Naples, Florida

February 24-26
purse, $300,000

Par 36-36—72; 6,719 yards

	SCORES			TOTAL	MONEY
Gene Littler	70	70	69	209	$45,000
Harold Henning	70	70	71	211	26,000
Miller Barber	70	73	71	214	21,500
Bob Charles	74	69	72	215	16,250
Lou Graham	75	69	71	215	16,250
Chick Evans	70	73	73	216	10,550
Chi Chi Rodriguez	73	75	68	216	10,550
Dale Douglass	72	73	72	217	8,168.75
Bruce Crampton	70	72	75	217	8,168.75
Bruce Devlin	77	71	69	217	8,168.75
Phil Rodgers	72	76	69	217	8,168.75
Dick Hendrickson	72	78	68	218	5,860
George Lanning	73	71	74	218	5,860
Charles Sifford	73	76	69	218	5,860
Gary Player	71	78	69	218	5,860
Mike Hill	71	73	74	218	5,860
Robert Boldt	72	76	71	219	4,208.34
Arnold Palmer	75	74	70	219	4,208.34
Bobby Nichols	73	74	72	219	4,208.33
Ben Smith	77	70	72	219	4,208.33
Bert Yancey	72	76	71	219	4,208.33
Doug Dalziel	72	75	72	219	4,208.33
Don Massengale	71	76	73	220	3,425
Dave Hill	78	73	69	220	3,425
Bob Erickson	75	73	73	221	3,125
Bob Brue	79	71	71	221	3,125
Deray Simon	72	76	74	222	2,750
Orville Moody	75	77	70	222	2,750
Walter Zembriski	76	71	75	222	2,750
Butch Baird	71	75	77	223	2,412.50
Roberto De Vicenzo	75	75	73	223	2,412.50
Jim King	76	75	73	224	2,125.00
J.C. Goosie	77	74	73	224	2,125.00
Gay Brewer	76	76	72	224	2,125.00
Doug Ford	78	74	73	225	1,737.50
Gordon Jones	76	75	74	225	1,737.50
Joe Jimenez	75	74	76	225	1,737.50
Quinton Gray	76	76	73	225	1,737.50
Joe Lopez	72	75	78	225	1,737.50
Jimmy Powell	73	82	70	225	1,737.50

Vintage Chrysler Invitational

The Vintage Club, Mountain Course, Indian Wells, California
Par 36-36—72; 6,819 yards

March 2-5
purse, $370,000

		SCORES			TOTAL	MONEY
Miller Barber	70	70	72	69	281	$55,500
Don Bies	73	72	68	69	282	25,666.67
Larry Mowry	72	70	71	69	282	25,666.67
Bob Charles	68	71	73	70	282	25,666.66
J.C. Goosie	71	68	74	71	284	18,000
Bruce Crampton	73	71	74	68	286	15,000
Mike Hill	75	73	68	71	287	13,000
Dave Hill	74	73	73	68	288	10,080
Gene Littler	74	70	68	76	288	10,080
Dale Douglass	71	73	70	74	288	10,080
Orville Moody	72	71	72	73	288	10,080
Joe Jimenez	75	69	73	71	288	10,080
Gary Player	71	75	70	73	289	7,266.67
Tommy Aaron	79	72	70	68	289	7,266.67
Tom Shaw	71	70	73	75	289	7,266.66
George Lanning	74	70	73	73	290	6,400
Lou Graham	71	72	76	71	290	6,400
Al Geiberger	80	70	67	73	290	6,400
Rafe Botts	75	69	73	74	291	6,000
Butch Baird	76	74	75	67	292	5,700
Bobby Nichols	74	75	70	73	292	5,700
Dick Hendrickson	76	71	76	71	294	5,200
Don January	71	70	77	76	294	5,200
Charles Sifford	73	73	75	73	294	5,200
Don Massengale	76	72	74	73	295	4,500
Richard Rhyan	81	72	73	69	295	4,500
Bob Brue	75	77	72	71	295	4,500
Roberto De Vicenzo	76	72	73	74	295	4,500
Walter Zembriski	76	74	73	73	296	4,000
Ken Still	81	71	73	72	297	3,700
Charles Coody	79	74	72	72	297	3,700
Lee Elder	76	70	76	76	298	3,100
Gay Brewer	78	73	72	75	298	3,100
Al Chandler	78	73	74	73	298	3,100
Bruce Devlin	75	76	76	71	298	3,100
Gardner Dickinson	77	76	72	74	299	2,400
John Brodie	75	78	70	76	299	2,400
Doug Dalziel	80	71	77	71	299	2,400
Billy Casper	78	74	72	76	300	1,800
Bob Erickson	76	70	76	78	300	1,800
Jim Ferree	81	73	71	75	300	1,800

MONY Arizona Classic

The Pointe Golf Club, Phoenix, Arizona
Par 36-36—72; 6,617 yards

March 10-12
purse, $300,000

		SCORES		TOTAL	MONEY
Bruce Crampton	67	64	69	200	$45,000
Bobby Nichols	62	67	72	201	26,000
Al Geiberger	65	68	69	202	18,000
Gene Littler	67	65	70	202	18,000

	SCORES			TOTAL	MONEY
Robert Boldt	70	62	70	202	18,000
Miller Barber	66	67	70	203	9,718.75
Lou Graham	67	68	68	203	9,718.75
Bruce Devlin	70	65	68	203	9,718.75
Dale Douglass	73	65	65	203	9,718.75
J.C. Goosie	68	69	68	205	7,800
Charles Coody	67	69	70	206	6,240
Harold Henning	66	71	69	206	6,240
Walter Zembriski	69	66	71	206	6,240
Dave Hill	68	68	70	206	6,240
Babe Hiskey	70	70	66	206	6,240
Mike Hill	70	70	67	207	5,050
Bob Brue	69	68	70	207	5,050
Tom Shaw	73	67	68	208	4,070
Don Bies	70	70	68	208	4,070
Orville Moody	69	70	69	208	4,070
Dick Hendrickson	69	66	73	208	4,070
Butch Baird	68	69	71	208	4,070
Paul Moran	71	67	71	209	3,200
Don Massengale	72	66	71	209	3,200
Charles Owens	73	70	66	209	3,200
George Lanning	67	70	72	209	3,200
Al Chandler	68	69	72	209	3,200
Ben Smith	72	68	70	210	2,750
Ken Still	68	71	72	211	2,537.50
Tommy Aaron	66	74	71	211	2,537.50
Jim Ferree	71	69	72	212	2,181.25
Lee Elder	71	69	72	212	2,181.25
Billy Maxwell	73	69	70	212	2,181.25
Chick Evans	74	68	70	212	2,181.25
Joe Jimenez	70	76	67	213	1,850
John Paul Cain	68	69	76	213	1,850
Bob Erickson	69	74	70	213	1,850
Charles Sifford	72	68	74	214	1,625
Larry Mowry	68	70	76	214	1,625
John Brodie	73	67	74	214	1,625

Fuji Electric Grand Slam

Oak Hills Country Club, Katori, Japan
Par 36-36—72; 6,660 yards

March 24-26
purse, $370,000

	SCORES			TOTAL	MONEY
Bob Charles	67	71	69	207	$76,000
Larry Mowry	69	72	70	211	35,500
Charles Coody	74	69	68	211	35,500
Don January	71	71	69	211	35,500
Orville Moody	67	76	69	212	20,000
Tadashi Kitsuta	72	74	67	213	16,500
Arnold Palmer	68	75	71	214	13,250
Gene Littler	69	74	71	214	13,250
Bob Brue	74	73	68	215	9,500
Miller Barber	71	74	70	215	9,500
Bert Yancey	72	74	69	215	9,500
Masami Nishiyama	74	71	73	218	5,767
Ichio Sato	72	73	73	218	5,767
Chen Ching Po	74	74	73	218	5,767

	SCORES			TOTAL	MONEY
Chi Chi Rodriguez	75	72	72	219	4,550
Tommy Aaron	71	71	77	219	4,550
Masao Hara	75	74	71	220	3,900
Hideyo Sugimoto	70	77	73	220	3,900
Chen Chien Chung	72	75	73	220	3,900
Billy Casper	73	75	72	220	3,900
Sadao Ogawa	74	75	72	221	3,400
Ichiro Togawa	72	75	74	221	3,400
Lu Liang Huan	75	72	74	221	3,400
Hsieh Yung Yo	72	76	74	222	3,150
Jim O'Hern	73	72	77	222	3,150
Mitsuo Hirukawa	70	76	77	223	3,000
Takao Hara	76	80	68	224	2,900
Seiichi Sato	76	77	72	225	2,800
Kesahiko Uchida	75	79	72	226	2,450
Hideo Jibiki	75	76	75	226	2,450
Peter Thomson	75	74	77	226	2,450
Bob Boldt	74	74	78	226	2,450
Mitsuhiko Masuda	77	75	75	227	2,000
Dow Finsterwald	72	77	78	227	2,000
Shouri Miura	75	80	74	229	2,000
Doug Sanders	73	80	76	229	2,000
Shigeru Uchida	73	82	75	230	2,000
Agim Bardha	81	74	75	230	2,000
Tetsuo Ishii	78	79	77	234	2,000
Koichi Ono	81	81	76	238	2,000
Tomoo Ishii	79	89	76	244	2,000

Murata Seniors Reunion

Stonebriar Country Club, Frisco, Texas
Par 36-36—72; 6,800 yards

March 31-April 2
purse, $300,000

	SCORES			TOTAL	MONEY
Don Bies	68	67	73	208	$45,000
Harold Henning	73	71	70	214	26,000
Don January	75	69	73	217	21,500
Mike Hill	72	74	74	220	16,250
Al Geiberger	74	72	74	220	16,250
Bruce Crampton	71	72	78	221	11,100
Butch Baird	72	77	73	222	9,625
Dale Douglass	72	72	78	222	9,625
Gary Player	71	77	76	224	8,525
Walter Zembriski	73	78	74	225	7,450
Lou Graham	73	79	73	225	7,450
Rives McBee	76	76	74	226	6,400
Don Massengale	73	78	75	226	6,400
Orville Moody	72	79	77	228	5,800
Phil Rodgers	74	79	76	229	5,200
Homero Blancas	77	78	74	229	5,200
Rafe Botts	73	80	76	229	5,200
John Paul Cain	76	78	76	230	4,600
Bob Brue	74	76	81	231	4,033.34
Paul Moran	77	80	74	231	4,033.33
Charles Coody	74	82	75	231	4,033.33
Jim O'Hern	79	72	81	232	3,650
Robert Boldt	73	83	77	233	3,125

	SCORES			TOTAL	MONEY
Jim King	76	78	79	233	3,125
Richard Rhyan	80	76	78	234	3,125
Jack Fleck	79	77	78	234	3,125
Deray Simon	73	81	81	235	2,750
Ben Smith	81	77	77	235	2,750
Quinton Gray	81	79	75	235	2,750
Bobby Nichols	77	82	77	236	2,350
Bob Erickson	77	80	79	236	2,350
Doug Ford	76	82	78	236	2,350
Jim Ferree	79	80	78	237	2,075
J.C. Goosie	76	82	79	237	2,075
Tom Shaw	81	77	80	238	1,737.50
Charles Sifford	78	79	81	238	1,737.50
Jesse Whittenton	83	75	80	238	1,737.50
Cotton Dunn	81	76	81	238	1,737.50
Chick Evans	81	79	78	238	1,737.50
Fred Hawkins	78	80	80	238	1,737.50

The Tradition At Desert Mountain

The Golf Club at Desert Mountain, Cochise Course,
Scottsdale, Arizona
Par 36-36—72; 6,837 yards

April 14-16
purse, $600,000

	SCORES				TOTAL	MONEY
Don Bies	71	70	68	66	275	$90,000
Gary Player	67	69	72	68	276	52,000
Harold Henning	70	70	70	70	280	45,000
Bob Charles	69	71	73	68	281	34,000
Charles Coody	73	67	72	69	281	34,000
Bob Erickson	69	70	70	73	282	25,000
Al Geiberger	71	69	71	73	284	18,333.34
Gene Littler	66	70	73	75	284	18,333.33
Chi Chi Rodriguez	72	70	70	72	284	18,333.33
Gay Brewer	72	70	71	72	285	15,000
Joe Jimenez	73	70	71	71	285	15,000
Chick Evans	73	68	71	73	285	15,000
Bobby Nichols	76	72	68	70	286	11,500
Dave Hill	71	70	69	76	286	11,500
Bruce Crampton	74	73	68	71	286	11,500
Bruce Devlin	70	70	76	70	286	11,500
Orville Moody	72	69	76	70	287	8,500
Tom Shaw	74	76	69	68	287	8,500
Dick Hendrickson	76	71	71	69	287	8,500
Billy Casper	73	72	71	71	287	8,500
Lou Graham	72	73	70	72	287	8,500
Tommy Aaron	73	70	75	70	288	6,500
Butch Baird	70	70	73	75	288	6,500
Dale Douglass	74	71	72	71	288	6,500
Ken Still	75	74	66	74	289	5,750
Richard Rhyan	74	73	69	74	290	5,250
Arnold Palmer	72	76	69	73	290	5,250
Paul Moran	74	75	71	70	290	5,250
Walter Zembriski	68	75	69	79	291	4,500
Charles Owens	71	77	73	70	291	4,500
Don Massengale	71	74	73	73	291	4,500
Mike Hill	71	74	71	75	291	4,500

	SCORES				TOTAL	MONEY
Billy Maxwell	77	70	72	73	292	4,000
Phil Rodgers	69	74	77	73	293	3,500
Miller Barber	74	69	74	76	293	3,500
Lee Elder	74	74	71	74	293	3,500
J.C. Goosie	74	72	73	74	293	3,500
Ray Beallo	79	74	70	71	294	2,850
Bob Brue	72	73	71	78	294	2,850
Jim Ferree	75	73	73	73	294	2,850
Quinton Gray	76	77	72	69	294	2,850

Chrysler Cup

TPC at Prestancia, Sarasota, Florida   April 21-23
Par 36-36—72; 6,763 yards   purse, $600,000

FINAL RESULT: United States 71, International 29

FIRST ROUND
Four-Ball Match

Bruce Crampton-Roberto De Vicenzo (Int.) defeated Walter Zembriski-Chi Chi
   Rodriguez, 2 and 1.
Gene Littler-Al Geiberger (U.S.) defeated Harold Henning-Bruce Devlin, 3 and 1.
Orville Moody-Dave Hill (U.S.) defeated Bob Charles-Peter Thomson, 2 and 1.
Arnold Palmer-Miller Barber (U.S.) halved with Gary Player-Doug Dalziel.

STANDINGS: United States 10, International 6.

SECOND ROUND
Singles Match

Rodriguez (U.S.) defeated Dalziel, 1 up.
Henning (Int.) defeated Zembriski, 3 and 2.
Littler (U.S.) defeated Player, 3 and 2.
Charles (Int.) defeated Hill, 2 and 1.
Palmer (U.S.) halved with De Vicenzo.
Moody (U.S.) defeated Crampton, 1 up.
Barber (U.S.) defeated Devlin, 5 and 4.
Geiberger (U.S.) defeated Thomson, 1 up.

STANDINGS: United States 21, International 11.

THIRD ROUND
Four-Ball Stroke

Geiberger-Moody (U.S.) defeated Charles-Crampton, 69-70.
Rodriguez-Barber (U.S.) halved with Player-Henning, 65-65.
Palmer-Hill (U.S.) defeated De Vicenzo-Dalziel, 65-68.
Devlin-Thomson (Int.) defeated Littler-Zembriski, 63-88.

STANDINGS: United States 38-1/2, International 21-1/2.

FOURTH ROUND
Singles Stroke

Rodriguez (U.S.) defeated Crampton, 60-73.
Geiberger (U.S.) defeated Henning, 68-81.
Zembriski (U.S.) defeated Dalziel, 70-71.

Thomson (Int.) defeated Littler, 69-72.
Palmer (U.S.) defeated Devlin, 70-74.
Moody (U.S.) halved with De Vicenzo, 68-68.
Barber (U.S.) defeated Player, 69-70.
Hill (U.S.) defeated Charles, 66-71.

Each member of the United States team received $50,000; each member of the
International team received $25,000.

Liberty Mutual Legends of Golf

Onion Creek Country Club, Austin, Texas   April 27-30
Par 35-35—70; 6,367 yards   purse, $650,000
                                                                              (unofficial)

	SCORES				TOTAL	MONEY
						(Team)
Al Geiberger/Harold Henning	61	61	62	67	251	$120,000
Bob Charles/Bruce Devlin	61	64	61	66	252	65,000
Dale Douglass/Charles Coody	65	65	63	60	253	50,000
Bruce Crampton/Orville Moody	63	63	64	64	254	37,500
Gardner Dickinson/Dave Hill	62	64	64	64	254	37,500
Tommy Aaron/Lou Graham	66	64	63	65	258	28,500
Billy Casper/Gay Brewer	63	64	63	68	258	28,500
Arnold Palmer/Miller Barber	68	62	67	62	259	20,000
Homero Blancas/Don Massengale	65	64	64	67	260	15,000
Don January/Gene Littler	65	65	64	66	260	15,000
Tommy Jacobs/Ken Still	63	63	68	67	261	11,500
Peter Thomson/Jim Ferree	66	65	64	64	261	11,500
Bobby Nichols/Butch Baird	68	64	66	66	262	10,000
Dow Finsterwald/Don Bies	66	65	69	63	263	10,000
Chi Chi Rodriguez/Lee Elder	63	66	66	69	264	10,000
Jack Burke/Mike Hill	65	63	69	68	265	10,000
Doug Sanders/Larry Mowry	70	63	66	66	265	10,000
Charles Owens/Billy Maxwell	70	68	68	69	275	10,000

RJR At The Dominion

Dominion Country Club, San Antonio, Texas   May 5-7
Par 36-36—72; 6,814 yards   purse, $250,000

	SCORES			TOTAL	MONEY
Larry Mowry	66	67	68	201	$37,500
Gay Brewer	65	69	68	202	21,500
Miller Barber	66	70	68	204	17,800
Billy Casper	70	69	67	206	14,800
Harold Henning	71	65	71	207	10,500
Lou Graham	66	71	70	207	10,500
Dave Hill	70	70	68	208	8,400
Bobby Nichols	69	71	69	209	7,400
Charles Coody	72	69	68	209	7,400
Walter Zembriski	69	70	71	210	6,162.50
Ben Smith	69	70	71	210	6,162.50
Chi Chi Rodriguez	69	71	71	211	4,825
Gene Littler	69	71	71	211	4,825
Don Massengale	66	73	72	211	4,825
Robert Rawlins	69	70	72	211	4,825

	SCORES			TOTAL	MONEY
Jim Ferree	71	72	68	211	4,825
Don Bies	69	71	72	212	3,570
Mike Hill	71	72	69	212	3,570
Bob Brue	70	73	69	212	3,570
Bruce Crampton	72	72	68	212	3,570
Dick Hendrickson	71	70	71	212	3,570
Ken Still	69	73	71	213	2,900
Doug Dalziel	71	71	71	213	2,900
Al Geiberger	72	70	71	213	2,900
Butch Baird	72	70	72	214	2,587.50
Joe Jimenez	70	72	72	214	2,587.50
Phil Rodgers	75	71	69	215	2,150
John Paul Cain	74	70	71	215	2,150
Lee Elder	74	72	69	215	2,150
Bob Erickson	76	71	68	215	2,150
J.C. Goosie	71	73	71	215	2,150
Tom Shaw	70	73	73	216	1,637.50
Charles Owens	72	74	70	216	1,637.50
Deray Simon	73	76	67	216	1,637.50
Tommy Aaron	72	76	68	216	1,637.50
Frank Beard	76	70	70	216	1,637.50
Babe Hiskey	72	74	70	216	1,637.50
Quinton Gray	72	70	75	217	1,300
Al Chandler	73	70	74	217	1,300
Bill Collins	74	73	70	217	1,300
Dale Douglass	74	71	72	217	1,300

Bell Atlantic St. Christopher's Classic

Chester Valley Golf Club, Malvern, Pennsylvania
Par 35-35—70; 6,406 yards

May 12-14
purse, $400,000

	SCORES			TOTAL	MONEY
Dave Hill	72	66	68	206	$60,000
Chi Chi Rodriguez	67	72	67	206	35,000
(Hill defeated Rodriguez on third extra hole.)					
Harold Henning	70	69	68	207	29,000
Don Bies	69	71	69	209	21,800
Jim Dent	69	69	71	209	21,800
Bob Charles	70	69	71	210	14,700
Mike Hill	68	71	72	211	13,600
Orville Moody	68	71	73	212	11,025
Miller Barber	70	73	69	212	11,025
Joe Jimenez	70	74	68	212	11,025
Dale Douglass	69	70	73	212	11,025
Charles Coody	69	76	68	213	8,800
Billy Maxwell	70	72	72	214	8,200
Ben Smith	72	74	69	215	7,800
Deray Simon	68	74	74	216	6,400
Jerry Barber	71	72	73	216	6,400
Al Kelley	73	71	72	216	6,400
Jim King	73	72	71	216	6,400
Billy Casper	73	71	72	216	6,400
Bruce Crampton	73	71	72	216	6,400
Charles Owens	72	74	71	217	4,600
George Lanning	75	71	71	217	4,600
Frank Beard	70	70	77	217	4,600

	SCORES			TOTAL	MONEY
Lee Elder	69	74	74	217	4,600
Bob Erickson	75	70	72	217	4,600
Lou Graham	75	68	74	217	4,600
Walter Zembriski	70	74	74	218	3,600
Tommy Aaron	68	74	76	218	3,600
Larry Mowry	73	73	72	218	3,600
Dick Hendrickson	70	77	71	218	3,600
Don Massengale	74	74	71	219	3,037.50
Bob Brue	74	72	73	219	3,037.50
J.C. Goosie	74	75	71	220	2,875
Charles Sifford	76	71	74	221	2,475
Ken Still	72	75	74	221	2,475
Bob Thatcher	72	77	72	221	2,475
Tom Shaw	77	69	75	221	2,475
Arnold Palmer	72	73	76	221	2,475
John Paul Cain	71	75	75	221	2,475
Doug Dalziel	76	75	70	221	2,475

NYNEX/Golf Digest Commemorative

Sleepy Hollow Country Club, Scarborough, New York   May 19-21
Par 35-35—70; 6,545 yards   purse, $300,000

	SCORES			TOTAL	MONEY
Bob Charles	63	65	65	193	$45,000
Don Bies	65	67	66	198	23,750
Bruce Crampton	68	64	66	198	23,750
Charles Coody	69	67	65	201	18,000
Harold Henning	69	68	65	202	12,800
Dave Hill	66	67	69	202	12,800
Walter Zembriski	68	68	68	204	10,000
Chi Chi Rodriguez	72	65	68	205	8,525
Dan Morgan	70	65	70	205	8,525
Lee Elder	69	65	71	205	8,525
Ben Smith	67	70	69	206	6,850
Dale Douglass	71	69	66	206	6,850
Gary Player	70	69	68	207	5,366.67
George Lanning	70	68	69	207	5,366.67
Tom Shaw	71	68	68	207	S,366.67
Terrance Dill	69	68	70	207	5,366.67
Billy Casper	65	71	71	207	5,366.66
Lou Graham	68	67	72	207	5,366.66
Richard Rhyan	66	72	70	208	3,766.67
Gene Littler	70	69	69	208	3,766.67
Miller Barber	70	69	69	208	3,766.67
Gay Brewer	70	69	69	208	3,766.67
Frank Beard	65	73	70	208	3,766.66
Joe Jimenez	70	68	70	208	3,766.66
Orville Moody	71	71	67	209	3,050
Mike Hill	70	68	71	209	3,050
Jim Ferree	71	65	73	209	3,050
Dick Hendrickson	69	72	69	210	2,608.34
Jim Cochran	71	68	71	210	2,608.33
Bruce Devlin	74	67	69	210	2,608.33
Ken Still	73	70	68	211	2,350
Jim Dent	72	69	71	212	2,175
J.C. Goosie	69	68	75	212	2,175

	SCORES			TOTAL	MONEY
Jim King	71	70	72	213	1,855
Jim O'Hern	69	71	73	213	1,855
Al Kelley	71	79	63	213	1,855
Doug Dalziel	71	72	70	213	1,855
Jimmy Powell	67	74	72	213	1,855
Ralph Terry	72	69	73	214	1,512.50
Mike Joyce	72	70	72	214	1,512.50
Don Massengale	72	70	72	214	1,512.50
Bob Erickson	73	73	68	214	1,512.50

Southwestern Bell Classic

Quail Creek Golf and Country Club, Oklahoma City, Oklahoma   May 26-28
Par 36-36—72; 6,708 yards   purse, $300,000

	SCORES			TOTAL	MONEY
Bobby Nichols	69	69	71	209	$45,000
Orville Moody	69	70	70	209	26,000
(Nichols defeated Moody on third extra hole.)					
Jimmy Powell	72	68	72	212	19,750
Al Geiberger	66	71	75	212	19,750
Bob Charles	73	70	70	213	12,800
Jim Dent	69	70	74	213	12,800
Deray Simon	69	72	73	214	9,625
Gary Player	72	70	72	214	9,625
Lou Graham	71	72	72	215	7,808.34
Walter Zembriski	72	72	71	215	7,808.33
Mike Hill	74	70	71	215	7,808.33
Paul Moran	74	65	77	216	6,200
Butch Baird	72	71	73	216	6,200
Terrance Dill	73	70	73	216	6,200
Tom Shaw	74	72	71	217	5,350
Gordon Jones	74	72	71	217	5,350
Dudley Wysong	72	73	73	218	4,600
Don Massengale	74	72	72	218	4,600
Jim O'Hern	75	71	72	218	4,600
Robert Rawlins	76	72	71	219	3,737.50
Rafe Botts	73	73	73	219	3,737.50
Joe Jimenez	70	77	72	219	3,737.50
Harold Henning	74	71	74	219	3,737.50
Charles Sifford	76	75	69	220	3,050
Ben Smith	73	75	72	220	3,050
Jerry Barber	73	69	78	220	3,050
Gay Brewer	71	73	76	220	3,050
Dave Hill	76	70	74	220	3,050
Billy Maxwell	77	71	73	221	2,537.50
Rives McBee	74	72	75	221	2,537.50
Ralph Terry	72	77	73	222	2,130
Jesse Whittenton	75	75	72	222	2,130
Jim Cochran	74	76	72	222	2,130
George Lanning	72	75	75	222	2,130
Dick Hendrickson	76	75	71	222	2,130
Ken Still	70	76	77	223	1,737.50
Richard Rhyan	73	76	74	223	1,737.50
Miller Barber	74	73	76	223	1,737.50
Bob Brue	72	73	78	223	1,737.50
Bob Erickson	74	71	79	224	1,550

Doug Sanders Kingwood Celebrity Classic

Deerwood Club, Houston, Texas
Par 36-36—72; 6,564 yards

June 2-4
purse, $300,000

	SCORES			TOTAL	MONEY
Homero Blancas	73	65	70	208	$45,000
Walter Zembriski	70	71	69	210	24,750
Bob Charles	71	71	68	210	24,750
Gary Player	67	70	74	211	16,875
Charles Coody	72	69	70	211	16,875
Butch Baird	71	70	71	212	10,125
Bruce Crampton	72	70	70	212	10,125
Dale Douglass	72	69	71	212	10,125
Al Geiberger	68	69	75	212	10,125
Tom Shaw	70	70	73	213	7,331.25
Orville Moody	72	69	72	213	7,331.25
Bobby Nichols	70	74	69	213	7,331.25
Lou Graham	72	67	74	213	7,331.25
Gay Brewer	71	77	66	214	5,887.50
Jim Ferree	69	72	73	214	5,887.50
Charles Sifford	69	72	74	215	5,250
Arnold Palmer	72	72	71	215	5,250
Frank Beard	71	72	73	216	4,650
Bruce Devlin	68	74	74	216	4,650
George Lanning	73	74	70	217	3,950
Larry Mowry	69	75	73	217	3,950
Roberto De Vicenzo	73	73	71	217	3,950
Billy Maxwell	72	73	73	218	3,525
Jim Dent	69	78	71	218	3,525
Miller Barber	75	75	70	220	3,225
Ben Smith	77	71	72	220	3,225
Don Massengale	71	77	73	221	2,850
Lee Elder	79	73	69	221	2,850
J.C. Goosie	72	75	74	221	2,850
Richard Rhyan	72	75	75	222	2,550
Bert Yancey	74	68	81	223	2,400
Doug Sanders	74	79	71	224	2,025
Bob Brue	78	73	73	224	2,025
Ralph Terry	78	73	73	224	2,025
Bob Erickson	75	70	79	224	2,025
Jack Fleck	71	80	73	224	2,025
Charles Owens	73	76	75	224	2,025
Jimmy Powell	76	73	75	224	2,025
John Paul Cain	74	75	76	225	1,687.50
Gardner Dickinson	75	74	76	225	1,687.50

Mazda Senior Tournament Players Championship

TPC at Sawgrass, Valley Course, Ponte Vedra, Florida
Par 36-36—72; 6,646 yards

June 8-11
purse, $700,000

	SCORES				TOTAL	MONEY
Orville Moody	67	69	64	71	271	$105,000
Charles Coody	70	70	66	67	273	60,000
Gary Player	68	66	72	68	274	48,000
Arnold Palmer	67	69	75	67	278	29,600
Miller Barber	68	68	73	69	278	29,600

	SCORES				TOTAL	MONEY
Bob Charles	70	69	71	68	278	29,600
Lou Graham	67	72	67	72	278	29,600
Al Geiberger	69	71	69	69	278	29,600
Harold Henning	70	73	68	68	279	20,000
Walter Zembriski	72	71	69	69	281	16,200
Don Massengale	70	72	70	69	281	16,200
Chi Chi Rodriguez	71	71	69	70	281	16,200
Butch Baird	67	68	74	72	281	16,200
Don Bies	73	75	66	68	282	13,600
Tom Shaw	67	72	73	71	283	11,600
Gay Brewer	71	73	69	70	283	11,600
Bruce Crampton	70	74	70	69	283	11,600
Ben Smith	70	72	72	70	284	9,000
Mike Hill	69	72	73	70	284	9,000
Doug Dalziel	70	68	73	73	284	9,000
Dale Douglass	70	73	69	72	284	9,000
Homero Blancas	71	68	71	75	285	7,800
Jim Ferree	68	73	72	72	285	7,800
Gardner Dickinson	69	80	70	67	286	7,400
Dave Hill	69	72	75	71	287	6,800
Gene Littler	72	69	74	72	287	6,800
Billy Casper	71	73	70	73	287	6,800
Jim Dent	71	76	71	69	287	6,800
Bruce Devlin	73	73	70	71	287	6,800
Ralph Terry	73	71	68	76	288	6,100
Richard Rhyan	72	71	69	76	288	6,100
Deray Simon	73	72	70	74	289	5,700
Dick Hendrickson	70	70	74	75	289	5,700
Don January	73	72	73	72	290	5,200
Gordon Jones	72	69	76	73	290	5,200
Mike Fetchick	74	73	71	72	290	5,200
Charles Sifford	73	74	71	73	291	4,200
J.C. Goosie	73	73	72	73	291	4,200
Joe Lopez	75	71	73	72	291	4,200
Bob Brue	70	76	74	71	291	4,200
Al Chandler	75	69	75	72	291	4,200
Bobby Nichols	74	70	70	77	291	4,200
Bob Erickson	72	70	76	73	291	4,200

Northville Long Island Classic

Meadow Brook Club, Jericho, New York
Par 36-36—72; 6,595 yards

June 16-18
purse, $350,000

	SCORES			TOTAL	MONEY
Butch Baird	58	62	63	183	$52,500
Frank Beard	59	63	61	183	24,666.67
Orville Moody	59	63	61	183	24,666.67
Don Bies	59	62	62	183	24,666.66
(Baird defeated Beard, Moody and Bies on first extra hole.)					
Lou Graham	62	60	63	185	15,500
George Lanning	59	61	65	185	15,500
Mike Hill	61	64	61	186	11,500
Bob Charles	60	59	67	186	11,500
Terry Dill	62	63	62	187	10,000
Jim Ferree	61	65	62	188	7,840
Charles Coody	62	64	62	188	7,840
Billy Casper	65	61	62	188	7,840

	SCORES			TOTAL	MONEY
John Paul Cain	63	63	62	188	7,840
Paul Moran	59	64	65	188	7,840
Bruce Crampton	68	60	62	190	5,550
Chick Evans	63	64	63	190	5,550
Bob Erickson	63	63	64	190	5,550
Bob Boldt	61	60	69	190	5,550
J.C. Goosie	63	64	64	191	4,300
Dale Douglass	62	65	64	191	4,300
Jimmy Powell	63	62	66	191	4,300
Joe Jimenez	63	62	66	191	4,300
Gary Brewer	64	64	64	192	3,600
Charles Sifford	63	65	64	192	3,600
Dave Hill	66	63	63	192	3,600
Bob Brue	62	65	65	192	3,600
Harold Henning	66	60	66	192	3,600
Richard Rhyan	65	65	63	193	3,100
Roberto De Vicenzo	62	65	66	193	3,100
Al Chandler	64	63	66	193	3,100
Miller Barber	64	63	66	193	3,100
Gene Littler	62	63	68	193	3,100
Billy Maxwell	64	65	65	194	2,750
Don January	64	62	68	194	2,750
Tom Shaw	65	64	66	195	2,450
Don Massengale	68	62	65	195	2,450
Dick Hendrickson	64	66	65	195	2,450
Jim Dent	69	64	62	195	2,450
Charlie Huckaby	67	63	66	196	2,100
Jim O'Hern	67	64	68	196	2,100
Ben Smith	68	65	63	196	2,100

MONY Syracuse Classic

Lafayette Country Club, Syracuse, New York
Par 36-36—72; 6,540 yards

June 23-25
purse, $300,000

	SCORES			TOTAL	MONEY
Jim Dent	69	68	64	201	$45,000
Al Geiberger	73	66	63	202	26,000.00
Dick Hendrickson	66	66	71	203	21,500.00
Gene Littler	72	66	67	205	18,000.00
Phil Rodgers	70	66	71	207	11,212.50
Ray Beallo	69	70	68	207	11,212.50
Terrance Dill	70	69	68	207	11,212.50
Lou Graham	69	70	68	207	11,212.50
Jimmy Powell	74	65	69	208	7,506.25
Mike Hill	68	72	68	208	7,506.25
Harold Henning	68	68	72	208	7,506.25
Dave Hill	72	70	66	208	7,506.25
Richard Rhyan	71	68	70	209	5,833.34
Walter Zembriski	70	68	71	209	5,833.33
Frank Beard	72	67	70	209	5,833.33
Dan Morgan	73	67	70	210	5,050.00
Mike Fetchick	72	69	69	210	5,050.00
Deray Simon	69	73	69	211	3,885.72
Rafe Botts	72	71	68	211	3,885.72
Bob Erickson	73	70	68	211	3,885.72

	SCORES			TOTAL	MONEY
Tom Shaw	70	71	70	211	3,885.71
Bill Johnston	70	70	71	211	3,885.71
Bob Brue	71	69	71	211	3,885.71
John Paul Cain	71	70	70	211	3,885.71
Robert Boldt	72	70	70	212	3,050.00
Doug Ford	72	73	67	212	3,050.00
Roger Ginsberg	69	72	71	212	3,050.00
Homero Blancas	72	68	73	213	2,543.75
Jim King	71	71	71	213	2,543.75
Bruce Crampton	73	71	69	213	2,543.75
J.C. Goosie	70	68	75	213	2,543.75
Peter Thomson	70	71	73	214	2,030.00
Casmere Jawor	70	74	70	214	2,030.00
Chick Evans	73	75	66	214	2,030.00
Charles Mehok	73	69	72	214	2,030.00
Jim O'Hern	76	70	68	214	2,030.00
Gordon Jones	72	71	72	215	1,550.00
George Lanning	71	73	71	215	1,550.00
Al Chandler	72	71	72	215	1,550.00
Bobby Nichols	72	74	69	215	1,550.00
Joe Jimenez	72	72	71	215	1,550.00
Fred Hawkins	74	69	72	215	1,550.00
Roland Stafford	68	74	73	215	1,550.00

USGA Senior Open

Laurel Valley Golf Club, Ligonier, Pennsylvania
Par 36-36—72; 6,691 yards

June 30-July 2
purse, $450,000

	SCORES				TOTAL	MONEY
Orville Moody	72	73	64	70	279	$80,000
Frank Beard	70	69	70	72	281	40,000
Dale Douglass	71	70	76	67	284	22,267
Jim Dent	71	73	70	70	284	22,267
Bobby Nichols	70	70	74	71	285	13,812
Charles Coody	72	72	71	70	285	13,812
Al Geiberger	68	72	76	70	286	10,955
Harold Henning	69	74	71	72	286	10,955
Gary Player	72	73	73	69	287	8,594
Jimmy Powell	74	71	73	69	287	8,594
Bob Charles	73	74	73	67	287	8,594
Bruce Crampton	72	72	69	74	287	8,594
Larry Mowry	71	73	73	71	288	7,391
Mike Hill	72	72	73	72	289	7,046
Butch Baird	73	72	69	76	290	6,553
Don Bies	74	66	77	73	290	6,553
Terrance Dill	70	76	72	74	292	6,101
Chi Chi Rodriguez	75	72	75	72	294	5,714.50
Dave Hill	70	72	73	79	294	5,714.50
Lou Graham	77	74	75	69	295	5,373
Peter Thomson	74	74	76	72	296	5,028
Ben Smith	74	74	77	71	296	5,028
Rives McBee	73	71	78	74	296	5,028
Al Kelley	77	74	72	74	297	4,692
Don Massengale	74	74	74	77	299	4,425.67
Al Chandler	76	76	74	73	299	4,425.67
Doug Dalziel	73	73	72	81	299	4,425.66

	SCORES				TOTAL	MONEY
Dick Hendrickson	72	74	82	72	300	4,103
Agim Bardha	80	72	73	75	300	4,103
*Jim McMurtrey	73	77	77	73	300	
Robert Rawlins	76	68	78	79	301	3,865.50
Richard Rhyan	75	79	76	71	301	3,865.50
Mike Joyce	78	75	72	77	302	3,692.50
Jim Cochran	73	74	77	78	302	3,692.50
Jim O'Hern	76	76	76	75	303	3,519
Bob Brue	76	75	82	70	303	3,519
Jack Fleck	77	73	79	75	304	3,347
Miller Barber	75	79	74	76	304	3,347
Carl Lohren	76	80	76	73	305	3,174.50
Quinton Gray	76	80	78	71	305	3,174.50
*Charles Ebner	77	76	79	73	305	
*Frank Boydston	69	76	78	82	305	
*Ron Eulenfeld	74	77	79	75	305	

Digital Classic

Nashawtuc Country Club, Concord, Massachusetts
Par 36-36—72; 6,449 yards

July 7-9
purse, $300,000

	SCORES			TOTAL	MONEY
Bob Charles	65	70	65	200	$45,000
Mike Hill	65	69	69	203	26,000
Bruce Crampton	66	67	71	204	19,750
Dale Douglass	64	69	71	204	19,750
Miller Barber	66	72	67	205	12,800
Jim Ferree	69	71	65	205	12,800
Terrance Dill	71	68	67	206	10,000
Walter Zembriski	66	72	69	207	9,250
Larry Mowry	69	69	70	208	7,245
Orville Moody	72	69	67	208	7,245
Dan Morgan	71	71	66	208	7,245
Frank Beard	68	69	71	208	7,245
Homero Blancas	72	68	68	208	7,245
Bobby Nichols	69	74	66	209	5,500
Harold Henning	70	69	70	209	5,500
Mike Fetchick	68	70	71	209	5,500
Tom Shaw	72	70	68	210	4,208.34
Dick Hendrickson	73	70	67	210	4,208.34
Peter Thomson	69	71	70	210	4,208.33
Gary Player	71	69	70	210	4,208.33
Don Bies	67	70	73	210	4,208.33
Lee Elder	69	72	69	210	4,208.33
Jimmy Powell	69	75	67	211	3,200
Charles Owens	69	69	73	211	3,200
Ben Smith	70	69	72	211	3,200
Doug Dalziel	72	72	67	211	3,200
Chick Evans	70	73	68	211	3,200
Bert Yancey	74	69	69	212	2,480
Richard Rhyan	72	68	72	212	2,480
Babe Hiskey	70	72	70	212	2,480
Bob Brue	74	72	66	212	2,480
Charles Coody	72	70	70	212	2,480
Chi Chi Rodriguez	69	72	72	213	2,025
Gordon Jones	74	70	69	213	2,025

	SCORES			TOTAL	MONEY
George Lanning	71	68	74	213	2,025
Ralph Terry	73	71	70	214	1,662.50
Charles Sifford	70	72	72	214	1,662.50
Butch Baird	74	71	69	214	1,662.50
Don Massengale	71	73	70	214	1,662.50
Jim O'Hern	72	72	70	214	1,662.50
Joe Jimenez	68	69	77	214	1,662.50

Greater Grand Rapids Open

Elks Country Club, Grand Rapids, Michigan
Par 36-35—71; 6,543 yards

July 14-16
purse, $300,000

	SCORES			TOTAL	MONEY
John Paul Cain	69	68	66	203	$45,000
Charles Sifford	70	69	65	204	23,750
Dave Hill	65	71	68	204	23,750
Walter Zembriski	68	66	71	205	16,250
Al Geiberger	69	70	66	205	16,250
Orville Moody	64	70	72	206	10,550
Frank Beard	69	67	70	206	10,550
Mike Hill	69	70	68	207	7,325
Jimmy Powell	72	67	68	207	7,325
Gene Littler	71	69	67	207	7,325
Peter Thomson	71	70	66	207	7,325
Bob Brue	70	68	69	207	7,325
Bruce Crampton	70	67	70	207	7,325
Dale Douglass	66	69	72	207	7,325
Butch Baird	71	67	70	208	5,200
Harold Henning	67	73	68	208	5,200
Joe Jimenez	69	70	69	208	5,200
Ralph Terry	69	71	69	209	4,175
Bobby Nichols	67	69	73	209	4,175
Ben Smith	72	66	71	209	4,175
Jim Dent	71	68	70	209	4,175
Don Massengale	73	69	68	210	3,350
Doug Sanders	70	70	70	210	3,350
Deray Simon	71	67	72	210	3,350
Homero Blancas	70	69	71	210	3,350
Bruce Devlin	68	69	73	210	3,350
Agim Bardha	67	74	70	211	2,825
George Lanning	72	70	69	211	2,825
Quinton Gray	73	66	73	212	2,537.50
Jim King	71	68	73	212	2,537.50
Al Chandler	70	76	67	213	2,233.34
Dan Morgan	70	71	72	213	2,233.33
Gordon Jones	72	72	69	213	2,233.33
Bert Yancey	72	72	70	214	1,627.28
Paul Moran	76	69	69	214	1,627.28
Charles Mehok	71	73	70	214	1,627.28
Miller Barber	69	73	72	214	1,627.27
Jim O'Hern	74	68	72	214	1,627.27
Charles Owens	72	70	72	214	1,627.27
Rafe Botts	70	73	71	214	1,627.27
Gay Brewer	72	71	71	214	1,627.27
Terrance Dill	67	72	75	214	1,627.27
Phil Rodgers	70	68	76	214	1,627.27
Fred Haas	72	69	73	214	1,627.27

Ameritech Open

Canterbury Golf Club, Cleveland, Ohio
Par 36-36—72; 6,615 yards

July 21-23
purse, $500,000

	SCORES			TOTAL	MONEY
Bruce Crampton	70	67	68	205	$75,000
Orville Moody	71	68	67	206	40,500
Jim Ferree	70	72	64	206	40,500
Mike Hill	69	70	68	207	31,000
Larry Mowry	68	71	69	208	21,000
Charles Coody	67	71	70	208	21,000
Harold Henning	67	68	73	208	21,000
Bob Charles	70	69	70	209	14,850
Dale Douglass	73	68	68	209	14,850
Jimmy Powell	68	68	74	210	12,000
Tom Shaw	73	67	70	210	12,000
Dave Hill	70	69	71	210	12,000
Lee Elder	71	73	69	213	9,750
Chick Evans	66	74	73	213	9,750
Walter Zembriski	71	72	71	214	7,850
Jim Dent	70	72	72	214	7,850
Bruce Devlin	72	71	71	214	7,850
Dick Hendrickson	76	69	69	214	7,850
Al Geiberger	75	70	69	214	7,850
J.C. Goosie	71	69	74	214	7,850
Frank Beard	72	72	71	215	5,564.29
Al Kelley	74	75	66	215	5,564.29
Joe Jimenez	72	73	70	215	5,564.29
Lou Graham	72	71	72	215	5,564.29
Charles Sifford	69	72	74	215	5,564.28
Homero Blancas	72	67	76	215	5,564.28
Bob Erickson	69	72	74	215	5,564.28
Ralph Terry	71	74	71	216	4,300
Charles Owens	76	71	69	216	4,300
Gay Brewer	73	71	72	216	4,300
Bob Brue	78	72	66	216	4,300
Chi Chi Rodriguez	72	74	71	217	3,242.86
Don Massengale	75	72	70	217	3,242.86
Bobby Nichols	68	76	73	217	3,242.86
Bill Collins	75	70	72	217	3,242.86
Don January	74	74	69	217	3,242.86
Butch Baird	74	69	74	217	3,242.85
Don Bies	71	73	73	217	3,242.85
Bert Yancey	73	73	72	218	2,450
Miller Barber	72	76	70	218	2,450
Richard Rhyan	66	75	77	218	2,450
Phil Rodgers	74	74	70	218	2,450
Gordon Jones	71	75	72	218	2,450
Jim King	75	69	74	218	2,450

Newport Cup

Newport Country Club, Newport, Rhode Island
Par 36-36—72; 6,566 yards

July 28-30
purse, $275,000

	SCORES			TOTAL	MONEY
Jim Dent	67	73	66	206	$41,500
Harold Henning	70	65	72	207	25,000
Tom Shaw	71	67	70	208	20,500
Gay Brewer	72	70	68	210	15,750
Chick Evans	70	68	72	210	15,750
Charles Coody	73	68	70	211	10,600
Al Kelley	68	71	72	211	10,600
Miller Barber	70	70	72	212	7,041.67
Jimmy Powell	73	71	68	212	7,041.67
John Paul Cain	71	73	68	212	7,041.67
Larry Mowry	75	68	69	212	7,041.67
Jim Ferree	69	70	73	212	7,041.66
Dick Hendrickson	69	68	75	212	7,041.66
Jim Cochran	69	72	72	213	5,375
Paul Moran	69	73	71	213	5,375
Chi Chi Rodriguez	72	70	72	214	4,900
Bob Goalby	72	69	73	214	4,900
Jerry Barber	72	70	73	215	4,400
Al Chandler	73	75	67	215	4,400
Terrance Dill	69	72	74	215	4,400
Lou Graham	73	69	74	216	3,900
George Lanning	73	71	72	216	3,900
Lee Elder	72	70	75	217	3,600
Bill Collins	79	71	68	218	3,300
Quinton Gray	70	71	77	218	3,300
Jim O'Hern	73	72	74	219	2,800
Deray Simon	75	71	73	219	2,800
Phil Rodgers	73	74	72	219	2,800
Walter Zembriski	73	72	75	220	2,200
Dan Morgan	69	75	76	220	2,200
Gordon Jones	67	77	76	220	2,200
Tommy Aaron	75	74	72	221	1,800
Charles Sifford	73	75	73	221	1,800
Bob Erickson	75	73	73	221	1,800
Gardner Dickinson	74	80	68	222	1,525
Bill Johnston	77	73	72	222	1,525
Charles Owens	72	79	71	222	1,525
Jim King	71	73	78	222	1,525
Richard Rhyan	78	70	75	223	1,300
Bob Brue	75	76	72	223	1,300
Billy Maxwell	71	75	77	223	1,300
Mike Fetchick	76	73	74	223	1,300
Doug Ford	72	72	79	223	1,300

Volvo Seniors British Open

Turnberry Hotel, Ailsa Course, Turnberry, Scotland
Par 35-35—70; 6,480 yards

July 27-30
purse, £150,000

	SCORES				TOTAL	MONEY
Bob Charles	70	68	65	66	269	£25,000
Billy Casper	67	69	65	75	276	16,400
Babe Hiskey	71	71	65	72	279	9,150
Gary Player	74	68	69	71	282	6,750
David Butler	72	74	67	69	282	6,750
Neil Coles	70	74	70	69	283	5,100
Christy O'Connor	76	70	70	68	284	4,340
Arnold Palmer	74	72	70	70	286	3,610
Anthony Grubb	73	72	70	73	288	3,235
Bert Yancey	75	68	71	75	289	2,716.67
Larry Mancour	72	68	73	76	289	2,716.67
Doug Dalziel	72	76	71	70	289	2,716.67
Ross Whitehead	73	73	68	76	290	2,430
Jack O'Keefe	76	74	71	70	291	2,200
Art Silvestrone	73	74	73	71	291	2,200
Agim Bardha	70	77	69	75	291	2,200
Austin Skerritt	76	70	74	72	292	1,870
George Will	72	72	70	78	292	1,870
Kyle Burton	75	78	73	66	292	1,870
Mohamed Moussa	73	73	71	75	292	1,870
Hugh Boyle	77	74	69	73	293	1,640
Frank Rennie	73	72	76	72	293	1,640
Paul Kelly	73	75	74	71	293	1,640
Michael Plumbridge	74	72	72	75	293	1,640
Al Balding	77	71	76	70	294	1,540
Doug Sanders	78	72	72	73	295	1,480
Alec Bickerdike	72	74	73	76	295	1,480
Lou Garrison	75	76	70	75	296	1,340
Al Johnston	74	77	73	72	296	1,340
Roger Fidler	74	76	69	77	296	1,340
Ernie Jones	73	71	73	79	296	1,340
Douglas Beattie	79	72	72	73	296	1,340
David Snell	76	70	74	77	297	1,200
Jimmy Kinsella	76	77	68	76	297	1,200
Charles Mehok	72	73	74	79	298	1,080
John Taylor	74	73	75	76	298	1,080
Dean Refram	73	76	75	74	298	1,080
Hedley Muscroft	77	74	73	74	298	1,080
Terence Westbrook	78	75	77	69	299	960
Frederick Boobyer	77	70	74	78	299	960
*Charles Green	80	71	75	73	299	
*Gordon Clark	76	74	74	75	299	

Showdown Classic

Jeremy Ranch Golf Club, Park City, Utah
Par 36-36—72; 7,103 yards

August 4-6
purse, $350,000

	SCORES			TOTAL	MONEY
Tom Shaw	69	68	70	207	$52,500
Larry Mowry	73	66	69	208	30,000
Homero Blancas	69	72	69	210	22,000

	SCORES			TOTAL	MONEY
Lou Graham	68	72	70	210	22,000
Gene Littler	67	75	69	211	17,000
Jimmy Powell	71	73	68	212	11,750
Don Bies	74	65	73	212	11,750
Billy Casper	69	73	70	212	11,750
Dale Douglass	68	71	73	212	11,750
Walter Zembriski	71	70	72	213	8,100
Ralph Terry	72	71	70	213	8,100
Bobby Nichols	69	74	70	213	8,100
Chick Evans	71	71	71	213	8,100
Don Massengale	75	69	70	214	6,550
Bruce Devlin	70	71	73	214	6,550
Orville Moody	69	73	73	215	5,550
Miller Barber	74	70	71	215	5,550
Deray Simon	73	69	74	216	4,600
George Lanning	77	72	67	216	4,600
Al Kelley	69	73	74	216	4,600
Jesse Whittenton	77	71	69	217	3,925
Phil Rodgers	75	72	70	217	3,925
Rives McBee	74	69	74	217	3,925
Bill Johnston	74	70	73	217	3,925
Paul Moran	74	72	72	218	3,400
Richard Rhyan	75	71	72	218	3,400
Gordon Waldespuhl	72	76	70	218	3,400
Joe Jimenez	72	75	71	218	3,400
Quinton Gray	71	76	71	218	3,400
Bob Toski	72	77	70	219	2,950
Charles Sifford	74	73	72	219	2,950
Robert Rawlins	75	73	71	219	2,950
Tommy Aaron	72	74	73	219	2,950
Bob Rosburg	77	69	74	220	2,600
Ben Smith	74	70	76	220	2,600
Bob Brue	73	72	75	220	2,600
Ken Still	72	74	75	221	2,150
Butch Baird	76	72	73	221	2,150
Harold Henning	74	76	71	221	2,150
Jim Cochran	73	74	74	221	2,150
Bob Erickson	77	71	73	221	2,150
J.C. Goosie	73	73	75	221	2,150

Rancho Murieta Gold Rush

Rancho Murieta Country Club, Rancho Murieta, California
Par 36-36—72; 6,674 yards

August 11-13
purse, $350,000

	SCORES			TOTAL	MONEY
Dave Hill	69	70	68	207	$52,500
Orville Moody	72	68	68	208	30,000
Don Bies	75	69	65	209	24,000
Ken Still	68	71	72	211	15,750
Phil Rodgers	69	73	69	211	15,750
Quinton Gray	71	68	72	211	15,750
Al Geiberger	70	73	68	211	15,750
Gene Littler	72	75	67	214	9,575
Bruce Crampton	71	72	71	214	9,575
Dale Douglass	73	69	72	214	9,575
Chick Evans	73	67	74	214	9,575

	SCORES			TOTAL	MONEY
Tom Shaw	72	70	73	215	6,800
Walter Zembriski	72	70	73	215	6,800
John Paul Cain	67	72	76	215	6,800
Bob Charles	73	73	69	215	6,800
Lou Graham	72	71	72	215	6,800
Larry Mowry	74	70	72	216	5,050
Chi Chi Rodriguez	71	70	75	216	5,050
Richard Rhyan	73	73	71	217	4,116.67
Bruce Devlin	71	74	72	217	4,116.67
Lee Elder	73	74	70	217	4,116.67
Bob Erickson	70	77	70	217	4,116.67
John Brodie	73	71	73	217	4,116.66
Bill Collins	71	73	73	217	4,116.66
Gay Brewer	75	74	69	218	3,450
Charles Coody	74	72	72	218	3,450
Joe Jimenez	75	75	68	218	3,450
Dick Hendrickson	75	72	71	218	3,450
Charles Sifford	73	75	71	219	3,000
Jimmy Powell	75	71	73	219	3,000
Bobby Nichols	74	69	76	219	3,000
Butch Baird	72	74	73	219	3,000
George Lanning	73	73	73	219	3,000
Bert Yancey	69	74	77	220	2,550
Bob Brue	71	74	75	220	2,550
Al Chandler	75	75	70	220	2,550
Gordon Jones	77	74	69	220	2,550
Frank Beard	74	72	75	221	2,200
Don Massengale	76	70	75	221	2,200
Mike Hill	76	74	71	221	2,200

GTE Northwest Classic

Inglewood Country Club, Kenmore, Washington
Par 36-36—72; 6,501 yards

August 18-20
purse, $350,000

	SCORES			TOTAL	MONEY
Al Geiberger	68	68	68	204	$52,500
Frank Beard	69	70	68	207	30,000
Orville Moody	70	72	66	208	24,000
Miller Barber	65	74	70	209	15,750
Harold Henning	70	70	69	209	15,750
Mike Hill	72	66	71	209	15,750
Bruce Crampton	69	71	69	209	15,750
Dave Hill	68	70	72	210	11,000
Phil Rodgers	76	68	68	212	8,775
Butch Baird	73	68	71	212	8,775
Don Bies	71	69	72	212	8,775
Homero Blancas	74	69	69	212	8,775
Larry Mowry	71	70	72	213	6,550
Don Massengale	68	75	70	213	6,550
Bob Charles	72	68	73	213	6,550
Dick Hendrickson	71	70	72	213	6,550
Larry Ziegler	73	73	68	214	4,900
Jim Dent	71	72	71	214	4,900
Dale Douglass	69	74	71	214	4,900
Arnold Palmer	70	74	71	215	4,300
Charles Coody	75	70	70	215	4,300

	SCORES			TOTAL	MONEY
Bob Erickson	73	66	77	216	4,000
Richard Rhyan	74	70	73	217	3,500
Tom Shaw	73	70	74	217	3,500
Joe Jimenez	74	69	74	217	3,500
Robert Boldt	77	71	69	217	3,500
Roberto De Vicenzo	73	73	71	217	3,500
Lee Elder	71	74	72	217	3,500
Chick Evans	73	73	71	217	3,500
Chi Chi Rodriguez	72	72	74	218	3,000
John Paul Cain	75	68	75	218	3,000
Quinton Gray	71	74	73	218	3,000
Ken Still	75	68	76	219	2,450
Al Kelley	71	74	74	219	2,450
Gay Brewer	73	74	72	219	2,450
Bob Brue	73	76	70	219	2,450
Jim O'Hern	72	75	72	219	2,450
Bill Collins	75	73	71	219	2,450
Doug Dalziel	71	76	72	219	2,450
Bruce Devlin	77	71	71	219	2,450

Sunwest Bank/Charley Pride Classic

Four Hills Country Club, Albuquerque, New Mexico
Par 36-36—72; 6,722 yards

August 25-27
purse, $300,000

	SCORES			TOTAL	MONEY
Bob Charles	66	69	68	203	$45,000
Charles Coody	66	70	68	204	26,000
Mike Hill	69	72	65	206	21,500
Gene Littler	73	69	65	207	16,250
Al Geiberger	70	69	68	207	16,250
Jim Dent	67	69	72	208	11,100
Bobby Nichols	67	71	71	209	9,625
Dick Hendrickson	71	71	67	209	9,625
Frank Beard	71	72	68	211	8,525
Butch Baird	72	70	70	212	6,314.29
Miller Barber	68	74	70	212	6,314.29
John Paul Cain	71	71	70	212	6,314.29
Lou Graham	72	70	70	212	6,314.29
Larry Ziegler	75	67	70	212	6,314.28
Doug Dalziel	71	69	72	212	6,314.28
Al Kelley	72	69	71	212	6,314.28
Don Massengale	72	71	70	213	4,320
Bob Toski	69	70	74	213	4,320
Homero Blancas	68	72	73	213	4,320
Bob Brue	70	69	74	213	4,320
Harold Henning	71	74	68	213	4,320
Deray Simon	72	70	72	214	3,575
Don Bies	76	70	68	214	3,575
Ben Smith	73	71	71	215	3,275
Jimmy Powell	69	72	74	215	3,275
Tom Shaw	68	76	72	216	2,687.50
Ray Beallo	72	76	68	216	2,687.50
Robert Boldt	73	72	71	216	2,687.50
Chick Evans	70	76	70	216	2,687.50
Gordon Jones	72	74	70	216	2,687.50
Orville Moody	71	69	76	216	2,687.50

	SCORES			TOTAL	MONEY
Ken Still	71	74	72	217	2,125
Quinton Gray	73	73	71	217	2,125
Jim Cochran	72	70	75	217	2,125
Bob Goalby	70	75	73	218	1,925
Terrance Dill	75	73	71	219	1,775
Mike Fetchick	74	73	72	219	1,775
J.C. Goosie	71	75	73	219	1,775
Jesse Whittenton	71	72	77	220	1,550
Bill Johnston	75	72	73	220	1,550
Bob Erickson	71	76	73	220	1,550

RJR Bank One Classic

Griffin Gate Golf Club, Lexington, Kentucky
Par 35-35—70; 6,595 yards

September 1-3
purse, $300,000

	SCORES			TOTAL	MONEY
Rives McBee	68	65	69	202	$45,000
Harold Henning	68	66	70	204	26,000
Larry Ziegler	68	70	67	205	21,500
Orville Moody	67	71	68	206	18,000
Mike Hill	69	69	69	207	11,866.67
Bob Charles	71	67	69	207	11,866.67
Jim O'Hern	66	71	70	207	11,866.66
Dave Hill	74	65	69	208	8,168.75
Ben Smith	67	71	70	208	8,168.75
Jimmy Powell	69	72	67	208	8,168.75
Gene Littler	72	69	67	208	8,168.75
George Lanning	71	69	69	209	5,860
Ralph Terry	69	71	69	209	5,860
Gordon Waldespuhl	69	71	69	209	5,860
Walter Zembriski	66	70	73	209	5,860
Dale Douglass	73	68	68	209	5,860
Miller Barber	69	71	70	210	4,450
Billy Casper	69	72	69	210	4,450
Bruce Crampton	70	69	71	210	4,450
Lou Graham	67	71	72	210	4,450
Tom Shaw	70	72	69	211	3,350
Deray Simon	72	70	69	211	3,350
Frank Beard	70	70	71	211	3,350
Robert Boldt	68	75	68	211	3,350
Bob Erickson	69	69	73	211	3,350
Joe Jimenez	74	67	70	211	3,350
Quinton Gray	74	66	71	211	3,350
Bobby Nichols	72	71	69	212	2,480
Gay Brewer	75	68	69	212	2,480
Jim King	73	71	68	212	2,480
Henry Brown	74	69	69	212	2,480
Al Kelley	70	71	71	212	2,480
Tommy Aaron	71	70	72	213	2,125
Mike Fetchick	69	70	75	214	1,975
J.C. Goosie	71	71	72	214	1,975
Richard Rhyan	70	74	71	215	1,700
Bill Collins	74	70	71	215	1,700
Lee Elder	73	69	73	215	1,700
Chick Evans	73	72	70	215	1,700
Fred Haas	72	73	70	215	1,700

GTE North Classic

Broadmoor Country Club, Indianapolis, Indiana
Par 35-37—72; 6,670 yards
(Saturday round rained out.)

September 7-10
purse, $350,000

	SCORES		TOTAL	MONEY
Gary Player	67	68	135	$52,500
Joe Jimenez	68	68	136	24,666.67
Al Geiberger	68	68	136	24,666.67
Billy Casper	67	69	136	24,666.66
Mike Hill	67	70	137	14,333.34
Jim Dent	67	70	137	14,333.33
Dale Douglass	67	70	137	14,333.33
Gay Brewer	69	69	138	10,500
Bruce Crampton	69	69	138	10,500
Jimmy Powell	70	69	139	7,840
Larry Mowry	68	71	139	7,840
Walter Zembriski	67	72	139	7,840
Bob Charles	68	71	139	7,840
Dave Hill	68	71	139	7,840
Gene Littler	67	73	140	6,050
Bob Erickson	71	69	140	6,050
Tommy Aaron	68	73	141	4,350
Butch Baird	72	69	141	4,350
Miller Barber	69	72	141	4,350
Frank Beard	70	71	141	4,350
Don Bies	72	69	141	4,350
Bob Brue	70	71	141	4,350
Charles Coody	70	71	141	4,350
Terrance Dill	69	72	141	4,350
Arnold Palmer	71	71	142	3,550
Quinton Gray	71	71	142	3,550
Al Chandler	74	69	143	3,400
Ken Still	72	72	144	3,100
Jim King	70	74	144	3,100
Jim O'Hern	72	72	144	3,100
Rafe Botts	69	75	144	3,100
Orville Moody	72	72	144	3,100
Doug Sanders	72	73	145	2,500
Ben Smith	71	74	145	2,500
Chi Chi Rodriguez	75	70	145	2,500
Charles Sifford	71	74	145	2,500
Harold Henning	71	74	145	2,500
John Brodie	72	73	145	2,500
J.C. Goosie	73	72	145	2,500
Larry Ziegler	73	73	146	1,950
Rives McBee	72	74	146	1,950
Bruce Devlin	70	76	146	1,950
Dick Hendrickson	73	73	146	1,950

Crestar Classic

Hermitage Country Club, Manakin-Sabot, Virginia
Par 36-36—72; 6,644 yards

September 15-17
purse, $350,000

	SCORES			TOTAL	MONEY
Chi Chi Rodriguez	66	69	68	203	$52,500
Richard Rhyan	66	68	70	204	27,000
Jim Dent	65	70	69	204	27,000
Bob Charles	66	69	70	205	15,750
Jim Ferree	67	66	72	205	15,750
Harold Henning	69	67	69	205	15,750
Mike Hill	72	67	66	205	15,750
Arnold Palmer	70	67	69	206	11,000
Rives McBee	72	67	69	208	8,480
Butch Baird	69	67	72	208	8,480
John Paul Cain	72	68	68	208	8,480
Bruce Crampton	71	70	67	208	8,480
Al Geiberger	68	68	72	208	8,480
Homero Blancas	69	68	72	209	6,800
Tom Shaw	72	65	73	210	5,550
Larry Ziegler	70	72	68	210	5,550
Walter Zembriski	69	69	72	210	5,550
Ralph Terry	70	72	68	210	5,550
Don Massengale	74	68	69	211	4,300
Phil Rodgers	70	71	70	211	4,300
Larry Mowry	70	67	74	211	4,300
Dale Douglass	71	70	70	211	4,300
Orville Moody	74	67	71	212	3,600
Bobby Nichols	73	70	69	212	3,600
Ray Beallo	71	72	69	212	3,600
Joe Jimenez	72	69	71	212	3,600
Bruce Devlin	75	67	70	212	3,600
Dan Morgan	70	71	72	213	3,100
Robert Boldt	73	70	70	213	3,100
George Lanning	70	71	72	213	3,100
Charles Coody	72	69	72	213	3,100
Doug Dalziel	72	71	70	213	3,100
Gary Player	72	71	71	214	2,650
Mike Fetchick	73	69	72	214	2,650
J.C. Goosie	71	69	74	214	2,650
Lou Graham	70	73	71	214	2,650
Bert Yancey	73	71	71	215	2,200
Jimmy Powell	73	72	70	215	2,200
Rafe Botts	73	69	73	215	2,200
Al Chandler	72	75	68	215	2,200
Paul Moran	72	73	70	215	2,200

PaineWebber Invitational

Quail Hollow Country Club, Charlotte, North Carolina
Par 36-36—72; 6,826 yards

September 22-24
purse, $325,000

Tournament cancelled because of Hurricane Hugo damage early on September 22nd.

Fairfield Barnett Space Coast Classic

Suntree Country Club, Melbourne, Florida
Par 36-36—72; 6,590 yards

September 29-October 1
purse, $300,000

	SCORES			TOTAL	MONEY
Bob Charles	66	70	67	203	$45,000
Butch Baird	67	70	72	209	26,000
Larry Mowry	68	72	70	210	19,750
Harold Henning	69	73	68	210	19,750
Gary Player	70	72	69	211	14,500
Jim O'Hern	70	71	71	212	10,550
Al Geiberger	72	67	73	212	10,550
Bruce Devlin	68	74	71	213	9,250
Rives McBee	76	71	67	214	7,004.17
Phil Rodgers	70	75	69	214	7,004.17
Homero Blancas	71	73	70	214	7,004.17
J.C. Goosie	74	71	69	214	7,004.17
George Lanning	71	72	71	214	7,004.16
Jim Dent	68	70	76	214	7,004.16
Walter Zembriski	71	72	72	215	5,350
Larry Ziegler	71	72	72	215	5,350
Dave Hill	71	73	72	216	4,600
Bob Brue	72	70	74	216	4,600
Charles Coody	73	72	71	216	4,600
Jimmy Powell	71	72	74	217	3,660
Charles Mehok	70	76	71	217	3,660
Ken Still	72	72	73	217	3,660
Frank Beard	70	74	73	217	3,660
Billy Casper	74	71	72	217	3,660
Miller Barber	73	71	74	218	3,050
John Paul Cain	69	78	71	218	3,050
Quinton Gray	70	75	73	218	3,050
Charles Sifford	74	72	73	219	2,543.75
Dan Morgan	72	71	76	219	2,543.75
Dick Hendrickson	75	71	73	219	2,543.75
Mike Hill	70	71	78	219	2,543.75
Bobby Nichols	73	74	73	220	2,075
Alexander Sutton	73	77	70	220	2,075
Ralph Terry	73	73	74	220	2,075
Lou Graham	73	74	73	220	2,075
Tom Shaw	76	72	73	221	1,662.50
Gay Brewer	75	74	72	221	1,662.50
Doug Dalziel	75	71	75	221	1,662.50
Roberto De Vicenzo	72	76	73	221	1,662.50
Bob Erickson	74	74	73	221	1,662.50
Bob Goalby	69	80	72	221	1,662.50

RJR Championship

Tanglewood Park, Championship Course,
Clemmons, North Carolina
Par 35-35—70; 6,606 yards

October 6-8
purse, $1,350,000

	SCORES			TOTAL	MONEY
Gary Player	65	71	71	207	$202,500
Rives McBee	68	67	73	208	145,000
Dave Hill	70	70	70	210	107,000

	SCORES			TOTAL	MONEY
Mike Hill	73	72	66	211	78,333.34
Bob Charles	73	69	69	211	78,333.33
Orville Moody	71	71	69	211	78,333.33
Quinton Gray	67	76	69	212	55,000
Al Geiberger	73	73	67	213	47,500
Tom Shaw	70	73	70	213	47,500
Bruce Crampton	74	68	72	214	37,500
Larry Ziegler	72	69	73	214	37,500
Bob Brue	72	74	69	215	24,833.34
Robert Boldt	71	74	70	215	24,833.33
Jim Dent	75	69	71	215	24,833.33
Charles Coody	71	70	75	216	17,250
Don January	69	76	71	216	17,250
Jimmy Powell	72	73	71	216	17,250
Ben Smith	68	75	73	216	17,250
Doug Dalziel	70	69	78	217	12,750
Roberto De Vicenzo	69	78	70	217	12,750
Lou Graham	72	72	73	217	12,750
Paul Moran	67	77	73	217	12,750
Ken Still	75	71	71	217	12,750
Homero Blancas	69	73	76	218	9,725
Harold Henning	76	68	74	218	9,725
Don Massengale	73	72	73	218	9,725
Walter Zembriski	72	73	73	218	9,725
Gay Brewer	77	70	72	219	8,550
John Paul Cain	70	76	73	219	8,550
Terrance Dill	74	73	72	219	8,550
Dale Douglass	75	70	74	219	8,550
Lee Elder	71	74	74	219	8,550
Dan Morgan	74	72	73	219	8,550
Chi Chi Rodriguez	70	78	71	219	8,550
George Lanning	72	73	75	220	7,650
Deray Simon	73	74	73	220	7,650
Miller Barber	70	73	78	221	7,150
Bob Erickson	76	75	70	221	7,150
Larry Mowry	75	73	73	221	7,150
Frank Beard	76	75	71	222	6,150
Bruce Devlin	70	74	78	222	6,150
Jim Ferree	78	71	73	222	6,150
Dick Hendrickson	70	76	76	222	6,150
Joe Jimenez	74	73	75	222	6,150
Jim King	74	71	77	222	6,150
Bobby Nichols	71	76	75	222	6,150

Gatlin Brothers Southwest Classic

Fairway Oaks Golf and Racquet Club, Abilene, Texas
Par 36-36—72; 6,700 yards

October 13-15
purse, $300,000

	SCORES			TOTAL	MONEY
George Archer	69	72	68	209	$45,000
Orville Moody	70	70	69	209	23,750
Jimmy Powell	72	71	66	209	23,750
(Archer defeated Moody and Powell on second extra hole.)					
John Paul Cain	70	70	70	210	12,570
Bruce Crampton	71	68	71	210	12,570
Jim Dent	72	68	70	210	12,570

	SCORES			TOTAL	MONEY
Mike Hill	69	67	74	210	12,570
Gary Player	68	72	70	210	12,570
Larry Ziegler	74	66	71	211	8,525
Butch Baird	68	71	73	212	7,450
Charles Coody	74	68	70	212	7,450
Tommy Aaron	73	71	69	213	6,200
Chi Chi Rodriguez	71	71	71	213	6,200
Walter Zembriski	71	69	73	213	6,200
Terrance Dill	72	71	71	214	5,200
Dale Douglass	74	70	70	214	5,200
Rives McBee	75	68	71	214	5,200
Gay Brewer	74	67	74	215	4,070
Al Kelley	70	71	74	215	4,070
Don Massengale	72	68	75	215	4,070
Bobby Nichols	71	72	72	215	4,070
Tom Shaw	76	65	74	215	4,070
Paul Moran	74	67	75	216	3,425
Dewitt Weaver	73	70	73	216	3,425
Bob Brue	72	71	74	217	3,125
Jim Ferree	74	71	72	217	3,125
Doug Dalziel	76	71	71	218	2,750
Charles Mehok	72	72	74	218	2,750
Bert Yancey	75	70	73	218	2,750
Lou Garrison	74	71	74	219	2,412.50
Harold Henning	74	71	74	219	2,412.50
Miller Barber	71	76	73	220	2,075
Homero Blancas	76	72	72	220	2,075
Bruce Devlin	73	71	76	220	2,075
Richard Rhyan	73	75	72	220	2,075
Charles Sifford	72	74	75	221	1,850
John Brodie	72	68	82	222	1,625
George Lanning	74	73	75	222	1,625
Robert Rawlins	74	72	76	222	1,625
Roland Stafford	75	69	78	222	1,625
Bob Toski	75	70	77	222	1,625

Transamerica Championship

Silverado Country Club, South Course, Napa, California
Par 35-37—72; 6,632 yards

October 20-22
purse, $400,000

	SCORES			TOTAL	MONEY
Billy Casper	69	70	68	207	$60,000
Al Geiberger	70	69	71	210	35,000
Charles Coody	67	72	72	211	26,600
Larry Ziegler	71	70	70	211	26,600
Bob Charles	70	70	72	212	19,400
Dave Hill	69	70	74	213	14,700
Mike Hill	70	74	70	214	12,533.34
Jim Dent	71	73	70	214	12,533.33
Jim Ferree	72	68	74	214	12,533.33
George Archer	72	70	73	215	8,237.50
Miller Barber	72	73	70	215	8,237.50
Robert Boldt	71	76	68	215	8,237.50
Bruce Devlin	69	72	74	215	8,237.50
Dale Douglass	76	69	70	215	8,237.50
Lou Graham	74	74	67	215	8,237.50

	SCORES			TOTAL	MONEY
Gene Littler	73	73	69	215	8,237.50
Arnold Palmer	70	73	72	215	8,237.50
Don Bies	72	72	72	216	5,800
John Brodie	70	73	73	216	5,800
Gary Player	72	70	74	216	5,800
Gay Brewer	75	72	70	217	4,400
Doug Dalziel	72	74	71	217	4,400
Dick Hendrickson	67	75	75	217	4,400
Harold Henning	74	76	67	217	4,400
Joe Jimenez	71	74	72	217	4,400
Don Massengale	71	72	74	217	4,400
Larry Mowry	73	72	72	217	4,400
Ken Still	72	76	69	217	4,400
Butch Baird	75	71	72	218	3,300
Bobby Nichols	72	73	73	218	3,300
Doug Sanders	71	73	74	218	3,300
Bruce Crampton	75	73	71	219	2,675
Rives McBee	71	73	75	219	2,675
Jim O'Hern	75	73	71	219	2,675
Phil Rodgers	72	74	73	219	2,675
Chi Chi Rodriguez	73	74	72	219	2,675
Ben Smith	72	72	75	219	2,675
Walter Zembriski	74	73	72	219	2,675
Frank Beard	72	74	74	220	2,125
Bob Erickson	75	75	70	220	2,125
Rocky Thompson	74	73	73	220	2,125
Bert Yancey	75	73	72	220	2,125

General Tire Classic

Desert Inn Country Club, Las Vegas, Nevada
Par 36-36—72; 7,111 yards

October 28-30
purse, $300,000

	SCORES			TOTAL	MONEY
Charles Coody	67	69	69	205	$45,000
Bob Charles	71	67	67	205	24,625
Chi Chi Rodriguez	70	69	66	205	24,625
(Coody defeated Charles and Rodriguez on second extra hole.)					
Dave Hill	71	68	68	207	18,500
Al Geiberger	69	68	72	209	15,000
George Archer	67	74	69	210	11,000
Orville Moody	70	72	69	211	9,666.67
Larry Mowry	73	70	68	211	9,666.67
Lee Elder	69	70	72	211	9,666.66
Mike Hill	74	70	68	212	8,250
Gene Littler	66	74	73	213	7,275
Tom Shaw	70	67	76	213	7,275
Bob Brue	71	72	71	214	6,300
John Paul Cain	70	73	71	214	6,300
Doug Dalziel	75	69	71	215	5,550
Ben Smith	70	71	74	215	5,550
Miller Barber	73	72	71	216	4,650
Bruce Crampton	72	75	69	216	4,650
Dale Douglass	74	73	69	216	4,650
Lou Graham	70	75	71	216	4,650
Frank Beard	76	69	72	217	3,825
Walter Zembriski	72	72	73	217	3,825

	SCORES			TOTAL	MONEY
Jim Dent	75	73	70	218	3,225
Bruce Devlin	76	72	70	218	3,225
Jim Ferree	72	72	74	218	3,225
George Lanning	72	74	72	218	3,225
Charles Sifford	74	73	71	218	3,225
Larry Ziegler	72	74	72	218	3,225
Butch Baird	76	71	72	219	2,415
Gay Brewer	71	73	75	219	2,415
Howie Johnson	74	74	71	219	2,415
Don Massengale	72	73	74	219	2,415
Rives McBee	72	71	76	219	2,415
Joe Jimenez	77	72	71	220	2,100
Harold Henning	74	73	74	221	1,950
Richard Rhyan	74	74	73	221	1,950
Bert Yancey	71	74	76	221	1,950
Ken Still	80	70	73	223	1,800
Billy Casper	78	73	73	224	1,725
Martin Roesink	72	73	80	225	1,650

Du Pont Cup

Tournament Players Club, Batoh   November 17-19
Par 72; 6,640 yards   purse, $450,000

FIRST ROUND

UNITED STATES: Charles Coody, 69; Don Bies, 69; Frank Beard, 71; Rives McBee, 71; Larry Mowry, 73; Orville Moody, 72; Dale Douglass, 75.
TOTAL—503.

JAPAN: Teruo Sugihara, 70; Hideo Jibiki, 72; Kesahiko Uchida, 73; Shigeru Uchida, 73; Kiyokuni Kimoto, 74; Hisashi Suzumura, 75; Tadashi Kitta, 76.
TOTAL—513.

SECOND ROUND

UNITED STATES: Orville Moody, 68; Rives McBee, 68; Tom Shaw, 68; Dale Douglass, 69; Charles Coody, 69; Frank Beard, 70; Larry Mowry, 71.
TOTAL—483 - 986.

JAPAN: Kesahiko Uchida, 69; Teruo Sugihara, 70; Shigeru Uchida, 70; Hisashi Suzumura, 71; Seiichi Satoh, 71; Tetsuhiro Ueda, 71; Hideo Jibiki, 73.
TOTAL—495 - 1,008.

THIRD ROUND

UNITED STATES: Don Bies, 70; Tom Shaw, 72; Rives McBee, 72; Charles Coody, 72; Frank Beard, 73; Lou Graham, 74; Larry Mowry, 74.
TOTAL—507 - 1,493.

JAPAN: Teruo Sugihara, 70; Hisashi Suzumura, 73; Kesahiko Uchida, 74; Hideo Jibiki, 75; Shigeru Uchida, 75; Hideyo Sugimoto, 76; Seiichi Satoh, 76.
TOTAL—519 - 1,527.

(Each U.S. player received $27,000; each Japanese player received $13,000.)

GTE West Classic

Ojai Valley Inn and Country Club, Ojai, California
Par 35-35—70; 6,190 yards

November 30-December 2
purse, $300,000

	SCORES			TOTAL	MONEY
Walter Zembriski	64	68	65	197	$52,500
George Archer	69	64	66	199	27,000
Jim Dent	66	69	64	199	27,000
Bob Charles	66	70	66	202	20,000
Chi Chi Rodriguez	67	69	67	203	17,000
Butch Baird	71	70	63	204	11,750
Homero Blancas	64	72	68	204	11,750
Rafe Botts	69	69	66	204	11,750
Rocky Thompson	71	64	69	204	11,750
Don Bies	71	70	64	205	8,366.67
Al Geiberger	69	68	68	205	8,366.67
Al Kelley	67	66	72	205	8,366.66
Deray Simon	67	71	68	206	7,300
Charles Coody	69	68	70	207	6,550
Jim Ferree	68	68	71	207	6,550
Bob Brue	71	66	71	208	5,300
Dick Hendrickson	69	70	69	208	5,300
Larry Mowry	73	65	70	208	5,300
Frank Beard	66	69	74	209	3,975
Dale Douglass	72	67	70	209	3,975
Joe Jimenez	72	67	70	209	3,975
Bill Johnston	67	70	72	209	3,975
Gene Littler	72	71	66	209	3,975
Phil Rodgers	71	69	69	209	3,975
Tom Shaw	73	68	68	209	3,975
Larry Ziegler	67	72	70	209	3,975
Bruce Devlin	69	70	71	210	3,350
Bob Erickson	70	67	73	210	3,350
Al Chandler	69	71	71	211	2,900
Terrance Dill	68	73	70	211	2,900
Harold Henning	74	69	68	211	2,900
Billy Maxwell	70	72	69	211	2,900
Arnold Palmer	72	70	69	211	2,900
Ben Smith	70	72	69	211	2,900
Bert Yancey	71	69	71	211	2,900
John Paul Cain	69	70	73	212	2,200
Bill Collins	67	75	70	212	2,200
Chick Evans	72	70	70	212	2,200
Mike Fetchick	72	68	72	212	2,200
Rives McBee	73	72	67	212	2,200
Orville Moody	67	70	75	212	2,200
Ralph Terry	70	73	69	212	2,200

GTE Kaanapali Classic

Royal Kaanapali Golf Club, Maui, Hawaii
Par 35-37—72; 6,704 yards

December 7-9
purse, $300,000

(Final round cancelled - rain)

	SCORES		TOTAL	MONEY
Don Bies	68	64	132	$45,000
Dale Douglass	66	67	133	26,000
Charles Coody	70	65	135	19,750
Tom Shaw	69	66	135	19,750
Joe Jimenez	64	73	137	12,800
Gene Littler	69	68	137	12,800
Harold Henning	72	66	138	9,258.34
Miller Barber	69	69	138	9,258.33
Lee Trevino	69	69	138	9,258.33
Homero Blancas	68	71	139	7,800
Jim Dent	70	70	140	6,850
Jim Ferree	71	69	140	6,850
Al Geiberger	71	70	141	5,675
Al Kelley	70	71	141	5,675
Bobby Nichols	72	69	141	5,675
Arnold Palmer	73	68	141	5,675
Billy Casper	74	68	142	4,450
Rives McBee	70	72	142	4,450
Ralph Terry	73	69	142	4,450
Walter Zembriski	70	72	142	4,450
George Archer	70	73	143	3,425
Robert Boldt	68	75	143	3,425
Jim O'Hern	71	72	143	3,425
Richard Rhyan	73	70	143	3,425
Ben Smith	69	74	143	3,425
Rocky Thompson	70	73	143	3,425
Bob Brue	72	72	144	2,550
Lee Elder	70	74	144	2,550
Mike Hill	72	72	144	2,550
Chi Chi Rodriguez	74	70	144	2,550
Allan Yamamoto	72	72	144	2,550
Larry Ziegler	74	70	144	2,550
Frank Beard	75	70	145	1,981.25
Bill Johnston	71	74	145	1,981.25
George Lanning	70	75	145	1,981.25
Shigeru Uchida	72	73	145	1,981.25
Butch Baird	75	71	146	1,662.50
Al Chandler	73	73	146	1,662.50
Bob Erickson	73	73	146	1,662.50
Don Massengale	75	71	146	1,662.50

Mauna Lani Challenge

Mauna Lani Golf Club, Kohala Coast, Hawaii
Par 36-36—72; 6,728 yards

December 13-15
purse, $300,000

	SCORES			TOTAL	MONEY
Dale Douglass	69	70	70	209	$45,000
Jim Ferree	71	68	70	209	20,000
(Douglass defeated Ferree on first extra hole.)					
George Archer	60	70	73	212	15,000
Al Kelley	70	72	71	213	8,750
Bob Brue	73	69	71	213	8,750
Howie Johnson	74	69	74	217	4,930
Lee Elder	71	75	71	217	4,930
Bob Erickson	72	74	71	217	4,930
Tom Shaw	72	75	70	217	4,930
Mike Fetchick	74	73	70	217	4,930
Bob Rawlins	70	75	73	218	3,000
Don Massengale	71	73	74	218	3,000
Butch Baird	75	71	73	219	2,550
Bobby Nichols	73	75	71	219	2,550
Kyle Burton	77	72	71	220	2,317
Charles Sifford	74	73	73	220	2,317
Tommy Bolt	75	72	73	220	2,317
Pat Chartrand	71	78	72	221	2,175
Ed Rieu	75	71	75	221	2,175
Allan Yamamoto	74	73	75	222	2,050
Bill Johnston	75	73	74	222	2,050
Dow Finsterwald	75	75	72	222	2,050
Doug Ford	75	72	76	223	1,900
Rafe Botts	75	76	73	224	1,800
Lanny Nielsen	78	74	73	225	1,750
Jerry Barber	75	73	78	226	1,675
Bruce Devlin	71	77	78	226	1,675
Gordon Jones	76	76	76	228	1,600
Eldridge Miles	73	80	77	230	1,525
Bob Spencer	77	76	77	230	1,525

Mazda Champions

Hyatt Dorado Beach, Dorado, Puerto Rico
Par 36-36—72; 6,740 yards - men, 6,265 yards - ladies

December 15-17
purse, $900,000

	SCORES			TOTAL	MONEY (Each)
Mike Hill/Patty Rizzo	65	60	66	191	$250,000
Don Bies/Tammy Green	61	65	66	192	42,500
Charles Coody/Sherri Turner	63	64	65	192	42,500
Orville Moody/Beth Daniel	63	63	67	193	25,000
Gene Littler/Jane Geddes	64	62	68	194	17,500
Dave Hill/Pat Bradley	66	65	63	194	17,500
Bob Charles/Betsy King	68	65	62	195	11,000
Chi Chi Rodriguez/Colleen Walker	65	67	63	195	11,000
Miller Barber/Cindy Rarick	64	65	66	195	11,000
Al Geiberger/Nancy Lopez	63	68	65	196	8,000
Harold Henning/Patty Sheehan	66	65	68	199	7,000
Billy Casper/Laura Davies	64	67	68	199	7,000

The European Tour

Tenerife Open

Golf Del Sur, Tenerife, The Azores
Par 36-36—72; 6,384 yards

February 23-26
purse, £200,000

	SCORES				TOTAL	MONEY
Jose-Maria Olazabal	69	68	68	70	275	£33,330
David Gilford	72	70	69	67	278	17,360
Jose-Maria Canizares	70	66	70	72	278	17,360
Michael King	74	70	69	67	280	7,867
Philip Walton	70	70	68	72	280	7,867
Juan Quiros	70	73	69	68	280	7,867
Johan Rystrom	72	72	68	68	280	7,867
Jose Rivero	70	72	68	71	281	4,290
Mark Roe	68	69	69	75	281	4,290
Des Smyth	66	75	68	72	281	4,290
Roger Chapman	74	70	67	70	281	4,290
Santiago Luna	72	75	70	65	282	2,905
Jim Rutledge	64	72	72	74	282	2,905
Marc Farry	76	70	67	69	282	2,905
David Jones	71	70	70	71	282	2,905
Peter Teravainen	66	73	68	75	282	2,905
Denis Durnian	68	72	71	71	282	2,905
Mark James	71	71	70	70	282	2,905
Ronan Rafferty	72	70	70	70	282	2,905
Eamonn Darcy	73	68	70	72	283	2,280
David Williams	71	70	73	69	283	2,280
Jean Van De Velde	70	67	75	71	283	2,280
Kevin Dickens	70	77	66	70	283	2,280
Malcolm Mackenzie	73	71	71	68	283	2,280
Bernard Gallacher	72	70	70	72	284	1,980
Juan Rosa	74	72	69	69	284	1,980
Martin Poxon	71	71	71	71	284	1,980
Howard Clark	71	71	72	70	284	1,980
Manuel Pinero	70	72	71	71	284	1,980
Emmanuel Dussart	72	72	69	72	285	1,740
Ronald Stelten	70	73	69	73	285	1,740
Jose Davila	74	71	67	73	285	1,740
Mike Miller	74	72	69	71	286	1,560
Sam Torrance	73	71	69	73	286	1,560
Ian Woosnam	65	73	77	71	286	1,560
Magnus Persson	70	72	70	74	286	1,560
Charles Bolling, Jr.	75	71	69	71	286	1,560
Grant Turner	71	72	71	73	287	1,380
Anders Sorensen	73	69	77	68	287	1,380
Mark Davis	72	73	73	69	287	1,380
Christy O'Connor, Jr.	71	74	70	72	287	1,380
Eduardo Romero	74	69	72	73	288	1,160
Bill Malley	71	72	74	71	288	1,160
David Llewellyn	71	74	72	71	288	1,160
Vijay Singh	74	71	67	76	288	1,160
Philip Harrison	69	74	71	74	288	1,160
Brian Waites	75	68	74	71	288	1,160
Magnus Sunesson	71	72	75	70	288	1,160
Jamie Howell	72	75	72	70	289	920

	SCORES				TOTAL	MONEY
Mats Lanner	75	71	72	71	289	920
Antonio Garrido	71	70	75	73	289	920
Michael Allen	73	72	72	72	289	920
Paul Carrigill	71	76	71	71	289	920

Karl Litten Desert Classic

Emirates Golf Club, Dubai
Par 35-37—72; 7,100 yards

March 2-5
purse, £250,000

	SCORES				TOTAL	MONEY
Mark James	69	68	72	68	277	£41,660
Peter O'Malley	71	68	68	70	277	27,760
(James defeated O'Malley on first extra hole.)						
Paul Broadhurst	72	66	70	72	280	15,660
Brett Ogle	77	69	67	69	282	12,500
Magnus Persson	67	72	72	72	283	10,600
Emmanuel Dussart	71	71	72	70	284	6,620
Barry Lane	71	73	73	67	284	6,620
Mike Miller	72	74	67	71	284	6,620
Jim Rutledge	73	70	70	71	284	6,620
Sam Torrance	70	71	71	72	284	6,620
Gordon J. Brand	77	68	70	70	285	4,450
Denis Durnian	75	69	68	73	285	4,450
Anders Sorensen	70	71	72	73	286	4,020
Alberto Binaghi	68	74	71	74	287	3,522
David Feherty	72	73	72	70	287	3,522
Joe Higgins	70	72	70	75	287	3,522
Stephen McAllister	73	74	73	67	287	3,522
Jean Van De Velde	76	72	67	72	287	3,522
Peter Baker	71	74	72	71	288	2,930
Gordon Brand, Jr.	71	71	71	75	288	2,930
Howard Clark	74	69	76	69	288	2,930
Des Smyth	70	72	75	71	288	2,930
Steen Tinning	66	73	74	75	288	2,930
Vicente Fernandez	75	74	69	71	289	2,550
Robin Mann	74	73	76	66	289	2,550
Martin Poxon	72	71	77	69	289	2,550
Ronan Rafferty	71	72	77	69	289	2,550
David Williams	68	72	76	73	289	2,550
Paul Carrigill	73	72	72	73	290	2,150
Eugene Elliott	71	75	71	73	290	2,150
Anders Forsbrand	71	71	71	77	290	2,150
John Slaughter	76	70	70	74	290	2,150
Grant Turner	73	73	76	68	290	2,150
Philip Walton	70	76	70	74	290	2,150
Mats Hallberg	71	76	71	73	291	1,875
Leif Hederstrom	72	73	74	72	291	1,875
Wayne Stephens	77	71	73	70	291	1,875
Peter Teravainen	68	76	76	71	291	1,875
Mark Davis	73	74	72	73	292	1,650
David Gilford	74	73	73	72	292	1,650
Malcolm Mackenzie	68	76	75	73	292	1,650
Chris Moody	73	70	77	72	292	1,650
Eduardo Romero	74	73	75	70	292	1,650
Richard Fish	75	74	70	74	293	1,325
Mats Lanner	70	79	72	72	293	1,325

	SCORES			TOTAL	MONEY
Bill Longmuir	73	74	76	70	293	1,325
Ossie Moore	73	76	73	71	293	1,325
Frederic Regard	71	74	76	72	293	1,325
David A. Russell	74	72	72	75	293	1,325
Johan Rystrom	69	79	73	72	293	1,325
Sandy Stephen	74	73	70	76	293	1,325

Renault Open de Baleares

Santa Ponsa Golf Club, Majorca
Par 36-36—72; 7,152 yards

March 10-13
purse, £225,000

	SCORES			TOTAL	MONEY
Ove Sellberg	68	71	69	71	279	£37,500
Mark McNulty	69	70	71	71	281	16,773.33
Jose-Maria Olazabal	71	75	68	67	281	16,773.33
Philip Parkin	71	71	69	70	281	16,773.33
Denis Durnian	71	72	69	70	282	6,523.33
Jamie Howell	68	74	70	70	282	6,523.33
Bill Malley	69	70	70	73	282	6,523.33
Brett Ogle	70	70	71	71	282	6,523.33
Juan Quiros	71	70	71	70	282	6,523.33
Ronan Rafferty	72	69	69	72	282	6,523.33
Jose-Maria Canizares	73	71	70	69	283	4,100
Bill Longmuir	73	72	72	67	284	3,890
Tony Charnley	67	69	74	75	285	3,487.50
Anders Forsbrand	67	73	72	73	285	3,487.50
Barry Lane	74	72	67	72	285	3,487.50
Eduardo Romero	69	75	70	71	285	3,487.50
Alberto Binaghi	75	71	71	69	286	3,050
Ron Commans	73	72	72	69	286	3,050
Ulf Nilsson	72	71	72	72	287	2,766.67
Jim Rutledge	75	70	72	70	287	2,766.67
Mike Smith	69	74	71	73	287	2,766.67
Juan Anglada	72	75	71	70	288	2,520
Emmanuel Dussart	71	72	74	71	288	2,520
Mark Roe	71	73	74	70	288	2,520
Eamonn Darcy	71	72	74	72	289	2,520
Mark Davis	68	74	72	75	289	2,185
David Feherty	71	73	73	72	289	2,185
Jerry Haas	73	73	71	72	289	2,185
Mats Lanner	73	69	77	70	289	2,185
Peter Mitchell	72	72	71	74	289	2,185
Mariano Aparicio	71	75	72	72	290	1,776.67
Jose Carriles	74	73	73	70	290	1,776.67
Vicente Fernandez	72	75	72	71	290	1,776.67
Manuel Pinero	73	71	73	73	290	1,776.67
Philip Walton	75	69	71	75	290	1,776.67
Ian Woosnam	73	71	75	71	290	1,776.67
Antonio Garrido	75	71	73	72	291	1,520
Joe Higgins	74	73	71	73	291	1,520
Chris Moody	72	75	70	74	291	1,520
Jose Rivero	72	75	72	72	291	1,520
Peter Teravainen	75	71	71	74	291	1,520
Paul Carrigill	72	74	71	75	292	1,320
Carlos Franco	75	71	75	71	292	1,320
Colin Montgomerie	70	72	72	78	292	1,320

	SCORES				TOTAL	MONEY
John Morgan	73	72	72	75	292	1,320
Wayne Stephens	72	75	71	74	292	1,320
Ossie Moore	73	70	75	75	293	1,120
Bryan Norton	68	77	73	75	293	1,120
Jesper Parnevik	71	74	74	74	293	1,120
David A. Russell	74	73	73	73	293	1,120
Des Smyth	74	72	74	73	293	1,120

Massimo Dutti Catalan Open

Club Golf de Pals   March 16-19
Par 36-37—73; 6,804 yards   purse, £200,000

	SCORES				TOTAL	MONEY
Mark Roe	69	70	69	71	279	£33,330
Gordon Brand, Jr.	73	67	70	70	280	14,906.67
Colin Montgomerie	73	68	72	67	280	14,906.67
Jose-Maria Olazabal	70	71	68	71	280	14,906.67
Denis Durnian	73	68	71	69	281	8,470
Howard Clark	72	68	70	72	282	6,000
Peter O'Malley	72	69	69	72	282	6,000
Grant Turner	73	66	70	73	282	6,000
Manuel Calero	68	76	69	71	284	4,480
David Ecob	68	72	75	70	285	3,840
Magnus Persson	72	72	71	70	285	3,840
Manuel Pinero	72	71	72	71	286	3,330
Eduardo Romero	73	69	72	72	286	3,330
Vicente Fernandez	72	72	71	73	287	2,940
David A. Russell	72	71	72	72	287	2,940
Jim Rutledge	75	69	71	72	287	2,940
Ron Commans	72	73	69	74	288	2,428.57
John Jacobs	70	70	73	75	288	2,428.57
Malcolm Mackenzie	70	72	71	75	288	2,428.57
John Morgan	70	72	68	78	288	2,428.57
Jose Rivero	72	71	73	72	288	2,428.57
Mike Smith	72	70	75	71	288	2,428.57
Sam Torrance	71	73	72	72	288	2,428.57
Ross Drummond	69	75	71	74	289	2,040
Neil Hansen	72	70	74	73	289	2,040
Martin Poxon	72	73	70	74	289	2,040
Ronan Rafferty	72	73	72	72	289	2,040
David Williams	72	72	72	73	289	2,040
David Feherty	74	71	72	73	290	1,720
David Gilford	72	70	74	74	290	1,720
Leif Hederstrom	71	72	75	72	290	1,720
Mark McNulty	71	74	74	71	290	1,720
Mark Mouland	79	67	71	73	290	1,720
Peter Teravainen	73	67	76	74	290	1,720
Jerry Anderson ·	69	73	73	76	291	1,500
Emmanuel Dussart	72	73	71	75	291	1,500
Manuel Moreno	76	71	71	73	291	1,500
Philip Parkin	74	71	70	76	291	1,500
Jamie Howell	74	72	73	73	292	1,400
Gordon J. Brand	72	71	74	76	293	1,260
David Jones	72	73	73	75	293	1,260
Mikael Krantz	76	69	76	72	293	1,260
Bill Longmuir	76	69	76	72	293	1,260

	SCORES			TOTAL	MONEY
Emilio Rodriguez	72	72 73	76	293	1,260
Jose Romero	76	70 72	75	293	1,260
Steven Bottomley	74	73 69	78	294	920
Jose Davila	74	71 73	76	294	920
Barry Lane	74	70 74	76	294	920
Brian Marchbank	77	68 76	73	294	920
Peter Mitchell	76	70 73	75	294	920
Ian Mosey	71	74 75	74	294	920
Christy O'Connor, Jr.	69	73 76	76	294	920
Jose Rozadilla	72	72 76	74	294	920
Ove Sellberg	72	75 72	75	294	920
Vijay Singh	75	69 76	74	294	920
Philip Walton	75	71 70	78	294	920

AGF Open

La Grande Motte, Montpelier, France
Par 36-36—72; 6,704 yards

March 24-27
purse, £137,457

	SCORES			TOTAL	MONEY
Mark James	69	67 69	72	277	£22,909.51
Mark Mouland	72	73 70	65	280	15,266.90
Bryan Norton	70	70 70	71	281	8,604.81
Vijay Singh	73	68 73	68	282	5,408.94
Ronald Stelten	65	68 72	77	282	5,408.94
Sam Torrance	68	67 73	74	282	5,408.94
Grant Turner	73	73 65	71	282	5,408.94
Jamie Howell	70	75 70	68	283	3,257.74
Andrew Sherborne	72	70 70	71	283	3,257.74
Mariano Aparicio	74	72 73	65	284	2,327.61
Stephen Bennett	70	71 71	72	284	2,327.61
Michel Besanceney	72	72 70	70	284	2,327.61
Juan Quiros	69	69 72	74	284	2,327.61
Glenn Ralph	72	71 67	74	284	2,327.61
David A. Russell	74	73 66	71	284	2,327.61
Brian Evans	72	74 69	70	285	1,933.56
Denis Durnian	71	72 68	75	286	1,718.21
Eugene Elliott	72	69 71	74	286	1,718.21
David Gilford	69	73 70	74	286	1,718.21
Armando Saavedra	69	73 73	71	286	1,718.21
Mike Smith	74	74 67	71	286	1,718.21
Mark Davis	68	70 75	74	287	1,505.16
Michael McLean	70	74 71	72	287	1,505.16
Andrew Murray	72	73 74	68	287	1,505.16
Wayne Riley	73	69 72	73	287	1,505.16
Steven Bottomley	73	72 70	73	288	1,319.59
Richard Fish	71	69 76	72	288	1,319.59
David James	76	71 68	73	288	1,319.59
Mike Miller	75	71 70	72	288	1,319.59
Peter O'Malley	74	72 71	71	288	1,319.59
Paul Broadhurst	72	72 74	71	289	1,129.90
Paul Carman	69	74 75	71	289	1,129.90
Paul Carrigill	75	70 78	66	289	1,129.90
Ron Commans	72	70 76	71	289	1,129.90
Silvio Grappasonni	74	72 69	74	289	1,129.90
Simon Bishop	74	71 74	71	290	1,003.44
Gordon J. Brand	74	67 75	74	290	1,003.44

	SCORES				TOTAL	MONEY
Neil Hansen	73	73	74	70	290	1,003.44
Mark Roe	72	72	75	71	290	1,003.44
Juan Anglada	73	73	75	70	291	879.73
Mats Hallberg	70	72	75	74	291	879.73
John Hawksworth	70	70	76	75	291	879.73
David Llewellyn	69	75	76	71	291	879.73
Malcolm Mackenzie	78	70	67	76	291	879.73
Tony Charnley	68	78	75	71	292	728.52
Mike Clayton	74	72	75	71	292	728.52
Marco Durante	72	75	73	72	292	728.52
Wayne Stephens	73	74	72	73	292	728.52
Johan Tumba	76	72	73	71	292	728.52
Philip Walton	69	72	75	76	292	728.52

Volvo Open

Is Molas Golf Club, Sardinia
Par 35-37—72; 7,080 yards

March 30 - April 2
purse, £200,000

	SCORES				TOTAL	MONEY
Vijay Singh	72	68	68	68	276	£33,330
Peter Fowler	71	69	71	68	279	22,200
Gordon J. Brand	69	72	70	72	283	11,260
Bill Longmuir	71	69	72	71	283	11,260
Charles Bolling, Jr.	68	72	71	73	284	7,735
Christy O'Connor, Jr.	70	72	69	73	284	7,735
Massimo Mannelli	73	72	71	69	285	4,870
Peter O'Malley	72	70	68	75	285	4,870
Ronan Rafferty	72	68	71	74	285	4,870
David Williams	73	72	72	68	285	4,870
Mats Hallberg	75	69	73	69	286	3,268
John Morgan	70	71	70	75	286	3,268
Jesper Parnevik	71	70	73	72	286	3,268
Jacob Rasmussen	71	74	72	69	286	3,268
Jose Rivero	74	71	69	72	286	3,268
Richard Boxall	72	68	72	75	287	2,645
Vicente Fernandez	70	70	73	74	287	2,645
Magnus Jonsson	72	71	72	72	287	2,645
Carl Mason	68	71	70	78	287	2,645
Steven Bottomley	71	72	72	73	288	2,310
Mats Lanner	71	73	70	74	288	2,310
Malcolm Mackenzie	74	72	72	70	288	2,310
Juan Rosa	73	70	73	72	288	2,310
Giuseppe Cali	75	70	71	73	289	2,010
Andrew Chandler	69	69	75	76	289	2,010
David Gilford	72	72	73	72	289	2,010
Jamie Howell	73	70	71	75	289	2,010
Frederic Regard	70	74	72	73	289	2,010
Andrew Sherborne	73	71	69	76	289	2,010
Mike Clayton	75	73	73	69	290	1,770
Neil Hansen	77	69	73	71	290	1,770
Neal Briggs	71	73	72	75	291	1,580
Andrea Canessa	72	71	70	78	291	1,580
Eugene Elliott	73	73	73	72	291	1,580
John Hawksworth	75	70	71	75	291	1,580
Ove Sellberg	70	74	72	75	291	1,580
Steen Tinning	72	75	74	70	291	1,580

	SCORES				TOTAL	MONEY
Carlos Franco	72	73	73	74	292	1,340
Gavin Levenson	76	70	72	74	292	1,340
Thomas Levet	73	71	72	76	292	1,340
Colin Montgomerie	74	72	71	75	292	1,340
Juan Quiros	70	74	71	77	292	1,340
Peter Teravainen	78	68	70	76	292	1,340
Derrick Cooper	73	72	74	74	293	1,120
Eamonn Darcy	70	76	73	74	293	1,120
Constantino Rocca	73	72	74	74	293	1,120
Armando Saavedra	75	72	71	75	293	1,120
Ian Young	71	74	75	73	293	1,120
Paul Carrigill	77	71	73	73	294	940
Bill Malley	73	72	74	75	294	940
Mike Miller	71	72	75	76	294	940
Keith Waters	73	72	73	76	294	940

Jersey European Airways Open

La Moye Golf Club, Jersey
Par 36-36—72; 6,797 yards

April 6-9
purse, £147,000

	SCORES				TOTAL	MONEY
Christy O'Connor, Jr.	73	70	66	72	281	£24,490
Denis Durnian	70	71	67	73	281	16,315
(O'Connor defeated Durnian on first extra hole.)						
Mats Lanner	71	69	70	72	282	8,275
Paul Broadhurst	73	69	71	69	282	8,275
Des Smyth	74	69	71	69	283	4,552
Colin Montgomerie	69	75	68	71	283	4,552
Bernard Gallacher	71	70	70	72	283	4,552
Sam Torrance	72	70	69	72	283	4,552
Ronan Rafferty	74	69	68	72	283	4,552
Barry Lane	76	70	65	73	284	2,822.50
Peter Fowler	74	71	69	70	284	2,822.50
David J. Russell	73	71	72	69	285	2,381.67
David A. Russell	69	70	71	75	285	2,381.67
Rick Hartmann	69	72	75	69	285	2,381.67
Mark Roe	73	72	70	71	286	2,117.50
David James	71	71	72	72	286	2,117.50
Jesper Parnevik	75	67	70	75	287	1,838
David Feherty	69	72	71	75	287	1,838
Glenn Ralph	70	74	76	67	287	1,838
Magnus Persson	73	69	71	74	287	1,838
Tony Charnley	72	72	69	74	287	1,838
Wayne Stephens	76	69	70	73	288	1,588
Paul Way	73	74	70	71	288	1,588
David Llewellyn	70	69	73	76	288	1,588
Andrew Murray	72	74	72	70	288	1,588
Ron Commans	71	70	71	76	288	1,588
Ross McFarlane	73	74	70	72	289	1,325
Carl Mason	73	69	73	74	289	1,325
Joe Higgins	76	69	69	75	289	1,325
David Ray	74	70	72	73	289	1,325
Andrew Oldcorn	71	71	73	74	289	1,325
Richard Boxall	71	73	74	71	289	1,325
Philip Walton	73	71	69	76	289	1,325
Sandy Stephen	71	69	73	77	290	1,131.25

	SCORES				TOTAL	MONEY
Paul Curry	73	72	68	77	290	1,131.25
Gordon Brand, Jr.	72	71	76	71	290	1,131.25
Andrew Sherborne	70	72	73	75	290	1,131.25
Peter Mitchell	69	72	75	75	291	1,060
Jose-Maria Canizares	74	73	70	75	292	1,000
Paul Kent	73	70	76	73	292	1,000
Mark Mouland	72	73	73	74	292	1,000
Robert Lee	71	73	73	76	293	882
David Jones	72	71	72	78	293	882
Marc Pendaries	72	76	72	73	293	882
Ross Drummond	77	69	74	73	293	882
Martin Poxon	72	74	72	75	293	882
Jerry Haas	77	70	71	76	294	705
Jimmy Heggarty	72	76	71	75	294	705
Greg J.Turner	73	70	77	74	294	705
John Jacobs	70	70	76	78	294	705
David Williams	74	73	74	73	294	705
Ian Young	75	72	73	74	294	705
Stephen Bennett	71	73	75	75	294	705

Credit Lyonnais Cannes Open

Cannes Mougins Golf Club, Cannes, France　　　　　　　　　　April 13-16
Par 36-36—72; 6,786 yards　　　　　　　　　　　　　　　　purse, £209,110

(Shortened to 54 holes, flooded course Sunday.)

	SCORES			TOTAL	MONEY
Paul Broadhurst	65	70	72	207	£34,851.30
Jimmy Heggarty	69	72	67	208	15,588.60
Brett Ogle	71	68	69	208	15,588.60
Peter Senior	70	66	72	208	15,598.60
Ronan Rafferty	72	67	70	209	8,829.00
Jean Van De Velde	71	69	70	210	5,845.73
Tony Charnley	71	68	71	210	5,845.73
Mark McNulty	71	70	69	210	5,845.73
Derrick Cooper	73	64	73	210	5,845.73
Des Smyth	70	72	69	211	3,671
Jose Rivero	72	68	71	211	3,671
Manuel Calero	70	66	75	211	3,671
Philip Walton	74	71	66	211	3,671
Magnus Persson	68	68	75	211	3,671
Colin Montgomerie	71	73	68	212	2,905.20
Juan Anglada	67	71	74	212	2,905.20
Bryan Norton	70	71	71	212	2,905.20
Stephen Hamill	68	68	76	212	2,905.20
Bill Malley	69	73	70	212	2,905.20
Mats Lanner	69	72	72	213	2,527.89
Ian Woosnam	72	73	68	213	2,527.89
Eduardo Romero	72	68	74	214	2,134.45
Bill Glasson	71	73	70	214	2,134.45
Mark Roe	75	69	70	214	2,134.45
Keith Waters	71	73	70	214	2,134.45
Richard Boxall	67	73	74	214	2,134.45
Stephen Bennett	70	70	74	214	2,134.45
David Llewellyn	69	73	72	214	2,134.45
Barry Lane	67	75	72	214	2,134.45

	SCORES			TOTAL	MONEY
Roger Chapman	69	72	73	214	2,134.45
Steen Tinning	69	76	70	215	1,627.72
Emmanuel Dussart	71	73	71	215	1,627.72
Paul Hoad	70	72	73	215	1,627.72
David A. Russell	73	69	73	215	1,627.72
David Williams	73	70	72	215	1,627.72
Gordon J. Brand	71	72	72	215	1,627.72
Greg J. Turner	74	67	74	215	1,627.72
Robert Lee	70	70	76	216	1,319.70
Stephen McAllister	72	68	76	216	1,319.70
Emilio Rodriguez	72	71	73	216	1,319.70
Jamie Howell	74	69	73	216	1,319.70
Rick Hartmann	70	72	74	216	1,319.70
Luis Carbonetti	70	73	73	216	1,319.70
Ian Young	71	71	74	216	1,319.70
Jesper Parnevik	71	71	74	216	1,319.70
Alberto Binaghi	75	67	75	217	1,022.31
Armando Saavedra	68	77	72	217	1,022.31
Sam Torrance	73	71	73	217	1,022.31
Jerry Haas	72	73	72	217	1,022.31
Ove Sellberg	72	71	74	217	1,022.31
Antonio Garrido	74	70	73	217	1,022.31
Mark Davis	75	70	72	217	1,022.31
Peter Teravainen	69	76	72	217	1,022.31

Cepsa Madrid Open

Puerta de Hierro Golf Club, Madrid, Spain
Par 36-36—72; 6,941 yards

April 20-23
purse, £225,000

	SCORES				TOTAL	MONEY
Severiano Ballesteros	67	67	69	69	272	£37,500
Howard Clark	65	68	70	70	273	25,000
Philip Walton	70	67	70	68	275	14,070
Mats Lanner	70	70	68	68	276	11,250
Derrick Cooper	67	72	67	71	277	9,500
Tony Charnley	70	69	70	69	278	7,850
Rodger Davis	69	72	70	68	279	6,150
Magnus Persson	64	70	75	70	279	6,150
Emmanuel Dussart	69	71	68	72	280	4,370
Carl Mason	70	68	71	71	280	4,370
Mark James	70	68	68	74	280	4,370
Mike Smith	69	72	69	70	280	4,370
Jesper Parnevik	64	71	75	71	281	3,487.50
Manuel Pinero	71	68	69	73	281	3,487.50
Bob Shearer	68	73	71	69	281	3,487.50
Richard Boxall	69	69	71	72	281	3,487.50
Johan Rystrom	70	71	68	73	282	2,702.22
Eamonn Darcy	67	76	69	70	282	2,702.22
Jose-Maria Olazabal	71	68	70	73	282	2,702.22
Ian Woosnam	72	67	72	71	282	2,702.22
Antonio Garrido	69	70	68	75	282	2,702.22
Chris Moody	70	71	69	72	282	2,702.22
Colin Montgomerie	73	69	72	68	282	2,702.22
Peter Fowler	68	73	72	69	282	2,702.22
David Williams	70	69	71	72	282	2,702.22
*Yago Beamonte	70	70	68	74	282	

	SCORES				TOTAL	MONEY
Mats Hallberg	72	71	68	72	283	2,080
Neil Hansen	71	70	70	72	283	2,080
Manuel Moreno	71	71	71	70	283	2,080
Christy O'Connor, Jr.	70	68	75	70	283	2,080
Vicente Fernandez	69	67	77	70	283	2,080
Calvin Peete	68	72	72	71	283	2,080
Denis Durnian	75	67	68	73	283	2,080
Jose-Maria Canizares	69	72	67	76	284	1,668.33
Jean Van De Velde	69	74	71	70	284	1,668.33
Mike Clayton	70	74	73	67	284	1,668.33
Stephen Bennett	71	73	68	72	284	1,668.33
Michael Allen	69	69	76	70	284	1,668.33
Jose Davilla	70	72	68	74	284	1,668.33
Mark Roe	74	70	71	70	285	1,440
Barry Lane	70	72	69	74	285	1,440
Daniel Lozano	68	71	73	73	285	1,440
Philip Parkin	73	71	70	71	285	1,440
Ulf Nilsson	69	70	69	77	285	1,440
Paul Carrigill	72	71	67	76	286	1,180
Mark Mouland	70	71	73	72	286	1,180
Juan Anglada	69	71	72	74	286	1,180
Santiago Luna	72	71	72	71	286	1,180
Miguel Angel Jimenez	75	66	72	73	286	1,180
Ove Sellberg	70	74	72	70	286	1,180
Malcolm Mackenzie	72	70	72	72	286	1,180
Armando Saavedra	70	71	70	75	286	1,180

Peugeot Spanish Open

El Saler Golf Club, Valencia, Spain
Par 36-36—72; 7,092 yards

April 27-30
purse, £250,000

	SCORES				TOTAL	MONEY
Bernhard Langer	70	72	67	72	281	£41,660
Jose-Maria Canizares	72	72	70	70	284	21,705
Paul Carrigill	70	69	72	73	284	21,705
Jose-Maria Olazabal	70	72	70	73	285	12,500
Mats Lanner	71	72	71	72	286	10,600
Gordon Brand, Jr.	71	73	69	74	287	8,125
Barry Lane	72	69	75	71	287	8,125
David Feherty	70	70	74	74	288	6,250
Severiano Ballesteros	75	68	74	72	289	5,300
Johan Rystrom	72	73	72	72	289	5,300
Denis Durnian	74	71	71	74	290	4,600
Tony Charnley	73	74	72	72	291	4,160
Sam Torrance	74	73	69	75	291	4,160
Gordon J. Brand	73	71	75	73	292	3,745
Derrick Cooper	66	75	76	75	292	3,745
Emmanuel Dussart	74	74	71	74	293	3,305
Paul Way	73	75	70	75	293	3,305
Christy O'Connor, Jr.	73	73	72	75	293	3,305
Ronan Rafferty	74	74	71	74	293	3,305
Brian Marchbank	72	75	73	74	294	2,812.50
Jerry Haas	73	72	76	73	294	2,812.50
Mike Harwood	71	75	76	72	294	2,812.50
Vicente Fernandez	75	74	73	72	294	2,812.50
Richard Fish	71	70	80	73	294	2,812.50

	SCORES			TOTAL	MONEY
Antonio Garrido	74	74	75	71	294	2,812.50
David Williams	72	75	75	73	295	2,437.50
Juan Anglada	77	72	76	70	295	2,437.50
Eamonn Darcy	74	75	75	71	295	2,437.50
Howard Clark	73	74	73	75	295	2,437.50
Mark McNulty	73	75	73	75	296	2,212.50
Frank Nobilo	73	74	75	74	296	2,212.50
Mark Davis	69	81	75	72	297	2,000
Ian Woosnam	78	70	73	76	297	2,000
Manuel Pinero	75	74	78	70	297	2,000
Jesper Parnevik	73	73	77	74	297	2,000
Malcolm Mackenzie	72	77	77	71	297	2,000
Keith Waters	79	71	76	72	298	1,675
Mike Smith	74	74	78	72	298	1,675
Eduardo Romero	71	76	72	79	298	1,675
Jose Davila	75	74	74	75	298	1,675
David Llewellyn	74	76	73	75	298	1,675
Grant Turner	73	74	74	77	298	1,675
Paul Kent	72	78	76	72	298	1,675
Jamie Howell	73	72	77	76	298	1,675
Neil Hansen	74	72	77	76	299	1,375
Manuel Calero	71	77	72	79	299	1,375
Jim Rutledge	73	72	78	76	299	1,375
Peter Mitchell	77	72	71	79	299	1,375
Marc Farry	70	76	81	73	300	1,175
Jean Van De Velde	76	73	77	74	300	1,175
Philip Walton	76	71	76	77	300	1,175
David James	78	72	76	74	300	1,175

Epson Grand Prix of Europe Match Play Championship

St. Pierre Golf and Country Club, Chepstow, England — May 4-7
Par 35-36—71; 6,859 yards — purse, £300,000

FIRST ROUND

Mike Clayton defeated Miguel Angel Martin, 3 and 2.
Frank Nobilo defeated Wayne Riley, 1 up.
Michael Allen defeated Peter Senior, 2 and 1.
Jeff Hawkes defeated Ronan Rafferty, 2 and 1.
Jose-Maria Canizares defeated Stephen Bennett, 1 up, 19 holes.
Mark Mouland defeated Derrick Cooper, 4 and 2.
Mike Harwood defeated David Williams, 1 up, 19 holes.
Tony Johnstone defeated David Whelan, 5 and 4.
David J. Russell defeated Peter Baker, 1 up.
Howard Clark defeated Sam Torrance, 1 up.
Roger Chapman defeated Chris Moody, 3 and 1.
Richard Boxall defeated Eduardo Romero, 4 and 3.
Philip Walton defeated Mike Smith, 4 and 3.
Gordon J. Brand defeated Anders Forsbrand, 3 and 1.
Carl Mason defeated Barry Lane, 1 up.
Gordon Brand, Jr. defeated Andrew Murray, 5 and 4.
Peter Fowler defeated Colin Montgomerie, 2 and 1.
Mark Roe defeated David Llewellyn, 3 and 2.
Mats Lanner defeated Manuel Pinero, 8 and 6.
Denis Durnian defeated Rodger Davis, 1 up.
Jose Rivero defeated David Feherty, 1 up.
Tony Charnley defeated Eamonn Darcy, 2 and 1.

Ken Brown defeated Ove Sellberg, 3 and 2.
Christy O'Connor, Jr. defeated John Morgan, 2 and 1.
(All first-round losers received £1,920.)

SECOND ROUND

Severiano Ballesteros defeated Clayton, 4 and 3.
Allen defeated Nobilo, 2 and 1.
Canizares defeated Hawkes, 1 up.
Mouland defeated Masahiro Kuramoto, 5 and 4.
Harwood defeated Mark McNulty, 2 and 1.
Johnstone defeated Russell, 4 and 3.
Clark defeated Chapman, 4 and 3.
Ian Woosnam defeated Boxall, 1 up, 19 holes.
Jose-Maria Olazabal defeated Walton, 4 and 2.
Gordon J. Brand defeated Mason, 4 and 3.
Fowler defeated Gordon Brand, Jr., 4 and 3.
Des Smyth defeated Roe, 1 up, 19 holes.
Mark James defeated Lanner, 2 up.
Durnian defeated Rivero, 2 up.
Brown defeated Charnley, 1 up.
Bernhard Langer defeated O'Connor, 2 and 1.
(All second-round losers received £3,450.)

THIRD ROUND

Ballesteros defeated Allen, 8 and 6.
Mouland defeated Canizares, 2 and 1.
Harwood defeated Johnstone, 1 up.
Woosnam defeated Clark, 2 up.
Olazabal defeated Brand, 4 and 3.
Smyth defeated Fowler, 2 and 1.
Durnian defeated James, 2 and 1.
Brown defeated Langer, 2 and 1.
(All third-round losers received £5,500.)

QUARTER-FINALS

Ballesteros defeated Mouland, 2 up.
Harwood defeated Woosnam, 1 up.
Smyth defeated Olazabal, 1 up.
Durnian defeated Brown, 3 and 2.
(All quarter-final losers received £9,900.)

SEMI-FINALS

Ballesteros defeated Harwood, 6 and 5.
Durnian defeated Smyth, 4 and 3.

PLAYOFF FOR THIRD-FOURTH PLACE

Smyth defeated Harwood, 1 up.
(Smyth received £18,370, Harwood £14,750.)

FINAL

Ballesteros defeated Durnian, 4 and 3.
(Ballesteros received £50,000, Durnian £32,000.)

Volvo Belgian Open

Royal Waterloo Golf Club, Brussels, Belgium
Par 35-37—72; 6,803 yards

May 11-14
purse, £200,000

	SCORES			TOTAL	MONEY
Gordon J. Brand	67	69	68	69	273	£33,330
Kevin Dickens	70	67	67	73	277	22,200
Mark Davis	68	73	70	67	278	12,520
Jesper Parnevik	74	70	67	68	279	10,000
Richard Boxall	69	70	66	75	280	6,190
Marc Farry	69	69	71	71	280	6,190
Ronan Rafferty	70	73	67	70	280	6,190
Malcolm Mackenzie	70	72	71	67	280	6,190
Derrick Cooper	71	71	71	67	280	6,190
Eamonn Darcy	68	72	72	69	281	3,480
Andrew Murray	72	71	69	69	281	3,480
David Williams	71	70	72	68	281	3,480
Grant Turner	74	70	70	67	281	3,480
Philip Walton	75	69	70	67	281	3,480
Peter McWhinney	67	74	71	70	282	2,940
Peter Baker	73	74	65	71	283	2,596
Mark McNulty	71	69	72	71	283	2,596
Emmanuel Dussart	69	72	71	71	283	2,596
Miguel Angel Jimenez	70	72	72	69	283	2,596
Mike Clayton	71	72	72	68	283	2,596
Bernhard Langer	73	70	72	69	284	2,310
Stephen Bennett	73	72	71	68	284	2,310
David J. Russell	72	69	70	74	285	2,040
Charles Bolling, Jr.	72	71	71	71	285	2,040
Carl Mason	74	70	70	71	285	2,040
Anders Forsbrand	68	74	73	70	285	2,040
Paul Kent	73	72	71	69	285	2,040
Vijay Singh	69	76	73	67	285	2,040
Chris Moody	72	75	72	66	285	2,040
Santiago Luna	68	71	74	73	286	1,648.57
Paul Curry	74	72	68	72	286	1,648.57
Brian Marchbank	70	75	70	71	286	1,648.57
Jean Van De Velde	71	74	73	68	286	1,648.57
Gordon Brand, Jr.	72	75	71	68	286	1,648.57
Paul Carrigill	76	71	71	68	286	1,648.57
Jose-Maria Olazabal	75	71	73	67	286	1,648.57
Steven Bottomley	68	76	73	70	287	1,420
David James	70	74	74	69	287	1,420
Neil Hansen	70	74	75	68	287	1,420
Vicente Fernandez	71	74	74	68	287	1,420
Juan Quiros	71	76	68	73	288	1,200
Ken Brown	69	72	74	73	288	1,200
Rick Hartmann	68	77	71	72	288	1,200
Mark Nichols	70	74	73	71	288	1,200
Paul Broadhurst	68	76	74	70	288	1,200
Manuel Calero	72	72	74	70	288	1,200
Eduardo Romero	74	73	73	68	288	1,200
Tony Charnley	75	72	69	73	289	1,000
Bob E. Smith	76	71	70	72	289	1,000
David A. Russell	71	75	73	70	289	1,000

Lancia Italian Open

Monticello Golf Course, Como, Italy
Par 36-36—72; 6,960 yards

May 18-21
purse, £255,450

	SCORES				TOTAL	MONEY
Ronan Rafferty	71	69	68	65	273	£42,589
Sam Torrance	69	70	65	70	274	28,371.09
Magnus Persson	66	72	69	68	275	15,995.69
Robert Lee	66	73	69	69	277	12,772.39
Paul Carman	70	69	67	72	278	9,885.66
Andrew Sherborne	72	70	65	71	278	9,885.66
David Feherty	65	72	69	73	279	5,915.86
Severiano Ballesteros	71	69	68	71	279	5,915.86
Luis Carbonetti	76	68	67	68	279	5,915.86
Frank Nobilo	71	70	71	67	279	5,915.86
Neil Hansen	71	72	71	65	279	5,915.86
Mark James	70	71	69	70	280	4,135
Philip Parkin	74	68	68	70	280	4,135
Constantino Rocca	69	76	72	63	280	4,135
Marc Pendaries	72	70	70	69	281	3,674.92
Mike Harwood	72	68	73	68	281	3,674.92
Craig Parry	70	71	70	71	282	3,193.10
Carl Magnus Stromberg	69	70	74	69	282	3,193.10
Ruud Bos	70	71	73	68	282	3,193.10
Jose Davila	76	68	70	68	282	3,193.10
Massimo Mannelli	70	71	74	67	282	3,193.10
Mariano Aparicio	68	72	70	73	283	2,834.95
Ross McFarlane	69	68	75	71	283	2,834.95
Giuseppe Cali	70	70	73	70	283	2,834.95
Gordon J. Brand	70	72	69	73	284	2,567.43
Paul Hoad	71	72	71	70	284	2,567.43
Paul Curry	69	74	72	69	284	2,567.43
Mark Roe	68	73	75	68	284	2,567.43
Jesper Parnevik	70	72	69	74	285	2,259.98
Roger Chapman	72	71	68	74	285	2,259.98
Noel Ratcliffe	72	71	72	70	285	2,259.98
Steven Bottomley	71	74	72	68	285	2,259.98
Barry Lane	71	72	68	75	286	1,966.92
Jacob Rasmussen	71	74	70	71	286	1,966.92
Keith Waters	71	70	74	71	286	1,966.92
Peter McWhinney	71	72	72	71	286	1,966.92
Eduardo Romero	71	74	70	71	286	1,966.92
Wayne Stephens	74	69	73	70	286	1,966.92
David Ray	72	73	69	73	287	1,684.57
Miguel Angel Jimenez	70	75	70	72	287	1,684.57
Jamie Howell	73	72	72	70	287	1,684.57
Vijay Singh	73	70	74	70	287	1,684.57
Peter Senior	72	72	73	70	287	1,684.57
Neal Briggs	70	71	72	75	288	1,404.53
Peter Mitchell	71	74	70	73	288	1,404.53
Baldovino Dassu	69	74	72	73	288	1,404.53
Delio Lovato	74	71	71	72	288	1,404.53
Mark Davis	69	74	75	70	288	1,404.53
Jerry Anderson	70	75	74	69	288	1,404.53
Michael Allen	73	69	75	72	289	1,199.57
Jeremy Bennett	74	71	73	71	289	1,199.57

Volvo PGA Championship

Wentworth Club, West Course, Surrey, England
Par 35-37—72; 6,945 yards

May 26-29
purse, £350,000

	SCORES				TOTAL	MONEY
Nick Faldo	67	69	69	67	272	£58,330
Ian Woosnam	67	72	68	67	274	38,860
Craig Parry	68	68	69	71	276	21,910
Severiano Ballesteros	73	74	65	66	278	14,860
Mark McNulty	70	69	69	70	278	14,860
Christy O'Connor, Jr.	71	68	74	65	278	14,860
Denis Durnian	73	68	69	69	279	10,500
Vijay Singh	71	70	71	68	280	7,863.33
Mark James	71	75	68	66	280	7,863.33
Gordon J. Brand	74	72	65	69	280	7,863.33
Jeff Hawkes	75	70	66	70	281	5,860
Jose-Maria Olazabal	72	74	69	66	281	5,860
Gavin Levenson	70	69	69	73	281	5,860
Neil Hansen	69	70	72	70	281	5,860
Ronan Rafferty	72	69	71	70	282	5,140
Jesper Parnevik	72	70	67	74	283	4,930
Peter Fowler	71	70	74	69	284	4,526.67
Paul Curry	68	72	73	71	284	4,526.67
Eamonn Darcy	72	71	71	70	284	4,526.67
Brett Ogle	68	73	70	74	285	3,990
Sam Torrance	71	75	70	69	285	3,990
Bernhard Langer	73	69	68	75	285	3,990
Eduardo Romero	71	73	70	71	285	3,990
Glenn Ralph	72	71	71	71	285	3,990
Philip Walton	73	70	71	72	286	3,360
Stephen McAllister	71	74	69	72	286	3,360
Stephen Hamill	71	72	70	73	286	3,360
Michael Allen	73	72	73	68	286	3,360
Gordon Brand, Jr.	72	74	69	71	286	3,360
Roger Chapman	77	69	68	72	286	3,360
Carl Mason	69	76	74	67	286	3,360
Bernard Gallacher	74	73	70	70	287	2,800
Andrew Murray	70	71	73	73	287	2,800
Johan Rystrom	73	74	67	73	287	2,800
Malcolm Mackenzie	75	71	69	72	287	2,800
Ross McFarlane	70	70	74	73	287	2,800
Michael McLean	76	69	75	68	288	2,520
Howard Clark	75	66	74	73	288	2,520
Mike Smith	74	73	71	70	288	2,520
Magnus Persson	74	72	69	74	289	2,380
Ken Brown	71	73	69	77	290	2,170
Philip Harrison	76	69	74	71	290	2,170
Bill Longmuir	69	72	73	76	290	2,170
Gerry Taylor	72	73	68	77	290	2,170
Mike Harwood	72	72	70	76	290	2,170
Paul Kent	79	68	72	72	291	1,855
Ove Sellberg	71	73	71	76	291	1,855
Jerry Haas	73	73	73	72	291	1,855
Kevin Dickens	74	73	73	71	291	1,855
Mike Clayton	74	73	75	70	292	1,610
Ian Young	71	75	74	72	292	1,610
Peter Senior	71	74	73	74	292	1,610

Dunhill British Masters

Woburn Golf and Country Club, Bow Brickhill, England
Par 34-38—72; 6,940 yards

June 1-4
purse, £300,000

	SCORES				TOTAL	MONEY
Nick Faldo	71	65	65	66	267	£50,000
Ronan Rafferty	70	65	67	69	271	33,300
Christy O'Connor, Jr.	69	66	73	68	276	15,493.33
Ove Sellberg	71	66	70	69	276	15,493.33
Mike Harwood	69	70	66	71	276	15,493.33
Ian Woosnam	71	70	70	66	277	9,000
Rick Hartmann	70	69	71	67	277	9,000
Mike Smith	71	69	66	71	277	9,000
Mark James	69	68	70	71	278	6,080
Peter Senior	74	66	66	72	278	6,080
Peter Mitchell	67	73	64	74	278	6,080
Jose-Maria Olazabal	69	71	71	68	279	4,860
Jose-Maria Canizares	69	67	71	72	279	4,860
Jeff Hawkes	73	65	69	72	279	4,860
Gordon Brand, Jr.	72	73	67	68	280	4,320
Jose Rivero	69	70	71	70	280	4,320
Ian Mosey	70	73	69	69	281	3,810
Mike Clayton	72	70	70	69	281	3,810
Bob Shearer	72	71	69	69	281	3,810
Ross McFarlane	72	73	65	71	281	3,810
Mark Mouland	71	70	72	69	282	3,465
Peter O'Malley	73	70	69	70	282	3,465
Sam Torrance	73	69	68	73	283	3,240
Richard Boxall	71	72	69	71	283	3,240
Frank Nobilo	70	75	69	69	283	3,240
Mark McNulty	72	70	66	76	284	2,880
Des Smyth	70	73	69	72	284	2,880
Peter Fowler	71	67	71	75	284	2,880
Paul Curry	66	76	69	73	284	2,880
Tony Johnstone	71	70	70	73	284	2,880
Neil Hansen	71	70	70	74	285	2,497.50
David Feherty	71	73	70	71	285	2,497.50
Colin Montgomerie	70	73	70	72	285	2,497.50
Carl Mason	72	70	71	72	285	2,497.50
Eamonn Darcy	68	70	73	75	286	2,070
Anders Forsbrand	73	71	68	74	286	2,070
Vicente Fernandez	73	71	70	72	286	2,070
Martin Poxon	71	72	70	73	286	2,070
Manuel Calero	72	72	69	73	286	2,070
Eduardo Romero	74	69	72	71	286	2,070
Tony Charnley	70	68	71	77	286	2,070
Philip Walton	71	69	72	74	286	2,070
Bernard Gallacher	77	67	69	73	286	2,070
Mark Roe	70	71	70	75	286	2,070
Mark Davis	73	71	69	74	287	1,620
Craig Parry	70	73	74	70	287	1,620
Paul Kent	71	72	70	74	287	1,620
Denis Durnian	71	70	76	70	287	1,620
Ross Drummond	71	71	74	71	287	1,620
Armando Saavedra	69	71	76	72	288	1,380
Hugh Baiocchi	72	71	71	74	288	1,380
Keith Waters	70	73	70	75	288	1,380

Wang Four Stars National Pro-Celebrity

Moor Park Golf Club, Richmansworth, England
Par 37-35—72; 6,855 yards

June 8-11
purse, £200,000

	SCORES				TOTAL	MONEY
Craig Parry	67	71	66	69	273	£32,000
Ian Woosnam	67	72	68	66	273	21,900
(Parry defeated Woosnam on first extra hole.)						
David Gilford	71	69	65	69	274	11,150
Mike Harwood	66	72	67	69	274	11,150
Barry Lane	72	68	68	68	276	7,650
Gordon Brand, Jr.	72	67	72	65	276	7,650
Jerry Anderson	70	69	69	69	277	5,800
Brian Marchbank	73	69	67	69	278	3,818
Peter Senior	72	67	68	71	278	3,818
Bob Shearer	69	72	65	72	278	3,818
Jeff Hawkes	71	70	66	71	278	3,818
Ross McFarlane	68	74	67	69	278	3,818
Michael McLean	67	70	73	69	279	2,650
Anders Sorensen	73	67	67	72	279	2,650
Sam Torrance	74	72	64	69	279	2,650
Denis Durnian	69	70	68	73	280	2,273.33
Michael King	75	72	66	67	280	2,273.33
Andrew Chandler	69	71	72	68	280	2,273.33
Des Smyth	73	69	67	71	280	2,273.33
David Williams	68	68	71	73	280	2,273.33
Peter Mitchell	70	75	67	68	280	2,273.33
Neil Hansen	70	73	68	70	281	1,877.50
Mark Roe	72	70	68	71	281	1,877.50
Tommy Horton	68	73	71	69	281	1,877.50
Paul Curry	71	72	69	69	281	1,877.50
Colin Montgomerie	73	68	72	69	282	1,608.57
Jose-Maria Canizares	73	70	68	71	282	1,608.57
John Bland	71	71	74	66	282	1,608.57
Stephen Bennett	71	69	67	75	282	1,608.57
Ossie Moore	71	73	71	67	282	1,608.57
Tony Charnley	72	70	69	71	282	1,608.57
Frank Nobilo	70	70	70	72	282	1,608.57
Roger Chapman	72	71	69	71	283	1,380
Bill Malley	70	70	73	70	283	1,380
Peter Fowler	72	72	68	71	283	1,380
Michael Allen	71	74	68	70	283	1,380
David Feherty	69	72	69	74	284	1,200
Eamonn Darcy	72	72	72	68	284	1,200
Armando Saavedra	75	68	70	71	284	1,200
Glenn Ralph	73	68	74	69	284	1,200
Bernard Gallacher	73	71	68	72	284	1,200
Ian Mosey	70	75	67	73	285	965
Bob E. Smith	71	72	72	70	285	965
Stephen McAllister	73	71	72	69	285	965
Ian Young	75	66	70	74	285	965
Martin Poxon	70	74	67	74	285	965
Paul Broadhurst	71	68	75	71	285	965
Brian Waites	69	72	70	74	285	965
David Jones	72	65	75	73	285	965
Brian Barnes	70	74	70	72	286	820
Gavin Levenson	73	74	72	67	286	820
Ron Commans	75	72	70	69	286	820
Jose Rivero	71	75	70	70	286	820
Philip Harrison	71	72	71	72	286	820

NM English Open

The Belfry Golf and Country Club, Brabazon Course,
Sutton Coldfield, England
Par 36-36—72; 7,202 yards

June 15-18
purse, £250,000

	SCORES				TOTAL	MONEY
Mark James	72	70	69	68	279	£41,660
Eamonn Darcy	70	71	67	72	280	18,636.67
Craig Parry	66	74	73	67	280	18,636.67
Sam Torrance	66	73	70	71	280	18,636.67
Bryan Norton	74	70	67	71	282	9,675
John Bland	69	70	70	73	282	9,675
Martin Poxon	69	72	69	73	283	6,450
Peter Teravainen	71	75	69	68	283	6,450
Christy O'Connor, Jr.	71	73	68	71	283	6,450
Jose Davila	68	75	73	68	284	4,235
Ronan Rafferty	72	67	73	72	284	4,235
Mats Lanner	72	71	69	72	284	4,235
Jeff Hawkes	67	71	73	73	284	4,235
Roger Chapman	73	72	73	66	284	4,235
Steen Tinning	66	78	71	69	284	4,235
*Russell Claydon	72	71	71	70	284	
Jean Van De Velde	73	70	72	70	285	3,190.83
Howard Clark	71	75	68	71	285	3,190.83
Peter Mitchell	74	71	70	70	285	3,190.83
Mark Davis	71	69	71	74	285	3,190.83
Bill Malley	71	72	73	69	285	3,190.83
Mark Mouland	65	74	69	74	285	3,190.83
Jose-Maria Canizares	71	74	67	74	286	2,700
Kevin Dickens	70	71	72	73	286	2,700
Brian Evans	71	70	71	74	286	2,700
Alberto Binaghi	74	71	72	69	286	2,700
Tony Johnstone	72	72	70	72	286	2,700
Tony Charnley	72	69	73	73	287	2,253.57
Ossie Moore	70	73	73	71	287	2,253.57
David Feherty	71	75	69	72	287	2,253.57
Keith Waters	68	72	74	73	287	2,253.57
Manuel Pinero	73	70	72	72	287	2,253.57
Ken Brown	71	69	70	77	287	2,253.57
Miguel Angel Martin	74	68	74	71	287	2,253.57
Barry Lane	71	74	70	73	288	1,850
Ross McFarlane	73	71	75	69	288	1,850
Brian Marchbank	71	74	69	74	288	1,850
Frank Nobilo	72	71	70	75	288	1,850
David Ray	72	70	74	72	288	1,850
Peter Senior	74	71	72	71	288	1,850
Richard Boxall	75	70	70	73	288	1,850
Michael McLean	72	71	73	73	289	1,600
David Williams	71	73	74	71	289	1,600
Mark Roe	70	71	73	75	289	1,600
Carl Mason	74	70	77	69	290	1,425
Paul Hoad	71	70	75	74	290	1,425
Mike Smith	71	72	74	73	290	1,425
David A. Russell	75	70	72	73	290	1,425
Ross Drummond	74	71	72	74	291	1,300
Ove Sellberg	71	73	73	75	292	1,250
Brian Barnes	74	69	73	77	293	1,000
Bernard Gallacher	69	74	72	78	293	1,000
Bob E. Smith	70	73	75	75	293	1,000

	SCORES				TOTAL	MONEY
Robert Lee	73	72	74	74	293	1,000
David Gilford	73	73	70	77	293	1,000
Neil Hansen	69	72	77	75	293	1,000
David Jones	70	76	73	74	293	1,000
Jamie Howell	72	74	72	75	293	1,000
Juan Rosa	72	68	79	74	293	1,000

Carrolls Irish Open

Portmarnock Golf Club, Dublin, Ireland
Par 36-36—72; 7,102 yards

June 22-25
purse, £262,697

	SCORES				TOTAL	MONEY
Ian Woosnam	70	67	71	70	278	£43,782.84
Philip Walton	68	69	69	72	278	29,159.37
(Woosnam defeated Walton on first extra hole.)						
Brett Ogle	69	69	74	70	282	13,566.84
Ronan Rafferty	67	71	72	72	282	13,566.84
Mark McNulty	71	67	71	73	282	13,566.84
Sam Torrance	71	70	72	70	283	7,381.79
Jose-Maria Olazabal	69	70	73	71	283	7,381.79
Mark Davis	73	71	66	73	283	7,381.79
Peter McWhinney	70	68	73	72	283	7,381.79
Eamonn Darcy	71	70	69	74	284	5,253.94
Bob E. Smith	69	71	73	72	285	4,527.15
Christy O'Connor, Jr.	68	71	71	75	285	4,527.15
Peter Senior	68	70	76	71	285	4,527.15
Mark Roe	73	72	70	71	286	4,019.26
Mark Mouland	67	73	73	74	287	3,426.32
Ossie Moore	68	74	75	70	287	3,426.32
Mike Miller	71	70	75	71	287	3,426.32
Bill Longmuir	69	72	72	74	287	3,426.32
Sandy Lyle	64	73	74	76	287	3,426.32
Martin Sludds	73	72	69	73	287	3,426.32
Ove Sellberg	69	72	72	74	287	3,426.32
Manuel Pinero	70	73	70	75	288	2,797.73
Wayne Riley	69	72	74	73	288	2,797.73
Luis Carbonetti	73	71	68	76	288	2,797.73
Howard Clark	69	70	74	75	288	2,797.73
Des Smyth	71	72	68	77	288	2,797.73
Martin Poxon	69	71	72	76	288	2,797.73
Brian Marchbank	72	71	75	71	289	2,443.08
Bernhard Langer	73	69	70	77	289	2,443.08
Gordon Brand, Jr.	69	71	74	75	289	2,443.08
Christy O'Connor, Jr.	72	72	70	76	290	2,186.95
Magnus Jonsson	72	69	77	72	290	2,186.95
Lyndsay Stephen	71	71	73	75	290	2,186.95
Lee Jones	73	69	73	75	290	2,186.95
Magnus Persson	70	75	73	73	291	1,943.96
Richard Boxall	69	70	75	77	291	1,943.96
Jimmy Heggarty	72	73	70	76	291	1,943.96
Frank Nobilo	73	72	71	75	291	1,943.96
Wayne Stephens	69	69	76	77	291	1,943.96
David Feherty	72	71	74	75	292	1,707.53
Sandy Stephen	71	69	74	78	292	1,707.53
Andrew Chandler	71	74	70	77	292	1,707.53
Kevin Dickens	74	68	74	76	292	1,707.53

	SCORES				TOTAL	MONEY
Paul Carrigill	70	72	73	78	293	1,471.10
Jim Thorpe	73	71	75	74	293	1,471.10
Paul Broadhurst	72	73	73	75	293	1,471.10
David Jones	69	73	71	80	293	1,471.10
Andrew Sherborne	72	72	72	77	293	1,471.10
John Morgan	73	72	72	77	294	1,208.41
David A. Russell	73	72	71	78	294	1,208.41
John McHenry	69	73	75	77	294	1,208.41
Barry Lane	72	72	74	76	294	1,208.41
Bill Malley	65	74	78	77	294	1,208.41

Peugeot French Open

Chantilly Golf Club, Paris, France
Par 35-35—70; 7,016 yards

June 29-July 2
purse, £313,405

	SCORES				TOTAL	MONEY
Nick Faldo	70	70	64	69	273	£52,233.36
Hugh Baiocchi	69	67	68	70	274	23,359.37
Mark Roe	69	68	67	70	274	23,359.37
Bernhard Langer	70	67	71	66	274	23,359.37
Mark James	70	70	66	69	275	10,368.85
Ian Woosnam	67	70	69	69	275	10,368.85
Mike Harwood	68	68	69	70	275	10,368.85
Philip Parkin	71	68	72	64	275	10,368.85
Ronan Rafferty	69	67	66	74	276	6,351.65
Mark McNulty	70	70	70	66	276	6,351.65
Gordon Brand, Jr.	69	67	69	71	276	6,351.65
Carl Mason	70	70	66	71	277	5,076.82
Severiano Ballesteros	71	64	71	71	277	5,076.82
Grant Turner	72	67	75	63	277	5,076.82
Richard Boxall	69	73	67	69	278	4,237.03
Barry Lane	72	67	73	66	278	4,237.03
Jose-Maria Olazabal	66	70	72	70	278	4,237.03
Miguel Angel Martin	68	70	71	69	278	4,237.03
Des Smyth	71	70	72	65	278	4,237.03
Jose Rivero	72	68	68	71	279	3,525.80
Peter Mitchell	72	72	69	66	279	3,525.80
John Bland	70	66	71	72	279	3,525.80
Miguel Angel Jimenez	69	69	69	72	279	3,525.80
Roger Chapman	73	68	71	67	279	3,525.80
Michael Allen	67	69	69	74	279	3,525.80
Ian Mosey	72	69	68	71	280	3,149.71
David Williams	71	72	67	70	280	3,149.71
Eduardo Romero	73	70	68	70	281	2,740.05
David Jones	72	70	69	70	281	2,740.05
Keith Waters	70	71	73	67	281	2,740.05
Bill Malley	75	69	69	68	281	2,740.05
Sam Torrance	74	68	67	72	281	2,740.05
Andrew Murray	69	73	67	72	281	2,740.05
Jeff Hawkes	71	71	68	71	281	2,740.05
Bryan Norton	69	71	72	70	282	2,225.17
Jean Van De Velde	70	72	73	67	282	2,225.17
Howard Clark	71	69	73	69	282	2,225.17
David Feherty	71	68	71	72	282	2,225.17
Manuel Pinero	72	72	69	69	282	2,225.17
Jimmy Heggarty	71	73	67	71	282	2,225.17

	SCORES				TOTAL	MONEY
Bob E. Smith	74	70	68	70	282	2,225.17
Alberto Binaghi	75	67	70	70	282	2,225.17
Vijay Singh	75	69	68	71	283	1,880.42
John Morgan	70	69	69	75	283	1,880.42
Magnus Persson	68	73	73	69	283	1,880.42
Mikael Krantz	72	67	71	74	284	1,723.72
Luis Carbonetti	71	70	70	73	284	1,723.72
Armando Saavedra	72	69	70	74	285	1,567.02
Denis Durnian	70	68	69	78	285	1,567.02
Anders Sorensen	73	67	74	71	285	1,567.02

Torras Monte Carlo Open

Mont Agel Golf Club, Monte Carlo   July 5-8
Par 34-35—69; 6,198 yards   purse, £289,715

	SCORES				TOTAL	MONEY
Mark McNulty	68	64	64	65	261	£48,285.85
Jeff Hawkes	64	72	67	64	267	25,147.28
Jose-Maria Canizares	68	66	65	68	267	25,147.28
Peter Senior	66	66	67	69	268	14,485.76
Robert Lee	68	70	69	64	271	11,202.32
Peter Mitchell	65	68	67	71	271	11,202.32
Peter Fowler	66	72	70	64	272	7,967.17
Luis Carbonetti	68	66	71	67	272	7,967.17
Gavin Levenson	70	70	67	66	273	5,452.44
Michael Allen	71	67	70	65	273	5,452.44
Bernhard Langer	66	68	71	68	273	5,452.44
Jose Rivero	67	71	67	68	273	5,452.44
Miguel Angel Jimenez	72	64	68	69	273	5,452.44
Mikael Krantz	66	69	70	70	275	4,002.90
Andrew Sherborne	65	71	73	66	275	4,002.90
Rodger Davis	69	69	69	68	275	4,002.90
Jim Rutledge	69	68	66	72	275	4,002.90
Neal Briggs	70	69	68	68	275	4,002.90
Denis Durnian	71	62	71	71	275	4,002.90
Antonio Garrido	68	70	68	70	276	3,259.30
Hugh Baiocchi	70	67	70	69	276	3,259.30
Miguel Angel Martin	66	67	69	74	276	3,259.30
Grant Turner	63	70	70	73	276	3,259.30
Raymond Floyd	67	68	70	71	276	3,259.30
Craig Parry	72	62	78	64	276	3,259.30
Ian Mosey	70	71	71	65	277	2,654.52
Mark Mouland	66	67	68	76	277	2,654.52
Jerry Haas	71	68	71	67	277	2,654.52
Alberto Binaghi	67	67	72	71	277	2,654.52
Mike Smith	70	68	72	67	277	2,654.52
Paul Hoad	69	71	72	65	277	2,654.52
David Williams	72	68	72	65	277	2,654.52
Philip Parkin	69	69	72	67	277	2,654.52
Paolo Quirici	66	70	71	71	278	2,201.83
Ronald Stelten	70	71	66	71	278	2,201.83
Jesper Parnevik	69	72	69	68	278	2,201.83
Peter McWhinney	69	71	69	69	278	2,201.83
John O'Leary	70	70	68	70	278	2,201.83
Stephen McAllister	68	68	73	70	279	1,883.15
Robin Mann	63	70	76	70	279	1,883.15

	SCORES				TOTAL	MONEY
Mike Harwood	71	69	68	71	279	1,883.15
Lee Jones	71	68	69	71	279	1,883.15
Paul Curry	69	68	69	73	279	1,883.15
Stephen Hamill	74	64	69	72	279	1,883.15
David Llewellyn	66	69	69	76	280	1,593.43
Bill Malley	70	71	69	70	280	1,593.43
Steven Bottomley	70	71	73	66	280	1,593.43
Jean Van De Velde	73	67	70	70	280	1,593.43
Silvio Grappasonni	69	70	69	73	281	1,361.66
Emanuele Bolognesi	66	69	74	72	281	1,361.66
Vijay Singh	72	69	73	67	281	1,361.66
Jose Davila	66	71	72	72	281	1,361.66

Bell's Scottish Open

Gleneagles Hotel, Kings Course, Gleneagles, Scotland
Par 35-36—71; 6,745 yards

July 12-15
purse, £300,000

	SCORES				TOTAL	MONEY
Michael Allen	73	66	70	63	272	£50,000
Jose-Maria Olazabal	67	70	68	69	274	26,040
Ian Woosnam	65	70	71	68	274	26,040
Ronan Rafferty	69	67	70	70	276	13,850
David Feherty	71	67	69	69	276	13,850
Mark McNulty	69	71	67	70	277	9,750
Eduardo Romero	72	66	70	69	277	9,750
Roger Chapman	69	70	70	69	278	7,110
Larry Rinker	73	66	68	71	278	7,110
Sandy Lyle	70	66	72	71	279	5,085
Martin Poxon	68	70	71	70	279	5,085
Des Smyth	67	72	74	66	279	5,085
Peter Fowler	72	69	68	70	279	5,085
Richard Boxall	72	69	69	69	279	5,085
Peter Senior	71	66	68	74	279	5,085
Mark James	72	69	69	70	280	3,967.50
Payne Stewart	72	70	70	68	280	3,967.50
Sam Torrance	71	71	69	69	280	3,967.50
Howard Clark	72	72	69	67	280	3,967.50
Brian Barnes	68	68	71	74	281	3,420
Jeff Hawkes	68	74	73	66	281	3,420
Jose Rivero	74	68	69	70	281	3,420
Barry Lane	72	69	72	68	281	3,420
Nick Faldo	70	72	72	67	281	3,420
Gordon Brand, Jr.	68	69	67	78	282	3,060
David Williams	75	67	68	72	282	3,060
Christy O'Connor, Jr.	72	70	68	72	282	3,060
Gavin Levenson	68	71	74	70	283	2,622.86
David Graham	71	70	73	69	283	2,622.86
David Gilford	68	68	73	74	283	2,622.86
Tony Charnley	70	74	66	73	283	2,622.86
Brett Ogle	70	71	72	70	283	2,622.86
Mike Clayton	69	71	73	70	283	2,622.86
Hugh Baiocchi	71	72	70	70	283	2,622.86
Craig Parry	71	69	71	73	284	2,220
Naomichi Ozaki	68	67	73	76	284	2,220
Lyndsay Stephen	73	70	72	69	284	2,220
Andrew Murray	73	70	70	71	284	2,220

	SCORES				TOTAL	MONEY
Vijay Singh	70	74	70	70	284	2,220
Ove Sellberg	73	68	75	69	285	1,890
Mark Davis	71	71	73	70	285	1,890
Derrick Cooper	73	71	70	71	285	1,890
James White	72	70	70	73	285	1,890
John Bland	74	69	73	69	285	1,890
Paul Mayo	73	71	70	71	285	1,890
Tommy Armour III	68	73	72	73	286	1,620
Stephen Bennett	72	71	73	70	286	1,620
Mark Roe	72	72	72	70	286	1,620
Paul Way	70	72	70	75	287	1,500
Keith Waters	73	69	72	74	288	1,410
Peter McWhinney	72	70	76	70	288	1,410

British Open Championship

Royal Troon Golf Club, Troon, Scotland   July 20-23
Par 36-36—72; 7,097 yards   purse, £771,300

	SCORES				TOTAL	MONEY
Mark Calcavecchia	71	68	68	68	275	£80,000
Wayne Grady	68	67	69	71	275	55,000
Greg Norman	69	70	72	64	275	55,000
(Playoff: Calcavecchia 4, 3, 3, 3; Norman 3, 3, 4, C; Grady 4, 4, 4, 4)						
Tom Watson	69	68	68	72	277	40,000
Jodie Mudd	73	67	68	70	278	30,000
Fred Couples	68	71	68	72	279	26,000
David Feherty	71	67	69	72	279	26,000
Eduardo Romero	68	70	75	67	280	21,000
Paul Azinger	68	73	67	72	280	21,000
Payne Stewart	72	65	69	74	280	21,000
Nick Faldo	71	71	70	69	281	17,000
Mark McNulty	75	70	70	66	281	17,000
Philip Walton	69	74	69	70	282	13,000
Howard Clark	72	68	72	70	282	13,000
Steve Pate	69	70	70	73	282	13,000
Roger Chapman	76	68	67	71	282	13,000
Mark James	69	70	71	72	282	13,000
Craig Stadler	73	69	69	71	282	13,000
Larry Mize	71	74	66	72	283	8,575
Derrick Cooper	69	70	76	68	283	8,575
Tom Kite	70	74	67	72	283	8,575
Don Pooley	73	70	69	71	283	8,575
Vijay Singh	71	73	69	71	284	6,733.33
Davis Love III	72	70	73	69	284	6,733.33
Jose-Maria Olazabal	68	72	69	75	284	6,733.33
Stephen Bennett	75	69	68	73	285	5,800
Lanny Wadkins	72	70	69	74	285	5,800
Chip Beck	75	69	68	73	285	5,800
Scott Simpson	73	66	72	74	285	5,800
Jeff Hawkes	75	67	69	75	286	4,711.11
Gary Koch	72	71	74	69	286	4,711.11
Jack Nicklaus	74	71	71	70	286	4,711.11
Peter Jacobsen	71	74	71	70	286	4,711.11
Brian Marchbank	69	74	73	70	286	4,711.11
Miguel Angel Martin	68	73	73	72	286	4,711.11
Ian Baker-Finch	72	69	70	75	286	4,711.11

	SCORES				TOTAL	MONEY
Masashi Ozaki	71	73	70	72	286	4,711.11
Mark Davis	77	68	67	74	286	4,711.11
Mike Harwood	71	72	72	72	287	4,100
Tommy Armour III	70	71	72	74	287	4,100
Jeff Woodland	74	67	75	71	287	4,100
Mark O'Meara	72	74	69	73	288	3,725
Lee Trevino	68	73	73	74	288	3,725
Raymond Floyd	73	68	73	74	288	3,725
Jose Rivero	71	75	72	70	288	3,725
Mark McCumber	71	68	70	80	289	3,550
Sandy Lyle	73	73	71	72	289	3,550
Naomichi Ozaki	71	71	69	78	289	3,550
Johnny Miller	72	69	76	73	290	3,400
Ian Woosnam	74	72	73	71	290	3,400
Christy O'Connor, Jr.	71	73	72	74	290	3,400
Brett Ogle	74	70	76	71	291	3,100
Mark Roe	74	71	73	73	291	3,100
Tateo Ozaki	75	71	73	72	291	3,100
Michael Allen	74	67	76	74	291	3,100
Tony Johnstone	71	71	74	75	291	3,100
Emmanuel Dussart	76	68	73	74	291	3,100
Richard Boxall	74	68	73	76	291	3,100
Gene Sauers	70	73	72	76	291	3,100
Ben Crenshaw	73	73	74	71	291	3,100
Curtis Strange	70	74	74	74	292	2,675
David Graham	74	72	69	77	292	2,675
Ken Green	75	71	68	78	292	2,675
Paul Hoad	72	71	77	72	292	2,675
Bob Tway	76	70	71	75	292	2,675
Ronan Rafferty	70	72	74	76	292	2,675
Mike Reid	74	72	73	73	292	2,675
Wayne Stephens	66	72	76	78	292	2,675
Luis Carbonetti	71	72	74	76	293	2,425
Sandy Stephen	71	74	71	77	293	2,425
*Russell Claydon	70	74	74	75	293	
Colin Gillies	72	74	74	74	294	2,400
Brad Faxon	72	72	75	76	295	2,400
Peter Teravainen	72	73	72	78	295	2,400
Emlyn Aubrey	72	73	73	78	296	2,400
Martin Sludds	72	74	73	78	297	2,400
Severiano Ballesteros	72	73	76	78	299	2,400
*Robert Karlsson	75	70	76	78	299	
Gavin Levenson	69	76	77	79	301	2,400
Bernhard Langer	71	73	83	82	309	2,400

Out of Final 36 Holes

	SCORES		TOTAL
Stephen Hamill	74	73	147
Neil Hansen	73	74	147
Paul Affleck	72	75	147
Neil Briggs	77	70	147
Barry Lane	74	73	147
Peter Senior	74	73	147
Des Smyth	78	69	147
Tom Weiskopf	74	73	147
John Bland	72	75	147
Bob E. Smith	70	77	147
David Ray	73	74	147
Mike Smith	76	71	147
Stephen Field	76	71	147

	SCORES		TOTAL
Sam Torrance	70	77	147
Nick Price	74	73	147
Larry Nelson	73	74	147
Martin Poxon	71	76	147
Andy Bean	73	75	148
Paul Mayo	75	73	148
Brian Barnes	73	75	148
Gordon Brand, Jr.	76	72	148
Mike Clayton	74	74	148
Fuzzy Zoeller	73	75	148
*Ernie Els	72	76	148
Charles Bolling, Jr.	73	76	149
Wayne Henry	76	73	149
Denis Durnian	75	74	149
Peter Baker	74	75	149
*Gary Evans	73	76	149
Steen Tinning	78	72	150
Philip Parkin	73	77	150
Ross McFarlane	73	77	150
Paul Carrigill	78	72	150
Anders Sorensen	74	76	150
Keith Waters	74	76	150
Peter Mitchell	75	75	150
David Llewellyn	78	72	150
Steve Jones	73	77	150
Larry Rinker	75	75	150
Jonathan Sewell	78	72	150
Gary Emerson	75	75	150
Andrew Stubbs	72	78	150
Vicente Fernandez	75	76	151
Jeff Sluman	78	73	151
Gordon J. Brand	78	73	151
Paul Carman	76	75	151
Bryant Hiskey	75	77	152
Mark Mouland	77	75	152
Ken Brown	74	78	152
Eamonn Darcy	75	77	152
Gary Player	79	73	152
David Williams	77	75	152
Daniel Lozano	79	74	153
Wayne Riley	76	77	153
Paul Eales	74	79	153
John Price	80	73	153
David Frost	75	79	154
Chris Moody	81	73	154
*Stephen Dodd	79	75	154
*Gary Milne	79	75	154
Peter Cowen	81	74	155
Philip Harrison	79	76	155
*Andrew Hare	73	82	155
*Jerome O'Shea	80	75	155
Gordon Townhill	79	77	156
Paul Broadhurst	73	84	157
Rodger Davis	78	79	157
Tony Jacklin	80	77	157
Nobuo Serizawa	79	78	157
Paul Kent	78	79	157
David J. Russell	80	78	158
Johan Rystrom	79	79	158

	SCORES				TOTAL
*James Noon	81	77			158
John Garner	78	81			159
*Eric Meeks	81	80			161
Arnold Palmer	82	82			164

(All professionals who did not complete 72 holes received £500.)

KLM Open

Kennemer Golf & Country Club, Kennemer, Holland
Par 36-34—70; 6,634 yards

July 27-30
purse, £275,000

	SCORES				TOTAL	MONEY
Jose-Maria Olazabal	67	66	68	76	277	£45,830
Roger Chapman	70	67	71	69	277	23,875
Ronan Rafferty	72	66	66	73	277	23,875
(Olazabal defeated Chapman on first extra hole, Rafferty on ninth extra hole.)						
Jesper Parnevik	69	67	72	70	278	13,750
Gordon Brand, Jr.	65	68	74	72	279	11,665
Sam Torrance	69	70	72	69	280	8,937.50
Craig Parry	69	65	70	76	280	8,937.50
Des Smyth	71	68	70	72	281	6,180
Miguel Angel Martin	68	71	71	71	281	6,180
David Feherty	72	69	68	72	281	6,180
Severiano Ballesteros	67	76	72	67	282	5,050
Peter Fowler	70	70	68	75	283	4,483.33
Eamonn Darcy	66	73	76	68	283	4,483.33
Carl Mason	68	71	69	75	283	4,483.33
Mark Roe	68	72	70	74	284	3,891.67
Christy O'Connor, Jr.	71	69	68	76	284	3,891.67
Michael King	69	73	68	74	284	3,891.67
David Jones	70	70	71	74	285	3,560
Sandy Lyle	71	67	71	77	286	2,967.73
Tony Charnley	70	74	72	70	286	2,967.73
Stephen McAllister	74	68	69	75	286	2,967.73
Michael Allen	75	64	70	77	286	2,967.73
Lyndsay Stephen	67	70	74	75	286	2,967.73
David Williams	69	70	79	68	286	2,967.73
Barry Lane	70	68	73	75	286	2,967.73
Colin Montgomerie	67	72	72	75	286	2,967.73
Philip Harrison	69	69	77	71	286	2,967.73
Bryan Norton	70	71	70	75	286	2,967.73
Eduardo Romero	71	68	77	70	286	2,967.73
John Woof	70	69	71	77	287	2,300
Andrew Sherborne	72	70	73	72	287	2,300
Jamie Howell	73	69	73	72	287	2,300
Glenn Ralph	70	74	72	71	287	2,300
Sandy Stephen	76	68	71	72	287	2,300
Mike Miller	70	69	71	77	287	2,300
John O'Leary	70	73	70	75	288	1,990
Vicente Fernandez	73	70	72	73	288	1,990
Philip Walton	68	74	71	75	288	1,990
Anders Sorensen	72	71	74	71	288	1,990
Bob Shearer	71	73	70	75	289	1,618.89
Lee Jones	74	69	76	70	289	1,618.89
Andrew Murray	73	69	74	73	289	1,618.89
Mike Colandro	72	67	78	72	289	1,618.89

	SCORES				TOTAL	MONEY
Jonas Saxton	75	68	74	72	289	1,618.89
Jimmy Heggarty	72	68	73	76	289	1,618.89
Grant Turner	74	70	72	73	289	1,618.89
Paul Carman	67	72	75	75	289	1,618.89
Wayne Riley	69	70	73	77	289	1,618.89
Steen Tinning	73	66	75	76	290	1,235
Magnus Persson	70	71	74	75	290	1,235
Marc Pendaries	69	73	74	74	290	1,235
Leif Hederstrom	72	71	72	75	290	1,235
Marc Antoine Farry	70	71	72	77	290	1,235
Bob E. Smith	70	70	73	77	290	1,235

Scandinavian Enterprise Open

Drottingholm Golf Club, Stockholm, Sweden
Par 36-36—72; 6,747 yards

August 3-6
purse, £335,000

	SCORES				TOTAL	MONEY
Ronan Rafferty	70	69	64	65	268	£55,810
Michael Allen	67	71	67	65	270	37,180
Peter Senior	64	70	73	67	274	20,970
Gordon Brand, Jr.	70	70	66	69	275	15,475
Vijay Singh	69	70	67	69	275	15,475
Brett Ogle	68	70	70	68	276	10,887.50
Derrick Cooper	70	70	69	67	276	10,887.50
David Whelan	68	73	72	64	277	7,526.67
Mark Mouland	70	71	67	69	277	7,526.67
Jerry Haas	71	68	68	70	277	7,526.67
Joakim Haggman	70	73	69	66	278	5,962.50
Mats Lanner	68	72	72	66	278	5,962.50
Philip Harrison	64	71	71	73	279	4,939
Alberto Binaghi	70	69	70	70	279	4,939
Johan Tumba	67	70	71	71	279	4,939
Ossie Moore	72	71	66	70	279	4,939
David Feherty	72	70	71	66	279	4,939
Magnus Jonsson	71	71	68	70	280	3,886.88
Bob Shearer	72	70	71	67	280	3,886.88
Paul Hoad	69	69	71	71	280	3,886.88
Grant Turner	69	69	73	69	280	3,886.88
Ove Sellberg	69	70	71	70	280	3,886.88
Andrew Murray	74	67	70	69	280	3,886.88
John Slaughter	73	67	68	72	280	3,886.88
Jose-Maria Canizares	72	68	72	68	280	3,886.88
Anders Sorensen	73	69	71	68	281	3,025.56
Richard Boxall	69	70	72	70	281	3,025.56
Marc Antoine Farry	71	70	71	69	281	3,025.56
Peter Teravainen	67	72	72	70	281	3,025.56
Carl Mason	69	69	72	71	281	3,025.56
Andrew Sherborne	70	71	70	70	281	3,025.56
Eamonn Darcy	71	69	68	73	281	3,025.56
Jesper Parnevik	69	73	72	67	281	3,025.56
Christy O'Connor, Jr.	70	73	66	72	281	3,025.56
Mark Davis	71	69	74	68	282	2,445.83
Magnus Persson	71	70	73	68	282	2,445.83
Philip Walton	72	68	71	71	282	2,445.83
Des Smyth	72	68	71	71	282	2,445.83
Juan Anglada	68	70	74	70	282	2,445.83

	SCORES				TOTAL	MONEY
David Llewellyn	73	70	70	69	282	2,445.83
Andrew Canessa	69	73	70	71	283	2,110
Jon Heimer	69	71	74	69	283	2,110
Frank Nobilo	70	70	72	71	283	2,110
Mike Harwood	72	69	70	72	283	2,110
Leif Hederstrom	69	72	70	73	284	1,809
Brian Marchbank	68	74	72	70	284	1,809
Marc Pendaries	70	69	73	72	284	1,809
Gary Koch	71	71	68	74	284	1,809
Manuel Calero	70	73	73	68	284	1,809
David James	68	70	72	75	285	1,474
Rick Hartmann	72	70	73	70	285	1,474
Mariano Aparicio	75	67	71	72	285	1,474
Magnus Granqvist	68	72	72	73	285	1,474
Mark Roe	73	69	68	75	285	1,474

Benson & Hedges International Open

Fulford Golf Club, York, England
Par 36-36—72; 6,807 yards

August 10-13
purse, £300,000

	SCORES				TOTAL	MONEY
Gordon Brand, Jr.	64	72	72	64	272	£50,000
Derrick Cooper	67	66	68	72	273	33,300
Malcolm Mackenzie	66	68	71	69	274	18,780
Jose-Maria Canizares	65	72	70	69	276	15,000
Craig Parry	68	72	67	70	277	9,925
Howard Clark	69	67	69	72	277	9,925
Ian Mosey	69	67	69	72	277	9,925
John Bland	67	68	70	72	277	9,925
Peter Fowler	69	71	70	68	278	6,360
Bradley Hughes	62	71	71	74	278	6,360
Des Smyth	67	73	69	70	279	5,520
Philip Harrison	71	69	70	70	280	4,747.50
Jose Rivero	69	72	68	71	280	4,747.50
Gary Player	69	67	73	71	280	4,747.50
Eamonn Darcy	67	72	71	70	280	4,747.50
Andrew Oldcorn	72	71	66	72	281	4,140
Brett Ogle	72	69	68	72	281	4,140
Peter Senior	64	72	72	74	282	3,730
Jerry Haas	67	72	72	71	282	3,730
Antonio Garrido	70	70	70	72	282	3,730
David Jones	73	69	70	71	283	3,375
Gavin Levenson	69	74	70	70	283	3,375
Emmanuel Dussart	66	72	73	72	283	3,375
Tony Johnstone	73	69	69	72	283	3,375
David Williams	71	71	69	73	284	2,925
John O'Leary	68	74	70	72	284	2,925
Peter Baker	68	75	67	74	284	2,925
Richard Boxall	70	71	70	73	284	2,925
Andrew Murray	72	69	69	74	284	2,925
Andrew Stubbs	70	72	68	74	284	2,925
Philip Walton	71	65	75	74	285	2,466
David A. Russell	69	73	69	74	285	2,466
Carl Mason	69	74	71	71	285	2,466
Bernard Gallacher	67	72	74	72	285	2,466
Ross Drummond	72	68	72	73	285	2,466

	SCORES				TOTAL	MONEY
Bob E. Smith	70	72	72	72	286	2,100
Joe Higgins	71	71	69	75	286	2,100
Peter Allan	72	71	73	70	286	2,100
Rick Hartmann	67	68	78	73	286	2,100
Peter Mitchell	68	72	74	72	286	2,100
Ross McFarlane	66	74	71	75	286	2,100
Ken Brown	69	69	76	72	286	2,100
Mark Roe	71	72	71	73	287	1,740
Mark McNulty	66	73	76	72	287	1,740
Ignacio Gervas	72	69	70	76	287	1,740
Neil Hansen	71	70	73	73	287	1,740
David J. Russell	70	73	74	70	287	1,740
Armando Saavedra	71	70	73	74	288	1,500
Mike Clayton	71	72	75	70	288	1,500
Chris Moody	69	69	76	74	288	1,500

PLM Open

Bokskogen Golf Club, Malmo, Sweden
Par 36-36—72; 6,889 yards

August 17-20
purse, £300,000

	SCORES				TOTAL	MONEY
Mike Harwood	66	70	67	68	271	£50,000
Peter Senior	68	67	65	72	272	33,300
Sam Torrance	71	67	65	70	273	18,780
Mats Lanner	70	68	69	67	274	13,850
Bernhard Langer	68	66	69	71	274	13,850
Ronan Rafferty	69	69	66	72	276	9,750
Philip Walton	67	72	66	71	276	9,750
Ove Sellberg	69	73	65	70	277	7,110
Leif Hederstrom	71	66	70	70	277	7,110
Manuel Moreno	68	68	73	69	278	6,000
Jose-Maria Olazabal	70	70	70	69	279	4,790
Derrick Cooper	69	71	68	71	279	4,790
Mike Clayton	68	73	67	71	279	4,790
Jeremy Bennett	70	70	68	71	279	4,790
Roger Chapman	69	71	67	72	279	4,790
Frank Nobilo	71	71	67	70	279	4,790
Howard Clark	69	71	70	70	280	3,960
Barry Lane	64	74	70	72	280	3,960
Robin Mann	70	70	71	70	281	3,610
Ruud Bos	67	72	72	70	281	3,610
Jose Rivero	73	67	69	72	281	3,610
Lyndsay Stephen	68	73	71	70	282	3,150
Ian Woosnam	69	72	68	73	282	3,150
Wayne Riley	71	70	71	70	282	3,150
Mark Roe	70	74	70	68	282	3,150
Johan Rystrom	69	66	72	75	282	3,150
Mark James	73	71	69	69	282	3,150
Rodger Davis	71	71	70	70	282	3,150
Clive Tucker	69	69	71	74	283	2,580
Craig Parry	71	72	72	68	283	2,580
Daniel Lozano	71	71	73	68	283	2,580
Kevin Dickens	70	73	66	74	283	2,580
Anders Forsbrand	67	75	72	69	283	2,580
Grant Turner	70	69	73	71	283	2,580
Peter Baker	69	70	71	74	284	2,250

	SCORES				TOTAL	MONEY
Vijay Singh	73	70	71	70	284	2,250
Magnus Sunesson	71	69	72	72	284	2,250
Gordon Brand, Jr.	71	71	70	72	284	2,250
Neil Hansen	69	71	70	75	285	1,920
David Ecob	72	72	72	69	285	1,920
Fredrik Lindgren	69	73	71	72	285	1,920
Jean Van De Velde	72	71	70	72	285	1,920
Ronald Stelten	72	72	67	74	285	1,920
Steven Bottomley	69	71	73	72	285	1,920
Paul Hunstone	72	70	71	72	285	1,920
Joakim Haggman	69	74	77	66	286	1,620
Jerry Haas	72	70	71	73	286	1,620
Denis Durnian	70	70	73	73	286	1,620
Christy O'Connor, Jr.	72	71	72	72	287	1,350
Mark Davis	67	73	74	73	287	1,350
Tony Charnley	71	73	70	73	287	1,350
Magnus Jonsson	69	71	72	75	287	1,350
Ossie Moore	72	70	72	73	287	1,350
Stephen McAllister	70	73	73	71	287	1,350

German Open

Frankfurter Golf Club, Frankfurt, West Germany
Par 35-36—71; 6,686 yards

August 24-27
purse, £325,470

	SCORES				TOTAL	MONEY
Craig Parry	66	70	66	64	266	£54,222.95
Mark James	65	66	65	70	266	36,126.93
Michael Allen	68	66	64	69	267	20,374.29
Mike Harwood	65	65	68	70	268	16,273.39
Jose-Maria Canizares	66	72	62	69	269	10,772.99
Jerry Haas	66	69	64	70	269	10,772.99
Gordon Brand, Jr.	71	66	67	65	269	10,772.99
Bernhard Langer	68	69	67	65	269	10,772.99
Rick Hartmann	67	70	64	69	270	6,596.15
Brett Ogle	66	67	68	69	270	6,596.15
Jose Rivero	69	68	66	67	270	6,596.15
*Sven Struever	73	62	66	69	270	
Bill Malley	65	68	69	69	271	5,419.04
Ken Brown	66	70	65	70	271	5,419.04
Peter Senior	67	70	64	71	272	4,784.38
David Feherty	68	70	67	67	272	4,784.38
Derrick Cooper	71	65	69	67	272	4,784.38
Eduardo Romero	67	68	69	69	273	4,133.44
Luis Carbonetti	65	68	68	72	273	4,133.44
Carl Mason	68	69	66	70	273	4,133.44
Howard Clark	69	73	67	64	273	4,133.44
Richard Boxall	67	71	66	70	274	3,563.87
Barry Lane	71	71	64	68	274	3,563.87
Mark Davis	68	71	65	70	274	3,563.87
Mark McNulty	68	71	65	70	274	3,563.87
Colin Montgomerie	74	65	68	67	274	3,563.87
Mats Lanner	68	68	71	67	274	3,563.87
Magnus Persson	72	66	69	68	275	2,978.03
Christy O'Connor, Jr.	70	70	68	67	275	2,978.03
Miguel Angel Jimenez	72	69	69	65	275	2,978.03
Armando Saavedra	69	67	71	68	275	2,978.03

	SCORES				TOTAL	MONEY
John Bland	69	70	68	68	275	2,978.03
Stephen Bennett	66	74	64	71	275	2,978.03
Malcolm Mackenzie	69	73	66	68	276	2,538.65
Marc Antoine Farry	67	73	68	68	276	2,538.65
Ross Drummond	68	69	69	70	276	2,538.65
Hugh Baiocchi	71	67	66	72	276	2,538.65
Jean Van De Velde	67	71	68	70	276	2,538.65
Torsten Giedeon	70	69	67	71	277	2,245.73
Severiano Ballesteros	70	69	66	72	277	2,245.73
Roger Chapman	67	72	69	69	277	2,245.73
Martin Poxon	68	71	66	72	277	2,245.73
Mikael Krantz	67	69	71	71	278	2,017.90
Gavin Levenson	70	71	69	68	278	2,017.90
Frank Nobilo	69	73	65	71	278	2,017.90
David Ray	70	70	70	69	279	1,724.98
Paul Curry	70	65	72	72	279	1,724.98
Andrew Murray	67	67	74	71	279	1,724.98
Wayne Riley	73	69	67	70	279	1,724.98
Rodger Davis	69	72	69	69	279	1,724.98
Sandy Stephen	70	72	69	68	279	1,724.98

Ebel European Masters - Swiss Open

Crans-Sur-Sierre Golf Club, Sierre, Switzerland
Par 36-36—72; 6,811 yards

August 31-September 3
purse, £414,315

	SCORES				TOTAL	MONEY
Severiano Ballesteros	65	68	66	67	266	£69,024.48
Craig Parry	66	69	66	67	268	45,988.70
Stephen Bennett	65	67	66	71	269	25,935.97
Jose Rivero	66	64	67	73	270	19,141.24
Paolo Quirici	72	67	66	65	270	19,141.24
Barry Lane	67	65	67	72	271	14,500.94
Colin Montgomerie	68	66	67	71	272	12,429.38
Gavin Levenson	68	66	71	68	273	9,308.22
Mats Lanner	65	72	65	71	273	9,308.22
Jose-Maria Olazabal	69	70	69	65	273	9,308.22
Ossie Moore	66	70	68	73	277	6,769.87
Derrick Cooper	67	68	74	68	277	6,769.87
Manuel Garcia	68	69	70	70	277	6,769.87
Eduardo Romero	71	66	69	71	277	6,769.87
Jose-Maria Canizares	69	70	71	67	277	6,769.87
David Jones	67	68	71	72	278	5,377.78
Richard Boxall	70	70	67	71	278	5,377.78
Miguel Angel Jimenez	69	67	71	71	278	5,377.78
John Bland	69	68	70	71	278	5,377.78
Jerry Haas	66	68	72	72	278	5,377.78
Mariano Aparicio	73	66	72	68	279	4,474.58
Brian Marchbank	68	72	70	69	279	4,474.58
Massimo Mannelli	67	68	75	69	279	4,474.58
Alberto Binaghi	68	72	72	67	279	4,474.58
Magnus Persson	68	70	71	70	279	4,474.58
Malcolm Mackenzie	68	70	72	69	279	4,474.58
Keith Waters	69	72	67	71	279	4,474.58
Sandy Lyle	70	69	72	69	280	3,790.96
Carl Mason	68	73	70	69	280	3,790.96
Peter McWhinney	73	64	74	69	280	3,790.96

	SCORES				TOTAL	MONEY
Mark McNulty	70	71	67	72	280	3,790.96
Roger Chapman	72	69	71	69	281	3,148.78
Paul Carrigill	70	72	70	69	281	3,148.78
Leif Hederstrom	68	73	72	68	281	3,148.78
Paul Curry	68	73	71	69	281	3,148.78
David A. Russell	69	68	72	72	281	3,148.78
Jeff Hawkes	70	69	68	74	281	3,148.78
Ken Brown	65	72	75	69	281	3,148.78
Tony Charnley	73	69	68	71	281	3,148.78
Mike Harwood	66	74	71	70	281	3,148.78
Ron Commans	71	70	73	68	282	2,568.74
Bernhard Langer	65	75	73	69	282	2,568.74
Lyndsay Stephen	67	70	75	70	282	2,568.74
Philip Walton	70	71	70	71	282	2,568.74
Michael Allen	72	68	73	69	282	2,568.74
Ronald Stelten	67	69	71	76	283	2,237.29
Bob E. Smith	70	72	71	70	283	2,237.29
Juan Anglada	69	70	72	72	283	2,237.29
Aaron Meeks	69	69	74	72	284	1,822.98
Frank Nobilo	68	72	71	73	284	1,822.98
Gordon J. Brand	67	72	75	70	284	1,822.98
Mikael Krantz	68	71	73	72	284	1,822.98
Bill Longmuir	66	74	73	71	284	1,822.98
Manuel Moreno	68	71	73	72	284	1,822.98
Michael King	68	69	78	69	284	1,822.98

Panasonic European Open

Walton Heath Golf Club, Surrey, England
Par 36-36—72; 7,108 yards

September 7-10
purse, £350,000

	SCORES				TOTAL	MONEY
Andrew Murray	66	68	71	72	277	£58,330
Frank Nobilo	70	69	69	70	278	38,860
Sam Torrance	70	71	69	70	280	21,910
Craig Parry	73	72	70	66	281	16,165
Ian Woosnam	71	68	70	72	281	16,165
Russell Claydon	70	68	71	74	283	11,375
Ross Drummond	70	69	71	73	283	11,375
Sandy Lyle	69	74	71	70	284	7,863.33
Rodger Davis	69	73	72	70	284	7,863.33
David Feherty	72	71	71	70	284	7,863.33
Mark James	70	73	75	67	285	6,230
Scott Hoch	69	69	77	70	285	6,230
Peter Fowler	67	72	79	68	286	4,947.14
Martin Poxon	70	71	72	73	286	4,947.14
Michael Allen	74	69	76	67	286	4,947.14
Vijay Singh	74	70	73	69	286	4,947.14
Derrick Cooper	72	69	70	75	286	4,947.14
John Bland	73	73	71	69	286	4,947.14
Peter Senior	70	68	71	77	286	4,947.14
Eduardo Romero	70	73	74	71	288	3,990
Roger Chapman	71	67	78	72	288	3,990
Nick Faldo	72	73	73	70	288	3,990
Tony Johnstone	71	76	71	70	288	3,990
Rick Hartmann	70	70	76	72	288	3,990
Colin Montgomerie	71	70	76	72	289	3,622.50

	SCORES				TOTAL	MONEY
Howard Clark	70	72	77	70	289	3,622.50
Jesper Parnevik	73	74	72	71	290	3,155
Peter Teravainen	72	75	76	67	290	3,155
Ronan Rafferty	74	72	74	70	290	3,155
Hugh Baiocchi	73	67	75	75	290	3,155
Paul Kent	74	69	74	73	290	3,155
Des Smyth	73	68	76	73	290	3,155
Joe Higgins	71	75	77	67	290	3,155
Masahiro Kuramoto	68	75	72	76	291	2,765
Ken Brown	72	73	76	70	291	2,765
Jean Van De Velde	70	71	80	71	292	2,450
Steen Tinning	71	71	79	71	292	2,450
Stephen McAllister	69	72	73	78	292	2,450
Ron Commans	71	73	74	74	292	2,450
Marc Pendaries	71	74	75	72	292	2,450
David Llewellyn	71	72	75	74	292	2,450
Gordon Brand, Jr.	69	74	77	72	292	2,450
Wayne Riley	72	75	77	69	293	2,065
Stephen Bennett	71	71	76	75	293	2,065
Tony Charnley	75	68	77	73	293	2,065
Gordon J. Brand	73	73	71	76	293	2,065
Jamie Howell	72	74	77	71	294	1,750
Richard Boxall	75	72	73	74	294	1,750
Luis Carbonetti	74	73	77	70	294	1,750
John Slaughter	72	72	80	70	294	1,750
Denis Durnian	75	70	77	72	294	1,750

Lancome Trophy

St. Nom la Breteche, Versailles, France
Par 35-35—70; 6,756 yards

September 14-17
purse, £410,000

	SCORES				TOTAL	MONEY
Eduardo Romero	69	65	66	66	266	£68,330
Bernhard Langer	68	68	66	65	267	35,585
Jose-Maria Olazabal	67	70	65	65	267	35,585
Peter Fowler	66	64	68	70	268	20,600
David Feherty	68	69	67	65	269	17,400
Vijay Singh	70	71	66	67	274	12,320
Howard Clark	69	74	67	64	274	12,320
Craig Parry	68	69	68	69	274	12,320
Sam Torrance	72	68	69	66	275	8,306.67
Andrew Murray	64	78	68	65	275	8,306.67
Mats Lanner	72	74	62	67	275	8,306.67
Brett Ogle	71	72	67	66	276	6,467.50
Ronan Rafferty	67	74	66	69	276	6,467.50
Frank Nobilo	72	65	72	67	276	6,467.50
Rodger Davis	70	68	71	67	276	6,467.50
Barry Lane	72	69	68	68	277	5,340
Des Smyth	70	74	67	66	277	5,340
Greg Norman	66	74	69	68	277	5,340
Curtis Strange	67	70	72	68	277	5,340
Vicente Fernandez	73	67	71	67	278	4,550
Severiano Ballesteros	70	68	71	69	278	4,550
Tony Johnstone	71	69	71	67	278	4,550
Christy O'Connor, Jr.	70	69	69	70	278	4,550
David Williams	70	68	73	67	278	4,550

	SCORES				TOTAL	MONEY
Jose Rivero	75	68	69	66	278	4,550
Mark Davis	72	66	68	73	279	4,010
Masahiro Kuramoto	73	69	72	65	279	4,010
Colin Montgomerie	66	69	74	70	279	4,010
Nick Faldo	71	70	69	70	280	3,590
Roger Chapman	66	72	72	70	280	3,590
John Bland	71	73	68	68	280	3,590
Jean Van De Velde	67	73	72	68	280	3,590
Gordon J. Brand	70	72	71	68	281	3,170
Philip Walton	72	66	72	71	281	3,170
Eamonn Darcy	72	72	70	67	281	3,170
Mark Roe	69	73	69	70	281	3,170
Michael King	72	69	70	70	281	3,170
Malcolm Mackenzie	73	75	68	66	282	2,930
Mark McNulty	70	74	69	70	283	2,770
Mark James	73	71	69	70	283	2,770
Jesper Parnevik	72	70	72	69	283	2,770
Jeff Hawkes	75	75	66	68	284	2,490
Magnus Persson	71	72	72	69	284	2,490
Jose-Maria Canizares	71	73	70	70	284	2,490
Stephen Bennett	70	72	71	71	284	2,490
Mark Mouland	70	74	73	68	285	2,250
Richard Boxall	74	72	72	67	285	2,250
Carl Mason	67	71	76	72	286	2,050
Marc Farry	75	73	70	68	286	2,050
Emmanuel Dussart	74	73	74	65	286	2,050

Ryder Cup

The Belfry, Sutton, Coldfield, England
Par 36-36—72; 7,176 yards

September 22-24

FINAL SCORE: Europe 14, United States 14 (Europe retains Cup)

FRIDAY

Foursomes:
Tom Kite and Curtis Strange (US) halved with Nick Faldo and Ian Woosnam.
Lanny Wadkins and Payne Stewart (US) defeated Howard Clark and Mark James, 1
up.
Tom Watson and Chip Beck (US) halved with Severiano Ballesteros and Jose-Maria
Olazabal.
Mark Calcavecchia and Ken Green (US) defeated Bernhard Langer and Ronan
Rafferty, 2 and 1.

Fourball:
Sam Torrance and Gordon Brand Jr. (E) defeated Curtis Strange and Paul Azinger, 1
up.
Howard Clark and Mark James (E) defeated Fred Couples and Lanny Wadkins, 3 and
2.
Nick Faldo and Ian Woosnam (E) defeated Mark Calcavecchia and Mark McCumber,
2 up.
Severiano Ballesteros and Jose-Maria Olazabal (E) defeated Tom Watson and Mark
O'Meara, 6 and 5.
EUROPE LEADS, 5-3.

SATURDAY

Foursomes:
Woosnam and Faldo (E) defeated Wadkins and Stewart, 3 and 2.
Beck and Azinger (US) defeated Brand and Torrance, 4 and 3.
Calcavecchia and Green (US) defeated Christy O'Connor Jr. and Rafferty, 3 and 2.
Ballesteros and Olazabal (E) defeated Kite and Strange, 1 up.

Fourball:
Beck and Azinger (US) defeated Faldo and Woosnam, 2 and 1.
Kite and McCumber (US) defeated Langer and Jose-Maria Canizares, 2 and 1.
Clark and James (E) defeated Stewart and Strange, 1 up.
Ballesteros and Olazabal (E) defeated Calcavecchia and Green, 4 and 2.
EUROPE LEADS, 9-7.

SUNDAY

Singles:
Azinger (US) defeated Ballesteros, 1 up.
Beck (US) defeated Langer, 3 and 2.
Olazabal (E) defeated Stewart, 1 up.
Rafferty (E) defeated Calcavecchia, 1 up.
Kite (US) defeated Clark, 8 and 7.
James (E) defeated O'Meara, 3 and 2.
O'Connor (E) defeated Couples, 1 up.
Canizares (E) defeated Green, 1 up.
McCumber (US) defeated Brand, 1 up.
Watson (US) defeated Torrance, 3 and 1.
Wadkins (US) defeated Faldo, 1 up.
Strange (US) defeated Woosnam, 2 up.

Dunhill Cup

Old Course, St. Andrews, Scotland
Par 36-36—72; 6,933 yards

September 28-October 1
purse, US$1,018,000

PRELIMINARY ROUND

KOREA DEFEATED COLOMBIA, 3-0
Park Nam Shin (K) defeated Liborio Zapata, 67-74; Choi Sang Ho (K) defeated Ivan
Rengifo, 74-81; Choi Yoon Soo (K) defeated Juan Pinzon, 73-80.

ITALY DEFEATED ZIMBABWE, 3-0
Massimo Mannelli (I) defeated Anthony Edwards, 72-73; Alberto Binaghi (I) defeated
Tim Price, 67-74; Costantino Rocca (I) defeated Morgan Shumba, 73-84.

(Each member of each losing team received US$3,000.)

FIRST ROUND

ARGENTINA DEFEATED WALES, 2-1/2—1/2
Eduardo Romero (A) defeated Philip Parkin, 68-75; Vicente Fernandez (A) halved
with Mark Mouland, 70-70; Miguel Fernandez (A) defeated Ian Woosnam, 69-72.

UNITED STATES DEFEATED KOREA, 2-1
Park Nam Shin (K) defeated Mark Calcavecchia, 70-71; Tom Kite (U) defeated Choi
Yoon Soo, 72-75; Curtis Strange (U) defeated Choi Sang Ho, 67-79.

SWEDEN DEFEATED SPAIN, 2-1
Jose-Maria Olazabal (S) defeated Mats Lanner, 67-70; Ove Sellberg (Sw) defeated Jose-Maria Canizares, 71-72; Magnus Persson (Sw) defeated Jose Rivero, 71-72.

IRELAND DEFEATED CHINA, 2-1
Philip Walton (I) defeated Lu Chien Soon, 69-76; Yu Chin Han (C) defeated Ronan Rafferty, 71-73; Christy O'Connor Jr. defeated Hsieh Chin Sheng, 73-73, 22nd hole.

SCOTLAND DEFEATED NEW ZEALAND, 2-1
Simon Owen (NZ) defeated Gordon Brand Jr., 72-76; Sam Torrance (S) defeated Grant Waite, 67-70; Sandy Lyle (S) defeated Frank Nobilo, 65-70.

JAPAN DEFEATED ITALY, 2-1
Koichi Suzuki (J) defeated Mannelli, 74-76; Naomichi Ozaki (J) defeated Rocca, 68-73; Binaghi (I) defeated Hajime Meshiai, 72-73.

FRANCE DEFEATED AUSTRALIA, 2-1
Emmanuel Dussart (F) defeated Ian Baker-Finch, 72-73; Marc Pendaries (F) defeated Greg Norman, 71-73; Wayne Grady (A) defeated Gery Watine, 67-70.

ENGLAND DEFEATED CANADA, 2-1
Denis Durnian (E) defeated Richard Zokol, 72-72, 20th hole; Dave Barr (C) defeated Mark James, 71-73; Howard Clark (E) defeated Dan Halldorson, 71-72.

(Each member of each losing team received US$7,500.)

QUARTER-FINALS

JAPAN DEFEATED FRANCE, 3-0
Ozaki (J) defeated Dussart, 71-73; Suzuki (J) defeated Pendaries, 73-75; Meshiai (J) defeated Watine, 72-74.

UNITED STATES DEFEATED ARGENTINA, 3-0
Kite (U) defeated Fernandez, 70-72; Calcavecchia (U) defeated Fernandez, 72-77; Strange (U) defeated Romero, 68-70.

IRELAND DEFEATED SWEDEN, 3-0
Walton (I) defeated Lanner, 72-74; Rafferty (I) defeated Sellberg, 68-78; O'Connor (I) defeated Persson, 73-76.

ENGLAND DEFEATED SCOTLAND, 2-1
Clark (E) defeated Torrance, 67-69; Brand (S) defeated Durnian, 71-78; James (E) defeated Lyle, 70-70, 19th hole.

(Each member of each losing team received US$15,000.)

SEMI-FINALS

UNITED STATES DEFEATED IRELAND, 2-1
Calcavecchia (U) defeated Walton, 69-71; Kite (U) defeated O'Connor, 71-71, 19th hole; Rafferty (I) defeated Strange, 71-72.

JAPAN DEFEATED ENGLAND, 2-1
Ozaki (J) defeated Durnian, 70-72; Suzuki (J) defeated Clark, 66-70; James (E) defeated Meshiai, 71-73.

PLAYOFF FOR THIRD-FOURTH PLACES

ENGLAND DEFEATED IRELAND, 2-1
Walton (I) defeated Durnian, 71-72; Clark (E) defeated Rafferty, 72-75; James (E) defeated O'Connor, 69-76.

(Each English player received US$36,666; each Irish player received US$26,666.)

FINAL

UNITED STATES DEFEATED JAPAN, 3-1/2—2-1/2
Calcavecchia (U) defeated Meshiai, 67-68; Kite (U) halved with Ozaki, 68-68;
Strange (U) defeated Suzuki, 72-75 . . . Calcavecchia (U) defeated Meshiai, 66-68;
Suzuki (J) defeated Kite, 71-74; Ozaki (J) defeated Strange, 69-71.

(Each U.S. player received US$100,000; each Japanese player received US$50,000.)

Motorola Classic

Burnham and Berrow Golf Club, Burnham-on-Sea, England   September 28-October 1
Par 36-35—71; 6,680 yards   purse, £69,000

	SCORES				TOTAL	MONEY
David Llewellyn	64	69	72	67	272	£10,500
David Williams	70	68	61	71	276	7,100
Russell Weir	70	67	71	69	277	5,100
Paul Carrigill	71	71	71	65	278	4,100
Darren Prosser	71	69	69	70	279	3,450
Ronald Stelten	70	69	72	69	280	2,700
Brian Barnes	73	66	68	73	280	2,700
Steven Richardson	71	70	69	71	281	2,100
Peter Teravainen	71	68	72	71	282	1,800
David Jagger	69	70	73	71	283	1,600
Bobby Mitchell	72	69	72	71	284	1,332.50
Paul Mayo	72	70	73	69	284	1,332.50
John Morgan	70	74	73	67	284	1,332.50
Andrew Sherborne	72	74	70	68	284	1,332.50
Mike Clayton	74	71	69	70	284	1,332.50
David J. Russell	73	74	72	65	284	1,332.50
Kevin Dickens	69	78	69	68	284	1,332.50
Ross McFarlane	75	71	70	68	284	1,332.50
Martin Sludds	73	73	73	67	286	1,080
Malcolm Mackenzie	72	73	71	70	286	1,080
Paul Hoad	74	72	73	67	286	1,080
Glyn Davies	72	71	72	71	286	1,080
John Lower	71	72	71	73	287	980
Chris Moody	73	71	66	78	288	920
Richard Fish	70	69	75	74	288	920
Willie Milne	73	71	73	72	289	820
Kevin Spurgeon	75	71	71	72	289	820
Mark Stokes	72	70	74	73	289	820
Scott Taylor	71	71	74	74	290	687.50
Craig Maltman	72	68	74	76	290	687.50
Chris Platts	76	68	75	71	290	687.50
Neil Roderick	71	75	72	72	290	687.50
Andrew Stubbs	71	75	71	74	291	595
Michael Lord	74	73	75	69	291	595
Mark Thomas	69	78	72	73	292	490
Wayne Riley	69	71	78	74	292	490
Lyndsay Stephen	72	74	72	74	292	490
Lucian Tinkler	71	75	73	73	292	490
John Jacobs	72	71	72	77	292	490
Jeff Hall	74	73	73	74	294	400

German Masters

Stuttgarter Golf Club, Monsheim, West Germany
Par 36-36—72; 6,839 yards

October 5-8
purse, £331,950

	SCORES				TOTAL	MONEY
Bernhard Langer	67	71	70	68	276	£55,302.90
Payne Stewart	69	67	70	71	277	28,813.28
Jose-Maria Olazabal	73	66	69	69	277	28,813.28
Brett Ogle	73	68	71	68	280	15,336.10
Fred Couples	69	72	73	66	280	15,336.10
Derrick Cooper	70	72	71	68	281	11,618.26
Stephen Bennett	72	70	70	70	282	8,564.32
Bernard Gallacher	73	71	70	68	282	8,564.32
Nick Faldo	69	66	74	73	282	8,564.32
Rodger Davis	68	69	72	74	283	6,639
Mike Harwood	72	70	74	68	284	6,107.88
Eduardo Romero	70	72	69	74	285	5,377.59
Andrew Sherborne	71	69	74	71	285	5,377.59
Barry Lane	72	69	76	68	285	5,377.59
Eamonn Darcy	74	72	68	72	286	4,780.09
Magnus Persson	70	73	69	74	286	4,780.09
Bill Longmuir	74	66	79	68	287	4,088.52
Vijay Singh	74	74	72	67	287	4,088.52
Miguel Angel Martin	69	71	74	73	287	4,088.52
Richard Boxall	68	73	74	72	287	4,088.52
Jimmy Heggarty	71	70	79	67	287	4,088.52
Keith Waters	68	71	76	72	287	4,088.52
Brian Marchbank	74	72	71	71	288	3,485.48
Mark McNulty	73	73	72	70	288	3,485.48
Malcolm Mackenzie	74	70	72	72	288	3,485.48
Bob E. Smith	72	68	74	74	288	3,485.48
Chris Moody	74	68	73	73	288	3,485.48
Tom Purtzer	73	70	74	72	289	2,943.29
David Llewellyn	68	76	69	76	289	2,943.29
Anders Sorensen	76	71	71	71	289	2,943.29
Peter Senior	72	76	70	71	289	2,943.29
Ove Sellberg	73	72	72	72	289	2,943.29
Philip Walton	73	71	71	74	289	2,943.29
Antonio Garrido	70	73	77	70	290	2,489.63
Tony Charnley	70	70	71	79	290	2,489.63
Peter Fowler	76	71	72	71	290	2,489.63
Paul Way	71	69	73	77	290	2,489.63
Vicente Fernandez	73	74	71	72	290	2,489.63
Jose Rivero	73	75	71	71	290	2,489.63
Denis Durnian	76	70	73	72	291	2,224.07
Michael Allen	73	72	73	73	291	2,224.07
David A. Russell	72	76	71	73	292	2,024.90
David Gilford	77	69	75	71	292	2,024.90
Mark Mouland	72	74	72	74	292	2,024.90
Peter Baker	76	71	74	71	292	2,024.90
Ron Commans	71	74	74	74	293	1,659.75
Armando Saavedra	73	75	71	74	293	1,659.75
Stephen McAllister	72	74	74	73	293	1,659.75
David Ray	69	74	76	74	293	1,659.75
Ian Baker-Finch	75	73	73	72	293	1,659.75
Craig Parry	73	73	72	75	293	1,659.75
Ruud Bos	73	74	71	75	293	1,659.75

Suntory World Match Play Championship

Wentworth Club, West Course
Virginia Water, Surrey, England
Par 434 534 444—35; 345 434 455—37—72; 6,945 yards

October 12-15
purse, £330,000

FIRST ROUND

Ronan Rafferty defeated Mike Reid, 3 and 2

Rafferty	424	334	544	33	344	333	544	33	66
Reid	435	433	434	33	444	423	445	34	67

Rafferty leads, 1 up

Rafferty	445	333	433	32	334	433	4	
Reid	434	433	44C	X	244	434	4	

Jose-Maria Olazabal defeated Scott Hoch, 4 and 2

Olazabal	535	433	546	38	243	534	454	34	72
Hoch	535	534	444	37	344	434	465	37	74

Olazabal leads, 2 up

Olazabal	434	434	534	34	344	424	3	
Hoch	534	523	435	34	344	434	4	

Chip Beck defeated Aki Ohmachi, 8 and 6

Beck	425	523	443	32	345	433	454	35	67
Ohmachi	434	433	445	34	245	346	455	38	72

Beck leads, 2 up

Beck	434	534	534	35	333	
Ohmachi	435	544	535	38	444	

David Frost defeated Ian Baker-Finch, 4 and 3

Frost	434	444	445	36	344	443	454	35	71
Baker-Finch	445	544	444	38	255	345	445	37	75

Frost leads, 3 up

Frost	435	423	443	32	344	434
Baker-Finch	434	423	443	31	344	544

SECOND ROUND

Ronan Rafferty defeated Sandy Lyle, 1 hole

Rafferty	524	534	334	33	344	334	C54	X	X
Lyle	424	434	344	32	344	434	345	34	66

Lyle leads, 1 up

Rafferty	435	C44	344	X	244	424	W54	X	X
Lyle	434	344	444	34	354	434	C44	X	X

Ian Woosnam defeated Jose-Maria Olazabal, 3 and 2

Woosnam	334	424	444	32	445	42C	355	X	X
Olazabal	435	334	444	34	345	423	354	33	67

Olazabal leads, 1 up

Woosnam	434	443	443	33	234	424	4	
Olazabal	434	544	444	36	334	433	4	

Seve Ballesteros defeated Chip Beck, 9 and 8

Ballesteros	434	433	344	32	244	534	345	34	66
Beck	434	444	444	35	335	435	445	36	71

Ballesteros leads, 5 up

Ballesteros	424	434	434	32	3
Beck	535	444	533	36	3

Nick Faldo defeated David Frost at 38th hole

Faldo	434	434	543	34	244	434	444	33	67
Frost	324	434	544	33	254	434	344	33	66

Frost leads, 1 up

Faldo	424	434	444	33	234	434	445	33	66
Frost	434	333	354	32	344	434	454	35	67

Match all-square

Faldo	42
Frost	43

SEMI-FINALS

Ian Woosnam defeated Ronan Rafferty, 2 and 1

Woosnam	525	434	334	33	243	434	454	33	66
Rafferty	435	334	344	33	244	534	445	35	68

Woosnam leads, 2 up

Woosnam	435	434	434	34	345	424	44
Rafferty	435	433	543	34	245	434	44

Nick Faldo defeated Seve Ballesteros, 6 and 5

Faldo	434	533	443	33	345	423	434	32	65
Ballesteros	525	534	443	35	343	434	4C	4X	X

Faldo leads, 4 up

Faldo	324	434	433	30	344	4	
Ballesteros	423	534	444	33	244	4	

FINAL

Nick Faldo defeated Ian Woosnam, 1 hole

Faldo	434	434	444	34	345	433	335	33	67
Woosnam	425	424	344	32	343	43C	444	X	X

Woosnam leads, 1 up

Faldo	435	333	445	34	343	334	343	30	64
Woosnam	434	425	344	33	344	534	444	35	68

THIRD PLACE

Seve Ballesteros defeated Ronan Rafferty, 5 and 3

Ballesteros	335	423	543	32	244	433	
Rafferty	435	534	434	35	344	434	

PRIZE MONEY: Faldo £100,000; Woosnam £60,000; Ballesteros £30,000; Rafferty £20,000; Lyle, Olazabal, Beck, Frost £17,500 each; Reid, Hoch, Ohmachi, Baker-Finch £12,500 each.

LEGEND: C—conceded hole to opponent; W—won hole by concession without holing out; X—no total score.

BMW International Open

Golfplatz Munchen, Nord-Eichenried, Munich, West Germany   October 12-15
Par 36-36—72; 6,910 yards   purse, £275,000

	SCORES				TOTAL	MONEY
David Feherty	62	66	68	73	269	£45,820
Fred Couples	68	69	67	70	274	30,540
Philip Walton	67	70	68	70	275	17,210
Eamonn Darcy	70	69	70	67	276	13,750
Mark Mouland	70	70	68	69	277	10,645

	SCORES				TOTAL	MONEY
Mike Harwood	70	71	66	70	277	10,645
Gordon J. Brand	68	68	70	72	278	7,500
Tom Purtzer	69	69	69	71	278	7,500
Davis Love III	65	73	70	71	279	5,750
Ove Sellberg	66	71	70	72	279	5,750
Denis Durnian	73	69	68	70	280	4,796.67
Torsten Giedeon	71	70	69	70	280	4,796.67
Craig Parry	69	71	70	70	280	4,796.67
Rodger Davis	69	69	73	70	281	4,190
Gordon Brand, Jr.	73	67	69	72	281	4,190
Magnus Persson	67	70	71	74	282	3,680
Howard Clark	66	72	73	71	282	3,680
Johan Rystrom	71	72	72	67	282	3,680
Peter Fowler	66	74	70	72	282	3,680
Russell Claydon	70	70	70	72	282	3,680
Peter Mitchell	67	67	78	71	283	3,200
Keith Waters	69	67	75	72	283	3,200
Carl Mason	68	71	73	71	283	3,200
Anders Forsbrand	69	72	68	75	284	2,845
Miguel Angel Jimenez	71	69	74	70	284	2,845
Peter Senior	72	71	70	71	284	2,845
Bryan Norton	67	73	71	73	284	2,845
Mats Lanner	71	66	70	78	285	2,492.50
Paul Way	69	70	74	72	285	2,492.50
Mark McNulty	73	70	73	69	285	2,492.50
Des Smyth	71	69	72	73	285	2,492.50
Richard Boxall	69	69	74	74	286	2,030
Lyndsay Stephen	68	70	76	72	286	2,030
Mark James	71	68	71	76	286	2,030
Paul Carrigill	70	67	77	72	286	2,030
Tony Charnley	72	71	72	71	286	2,030
David A. Russell	67	72	73	74	286	2,030
Peter Baker	69	73	72	72	286	2,030
David Gilford	72	71	70	73	286	2,030
Stephen Bennett	69	71	72	74	286	2,030
Derrick Cooper	69	73	69	75	286	2,030
Paul Kent	70	69	75	73	287	1,497.50
David Williams	72	69	72	74	287	1,497.50
Philip Harrison	69	74	72	72	287	1,497.50
David Ray	70	72	73	72	287	1,497.50
Vicente Fernandez	70	70	73	74	287	1,497.50
Ross Drummond	69	71	72	75	287	1,497.50
Mark Davis	68	74	70	75	287	1,497.50
Glenn Ralph	72	71	72	72	287	1,497.50
Chris Moody	71	70	72	75	288	1,131.43
Mike Clayton	73	70	74	71	288	1,131.43
Sandy Stephen	71	71	73	73	288	1,131.43
Malcolm Mackenzie	70	72	72	74	288	1,131.43
Alberto Binaghi	69	74	75	70	288	1,131.43
Eduardo Romero	69	71	71	77	288	1,131.43
Juan Anglada	69	74	70	75	288	1,131.43

Portuguese Open - TPC Championship

Quinta do Lago Golf Club, Almancil, Algarve, Portugal
Par 36-36—72; 7,095 yards

October 19-22
purse, £275,000

	SCORES				TOTAL	MONEY
Colin Montgomerie	67	65	69	63	264	£45,825
Mike Smith	70	69	66	70	275	20,498.33
Manuel Moreno	71	69	69	66	275	20,498.33
Rodger Davis	66	72	69	68	275	20,498.33
Manuel Pinero	68	70	72	66	276	10,640
Christy O'Connor, Jr.	69	68	71	68	276	10,640
Sandy Stephen	71	69	68	69	277	6,095.83
David Feherty	70	71	67	69	277	6,095.83
Gordon J. Brand	70	71	67	69	277	6,095.83
Peter Senior	73	65	71	68	277	6,095.83
Antonio Garrido	69	71	67	70	277	6,095.83
Peter Fowler	69	68	73	67	277	6,095.83
Luis Carbonetti	67	69	72	70	278	4,052
David Whelan	72	73	65	68	278	4,052
Armando Saavedra	70	70	67	71	278	4,052
Ove Sellberg	73	69	68	68	278	4,052
Ronan Rafferty	73	68	69	68	278	4,052
Peter Baker	68	72	70	69	279	3,420
Mark Davis	74	71	65	69	279	3,420
Jose Rivero	68	72	69	70	279	3,420
David Ray	69	74	67	70	280	2,887.22
Des Smyth	69	72	71	68	280	2,887.22
Mark McNulty	68	70	72	70	280	2,887.22
Wayne Riley	74	70	68	68	280	2,887.22
Gordon Brand, Jr.	70	69	68	73	280	2,887.22
Sam Torrance	75	70	68	67	280	2,887.22
Craig Parry	72	70	67	71	280	2,887.22
Ken Brown	72	69	68	71	280	2,887.22
Peter Teravainen	70	71	70	69	280	2,887.22
Mark Roe	69	68	75	69	281	2,237.50
Juan Quiros	69	67	72	73	281	2,237.50
Emilio Rodriguez	72	70	71	68	281	2,237.50
David Williams	69	72	70	70	281	2,237.50
Mark Mouland	67	69	73	72	281	2,237.50
Eduardo Romero	71	70	71	69	281	2,237.50
Jose-Maria Canizares	73	72	67	69	281	2,237.50
Ron Commans	69	69	71	72	281	2,237.50
Mike Harwood	69	73	70	70	282	1,952.50
Roger Chapman	74	69	69	70	282	1,952.50
Bryan Norton	72	73	68	70	283	1,787.50
Miguel Angel Martin	75	70	68	70	283	1,787.50
Stephen Bennett	73	72	68	70	283	1,787.50
Ross Drummond	70	69	70	74	283	1,787.50
Marc Pendaries	69	76	71	68	284	1,485
Daniel Silva	72	70	72	70	284	1,485
Martin Poxon	73	69	69	73	284	1,485
Alberto Binaghi	71	73	74	66	284	1,485
Bill Longmuir	74	70	65	75	284	1,485
Paul Carrigill	74	70	70	70	284	1,485
Peter Mitchell	71	70	72	71	284	1,485

Volvo Masters

Valderrama Golf Club, Sotogrande, Spain
Par 36-36—72; 7,020 yards

October 26-29
purse, £400,000

	SCORES			TOTAL	MONEY
Ronan Rafferty	72	69	70	71	282	£66,660
Nick Faldo	74	68	72	69	283	44,425
Jose-Maria Olazabal	69	70	74	74	287	25,040
Sandy Lyle	70	76	69	74	289	20,000
Peter Fowler	75	72	69	74	290	14,316.67
Mark James	77	70	71	72	290	14,316.67
Howard Clark	73	70	74	73	290	14,316.67
Craig Parry	73	68	75	75	291	10,000
Vicente Fernandez	75	73	73	71	292	8,106.67
Eduardo Romero	73	73	74	72	292	8,106.67
Ove Sellberg	75	74	73	70	292	8,106.67
Andrew Murray	75	71	72	75	293	6,190
Roger Chapman	73	72	77	71	293	6,190
Peter Senior	73	78	68	74	293	6,190
Ian Woosnam	71	69	75	78	293	6,190
Jose-Maria Canizares	75	73	75	70	293	6,190
Tony Charnley	76	75	73	71	295	5,171.67
Mark McNulty	72	73	75	75	295	5,171.67
Christy O'Connor, Jr.	72	74	72	77	295	5,171.67
Luis Carbonetti	74	71	75	76	296	4,620
Peter Teravainen	72	74	78	72	296	4,620
Richard Boxall	78	73	74	71	296	4,620
Miguel Angel Martin	74	75	74	73	296	4,620
Brett Ogle	75	71	78	73	297	3,960
Michael Allen	76	73	73	75	297	3,960
Rick Hartmann	75	77	75	70	297	3,960
Mike Smith	72	75	77	73	297	3,960
Derrick Cooper	76	69	77	75	297	3,960
Bill Longmuir	74	77	72	74	297	3,960
Jean Van De Velde	74	74	75	74	297	3,960
David Gilford	79	73	73	73	298	3,420
David Williams	75	73	76	74	298	3,420
Manuel Pinero	74	75	73	77	299	3,240
Mats Lanner	73	73	76	77	299	3,240
Mark Mouland	79	72	76	73	300	2,920
Mike Harwood	75	72	77	76	300	2,920
David Feherty	74	73	76	77	300	2,920
Paul Carrigill	73	77	71	79	300	2,920
Vijay Singh	76	72	75	77	300	2,920
Keith Waters	75	72	80	73	300	2,920
Philip Parkin	74	74	76	77	301	2,600
Andrew Sherborne	75	74	76	76	301	2,600
Bryan Norton	74	77	75	76	302	2,440
Paul Way	81	71	76	74	302	2,440
Sam Torrance	73	78	75	77	303	2,240
Emmanuel Dussart	77	74	76	76	303	2,240
Bernard Gallacher	72	78	74	79	303	2,240
Frank Nobilo	75	75	76	78	304	2,040
Mike Clayton	76	74	81	73	304	2,040
Philip Walton	81	71	78	76	306	1,880
Miguel Angel Jimenez	78	72	80	76	306	1,880

Benson & Hedges Trophy

Aloha Golf Club, Marbella, Spain
Par 36-36—72; 6,734 yards - men, 6,211 yards - women

November 9-12
purse, £140,000

	SCORES				TOTAL	MONEY (Team)
Miguel Angel Jimenez/ Xonia Wunsch-Ruiz	70	68	71	72	281	£23,400
Carl Mason/Gillian Stewart	67	69	71	76	283	17,500
Gordon J. Brand/Florence Descampe	69	71	72	72	284	13,400
Andrew Sherborne/Kitrina Douglas	74	70	74	68	286	7,380
Ian Mosey/Patricia Gonzalez	72	70	73	71	286	7,380
David Jones/Cathy Panton	71	72	71	72	286	7,380
Jose-Maria Canizares/Tania Abitbol	72	73	68	73	286	7,380
Manuel Pinero/Marta Figueras-Dotti	72	70	70	74	286	7,380
Derrick Cooper/Peggy Conley	71	71	74	71	287	4,020
Mark Mouland/Alison Nicholas	71	71	73	72	287	4,020
David Llewellyn/Mickey Walker	68	69	74	76	287	4,020
Richard Boxall/Dennise Hutton	73	71	74	70	288	2,834
Emilio Rodriguez/Jane Connachan	75	71	72	70	288	2,834
Philip Parkin/Sue Strudwick	68	74	74	72	288	2,834
Juan Quiros/Alicia Dibos	72	72	72	72	288	2,834
Mark Roe/Corinne Dibnah	71	71	73	73	288	2,834
Bernard Gallacher/Janet Soulsby	73	73	73	70	289	2,106.66
Anders Forsbrand/Corinne Soules	70	73	72	74	289	2,106.66
Ove Sellberg/Sofia Gronberg	72	72	71	74	289	2,106.66
Baldovino Dassu/Federica Dassu	70	72	76	72	290	1,790
Glenn Ralph/Rae Hast	73	69	72	76	290	1,790
David Williams/Susan Moon	69	74	74	74	291	1,650
Jose Luis Mangas/ Maria Navarro Corbachio	74	75	70	74	293	1,570
Steen Tinning/Barbara Helbig	74	74	74	72	294	1,500
*Diego Borrego/ *Macarena Campomanes	75	76	75	68	294	
Paul Way/Karen Lunn	70	78	70	77	295	1,440
Wayne Stephens/Diane Barnard	78	70	77	71	296	1,365
Paul Carrigill/Maureen Garner	72	72	79	73	296	1,365
Ross McFarlane/Cindy Scholefield	73	72	76	77	298	1,300
Sam Torrance/Regine Lautens	79	76	74	72	301	1,260
*Tomas Jesus Munoz/*Sonia Navarro	77	81	77	75	310	
Tony Charnley/Dale Reid	72	74	DQ			1,220

World Cup

Las Brisas Golf Club, Marbella, Spain
Par 72

November 16-19
purse, $910,000

	INDIVIDUAL SCORES		TOTAL
AUSTRALIA (278)—$240,000			
Peter Fowler	66	71	137
Wayne Grady	68	73	141
SPAIN (281)—$120,000			
Jose-Maria Olazabal	70	73	143
Jose-Maria Canizares	71	67	138

UNITED STATES (287)—$76,000

Paul Azinger	70	71	141
Mark McCumber	73	73	146

SWEDEN (287)—$76,000

Mats Lanner	69	73	142
Ove Sellberg	73	72	145

WALES (288)—$50,000

Philip Parkin	72	72	144
Mark Mouland	75	69	144

ARGENTINA (290)—$35,000

Miguel Fernandez	71	69	140
Jose Coceres	77	73	150

NEW ZEALAND (290)—$35,000

Simon Owen	72	72	144
Greg Turner	73	73	146

DENMARK (291)—$21,000

Anders Sorensen	70	68	138
Steen Tinning	78	75	153

ENGLAND (291)—$21,000

Mark Roe	71	70	141
Denis Durnian	74	76	150

IRELAND (294)—$16,000

Des Smyth	72	76	148
Christy O'Connor, Jr.	73	73	146

SCOTLAND (295)—$14,000

Gordon Brand, Jr.	74	74	148
Sam Torrance	75	72	147

WEST GERMANY (296)—$10,000

Hans-Peter Thuel	72	73	145
Torsten Gideon	76	75	151

FRANCE (296)—$10,000

Jean Van de Velde	73	75	148
Emmanuel Dussart	75	73	148

ITALY (296)—$10,000

Messimo Mannelli	74	74	148
Alberto Binaghi	74	74	148

CANADA (298)—$7,000

Jerry Anderson	75	75	150
Dave Barr	76	72	148

JAPAN (299)—$7,000

Yoshimi Niizeki	72	77	149
Yoshiyuki Isomura	77	73	150

PHILIPPINES (300)—$7,000

Frankie Minoza	72	73	145
Mario Siodina	80	75	155

	INDIVIDUAL SCORES		TOTAL
VENEZUELA (303)—$7,000			
Francisco Alvarado	71	76	147
Ramon Munoz	81	75	146
SWITZERLAND (306)—$7,000			
Karim Barabie	74	77	151
Paolo Quirici	76	79	155
COLOMBIA (306)—$7,000			
Eduardo Herrera	77	74	151
Ivan Rengifo	82	73	155
SOUTH KOREA (308)—$7,000			
Nam Shin Park	78	73	151
Yoon Soo Choi	79	78	157
GREECE (310)—$7,000			
Craigen Pappas	76	74	150
Victor Karatzlas	80	80	160
BRAZIL (311)—$7,000			
Antonio Nascimento	74	83	157
Rafael Navarro	77	77	154
TAIWAN (311)—$7,000			
Yu Chin Ran	73	78	151
Lu Chien Soon	83	77	160
URUGUAY (315)—$7,000			
Alvaro Canessa	77	75	152
Enrique Fernandez	83	80	163
MEXICO (316)—$7,000			
Feliciano Esparza	77	79	156
Carlos Espinoza	78	82	160
NORWAY (316)—$7,000			
Per Haugsrud	74	72	146
Tom Vollan	85	85	170
NETHERLANDS (316)—$7,000			
Ruud Bos	78	74	152
C. van der Velde	82	82	164
PORTUGAL (317)—$7,000			
Daniel Silva	74	77	151
Rogehrio Valente	87	79	166
THAILAND (320)—$7,000			
Boonchu Ruengkit	78	77	155
Thaworn Wiratchant	80	85	165
AUSTRIA (323)—$7,000			
Johannes Lamberg	81	85	166
Franz Laimer	81	76	157
BELGIUM (336)—$7,000			
Andre Van Damme	83	81	164
Olivier Buysse	89	83	172

INTERNATIONAL TROPHY

WINNER—Fowler - 137 - $50,000. ORDER OF FINISH: Canizares, Sorensen - 138; Fernandez - 140; Grady, Azinger, Roe - 141; Lanner - 142; Olazabal - 143; Parkin, Mouland, Owen - 144; Sellberg, Thuel, Minoza - 145; McCumber, Turner, O'Connor, Haugsrud - 146; Torrance, Alvarado - 147; Smyth, Brand, Van de Velde, Dussart, Mannelli, Binaghi, Barr - 148; Niizeki - 149; Coceres, Durnian, Anderson, Isomura, Pappas - 150; Gideon, Barabie, Herrera, Park, Yu, Silva - 151; Bos - 152; Tinning - 153; Navarro - 154; Siodina, Quirici, Rengifo, Ruengkit - 155; Munoz, Esparza, Laimer - 156; Choi, Nascimento - 157; Karatzias, Espinoza, Lu - 160; Van der Velde, Van Damme - 164; Wiratchant - 165; Valente, Lamberg - 166; Vollan - 170; Buysse - 172.

The African Tours

Dewars White Label Trophy

Durban Country Club, Durban, South Africa
Par 36-36—72; 6,558 yards

January 4-7
purse, R250,000

	SCORES				TOTAL	MONEY
John Bland	70	66	71	66	273	R40,000
Tony Johnstone	67	70	69	68	274	28,750
Stuart Smith	68	69	68	70	275	17,500
John Daly	65	75	69	67	276	11,500
Carl Cooper	70	68	68	70	276	11,500
Gavin Levenson	66	72	69	71	278	8,250
Alan Pate	68	67	70	73	278	8,250
Jeff Hawkes	69	71	68	71	279	6,250
Andre Cruse	68	70	72	70	280	5,500
Phillip Hatchett	67	72	72	70	281	4,750
Kelly Gibson	69	74	69	69	281	4,750
Simon Hobday	70	69	74	69	282	4,125
Malcolm McKenzie	72	68	70	72	282	4,125
Hugh Baiocchi	68	72	72	71	283	3,500
Wayne Westner	69	70	73	71	283	3,500
Andrew Morse	70	74	69	70	283	3,500
Bob McDonnell	71	72	68	72	283	3,500
Phil Simmons	67	69	71	76	283	3,500
Trevor Dodds	68	74	72	70	284	3,008.33
Ian Mosey	73	72	69	70	284	3,008.33
Mark Wiltshire	70	67	71	76	284	3,008.33
Chris Moody	71	73	73	68	285	2,712.50
Marty Schiene	75	71	70	69	285	2,712.50
Wilhelm Winsnes	70	72	72	71	285	2,712.50
Jon Chaffee	72	73	68	72	285	2,712.50

	SCORES				TOTAL	MONEY
Andrew Chandler	67	71	69	69	286	2,271.88
David Armor	71	70	74	71	286	2,271.88
Steve van Vuuren	70	71	72	73	286	2,271.88
Brian Evans	72	71	70	73	286	2,271.88
Robbie Stewart	72	70	71	73	286	2,271.88
J.C. Anderson	75	68	68	75	286	2,271.88
Bob Smith	71	70	69	76	286	2,271.88
Ben Fouchee	66	70	73	77	286	2,271.88

ICL International

Zwartkops Country Club, Pretoria, South Africa
Par 36-36—72; 7,125 yards

January 11-14
purse, R250,000

	SCORES				TOTAL	MONEY
Chris Williams	64	68	69	71	272	R40,000
J.C. Anderson	66	70	69	68	273	28,750
Timothy Robinson	71	69	68	66	274	13,500
David Feherty	71	68	68	67	274	13,500
Jon Chaffee	68	69	67	70	274	13,500
Jeff Hawkes	67	71	72	65	275	8,250
Bob McDonnell	70	68	67	70	275	8,250
Mark James	70	70	72	64	276	6,250
Gavin Levenson	69	75	65	68	277	5,500
Ben Fouchee	67	69	75	67	278	4,437.50
Fred Wadsworth	70	72	67	69	278	4,437.50
John Bland	65	72	72	69	278	4,437.50
Hugh Baiocchi	68	66	70	74	278	4,437.50
Desmond Terblanche	72	70	70	67	279	3,750
Tony Johnstone	68	72	72	68	280	3,312.50
Brian Evans	71	73	67	69	280	3,312.50
Marty Schiene	73	66	72	69	280	3,312.50
Bruce Vaughan	68	71	71	70	280	3,312.50
Wayne Westner	71	71	67	71	280	3,312.50
Trevor Dodds	74	67	67	72	280	3,312.50
Scott Dunlap	68	72	74	67	281	2,825
Carl Cooper	73	69	72	67	281	2,825
Jay Townsend	73	70	68	70	281	2,825
Jimmy Johnson	67	75	73	67	282	2,487.50
John Fourie	69	74	71	68	282	2,487.50
Jim Johnson	73	69	70	70	282	2,487.50
Phil Harrison	70	74	68	70	282	2,487.50
Ian Palmer	71	73	67	71	282	2,487.50
Craigen Pappas	73	70	67	72	282	2,487.50
Tom Lehman	70	73	72	68	283	1,977.50
Andrew Morse	74	69	73	67	283	1,977.50
Bob Ford	69	74	72	68	283	1,977.50
Stuart Smith	71	72	73	67	283	1,977.50
Don Robertson	70	74	70	69	283	1,977.50
Alan Pate	69	74	70	70	283	1,977.50
Malcolm McKenzie	73	68	72	70	283	1,977.50
Phillip Hatchett	69	71	72	71	283	1,977.50
Teddy Webber	69	75	68	71	283	1,977.50
Eamonn Darcy	70	72	68	73	283	1,977.50

Lexington PGA Championship

Wanderers Golf Club, Johannesburg, South Africa
Par 35-35—70; 6,960 yards

January 18-21
purse, R250,000

	SCORES				TOTAL	MONEY
Tony Johnstone	71	65	66	67	269	R40,000
Chris Williams	67	68	67	67	269	28,750
(Johnstone defeated Williams on first extra hole.)						
Mark Wiltshire	69	63	67	71	270	17,500
John Daly	70	69	68	66	273	10,666.67
Fred Wadsworth	72	67	68	66	273	10,666.67
J.C. Anderson	70	64	68	71	273	10,666.67
David Feherty	60	71	60	63	274	5,750
John Bland	68	71	69	66	274	5,750
Chris Moody	70	66	71	67	274	5,750
Jeff Hawkes	69	69	68	68	274	5,750
Bruce Vaughan	65	69	71	69	274	5,750
Sean Pappas	71	67	69	68	275	4,250
Jay Townsend	66	71	74	65	276	3,718.75
Jon Chaffee	67	72	71	66	276	3,718.75
Phil Jonas	64	74	70	68	276	3,718.75
Don Walsworth	63	74	68	71	276	3,718.75
William Kane	71	70	70	66	277	3,032.14
Robert Friend	60	68	72	67	277	3,032.14
Frank Edmunds	76	67	67	67	277	3,032.14
Simon Hobday	68	68	73	68	277	3,032.14
Wayne Westner	69	67	71	70	277	3,032.14
Trevor Dodds	73	65	68	71	277	3,032.14
Andre Cruse	68	71	67	71	277	3,032.14
Jim Vernon	70	72	72	64	278	2,525
Andrew Chandler	66	71	73	68	278	2,525
Stuart Smith	70	69	71	68	278	2,525
Wayne Bradley	70	69	70	69	278	2,525
Brian Evans	69	68	71	70	278	2,525
Mark Davis	65	73	71	70	279	2,193.75
Hugh Royer	67	72	69	71	279	2,193.75
Alan Pate	69	69	68	73	279	2,193.75
Steve Thomas	67	68	70	74	279	2,193.75

Palabora Classic

Hans Merensky Golf Club, Phalaborwa, South Africa
Par 36-36—72; 6,727 yards

January 25-28
purse, R250,000

	SCORES				TOTAL	MONEY
Stuart Smith	70	65	71	68	274	R40,000
Ian Palmer	68	67	68	71	274	28,750
(Smith defeated Palmer on first extra hole.)						
Trevor Dodds	74	65	70	66	275	17,500
Wayne Westner	68	73	71	64	276	11,500
David Feherty	70	69	67	70	276	11,500
John Bland	73	71	70	65	279	6,650
Scott Dunlap	67	70	73	69	279	6,650
Alan Pate	72	68	70	69	279	6,650
Robbie Stewart	73	69	68	69	279	6,650
Mark Davis	73	67	68	71	279	6,650

	SCORES	TOTAL	MONEY
Marty Schiene	74 68 72 66	280	4,250
Bruce Vaughan	73 71 69 67	280	4,250
Don Robertson	71 73 69 67	280	4,250
Justin Hobday	72 70 69 70	281	3,437.50
Craigen Pappas	70 69 71 71	281	3,437.50
Steve Thomas	72 68 70 71	281	3,437.50
Bobby Cole	70 71 68 72	281	3,437.50
Jeff Hawkes	68 72 68 73	281	3,437.50
Tony Johnstone	70 69 69 73	281	3,437.50
Fred Wadsworth	71 68 73 70	282	3,000
Jim Vernon	68 70 72 73	283	2,900
Francis Quinn	71 72 72 69	284	2,637.50
Jannie le Grange	71 72 72 69	284	2,637.50
Desmond Terblanche	73 70 71 70	284	2,637.50
Robert Friend	75 68 70 71	284	2,637.50
David Abell	70 70 72 72	284	2,637.50
Bob McDonnell	73 69 68 73	284	2,637.50
Sean Pappas	74 71 72 68	285	2,262.50
Robert Richardson	73 68 74 70	285	2,262.50
Jon Chaffee	72 70 72 71	285	2,262.50
Schalk van der Merwe	68 77 69 71	285	2,265.50

Zimbabwe Open

Royal Harare Golf Club, Harare, Zimbabwe
Par 36-36—72; 7,036 yards

January 26-29
purse, £49,550

	SCORES	TOTAL	MONEY
Vijay Singh	72 67 71 72	282	£8,168.12
Mark Mouland	73 71 67 73	284	5,420.29
David Wood	67 75 75 68	285	3,072.46
Gordon J. Brand	73 69 73 72	287	2,077.30
Wayne Stephens	73 68 72 74	287	2,077.30
John Vingoe	72 70 70 75	287	2,077.30
Mark Roe	72 73 74 69	288	1,478.26
Ross Drummond	71 75 72 72	290	1,106.28
Stephen Hamill	71 73 74 72	290	1,106.28
James Spence	73 74 73 70	290	1,106.28
Joe Higgins	74 71 73 73	291	913.04
Mats Hallberg	68 77 75 72	292	768.70
Jerry Anderson	73 75 69 75	292	768.70
Ronald Gregan	72 71 74 75	292	768.70
William Koen	75 73 72 72	292	768.70
Anthony Edwards	72 72 74 74	292	768.70
David Llewellyn	71 72 78 72	293	622.03
Wraith Grant	72 72 76 73	293	622.03
David R. Jones	73 74 73 73	293	622.03
Tony Stevens	74 72 74 73	293	622.03
Craig Maltman	75 69 74 75	293	622.03
David Williams	75 73 74 72	294	572.46
Andrew Stubbs	76 75 73 71	295	500.72
Nick Godin	70 80 74 71	295	500.72
Clive Tucker	75 76 74 70	295	500.72
Andrew Cotton	75 72 74 74	295	500.72
John Morgan	71 74 76 74	295	500.72
James Annable	74 72 74 75	295	500.72
Paul Kent	72 71 74 78	295	500.72
Morgan Shumba	73 77 73 72	295	500.72

Protea Assurance South African Open

Glendower Golf Club, Bedfordview, Johannesburg
Par 36-36—72; 7,370 yards

February 1-4
purse, R300,000

	SCORES				TOTAL	MONEY
Fred Wadsworth	72	68	70	68	278	R48,000
Tom Lehman	72	66	68	73	279	34,500
Jack Ferenz	75	71	68	67	281	21,000
Tony Johnstone	69	67	74	73	283	15,000
Jeff Hawkes	71	69	71	73	284	12,600
Bruce Vaughan	73	71	72	69	285	9,900
Charlie Bolling	73	67	70	75	285	9,900
Justin Hobday	72	73	69	72	286	7,050
Greg Cesario	72	74	67	73	286	7,050
Andre Cruse	70	65	76	76	287	6,000
Simon Hobday	72	73	73	70	288	4,830
Clayton Simmons	73	73	72	70	288	4,830
John Daly	74	75	67	72	288	4,830
Mark James	73	70	72	73	288	4,830
Chris Williams	71	73	70	74	288	4,830
J.C. Anderson	75	69	74	71	289	4,050
Phil Jonas	72	73	73	71	289	4,050
Stuart Smith	70	71	74	74	289	4,050
Teddy Webber	74	73	73	70	290	3,675
Gavin Levenson	73	74	69	74	290	3,675
Mark Wiltshire	67	76	74	74	291	3,390
Richard Parker	70	74	72	75	291	3,390
David Feherty	69	71	74	77	291	3,390
Bob McDonnell	71	69	80	72	292	2,940
Schalk van der Merwe	76	71	73	72	292	2,940
Timothy Robinson	72	73	74	73	292	2,940
Derek James	73	70	75	74	292	2,940
Alan Pate	74	71	73	74	292	2,940
Brian Evans	74	68	73	77	292	2,940
Wayne Westner	74	70	71	77	292	2,940

Zambian Open

Lusaka Golf Club, Lusaka, Zambia
Par 35-38—73; 7,216 yards

February 2-5
purse, £75,000

(Shortened to three rounds, rain; final round 17 holes, par 69—215)

	SCORES			TOTAL	MONEY
Craig Maltman	67	76	72	215	£12,500
Mark Roe	76	71	70	217	8,320
Gordon J. Brand	76	72	70	218	4,690
Vijay Singh	75	73	72	220	3,745
Andrew Cotton	75	76	70	221	2,897.50
Jeffrey Pinsent	72	74	75	221	2,897.50
Jerry Anderson	77	73	72	222	2,062.50
Adam Hunter	73	78	71	222	2,062.50
James Spence	75	75	73	223	1,680
Anthony Edwards	79	74	71	224	1,500
Paul Carrigill	75	74	76	225	1,171.43
Peter Cowen	73	81	71	225	1,171.43
Ross Drummond	81	74	70	225	1,171.43

	SCORES			TOTAL	MONEY
Stephen Hamill	74	75	76	225	1,171.43
Lee Jones	73	79	73	225	1,171.43
Glenn Ralph	75	77	73	225	1,171.43
David Williams	77	75	73	225	1,171.43
Paul Carman	76	78	72	226	894.16
Wraith Grant	79	71	76	226	894.16
David R. Jones	76	76	74	226	894.16
David Llewellyn	76	75	75	226	894.16
Mark Mouland	76	75	75	226	894.16
Tim Price	79	74	73	226	894.16
Mike Miller	77	78	72	227	810
David Jones	74	79	75	228	743
Stephen McAllister	73	74	81	228	743
John Morgan	77	75	76	228	743
Ian Spencer	74	79	75	228	743
Wayne Stephens	76	81	71	228	743
Andrew Clapp	77	76	76	229	651.67
Chris Gray	74	78	77	229	651.67
Mark Litton	76	82	71	229	651.67

AECI Charity Classic

Rand Park Golf Club, Johannesburg, South Africa
Par 36-36—72; 7,320 yards

February 8-11
purse, R250,000

(Final round cancelled - rain.)

	SCORES			TOTAL	MONEY
Jeff Hawkes	67	64	70	201	R40,000
Tony Johnstone	66	68	69	203	28,750
Hugh Baiocchi	66	67	72	205	15,000
Stuart Smith	69	63	73	205	15,000
Ian Palmer	70	66	71	207	10,500
Phil Jonas	72	68	68	208	6,650
John Bland	71	68	69	208	6,650
Marty Schiene	71	67	70	208	6,650
Ashley Roestoff	68	69	71	208	6,650
Schalk van der Merwe	69	64	75	208	6,650
Bruce Vaughan	73	68	68	209	3,857.14
Allan Henning	71	69	69	209	3,857.14
Mark James	69	70	70	209	3,857.14
John Daly	67	72	70	209	3,857.14
Dale Hayes	70	67	72	209	3,857.14
Brian Evans	69	66	74	209	3,857.14
Phillip Hatchett	71	65	73	209	3,857.14
Douglas Wherry	67	73	70	210	3,020
Scott Dunlap	68	72	70	210	3,020
John Mashego	70	70	70	210	3,020
Tertius Claassens	72	67	71	210	3,020
Wayne Westner	69	67	74	210	3,020
Tom Lehman	70	71	70	211	2,562.50
Brian Mahon	72	68	71	211	2,562.50
Bob McDonnell	70	70	71	211	2,562.50
Jim Vernon	70	69	72	211	2,562.50
Chris Williams	67	71	73	211	2,562.50
Thomas Tolles, Jr.	67	67	77	211	2,562.50
Gavin Levenson	72	70	70	212	2,006.82

	SCORES			TOTAL	MONEY
Hendrik Buhrmann	69	73	70	212	2,006.82
Bobby Cole	72	70	70	212	2,006.82
Hugh Royer	72	69	71	212	2,006.82
Don Robertson	71	70	71	212	2,006.82
Don Walsworth	67	73	72	212	2,006.82
Wilhelm Winsnes	69	71	72	212	2,006.82
Craigen Pappas	72	67	73	212	2,006.82
Richard Kaplan	69	69	73	212	2,006.82
Bobby Lincoln	68	71	73	212	2,006.82
Teddy Webber	68	70	74	212	2,006.82

Kenya Open

Muthaiga Golf Club, Nairobi, Kenya
Par 36-35—71; 6,766 yards

February 9-12
purse, £69,230

	SCORES				TOTAL	MONEY
David Jones	69	69	65	68	271	£11,230.77
Mark Mouland	67	69	71	67	274	7,615.38
James Spence	70	71	65	69	275	4,246.15
Clive Tucker	70	66	71	69	276	3,092.31
Vijay Singh	70	68	70	68	276	3,092.31
Kyle Kelsall	71	71	71	64	277	2,338.46
David Wood	71	69	72	67	279	1,692.69
Wayne Stephens	70	71	69	69	279	1,692.69
Mikael Krantz	68	70	68	73	279	1,692.69
Craig Maltman	67	70	74	68	279	1,692.69
Stephen McAllister	72	72	66	71	281	1,298.46
Malcolm Gregson	72	70	72	68	282	1,179.23
Paul Carman	74	72	68	68	282	1,179.23
Richard Fish	70	71	73	69	283	1,002.69
Gordon J. Brand	69	70	70	74	283	1,002.69
Tony Stevens	69	74	70	70	283	1,002.69
Glenn Ralph	71	71	71	70	283	1,002.69
Jerry Anderson	73	69	74	68	284	898.46
Peter Cowen	74	70	70	71	285	839.23
David Llewellyn	75	71	67	72	285	839.23
John Vingoe	73	74	71	68	286	745.77
David R. Jones	74	68	73	71	286	745.77
John Morgan	75	70	69	72	286	745.77
Ronald Gregan	73	72	72	69	286	745.77
*John Mucheru	74	72	72	69	287	
Andrew Stubbs	72	72	73	70	287	676.92
Paul Carrigill	73	69	73	73	288	632.31
Andrew Cotton	71	73	73	71	288	632.31
David Blakeman	67	74	74	73	288	632.31
Anthony Edwards	74	72	73	70	289	546.37
Mats Hallberg	71	72	73	73	289	546.37
Johnny Young	74	71	70	74	289	546.37
Peter Harrison	72	70	74	73	289	546.37
Ross Drummond	72	74	73	70	289	546.37
Ben Porter	74	71	74	70	289	546.37
Ian Spencer	71	72	71	75	289	546.37

Hosken Hollard Swazi Sun Classic

Royal Swazi Golf Club, Mbabane, Swaziland
Par 36-36—72; 6,708 yards

February 17-19
purse, R250,000

(Final round cancelled - rain.)

	SCORES			TOTAL	MONEY
Jeff Hawkes	67	66	69	202	R40,000
Joe Dlamini	67	69	67	203	23,125
John Daly	67	67	69	203	23,125
Chris Williams	70	69	65	204	10,666.67
Brian Mahon	67	69	68	204	10,666.67
Alan Pate	68	72	64	204	10,666.67
Kevin Stone	70	70	65	205	6,416.67
Jay Townsend	72	68	65	205	6,416.67
Marty Schiene	67	67	71	205	6,416.67
Timothy Robinson	71	69	66	206	4,503.33
Chip Holcombe	68	71	67	206	4,503.33
Ian Palmer	68	70	68	206	4,503.33
Bob McDonnell	71	68	68	207	3,583.33
Brandt Jobe	71	68	68	207	3,583.33
Bruce Vaughan	72	67	68	207	3,583.33
Phil Simmons	66	71	70	207	3,583.33
Dale Hayes	68	68	71	207	3,583.33
Jon Chaffee	68	68	71	207	3,583.33
Wilhelm Winsnes	68	71	69	208	2,920
Wayne Westner	67	72	69	208	2,920
Jack Ferenz	70	69	69	208	2,920
Phil Jonas	70	68	70	208	2,920
Tom Lehman	69	69	71	208	2,920
Allan Henning	73	67	69	209	2,525
Hendrik Buhrmann	71	72	66	209	2,525
Angus Baker	71	67	71	209	2,525
Jim Moodie	67	70	72	209	2,525
Bobby Lincoln	71	70	68	209	2,525
Francis Quinn	74	69	67	210	2,110.71
Steve van Vuuren	70	73	67	210	2,110.71
John Bland	72	71	67	210	2,110.71
Nico von Rensburg	70	69	71	210	2,110.71
Robert Richardson	69	73	68	210	2,110.71
William Kane	69	69	72	210	2,110.71
Andre Cruse	70	71	69	210	2,110.71

Trust Bank Tournament of Champions

Kensington Golf Club, Johannesburg, South Africa
Par 35-37—72; 6,716 yards

February 22-25
purse, R250,000

	SCORES				TOTAL	MONEY
Jay Townsend	67	70	67	71	275	R40,000
Bruce Vaughan	71	71	70	65	277	28,750
Ian Palmer	73	68	73	65	279	12,375
John Bland	70	71	71	67	279	12,375
Gavin Levenson	73	69	69	68	279	12,375
Jeff Hawkes	69	69	71	70	279	12,375
Timothy Robinson	72	71	71	67	281	5,750
Chip Holcombe	72	72	69	68	281	5,750

	SCORES			TOTAL	MONEY
Bob McDonnell	70	72	68	71	281	5,750
Jon Chaffee	66	72	70	73	281	5,750
Hugh Royer	71	74	63	73	281	5,750
Wayne Westner	70	70	74	68	282	3,825
Schalk van der Merwe	73	73	67	69	282	3,825
John Daly	71	70	70	71	282	3,825
Tony Johnstone	68	73	69	72	282	3,825
Frank Edmonds	69	69	70	74	282	3,825
Don Robertson	73	71	68	71	283	3,375
Justin Hobday	73	69	71	71	284	3,125
J.C. Anderson	71	67	73	73	284	3,125
Teddy Webber	71	70	69	74	284	3,125
Jim Vernon	70	76	68	71	285	2,825
Marty Schiene	68	74	70	73	285	2,825
Andre Cruse	69	75	67	74	285	2,825
Dale Hayes	73	72	70	71	286	2,562.50
Jack Ferenz	73	70	67	74	286	2,562.50
Allan Henning	72	73	67	74	286	2,562.50
Carl Cooper	70	70	68	78	286	2,562.50
Mark Hartness	75	70	73	69	287	2,063.64
Fred Wadsworth	70	72	74	71	287	2,063.64
Thomas Tolles, Jr.	71	75	70	71	287	2,063.64
Robert Friend	72	73	71	71	287	2,063.64
Ben Fouchee	76	71	69	71	287	2,063.64
Gert von Biljon	72	69	74	72	287	2,063.64
Wayne Bradley	71	68	76	72	287	2,063.64
Hugh Baiocchi	72	75	69	71	287	2,063.64
Andrew Morse	70	72	72	73	287	2,063.64
Kelly Gibson	72	74	69	72	287	2,063.64
Phil Jonas	70	73	71	73	287	2,063.64

Railfreight Bloemfontein Classic

Schoeman Park Golf Club, Bloemfontein
Par 35-35—70; 6,706 yards

November 15-18
purse, R250,000

	SCORES			TOTAL	MONEY
Desmond Terblanche	74	67	67	70	278	R40,000
Wayne Westner	70	69	74	67	280	23,125
John Bland	69	69	73	69	280	23,125
Justin Hobday	73	71	68	70	282	12,500
Jeff Hawkes	69	73	67	74	283	9,000
Chris Williams	71	72	68	72	283	9,000
Tony Johnstone	69	72	67	75	283	9,000
Fred Wadsworth	69	70	68	77	284	6,250
Jannie Le Grange	70	74	71	70	285	4,650
Dale Hayes	73	72	70	70	285	4,650
Schalk van der Merwe	70	75	69	71	285	4,650
Jimmy Johnson	72	70	69	74	285	4,650
Peter van der Riet	73	71	67	74	285	4,650
De Wet Basson	70	78	69	69	286	3,625
Simon Hobday	73	75	69	69	286	3,625
Rick Hartman	71	69	72	74	286	3,625
Hugh Baiocchi	73	75	70	69	287	3,130
Richard Kaplan	72	72	72	71	287	3,130
Phil Simmons	75	71	69	72	287	3,130
Mark Wiltshire	71	71	73	72	287	3,130

	SCORES	TOTAL	MONEY
Bobby Lincoln	69 71 74 73	287	3,130
Allan Henning	73 73 74 68	288	2,750
Nico van Rensburg	71 68 78 71	288	2,750
Wilhelm Winsnes	73 70 73 72	288	2,750
Jim Johnson	72 75 72 70	289	2,562.50
Hendrik Buhrmann	75 70 71 73	289	2,562.50
Thomas Tolles, Jr.	73 75 74 68	290	2,337.50
Glenn James	72 72 73 73	290	2,337.50
Kevin Stone	70 71 75 74	290	2,337.50
Ernie Els	74 72 70 74	290	2,337.50

First Bank Nigerian Open

Ikoyi Golf Club, Lagos, Nigeria
Par 36-35—71; 6,389 yards

November 16-19
purse, £63,211

	SCORES	TOTAL	MONEY
Vijay Singh	71 68 72 68	279	£10,530.97
Gordon J. Brand	69 71 70 70	280	4,711.34
Ian Spencer	73 69 71 67	280	4,711.34
Jeffrey Pinsent	71 70 68 71	280	4,711.34
Chris Platts	68 68 74 71	281	2,680.15
David Llewellyn	73 67 73 70	283	2,212.39
David Jagger	71 71 71 71	284	1,896.33
John Morgan	71 69 73 72	285	1,498.11
Steven Richardson	69 76 74 66	285	1,498.11
Paul Hoad	73 74 69 70	286	1,213.65
Philip Talbot	71 73 71 71	286	1,213.65
*Marcel Soumahoro	73 69 74 70	286	
Stephen Hamill	72 67 73 75	287	1,024.02
Bello Seibidor	74 71 72 70	287	1,024.02
Peter Akakasiaka	71 69 73 74	287	1,024.02
Jacob Omoruah	72 72 74 70	288	929.20
Mike Miller	70 71 70 78	289	891.28
Tony Uduimoh	73 71 75 71	290	834.39
Tony Stevens	73 70 72 75	290	834.39
Paul Osanebi	71 76 71 73	291	771.18
John Vingoe	76 72 69 74	291	771.18
David Owoyemi	80 68 72 72	292	730.09
S. Okpe	71 70 74 77	292	730.09
Charles Giddins	74 73 74 72	293	692.16
I. Baliya	73 71 76 73	293	692.16
*Richard Omoyi	72 73 74 74	293	
Christian Okwu	75 73 74 72	294	625.79
James Lebbie	72 72 77 73	294	625.79
Festus Makelemi	77 71 73 73	294	625.79
John Ngugi	75 69 76 74	294	625.79
Pender Umuebu	72 76 71 75	294	625.79
Richard Fish	76 75 73 71	295	559.42
Brave Mensah	71 78 73 73	295	559.42

Ivory Coast Open

President Golf Club, Yamoussoukro, Ivory Coast
Par 36-36—72; 6,476 yards

November 23-26
purse, £82,858.74

	SCORES				TOTAL	MONEY
Vijay Singh	70	65	65	74	274	£13,808.39
Jeffrey Pinsent	69	65	70	71	275	9,197.31
John Morgan	69	69	69	72	279	4,664.94
Gordon J. Brand	68	70	70	71	279	4,664.94
Paul Hoad	70	70	74	67	281	3,204.56
Ramuncho Artola	74	64	73	70	281	3,204.56
David Llewellyn	71	66	75	70	282	2,485.76
John Vingoe	75	68	73	69	285	2,071.47
Mike Miller	74	72	67	74	287	1,679.27
Stephen McAllister	75	73	72	67	287	1,679.27
Chris Gray	71	76	76	64	287	1,679.27
Chris Platts	69	69	75	75	288	1,425.17
Stephen Hamill	69	74	72	74	289	1,300.88
Richard Fish	76	68	72	73	289	1,300.88
Steven Richardson	75	71	74	70	290	1,218.02
Philip Talbot	69	74	78	70	291	1,143.45
David Jagger	74	76	72	69	291	1,143.45
Robert Green	73	71	76	72	292	1,048.17
Pascal Ferran	72	76	77	67	292	1,048.17
Ben Porter	69	76	75	73	293	981.88
Phil Golding	73	74	75	71	293	981.88
*Siaka Kone	70	72	73	78	293	
Jerry Mulubah	76	74	73	72	295	932.16
Bello Seibidor	72	75	73	75	295	932.16
*Marcel Soumahoro	77	74	74	70	295	
Fabrice Honnorat	78	77	69	73	297	857.59
Tony Stevens	76	77	71	73	297	857.59
S. Okpe	77	73	74	73	297	857.59
Charles Chichi	78	74	76	69	297	857.59
Ian Campbell	73	70	80	75	298	783.02
Hyacinthe Gnaba	73	80	72	73	298	783.02
Amos Korblah	71	77	73	78	299	733.30
Bradley Smith	77	69	78	75	299	733.30

Million Dollar Challenge

Gary Player Country Club, Sun City, Bophuthatswana
Par 36-36—72; 7,665 yards

December 7-10
purse $2,360,000

	SCORES				TOTAL	MONEY
David Frost	67	66	75	68	276	$1,000,000
Scott Hoch	67	72	71	69	279	300,000
Tim Simpson	67	69	72	72	280	250,000
Don Pooley	73	71	76	71	291	200,000
Chip Beck	72	70	76	76	294	150,000
Andy Bean	81	74	71	69	295	120,000
Sandy Lyle	75	73	76	74	298	100,000
Fulton Allem	76	75	70	78	299	90,000
Ken Green	72	77	75	77	301	75,000
Scott Simpson	72	75	80	74	301	75,000

Twee Jongegezellen Masters

Stellenbosch Golf Club, Cape Town
Par 37-35—72; 7,036 yards

December 15-18
purse, R252,750

	SCORES				TOTAL	MONEY
Hugh Baiocchi	67	68	74	70	281	R40,000
Rick Hartman	71	73	71	67	282	19,500.33
Tertius Classens	71	71	70	70	282	19,500.33
Ernie Els	76	68	65	73	282	19,500.33
Thomas Tolles, Jr.	72	67	71	73	283	10,500
John Bland	69	70	75	71	285	8,250
Tony Johnstone	69	71	69	76	285	8,250
Andre Cruse	73	75	68	70	286	5,875
Fulton Allem	74	70	72	70	286	5,875
De Wet Basson	72	77	69	69	287	4,750
Desmond Terblanche	74	68	71	74	287	4,750
Peter Van Der Riet	72	72	74	70	288	4,000
Gavin Levinson	76	70	69	73	288	4,000
Teddy Webber	73	71	70	74	288	4,000
Ian Palmer	72	78	73	66	289	3,437.50
Mervyn Galant	73	70	76	70	289	3,437.50
Robbie Stewart	77	69	72	71	289	3,437.50
Jeff Hawkes	70	74	73	72	289	3,437.50
Ben Fouchee	76	71	74	69	290	2,920
Phil Jonas	76	70	73	71	290	2,920
Wayne Player	76	69	73	72	290	2,920
Denis Durnian	74	68	74	74	290	2,920
Bobby Lincoln	72	69	73	76	290	2,920
Wayne Bradley	73	71	75	72	291	2,600
Wayne Westner	73	71	74	73	291	2,600
Steve Van Vuuren	71	69	74	77	291	2,600
Phil Simmons	79	69	73	71	292	2,300
Simon Hobday	78	72	71	71	292	2,300
Steven Burnett	73	74	72	73	292	2,300
Richard Kaplan	74	72	72	74	292	2,300
Derek James	70	75	73	74	292	2,300

The Australasian Tour

Daikyo Palm Meadows Cup

Palm Meadows Golf Club, Gold Coast, Queensland
Par 36-36—72; 6,973 yards

January 12-15
purse, A$600,000

	SCORES				TOTAL	MONEY
Curtis Strange	66	70	71	73	280	A$108,000
Ray Floyd	71	68	70	73	282	64,800
Terry Price	74	65	70	74	283	41,400
Peter Fowler	70	70	70	74	284	29,880
George Serhan	70	70	73	72	285	22,800
Jeff Maggert	67	71	74	73	285	22,800
Isao Aoki	69	72	69	75	285	22,800
Ossie Moore	74	73	70	70	287	16,080
Rodger Davis	71	71	73	72	287	16,080
Brett Ogle	68	71	73	75	287	16,080
Yutaka Hagawa	71	71	75	71	288	10,440
Roger Mackay	72	71	71	74	288	10,440
Michael Bradley	73	71	70	74	288	10,440
Masashi Ozaki	72	68	72	76	288	10,440
David Smith	74	66	75	74	289	8,160
Lyndsay Stephen	71	74	69	75	289	8,160
Ken Dukes	74	71	74	71	290	7,380
Ian Stanley	71	74	73	72	290	7,380
John O'Neill	72	72	74	73	291	6,000
Mark K. Nash	74	71	73	73	291	6,000
Kirk Triplett	71	73	73	74	291	6,000
Jeff Woodland	71	72	73	75	291	6,000
Greg Norman	75	68	73	75	291	6,000
David Graham	68	71	76	76	291	6,000
Grant Waite	72	72	71	76	291	6,000
Peter Senior	69	73	72	77	291	6,000
Mike Ferguson	73	73	76	70	292	4,160
Andrew La'Brooy	74	72	74	72	292	4,160
Peter McWhinney	71	74	74	73	292	4,160
Tim Elliott	74	72	72	74	292	4,160
Steve Rintoul	74	73	71	74	292	4,160
Simon Owen	70	74	73	75	292	4,160
Hajime Meshiai	67	72	76	77	292	4,160
Tateo Ozaki	74	70	70	78	292	4,160
Tsukasa Watanabe	77	68	67	80	292	4,160

Coca-Cola Golf Classic

Royal Melbourne Golf Club, Composite Course,
Melbourne, Victoria
Par 35-37—72; 6,945 yards

January 19-22
purse, A$600,000

	SCORES				TOTAL	MONEY
Isao Aoki	69	73	66	71	279	A$108,000
Peter Fowler	71	68	73	68	280	40,260

	SCORES				TOTAL	MONEY
Tsuneyuki Nakajima	69	69	75	67	280	40,260
Peter O'Malley	64	70	77	69	280	40,260
Rodger Davis	68	70	71	71	280	40,260
Scott Simpson	73	70	71	67	281	21,720
Grant Waite	71	69	69	72	281	21,720
Ian Baker-Finch	72	72	68	70	282	17,880
Peter Senior	71	71	72	69	283	15,180
Masahiro Kuramoto	70	71	74	68	283	15,180
Ossie Moore	69	71	74	70	284	11,520
Anthony Gilligan	69	76	69	70	284	11,520
Brett Ogle	70	73	72	70	285	9,360
Lyndsay Stephen	69	69	73	74	285	9,360
Nobumitsu Yuhara	68	74	74	71	287	8,160
Bryan Watts	66	73	73	75	287	8,160
John Clifford	70	72	75	71	288	7,560
Bob Shearer	71	77	72	69	289	7,020
Tim Elliott	69	74	74	72	289	7,020
Jim Woodward	67	73	77	73	290	6,000
David De Long	67	73	77	73	290	6,000
Terry Gale	72	70	75	73	290	6,000
Mike Harwood	68	75	74	73	290	6,000
Donnie Hammond	72	72	72	74	290	6,000
Ronan Rafferty	72	73	72	73	290	6,000
Ian Stanley	67	75	78	71	291	4,680
Ken Trimble	72	74	74	71	291	4,680
Kirk Triplett	70	75	73	73	291	4,680
Jeff Woodland	70	73	74	74	291	4,680
Anders Forsbrand	72	70	73	76	291	4,680

Asthma Foundation Victorian PGA

Keysborough Golf Club, Melbourne, Victoria
Par 36-37—73; 6,889 yards

January 26-29
purse, A$100,000

	SCORES				TOTAL	MONEY
David Ecob	72	69	71	67	279	A$18,000
Peter Senior	69	69	71	71	280	10,800
Mike Harwood	71	67	71	74	283	6,900
John Clifford	71	69	73	71	284	4,320
Louis Brown	71	70	70	73	284	4,320
Peter McWhinney	71	70	70	73	284	4,320
Michael Bradley	68	72	72	73	285	3,420
Simon Owen	70	68	73	75	286	2,680
Richard Gilkey	69	72	72	73	286	2,680
Jack Larkin	70	74	68	74	286	2,680
Tim Elliott	69	71	75	72	287	2,040
Craig Parry	70	75	76	67	288	1,800
Glenn Joyner	72	70	73	74	289	1,640
Kirk Triplett	74	72	72	72	290	1,365
Johan Rystrom	73	71	73	73	290	1,365
David Smith	73	70	74	73	290	1,365
Ken Trimble	72	73	70	75	290	1,365
Bob Shearer	75	70	75	71	291	1,104
Grant Waite	68	77	75	71	291	1,104
Steve Rintoul	72	71	75	73	291	1,104
David De Long	73	70	75	73	291	1,104
Gordon Smith	69	72	75	75	291	1,104
Jeff Senior	73	72	75	72	292	806

	SCORES				TOTAL	MONEY
Jason Deep	70	77	72	73	292	806
Terry Gale	73	75	71	73	292	806
Jon Diggetts	72	70	76	74	292	806
Mike Colandro	76	69	73	74	292	806
Jeff Woodland	71	71	75	75	292	806
Mark Keating	75	68	73	76	292	806
Kris Moe	73	72	71	76	292	806
David Merriman	73	73	70	76	292	806
Wayne Smith	69	73	71	79	292	806

Victorian Open

Kingston Heath Golf Club, Melbourne, Victoria
Par 36-36—72; 6,814 yards

February 2-5
purse, A$100,000

	SCORES				TOTAL	MONEY
Mike Clayton	69	67	75	74	285	A$18,000
Ossie Moore	71	70	77	69	287	10,800
Wayne Smith	67	70	76	75	288	6,900
Brent Franklin	70	75	72	72	289	4,570
Craig Parry	70	73	71	75	289	4,570
Steve Rintoul	74	70	72	74	290	3,620
Peter Fowler	74	69	72	75	290	3,620
Louis Brown	73	73	74	71	291	2,376
Brett Officer	68	76	75	72	291	2,376
Brett Ogle	71	73	73	74	291	2,376
Bob Shearer	69	73	73	76	291	2,376
Lucien Tinkler	72	69	69	81	291	2,376
Mike Harwood	71	70	76	75	292	1,460
Gerry Taylor	71	72	75	74	292	1,460
Peter Senior	71	72	74	75	292	1,460
Cameron Howell	70	72	75	75	292	1,460
Ian Stanley	76	72	73	72	293	1,230
Peter Jones	71	73	73	76	293	1,230
*Stephen McCraw	71	69	78	75	293	
Peter McWhinney	74	68	80	72	294	1,080
Lyndsay Stephen	74	72	75	73	294	1,080
Ronan Rafferty	72	69	78	75	294	1,080
David Merriman	71	67	74	82	294	1,080
Anthony Gilligan	74	72	76	73	295	940
Brad Hughes	74	72	71	78	295	940
Kris Moe	69	68	79	79	295	940
Mark K. Nash	72	73	79	72	296	748.57
Jeff Maggert	72	72	79	73	296	748.57
Jason Deep	73	73	75	75	296	748.57
David Smith	78	69	72	77	296	748.57
John Brellenthin	72	69	77	78	296	748.57
Ken Trimble	76	67	73	80	296	748.57
John Clifford	71	73	69	83	296	748.57

Australian Match Play Championship

Kingston Heath Golf Club, Melbourne, Victoria
Par 36-36—72; 6,814 yards

February 9-12
purse, A$150,000

FIRST ROUND

Anthony Gilligan defeated David Ecob, 1 up
Mike Ferguson defeated Anthony Painter, 6 and 4
Paul Foley defeated Lindsay Stephen, 3 and 2
John Clifford defeated Ian Baker-Finch, 3 and 2
Ken Trimble defeated Simon Owen, 4 and 2
Ossie Moore defeated David Merriman, 4 and 3
Mike Clayton defeated Terry Gale, 3 and 2
Roger Mackay defeated Grant Waite, 3 and 2
Wayne Riley defeated *Stuart Bouvier, 2 up
Vaughan Somers defeated Brett Ogle, w/o
Mike Harwood defeated Ian Stanley, 2 up
David Smith defeated Mike Colandro, 1 up
Bob Shearer defeated Brad Hughes, 1 up
Peter Fowler defeated Noel Ratcliffe, 4 and 2
Frank Nobilo defeated Jeff Woodland, 1 up
Ronan Rafferty defeated Wayne Smith, 1 up
(Each losing player received A$1,500.)

SECOND ROUND

Rafferty defeated Nobilo, 2 and 1
Fowler defeated Shearer, 1 up, 20 holes
Smith defeated Harwood, 1 up
Riley defeated Somers, 1 up
Clayton defeated Mackay, 5 and 4
Moore defeated Trimble, 5 and 4
Clifford defeated Foley, 1 up, 19 holes
Gilligan defeated Ferguson, 3 and 2
(Each losing played received A$3,000.)

QUARTER-FINALS

Clifford defeated Gilligan, 4 and 3
Moore defeated Clayton, 3 and 2
Smith defeated Riley, 3 and 2
Fowler defeated Rafferty, 2 up
(Each losing player received A$6,000.)

SEMI-FINALS

Fowler defeated Smith, 4 and 2
Moore defeated Clifford, 3 and 2

THIRD-FOURTH PLACE PLAYOFF

Clifford defeated Smith, 4 and 2

FINAL

Moore defeated Fowler, 1 up
(Moore received A$32,000, Fowler A$18,000, Clifford A$12,000, Smith A$8,500.)

Australian Masters

Huntingdale Golf Club, Melbourne, Victoria
Par 37-36—73; 6,955 yards

February 16-19
purse, A$450,000

	SCORES				TOTAL	MONEY
Greg Norman	69	69	74	68	280	A$81,000
*Russell Claydon	66	69	75	75	285	
Craig Parry	68	67	79	72	286	39,825
Bob Shearer	67	69	74	76	286	39,825
Grant Waite	67	71	76	73	287	22,410
Peter Fowler	67	68	80	73	288	18,720
Brent Franklin	71	70	75	73	289	13,752
Ossie Moore	69	72	74	74	289	13,752
Mike Harwood	69	71	78	71	289	13,752
Mike Clayton	72	70	73	74	289	13,752
Tsuyoshi Yoneyama	71	70	70	78	289	13,752
David Graham	76	68	72	74	290	9,180
Jack Nicklaus	70	72	72	77	291	8,100
Brad King	74	73	74	71	292	6,390
Kel Devlin	73	73	75	71	292	6,390
John Clifford	71	72	74	75	292	6,390
Wayne Smith	72	72	73	75	292	6,390
Frank Nobilo	70	70	78	74	292	6,390
Lucien Tinkler	75	71	74	73	293	5,265
Peter O'Malley	72	75	72	74	293	5,265
David Ecob	73	70	78	73	294	4,680
Terry Gale	73	72	74	75	294	4,680
Mike Colandro	73	71	75	75	294	4,680
Brian Jones	70	73	74	77	294	4,680
Stewart Ginn	75	72	75	73	295	3,780
Ray Picker	74	70	76	75	295	3,780
David De Long	78	68	74	75	295	3,780
Ian Baker-Finch	69	74	76	76	295	3,780
Peter McWhinney	73	71	74	77	295	3,780
Robert Stephens	73	69	76	77	295	3,780

Tournament Players' Championship

Riverside Oaks PGA National, Cattai, New South Wales
Par 36-36—72; 6,950 yards

February 23-26
purse, A$500,000

	SCORES				TOTAL	MONEY
Greg Norman	70	70	69	67	276	A$90,000
Roger Mackay	67	73	69	69	278	54,000
Rodger Davis	72	67	72	69	280	29,700
David De Long	68	70	70	72	280	29,700
Peter Fowler	71	69	71	70	281	19,950
Craig Parry	70	70	70	71	281	19,950
Frank Nobilo	69	74	70	69	282	15,166.66
Peter Senior	73	70	67	72	282	15,166.66
Jeff Woodland	69	70	67	72	282	15,166.66
Bob Shearer	70	71	76	66	283	10,333.33
Brad Hughes	78	68	68	69	283	10,333.33
Greg Hohnen	70	71	70	72	283	10,333.33
Ken Trimble	73	70	71	70	284	8,200
Simon Owen	73	70	72	70	285	7,200

	SCORES				TOTAL	MONEY
Kirk Triplett	72	73	66	74	285	7,200
Anthony Painter	75	73	71	67	286	5,675
Graham Marsh	73	71	74	68	286	5,675
John O'Neill	76	72	70	68	286	5,675
Mike Harwood	73	71	72	70	286	5,675
Ian Baker-Finch	69	70	74	73	286	5,675
Terry Gale	74	72	67	73	286	5,675
Michael Springer	71	70	70	75	286	5,675
Brett Ogle	75	67	69	75	286	5,675
Robert McNamara	77	68	73	69	287	4,400
Mike Clayton	74	71	72	70	287	4,400
Brad King	75	71	70	71	287	4,400
Brian Jones	73	70	71	73	287	4,400
Jason Deep	73	75	69	71	288	3,800
Terry Price	76	72	69	71	288	3,800
John Clifford	74	73	70	72	289	3,400
Lyndsay Stephen	70	73	73	73	289	3,400
Jon Heimer	75	69	72	73	289	3,400

Monro Interiors Nedlands Masters

Nedlands Golf Club, Perth, Western Australia
Par 36-36—72; 6,289 yards

March 9-12
purse, A$100,000

	SCORES				TOTAL	MONEY
Louis Brown	70	68	68	68	274	A$18,000
Ken Trimble	68	70	71	66	275	7,560
Wayne Smith	64	72	68	71	275	7,560
Garry Merrick	70	67	67	71	275	7,560
Roger Mackay	70	68	69	69	276	3,990
Jeff Woodland	75	64	66	71	276	3,990
Bob Shearer	68	70	68	71	277	3,200
Terry Gale	73	63	68	73	277	3,200
Peter Senior	67	72	67	72	278	2,700
Brad King	69	69	71	70	279	2,360
Lyndsay Stephen	65	74	70	71	280	2,040
Richard Gilkey	69	67	75	70	281	1,640
Mike Harwood	71	66	72	72	281	1,640
Grant Waite	68	72	65	76	281	1,640
Brad Hughes	71	65	76	70	282	1,264
Magnus Grankvist	69	72	69	72	282	1,264
Ken Collins	66	69	74	73	282	1,264
Mike Colandro	72	69	69	72	282	1,264
Craig Parry	70	71	68	73	282	1,264
Jon Evans	73	73	67	70	283	1,100
George Serhan	69	72	74	69	284	1,060
Brett Officer	71	70	73	71	285	1,000
Steve Rintoul	73	70	70	72	285	1,000
Peter McWhinney	72	70	74	70	286	940
Jeff Senior	74	70	74	69	287	820
Tony Brigstock	72	70	72	73	287	820
Ian Roberts	69	72	74	72	287	820
Wayne Case	70	70	71	76	287	820
Kirk Triplett	69	73	69	76	287	820
John Clifford	71	71	74	72	288	680
Robert Stephens	69	75	72	72	288	680
Craig Warren	74	70	70	74	288	680

Town & Country Joondalup PGA Classic

Joondalup Country Club, Perth, Western Australia
Par 36-36—72; 6,754 yards

March 16-19
purse, A\$100,000

	SCORES				TOTAL	MONEY
Brad King	74	65	64	68	271	A\$18,000
Ken Trimble	71	70	67	72	280	8,850
Peter Senior	71	70	66	73	280	8,850
Jon Evans	75	73	65	70	283	4,570
Roger Mackay	71	73	68	71	283	4,570
Lucien Tinkler	74	69	73	68	284	3,820
Glenn Joyner	68	73	72	72	285	3,200
Graham Marsh	69	72	71	73	285	3,200
Mike Colandro	72	72	73	69	286	2,700
Paul Foley	72	75	68	73	288	2,200
Craig Parry	71	68	75	74	288	2,200
Robert Stephens	74	76	68	72	290	1,720
Jeff Woodland	66	71	79	74	290	1,720
Louis Brown	73	75	75	68	291	1,400
Ian Roberts	73	71	76	71	291	1,400
David Merriman	71	76	73	71	291	1,400
Philip Baird	73	76	74	69	292	1,230
Anthony Painter	75	68	77	72	292	1,230
Bob Shearer	77	74	72	70	293	1,080
Garry Merrick	70	76	75	72	293	1,080
Ray Picker	73	73	72	75	293	1,080
Terry Gale	73	74	72	74	293	1,080
Michael Springer	77	73	73	71	294	960
Peter McWhinney	73	75	73	73	294	960
Ken Collins	76	76	74	69	295	840
Jack Larkin	73	79	72	71	295	840
Steve Rintoul	75	71	77	72	295	840
Richard Gilkey	73	76	74	72	295	840
Hank Baran	71	78	75	73	297	740
Brad Andrews	75	74	77	72	298	660
Timothy Petrovic	73	77	76	72	298	660
Brad Hughes	77	73	72	76	298	660
John Brellenthin	75	71	75	77	298	660
Craig Warren	71	73	75	79	298	660

Tattersall Tasmanian Open

Devonport Golf Club, Devonport, Tasmania
Par 35-35—70; 6,424 yards

October 19-22
purse, A\$100,000

	SCORES				TOTAL	MONEY
Ian Stanley	68	69	73	69	279	A\$18,000
Peter O'Malley	72	73	67	67	279	10,800
(Stanley defeated O'Malley on first hole of playoff.)						
Zoran Zorkic	72	69	72	68	281	5,940
Jeff Woodland	70	69	71	71	281	5,940
Jeff Wagner	69	70	71	72	282	4,160
Tod Power	68	70	73	72	283	3,820
Ian Roberts	68	70	78	69	285	2,700
Mike Colandro	70	74	69	72	285	2,700
Roy Hunter	67	66	76	76	285	2,700

	SCORES				TOTAL	MONEY
Ken Dukes	68	74	68	75	285	2,700
Stephen Taylor	72	69	67	77	285	2,700
Steve Rintoul	72	72	72	70	286	1,720
Peter Lonard	75	68	72	71	286	1,720
Glenn Joyner	72	75	74	66	287	1,332
Brad Hughes	76	70	72	69	287	1,332
Bob Shearer	71	72	71	73	287	1,332
Darryl Purchase	71	72	71	73	287	1,332
Hank Baran	67	72	71	77	287	1,332
Wayne Case	71	73	73	71	288	1,040
Kevin Burton	68	72	75	73	288	1,040
Rob McNaughton	70	73	73	72	288	1,040
Charles Henderson	73	73	68	74	288	1,040
John Clifford	73	69	72	74	288	1,040
Ben Jackson	71	70	69	78	288	1,040
Robert Farley	74	72	72	71	289	860
Neil Kerry	73	69	73	74	289	860
Sam Wigan	75	73	69	72	289	860
Kale Reynolds	74	73	73	70	290	712
Philip Baird	70	74	75	71	290	712
Ray Picker	74	71	74	71	290	712
Vaughan Somers	73	73	70	74	290	712
Martin Gates	71	70	70	79	290	712

Air New Zealand-Shell Open

Titirangi Golf Club, Auckland
Par 35-35—70; 6,311 yards

October 26-29
Purse, NZ$200,000

	SCORES				TOTAL	MONEY
Don Bies	70	71	69	65	275	NZ$36,000
Brad Andrews	70	73	72	64	279	17,700
Glenn Joyner	71	68	72	68	279	17,700
Kevin Burton	72	69	71	68	280	8,640
Stewart Ginn	69	71	68	72	280	8,640
Tony Maloney	69	66	72	73	280	8,640
Peter O'Malley	64	70	75	72	281	6,840
Garry Merrick	67	71	73	71	282	5,040
Peter Lonard	71	69	69	73	282	5,040
Craig Warren	70	69	70	73	282	5,040
Peter McWhinney	69	65	74	74	282	5,040
Rob McNaughton	73	68	73	69	283	3,600
Chris Rutherford	70	73	75	66	284	2,766.66
Bob Shearer	70	69	75	70	284	2,766.66
Graeme Trew	71	68	74	71	284	2,766.66
Roy Hunter	69	74	69	72	284	2,766.66
Hank Baran	73	72	68	71	284	2,766.66
George Serhan	70	73	70	71	284	2,766.66
Paul Foley	68	70	77	70	285	2,160
John Wilson	65	74	71	75	285	2,160
Anthony Painter	70	69	72	74	285	2,160
John Clifford	77	71	68	74	285	2,160
Jon Evans	75	70	70	71	286	1,960
Brad King	70	75	72	70	287	1,800
Bob Charles	70	72	74	71	287	1,800
Kale Reynolds	72	71	72	72	287	1,800
Grant Percy	69	75	76	68	288	1,460

	SCORES				TOTAL	MONEY
Steve Rintoul	70	69	79	70	288	1,460
Stephen Taylor	73	73	70	72	288	1,460
Martin Gates	70	69	76	73	288	1,460
Grant Kenny	70	73	71	74	288	1,460
David De Long	74	71	67	76	288	1,460

AMP New Zealand Open

Paraparaumu Beach Golf Club, Paraparaumu
Par 35-36—71; 6,492 yards

November 2-5
purse, NZ$150,000

	SCORES				TOTAL	MONEY
Greg Turner	70	72	69	66	277	NZ$27,000
Richard Gilkey	71	74	66	72	283	16,200
Graeme Trew	75	70	70	69	284	8,910
Jim Benepe	70	73	69	72	284	8,910
Martin Gates	72	71	74	68	285	5,985
Glenn Joyner	74	67	73	71	285	5,985
Peter O'Malley	74	68	76	68	286	4,050
Greg Carroll	72	72	73	69	286	4,050
Russell Swanson	72	72	71	71	286	4,050
Peter McWhinney	70	69	75	72	286	4,050
David De Long	73	72	67	74	286	4,050
*Steven Alker	70	70	74	72	286	
Jack Oliver	75	70	73	69	287	2,370
Simon Owen	78	70	69	70	287	2,370
Lucien Tinkler	74	72	69	72	287	2,370
Frank Nobilo	66	72	71	78	287	2,370
John Clifford	72	69	77	70	288	1,806
Peter Lonard	69	74	73	72	288	1,806
Wayne Case	71	72	71	74	288	1,806
Gerry Taylor	71	71	70	76	288	1,806
Mike Colandro	72	69	69	78	288	1,806
David Sheather	71	74	72	72	289	1,470
Tony Mahoney	72	74	71	72	289	1,470
Cameron Howell	72	74	69	74	289	1,470
Tim Elliott	72	69	71	77	289	1,470
Grant Kenny	69	73	71	76	289	1,470
*Tony Christie	76	70	71	72	289	
Rob McNaughton	72	76	70	72	290	1,230
Chris Rutherford	70	75	72	73	290	1,230
Ossie Moore	70	71	75	74	290	1,230

Australian PGA Championship

PGA National Riverside Oaks, Cattai, New South Wales
Par 36-36—72; 7,029 yards

November 9-12
purse, A$500,000

	SCORES				TOTAL	MONEY
Peter Senior	67	68	68	71	274	A$90,000
Jim Benepe	72	66	65	72	275	54,000
Mike Harwood	68	69	71	69	277	34,500
Rodger Davis	69	70	72	67	278	22,850
Peter Fowler	67	71	72	68	278	22,850
Wayne Riley	72	70	68	69	279	19,100

	SCORES				TOTAL	MONEY
Frank Nobilo	73	69	68	70	280	16,000
John Wilson	68	69	72	71	280	16,000
Cameron Howell	70	72	69	70	281	13,500
Ian Woosnam	70	70	71	71	282	11,000
Fred Couples	73	69	68	72	282	11,000
Peter O'Malley	70	69	75	69	283	7,416.66
Mike Clayton	73	69	72	69	283	7,416.66
Tony Wolsey	74	70	70	69	283	7,416.66
Brad Hughes	70	70	73	70	283	7,416.66
Michael Wilkerson	71	74	68	70	283	7,416.66
Brent Franklin	69	72	69	73	283	7,416.66
Tim Elliott	74	65	72	73	284	6,000
Brett Ogle	69	78	71	67	285	5,200
Wayne Grady	73	72	72	68	285	5,200
Peter McWhinney	74	73	69	69	285	5,200
Terry Gale	70	75	69	71	285	5,200
Lucien Tinkler	72	67	73	73	285	5,200
Doug Martin	69	70	70	76	285	5,200
Ken Trimble	73	74	70	69	286	4,500
Simon Owen	75	72	70	70	287	4,100
David Tentis	73	71	72	71	287	4,100
Hank Baran	68	72	71	76	287	4,100
Andrew La'Brooy	71	75	74	70	290	3,600
Russell Swanson	75	71	72	72	290	3,600

Ford New South Wales Open

The Lakes Golf Club, Sydney, New South Wales
Par 36-37—73; 6,856 yards

November 16-19
purse, A$300,000

	SCORES				TOTAL	MONEY
Rodger Davis	71	65	71	70	277	A$54,000
Brad Hughes	75	64	72	75	286	32,400
Mike Colandro	71	67	76	73	287	20,700
David Smith	70	70	75	73	288	13,710
Jeff Maggert	67	69	75	77	288	13,710
Peter McWhinney	73	70	77	69	289	10,860
Chris Rutherford	73	74	71	71	289	10,860
Wayne Smith	68	71	78	73	290	8,520
Kyi Hla Han	71	74	72	73	290	8,520
David Graham	73	72	74	72	291	5,880
Ossie Moore	74	72	71	74	291	5,880
Ian Woosnam	69	72	75	75	291	5,880
Bob Shearer	69	69	74	79	291	5,880
John Morse	74	70	73	75	292	4,444
Glenn Joyner	74	70	75	74	293	3,885
Doug Martin	70	70	76	77	293	3,885
Nick Price	70	72	74	77	293	3,885
Mike Clayton	71	72	73	77	293	3,885
Jeff Wagner	74	71	76	73	294	3,885
Brent Franklin	71	68	78	77	294	3,120
Richard Gilkey	70	76	72	76	294	3,120
Ian Stanley	73	65	78	78	294	3,120
Brad King	73	68	74	79	294	3,120
Hank Baran	72	72	69	81	294	3,120
Jeff Woodland	71	73	75	76	295	2,640
Lyndsay Stephen	70	73	76	76	295	2,640

	SCORES				TOTAL	MONEY
*Stuart Bouvier	69	69	75	82	295	
Anthony Painter	75	72	73	76	296	2,280
Jon Evans	72	72	76	76	296	2,280
Ray Picker	72	75	74	75	296	2,280
George Serhan	74	72	73	77	296	2,280
*Matthew King	71	72	73	80	296	

West End South Australian Open

Royal Adelaide Golf Club, Adelaide, South Australia
Par 37-36—73; 6,985 yards

November 23-26
purse, A$150,000

	SCORES				TOTAL	MONEY
Nick Price	70	71	67	69	277	A$27,000
Lucien Tinkler	71	73	68	70	282	13,275
Paul Foley	73	67	70	72	282	13,275
Peter O'Malley	73	71	69	71	284	7,470
Jon Evans	71	69	73	73	286	5,985
Tim Elliott	74	69	71	72	286	5,985
Max Stevens	66	75	73	73	287	5,130
Jeff Woodland	73	68	77	70	288	4,260
Mike Harwood	72	69	76	71	288	4,260
Michael Winfrey	74	73	69	73	289	3,540
Anthony Edwards	73	73	72	72	290	2,880
Wayne Grady	70	77	73	70	290	2,880
Noel Ratcliffe	78	69	67	77	291	2,340
Peter Senior	74	73	69	75	291	2,340
Brad Hughes	67	76	76	73	292	1,942.50
Kyi Hla Han	73	76	74	69	292	1,942.50
Lyndsay Stephen	74	69	75	74	292	1,942.50
Mike Clayton	74	75	73	70	292	1,942.50
Stephen Bennett	73	77	74	69	293	1,710
Frank Nobilo	71	79	72	72	294	1,500
Ian Roberts	76	72	73	73	294	1,500
Jim Kennedy	71	74	76	73	294	1,500
John Clifford	74	75	71	74	294	1,500
Peter Lonard	76	73	72	73	294	1,500
Simon Owen	77	73	71	73	294	1,500
Anthony Painter	77	70	75	73	295	1,170
Darryl Purchase	74	71	80	70	295	1,170
Mike Colandro	76	75	73	71	295	1,170
Peter McWhinney	75	74	74	72	295	1,170
Steve Rintoul	71	74	73	77	295	1,170

Australian Open Championship

Kingston Heath Golf Club, Melbourne, Victoria
Par 36-36—72; 6,814 yards

November 30-December 3
purse, A$500,000

	SCORES				TOTAL	MONEY
Peter Senior	66	66	69	70	271	A$90,000
Peter Fowler	68	70	71	69	278	54,000
Brett Ogle	66	71	73	69	279	34,500
Mark Calcavecchia	67	69	69	75	280	24,900
Nick Faldo	68	67	74	72	281	20,800

	SCORES				TOTAL	MONEY
Jeff Woodland	66	69	73	74	282	19,100
Gordon Brand, Jr.	68	69	71	75	283	16,000
Mike Harwood	71	67	71	74	283	16,000
Curtis Strange	65	71	73	75	284	11,833.33
Frank Nobilo	71	72	70	71	284	11,833.33
Howard Clark	68	75	72	69	284	11,833.33
Roger Mackay	71	72	75	67	285	8,200
Ian Baker-Finch	71	72	68	74	285	8,200
Steve Bann	67	73	72	73	285	8,200
Kyi Hla Han	70	70	72	74	286	6,800
Stephen Bennett	73	70	72	71	286	6,800
Mike Colandro	73	70	70	74	287	6,300
*Stuart Bouvier	68	71	75	73	287	
Colin Montgomerie	72	65	70	81	288	5,520
Jim Benepe	72	72	72	72	288	5,520
Simon Owen	73	67	71	77	288	5,520
Bob Shearer	69	75	73	71	288	5,520
Wayne Grady	73	67	78	70	288	5,520
David Graham	72	73	71	73	289	4,400
Peter McWhinney	71	73	70	75	289	4,400
Russell Swanson	68	71	77	73	289	4,400
David Smith	71	73	74	71	289	4,400
John Morse	69	72	77	71	289	4,400
Zoran Zorkic	72	70	76	71	289	4,400
Greg Norman	72	70	71	77	290	3,600
Anthony Painter	69	72	78	71	290	3,600
Terry Gale	71	69	75	76	291	3,300
Ian Stanley	71	74	74	72	291	3,300
Peter O'Malley	71	72	76	72	291	3,300
*Lucas Parsons	68	74	75	74	291	
Peter Lonard	76	69	75	72	292	3,000
Steve Elkington	69	72	79	72	292	3,000
Wayne Smith	69	74	75	74	292	3,000
*Chris Gray	68	73	75	77	293	
Dave Eichelberger	71	74	74	74	293	2,650
Louis Brown	68	74	75	76	293	2,650
Michael Barry	74	71	76	72	293	2,650
Mike Clayton	69	74	77	73	293	2,650
Anthony Edwards	68	72	79	75	294	2,250
Darren Spencer	70	74	75	75	294	2,250
*David Podlich	69	76	78	71	294	
Richard Gilkey	70	74	79	71	294	2,250
Sam Torrance	70	74	77	73	294	2,250
Lyndsay Stephen	68	74	79	74	295	2,000
Lucien Tinkler	66	71	79	80	296	1,900

Johnnie Walker Classic

Royal Melbourne Composite Course, Melbourne, Victoria
Par 35-37—72; 6,944 yards

December 7-10
purse, A$1,000,000

	SCORES				TOTAL	MONEY
Peter Senior	65	72	70	69	276	A$180,000
Greg Norman	73	71	70	67	281	108,000
Howard Clark	70	72	69	71	282	69,000
Nick Faldo	71	72	71	69	283	43,200
Bob Shearer	72	71	71	69	283	43,200

	SCORES				TOTAL	MONEY
Frank Nobilo	69	70	72	72	283	43,200
Terry Gale	70	74	68	72	284	43,200
Peter Fowler	72	72	71	69	284	43,200
John Cook	72	73	71	69	285	32,000
Mike Clayton	69	69	77	70	285	23,666.66
Rodger Davis	69	73	68	75	285	23,666.66
Jim Benepe	68	73	70	75	286	17,200
Louis Brown	74	73	69	70	286	17,200
Cameron Howell	74	74	69	70	287	13,650
Lyndsay Stephen	70	71	75	71	287	13,650
Mike Harwood	70	72	74	71	287	13,650
Michael Bradley	74	69	71	73	287	13,650
Ian Baker-Finch	71	72	73	72	288	11,250
Paul Foley	73	73	70	72	288	11,250
Terry Price	73	67	75	73	288	11,250
Wayne Smith	73	72	70	73	288	11,250
John Clifford	76	71	72	70	289	9,600
Simon Owen	73	72	73	71	289	9,600
Wayne Case	75	73	69	72	289	9,600
Wayne Riley	75	70	70	74	289	9,600
Craig Warren	76	72	71	71	290	7,800
Glenn Joyner	75	72	74	69	290	7,800
Sam Torrance	73	73	71	73	290	7,800
Stephen Bennett	74	69	73	74	290	7,800
Gordon Brand, Jr.	73	73	68	76	290	7,800
Graeme Trew	75	72	67	77	291	6,100
Chris Moody	68	71	75	77	291	6,100
David Feherty	72	71	77	71	291	6,100
Ken Dukes	71	75	73	72	291	6,100
Kirk Triplett	75	70	71	75	291	6,100
Lucien Tinkler	73	74	70	74	291	6,100
Richard Gilkey	77	71	70	73	291	6,100
Stewart Ginn	74	73	73	71	291	6,100
Brad King	71	73	75	73	292	4,900
Gary Hallberg	70	76	71	75	292	4,900
Jeff Maggert	72	76	69	75	292	4,900
Tim Elliott	72	72	73	75	292	4,900
Doug Martin	69	78	68	78	293	4,100
Jeff Woodland	71	70	73	79	293	4,100
John Wilson	73	72	79	69	293	4,100
Peter Jones	70	74	75	74	293	4,100
Brad Andrews	75	73	75	71	294	3,300
Craig Parry	75	70	76	73	294	3,300
David Smith	72	76	73	73	294	3,300
Ossie Moore	74	73	73	74	294	3,300

Mirage Queensland Open

Royal Queensland Golf Club, Brisbane, Queensland
Par 36-37—73; 6,970 yards

December 14-17
purse, A$300,000

	SCORES				TOTAL	MONEY
Brett Ogle	66	68	71	73	278	A$54,000
John Clifford	68	69	70	74	281	32,400
Peter Senior	71	72	69	72	284	20,700
Wayne Grady	70	70	72	73	285	12,960
Ian Baker-Finch	69	73	70	73	285	12,960

	SCORES				TOTAL	MONEY
Mike Harwood	71	69	74	71	285	12,960
Zoran Zorkic	71	70	71	74	286	10,260
Ken Dukes	69	68	76	74	287	8,940
Stephen Bennett	69	69	74	76	288	8,100
Wayne Smith	69	72	74	74	289	7,080
Stewart Ginn	70	77	70	73	290	5,480
Danny Mijovic	77	68	70	75	290	5,480
Peter McWhinney	69	74	71	76	290	5,480
*Wayne Stewart	71	73	75	72	291	
Mark Officer	75	73	70	73	291	3,900
Chris Rutherford	73	75	70	73	291	3,900
Greg Hohnen	72	68	77	74	291	3,900
James Heninger	71	71	75	74	291	3,900
Mark K. Nash	73	74	70	74	291	3,900
Terry Price	70	72	71	78	291	3,900
*Steve Conran	73	73	78	68	292	
Mike Mills	72	71	74	75	292	3,120
Hank Baran	73	69	74	76	292	3,120
David De Long	70	73	78	72	293	2,700
Kyi Hla Han	73	72	73	75	293	2,700
*Darren Barnes	72	76	70	75	293	
Brad King	72	72	71	78	293	2,700
Kirk Triplett	74	72	71	77	294	2,400
Anthony Gilligan	74	72	70	78	294	2,400
Peter Lonard	72	71	79	73	295	2,052

The Asia/Japan Tour

San Miguel/Coca Cola Philippines Open

Puerto Azul Beach and Country Club, Ternate
Par 71; 6,794 yards

February 9-12
purse, US$140,000

	SCORES				TOTAL	MONEY
Emlyn Aubrey	69	71	69	67	276	US$23,324
Mario Siodina	74	66	73	65	278	15,554
Mats Lanner	68	70	65	77	280	7,882
Craig McClellan	70	69	71	70	280	7,882
Frankie Minosa	71	67	70	73	281	5,936
Steve Bowman	73	73	68	68	282	3,934
Jeff Cook	70	70	70	72	282	3,934
Lu Hsi Chuen	71	68	72	71	282	3,934
Brian Mogg	70	67	74	71	282	3,934
Mark Aebli	69	68	71	75	283	2,613.33
Chen Tze Ming	77	67	69	70	283	2,613.33
Katsuyoshi Tomori	71	71	73	68	283	2,613.33

	SCORES				TOTAL	MONEY
Brian Claar	76	70	71	67	284	2,261
Brian Watts	73	68	69	74	284	2,261
Hsieh Yu Shu	70	73	70	72	285	2,023
Steve Veriato	75	69	66	75	285	2,023
Rafael Alarcon	70	75	69	72	286	1,771
Carlos Espinosa	70	73	70	73	286	1,771
Denny Hepler	70	77	68	71	286	1,771
Norikazu Kawakami	75	68	71	72	286	1,771
Hsieh Chin Sheng	67	76	71	73	287	1,596
Rafael Navarro	71	70	77	69	287	1,596
Takeru Shibata	74	73	69	71	287	1,596
Michael McLean	68	71	72	77	288	1,526
Feliciano Esparsa	71	70	74	74	289	1,360
Han Kyi Hla	75	71	70	73	289	1,360
Don Klenk	70	73	72	74	289	1,360
Lin Chia	71	70	74	74	289	1,360
George Olaybar	71	75	75	68	289	1,360
Anders Sorenson	75	72	73	69	289	1,360
Gary Webb	70	70	74	75	289	1,360

Johnnie Walker Hong Kong Open

Royal Hong Kong Golf Club, Composite Course, Kowloon
Par 35-35—70; 6,692 yards

February 16-19
purse, US$175,000

	SCORES				TOTAL	MONEY
Brian Claar	70	68	69	67	274	US$29,155
Mats Lanner	72	68	69	66	275	15,198.50
Gary Rusnak	74	69	65	67	275	15,198.50
Todd Hamilton	67	69	71	69	276	6,886.50
Hsieh Yu Shu	68	68	68	72	276	6,886.50
Jean-Louis Lamarre	69	69	70	68	276	6,886.50
Howard Clark	69	70	64	73	276	6,886.50
Lin Chie Hsiang	70	71	69	68	278	4,147.50
Tim Fleming	70	70	67	71	278	4,147.50
Takeru Shibata	70	69	70	70	279	3,010
Kuo Chi Hsiung	72	70	67	70	279	3,010
Lai Chung Jen	69	69	70	71	279	3,010
Craig McClellan	71	66	70	72	279	3,010
Scott Taylor	74	71	67	67	279	3,010
Steve Veriato	73	69	68	69	279	3,010
Hsieh Chin Sheng	74	69	67	70	280	2,161
Li Wen Sheng	68	71	70	71	280	2,161
Emlyn Aubrey	72	65	71	72	280	2,161
Glen Day	72	65	71	72	280	2,161
Hsu Sheng San	75	69	66	70	280	2,161
Chris Endres	68	70	70	72	280	2,161
Eduardo Herrera	73	71	66	70	280	2,161
Lu Chien Soon	70	72	70	68	280	2,161
Steve Bowman	72	68	71	70	281	1,802.50
Choi Yoon Soo	70	71	68	72	281	1,802.50
Lin Chia	71	73	68	69	281	1,802.50
Carlos Espinosa	73	66	73	69	281	1,802.50
Isamu Suguta	71	70	69	71	281	1,802.50
Gary Webb	71	71	70	70	282	1,522.50
Mark McNulty	69	71	73	69	282	1,522.50
Katsuyoshi Tomori	71	69	72	70	282	1,522.50

	SCORES				TOTAL	MONEY
Jeff Maggert	71	68	73	70	282	1,522.50
Park Nam Sin	72	71	69	70	282	1,522.50
Tsao Chien Teng	73	69	70	70	282	1,522.50

Thai International Thailand Open

Pinehurst Golf and Country Club, Bangkok, Thailand
Par 36-36—72; 6,854 yards

February 23-26
purse, US$150,000

	SCORES				TOTAL	MONEY
Brian Claar	66	67	68	71	272	US$25,000
E.J. Pfister	68	70	69	68	275	16,665
Gary Webb	67	69	69	72	277	9,390
Esteban Toledo	74	67	67	70	278	6,930
Emlyn Aubrey	70	70	70	68	278	6,930
Frankie Minosa	67	71	72	69	279	5,250
Chen Liang Hsi	67	70	72	71	280	4,125
Lu Hsi Chuen	71	67	69	73	280	4,125
Remi Bouchard	71	73	69	68	281	3,050
Hiroshi Ueda	63	71	70	77	281	3,050
Mike Hammond	67	67	74	73	281	3,050
Han Kyi Hla	65	71	71	75	282	2,113.50
Rick Gibson	69	68	74	71	282	2,113.50
Chen Tze Ming	65	72	70	75	282	2,113.50
Chung Chun Hsing	71	70	71	70	282	2,113.50
Li Wen Sheng	66	72	71	73	282	2,113.50
Wang Ter Chang	69	68	71	74	282	2,113.50
Steve Bowman	68	69	72	73	282	2,113.50
Jeff Cook	72	70	69	71	282	2,113.50
Chris Endres	67	68	72	75	282	2,113.50
Craig McClellan	69	74	72	67	282	2,113.50
Tim Fleming	70	72	71	70	283	1,687.50
Mark Trauner	69	70	70	74	283	1,687.50
Harumitsu Hamano	70	71	71	72	284	1,612.50
Gary Rusnak	69	73	67	75	284	1,612.50
Atsushi Ishikawa	70	69	76	70	285	1,455
Toshihiko Ohtsuka	69	69	75	72	285	1,455
Mario Siodina	70	71	70	74	285	1,455
Kuo Chi Hsiung	71	69	74	71	285	1,455
Casey Nakama	70	72	74	69	285	1,455

Pakistan Open

Lahore Gymkhana Golf Club, Lahore, Pakistan
Par 36-36—72; 6,497 yards

March 2-5
purse, US$120,000

	SCORES				TOTAL	MONEY
Frankie Minosa	74	77	65	70	286	US$19,992
Tray Tyner	69	72	72	74	287	13,332
Eddie Kirby	76	70	73	71	290	7,512
Brian Claar	71	73	74	74	292	5,544
Jean-Louis Lamarre	72	75	72	73	292	5,544
Jeff Cook	70	75	76	72	293	3,900
Mark Trauner	74	70	71	78	293	3,900
E.J. Pfister	72	77	73	74	294	3,000

	SCORES				TOTAL	MONEY
Chris Endres	79	70	71	75	295	2,440
Jerry Smith	74	72	77	72	295	2,440
Don Walsworth	77	69	72	77	295	2,440
Emlyn Aubrey	71	79	72	74	296	1,938
Kyle Coody	79	72	71	74	296	1,938
Tim Fleming	73	71	79	73	296	1,938
Peter Smith	76	77	70	73	296	1,938
Mark Aebli	73	75	73	76	297	1,526
Carlos Espinosa	76	72	77	72	297	1,526
Bob Lendzion	76	77	69	75	297	1,526
Ghulam Nabi	71	74	74	78	297	1,526
Seiki Okuda	73	77	74	73	297	1,526
Hiroshi Ueda	72	77	73	75	297	1,526
Remi Bouchard	69	83	75	71	298	1,251
Steve Chapman	74	79	74	71	298	1,251
Harumitsu Hamano	74	76	75	73	298	1,251
Tishiomi Inaba	74	74	77	73	298	1,251
Lin Chie Chen	72	73	75	76	298	1,251
Gohei Satoh	72	70	81	75	298	1,251
Scott Taylor	72	74	80	72	298	1,251
Gary Webb	75	76	74	75	298	1,251
Danny Mijovic	74	72	74	79	299	1,092

Wills Indian Open

Delhi Golf Club, New Delhi, India
Par 36-36—72; 6,869 yards

March 9-12
purse, US$120,000

	SCORES				TOTAL	MONEY
Remi Bouchard	73	64	72	70	279	US$19,992
Carlos Espinosa	65	75	71	69	280	13,332
Steve Bowman	70	74	70	72	286	6,756
Greg Bruckner	68	70	72	76	286	6,756
Emlyn Aubrey	73	72	71	71	287	4,644
Gary Rusnak	71	68	71	77	287	4,644
Glen Day	74	74	67	73	288	3,096
Scott Taylor	73	74	72	69	288	3,096
Wang Ter Chang	72	75	71	70	288	3,096
Eddie Kirby	70	78	73	69	290	2,316
Lin Chie Chen	71	73	75	71	290	2,316
Jeff Cook	72	69	77	73	291	1,988
Neil Hickerson	71	74	71	75	291	1,988
Esteban Toledo	70	77	73	71	291	1,988
Tom Eubanks	70	74	72	76	292	1,620
Rick Gibson	71	71	70	80	292	1,620
Bob Lendzion	73	75	72	72	292	1,620
Mario Siodina	73	73	77	69	292	1,620
Seiki Okuda	73	75	69	75	292	1,620
Kyle Coody	74	70	71	78	293	1,370
Danny Mijovic	73	74	74	72	293	1,370
Ghulan Nabi	73	74	73	73	293	1,370
Mark Trauner	70	72	72	79	293	1,370
Cheng Yun Hsieng	73	76	71	73	293	1,370
Chris Endres	72	75	74	73	294	1,236
Ajay Guputa	71	76	74	73	294	1,236
Gohei Satoh	78	72	72	72	294	1,236
Brandon De Souza	75	74	73	73	295	1,113

	SCORES				TOTAL	MONEY
Andrew Debusk	76	74	70	75	295	1,113
Mark Diamond	70	70	80	75	295	1,113
Moritaka Terasawa	75	74	74	72	295	1,113

Singapore Open

Tanah Merah Country Club, Singapore
Par 36-36—72; 7,059 yards

March 16-19
purse, US$220,000

	SCORES				TOTAL	MONEY
Lu Chien Soon	69	69	67	72	277	US$36,652
Carlos Espinosa	70	67	69	72	278	24,442
E.J. Pfister	65	71	71	75	282	13,772
Scott Taylor	69	71	70	73	283	10,164
Esteban Toledo	71	69	71	72	283	10,164
Brian Claar	72	70	69	74	285	5,292
Ian Doig	71	70	75	69	285	5,292
Han Kyi Hla	75	71	67	72	285	5,292
Kuo Chi Hsiung	74	70	69	72	285	5,292
Danny Mijovic	71	71	71	72	285	5,292
Mario Siodina	70	70	72	73	285	5,292
Kirk Triplett	67	72	71	75	285	5,292
Jeff Cook	72	73	70	71	286	3,461
Lai Chung Jen	71	70	71	74	286	3,461
Simon Owen	73	70	69	74	286	3,461
Poh Eing Chong	70	69	71	77	287	2,948
Jeff Senior	70	70	73	74	287	2,948
Brian Watts	70	73	68	76	287	2,948
Choi Yoon Soo	72	71	73	72	288	2,517
Chung Chun Hsing	72	74	71	71	288	2,517
Stewart Ginn	75	71	71	71	288	2,517
Lin Chie Hsiang	70	72	73	73	288	2,517
Craig McClellan	73	71	72	72	288	2,517
Aaron Meeks	73	71	73	71	288	2,517
Hiroshi Ueda	74	69	70	75	288	2,517
Lin Chia	72	72	75	70	289	2,071
Lu Ho Tsai	70	74	71	74	289	2,071
Jeff Maggert	76	68	72	73	289	2,071
Daniel Nishimoto	75	68	74	72	289	2,071
Arjin Sophon	72	70	72	75	289	2,071
Mark Trauner	71	76	71	71	289	2,071
Yu Chin Han	69	68	74	78	289	2,071

Shizuoka Open

Shizuoka Country Club, Hamaoka Course, Hamaoka
Par 72; 6,821 yards

March 16-19
purse, ¥40,000,000

	SCORES				TOTAL	MONEY
Koichi Suzuki	67	78	69	71	285	¥7,200,000
Naomichi Ozaki	71	75	71	69	286	3,360,000
Nobumitsu Yuhara	74	71	71	70	286	3,360,000
Eduardo Herrera	69	74	73	72	288	1,920,000
Seiichi Kanai	73	74	74	68	289	1,440,000
Toshimitsu Kai	72	78	70	69	289	1,440,000

	SCORES				TOTAL	MONEY
Yoshitaka Yamamoto	72	75	70	72	289	1,440,000
Toru Nakamura	70	72	75	73	290	931,000
Yoshikazu Yokoshima	70	72	76	72	290	931,000
Katsuji Hasegawa	70	75	74	71	290	931,000
Kazuo Kanayama	75	72	75	68	290	931,000
Eitaro Deguchi	73	74	71	72	290	931,000
Isao Isozaki	68	74	77	72	291	576,000
Junji Hashizoe	76	71	76	68	291	576,000
Shigeru Kawamata	71	75	72	73	291	576,000
Katsuyoshi Tomori	70	75	74	72	291	576,000
Tadao Nakamura	71	75	77	68	291	576,000
Saburo Fujiki	69	79	75	69	292	448,000
Hisayuki Sasaki	75	73	75	70	293	400,000
Jun Murota	76	71	76	70	293	400,000
Takeshi Shibata	73	75	73	72	293	400,000
Kiyoshi Maita	75	73	76	70	294	360,000
Joji Furuki	71	73	79	71	294	360,000
Yoshimi Niizeki	72	79	72	72	295	340,000
Hsieh Min Nan	74	75	73	73	295	340,000
Masanobu Kimura	74	77	73	72	296	300,000
Kazushige Kono	70	79	71	76	296	300,000
Takashi Iwai	73	74	75	74	296	300,000
Pete Izumikawa	74	74	76	72	296	300,000
Norikazu Kawakami	70	76	77	73	296	300,000
Namio Takasu	73	78	73	72	296	300,000
Kenji Mori	71	77	75	73	296	300,000
Tsuyoshi Yoneyama	77	72	73	74	296	300,000

Indonesia Open

Jakarta Golf Club, Jakarta, Indonesia
Par 35-35—70

March 22-25
purse, US$120,000

	SCORES				TOTAL	MONEY
Kasiyadi	68	68	67	66	269	US$19,992
Frankie Minosa	67	70	67	67	271	10,422
Kirk Triplett	70	64	68	69	271	10,422
Anthony Gilligan	72	64	67	71	272	6,000
Han Kyi Hla	68	64	73	68	273	4,644
Jeff Maggert	65	64	70	74	273	4,644
Emlyn Aubrey	68	69	65	72	274	2,784
Brian Claar	68	67	68	71	274	2,784
Feliciano Esparsa	68	68	72	66	274	2,784
Stewart Ginn	70	65	69	70	274	2,784
Mario Siodina	68	72	69	65	274	2,784
Andrew Debusk	67	69	66	73	275	1,938
Roger Thorn	70	72	67	66	275	1,938
Esteban Toledo	68	71	68	68	275	1,938
Brian Watts	69	79	68	68	275	1,938
Carlos Espinosa	71	67	69	69	276	1,550
Liao Kuo Chie	70	69	66	71	276	1,550
Li Wen Sheng	70	66	71	69	276	1,550
Tray Tyner	68	68	68	72	276	1,550
Don Walsworth	71	71	65	69	276	1,550
Lin Chia	71	68	70	68	277	1,404
Chen Liang Hsi	67	67	70	74	278	1,268
Jeff Cook	67	67	68	76	278	1,268

	SCORES				TOTAL	MONEY
Harumitsu Hamano	70	70	68	70	278	1,268
Lu Hsi Chuen	73	67	70	68	278	1,268
Scott Taylor	70	71	68	69	278	1,268
Paul Foley	70	70	68	70	278	1,268
Bauri	68	68	73	69	278	1,268
Remi Bouchard	73	67	69	70	279	1,128
Michael Blewett	73	70	72	65	280	1,060
Lin Chie Chen	72	69	72	67	280	1,060
Jeff Senior	71	69	68	72	280	1,060

Setonaikai Open

Shido Country Club, Shidocho
Par 72; 6,452 yards

March 23-26
purse, ¥40,000,000

	SCORES				TOTAL	MONEY
Naomichi Ozaki	68	74	69	71	282	¥9,000,000
Kinpachi Yoshimura	70	73	72	69	284	5,000,000
Tsutomu Irie	71	73	72	69	285	2,900,000
Fujio Kobayashi	73	74	71	67	285	2,900,000
Nobumitsu Yuhara	70	69	72	75	286	1,900,000
Masaji Kusakabe	70	72	72	72	286	1,900,000
Pete Izumikawa	71	69	73	74	287	1,525,000
Yoshiyuki Isomura	73	74	68	72	287	1,525,000
Jun Murota	71	75	71	71	288	1,225,000
Yoshimi Nizeki	72	75	71	70	288	1,225,000
Takeshi Shibata	73	76	72	68	289	885,000
Seiji Ebihara	60	72	75	73	289	885,000
Tateo Ozaki	73	74	68	74	289	885,000
Miyuki Omori	73	73	73	70	289	885,000
Yoshinori Kaneko	69	74	74	73	290	690,000
Haruo Yasuda	70	73	75	72	290	690,000
Yoshitaka Yamamoto	69	74	76	72	291	520,000
Seiichi Kanai	74	74	71	72	291	520,000
Wayne Smith	75	72	72	72	291	520,000
Koji Kobayashi	74	74	72	71	291	520,000
Teruo Sugihara	72	72	73	74	291	520,000
Brent Franklin	74	74	69	74	291	520,000
Yoshikazu Yokoshima	70	70	79	73	292	425,000
Ichiro Teramoto	72	74	72	74	292	425,000
Shinsaku Maeda	73	71	75	73	292	425,000
Hiromichi Namiki	72	75	71	74	292	425,000
Katsuji Hasegawa	72	75	71	75	293	380,000
Kawamata Shigeru	75	74	73	71	293	380,000
Katsunari Takahashi	76	73	71	73	293	380,000
Norio Adachi	73	75	71	74	293	380,000
Norio Mikami	74	75	67	77	293	380,000

Benson & Hedges Malaysian Open

Ayer Keroh Country Club, Malacca, Malaysia
Par 36-36—72

March 30 - April 2
purse, US$175,000

	SCORES				TOTAL	MONEY
Jeff Maggert	71	73	71	68	283	US$29,155
Greg Bruckner	75	69	67	77	288	11,641
Bob Lendzion	75	69	73	71	288	11,641
Craig McClellan	72	69	71	76	288	11,641
Casey Nakama	71	73	73	71	288	11,641
Lu Hsi Chuen	73	73	70	73	289	5,688
Frankie Minosa	73	69	77	70	289	5,688
Liao Kuo Chie	74	68	73	75	290	4,375
Jeff Cook	77	74	73	67	291	3,710
Grant Waite	70	76	71	74	291	3,710
Brian Claar	73	74	72	73	292	2,988
Han Kyi Hla	73	72	73	74	292	2,988
Lu Chien Soon	69	77	73	73	292	2,988
Jeff Woodland	72	74	73	73	292	2,988
Emlyn Aubrey	75	75	70	73	293	2,409
Lin Chia	75	70	74	74	293	2,409
E.J. Pfister	73	74	73	73	293	2,409
Thaworn Wiratchant	77	71	71	74	293	2,409
Jean-Louise Lamarre	75	76	72	71	294	2,078
Lin Chie Hsiang	72	71	75	76	294	2,078
Jeff Senior	71	75	73	75	294	2,078
Mario Siodina	74	70	76	74	294	2,078
Mike Cunning	74	72	73	76	295	1,824
Hsieh Yu Shu	72	74	74	75	295	1,824
Kuo Chi Hsiung	74	74	72	75	295	1,824
Li Wen Sheng	72	75	74	74	295	1,824
Paul Foley	74	77	68	76	295	1,824
Anthony Gilligan	73	75	72	75	295	1,824
Terry Budzinski	75	72	75	74	296	1,496
Carlos Espinosa	76	74	75	71	296	1,496
Lin Chie Chen	68	76	78	74	296	1,496
Keiichi Nagata	74	76	77	69	296	1,496
Esteban Toledo	72	77	74	71	296	1,496
Tsunehisa Yamamoto	75	73	70	78	296	1,496
John Clifford	75	72	77	72	296	1,496

Republic of China Open

Linkou International Golf and Country Club, Taipei, Taiwan
Par 36-36—72; 7,008 yards

April 6-9
purse, US$200,000

(Fourth round cancelled - fog.)

	SCORES			TOTAL	MONEY
Lu Chien Soon	70	69	68	207	US$33,320
Chen Liang Hsi	70	68	70	208	22,220
Liao Kuo Chie	69	70	70	209	12,520
Li Wen Sheng	75	68	67	210	7,296
Carlos Espinosa	72	68	70	210	7,296
Lu Hsi Chuen	70	70	70	210	7,296
Hsieh Chin Sheng	69	70	71	210	7,296
George Serhan	64	70	76	210	7,296

	SCORES		TOTAL	MONEY
Lin Chia	71 70 70		211	4,240
Andrew Debusk	69 69 73		211	4,240
Chung Chun Hsing	70 73 69		212	3,085
Chen Tze Ming	70 72 70		212	3,085
Lu Wen Teh	71 71 70		212	3,085
Lin Chie Chen	72 69 71		212	3,085
Kirk Triplett	71 70 71		212	3,085
Hsieh Yu Shu	71 69 72		212	3,085
Remi Bouchard	69 71 72		212	3,085
Kuo Chi Hsiung	68 70 74		212	3,085
Michael Blewett	73 70 70		213	2,440
Greg Bruckner	70 72 71		213	2,440
Kyle Coody	68 75 71		214	2,228
Shen Chung Shyan	71 72 71		214	2,228
Mark Aebli	72 70 72		214	2,228
Casey Nakama	68 73 73		214	2,228
Jeff Maggert	69 71 74		214	2,228
Lin Chie Hsiang	70 73 72		215	1,940
Jay Nickols	73 70 72		215	1,940
Brian Claar	72 73 70		215	1,940
Steve Veriato	68 73 74		215	1,940
Yu Chin Han	70 74 71		215	1,940

Pocari Sweat Open

Hakuryuko Country Club, Daiwacho
Par 71; 6,780 yards

April 6-9
purse, ¥50,000,000

	SCORES				TOTAL	MONEY
Yoshikazu Yokoshima	67	68	69	70	274	¥9,000,000
Naomichi Ozaki	66	65	73	71	275	5,000,000
Nobumitsu Yuhara	67	65	72	72	276	2,900,000
Noboru Sugai	68	67	75	66	276	2,900,000
Kinpachi Yoshimura	63	70	72	73	278	1,800,000
Craig Parry	71	66	73	68	278	1,800,000
Satoshi Azuma	70	69	71	68	278	1,800,000
Yoshimi Niizeki	71	65	74	69	279	1,164,000
Yoshiyuki Isomura	71	70	70	68	279	1,164,000
Toshimitsu Kai	68	74	69	68	279	1,164,000
Wayne Smith	72	69	72	66	279	1,164,000
Yoshimi Ueno	70	69	69	71	279	1,164,000
*Takahiro Nakagawa	69	71	71	68	279	
Haruo Yasuda	68	71	72	69	280	840,000
Toru Nakamura	70	66	74	71	281	690,000
Nobuo Serizawa	74	69	69	69	281	690,000
Teruo Nakamura	70	66	73	72	281	690,000
Ikuo Shirahama	65	68	75	73	281	690,000
Koichi Suzuki	71	69	71	71	282	493,000
Toshitaka Yamamoto	71	70	71	70	282	493,000
Hiroshi Makino	66	71	73	72	282	493,000
Roger Mackay	70	69	71	72	282	493,000
Motomasa Aoki	68	72	70	72	282	493,000
David Ishii	70	70	70	72	282	493,000
Tateo Ozaki	67	72	72	72	283	415,000
Akiyoshi Omachi	73	69	71	70	283	415,000
Akihito Yokoyama	73	70	72	68	283	415,000
Terry Gale	66	69	74	74	283	415,000

	SCORES				TOTAL	MONEY
Seiichi Kanai	69	73	72	70	284	343,000
Shigeru Kawamata	65	72	75	72	284	343,000
Hisayuki Sasaki	68	73	75	68	284	343,000
Ichiro Teramoto	69	70	72	73	284	343,000
Katsunari Takahashi	71	68	73	72	284	343,000
Tsuyoshi Yoneyama	70	69	69	76	284	343,000
Shinsaku Maeda	69	69	73	73	284	343,000
Seiichi Koizuma	72	70	70	72	284	343,000
Hideto Shigenobu	67	70	76	71	284	343,000
Taisei Inagaki	69	71	73	71	284	343,000
Yutaka Hagawa	73	67	73	71	284	343,000

Maekyung Korean Open

Nam Seoul Country Club, Seoul, Korea
Par 36-36—72; 6,862 yards

April 13-16
purse, US$150,000

	SCORES				TOTAL	MONEY
Lu Hsi Chuen	67	69	70	71	277	US$26,656
Chen Liang Hsi	68	72	66	72	278	17,776
Rick Gibson	70	72	69	69	280	10,106
Bong Tae Ha	71	68	68	74	281	6,794
Craig McClellan	71	72	69	69	281	6,794
Brian Claar	70	68	73	70	281	6,794
Chung Chun Hsing	71	71	74	67	283	3,712
Ho Ming Chung	75	69	68	71	283	3,712
Jeff Maggert	71	73	70	69	283	3,712
Tsao Chien Teng	72	69	73	69	283	3,712
Koichi Suzuki	68	74	66	75	283	3,712
Lim Jin Han	68	74	72	70	284	2,584
Emlyn Aubrey	75	68	69	72	284	2,584
Steve Veriato	72	72	69	71	284	2,584
Gary Webb	68	75	69	72	284	2,584
Chen Tze Ming	72	67	71	75	285	2,034
Steve Bowman	67	74	68	76	285	2,034
Li Wen Sheng	71	71	72	71	285	2,034
Lin Chia	74	70	71	70	285	2,034
Lin Chie Hsiang	75	70	71	69	285	2,034
Kirk Triplett	70	73	67	75	285	2,034
Hahn Chang Sang	70	73	73	70	286	1,691
Choi Kwan Soo	70	70	71	75	286	1,691
Aaron Meeks	67	72	71	76	286	1,691
Michael Blewett	72	72	71	71	286	1,691
Lu Chien Soon	69	74	72	71	286	1,691
Shigeo Kinoshita	71	72	73	70	286	1,691
Brian Watts	69	76	69	72	286	1,691
Chung Do Mahn	72	70	70	75	287	1,392
Kim Young Il	70	72	71	74	287	1,392
Park Nam Shin	70	74	66	77	287	1,392
George Serhan	69	70	75	73	287	1,392
Stewart Ginn	73	67	75	72	287	1,392
Jay Nickols	71	74	72	70	287	1,392

Bridgestone Open

Aso Golf Club, Aso, Kumamoto
Par 72; 7,037 yards

April 13-16
purse, ¥40,000,000

	SCORES				TOTAL	MONEY
Craig Parry	67	69	70	66	272	¥7,200,000
Yoshiyuki Isomura	68	69	68	73	278	4,000,000
Fujio Kobayashi	71	67	68	74	280	2,320,000
Toru Nakamura	67	72	69	72	280	2,320,000
Tadami Ueno	68	71	71	72	282	1,600,000
Haruo Yasuda	69	76	67	72	284	1,360,000
Eitaro Deguchi	73	70	70	71	284	1,360,000
Nobuo Serizawa	70	72	70	74	286	980,000
Roger Mackay	71	73	68	74	286	980,000
Futoshi Irino	73	67	72	74	286	980,000
Mitsunobu Hatsumi	70	71	72	73	286	980,000
Eduardo Herrera	72	68	70	77	287	704,000
Yukio Noguchi	71	70	72	74	287	704,000
Yoshimi Niizeki	73	70	72	73	288	576,000
Hideyuki Sato	72	71	73	72	288	576,000
Terry Gale	70	72	69	77	288	576,000
Yoshinori Kaneko	72	70	72	75	289	406,000
Kiyoshi Maita	68	71	73	77	289	406,000
David Ishii	68	72	74	75	289	406,000
Hideto Shigenobu	71	72	72	74	289	406,000
Toru Nakayama	72	74	67	76	289	406,000
Nobuhiro Yoshino	72	73	75	69	289	406,000
Tsukasa Watanabe (E)	69	74	75	71	289	406,000
Nobumitsu Yuhara	71	68	74	77	290	324,000
Pete Izumikawa	69	74	71	76	290	324,000
Kazuo Kanayama	73	67	75	75	290	324,000
Saburo Fujiki	74	68	74	74	290	324,000
Hajime Meshiai	73	72	69	76	290	324,000
Yasuo Sone	72	73	72	73	290	324,000
Toshimitsu Kai	71	70	78	72	291	288,000
Katsuji Hasegawa	72	69	74	76	291	288,000
Norio Mikami	73	72	70	76	291	288,000
*Kenichi Tsurumoto	72	74	72	73	291	

Dunlop Open

Ibaraki Golf Club, West Course, Inamachi
Par 72; 7,052 yards

April 20-23
purse, ¥60,000,000

	SCORES				TOTAL	MONEY
Terry Gale	73	74	68	69	284	¥10,800,000
Peter Senior	71	69	72	73	285	5,040,000
Chen Tze Ming	72	73	68	72	285	5,040,000
Yoshimi Niizeki	72	71	72	71	286	2,110,000
Haruo Yasuda	72	71	71	72	286	2,110,000
Katsuyoshi Tomori	73	71	73	69	286	2,110,000
Masashi Ozaki	70	67	72	77	286	2,110,000
Ian Baker-Finch	70	71	72	73	286	2,110,000
Greg Bruckner	68	71	75	72	286	2,110,000
Isamu Sugita	69	75	69	74	287	1,290,000
Masahiro Kuramoto	71	72	76	68	287	1,290,000
David Ishii	69	72	73	74	288	1,016,000
Jeff Cook	72	74	73	69	288	1,016,000

	SCORES				TOTAL	MONEY
Brian Claar	71	70	73	74	288	1,016,000
Yoshikazu Yokoshima	72	69	73	75	289	762,000
Steve Bowman	68	74	73	74	289	762,000
Chen Tze Chung	69	74	70	76	289	762,000
Hsieh Chin Seng	73	65	78	73	289	762,000
Wayne Smith	78	69	74	69	290	588,000
Andrew Labrooy	76	71	73	70	290	588,000
Chris Endres	71	75	70	74	290	588,000
Jeff Maggert	75	73	70	72	290	588,000
Nobuo Serizawa	72	76	72	71	291	516,000
Tadao Nakamura	73	73	72	73	291	516,000
Li Wen Sheng	76	69	74	72	291	516,000
Naomichi Ozaki	71	72	76	73	292	468,000
Toru Nakayama	75	70	76	71	292	468,000
Rick Gibson	77	71	72	72	292	468,000
Kirk Triplett	75	71	73	73	292	468,000
Lucien Tinkler	71	74	74	73	292	468,000

Chunichi Crowns

Nagoya Golf Club, Wago Course, Nagoya
Par 70; 6,473 yards

April 27-30
purse, ¥100,000,000

	SCORES				TOTAL	MONEY
Greg Norman	65	68	71	68	272	¥18,000,000
Koichi Suzuki	66	67	71	71	275	8,400,000
Blaine McCallister	67	70	65	73	275	8,400,000
Tateo Ozaki	68	71	72	68	279	4,400,000
Mike Reid	69	71	69	70	279	4,400,000
Craig Parry	71	68	70	71	280	3,075,000
Yoshinori Kaneko	69	69	71	71	280	3,075,000
Chen Tze Chung	70	67	69	74	280	3,075,000
Graham Marsh	71	66	73	70	280	3,075,000
Masashi Ozaki	73	71	70	67	281	2,300,000
Peter Senior	69	73	71	69	282	1,840,000
Toru Nakamura	71	69	69	73	282	1,840,000
Shigeru Kawamata	70	71	66	75	282	1,840,000
Nobuo Serizawa	74	72	66	71	283	1,440,000
Saburo Fujiki	69	71	72	71	283	1,440,000
Tsukasa Watanabe (E)	70	73	71	69	283	1,440,000
Terry Gale	73	75	66	70	284	1,120,000
Haruo Yasuda	67	70	75	72	284	1,120,000
Motomasa Aoki	73	74	67	70	284	1,120,000
Masahiro Kuramoto	70	75	70	70	285	940,000
Tadao Nakamura	65	76	71	73	285	940,000
Yutaka Hagawa	69	71	69	76	285	940,000
Akihito Yokoyama	71	76	67	71	285	940,000
Katsuji Hasegawa	70	73	69	74	286	850,000
Katsunari Takahashi	71	70	74	71	286	850,000
Seiichi Kanai	73	74	71	69	287	741,000
Ian Baker-Finch	68	77	71	71	287	741,000
David Ishii	72	73	71	71	287	741,000
Teruo Nakamura	70	77	70	70	287	741,000
Namio Takasu	72	75	71	69	287	741,000
Tomohiro Maruyama	69	75	69	64	287	741,000
Tsuneyuki Nakajima	71	72	73	71	287	741,000
Takashi Murakami	71	77	71	68	287	741,000
Hsieh Yung Yo	71	68	76	72	287	741,000

Fuji Sankei Classic

Kawana Hotel, Fuji Course, Ito
Par 71; 6,694 yards

May 4-7
purse, ¥60,000,000

	SCORES				TOTAL	MONEY
Masashi Ozaki	68	68	70	76	282	¥10,800,000
Katsunari Takahashi	68	73	72	71	284	6,000,000
Eduardo Herrera	70	71	71	74	286	3,120,000
Masanobu Kimura	67	71	73	75	286	3,120,000
Jeff Sluman	68	71	73	74	286	3,120,000
Naomichi Ozaki	72	69	73	73	287	1,845,000
Yoshiyuki Isomura	72	71	70	74	287	1,845,000
Chen Tze Chung	72	71	72	72	287	1,845,000
Namio Takasu	72	70	72	73	287	1,845,000
Yoshimi Niizeki	69	76	68	75	288	1,173,000
Chen Tze Ming	72	71	71	74	288	1,173,000
Katsuji Hasegawa	73	71	71	73	288	1,173,000
Yoshitaka Yamamoto	69	72	74	73	288	1,173,000
Toru Nakamura	72	70	76	71	289	768,000
Graham Marsh	73	73	73	70	289	768,000
Tadao Nakamura	69	74	73	73	289	768,000
Kikuo Arai	72	71	71	75	289	768,000
Hajime Meshiai	71	73	70	75	289	768,000
Ikuo Shirahama	69	67	73	80	289	768,000
Brian Jones	71	71	74	74	290	588,000
Takumi Asao	72	71	76	71	290	588,000
Nobuo Serizawa	69	76	73	73	291	525,000
Roger Mackay	71	72	75	73	291	525,000
Yutaka Hagawa	75	70	71	75	291	525,000
Norio Mikami	70	72	75	74	291	525,000
Kiyoshi Muroda	71	71	74	76	292	480,000
Tsukasa Watanabe (E)	68	75	70	79	292	480,000
Seiji Ebihara	67	75	76	74	292	480,000
Fujio Kobayashi	68	75	77	73	293	438,000
Toshiaki Sudo	70	76	74	73	293	438,000
Shoji Kikuchi	70	71	76	76	293	438,000

Japan Match Play Championship

Green Academy Country Club, Ishikawa
Par 72; 7,038 yards

May 11-14
purse, ¥50,000,000

FIRST ROUND

Masashi Ozaki defeated Haruo Yasuda, 5 and 4
Tomohiro Maruyama defeated Seiichi Kanai, 4 and 3
Toru Nakamura defeated Tadami Ueno, 1 up
Noboru Sugai defeated Yoshimi Niizeki, 1 up
Toshimitsu Kai defeated Masanobu Kimura, 2 and 1
Nobumitsu Yuhara defeated Teruo Nakamura, 1 up
Yoshiyuki Isomura defeated Brian Jones, 2 and 1
Tsukasa Watanabe (W) defeated Katsuji Hasegawa, 2 and 1
Kinpachi Yoshimura defeated Naomichi Ozaki, 2 and 1
Saburo Fujiki defeated Yoshikazu Yokoshima, 3 and 2
Yutaka Hagawa defeated Tateo Ozaki, 4 and 2
Hajime Meshiai defeated Katsuyoshi Tomori, 2 and 1
Yoshitaka Yamamoto defeated David Ishii, 1 up, 24th hole

Nobuo Serizawa defeated Koichi Suzuki, 2 and 1
Katsunari Takahashi defeated Chen Tze Ming, 1 up
Hiroshi Makino defeated Ikuo Shirahama, 1 up
(Each defeated player received ¥250,000)

SECOND ROUND

Ozaki defeated Maruyama, 4 and 3
Sugai defeated Nakamura, 2 and 1
Yuhara defeated Kai, 2 and 1
Isomura defeated Watanabe, 5 and 4
Fujiki defeated Yoshimura, 3 and 2
Meshiai defeated Hagawa, 2 and 1
Yamamoto defeated Serizawa, 1 up, 21 holes
Makino defeated Takahashi, 2 and 1
(Each defeated player received ¥500,000)

QUARTER-FINALS

Ozaki defeated Sugai, 4 and 3
Yuhara defeated Isomura, 2 and 1
Fujiki defeated Meshiai, 2 and 1
Makino defeated Yamamoto, 5 and 3
(Each defeated player received ¥1,000,000)

SEMI-FINALS

Ozaki defeated Yuhara, 5 and 4
Makino defeated Fujiki, 2 up

THIRD-FOURTH PLACE PLAYOFF

Fujiki defeated Yuhara, 4 and 3
(Fujiki received ¥3,500,000; Yuhara ¥2,500,000)

FINAL

Ozaki defeated Makino, 3 and 2
(Ozaki received ¥14,000,000; Makino ¥7,000,000)

Pepsi Ube Kosan

Ube Country Club, Mannenike East Course, Ajisucho   May 18-21
Par 72; 6,595 yards   purse, ¥50,000,000

(Friday round cancelled - rain)

	SCORES			TOTAL	MONEY
Akihito Yokoyama	67	69	67	203	¥6,750,000
Yoshimi Niizeki	66	69	68	203	3,750,000
(Yokoyama defeated Niizeki on second extra hole.)					
Nobuo Serizawa	66	71	67	204	2,175,000
Tadami Ueno	67	65	72	204	2,175,000
Katsunari Takahashi	71	66	68	205	1,500,000
Tadao Nakamura	71	68	68	207	1,212,000
Tsuyoshi Yoneyama	66	70	71	207	1,212,000
Kiiji Teshima	72	67	68	207	1,212,000
Yoshinori Kaneko	71	71	67	209	862,000
Nozomu Kamatsu	70	69	70	209	862,000

	SCORES			TOTAL	MONEY
Tsukasa Watanabe (W)	69	71	69	209	862,000
Katsuji Hasegawa	67	74	69	210	690,000
Chen Tze Ming	69	72	70	211	501,000
Haruo Yasuda	67	75	69	211	501,000
Tsukasa Watanabe (E)	72	65	74	211	501,000
Wayne Smith	64	75	72	211	501,000
Toshiaki Sudo	69	70	72	211	501,000
Hajime Matsui	69	72	70	211	501,000
Eiichi Itai	69	71	71	211	501,000
Toshimitsu Kai	68	73	71	212	352,000
Kiyoshi Murota	71	67	74	212	352,000
Teruo Nakamura	71	72	69	212	352,000
Ryoichi Takamoto	71	70	71	212	352,000
Koichi Suzuki	67	75	71	213	300,000
Seiji Ebihara	71	72	70	213	300,000
Brian Jones	72	71	70	213	300,000
Kenji Mori	69	70	74	213	300,000
Akiyoshi Omachi	70	71	72	213	300,000
Mitsuyasu Kojima	69	70	74	213	300,000
Norio Suzuki	75	68	70	213	300,000

Mitsubishi Galant

Kumamoto Airport Country Club, Kikuyomachi
Par 72; 7,028 yards

May 25-28
purse, ¥70,000,000

	SCORES				TOTAL	MONEY
Tateo Ozaki	72	67	74	71	284	¥12,600,000
Masanobu Kimura	69	74	72	71	286	7,000,000
Yoshimi Niizeki	69	73	78	67	287	3,640,000
Masahiro Kuramoto	75	73	70	69	287	3,640,000
Ikuo Shirahama	71	73	72	71	287	3,640,000
Graham Marsh	75	70	71	72	288	2,520,000
Haruo Yasuda	72	71	72	74	289	2,135,000
Tsuyoshi Yoneyama	74	71	73	71	289	2,135,000
Koichi Suzuki	72	70	76	72	290	1,458,000
Tadami Ueno	71	70	75	74	290	1,458,000
Tadao Nakamura	73	71	75	71	290	1,458,000
David Ishii	73	72	70	75	290	1,458,000
Seiji Ebihara	72	74	74	70	290	1,458,000
Katsunari Takahashi	70	71	75	75	291	1,008,000
Nobuo Serizawa	76	72	72	71	291	1,008,000
Eitaro Deguchi	70	77	76	68	291	1,008,000
Akihito Yokoyama	73	71	76	72	292	728,000
Kiyoshi Murota	76	72	70	74	292	728,000
Yutaka Hagawa	75	72	72	73	292	728,000
Futoshi Irino	75	74	71	72	292	728,000
Motomasa Aoki	70	74	77	71	292	728,000
Toshiaki Sudo	75	70	74	73	292	728,000
Katsuyoshi Tomori	71	76	72	74	293	616,000
Naomichi Ozaki	73	75	75	71	294	574,000
Toru Nakamura	73	71	76	74	294	574,000
Shigeru Kawamata	72	74	76	72	294	574,000
Brian Jones	72	72	76	74	294	574,000
Akiyoshi Omachi	76	72	73	73	294	574,000
Chen Tze Chung	73	71	75	76	295	518,000
Hajime Meshiai	71	73	74	77	295	518,000
Satoshi Higashi	72	73	76	74	295	518,000

Sendai Hoso Classic

Omote Zeo Golf Club, Shibatamachi
Par 71; 6,622 yards

June 1-4
purse, ¥45,000,000

	SCORES				TOTAL	MONEY
Masashi Ozaki	70	65	71	66	272	¥9,000,000
Katsunari Takahashi	68	71	70	66	275	4,200,000
Tsuneyuki Nakajima	77	65	68	65	275	4,200,000
Nobuo Serizawa	71	66	70	70	277	1,850,000
Eitaro Deguchi	67	69	75	66	277	1,850,000
Hajime Meshiai	66	70	70	71	277	1,850,000
Norio Mikami	67	71	67	72	277	1,850,000
Takeshi Kubota	68	71	73	65	277	1,850,000
Terry Gale	72	69	68	69	278	1,225,000
Toru Nakamura	74	67	66	71	278	1,225,000
Yoshitaka Yamamoto	71	72	67	69	279	885,000
Roger Mackay	65	74	69	71	279	885,000
Hiroya Kamide	70	69	72	68	279	885,000
Yoshio Fumiyama	72	69	70	68	279	885,000
Graham Marsh	74	68	69	69	280	690,000
Toshimitsu Kai	71	71	69	69	280	690,000
Ikuo Shirahama	71	69	72	69	281	600,000
Kiyoshi Murota	69	69	70	74	282	504,000
Wayne Smith	73	71	71	67	282	504,000
Namio Takasu	72	70	71	69	282	504,000
Brian Jones	71	71	73	67	282	504,000
Keiji Tejima	70	70	70	72	282	504,000
Hiroshi Makino	72	70	67	74	283	430,000
Tadami Ueno	69	72	71	71	283	430,000
Tsukasa Watanabe (E)	72	69	72	70	283	430,000
Masanobu Kimura	74	70	70	70	284	390,000
Haruo Yasuda	71	71	72	70	284	390,000
Yutaka Hagawa	69	72	71	72	284	390,000
Hajime Matsui	70	73	68	73	284	390,000
Hisao Inoue	72	72	69	71	284	390,000

Sapporo Tokyu Open

Sapporo Kokusai Country Club, Hiroshimacho
Par 72; 6,949 yards

June 8-11
purse, ¥50,000,000

	SCORES				TOTAL	MONEY
Graham Marsh	71	65	76	70	282	¥9,000,000
Tsuneyuki Nakajima	71	73	74	67	285	4,200,000
Katsuji Hasegawa	72	71	73	69	285	4,200,000
Naomichi Ozaki	75	69	73	70	287	2,066,666
David Ishii	72	71	77	67	287	2,066,666
Tsukasa Watanabe (E)	74	72	71	70	287	2,066,666
Terry Gale	78	69	70	71	288	1,450,000
Roger Mackay	76	71	74	67	288	1,450,000
Yurio Akitomi	75	70	71	72	288	1,450,000
Haruo Yasuda	73	71	77	68	289	1,023,333
Noboru Sugai	75	71	74	69	289	1,023,333
Katsuyoshi Tomori	70	74	74	71	289	1,023,333
Yoshitaka Yamamoto	71	72	73	74	290	810,000
Namio Takasu	77	73	72	68	290	810,000
Yasuo Sone	71	71	78	71	291	720,000

	SCORES			TOTAL	MONEY
Norio Mikami	74	70 74	74	292	585,000
Takeshi Shibata	74	70 75	73	292	585,000
Isamu Sugita	72	73 76	71	292	585,000
Motomasa Aoki	73	72 73	74	292	585,000
Yoshiyuki Isomura	71	74 77	71	293	462,000
Tadao Nakamura	74	73 75	71	293	462,000
Futoshi Irino	76	73 73	71	293	462,000
Kiyoshi Maita	77	71 73	72	293	462,000
Masakatsu Sano	78	70 70	75	293	462,000
Tadami Ueno	76	74 75	69	294	400,000
Kikuo Arai	77	73 70	74	294	400,000
Kazuo Kanayama	72	71 77	72	294	400,000
Junji Hashizoe	74	73 76	71	294	400,000
Yoshihisa Iwashita	74	71 77	72	294	400,000
Chen Tze Ming	78	68 74	75	295	360,000
Ikuo Shirahama	76	70 73	76	295	360,000
Hideyuki Satoh	77	71 77	70	295	360,000

Yomiuri Sapporo Beer Open

Yomiuri Country Club, Nishinomiya
Par 72; 7,023 yards

June 15-18
purse, ¥70,000,000

(Second round cancelled - rain.)

	SCORES			TOTAL	MONEY
Hajime Meshiai	64	71	70	205	¥9,450,000
Naomichi Ozaki	66	72	69	207	5,250,000
Chen Tze Chung	71	67	70	208	3,045,000
Brian Jones	70	72	66	208	3,045,000
Graham Marsh	68	72	69	209	1,995,000
Shinsaku Maeda	71	68	70	209	1,995,000
Yoshitaka Yamamoto	69	69	72	210	1,443,000
Yoshinori Kaneko	67	71	72	210	1,443,000
Kiyoshi Murota	69	73	68	210	1,443,000
Shoichi Yamamoto	70	70	70	210	1,443,000
Namio Takasu	72	68	71	211	966,000
Teruo Sugihara	73	70	68	211	966,000
Yoshihisa Iwashita	70	72	69	211	966,000
Nobuo Serizawa	72	70	70	212	600,000
Tsuneyuki Nakajima	71	70	71	212	600,000
Chen Tze Ming	71	73	68	212	600,000
Eitaro Deguchi	72	70	70	212	600,000
Yutaka Hagawa	71	72	69	212	600,000
Isamu Sugita	71	69	72	212	600,000
Mitsunobu Hataumi	71	71	70	212	600,000
Taisei Inagaki	69	75	68	212	600,000
Toyotake Nakao	68	72	72	212	600,000
Toshihiko Otsuka	69	72	71	212	600,000
Katsunari Takahashi	71	70	72	213	409,000
Yoshimi Niizeki	69	72	72	213	409,000
Ikuo Shirahama	72	70	71	213	409,000
Masahiro Kuramoto	69	70	74	213	409,000
Toshimitsu Kai	73	71	69	213	409,000
Teruo Nakamura	70	74	69	213	409,000
Akiyoshi Omachi	75	67	71	213	409,000
Masakatsu Sano	73	70	70	213	409,000
Hisao Inoue	75	68	70	213	409,000

Mizuno Open

Tokinodai Country Club, Mijodai Course, Hakui
Par 72; 6,799 yards

June 22-25
purse, ¥65,000,000

	SCORES				TOTAL	MONEY
Akiyoshi Omachi	70	72	72	69	283	¥11,700,000
Tsuneyuki Nakajima	72	74	67	72	285	4,160,000
Fujio Kobayashi	67	73	74	71	285	4,160,000
Masahiro Kuramoto	72	73	69	71	285	4,160,000
Brian Jones	73	73	68	71	285	4,160,000
Yoshimi Niizeki	70	73	70	73	286	2,101,000
Chen Tze Ming	69	74	69	74	286	2,101,000
Satoshi Higashi	71	75	70	70	286	2,101,000
Akihito Yokoyama	72	74	70	72	288	1,495,000
Kiyoshi Maita	76	73	69	70	288	1,495,000
Eiichi Itai	71	72	70	75	288	1,495,000
Futoshi Irino	67	71	79	72	289	1,196,000
Katsuji Hasegawa	72	74	69	75	290	936,000
Toshimitsu Kai	68	74	73	75	290	936,000
Toshiaki Sudo	68	77	74	71	290	936,000
Norikazu Kawakami	72	76	69	73	290	936,000
Frankie Minosa	70	73	72	75	290	936,000
Yoshikazu Yokoshima	72	73	68	78	291	641,000
Toru Nakamura	70	74	72	75	291	641,000
Tadami Ueno	73	72	71	75	291	641,000
Tadao Nakamura	76	70	73	72	291	641,000
Tsukasa Watanabe (E)	71	73	72	75	291	641,000
Pete Izumikawa	70	76	75	70	291	641,000
David Ishii	76	73	69	74	292	539,000
Shinsaku Maeda	68	78	73	73	292	539,000
Teruo Sugihara	70	74	70	78	292	539,000
Taijiro Tanaka	70	75	73	74	292	539,000
*Yoshikane Kawagishi	73	78	65	76	292	
Seiichi Kanai	75	71	74	73	293	507,000
Nobuo Serizawa	71	72	75	76	294	481,000
Yutaka Hagawa	75	73	74	72	294	481,000
Norio Mikami	68	80	73	74	294	481,000

Kanto PGA Championship

Prestige Country Club, Tochigi
Par 72; 7,094 yards

June 29-July 2
purse, ¥40,000,000

	SCORES				TOTAL	MONEY
Saburo Fujiki	69	68	70	70	277	¥7,200,000
Akiyoshi Omachi	68	70	67	73	278	4,000,000
Yoshimi Niizeki	70	69	70	71	280	2,320,000
Noboru Sugai	69	69	68	74	280	2,320,000
Koichi Suzuki	70	70	72	70	282	1,240,000
Nobumitsu Yuhara	68	71	71	72	282	1,240,000
Katsuji Hasegawa	70	68	70	74	282	1,240,000
David Ishii	70	74	69	69	282	1,240,000
Yutaka Hagawa	68	69	74	71	282	1,240,000
Takumi Asao	67	71	73	71	282	1,240,000
Mitsunobu Hatsumi	70	72	71	71	284	736,000
Ichiro Ino	69	70	73	72	284	736,000
Yasunori Uehara	74	68	68	74	284	736,000

	SCORES				TOTAL	MONEY
Tsukasa Watanabe (E)	74	69	70	72	285	600,000
Kiyoshi Murota	67	73	71	74	285	600,000
Gohei Satoh	71	69	69	77	286	528,000
Katsunari Takahashi	70	71	70	76	287	436,000
Seiji Ebihara	72	73	68	74	287	436,000
Norio Adachi	70	70	75	72	287	436,000
Hiroshi Tominaga	73	73	69	72	287	436,000
Haruo Yasuda	72	71	73	72	288	368,000
Hiroshi Makino	74	71	72	71	288	368,000
Hiroshi Ueda	69	73	71	75	288	368,000
Tsuyoshi Yoneyama	72	74	70	73	289	328,000
Hisayuki Sasaki	75	68	74	72	289	328,000
Ryoichi Takamoto	71	73	71	74	289	328,000
Hideki Kase	73	69	75	72	289	328,000
Yoshinori Mizumaki	73	67	76	73	289	328,000
Shigeru Kawamata	73	72	69	76	290	284,000
Satoshi Higashi	72	74	73	71	290	284,000
Taisei Inagaki	71	74	73	72	290	284,000
Nozomu Kamatsu	70	75	68	77	290	284,000
Takao Kage	72	72	70	76	290	284,000
Yoshiharu Ota	75	69	69	77	290	284,000

Kansai PGA Championship

Yamaguchi Golf and Country Club, Toyota
Par 72; 6,688 yards

June 29-July 2
purse, ¥30,000,000

	SCORES				TOTAL	MONEY
Hajime Matsui	70	68	70	68	276	¥5,400,000
Nobuhiro Yoshino	69	70	69	71	279	3,000,000
Toru Nakamura	68	69	67	79	283	1,560,000
Tadao Nakamura	71	67	69	76	283	1,560,000
Hisashi Kaji	70	71	70	72	283	1,560,000
Yoshiyuki Isomura	70	76	66	72	284	922,000
Teruo Sugihara	70	72	72	70	284	922,000
Tatsuo Takasaki	68	72	70	74	284	922,000
Hiroaki Uenishi	67	73	71	73	284	922,000
Masahiro Kuramoto	72	71	70	72	285	645,000
Toshimitsu Kai	71	71	72	71	285	645,000
Tadami Ueno	72	70	70	74	286	508,000
Toyotake Nakao	72	72	72	70	286	508,000
Takuo Terashima	70	72	73	71	286	508,000
Hiroya Kamide	71	69	69	78	287	396,000
Takenori Hiraishi	70	73	71	73	287	396,000
Seiki Okuda	73	71	71	72	287	396,000
Tsutomu Irie	69	73	72	74	288	324,000
Keizo Yamada	70	71	76	71	288	324,000
Eitaro Deguchi	73	71	72	73	289	288,000
Teruo Nakamura	69	69	79	72	289	288,000
Shoichi Yamamoto	68	74	72	75	289	288,000
Norikazu Kawakami	69	75	72	74	290	261,000
Toshiaki Nakagawa	74	70	73	73	290	261,000
Masanobu Kimura	67	71	79	74	291	225,000
Katsuyoshi Tomori	75	69	69	78	291	225,000
Hideto Shigenobu	70	74	72	75	291	225,000
Yasuhiro Okumura	70	72	73	76	291	225,000
Yoshinori Sasayama	73	72	72	74	291	225,000
Tsutomu Fukasawa	74	72	74	71	291	225,000

	SCORES				TOTAL	MONEY
Katsumi Hara	71	73	74	73	291	225,000
Hideo Hashimoto	70	73	75	73	291	225,000
Shigeo Kinoshita	73	72	71	75	291	225,000
Yoshio Ichikawa	71	74	78	68	291	225,000

Yonex Hiroshima Open

Hiroshima Country Club, Happonmatsu Course, Higashi Hiroshima   July 6-9
Par 72; 6,865 yards   purse, ¥50,000,000

	SCORES				TOTAL	MONEY
Masashi Ozaki	69	67	68	66	270	¥10,800,000
Nobuo Serizawa	63	72	71	70	276	4,320,000
Seiichi Kanai	68	71	68	69	276	4,320,000
Seiji Ebihara	70	67	70	69	276	4,320,000
Satoshi Higashi	67	71	68	72	278	2,400,000
Pete Izumikawa	66	74	67	73	280	2,040,000
Hiroshi Ueda	67	69	74	70	280	2,040,000
Masaji Kusakabe	69	70	71	71	281	1,740,000
Haruo Yasuda	72	71	72	67	282	1,311,000
Tadami Ueno	69	73	70	70	282	1,311,000
Yutaka Hagawa	71	68	69	74	282	1,311,000
Seiki Okuda	67	76	67	72	282	1,311,000
Akihito Yokoyama	71	68	69	75	283	832,000
David Ishii	70	72	72	69	283	832,000
Noboru Sugai	71	69	74	69	283	832,000
Toshiaki Sudo	72	72	72	67	283	832,000
Yoshihisa Iwashita	73	70	69	71	283	832,000
Ichiro Teramoto	72	72	66	73	283	832,000
Akiyoshi Omachi	70	71	72	71	284	588,000
Yoshikazu Yokoshima	71	72	70	71	284	588,000
Satoshi Furuyama	70	71	74	69	284	588,000
Hikaru Emoto	67	73	71	73	284	588,000
Naomichi Ozaki	69	71	74	71	285	504,000
Toru Nakamura	71	68	72	74	285	504,000
Eitaro Deguchi	70	72	70	73	285	504,000
Ichiro Ino	71	72	68	74	285	504,000
Tsukasa Watanabe (W)	73	71	69	72	285	504,000
Teruo Sugihara	66	77	70	73	286	450,000
Hisao Inoue	71	69	71	75	286	450,000
Gohei Sato	73	67	75	71	286	450,000
Kenji Sogame	74	70	68	74	286	450,000

NST Niigata Open

Dainiigata Country Club, Sanjo Course, Shitadamura   July 27-30
Par 72; 6,930 yards   purse, ¥50,000,000

	SCORES				TOTAL	MONEY
Katsuyoshi Tomori	71	70	76	71	288	¥9,000,000
Tomohiro Maruyama	73	69	76	71	289	5,000,000
Seiichi Kanai	75	72	71	72	290	2,600,000
Teruo Sugihara	78	70	71	71	290	2,600,000
Kikuo Arai	75	72	74	69	290	2,600,000
Shigeru Kawamata	72	74	71	74	291	1,616,000

	SCORES				TOTAL	MONEY
Shoichi Yamamoto	74	74	76	67	291	1,616,000
Toru Nakayama	73	68	74	76	291	1,616,000
Ikuo Shirahama	71	73	74	74	292	1,042,000
Yurio Akitomi	72	70	79	71	292	1,042,000
Hsieh Min Nan	76	71	74	71	292	1,042,000
Yoshinori Mizumaki	72	72	75	73	292	1,042,000
Yukiyoshi Idoki	71	72	77	72	292	1,042,000
Yoshimi Niizeki	74	73	75	71	293	640,000
Toshiaki Sudo	78	69	72	74	293	640,000
Shinsaku Maeda	77	73	74	69	293	640,000
Nobuhiro Yoshino	74	72	75	72	293	640,000
Takeshi Shibata	73	72	76	72	293	640,000
Norikazu Kawakami	77	72	72	72	293	640,000
Masanobu Kimura	73	77	75	69	294	470,000
Akihito Yokoyama	76	70	75	73	294	470,000
Yoshiyuki Isomura	73	77	75	69	294	470,000
Norio Mikami	73	77	71	73	294	470,000
Toru Nakamura	74	73	78	70	295	405,000
Brian Jones	76	72	75	72	295	405,000
Tadao Nakamura	76	73	72	74	295	405,000
Teruo Nakamura	75	73	77	70	295	405,000
Keiji Teshima	72	75	78	70	295	405,000
Hideki Kase	74	77	72	72	295	405,000
Pete Izumikawa	72	74	78	72	296	370,000

Japan PGA Championship

Karasuyamajo Country Club, Karasuyama
Par 71; 6,968 yards

August 3-6
purse, ¥70,000,000

	SCORES				TOTAL	MONEY
Masashi Ozaki	68	68	71	71	278	¥12,600,000
Hideki Kase	72	69	72	66	279	7,000,000
Naomichi Ozaki	70	71	74	69	284	3,640,000
Katsuyoshi Tomori	72	71	71	70	284	3,640,000
Saburo Fujiki	68	73	69	74	284	3,640,000
Yoshinori Kaneko	68	74	71	72	285	2,263,000
Roger Mackay	71	68	71	75	285	2,263,000
Toyotake Nakao	69	69	74	73	285	2,263,000
Akiyoshi Omachi	70	71	71	74	286	1,715,000
Hajime Meshiai	72	72	72	70	286	1,715,000
Graham Marsh	74	67	70	76	287	1,239,000
Eitaro Deguchi	70	71	71	75	287	1,239,000
Tsuyoshi Yoneyama	68	71	74	74	287	1,239,000
Isao Aoki	73	72	70	72	287	1,239,000
Haruo Yasuda	70	68	74	76	288	889,000
Tsudasa Watanabe	69	70	75	74	288	889,000
Kiyoshi Murota	71	74	73	70	288	889,000
Futoshi Iruino	72	68	72	76	288	889,000
Yoshikazu Yokoshima	71	73	73	72	289	631,000
Toru Nakamura	67	70	72	80	289	631,000
Brian Jones	70	72	74	73	289	631,000
Yoshitaka Yamamoto	72	68	76	73	289	631,000
Masaji Kusakabe	73	71	70	75	289	631,000
Kazuo Kanayama	69	72	71	77	289	631,000
Kenji Nakamura	72	73	70	74	289	631,000
Tatsuya Shiraishi	72	71	71	75	289	631,000

	SCORES				TOTAL	MONEY
Yoichi Yamamoto	75	67	73	74	289	631,000
Tsuneyuki Nakajima	70	75	72	73	290	525,000
Shigeru Kawamata	73	71	71	75	290	525,000
Yoshihisa Iwashita	73	71	72	74	290	525,000
Nozomu Kamatsu	65	76	74	75	290	525,000

Nikkei Cup

Izu Nirayama Country Club, Nirayama
Par 70; 6,617 yards

August 10-13
purse, ¥60,000,000

	SCORES				TOTAL	MONEY
Yoshimi Niizeki	66	69	68	68	271	¥10,800,000
Saburo Fujiki	65	70	68	68	271	6,000,000
(Niizeki defeated Fujiki on first extra hole.)						
Yutaka Hagawa	69	65	67	73	274	4,080,000
Yoshiyuki Isomura	65	69	70	71	275	2,640,000
Norikazu Kawakami	68	66	67	74	275	2,640,000
Yoshitaka Yamamoto	68	74	69	65	276	2,160,000
Tsuneyuki Nakajima	71	67	69	70	277	1,650,000
Tsukasa Watanabe (E)	68	75	66	68	277	1,650,000
Hiroya Kamide	68	70	70	69	277	1,650,000
Masakatsu Sano	71	73	65	68	277	1,650,000
Hajime Meshiai	69	72	68	70	279	1,022,000
Terry Gale	72	68	69	70	279	1,022,000
Hajime Matsui	66	72	72	69	279	1,022,000
Mitsunobu Hatsumi	72	69	68	70	279	1,022,000
Kazuo Kanayama	69	68	72	70	279	1,022,000
Takeshi Shibata	70	70	68	72	280	756,000
Yoichi Yamamoto	71	67	67	75	280	756,000
Yoshinori Kaneko	65	71	70	75	281	632,000
Keiji Teshima	67	72	69	73	281	632,000
Norihiko Matsumoto	71	72	63	75	281	632,000
Koichi Suzuki	69	71	70	72	282	535,000
Seiichi Kanai	71	72	70	69	282	535,000
Ikuo Shirahama	68	72	68	74	282	535,000
Mitsuo Harada	71	70	74	67	282	535,000
Mamoru Takahashi	72	69	70	71	282	535,000
Roger Mackay	64	72	67	80	283	474,000
Hisayuki Sasaki	72	71	65	75	283	474,000
Hsieh Min Nan	73	71	72	67	283	474,000
Gohei Sato	69	72	65	77	283	474,000
Toshimitsu Kai	60	74	72	69	284	426,000
Namio Takasu	71	72	71	70	284	426,000
Kiyoshi Maita	69	73	71	71	284	426,000
Yurio Akitomi	70	72	69	73	284	426,000

Maruman Open

Higashi Matsuyama Country Club, Hatoyamamachi
Par 72; 7,082 yards

August 17-20
purse, ¥80,000,000

	SCORES				TOTAL	MONEY
Koichi Suzuki	70	63	71	74	278	¥14,400,000
Tsukasa Watanabe (E)	66	71	72	70	279	6,720,000

	SCORES				TOTAL	MONEY
Satoshi Higashi	69	70	71	69	279	6,720,000
Masashi Ozaki	74	68	72	66	280	3,840,000
Toru Nakayama	67	72	72	70	281	3,200,000
Yoshimi Niizeki	71	74	70	69	284	2,586,000
Ikuo Shirahama	72	71	67	74	284	2,586,000
Taijiro Tanaka	71	68	68	77	284	2,586,000
Tsuneyuki Nakajima	73	71	69	72	285	1,597,000
Nobuo Serizawa	70	72	73	70	285	1,597,000
Yoshikazu Yokoshima	72	75	71	67	285	1,597,000
Yutaka Hagawa	72	72	72	69	285	1,597,000
Roger Mackay	70	71	70	74	285	1,597,000
Kiyoshi Maita	73	71	71	70	285	1,597,000
Nobumitsu Yuhara	69	71	72	74	286	979,000
Masahiro Kuramoto	73	72	70	71	286	979,000
Yoshitaka Yamamoto	69	73	73	71	286	979,000
Hiroshi Makino	70	73	73	70	286	979,000
Muroda Kiyoshi	72	72	71	71	286	979,000
Tomohiro Maruyama	72	75	70	70	287	784,000
Seiki Okuda	74	71	70	72	287	784,000
Tateo Ozaki	72	68	76	72	288	691,000
Masanobu Kimura	68	73	76	71	288	691,000
Yoshihisa Iwashita	70	75	70	73	288	691,000
Hideyuki Sato	70	75	70	73	288	691,000
Norio Hirayama	73	70	74	71	288	691,000
Brian Jones	74	69	74	72	289	616,000
Yurio Akitomi	72	73	72	72	289	616,000
Koji Kobayashi	72	75	72	70	289	616,000
Yasuo Nukaga	73	74	68	74	289	616,000
Toru Nakamura	72	72	74	72	290	547,000
Seiichi Kanai	72	72	73	73	290	547,000
Yoshinori Kaneko	77	70	73	70	290	547,000
Toshimitsu Kai	72	74	71	73	290	547,000
Shigenori Mori	72	74	72	72	290	547,000

Daiwa KBC Augusta

Kyushu Shima Country Club, Shima
Par 72; 7,130 yards

August 24-27
purse, ¥100,000,000

	SCORES				TOTAL	MONEY
Teruo Sugihara	70	72	71	68	281	¥18,000,000
Graham Marsh	74	70	71	68	283	8,400,000
Tsuneyuki Nakajima	71	69	73	70	283	8,400,000
Masashi Ozaki	69	69	78	68	284	4,400,000
Yoshitaka Yamamoto	70	71	70	73	284	4,400,000
Hideki Kase	74	68	70	73	285	3,400,000
Harumitsu Hamano	70	68	71	76	285	3,400,000
Koichi Suzuki	68	72	71	75	286	2,328,000
Masanobu Kimura	75	69	69	73	286	2,328,000
Takeshi Shibata	71	75	71	69	286	2,328,000
Hiroshi Ueda	67	72	70	77	286	2,328,000
Isao Aoki	72	71	72	71	286	2,328,000
Toru Nakamura	69	70	71	77	287	1,560,000
Roger Mackay	73	71	69	74	287	1,560,000
Hiroya Kamide	71	72	71	73	287	1,560,000
Saburo Fujiki	73	70	73	72	288	1,213,000
Hajime Meshiai	68	74	73	73	288	1,213,000

	SCORES			TOTAL	MONEY
Kiyoshi Murota	69	68	74	77	288	1,213,000
Yutaka Hagawa	72	69	70	78	289	928,000
Brian Jones	73	69	73	74	289	928,000
Hiroshi Makino	73	72	67	77	289	928,000
Tadami Ueno	72	69	74	74	289	928,000
Tomohiro Maruyama	72	73	68	76	289	928,000
Norio Mikami	71	67	72	79	289	928,000
Toyotake Nakao	72	73	71	73	289	928,000
Satoshi Higashi	70	73	74	73	290	790,000
Seiichi Kanai	72	74	68	76	290	790,000
Norikazu Kawakami	71	71	75	73	290	790,000
Masaji Kusakabe	71	74	73	72	290	790,000
Yoshikazu Yokoshima	71	75	73	72	291	694,000
Nobumitsu Yuhara	71	70	74	76	291	694,000
Shigeru Kawamata	74	71	74	72	291	694,000
Toshiaki Sudo	74	65	73	79	291	694,000
Yoichi Yamamoto	75	68	74	74	291	694,000
David Graham	74	70	72	75	291	694,000

Kanto Open

Hidaka Country Club
Par 72; 6,726 yards

August 31-September 3
purse, ¥30,000,000

	SCORES			TOTAL	MONEY
Yoshinori Mizumaki	68	69	74	70	281	¥6,000,000
Isao Aoki	69	71	71	71	282	3,000,000
Yoshikazu Yokoshima	71	68	71	76	286	1,800,000
Ikuo Shirahama	72	69	72	74	287	1,200,000
Akihiro Yokoyama	68	71	69	81	289	1,000,000
Koichi Suzuki	69	73	76	72	290	850,000
Hiroshi Makino	73	71	71	75	290	850,000
Noboru Sugai	71	69	75	78	293	725,000
Tsuyoshi Yoneyama	71	71	75	76	293	725,000
Shinji Ikeuchi	73	77	71	73	294	590,000
Seiichi Kanai	76	69	74	75	294	590,000
Eiichi Itai	73	74	70	77	294	590,000
Shigeru Kawamata	72	72	72	78	294	590,000
Masaji Kusakabe	71	80	72	72	295	480,000
Tsuneyuki Nakajima	73	74	74	74	295	480,000
Taiji Shimizu	73	74	74	74	295	480,000
Hideki Kase	73	76	71	76	296	396,000
Hiroshi Tominaga	75	74	73	74	296	396,000
Katsuji Hasegawa	72	76	75	73	296	396,000
Satoshi Higashi	74	73	70	79	296	396,000
Minoru Hatsumi	72	74	71	79	296	396,000
Shuichi Sano	74	70	76	77	297	350,000
Gohei Sato	74	74	72	77	297	350,000
Nozomu Kamatsu	77	71	74	75	297	350,000
Toru Nakayama	73	74	73	78	298	310,000
Takaaki Fukuzawa	69	79	74	76	298	310,000
Tetsu Nishikawa	68	75	80	75	298	310,000
Tokuo Hirayama	73	74	77	74	298	310,000
Tomohiro Maruyama	71	79	74	74	298	310,000

Kansai Open

Hanayashiki Golf Club
Par 72; 6,740 yards

August 31-September 3
purse, ¥20,000,000

	SCORES			TOTAL	MONEY
Yoshitaka Yamamoto	67	74	70	211	¥3,750,000
Toro Nakamura	73	71	68	212	1,225,000
Kazuo Kanayama	69	69	74	212	1,225,000
Toshiaki Nakagawa	68	68	76	212	1,225,000
Takenori Hiraishi	71	73	70	214	675,000
Koji Kobayashi	72	71	73	216	562,500
Shinsaku Maeda	73	74	69	216	562,500
Hisao Inoue	73	73	71	217	412,500
Masanobu Kimura	75	73	69	217	412,500
Yoshiyuki Isomura	75	71	71	217	412,500
Tatsuo Nakagami	72	71	75	218	318,750
Takeshi Kitadai	73	69	76	218	318,750
Hisashi Terada	75	72	72	219	243,750
Yasuo Sone	70	75	74	219	243,750
Toshiji Kusaka	73	76	71	220	168,750
Yoshio Ichikawa	73	75	72	220	168,750
Kenji Tokuyama	72	75	74	221	150,000
Kiyoshi Sakamoto	72	76	73	221	150,000
Keiichi Kobayashi	75	73	73	221	150,000
Yoshinori Ichioka	72	74	76	222	150,000
Koji Okuno	74	78	71	223	120,000
Tsutomu Irie	71	76	76	223	120,000
Teruo Sugihara	76	74	73	223	120,000
Yoichi Yamamoto	75	73	75	223	120,000
Hisashi Kaji	74	72	77	223	120,000
Toyotake Nakao	72	76	76	224	97,500
Kenji Kataoka	73	78	73	224	97,500
Mikio Nakamatsu	72	74	78	224	97,500

Chu-Shikoku Open

Kamo Country Club
Par 72; 7,005 yards

August 31-September 3
purse, ¥20,000,000

	SCORES				TOTAL	MONEY
Tadami Ueno	69	69	71	74	283	¥5,000,000
Norio Mikami	70	66	77	71	284	2,050,000
Yoshikazu Sakamoto	70	75	71	68	284	2,050,000
Kazunari Matsunaga	72	71	70	75	288	1,100,000
Masahiro Kuramoto	75	76	72	68	291	762,500
Seiki Okuda	71	69	78	73	291	762,500
Kiminori Kato	74	74	73	70	291	762,500
Masayuki Kawamura	71	71	75	74	291	762,500
Atsuo Suemura	73	75	77	68	293	475,000
Kenji Sogame	72	72	78	71	293	475,000
Takeshi Nakatani	72	71	76	76	295	400,000
Hiroshi Taninaka	75	76	74	71	296	325,000
Yasuhiro Daio	72	78	76	70	296	325,000
Tsukasa Watanabe	69	80	74	74	297	250,000
Hideto Shigenobu	80	74	73	71	298	195,000
Satoshi Haga	74	73	76	75	298	195,000
Takfumi Ogawa	71	79	74	75	299	165,000

	SCORES				TOTAL	MONEY
Katsumi Hara	76	74	72	77	299	165,000
Nobuhiro Yoshino	72	78	74	75	299	165,000
Nobuo Sato	77	75	74	73	299	165,000
Masami Nishiyama	74	75	78	73	300	140,000
Takashi Watanabe	71	77	77	76	301	140,000
Kazuo Yamamoto	77	75	74	75	301	140,000
Kazuki Nagao	72	79	74	77	302	134,000
Shigeru Yamada	77	77	73	75	302	134,000
Mitoshi Tomita	73	79	79	71	302	134,000
Koji Tanaka	68	81	77	76	302	134,000
Hideo Hashimoto	75	76	78	73	302	134,000
Seiichi Suzuki	78	76	74	75	303	130,000
Koji Inaba	75	77	79	72	303	130,000

Hokkaido Open

Barato Country Club
Par 72; 6,790 yards

August 31-September 3
purse, ¥10,000,000

	SCORES				TOTAL	MONEY
Mamoru Takahashi	67	78	71	69	285	¥3,000,000
Katsunari Takahashi	67	74	72	72	285	1,500,000
(Mamoru Takahashi won playoff.)						
Koichi Uehara	72	72	72	70	286	1,000,000
Kazuhiro Takami	71	75	70	72	288	600,000
Shoichi Sato	74	72	72	71	289	450,000
Kesahiko Uchida	75	74	73	70	292	290,000
Jun Nobechi	74	76	72	70	292	290,000
Kenji Noma	71	73	73	75	292	290,000
Fumio Tanaka	73	71	76	73	293	200,000
Fukuji Kikuchi	70	70	79	75	294	142,500
Masaaki Shiraishi	76	68	75	75	294	142,500
Ryoichi Takamoto	76	71	74	73	294	142,500
Susumu Mori	74	70	78	72	294	142,500
Satoshi Sudo	75	76	74	70	295	130,000
Hiroshi Yamada	69	76	75	75	295	130,000
Kenji Takeda	76	73	76	71	296	100,000
Akihiko Kojima	74	75	73	75	297	100,000
Mitsuyoshi Goto	77	76	74	71	298	100,000
Masaru Sato	74	74	73	77	298	100,000
Masaaki Fujii	74	74	75	75	298	100,000
Yasuo Kininaka	77	72	77	73	299	100,000
Toshiaki Nakamura	74	78	73	76	301	100,000
Takayuki Shiotani	70	77	77	77	301	100,000
Yoshitaka Igawa	72	79	75	75	301	100,000
Hiroshi Todate	76	81	75	71	303	100,000
Toshinori Horiki	74	74	78	77	303	100,000
Yoshiharu Takai	73	79	80	72	304	100,000
Noritaka Shiraishi	72	78	83	75	308	100,000
Kazuyoshi Takai	74	78	81	75	308	100,000
Masaaki Yamamoto	76	76	85	71	308	100,000
Horonori Yuda	77	77	78	76	308	100,000

Chubu Open

Three Lakes Country Club
Par 72; 6,900 yards

August 31-September 3
purse, ¥15,000,000

	SCORES			TOTAL	MONEY
Tadao Nakamura	72	68	70	210	¥3,000,000
Masahiro Shioda	71	68	72	211	1,500,000
Hiroto Ieda	73	70	72	215	900,000
Masami Ito	72	72	72	216	435,000
Norihiko Matsumoto	71	70	75	216	435,000
Eitaro Deguchi	74	72	70	216	435,000
Jun Hattori	75	73	68	216	435,000
Shigeru Uchida	70	73	73	216	435,000
Takuo Terashima	71	72	74	217	262,000
Takeru Shibata	77	68	73	218	178,125
Hiroaki Uenishi	71	72	75	218	178,125
Yutaka Suzuki	75	71	72	218	178,125
Teruo Nakamura	74	69	75	218	178,125
Toshiki Matsui	70	72	78	220	135,000
Toshihiko Kikuichi	74	75	72	221	127,500
Hisashi Suzumura	75	73	74	222	108,750
Toshio Takeuchi	77	69	76	222	108,750
Mitsuo Hirukawa	73	73	76	222	108,750
Kakuji Matsui	74	73	75	222	108,750
Masamitsu Koguri	73	78	72	223	90,000
Tatsuo Ukai	76	74	74	224	82,500
Yoshihiro Nakamura	75	74	76	225	82,500
Kiyoshi Nakagawa	73	75	77	225	82,500
Hideo Kamiya	75	74	77	225	82,500
Motoi Nakamura	75	72	78	225	82,500
Hatsutoshi Sakai	75	74	77	226	75,000
Kazumi Nakao	78	74	75	227	75,000
Kazutomo Niwa	76	74	77	227	75,000
Noriyoshi Mabuchi	73	73	81	227	75,000
Yoshihisa Kosaka	72	71	85	228	75,000

Kyushu Open

Kumamoto Chuo Country Club
Par 72; 7,132 yards

August 31-September 3
purse, ¥20,000,000

	SCORES				TOTAL	MONEY
Shinji Kuraoka	69	76	71	71	287	¥5,000,000
Katsuyoshi Tomori	71	73	69	74	287	2,500,000
(Kuraoka won playoff.)						
Yurio Akitomi	75	72	71	71	289	1,500,000
Kinpachi Yoshimura	72	72	73	73	290	1,100,000
Makoto Nanbu	74	75	70	72	291	900,000
Atsushi Ikehara	77	74	77	68	296	600,000
Isamu Sugita	77	76	70	73	296	600,000
Toshiro Yoshitake	79	72	71	74	296	600,000
Kenji Teshima	77	74	71	75	297	500,000
Takida Tsugiomi	71	79	75	73	298	450,000
Masahiro Nakajima	75	71	75	78	299	325,000
Norikazu Kawakami	73	76	82	68	299	325,000
Takamasa Sakai	77	76	75	71	299	325,000

	SCORES				TOTAL	MONEY
Kuniharu Nakagawara	77	71	76	75	299	325,000
Noboru Shibata	75	77	74	74	300	173,333
Yoshinori Onishi	74	76	74	76	300	173,333
Reiji Bando	75	76	75	74	300	173,333

Suntory Open

Narashino Country Club, Inzaimachi
Par 72; 7,086 yards

September 7-10
purse, ¥80,000,000

		SCORES			TOTAL	MONEY
Larry Nelson	69	67	70	70	276	¥14,400,000
Saburo Fujiki	68	68	70	70	276	8,000,000
(Nelson defeated Fujiki on first extra hole.)						
Graham Marsh	69	72	70	71	282	4,640,000
Satoshi Furuyama	70	72	67	73	282	4,640,000
Brian Jones	71	67	71	74	283	2,740,000
Noboru Sugai	73	68	75	67	283	2,740,000
Chen Tze Chung	69	67	70	77	283	2,740,000
Isao Aoki	73	69	69	72	283	2,740,000
Teruo Sugihara	73	70	68	73	284	1,748,000
Tateo Ozaki	74	72	70	68	284	1,748,000
Seiichi Kanai	70	69	73	72	284	1,748,000
Tadao Nakamura	72	70	73	69	284	1,748,000
Yoshitaka Yamamoto	69	73	72	71	285	1,296,000
Shinsaku Maeda	73	74	65	73	285	1,296,000
Norio Hirayama	74	71	73	68	286	1,016,000
Yoichi Yamamoto	70	72	72	72	286	1,016,000
Hiroshi Tominaga	72	69	75	70	286	1,016,000
Bob Tway	73	70	72	71	286	1,016,000
Tsuneyuki Nakajima	74	69	73	71	287	784,000
Akira Higashi	69	71	74	73	287	784,000
Katsuji Hasegawa	71	73	69	74	287	784,000
Toshiaki Sudo	69	71	77	70	287	784,000
Katsuyoshi Tomori	72	74	73	69	288	680,000
Hajime Meshiai	74	69	70	75	288	680,000
Nobumitsu Yuhara	73	70	75	70	288	680,000
Tomohiro Maruyama	71	73	74	70	288	680,000
Koichi Suzuki	73	74	70	72	289	632,000
Fujio Kobayashi	75	67	70	77	289	632,000
Roger Mackay	73	73	71	73	290	592,000
Norikazu Kawakami	71	74	72	73	290	592,000
Shigenori Mori	71	72	71	76	290	592,000

All Nippon Airways Open

Sapporo Golf Club, Hiroshimacho
Par 72; 7,100 yards

September 14-17
purse, ¥70,000,000

	SCORES				TOTAL	MONEY
Masashi Ozaki	71	70	68	71	280	¥12,600,000
Ian Woosnam	74	67	72	73	286	7,000,000
Tsukasa Watanabe (E)	72	68	76	71	287	4,060,000
Brian Jones	73	73	70	71	287	4,060,000
Toru Nakamura	73	75	72	68	288	2,800,000

	SCORES				TOTAL	MONEY
Yoshinori Kaneko	75	72	73	69	289	2,380,000
Seiji Ebihara	72	75	70	72	289	2,380,000
Tateo Ozaki	72	73	75	70	290	1,820,000
Akiyoshi Omachi	73	70	72	75	290	1,820,000
Kiyoshi Muroda	74	73	69	74	290	1,820,000
Takashi Kubota	73	69	76	73	291	1,400,000
Hajime Meshiai	78	71	74	69	292	1,232,000
Hiroshi Makino	72	73	72	75	292	1,232,000
Norikazu Kawakami	70	72	80	71	293	1,092,000
Yoshitaka Yamamoto	75	74	72	73	294	1,031,000
Yoshinori Mizumaki	74	75	73	72	294	1,031,000
Yoshiyuki Isomura	76	73	72	74	295	748,000
Akihito Yokoyama	72	71	76	76	295	748,000
Tomohiro Maruyama	76	76	73	70	295	748,000
Mitsunobu Hatsumi	76	73	73	73	295	748,000
Hidenori Nakajima	75	76	71	73	295	748,000
Roger Mackay	78	70	76	72	296	612,000
David Ishii	78	71	75	72	296	612,000
Pete Izumikawa	74	70	77	75	296	612,000
Kiyoshi Maita	76	75	72	73	296	612,000
Toru Nakayama	78	70	75	74	297	574,000
Teruo Sugihara	76	71	77	74	298	546,000
Ysuyoshi Yoneyama	75	70	72	81	298	546,000
Hal Sutton	73	74	73	78	298	546,000
Tetsu Nishikawa	77	72	72	78	299	504,000
Hiroshi Goda	75	77	75	72	299	504,000
Misao Hieda	78	73	74	74	299	504,000

Jun Classic

Tochigi Jun Classic Country Club, Ogawacho
Par 72; 7,091 yards

September 21-24
purse, ¥70,000,000

	SCORES				TOTAL	MONEY
Tateo Ozaki	73	70	70	66	279	¥12,600,000
Naomichi Ozaki	70	71	69	69	279	7,000,000
(Tateo Ozaki defeated Naomichi Ozaki in playoff.)						
Yoshikazu Yokoshima	67	74	72	68	281	4,060,000
Seiji Ebihara	73	71	69	68	281	4,060,000
Toru Nakamura	73	71	68	70	282	2,800,000
Masashi Ozaki	70	74	69	72	285	2,263,000
Tsuyoshi Yoneyama	69	72	71	73	285	2,263,000
Norio Mikami	69	71	73	72	285	2,263,000
Brian Jones	74	69	71	72	286	1,529,000
Hiroshi Makino	74	70	72	70	286	1,529,000
Masahiro Kuramoto	69	72	73	72	286	1,529,000
Eduardo Herrera	71	75	69	71	286	1,529,000
Yoshitaka Yamamoto	70	77	69	71	287	1,092,000
Nobumitsu Yuhara	72	69	70	76	287	1,092,000
Hisayuki Sasaki	72	73	70	72	287	1,092,000
Taisei Inagaki	74	72	72	70	288	924,000
Koichi Suzuki	71	69	73	76	289	784,000
Hideki Kase	72	71	73	73	289	784,000
Shoichi Yamamoto	73	73	71	72	289	784,000
Ikuo Shirahama	71	74	74	71	290	672,000
David Ishii	71	73	74	72	290	672,000
Toru Nakayama	71	71	76	72	290	672,000

	SCORES				TOTAL	MONEY
Tsuneyuki Nakajima	70	74	75	72	291	581,000
Teruo Sugihara	74	75	71	71	291	581,000
Katsuji Hasegawa	72	76	69	74	291	581,000
Haruo Yasuda	73	75	69	74	291	581,000
Roger Mackay	73	72	71	75	291	581,000
Eiichi Itai	73	71	74	73	291	581,000
Saburo Fujiki	72	75	72	73	292	492,000
Hajime Meshiai	73	75	68	76	292	492,000
Nobuo Serizawa	74	72	72	74	292	492,000
Noboru Sugai	72	72	71	77	292	492,000
Yoshinori Mizumaki	70	72	73	77	292	492,000
Isao Aoki	75	72	69	76	292	492,000
Norikazu Kawakami	72	75	72	73	292	492,000

Tokai Classic

Miyoshi Country Club, West Course, Miyoshicho
Par 72; 7,089 yards

September 28-October 1
purse, ¥60,000,000

	SCORES				TOTAL	MONEY
Isao Aoki	67	69	71	68	275	¥10,800,000
Pete Izumikawa	72	64	70	74	280	6,000,000
Tsuneyuki Nakajima	70	69	71	71	281	3,480,000
Akiyoshi Omachi	76	69	67	69	281	3,480,000
Eitaro Deguchi	70	76	69	70	285	2,400,000
Yoshikazu Yokoshima	72	74	71	69	286	1,752,000
Tadao Nakamura	72	72	73	69	286	1,752,000
Nobumitsu Yuhara	75	71	65	75	286	1,752,000
Tadami Ueno	76	72	68	70	286	1,752,000
Hajime Matsui	70	71	74	71	286	1,752,000
Graham Marsh	72	68	74	73	287	1,152,000
Mark O'Meara	74	71	71	71	287	1,152,000
Brian Jones	72	73	72	71	288	900,000
Masanobu Kimura	73	74	69	72	288	900,000
Hiroshi Makino	74	70	72	72	288	900,000
Kiyoshi Muroda	71	72	71	74	288	900,000
Seiji Ebihara	71	73	74	72	290	672,000
Chen Tze Ming	74	67	73	76	290	672,000
Yoshinori Mizumaki	72	74	72	72	290	672,000
Nobuo Serizawa	74	74	70	73	291	554,000
Tadao Nakamura	71	72	75	73	291	554,000
Fujio Kobayashi	76	67	73	75	291	554,000
Kazuo Kanayama	72	77	65	77	291	554,000
Andrew Murray	74	74	71	72	291	554,000
Noboru Sugai	74	75	72	71	292	498,000
Hsieh Min Nan	71	73	75	73	292	498,000
Saburo Fujiki	71	73	75	74	293	450,000
Akihito Yokoyama	69	77	74	73	293	450,000
Hideki Kase	73	70	74	76	293	450,000
Shigeru Kamata	71	75	76	71	293	450,000
Seiki Okuda	77	72	71	73	293	450,000
Carlos Espinosa	71	74	70	78	293	450,000

Japan Open

Nagoya Golf Club, Wago Course, Nagoya
Par 70; 6,473 yards

October 5-8
purse, ¥60,000,000

	SCORES				TOTAL	MONEY
Masashi Ozaki	66	68	67	73	274	¥10,000,000
Brian Jones	67	68	69	71	275	6,000,000
Akihito Yokoyama	67	69	70	72	278	4,000,000
Isao Aoki	71	71	66	73	281	2,750,000
Tadami Ueno	70	70	69	72	281	2,750,000
Noboru Sugai	69	67	70	76	282	2,200,000
Seiichi Kanai	68	74	69	72	283	1,900,000
Eitaro Deguchi	71	66	73	73	283	1,900,000
Kiyoshi Muroda	68	74	71	71	284	1,500,000
Tomohiro Maruyama	68	72	69	75	284	1,500,000
Hsieh Min Nan	71	72	70	71	284	1,500,000
Saburo Fujiki	69	72	72	72	285	1,200,000
Tsuneyuki Nakajima	73	70	66	76	285	1,200,000
Hideki Kase	71	72	65	77	285	1,200,000
Yoshimi Niizeki	74	71	70	71	286	775,000
Teruo Sugihara	74	73	69	70	286	775,000
Yoshikazu Yokoshima	72	70	69	75	286	775,000
Haruo Yasuda	71	70	69	76	286	775,000
Yoichi Yamamoto	73	74	69	70	286	775,000
Jeff Maggert	76	67	73	70	286	775,000
Koichi Suzuki	76	70	67	74	287	540,000
Hiroshi Makino	72	71	70	74	287	540,000
Katsuji Hasegawa	72	70	70	75	287	540,000
Shigeru Kawamata	71	75	69	72	287	540,000
Futoshi Irino	72	72	69	74	287	540,000
Graham Marsh	74	71	72	71	288	470,000
Kinpachi Takahashi	73	74	65	76	288	470,000
Chen Tze Chung	69	74	76	69	288	470,000
Kazuo Kanayama	68	75	74	71	288	470,000
Kan Takahashi	71	74	68	75	288	470,000
Naomichi Ozaki	73	71	70	75	289	415,000
Yoshinori Kaneko	74	68	71	76	289	415,000
David Ishii	71	74	72	72	289	415,000
Yoshinori Mizumaki	70	73	71	75	289	415,000
Toru Nakayama	75	72	71	71	289	415,000
Nozomi Yoshimatsu	73	73	70	73	289	415,000
Masanobu Kimura	73	74	73	70	290	317,000
Tadao Nakamura	70	76	70	74	290	317,000
Tsuyoshi Yoneyama	74	72	73	71	290	317,000
Kinpachi Yoshimura	70	73	74	73	290	317,000
Hajime Matsui	74	71	73	72	290	317,000
Toshimitsu Kai	75	69	68	78	290	317,000
Hiroya Kamide	73	72	74	71	290	317,000
Masaji Kusakabe	77	69	69	75	290	317,000
Hiroshi Tominaga	78	68	71	73	290	317,000
Hiromichi Namiki	72	71	74	73	290	317,000
Frankie Minosa	71	76	73	70	290	317,000
Y. Kazuoka	71	73	75	71	290	317,000
Emlyn Aubrey	72	74	73	71	290	317,000
Mike Colandro	77	69	72	72	290	317,000

Polaroid Cup Golf Digest

Tomei Country Club, Susono
Par 71; 6,770 yards

October 12-15
purse, ¥60,000,000

	SCORES				TOTAL	MONEY
Yoshikazu Yokoshima	67	67	65	69	268	¥12,600,000
Kiyoshi Muroda	67	69	68	70	274	5,040,000
Masaji Kusakabe	66	69	70	69	274	5,040,000
Bill Glasson	69	68	69	68	274	5,040,000
Akihito Yokoyama	68	66	69	72	275	2,397,000
Nobuo Serizawa	71	70	67	67	275	2,397,000
Katsuji Hasegawa	71	68	69	67	275	2,397,000
Seiki Okuda	70	68	67	70	275	2,397,000
Nobumitsu Yuhara	67	70	69	70	276	1,715,000
David Ishii	68	68	72	68	276	1,715,000
Kiyoshi Maita	68	75	63	71	277	1,344,000
Takeshi Kubota	66	73	71	67	277	1,344,000
Graham Marsh	66	73	68	71	278	1,050,000
Masanobu Kimura	71	70	69	68	278	1,050,000
Pete Izumikawa	69	68	71	70	278	1,050,000
Norikazu Kawakami	66	68	72	72	278	1,050,000
Tateo Ozaki	72	70	73	64	279	812,000
Hideyuki Satoh	73	70	69	67	279	812,000
Eduardo Herrera	67	76	74	63	280	660,000
Futoshi Irino	70	72	72	66	280	660,000
Shoichi Yamamoto	69	68	71	72	280	660,000
Yoichi Yamamoto	67	72	71	70	280	660,000
Nozomu Kamatsu	75	68	67	70	280	660,000
Tatsuya Shiraishi	69	73	71	67	280	660,000
Toru Nakamura	71	69	70	71	281	532,000
Hajime Meshiai	71	72	69	69	281	532,000
Seiichi Kanai	72	69	70	70	281	532,000
Noboru Sugai	70	68	69	74	281	532,000
Ikuo Shirahama	70	68	70	73	281	532,000
Chen Tze Ming	66	68	72	75	281	532,000
Taijiro Tanaka	73	68	68	72	281	532,000
Motomasa Aoki	67	72	71	71	281	532,000
Ichiro Teramoto	70	70	70	71	281	532,000

Bridgestone

Sodegaura Country Club, Chiba
Par 72; 7,120 yards

October 19-22
purse, ¥80,000,000

	SCORES				TOTAL	MONEY
Roger Mackay	66	70	68	73	277	¥18,000,000
Yoshitaka Yamamoto	69	69	70	70	278	10,000,000
Brian Jones	64	71	69	75	279	4,800,000
Katsuji Hasegawa	73	67	68	71	279	4,800,000
Tadao Nakamura	68	68	75	68	279	4,800,000
Bill Glasson	73	66	68	72	279	4,800,000
Chen Tze Chung	73	68	70	69	280	3,200,000
Saburo Fujiki	71	71	73	66	281	2,900,000
Isao Aoki	68	71	71	72	282	2,300,000
Yoshinori Kaneko	73	72	68	69	282	2,300,000
Hikaru Emoto	70	70	73	69	282	2,300,000
Naomichi Ozaki	72	69	73	69	283	1,568,000

	SCORES				TOTAL	MONEY
Noboru Sugai	70	71	73	69	283	1,568,000
Ikuo Shirahama	70	68	76	69	283	1,568,000
Kinpachi Yoshimura	73	66	68	76	283	1,568,000
Seiki Okuda	72	72	69	70	283	1,568,000
Yoshikazu Yokoshima	72	72	72	68	284	1,120,000
Hiroshi Makino	71	72	70	71	284	1,120,000
Masahiro Kuramoto	69	73	75	67	284	1,120,000
Yoshimi Niizeki	70	73	73	69	285	960,000
Teruo Sugihara	71	73	70	71	285	960,000
Nobumitsu Yuhara	72	71	74	68	285	960,000
Masashi Ozaki	71	71	70	74	286	850,000
Masanobu Kimura	71	73	71	71	286	850,000
Hsieh Min Nan	70	75	73	68	286	850,000
Tetsuya Tsuda	70	74	75	67	286	850,000
Toru Nakamura	71	73	73	70	287	740,000
Hajime Meshiai	72	72	75	68	287	740,000
David Ishii	69	71	72	75	287	740,000
Shigeru Kawamata	69	73	70	75	287	740,000
Kikuo Arai	69	73	74	71	287	740,000
Tetsu Nishikawa	74	71	72	70	287	740,000
Kazuhiro Takami	72	71	72	72	287	740,000

Lark Cup

ABC Golf Club, Tojocho
Par 72; 7,156 yards

October 26-29
purse, ¥160,000,000

	SCORES				TOTAL	MONEY
Brian Jones	70	69	69	72	280	¥28,800,000
Toshiaki Sudo	70	74	66	74	284	16,000,000
Naomichi Ozaki	74	69	69	73	285	9,280,000
Hiroshi Makino	71	73	66	75	285	9,280,000
Nobuo Serizawa	73	71	71	71	286	6,080,000
David Ishii	69	71	72	74	286	6,080,000
Masashi Ozaki	73	72	69	73	287	4,160,000
Graham Marsh	69	77	71	70	287	4,160,000
Tsuneyuki Nakajima	74	71	70	72	287	4,160,000
Katsuji Hasegawa	73	70	69	75	287	4,160,000
Hale Irwin	76	72	67	72	287	4,160,000
Saburo Fujiki	70	75	69	74	288	2,944,000
Tsuyoshi Yoneyama	72	72	69	76	289	2,400,000
Bob Gilder	73	70	72	74	289	2,400,000
Doug Tewell	67	71	72	79	289	2,400,000
Hiroshi Chosa	75	72	69	73	289	2,400,000
Yoshikazu Yokoshima	68	74	72	76	290	1,596,000
Roger Mackay	71	72	73	74	290	1,596,000
Katsuyoshi Tomori	72	73	73	72	290	1,596,000
Seiichi Kanai	70	71	70	79	290	1,596,000
Terry Gale	76	72	71	71	290	1,596,000
Chen Tze Ming	69	69	76	76	290	1,596,000
Toshimitsu Kai	69	75	71	75	290	1,596,000
Wayne Smith	76	72	68	74	290	1,596,000
Satoshi Higashi	71	68	75	77	291	1,312,000
Peter Izumikawa	73	74	71	73	291	1,312,000
Yasuhiro Funatogawa	69	70	72	80	291	1,312,000
Tateo Ozaki	71	72	75	74	292	1,184,000
Chen Tze Chung	75	67	74	76	292	1,184,000

	SCORES				TOTAL	MONEY
Hideki Kase	71	71	77	73	292	1,184,000
Hsieh Min Nan	67	72	72	81	292	1,184,000
Motomasa Aoki	71	74	71	76	292	1,184,000
Masanobu Kimura	68	79	69	77	293	1,068,000
Tadao Nakamura	72	74	72	75	293	1,068,000
Yoshinori Kaneko	73	72	73	75	293	1,068,000
Nobumitsu Yuhara	75	73	71	75	294	992,000
Noboru Sugai	70	71	79	74	294	992,000
Yutaka Hagawa	71	75	72	76	294	992,000
Yoshiyuki Isomura	72	73	76	74	295	915,000
Eitaro Deguchi	74	74	71	76	295	915,000
Shigeru Kawamata	69	74	69	83	295	915,000
Akiyoshi Omachi	75	70	73	78	296	851,000
Teruo Nakamura	72	73	73	78	296	851,000
Teruo Sugihara	72	72	70	83	297	787,000
Ikuo Shirahama	79	69	70	79	297	787,000
Futoshi Irino	74	72	73	78	297	787,000
Akihito Yokoyama	72	74	74	78	298	723,000
Tetsu Nishikawa	69	74	77	78	298	723,000
Shinji Nishikawa	71	74	78	75	298	723,000
Hajime Meshiai	74	74	71	80	299	691,000
Kiyoshi Muroda	71	74	74	80	299	691,000
Yoshihisa Iwashita	76	72	75	76	299	691,000
Toshiaki Nakagawa	69	78	74	78	299	691,000
Shozo Miyamoto	74	73	70	82	299	691,000

Asahi Glass Four Tours World Championship

Yomiuri Country Club, Inagi
Par 36-36—72; 7,017 yards

November 2-5
purse, US$1,020,000

FIRST ROUND

POINTS: UNITED STATES 6, EUROPE 6
Ken Green (US) defeated Ian Woosnam (E), 70-73.
Mark Calcavecchia (US) defeated Jose-Maria Olazabal (E), 72-73.
Bernhard Langer (E) defeated Payne Stewart (US), 70-73.
Gordon Brand, Jr. (E) defeated Chip Beck (US), 68-69.
Ronan Rafferty (E) defeated Tom Kite (US), 69-70.
Curtis Strange (US) defeated Mark James (E), 65-71.

POINTS: AUSTRALIA/NEW ZEALAND 8, JAPAN 4
Wayne Grady (A/NZ) defeated Koichi Suzuki (J), 73-75.
Naomichi Ozaki (J) defeated Peter Senior (A/NZ), 68-76.
Ian Baker-Finch (A/NZ) defeated Katsunari Takahashi (J), 71-74.
Greg Norman (A/NZ) defeated Tateo Ozaki (J), 68-77.
Brian Jones (A/NZ) defeated Toru Nakamura (J), 71-73.
Masashi Ozaki (J) defeated Craig Parry (A/NZ), 71-73.

SECOND ROUND

POINTS: UNITED STATES 10, AUSTRALIA/NEW ZEALAND 2
Calcavecchia defeated Jones, 67-70.
Green defeated Parry, 67-71.
Stewart halved with Grady, 69-69.
Kite halved with Senior, 69-69.
Strange defeated Baker-Finch, 68-74.
Beck defeated Norman, 69-71.

POINTS: EUROPE 9, JAPAN 3
James halved with Suzuki, 72-72.
Langer defeated N. Ozaki, 69-72.
Brand defeated T. Ozaki, 71-75.
Rafferty defeated Takahashi, 66-69.
Olazabal defeated Nakamura, 67-69.
M. Ozaki defeated Woosnam, 66-72.

THIRD ROUND

POINTS: EUROPE 7, AUSTRALIA/NEW ZEALAND 5
James defeated Parry, 69-71.
Langer defeated Senior, 66-69.
Baker-Finch defeated Brand, 73-75.
Norman defeated Rafferty, 64-69.
Olazabal defeated Jones, 69-74.
Woosnam halved with Grady, 68-68.

POINTS: UNITED STATES 10, JAPAN 2
Calcavecchia halved with N. Ozaki, 67-67.
Green halved with Suzuki, 68-68.
Stewart defeated T. Ozaki, 67-70.
Beck defeated Takahashi, 65-70.
Kite defeated Nakamura, 69-73.
Strange defeated M. Ozaki, 68-70.

THIRD/FOURTH PLACE PLAYOFF

POINTS: JAPAN 9, AUSTRALIA/NEW ZEALAND 3
N. Ozaki defeated Senior, 67-71.
Suzuki halved with Baker-Finch, 68-68.
T. Ozaki defeated Jones, 69-71.
Takahashi defeated Parry, 70-71.
Nakamura defeated Grady, 70-71.
Norman defeated M. Ozaki, 65-68.

FINAL

POINTS: UNITED STATES 6, EUROPE 6
Rafferty defeated Green, 66-70.
Brand defeated Stewart, 69-70.
Calcavecchia defeated James, 68-74.
Beck defeated Langer, 62-68.
Kite defeated Woosnam, 65-71.
Olazabal defeated Strange, 68-69.
(UNITED STATES wins tie-breaker for championship, 404 strokes to 416 strokes.)

FINAL STANDINGS AND MONEY

	POINTS	STROKES	MONEY (Team)
United States	32	1,636	US$390,000
Europe	28	1,673	240,000
Japan	18	1,691	210,000
Australia/New Zealand	18	1,692	180,000

Visa Taiheiyo Club Masters

Taiheiyo Club, Gotemba Course, Gotemba
Par 72; 7,072 yards

November 10-12
purse, ¥100,000,000

(Thursday round cancelled - rain)

	SCORES			TOTAL	MONEY
Jose-Maria Olazabal	66	70	67	203	¥16,200,000
Naomichi Ozaki	70	66	70	206	7,560,000
Isao Aoki	71	70	65	206	7,560,000
Nobuo Serizawa	69	67	71	207	3,720,000
Barry Lane	67	72	68	207	3,720,000
Ken Green	71	65	71	207	3,720,000
Graham Marsh	70	69	69	208	2,610,000
Chen Tze Ming	71	67	70	208	2,610,000
Ryoken Kawagishi	69	67	72	208	2,610,000
Jeff Sluman	73	69	67	209	2,070,000
Masashi Ozaki	73	70	67	210	1,476,000
Koichi Suzuki	70	67	73	210	1,476,000
Hajime Meshiai	70	69	71	210	1,476,000
Ronan Rafferty	70	71	69	210	1,476,000
Scott Hoch	70	67	73	210	1,476,000
Don Pooley	71	68	71	210	1,476,000
Masahiro Kuramoto	71	71	69	211	957,000
Futoshi Irino	68	74	69	211	957,000
Mike Reid	70	70	71	211	957,000
Yasuhiro Funatogawa	73	69	69	211	957,000
Ian Baker-Finch	68	73	70	211	957,000
Toru Nakamura	69	72	71	212	787,000
Seiichi Kanai	69	74	69	212	787,000
Craig Parry	69	69	74	212	787,000
Steve Jones	71	67	74	212	787,000
Brian Jones	68	73	72	213	693,000
Tateo Ozaki	71	69	73	213	693,000
Teruo Sugihara	73	73	67	213	693,000
David Ishii	72	70	71	213	693,000
Toshimitsu Kai	72	72	69	213	693,000
Teruo Nakamura	72	70	71	213	693,000
Roger Mackay	72	70	72	214	615,000
Tadao Nakamura	71	68	75	214	615,000
Hajime Meshiai	71	73	70	214	615,000
Yoshitaka Yamamoto	73	68	74	215	550,000
Toshiaki Sudo	69	74	72	215	550,000
Akihito Yokoyama	70	73	72	215	550,000
Yoshiyuki Isomura	67	72	76	215	550,000
Ikuo Shirahama	72	70	73	215	550,000
Haruo Yasuda	70	74	71	215	550,000
Katsuyoshi Tomori	73	72	71	216	478,000
Seiji Ebihara	71	72	73	216	478,000
Norio Mikami	71	71	74	216	478,000
Bobby Wadkins	71	72	73	216	478,000
*Takahiro Nakagawa	70	73	73	216	
Saburo Fujiki	72	73	72	217	418,000
Tsuneyuki Nakajima	70	73	74	217	418,000
Noboru Sugai	72	73	72	217	418,000
Chen Tze Chung	75	69	73	217	418,000
Kinpachi Yoshimura	71	75	71	217	418,000

Dunlop Phoenix

Phoenix Country Club, Miyazaki
Par 72; 6,993 yards

November 16-19
purse, ¥160,000,000

	SCORES			TOTAL	MONEY
Larry Mize	69	64	71	68	272	¥28,800,000
Naomichi Ozaki	66	70	69	71	276	16,000,000
Blaine McCallister	68	69	72	69	278	10,880,000
Tateo Ozaki	72	66	71	70	279	7,680,000
Mike Reid	71	69	70	70	280	6,080,000
Jeff Sluman	69	70	70	71	280	6,080,000
Yoshikazu Yokoshima	68	69	70	75	282	4,880,000
Larry Nelson	73	67	72	70	282	4,880,000
Akihito Yokoyama	72	70	70	71	283	3,920,000
Seve Ballesteros	73	68	69	73	283	3,920,000
Masashi Ozaki	70	71	73	70	284	2,832,000
Graham Marsh	71	71	69	73	284	2,832,000
David Ishii	70	72	70	72	284	2,832,000
Ian Baker-Finch	72	73	71	68	284	2,832,000
Nobuo Serizawa	71	72	67	75	285	1,898,000
Terry Gale	73	71	69	72	285	1,898,000
Dave Rummells	72	73	71	69	285	1,898,000
Tom Byrum	78	67	68	72	285	1,898,000
Scott Simpson	70	72	71	72	285	1,898,000
Craig Stadler	71	72	71	71	285	1,898,000
Chen Tze Chung	69	66	75	76	286	1,448,000
Ken Green	68	75	69	74	286	1,448,000
Ronan Rafferty	73	69	73	71	286	1,448,000
Bobby Wadkins	71	67	74	74	286	1,448,000
Tomohiro Maruyama	73	68	76	70	287	1,312,000
Tom Watson	67	73	72	75	287	1,312,000
Hubert Green	69	71	69	78	287	1,312,000
Isao Aoki	71	72	73	72	288	1,216,000
Teruo Nakamura	73	69	74	72	288	1,216,000
Ryoken Kawagishi	73	67	71	77	288	1,216,000
Nobumitsu Yuhara	71	71	75	72	289	1,122,000
Tadami Ueno	69	72	74	74	289	1,122,000
Nick Faldo	72	72	73	72	289	1,122,000
Tsuneyuki Nakajima	74	70	73	73	290	1,030,000
Seiichi Kanai	73	71	74	72	290	1,030,000
Greg Bruckner	73	69	73	75	290	1,030,000
Scott Hoch	76	70	68	76	290	1,030,000
Masanobu Kimura	75	71	73	72	291	928,000
Tadao Nakamura	71	75	72	73	291	928,000
Masahiro Kuramoto	76	70	72	73	291	928,000
Peter Senior	73	68	77	73	291	928,000
Akiyoshi Omachi	72	71	74	75	292	838,000
Chen Tze Ming	72	73	71	76	292	838,000
Seiji Ebihara	69	76	73	74	292	838,000
Hajime Meshiai	70	73	74	76	293	761,000
Katsuyoshi Tomori	72	69	77	75	293	761,000
Hajime Matsui	71	73	70	79	293	761,000
Yoshitaka Yamamoto	70	73	74	77	294	712,000
Hiroshi Makino	71	73	77	73	294	712,000
Pete Izumikawa	73	70	72	79	294	712,000

Casio World Open

Ibusuki Golf Club, Kaimoncho
Par 72; 7,014 yards

November 23-26
purse, ¥100,000,000

	SCORES				TOTAL	MONEY
Isao Aoki	70	70	65	69	274	¥18,000,000
Larry Mize	67	71	67	70	275	10,000,000
Graham Marsh	68	71	67	70	276	6,800,000
Mark Calcavecchia	69	69	70	69	277	4,800,000
Chen Tze Chung	68	72	68	70	278	4,000,000
Naomichi Ozaki	66	70	74	69	279	2,920,000
Tadao Nakamura	71	69	71	68	279	2,920,000
Blaine McCallister	70	70	69	70	279	2,920,000
Scott Simpson	74	68	68	69	279	2,920,000
Hubert Green	68	67	69	75	279	2,920,000
Masashi Ozaki	69	71	72	68	280	2,000,000
Eitaro Deguchi	73	70	67	72	282	1,840,000
Tsuneyuki Nakajima	73	68	71	71	283	1,560,000
Akiyoshi Omachi	70	75	67	71	283	1,560,000
Teruo Nakamura	71	69	72	71	283	1,560,000
Yoshinori Kaneko	69	77	70	68	284	1,213,000
Mike Donald	71	69	71	73	284	1,213,000
Howard Clark	72	73	69	70	284	1,213,000
Brian Jones	73	71	68	73	285	980,000
Masahiro Kuramoto	73	70	73	69	285	980,000
Yutaka Hagawa	76	71	73	65	285	980,000
Taijiro Tanaka	76	70	69	70	285	980,000
Futoshi Irino	71	71	69	75	286	880,000
Yoshitaka Yamamoto	74	72	68	73	287	790,000
Hajime Meshiai	67	77	75	68	287	790,000
David Ishii	70	72	74	71	287	790,000
Tsukasa Watanabe	70	72	70	75	287	790,000
Kiyoshi Muroda	72	72	70	73	287	790,000
Hideki Kase	69	74	72	72	287	790,000
Dave Rummells	71	72	70	74	287	790,000
Ove Sellberg	69	72	72	74	287	790,000
Koichi Suzuki	70	70	72	76	288	684,000
Yoshinori Mizumaki	73	70	71	74	288	684,000
Norikazu Kawakami	74	73	71	70	288	684,000
Tateo Ozaki	72	71	73	73	289	588,000
Yoshimi Niizeki	71	74	71	73	289	588,000
Akihito Yokoyama	72	74	71	72	289	588,000
Toru Nakamura	70	67	77	75	289	588,000
Tadami Ueno	72	73	72	72	289	588,000
Pete Izumikawa	73	67	75	74	289	588,000
Eduardo Herrera	72	71	74	72	289	588,000
Namio Takasu	73	74	70	72	289	588,000
Gregory Mayer	74	73	69	73	289	588,000
Teruo Sugihara	72	70	74	74	290	508,000
Toshiaki Sudo	72	72	73	74	291	476,000
Shigeru Kawamata	75	72	74	70	291	476,000
Wayne Smith	75	71	71	74	291	476,000
Chen Tze Ming	73	74	72	73	292	445,000
Tomohiro Maruyama	73	72	73	74	292	445,000
Takeru Shibata	72	72	72	76	292	445,000

Japan Series Hitachi Cup

Yomiuri Country Club, Osaka
Par 72; 7,039 yards

November 29-30

Yomiuri Country Club, Tokyo
Par 72; 7,017 yards

December 2-3
purse, ¥60,000,000

	SCORES				TOTAL	MONEY
Akiyoshi Omachi	70	73	69	66	278	¥15,000,000
Tsuneyuki Nakajima	69	68	68	75	280	6,650,000
Katsuyoshi Tomori	71	71	67	71	280	6,650,000
Toru Nakamura	73	72	68	68	281	3,450,000
Larry Nelson	73	71	66	71	281	3,450,000
Brian Jones	70	70	73	69	282	2,600,000
Masashi Ozaki	74	69	69	72	284	2,150,000
Nobuo Serizawa	75	75	65	69	284	2,150,000
Akihiro Yokoyama	74	73	72	67	286	1,800,000
Yoshikazu Yokoshima	71	71	72	73	287	1,500,000
Yoshimi Niizeki	72	75	69	71	287	1,500,000
Hajime Meshiai	73	69	73	72	287	1,500,000
Graham Marsh	71	69	72	76	288	1,200,000
Yoshitaka Yamamoto	77	72	70	69	288	1,200,000
Yoshinori Mizumaki	73	74	71	70	288	1,200,000
Teruo Sugihara	76	77	67	69	289	1,000,000
Koichi Suzuki	71	81	70	68	290	900,000
Naomichi Ozaki	74	75	69	73	291	800,000
Isao Aoki	77	71	72	74	294	700,000
Hajime Matsui	76	77	71	76	300	600,000
Saburo Fujiki	75	77	75	74	301	515,000
Hiroshi Makino	75	76	74	76	301	515,000
Tateo Ozaki	74	81	73	74	302	450,000

Daikyo Open

Daikyo Country Club, Okinawa
Par 72; 6,273 yards

December 7-10
purse, ¥80,000,000

	SCORES				TOTAL	MONEY
Nobuo Serizawa	67	67	67	70	271	¥14,400,000
David Ishii	68	74	66	67	275	8,000,000
Masahiro Kuramoto	71	75	64	68	278	5,440,000
Atsushi Ikehara	71	70	70	68	279	3,840,000
Brian Jones	67	73	71	69	280	3,200,000
Hiroshi Makino	69	71	70	71	281	2,720,000
Chen Chung Ming	68	74	71	68	281	2,720,000
Tateo Ozaki	70	75	70	67	282	2,200,000
Yoshimi Niizeki	70	70	70	72	282	2,200,000
Toru Nakamura	69	73	70	71	283	1,637,000
Noriichi Kawakami	67	75	70	71	283	1,637,000
Taijiro Tanaka	70	76	70	67	283	1,637,000
Seiji Ebihara	71	75	70	68	284	1,296,000
Tsuyoshi Yoneyama	72	73	72	67	284	1,296,000
Akihito Yokoyama	72	71	70	72	285	1,056,000
Kinpachi Yoshimura	72	74	71	68	285	1,056,000
Motomasa Aoki	67	76	71	71	285	1,056,000
Yoshikazu Yokoshima	70	76	71	69	286	806,000

	SCORES			TOTAL	MONEY
Yoshitaka Yamamoto	68	75	69	74	286	806,000
Eduardo Herrera	78	70	68	70	286	806,000
Teruo Nakamura	71	72	69	74	286	806,000
Brent Franklin	70	75	69	72	286	806,000
Futoshi Irino	69	77	70	71	287	688,000
Hisao Inoue	70	71	74	72	287	688,000
Hideto Shigenobu	70	75	69	73	287	688,000
Hajime Meshiai	68	78	75	67	288	648,000
Hiroshi Tominaga	71	76	68	73	288	648,000
Kiyoshi Maita	70	77	74	68	289	608,000
Hsieh Min Nan	71	72	76	70	289	608,000
Tsutomu Higa	73	73	74	69	289	608,000

The Women's Tours

Jamaica Classic

Tryall Golf and Beach Club, Sandy Bay, Jamaica
Par 34-37—71; 6,191 yards

January 13-15
purse, $500,000

	SCORES			TOTAL	MONEY
Betsy King	64	68	70	202	$75,000
Nancy Lopez	69	70	69	208	46,250
Lori Garbacz	70	71	69	210	30,000
Martha Nause	71	71	68	210	30,000
Hollis Stacy	69	71	71	211	17,834
Beth Daniel	76	66	69	211	17,833
Rosie Jones	73	71	67	211	17,833
Robin Walton	71	70	71	212	11,194
Colleen Walker	71	72	69	212	11,194
Sherri Turner	70	74	68	212	11,194
Judy Dickinson	73	71	68	212	11,194
Nancy Brown	70	71	72	213	8,276
Danielle Ammaccapane	71	70	72	213	8,276
Cathy Morse	69	76	68	213	8,276
Carolyn Hill	72	71	71	214	6,860
Cindy Rarick	73	72	69	214	6,859
Vicki Fergon	72	74	68	214	6,859
Marta Figueras-Dotti	71	73	71	215	5,901
Sally Little	72	72	71	215	5,901
Jan Stephenson	72	73	70	215	5,901
Ayako Okamoto	72	74	69	215	5,901
Alice Ritzman	72	73	71	216	4,983
Debbie Massey	75	70	71	216	4,982
JoAnne Carner	76	70	70	216	4,982
Shirley Furlong	70	77	69	216	4,982
Penny Hammel	76	70	71	217	4,501
Allison Finney	79	67	71	217	4,501
Dottie Mochrie	70	72	76	218	3,914

	SCORES			TOTAL	MONEY
Heather Farr	70	74	74	218	3,914
Kathryn Young	70	77	71	218	3,914
Jody Rosenthal	71	77	70	218	3,913
Susan Sanders	76	73	69	218	3,913
Dot Germain	76	74	68	218	3,913

Oldsmobile Classic

Stonebridge Golf & Country Club, Boca Raton, Florida
Par 36-36—72; 6,333 yards

January 26-29
purse, $300,000

	SCORES				TOTAL	MONEY
Dottie Mochrie	69	74	67	69	279	$45,000
Beth Daniel	69	68	72	70	279	27,750
(Mochrie defeated Daniel on fifth extra hole.)						
Nancy Lopez	72	68	69	71	280	20,250
Sandra Palmer	73	72	69	69	283	15,750
Shirley Furlong	72	72	70	71	285	10,700
Jane Geddes	75	67	69	74	285	10,700
Jody Rosenthal	69	71	71	74	285	10,700
Kathy Guadagnino	72	74	69	71	286	7,050
Jan Stephenson	75	70	69	72	286	7,050
Nancy Brown	73	70	71	72	286	7,050
Tammie Green	75	72	71	69	287	5,701
Kim Williams	72	75	73	68	288	4,415
Lori Garbacz	75	73	70	70	288	4,415
Dot Germain	68	72	77	71	288	4,414
Hollis Stacy	74	72	70	72	288	4,414
Amy Benz	74	73	68	73	288	4,414
Lynn Connelly	78	70	66	74	288	4,414
Martha Nause	71	69	73	75	288	4,414
Deb Richard	75	73	69	72	289	3,450
Debbie Massey	76	71	70	72	289	3,450
Cathy Johnston	72	72	73	72	289	3,450
Muffin Spencer-Devlin	76	73	73	68	290	2,693
Ayako Okamoto	74	75	73	68	290	2,693
Betsy King	71	72	77	70	290	2,693
Chris Johnson	70	69	81	70	290	2,693
Mitzi Edge	75	73	71	71	290	2,693
Cindy Figg-Currier	75	73	71	71	290	2,692
Marta Figueras-Dotti	72	76	71	71	290	2,692
Cindy Rarick	72	75	72	71	290	2,692
Pamela Wright	72	73	72	73	290	2,692
Susie Redman	71	69	72	78	290	2,692

Orix Hawaiian Open

Turtle Bay Country Club, Oahu, Hawaii
Par 36-36—72; 6,267 yards

February 16-18
purse, $300,000

	SCORES			TOTAL	MONEY
Sherri Turner	70	69	66	205	$45,000
Sara Anne McGetrick	69	69	71	209	27,750
Deb Richard	68	74	68	210	18,000
Colleen Walker	71	70	69	210	18,000
Liselotte Neumann	72	70	69	211	10,700

	SCORES			TOTAL	MONEY
Jane Geddes	69	73	69	211	10,700
Alice Ritzman	69	69	73	211	10,700
Danielle Ammaccapane	71	72	69	212	7,425
Patty Sheehan	68	74	70	212	7,425
Laura Davies	72	73	68	213	5,551
Myra Blackwelder	70	73	70	213	5,550
Penny Hammel	70	71	72	213	5,550
Amy Benz	69	70	74	213	5,550
Martha Nause	72	70	72	214	4,500
Shelley Hamlin	70	71	73	214	4,500
Missie Berteotti	71	74	70	215	3,600
Betsy King	69	76	70	215	3,600
Allison Finney	75	69	71	215	3,600
Sandra Palmer	74	70	71	215	3,600
Tammie Green	72	71	72	215	3,600
Martha Foyer	73	69	73	215	3,600
Val Skinner	72	70	73	215	3,600
Heather Farr	73	72	71	216	2,778
Shirley Furlong	72	72	72	216	2,778
Elaine Crosby	69	74	73	216	2,778
Hiromi Kobayashi	73	69	74	216	2,777
Mindy Moore	73	69	74	216	2,777
Muffin Spencer-Devlin	70	71	75	216	2,777
Pat Bradley	74	72	71	217	2,289
Lori Garbacz	75	70	72	217	2,289
Jenny Lidback	74	71	72	217	2,289
Connie Baker	74	70	73	217	2,289
Julie Cole	72	70	75	217	2,289

Women's Kemper Open

Princeville Makai Golf Course, Kauai, Hawaii
Par 36-36—72; 6,171 yards

February 24-26
purse, $400,000

	SCORES			TOTAL	MONEY
Betsy King	63	72	67	202	$60,000
Jane Geddes	65	69	70	204	37,000
Beth Daniel	67	68	70	205	24,000
Nancy Lopez	65	70	70	205	24,000
Cathy Morse	66	70	71	207	14,267
Jenny Lidback	64	72	71	207	14,267
Hollis Stacy	64	72	71	207	14,266
Jill Briles	66	74	68	208	8,241
Susan Sanders	69	70	69	208	8,241
Carolyn Hill	64	75	69	208	8,240
Lori Garbacz	67	71	70	208	8,240
Patty Sheehan	65	71	72	208	8,240
Colleen Walker	64	69	75	208	8,240
Myra Blackwelder	68	73	68	209	5,534
Cindy Rarick	67	72	70	209	5,534
Laurie Rinker	64	75	70	209	5,534
Nina Foust	65	73	71	209	5,534
Nancy Brown	64	68	77	209	5,534
Caroline Keggi	67	74	69	210	4,331
Juli Inkster	65	74	71	210	4,330
Michelle McGann	64	75	71	210	4,330
Danielle Ammaccapane	66	72	72	210	4,330
Julie Cole	65	73	72	210	4,330

	SCORES			TOTAL	MONEY
Laura Davies	65	73	72	210	4,330
Chris Johnson	69	73	69	211	3,533
Robin Hood	65	74	72	211	3,533
Barb Thomas	65	73	73	211	3,533
Marci Bozarth	64	74	73	211	3,533
Marta Figueras-Dotti	68	69	74	211	3,533
Shirley Furlong	68	74	70	212	2,509
Cathy Gerring	67	75	70	212	2,509
Kristi Albers	69	72	71	212	2,509
Chihiro Nakajima	68	73	71	212	2,509
Nancy Taylor	67	74	71	212	2,509
Rosie Jones	66	75	71	212	2,509
Kim Bauer	67	73	72	212	2,509
Robin Walton	68	71	73	212	2,509
Terry-Jo Myers	66	73	73	212	2,509
Martha Foyer	66	73	73	212	2,509
Jan Stephenson	65	74	73	212	2,508
Kim Shipman	67	71	74	212	2,508
Shelley Hamlin	66	72	74	212	2,508
Missie Berteotti	65	71	76	212	2,508

Circle K Tucson Open

Randolph North Golf Course, Tucson, Arizona
Par 36-36—72; 6,243 yards

March 16-19
purse, $300,000

	SCORES				TOTAL	MONEY
Lori Garbacz	69	68	67	70	274	$45,000
Nancy Lopez	69	70	72	67	278	27,750
Kristi Albers	70	69	72	68	279	14,813
Jody Rosenthal	69	70	70	70	279	14,813
Jan Stephenson	68	69	71	71	279	14,812
Martha Nause	66	69	71	73	279	14,812
Colleen Walker	69	72	71	68	280	8,850
Alice Ritzman	73	70	69	69	281	7,050
Vicki Fergon	68	71	73	69	281	7,050
Laura Davies	68	71	70	72	281	7,050
Betsy King	73	74	68	67	282	5,001
Missie McGeorge	70	76	69	67	282	5,001
Cindy Rarick	70	71	72	69	282	5,001
Lynn Connelly	70	69	72	71	282	5,001
Sherri Turner	70	73	67	72	282	5,001
Sandra Haynie	71	72	71	69	283	3,846
Meg Mallon	70	72	70	71	283	3,846
Amy Alcott	72	69	71	71	283	3,846
Dale Eggeling	69	72	69	73	283	3,846
Nina Foust	71	71	74	68	284	3,186
Sherri Steinhauer	72	73	69	70	284	3,186
Jane Geddes	72	68	73	71	284	3,186
Mei Chi Cheng	72	71	68	73	284	3,186
Missie Berteotti	67	72	70	75	284	3,186
Mindy Moore	71	74	70	70	285	2,616
Terry-Jo Myers	71	73	71	70	285	2,616
Allison Finney	70	69	75	71	285	2,616
Patty Sheehan	69	71	72	73	285	2,616
Danielle Ammaccapane	71	69	71	74	285	2,616
Cindy Mackey	68	72	70	75	285	2,616

Standard Register Turquoise Classic

Moon Valley Country Club, Phoenix, Arizona
Par 36-37—73; 6,514 yards

March 23-26
purse, $400,000

		SCORES			TOTAL	MONEY
Allison Finney	66	69	74	73	282	$60,000
Beth Daniel	68	70	70	75	283	37,000
Jody Rosenthal	70	73	72	70	285	27,000
Rosie Jones	72	72	69	74	287	19,000
Patti Rizzo	71	68	73	75	287	19,000
Pat Bradley	79	66	72	71	288	10,800
Dottie Mochrie	75	70	72	71	288	10,800
Amy Alcott	72	72	72	72	288	10,800
Jane Geddes	73	71	72	72	288	10,800
Penny Hammel	69	72	69	78	288	10,800
Alice Ritzman	72	74	70	73	289	6,886
Mei Chi Cheng	73	71	72	73	289	6,886
Kim Shipman	71	73	71	74	289	6,886
Ok Hee Ku	71	70	74	74	289	6,886
Bonnie Lauer	77	72	70	71	290	5,503
Kristi Albers	74	71	70	75	290	5,503
Nancy Brown	74	71	70	75	290	5,502
Val Skinner	73	73	72	73	291	4,936
Sandra Haynie	73	69	73	76	291	4,936
Marta Figueras-Dotti	73	72	74	73	292	4,108
Colleen Walker	72	71	76	73	292	4,108
Vicki Fergon	74	71	73	74	292	4,108
Cathy Morse	74	71	72	75	292	4,107
Mindy Moore	74	68	75	75	292	4,107
Tammie Green	71	74	71	76	292	4,107
Patty Sheehan	72	69	75	76	292	4,107
Sally Little	74	74	72	73	293	3,260
Jill Briles	75	71	74	73	293	3,260
Nancy Lopez	75	71	74	73	293	3,259
Ayako Okamoto	73	75	71	74	293	3,259
Connie Chillemi	75	73	70	75	293	3,259
Heather Farr	73	72	73	75	293	3,259

Nabisco Dinah Shore

Mission Hills Country Club, Rancho Mirage, California
Par 36-36—72; 6,441 yards

March 30-April 2
purse, $500,000

		SCORES			TOTAL	MONEY
Juli Inkster	66	69	73	71	279	$80,000
Tammie Green	72	68	75	69	284	34,000
JoAnne Carner	71	71	71	71	284	34,000
Betsy King	73	75	68	71	287	19,750
Jody Rosenthal	69	72	72	74	287	19,750
Pat Bradley	70	75	75	68	288	12,511
Amy Benz	74	74	71	69	288	12,511
Cathy Morse	72	72	73	71	288	12,511
Janet Coles	72	70	73	73	288	12,511
Beth Daniel	69	70	76	73	288	12,510
Kathy Guadagnino	76	71	72	70	289	7,960
Colleen Walker	73	74	69	73	289	7,960

	SCORES				TOTAL	MONEY
Danielle Ammaccapane	72	69	74	74	289	7,960
Lynn Adams	74	70	69	76	289	7,960
Patti Rizzo	77	73	71	69	290	6,357
Missie McGeorge	76	70	72	72	290	6,357
Dale Eggeling	68	73	75	74	290	6,357
Nancy Lopez	72	75	73	71	291	5,353
Val Skinner	74	72	74	71	291	5,353
Sherri Turner	71	73	75	72	291	5,352
Sandra Haynie	74	74	70	73	291	5,352
Alice Ritzman	72	74	72	73	291	5,352
Patty Sheehan	73	72	74	73	292	4,455
Debbie Massey	74	72	72	74	292	4,455
Allison Finney	74	71	73	74	292	4,454
Liselotte Neumann	69	73	76	74	292	4,454
Martha Nause	72	78	75	68	293	3,962
Cindy Rarick	71	73	73	76	293	3,962
Lori Garbacz	69	74	73	77	293	3,962
Kathy Postlewait	73	76	75	70	294	3,684
Myra Blackwelder	75	75	73	72	295	3,314
Hollis Stacy	75	73	73	74	295	3,314
Penny Hammel	71	76	73	75	295	3,314
Cindy Mackey	72	74	73	76	295	3,313
Laurie Rinker	74	70	74	77	295	3,313
Alison Nicholas	73	74	79	70	296	2,677
Cathy Johnston	76	75	73	72	296	2,677
Sherri Steinhauer	74	74	76	72	296	2,676
Muffin Spencer-Devlin	71	76	76	73	296	2,676
Connie Chillemi	77	71	74	74	296	2,676
Ok Hee Ku	72	72	77	75	296	2,676
Laura Davies	77	74	73	73	297	2,063
Janet Anderson	73	76	75	73	297	2,063
Jan Stephenson	75	74	74	74	297	2,062
Deb Richard	73	77	72	75	297	2,062
Kathy Whitworth	75	74	73	75	297	2,062
Kathryn Young	71	74	75	77	297	2,062
Kristi Albers	76	71	79	72	298	1,646
Marie-Laure de Lorenzi	74	75	74	75	298	1,645
Sally Little	80	67	75	76	298	1,645

Red Robin Kyocera Inamori Classic

StoneRidge Country Club, San Diego, California
Par 35-36—71; 6,042 yards

April 6-9
purse, $300,000

	SCORES				TOTAL	MONEY
Patti Rizzo	73	67	68	69	277	$45,000
Martha Nause	69	68	72	70	279	27,750
Jane Crafter	71	71	68	70	280	18,000
Juli Inkster	71	69	70	70	280	18,000
Mitzi Edge	72	71	69	69	281	9,975
Sherri Turner	69	73	70	69	281	9,975
Amy Alcott	70	69	72	70	281	9,975
Penny Hammel	74	69	67	71	281	9,975
Laura Davies	69	67	76	70	282	6,675
Cindy Rarick	68	70	73	71	282	6,675
Pat Bradley	69	70	75	69	283	4,826
Barb Thomas	71	74	67	71	283	4,825

	SCORES				TOTAL	MONEY
Rosie Jones	71	73	68	71	283	4,825
Gina Hull	70	72	70	71	283	4,825
Sherri Steinhauer	69	73	70	71	283	4,825
Dale Eggeling	68	70	74	71	283	4,825
Marlene Floyd	74	70	70	70	284	3,525
Lenore Rittenhouse	74	71	68	71	284	3,525
Tracy Kerdyk	72	70	71	71	284	3,525
Missie McGeorge	72	69	71	72	284	3,525
Amy Benz	70	70	71	73	284	3,525
Nancy Brown	69	67	70	78	284	3,525
Elaine Crosby	71	71	74	69	285	2,915
Danielle Ammaccapane	70	70	74	71	285	2,915
Alice Ritzman	75	68	70	72	285	2,915
Caroline Keggi	71	75	70	70	286	2,640
Val Skinner	70	73	72	71	286	2,640
Therese Hession	71	70	72	73	286	2,640
Susie Redman	72	75	75	65	287	2,174
Myra Blackwelder	72	74	72	69	287	2,173
Pamela Wright	70	72	75	70	287	2,173
Deedee Lasker	68	74	75	70	287	2,173
Sally Little	72	72	72	71	287	2,173
Barb Mucha	71	71	74	71	287	2,173
Missie Berteotti	69	72	75	71	287	2,173
Cindy Mackey	73	73	66	75	287	2,173

Al Star/Centinela Hospital Classic

Rancho Park Golf Course, Los Angeles, California
Par 37-35—72; 6,213 yards

April 14-16
purse, $450,000

	SCORES			TOTAL	MONEY
Pat Bradley	72	69	67	208	$67,500
Hollis Stacy	70	71	68	209	36,000
Nancy Lopez	67	73	69	209	36,000
Beth Daniel	71	74	66	211	21,375
Alice Ritzman	69	72	70	211	21,375
Colleen Walker	67	75	70	212	13,575
Martha Nause	68	71	73	212	13,575
Danielle Ammaccapane	72	67	73	212	13,575
Jane Geddes	70	71	72	213	9,113
Myra Blackwelder	68	73	72	213	9,113
Ok Hee Ku	69	71	73	213	9,113
Sherri Turner	71	68	74	213	9,113
Heather Farr	73	72	69	214	6,001
Tracy Kerdyk	76	68	70	214	6,001
Ayako Okamoto	72	71	71	214	6,001
Janet Anderson	71	72	71	214	6,001
Cindy Rarick	70	72	72	214	6,001
Laura Hurlbut	74	68	72	214	6,001
Susan Sanders	67	74	73	214	6,001
Robin Walton	70	70	74	214	6,001
Shelley Hamlin	70	70	74	214	6,001
Dawn Coe	75	70	70	215	4,246
Cathy Morse	75	69	71	215	4,246
Jenny Lidback	73	70	72	215	4,246
Sherrin Smyers	69	73	73	215	4,246
Deborah McHaffie	74	67	74	215	4,246

	SCORES			TOTAL	MONEY
Patti Rizzo	71	69	75	215	4,246
Juli Inkster	70	70	75	215	4,246
Dottie Mochrie	70	75	71	216	3,434
Deedee Lasker	74	71	71	216	3,434
Janet Coles	71	73	72	216	3,433
Deb Richard	71	72	73	216	3,433
Sandra Palmer	72	71	73	216	3,433

USX Classic

Pasadena Yacht & Country Club, St. Petersburg, Florida
Par 36-36—72; 6,016 yards

April 20-23
purse, $250,000

	SCORES				TOTAL	MONEY
Betsy King	67	70	72	66	275	$37,500
Lynn Adams	69	68	68	70	275	23,125
(King defeated Adams on first extra hole.)						
Lori Garbacz	64	73	71	69	277	16,875
Jan Stephenson	70	68	71	70	279	11,875
Kathy Postlewait	67	69	73	70	279	11,875
Ok Hee Ku	71	68	72	69	280	8,063
Liselotte Neumann	72	68	69	71	280	8,062
Gina Hull	71	73	69	68	281	5,147
Dale Eggeling	69	70	73	69	281	5,147
Martha Nause	70	72	69	70	281	5,146
Lori West	65	74	71	71	281	5,146
Chris Johnson	72	69	68	72	281	5,146
Rosie Jones	68	68	71	74	281	5,146
Dottie Mochrie	71	71	71	69	282	3,533
Lenore Rittenhouse	70	71	70	71	282	3,532
Jill Briles	67	72	72	71	282	3,532
Penny Hammel	70	69	71	72	282	3,532
Connie Chillemi	73	71	71	68	283	3,064
Nina Foust	68	70	73	72	283	3,063
Sally Quinlan	69	70	73	72	284	2,814
Amy Benz	70	70	71	73	284	2,813
Caroline Pierce	68	73	73	71	285	2,521
Colleen Walker	74	71	68	72	285	2,521
Meg Mallon	69	68	76	72	285	2,520
Carolyn Hill	72	74	72	68	286	2,275
Cindy Hill	70	71	73	72	286	2,275
Jane Geddes	70	69	75	72	286	2,275
Nancy Ramsbottom	75	73	71	68	287	1,911
Lisa Walters	75	71	71	70	287	1,911
Elaine Crosby	73	73	71	70	287	1,911
Jenny Lidback	73	69	75	70	287	1,911
JoAnne Carner	73	73	70	71	287	1,910
Donna Cusano-Wilkins	72	70	73	72	287	1,910
Tina Barrett	73	71	69	74	287	1,910

Sara Lee Classic

Hermitage Golf Course, Nashville, Tennessee
Par 36-36—72; 6,242 yards

April 28-30
purse, $425,000

	SCORES			TOTAL	MONEY
Kathy Postlewait	68	66	69	203	$63,750
Val Skinner	68	67	69	204	39,312
Patty Sheehan	66	74	67	207	25,500
Nancy Lopez	66	71	70	207	25,499
Tracy Kerdyk	71	70	68	209	15,158
Beth Daniel	67	71	71	209	15,158
Colleen Walker	66	70	73	209	15,158
Joan Delk	72	72	66	210	9,512
Mindy Moore	69	72	69	210	9,511
JoAnne Carner	70	69	71	210	9,511
Betsy King	67	68	75	210	9,511
Tammie Green	69	74	68	211	6,595
Sandra Haynie	69	73	69	211	6,595
Patti Rizzo	72	67	72	211	6,595
Sherri Turner	70	69	72	211	6,595
Mitzi Edge	70	68	73	211	6,595
Missie McGeorge	73	71	68	212	4,550
Ok Hee Ku	71	73	68	212	4,550
Amy Alcott	73	70	69	212	4,550
Gina Hull	72	71	69	212	4,550
Meg Mallon	68	75	69	212	4,549
Hollis Stacy	70	72	70	212	4,549
Danielle Ammaccapane	73	67	72	212	4,549
Pat Bradley	69	71	72	212	4,549
Jody Rosenthal	69	71	72	212	4,549
Kay Cockerill	69	70	73	212	4,549
Alice Ritzman	68	71	73	212	4,549
Donna White	74	70	69	213	3,036
Kathy Guadagnino	75	68	70	213	3,036
Cindy Rarick	74	69	70	213	3,036
Cindy Mackey	71	72	70	213	3,036
Jan Stephenson	69	74	70	213	3,036
Chihiro Nakajima	71	71	71	213	3,036
Cindy Schreyer	71	70	72	213	3,036
Jenny Lidback	71	69	73	213	3,036
Missie Berteotti	66	74	73	213	3,035
Pamela Wright	71	67	75	213	3,035
Deborah McHaffie	68	70	75	213	3,035

Crestar Classic

Greenbrier Country Club, Chesapeake, Virginia
Par 36-36—72; 6,275 yards

May 5-7
purse, $300,000

	SCORES			TOTAL	MONEY
Juli Inkster	69	72	69	210	$45,000
Beth Daniel	75	66	74	215	24,000
Liselotte Neumann	74	67	74	215	24,000
Amy Benz	76	72	68	216	11,130
Debbie Massey	72	74	70	216	11,130
Jane Geddes	72	73	71	216	11,130
Jan Stephenson	75	69	72	216	11,130

	SCORES			TOTAL	MONEY
Cindy Figg-Currier	72	68	76	216	11,130
Colleen Walker	75	72	70	217	6,357
Kristi Albers	72	72	73	217	6,357
Jody Rosenthal	74	66	77	217	6,357
Penny Hammel	71	75	72	218	5,271
Marta Figueras-Dotti	74	75	70	219	4,671
Lynn Adams	77	71	71	219	4,671
Tammie Green	72	74	73	219	4,671
Laura Davies	78	70	72	220	3,621
Heather Farr	75	73	72	220	3,621
Missie McGeorge	72	75	73	220	3,621
Amy Alcott	74	72	74	220	3,621
Alice Ritzman	72	74	74	220	3,621
Betsy King	69	77	74	220	3,621
Janet Anderson	71	73	76	220	3,621
Cathy Morse	72	75	74	221	2,984
Vicki Fergon	74	72	75	221	2,983
Janice Gibson	75	73	74	222	2,751
Sherri Steinhauer	74	73	75	222	2,751
Cindy Rarick	74	72	76	222	2,751
Chihiro Nakajima	77	73	73	223	2,236
Sue Ertl	76	74	73	223	2,236
Marlene Hagge	77	72	74	223	2,236
Lisa Lewis	76	73	74	223	2,236
Pat Bradley	76	73	74	223	2,236
Patty Jordan	74	75	74	223	2,236
Mizzi Edge	73	76	74	223	2,236
Patti Rizzo	74	71	78	223	2,236
Sandra Haynie	72	73	78	223	2,236

Chrysler Plymouth Classic

Bamm Hollow Country Club, Lincroft, New Jersey
Par 37-36—73; 6,410 yards

May 12-14
purse, $275,000

	SCORES			TOTAL	MONEY
Cindy Rarick	70	72	72	214	$41,250
Laura Davies	70	72	74	216	25,437
Alice Ritzman	72	73	72	217	16,500
Nancy Lopez	71	73	73	217	16,499
Barb Mucha	74	75	69	218	8,608
Kristi Albers	76	71	71	218	8,607
Caroline Keggi	72	74	72	218	8,607
Betsy King	76	68	74	218	8,607
Sherri Steinhauer	71	71	76	218	8,607
Jane Geddes	75	74	70	219	5,272
Colleen Walker	73	75	71	219	5,271
Marlene Floyd	73	71	75	219	5,271
Amy Alcott	75	68	77	220	4,538
Trish Johnson	74	73	74	221	4,263
Marci Bozarth	70	77	75	222	3,988
Rosie Jones	76	75	72	223	3,576
Nancy Brown	72	76	75	223	3,576
Cindy Figg-Currier	73	74	76	223	3,575
Sue Ertl	76	74	74	224	3,164
Robin Walton	77	72	75	224	3,163
Lori West	75	74	75	224	3,163

	SCORES			TOTAL	MONEY
Susan Sanders	80	73	72	225	2,682
Caroline Pierce	76	74	75	225	2,682
Becky Pearson	76	73	76	225	2,682
Mitzi Edge	73	75	77	225	2,682
Nancy Taylor	72	75	78	225	2,681
Pam Allen	77	74	75	226	2,256
Shirley Furlong	75	76	75	226	2,256
Kate Rogerson	76	73	77	226	2,256
Sally Little	73	75	78	226	2,256
Karin Mundinger	74	73	79	226	2,255

Mazda LPGA Championship

Jack Nicklaus Sports Center, Kings Island, Ohio
Par 36-36—72; 6,359 yards

May 18-21
purse, $500,000

	SCORES				TOTAL	MONEY
Nancy Lopez	71	69	68	66	274	$75,000
Ayako Okamoto	69	68	69	71	277	46,250
Susan Sanders	72	67	71	68	278	33,750
Allison Finney	72	72	66	73	283	23,750
Pat Bradley	67	72	71	73	283	23,750
Jane Geddes	69	73	71	71	284	17,500
Patty Sheehan	69	72	66	78	285	14,750
Sherri Turner	72	70	74	70	286	12,375
Betsy King	69	67	72	78	286	12,375
Liselotte Neumann	73	73	72	70	288	10,023
Tammie Green	75	70	68	75	288	10,022
Missie McGeorge	71	73	72	73	289	8,545
Chris Johnson	74	74	67	74	289	8,545
Nancy Brown	73	75	72	70	290	6,379
Deb Richard	69	78	72	71	290	6,379
Lauri Merten	73	73	73	71	290	6,379
Jody Rosenthal	72	72	75	71	290	6,378
Carolyn Hill	72	75	71	72	290	6,378
Debbie Massey	70	77	71	72	290	6,378
Pamela Wright	73	75	69	73	290	6,378
Beth Daniel	74	72	70	74	290	6,378
Amy Alcott	72	70	74	74	290	6,378
Patti Rizzo	74	75	69	73	291	4,675
Colleen Walker	75	71	72	73	291	4,674
Donna White	75	71	71	74	291	4,674
Caroline Keggi	71	71	75	74	291	4,674
Dawn Coe	73	72	69	77	291	4,674
Sandra Haynie	67	73	74	77	291	4,674
Judy Dickinson	73	75	71	73	292	3,860
Meg Mallon	74	73	72	73	292	3,860
Deborah McHaffie	72	73	71	76	292	3,860
Cathy Morse	70	75	71	76	292	3,860
Susie Redman	68	71	77	76	292	3,860
Kristi Albers	73	74	72	74	293	3,220
Vicki Fergon	70	75	74	74	293	3,220
Ok Hee Ku	75	72	71	75	293	3,220
Caroline Pierce	73	72	73	75	293	3,220
Tracy Kerdyl	74	71	71	77	293	3,220
Dottie Mochrie	71	78	74	71	294	2,664
Kim Bauer	73	71	78	72	294	2,664

	SCORES				TOTAL	MONEY
Dale Eggeling	71	76	74	73	294	2,664
Shelley Hamlin	71	73	72	78	294	2,663
Hollis Stacy	73	73	76	73	295	2,045
Lynn Adams	75	74	72	74	295	2,045
Janet Anderson	74	73	74	74	295	2,045
Bonnie Lauer	72	77	70	76	295	2,045
Elaine Crosby	68	75	76	76	295	2,045
Kris Tschetter	74	70	74	77	295	2,045
Diana Heinicke-Rauch	73	70	74	78	295	2,045
Danielle Ammaccapane	70	74	71	80	295	2,045

Corning Classic

Corning Country Club, Corning, New York
Par 35-36—71; 6,006 yards

May 25-28
purse, $325,000

	SCORES				TOTAL	MONEY
Ayako Okamoto	69	66	67	70	272	$48,750
Beth Daniel	70	66	71	71	278	30,062
Dawn Coe	67	72	72	70	281	21,937
Patty Sheehan	72	70	69	72	283	17,062
Betsy King	71	71	72	70	284	13,812
Amy Benz	74	71	71	69	285	9,804
Pamela Wright	75	67	73	70	285	9,804
Ok Hee Ku	72	74	67	72	285	9,804
Pat Bradley	70	70	69	77	286	7,637
Cindy Rarick	71	70	75	71	287	6,825
Kathy Postlewait	72	70	73	73	288	5,948
Danielle Ammaccapane	74	70	69	75	288	5,948
Cindy Mackey	73	72	71	73	289	5,054
Heather Farr	71	70	74	74	289	5,054
Dale Eggeling	72	68	75	74	289	5,054
Penny Hammel	73	68	78	71	290	4,080
Tracy Kerdyk	68	71	80	71	290	4,079
Vicki Fergon	77	71	70	72	290	4,079
Debbie Massey	73	73	70	74	290	4,079
Sherri Turner	72	70	74	74	290	4,079
Missie McGeorge	77	71	71	72	291	3,511
Chris Johnson	74	69	74	74	291	3,510
Rosie Jones	75	73	74	70	292	2,832
Hollis Stacy	73	73	74	72	292	2,832
Marlene Floyd	74	72	73	73	292	2,831
JoAnne Carner	74	71	74	73	292	2,831
Mei Chi Cheng	74	71	73	74	292	2,831
Caroline Keggi	72	74	71	75	292	2,831
Sandra Palmer	73	70	72	77	292	2,831
Caroline Gowan	70	71	74	77	292	2,831
Jenny Lidback	74	70	70	78	292	2,831
Donna Cusano-Wilkins	73	70	70	79	292	2,831

Rochester International

Locust Hill Country Club, Pittsford, New York
Par 35-37—72; 6,162 yards

June 1-4
purse, $300,000

	SCORES				TOTAL	MONEY
Patty Sheehan	68	73	66	71	278	$45,000
Ayako Okamoto	69	72	69	68	278	27,750
(Sheehan defeated Okamoto on first extra hole.)						
Nancy Lopez	73	69	72	66	280	18,000
Sherri Turner	70	69	69	72	280	18,000
Betsy King	70	69	76	71	286	12,750
Beth Daniel	73	73	71	70	287	9,675
Patti Rizzo	70	74	68	75	287	9,675
Barb Mucha	73	72	71	72	288	7,800
Kristi Albers	72	72	72	73	289	7,050
Dale Eggeling	77	72	77	64	290	6,014
Nancy Brown	75	72	69	74	290	6,013
Chris Johnson	72	74	73	72	291	4,977
Dottie Mochrie	75	70	73	73	291	4,977
Val Skinner	73	71	70	77	291	4,977
Caroline Keggi	72	78	70	72	292	4,127
Danielle Ammaccapane	72	72	75	73	292	4,127
Missie McGeorge	72	71	75	74	292	4,127
Elaine Crosby	72	77	76	68	293	3,777
Kris Monaghan	75	74	74	71	294	3,096
Laurie Rinker	75	77	70	72	294	3,096
Nicky LeRoux	79	70	73	72	294	3,096
Heather Drew	75	75	71	73	294	3,095
Lisa Walters	73	77	71	73	294	3,095
Sue Ertl	73	74	73	74	294	3,095
Lauri Merten	72	73	75	74	294	3,095
Vicki Fergon	74	71	74	75	294	3,095
Cathy Marino	73	70	76	75	294	3,095
Pamela Wright	76	75	72	72	295	2,360
Caroline Pierce	73	77	71	74	295	2,360
Lynn Adams	75	72	74	74	295	2,360
Cathy Morse	73	74	74	74	295	2,359
Liselotte Neumann	73	74	73	75	295	2,359
Cindy Rarick	76	71	72	76	295	2,359

Planters Pat Bradley International

Willow Creek Golf Club, High Point, North Carolina
Par 36-36—72; 6,260 yards

June 9-11
purse, $400,000

36-HOLE QUALIFIERS

28 Patti Rizzo.
26 Myra Blackwelder.
24 Pat Bradley.
23 Tammie Green.
20 Jody Rosenthal.
19 Ayako Okamoto.
18 Amy Alcott, Cindy Mackey.
17 Shelly Hamlin, Jane Geddes.
16 Sherri Steinhauer, Cathy Gerring.
15 Ok Hee Ku, Susan Sanders, Kathy Postlewait, Amy Benz, Colleen Walker.

14 Chris Johnson, Mitzi Edge, Sara Anne McGetrick, Missie McGeorge.
13 Meg Mallon, Dot Germain, Kristi Albers, Loretta Alderete.
12 Dale Eggeling, Nina Foust, Cindy Rarick, Cathy Morse.
11 JoAnne Carner.
10 Barb Mucha, Lenore Rittenhouse, Nancy Brown, Gina Hull.
9   Alice Ritzman, Robin Hood, Marlene Floyd.
8   Laura Baugh, Elaine Crosby, Sherrin Smyers, Dawn Coe, Lauri Merten, Kris Monaghan, Sue Ertl.
7   Heather Farr, Heather Drew, Jan Stephenson, Martha Foyer, Deborah McHaffie, Yuka Irie, Lori Garbacz, Laurie Rinker, Sandra Haynie.
6   Mary Dwyer, Nicky LaRoux, Caroline Gowan, Susie Berning, Muffin Spencer-Devlin, Lisa Walters.
5   Mei Chi Cheng, Allison Finney, Cindy Hill, Jane Crafter, Denise Heinicke-Rauch.
4   Debbie Massey, Lynn Adams, Tina Barrett, Julie Cole, Michelle McGann, Mina Hardin.
3   Martha Nause, Kris Tschetter, Lori West, Jenny Lidbeck, Janet Anderson.

54-HOLE QUALIFIERS

13 Massey.
12 Foust.
10 Postlewait, Walters, Doe.
9   McGetrick.
8   Rinker, Alcott, Merten, Johnson, Berning.
7   Baugh, Carner.
6   Mucha, McGeorge.
5   Rizzo, Crafter, Barrett, Ertl, Floyd, Gerring, Green, Edge, Okamoto.
4   Adams, Garbacz, McGann, Mackey, Rosenthal, Bradley, Rarick, Walker, Steinhauer.
3   Irie, Albers, Hood.

FINAL ROUND

16 Hood, $62,500.
11 Rizzo, Postlewait, $30,000 each.
10 Baugh, $19,000.
9   Rinker, $15,000.
8   Massey, Rosenthal, Rarick, $10,300 each.
7   Walker, Floyd, $7,200 each.
6   Albers, Bradley, $5,600 each.
5   Mackey, Adams, Merten, Coe, Foust, $4,140 each.
4   Edge, Barrett, McGetrick, $3,300 each.
3   Johnson, $3,100.
1   Crafter, Mucha, Alcott, $2,950 each.
0   Okamoto, Green, $2,700 each.
-1 Steinhauer, Garbacz, McGann, Ertl, Carner, $2,350 each.
-2 Gerring, Berning, $2,000 each.
-4 McGeorge, $1,850.
-5 Walters, Irie, $1,725 each.

Lady Keystone Open

Hershey Country Club, Hershey, Pennsylvania
Par 36-36—72; 6,348 yards

June 16-18
purse, $300,000

	SCORES			TOTAL	MONEY
Laura Davies	67	73	67	207	$45,000
Pat Bradley	69	71	68	208	21,750

	SCORES			TOTAL	MONEY
Liselotte Neumann	70	69	70	209	18,000
Betsy King	69	69	71	209	18,000
Beth Daniel	71	70	70	211	11,625
Patty Sheehan	70	71	70	211	11,625
Ok Hee Ku	68	70	74	212	8,850
Val Skinner	73	69	71	213	7,425
Marta Figueras-Dotti	71	70	72	213	7,425
Kim Shipman	72	74	68	214	6,001
Danielle Ammaccapane	72	69	73	214	6,000
Cindy Rarick	70	75	70	215	4,525
Rosie Jones	72	72	71	215	4,525
Martha Nause	72	71	72	215	4,525
Shelley Hamlin	72	71	72	215	4,525
Sherri Steinhauer	70	73	72	215	4,525
Mei Chi Cheng	69	72	74	215	4,525
Susan Sanders	73	75	68	216	3,378
Barb Mucha	72	71	73	216	3,378
Elaine Crosby	70	73	73	216	3,378
Patti Rizzo	73	69	74	216	3,377
Kathy Postlewait	70	72	74	216	3,377
Marci Bozarth	69	73	74	216	3,377
Meg Mallon	71	76	70	217	2,730
Shirley Furlong	70	76	71	217	2,730
Caroline Keggi	74	71	72	217	2,730
Laura Baugh	71	74	72	217	2,730
Dawn Coe	70	72	75	217	2,730
Kris Tschetter	74	74	70	218	2,022
Cindy Schreyer	76	71	71	218	2,022
Jennifer Wyatt	75	72	71	218	2,022
Jane Geddes	73	74	71	218	2,021
Cathy Marino	72	75	71	218	2,021
Janice Gibson	72	74	72	218	2,021
Tracy Kerdyk	74	71	73	218	2,021
Susie Redman	73	72	73	218	2,021
Jan Stephenson	72	73	73	218	2,021
Sherrin Smyers	69	76	73	218	2,021
Alice Ritzman	73	71	74	218	2,021
Connie Chillemi	72	72	74	218	2,021

McDonald's Championship

DuPont Country Club, Wilmington, Delaware
Par 36-36—72; 6,386 yards

June 22-25
purse, $ 550,000

	SCORES				TOTAL	MONEY
Betsy King	69	65	71	67	272	$82,500
Pat Bradley	69	66	71	68	274	44,000
Shirley Furlong	66	69	66	73	274	44,000
Deborah McHaffie	68	69	69	70	276	28,875
Allison Finney	69	71	69	69	278	19,617
Patty Sheehan	69	72	67	70	278	19,617
JoAnne Carner	71	70	66	71	278	19,616
Sherri Turner	71	69	73	66	279	12,925
Colleen Walker	73	71	67	68	279	12,925
Patti Rizzo	74	70	66	69	279	12,925
Tammie Green	70	73	67	70	280	9,420
Elaine Crosby	69	69	72	70	280	9,420

	SCORES				TOTAL	MONEY
Chris Johnson	69	71	69	71	280	9,420
Beth Daniel	70	66	72	72	280	9,419
Ayako Okamoto	70	74	69	68	281	7,518
Nancy Brown	73	68	69	71	281	7,518
Missie Berteotti	67	70	73	71	281	7,517
Jane Geddes	71	71	70	70	282	6,601
Vicki Fergon	70	72	70	70	282	6,601
Danielle Ammaccapane	70	70	70	72	282	6,601
Cathy Marino	71	70	70	72	283	5,672
Lenore Rittenhouse	71	71	68	73	283	5,672
Caroline Pierce	71	70	69	73	283	5,672
Susan Sanders	68	71	70	74	283	5,672
Donna White	74	68	70	72	284	5,088
Nancy Ramsbottom	67	73	70	74	284	5,087
Lori Garbacz	75	69	71	70	285	4,510
Marci Bozarth	73	69	73	70	285	4,510
Cindy Rarick	70	71	74	70	285	4,510
Missie McGeorge	70	71	70	74	285	4,510
Amy Alcott	69	70	71	75	285	4,510

du Maurier Classic

Beaconsfield Golf Club, Pointe Claire, Canada
Par 36-36—72; 6,261 yards

June 29-July 2
purse, $600,000

	SCORES				TOTAL	MONEY
Tammie Green	68	69	70	72	279	$90,000
Pat Bradley	69	75	69	67	280	48,000
Betsy King	67	69	74	70	280	48,000
Patty Sheehan	69	74	69	69	281	26,000
Amy Alcott	70	70	72	69	281	26,000
Penny Hammel	71	71	68	71	281	26,000
Nancy Brown	70	74	70	68	282	16,650
Beth Daniel	71	69	71	71	282	16,650
Nancy Lopez	72	67	72	72	283	14,100
Dawn Coe	71	73	73	67	284	10,740
Nina Foust	75	73	68	68	284	10,740
JoAnne Carner	73	71	72	68	284	10,740
Colleen Walker	71	70	73	70	284	10,740
Jane Geddes	69	71	70	74	284	10,740
Amy Benz	71	73	71	70	285	8,400
Cathy Reynolds	71	72	71	71	285	8,400
Laura Davies	71	69	72	74	286	7,800
Dottie Mochrie	74	70	72	71	287	7,200
Patti Rizzo	73	68	75	71	287	7,200
Jody Rosenthal	72	71	70	74	287	7,200
Kate Rogerson	75	71	71	71	288	6,310
Myra Blackwelder	73	72	70	73	288	6,310
Alice Ritzman	69	75	70	74	288	6,310
Marci Bozarth	72	74	73	70	289	5,550
Donna White	72	73	74	70	289	5,550
Ayako Okamoto	73	71	71	74	289	5,550
Hollis Stacy	69	72	69	79	289	5,550
Tracy Kerdyk	75	69	77	69	290	4,508
Susie Redman	74	73	72	71	290	4,508
Robin Walton	72	75	72	71	290	4,508
Kay Cockerill	73	73	72	72	290	4,508

	SCORES				TOTAL	MONEY
Mina Rodriguez-Hardin	75	70	72	73	290	4,507
Trish Johnson	75	72	69	74	290	4,507
Shirley Furlong	73	72	71	74	290	4,507
Cindy Rarick	73	71	71	75	290	4,507
Lauri Merten	73	74	73	71	291	3,585
Ok Hee Ku	74	72	74	71	291	3,585
Lynn Adams	69	77	72	73	291	3,585
Sherri Turner	72	71	70	78	291	3,585
Diana Heinicke-Rauch	78	70	74	70	292	2,885
Kathy Guadagnino	75	73	73	71	292	2,885
Tina Barrett	71	71	78	72	292	2,885
Kathy Whitworth	74	71	73	74	292	2,885
Kristi Albers	69	72	76	75	292	2,885
Caroline Pierce	73	71	71	77	292	2,885
Rosie Jones	71	76	77	69	293	2,113
Sue Thomas	72	76	72	73	293	2,113
Heather Farr	74	73	73	73	293	2,113
Cindy Schreyer	71	74	75	73	293	2,113
Sandra Haynie	75	72	72	74	293	2,113
Deborah McHaffie	70	71	77	75	293	2,113
Deb Richard	69	70	76	78	293	2,112

Jamie Farr Toledo Classic

Highland Meadows Golf Club, Sylvania, Ohio
Par 34-37—71; 6,270 yards

July 7-9
purse, $275,000

	SCORES			TOTAL	MONEY
Penny Hammel	69	66	71	206	$41,250
Hollis Stacy	72	68	68	208	19,479
Nancy Lopez	70	70	68	208	19,479
Liselotte Neumann	68	69	71	208	19,478
Chris Johnson	70	75	64	209	9,808
Lauri Merten	72	71	66	209	9,808
Betsy King	68	70	71	209	9,808
Deborah McHaffie	71	71	68	210	7,150
Laura Davies	73	72	66	211	5,582
Heather Drew	71	74	66	211	5,582
Jennifer Wyatt	71	70	70	211	5,581
Caroline Keggi	71	70	70	211	5,581
Muffin Spencer-Devlin	73	71	68	212	4,151
Deb Richard	73	70	69	212	4,151
Susan Sanders	67	76	69	212	4,150
Dale Eggeling	70	70	72	212	4,150
Diana Heinicke-Rauch	72	71	70	213	3,395
Chihiro Nakajima	72	69	72	213	3,395
Bonnie Lauer	72	69	72	213	3,394
Sara Anne McGetrick	69	69	75	213	3,394
Barb Thomas	74	72	68	214	2,674
Nina Foust	75	69	70	214	2,674
Carolyn Hill	72	72	70	214	2,674
Elaine Crosby	71	72	71	214	2,673
Sandra Haynie	69	74	71	214	2,673
Martha Nause	73	69	72	214	2,673
Caroline Pierce	71	71	72	214	2,673
Laura Hurlbut	70	71	73	214	2,673
Myra Blackwelder	73	74	68	215	2,052

	SCORES	TOTAL	MONEY
Cathy Gerring	74 72 69	215	2,052
Allison Finney	72 74 69	215	2,052
Cindy Mackey	72 72 71	215	2,052
Cindy Figg-Currier	71 72 72	215	2,052
Cathy Marino	69 74 72	215	2,052
Tammie Green	73 69 73	215	2,051

U.S. Women's Open Championship

Indianwood Golf & Country Club, Lake Orion, Michigan   July 13-16
Par 35-36—71; 6,109 yards   purse, $450,000

	SCORES	TOTAL	MONEY
Betsy King	67 71 72 68	278	$80,000
Nancy Lopez	73 70 71 68	282	40,000
Penny Hammel	74 73 69 67	283	24,250
Pat Bradley	73 74 68 68	283	24,250
Dottie Mochrie	72 70 75 67	284	15,043
Lori Garbacz	71 70 73 70	284	15,043
Laura Davies	73 71 75 66	285	11,931
Vicki Fergon	72 74 69 70	285	11,931
Jane Geddes	70 72 72 72	286	9,974
Colleen Walker	72 69 71 74	286	9,974
Ayako Okamoto	76 72 74 65	287	8,304
Danielle Ammaccapane	73 70 74 70	287	8,304
Myra Blackwelder	76 68 71 72	287	8,304
Marie-Laure de Lorenzi	68 74 71 74	287	8,304
Kim Bauer	72 72 73 71	288	7,137
Marta Figueras-Dotti	75 70 70 73	288	7,137
Gina Hull	74 72 72 71	289	6,374
JoAnne Carner	76 69 71 73	289	6,374
Patty Sheehan	74 67 69 79	289	6,374
Shirley Furlong	74 75 73 68	290	5,392
Beth Daniel	73 73 71 73	290	5,392
Caroline Keggi	71 73 73 73	290	5,391
Liselotte Neumann	71 71 75 73	290	5,391
Kathy Postlewait	77 70 70 73	290	5,391
Donna Cusano-Wilkins	71 72 71 76	290	5,391
Sally Quinlan	78 71 73 69	291	4,680
Amy Alcott	73 71 73 74	291	4,680
Kim Shipman	74 69 74 74	291	4,680
Donna White	75 73 74 70	292	4,172
Chris Johnson	73 73 75 71	292	4,172
Nancy Taylor	74 73 73 72	292	4,172
Patti Rizzo	77 69 73 73	292	4,172
Debbie Massey	71 72 75 74	292	4,172
Jody Rosenthal	80 69 76 69	294	3,786
Deborah McHaffie	71 73 80 70	294	3,786
Cindy Rarick	75 73 73 73	294	3,786
Amy Benz	71 76 76 72	295	3,458
Hollis Stacy	78 70 73 74	295	3,458
Kristi Albers	71 73 75 76	295	3,458
Sandra Haynie	72 73 74 76	295	3,458
Lenore Rittenhouse	73 72 72 79	296	3,178
Linda Hunt	71 72 74 79	296	3,177
Allison Finney	74 74 76 73	297	2,758
Kathy Guadagnino	76 74 74 73	297	2,758

	SCORES				TOTAL	MONEY
Missie McGeorge	74	73	77	73	297	2,758
Peggy Kirsch	76	70	77	74	297	2,758
Maggie Will	74	75	74	74	297	2,758
Tammie Green	77	67	77	76	297	2,758
Alice Ritzman	71	75	74	77	297	2,758
Val Skinner	78	72	74	74	298	2,292
Lori West	76	73	75	74	298	2,292
Alison Nicholas	74	73	75	76	298	2,292

Boston Five Classic

Sheraton Tara Hotel at Ferncroft Village, Danvers, Massachusetts   July 20-23
Par 35-37—72; 6,008 yards   purse, $350,000

	SCORES				TOTAL	MONEY
Amy Alcott	68	68	68	68	272	$52,500
Cathy Marino	69	67	71	68	275	32,375
Marta Figueras-Dotti	74	68	66	68	276	23,625
Beth Daniel	69	68	73	67	277	16,625
Shirley Furlong	70	66	70	71	277	16,625
Ayako Okamoto	73	66	71	68	278	12,250
Patti Rizzo	70	73	70	66	279	9,713
Patty Sheehan	70	69	68	72	279	9,712
Colleen Walker	70	69	69	72	280	7,788
Jodi Rosenthal	69	70	68	73	280	7,787
Kristi Albers	70	72	73	67	282	5,811
Jane Geddes	74	70	68	70	282	5,811
Dottie Mochrie	70	71	71	70	282	5,811
Kathy Postlewait	67	71	72	72	282	5,811
Cindy Rarick	68	70	71	73	282	5,811
Dawn Coe	70	74	68	71	283	4,464
Donna Cusano-Wilkins	69	72	71	71	283	4,464
Sally Quinlan	72	68	70	73	283	4,463
Penny Hammel	67	69	72	75	283	4,463
Alice Ritzman	74	67	72	71	284	4,026
Kim Shipman	74	72	69	70	285	3,486
Sarah McGuire	72	68	75	70	285	3,486
Sandra Haynie	70	71	73	71	285	3,486
Cathy Reynolds	69	71	74	71	285	3,485
Kris Monaghan	71	68	75	71	285	3,485
Lynn Adams	71	71	71	72	285	3,485
Lauri Merten	76	71	71	68	286	2,975
Donna White	68	72	75	71	286	2,975
Mitzi Edge	72	75	67	72	286	2,975
Mina Rodriguez-Hardin	71	73	74	69	287	2,444
Vicki Fergon	73	72	71	71	287	2,444
Heather Drew	72	71	73	71	287	2,443
Gina Hull	76	71	68	72	287	2,443
Tina Barrett	68	75	72	72	287	2,443
Nancy Ramsbottom	71	71	72	73	287	2,443
Danielle Ammaccapane	72	71	68	76	287	2,443
Rosie Jones	71	69	71	76	287	2,443

Atlantic City Classic

Sands Country Club, Somers Point, New Jersey
Par 35-35—70; 6,020 yards

July 28-30
purse, $225,000

	SCORES			TOTAL	MONEY
Nancy Lopez	67	70	69	206	$33,750
Vicki Fergon	70	66	71	207	18,000
Chris Johnson	68	68	71	207	17,999
Jennifer Wyatt	69	70	69	208	11,812
Elaine Crosby	68	73	68	209	8,025
Pat Bradley	71	69	69	209	8,025
Rosie Jones	69	69	71	209	8,024
Cathy Marino	72	69	69	210	5,569
Beth Daniel	71	69	70	210	5,568
Amy Benz	71	71	69	211	4,163
Amy Alcott	71	67	73	211	4,163
Susan Sanders	70	68	73	211	4,163
Betsy King	68	70	73	211	4,163
Cindy Figg-Currier	76	67	69	212	3,179
Sally Quinlan	73	70	69	212	3,179
Nancy Taylor	72	70	70	212	3,179
Debbie Massey	70	70	72	212	3,178
Nancy Ramsbottom	73	72	68	213	2,438
Deedee Lasker	73	71	69	213	2,438
Val Skinner	72	72	69	213	2,438
Cathy Gerring	72	70	71	213	2,438
Muffin Spencer-Devlin	73	68	72	213	2,438
Hollis Stacy	72	69	72	213	2,438
Gina Hull	71	70	72	213	2,437
Kathy Postlewait	70	70	73	213	2,437
Danielle Ammaccapane	71	73	70	214	1,947
Nancy Brown	69	74	71	214	1,947
Kris Monaghan	72	70	72	214	1,947
Sandra Haynie	69	71	74	214	1,547
Barb Thomas	72	74	69	215	1,544
Shirley Furlong	70	76	69	215	1,543
Shelley Hamlin	78	67	70	215	1,543
Kathy Whitworth	72	73	70	215	1,543
Kim Bauer	73	71	71	215	1,543
Lynn Connelly	69	75	71	215	1,543
Lenore Rittenhouse	70	72	73	215	1,543
Lynn Adams	72	68	75	215	1,543
Sherrin Smyers	69	70	76	215	1,543

Greater Washington Open

Bethesda Country Club, Bethesda, Maryland
Par 36-35—71; 6,250 yards

August 4-6
purse, $300,000

	SCORES			TOTAL	MONEY
Beth Daniel	66	68	71	205	$45,000
Sherri Turner	73	71	65	209	27,750
Danielle Ammaccapane	74	70	66	210	18,000
Betsy King	70	72	68	210	18,000
Debbie Massey	70	72	70	212	12,750
Alice Ritzman	75	71	67	213	8,100
Kathy Postlewait	74	71	68	213	8,100

	SCORES			TOTAL	MONEY
Cindy Mackey	72	72	69	213	8,100
Rosie Jones	67	75	71	213	8,100
Pat Bradley	71	70	72	213	8,100
Cindy Rarick	72	72	70	214	5,476
Hollis Stacy	70	71	73	214	5,475
Dottie Mochrie	74	71	70	215	4,650
Pam Allen	72	68	75	215	4,650
Penny Hammel	70	68	77	215	4,650
Nina Foust	73	74	69	216	3,600
Dawn Coe	70	73	73	216	3,600
Chris Johnson	70	73	73	216	3,600
Meg Mallon	70	72	74	216	3,600
Val Skinner	74	68	74	216	3,600
Lynn Adams	71	70	75	216	3,600
Amy Alcott	71	70	75	216	3,600
Sue Ertl	74	74	69	217	2,642
Kris Tschetter	76	72	69	217	2,642
Susan Sanders	71	75	71	217	2,642
Sherri Steinhauer	75	71	71	217	2,642
Deb Richard	73	72	72	217	2,642
Laura Baugh	72	72	73	217	2,642
Shirley Furlong	71	73	73	217	2,641
Jennifer Wyatt	73	71	73	217	2,641
Missie McGeorge	68	74	75	217	2,641

Nestle World Championship

Stouffer PineIsle Resort, Buford, Georgia
Par 36-36—72; 6,107 yards

August 24-27
purse, $265,000

	SCORES				TOTAL	MONEY
Betsy King	66	71	70	68	275	$83,500
Pat Bradley	74	66	68	70	278	34,750
Patty Sheehan	70	66	72	70	278	34,750
Laura Davies	70	72	68	69	279	17,500
Beth Daniel	70	69	71	69	279	17,500
Rosie Jones	66	72	74	70	282	10,500
Jane Geddes	71	67	76	69	283	8,500
Sherri Turner	73	73	69	69	284	6,225
Patti Rizzo	70	71	69	74	284	6,225
Colleen Walker	70	72	73	71	286	4,750
Hiromi Kobayashi	71	71	72	72	286	4,750
Juli Inkster	72	67	75	73	287	4,000
Marie-Laure de Lorenzi	70	73	72	75	290	3,750
Tammie Green	75	68	75	73	291	3,500
Nancy Lopez	72	71	72	77	292	3,250
Penny Hammel	73	74	73	75	295	3,000

Mitsubishi Motors Ocean State Open

Alpine Country Club, Cranston, Rhode Island
Par 36-36—72; 6,210 yards

August 25-27
purse, $150,000

	SCORES			TOTAL	MONEY
Tina Barrett	67	73	70	210	$22,500
Nancy Brown	72	69	71	212	13,875

	SCORES			TOTAL	MONEY
Maggie Will	72	73	68	213	8,125
Missie Berteotti	70	73	70	213	8,125
Jill Briles	72	69	72	213	8,125
Deborah McHaffie	72	71	71	214	4,525
Nancy Rubin	69	73	72	214	4,525
Dottie Mochrie	73	67	74	214	4,525
Cindy Figg-Currier	73	74	68	215	3,176
Martha Nause	72	74	69	215	3,176
Pamela Wright	75	69	71	215	3,176
Cindy Mackey	75	72	69	216	2,403
Kate Rogerson	70	74	72	216	2,403
Lynn Connelly	71	73	72	216	2,403
Nina Foust	70	72	74	216	2,403
Laurel Kean	73	74	70	217	1,878
Susie Redman	75	70	72	217	1,878
M.J. Smith	72	72	73	217	1,878
Barb Mucha	71	72	74	217	1,878
Elaine Crosby	72	71	74	217	1,878
Nicky LeRoux	77	72	69	218	1,550
Martha Foyer	74	75	69	218	1,550
Chihiro Nakajima	74	71	73	218	1,550
Margaret Ward	74	70	74	218	1,549
Trish Johnson	77	72	70	219	1,278
Janice Gibson	76	72	71	219	1,278
Joan Delk	74	74	71	219	1,278
Cathy Johnston	75	72	72	219	1,278
Caroline Keggi	73	74	72	219	1,278
Sally Quinlan	70	76	73	219	1,278
Jane Crafter	75	71	73	219	1,278

Rail Charity Classic

Rail Golf Course, Springfield, Illinois
Par 36-36—72; 6,403 yards

September 2-4
purse, $275,000

	SCORES			TOTAL	MONEY
Beth Daniel	69	70	64	203	$41,250
Betsy King	71	66	69	206	22,000
Alice Ritzman	69	66	71	206	21,999
Penny Hammel	70	68	69	207	14,437
Muffin Spencer-Devlin	73	68	67	208	10,656
Meg Mallon	71	67	70	208	10,656
Cindy Rarick	69	71	69	209	6,875
Marci Bozarth	71	68	70	209	6,875
Danielle Ammaccapane	71	68	70	209	6,875
Cathy Gerring	68	69	72	209	6,874
Sue Ertl	70	74	66	210	4,859
Martha Nause	72	71	67	210	4,859
Sherri Turner	72	70	68	210	4,859
Pat Bradley	72	71	68	211	3,796
Barb Thomas	72	68	71	211	3,796
Kris Tschetter	69	71	71	211	3,796
Lynn Connelly	70	69	72	211	3,795
Connie Chillemi	69	70	72	211	3,795
Sarah McGuire	72	72	68	212	3,095
Pamela Wright	72	71	69	212	3,095
Amy Benz	72	71	69	212	3,094

	SCORES			TOTAL	MONEY
Shirley Furlong	69	73	70	212	3,094
Jenny Lidbeck	72	75	66	213	2,383
Heather Drew	74	70	69	213	2,383
Elaine Crosby	71	73	69	213	2,382
Barb Mucha	72	71	70	213	2,382
Nancy Taylor	72	71	70	213	2,382
Jill Briles	72	70	71	213	2,382
Susie Redman	71	71	71	213	2,382
Maggie Will	72	69	72	213	2,382
Nina Foust	72	69	72	213	2,382
Tracy Kerdyk	70	69	74	213	2,382

Cellular One-Ping Championship

Riverside Golf and Country Club, Portland, Oregon   September 8-10
Par 36-36—72; 6,258 yards   purse, $300,000

	SCORES			TOTAL	MONEY
Muffin Spencer-Devlin	74	69	71	214	$45,000
Nancy Lopez	74	72	69	215	19,125
Tammie Green	71	74	70	215	19,125
Susan Sanders	71	72	72	215	19,125
Dawn Coe	68	71	76	215	19,125
Betsy King	72	72	72	216	9,675
Amy Benz	71	73	72	216	9,675
Patti Rizzo	71	74	72	217	6,713
Shelley Hamlin	69	76	72	217	6,713
Joan Pitcock	75	69	73	217	6,713
Val Skinner	71	73	73	217	6,712
Myra Blackwelder	72	72	74	218	4,950
Cindy Figg-Currier	71	73	74	218	4,950
Alice Ritzman	71	73	74	218	4,950
Kathy Postlewait	73	74	72	219	3,930
Dottie Mochrie	73	73	73	219	3,930
Nancy Brown	70	76	73	219	3,930
Cathy Gerring	73	72	74	219	3,930
Patty Sheehan	73	70	76	219	3,930
Deborah McHaffie	74	75	71	220	3,229
Caroline Keggi	69	80	71	220	3,229
Colleen Walker	76	72	72	220	3,229
Martha Nause	70	73	77	220	3,228
Sue Ertl	75	76	70	221	2,552
Hollis Stacy	75	75	71	221	2,552
Liselotte Neumann	76	73	72	221	2,552
Pamela Wright	73	75	73	221	2,552
Allison Finney	72	75	74	221	2,552
Heather Drew	72	75	74	221	2,552
Cindy Mackey	75	71	75	221	2,551
Chris Johnson	72	74	75	221	2,551
Tracy Kerdyk	73	72	76	221	2,551

Safeco Classic

Meridian Valley Country Club, Seattle, Washington
Par 36-36—72; 6,222 yards

September 14-17
purse, $300,000

	SCORES				TOTAL	MONEY
Beth Daniel	69	69	65	70	273	$45,000
Cindy Rarick	68	69	73	69	279	27,750
Pat Bradley	70	67	70	73	280	20,250
Betsy King	71	70	74	66	281	13,000
Jane Geddes	74	70	68	69	281	13,000
Juli Inkster	68	71	70	72	281	13,000
Lenore Rittenhouse	70	70	69	73	282	8,850
Maggie Will	72	69	73	70	284	6,421
Dawn Coe	71	70	71	72	284	6,420
Patty Sheehan	70	70	72	72	284	6,420
Patti Rizzo	70	70	70	74	284	6,420
Danielle Ammaccapane	67	71	70	76	284	6,420
Barb Thomas	68	74	72	71	285	4,800
Nancy Brown	70	71	70	74	285	4,800
Lisa Walters	71	77	72	66	286	4,100
Chris Johnson	66	75	73	72	286	4,100
Val Skinner	73	69	68	76	286	4,100
Cathy Johnston	71	69	77	70	287	3,600
Amy Alcott	73	73	70	71	287	3,600
Shirley Furlong	66	76	72	73	287	3,600
Shelley Hamlin	75	71	74	68	288	3,155
Susan Sanders	70	74	72	72	288	3,155
Susie Redman	75	72	68	73	288	3,155
Muffin Spencer-Devlin	71	74	71	73	289	2,775
Janet Coles	72	72	70	75	289	2,775
Kathy Postlewait	70	73	71	75	289	2,775
Stephanie Lowe	71	69	73	76	289	2,775
Dottie Mochrie	72	69	78	71	290	2,505
Rosie Jones	74	72	71	73	290	2,505
Sue Ertl	68	77	73	73	291	2,285
Colleen Walker	73	74	70	74	291	2,285
Cindy Figg-Currier	71	74	72	74	291	2,285

Nippon Travel-MBS Classic

Los Coyotes Country Club, Buena Park, California
Par 36-36—72; 6,351 yards

September 21-24
purse, $300,000

	SCORES				TOTAL	MONEY
Nancy Lopez	73	69	65	70	277	$45,000
Alice Ritzman	70	72	70	67	279	24,000
Pamela Wright	70	69	67	73	279	24,000
Pat Bradley	69	69	73	69	280	13,000
Beth Daniel	74	67	69	70	280	13,000
Colleen Walker	71	69	69	71	280	13,000
Shelley Hamlin	73	69	70	69	281	8,850
Patti Rizzo	69	74	68	71	282	7,050
Amy Alcott	69	69	73	71	282	7,050
Cindy Rarick	70	68	70	74	282	7,050
Kathy Postlewait	74	71	72	66	283	5,138
Allison Finney	72	73	70	68	283	5,138

	SCORES				TOTAL	MONEY
Nancy Brown	73	70	72	68	283	5,138
Dawn Coe	70	74	70	69	283	5,137
Jenny Lidback	74	68	72	70	284	4,013
Elaine Crosby	72	70	72	70	284	4,013
Danielle Ammaccapane	72	69	72	71	284	4,012
Myra Blackwelder	72	67	73	72	284	4,012
Vicki Fergon	71	74	73	67	285	3,238
Lynn Connelly	73	72	70	70	285	3,238
Missie McGeorge	72	70	73	70	285	3,238
Cathy Gerring	75	70	68	72	285	3,237
Sherri Turner	67	75	71	72	285	3,237
Rosie Jones	70	72	65	78	285	3,237
Shirley Furlong	74	74	70	68	286	2,685
Jan Stephenson	72	73	70	71	286	2,685
Tracy Kerdyk	75	68	70	73	286	2,685
Lisa Walters	67	72	74	73	286	2,685
Barb Thomas	75	72	69	71	287	2,329
Barb Mucha	73	71	72	71	287	2,329
Jill Briles	69	75	69	74	287	2,329
Dale Eggeling	70	70	72	75	287	2,328

Konica San Jose Classic

Almaden Golf and Country Club, San Jose, California
Par 36-36—72; 6,370 yards

September 29-October 1
purse, $325,000

	SCORES			TOTAL	MONEY
Beth Daniel	65	67	73	205	$48,750
Pat Bradley	66	69	71	206	30,062
Vicki Fergon	71	68	70	209	21,937
Cindy Mackey	68	73	69	210	17,062
Lynn Connelly	70	71	70	211	12,594
Lenore Rittenhouse	69	69	73	211	12,593
Myra Blackwelder	73	73	66	212	8,558
Barb Mucha	74	71	67	212	8,558
Nancy Lopez	67	72	73	212	8,558
Alice Ritzman	70	72	71	213	6,501
Pamela Wright	74	67	72	213	6,500
Nancy Brown	72	69	73	214	5,688
Patty Sheehan	72	72	71	215	5,201
Kathy Postlewait	68	73	74	215	5,200
Shirley Furlong	74	75	67	216	4,259
Danielle Ammaccapane	74	72	70	216	4,258
Lisa Walters	71	75	70	216	4,258
Dawn Coe	71	71	74	216	4,258
Mitzi Edge	73	67	76	216	4,258
Anne-Marie Palli	74	72	71	217	3,430
Martha Nause	70	76	71	217	3,430
Marta Figueras-Dotti	74	71	72	217	3,429
Susan Tonkin	73	72	72	217	3,429
Jenny Lidback	73	71	73	217	3,429
Robin Walton	76	73	69	218	2,812
Colleen Walker	75	73	70	218	2,812
Tracy Kerdyk	75	72	71	218	2,812
Missie McGeorge	73	71	74	218	2,812
Patti Rizzo	68	75	75	218	2,812
Muffin Spencer-Devlin	67	76	75	218	2,812

Nichieri Cup

Tsukuba Country Club, Ibaraki, Japan   October 27-29
Par 72, 6,268 yards   purse, US$280,000

	SCORES			TOTAL	MONEY
Colleen Walker	69	70	71	210	$80,000
Hiromi Kobayashi	71	67	72	210	40,000
(Walker defeated Kobayashi on sixth extra hole.)					
Kathy Postlewait	71	69	71	211	28,455
Allison Finney	73	68	73	214	21,035
Jody Rosenthal	73	73	69	215	16,625
Patti Rizzo	72	69	74	215	16,625
Alice Ritzman	70	74	72	216	13,125
Fukumi Tani	74	69	73	216	13,125
Penny Hammel	71	68	78	217	10,500
Sherri Turner	74	74	70	218	8,050
Cindy Rarick	74	73	71	218	8,050
Lori Garbacz	74	72	73	219	6,300
Laura Davies	71	75	73	219	6,300
Martha Nause	76	69	74	219	6,300
Jane Geddes	71	80	70	221	4,900
Fusako Nagata	76	72	73	221	4,900
Mayumi Hirase	74	72	75	221	4,900
Holly Hartley	72	73	76	221	4,900
Tomeko Ikebuchi	77	72	73	222	3,990
Ming Yeh Wu	80	67	75	222	3,990
Ayako Okamoto	77	74	72	223	3,850
Yueh Chyn Huang	72	75	76	223	3,850
Aiko Takasu	78	72	74	224	3,745
Dottie Mochrie	78	72	76	226	3,640
Danielle Ammaccapane	78	71	77	226	3,640
Ikuyo Shiotani	73	75	78	226	3,640
Haruyo Miyazawa	77	74	76	227	3,552
Norimi Terasawa	77	74	76	227	3,552
Junko Yasui	77	74	77	228	3,500
Megumi Ishikawa	79	71	80	230	3,470
Akemi Yamaoka	78	78	76	232	3,440

Mazda Japan Classic

Seta Golf Course, Otsu, Japan   November 3-5
Par 36-36—72; 6,543 yards   purse, $500,000

	SCORES			TOTAL	MONEY
Elaine Crosby	71	64	70	205	$75,000
Dawn Coe	69	69	70	208	46,250
Laura Davies	67	73	69	209	33,750
Ayako Okamoto	70	67	73	210	26,250
Colleen Walker	71	70	70	211	19,375
Cindy Rarick	67	73	71	211	19,375
Pat Bradley	71	69	72	212	14,750
Shirley Furlong	73	72	68	213	11,192
Nancy Brown	72	71	70	213	11,192
Alice Ritzman	71	70	72	213	11,192
Deb Richard	71	70	72	213	11,191
Dottie Mochrie	73	73	68	214	7,375

	SCORES			TOTAL	MONEY
Nayoko Yoshikawa	75	70	69	214	7,374
Haruyo Miyazawa	70	75	69	214	7,374
Sherri Turner	70	73	71	214	7,374
Hiromi Kobayashi	71	71	72	214	7,374
Susan Sanders	70	72	72	214	7,374
Deborah McHaffie	68	71	75	214	7,374
Shihomi Suzuki	74	70	71	215	5,522
Amy Benz	72	72	71	215	5,522
Liselotte Neumann	74	68	73	215	5,522
Martha Nause	72	69	74	215	5,522
Chris Johnson	69	71	75	215	5,522
Kathy Postlewait	75	71	70	216	4,492
Val Skinner	72	73	71	216	4,492
Mayumi Hirase	71	74	71	216	4,492
Amy Alcott	72	72	72	216	4,492
Nancy Lopez	71	72	73	216	4,492
Debbie Massey	71	71	74	216	4,492
Pamela Wright	73	74	70	217	3,445
Vicki Fergon	72	74	71	217	3,445
Hiromi Takamura	75	70	72	217	3,445
Bie Shyun Huang	75	70	72	217	3,445
Hollis Stacy	74	71	72	217	3,445
Ok Hee Ku	72	73	72	217	3,445
Yuko Moriguchi	70	75	72	217	3,445
Myra Blackwelder	72	72	73	217	3,444
Tracy Kerdyk	70	74	73	217	3,444

The Women's European Tour

Rome Ladies Classic

Ogliata Golf Club, Rome, Italy
Par 36-35—71, 5,917 yards

April 12-16
purse, £65,000

	SCORES			TOTAL	MONEY
Sofia Gronberg	70	71	69	210	£9,750
Marie-Laure de Lorenzi	71	72	68	211	6,600
Gillian Stewart	75	65	72	212	4,550
Laurette Maritz	76	69	68	213	3,133
Florence Descampe	71	73	69	213	3,133
Tania Abitbol	72	75	70	217	2,112.50
Maureen Garner	75	72	70	217	2,112.50
Kitrina Douglas	71	70	77	218	1,460.33
Debbie Dowling	70	69	79	218	1,460.33
Dale Reid	72	71	75	218	1,460.33
Regine Lautens	72	73	75	220	1,120
Alison Nicholas	75	72	73	220	1,120

	SCORES			TOTAL	MONEY
Maria Navarro Corbachio	76	73	71	220	1,120
Brenda Lunsford	75	75	71	221	991
Suzanne Strudwick	76	68	77	221	921
Alison Sheard	70	75	77	222	923
Corinne Soules	74	73	75	222	923
Melissa McNamara	73	76	73	222	923
Tracy Hammond	77	72	74	223	858
Xonia Wunsch-Ruiz	75	76	72	223	858
Jane Connachan	74	74	75	224	775
Corinne Dibnah	74	75	75	224	775
Sonja Van Wyk	74	76	74	224	775
Alicia Dibos	79	74	71	224	775
Susan Shapcott	74	75	75	224	775
Sherry Andonian-Smith	77	75	72	224	775
Karine Espinasse	74	76	75	225	655.16
Patricia Gonzalez	76	75	74	225	655.16
Caroline Griffiths	75	75	75	225	655.16
Diane Martin	81	71	73	225	655.16
Susan Moon	77	72	76	225	655.16
Catherine Panton	78	74	73	225	655.16

Ford Ladies Classic

Woburn Golf and Country Club, Duke's Course,
Bow Brickhill, England
Par 36-38—74; 6,060 yards

April 26-29
purse, £50,000

	SCORES				TOTAL	MONEY
Marie-Laure de Lorenzi	67	74	73	72	286	£7,500
Gillian Stewart	73	74	76	71	294	5,075
Sofia Gronberg	74	79	74	71	298	3,100
Mickey Walker	73	75	76	74	298	3,100
Barbara Helbig	76	76	76	71	299	1,790
Karen Lunn	73	78	79	69	299	1,790
Janet Soulsby	73	74	75	77	299	1,790
Alison Nicholas	77	74	77	72	300	1,185
Suzanne Strudwick	78	79	70	73	300	1,185
Laura Davies	74	75	79	75	303	926.66
Regine Lautens	77	78	74	74	303	926.66
Anne Jones	80	77	73	73	303	926.66
Jane Forrest	77	73	76	78	304	765
Penny Grice-Whittaker	78	77	74	75	304	765
Caroline Griffiths	76	77	75	76	304	765
Julie Kintz	81	79	72	72	304	765
Maureen Garner	73	79	76	77	305	690
Melissa McNamara	78	79	76	72	305	690
Denise Baldwin	76	77	75	77	305	690
Kitrina Douglas	74	77	75	80	306	627.50
Debbie Dowling	76	75	79	75	306	627.50
Beverly New	71	80	80	75	306	627.50
Alison Sheard	79	72	80	75	306	627.50
Tania Abitbol	78	80	73	76	307	530
Julie Brown	75	79	77	76	307	530
Corinne Dibnah	83	74	73	77	307	530
Beverly Huke	75	82	74	75	307	530
Laurette Maritz	76	82	73	76	307	530
Sonja Van Wyk	78	77	72	80	307	530

	SCORES				TOTAL	MONEY
Florence Descampe	78	79	81	74	307	530
Nathalie Jeanson Desres	79	81	76	71	307	530
Helen Alfredsson	77	79	73	78	307	530

Hennessy Ladies Cup

St. Germain Golf Club, Paris, France
Par 35-37—72; 6,039 yards

May 25-28
purse, £80,000

	SCORES				TOTAL	MONEY
Marie-Laure de Lorenzi	68	66	72	73	279	£12,000
Corinne Dibnah	67	71	70	73	281	6,860
Jody Rosenthal	70	71	70	70	281	6,860
Laura Davies	69	68	70	75	282	4,320
Laurette Maritz	71	72	74	70	287	3,392
Alicia Dibos	71	72	72	73	288	2,800
Corinne Soules	71	71	74	73	289	2,064
Florence Descampe	75	71	71	72	289	2,064
Lori Garbacz	75	72	69	73	289	2,064
Diane Barnard	71	76	71	76	294	1,434
Judy Greco	70	76	73	75	294	1,434
Alison Nicholas	71	75	72	76	294	1,434
Helen Alfredsson	70	72	79	73	294	1,434
Susan Moon	75	78	73	69	295	1,202.66
Gillian Stewart	74	75	75	71	295	1,202.66
Anne Jones	71	73	78	73	295	1,202.66
Tracy Chapman	75	76	70	75	296	1,136
Tania Abitbol	79	72	75	71	297	1,044.80
Rica Comstock	73	76	71	77	297	1,044.80
Suzanne Strudwick	78	72	74	73	297	1,044.80
Kris Hanson	77	73	70	77	297	1,044.80
Catrin Nilsmark	76	74	72	75	297	1,044.80
Kitrina Douglas	69	76	77	76	298	932
Rae Hast	76	73	74	75	298	932
Beverly New	73	76	73	76	298	932
Catherine Panton	70	76	78	74	298	932
Brenda Lunsford	79	69	79	72	299	860
Patti Liscio	72	76	74	77	299	860
Dale Reid	70	72	76	73	300	800
Mickey Walker	75	72	79	74	300	800
Julie Hennessy	75	73	77	75	300	800

BMW Ladies Classic

Hubbelrath Golf Club, Dusseldorf, West Germany
Par 36-36—72; 5,896 yards

June 1-4
purse, £70,000

	SCORES				TOTAL	MONEY
Marie-Laure de Lorenzi	70	72	68	67	277	£10,500
Dennise Hutton	69	69	70	70	278	7,105
Corinne Dibnah	70	70	68	72	280	4,900
Corinne Soules	67	69	74	72	282	3,780
Susan Moon	67	72	71	73	283	2,968
Florence Descampe	68	75	67	74	284	2,450
Marie Wennersten-From	69	72	71	73	285	2,100

	SCORES				TOTAL	MONEY
Suzanne Strudwick	71	73	75	67	286	1,750
Catherine Panton	74	72	71	70	287	1,568
Regine Lautens	69	74	74	71	288	1,297.33
Alison Nicholas	74	75	69	70	288	1,297.33
Alicia Dibos	74	71	69	74	288	1,297.33
Judy Greco	72	72	74	71	289	1,106
Julie Hennessy	75	71	70	73	289	1,106
Cindy Scholefield	72	71	75	72	290	1,050
Diane Barnard	74	73	70	74	291	1,008
Barbara Helbig	72	72	73	74	291	1,008
Kitrina Douglas	72	73	74	73	292	966
Laura Davies	71	74	75	73	293	901.25
Brenda Lunsford	71	73	74	75	293	901.25
Laurette Maritz	73	71	73	76	293	901.25
Janet Soulsby	79	71	71	72	293	901.25
Jane Connachan	71	76	75	72	294	805
Debbie Dowling	76	71	76	71	294	805
Dale Reid	75	72	76	71	294	805
Kerri Clark	71	74	75	74	294	805
Julie Ralls	74	75	73	72	294	805
Majorie Jones	73	74	73	75	295	742
Maureen Garner	76	73	71	76	296	679
Sofia Gronberg	75	72	73	76	296	679
Diane Pavich	74	74	74	74	296	679
Jennifer Graff	77	72	68	79	296	679
Helen Alfredsson	76	71	75	74	296	679

Ladies French Open

Fourquex Golf Club, Fourquex, France
Par 37-35—72; 5,830 yards

June 15-18
purse, £60,000

	SCORES				TOTAL	MONEY
Suzanne Strudwick	70	69	74	72	285	£9,000
Marie-Laure de Lorenzi	78	73	64	70	285	6,090
(Strudwick defeated de Lorenzi on first extra hole.)						
Debbie Petrizzi	72	73	73	72	290	4,200
Sue Nyhus	73	73	74	71	291	3,240
Rica Comstock	73	74	74	71	292	2,148
Claire Duffy	74	72	72	74	292	2,148
Laurette Maritz	69	76	75	72	292	2,148
Catherine Panton	75	75	72	71	293	1,348
Dale Reid	76	71	71	75	293	1,348
Maria Navarro Corbachio	71	76	71	75	293	1,348
*Caroline Bourtayre	77	69	74	73	293	
Debbie Dowling	74	72	75	73	294	1,034
Dennise Hutton	78	68	74	74	294	1,034
Gillian Stewart	74	73	76	71	294	1,034
Maureen Garner	72	76	71	76	295	889.50
Elizabeth Glass	74	75	72	74	295	889.50
Majorie Jones	75	73	71	76	295	889.50
Judy Statham	74	74	71	76	295	889.50
Corinne Dibnah	75	74	73	74	296	774
Rae Hast	72	73	74	72	296	774
Louise Mullard	78	73	71	74	296	774
Page Dunlap	77	73	73	73	296	774
Karen Davies	77	75	69	75	296	774

	SCORES				TOTAL	MONEY
Denise Baldwin	74	69	78	75	296	774
Florence Descampe	75	76	71	75	297	699
Cindy Scholefield	76	69	77	75	297	699
Sonja Van Wyk	76	76	75	71	298	663
Jennifer Graff	77	73	74	74	298	663
Beverly New	72	73	81	73	299	627
Kay Cornelius	73	76	78	72	299	627

St. Moritz Ladies Classic

Engadine Golf Club, St. Moritz, Switzerland
Par 37-35—72; 5,961 yards

June 29-July 2
purse, £70,000

	SCORES				TOTAL	MONEY
Kitrina Douglas	74	71	71	70	286	£10,500
Suzanne Strudwick	74	68	75	69	286	7,105
(Douglas defeated Strudwick on first extra hole.)						
Nicole Lowien	75	72	69	72	288	4,900
Dennise Hutton	74	71	75	69	289	2,284.50
Laurette Maritz	73	71	71	74	289	2,284.50
Catherine Panton	71	75	74	69	289	2,284.50
Kris Hanson	73	71	74	71	289	2,284.50
Diane Barnard	71	72	75	72	290	1,442
Marie-Laure de Lorenzi	76	72	76	66	290	1,442
Marie Wennersten-From	70	75	73	72	290	1,442
Florence Descampe	72	69	73	76	290	1,442
Melissa McNamara	72	72	75	71	290	1,442
Regine Lautens	75	76	72	68	291	1,106
Xonia Wunsch-Ruiz	73	69	77	72	291	1,106
Susan Moon	73	76	72	71	292	1,036
Page Dunlap	77	71	72	72	292	1,036
Alison Nicholas	81	71	70	71	293	980
Elisabeth Quelhas	74	70	70	79	293	980
Janet Soulsby	75	71	74	74	294	924
Alicia Dibos	75	73	71	75	294	924
Rica Comstock	74	75	74	72	295	878.50
Muriel Thomson	77	73	73	72	295	878.50
Tania Abitbol	78	73	76	69	296	794.50
Corinne Dibnah	76	73	76	71	296	794.50
Marjorie Jones	75	71	76	74	296	794.50
Alison Sheard	76	70	77	73	296	794.50
Debbie Petrizzi	74	76	71	75	296	794.50
Leigh Mills	75	75	75	71	296	794.50
Li Wen Lin	74	72	73	78	297	721
Janice Arnold	76	74	75	73	298	668.50
Federica Dassu	73	75	76	74	298	668.50
Dale Reid	78	73	75	72	298	668.50
Gillian Stewart	78	71	73	76	298	668.50

TEC Players Championship

Tytherington Golf Club, MacClesfield, England
Par 36-36—72; 5,566 yards

July 6-9
purse, £75,000

	SCORES				TOTAL	MONEY
Anna Oxenstierna-Rhodin	75	74	66	71	286	£11,250
Laurette Maritz	69	73	73	73	288	7,610
Mickey Walker	73	72	74	72	291	5,250
Jane Connachan	73	76	73	70	292	3,285
Sofia Gronberg	74	78	70	70	292	3,285
Susan Moon	74	75	74	69	292	3,285
Peggy Conley	73	77	75	69	294	1,737
Corinne Dibnah	72	73	74	75	294	1,737
Kitrina Douglas	74	73	75	72	294	1,737
Maureen Garner	74	74	73	73	294	1,737
Suzanne Strudwick	76	70	75	73	294	1,737
Tracy Hammond	73	76	73	73	295	1,248.50
Dale Reid	75	73	74	73	295	1,248.50
Tania Abitbol	76	75	73	72	296	1,081.16
Marjorie Jones	77	72	73	74	296	1,081.16
Catherine Panton	75	77	71	73	296	1,081.16
Corinne Soules	76	76	72	72	296	1,081.16
Julie Hennessy	70	72	75	79	296	1,081.16
Susan Shapcott	74	77	71	74	296	1,081.16
Diane Barnard	74	75	73	75	297	940.50
Sonja Van Wyk	75	77	74	71	297	940.50
Debbie Petrizzi	73	74	74	76	297	940.50
Helen Alfredsson	72	69	80	76	297	940.50
Debbie Dowling	71	76	75	76	298	860
Jane Howard	78	72	73	75	298	860
Dennise Hutton	74	75	73	76	298	860
Rae Hast	70	75	76	78	299	779.50
Janet Soulsby	75	76	75	73	299	779.50
Gillian Stewart	71	76	74	78	299	779.50
Mardi Lunn	71	77	75	76	299	779.50

Bloor Homes Eastleigh Classic

Fleming Park Golf Club, Eastleigh, England
Par 34-32—66; 4,456 yards

July 13-16
purse, £60,000

(Final round played at par 65)

	SCORES				TOTAL	MONEY
Debbie Dowling	69	65	65	62	261	£9,000
Rae Hast	67	67	64	63	261	4,510
Catherine Panton	66	65	63	67	261	4,510
Melissa McNamara	64	66	65	66	261	4,510
(Dowling defeated Hast, Panton and McNamara on third extra hole.)						
Diane Barnard	67	66	67	62	262	1,986
Peggy Conley	67	64	68	63	262	1,986
Anna Oxenstierna-Rhodin	66	66	67	63	262	1,986
Diane Pavich	66	65	66	65	262	1,986
Kitrina Douglas	66	66	65	66	263	1,344
Maureen Garner	68	64	63	69	264	1,200
Claire Duffy	68	69	67	63	267	986.40

	SCORES				TOTAL	MONEY
Dennise Hutton	67	65	68	67	267	986.40
Janet Soulsby	67	66	66	68	267	986.40
Debbie Petrizzi	65	65	67	70	267	986.40
Cindy Scholefield	72	66	66	63	267	986.40
Sue Nyhus	66	74	63	65	268	864
Susan Moon	62	71	67	68	268	864
Alison Munt	66	69	70	64	269	804
Kay Cornelius	66	74	65	64	269	804
Karen Davies	64	71	66	68	269	804
Janice Arnold	67	68	68	67	270	744
Tracy Hammond	70	68	64	68	270	744
Laurette Maritz	66	67	68	69	270	744
Lillian Behan	69	69	66	67	271	663
Maxine Burton	69	64	68	70	271	663
Beverly Huke	70	71	65	65	271	663
Dale Reid	70	69	64	68	271	663
Julie Hennessy	75	65	65	66	271	663
Nicola Way	67	66	65	73	271	663
Rica Comstock	67	74	66	65	272	546
Jane Howard	69	68	66	69	272	546
Louise Mullard	70	68	67	67	272	546
Alicia Dibos	65	70	68	69	272	546
Tracey Craik	68	66	71	67	272	546
Sally Prosser	74	65	68	65	272	546
Susan Shapcott	67	71	69	65	272	546

Lufthansa German Open

Worthsee Golf Club, Munich, West Germany
Par 36-36—72; 5,628 yards

July 27-30
purse, £80,000

	SCORES				TOTAL	MONEY
Alison Nicholas	67	69	68	65	269	£12,000
Patricia Gonzalez	68	71	66	69	274	8,120
Suzanne Strudwick	69	68	71	71	279	4,960
Patti Rizzo	67	68	71	73	279	4,960
Diane Barnard	70	70	70	70	280	3,096
Marie-Laure de Lorenzi	70	70	69	71	280	3,096
Laurette Maritz	69	72	70	70	281	1,948
Florence Descampe	70	69	71	71	281	1,948
Martha Nause	75	69	68	69	281	1,948
Helen Alfredsson	70	66	74	71	281	1,948
Jane Geddes	67	71	73	71	282	1,472
Karine Espinasse	70	71	73	70	284	1,332
Marta Figueras-Dotti	69	71	74	70	284	1,332
Tania Abitbol	75	67	72	71	285	1,202.66
Peggy Conley	74	74	69	68	285	1,202.66
Kelly Leadbetter	69	70	73	73	285	1,202.66
Sofia Gronberg	74	74	69	69	286	1,104
Gillian Stewart	72	69	72	73	286	1,104
Xonia Wunsch-Ruiz	71	72	71	72	286	1,104
Debbie Dowling	71	77	68	71	287	980
Dennise Hutton	70	73	70	74	287	980
Regine Lautens	72	67	74	74	287	980
Alison Sheard	74	70	72	71	287	980
Janet Soulsby	70	73	72	72	287	980
Susan Shapcott	70	69	73	75	287	980

	SCORES				TOTAL	MONEY
Kitrina Douglas	72	73	71	72	288	872
Rae Hast	71	74	71	72	288	872
Louise Mullard	79	70	67	72	288	872
Dale Reid	75	71	73	70	289	800
Catrin Nilsmark	72	68	74	75	289	800
Cindy Scholefield	70	69	80	70	289	800

Weetabix Ladies British Open

Ferndown Golf Club, Dorset, England
Par 36-36—72; 5,975 yards

August 3-6
purse, £120,000

	SCORES				TOTAL	MONEY
Jane Geddes	67	67	72	68	274	£18,000
Florence Descampe	73	66	70	67	276	12,340
Marie-Laure de Lorenzi	68	71	67	72	278	6,880
Patti Rizzo	71	69	68	71	279	6,480
Muffin Spencer-Devlin	72	69	67	71	279	6,480
Peggy Conley	70	67	76	67	280	4,860
Xonia Wunsch-Ruiz	69	73	72	67	281	4,140
Kitrina Douglas	71	70	71	70	282	3,540
Alicia Dibos	67	75	72	69	283	3,060
Ray Bell	71	68	74	72	285	2,480
Marta Figueras-Dotti	69	71	72	73	285	2,480
Helen Alfredsson	73	70	69	73	285	2,480
Laurette Maritz	67	74	71	74	286	2,160
Laura Davies	76	71	69	71	287	1,924
Rae Hast	73	71	73	70	287	1,924
Alison Nicholas	71	69	71	76	287	1,924
Melissa McNamara	73	70	72	72	287	1,924
Cindy Scholefield	75	72	71	69	287	1,924
Debbie Dowling	69	76	72	71	288	1,710
Joanne Furby	71	72	70	75	288	1,710
Trish Johnson	72	75	69	73	289	1,560
Suzanne Strudwick	70	74	69	76	289	1,560
Karen Davies	73	70	72	74	289	1,560
Nicole Lowien	71	70	79	70	290	1,440
Jane Connachan	72	75	69	75	291	1,290
Federica Dassu	74	72	73	72	291	1,290
Susan Moon	75	71	77	68	291	1,290
Alison Munt	73	70	73	75	291	1,290
Marjorie Jones	74	75	70	73	292	1,110
Liselotte Neumann	71	72	75	74	292	1,110

Ladies Danish Open

Rungsted Golf Club, Copenhagen, Denmark
Par 35-37—72; 6,034 yards

August 17-20
purse, £65,000

	SCORES				TOTAL	MONEY
Tania Abitbol	69	69	73	74	285	£9,750
Marie-Laure de Lorenzi	75	70	68	72	285	6,650
(Abitbol defeated de Lorenzi on third extra hole.)						
Alison Nicholas	74	71	73	69	287	4,570
Suzanne Strudwick	75	67	77	70	289	3,510

	SCORES				TOTAL	MONEY
Peggy Conley	69	69	74	80	292	2,151.50
Kitrina Douglas	75	73	70	74	292	2,151.50
Sofia Gronberg	75	73	73	71	292	2,151.50
Gillian Stewart	72	72	73	75	292	2,151.50
Dennise Hutton	73	71	76	73	293	1,317.33
Dale Reid	72	72	72	77	293	1,317.33
Corinne Soules	75	74	74	70	293	1,317.33
Jane Connachan	73	75	73	73	294	1,057
Catherine Panton	69	76	75	74	294	1,057
Xonia Wunsch-Ruiz	74	73	72	75	294	1,057
Janice Arnold	76	73	71	76	296	962
Alicia Dibos	74	79	70	73	296	962
Beverly New	77	75	70	75	297	910
Malin Landehag	76	74	74	73	297	910
Lillian Behan	73	79	73	73	298	826.20
Federica Dassu	73	71	77	77	298	826.20
Patricia Gonzalez	74	77	76	71	298	826.20
Anna Oxenstierna-Rhodin	74	77	69	78	298	826.20
Marie Wennersten-From	75	73	77	73	298	826.20
Diane Barnard	71	74	78	76	299	735
Rae Hast	77	76	73	73	299	735
Susan Moon	76	72	73	78	299	735
Kelley Spooner	72	78	72	77	299	735
Corinne Dibnah	76	76	76	73	301	645.20
Maureen Garner	74	76	77	74	301	645.20
Anne Jones	80	76	73	72	301	645.20
Catrin Nilsmark	76	76	74	75	301	645.20
Cindy Scholefield	76	77	74	74	301	645.20

Gislaved Open

Isaberg Golf Club, Gislaved, Sweden
Par 36-36—72; 5,835 yards

August 24-27
purse, £65,000

	SCORES				TOTAL	MONEY
Alison Nicholas	73	72	69	74	288	£9,750
Liselotte Neumann	77	68	74	71	290	6,600
Maxine Burton	77	75	71	69	292	4,030
Peggy Conley	73	73	71	75	292	4,030
Jane Connachan	73	72	74	75	294	2,515.50
Dennise Hutton	77	70	72	75	294	2,515.50
Federica Dassu	74	72	71	78	295	1,505.40
Debbie Dowling	73	75	73	74	295	1,505.40
Maureen Garner	80	69	73	73	295	1,505.40
Xonia Wunsch-Ruiz	76	72	72	75	295	1,505.40
Cindy Scholefield	76	73	72	74	295	1,505.40
Tania Abitbol	78	77	67	74	296	1,057
Corinne Dibnah	75	73	73	75	296	1,057
Corinne Soules	77	73	70	76	296	1,057
Regine Lautens	74	75	71	78	298	936
Pia Nilsson	79	73	70	76	298	936
Jo Rumsey	73	82	72	71	298	936
Gillian Stewart	77	76	68	77	298	936
Karine Espinasse	76	75	73	75	299	836.50
Beverly New	75	75	74	75	299	836.50
Janet Soulsby	73	78	74	74	299	836.50
Marie Wennersten-From	77	76	72	74	299	836.50

	SCORES				TOTAL	MONEY
Janice Arnold	74	76	76	74	300	735
Diane Barnard	75	75	71	79	300	735
Anne Jones	77	79	74	70	300	735
Debbie Petrizzi	79	71	73	77	300	735
Helen Alfredsson	73	79	73	75	300	735
Malin Landehag	80	75	69	76	300	735
Diane Martin	77	72	77	75	301	655
Catherine Panton	77	75	74	75	301	655

Variety Club Celebrity Classic

Calcot Park Golf Club, Reading, England
Par 37-36—73; 5,839 yards

August 31-September 3
purse, £50,000

	SCORES				TOTAL	MONEY
Corinne Dibnah	68	70	70	71	279	£6,500
Peggy Conley	68	71	72	70	281	4,400
Sally Prosser	71	76	71	65	283	3,400
Jane Connachan	70	72	74	70	286	2,166.66
Alison Nicholas	71	72	73	70	286	2,166.66
Sonja Van Wyk	72	71	75	68	286	2,166.66
Dale Reid	73	71	75	68	287	1,350
Kitrina Douglas	75	69	74	70	288	1,012.50
Dennise Hutton	72	66	76	74	288	1,012.50
Maureen Garner	70	70	78	71	289	783.33
Rae Hast	70	66	74	79	289	783.33
Karen Lunn	70	72	72	75	289	783.33
Diane Barnard	76	70	72	72	290	700
Suzanne Strudwick	73	71	73	73	290	700
Joanne Furby	70	71	76	73	290	700
Janice Arnold	77	72	72	70	291	630
Susan Moon	72	77	72	70	291	630
Anne Jones	72	73	73	73	291	630
Debbie Dowling	75	73	70	74	292	570
Janet Soulsby	70	79	70	73	292	570
Karen Davies	75	74	71	72	292	570
Laurence Blondin	74	71	73	75	293	520
Jane Forrest	74	75	70	74	293	520
Catherine Panton	74	73	73	73	293	520
Caroline Griffiths	76	75	72	71	294	460
Laurette Maritz	74	73	74	73	294	460
Louise Mullard	72	74	75	73	294	460
Diane Pavich	71	74	75	74	294	460
Li Wen-Lin	71	72	77	74	294	460
Claire Duffy	73	73	76	73	295	415

Godiva European Masters

Golf du Bercuit, Brussels, Belgium
Par 35-37—72; 5,615 yards

September 7-10
purse, £110,000

	SCORES				TOTAL	MONEY
Kitrina Douglas	69	75	73	70	287	£16,500
Marie-Laure de Lorenzi	69	72	76	70	287	11,125

(Douglas defeated de Lorenzi on second extra hole.)

	SCORES				TOTAL	MONEY
Helene Andersson	72	72	75	70	289	7,700
Laurette Maritz	75	72	73	71	291	5,302
Alison Nicholas	73	74	74	70	291	5,302
Karine Espinasse	75	73	74	70	292	3,850
Jane Connachan	76	71	74	73	294	3,300
Caroline Griffiths	76	75	75	69	295	2,471.33
Suzanne Strudwick	78	75	71	71	295	2,471.33
Florence Descampe	74	75	71	75	295	2,471.33
Laura Davies	75	76	74	71	296	2,024
Julie Brown	75	71	77	74	297	1,754.50
Corinne Dibnah	74	74	74	75	297	1,754.50
Janet Soulsby	77	74	73	73	297	1,754.50
Evelyn Orley	73	78	73	73	297	1,754.50
Rae Hast	75	77	74	73	299	1,565.33
Susan Moon	76	77	74	72	299	1,565.33
Gillian Stewart	73	76	78	72	299	1,565.33
Federica Dassu	74	76	73	77	300	1,433.66
Joanne Furby	78	73	74	75	300	1,433.66
Helen Alfredsson	76	72	79	73	300	1,433.66
Tiru Fernando	76	72	76	77	301	1,347.50
Karen Davies	75	78	76	72	301	1,347.50
Jane Howard	76	78	75	73	302	1,281.50
Marie Wennersten-From	77	73	73	79	302	1,281.50
*Sylvie Clausset	71	76	78	77	302	
Debbie Dowling	78	77	77	71	303	1,182.50
Maureen Garner	78	74	76	75	303	1,182.50
Mickey Walker	79	76	76	72	303	1,182.50
Sally Prosser	77	79	70	77	303	1,182.50

Expedier European Open

Kingswood Golf Club, England
Par 36-36—72; 5,819 yards

September 14-17
purse, £70,000

	SCORES				TOTAL	MONEY
Jane Connachan	65	73	70	71	279	£10,500
Gillian Stewart	75	69	71	67	282	7,105
Karen Lunn	73	76	71	65	285	4,340
Sonja Van Wyk	70	73	75	67	285	4,340
Maureen Garner	69	75	71	71	286	2,968
Jane Howard	75	73	71	68	287	2,100
Corinne Soules	72	72	75	68	287	2,100
Karen Davies	72	69	73	73	287	2,100
Peggy Conley	69	72	75	72	288	1,418.66
Claire Duffy	71	74	71	72	288	1,418.66
Anne Jones	69	76	72	71	288	1,418.66
Debbie Dowling	71	75	70	73	289	1,204
Suzanne Strudwick	70	74	74	72	290	1,127
Laura Davies	72	76	72	71	291	1,052.33
Karen Espinasse	76	74	70	71	291	1,052.33
Diane Pavich	71	72	71	77	291	1,052.33
Barbara Helbig	75	70	72	75	292	939.40
Susan Moon	74	73	75	70	292	939.40
Dale Reid	70	80	72	70	292	939.40
Mickey Walker	73	74	71	74	292	939.40
Alicia Dibos	71	76	74	71	292	939.40
Kitrina Douglas	75	71	76	71	293	847

	SCORES				TOTAL	MONEY
Alison Sheard	75	75	70	73	293	847
Xonia Wunsch-Ruiz	70	72	76	75	293	847
Corinne Dibnah	76	75	70	73	294	773.50
Patricia Gonzalez	73	71	74	76	294	773.50
Judy Greco	69	81	71	73	294	773.50
Trish Johnson	79	72	73	70	294	773.50
Diane Barnard	71	73	74	77	295	679
Lillian Behan	69	72	76	78	295	679
Diane Patterson	70	76	77	72	295	679
Judy Statham	73	70	73	73	295	679
Susan Shapcott	72	75	74	74	295	679

Italian Open

Carimate Golf Club, Milan, Italy
Par 36-35—71; 5,948 yards

September 28-October 1
purse, £80,000

	SCORES				TOTAL	MONEY
Xonia Wunsch-Ruiz	68	70	72	68	278	£12,000
Jane Connachan	67	69	73	71	280	8,120
Trish Johnson	67	71	71	74	283	5,600
Susan Moon	71	67	73	73	284	3,856
Alicia Dibos	70	70	74	70	284	3,856
Regine Lautens	70	70	72	73	285	2,600
Alison Nicholas	71	73	69	72	285	2,600
Suzanne Strudwick	68	72	73	73	286	2,000
Laurette Maritz	73	74	71	70	288	1,792
Gillian Stewart	71	71	74	73	289	1,536
Catrin Nilsmark	71	74	73	71	289	1,536
Federica Dassu	76	74	72	68	290	1,301.33
Marie-Laure de Lorenzi	69	74	73	74	290	1,301.33
Stefania Croce	73	69	75	73	290	1,301.33
Li Wen-Lin	75	73	70	73	291	1,200
Karine Espinasse	76	71	73	72	292	1,152
Sofia Gronberg	72	70	77	73	292	1,152
Corinne Dibnah	73	73	73	74	293	1,072
Maureen Garner	76	72	70	75	293	1,072
Dale Reid	73	76	72	72	293	1,072
Maxine Burton	74	75	70	75	294	980
Peggy Conley	73	73	75	73	294	980
Catherine Panton	79	73	72	70	294	980
Sonja Van Wyk	72	74	75	73	294	980
Kitrina Douglas	78	73	75	69	295	920
Ray Bell	75	73	76	72	296	860
Laura Davies	72	74	77	73	296	860
Elizabeth Glass	77	70	73	76	296	860
Patricia Gonzalez	72	73	81	70	296	860
Debbie Dowling	74	72	73	78	297	764
Anna Oxenstierna-Rhodin	73	77	73	74	297	764
Corinne Soules	78	73	73	73	297	764
Anne Rogerson	77	72	72	76	297	764

Laing Ladies Classic

Stoke Poges Golf Club, Stoke Poges, England
Par 37-36—73; 5,741 yards

October 12-15
purse, £60,000

	SCORES				TOTAL	MONEY
Laura Davies	72	64	72	68	276	£9,000
Jane Connachan	73	68	70	68	279	4,018.50
Corinne Dibnah	71	68	73	67	279	4,018.50
Susan Moon	67	70	72	70	279	4,018.50
Dale Reid	69	70	72	68	279	4,018.50
Peggy Conley	70	72	72	66	280	2,100
Cindy Scholefield	70	70	70	71	281	1,800
Federica Dassu	73	70	70	69	282	1,500
Karen Lunn	74	70	70	70	284	1,272
Xonia Wunsch-Ruiz	68	70	72	74	284	1,272
Diane Barnard	72	72	74	67	285	1,034
Laurette Maritz	75	69	73	68	285	1,034
Susan Shapcott	72	71	71	71	285	1,034
Karine Espinasse	71	74	72	69	286	930
Kitrina Douglas	71	72	72	72	287	852
Beverly Huke	70	71	75	71	287	852
Trish Johnson	72	70	75	70	287	852
Pat Saillie	72	70	69	76	287	852
Anne Jones	72	73	73	69	287	852
Maureen Garner	72	72	71	73	288	744
Barbara Helbig	78	69	71	70	288	744
Nicola McCormack	74	72	68	74	288	744
Diane Pavich	71	74	71	72	288	744
Gillian Stewart	71	71	73	73	288	744
Debbie Dowling	69	74	72	74	289	654
Patricia Gonzalez	71	75	73	70	289	654
Susan Moorcraft	74	73	69	73	289	654
Suzanne Strudwick	73	71	73	72	289	654
Alicia Dibos	72	74	73	70	289	654
Regine Lautens	71	73	72	74	290	582
Corinne Soules	73	73	70	74	290	582
Tracey Craik	72	71	73	74	290	582

Woolmark Ladies Match Play Championship

Vallromanas Golf Club, Barcelona, Spain
Par 36-36—72; 5,885 yards

October 19-22
purse, £70,000

FIRST ROUND

Marie-Laure de Lorenzi defeated Malin Landehag, 4 and 2
Margie Jones defeated Claire Duffy, 1 up, 19 holes
Debbie Petrizzi defeated Tracey Craik, 2 and 1
Karen Lunn defeated Alicia Dibos, 1 up
Debbie Dowling defeated Janet Soulsby, 3 and 2
Helen Alfredsson defeated Li Wen Lin, 1 up
Caroline Griffiths defeated Trish Johnson, 3 and 2
Xonia Wunsch-Ruiz defeated Barbara Helbig, 3 and 2
Corinne Dibnah defeated Julie Ralls, 6 and 5
Susan Shapcott defeated Judy Greco, 2 and 1
Tiru Fernando defeated Beverley New, 2 and 1
Dennise Hutton defeated Tracy Hammond, 1 up

Tania Abitbol defeated Mardi Lunn, 1 up
Louise Mullard defeated Stefania Croce, 1 up
Rae Hast defeated Kerri Clark, 2 and 1
Elizabeth Glass defeated Suzanne Strudwick, 1 up, 20 holes
Kitrina Douglas defeated Leigh Mills, 1 up, 21 holes
Maxine Burton defeated Ray Bell, 6 and 5
Laura Davies defeated Kim Lasken, 6 and 5
Patricia Gonzalez defeated Catherine Panton, 2 up
Susan Moon defeated Rica Comstock, 4 and 3
Anne Jones defeated Corinne Soules, 2 and 1
Dale Reid defeated Jo Rumsey, 2 and 1
Gillian Stewart defeated Cindy Scholefield, 4 and 3
Florence Descampe defeated Diane Barnard, 6 and 5
Karine Espinasse defeated Judy Statham, 5 and 4
Sally Prosser defeated Diane Pavich, 2 and 1
Kay Cornelius defeated Karyn Dallas, 1 up
Maureen Garner defeated Federica Dassu, 2 up
Linda Percival defeated Sarah Duhig, 2 up
Regine Lautens defeated Catrin Nilsmark, 4 and 3
Alison Nicholas defeated Jane Howard, 1 up, 19 holes

SECOND ROUND

de Lorenzi defeated Margie Jones, 1 up, 23 holes
Lunn defeated Petrizzi, 3 and 2
Alfredsson defeated Dowling, 3 and 2
Wunsch-Ruiz defeated Griffiths, 4 and 3
Dibnah defeated Shapcott, 4 and 3
Hutton defeated Fernando, 2 and 1
Abitbol defeated Mullard, 1 up
Hast defeated Glass, 5 and 4
Douglas defeated Burton, 3 and 2
Gonzalez defeated Davies, 1 up
Anne Jones defeated Moon, 4 and 3
Reid defeated Stewart, 3 and 1
Espinasse defeated Descampe, 3 and 2
Cornelius defeated Prosser, 1 up
Garner defeated Percival, 3 and 2
Nicholas defeated Lautens, 6 and 4
(All second-round losers received £600.)

THIRD ROUND

de Lorenzi defeated Lunn, 1 up
Alfredsson defeated Wunsch-Ruiz, 3 and 2
Hutton defeated Dibnah, 4 and 3
Abitbol defeated Hast, 4 and 3
Douglas defeated Gonzalez, 4 and 3
Anne Jones defeated Reid, 2 and 1
Espinasse defeated Cornelius, 4 and 3
Garner defeated Nicholas, 1 up
(All third-round losers received £1,000.)

QUARTER-FINALS

Alfredsson defeated de Lorenzi, 3 and 2
Hutton defeated Abitbol, 5 and 4
Anne Jones defeated Douglas, 2 and 1
Garner defeated Espinasse, 2 and 1
(All quarter-finals losers received £2,400.)

SEMI-FINALS

Hutton defeated Alfredsson, 1 up, 20 holes
Garner defeated Anne Jones, 7 and 6
(Alfredsson and Jones each received £5,000.)

FINAL

Hutton defeated Garner, 2 up
(Hutton received £12,000; Garner £8,000.)

AGF Biarritz Open

Biarritz Golf Club, Biarritz, France
Par 35-34—69; 4,967 yards

October 26-29
purse, £60,000

	SCORES			TOTAL	MONEY
Dennise Hutton	68	73	66	67	274	£9,000
Peggy Conley	70	64	70	70	274	6,090
(Hutton defeated Conley on first extra hole.)						
Alison Nicholas	69	71	70	67	277	3,720
Helen Alfredsson	64	72	74	67	277	3,720
*Sandrine Mendiburu	69	70	72	66	277	
Corinne Soules	70	70	70	68	278	2,544
Diane Barnard	71	68	73	67	279	1,800
Caroline Griffiths	71	71	68	69	279	1,800
Sally Prosser	71	72	68	68	279	1,800
Trish Johnson	73	73	66	68	280	1,272
Regine Lautens	72	70	68	70	280	1,272
Leigh Mills	71	70	72	68	281	1,104
Tania Abitbol	67	71	70	74	282	999
Susan Moon	75	70	72	65	282	999
Maureen Garner	68	69	76	71	284	930
Corinne Dibnah	72	67	70	76	285	876
Kitrina Douglas	73	72	70	70	285	876
Tracey Craik	73	70	71	71	285	876
Gillian Stewart	70	73	72	71	286	783.60
Florence Descampe	76	69	75	66	286	783.60
Alicia Dibos	67	77	73	69	286	783.60
Melissa McNamara	72	74	69	71	286	783.60
Susan Shapcott	66	73	76	71	286	783.60
Patricia Gonzalez	76	69	69	74	288	717
Karyn Dallas	69	77	73	69	288	717
Janice Arnold	70	73	74	72	289	681
Suzanne Strudwick	72	73	71	73	289	681
Tiru Fernando	71	71	73	75	290	645
Tina Yarwood	75	73	70	72	290	645
Jane Howard	72	77	69	73	291	582
Karen Lunn	77	74	68	72	291	582
Catherine Panton	73	71	75	72	291	582
Sonja Van Wyk	66	72	78	75	291	582
Karen Davies	72	76	72	71	291	582

Qualitair Ladies Classic

La Manga Golf Club, Cartagena, Spain
Par 36-37—73; 6,075 yards

November 1-3
purse, £50,000

	SCORES			TOTAL	MONEY
Alison Nicholas	69	74	70	213	£7,500
Peggy Conley	69	76	70	215	4,287.50
Sofia Gronberg	70	76	69	215	4,287.50
Caroline Griffiths	74	72	70	216	2,410
Dale Reid	77	69	70	216	2,410
Regine Lautens	74	74	69	217	1,500
Florence Descampe	74	73	70	217	1,500
Tina Yarwood	74	71	72	217	1,500
Diane Barnard	74	71	73	218	913.33
Debbie Dowling	72	72	74	218	913.33
Barbara Helbig	72	80	66	218	913.33
Jane Howard	75	72	71	218	913.33
Gillian Stewart	70	73	75	218	913.33
Alicia Dibos	71	74	73	218	913.33
Tania Abitbol	76	70	73	219	730
Rae Hast	72	76	71	219	730
Kerri Clark	71	74	74	219	730
Ray Bell	76	74	70	220	645
Jo Rumsey	73	77	70	220	645
Julie Ralls	77	75	68	220	645
Catrin Nilsmark	71	78	71	220	645
Karen Davies	74	75	71	220	645
Susan Shapcott	73	72	75	220	645
Janice Arnold	74	75	72	221	560
Rica Comstock	74	72	75	221	560
Kitrina Douglas	74	74	73	221	560
Suzanne Strudwick	68	75	78	221	560
Stefania Croce	71	75	75	221	560
Patricia Gonzalez	79	72	71	222	470
Dennise Hutton	71	77	74	222	470
Corinne Soules	74	74	74	222	470
Xonia Wunsch-Ruiz	75	73	74	222	470
Debbie Petrizzi	75	74	73	222	470
Anne Marie Palli	75	70	77	222	470
Leigh Mills	76	70	76	222	470